Human Development

A LIFESPAN VIEW

Second Edition

Robert V. Kail
University of Maryland,
College Park

John C. Cavanaugh
University of North Carolina
at Wilmington

Wadsworth
Thomson Learning™

Australia • Canada • Denmark • Japan • Mexico • New Zealand • Philippines • Puerto Rico
Singapore • South Africa • Spain • United Kingdom • United States

Psychology Editor: *Stacey Purviance*
Development Editor: *Jim Strandberg*
Assistant Editor: *Jennifer Wilkinson*
Editorial Assistant: *Amy Wood*
Marketing Manager: *Lauren Harp*
Editorial Production Supervisor: *John Walker*
Print Buyer: *Karen Hunt*
Permissions Editor: *Linda L Rill*
Production Service: *Joan Keyes, Dovetail Publishing Services*
Text Designer: *Jeanne Calabrese Design*
Photo Researcher: *Linda L Rill*

Closer Look Photo Researcher: *Myrna Engler*
Copy Editor: *Luana Richards*
Illustrators: *Suffolk Technical Illustrators, Wayne Clark, Stan Maddock*
Cover Designer: *Jeanne Calabrese Design*
Cover Printer: *Phoenix Color Corp.*
Signing Representatives: *Jay Honeck, Ron Shelly*
Compositor: *G&S Typesetters, Inc.*
Printer/Binder: *World Color, Versailles*

Photo and figure credits are provided beginning on page 673.

Printed in the United States of America
2 3 4 5 6 03 02 01 00

Library of Congress Cataloging-in-Publication Data

Kail, Robert V.
    Human development : a life span view / Robert V. Kail, John C. Cavanaugh. — 2nd ed.
        p.   cm.
    Includes bibliographical references and index.
    ISBN 0-534-35696-6 (alk. paper)
    1. Developmental psychology.   I. Cavanaugh, John C.
    II. Title.
BF713.K336   2000
155—DC21   99-34477

For more information, contact
Wadsworth/Thomson Learning
10 Davis Drive
Belmont, CA 94002-3098
USA
www.wadsworth.com

International Headquarters
Thomson Learning
290 Harbor Drive, 2nd Floor
Stamford, CT 06902-7477
USA

UK/Europe/Middle East
Thomson Learning
Berkshire House
168-173 High Holborn
London WC1V 7AA
United Kingdom

Asia
Thomson Learning
60 Albert Street #15-01
Albert Complex
Singapore 189969

Canada
Nelson/Thomson Learning
1120 Birchmount Road
Scarborough, Ontario M1K 5G4
Canada

To Dea and Patrice

BRIEF CONTENTS

CHAPTER 1   The Study of Human Development   1

PART ONE   PRENATAL DEVELOPMENT, INFANCY, AND EARLY CHILDHOOD   42

CHAPTER 2   Biological Foundations   45

CHAPTER 3   Tools for Exploring the World   82

CHAPTER 4   The Emergence of Thought and Language   122

CHAPTER 5   Entering the Social World   160

PART TWO   SCHOOL-AGE CHILDREN AND ADOLESCENTS   200

CHAPTER 6   Off to School   203

CHAPTER 7   Expanding Social Horizons   237

CHAPTER 8   Rites of Passage to Young Adulthood   277

PART THREE   YOUNG AND MIDDLE ADULTHOOD   318

CHAPTER 9   Becoming an Adult   321

CHAPTER 10   Relationships in Adulthood   363

CHAPTER 11   Work and Leisure   403

CHAPTER 12   Experiencing Middle Age   443

PART FOUR   LATE LIFE   484

CHAPTER 13   The Personal Context of Later Life   487

CHAPTER 14   Social Aspects of Later Life   529

CHAPTER 15   Dying and Bereavement   573

CONTENTS

CHAPTER 1
The Study of Human Development   1

How to Use This Book   2
Learning and Study Aids   2
Terminology   3
Organization   3
Thinking About Development   5
Recurring Issues in Human Development   5
Basic Forces in Human Development: The Biopsycho-
   social Framework   8
Developmental Theories   14
Psychodynamic Theory   16
Learning Theory   18
Cognitive-Developmental Theory   20
The Ecological and Systems Approach   23
Life-Span and Life-Cycle Theories   25
The Big Picture   26
Doing Developmental Research   27
Measurement in Human Development Research   28
General Designs for Research   31
Designs for Studying Development   33
Conducting Research Ethically   36
Communicating Research Results   37
Summary   39
Key Terms   40
If You'd Like to Learn More   41

PART ONE

**PRENATAL DEVELOPMENT, INFANCY,
AND EARLY CHILDHOOD**   42

A Closer Look: Tiger Woods   42

CHAPTER 2
Biological Foundations   45

In the Beginning: 23 Pairs of Chromosomes   46
Mechanisms of Heredity   47
Genetic Disorders   51
Heredity Is Not Destiny: Genes and Environments   53

REAL PEOPLE
Ben and Matt Pick Their Niches   55

From Conception to Birth   56
Period of the Zygote (Weeks 1–2)   56

CURRENT CONTROVERSIES
Conception in the 21st Century   57

Period of the Embryo (Weeks 3–8)   59

Period of the Fetus (Weeks 9–38)   60

Influences on Prenatal Development   62

General Risk Factors   63

Teratogens: Drugs, Diseases, and Environmental
Hazards   63

SPOTLIGHT ON RESEARCH
Industrial Toxins and Mental Development   66

How Teratogens Influence Prenatal Development   67

Prenatal Diagnosis and Treatment   69

Labor and Delivery   72

Stages of Labor   73

Approaches to Childbirth   73

Birth Complications   75

FORCES IN ACTION
*What Determines Life Outcomes for Low-Birth-Weight
Babies?*   76

Infant Mortality   76

Putting It All Together   77

Summary   77

Key Terms   79

If You'd Like to Learn More   80

CHAPTER 3
Tools for Exploring the World   83

The Newborn   84

The Newborn's Reflexes   85

Assessing the Newborn   86

The Newborn's States   86

Temperament   88

SEE FOR YOURSELF
Visit a Newborn Nursery   90

Physical Development   91

Growth of the Body   91

FORCES IN ACTION
Fostering Development in Malnourished Children   94

The Emerging Nervous System   94

Moving and Grasping—Early Motor Skills   98

Locomotion   99

Fine-Motor Skills   101

Maturation and Experience Both Influence
Motor Skill   102

YOU MAY BE WONDERING
Toilet Training   104

Coming to Know the World: Perception   106

Smell and Taste   106

Touch and Pain   107

Hearing   108

Seeing   108

Integrating Sensory Information   111

SPOTLIGHT ON RESEARCH
Integrating Sight and Sound   112

Becoming Self-Aware   114

Origins of Self-Concept   115

Theory of Mind   116

REAL PEOPLE
"Seeing Is Believing . . ." for 3-year-olds   117

Putting It All Together   118

Summary   118

Key Terms   120

If You'd Like to Learn More   121

CHAPTER 4
The Emergence of Thought and Language   123

The Onset of Thinking: Piaget's Account   124

Basic Principles of Cognitive Development   124

Sensorimotor Thinking   126

Preoperational Thinking   129

REAL PEOPLE
Christine, Egocentrism, and Animism   129

SEE FOR YOURSELF
Preoperational Thinking in Action   131

Evaluating Piaget's Theory   132

**Information Processing During Infancy and Early
Childhood**   135

General Principles of Information Processing   135

Attention   136

Memory   136

CURRENT CONTROVERSIES
Preschoolers on the Witness Stand   137

Quantitative Knowledge   139

Mind and Culture: Vygotsky's Theory   141

The Zone of Proximal Development   142

Scaffolding   142

SPOTLIGHT ON RESEARCH
How Do Mothers in Different Cultures Scaffold
Children's Learning?   143

Private Speech   144
Language   145
The Road to Speech   145
First Words and Many More   148
Speaking in Sentences: Grammatical Development   151

FORCES IN ACTION
How Children Learn Grammar   153

Communicating with Others   153
Putting It All Together   156
Summary   156
Key Terms   158
If You'd Like to Learn More   159

CHAPTER 5
Entering the Social World   161

Beginnings: Trust and Attachment   162
Erikson's Stages of Early Psychosocial Development   162
The Growth of Attachment   163

FORCES IN ACTION
What Determines Quality of Attachment?   168

Attachment, Work, and Alternative Caregiving   169

REAL PEOPLE
Lois, Bill, and Sarah   171

Emerging Emotions   172
Basic Emotions   172
Complex Emotions   174
Recognizing and Using Others' Emotions   175
Interacting with Others   177
The Joys of Play   177
Learning to Cooperate   180

SEE FOR YOURSELF
Children Cooperating and Competing   181

Helping Others   182

SPOTLIGHT ON RESEARCH
Are Empathic Children More Likely to Help?   183

Gender Roles and Gender Identity   186
Images of Men and Women: Facts and Fantasy   187
Gender Typing   189

Evolving Gender Roles   192

YOU MAY BE WONDERING
Children of Gay and Lesbian Parents   193

Putting It All Together   194
Summary   195
Key Terms   196
If You'd Like to Learn More   197
Snapshots of Development: A Visual Summary   198

PART TWO

School-Age Children and Adolescents   200

A Closer Look: Janet Jackson   200

CHAPTER 6
Off to School   203

Cognitive Development   204
More Sophisticated Thinking: Piaget's Version   204

REAL PEOPLE
Combinatorial Reasoning Goes to the Races   206

Information-Processing Strategies for Learning and
  Remembering   207
Aptitudes for School   210
Binet and the Development of Intelligence Testing   210
Do Tests Work?   211
The Elements of Intelligence   212

The Impact of Race, Ethnicity, and Social Class   214
Hereditary and Environmental Factors   215

SPOTLIGHT ON RESEARCH
The Carolina Abecedarian Project   216

Special Children, Special Needs   218
Gifted and Creative Children   219
Children with Mental Retardation   220

REAL PEOPLE
Little David—the Rest of the Story   221

Children with Learning Disability   221
Attention-Deficit Hyperactivity Disorder   222

FORCES IN ACTION
Treating ADHD   224

Learning in School   225
Grading U.S. Schools   225
Effective Schools, Effective Teachers   227

CURRENT CONTROVERSIES
Computers in the Classroom   228

SEE FOR YOURSELF
Recognizing Good Teaching   230

Putting It All Together   231
Summary   232
Key Terms   233
If You'd Like to Learn More   233

CHAPTER 7
Expanding Social Horizons   237

Family Relationships   238
Dimensions and Styles of Parenting   238
Siblings   244

FORCES IN ACTION
When Do Siblings Get Along?   245

Divorce and Remarriage   246
Parent-Child Relationships Gone Awry: Child Abuse   250
Peers   253
Friendships   253
Groups   255

SEE FOR YOURSELF
Identifying School Crowds   256

Popularity and Rejection   258

SPOTLIGHT ON RESEARCH
Long-Term Consequences of Popularity and Rejection   259

Television: Boob Tube or Window on the World?   261
Influence on Attitudes and Social Behavior   262

YOU MAY BE WONDERING
No More Child Couch Potatoes!   265

Influences on Cognition   266
Understanding Others   267
Describing Others   268

REAL PEOPLE
Tell Me About a Girl That You Like a Lot   268

Understanding What Others Think   269
Prejudice   271
Putting It All Together   272
Summary   273
Key Terms   275
If You'd Like to Learn More   275

CHAPTER 8
Rites of Passage to Young Adulthood   277

Farewell to Childhood: Puberty   278
Physical Growth   278
Eating Disorders   281

FORCES IN ACTION
What Causes Anorexia and Bulimia?   282

Who Am I? The Search for Identity   283
Identity Versus Role Confusion   284
Resolving the Identity Crisis   285
Ethnic Identity   287

SPOTLIGHT ON RESEARCH
Identity in Children of Transracial Adoptions   288

The Myth of Storm and Stress   289
Flipping Burgers and Waiting Tables: Entering the World of Work   291
Part-Time Work   292
Career Development   294

REAL PEOPLE
"The Life of Lynne," a Drama in Three Acts   295

"How Do I Love Thee?"—Romantic Relationships   298
Dating
Awakening of Sexual Interests   300

SEE FOR YOURSELF
Promoting Greater Awareness on Campus About Sexual Assault   304

A Look at the Dark Side: Problems of Adolescent Development   305
Use of Drugs   305
Depression   306

YOU MAY BE WONDERING
Preventing Teen Suicides   308

Delinquency   308

CURRENT CONTROVERSIES
When Juveniles Commit Serious Crimes, Should They Be Tried as Adults?   311

Putting It All Together   312
Summary   312
Key Terms   314
If You'd Like to Learn More   314
Snapshots of Development: A Visual Summary   316

PART THREE

Young and Middle Adulthood   318

A Closer Look: Debbi Fields   318

CHAPTER 9
Becoming an Adult   321

When Does Adulthood Begin?   322
Role Transitions Marking Adulthood   322

Going to College   324

YOU MAY BE WONDERING
Individuals with Learning Disabilities and the Transition to College   325
Psychological Views   325
So When Do People Become Adults?   326
Physical Development and Health   327
Growth, Strength, and Physical Functioning   327
Health Status   328
Life-Style Factors   328

CURRENT CONTROVERSIES
Binge Drinking on College Campuses   330

Social, Gender, and Ethnic Issues in Health   332

FORCES IN ACTION
Healthy Adulthood   334

Cognitive Development   335
How Should We View Intelligence in Adults?   335
What Happens to Intelligence in Adulthood?   336

SPOTLIGHT ON RESEARCH
The Seattle Longitudinal Study   337

Going Beyond Formal Operations: Thinking in Adulthood   341
Moral Reasoning   345
Kohlberg's Theory   346

REAL PEOPLE
Schindler's List   348

Alternatives to Justice   349
Cultural Differences in Moral Reasoning   350
Who Do You Want to Be? Personality in Young Adulthood   352
Creating Scenarios and Life Stories   352

SEE FOR YOURSELF
When I Was 35, It Was a Very Good Year   353

Possible Selves   354
Self-Concept   356
Personal Control Beliefs   356
Putting It All Together   358
Summary   358
Key Terms   360
If You'd Like to Learn More   360

CHAPTER 10
Relationships in Adulthood   363

Relationships   364
Friendships   364
Love Relationships   366

SPOTLIGHT ON RESEARCH
The Mating Game Around the World   369

The Dark Side of Relationships: Violence   371

FORCES IN ACTION
Influences on Relationships in Adulthood   374

Life-Styles   375
Singlehood   375
Cohabitation   376
Gay and Lesbian Couples   378

REAL PEOPLE
Maggie O'Carroll's Story   378

Marriage   379
The Family Life Cycle   384
Family Life-Cycle Stages   384
Deciding Whether to Have Children   385

YOU MAY BE WONDERING
The Cost of Raising a Child   386

The Parental Role   387
Divorce and Remarriage   390
Divorce   391

CURRENT CONTROVERSIES
"Covenant Marriage," A Way to Keep Couples Together?   392

SEE FOR YOURSELF
The Effects of Divorce on Adult Children   396

Remarriage   396
Putting It All Together   397
Summary   398
Key Terms   399
If You'd Like to Learn More   399

CHAPTER 11
Work and Leisure   403

Occupational Selection and Development   404
The Meaning of Work   404
Holland's Theory of Occupational Choice Revisited   406
Occupational Development   407
Job Satisfaction   410

SPOTLIGHT ON RESEARCH
Periodicity and Job Satisfaction   411

Gender, Ethnicity, and Discrimination Issues   414
Gender Differences in Occupational Selection   414
Women and Occupational Development   417
Ethnicity and Occupational Development   417
Bias and Discrimination   418

CURRENT CONTROVERSIES
Sexual Harassment in the Workplace   422

FORCES IN ACTION
Occupational Success Is More Than Just Hard Work   424

Occupational Transitions   425

REAL PEOPLE
Changing Occupations to Find Satisfying Work   425

Retraining Workers   426
Occupational Insecurity   427
Coping with Unemployment   427
Work and Family   429
The Dependent Care Dilemma   429
Juggling Multiple Roles   432

YOU MAY BE WONDERING
How Do Dual-Earner Couples Handle Division of Labor and Work-Family Conflict?   433

Time to Relax: Leisure Activities   435

SEE FOR YOURSELF
Varieties of Leisure Activity in Adulthood   436

Types of Leisure Activities   436
Developmental Changes in Leisure   437
Consequences of Leisure Activities   437
Putting It All Together   438
Summary   439
Key Terms   440
If You'd Like to Learn More   440

CHAPTER 12
Experiencing Middle Age   443

Physical Changes and Health   443

Changes in Appearance   445

SEE FOR YOURSELF
Dealing with Physical Aging   445

Reproductive Changes   446

CURRENT CONTROVERSIES
Having Babies After Menopause   448

Stress and Health   449

Exercise   452

Cognitive Development   453

Practical Intelligence   454

Becoming an Expert   456

Lifelong Learning   457

REAL PEOPLE
College at Midlife   458

Personality   460

Stability Is the Rule: The Five-Factor Model   461

Change Is the Rule: Changing Priorities in Midlife   462

YOU MAY BE WONDERING
Does Everyone Have a Midlife Crisis?   465

Family Dynamics and Middle Age   467

Letting Go: Middle-Aged Adults and Their Children   468

SPOTLIGHT ON RESEARCH
How Do You Think Your Children Turned Out?   469

Giving Back: Middle-Aged Adults and Their Aging
  Parents   470

FORCES IN ACTION
The Complexities of Caring for Older Parents   473

Grandparenthood   474

Putting It All Together   477

Summary   477

Key Terms   479

If You'd Like to Learn More   479

Snapshots of Development: A Visual Summary   482

PART FOUR

Late Life   484

A Closer Look: John Glenn   484

CHAPTER 13
The Personal Context of Later Life   487

What Are Older Adults Like?   488

The Demographics of Aging   488

How Long Will You Live?   491

Physical Changes and Health   494

Biological Theories of Aging   494

Physiological Changes   495

YOU MAY BE WONDERING
Preventing Accidents Involving Older Adults   500

Health Issues   500

Cognitive Processes   502

Information Processing   502

CURRENT CONTROVERSIES
*Information Processing in Everyday Life:
Older Drivers*   504

Memory   505

SEE FOR YOURSELF
Helping People Remember   509

Training Intellectual Abilities   509
Creativity and Wisdom   510

FORCES IN ACTION
Cognitive Changes in Later Life   512

Mental Health and Intervention   513
Depression   514
Anxiety Disorders   516
Dementia: Alzheimer's Disease   517

REAL PEOPLE
What's the Matter with Mary?   517

SPOTLIGHT ON RESEARCH
What's Her Name? Memory Training in Alzheimer's Disease   521

Putting It All Together   522
Summary   523
Key Terms   525
If You'd Like to Learn More   525

CHAPTER 14
Social Aspects of Later Life   529

Theories of Psychosocial Aging   530
Continuity Theory   530
Competence and Environmental Press   531

FORCES IN ACTION
Finding Where You Fit   533

Personality Development in Later Life   533
Integrity Versus Despair   534
Well-Being and Possible Selves in Later Life   535

SPOTLIGHT ON RESEARCH
Views of a Life: Well-Being and Aging   536

Religiosity and Spiritual Support   538
I Used to Work at . . . : Living in Retirement   539
What Does Being Retired Mean?   540

SEE FOR YOURSELF
Are You Retired?   541

Why Do People Retire?   542
Adjustment to Retirement   543
Interpersonal Ties   544
Friends and Family in Late Life   546

Friends and Siblings   547
Marriage   549
Caring for a Partner   549

REAL PEOPLE
'Til Death Do Us Part: Spousal Caregiving   550

Widowhood   551
Great-Grandparenthood   553
Social Issues and Aging   554
Frail Older Adults   555
Living in Nursing Homes   556

YOU MAY BE WONDERING
How Do You Respond to a Nursing Home Resident?   558

Elder Abuse and Neglect   560

CURRENT CONTROVERSIES
Which Older People Are Abused and Why?   561

Public Policy Issues and Older Adults   562
Putting It All Together   566
Summary   567
Key Terms   569
If You'd Like to Learn More   569

CHAPTER 15
Dying and Bereavement   573

Definitions and Ethical Issues   574
Sociocultural Definitions of Death   574

SEE FOR YOURSELF
Funerals   576

Legal and Medical Definitions   576
Ethical Issues   577

CURRENT CONTROVERSIES
Physician-Assisted Suicide   578

Ideas About Death Through the Life Span   580
Childhood   581
Adolescence   582
Young Adulthood   583
Middle Age   583
Late Adulthood   583

FORCES IN ACTION
Understanding Death   584

The Process of Dying   585
Death Anxiety   585

The Stage Theory of Dying   586

Alternative Views   587

Dying with Dignity: Hospice   588

YOU MAY BE WONDERING

The Hospice Alternative   589

A Life-Span Developmental Perspective on Dying   590

Surviving the Loss: The Grieving Process   591

The Grief Process   592

Normal Grief Reactions   594

SPOTLIGHT ON RESEARCH

Family Stress and Adaptation Before and After Bereavement   596

Abnormal Grief Reactions   597

Dealing with Different Types of Loss   598

Death of One's Parent   599

Death of One's Child   599

REAL PEOPLE

The Grief of Miscarriage   600

Death of One's Partner   600

Comparisons of Types of Loss   602

Putting It All Together   603

Summary   603

Key Terms   605

If You'd Like to Learn More   605

Snapshots of Development: A Visual Summary   608

Glossary   611

References   621

Credits   673

Name Index   679

Subject Index   692

PREFACE

"To boldly go where no one has gone before" is a phrase familiar to millions of *Star Trek* fans around the world. The desire to explore the unknown to further our knowledge and understanding is a fundamental characteristic of being human. Boldly going into the unknown is also what each of us does in the course of our development. None of us has been where we are headed; indeed, in a real sense, we create our own destinies.

Just as all good starship captains rely on computer data banks and technical manuals to help guide them through the galaxy, *Human Development: A Lifespan View, Second Edition* serves as a resource to describe aspects of your past and point you toward your future. Human development is both the most fascinating and most complex science there is. Our text introduces you to the issues, forces, and outcomes that make us who we are.

Contemporary research and theory on human development consistently emphasize the multidisciplinary approach needed to describe and explain how people change (and how they stay the same) over time. Moreover, the great diversity of people requires an appreciation for individual differences in the course of development. *Human Development: A Lifespan View, Second Edition* incorporates both, and aims to address three specific goals:

- To provide a comprehensive, yet highly readable, account of human development across the life span.

- To provide theoretical and empirical foundations that enable students to become educated and critical interpreters of developmental information.

- To provide a blend of basic and applied research, as well as controversial topics and emergent trends, to demonstrate connections between the laboratory and life and the dynamic science of human development.

ORGANIZATION

A Modified Chronological Approach. The great debate among authors and instructors in the field of human development is whether to approach the study from a *chronological approach* (focusing on functioning at specific stages of the life span, such as infancy, adolescence, and middle adulthood), or from a *topical approach* (following a specific aspect of development, such as personality, throughout the life span). Both approaches have their merits. We have chosen a modified chronological approach that we believe combines the best aspects of both. The overall organization of the text is chronological: We trace development from conception through late life in sequential order, and dedicate several chapters to topical issues pertaining to particular points in the life span (such as infancy and early childhood, adolescence, young adulthood, middle adulthood, and late life).

But because the developmental continuity of topics such as social and cognitive development gets lost with narrowly defined, artificial age-stage divisions, we dedicate some chapters to tracing their development over larger segments of the life span. These chapters provide a much more coherent description of important developmental changes, emphasize the fact that development is not easily divided into "slices," and provide students with more understandable explications of developmental theories.

Balanced Coverage of the Entire Life Span. A primary difference between *Human Development: A Lifespan View, Second Edition* and similar texts is that this book provides a much richer and more complete description of adult development and aging. Following the introductory chapter, the remaining fourteen chapters of the text are evenly divided between those covering childhood and adolescence, and those covering adulthood and aging. This even treatment reflects the rapid emergence of adult development and aging as a major emphasis in the science of human development, and a recognition that roughly three-fourths of most people's lives occurs beyond adolescence.

As a reflection of our modified chronological approach, *Human Development: A Lifespan View, Second Edition* is divided into four main parts. After an introduction to the science of human development (Chapter 1), Part One includes a discussion of the biological foundations of life (Chapter 2) and development during infancy and early childhood (Chapters 3–5). Part Two focuses on development during middle childhood and adolescence (Chapters 6–8). Part Three (Chapters 9–12) focuses on young and middle adulthood. Part Four examines late adulthood (Chapters 13 and 14), and concludes with a consideration of dying and bereavement (Chapter 15).

Users and reviewers gave us high marks for the organization of the first edition of *Human Development*. For the second edition, we have made a few organizational changes of note:

- The section on How to Use This Book in Chapter 1 has been moved from the end of the chapter to the beginning.
- The section on The Newborn has moved from the end of Chapter 2 to the beginning of Chapter 3.
- The section on Divorce and Remarriage in Chapter 10 has been moved to follow, rather than precede, the section on The Family Life Cycle.
- More subheads have been added to several sections throughout the book to help break up the coverage into more manageable chunks.

CONTENT AND APPROACH

The Biopsychosocial Emphasis. Our text provides comprehensive, up-to-date coverage of research and theory from conception to old age and death. We explicitly adopt the biopsychosocial framework as an organizing theme, describing it in depth in Chapter 1, then integrate it throughout the text— often in combination with other developmental theories.

An Engaging Personal Style. On several occasions, we communicate our personal involvement with the issues being discussed as illustrations of how human development plays itself out in people's lives. For instance, Rob Kail provides several examples from his children's developmental experiences, and John Cavanaugh shares his and his wife's experiences with miscarriage. Additionally, every major section of a chapter opens with a short vignette, helping to personalize a concept just before it is discussed. Other rich examples are integrated throughout the text narrative, and showcased in the Real People feature in nearly every chapter. Finally, we encourage students to find their own real-life examples of developmental issues through the See for Yourself features.

Emphasis on Inclusiveness. In content coverage, in the personalized examples used, and in the photo program, we emphasize diversity—within the U.S. and around the world—in ethnicity, gender, race, age, ability, and sexual orientation.

Changes in the Second Edition. Besides updating the second edition with several hundred new reference citations to works from the past four years, we have made significant changes in every chapter. Of particular note are these additions in coverage:

- A full new section added to the end of Chapter 3 on Becoming Self-Aware, with coverage of the origins of self-concept, and children's "theory of mind."

- A major new section added to Chapter 5 on Emerging Emotions, covering basic and complex emotions among infants and young children, and including a subsection on Recognizing and Using Others' Emotions.

- In Chapter 7, an entire new section has been added on Understanding Others, including coverage of children's description and understanding of others, and research on prejudice among children.

- The section on Friendships in Chapter 10 has been expanded, with a new subsection on the meaning of friendship, and new material on themes in adult friendships.

- In Chapter 13, significant new research on the concept of working memory in older adults has been added as a new subsection.

- A new Public Policy Issues and Older Adults section has been added to Chapter 14, with new subsections on The Political Landscape, Political Activity, Social Security and Medicare.

To provide an extensive guide to improvements made throughout the second edition, we continue with a substantial list of changes by chapter.

Chapter 1: The Study of Human Development

- How to Use This Book section moved from the end of the chapter to the beginning.

- Doing Developmental Research section revised completely and expanded, with an increased emphasis on the actual steps taken by researchers. This focus on the actual process of research is also the basis for how the Spotlight on Research features are formatted in the second edition, providing a more realistic look at the series of decisions that researchers make.

- Coverage of Erikson, learning theory, and Piaget revised thoroughly for clarity.

- The Conducting Research Ethically section has been revised and expanded, with a stronger emphasis on the key guidelines employed by professional research organizations.
- All new vignettes added to open each section of this chapter, providing readers an accessible scenario to help lead them into the material that follows.

Chapter 2: Biological Foundations

- Opening section on genetics reorganized and streamlined.
- Two new figures added to the From Conception to Birth section—the first graphically depicts the early stages of fertilization, zygote growth, and implantation in the uterine wall; the second provides a detailed look at the growing embryo's environment.
- Updated coverage of fetal alcohol syndrome, citing recent research on alcohol's teratogenic effects.
- The Approaches to Childbirth section revised to provide more detail about childbirth classes and information about home delivery.
- New subsection added on Infant Mortality, noting the lack of good pre-natal care as the primary reason why the infant mortality rate in the United States is so high relative to other industrialized nations.
- Labor and Delivery section now concludes the chapter, with coverage of The Newborn moved to become the opening section in Chapter 3.

Chapter 3: Tools for Exploring the World

- Chapter now opens with material on The Newborn, moved here from Chapter 2.
- Entire new major section added on Becoming Self-Aware, including material on the development of self-recognition, theory of mind, and self-concept.
- New Real People feature on "Seeing Is Believing . . ." for 3-Year-Olds, focusing on how preschoolers come to recognize that people's behavior is sometimes guided by mistaken beliefs.
- New subsection added on Sudden Infant Death Syndrome (SIDS), with advice to parents and caregivers on reducing the known environmental risk factors.

Chapter 4: The Emergence of Thought and Language

- Introduction to the section on Piaget's theory (Basic Principles of Cognitive Development) revamped, and subsection on Evaluating Piaget's Theory includes some positive reconsiderations of his theory instead of only criticisms.
- New Spotlight on Research feature on How Do Mothers in Different Cultures Scaffold Children's Learning?
- A new See for Yourself feature on Preoperational Thinking in Action, encouraging the reader to conduct his or her own Piaget conservation experiment with 3- or 4-year-olds.
- New summary table added showing milestones of language acquisition.

Chapter 5: Entering the Social World

- An entire new section has been added on Emerging Emotions, covering basic and complex emotions.
- New Spotlight on Research feature on altruism, titled Are Empathic Children More Likely to Help?
- Section on the impact of day care rewritten, emphasizing findings of the NICHD Early Child Care Study.
- The section on The Joys of Play reorganized, and a new subsection added on parental influence on children's play.
- New material on make-believe describes age and cultural differences.
- Updated information on the demographics of day care.
- The Gender Typing (formerly Sex Typing) subsection now includes new material on the influence of peers, and new material has been added on Gender Identity.

Chapter 6: Off to School

- Major reorganization of material on schools, with two major sections from the first edition (Effective Schools and Effective Teachers, and Grading U.S. Schools) now combined into one section titled Learning in School, and reorganized, focusing on what characteristics define good schools and what characteristics define good teachers.
- New Current Controversies feature on Computers in the Classroom, based upon what was a subsection in the first edition, describing the opportunities afforded by such computer use as well as addressing concerns about potential negative effects on students.
- Updated and revised coverage in sections on monitoring, Gardner's theory of multiple intelligences, hereditary and environmental influences on intelligence, and mental retardation.

Chapter 7: Expanding Social Horizons

- Major new section added on Understanding Others, including work on children's descriptions and understanding of others, and research on prejudice among children.
- Added coverage of Harry Stack Sullivan's early theory of how interpersonal friendships follow a stagelike sequence.
- New Spotlight on Research feature on Long-Term Consequences of Popularity and Rejection.
- New Real People feature on Tell Me About a Girl That You Like A Lot added to the new Understanding Others section. This feature compares the thoughts of the same girl at three ages (7, 10, and 16) in terms of who she finds to be the most likeable girl she knows, and why.
- Reorganized material on child abuse.

Chapter 8: Rites of Passage to Young Adulthood

- Bulimia now discussed along with anorexia in the subsection on Eating Disorders.
- New Spotlight on Research feature focuses on Identity in Children of Transracial Adoptions.

- Subsection on Sexual Orientation now includes new information about some of the special challenges faced by gay and lesbian youth.
- New See for Yourself feature on Promoting Greater Awareness on Campus About Sexual Assault.
- Causes of Delinquency coverage completely reorganized, emphasizing distinction between adolescent-limited and life-course persistent antisocial behavior.
- New Current Controversies feature highlights When Juveniles Commit Serious Crimes, Should They Be Tried as Adults?

Chapter 9: Becoming an Adult

- New Current Controversies feature added on Binge Drinking on College Campuses, and includes some basic strategies to try to address this dangerous, widespread phenomenon.
- In the section on What Happens to Intelligence in Adulthood? more explicit discussion now included on the hypothetical nature of primary and secondary mental abilities.

Chapter 10: Relationships in Adulthood

- Section on Friendships significantly expanded, with new section on the meaning of friendship and new material on themes in adult friendships.
- Subsections on Singlehood and Cohabitation significantly revised, with cohabitation coverage updated to include weaker link between it and marital instability.
- The section on Marriage now includes discussion of the complex data concerning effects on marital satisfaction of the birth of a child, physical illness, communication, and work-family demands.
- Additional research cited on successful outcomes by most children of gay and lesbian parents.
- Mate Selection subsection now includes material on assortative mating, stimulus-value-role theory, and attachment in adulthood.
- New Current Controversies feature on Covenant Marriage, a new option in Louisiana aimed at keeping couples together.
- Discussion of being child-free now includes differentiation between voluntary and involuntary causes.

Chapter 11: Work and Leisure

- New Real People feature on Changing Occupations to Find Satisfying Work.
- Specific new research findings added to You May Be Wondering feature on How Do Dual-Earner Couples Handle Division of Labor and Work-Family Conflict?
- Bias and Discrimination section heavily revised and updated, with new data and graphs concerning the gender wage gap and developmental issues related to it.
- Discussion of new research on sexual harassment and its effects, and discussion of sexual harassment in academic settings.
- Section on Work and Family heavily revised, with The Dependent Care Dilemma subsection now focusing on dependent care of both children

and older parent; new subsection on employer responses to dependent caregiving; new focus on effects on workers of caring for their dependents; reorganization of multiple roles and role conflict sections; more research on the effects of work-family conflict.

- The discontinuous nature of women's participation in the workforce is examined.

Chapter 12: Experiencing Middle Age

- The osteoporosis section has been rewritten.
- New findings related to estrogen and hormone replacement therapy incorporated into heavily revised section on The Climacteric and Menopause.
- Added solution style to Practical Intelligence section.
- The section on Personality has been refocused, reorganized, and heavily revised, with a new subsection on What Are Generative People Like?
- The subsection on Life Transition Theories and the Midlife Crisis has been refocused on transition process, and new research has been incorporated; ego resilience now described and added as a key term in the revised coverage.
- More emphasis now given to women as adult children caregivers, with ethnic differences noted, and the findings of several recent research studies cited and described.
- Coverage of styles of grandparenting rewritten.

Chapter 13: The Personal Context of Later Life

- In The Demographics of Aging section, a new graph charts recent U.S. Census projections on the expected increase in the populations of elderly Americans into the mid-21st century, broken down by ethnic group.
- New Current Controversies feature on Information Processing in Everyday Life: Older Drivers, including the importance of measuring the Useful Field of View of elderly drivers.
- New subsection added on Working Memory, citing recent research.
- Memory section revised and updated, with new examples and a table added of implicit-external and implicit-internal memory aids.
- New subsection added on Creativity, with a new graph showing peak years of productivity in several disciplines, and drawing upon recent research studies.
- New material on Alzheimer's disease added, including the links to estrogen levels, recent genetic research, normal pressure hydrocephalus as a condition to be differentially diagnosed from Alzheimer's disease, and the difference in course and diagnosis of vascular dementia and Alzheimer's.

Chapter 14: Social Aspects of Later Life

- Added concept of spiritual support to religiosity section.
- Added concepts of "crisp" and "blurred" types of retirement, with new data included on adjustment to retirement.
- Section on Gender Differences in Retirement thoroughly rewritten.
- Concept of socioemotional selectivity added to Friendships subsection.

- Public Policy Issues and Older Adults section added, with four new sub-sections on The Political Landscape, Political Activity, Social Security, and Medicare.
- Discussion of patronizing speech and infantilization added to coverage of nursing homes, and new information provided on selecting a nursing home.

Chapter 15: Dying and Bereavement

- Subsection on euthanasia revised to include recent U.S. Supreme Court decisions and the Oregon Death with Dignity law, and to describe "Do Not Resuscitate" order.
- Current Controversies feature revised to focus on physician-assisted suicide.
- More material on adolescent experience with death added.
- Attachment theory as a framework for understanding grief is noted.
- New subsection on Death Anxiety now included in the Processes of Dying section.
- The task approach to dying added as an alternative to Kübler-Ross.
- New See for Yourself feature on Funerals, encouraging students to visit a funeral home to learn about different options and costs.
- Section on grief revised to emphasize the process rather than the stage theory of grief, additional details included on anticipatory grief.

SPECIAL FEATURES

Six special features are a significant reason why this textbook is so unique. These features are woven seamlessly into the narrative, signaled by a distinct icon for each—not boxed off from the flow of the chapter. These six features are:

- **Spotlight on Research**
- **You May Be Wondering**
- **Current Controversies**
- **See for Yourself**
- **Real People**
- **Forces in Action**

These features are described in the How to Use This Book section of Chapter 1, and each one appears in nearly every chapter thereafter.

For the second edition, each Spotlight on Research feature has been reformatted to emphasize the methodology employed in all developmental research. Each Spotlight on Research now follows the same format to show readers the main questions that need to be considered in evaluating every developmental research study:

- What was the aim of the study and who were the investigators?
- How did the investigators measure the topic of interest?
- Who were the participants in the study?
- What was the design of the study?
- Were there ethical concerns with the study?
- What were the results?
- What did the investigators conclude?

In this new edition, another enhancement is that in the margin next to each of the Current Controversies features you will see an **InfoTrac College Edition®** icon and a brief prompt, with a keyword suggested. For example, in Chapter 2, the Current Controversies feature is on Conception in the 21st Century, and the keyword is "fertilization in vitro." For those students whose professors choose to adopt the textbook with InfoTrac, students will receive a four-month subscription to this online library of hundreds of periodicals, and can access actual articles (not just references to useful articles) relevant to a topic covered (e.g., fertilization in vitro) in the Current Controversies feature. This provides an exceptional opportunity to search InfoTrac's substantial database of journals and periodicals to find *very* recent articles.

Many of the specific features have been updated and revised in the second edition, and a significant number have been replaced or added. New to this edition:

- In Chapter 3, a new Real People feature on "Seeing Is Believing . . ." for 3-Year-Olds.
- In Chapter 4, a new Spotlight on Research feature on How Do Mothers in Different Cultures Scaffold Children's Learning? and a new See for Yourself feature on Preoperational Thinking in Action.
- In Chapter 5, a new Spotlight on Research feature on Are Empathic Children More Likely to Help?
- In Chapter 6, a new Current Controversies feature on Computers in the Classroom.
- In Chapter 7, a new Spotlight on Research feature on Long-Term Consequences of Popularity and Rejection, and a new Real People feature titled Tell Me About a Girl That You Like a Lot.
- In Chapter 8, a new Spotlight on Research feature on Identity in Children of Transracial Adoptions, a new See for Yourself on Promoting Greater Awareness on Campus About Sexual Assault, and a new Current Controversies on When Juveniles Commit Serious Crimes, Should They Be Tried as Adults?
- In Chapter 9, a new Current Controversies feature on Binge Drinking on College Campuses.
- In Chapter 10, a new Current Controversies feature on Covenant Marriage.
- In Chapter 11, a new Real People feature on Changing Occupations to Find Satisfying Work.
- In Chapter 13, a new Current Controversies feature on Information Processing in Everyday Life: Older Drivers.
- In Chapter 15, a new See for Yourself feature on Funerals.

NEW FEATURES IN THE SECOND EDITION

For this new edition, we have added two new features, both of which serve to illustrate important themes. The first, *A Closer Look,* opens each of the book's four main parts with a short photo essay on the development of a particular individual within the age range covered in that part. For example, astronaut-turned-senator-turned-astronaut John Glenn is featured in the A Closer Look opening to Part Four. While the individuals highlighted are well-known and truly extraordinary, their successes at different stages of life are exemplary of human development throughout the life span.

A second feature new to this edition closes each of the four major parts of our text: *Snapshots of Development: A Visual Summary.* These visual spreads briefly summarize the biological, psychological, and sociocultural forces that contribute to development over the chronological span covered in that part. By succinctly describing the result of these forces, then using representative photos from the chapters just covered, Snapshots of Development reinforce the major biopsychosocial development themes of each part through visual cues.

PEDAGOGICAL FEATURES

Among the most important aspects of *Human Development: A Lifespan View, Second Edition* is its exceptional integration of pedagogical features, designed to help students maximize their learning.

- *Integration of Photos, Art, Features, and Key Terms.* One of the first things you may notice in paging through this text is that figures, tables, and photos are not captioned, but are described directly in the text narrative where they appear. Similarly, the six special features described earlier, which are normally set apart in boxes in other texts (boxes that students often skip!), are integrated directly into the narrative. Continuing with this integrative theme, definitions of key terms are provided in context within the chapter narrative. Key terms themselves are in red (new to this edition) and the definition sentences are in italics. This *unrivaled* integration is meant to help the student stay focused, providing a seamless presentation of human development across the life span.

- *Section-by-Section Pedagogy.* Each major section (every chapter has four or five) has been carefully crafted: It opens with a set of **learning objectives,** a **vignette,** and a **mini-table of contents** for the section, typically includes one or more **Think About It** questions in the margin (new to the second edition), and ends with a set of questions called **Test Yourself** that reinforces key elements of the section.

- *Chapter-by-Chapter Pedagogy.* Each chapter opens with a **table of contents** and a brief **Introduction.** A **Putting It All Together** section follows the chapter's final section to tie major chapter themes together (usually referring back to the individuals described in the section vignettes as well), and includes a bulleted, detailed **Summary** (broken down by section), followed by a list of **Key Terms** (with page references), and **If You'd Like to Learn More.** For the second edition, we have expanded the If You'd Like to Learn More resources to include **InfoTrac College Edition** (the online college library), a set of annotated **Web Sites** pertinent to the chapter's content, and a referral for additional resources to the **Wadsworth Psychology Study Center Web Site.**

In sum, we believe that our integrated pedagogical system will give the student all the tools she or he needs to comprehend the material and study for tests.

SUPPLEMENTARY MATERIALS

An extensive array of supplemental materials are available to accompany this text:

For the Instructor:

- *Instructor's Manual.* The Instructor's Manual for the Second Edition has been prepared by Jessica Miller of Mesa State College. It includes a wealth of material, including Instructional Goals and Teaching Strategies, Chapter Outlines, Learning Objectives, Lecture Expanders, Classroom Activities, Questions to Stimulate Critical Thinking, Web Activities, InfoTrac College Edition Tie-Ins, and Video Recommendations. The Instructor's Manual also includes transition guides to help instructors switch easily from a major competing text to our Second Edition.

- *Electronic Instructor's Manual.* The Instructor's Manual is also available (Windows® and Macintosh® versions) in ASCII format.

- *Transparency Acetates.* Approximately 100 full-color illustrations of concepts presented in the text are available to qualifying instructors who adopt the Second Edition.

- *Electronic Transparencies.* A dual-platform CD-ROM providing the full set of color transparencies as an Acrobat slide presentation, is also available.

- *Test Items.* Bradley Caskey and Richard Seefeldt, both of the University of Wisconsin-River Falls, have prepared the Test Bank for the Second Edition. One hundred twenty multiple-choice questions are provided for each chapter, and each is identified by learning objective, page reference, classification (conceptual, factual, or applied), and level of difficulty. Ten additional multiple-choice items are provided and identified as those which appear on the book's Web site, where students can take an interactive quiz with instant feedback.

- *Thomson World Class Learning Testing Tools.* Available in both Windows® and Macintosh® formats, Thomson World Class Learning Testing Tools offer a fully integrated suite of test creation, delivery, and classroom management tools, including World Class Test, Test Online, and World Class Management software. World Class Learning Testing Tools allows professors to deliver tests via print, floppy, hard drive, LAN, or Internet.

- *InfoTrac College Edition.* Instructors who adopt the Second Edition (and their students) will have access to this online database of full-text articles from 900 scholarly and popular publications.

For the Student:

- *Study Guide.* Dea DeWolff of Purdue University and Terri Combs of Indiana University-Purdue University, Indianapolis, have revised their dynamic Study Guide to accompany the Second Edition. The Study Guide provides detailed chapter outlines, learning objectives, key terms, true/false questions, multiple-choice questions, essay questions, and answer keys cross-referenced to appropriate pages of the text.

- *Electronic Study Guide.* Questions and answers in an interactive format are provided in the Electronic Study Guide Available in both Windows and Macintosh format.

- *InfoTrac College Edition.* Students whose instructors adopt *Human Development: A Lifespan View, Second Edition* with InfoTrac College Edition have 24-hour access to a fully searchable online database. Offering full-text
articles from more than 900 scholarly and popular periodicals, InfoTrac College Edition—available only in higher education institutions in North America—offers authoritative sources, updated daily.

ACKNOWLEDGMENTS

Textbook authors do not produce books on their own. We would like to thank the many reviewers who have generously given their time and effort to help us sharpen our thinking about human development and, in so doing, shape the development of this text.

We also deeply appreciate the strong support we received from our Wadsworth megateam: Jim Brace-Thompson, who got us going on the second edition and whose sage advice is clearly discernible; Stacey Purviance, who took over the reins and provided strong guidance; Jim Strandberg, a truly excellent developmental editor whom "we" thank for all his help; and Joan Keyes, who guided the book through production. To all these people, many thanks.

First Edition Reviewers

Polly Applefield
University of North Carolina at Wilmington

Daniel R. Bellack
Trident Technical College

David Bishop
Luther College

Lanthan Camblin, Jr.
University of Cincinnati

Kenneth Elliott
University of Maine at Augusta

Martha Ellis
Collin County Community College

Linda Flickinger
St. Clair County Community College

Steve Fulks
University of Tennessee

Rebecca Glover
University of North Texas

J. A. Greaves
Jefferson State Community College

Patricia Guth
Westmoreland County Community College

Phyllis Heath
Central Michigan University

Myra Heinrich
Mesa State College

Sandra Hellyer
Indiana University-Purdue University at Indianapolis

Shirley-Anne Hensch
University of Wisconsin Center

Thomas Hess
North Carolina State University

Kathleen Hurlburt
University of Massachusetts-Lowell

Heidi Inderbitzen
University of Nebraska at Lincoln

Sanford Lopater
Christopher Newport University

Bill Meredith
University of Nebraska at Omaha

Maribeth Palmer-King
Broome Community College

Harve Rawson
Franklin College

Virginia Wyly
State University of New York College at Buffalo

Second Edition Reviewers

Gary L. Allen
University of South Carolina

Ann MB Austin
Utah State University

David Bishop
Luther College

Elizabeth M. Blunk
Southwest Texas State University

Josette Bonewitz
Vincennes University

Lanthan D. Camblin, Jr.
University of Cincinnati

Shelley M. Drazen
SUNY, Binghampton

Kenneth Elliott
University of Maine, Augusta

Nolen Embry
Lexington Community College

James Garbarino
Cornell University

Catherine Hackett Renner
West Chester University

Sandra Hellyer
Indiana University-Purdue University at Indianapolis

John Klein
Castleton State College

Wendy Kliewer
Virginia Commonwealth University

Nancy Macdonald
University of South Carolina, Sumter

Lisa McGuire
Allegheny College

Martin D. Murphy
University of Akron

John Pfister
Dartmouth College

Bradford Pillow
Northern Illinois University

Gary Popoli
Hartford Community College

Robert Poresky
Kansas State University

Joseph M. Price
San Diego State University

Rosemary Rosser
University of Arizona

Timothy O. Shearon
Albertson College of Idaho

Marcia Somer
University of Hawaii-Kapiolani Community College

Nanci Stewart Woods
Austin Peay State University

Anne Watson
West Virginia University

Fred A. Wilson
Appalachian State University

Karen Yanowitz
Arkansas State University

Christine Ziegler
Kennesaw State University

ABOUT THE AUTHORS

ROBERT V. KAIL

Robert V. Kail is Professor of Psychology at the University of Maryland, College Park. His undergraduate degree is from Ohio Wesleyan University and he received his Ph.D. from the University of Michigan. Kail is currently the Associate Editor of the *Journal of Experimental Child Psychology* and co-editor of *Advances in Child Development and Behavior*. He received the McCandless Young Scientist Award from the American Psychological Association, was named the Distinguished Sesquicentennial Alumnus in Psychology by Ohio Wesleyan University, and is a fellow of the American Psychological Society. Kail has also written *The Development of Memory in Children* and *Children and Their Development*. His research interests are in the area of cognitive development during childhood and adolescence. Away from the office, he enjoys flying, working out, coaching his daughter's soccer team, and watching his young adult sons on stage.

JOHN C. CAVANAUGH

John C. Cavanaugh is Provost and Vice Chancellor for Academic Affairs, as well as Professor of Psychology, at the University of North Carolina at Wilmington. He received his undergraduate degree from the University of Delaware, and his Ph.D. from the University of Notre Dame. Cavanaugh is a fellow of the American Psychological Association, the American Psychological Society, and the Gerontological Society of America. He has been an American Council of Education Fellow, and has served as President of the Adult Development and Aging Division (Division 20) of the APA. Cavanaugh has also written *Adult Development and Aging*. His research interests in gerontology concern family caregiving as well as the role of beliefs in older adults' cognitive performance. For enjoyment he backpacks, writes poetry, and, while eating chocolate, ponders the relative administrative abilities of James T. Kirk, Jean-Luc Picard, Kathryn Janeway, and Benjamin Sisko.

THE STUDY OF HUMAN DEVELOPMENT

How to Use This Book
Learning and Study Aids
Terminology
Organization

Thinking About Development
Recurring Issues in Human
    Development
Basic Forces in Human Development:
    The Biopsychosocial Framework

Developmental Theories
Psychodynamic Theory
Learning Theory
Cognitive-Developmental Theory
The Ecological and Systems Approach
Life-Span and Life-Cycle Theories
The Big Picture

Doing Developmental Research
Measurement in Human Development
    Research
General Designs for Research
Designs for Studying Development
Conducting Research Ethically
Communicating Research Results

Summary

If You'd Like to Learn More

You are about to begin an exciting personal journey. In this course, you will have the opportunity to ask some of the most basic questions there are: How did your life begin? How did you go from a single cell, about the size of the period at the end of a sentence in this text, to the fully grown, complex adult person you are today? Will you be the same or different by the time you reach late life? How do you influence other people's lives? How do they influence yours? How do the various roles you have throughout life—child, teenager, partner, spouse, parent, worker, grandparent—shape your development? How do we deal with our own and others' deaths?

These are examples of the questions that create the scientific foundation of human development, *the multidisciplinary study of how people change and how they remain the same over time.* Answering them requires us to draw on theories and research in the physical and social sciences, including biology, genetics, chemistry, medicine, psychology, sociology, demography, ethnography, economics, and anthropology. The science of human development reflects the complexity and uniqueness of each person and each person's experiences, as well as commonalities and patterns across people. As a science, human development is firmly grounded in theory and research and seeks to understand human behavior.

Before our journey begins, there are some things you need to have to make the trip more rewarding. In this chapter, we pick up the necessary road maps that point us in the proper direction: tips on how to use this book, a framework to organize theories and research, common issues and influences on development, and the methods developmentalists use to make discoveries. Pack well, and bon voyage.

HOW TO USE THIS BOOK

Human Development is written with you, the student, in mind. In the next few pages, we describe several features of the book that will make it easier for you to learn. Please don't skip this material; it will save you time in the long run.

LEARNING AND STUDY AIDS

Each chapter includes several distinctive features to help you learn the material and organize your studying.

- Each chapter opens with an overview of the main topics and a detailed outline.
- Each major section within a chapter begins with a mini-outline that lists the major subheadings of the section and a set of learning objectives. There is also a brief vignette that introduces one of the topics to be covered in that section and provides an example of the developmental issues that people face.
- When key terms are introduced in the text, they appear in red. The definition of the key term appears in *italics*. This should make key terms easier to find and learn.
- Data tables, photographs, and cartoons are integrated into the text where they are discussed, eliminating the need to search for them on other pages. This integration will help you tie the graphic material with the text.
- Key developmental theories are introduced in Chapter 1, and are referred to throughout the text.
- Critical thinking questions are listed in the margins. These questions are designed to help you make connections across sections within a chapter or across chapters.
- The end of each section includes a feature called Test Yourself, which will help you check your knowledge of major ideas you just read about. The Test Yourself questions serve two purposes. First, they give you a chance to spot-check your understanding of the material. Second, at times the questions will relate the material you have just read to other facts, theories, or the biopsychosocial framework you read about earlier.
- Text features that expand or highlight a specific topic are integrated with the rest of the material. This book includes six different types of features, each identified by a distinctive icon. The list below describes the types of features and shows the respective icons.

 SPOTLIGHT ON RESEARCH elaborates a specific research study discussed in the text and offers more details on the design and methods used.

 CURRENT CONTROVERSIES offers thought-provoking questions about difficult issues that warrant further discussion.

 REAL PEOPLE is a case study that illustrates how an issue in human development is manifested in the life of a real person.

YOU MAY BE WONDERING gives answers to common questions people have about development, often based in everyday experiences.

 SEE FOR YOURSELF provides ways for you to explore issues in human development on your own.

 FORCES IN ACTION describes how the biopsychosocial framework is used to understand a particular issue in development.

• The end of each chapter includes several special study tools. Putting It All Together returns to each vignette to reprise the major topics of the chapter. A Summary organized by major section headings provides a review of the key ideas in the chapter. Next is a list of key terms that appear in the chapter. Drawing the chapter to a close is If You'd Like to Learn More, which contains reading material and Web sites where you can find more information about human development.

We strongly encourage you to take advantage of these learning and study aids as you read the book. We have also left room in the margins for you to make notes to yourself on the material, so you can more easily integrate the text with your class and lecture material.

TERMINOLOGY

A few words about terminology before we embark. Certain terms will be used to refer to different periods of the life span. Although you may already be familiar with the terms, we would like to clarify how they will be used in this text. The following terms will refer to a specific range of ages:

Newborn	birth to 1 month
Infant	1 month to 1 year
Toddler	1 year to 2 years
Preschooler	2 years to 6 years
School-age child	6 years to 12 years
Adolescent	12 years to 20 years
Young adult	20 years to 40 years
Middle-aged adult	40 years to 60 years
Young-old adult	60 years to 80 years
Old-old adult	80 years and beyond

Sometimes, for the sake of variety, we will use other terms that are less tied to specific ages, such as babies, youngsters, and older adults. However, you will be able to determine the specific ages from the context.

ORGANIZATION

Authors of textbooks on human development always face the problem of deciding how to organize the material into meaningful segments across the life span. This book is organized in four parts: Prenatal Development, Infancy, and Early

Childhood; School-Age Children and Adolescents; Early and Middle Adulthood; and Later Adulthood. We believe that this organization achieves two major goals. First, it divides the life span in ways that relate to the divisions encountered in everyday life. Second, it allows this book to provide a more complete account of adulthood than other books do.

Because some developmental issues pertain only to a specific point in the life span, some chapters are organized around specific ages. Overall, the text begins with conception and proceeds through childhood, adolescence, adulthood, and old age to death. But because some developmental processes unfold over longer periods of time, some of the chapters are organized around specific topics.

Part I covers prenatal development, infancy, and early childhood. Here we will see how genetic inheritance operates and how the prenatal environment affects a person's future development. During the first two years of life, the rate of change in both motor and perceptual arenas is amazing. How young children acquire language and begin to think about their world is as intriguing as it is rapid. Early childhood also marks the emergence of social relationships, as well as an understanding of gender roles and identity. By the end of this period, a child is reasonably proficient as a thinker, uses language in sophisticated ways, and is ready for the major transition into formal education.

Part II covers the years from elementary school through high school. In middle childhood and adolescence, the cognitive skills formed earlier in life evolve to adultlike levels in many areas. Family and peer relationships expand. During adolescence, there is increased attention to work, and sexuality emerges. The young person begins to learn how to face difficult issues in life. By the end of this period, a person is on the verge of legal adulthood. The typical individual uses logic and has been introduced to most of the issues that adults face.

Part III covers young adulthood and middle age. During this period, most people achieve their most advanced modes of thinking, achieve peak physical performance, form intimate relationships, start families of their own, begin and advance within their occupations, manage to balance many conflicting roles, and begin to confront aging. Over these years, many people go from breaking away from their families to having their children break away from them. Relationships with parents get redefined, and the pressures of being caught between the younger and the older generations are felt. By the end of this period, most people have shifted focus from time since birth to time until death.

Part IV covers the last decades of life. The biological, physical, cognitive, and social changes associated with aging become apparent. Although many changes reflect decline, many other aspects of old age represent positive elements: wisdom, retirement, friendships, and family relationships. We conclude this section, and the text, with a discussion of the end of life. Through our consideration of death, we will gain additional insights into the meaning of life and human development.

We hope that the organization and learning features of the text are helpful to you—that they make it easier for you to learn about human development. After all, this book tells the story of people's lives, and understanding the story is what it's all about.

THINKING ABOUT DEVELOPMENT

Learning Objectives

- **What are the fundamental issues of development that scholars have addressed throughout history?**

- **What are the basic forces in the biopsychosocial framework? How does the timing of these forces make a difference in their impact?**

Thinking About Development

Recurring Issues in Human
Development

Basic Forces in Human Development:
The Biopsychosocial Framework

*J*AVIER SUAREZ *smiled broadly as he held his newborn grandson for the first time. So many thoughts rushed into his mind—What would Ricardo experience growing up? Would the poor neighborhood they live in prevent him from reaching his potential? Would the family genes for good health be passed on? How would Ricardo's life growing up as a Chicano in the United States be different compared to Javier's own experiences in Mexico?*

Like many grandparents, Javier wonders what the future holds for his grandson. The questions that he asks are interesting in their own right, but they are important for another reason: They bear on general issues of human development that have intrigued philosophers and scientists for centuries. In the next few pages, we introduce some of these issues, which surface no matter which specific aspect of development is being investigated.

RECURRING ISSUES IN HUMAN DEVELOPMENT

Do genes or experience really determine how smart a person becomes? If a 5-year-old is outgoing, does this mean that the child will be outgoing as an adult? Is human development much the same everywhere around the world? These and similar questions have occupied some of the greatest philosophers in history: Plato, Aristotle, René Descartes, John Locke, John Stuart Mill, and Ludwig Wittgenstein, among many others. Three main issues in human development have captured the most attention: nature versus nurture, continuity versus discontinuity, and universal versus context-specific development. These issues cut across virtually all of the topics we discuss in this book, so let's examine each one briefly.

Nature Versus Nurture

Think for a minute about a particular characteristic that you and several people in your family have, such as intelligence, good looks, or a friendly, outgoing personality. Why do you think this trait is so prevalent? Do you think it's because you inherited the trait from your parents? Or is it because of where and how you and your parents were brought up?

Various answers to these questions illustrate different positions on the nature-nurture issue, *which involves the degree to which genetic or hereditary influences (nature) and experiential or environmental influences (nurture) determine the kind of person you are.* Scientists once hoped to answer these questions by identifying either heredity or environment as *the* cause of a particular aspect of development. The goal was to be able to say, for example, that intelligence was

? THINK ABOUT IT
Think of some common, every-day behaviors, such as getting together with your friends. How do nature and nurture influence these behaviors?

due to heredity or that personality was due to experience. Today, however, we know that virtually no features of life-span development are due exclusively to either heredity or environment. Instead, development is always shaped by both; nature and nurture are mutually interactive influences. For example, in Chapter 2 you will see that some individuals inherit a disease that leads to mental retardation if they eat dairy products. However, if their environment contains no dairy products, they develop normal intelligence. Similarly, in Chapter 9 you will learn that one risk factor for cardiovascular disease is heredity, but that life-style factors such as diet and smoking play important roles in determining who has heart attacks. So Ricardo's development will surely be shaped by the genes that he inherited from his parents and the experiences that he will have.

As these examples illustrate, a major aim of modern developmental science is to understand how heredity and environment jointly determine the development of thought, personality, and social behavior. Throughout this text, we will provide numerous examples of how the interaction between nature and nurture shapes our lives.

Continuity Versus Discontinuity

Think of some ways in which you remain similar to how you were as a 5-year-old. Maybe you were outgoing and friendly at that age and remain outgoing and friendly today. Perhaps you were very bright then and remain so today. Examples like these suggest a great deal of continuity in development. Once a person begins down a particular developmental pathway—for example, toward friendliness or intelligence—he or she stays on that path throughout life. According to this view, if Ricardo is a friendly and smart 5-year-old, he should be friendly and smart as a 25- and 75-year-old.

The other view—that development is not always continuous—is illustrated in the cartoon. Sweet and cooperative Trixie has become assertive and demanding. In this view, people can change from one developmental path to another, perhaps several times in their lives. Consequently, Ricardo might be smart and friendly at age 5, smart but obnoxious at 25, and wise but aloof at 75!

Hi and Lois

The continuity-discontinuity issue *concerns whether a particular developmental phenomenon represents a smooth progression throughout the life span (continuity) or a series of abrupt shifts (discontinuity).* Continuity approaches usually focus on the amount of a characteristic a person has, whereas discontinuity approaches usually focus on the kinds of characteristics a person has. Throughout this book, you will find examples of both continuities and discontinuities in development. For example, in Chapter 5 you will see evidence of continuity: Infants who have satisfying emotional relationships with their parents typically become children with satisfying peer relationships. But in Chapter 14 you will see an instance of discontinuity: After spending most of adulthood trying to ensure the success of the next generation and to leave a legacy, older adults turn to evaluating their own lives, in search of closure and a sense that what they have done has been worthwhile.

Universal Versus Context-Specific Development

The universal versus context-specific development issue *concerns whether there is just one path of development or several.* In some cities in Brazil, 10- to 12-year-olds like the boy in the photo sell fruit and candy to pedestrians and passengers on buses. They purchase and sell goods, make change for customers, and monitor their sales. Even though they have little formal education and often cannot identify the numbers on the money, they handle money proficiently (Saxe, 1988).

Life for Brazilian street vendors contrasts sharply with childhood in the United States, where 10- to 12-year-olds are formally taught at home or school to identify numbers and to perform the kinds of arithmetic needed to handle money. Is it possible for one theory to explain development in both groups of children? Perhaps. Some theorists would argue that despite what look like differences in development, there is really only one fundamental developmental process for everyone. According to this view, differences in development are simply variations on a fundamental developmental process, in much the same way that cars as different as a Chevrolet, a Honda, and a Porsche are all products of fundamentally the same manufacturing process.

The opposing view, of course, is that differences among people may not be just variations on a theme. Advocates of this view argue that human development is inextricably intertwined with the context within which it occurs. A person's development is a product of complex interaction with the environment, and that interaction is *not* fundamentally the same in all environments. Each environment has its own set of unique procedures that shape development, just as the "recipes" for cars, milkshakes, and fly swatters have little in common.

Putting all three issues together, and using personality to illustrate, we can ask how heredity and environment interact to influence the development of personality, whether the development of personality is continuous or discontinuous, and whether personality develops in much the same way around the world. Of course, *answers* to these questions are what really interest us; let's begin our search for answers by looking at the forces that combine to shape development.

BASIC FORCES IN HUMAN DEVELOPMENT: THE BIOPSYCHOSOCIAL FRAMEWORK

We've seen that developmentalists deal with three fundamental issues in an effort to frame the general discussion of human development. These issues are fundamental because they set the stage for asking much grander questions: What specific forces make us who we are? Why do some people become creative artists, whereas others work on assembly lines? Why are some people conservatives and others liberals? How can siblings who grow up in the same family turn out very different from each other? What creates the wonderful range of diversity that is humanity? To provide cohesive explanations of people's characteristics and behaviors across the life span, developmentalists usually consider combinations of four interactive forces:

- Biological forces *include all genetic and health-related factors that affect development.*
- Psychological forces *include all internal perceptual, cognitive, emotional, and personality factors that affect development.*
- Sociocultural forces *include interpersonal, societal, cultural, and ethnic factors that affect development.*
- Life-cycle forces *reflect differences in how the same event affects people of different ages.*

Each person is a product of a unique combination of these forces. No two individuals, even in the same family, experience these forces in the same way; even identical twins eventually have different friendship networks, partners, and occupations.

To see why each of these forces is important, let's imagine that you wanted to know how a mother decides whether to breast-feed her infant. You would need to consider a number of biologically based variables, such as the mother's general health and the quality and amount of milk she produces. You would also want to ask about the mother's beliefs and attitudes about the virtues of breast-feeding. You would want to know the influences of other people, such as the father, and what the mother's culture says about appropriate ways to feed infants. Additionally, you would want to know how old the mother is, because she might have been influenced by the beliefs of a certain period. Focusing on only one of these forces would give you an inadequate, distorted view of the mother's decision.

One useful way to organize the biological, psychological, and sociocultural forces on human development is with the biopsychosocial framework. As you can see in the figure at the top of page 9, the biopsychosocial framework emphasizes that human development is more than any one of the basic forces considered alone. Rather, each force interacts with the others to make up development. Let's look at the different elements of the biopsychosocial model in more detail.

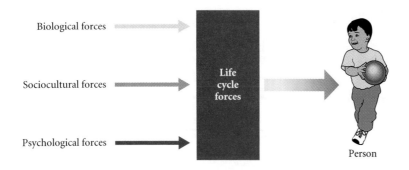

Biological forces

Sociocultural forces

Psychological forces

Life cycle forces

Person

Biological Forces

Did you ever wonder why members of the same family have different color eyes? Or why you don't seem to do as well on exams when you are not feeling well? Or how eating the right diet may help you live longer? Questions such as these highlight the important role that biological forces play in shaping the course of human development.

Biological forces include such diverse events as the sequence of prenatal development, brain maturation, puberty, menopause, facial wrinkling, and changes in the cardiovascular and other major body systems. Many of these biological forces are determined by our genetic code, which is discussed in Chapters 2, 3, 8, and 13. For example, looking at the children in the photo, you can see that they resemble their parents, which shows biological influences on development. But biological forces also include the effects of life-style factors, such as diet and exercise; these and other examples are explored in Chapters 2, 8, and 9.

As is true of all forces, some biological forces are experienced universally—either by all people or, in the case of reproductive changes, by all males or all females. *Forces like these, which affect people at a similar point in the life span, and have done so across generations, are termed* normative age-graded influences. One example of a normative age-graded influence is puberty, which occurs in early to mid-adolescence in virtually all people. Another is menopause, which occurs between the ages of 40 and 55 in most women. These normative age-graded influences create markers that are used to divide the life span into different segments.

Sometimes, though, forces act on only a specific generation. *Forces that only influence people in a certain generation at a particular point in historical time are termed* normative history-graded influences. One example of a normative history-graded biological influence is the worldwide flu epidemic in the years immediately after World War I. People who survived this epidemic had lifelong memories of seeing people die from what typically is a less serious illness.

Still other influences are rare, affecting only a handful of people. *When a force is experienced by only a few people, it is called a* nonnormative influence. For example, a progressive and fatal brain disease called kuru occurs only on certain islands in the South Pacific.

Collectively, biological forces can be viewed as providing the raw material necessary (in the case of genetics) and as setting the boundary conditions (in the case of one's general health) for development.

Psychological Forces

You probably have an intuitive understanding of psychological forces, because they are the ones used most often to describe the characteristics of a person. For example, think about how you respond when asked to describe yourself when you meet someone new. Most of us say that we have a nice personality and are intelligent, honest, self-confident, or something along those lines. Concepts like these reflect psychological forces.

In general, psychological forces are all the internal cognitive, emotional, personality, perceptual, and related factors that influence behavior. Psychological forces have received the most attention of the three main developmental forces. Much of what we discuss throughout the text reflects psychological forces. For example, we will see how the development of intelligence enables individuals to experience and think about their world in different ways. We'll also see how the emergence of self-esteem is related to the beliefs people have about their abilities, which in turn influence what they do.

Like biological forces, different psychological forces have different types of effects. Some, such as language, have normative age-graded influences; children around the world begin to acquire language during their second year of life, as discussed in Chapter 4. Other psychological forces, such as expertise in certain computer programs, may be specific to a particular generation. Still others, such as depression or other mental disorders, may affect only a relatively small number of people.

Collectively, psychological factors provide the things we notice most about what makes people the way they are, as well as the interesting variations that make us individuals.

Sociocultural Forces

People develop in the world, not in a vacuum. If we want to understand human development, we need to know how people and their environments interact and relate to each other. In other words, we need to view an individual's development as part of a much larger system, in which no part of the system can act without influencing all other aspects of the system. This larger system includes one's parents, children, and siblings as well as important individuals outside of the family, such as friends, teachers, and co-workers. The system also includes institutions that influence development, such as schools, television, and the workplace.

All of these people and institutions fit together to form a person's culture— the knowledge, attitudes, and behavior associated with a group of people. Culture can be linked to a particular country or people (e.g., French culture), to a specific point in time (e.g., popular culture of the 1990s), or to groups of individuals who maintain specific, identifiable cultural traditions (e.g., African Americans). Knowing the culture from which a person comes provides some general information about important influences that may appear throughout the life span. The United States, for example, includes many different ethnic groups, creating a diverse population that has a wide variety of experiences across the life span. By looking at human development in these different groups and in other groups around the world, we can understand how sociocultural forces influence human development.

As is the case with biological and psychological forces, many sociocultural forces influence all people at a particular age. A good example of such a normative age-graded influence is the fact that, throughout the United States, children begin kindergarten at approximately 5 years of age. Other sociocultural forces are specific to a particular generation: Growing up in the United States during the Great Depression is an example of such a normative history-graded influence. Finally, some sociocultural influences are nonnormative: A small percentage of American children, for instance, are educated at home rather than in school.

In trying to describe sociocultural influences on development, we confront a practical problem. Most investigators tend to study groups of people who are relatively easy to contact, and much of the research we describe in this text was conducted on middle-class European Americans. Accordingly, we must be careful *not* to assume that findings from this group necessarily apply to people in other groups. You may find yourself feeling frustrated at times, wondering whether a particular set of results obtained with one group is applicable to other groups as well. Indeed, there is a great need for research on different cultural groups. Perhaps, as a result of taking this course, you will help fill this need by becoming a developmental researcher yourself.

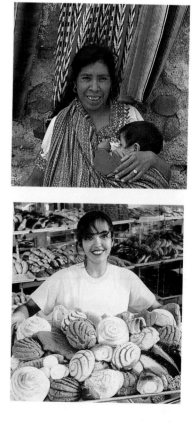

Another practical problem that we face is deciding the most appropriate term to describe each group. Terminology changes over time. For example, the terms *colored people, Negroes, black Americans,* and *African Americans* have all been used to describe Americans of African ancestry. In this book, we use the term *African American* because it emphasizes the unique cultural heritage of that group of people. Following the same line of reasoning, we use the terms *European American* (instead of *Caucasian* or *white*), *Native American* (instead of *Indian* or *American Indian*), *Asian American,* and *Hispanic American.*

These labels are not perfect. In some cases, they blur distinctions within ethnic groups. For example, the people in the photos are from Guatemala and Mexico, so we would describe their heritage as Hispanic. However, their cultural backgrounds vary on several important dimensions, so we should not view them as being from a homogenous group. Similarly, the term *European American* ignores differences between individuals of northern or southern European ancestry; the term *Asian American* blurs variations among people whose heritage is, for example, Japanese, Chinese, or Korean. Whenever researchers have identified the subgroups in their research sample, we will use the more specific terms in describing results. When we use the more general terms, you should remember that conclusions may not apply to all subgroups within the more general term.

The sociocultural forces in development provide most of the labels we use to identify people, whether referring to the kind of occupation a person has ("She's an engineer, and you know what *they're* like") or to a person's ethnicity or other demographic category. In sum, sociocultural forces provide the broader context or backdrop for development. In a real sense, they provide the stage upon which development gets played out.

The Forces Interact

So far, we've described biological, psychological, and sociocultural forces in the biopsychosocial framework as if they were independent of the others. But as we pointed out earlier in introducing the notion of the biopsychosocial framework, each shapes the others. Consider eating habits. When the authors of this text were growing up, a "red meat and potatoes" diet was typical. Based on dietary evidence of the day, such a diet was thought to be healthy. Subsequently, it became known that high-fat diets can lead to cardiovascular disease and some forms of cancer. (We will consider this in greater depth in Chapter 9.) Consequently, social pressures were brought to bear to change what people eat; advertising campaigns were begun; and restaurants began to indicate which menu items were low in fat. Thus, the biological forces of fat in the diet were influenced by the social forces of the times, whether in support of (or in opposition to) having beef every evening. Finally, as your authors became more educated about the whole issue of diets and their effects on health, the psychological forces of thinking and reasoning also influenced their choice of diets. (We must confess, however, that chocolate remains a passion for one of us!)

This example illustrates that no aspect of human development can be fully understood by examining only one or two of the forces. All three must be considered in interaction. In order to understand the effects of genetic variation, we may need to examine some specific aspect of behavior in a particular social context. Or to understand the effects of a sociocultural force such as poverty, we may need to look at how poverty affects people's health. In fact, we'll see later in this chapter that integration across the three major forces of the biopsychosocial framework is one criterion by which the adequacy of a developmental theory can be judged. Before we do that, however, we need to consider one more aspect of this framework: The point in life at which a specific combination of biological, psychological, and sociocultural forces operates matters a great deal.

Timing Is Everything: Life-Cycle Forces

Consider the following two situations. Jacqui, the 32-year-old woman in the photo below, has been happily married for 6 years. She and her husband have a steady income. After talking it over, they decide to start a family, and a month later, Jacqui learns she is pregnant. Jenny, the 14-year-old girl in the left photo, lives in the same neighborhood as Jacqui. She has been sexually active for about six months but is not in a stable relationship. After missing her period, Jenny took a pregnancy test and discovered that she is pregnant.

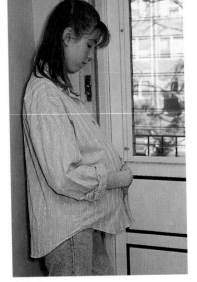

Despite the fact that both Jacqui and Jenny became pregnant, you probably would not conclude that the pregnancies had the exact same effect on them. Rather, you would probably conclude that the outcome would be affected by the other factors in each of their situations such as their age, financial situation, and extent of their social support systems. And you probably would be right.

The example illustrates another key fact in the process of human development: The same event can have different effects, depending on when it happens. Life-cycle forces refer to the fact that the meaning of any event depends on the person and the timing of the event. In the scenarios with Jacqui and Jenny, the same event—pregnancy—produces happiness and eager anticipation for one woman but anxiety and concern for the other.

? **THINK ABOUT IT**
The death of a spouse is another event that would have different effects based on when it happened in a person's life. Can you think of other events like these?

Jacqui and Jenny's different experiences show how life-cycle forces help shape the effects of the remaining three forces. One way to depict this influence is to show the biological, psychological, and sociocultural forces as a unified spiral. The spiral illustrates how a particular issue or event may recur, as indicated by the X's on the spiral, and how a person's accumulated experience, represented by the vertical arrow labeled "development," comes into play. For example, trust is an issue that is addressed throughout life (Erikson, 1982). From its beginnings as the trust infants have in their parents, represented by the lower "X" on the spiral, it develops into progressively more complex forms of trust over the life span for friends and for lovers, as Jacqui can attest and Jenny will ultimately learn. Each time a person revisits trust issues, he or she builds on past experiences in light of intervening development. This accumulated experience means that the person will deal with trust in a new way and that trust is shown in different ways across the life span.

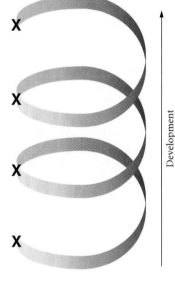

By combining the four developmental forces, we can take a view of human development that encompasses the life span, appreciating the unique aspects of each phase of life. Indeed, the remainder of the book is based on this combination.

TEST YOURSELF

1. The nature-nurture issue involves the degree to which _____ and the environment influence human development.

2. Azar remarked that her 14-year-old son is incredibly shy and has been ever since he was a little baby. This illustrates the _____ of development.

3. _____ forces include genetic and health factors.

4. How does the biopsychosocial framework provide insight into the recurring issues of development (nature-nurture, continuity-discontinuity, universal–context-specific)?

Answers: (1) genetics, (2) continuity, (3) Biological

DEVELOPMENTAL THEORIES

Developmental Theories

Psychodynamic Theory

Learning Theory

Cognitive-Developmental Theory

The Ecological and Systems Approach

Life-Span and Life-Cycle Theories

The Big Picture

Learning Objectives

- **How do psychodynamic theories account for development?**
- **What is the focus of learning theories of development?**
- **How do cognitive-developmental theories explain changes in thinking?**
- **What are the main points in the ecological and systems approach?**
- **What are the major tenets of life-span and life-cycle theories?**

*M*ARCUS *has just graduated from high school, first in his class. For his proud mother, Betty, this was a time to reflect on her son's past and ponder his future. Marcus has always been a happy, easygoing child—a joy to rear. And he's constantly been interested in learning. Betty wonders why he is so perpetually good-natured and so curious. If she knew the secret, she laughed, she could write a best-selling book and be a guest on Oprah!*

To answer Betty's questions about her son's growth, developmental researchers would provide a theory of his development. Unfortunately, for many people, the word *theory* means "boring." But that's not true. If you want to understand human development, theories are essential because they provide the "why's" for development. What is a theory? *In human development, a* theory *is an organized set of ideas that is designed to explain development.* For example, suppose friends of yours have a baby who cries often. You could imagine several explanations for her crying. Maybe the baby cries because she's hungry; maybe she cries to get her parents to hold her; maybe she cries because she's simply a cranky, unhappy baby. Each of these explanations is a very simple theory: It tries to explain why the baby cries so much. Of course, actual sophisticated theories in human development are much more complicated, but the purpose is the same—to explain behavior and development.

Theories lead to predictions that we can test in research; in the process, the theory is supported or not. Think about the different explanations for the crying baby. Each one leads to unique predictions. If, for example, the baby is crying because she's hungry, we predict that feeding her more often should stop the crying. When results of research match the predictions, this supports the theory. When results differ from the predictions, this shows that the theory is incorrect and needs to be revised.

Perhaps now you see why theories are essential for human development research: They are the source for predictions for research, which often lead to changes in the theories. These revised theories then provide the basis for new predictions, which lead to new research, and the cycle continues.

Many theories guide research and thinking about human development. Just as lumber, bricks, pipes, and wires can be used to build an incredible variety of houses, the basic elements of the biopsychosocial framework have been assembled to form an incredible assortment of theories. Some theories attempt to explain a range of behaviors, whereas others focus on specific aspects. Additionally, some theories only consider development at particular points in the life span, while others take a more holistic view. No modern theories of human development are truly comprehensive in attempting to cover all aspects of human behavior throughout the life span (Cavanaugh, 1981), so we will draw upon many different theories throughout the book.

Some of these theories share many ideas and assumptions about human development but differ in their details. These theories are often grouped together to form a theoretical perspective. The table lists five perspectives that guide contemporary thinking and research about development and describes the key aspects of each perspective. It also gives examples of theories, their main points, what aspects of the biopsychosocial framework they emphasize, and their positions on the recurring developmental issues of nature-nurture, continuity-discontinuity, and universal versus context-specific development.

THEORETICAL PERSPECTIVES ON HUMAN DEVELOPMENT

Perspective	Examples	Main Ideas	Emphases in Biopsychosocial Framework	Positions on Developmental Issues
Psychodynamic	Erikson's psychosocial theory	Personality develops through sequence of stages	Psychological, social, and life-cycle forces crucial; less emphasis on biological	Nature-nurture interaction, discontinuity, universal sequence but individual differences in rate
Learning	Behaviorism (Watson, Skinner) Social learning theory (Bandura)	Environment controls behavior. People learn through modeling and observing	In all theories, some emphasis on biological and psychological, major focus on social, little recognition of life cycle	In all theories, strongly nurture, continuity, and universal principles of learning
Cognitive	Piaget's theory (and extensions) Kohlberg's moral reasoning theory	For Piaget and Kohlberg, thinking develops in a sequence of stages	For Piaget and Kohlberg, main emphasis on biological and social forces, less on psychological, little on life cycle	For Piaget and Kohlberg, strongly nature, discontinuity, and universal sequence of stages
	Information-processing theory	Thought develops by increases in efficiency at handling information	Emphasis on biological and psychological, less on social and life cycle	Nature-nurture interaction, continuity, individual differences in universal structures
Ecological and Systems	Bronfenbrenner's theory	Developing person embedded in a series of interacting systems	Low emphasis on biological, moderate on psychological and life cycle, heavy on social	Nature-nurture interaction, continuity, context-specific
	Competence–environmental press (Lawton and Nahemow)	Adaptation is optimal when ability and demands are in balance	Strong emphasis on biological, psychological, and social, moderate on life cycle	Nature-nurture interaction, continuity, context-specific
Life Span and Life Cycle	Riley's life-span perspective	Development is multiply determined	Strong emphasis on the interaction of all four forces; cannot consider any in isolation	Nature-nurture interaction, continuity and discontinuity, context-specific
	Family life-cycle theory (Duvall)	Families go through series of stages	Strong emphasis on all except biological	Nature-nurture interaction, continuity and discontinuity, universal series of stages

In the next few pages, we'll introduce the five perspectives briefly. As we describe each of them, keep in mind that they were created to provide broad frameworks for understanding development and stimulating insightful research questions.

PSYCHODYNAMIC THEORY

Psychodynamic theories *propose that human behavior is largely governed by motives and drives that are internal and often unconscious.* These hidden forces influence all aspects of our behavior, thought, and personality, essentially shaping every part of our lives. Psychodynamic theories postulate that development occurs in a sequence of universal stages. This perspective underlies the oldest of the modern theories of human development, tracing its roots to Freud's work in the late 19th and early 20th centuries. It also led to the development of the first comprehensive life-span view, Erik Erikson's psychosocial theory.

Freud's Theory

Psychodynamic theory argues that we are driven by unconscious motives and emotions, shaped by experiences very early in life. Historically, Sigmund Freud

(1856–1939) originated this view. He was convinced that people mature psychologically according to principles that apply universally, but also that each individual personality is shaped by experience in a social context. Freud insisted that early experiences establish patterns that endure through the entire life span.

Freud's psychoanalytic theory of personality focuses on three components: the id, ego, and superego. *The* id, *a reservoir of primitive drives, is present at birth; it is the force that presses for immediate gratification of bodily needs and wants. The* ego *is the practical, rational component of personality.* The ego begins to emerge during the first year of life, in response to the fact that the infant cannot always have what it wants. An example of the emerging ego is the child's learning other means for communicating his or her needs when crying does not work. *Between the third and fourth years of life, the* superego *or "moral agent" of personality develops as the child begins to incorporate adult standards of right and wrong.*

Freud also proposed that development occurs in universal stages that do not vary in sequence. These stages are largely determined by an innate tendency to reduce tension and maximize pleasure. Each stage is given its unique character by the development of sensitivity in a particular part of the body or *erogenous zone*—that is, an area that is particularly sensitive to erotic stimulation—at a particular time in the developmental sequence. Freud characterized these stages as *psychosexual.* In his theory, development results from successively focusing on, and reducing tension in, the erogenous zones that predominate at different times in life.

Freud believed that development proceeds best when children's psychosexual needs at each stage, which are summarized in the table at the top of page 17, are met but not exceeded. Children whose needs are not met adequately become frustrated and reluctant to move to other, more mature forms of stimulation. If children find one source of stimulation *too* satisfying, they see little need to progress to more advanced stages. In Freud's view, parents have the difficult task of satisfying children's needs without indulging them.

FREUD'S STAGES OF PSYCHOSEXUAL DEVELOPMENT

Stage	Ages	Description
Oral	0–1 year	Psychosexual needs are gratified orally (by sucking), fostering attachment to the mother.
Anal	1–3 years	Youngsters are urged to control their bladder and bowels, creating a conflict between biological urges and social demands for control.
Phallic	3–6 years	Psychosexual energy is directed to the genitals, prompting desires for the opposite-sex parent. Fear of retaliation from the same-sex parent causes children to identify with that parent and vicariously satisfy attraction to the opposite-sex parent.
Latency	6–12 years	A "quiet time" in which psychosexual energy is channeled into socially acceptable activities such as schoolwork and play with same-sex peers.
Genital	12 years and older	A period of sexual maturation in which psychosexual needs are directed toward heterosexual relationships.

Erikson's Theory

In Freud's view, development is largely complete by adolescence. In contrast, one of Freud's students, Erik Erikson (1902–1994) believed that development continues throughout life. Erikson took the foundation laid by Freud and extended it through adulthood and into late life.

In his psychosocial theory, *Erikson proposed that personality development is determined by the interaction of an internal maturational plan and external societal demands.* He proposed that the life cycle is composed of eight stages and that the order of the stages is biologically fixed. The complete theory included the eight stages that are shown in the table at the top of page 18. You can see that the name of each stage reflects the challenge that people face at a particular age. For example, the challenge for young adults is to become involved in a loving relationship. Challenges are met through a combination of both inner psychological and outer social influences. When challenges are met successfully, people are well prepared to meet the challenge of the next stage.

The sequence of stages in Erikson's theory is based on the epigenetic principle, *which means that each psychosocial strength has its own special time of ascendancy or period of particular importance.* The eight stages represent the order of this ascendancy. Because the stages extend across the whole life span, it takes a lifetime to acquire all of the psychosocial strengths. Moreover, Erikson realizes that present and future behavior must have its roots in the past, because later stages are built on the foundation laid in previous ones.

We examine each of Erikson's stages in more detail later in the book. In general, we can view them as a cycle that repeats (Logan, 1986): The first cycle goes from basic trust vs. mistrust through identity vs. identity confusion; the second cycle goes from intimacy vs. isolation through integrity vs. despair. In this view, the primary developmental progression is trust → achievement → wholeness. Throughout life, we first establish that we can trust others and ourselves, represented by basic trust vs. mistrust in the first cycle. In the second

THE EIGHT STAGES OF PSYCHOSOCIAL DEVELOPMENT IN ERIKSON'S THEORY

Psychosocial Stage	Age	Challenge
Basic trust vs. mistrust	Birth to 1 year	To develop a sense that the world is safe, a "good place"
Autonomy vs. shame and doubt	1–3 years	To realize that one is an independent person who can make decisions
Initiative vs. guilt	3–6 years	To develop the ability to try new things and to handle failure
Industry vs. inferiority	6 years–adolescence	To learn basic skills and to work with others
Identity vs. identity confusion	Adolescence	To develop a lasting, integrated sense of self
Intimacy vs. isolation	Young adulthood	To commit to another in a loving relationship
Generativity vs. stagnation	Middle adulthood	To contribute to younger people, through child rearing, child care, or other productive work
Integrity vs. despair	Late life	To view one's life as satisfactory and worth living

? THINK ABOUT IT
How do Erikson's eight stages of psychosocial development resemble Freud's four stages of psychosexual development? How do they differ?

cycle, we search for a person whom we can trust enough to establish a close relationship, represented by intimacy vs. isolation. In achievement, we have a need to create something of our own, seen in the first cycle in the initiative vs. guilt and industry vs. inferiority stages, and in the second cycle in the generativity vs. stagnation stage. Finally, we seek to answer the question of who we are, which in the first cycle is the identity vs. identity confusion stage, and in the second cycle the integrity vs. despair stage. From Erikson's perspective, there are only a few issues that face us in life, and we periodically return to them in order to reach higher resolutions of them. This return to certain key issues is a good example of the life-cycle forces we discussed earlier (pages 12–13).

Whether we call them challenges, crises, or conflicts, the psychodynamic perspective emphasizes that the trek to adulthood is difficult because the path is strewn with obstacles. Outcomes of development reflect the manner and ease with which children surmount life's barriers. When children overcome early obstacles easily, they are better able to handle the later ones. A psychodynamic theorist would tell Betty that her son's cheerful disposition and his academic record suggest that he has handled life's early obstacles well, which is a good sign for his future development.

LEARNING THEORY

In contrast to psychodynamic theory, learning theory concentrates on how learning influences a person's behavior. This perspective emphasizes the role of experience, emphasizing whether a person's behavior is rewarded or punished. This perspective also emphasizes that people learn from watching others around them. Two influential theories in this perspective are behaviorism and social learning theory.

Behaviorism

At about the same time in the early 20th century that psychodynamic theory was attracting increased attention, John Watson (1878–1958) was among the first psychologists to champion the English philosopher John Locke's view that the infant's mind is a blank slate on which experience writes. Watson argued that learning determines what children will be. He assumed that with the correct techniques, anything could be learned, by almost anyone. In other words, in Watson's view, experience was just about all that mattered in determining the course of development.

Watson did little research to support his claims; B. F. Skinner (1904–1990) filled this gap. *Skinner studied* operant conditioning, *in which the consequences of a behavior determine whether a behavior is repeated in the future.* Skinner showed that two kinds of consequences were especially influential. *A* reinforcement *is a consequence that increases the future likelihood of the behavior that it follows.* Positive reinforcement consists of giving a reward like chocolate, gold stars, or pay checks to increase the likelihood of a previous behavior. A father who wants to encourage his daughter to help with chores may reinforce her with praise, food treats, or money whenever she cleans her room. Negative reinforcement consists of rewarding people by taking away unpleasant things. The same father could use negative reinforcement by saying that whenever his daughter cleans her room she doesn't have to wash the dishes or fold laundry.

A punishment *is a consequence that decreases the future likelihood of the behavior that it follows.* Punishment suppresses a behavior by either adding something aversive or by withholding a pleasant event. Should the daughter fail to clean her room, the father may punish her by spanking (adding something aversive) or by not allowing her to watch television (withholding a pleasant event).

Skinner's research was done primarily with animals, but human development researchers soon showed that the principles of operant conditioning could be extended readily to people, too (Baer & Wolf, 1968). Applied properly, reinforcement and punishment are indeed powerful influences on children, adolescents, and adults.

Social Learning Theory

Researchers discovered that people sometimes learn in ways that are not readily explained by operant conditioning. The most important of these is that people sometimes learn without reinforcement or punishment. *People learn much by simply watching those around them, which is known as* imitation *or* observational learning. Imitation is occurring when one toddler throws a toy after seeing a peer do so or when a school-age child offers to help an older adult carry groceries because she's seen her parents do the same.

Perhaps imitation makes you think of "monkey-see, monkey-do," in which people simply mimic what they see. Early investigators had this view, too, but research quickly showed that this was wrong. People do not always imitate what they see around them. People are more likely to imitate if the person they see is popular, smart, or talented. They're also more likely to imitate when the behavior they see is rewarded than when it is punished. Findings like these imply that imitation is more complex than sheer mimicry. People are not mechanically copying what they see and hear; instead, they look to others for information about appropriate behavior. When popular, smart peers are reinforced for behaving in a particular way, it makes sense to imitate them.

Albert Bandura (1918–) based his social cognitive theory *on this more complex view of reward, punishment, and imitation.* Bandura's theory is "cognitive" because he believes that people actively try to understand what goes on in their world; the theory is "social" because, along with reinforcement and punishment, what other people do is an important source of information about the world.

Bandura also argues that experience gives people a sense of self-efficacy, *which refers to people's beliefs about their own abilities and talents.* Self-efficacy beliefs help to determine when people will imitate others. A child who sees herself as athletically untalented, for example, will not try to imitate Michael Jordan dunking a basketball, despite the fact that he is obviously talented and popular. Thus, whether people will imitate others depends on who the other person is, whether that person's behavior is rewarded, and the person's beliefs about his or her own talents.

Bandura's social cognitive theory is a far cry from Skinner's operant conditioning. The operant conditioned person who responds mechanically to reinforcement and punishment has been replaced by the social cognitive person who actively interprets these and other events. Nevertheless, Skinner, Bandura, and all learning theorists share the view that experience propels people along their developmental journeys. They would tell Betty that she can thank experience for making Marcus both happy and successful academically.

COGNITIVE-DEVELOPMENTAL THEORY

Still another way to approach development is to focus on thought processes and the construction of knowledge. In cognitive-developmental theory, the key is how people think and how thinking changes over time. Two distinct

approaches have developed. One approach postulates that thinking develops in a universal sequence of stages; Piaget's theory of cognitive development (and its recent extensions) and Kohlberg's theory of moral reasoning are two examples. The other approach proposes that people process information much like computers, becoming more efficient over much of the life span; information-processing theory is an example of this view.

Piaget's Theory

The cognitive-developmental perspective focuses on how children construct knowledge and how their constructions change over time. Jean Piaget (1896–1980), who was the most influential developmental psychologist of the 20th century, proposed the best known of these theories. Piaget believed that children naturally try to make sense of their world. Throughout infancy, childhood, and adolescence, youngsters want to understand the workings of both the physical and the social world. For example, infants want to know about objects: "What happens when I push this toy off the table?" And they want to know about people: "Who is this person who feeds and cares for me?"

Piaget argued that in their efforts to comprehend their world, children act like scientists in creating theories about the physical and social worlds. They try to weave all that they know about objects and people into a complete theory. Children's theories are tested daily by experience because their theories lead them to expect certain things to happen. As with real scientific theories, when the predicted events do occur, a child's belief in her theory grows stronger. When the predicted events do not occur, the child must revise her theory. For example, an infant's theory of objects might include the idea that "Toys pushed off the table fall to the floor." If the infant pushes some other object—a plate or an article of clothing—she will find that it, too, falls to the floor and can make the theory more general: "Objects pushed off the table fall to the floor."

Piaget also believed that at a few critical points in development, children begin to construct knowledge in new ways. When this happens, they revise their theories radically. These changes are so fundamental that the revised theory is, in many respects, a brand-new theory. Piaget claimed that these changes occurred three times in development: once at about age 2 years, a second time at about age 7, and a third time just before adolescence. These changes mean that children go through four distinct stages in cognitive development. Each stage represents a fundamental change in how children understand and organize their environment, and each stage is characterized by more sophisticated types of reasoning. For example, the sensorimotor stage begins at birth and lasts until about 2 years of age. As the name implies, sensorimotor thinking refers to an infant's constructing knowledge through sensory and motor skills. This stage and the three later stages are shown in the table.

? THINK ABOUT IT
Try to use the basic ideas of operant conditioning (page 19) to explain how children create theories of the physical and social worlds.

PIAGET'S FOUR STAGES OF COGNITIVE DEVELOPMENT

Stage	Approximate Age	Characteristics
Sensorimotor	Birth to 2 years	Infant's knowledge of the world is based on senses and motor skills. By the end of the period, uses mental representations.
Preoperational thought	2–6 years	Child learns how to use symbols such as words and numbers to represent aspects of the world, but relates to the world only through his or her perspective.
Concrete operational thought	7 years to early adolescence	Child understands and applies logical operations to experiences provided they are focused on the here and now.
Formal operational thought	Adolescence and beyond	Adolescent or adult thinks abstractly, deals with hypothetical situations, and speculates about what may be possible.

Piaget's theory has had an enormous influence on how developmentalists and practitioners think about cognitive development. The theory has been applied in many ways—from the creation of discovery learning toys for children to the ways teachers plan lessons. However, his theory has also been criticized. Some say that Piaget underestimated the abilities of infants and young children. Also, the universality of his sequence of stages is not entirely supported by evidence from different cultures. More recently, Piaget's theory has been extended to include important cognitive changes in adulthood. We consider these issues in more detail in Chapters 4, 6, and 9.

Kohlberg's Theory

Because Piaget's theory attempts to tie together maturation and experience on the one hand and cognitive and social development on the other, it has inspired developmentalists with a wide variety of interests. One of the most influential of these was Lawrence Kohlberg, who built his theory of moral reasoning on the foundation of Piaget's theory of overall cognitive development.

As we'll see in detail in Chapter 9, Kohlberg described a sequence of fixed stages that reflect the different ways people think about moral dilemmas. Kohlberg's theory is an excellent example of how a general theory of development, Piaget's theory, can be focused to deal with the more circumscribed issue of moral reasoning. Kohlberg's stages correspond fairly well to Piaget's stages, but they involve levels of thinking beyond Piaget's final stage. In this respect, Kohlberg's theory constitutes an extension of Piaget's work.

Information-Processing Theory

Not all cognitive-developmental theorists view development as a sequence of stages. Information-processing theorists, for example, draw heavily on how computers work to explain thinking and how it develops through childhood and adolescence. *Just as computers consist of both hardware (disk drives, random-access memory, and central processing unit) and software (the programs we use),* information-processing theory *proposes that human cognition consists of mental hardware and mental software.* Mental hardware refers to cognitive structures, including different memories where information is stored. Mental software includes organized sets of cognitive processes that allow children to complete specific tasks, such as reading a sentence, playing a video game, or hitting a baseball. For example, an information-processing psychologist would say that, for the girl in the photo to do well on an exam, she must encode the information as she studies, store it in memory, then retrieve the necessary information during the test.

How do information-processing psychologists explain developmental changes in thinking? To answer this question, think about improvements in personal computers. Today's personal computers can accomplish much more than computers built just a few years ago. Why? Because today's computers have better hardware (e.g., more memory and a faster central processing unit) and because they have more sophisticated software that takes advantage of the better hardware. Like modern computers, older children and adolescents have better hardware and better software than younger children, who are more like last year's out-of-date model. For example, older children typically solve math word problems better than younger children because they have greater memory capacity to store the facts in the problem and because their methods for performing arithmetic operations are more efficient.

Some researchers also point to deterioration of the mental hardware, along with declines in the mental software, as explanations of cognitive aging. We will see in Chapter 13, for example, that normal aging brings with it significant changes in people's ability to process information.

For Piaget, Kohlberg, and information-processing theorists, children's thinking becomes more sophisticated as they develop. Piaget and Kohlberg explain this change as resulting from the more sophisticated knowledge that children construct from more sophisticated thinking; information-processing psychologists attribute it to more sophisticated mental hardware and mental software. None of these theorists would have much to say to Betty about Marcus's good nature. As to his academic success, Piaget and Kohlberg would explain that all children naturally want to understand their worlds; Marcus is simply unusually skilled in this regard. An information-processing psychologist would point to superior hardware and superior software as the keys to his academic success.

THE ECOLOGICAL AND SYSTEMS APPROACH

Most developmentalists agree that the environment is an important force in many aspects of development. However, only ecological theories have focused on the complexities of environments and their links to development. *In ecological theory, which gets its name from the branch of biology dealing with the relation of living things to their environment and to one another, human development is inseparable from the environmental contexts in which a person develops.* The ecological approach is broad; it proposes that all aspects of development are interconnected, much like the threads of a spider's web are intertwined. Interconnectedness means that no aspect of development can be isolated from others and understood independently. An ecological theorist would emphasize that, if we want to understand why the adolescents in the photo behave as they do, we need to consider the many different systems that influence them, including parents, peers, teachers, television, the neighborhood, and social policy.

We will consider two examples of the ecological and systems approach: Bronfenbrenner's theory and the competence–environmental press framework.

Bronfenbrenner's Theory

The best-known proponent of the ecological approach is Urie Bronfenbrenner (1979, 1989, 1995), who proposes that the developing child is embedded in a series of complex and interactive systems. Bronfenbrenner divides the environment into the four levels shown in the diagram at the top of page 24: the microsystem, the mesosystem, the exosystem, and the macrosystem. *At any point in life, the* microsystem *consists of the people and objects in an individual's immediate environment.* These are the people closest to a child, such as parents or siblings. Some children may have more than one microsystem; for example, a young child might have the microsystems of the family and of the day care setting. As you can imagine, microsystems strongly influence development.

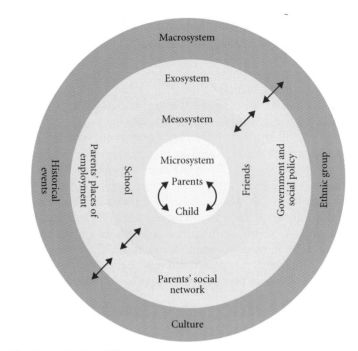

Adapted from Lopp and Krakow, 1982.

Microsystems themselves are connected to create the mesosystem. The meso-system provides connections across microsystems, because what happens in one microsystem is likely to influence others. Perhaps you've found that if you have a stressful day at work or school, you're often grouchy at home. This indicates that your mesosystem is alive and well; your microsystems of home and work are interconnected emotionally for you.

The exosystem *refers to social settings that a person may not experience first-hand but that still influence development.* For example, a mother may pay more attention to her child when her work situation is going well, and less attention when she's under a great deal of work-related stress. Although the influence of the exosystem is at least secondhand, its effects on the developing child can be quite strong.

The broadest environmental context is the macrosystem, *the subcultures and cultures in which the microsystem, mesosystem, and exosystem are embedded.* A mother, her workplace, her child, and the child's school are part of a larger cultural setting, such as Asian Americans living in Southern California or Italian Americans living in large cities on the East Coast. Members of these cultural groups share a common identity, a common heritage, and common values. The macrosystem evolves over time; what is true about a particular culture today may or may not have been true in the past and may or may not be true in the future. Thus, each successive generation of children may develop in a unique macrosystem.

Competence–Environmental Press Theory

A second, less complex approach that also emphasizes the interaction of individuals with their environment is Lawton and Nahemow's (1973) competence–environmental press theory. As we will see in greater detail in Chapter 14, this theory was originally proposed to account for the ways in which older adults function in their environment. Basically, according to the theory, how well people adapt depends on the match between their competence, or abilities, and the environmental press, or the demands put on them by the environment.

This notion of "best match" or "best fit" leading to adaptation could be extended across the life span. For example, how well a child's social skills match her peer group's demands could account for whether she will be accepted by the peer group or not. As with Bronfenbrenner's theory, competence–environmental press theory emphasizes that in order to understand people's functioning, it is essential to understand the systems in which they live.

Ecological theorists would agree with learning theorists in telling Betty that the environment has been pivotal in her son's amiable disposition and his academic achievements. However, the ecological theorist would insist that environment means much more than the reinforcements, punishments, and observations that are central to learning theory. The ecological theorist would emphasize the different levels of environmental influence on Marcus. Perhaps Betty's ability to balance home and work so skillfully (which meant that she was usually in a good mood herself) contributed positively to Marcus's development as did Betty's membership in a cultural group that emphasized the value of doing well in school.

LIFE-SPAN AND LIFE-CYCLE THEORIES

One criticism of most of the theories of human development we have considered thus far is that they pay little or no specific attention to the adult years of the life span. Historically, adulthood was downplayed due to the belief that it was a time when abilities had reached a plateau (rather than continuing to develop) and that adulthood was followed by inevitable decline in old age. However, the field of adult development and aging has evolved greatly since the late 1940s. As a result, new theoretical perspectives emphasize the importance of viewing human development as a lifelong process. Life-span and life-cycle theories view development in terms of where a person has been and where he or she is heading.

Life-Span Perspective

According to the life-span perspective, *human development is multiply determined and cannot be understood within the scope of a single framework.* Matilda Riley, the person most responsible for developing the life-span perspective, insists that human development must be viewed from the biopsychosocial framework. The basic premises of the life-span perspective, in which aging is viewed in the context of the rest of the life span, are as follows (Riley, 1979):

- Aging is a lifelong process of growing up and growing old, beginning with conception and ending with death. No single period of a person's life (such as childhood, adolescence, or middle age) can be understood apart from its origins and its consequences. To understand a specific period, we must know what came before and what comes after.

- How one's life is played out is affected by social, environmental, and historical change. Thus, the experiences of one generation may not be the same as those of another.

- New patterns of development can cause social change. For example, the realization over the past few decades that severe physical punishment harms psychological development resulted in the passage of laws restricting parents' rights to use this form of punishment. Thus, not only does social change influence people's development, but patterns of development influence society.

This perspective emphasizes that people continue to develop and change throughout their lives (Brim & Kagan, 1980). For example, the older adult in

the photo is furthering her development by returning to college. From this perspective, development involves the processes necessary to reach a person's potential in any domain, such as physical prowess, intellectual abilities, or social skills.

The life-span perspective is important because it argues for a holistic view of development by explicitly incorporating the biopsychosocial framework. In this holistic view, behaviors are *emergent*—that is, they cannot be understood or predicted by examining only their constituent parts. One cannot predict what a 67-year-old person will be like by only knowing what she was like in the past, or by breaking her behavior down into smaller units such as cognitive or personality components. Rather, some aspects of behavior will be consistent, whereas others will be new, reflecting discontinuities in development. The life-span perspective views nature and nurture as interactive. Individual differences in development are the rule; thus, development is context-specific.

Family Life-Cycle Theory

A key to the life-span perspective is knowing when certain events occur during life. This aspect emphasizes the importance of the life-cycle force in the biopsychosocial framework. This focus has led some researchers to develop life-cycle theories of development. One example of these theories, which we explore in more detail in Chapter 10, is Duvall's (1977) family life-cycle theory. This theory postulates that families go through a universal series of changes related to the ages of the children, not to the ages of the parents. Although each stage has its own characteristics, which indicates discontinuous development, families also show certain consistencies in all the stages in terms of how they deal with situations. This theory maintains that family development is multiply determined and that inherited abilities and experience interact to shape behavior.

Overall, life-span and life-cycle theories have greatly enhanced the general body of developmental theory by drawing attention to the role of aging in the broader context of human development. These theories have played a major role in conceptualizing adulthood and have greatly influenced the research we consider in Chapters 9–14. And life-span and life-cycle theorists would tell Betty that Marcus will continue to develop throughout his adult years, and that this developmental journey will be influenced by biopsychosocial forces, including his own family.

THE BIG PICTURE

Each of the theories provides ways of explaining how the biological, psychological, sociocultural, and life-cycle forces create human development. But because no single theory provides a complete explanation of all aspects of development, we must rely on the biopsychosocial framework to help piece together an account based on many different theories. Throughout the remainder of this text, you will read about many theories that differ in focus and in scope. To help you understand them better, each theory will be introduced in the context of the issues that it addresses.

Because one of the criteria for a theory is that it be testable, developmentalists have adopted certain methods to help accomplish this. The next section provides an overview of the methods by which developmentalists conduct research and test their theories.

1. _____ organize knowledge in order to provide testable explanations of human behaviors and the ways in which they change over time.

2. The _____ perspective proposes that people are governed by unconscious motives.

3. According to social cognitive theory, people learn from reinforcements, punishments, and through _____ .

4. Piaget's theory, Kohlberg's theory, and _____ theory are examples of the cognitive-developmental perspective.

5. According to Bronfenbrenner, development occurs in the context of the _____ , mesosystem, exosystem, and macrosystem.

6. A belief that understanding any given point in development requires knowing where a person has been and where the person is going is fundamental to the _____ perspective.

7. How are the psychodynamic perspective and Piaget's theory similar? How are they different?

Answers: (1) Theories, (2) psychodynamic, (3) observing others, (4) information-processing, (5) microsystem, (6) life-span and life-cycle

DOING DEVELOPMENTAL RESEARCH

Learning Objectives

- **How do scientists measure topics of interest in studying children's development?**

- **What general research designs are used in human development research? What designs are unique to human development research?**

- **What ethical procedures must researchers follow?**

Doing Developmental Research

Measurement in Human Development Research

General Designs for Research

Designs for Studying Development

Conducting Research Ethically

Communicating Research Results

*L*EAH AND JOAN *are both mothers of 10-year-old boys. Their sons have many friends, but the basis for the friendships is not obvious to the mothers. Leah believes that "opposites attract"—children form friendships with peers who have complementary interests and abilities. Joan doubts this; her son seems to seek out other boys who are near clones of himself in terms of interests and abilities.*

Suppose that Leah and Joan know that you're taking a course in human development, so they ask you to settle their argument. Leah believes that complementary children are more often friends, whereas Joan believes that similar children are more often friends. You know that research could show whose ideas are supported under which circumstances, but how? In fact, human development researchers must make several important decisions as they prepare to study a topic. They need to decide how to measure the topic of interest; they must design their study; they must choose a method for studying development; and they must decide whether their plan respects the rights of the individuals who would participate in the research.

Human development researchers do not always stick to this sequence of steps. For example, often researchers will consider the rights of research participants as they make the other decisions, perhaps rejecting a measurement procedure because it violates the rights of participants. Nevertheless, for simplicity, we will use this sequence as we describe each of the steps in doing developmental research.

MEASUREMENT IN HUMAN DEVELOPMENT RESEARCH

Research usually begins by deciding how to measure the topic or behavior of interest. For example, the first step toward answering Leah and Joan's question about friendships would be to decide how to measure friendships.

Human development researchers typically use one of three approaches: observing systematically, using tasks to sample behavior, and asking people for self reports.

Systematic Observation

As the name implies, systematic observation *involves watching people and carefully recording what they do or say.* Two forms of systematic observation are common. *In* naturalistic observation, *people are observed as they behave spontaneously in some real-life situation.* Of course, researchers can't keep track of everything that someone does, so beforehand they must decide what variables to record. For example, researchers studying friendship might decide to observe children at the start of the first year in a middle school (chosen because many children will be making new friends at this time). They could decide to record where children sit in the lunchroom and to record who talks to whom.

Structured observations *differ from naturalistic observations in that the researcher creates a setting that is particularly likely to elicit the behavior of interest.* Structured observations are particularly useful for studying behaviors that are difficult to observe naturally. Some phenomena occur rarely, such as emergencies. An investigator relying upon natural observations to study people's responses to emergencies wouldn't make much progress with naturalistic observation because, by definition, emergencies don't occur at predetermined times and locations. However, using a structured observation, an investigator might stage an emergency—perhaps by simulating an accident with the cooperation of authorities—to observe other people's responses.

Other behaviors are difficult for researchers to observe because they occur in private settings, not public ones. For example, much interaction between friends takes place at home, where it would be difficult for investigators to observe unobtrusively. However, friends could be asked to come to the researcher's laboratory, which might be furnished to resemble a family room in a typical house. Friends would then be asked to perform some activity typical of friends, such as discussing a problem together or deciding what movie to see. The researchers would then observe their activity from another room, through a one-way mirror, or by videotaping them.

Structured observations are valuable in allowing researchers to observe behavior(s) that would otherwise be difficult to study. However, investigators using this approach must be careful that the settings they create do not disturb the behavior of interest. For example, observing friends as they discuss a problem in a mock family room has many artificial aspects to it: The friends are not in their own homes, they were told in general terms what to do, and they know they're being observed. Any or all of these factors may cause friends to behave differently than they would in the real world. This issue relates to the validity of the research. For example, are observations of friends in a mock family room telling us about friends' interactions as they occur naturally? If they are, then they represent a valid measure of people's behavior. Investigators must take great care to document the validity of their measures.

Sampling Behavior with Tasks

When investigators can't observe a behavior directly, another popular alternative is to create tasks that are thought to sample the behavior of interest. One task often used to measure older adults' memory is digit span: Adults listen as a sequence of digits is presented aloud. After the last digit is presented, they try to repeat the digits in order. Another example is shown in the diagram. The child has been asked to look at the photographs and point to the face that looks happy. A child's answers on this sort of task are useful in determining children's ability to recognize emotions.

This approach is popular with human development researchers, primarily because it is so convenient. The main problem with this approach is validity: Does the task provide a realistic sample of the behavior of interest? For example, asking children to judge emotions from photographs may not be valid because it underestimates what they do in real life. Can you think of reasons why this might be the case? We mention several reasons on page 38, just after Test Yourself.

Self Reports

The last approach, self reports, is a special case of using tasks to measure people's behavior. Self reports *are simply people's answers to questions about the topic of interest.* When questions are posed in written form, the verbal report is a questionnaire; when questions are posed orally, the verbal report is an interview. In either format, questions are created that probe different aspects of the topic of interest. For example, if you believe that children are more often friends when they have interests in common, then you might tell your research participants the following:

> Tom and Dave just met each other at school. Tom likes to read, plays the clarinet in the school orchestra, and is not interested in sports; Dave likes to watch videos on MTV, tinkers with his car, and is a star on the football team. Do you think Tom and Dave will become friends?

? THINK ABOUT IT
If you were studying middle-aged adults caring for their aging parents, what would be the advantages of systematic observation, sampling behavior with tasks, and self reports?

The participants would then decide, perhaps using a rating scale, whether the boys are likely to become friends.

Self reports are useful because they can lead directly to information on the topic of interest. They are also relatively convenient, particularly when they can be administered to groups of subjects. However, self reports are not always valid measures of people's behavior because answers are sometimes inaccurate. Why? When asked about past events, people may not remember them accurately. For example, an older adult asked about adolescent friends may not remember those friendships well. Sometimes people answer incorrectly due to response bias. For many questions, some responses are more socially acceptable than others. People are more likely to select socially acceptable answers than socially unacceptable ones. For example, many people would be reluctant to admit that they have no friends at all. As long as investigators keep these weaknesses in mind, self report is a valuable tool for human development research.

The three approaches to measurement are summarized in the table.

MEASURING BEHAVIORS OF INTEREST IN HUMAN DEVELOPMENT RESEARCH

Method	Strength	Weakness
Systematic observation		
Naturalistic observation	Captures people's behavior in its natural setting	Difficult to use with behaviors that are rare or that typically occur in private settings
Structured observation	Can be used to study behaviors that are rare or that typically occur in private settings	May be invalid if structured setting distorts the behavior
Sampling behavior with tasks	Convenient—can be used to study most behaviors	May be invalid if the task does not sample behavior as it occurs naturally
Self reports	Convenient—can be used to study most behaviors	May be invalid because people answer incorrectly (due to either forgetting or response bias)

After researchers choose a method, they must show that it is both reliable and valid. *The reliability of a measure is the extent to which it provides a consistent index of a characteristic.* A measure of friendship, for example, is reliable to the extent that it gives a consistent estimate of a person's friendship network each time you administer it. All measures used in human development research must be shown to be reliable, or they cannot be used. *The validity of a measure refers to whether it really measures what researchers think it measures.* For example, a measure of friendship is valid only if it can be shown to actually measure friendship (and not love, for example). Validity is often established by showing that the measure in question is closely related to another measure known to be valid. Because it is possible to have a measure that is reliable but not valid (e.g., a ruler is a reliable measure of length but not a valid measure of friendship), researchers must ensure that their measures are both reliable and valid.

Throughout this book, you'll see many studies using different methods. In addition, you'll often see that studies of the same topic or behavior use different methods. That is, each of the approaches will be used in different studies. This can be particularly valuable: Because the approaches to measurement have different strengths and weaknesses, finding the same results regardless of the approach leads to particularly strong conclusions.

Representative Sampling

Valid measures also depend upon the people who are tested. *Researchers are usually interested in broad groups of people called* populations. Examples of populations would be all American 7-year-olds or all African American grandparents. *Virtually all studies include only a* sample *of people, which is a subset of the population.* Researchers must take care that their sample really is representative of the population of interest. An unrepresentative sample can lead to invalid research. For example, what would you think of a study of older adults' friendship if you learned that the sample consisted entirely of adults who had no siblings? You would, quite correctly, decide that this sample is not representative of the population of older adults and question whether its results apply to adults with siblings.

As you read on, you'll soon discover that much of the research we describe was conducted with samples of middle-class European American people. Are these samples representative of all people in the United States? Of all people in the world? Sometimes, but not always. Be careful *not* to assume that findings from this group necessarily apply to people in other groups. Additionally, some developmental issues have not been studied in all ethnic and racial groups. For example, the U.S. government does not consistently report its statistics for all ethnic groups.

In an effort to make samples more representative, some federal agencies now require the inclusion of certain groups unless there is a compelling reason not to do so. For example, the National Institutes of Health require the inclusion of ethnic minorities, women, and children in research funded by them. These steps may make it possible to obtain a broader view of developmental processes. Until we have representative samples in all developmental research, we cannot know whether a particular phenomenon applies only to the group studied or to people more generally.

GENERAL DESIGNS FOR RESEARCH

Having selected a way to measure the topic or behavior of interest, researchers next must embed this measure in a research design that yields useful, relevant results. Human development researchers rely upon two primary designs in planning their work: correlational and experimental studies.

Correlational Studies

In a correlational study, *investigators look at relations between variables as they exist naturally in the world.* In the simplest possible correlational study, a researcher would measure two variables, then see how they are related. Imagine a researcher who wants to test the idea that smarter people have more friends. To test this claim, the researcher would measure two variables for each person in the sample. One would be the number of friends that the person has; the other would be the person's intelligence.

The results of a correlational study are usually measured by calculating a correlation coefficient, *abbreviated* r, *which expresses the strength and direction of a relation between two variables.* Correlations can range from -1.0 to 1.0, and reflect three different relations between intelligence and the number of friends:

- When $r = 0$, two variables are completely unrelated: People's intelligence is unrelated to the number of friends they have.

- When r is greater than 0, scores are related positively: People who are smart tend to have more friends than people who are not as smart. That is, *more* intelligence is associated with having *more* friends.

- When r is less than 0, scores are related, but inversely: People who are smart tend to have fewer friends than people who are not as smart. That is, *more* intelligence is associated with having *fewer* friends.

A researcher conducting a correlational study can determine whether the variables are related. However, this design doesn't address the question of cause and effect between the variables. For example, suppose a researcher finds that the correlation between intelligence and number of friends is .7. This would mean that people who are smarter have more friends than people who are not as smart. How would you interpret this correlation? The diagram shows that three interpretations are possible. Maybe being smart causes people

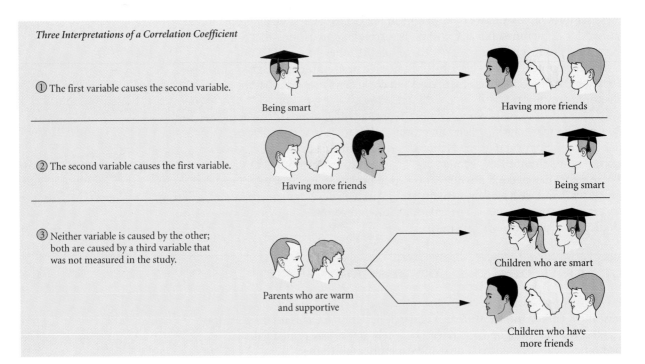

Three Interpretations of a Correlation Coefficient

① The first variable causes the second variable.

Being smart

Having more friends

② The second variable causes the first variable.

Having more friends

Being smart

③ Neither variable is caused by the other; both are caused by a third variable that was not measured in the study.

Parents who are warm and supportive

Children who are smart

Children who have more friends

to have more friends. Another interpretation is that having more friends causes people to be smarter. A third interpretation is that neither variable causes the other; instead, intelligence and number of friends are caused by a third variable that was not measured in the study. Perhaps parents who are warm and supportive tend to have children who grow up to both be smarter and have many friends. Any of these interpretations could be true. They cannot be distinguished in a correlational study. When investigators want to track down causes, they resort to a different design, an experimental study.

Experimental Studies

An experiment *is a systematic way of manipulating the key factor(s) that the investigator thinks causes a particular behavior. The factor being manipulated is called the* independent variable; *the behavior being observed is called the* dependent variable. In human development, an experiment requires that the investigator begin with one or more treatments, circumstances, or events (independent variables) that are thought to affect behavior. People are then assigned randomly to conditions that differ in the treatment they are given; then an appropriate measure (the dependent variable) is taken of all participants to see whether the treatment or treatments had the expected effect. Because each person has an equal chance of being assigned to each treatment condition (the definition of random assignment), the groups should be the same except in the treatment they have received. Any differences between the groups can be attributed to the differential treatment people received in the experiment, rather than to other factors.

Suppose, for example, that an investigator believes adolescents can learn more from a short story in a quiet room than in a room in which loud music is playing. The diagram shows how we might test this hypothesis. Adolescents come to the testing site (perhaps a room in a school) where they read a brief story prepared specially for the study. Based on random assignment, individual adolescents read the story either while the room is quiet or while loud music is played. The loud music is always the same music, played at the same volume, for all adolescents in the loud-music condition. All the participants read the identical story under circumstances held as constant as possible except for the presence or absence of the music. They all get the same amount of time to read the story, and are given the same test afterward. If scores on the test are, on average, better in the quiet condition than in the loud-music condition, the investigator may say with confidence that the music has an unfavorable effect on learning the story. Conclusions about cause and effect are possible in this example because the direct manipulation occurred under controlled conditions.

Human development researchers usually conduct experiments in laboratorylike settings, because this allows full control over the variables that may influence the outcome of the research. A shortcoming of laboratory work is that the behavior of interest is not studied in its natural setting. Consequently, there is always the potential problem that the results may be invalid because they are artificial—specific to the laboratory setting and not representative of the behavior in the "real world."

Each research design used by developmentalists has both strengths and weaknesses. There is no one best method. Consequently, no single investigation can definitely settle a question. Researchers rarely rely on one study or even one method to reach conclusions. Instead, they prefer to find converging evidence from as many different kinds of studies as possible.

> **? THINK ABOUT IT**
>
> Describe a correlational study that would examine the impact of exercise on health in older adults. Now describe an experimental study to look at the same topic. What are the advantages of each design?

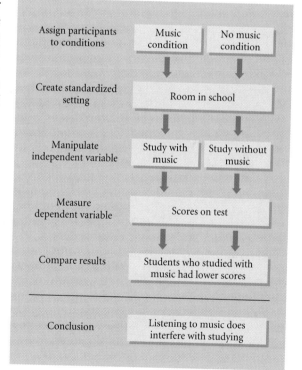

DESIGNS FOR STUDYING DEVELOPMENT

Sometimes human development research is directed at a single age group, such as the adolescent students in the example on the impact of music on studying.

Or we might study retirement planning in 55-year-olds or marital satisfaction in couples married 25 years. In each of these cases, after an investigator has decided how to measure the behavior of interest and whether the study will be correlational or experimental, the investigator could skip directly to the last step—determine if the study is ethical. However, much research in human development concerns changes that occur as people develop. In these cases, investigators must also choose one of two designs that allow them to examine development: longitudinal and cross-sectional studies.

Longitudinal Studies

In a longitudinal study, *the same individuals are observed or tested repeatedly at different points in their lives.* As the name implies, the longitudinal approach involves a lengthwise account of development, and is the most direct way to watch growth occur. The longitudinal approach is well suited to studying almost any aspect of the course of development. More important, it is the only way to answer certain questions about the stability or instability of behavior: Will characteristics such as aggression, dependency, or mistrust observed in infancy or early childhood persist into adulthood? How long will the beneficial effects of special academic training in the preschool years last? Will a regular exercise program begun in middle age have benefits in later life? Such questions can be explored only by testing people at one point in development and then retesting them later in their development.

The approach, however, has disadvantages that frequently offset its strengths. An obvious one is cost: The expense of merely keeping up with a large sample of individuals can be staggering. A related problem is the constancy of the sample over the course of the research. Experience has shown how difficult it is to maintain contact with people over several years (as long as several decades in some longitudinal studies!) in a highly mobile society. And even among those who do not move away, some lose interest and choose not to continue. These "dropouts" are often significantly different from their more research-minded peers, and this fact may also distort the outcome. For example, a group of older adults may seem to show intellectual stability late in life. What may have happened, however, is that those who found earlier testing most difficult quit the study and thereby raised the group average on the next round.

Even if the sample remains constant, though, the fact that people are given the same test many times may make them "test-wise." Improvement over time may be attributed to development when it actually stems from practice with a particular test. Changing the test from year to year solves the practice problem but raises the question of how to compare responses to different tests. Because of this and other problems with the longitudinal method, human development researchers often use cross-sectional studies instead.

Cross-Sectional Studies

In a cross-sectional study, *developmental differences are identified by testing people of different ages in the study.* Development is charted by noting the differences between individuals of different ages at the same point in calendar time. The cross-sectional approach avoids almost all the problems associated with repeated testing; it avoids costly record keeping and sample loss as well. But cross-sectional research has its own weaknesses. Because people are tested at only one point in their development, we learn nothing about the continuity of development. Consequently, we cannot tell whether an aggressive 14-year-old remains aggressive at age 30 because the person would be tested at age 14 or age 30, but not at both ages.

Cross-sectional studies are also affected by cohort effects, *meaning that differences between age groups (cohorts) may result as easily from environmental events as from developmental processes.* In a typical simple cross-sectional study, we compare people from two age groups. If we find differences, we attribute them to the difference in age, but this needn't be the case. Why? The cross-sectional study assumes that when the older people were younger, they resembled the people in the younger age group. This isn't always true and this may be responsible for differences between the groups, not the difference in age. An example of a cohort effect might come from a study measuring creativity in young and middle-aged adults. If the young adults were found to be more imaginative than middle-aged adults, should we conclude that imagination declines between these ages? Not necessarily. Perhaps a new curriculum to nourish creativity was introduced after the middle-aged adults completed school. Because the younger adults experienced the curriculum but the middle-aged adults did not, the difference between them is difficult to interpret.

When the two general research designs shown in the table are combined with the two designs that are unique to development, four prototypic designs

DESIGNS USED IN HUMAN DEVELOPMENT RESEARCH

Type of Design	Definition	Strengths	Weaknesses
General Designs			
Correlational	Observe variables as they exist in the world and determine their relations.	Behavior is measured as it occurs naturally.	Cannot determine cause and effect.
Experimental	Manipulate independent variable and determine effect on dependent variable.	Control of variables allows conclusions about cause and effect.	Work is often laboratory-based, which can be artificial.
Developmental Designs			
Longitudinal	One group of people is tested repeatedly as they develop.	Only way to chart an individual's development and look at the stability of behavior over time.	Expensive, participants drop out, and repeated testing can distort performance.
Cross-sectional	People of different ages are tested at the same time.	Convenient—solves all problems associated with longitudinal studies.	Cannot study stability of behavior; cohort effects complicate interpretation of differences between groups.

are possible: cross-sectional correlational studies, cross-sectional experimental studies, longitudinal-correlational studies, and longitudinal-experimental studies. You'll read about each of these designs in this book, although the two cross-sectional designs occur more frequently than the two longitudinal designs. Why? For most developmentalists, the ease of conducting cross-sectional studies more than compensates for their limitations.

Maybe all of these different steps in research seem tedious and involved to you. For a human development researcher, however, much of the fun of doing research is planning a study that no one has done before and that will provide useful information to other specialists. This is one of the most creative and challenging parts of human development research.

The Spotlight on Research features that appear in each chapter of this book are designed to convey both the creativity and the challenge of doing human development research. Each feature focuses on a specific study. Some are studies that have just appeared in the journals; others are classics that helped define a new area of investigation or provided definitive results in an existing area. In each of these features, we'll trace the decisions that researchers made as they planned their study. We focus on the research question addressed, the design of the study, the measures used, ethical concerns, key findings, and the researchers' conclusions. Some of the studies in this feature provide examples of difficult decisions researchers must make in designing good research, as well as constraints on investigators examining development in real world contexts. By reading these features, you'll see the ingenuity of researchers as they pursue questions of human development. You'll also see that any individual study has limitations; the way around these limits is to have converging evidence from different designs. We can have the most confidence when many studies—each using a unique combination of measurement methods and designs—all point to the same conclusion.

TEST YOURSELF

1. In _____ , people are observed as they behave spontaneously in a real-life setting.

2. A _____ is a group of individuals thought to be representative of some larger population of interest.

3. The _____ variable is measured in an experiment in order to evaluate the impact of the variable that was manipulated.

4. Problems of longitudinal studies research include the length of time to complete the work, loss of research participants over time, and _____ .

5. Human development researchers must submit their plans for research to a review board that determines whether the research _____ .

6. How could a longitudinal design be used to test Piaget's theory?

Answers: (1) naturalistic observation, (2) sample, (3) dependent, (4) influence of repeated testing on a person's performance, (5) preserves the rights of research participants

Problems with Using Photographs to Measure Understanding of Emotions

On page 29, we invited you to consider why asking children to judge emotions from photos may not be valid. Children's judgments of the emotions depicted in photographs may be less accurate than they would be in real life because (1) in real life, facial features are usually moving—not still as in the photographs—and movement may be one of the clues that children naturally use to judge emotions, (2) in real life, facial expressions are often accompanied by sounds and children use both sight and sound to judge emotions, and (3) in real life, children most often judge facial expressions of people that they know (parents, siblings, peers, teachers) and knowing the "usual" appearance of a face may help children judge emotions accurately.

SUMMARY

Thinking About Human Development

Recurring Issues in Human Development

• Three main issues are prominent in the study of human development. The nature-nurture issue involves the degree to which genetics and the environment influence human development. In general, theorists and researchers view nature and nurture as mutually interactive influences; development is always shaped by both. The continuity-discontinuity issue concerns whether the same explanations (continuity) or different explanations (discontinuity) must be used to explain changes in people over time. Continuity approaches emphasize quantitative change; discontinuity approaches emphasize qualitative change. In the issue of universal versus context-specific development, the question is whether development follows the same general path in all people or is fundamentally different, depending on the sociocultural context.

Basic Forces in Human Development: The Biopsychosocial Framework

• Development is based on the combined impact of four primary forces. Biological forces include all genetic and health-related factors that affect development. Some biological forces, such as puberty and menopause, are universal and affect people across generations, whereas others, such as diet or diseases, affect people in specific generations or occur only in a small number of people.

• Psychological forces include all internal cognitive, emotional, perceptual, and personality factors that influence development. Like biological forces, psychological forces may affect all individuals, only specific generations, or only a few individuals.

• Sociocultural forces include interpersonal, societal, cultural, and ethnic factors that affect development. Culture consists of the knowledge, attitudes, and behavior associated with a group of people. Overall, sociocultural forces provide the context or backdrop for development.

• Life-cycle forces provide a context for understanding how people perceive their current situation and its effects on them.

• The biopsychosocial framework emphasizes that the four forces are mutually interactive; development cannot be understood by examining the forces in isolation. Furthermore, the same event can have different effects, depending on when it happens.

Developmental Theories

Developmental theories organize knowledge so as to provide testable explanations of human behaviors and the ways in which they change over time. Current approaches to developmental theory focus on specific aspects of behavior. At present, there is no single unified theory of human development.

Psychodynamic Theories

• Psychodynamic theories propose that behavior is determined by unconscious motives. Freud claimed that development proceeds in a universal sequence of stages and that personality development is essentially complete by adolescence. Erikson proposed a life-span theory of psychosocial development, consisting of eight universal stages, each characterized by a particular struggle.

Learning Theory

• Learning theory focuses on the development of observable behavior. Operant conditioning is based on the notions of reinforcement, punishment, and environmental control of behavior. Social learning theory proposes that people learn by observing others.

Cognitive-Developmental Theory

• Cognitive-developmental theory focuses on thought processes. Piaget proposed a four-stage universal sequence based on the notion that, throughout development, people create their own theories to explain how the world works. According to information-processing theory, people deal with information like a computer does; development consists of increased efficiency in handling information.

The Ecological and Systems Approach

• Bronfenbrenner proposed that development occurs in the context of several interconnected systems of increasing complexity. The competence–environmental press theory postulates that there is a "best fit" between a person's abilities and the demands placed on that person by the environment.

Life-Span and Life-Cycle Theories

• According to the life-span perspective, development must be viewed in terms of all four forces in the biopsychosocial framework. Understanding any point in development requires knowing where the person came from and where the person is heading. In the life-cycle approach, the meaning of certain events depends on when in a person's life they are experienced. In family life-cycle theory, families go through stages based on their children's ages.

Doing Developmental Research

Measurement in Human Development Research

• Research typically begins by determining how to measure the topic of interest. Systematic observation involves recording people's behavior as it takes place, either in a natural environment (naturalistic observation) or a structured setting (structured observation). Researchers sometimes create tasks to obtain samples of behavior. In self reports, people answer questions posed by the experimenter. Researchers must determine that their measures are reliable and valid; they must also obtain a sample representative of some larger population.

General Designs for Research

• In correlational studies, investigators examine relations among variables as they occur naturally. This relation is often measured by a correlation coefficient, r, which can vary from -1 (strong inverse relation) to 0 (no relation) to $+1$ (strong positive relation). Correlational studies cannot determine cause and effect, so researchers do experimental studies in which an independent variable is manipulated and the impact of this manipulation on a dependent variable is recorded. Experimental studies allow conclusions about cause and effect, but the strict control of other variables that is required often makes the situation artificial. The best approach is to use both experimental and correlational studies to provide converging evidence.

Designs for Studying Development

• To study development, some researchers use a longitudinal design in which the same people are observed repeatedly as they grow. This approach provides evidence concerning actual patterns of individual growth but has several shortcomings as well: It is time-consuming, some people drop out of the project, and repeated testing can affect performance. An alternative, the cross-sectional design, involves testing people of different ages. This design avoids the problems of the longitudinal design but provides no information about individual growth. Also, what appear to be age differences may be cohort effects. Because neither design is problem-free, the best approach is to use both to provide converging evidence.

Conducting Research Ethically

• Planning research also involves selecting methods that preserve the rights of research participants. Experimenters must minimize the risks to potential research participants, describe the research so that potential participants can decide if they want to participate, avoid deception, and keep results anonymous or confidential.

Communicating Research Results

• Once research data are collected and analyzed, investigators publish the results in scientific outlets such as journals and books. Such results form the foundation of knowledge about human development.

KEY TERMS

human development (1)
nature-nurture issue (5)
continuity-discontinuity issue (6)
universal versus context-specific
  development issue (7)
biological forces (8)
psychological forces (8)

sociocultural forces (8)
life-cycle forces (8)
biopsychosocial framework (8)
normative age-graded influences
  (9)
normative history-graded
  influences (9)

nonnormative influence (9)
theory (14)
psychodynamic theories (16)
id (16)
ego (16)
superego (16)
psychosocial theory (17)

epigenetic principle (17)
operant conditioning (19)
reinforcement (19)
punishment (19)
imitation (observational learning)
    (19)
social cognitive theory (20)
self-efficacy (20)
information-processing theory (22)
ecological theory (23)
microsystem (23)

mesosystem (24)
exosystem (24)
macrosystem (24)
life-span perspective (25)
systematic observation (28)
naturalistic observation (28)
structured observations (28)
self reports (29)
reliability (30)
validity (30)
populations (31)

sample (31)
correlational study (31)
correlation coefficient (32)
experiment (33)
independent variable (33)
dependent variable (33)
longitudinal study (34)
cross-sectional study (34)
cohort effects (35)
sequential design (36)

IF YOU'D LIKE TO LEARN MORE

Readings

BALTES, P. B. (1987). Theoretical propositions of life-span developmental psychology: On the dynamics between growth and decline. *Developmental Psychology, 23*, 611–626. One of the classics in human development. This is an excellent overview of what it means to take a holistic view of life-span development. Written by one of the leading proponents of this approach, the article is moderately difficult reading.

BALTES, P. B., REESE, H. W., & NESSELROADE, J. R. (1977). *Life-span developmental psychology: Introduction to research methods.* Pacific Grove, CA: Brooks/Cole. This is one of the classic texts on developmental research methods, and still one of the best. It's very readable and an easily understood presentation of research designs and methods.

GARDINER, H. W., MUTTER, J. D., & KOSMITZKI, C. (1998). *Lives across cultures: Cross-cultural human development.* Boston: Allyn & Bacon. A readable introduction to how human development occurs in various world cultures. This book pulls together much of the available research.

LERNER, R. M. (1986). *Concepts and theories of human development* (2nd ed.). New York: Random House. Lerner's book is a very readable overview of the various philosophical assumptions underlying developmental theories. It includes summaries of several theories.

 For additional readings, explore Infotrac College Edition, your online library. Go to http://www.infotrac-college.com/wadsworth.

Web Sites

The Web site of the Society for Research in Child Development,

http://www.srcd.org/publica.htm

allows you to search for scientific articles by topic.

The AgeLine Database Web site,

http://www.aarp.org/resrch/ageline/

allows you to search for research articles and information about aging.

The Guidelines for the Conduct of Research Involving Human Subjects at the National Institutes of Health, at the Web site

http://helix.nih.gov:8001/ohsr/guidelines.phtml

are the foundation of all institutional review processes for such research.

Web site addresses are subject to change. The Wadsworth Study Center Web site listed below can be accessed for updated links.

The Wadsworth Psychology Study Center Web Site

See http://psychology.wadsworth.com/ for practice quiz questions, internet links, updates, critical thinking exercises, discussion forums and more! The Wadsworth Psychology Study Center provides a wealth of information fully organized and integrated by chapter.

PART ONE

PRENATAL DEVELOPMENT, INFANCY, AND EARLY CHILDHOOD

- CHAPTER 2

  Biological Foundations

- CHAPTER 3

  Tools for Exploring
  the World

- CHAPTER 4

  The Emergence of
  Thought and Language

- CHAPTER 5

  Entering the
  Social World

A CLOSER LOOK

On April 13, 1997, millions of people around the world watched in awe as Tiger Woods won the Masters golf tournament in Augusta, Georgia. Tiger's performance was extraordinary. He was the youngest golfer ever to win the Masters (20) and did so with the lowest score (270) and the biggest margin of victory (12) ever. Tiger's win was the first for a minority player at the Masters, a tournament that had its first African American player only two decades earlier. As impressive as this and Tiger's other golf achievements

have been, they are not completely unexpected when you realize that as a baby, Tiger was imitating his dad's golf swing, as a 2-year-old he showed his putting skill on TV, and as a 5-year-old he was featured in *Golf Digest* magazine.

In fact, though not many children match Tiger's accomplishments, the first five years of life are profoundly influential for all children. The events of these early years initiate and direct a lifelong developmental journey. In Chapters 2–5, you'll discover how biological, psychological, and social forces shape development from conception through 5 years of age.

CHAPTER 2

BIOLOGICAL FOUNDATIONS

In the Beginning:
23 Pairs of Chromosomes
Mechanisms of Heredity
Genetic Disorders
Heredity Is Not Destiny: Genes and
    Environments
Ben and Matt Pick Their Niches

From Conception to Birth
Period of the Zygote (Weeks 1–2)
Conception in the 21st Century
Period of the Embryo (Weeks 3–8)
Period of the Fetus (Weeks 9–38)

Influences on Prenatal Development
General Risk Factors
Teratogens: Drugs, Diseases, and
    Environmental Hazards
Industrial Toxins and Mental Development
How Teratogens Influence Prenatal
    Development
Prenatal Diagnosis and Treatment

Labor and Delivery
Stages of Labor
Approaches to Childbirth
Birth Complications
*What Determines Life Outcomes for
    Low-Birth-Weight Babies?*
Infant Mortality

Putting It All Together

Summary

If You'd Like to Learn More

*I*f you ask parents to name the most memorable experiences of their lives, many immediately mention the events associated with the birth of their children. From the initial exciting news that a woman is pregnant through birth nine months later, the entire experience of pregnancy and birth evokes awe and wonder.

The period before birth is the foundation for all human development and the focus of this chapter. Pregnancy begins when egg and sperm cells unite and exchange hereditary material. In the first section, you'll see how this exchange takes place and, in the process, learn about inherited factors that affect development. The second part of the chapter traces the events that transform sperm and egg into a living, breathing human being. You'll learn about the timetable that governs development before birth and, along the way, get answers to common questions about pregnancy. We'll also talk about some of the problems that can occur during development before birth. The last section of the chapter focuses on birth and the newborn baby. You'll find out how an expectant mother can prepare for birth and what labor and delivery are like.

IN THE BEGINNING: 23 PAIRS OF CHROMOSOMES

In the Beginning:
23 Pairs of Chromosomes

Mechanisms of Heredity

Genetic Disorders

Heredity Is Not Destiny:
    Genes and Environments

Learning Objectives

- **What are chromosomes and genes? How do they carry hereditary information from one generation to the next?**

- **What are common problems involving chromosomes and what are their consequences?**

- **How is children's heredity influenced by the environment in which they grow up?**

*L*ESLIE AND GLENN *are excited at the thought of starting their own family. At the same time, they're nervous because Leslie's grandfather had sickle-cell disease and died when he was just 20 years old. Leslie is terrified that her baby may inherit the disease that killed her grandfather. She and Glenn wish that someone could reassure them that their baby will be okay.*

How can we reassure Leslie and Glenn? For starters, we need to know more about sickle-cell disease. Red blood cells like the ones in the left photo carry oxygen and carbon dioxide to and from the body. When a person has sickle-cell disease, the red blood cells look like those in the right photo—they are long and curved like a sickle. These stiff, misshapen cells cannot pass through

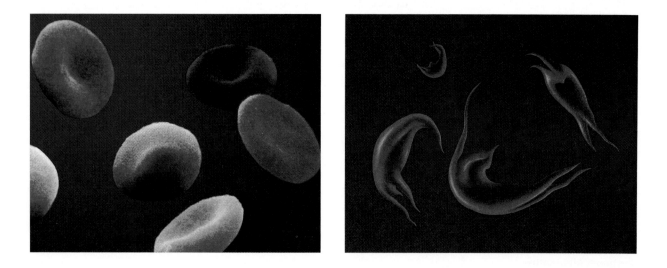

small capillaries, so oxygen cannot reach all parts of the body. The trapped sickle cells also block the way of white blood cells that are the body's natural defense against bacteria. As a result, many people with sickle-cell disease—including Leslie's grandfather and many other African Americans, who are more prone to this painful disease than other groups—often die from infections before the age of 20.

Sickle-cell disease is inherited and, because Leslie's grandfather had the disorder, it runs in her family. Will Leslie's baby inherit the disease? To answer this question, we need to examine the mechanisms of heredity.

MECHANISMS OF HEREDITY

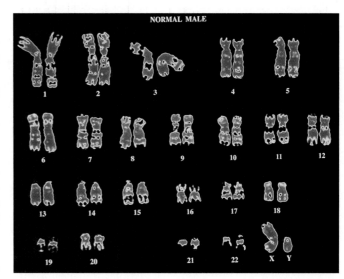

NORMAL MALE

At conception, egg and sperm unite to create a new organism that incorporates some characteristics of each parent. *Each egg and sperm cell has 23 chromosomes, threadlike structures in the nucleus that contain genetic material.* When a sperm penetrates an egg, their chromosomes combine to produce 23 pairs of chromosomes. The photo shows all 46 chromosomes, organized in pairs ranging from the largest to the smallest. *The first 22 pairs of chromosomes are called* autosomes. *The 23rd pair determines the sex of the child, so these are known as the* sex chromosomes. When the 23rd pair consists of an X and a Y chromosome, the result is a boy; two X chromosomes produce a girl.

Each chromosome actually consists of one molecule of deoxyribonucleic acid—*DNA for short.* To understand the structure of DNA, imagine four different colors of beads placed on two strings. The strings complement each other precisely: Wherever a red bead appears on one string, a blue bead appears on the other; wherever a green bead appears on one string, a yellow one appears on the other. DNA is organized this way, except that the four colors of beads are actually four different chemical compounds—adenine, thymine, guanine, and cytosine. The strings, which are made up of phosphates and sugars, wrap around each other, creating the double helix shown in the drawing.

The order in which the chemical compound "beads" appear is really a code that causes the cell to create specific amino acids, proteins, and enzymes—important biological building blocks. For example, three consecutive thymine "beads" make up the instruction to create the amino acid phenylalanine. *Each group of compounds that provides a specific set of biochemical instructions is a* gene. Thus, genes are the functional units of heredity, because they determine production of chemical substances that are, ultimately, the basis for all human characteristics and abilities.

Altogether, a child's 46 chromosomes include roughly 100,000 genes. Through biochemical instructions that are coded in DNA, genes regulate the development of all human characteristics and abilities. *The complete set of genes makes up a person's heredity and is known as the person's* genotype. *Genetic instructions, in conjunction with environmental influences, produce a* phenotype, *an individual's physical, behavioral, and psychological features.*

In the rest of this section, we'll see the ways in which the instructions contained in genes produce different phenotypes.

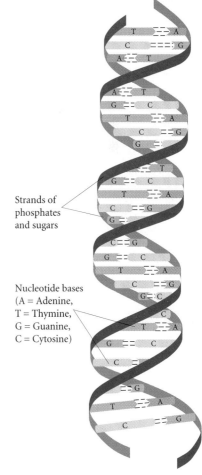

Strands of phosphates and sugars

Nucleotide bases (A = Adenine, T = Thymine, G = Guanine, C = Cytosine)

Single-Gene Inheritance

How do genetic instructions produce the misshapen red blood cells of sickle-cell disease? *Genes come in different forms that are known as* alleles. In the case of red blood cells, for example, two alleles can be present on chromosome 11.

One allele has instructions for normal red blood cells; another allele has instructions for sickle-shaped red blood cells. *The alleles in the pair of chromosomes are sometimes the same, which is known as being* homozygous. *The alleles sometimes differ, which is known as being* heterozygous. Leslie's baby would be homozygous if it had two alleles for normal cells *or* two alleles for sickle-shaped cells. The baby would be heterozygous if it had one allele of each type.

How does a genotype produce a phenotype? With sickle-cell disease, for example, how do genotypes lead to specific kinds of blood cells? The answer is simple if a person is homozygous. When both alleles are the same—and therefore have chemical instructions for the same phenotype—that phenotype results. If Leslie's baby had an allele for normal red blood cells on both of its 11th chromosomes, the baby would be almost guaranteed to have normal cells. If, instead, the baby had two alleles for sickle-shaped cells, her baby would almost certainly suffer from the disease.

When a person is heterozygous, the process is more complex. *Often one allele is* dominant, *which means that its chemical instructions are followed and those of the other,* recessive *allele are ignored.* In sickle-cell disease, the allele for normal cells is dominant, and the allele for sickle-shaped cells is recessive. This is good news for Leslie: As long as either she or Glenn contributes the allele for normal red blood cells, their baby will not develop sickle-cell disease.

The diagram summarizes what we've learned about sickle-cell disease: *A* denotes the allele for normal blood cells and *a* denotes the allele for sickle-shaped cells. Depending on the alleles in Leslie's egg and in the sperm that fertilizes that egg, three outcomes are possible. Only if the baby inherits two recessive alleles for sickle-shaped cells is it likely to develop sickle-cell disease.

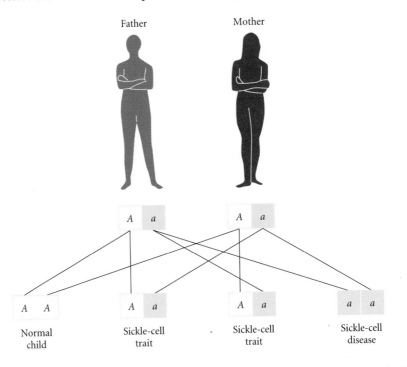

Father   Mother

A a   A a

A A   A a   A a   a a

Normal   Sickle-cell   Sickle-cell   Sickle-cell
child   trait   trait   disease

But this is unlikely in Glenn's case: He is positive no one in his family has had sickle-cell disease, so he almost certainly has the allele for normal blood cells on both of the chromosomes in his 11th pair.

Even though Glenn's sperm carries the gene for normal red blood cells, this doesn't guarantee that their baby will be healthy. Why? *Sometimes one allele does not dominate another completely, a situation known as* codominance. In codominance, the phenotype that results often falls between the phenotype associated with either allele. This is the case for the genes that control red blood cells. *Individuals with one dominant and one recessive allele have* sickle-cell trait: *In most situations they have no problems but when they are seriously short of oxygen, they suffer a temporary, relatively mild form of the disease.* Sickle-cell trait is likely to appear when the person exercises vigorously or is at high altitudes (Sullivan, 1987). Leslie and Glenn's baby will have sickle-cell trait if it inherits a recessive gene from Leslie and a dominant gene from Glenn.

The simple genetic mechanism responsible for sickle-cell disease, involving a single gene pair, with one dominant allele and one recessive allele, is also responsible for numerous other common traits, as shown in the table.

COMMON PHENOTYPES ASSOCIATED WITH SINGLE PAIRS OF GENES

Dominant Phenotype	Recessive Phenotype
Curly hair	Straight hair
Normal hair	Pattern baldness (men)
Dark hair	Blond hair
Thick lips	Thin lips
Cheek dimples	No dimples
Normal hearing	Some types of deafness
Normal vision	Nearsightedness
Farsightedness	Normal vision
Normal vision	Red-green color blindness
Type A blood	Type O blood
Type B blood	Type O blood
Rh-positive blood	Rh-negative blood

Source: McKusick, 1995.

In each of these instances, individuals with the recessive phenotype have two recessive alleles, one from each parent. Individuals with the dominant phenotype have at least one dominant allele.

You'll notice that the table includes many biological and medical phenotypes but lacks behavioral or psychological phenotypes. Behavioral and psychological characteristics can be inherited, but the genetic mechanism is usually more elaborate, as we'll see next.

Polygenic Inheritance

Traits that are controlled by single genes are usually "either-or" phenotypes. A person either has dimpled cheeks or not; a person either has normal color vision or red-green color blindness; a person's blood either clots normally or it does not. The genotypes are usually associated with two (or sometimes three) well-defined phenotypes.

Many important behavioral and psychological characteristics are *not* "either-or" cases. Instead, an entire range of different outcomes is possible. Take extroversion as an example. Imagine trying to classify ten people that you know well as either extroverts or introverts. This would be easy for a few

? **THINK ABOUT IT**
Introversion–extroversion is an example of a psychological characteristic that defines a continuum. Think of other psychological characteristics like this, in which outcomes are not "either-or" but represent a range.

extremely outgoing individuals (extroverts) and a few intensely shy persons (introverts). Most are probably neither extroverts nor introverts, but "in between." The result is a distribution of individuals ranging from extreme introversion at one end to extreme extroversion at the other.

Many behavioral and psychological characteristics are distributed in this fashion, including intelligence and many aspects of personality (Plomin, Owen, & McGuffin, 1994). *These phenotypes often reflect the combined activity of a number of separate genes, a pattern known as* polygenic inheritance.

Because many genes are involved in polygenic inheritance, we usually cannot trace the effects of each gene. However, the following *hypothetical* example shows how various genes could work together to produce a behavioral phenotype that spans a continuum. Let's suppose that extroversion is an inherited trait, that eight pairs of genes contribute to extroversion, and that the allele for extroversion is dominant. Thus, a person could inherit as many as 16 alleles for extroversion or as few as zero. Of course, these extremes would be rare, for the same reason that if you toss 16 coins, you rarely get 16 heads or 16 tails. Because each allele is equally likely to be present, most people will inherit about 8 dominant alleles for extroversion and 8 recessive alleles for introversion. The result is the distribution of extroversion shown in the diagram.

Remember, this example is completely hypothetical. Extroversion is *not* based on the combined influence of eight pairs of genes. However, the sample shows how several genes working together *could* produce a continuum of phenotypes. Something like our example is probably involved in the inheritance of many human behavioral traits, except that many more pairs of genes are involved. Moreover, the environment also influences the phenotype.

If many behavioral phenotypes involve countless genes, how can we hope to unravel the influence of heredity? Twins and adopted children provide some important clues to the role of heredity.

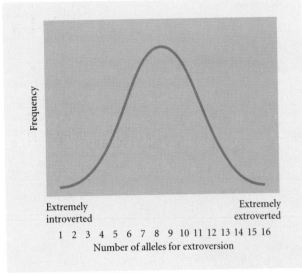

Frequency

Extremely introverted   Extremely extroverted

1 2 3 4 5 6 7 8 9 10 11 12 13 14 15 16
Number of alleles for extroversion

Studying Twins and Adopted Children

Identical twins are called monozygotic twins *because they come from a single fertilized egg that splits in two.* Because identical twins come from the same fertilized egg, the same genes control their body structure, height, and facial features, which explains why identical twins like those in the photo look alike. *In contrast, fraternal or* dizygotic twins *come from two separate eggs fertilized by two separate sperm.* Genetically, fraternal twins are just like any other siblings—on average, about half their genes are the same. In twin studies, scientists compare identical and fraternal twins to measure the influence of heredity. If identical twins are more alike than are fraternal twins, this implicates heredity (Phelps, Davis, & Schartz, 1997).

Much of this same logic is used in adoption studies, in which adopted children are compared with their biological parents and their adoptive parents. The idea here is that biological parents provide their child's genes, but adoptive parents provide the child's environment. Consequently, if a behavior has important genetic roots, then adopted children should behave more like their biological parents than their adoptive parents.

These and other methods are not foolproof. Maybe you thought of a potential flaw in twin studies: Parents and other people may treat monozygotic twins more similarly than they treat dizygotic twins. This would make monozygotic twins more similar than dizygotic twins in their experiences as well as in their genes. However, because each method has its unique pitfalls, when different methods converge on the same conclusion about the influence of heredity, we can be confident of that result. Throughout this book, you'll see many instances where twin studies and adoption studies have pointed to genetic influences on human development.

GENETIC DISORDERS

Some people are affected by heredity in a special way: They have genetic disorders that disrupt the usual pattern of development. Genetics can derail development in two ways. First, some disorders are inherited. Sickle-cell disease is one example of an inherited disorder. Second, sometimes eggs or sperm do not include the usual 23 chromosomes but have more or fewer chromosomes instead. In the next few pages, we'll see how inherited disorders and abnormal numbers of chromosomes can alter a person's development.

Inherited Disorders

You know that sickle-cell disease is a disorder that affects people who inherit two recessive alleles. *Another disorder that involves recessive alleles is* phenyl-ketonuria, *a disorder in which babies are born lacking an important liver enzyme.* This enzyme converts phenylalanine—a protein found in dairy products, bread, diet soda, and fish—into amino acids that are required for normal body functioning. Without this enzyme, phenylalanine accumulates and produces poisons that harm the nervous system, resulting in mental retardation (Diamond et al., 1997; Mange & Mange, 1990).

Most inherited disorders are like sickle-cell disease and PKU in that they are carried by recessive alleles. Relatively few serious disorders are caused by dominant alleles. Why? If the allele for the disorder is dominant, every person with at least one of these alleles would have the disorder. Individuals affected with these disorders typically do not live long enough to reproduce, so dominant alleles that produce fatal disorders soon vanish from the species. *An exception is* Huntington's disease, *a fatal disease characterized by progressive degeneration of the nervous system.* Huntington's disease is caused by a dominant allele found on chromosome 4. Individuals who inherit this disorder develop normally through childhood, adolescence, and young adulthood. However, during middle age, nerve cells begin to deteriorate, which produces symptoms such as muscle spasms, depression, and significant changes in personality (Shiwach, 1994). By this age, many adults with Huntington's disease have already reproduced, creating children who may well later display the disease themselves.

Abnormal Chromosomes

Sometimes individuals do not receive the normal complement of 46 chromosomes. If they are born with extra, missing, or damaged chromosomes, development is always disturbed. The best example is Down syndrome.

Like the boy in the photo, people with Down syndrome have almond-shaped eyes and a fold over the eyelid. Their head, neck, and nose are usually smaller than normal. During the first several months of life, development of babies with Down syndrome seems to be normal. Thereafter, their mental and

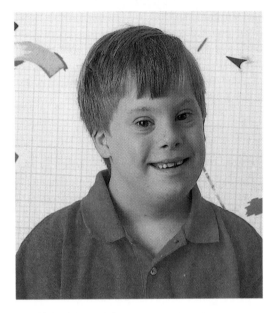

behavioral development begins to lag behind the average child's. For example, a child with Down syndrome might first sit up without help at about 1 year, walk at 2, and talk at 3, reaching each of these developmental milestones months or even years behind children without Down syndrome. By childhood, most aspects of cognitive and social development are seriously retarded (Cielinski et al., 1995; Rast & Meltzoff, 1995). Nevertheless, as you'll see in Chapter 6, many individuals with Down syndrome lead full, satisfying lives.

What causes Down syndrome? Individuals with Down syndrome typically have an extra 21st chromosome that is usually provided by the egg (Antonarakis et al., 1991). Why the mother provides two 21st chromosomes is unknown. However, the odds that a woman will bear a child with Down syndrome increases markedly as she gets older. For a woman in her late 20s, the risk of giving birth to a baby with Down syndrome is about 1 in 1,000; for a woman in her early 40s, the risk is about 1 in 50. Why? A woman's eggs have been in her ovaries since her own prenatal development. Eggs may deteriorate over time as part of aging or because an older woman has a longer history of exposure to hazards in the environment, such as X-rays, that may damage her eggs.

An extra autosome (as in Down syndrome), a missing autosome, or a damaged autosome always has far-reaching consequences for development because the autosomes contain huge amounts of genetic material. In fact, nearly half of all fertilized eggs abort spontaneously within two weeks, primarily because of abnormal autosomes. Thus, most eggs that cannot develop normally are removed naturally (Moore & Persaud, 1993).

Abnormal sex chromosomes can also disrupt development. The chart on page 53 lists four of the more frequent disorders associated with atypical numbers of X and Y chromosomes. Keep in mind that "frequent" is a relative term; although these disorders are more frequent than PKU or Huntington's disease, the chart shows that most are rare. Notice that there are no disorders consist-

COMMON DISORDERS ASSOCIATED WITH THE SEX CHROMOSOMES

Disorder	Chromosomes	Frequency	Characteristics
Klinefelter's syndrome	XXY	1 in 500 male births	Tall, small testicles, sterile, below-normal intelligence, passive
XYY complement	XYY	1 in 1,000 male births	Tall, some cases apparently have below-normal intelligence
Turner's syndrome	X	1 in 2,500–5,000 female births	Short, limited development of secondary sex characteristics, problems perceiving spatial relations
XXX syndrome	XXX	1 in 500–1,200 female births	Normal stature but delayed motor and language development

Source: Based on Bancroft et al., 1982; Downey et al., 1991; Linden et al., 1988; Plomin et al., 1990.

ing solely of Y chromosomes. The presence of an X chromosome appears to be necessary for life.

Fortunately, most of us receive the correct number of chromosomes and we do not inherit life-threatening illnesses. For most people, heredity reveals its power in creating a unique individual—a person unlike any other. Of course, heredity doesn't work alone. To fully understand how heredity influences development, we need to consider the environment, which we'll do next.

HEREDITY IS NOT DESTINY: GENES AND ENVIRONMENTS

Many people mistakenly view heredity as a set of phenotypes unfolding automatically from the genotypes that are set at conception. Nothing could be further from the truth. Although genotypes are fixed when the sperm fertilizes the egg, phenotypes are not. Instead, phenotypes depend on both the genotypes and the environment in which the child develops.

The Case of PKU

On page 51, we mentioned that when babies inherit PKU, poisons can damage the nervous system, producing mental retardation. Today, however, most American newborns are tested for PKU with a blood test. Newborns who have the disease are immediately placed on a diet that limits the intake of phenylalanine. The result is that mental retardation is avoided. Thus, a child who has the genotype for PKU becomes mentally retarded when exposed to phenylalanine but has normal intelligence when phenylalanine is avoided. (This explains the warning that appears on many products, such as diet soda: "Phenylketonurics: contains phenylalanine.") PKU illustrates that development depends on heredity *and* environmental factors such as medical care, educational opportunities, and diet.

Range of Reaction

PKU is *not* an isolated example. The general rule is that heredity and environment jointly determine the direction of development. *The term* reaction range *refers to the fact that a genotype can lead to a range of phenotypes, in reaction to the environment in which development takes place.* The graph illustrates this fact by showing how phenotypic intelligence might vary, depending on the environment. Look first at genotypic intelligence *A,* which has a small reaction

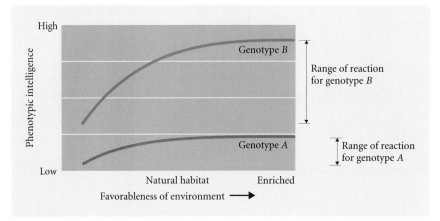

Gottesman, 1963.

range. This genotype leads to much the same phenotypic intelligence, no matter whether development takes place in an enriched environment filled with stimulation from parents, siblings, and books or in an impoverished environment that lacks all such stimulation. In contrast, genotype *B* has a larger reaction range: The enriched environment leads to a much greater phenotypic intelligence than does the impoverished environment. Thus, a single genotype can lead to a range of phenotypes, depending on the quality of the rearing environment.

Of course, what makes a "good" or "rich" environment is not the same for all facets of behavioral or psychological development. As you'll see throughout this book, children's mastery of different tasks—language, motor skills, and social skills, for example—is fostered by specific environmental influences (Wachs, 1983).

Gene-Environment Correlation

We have emphasized that experience can determine the impact of heredity. As strange as it may seem, the reverse is also true: Heredity can affect experience! Specifically, genotypes can determine the types of experiences that children have (Scarr & McCartney, 1983). For example, different genotypes may evoke different responses from the environment. Children who are naturally outgoing are more likely to find social interactions satisfying and pleasant. In contrast, children who are naturally shy are likely to find the same social interactions much less satisfying. *Furthermore, as children get older, they may deliberately seek environments that fit their heredity, a process known as* niche-picking. Extroverted youngsters will tend to seek environments in which they can socialize with others; shy youngsters will tend to seek quiet, private environments. The Real People feature shows such niche-picking in action.

? THINK ABOUT IT
How does the concept of reaction range help explain why nature and nurture are almost always involved in the developmental equation?

BEN AND MATT PICK THEIR NICHES

Ben and Matt Kail were born 25 months apart. Even as a young baby, Ben was always a "people person." He relished contact with other people and preferred play that involved others. From the beginning, Matt was different. He was more withdrawn and was quite happy to play alone. The first separation from parents was harder for Ben than for Matt, because Ben relished parental contact more. When they entered school, Ben enjoyed increasing the scope of his friendships; Matt liked all the different activities that were available and barely noticed the new faces. Though brothers, Ben and Matt are quite dissimilar in terms of their sociability, a characteristic known to have important genetic components (Braungart et al., 1992).

As Ben and Matt have grown up (they're now young adults), they have consistently sought environments that fit their differing needs for social stimulation. Ben was involved in team sports and now enjoys working in the theater. Matt took art and photography classes and now is happy when he's reading, drawing, or working at his computer. Ben and Matt have chosen very different niches, and their choices have been driven in part by the genes that regulate sociability. ●

Much of what we have said about genes, environment, and development is summarized in the diagram. Parents are the source of children's genes and, at least for young children, are also the primary source of children's experiences. Children's genes also influence the experiences that they have and the impact of those experiences on them. Together, heredity and environment determine behavioral and psychological development.

Most of this book is devoted to explaining the links between nature, nurture, and development. We can first see the interaction of nature and nurture during prenatal development, which we examine in the next section of this chapter.

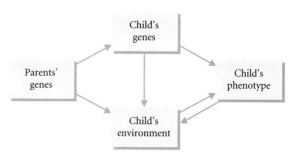

TEST YOURSELF

1. The first 22 pairs of chromosomes are called _____ .

2. _____ reflects the combined activity of a number of distinct genes.

3. Individuals with _____ have an extra 21st chromosome, usually inherited from the mother.

4. When a fertilized egg has defective autosomes, the usual result is that _____ .

5. Children who inherit PKU can develop normal intelligence if _____ .

6. The term _____ refers to the fact that the same genotype can be associated with many different phenotypes.

7. Explain how niche-picking might work in the domain of intelligence.

Answers: (1) autosomes, (2) Polygenic inheritance, (3) Down syndrome, (4) the fertilized egg is aborted spontaneously, (5) they have a special diet that is low in phenylalanine, (6) reaction range

FROM CONCEPTION TO BIRTH

From Conception to Birth

Period of the Zygote (Weeks 1–2)

Period of the Embryo (Weeks 3–8)

Period of the Fetus (Weeks 9–38)

Learning Objectives

- **What happens to a fertilized egg in the first two weeks after conception?**

- **When do body structures and internal organs emerge in prenatal development?**

- **When do body systems begin to function well enough to support life?**

Ɛ UN JUNG *has just learned that she is pregnant with her first child. Like many other parents-to-be, she and her husband Kinam are ecstatic. But they also soon realize how little they know about "what happens when" during pregnancy. Eun Jung is eager to visit her obstetrician to learn more about the normal timetable of events during pregnancy.*

Prenatal development begins when a sperm successfully fertilizes an egg. *The many changes that transform the fertilized egg into a newborn human are known as* prenatal development. Prenatal development takes an average of 38 weeks, which are divided into three periods: the period of the zygote, the period of the embryo, and the period of the fetus. Each period gets its name from the scientific term used to describe the baby-to-be at that point in prenatal development.

In this section, we'll trace the major developments of each of these periods. As we do, you'll learn the answers to the "what happens when" question that intrigues Eun Jung.

PERIOD OF THE ZYGOTE (WEEKS 1–2)

The teaspoon or so of seminal fluid produced during a fertile male's ejaculation contains from 200 to 500 million sperm. Of the sperm released into the vagina, only a few hundred will actually complete the 6- or 7-inch journey to the Fallopian tubes. Here, an egg arrives monthly, hours after it is released by an ovary. If an egg is present, many sperm will simultaneously begin to burrow their way through the cluster of nurturing cells that surround the egg. Two sperm cells are doing just this in the photo. Their tails can be seen clearly, but one sperm has burrowed so deeply that the head is barely visible. When this or some other sperm finally penetrates the cellular wall of the egg, chemical changes occur in the wall immediately, blocking out all other sperm. Then the nuclei of the egg and sperm fuse and the two independent sets of 23 chromosomes are interchanged. The development of a new human being is under way!

For nearly all of history, sexual intercourse was the only way for egg and sperm to unite and begin the development that results in a human being. This is no longer the only way, as we see in the Current Controversies feature.

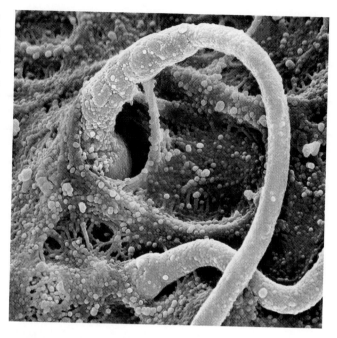

CONCEPTION IN THE 21ST CENTURY

More than 25 years ago, Louise Brown captured the world's attention as the first test-tube baby—conceived in a petri dish instead of in her mother's body. Today, this reproductive technology is no longer experimental; it is a multibillion-dollar business in the United States (Beck, 1994). Many new techniques are available to couples who cannot conceive a child through sexual intercourse. *The best known,* in vitro fertilization, *involves mixing sperm and egg together in a petri dish and then placing several fertilized eggs in the mother's uterus, with the hope that they will become implanted in the uterine wall.* Other methods include injecting many sperm directly into the Fallopian tubes or a single sperm directly into an egg.

The sperm and egg usually come from the prospective parents, but sometimes they are provided by donors. Typically, the fertilized eggs are placed in the uterus of the prospective mother, but sometimes they are placed in the uterus of a surrogate mother, who carries the baby to term. This means that a baby could have as many as five "parents": the man and woman who provided the sperm and egg; the surrogate mother who carried the baby; and the mother and father who will rear the baby.

For the many couples who have long yearned for a child, these techniques offer new hope. At the same time, they have led to much controversy because of some complex ethical issues associated with their use. One concerns the prospective parents' right to select particular egg and sperm cells; another involves who should be able to use this technology.

Pick your egg and sperm cells from a catalog? Until recently, prospective parents have known nothing about egg and sperm donors. Today, however, they are sometimes able to select egg and sperm based on physical and psychological characteristics of the donors, including appearance and race. Some claim that such prospective parents have a right to be fully informed about the person who provides the genetic material for their baby. *Others argue that this amounts to* eugenics, *which is the effort to improve the human species by allowing only certain people to mate and pass along their genes to subsequent generations.*

CURRENT CONTROVERSIES

INFOTRAC
COLLEGE EDITION

To learn more, enter the following search term: fertilization in vitro.

Available to all? Most couples who use *in vitro* fertilization are in their 30s and 40s, but a number of older women have begun to use the technology. Many of these women cannot conceive naturally, because they have gone through menopause and no longer ovulate. Some argue that it is unfair to a child to have parents who may not live until the child reaches adulthood. Others point out that people are living longer and that middle-aged (or older) adults make better parents. (We discuss this in more depth in Chapter 12.)

What do you think? Should prospective parents be allowed to browse a catalog with photos and biographies of prospective donors? Should new reproductive technologies be available to all, regardless of age? ●

Whether by artificial means like those we've just described or by natural means, fertilization begins the period of the zygote, which takes its name from zygote, *the technical term for the fertilized egg.* This period ends when the zygote implants itself in the wall of the uterus. During these two weeks, the zygote grows rapidly through cell division. The diagram traces the egg cell from the time it

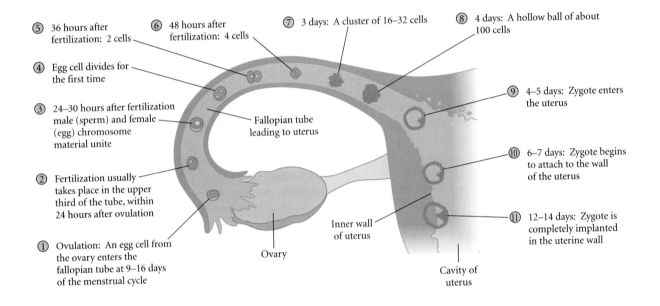

⑤ 36 hours after fertilization: 2 cells

⑥ 48 hours after fertilization: 4 cells

⑦ 3 days: A cluster of 16–32 cells

⑧ 4 days: A hollow ball of about 100 cells

④ Egg cell divides for the first time

③ 24–30 hours after fertilization male (sperm) and female (egg) chromosome material unite

② Fertilization usually takes place in the upper third of the tube, within 24 hours after ovulation

① Ovulation: An egg cell from the ovary enters the fallopian tube at 9–16 days of the menstrual cycle

Fallopian tube leading to uterus

Ovary

Inner wall of uterus

Cavity of uterus

⑨ 4–5 days: Zygote enters the uterus

⑩ 6–7 days: Zygote begins to attach to the wall of the uterus

⑪ 12–14 days: Zygote is completely implanted in the uterine wall

is released from the ovary until the zygote becomes implanted in the wall of the uterus. The zygote travels down the Fallopian tube toward the uterus. Within hours, the zygote divides for the first time, then continues to do so every 12 hours. Occasionally, the zygote separates into two clusters that develop into identical twins. Fraternal twins, which are more common, are created when two eggs are released and each is fertilized by a different sperm cell.

After about four days, the zygote includes about 100 cells and resembles a hollow ball. The inner part of the ball is destined to become the baby. The outer layer of cells will form a number of structures that provide a life-support system throughout prenatal development.

By the end of the first week, the zygote reaches the uterus. *The next step is* implantation, *in which the zygote burrows into the uterine wall and establishes connections with a woman's blood vessels.* Implantation takes about a week to complete and triggers hormonal changes that prevent menstruation, letting the woman know that she has conceived.

The implanted zygote, shown in the photo, is less than a millimeter in diameter. Yet its cells have already begun to differentiate. *A small cluster of cells near the center of the zygote, the* germ disc, *will eventually develop into the baby.* The other cells are destined to become structures that support, nourish, and protect the developing organism. *For example, the layer of cells closest to the uterus will become the* placenta, *a structure through which nutrients and wastes are exchanged between the mother and the developing organism.*

Implantation and differentiation of cells mark the end of the period of the zygote. Comfortably settled in the shelter of the uterus, the zygote is well prepared for the remaining 36 weeks of the marvelous trek leading up to birth.

PERIOD OF THE EMBRYO (WEEKS 3–8)

Once the zygote is completely embedded in the uterine wall, it is called an embryo. This new period typically begins the third week after conception and lasts until the end of the eighth week. During the period of the embryo, body structures and internal organs develop. At the beginning of this period, three layers begin to form in the embryo. *The outer layer or* ectoderm *becomes hair, the outer layer of skin, and the nervous system; the middle layer or* mesoderm *forms muscles, bones, and the circulatory system; the inner layer or* endoderm *forms the digestive system and the lungs.*

One dramatic way to see these changes is to compare a 3-week-old embryo with an 8-week-old embryo. The 3-week-old embryo shown in the left photo is about 2 millimeters long. Specialization of cells is under way, but the organism looks more like a salamander than a human being. However, growth and specialization proceed so rapidly that an 8-week-old embryo—shown in the right photo—looks very different: You can see eyes, jaw, arms, and legs. The brain and the nervous system are developing rapidly, and the heart has been

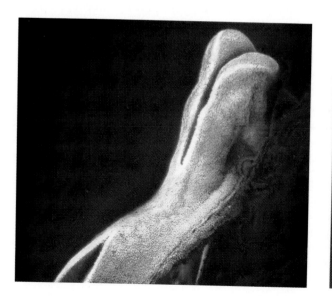

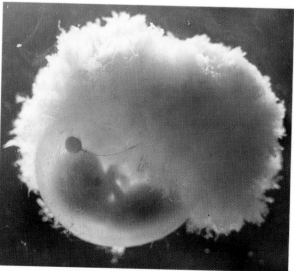

beating for nearly a month. Most of the organs found in a mature human are in place, in some form. (The sex organs are a notable exception.) Yet, being only an inch long and weighing a fraction of an ounce, the embryo is much too small for the mother to feel its presence.

The embryo's environment is shown in the diagram. *The embryo rests in a sac called the* amnion, *which is filled with* amniotic fluid *that cushions the embryo and maintains a constant temperature.* The embryo is linked to the

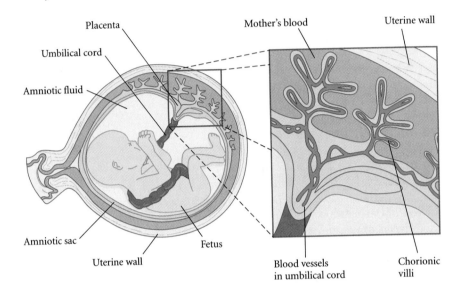

mother via two structures. *The* umbilical cord *houses blood vessels that join the embryo to the placenta.* In the placenta, the blood vessels from the umbilical cord run close to the mother's blood vessels, but aren't actually connected to them. The close proximity of the blood vessels allows nutrients, oxygen, vitamins, and waste products to be exchanged between mother and embryo.

Growth in the period of the embryo follows two important principles: First, the head develops before the rest of the body. *Such growth from the head to the base of the spine illustrates the* cephalocaudal principle. Second, arms and legs develop before hands and feet. *Growth of parts near the center of the body before those that are more distant illustrates the* proximodistal principle. Growth after birth also follows these principles.

With body structures and internal organs in place, the embryo has passed another major milestone in prenatal development. What's left is for these structures and organs to begin working properly. This is accomplished in the final period of prenatal development, as we'll see next.

PERIOD OF THE FETUS (WEEKS 9–38)

The final and longest phase of prenatal development, the period of the fetus, *begins at the ninth week (when cartilage begins to turn to bone) and ends at birth.* During this period, the baby-to-be becomes much larger and its bodily systems begin to work. The increase in size is remarkable. At the beginning of this period, the fetus weighs less than an ounce. At about four months, the fetus weighs roughly 4–8 ounces, which is large enough for the mother to feel its movements. In the last five months of pregnancy, the fetus will gain an additional 7 or 8 pounds before birth.

Also during this period, the finishing touches are placed on the many systems that are essential to human life, such as respiration, digestion, and vision. For example, by the fifth month, the billions of cells that make up the brain are in place and the brain has begun to function. Some simple reflexes like sucking and swallowing are present and mothers will sometimes feel the fetus hiccupping! The chart, which depicts the fetus at ⅛ its actual size, shows some highlights of this period.

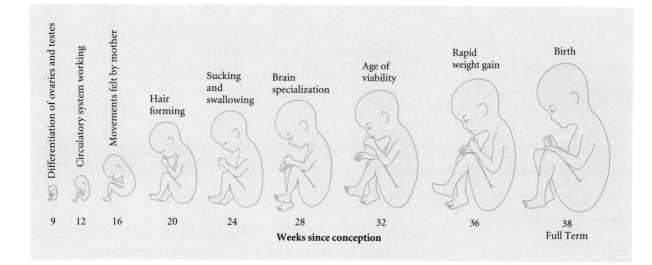

By about 7 months, most systems function well enough so that a fetus born at this age has a chance to survive, which is why 7 months is called the age of viability. At 7 months, the lungs are not yet fully mature, so babies born this early have trouble breathing. Also they cannot regulate their body temperature very well because they lack the insulating layer of fat that appears in the eighth month after conception. With modern neonatal intensive care, infants born this early can survive, but they face other challenges, as we'll see later in this chapter.

By the last two months of prenatal development, the fetus is so well developed that it has regular periods of activity and the eyes and ears have begun to function (Groome et al., 1997; Kisilevsky & Low, 1998). Of course, there's not much in the way of "visual experience" in the dark world of the uterus, but sounds abound. Microphones placed in the uterus reveal a noise level of about 75 decibels, which is the volume of normal conversation.

Remarkably, newborns apparently can recognize some of the sounds they experience during prenatal development. DeCasper and Spence (1986) had pregnant women read aloud the famous Dr. Seuss story *The Cat in the Hat* twice a day for the last 1½ months of pregnancy. As newborns, then, these babies had heard *The Cat in the Hat* more than 50 times! The newborns were then allowed to suck on a mechanical nipple connected to a tape recorder so that sucking could turn the tape on or off. Babies would suck to hear a tape of their mother reading *The Cat in the Hat* but not to hear her reading other stories. Evidently, newborns recognized the familiar, rhythmic quality of *The Cat in the Hat* from their prenatal story-times.

THINK ABOUT IT
Health care professionals often divide pregnancy into three 3-month trimesters. How do these three trimesters correspond to the periods of the zygote, embryo, and fetus?

Findings like these tell us that the last few months of prenatal development leave the fetus remarkably well prepared for independent living as a newborn baby. Unfortunately, not all babies arrive well prepared, because their prenatal development has been disrupted. Let's see how prenatal development sometimes goes awry.

TEST YOURSELF

1. The period of the zygote ends _____ .

2. Body structures and internal organs are created during the period of the _____ .

3. _____ is called the age of viability because this is when most body systems function well enough to support life.

4. An expert says, "Birth is when the environment starts to influence a child's development." Do you agree with the expert? Why or why not?

Answers: (1) at 2 weeks after conception (when the zygote is completely implanted in the wall of the uterus), (2) embryo, (3) Seven months

---

INFLUENCES ON PRENATAL DEVELOPMENT

Influences on Prenatal Development

General Risk Factors

Teratogens: Drugs, Diseases, and Environmental Hazards

How Teratogens Influence Prenatal Development

Prenatal Diagnosis and Treatment

Learning Objectives

- **How is prenatal development influenced by a pregnant woman's age, her nutrition, and the stress she experiences while pregnant?**

- **How do diseases, drugs, and environmental hazards sometimes affect prenatal development?**

- **What are some general principles affecting the ways that prenatal development can be harmed?**

- **How can prenatal development be monitored? Can abnormal prenatal development be corrected?**

*C*HLOE *was 2 months pregnant at her first prenatal checkup. As her appointment drew near, she began a list of questions to ask her obstetrician. "I spend much of my workday at a computer. Is radiation from the monitor harmful to my baby?" "When my husband and I get home from work, we'll have a glass of wine to help unwind from the stress of the day. Is moderate drinking like this okay?" "I'm 38. I know older women give birth to babies with mental retardation more often. Can I know if my baby will be mentally retarded?"*

Each of Chloe's questions concerns harm to her baby-to-be. She worries about the safety of her computer monitor, about her nightly glass of wine, and about her age. Chloe's concerns are well founded. Many factors influence the course of prenatal development and they are the focus of this section. If you're sure you can answer *all* of Chloe's questions, skip this section and go directly to page 72. Otherwise, read on to learn about problems that sometimes arise in pregnancy.

GENERAL RISK FACTORS

As the name implies, general risk factors can have widespread effects on prenatal development. Scientists have identified three such risk factors: parental age, nutrition, and stress.

Parental Age

The age of both the mother and the father can affect prenatal development. For women, the prime childbearing years are the 20s and early 30s. Teenage mothers as well as middle-aged (and older) mothers are more likely to have babies with birth defects, including mental retardation. For teenage mothers, problems are usually linked to poor health and to poor prenatal care (Goldenberg & Klerman, 1995). For older mothers, problems typically appear among women who are in poor health (Ales et al., 1990). Paternal age is also important; the odds that a damaged sperm will fertilize the egg increase steadily as men enter their 30s and 40s. For example, older men are more likely than younger men to contribute the extra 21st chromosome that leads to Down syndrome.

Maternal Nutrition

The mother is the sole source of nutrition throughout prenatal development, so a proper diet is vital. Proteins, vitamins, and iron are particularly important for pregnant women. When prenatal nourishment is not adequate, the baby is more likely to be born prematurely and to be underweight. Also, a poor diet can affect the development of the central nervous system and may leave babies vulnerable to illness (Guttmacher & Kaiser, 1986; Shaw et al., 1995).

Maternal Stress

Pregnant women who experience severe, prolonged stress often give birth to premature and irritable babies (Kalil et al., 1995; Schneider, Roughton, & Lubach, 1997). This may be because stress causes the secretion of hormones that reduce the flow of oxygen to the fetus while increasing its heart rate and activity level.

We can summarize these general factors by saying that prenatal development is most likely to proceed normally when women are in their 20s and 30s, have adequate health care and adequate nutrition, and lead lives that are free of chronic stress. However, even in these optimal cases, prenatal development can be disrupted by other, more specific influences.

TERATOGENS: DRUGS, DISEASES, AND ENVIRONMENTAL HAZARDS

In the late 1950s, many pregnant women in Germany took thalidomide, a drug that helped them sleep. Soon, however, came reports that many of these women were giving birth to babies with deformed arms, legs, hands, or fingers (Jensen, Benson, & Bobak, 1981). *Thalidomide is a powerful* teratogen, *an agent that causes abnormal prenatal development.* Ultimately, more than 7,000 babies worldwide were harmed before thalidomide was withdrawn from the market (Moore & Persaud, 1993).

Prompted by the thalidomide disaster, scientists began to study teratogens extensively. Today, we know a great deal about many teratogens that affect prenatal development. Most teratogens fall into one of three categories: drugs, diseases, and environmental hazards. Let's look at each.

Drugs

Thalidomide illustrates the harm that drugs can cause during prenatal development. The chart lists several other drugs that are known teratogens.

TERATOGENIC DRUGS AND THEIR CONSEQUENCES	
Drug	**Potential Consequences**
Alcohol	Fetal alcohol syndrome, cognitive deficits, heart damage, retarded growth
Aspirin	Deficits in intelligence, attention, and motor skill
Caffeine	Lower birth weight and decreased muscle tone
Cocaine and heroin	Retarded growth, irritability in newborns
Marijuana	Lower birth weight and less motor control
Nicotine	Retarded growth, facial deformities

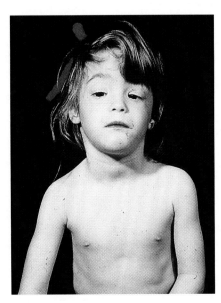

THINK ABOUT IT

A pregnant woman reluctant to give up her morning cup of coffee and nightly glass of wine says, "I drink so little coffee and wine that it couldn't possibly hurt my baby." What do you think?

Most of the drugs in the list are substances you may use routinely—alcohol, aspirin, caffeine, nicotine. Nevertheless, when consumed by pregnant women, they do present special dangers (Behnke & Eyler, 1993). Alcohol is a good example. *Pregnant women who consume large quantities of alcoholic beverages often give birth to babies with* fetal alcohol syndrome. Children with this syndrome usually grow more slowly than normal, have heart problems, and misshapen faces. Like the girl in the photo, youngsters with fetal alcohol syndrome often have a small head, a thin upper lip, a short nose, and widely spaced eyes. They are often mentally retarded and may have limited memory and motor skills (Church et al., 1997; Uecker & Nadel, 1996).

Fetal alcohol syndrome is most likely when pregnant women drink three or more ounces of alcohol daily. Does this mean that moderate drinking is safe? No. When women drink moderately throughout pregnancy, their children often have lower scores on tests of attention, memory, and intelligence (Streissguth et al., 1994).

Is there any amount of drinking that's safe during pregnancy? Maybe, but scientists have yet to determine one. This inconclusiveness stems from two factors. First, drinking is often estimated from women's responses to interviews or questionnaires. These replies may be incorrect, leading to inaccurate estimates of the harm associated with drinking. Second, any safe level of consumption is probably not the same for all women. Based on their health and heredity, some women may be able to consume more alcohol safely than others.

These factors make it impossible to offer guaranteed statements about safe levels of alcohol or any of the other drugs listed in the table above. For this reason, the best policy is for women to avoid all drugs throughout pregnancy.

Diseases

Sometimes women become ill while pregnant. Most diseases, such as colds and many strains of the flu, do not affect the fetus. However, several bacterial and viral infections can be quite harmful; five are listed in the chart.

TERATOGENIC DISEASES AND THEIR CONSEQUENCES	
Disease	**Potential Consequences**
AIDS	Frequent infections, neurological disorders, death
Cytomegalovirus	Deafness, blindness, abnormally small head, mental retardation
Genital herpes	Encephalitis, enlarged spleen, improper blood clotting
Rubella	Mental retardation, damage to eyes, ears, and heart
Syphilis	Damage to the central nervous system, teeth, and bones

Some diseases pass from the mother through the placenta to attack the embryo or fetus directly. AIDS, cytomegalovirus, rubella, and syphilis are examples of diseases that are transmitted through the placenta. Other diseases attack during birth: The virus is present in the lining of the birth canal and babies are infected as they pass through the canal. AIDS and genital herpes are two such diseases.

The only way to guarantee that these diseases will not harm prenatal development is for a woman to be sure that she does not contract the disease, before or during her pregnancy. Medicines that may help to treat a woman after she has become ill do not prevent the disease from damaging the fetus.

Environmental Hazards

As a by-product of life in an industrialized world, people are often exposed to toxins in food they eat, fluids they drink, and air they breathe. Chemicals associated with industrial waste are the most common form of environmentally based teratogen. The quantity involved is usually minute; however, as was true for drugs, amounts that go unnoticed in an adult can cause serious damage to the fetus. Several environmental hazards that are known teratogens are listed in the table.

ENVIRONMENTAL TERATOGENS AND THEIR CONSEQUENCES	
Hazard	**Potential Consequences**
Lead	Mental retardation
Mercury	Retarded growth, mental retardation, cerebral palsy
PCBs	Impaired verbal and memory skill
X-rays	Retarded growth, leukemia, mental retardation

You'll notice that although X-rays are included in the table, radiation associated with computer monitors or video-display terminals (VDTs) is not. Several major studies have examined the impact of exposure to the electromagnetic fields generated by VDTs. For example, Schnorr and her colleagues (1991) compared the outcomes of pregnancies in telephone operators who worked at VDTs at least 25 hours weekly with operators who never used VDTs. For both groups of women, about 15% of their pregnancies ended in miscarriage. Further, other studies have not found links between exposure to VDTs and birth defects (Parazzini et al., 1991). Evidently, VDTs can be used safely by pregnant women.

In the Spotlight on Research feature, we look at one of these environmental teratogens in detail.

SPOTLIGHT ON RESEARCH

INDUSTRIAL TOXINS AND MENTAL DEVELOPMENT

Who were the investigators and what was the aim of the study? For many years, polychlorinated biphenyls (PCBs) were used in electrical transformers and in paints. PCBs were banned by the U.S. government in the 1970s; however, like many industrial by-products, they have seeped into the waterways, where they can contaminate fish and wildlife. The amount of PCBs in a typical contaminated fish does not affect adults, but Joseph Jacobson, Sandra Jacobson, and Harold Humphrey (1990) wanted to determine whether this level of exposure is harmful to prenatal development. In particular, they knew from earlier work that substantial prenatal exposure to PCBs influenced infants' cognitive skills; they hoped to determine whether preschool children's cognitive skills were affected similarly.

How did the investigators measure the topic of interest? Jacobson and his colleagues needed to measure both cognitive skill and prenatal exposure to PCBs. To measure cognitive skill, they used a standardized test, the McCarthy Scales for Children's Abilities. This test measures children's abilities in five areas: verbal, perceptual, quantitative, memory, and motor abilities. To determine prenatal exposure to PCBs, they measured concentrations of PCBs in (a) blood obtained from the umbilical cord, and (b) for mothers who were breast-feeding, a sample of her breast milk.

Who were the participants in the study? The sample included 236 children who were born in western Michigan in 1980–1981. This region was chosen because, at the time, Lake Michigan contained many contaminated salmon and lake trout.

What was the design of the study? This study was correlational because the investigators were interested in the relation that existed naturally between two variables: exposure to PCBs and cognitive skill. The study was longitudinal because children were tested twice: Their exposure to PCBs was measured immediately after birth, and their cognitive skill was measured at 4 years of age.

Were there ethical concerns with the study? No. The children had been exposed to PCBs naturally, prior to the start of the study. (Obviously, it would not have been ethical to do an experimental study in which Jacobson and his colleagues deliberately asked pregnant women to eat contaminated fish.) The investigators obtained permission from the parents for the children to participate.

What were the results? On several tasks, exposure to PCBs did not affect performance. Specifically, PCB exposure was unrelated to performance on the perceptual, quantitative, and motor scales of the McCarthy tests. That is, children with high levels of PCB exposure were just as likely to get high scores on these tests as children with low levels of PCB exposure. However, PCB exposure did affect scores on the verbal and memory scales. Looking at the graphs, you can see that verbal and memory scores were highest for those with the least prenatal exposure to PCBs and lowest for the 4-year-olds with the greatest prenatal exposure. In other words, as prenatal exposure to PCBs increased, verbal and memory skills decreased.

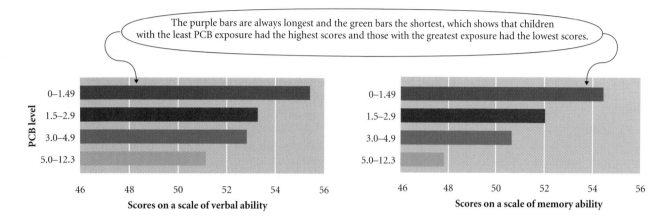

What did the investigators conclude? Prenatal exposure to PCBs does harm at least two aspects of cognitive development—verbal and memory skill. Children's scores were in the normal range. Nevertheless, because of their reduced verbal and memory skills, these youngsters will probably have some trouble in school, such as in learning to read. •

Environmental teratogens are treacherous because people are unaware of their presence in the environment. The women in the Jacobson, Jacobson, and Humphrey (1990) study, for example, did not realize that they were eating PCB-laden fish. This invisibility makes it more difficult for a pregnant woman to protect herself from environmental teratogens. The best advice is for a pregnant woman to be particularly careful of the foods she eats and the air she breathes. Be sure that all foods are cleaned thoroughly to rid them of insecticides. Avoid convenience foods, which often contain many chemical additives. Stay away from air that's been contaminated by household products such as cleansers, paint strippers, and fertilizers. Women in jobs such as housecleaning or hairdressing that require contact with potential teratogens should try to switch to less potent chemicals. For example, they should use baking soda instead of more chemically laden cleansers. And they should wear protective gloves, aprons, and masks to reduce their contact with potential teratogens. Finally, because environmental teratogens continue to increase, check with a health care provider to learn whether other materials should be avoided.

HOW TERATOGENS INFLUENCE PRENATAL DEVELOPMENT

By assembling all the evidence on the harm caused by drugs, diseases, and environmental hazards, scientists have identified four important general principles about how teratogens usually work (Hogge, 1990; Vorhees & Mollnow, 1987).

1. *The impact of a teratogen depends upon the genotype of the organism.* A substance may be harmful to one species but not to another. To determine its safety, thalidomide was tested on pregnant rats and rabbits, and their offspring

had normal limbs. Yet, when pregnant women took the same drug in comparable doses, many had children with deformed limbs. Moreover, some women who took thalidomide gave birth to babies with normal limbs while others, taking comparable doses of thalidomide at the same time in their pregnancies, gave birth to babies with deformed arms and legs. Apparently, heredity makes some individuals more susceptible than others to a teratogen.

2.   *The impact of teratogens changes over the course of prenatal development.* The timing of exposure to a teratogen is very important. Teratogens typically have different effects in the three periods of prenatal development. The chart shows how the consequences of teratogens differ for the periods of the zygote, embryo, and fetus. During the period of the zygote, exposure to teratogens usually results in spontaneous abortion of the fertilized egg. During the period of

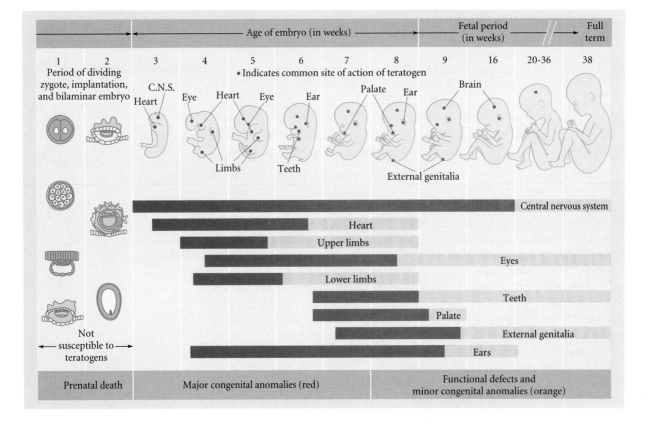

the embryo, exposure to teratogens produces major defects in bodily structure. For example, women who took thalidomide during the period of the embryo had babies with ill-formed or missing limbs. Women who contract rubella during the period of the embryo have babies with heart defects. During the period of the fetus, exposure to teratogens produces either minor defects in bodily structure or causes body systems to function improperly. For example, when women drink large quantities of alcohol during this period, the fetus develops fewer brain cells.

Even within the different periods of prenatal development, developing body parts and systems are more vulnerable at some times than others. The red shading in the chart indicates a time of maximum vulnerability; orange shading indicates a time when the developing organism is less vulnerable. The heart, for example, is most sensitive to teratogens during the first half of the embryonic period. Exposure to teratogens before this time rarely produces heart damage; exposure after results in milder damage.

3.   *Each teratogen affects a specific aspect (or aspects) of prenatal development.* Said another way, teratogens do not harm all body systems; instead, damage is selective. When women contract rubella, their babies often have problems with their eyes, ears, and heart, but they have normal limbs. When mothers consume PCB-contaminated fish, their babies typically have normal body parts and normal motor skill but below-average verbal and memory skills.

4.   *Damage from teratogens is not always evident at birth but may appear later in life.* In the case of malformed limbs or babies born addicted to cocaine, the effects of a teratogen are obvious immediately. Sometimes, however, the damage from a teratogen becomes evident only as the child develops. For example, when women ate PCB-contaminated fish, their babies were normal at birth. Their below-average cognitive skills were not evident until several months later.

An even more dramatic example of the delayed impact of a teratogen involves the drug diethylstilbestrol (DES). Between 1947 and 1971, many pregnant women took DES to prevent miscarriages. Their babies were apparently normal at birth. However, as adults, daughters of women who took DES are more likely to have a rare cancer of the vagina and to have difficulties becoming pregnant themselves. Sons of women who took DES may have abnormal seminal fluid and are at risk for cancer of the testes (Meyers, 1983). Here is a case in which the impact of the teratogen is not evident until decades after birth.

The Real World of Prenatal Risk

We have discussed risk factors individually, as if each was the only potential threat to prenatal development. In reality, many infants are exposed to multiple general risks and multiple teratogens. Pregnant women who drink often smoke and drink coffee (Barr et al., 1990). Pregnant women who are under stress often drink alcohol (Giberson & Weinberg, 1992). Many of these same women may have poor nutrition. When all of the risks are combined, unfortunately, prenatal development will rarely be optimal (Schneider et al., 1997).

From what we've said so far in this section, you may think that the developing child has little chance of escaping harm. But most babies *are* born in good health. Of course, a good policy for pregnant women is to avoid diseases, drugs, and environmental hazards that are known teratogens. This, coupled with thorough prenatal medical care and adequate nutrition, is the best recipe for normal prenatal development.

PRENATAL DIAGNOSIS AND TREATMENT

"I really don't care whether I have a boy or girl, just as long as it's healthy." Legions of parents worldwide have felt this way, but until recently, all they could do was hope for the best. Today, however, advances in technology mean that parents can have a much better idea whether their baby is developing normally.

Genetic Counseling

Often the first step in deciding whether a couple's baby is likely to be at risk is genetic counseling. A counselor asks about family medical history and constructs a family tree for each parent to assess the odds that their child would inherit a disorder. If the family tree suggests that a parent is likely to be a carrier of the disorder, blood tests can determine the parent's genotype. With this information, a genetic counselor then advises prospective parents about their choices. A couple might simply go ahead and attempt to conceive a child "naturally." Or, they may decide to use sperm or eggs from other people. Yet another choice might be adoption.

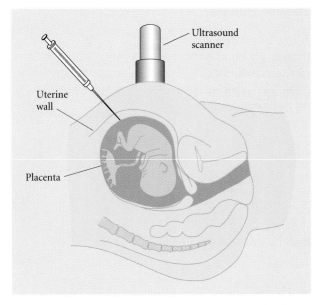

Prenatal Diagnosis

After a woman is pregnant, how can we know whether prenatal development is progressing normally? Traditionally, obstetricians tracked the progress of prenatal development by feeling the size and position of the fetus through a woman's abdomen. This technique was not very precise and, of course, couldn't be done at all until the fetus was large enough to feel. Today, however, several new techniques have revolutionized our ability to monitor prenatal growth and development. *A standard part of prenatal care in the United States is* ultrasound, *in which sound waves are used to generate a picture of the fetus.* In this procedure, shown in the photo, a tool about the size of a hair dryer is rubbed over the woman's abdomen; the image is shown on a nearby TV monitor. The pictures that are generated are hardly portrait quality; they are grainy and it takes an expert's eye to distinguish what's what. Nevertheless, parents are often thrilled to see their baby and to watch it move.

Ultrasound typically can be used as early as 4 or 5 weeks after conception; prior to this time the embryo is not large enough to generate an interpretable image. Ultrasound pictures are quite useful for determining the position of the fetus within the uterus and, at 16–20 weeks after conception, its sex. Ultrasound is also helpful in detecting twins or triplets. Finally, ultrasound is used to identify gross physical deformities, such as abnormal growth of the head.

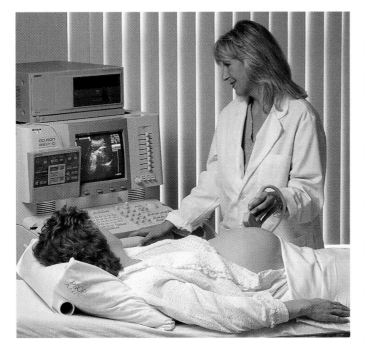

In pregnancies where a genetic disorder is suspected, two other techniques are particularly valuable because they provide a sample of fetal cells that can be analyzed. *In* amniocentesis, *a needle is inserted through the mother's abdomen to obtain a sample of the amniotic fluid that surrounds the fetus.* As you can see in the diagram, ultrasound is used to guide the needle into the uterus. The fluid contains skin cells that can be grown in a laboratory dish and then analyzed to determine the genotype of the fetus.

A drawback to amniocentesis is that although the amniotic fluid is extracted at about 16 weeks after conception, another three weeks must pass for the individual cells to grow sufficiently to allow testing. *A procedure that can be used much earlier in pregnancy is* chorionic villus sampling *in which a sample of tissue is obtained from part of the placenta.* The diagram shows that a small tube, inserted through the vagina and into the uterus, is used to collect a small plug of cells from the placenta. This procedure can be used within 8 or 9 weeks after conception, and results are available within 24 hours.

With the samples obtained from either amniocentesis or chorionic villus sampling, roughly 200 different genetic disorders, including Down syndrome, can be detected. These procedures are virtually error-free but at a price: Miscarriages are slightly more likely—1 or 2%—after amniocentesis or chorionic villus sampling (Cunningham, MacDonald, & Gant, 1989). A woman must decide whether the information gained from amniocentesis or chorionic villus sampling justifies the slight risks of a possible miscarriage.

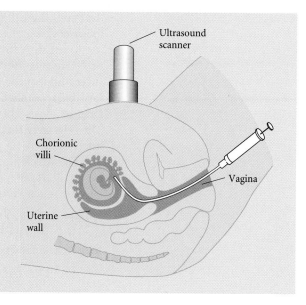

Fetal Medicine

Ultrasound, amniocentesis, and chorionic villus sampling have made it much easier to determine whether prenatal development is progressing normally. But what happens when it is not? Traditionally, a woman's options have been limited: She could continue the pregnancy or end it. However, the list of options is expanding. *A whole new field called* fetal medicine *is concerned with treating prenatal problems before birth.* One approach in fetal medicine is to treat disorders medically, by administering drugs or hormones to the fetus. In one case, ultrasound pictures showed a fetus with an enlarged thyroid gland that would have made delivery difficult. A hormone injected into the amniotic fluid caused the thyroid gland to shrink and resulted in a normal delivery (Davidson et al., 1991). In another case, amniocentesis revealed that a fetus had inherited a disorder in which the immune system did not work properly. This would leave a baby vulnerable to infection, so healthy immune cells were injected into the umbilical cord (Elmer-DeWitt, 1994).

Another approach is fetal surgery. Doctors partially remove the fetus from the uterus, perform corrective surgery, then return the fetus to the uterus. One example involves repairing the diaphragm, which separates the lungs from other organs in the abdomen. If the diaphragm does not develop properly, babies often die at birth because they cannot breathe properly. To correct an abnormal diaphragm, during the seventh or eighth month of pregnancy, surgeons cut through the mother's abdominal wall to expose the fetus, then through the fetal abdominal wall; the diaphragm is repaired and the fetus is returned to the uterus (Kolata, 1990). Surgery has also been used to correct some heart defects and blockages in the urinary tract (Ohlendorf-Moffat, 1992).

Yet another approach is genetic engineering in which defective genes are replaced by synthetic normal genes. Take PKU as an example. Remember that if a baby inherits the recessive allele for PKU from both parents, toxins that cause mental retardation accumulate. In theory, it should be possible to take a sample of cells from the fetus, remove the recessive genes, and replace them with the dominant genes. These "repaired" cells would then be injected into

? THINK ABOUT IT
Imagine that you are 42 years old and pregnant. Would you want to have amniocentesis or chorionic villus sampling to determine the genotype of the fetus? Why or why not?

the fetus, where they would multiply and cause enough enzyme to be produced to break down phenylalanine, thereby avoiding PKU (Verma, 1990).

Translating this idea into practice has been difficult, and there are many problems yet to be solved (Marshall, 1995). Nevertheless, gene therapy has been successful in a few cases. In one, a preschool girl was suffering from a hereditary disease of the immune system that left her unprotected against infection. Doctors took some of the girl's cells and inserted the immune gene into them. The cells were then injected into her bloodstream, where they help ward off infection.

These techniques are highly experimental and failures are common. However, this area of medicine is advancing rapidly, and prenatal treatment should become much more common in the 21st century.

Answers to Chloe's Questions. Now you can return to Chloe's questions in the section-opening vignette (page 62) and answer them for her. If you're not certain, here are the pages in this chapter where the answers appear:

- About her computer monitor—page 66
- About her nightly glass of wine—page 64
- About giving birth to a baby with mental retardation—page 71

TEST YOURSELF

1. General risk factors include parental age, _____, and maternal stress.

2. _____ are some of the most dangerous teratogens because a pregnant woman is often unaware of their presence.

3. During the period of the zygote, exposure to a teratogen typically results in _____ .

4. Two techniques used to determine whether a fetus has a hereditary disorder are amniocentesis and _____ .

5. Select three teratogens from those described on pages 63–67: one that represents a normative age-graded influence on development, one that represents a normative history-graded influence, and another that represents a nonnormative influence.

Answers: (1) the pregnant woman's nutrition, (2) Environmental hazards, (3) spontaneous abortion of the fertilized egg, (4) chorionic villus sampling

---

LABOR AND DELIVERY

Labor and Delivery

Stages of Labor

Approaches to Childbirth

Birth Complications

Infant Mortality

Learning Objectives

- **What are the different phases of labor and delivery?**
- **What are "natural" ways of coping with the pain of childbirth? Is childbirth at home safe?**
- **What are some complications that can occur during birth?**

ARLEA *is about to begin classes to prepare for her baby's birth. She is relieved that the classes are finally starting because this means the end of pregnancy is in sight. But all the talk she has heard about "breathing exercises" and "coaching" sounds pretty silly to her. Marlea would prefer to get knocked out for the delivery and wake up when everything is over.*

As women like Marlea near the end of pregnancy, they find that sleeping and breathing become more difficult, that they tire more rapidly, that they become constipated, and that their legs and feet swell. Women look forward to birth, both to relieve their discomfort and, of course, to see their baby. In this section, you'll see the different steps involved in birth, review different approaches to childbirth, and look at problems that can arise. Along the way, we'll look at classes like those Marlea will take and the exercises that she'll learn.

STAGES OF LABOR

Labor is an appropriate name for childbirth, which is the most intense, prolonged physical effort that humans experience. Labor is usually divided into the three stages shown in the diagram.

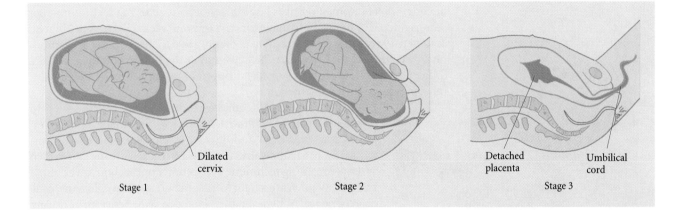

Dilated cervix

Detached placenta

Umbilical cord

Stage 1   Stage 2   Stage 3

- In stage 1, which may last from 12 to 24 hours for a first birth, the uterus starts to contract. The first contractions are weak and irregular. Gradually, they become stronger and more rhythmic, enlarging the cervix (the opening from the uterus to the vagina) to approximately 10 centimeters.

- In stage 2, the baby passes through the cervix and enters the vagina. The mother helps push the baby along by contracting muscles in her abdomen. *Soon the top of the baby's head appears, an event known as* crowning. Within about an hour, the baby is delivered.

- In stage 3, which lasts only minutes, the mother pushes a few more times to expel the placenta (also called, appropriately, the *afterbirth*).

The times given for each of the stages are only approximations; the actual times vary greatly among women. For most women, labor with their second and subsequent children is much more rapid. Stage 1 may last 4 – 6 hours, and stage 2 may be as brief as 20 minutes.

APPROACHES TO CHILDBIRTH

When your authors were born in the 1950s, women in labor were admitted to a hospital and administered a general anesthetic. Fathers waited anxiously in a nearby room for news of the baby. Since the 1960s, however, many people have tried more "natural" or prepared approaches to childbirth in which labor and delivery are seen as life events to be celebrated, not medical procedures to be endured. Prepared approaches to childbirth include many elements, but one of the fundamentals is the belief that birth is more likely to be problem-free and rewarding when mothers and fathers understand what's happening during pregnancy, labor, and delivery. Consequently, prepared childbirth means going to classes in which individuals learn basic facts about pregnancy and childbirth (not unlike the material presented in this chapter).

Childbirth classes also spend much time showing women how to handle the pain of childbirth. Natural methods of dealing with pain are emphasized over medication. Why? General anesthesia (medication that causes a woman to lose consciousness) or local anesthesia (medication that numbs the lower body) prevents women from using their abdominal muscles to help push the baby through the birth canal. Without this pushing, obstetricians sometimes have to use mechanical devices to pull the baby through the birth canal, a practice that involves some risk to the baby (Johanson et al., 1993). Also, drugs that reduce the pain of childbirth cross the placenta and affect the baby. Consequently, when a women receives large doses of pain-relieving medication, her baby is often withdrawn or irritable for days or even weeks (Brazelton, Nugent, & Lester, 1987; Emory, Schlackman, & Fiano, 1996). These effects are temporary; nevertheless, they may give the new mother the impression that she has a difficult baby. These problems make it important to minimize the use of pain-relieving drugs during birth.

Childbirth classes emphasize three related strategies to counter the pain of birth without drugs. One strategy is based on the fact that pain often feels greater when a person is tense. Consequently, pregnant women learn ways to relax during labor, such as deep-breathing techniques. A second approach involves visual imagery. Women are taught to imagine a reassuring, pleasant scene or experience. Whenever they begin to experience pain during labor, they focus intensely on this image instead of the pain. A third element is a supportive "coach." The father-to-be, a relative, or close friend attends childbirth classes with the mother-to-be. The coach learns the techniques for coping with pain and, like the man in the top photo, practices them with the pregnant woman. During labor and delivery, the coach helps the woman to use these techniques and offers support and encouragement.

Although Marlea, the pregnant woman in the vignette, may have her doubts about these classes, research shows that they *are* useful (Hetherington, 1990). Although most mothers who attend childbirth classes use some medication to reduce the pain of labor, they typically use less than mothers who do not attend childbirth classes. Also, mothers and fathers who attend childbirth classes feel more positively about labor and birth when compared to mothers and fathers who have not attended classes.

Another element of the trend to natural childbirth is the idea that birth need not always take place in a hospital. Virtually all babies in the United States are born in hospitals—only 1% are born at home. However, home birth is a common practice in Europe. In the Netherlands, for example, about one-third of all births take place at home. Advocates note that home delivery is less expensive and that most women are more relaxed during labor in their homes. Advocates also point out that many women enjoy the greater control they have over labor and birth in a home delivery. A health care professional is present in the home during labor and delivery. This is sometimes a doctor but is more often a trained nurse-midwife like the one in the photo.

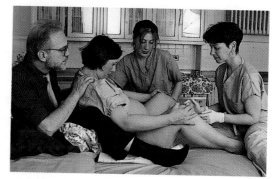

For Americans accustomed to hospital delivery, home delivery can seem like a risky proposition. Is home delivery safe? Yes, but with a very important catch. Birth problems are no more common in babies delivered at home than in babies delivered in a hospital, but only when the woman is healthy, her pregnancy has been problem-free, the labor and delivery are expected to be problem-free, and a trained health care professional assists with the delivery (Rooks et al., 1989). If there is *any* reason to believe that labor and delivery may encounter problems that require medical assistance, labor and delivery should take place in the hospital, not at home.

American women who are reluctant to give birth at home can turn to birth centers. These are typically smaller clinics that are independent of a hospital. A woman, her coach, and other family members and friends are assigned a birthing room that is often decorated to look more homelike. A doctor or nurse-midwife assists in labor and delivery, which takes place entirely in the birthing room, where it can be observed by all. Like home deliveries, birthing centers are best for deliveries that should be trouble-free.

BIRTH COMPLICATIONS

Birth requires that the newborn adjust rapidly to a new environment outside the uterus. Breathing is the most important of the many changes the newborn must make. Within moments after birth, babies must draw oxygen from their own lungs instead of from blood supplied from their mother, via the placenta. *If the umbilical cord connecting the baby to the placenta is pinched or tangled during delivery, or if the newborn's lungs do not react properly, the result is* anoxia, *lack of oxygen*. Lacking oxygen, cells begin to die, particularly those in the brain. Severe anoxia can cause mental retardation and cerebral palsy (Apgar & Beck, 1974).

Problems also arise when babies are born too early or too small. Normally, a baby spends about 38 weeks developing before being born. *Babies born before the 36th week are called* preterm *or* premature. In the first year or so, premature infants often lag behind full-term infants in many facets of development. However, by 2 or 3 years of age, such differences have vanished, and most premature infants develop normally (Greenberg & Crnic, 1988).

Prospects are usually not as bright for babies who are "small for date." Though born after a normal-length pregnancy, these babies are much smaller than normal, usually because the mother's nutrition was inadequate or because of congenital infections (Allen, 1984). *Newborns who weigh 2,500 grams (5.5 pounds) or less are said to have* low birth weight; *newborns weighing less than 1,500 grams (3.3 pounds) are said to have* very low birth weight; *and those weighing less than 1,000 grams (2.2 pounds) are said to have* extremely low birth weight.

Babies with very or extremely low birth weight do not fare well. Many do not survive; those who live often lag behind in the development of intellectual and motor skills (Sykes et al., 1997; Ventura et al., 1994). The odds are better for newborns who weigh more than 1,500 grams. Most survive. Some will develop normally, but others will always lag behind. Why? The Forces in Action feature provides some clues.

? **THINK ABOUT IT**
A friend of yours has just given birth 6 weeks prematurely. The baby is average size for a baby born prematurely and seems to be faring well, but your friend is concerned nonetheless. What could you say to reassure your friend?

WHAT DETERMINES LIFE OUTCOMES FOR LOW-BIRTH-WEIGHT BABIES?

Why do some low-birth-weight babies recover completely, but others do not? Biological forces are not the only factors determining whether low-birth-weight babies thrive. Sociocultural forces are critical: Low-birth-weight babies thrive *if* they receive excellent medical care and their home environment is supportive and stimulating. Unfortunately, not all low-birth-weight babies have optimal experiences. Many receive inadequate medical care because their families live in poverty. Others experience stress and disorder in their family life. For these low-birth-weight babies, development is usually delayed and sometimes permanently diminished.

The importance of a supportive environment for low-birth-weight babies is underscored by the results of a 30-year longitudinal study by Werner (1989), covering all children born on the Hawaiian island of Kauai in 1955. When low-birth-weight children grew up in stable homes—defined as the presence of two, mentally healthy parents throughout childhood—they were indistinguishable from children born without birth complications. However, when low-birth-weight children experienced an unstable family environment—defined as experiencing divorce, parental alcoholism, or parental mental illness—they lagged behind their peers in intellectual and social development.

Thus, when biological and sociocultural forces are both harmful—low birth weight *plus* inadequate medical care or family stress—the prognosis for babies is grim. The message to parents of low-birth-weight newborns is clear: Do not despair, because excellent caregiving can compensate for all but the most severe birth problems (Werner & Smith, 1992; Werner, 1994). ●

INFANT MORTALITY

In many respects, medical facilities in the United States are the finest in the world. Nevertheless, American babies don't fare well compared to infants from other countries. Infant mortality *is the number of infants out of 1,000 births who die before their first birthday.* In the United States, about 9 babies out of 1,000 — roughly 1% — live less than a year. This figure places the United States near the bottom of the industrialized countries of the world, as you can see in the graph (Wegman, 1994).

Why do so many American babies die? Low birth weight is part of the answer. The United States has more babies with low birth weight than any of the other countries listed in the graph, and we've already seen that low birth weight places an infant at risk. Low birth weight can usually be prevented when a pregnant woman has regular prenatal care, but many pregnant women in the United States receive inadequate or no prenatal care. Virtually all of the countries that rank ahead of the United States provide extensive prenatal care, at little or no cost. In addition, many of these countries provide for paid leaves of absence for pregnant women (Kamerman, 1993).

Prenatal development is the foundation of all development and only with regular prenatal checkups can we know whether this foundation is being laid properly. Pregnant women and the children they carry *need* this care.

Canada
Netherlands
Switzerland
Germany
Australia
France
Great Britain
Denmark
Austria
Spain
Ireland
Greece
New Zealand
Italy
Belgium
United States
Israel
Portugal
Cuba

0   5   10   15

Infant mortality
(Number of deaths per 1,000 births)

1. In the third stage of labor, the _____ is delivered.

2. Two problems with using anesthesia during labor are that a woman can't use her abdominal muscles to help push the baby down the birth canal and _____ .

3. Home delivery is safe when the pregnant woman is healthy, has had a problem-free pregnancy, expects to have a problem-free delivery, and _____ .

4. When the supply of oxygen to the fetus is disrupted because the umbilical cord is squeezed shut, _____ results.

5. Do studies on the long-term effects of prematurity and low birth weight provide evidence for continuity in development or discontinuity? Why?

Answers: (1) placenta, (2) the pain-relieving medication crosses the placenta and affects the baby, (3) when trained health care professionals are present to deliver the baby, (4) anoxia

PUTTING IT ALL TOGETHER

This chapter began with conception, covered 38 weeks of prenatal development, and ended with birth. You saw the mighty impact of the shuffling of genes that occurs at conception. Sometimes single genes influence development, as in the case of the sickle-cell disease that so frightens Leslie. More often, many genes work together to influence growth, with the outcome depending strongly on the impact of the environment. You learned that structures and processes unfold in a predictable sequence during prenatal development and this knowledge answered some of Eun Jung's questions about her pregnancy. You also learned how and why prenatal development sometimes goes awry and used this information to address Chloe's concerns about how her health and behavior might affect her baby's development. Finally, you looked at labor and delivery, including some of the advantages of a prepared childbirth such as Marlea plans to have.

This chapter, more than most of the others in this book, has emphasized the biological components of the biopsychosocial framework. Even here, however, biological forces do not operate in isolation but in interaction with the other elements of the framework. Prenatal development reflects biologically programmed events plus environmental influences on the fetus.

The development we have traced in this chapter serves as a prelude to the remainder of life-span human development. Each succeeding stage builds on the themes established in the prelude, as we'll see in the next chapter, which is devoted to infancy.

SUMMARY

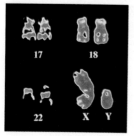

In the Beginning: 23 Pairs of Chromosomes

Mechanisms of Heredity

• At conception, the 23 chromosomes in the sperm merge with the 23 chromosomes in the egg. Each chromosome is one molecule of DNA; a section of DNA that provides specific biochemical instructions is called a gene.

• All of a person's genes make up a genotype; the phenotype refers to the physical, behavioral, and psychological characteristics that develop when the genotype is exposed to a specific environment.

• Different forms of the same gene are called alleles. A person who inherits the same allele on a pair of chromosomes is homozygous; in this case, the biochemical instructions on the allele are followed. A person who inherits different alleles is heterozygous; in this case, the instructions of the dominant allele are followed whereas those of the recessive allele are ignored.

• Behavioral and psychological phenotypes that reflect an underlying continuum (such as intelligence) often involve polygenic inheritance. In polygenic inheritance, the phenotype reflects the combined activity of many distinct genes. Polygenic inheritance is often examined by studying twins and adopted children. These studies indicate substantial influence of heredity on intelligence and personality.

Genetic Disorders

• Most inherited disorders are carried by recessive alleles. Examples include sickle-cell disease and phenylketonuria, in which toxins accumulate and cause mental retardation. Sometimes fertilized eggs do not have 46 chromosomes. Usually they are aborted spontaneously soon after conception. An exception is Down syndrome, in which individuals usually have an extra 21st chromosome. Down-syndrome individuals have a distinctive appearance and are mentally retarded. Disorders of the sex chromosomes are more common because these chromosomes contain less genetic material than autosomes.

Heredity Is Not Destiny: Genes and Environments

• PKU is an inherited disorder in which phenylalanine accumulates in the body, damaging the nervous system. The mental retardation that usually results can be avoided through a diet that is low in phenylalanine. This demonstrates the concept of reaction range—the outcome of heredity depends on the environment in which development occurs.

• Heredity can influence the types of experiences that children have. People seek environments that fit their genotype; this process is known as niche-picking.

From Conception to Birth

Period of the Zygote (Weeks 1–2)

• The first period of prenatal development lasts 2 weeks. It begins when the egg is fertilized by the sperm in the Fallopian tube and ends when the fertilized egg has implanted in the wall of the uterus. By the end of this period, cells have begun to differentiate.

Period of the Embryo (Weeks 3–8)

• The second period of prenatal development begins 2 weeks after conception and ends 8 weeks after. This is a period of rapid growth in which most major body structures are created. Growth in this period is cephalocaudal (the head develops first) and proximodistal (parts near the center of the body develop first).

Period of the Fetus (Weeks 9–38)

• The third period of prenatal development begins 8 weeks after conception and lasts until birth. The highlights of this period are a remarkable increase in the size of the fetus and changes in body systems that are necessary for life. By 7 months, most body systems function well enough to support life.

Influences on Prenatal Development

General Risk Factors

• Parents' age can affect prenatal development. Teenagers often have problem pregnancies mainly because they rarely receive adequate prenatal care. Older women in poor health are more likely to have problem pregnancies, and older men are more likely to have damaged sperm. Prenatal development can also be harmed if a pregnant mother has inadequate nutrition or experiences considerable stress.

Teratogens: Drugs, Diseases, and Environmental Hazards

• Teratogens are agents that can cause abnormal prenatal development. Many drugs that adults take are teratogens. For most drugs, scientists have not established amounts that can be consumed safely. Several diseases are teratogens. Only by avoiding these diseases entirely can a pregnant woman escape their harmful consequences. Environmental teratogens are particularly dangerous because a pregnant woman may not know that these substances are present in the environment.

How Teratogens Influence Prenatal Development

• The impact of teratogens depends upon the genotype of the organism, the period of prenatal development when the organism is exposed to the teratogen, and the amount of exposure. Sometimes the impact of a teratogen is not evident until later in life.

Prenatal Diagnosis and Treatment

• Many techniques are used to track the progress of prenatal development. A common component of prenatal care is ultrasound, which uses sound waves to generate a picture of the fetus. This picture can be used to determine the position of the fetus, its sex, and whether there are gross physical deformities. When genetic disorders are suspected, amniocentesis and chorionic villus sampling are used to determine the genotype of the fetus. Fetal medicine is a new field in which problems of prenatal development are corrected medically, with surgery, or using genetic engineering.

Labor and Delivery

Stages of Labor

• Labor consists of three stages. In stage 1, the muscles of the uterus contract. The contractions, which are weak at first and gradually become stronger, cause the cervix to enlarge. In stage 2, the baby moves through the birth canal. In stage 3, the placenta is delivered.

Approaches to Childbirth

• Natural or prepared childbirth is based on the assumption that parents should understand what takes place during pregnancy and birth. In natural childbirth, pain-relieving medications are avoided because this medication prevents women from pushing during labor and because it affects the fetus. Instead, women learn to cope with pain through relaxation, imagery, and with the help of a supportive coach.

• Most American babies are born in hospitals, but many European babies are born at home. Home delivery is safe when the mother is healthy, pregnancy and birth are trouble-free, and a health care professional is present to deliver the baby.

Birth Complications

• During labor and delivery, the flow of blood to the fetus can be disrupted because the umbilical cord is squeezed shut. This causes anoxia, a lack of oxygen to the fetus. Some babies are born prematurely and others are small for date. Premature babies develop more slowly at first but catch up by 2 or 3 years of age. Small-for-date babies often do not fare well, particularly if they weigh less than 1,500 grams at birth and if their environment is stressful.

Infant Mortality

• Infant mortality is relatively high in the United States, primarily due to low birth weight and inadequate prenatal care.

KEY TERMS

chromosomes (47)
autosomes (47)
sex chromosomes (47)
deoxyribonucleic acid (DNA) (47)
gene (47)
genotype (47)
phenotype (47)
alleles (47)
homozygous (48)
heterozygous (48)
dominant (48)
recessive (48)
codominance (49)
sickle-cell trait (49)
polygenic inheritance (50)
monozygotic twins (50)
dizygotic twins (50)
phenylketonuria (51)

Huntington's disease (51)
reaction range (54)
niche-picking (54)
prenatal development (56)
in vitro fertilization (57)
eugenics (57)
zygote (58)
implantation (58)
germ disc (59)
placenta (59)
embryo (59)
ectoderm (59)
mesoderm (59)
endoderm (59)
amnion (60)
amniotic fluid (60)
umbilical cord (60)
cephalocaudal principle (60)

proximodistal principle (60)
period of the fetus (60)
age of viability (61)
teratogen (63)
fetal alcohol syndrome (64)
ultrasound (70)
amniocentesis (70)
chorionic villus sampling (71)
fetal medicine (71)
crowning (73)
anoxia (75)
preterm (premature) (75)
low birth weight (75)
very low birth weight (75)
extremely low birth weight (75)
infant mortality (76)

IF YOU'D LIKE TO LEARN MORE

Readings

ALFRED, H. (1997). *Pregnancy and birth sourcebook.* Detroit: Omnigraphics. This is a comprehensive but readable reference book that covers all aspects of pregnancy, including genetic counseling, prenatal care, prenatal development, labor and delivery, and common disorders of pregnancy.

ALDRIDGE, S. (1996). *The thread of life: The story of genes and genetic engineering.* Cambridge, NY: Cambridge University Press. The author, a chemist turned professional writer, first provides an excellent account of the structure and functioning of DNA. Then she describes genetic engineering and shows how it may solve different genetic problems and may lead to the creation of new life forms.

NILSSON, L., & HAMBERGER, L. (1990). *A child is born.* New York: Delacorte. This book is the source of many of the photos of prenatal development in this chapter. Nilsson developed a variety of techniques to photograph the fetus as it was developing; Hamberger provides an entertaining and informative text to accompany the photos.

PLOMIN, R. (1990). *Nature and nurture.* Pacific Grove, CA: Brooks/Cole. This brief book provides a very readable introduction to modern research on the role of genetics in human behavior, written by one of the leading researchers in the field.

SHAPIRO, R. (1991). *The human blueprint: The race to unlock the secrets of our genetic script.* New York: St. Martin's Press. This book describes progress in genetics research by focusing on the Human Genome Project, which is designed to identify the exact location of all 100,000 human genes.

For additional readings, explore Infotrac College Edition, your online library. Go to http://www. infotrac-college.com/wadsworth.

Web Sites

The Web site of the New York Online Access to Health (NOAH),

http://www.noah.cuny.edu/pregnancy/pregnancy.html

provides a wealth of information about all aspects of pregnancy and prenatal care.

The Down Syndrome Web site,

http://www.nas.com/downsyn

includes information about children who have this genetic disorder.

At the Web site of the Human Genome Project,

http://www.ncbi.nlm.nih.gov/genemap98

you can see maps of each chromosome showing the location of known genes.

Web site addresses are subject to change. The Wadsworth Study Center Web site listed below can be accessed for updated links.

The Wadsworth Psychology Study Center Web Site

See http://psychology.wadsworth.com/ for practice quiz questions, internet links, updates, critical thinking exercises, discussion forums and more! The Wadsworth Psychology Study Center provides a wealth of information fully organized and integrated by chapter.

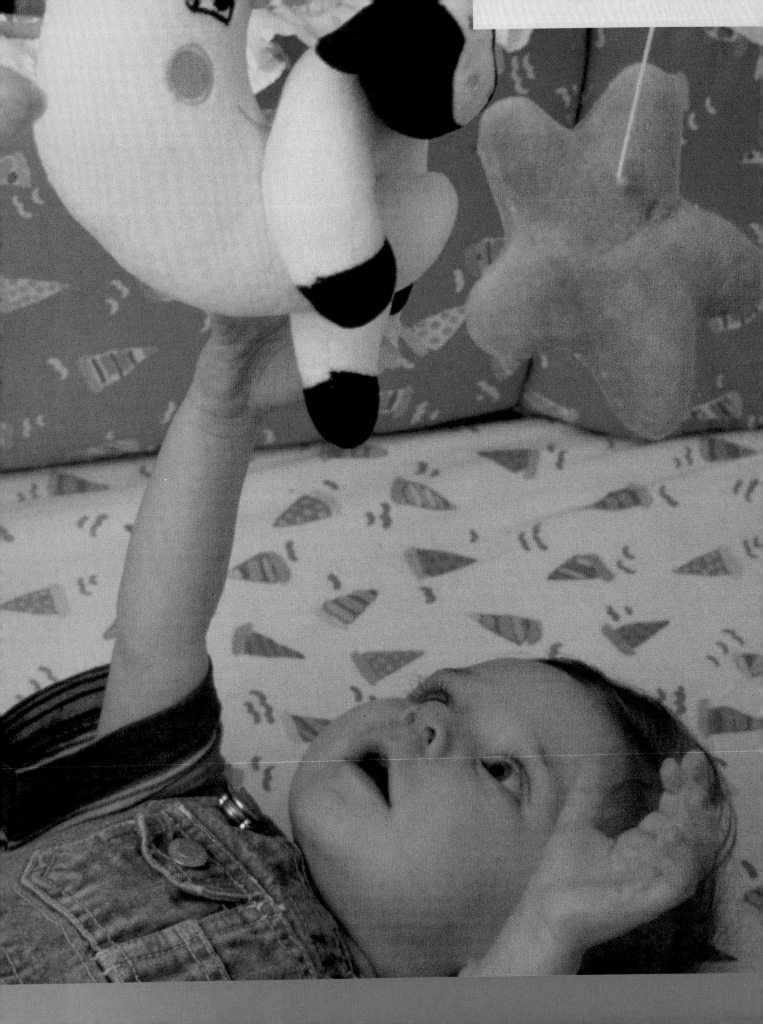

CHAPTER 3

TOOLS FOR EXPLORING THE WORLD

The Newborn
The Newborn's Reflexes
Assessing the Newborn
The Newborn's States
Temperament
Visit a Newborn Nursery

Physical Development
Growth of the Body
*Fostering Development in
   Malnourished Children*
The Emerging Nervous System

**Moving and Grasping—Early
Motor Skills**
Locomotion
Fine-Motor Skills
Maturation and Experience Both
   Influence Motor Skill
Toilet Training

**Coming to Know the World:
Perception**
Smell and Taste
Touch and Pain
Hearing
Seeing
Integrating Sensory Information
Integrating Sight and Sound

Becoming Self-Aware
Origins of Self-Concept
Theory of Mind
"Seeing Is Believing…" for 3-year-olds

Putting It All Together

Summary

If You'd Like to Learn More

Think about what you were like two years ago. Whatever you were doing, you probably look, act, think, and feel in much the same way today that you did then. Two years in an adult's life usually don't result in profound changes. But two years make a big difference early in life. The changes that occur in the first few years after birth are incredible. An infant is transformed from a seemingly helpless newborn into a talking, walking, havoc-wreaking toddler in less than two years. No changes at any other point in the life span come close to the drama and excitement of these early years.

In this chapter, our tour of these two years begins with the newborn, then moves to physical growth—changes in the body and the brain. The third section of the chapter concerns motor skills. You'll discover how babies learn to walk and how they learn to use their hands to hold and then manipulate objects. In the fourth section, we'll examine changes in infants' sensory abilities that allow them to comprehend their world.

As children begin to explore their world and learn more about it, they also learn more about themselves. They learn to recognize themselves and begin to understand more about their thoughts and others' thoughts. We'll explore these changes in the last section of the chapter.

THE NEWBORN

The Newborn

The Newborn's Reflexes

Assessing the Newborn

The Newborn's States

Temperament

Learning Objectives

- **How do reflexes help newborns interact with the world?**
- **How do we determine whether a baby is healthy and adjusting to life outside the uterus?**
- **What behavioral states are common among newborns?**
- **What are the different features of temperament? Do they change as children grow?**

*L*ISA AND STEVE, *proud but exhausted parents, are astonished at how their lives revolve around 10-day-old Dan's eating and sleeping. Lisa feels as if she is feeding Dan around the clock. When Dan naps, Lisa thinks of many things she should do, but usually naps herself because she is so tired. Steve wonders when Dan will start sleeping through the night, so that he and Lisa can get a good night's sleep themselves.*

The newborn baby that thrills parents like Lisa and Steve is actually rather homely, as shown in this photo of Ben Kail when he was 20 seconds old. Like

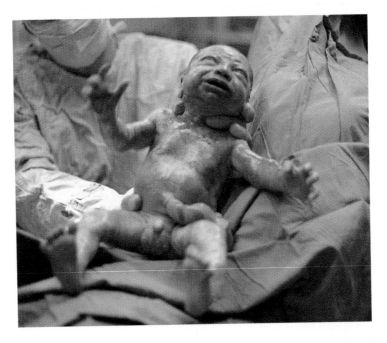

many newborns, he is covered with blood and vernix, a white-colored "wax" that protected his skin during the many months of prenatal development. Ben's head is temporarily distorted from its journey through the birth canal, he has a beer belly, and he is bow-legged.

What can newborns like Dan and Ben do? We'll answer that question in this section and, as we do, you'll learn when Lisa and Steve can expect to resume a full night's sleep.

THE NEWBORN'S REFLEXES

Most newborns are well prepared to begin interacting with their world. *The newborn is endowed with a rich set of* reflexes, *unlearned responses that are triggered by a specific form of stimulation.* The chart shows the variety of reflexes commonly found in newborn babies.

MAJOR REFLEXES FOUND IN NEWBORNS

Name	Response	Significance
Babinski	A baby's toes fan out when the sole of the foot is stroked from heel to toe.	Perhaps a remnant of evolution
Blink	A baby's eyes close in response to bright light or loud noise.	Protects the eyes
Moro	A baby throws its arms out and then inward (as if embracing) in response to loud noise or when its head falls.	May help a baby cling to its mother
Palmar	A baby grasps an object placed in the palm of its hand.	Precursor to voluntary grasping
Rooting	When a baby's cheek is stroked, it turns its head toward the cheek that was stroked and opens its mouth.	Helps a baby to find the nipple
Stepping	A baby who is held upright by an adult and is then moved forward begins to step rhythmically.	Precursor to voluntary walking
Sucking	A baby sucks when an object is placed in its mouth.	Permits feeding
Withdrawal	A baby withdraws its foot when the sole is pricked with a pin.	Protects a baby from unpleasant stimulation

You can see that some reflexes are designed to pave the way for newborns to get the nutrients that they need to grow: The rooting and sucking reflexes ensure that the newborn is well prepared to begin a new diet of life-sustaining milk. Others seem designed to protect the newborn from danger in the environment. The eye blink and withdrawal reflexes, for example, help newborns avoid unpleasant stimulation.

Still other reflexes serve as the foundation for larger, voluntary patterns of motor activity. For example, look at the baby in the photograph, who is showing us the stepping reflex. These motions look like precursors to walking, so it probably won't surprise you to learn that babies who practice the stepping reflex often learn to walk earlier than those who don't practice this reflex (Zelazo, 1993).

Reflexes are also important because they can be a useful way to determine whether the newborn's nervous system is working properly. For example, infants with damage to the sciatic nerve, which is found in the spinal cord, do not show the withdrawal reflex. As another example, infants who have problems with the lower part of the spine do not show the Babinski reflex. If these or other

reflexes are weak or missing altogether, a thorough physical and behavioral assessment is called for. Similarly, many of these reflexes normally vanish during infancy; if they linger, this too indicates the need for a thorough physical examination.

ASSESSING THE NEWBORN

Imagine that a mother has just asked you if her newborn baby is healthy. How would you decide? You would probably check to see whether the baby seems to be breathing and if her heart seems to be beating. In fact, breathing and heartbeat are two vital signs included in the Apgar score, which provides a quick, approximate assessment of the newborn's status, by focusing on the body systems needed to sustain life. The other vital signs are muscle tone, presence of reflexes such as coughing, and skin tone. Each of the five vital signs receives a score of 0, 1, or 2, with 2 being the optimal score. For example, a newborn whose muscles are completely limp receives a 0; a baby who shows strong movements of arms and legs receives a 2. The five scores are added together, with a score of 7 or more indicating a baby who is in good physical condition. A score of 4–6 means that the newborn needs special attention and care. A score of 3 or less signals a life-threatening situation that requires emergency medical care (Apgar, 1953).

For a comprehensive evaluation of the newborn's well-being, pediatricians and other child-development specialists sometimes administer the Neonatal Behavioral Assessment Scale or NBAS for short (Brazelton, 1984). This test evaluates a broad range of newborn abilities and behaviors that will help the infant to adjust to life outside of the uterus. The NBAS measures reflexes, hearing, vision, alertness, irritability, and consolability. The NBAS, along with a thorough physical examination, can determine whether the newborn is functioning normally. Scores from the NBAS can, for example, be used to diagnose disorders of the central nervous system (Brazelton, Nugent, & Lester, 1987).

THE NEWBORN'S STATES

Newborns spend most of each day alternating among four different states (St. James-Roberts & Plewis, 1996; Wolff, 1987):

- Alert inactivity—*The baby is calm with eyes open and attentive; the baby seems to be deliberately inspecting the environment.*

- Waking activity—*The baby's eyes are open but they seem unfocused; the arms or legs move in bursts of uncoordinated motion.*

- Crying—*The baby cries vigorously, usually accompanied by agitated but uncoordinated motion.*

- Sleeping—*The baby alternates from being still and breathing regularly to moving gently and breathing irregularly; eyes are closed throughout.*

Of these states, crying and sleeping have captured the attention of parents and researchers alike.

Crying

Newborns spend 2–3 hours each day crying or on the verge of crying. If you've not spent much time around newborns, you might think that all crying is pretty much alike. In fact, scientists and parents can identify three distinctive

? THINK ABOUT IT
Newborns seem to be extremely well prepared to begin to interact with their environments. Which of the theories described in Chapter 1 predict such preparedness? Which do not?

types of cries (Holden, 1988). *A basic cry starts softly, then gradually becomes more intense and usually occurs when a baby is hungry or tired; a mad cry is a more intense version of a basic cry; and a* pain cry *begins with a sudden, long burst of crying, followed by a long pause, and gasping.* Thus, crying represents the newborn's first venture into interpersonal communication; by crying, babies tell their parents that they are hungry or tired, angry or hurt. By responding to these cries, parents are encouraging their newborn's efforts to communicate.

Of course, parents are concerned when their baby cries. If they can't quiet a crying baby, their concern mounts and can easily give way to frustration and annoyance. For centuries, mothers have relied upon a number of different tricks for soothing their babies. Science hasn't contributed many new techniques, but it has told us which techniques work best and why. The first step should always be to determine why the baby began to cry. Is she hungry? Is her diaper wet? Addressing the needs that caused the crying will often quiet a baby. If crying persists, the best method is to lift the baby to the shoulder and rock or walk with her. This combination—being upright, restrained, and in physical contact with a person—helps calm babies. Also effective is swaddling—wrapping the baby tightly in a blanket—and then rocking it in a cradle or taking it for a ride in a baby carriage. Here, too, the key seems to be the combination of bodily restraint and movement. As the cartoon suggests, a modern variant is to strap the newborn into a car seat and go on a drive. This technique was used

Reprinted by permission of King Features Syndicate. Copyright © 1994 by King Features, Inc.

once as a last resort when Ben Kail was 10 days old and had been crying uncontrollably for more than an hour. After about the 12th time around the block, he finally fell asleep! Babies can also be soothed by giving them a pacifier; sucking apparently allows them to control their own level of arousal (Campos, 1989).

None of these techniques is foolproof. Some work well one day but not the next, and some seem to be better for one baby than for another. Sometimes you may need to combine techniques, such as holding a swaddled baby to your shoulder. If all of these fail, just put the baby down. Every so often, just to make you wonder, a baby will stop crying spontaneously and go right to sleep!

Sleeping

Crying may get parents' attention but sleep is what newborns do more than anything else. They sleep 16–18 hours daily. The problem for tired parents, like Lisa and Steve from the vignette, is that newborns sleep in naps taken round-the-clock. Newborns typically go through a cycle of wakefulness and sleep about every 4 hours. That is, they will be awake for about an hour, sleep for 3 hours, then start the cycle anew. During the hour when newborns are awake, they regularly move between the different waking states several times. Cycles of alert inactivity, waking activity, and crying are common.

As babies grow older, the sleep-wake cycle gradually begins to correspond to the day-night cycle (St. James-Roberts & Plewis, 1996). Most babies begin sleeping through the night by about 3 or 4 months of age, a major milestone for bleary-eyed parents like Lisa and Steve.

Roughly half of newborns' sleep is irregular or rapid-eye-movement (REM) sleep, *a time when the body is quite active.* During REM sleep, newborns move their arms and legs, they may grimace, and their eyes may dart beneath their eyelids. Brain waves register fast activity, the heart beats more rapidly, and breathing is more rapid. *In* regular or nonREM sleep, *breathing, heart rate, and brain activity are steady, and newborns lie quietly without the twitching associated with REM sleep.* REM sleep becomes less frequent as infants grow. By 4 months, only 40% of sleep is REM sleep. By the first birthday, REM sleep will drop to 25%, not far from the adult average of 20% (Halpern, MacLean, & Baumeister, 1995).

The function of REM sleep is still debated. Older children and adults dream during REM sleep, and brain waves during REM sleep resemble those of an alert, awake person. Consequently, many scientists believe that REM sleep provides stimulation for the brain that fosters growth in the nervous system (Halpern et al., 1995; Roffwarg, Muzio, & Dement, 1966).

Sudden Infant Death Syndrome

For many parents of young babies, however, sleep is a cause of concern. *In* sudden infant death syndrome (SIDS), *a healthy baby dies suddenly, for no apparent reason.* Approximately 1–3 of every 1,000 American babies dies from SIDS. Most of them are between 2 and 4 months of age (Wegman, 1994).

Scientists don't know the exact causes of SIDS, but they do know several contributing factors. Babies are more vulnerable to SIDS if they were born prematurely or with low birth weight. They are also more vulnerable if their parents smoke or if they have had respiratory infections. Furthermore, SIDS is more likely when babies sleep on their stomach (face down) than when they sleep on their back (face up). Finally, SIDS is more likely during winter when babies sometimes become overheated from too many blankets and too heavy sleepware (Carroll & Laughlin, 1994).

Evidently, some infants who are born prematurely or with low birth weight are less able to withstand physiological stresses and imbalances that are brought on by cigarette smoke, breathing that is temporarily interrupted, or by overheating. The best advice for parents—particularly those whose babies were premature or small for date—is to keep their babies away from smoke, to place infants on their backs at nap time, and not to overdress them or wrap them too tightly in blankets (Willinger, 1995).

TEMPERAMENT

So far, we've talked as if all babies are alike. But, if you've seen a number of babies together, you know this isn't true. Perhaps you've seen some babies who are quiet most of the time, alongside others who cried often and impatiently?

Maybe you've known infants who responded warmly to strangers next to others who seemed shy? *These characteristics of infants indicate a consistent style or pattern to an infant's behavior and, collectively, they define an infant's* temperament.

According to one important theory, proposed by Buss and Plomin (1984), temperament includes three primary dimensions: emotionality, activity, and sociability.

- Emotionality *refers to the strength of the infant's emotional response to a situation, the ease with which that response is triggered, and the ease with which the infant can be returned to a nonemotional state.* At one extreme are infants whose emotional responses are strong, easily triggered, and not easily calmed; at the other are infants whose responses are subdued, relatively difficult to elicit, and soothed readily.

- Activity *refers to the tempo and vigor of a child's activity.* Active infants are always busy, like to explore their environment, and enjoy vigorous play. Inactive infants have a more controlled behavioral tempo and are more likely to enjoy quiet play.

- Sociability *refers to a preference for being with other people.* Some infants relish contact with others, seek their attention, and prefer play that involves other people. Other infants, like the girl in the photo, enjoy solitude and are quite content to play alone with toys.

Not all developmentalists agree that these are the only dimensions of temperament (Goldsmith et al., 1987), but it is clear that temperament consists of a handful of biologically based dimensions.

Some temperamental characteristics are more common in some cultures than in others. Asian babies tend to be less emotional than European American babies. For instance, Asian babies cry less often and less intensely than European American babies (Kagan et al., 1994; Lewis, Ramsay, & Kawakami, 1993).

Why are Asian infants less emotional than their European American counterparts? Heredity may be involved. Perhaps the genes that contribute to emotionality are less common among Asians than among European Americans. But we can't overlook experience. Compared to European American mothers, Japanese mothers spend more time in close physical contact with their babies, constantly and gently soothing them; this may reduce the tendency to respond emotionally (Chen & Miyake, 1986; Lewis et al., 1993).

Regardless of where they grow up, are emotional newborns likely to be as emotional as 12-month-olds and as 12-year-olds? Yes, at least to some extent. Studies of temperamental dimensions reveal reasonable stability. For example, Stifter and Fox (1990) studied responses in two situations known to be moderately stressful to infants: As newborns, they were allowed to suck briefly on a pacifier, which was then taken away from them. Later, as 5-month-olds, mothers gently restrained their infant's arms, prohibiting all movement. Of the newborns who cried when the pacifier was removed, 53% cried when their hands were restrained; of the newborns who did not cry, 72% did not cry when their hands were restrained. In other words, emotional reactivity, as indicated by crying, was consistent from birth to 5 months of age.

This study is typical of research showing that temperament is somewhat stable (Belsky, Hsieh, & Crnic, 1996; Caspi & Silva, 1995). A young child's temperament does give clues to that child's temperament later in childhood. However, early temperament predicts later temperament only roughly, not precisely.

? THINK ABOUT IT
How would a learning theorist explain why children have different temperaments?

Mike, an emotional 1-year-old, is more likely to be emotional as a 12-year-old than Dave, an unemotional 1-year-old. However, it's not a "sure thing" that Mike will still be emotional as a 12-year-old. Instead, think of temperament as a predisposition. Some infants are naturally predisposed to be sociable, emotional, or active; others *can* act in these ways, too, but only if the behaviors are nurtured by parents and others (Nachmias et al., 1996).

Temperamental characteristics remind us that, although infants have many features in common, each baby also seems to have its own unique personality from the very start. The best way to appreciate this uniqueness is to experience it firsthand; the See for Yourself feature describes an excellent way to do this.

SEE FOR YOURSELF

VISIT A NEWBORN NURSERY

Words can hardly capture the miracle of a newborn baby. If you have never seen a newborn, you need to see one—or even better, a roomful. Arrange to visit the maternity ward of a local hospital, which will include a nursery for newborns. Through a large viewing window, you will be able to observe as many as 15 or 20 newborns. Almost all will be less than 3 days old because health insurance usually pays for only two nights in a hospital following childbirth. These babies will no longer be covered with blood or vernix, but you may be able to see how the newborn's head was distorted in its journey from the uterus.

As you watch the babies, look for reflexive behavior and changes in states. Watch while a baby sucks its fingers. Find a baby who seems to be awake and alert, then note how long the baby stays this way. When alertness wanes, watch for the behaviors that replace it. Finally, look for the temperamental characteristics described in the past few pages. See how newborns look and act differently from each other. Do all babies respond similarly to stimulation such as light and sound? When they're awake, are some babies more active than others? A recurring theme in this book is an appreciation of the wonderful variety and diversity found among human beings, and this is already evident in humans who are hours or days old. See for yourself! ●

TEST YOURSELF

1. Some reflexes help infants get necessary nutrients, other reflexes protect infants from danger, and still other reflexes _____ .

2. The _____ is based on five vital functions and provides a quick indication of a newborn's physical health.

3. A baby lying calmly with its eyes open and focused is in a state of _____ .

4. Newborns spend more time asleep than awake, and about half of this time asleep is spent in _____ , a time thought to foster growth in the central nervous system.

5. To protect infants from SIDS, parents should keep them away from smoke, not overdress them, and have them sleep _____ .

6. One prominent theory proposes three dimensions of temperament, including emotionality, _____ , and sociability.

7. Max, a father-to-be, says, "I'm sure I'll worry a lot about our baby, because babies are so helpless; they can't do anything." What can you tell Max to convince him that, all things considered, newborns are quite talented?

Answers: (1) serve as the basis for later motor behavior, (2) Apgar score, (3) alert inactivity, (4) REM sleep, (5) on their backs, (6) activity

PHYSICAL DEVELOPMENT

Learning Objectives

- **How do height and weight change from birth to 2 years of age?**

- **What nutrients do young children need? How are they best provided?**

- **What are the consequences of malnutrition? How can it be treated?**

- **What are nerve cells and how are they organized in the brain?**

- **How does the brain develop? When does it begin to function?**

Physical Development

Growth of the Body

The Emerging Nervous System

*W*HILE CROSSING THE STREET, *4-year-old Martin was struck by a passing car. He was in a coma for a week but then gradually became more alert. Now he seems to be aware of his surroundings. Needless to say, Martin's mother is grateful that he survived the accident, but she wonders what the future holds for her son.*

For parents and children alike, physical growth is a topic of great interest and a source of pride. Parents marvel at the speed with which babies add pounds and inches; 2-year-olds proudly proclaim, "I bigger now!" In this section, we examine some of the basic features of physical growth, see how the brain develops, and discover how the accident affected Martin's development.

GROWTH OF THE BODY

Growth is more rapid in infancy than during any other period after birth. Typically, infants double their birth weight by 3 months of age and triple it by their first birthday. This rate of growth is so rapid that if it continued throughout childhood, a typical 10-year-old boy would be nearly as long as an airliner and weigh almost as much (McCall, 1979).

Average heights and weights for young children are represented by the lines marked 50th percentile in the charts. An average girl weighs about 7 pounds at birth, about 21 pounds at age 12 months, and about 26 pounds at 24 months. If perfectly average, she would be 19–20 inches long at birth, grow to 29–30 inches at 12 months, and 34–35 inches at 24 months. Figures for an average boy are similar, but weights are slightly larger at ages 12 and 24 months.

These charts also highlight how much children of the same age vary

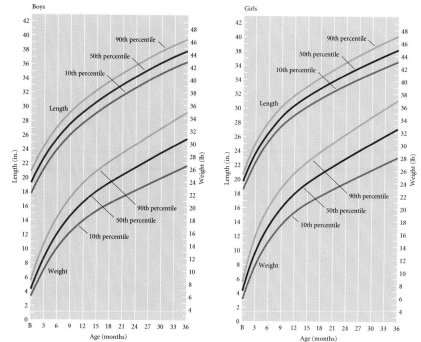

in weight and height. The lines marked 90th percentile on the charts on page 91 represent heights and weights for children who are larger than 90% of their peers; the lines marked 10th percentile represent heights and weights for children who are smaller than 90% of their peers. Any heights and weights between these lines are considered normal. At age 1, for example, normal weights for boys range from about 19 to 27 pounds. This means that an extremely light but normal boy weighs only two-thirds as much as his extremely heavy but normal peer!

The important message here is that average height and normal height are not one and the same. Many children are much taller or shorter than average but are still perfectly normal. This applies to all of the age norms that we mention in this book. Whenever we provide a typical or average age for a developmental milestone, remember that the normal range for passing the milestone is much wider.

Whether an infant is short or tall depends largely on heredity. Both parents contribute to their children's height. In fact, the correlation between the average of the two parents' heights and their child's height at 2 years of age is about .7 (Plomin, 1990). As a general rule, two tall parents will have tall offspring; two short parents will have short offspring; and, one tall parent and one short parent will have offspring of medium height.

So far, we have emphasized the quantitative aspects of growth, such as height. This ignores an important fact: Infants are not simply scaled-down versions of adults. The chart below shows that compared to adolescents and adults, infants and young children look top-heavy because their heads and trunks are disproportionately large. As growth of the hips, legs, and feet catches up later in childhood, their bodies take on more adult proportions. This pattern of growth, in which the head and trunk develop first, follows the cephalocaudal principle introduced in Chapter 2 (page 60).

> **? THINK ABOUT IT**
> In Chapter 2, we explained how polygenic inheritance is often involved when phenotypes form a continuum. Height is such a phenotype. Propose a simple polygenic model to explain how height might be inherited.

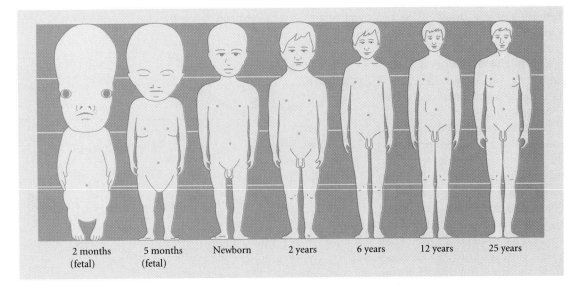

| 2 months (fetal) | 5 months (fetal) | Newborn | 2 years | 6 years | 12 years | 25 years |

Based on Eichorn, 1969.

Growth of this sort requires energy. Let's see how food and drink provide the fuel to grow.

"You Are What You Eat"—Nutrition and Growth

In a typical 2-month-old, roughly 40% of the body's energy is devoted to growth. Most of the remaining energy is used for basic bodily functions such as digestion and respiration. A much smaller portion is consumed in physical activity.

Because growth requires so much high energy, young babies must consume an enormous number of calories relative to their body weight. A typical, 12-pound 3-month-old, for example, should ingest about 600 calories daily, representing about 50 calories per pound of body weight. An adult, by contrast, needs to consume approximately 15–20 calories per pound, depending on the person's level of activity (National Research Council, 1989).

An infant's dietary needs are amply met by human milk, which contains the proper amounts of carbohydrates, fats, and protein, as well as necessary vitamins and minerals. Breast-feeding has other advantages as well: Breast milk contains antibodies that help fight disease; infants are less likely to develop allergies; and they are less likely to overeat than infants who are bottle-fed (Shelov, 1993; Sullivan & Birch, 1990). Bottle-feeding does allow other family members to experience the intimacy of feeding the baby, and modern formula does contain essentially the same proportion of nutrients as human milk. Consequently, a mother can choose either method—or use them both—knowing that they will meet her baby's nutritional needs.

Malnutrition

Unfortunately, an adequate diet is only a dream to many of the world's children. Worldwide, about one in three children under age 5 is malnourished, as indicated by being small for their age (World Health Organization, 1996). Many of these children are from Third World countries. However, malnutrition is regrettably common in industrialized countries, too. For example, many American children growing up homeless and in poverty are also malnourished.

Malnourished children tend to develop less rapidly than their peers. Malnourishment is especially damaging during infancy, because growth is ordinarily so rapid during these years. This is well illustrated by a longitudinal study conducted in Barbados in the West Indies (Galler & Ramsey, 1989; Galler, Ramsey, & Forde, 1986). Included were more than 100 children who were severely malnourished as infants, as well as 100 children whose family environments were similar but who had adequate nutrition as infants. The children who experienced malnutrition during infancy were indistinguishable from their peers physically—they were just as tall and weighed just as much. However, children with a history of infant malnutrition had much lower scores on intelligence tests. Also, many of the children who were malnourished during infancy had difficulty maintaining attention in school; they were easily distracted. Many similar studies suggest that malnourished youngsters tire easily, are more wary, and are often inattentive (Lozoff et al., 1998). In addition, malnutrition during rapid periods of growth may cause substantial and potentially irreversible damage to the brain (Morgane et al., 1993).

Malnutrition would seem to have a simple cure—an adequate diet. But as we see in the Forces in Action feature, the solution is more complex than you might expect.

FOSTERING DEVELOPMENT IN MALNOURISHED CHILDREN

Malnourished children are often listless and inactive (Ricciuti, 1993). They are unusually quiet and express little interest in what goes on around them. These behaviors *are* useful to children whose diet is inadequate, because they conserve limited energy. Unfortunately, these behaviors may also deprive youngsters of experiences that would further their development. For example, when children are routinely unresponsive and lethargic, parents often come to believe that their actions have little impact on the children. That is, when children do not respond to parents' efforts to stimulate their development, this discourages parents from providing additional stimulation in the future. Over time, parents tend to provide fewer experiences that foster their children's development. The result is a self-perpetuating cycle in which malnourished children are forsaken by parents who feel as if they can do little to contribute to their children's growth. A biological force (lethargy stemming from insufficient nourishment) causes a profound change in a sociocultural force (parental teaching), which, in turn, influences psychological development (children are less intelligent and less able to pay attention).

To break the vicious cycle, these children need more than an improved diet. Their parents must be taught how to foster their children's development and must be encouraged to do so. Programs that combine dietary supplements with parent training offer promise in treating malnutrition (Valenzuela, 1997). Children in these programs often catch up with their peers in physical and intellectual growth, showing that the best way to reduce the effect of malnutrition on psychological forces is by addressing both biological and sociocultural forces (Super, Herrera, & Mora, 1990).

THE EMERGING NERVOUS SYSTEM

The physical changes we see as infants grow are impressive. Even more awe-inspiring are the changes we cannot see—those involving the brain and the nervous system. An infant's feelings of hunger or pain, its smiles or laughs, and its efforts to sit upright or to hold a rattle all reflect the functioning of the brain and the rest of the emerging nervous system.

How does the brain accomplish these many tasks? To begin to answer this question, we need to look at the organization of the brain. *The basic unit in the brain and the rest of the nervous system is the* neuron, *a cell that specializes in receiving and transmitting information.* Neurons have the basic elements shown in the diagram. *The* cell body, *in the center of the cell, contains the basic biological machinery that keeps the neuron alive. The receiving end of the neuron, the* dendrite, *looks like a tree with its many branches.* This structure allows one neuron to receive input from thousands of other neurons (Morgan & Gibson, 1991). *The tubelike structure that emerges from the other side of the cell body, the* axon, *transmits information to other neurons. At the end of the axon are small knobs called* terminal buttons, *which release chemicals called* neurotransmitters. These

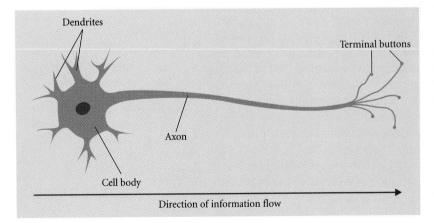

Dendrites

Terminal buttons

Axon

Cell body

Direction of information flow

neurotransmitters are the messengers that carry information to nearby neurons.

Take 50–100 billion neurons like these, and you have the beginnings of a human brain. An adult's brain, which weighs a little less than 3 pounds and would easily fit into your hands, is shown in the photo. *The wrinkled surface of the brain is the* cerebral cortex; *made up of 10 billion neurons, the cortex regulates many of the functions that we think of as distinctly human. The cortex consists of left and right halves, called* hemispheres, *linked by a thick bundle of neurons called the* corpus callosum. The characteristics you value the most—your engaging personality, your "way with words," or your uncanny knack for "reading" others' emotions—are all controlled by specific regions in the cortex. *For example, your personality and your ability to make and carry out plans are largely centered in an area in the front of the cortex called (appropriately enough) the* frontal cortex. For most people, the ability to produce and understand language is mainly housed in neurons in the left hemisphere of the cortex. When you recognize that others are happy or sad, neurons in your right hemisphere are usually at work.

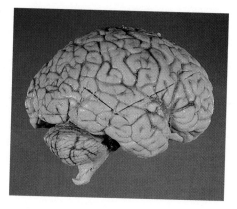

Now that we know a bit of the organization of the mature brain, let's look at how the brain grows and begins to function.

The Making of the Working Brain

The brain weighs only three-quarters of a pound at birth, which is roughly 25% of the weight of an adult brain. You can see from the figure that the brain grows rapidly during infancy and the preschool years. At 3 years of age, for example, the brain has achieved 80% of its ultimate weight.

Brain weight doesn't tell us much, however, about the fascinating sequence of changes that take place to create a working brain. Instead, we need to move back to prenatal development. *If you were to look at an embryo at roughly 3 weeks after conception, you would see a group of cells that form a flat structure known as the* neural plate. At 4 weeks, the neural plate folds to form a tube that is open at the ends. One end of this tube becomes the spinal cord; the other becomes the brain. Soon after the ends fuse shut, neurons are produced in one small region of the neural tube. Production of neurons begins at about 10 weeks after conception, and by 28 weeks the developing brain has virtually all of the neurons it will ever have. During these weeks, neurons form at the incredible rate of more than 4,000 per second (Kolb, 1989).

From the neuron-manufacturing site in the neural tube, neurons migrate to their final positions in the brain. The brain is built in stages, beginning with the innermost layers. Neurons in the deepest layer are positioned first, followed by neurons in the second layer, and

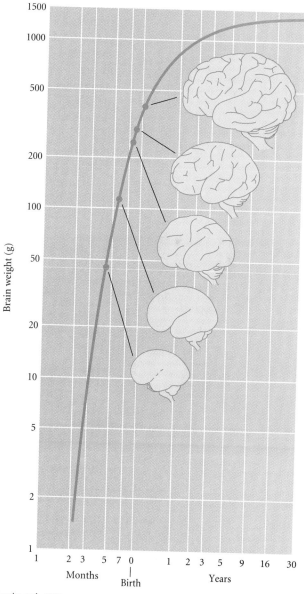

Lemire et al., 1975.

so on. This layering process continues until all six layers of the mature brain are in place, typically at about 7 months after conception (Huttenlocher, 1990).

When neurons reach their final position in the brain, their axons and neurons grow and synapses are created. Surprisingly, the brain produces many more neurons and synapses than necessary. Beginning after birth and continuing through childhood and adolescence, rarely used neurons and synapses simply disappear (Greenough & Black, 1992). The brain goes through its own version of "downsizing" in which unnecessary elements are weeded out.

Another important change is that neurons become wrapped in myelin, *a fatty sheath that allows them to transmit information more rapidly.* The boost in speed from myelin is like the difference between driving and flying: from about 6 feet per second to 50 feet per second. Myelinization begins in the fourth month of prenatal development and continues gradually into childhood and adolescence (Casear, 1993).

Because the brain grows so rapidly, it may not surprise you to learn that many areas of the cortex begin to function early in life. Take the left hemisphere's influence on language as an example. When children suffer damage to the brain, damage to the left hemisphere of the cortex typically produces greater loss of language ability than does a comparable injury to the right hemisphere of the cortex (Witelson, 1987). For example, after Martin (the preschooler in the vignette) was struck by a car, he spoke more slowly and deliberately than before, which was not surprising because the left hemisphere of Martin's brain had absorbed much of the force of the collision. The good news for Martin is that young children recover from brain damage more rapidly and more completely than adults.

Fortunately for children, such cases of brain damage are relatively uncommon. Consequently, scientists have devised other methods to study brain functioning in healthy children. One approach, shown in the photo, is to record

the brain's ongoing electrical activity. To do this, several metal electrodes are placed on an infant's scalp. *The combined output of the electrodes yields a pattern of waves known as an* electroencephalogram—*or simply an EEG.* Typically, a newborn infant's left hemisphere generates more electrical activity in response to speech than does the right hemisphere (Molfese & Burger-Judisch, 1991). Apparently, at birth, the left hemisphere of the cortex is uniquely prepared to process language. As we'll see in Chapter 4, this specialization allows language to develop rapidly during infancy.

Is the right hemisphere equally well prepared to function at birth? This is a difficult question to answer, in part because the right hemisphere influences so many different nonlinguistic functions. In addition to recognizing emotions, the right hemisphere influences understanding of spatial relations, identifying faces, and perceiving nonspeech sounds such as music (Kinsbourne, 1989). Music elicits greater electrical activity in the infant's right hemisphere than in the left hemisphere. Other functions, such as understanding spatial relations and recognizing faces, are under the right hemisphere's control by the preschool years (Hahn, 1987).

The frontal cortex also begins to function early. *Mapping the areas of activity and energy in the frontal cortex is possible with* positron emission tomography *or PET scan.* The energy that the brain needs to function is provided by glucose, a form of sugar. Consumption of glucose in different regions of the brain is related to the level of brain activity in those regions: Areas that are particularly active need more glucose than areas that are less active. The brain's consumption of glucose is measured by injecting a harmless radioactive form of glucose into a person's bloodstream. The levels of radioactivity measured in different regions of the brain indicate levels of glucose, which relate to the levels of brain activity in those regions. The photograph shown here, in which a computer has generated color codes for different levels of activity, reveals little activity in the frontal cortex of 5-day-old babies. Activity has increased considerably by 11 weeks of age and reaches adult levels by 7–8 months (Chugani & Phelps, 1986).

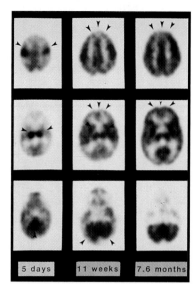

5 days   11 weeks   7.6 months

What is the frontal cortex regulating in PET scans like this one? Deliberate goal-oriented behavior is a good bet. To understand the research that leads to this conclusion, think back to a time when you had to make a permanent change in your regular routine. At the start of a new school year, perhaps you had a new locker, located in a different hallway in school. Nevertheless, for several days you may have turned down the old hallway, following last year's habit. To overcome this error, maybe you deliberately reminded yourself to turn at the new hallway, not the old one.

Overriding old responses that are now incorrect or inappropriate is an important part of deliberate, goal-directed behavior. Adults with damage to the frontal cortex often have great difficulty inhibiting responses that are no longer appropriate. The frontal cortex begins to regulate such inappropriate responses around the first birthday and gradually achieves greater control through the preschool and school years (Welsh, Pennington, & Groisser, 1991).

Not only does the frontal cortex regulate old, irrelevant responses; it also regulates our feelings of happiness, sadness, and fear. By distinguishing emotions associated with approaching or exploring a stimulus from those associated with avoiding or withdrawing from stimuli, we can pinpoint the regions of the frontal cortex that govern emotional responding. Among adults, the left frontal cortex regulates emotions stemming from the tendency to approach an object; the right frontal cortex regulates those stemming from avoidance.

Are these emotions regulated by the infant's frontal cortex? Yes. Scientists who have observed infants' emotions while measuring their EEGs have discovered that a happy baby has more electrical activity in the left frontal cortex than in the right. An angry baby like the one in the photo has more electrical activity in the right frontal cortex (Field et al., 1995; Fox, 1991).

In each region of the brain we have examined, the conclusion has been the same: Many of the distinguishing features of the mature brain can be recognized early in life. Language processing is associated primarily with the left hemisphere; recognizing nonspeech sounds, emotions, and faces is associated with the right hemisphere; and regulating emotions and intentional behavior is a function of the frontal cortex. Of course, this early specialization does not mean that the brain is functionally mature. Over the remainder of childhood and into adulthood, the brain continues to become more specialized. In Chapter 13, we'll see that some regions of the brain continue to develop into old age, whereas others are sometimes destroyed by diseases associated with aging.

? THINK ABOUT IT
When you're ecstatic because you discovered that you did well on a difficult exam, what part of your brain is probably particularly active?

TEST YOURSELF

1. Compared to older children and adults, an infant's head and trunk are _____ .

2. Because of the high energy demands of growth, infants need _____ calories per pound than adults.

3. The most effective treatment for malnutrition is improved diet and _____ .

4. The _____ is the part of the neuron that contains the basic machinery that keeps the cell alive.

5. The frontal cortex is the seat of personality and regulates _____ .

6. Human speech typically elicits the greatest electrical activity from the _____ of an infant's brain.

7. By measuring consumption of glucose, a _____ reveals activity in the frontal cortex by 3 months of age.

8. How does malnutrition illustrate the influence on development of life-cycle forces in the biopsychosocial framework?

Answers: (1) disproportionately large, (2) more, (3) parent training, (4) cell body, (5) goal-directed behavior, (6) left hemisphere, (7) PET scan

---

MOVING AND GRASPING—EARLY MOTOR SKILLS

Moving and Grasping— Early Motor Skills

Locomotion

Fine-Motor Skills

Maturation and Experience Both Influence Motor Skill

Learning Objectives

- **What are the component skills involved in learning to walk? At what age do infants master them?**

- **How do infants learn to coordinate the use of their hands?**

- **How do maturation and experience influence mastery of motor skills?**

ANCY *is 14 months old and a world-class crawler. Using hands and knees, she can go just about anywhere she wants to. Nancy does not walk and seems uninterested in learning how. Nancy's dad wonders whether he should be doing something to help Nancy progress beyond crawling. Deep down, he worries that perhaps he was negligent in not providing more exercise for Nancy when she was younger.*

Do you remember what it was like to learn to type, to drive a car with a stick shift, to play a musical instrument, or to play a sport? *Each of these activities involves* motor skills—*coordinated movements of the muscles and limbs.* Success demands that each movement be done in a precise way, in exactly the right sequence, and at exactly the right time. For example, if you don't give the car enough gas as you let out the clutch, you'll kill the engine. Too much gas, and the engine races and the car lurches forward.

These activities are demanding for adults, but think about similar challenges for infants. *Infants must learn to move about in the world: to* locomote. At first unable to move independently, infants soon learn to crawl, to stand, and to walk. Once the child can move through the environment upright, the arms and hands are free. To take advantage of this arrangement, the human hand has fully independent fingers (instead of a paw), with the thumb opposing the remaining four fingers. *Infants must learn the* fine-motor skills *associated with grasping, holding, and manipulating objects.* In the case of feeding, for example, infants progress from being fed by others, to holding a bottle, to feeding themselves with their fingers, to eating with utensils.

Together, locomotion and fine-motor skills give children access to an enormous variety of information about shapes, textures, and features in their environment. In this section, we'll see how locomotion and fine-motor skills develop and, as we do, we'll see whether Nancy's dad should worry about her lack of interest in walking.

LOCOMOTION

Advances in posture and locomotion transform the infant in little more than a year. The chart shows some of the important milestones in motor development and the age by which most infants have achieved them. By about 5 months of age, most babies will have rolled from back to front and will be able to sit upright with support. By 7 months, infants can sit alone, and by 10 months, they can creep. A typical 14-month-old is able to stand alone briefly and walk

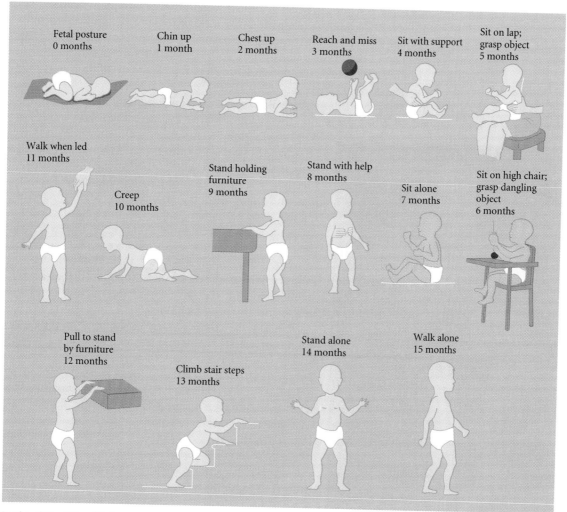

Based on Shirley, 1931 and Bayley, 1969.

with assistance. *This early, unsteady form of walking is called* toddling *(hence the term* toddler*)*. Of course, not all children walk at exactly the same age. Some walk before their first birthday; others, like Nancy, the world-class crawler in the vignette, take their first steps as late as 18 or 19 months of age. By 24 months, most children can climb steps, walk backwards, and kick a ball.

This sequence of milestones fails to do justice to the truly remarkable nature of the infant's accomplishments in learning to walk. Walking involves the maturity and coalescence of many essential skills. For example, the ability to maintain an upright posture is fundamental to walking. This is virtually impossible for newborns and young infants because of the shape of their body. Due to cephalocaudal growth, the infant is top-heavy and, consequently, inherently unstable: As soon as young infants start to lose their balance, they tumble over because of their top-heaviness. Only with growth of the legs and muscles can infants maintain an upright posture (Thelen, Ulrich, & Jensen, 1989).

When an infant can stand upright, he or she must continuously adjust posture to avoid falling down. By 4 months of age, infants are able to use cues from their inner ears to help them stay upright. If a 4-month-old is propped in a sitting position and starts to lose balance, he or she will nevertheless keep the head upright, using the muscles in the back of the neck. This happens even when the infant is blindfolded, which tells us that the essential cues are from the inner ears, not the eyes (Woollacott, Shumway-Cook, & Williams, 1989).

Another essential element in walking is moving the legs alternately—constantly transferring the weight of the body from one foot to the other. Children don't step spontaneously until approximately 10 months of age, because they must be able to stand in order to step. Can younger children step if they are held upright? Thelen and Ulrich (1991) devised a clever procedure to answer this question. Infants were placed on a treadmill and were held upright by an adult. When the belt on the treadmill started to move, the infants could have

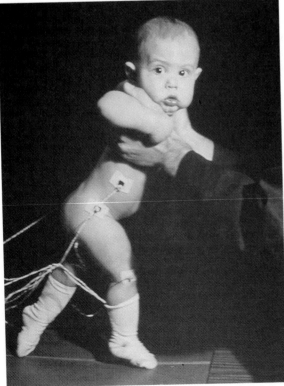

done several things. They might have simply let both legs be dragged rearward by the belt. Or they might have let their legs be dragged briefly, then moved them forward together in a hopping motion. Instead, some 3-month-olds and many 6- and 7-month-olds demonstrated the mature pattern of alternating steps on each leg, shown in the photograph. Even more amazing is that when the treadmill was equipped with separate belts for each leg, moving at different speeds, the babies adjusted, stepping more rapidly on the faster belt. Apparently, the alternate stepping motion that is essential for walking is present long before infants walk alone.

Findings like these remind us that each of the different motor milestones—from learning to sit to learning to walk—is not a unitary event. Instead, walking is a dynamic system of action that demands the orchestration of many individual skills (Thelen, 1996). Each must first be mastered alone and then integrated with the other skills, which is a general principle of motor development (Werner, 1948). *That is, mastery of intricate motions involves both* differentiation *of individual motions and their* integration *into a coherent, working whole.* In the case of walking, not until 12–15 months of age has control of component skills reached such a level of precision that they can be coordinated to allow independent, unsupported walking.

The first tentative steps are followed by others that are more skilled. Walking is joined by jumping, hopping, running, and skipping—a multitude of methods of locomotion that exhilarate children and parents alike (Whitall & Getchell, 1995). If you can recall the feelings of freedom that accompanied your first driver's license, you can imagine how the world expands for infants and toddlers as they learn to move independently. Much of youngsters' enthusiasm for their growing locomotive skills is because they are so useful (Biringen et al., 1995). Now toddlers can get to desired objects like toys, food, and books alone, without depending upon a parent. Of course, once the desired object is reached, another set of motor skills is called for. These we discuss next.

FINE-MOTOR SKILLS

Soon after birth, infants begin to grasp objects with their hands (Karniol, 1989). Initially, infants use one hand only, first holding an object and later moving it. By 3 months, they perform more complicated motions, such as shaking a toy. At about 4 months, infants use both hands. At first, these motions are not coordinated, as if each hand has a mind of its own. A toy may be held motionless in one hand while the other hand is used to shake a rattle. Soon, however, infants use both hands together in common actions, such as holding a large toy (Eppler, 1995).

At roughly 5 months of age, infants can coordinate the motions of their hands. The hands can now perform different actions that serve a common goal. A typical example would be grasping an object with one hand and manipulating it with the other. An infant might hold a toy animal in the right hand while petting it with the left (Kimmerle, Mick, & Michel, 1995).

These gradual changes in fine-motor coordination are well illustrated by the ways children feed themselves. Beginning at roughly 6 months of age, many infants experiment with "finger foods" such as sliced bananas and green beans. Infants can easily pick up such foods, but getting them into their mouths is another story. The hand grasping the food may be raised to the cheek, then moved to the edge of the lips, and finally shoved into the mouth. Mission accomplished, but only after many detours along the way! However, infants' eye/hand coordination improves rapidly, and foods varying in size, shape, and texture are soon placed directly in the mouth.

At about the first birthday, many parents allow their children to try eating with a spoon. Youngsters first simply play with the spoon, dipping it in and out of a dish filled with food or sucking on an empty spoon. Soon they learn to fill the spoon with food and place it in their mouth, but the motions are awkward. For example, most 1-year-olds fill a spoon by first placing it directly over a dish. Then, they lower it until the bowl of the spoon is full. In contrast, 2-year-olds typically scoop food from a dish by rotating their wrist, which is the same motion that adults use.

Fine-motor skills continue to progress beyond infancy. Most 18-month-olds can scribble with a pencil and build with blocks. During the preschool years, youngsters learn to draw simple geometric figures and the human body (Frankenburg & Dobbs, 1969). Soon, they master using scissors, buttoning shirts and coats, and tying shoelaces.

Each of these actions illustrates the principles of differentiation and integration that were introduced in our discussion of locomotion. Complex acts involve many constituent movements. Each must be performed correctly and in the proper sequence. Development involves first mastering the separate elements and then assembling them into a smoothly functioning whole.

> **? THINK ABOUT IT**
> How does learning to hop on one foot demonstrate differentiation and integration of motor skills?

Handedness

Are you right-handed or left-handed? If you're right-handed, you're in the majority. About 90% of the people worldwide prefer to use their right hand, although this figure varies somewhat from place to place, reflecting cultural influences. Most of the remaining 10% are left-handed; a relatively small percentage of people are truly ambidextrous.

A preference for one hand over the other does not seem to emerge until after the first birthday. Most 6- and 9-month-olds, for example, use their left and right hands interchangeably (McCormick & Maurer, 1988). They may shake a rattle with their left hand, but, moments later, pick up blocks with their right.

The emergence of handedness soon after the first birthday is illustrated in a study in which infants and toddlers were videotaped as they played with toys that could be manipulated with two hands, such as a pinwheel (Cornwell, Harris, & Fitzgerald, 1991). The 9-month-olds used their left and right hands

equally. However, by 13 months of age, most of the infants and toddlers acted like the one in the photograph: They first grasped the toy with their right hand, then used their left hand to steady the toy while the right hand manipulated the object.

This early preference for one hand becomes stronger and more consistent throughout the preschool years. By the time children are ready to enter kindergarten, handedness is well established and is very difficult to reverse (McManus et al., 1988).

Whether children become left- or right-handed is based, in part, on heredity (Corballis, 1997). Parents who are both right-handed tend to have children who are right-handed. Children who are left-handed generally have a left-handed parent or grandparent. But experience also contributes to handedness. Many aspects of modern industrial cultures favor right-handedness. School desks, scissors, and can openers, for example, are usually designed for right-handed people and can be used by left-handers only with difficulty. In some cultures, social values influence handedness. Islam dictates that the left hand is unclean, so its use is forbidden in eating and greeting others. Writing with the left hand is a cultural taboo in China, so virtually no Chinese youngsters write with the left hand. Nevertheless, when children of Chinese parents grow up in cultures that lack this prohibition, about 10% of them write with their left hand, which is a typical figure worldwide (Harris, 1983). In the United States, elementary school teachers used to encourage left-handed children to use their right hands; as this practice has diminished in the last 50 years, the percentage of left-handed children has risen steadily (Levy, 1976). Thus, handedness seems to involve a biological force (heredity) in conjunction with sociocultural forces (social values and experiences).

MATURATION AND EXPERIENCE: BOTH INFLUENCE MOTOR SKILL

For locomotion and fine-motor skill, the big picture is much the same. Infants' motor skills develop rapidly during the first year as fundamental skills are mastered; these are combined with other skills to generate even more complex behaviors. Are the changes we observe primarily due to maturation? Are we simply watching a gradual unfolding of skill that depends little on training, practice, or experience? As you might imagine, both maturation and experience contribute.

Let's begin with the impact of maturation on motor development, which is well documented. The sequence of motor development that we have described for locomotion and fine-motor skill holds for most cultures. That is, despite enormous variation in child-rearing practices across cultures, motor development proceeds in much the same way and at roughly the same rate worldwide.

This general point is well illustrated in a classic study of Hopi children by Dennis and Dennis (1940). Traditionally, infants in the Hopi culture are secured to cradle boards like the one shown in the photograph. Cradle boards prevent them from moving their hands or legs, rolling over, or raising their bodies. Infants feed and sleep while secured to the board; they are removed only for a change of clothes. This practice begins the day the infant is born and continues for the first three months. For the next several months, infants are allowed time in which they are not secured to the boards and are free to move about. This time increases gradually, but for most of the first year, infants sleep on cradle boards and are left there for some part of their waking hours.

Obviously, the cradle board strictly limits the infant's locomotion during much of the first year—a time when other infants are learning to sit, creep, and crawl. Nevertheless, the infants in this study learned to walk at approximately 15 months—about the same age as other Hopi children reared by parents who had adopted Western values and no longer used cradle boards.

More than 40 years later, the story remained the same. Chisholm (1983) studied Navajo infants who spent much of their infancy secured to cradle boards. They, too, learned to walk at about the same age as infants whose parents did not use cradle boards.

In both of these studies, a restrictive environment that massively reduced opportunities for practice had no apparent effect on the age at which children began walking. This suggests that the timing of an infant's first steps is determined more by an underlying genetic timetable than by specific experiences or practice. Thus, the worried father of the world-class crawler in the opening vignette needn't worry; his daughter's motor development is quite typical.

Maturation and experience are not, of course, mutually exclusive. The fact that maturation has been shown to figure in motor development does not imply that experience plays no role. In fact, practice and training do affect children's mastery of motor skills. Here, too, studies of other cultures are revealing. In some African countries, young infants have daily exercise sessions, in which they practice walking under the tutelage of a parent or sibling. In addition, many infants are carried by their parents piggyback style, as shown in the photo, which helps to develop muscles in the infants' trunk and legs. Apparently because of such experiences, these infants sometimes learn to walk months earlier than would be expected otherwise (Super, 1981).

? THINK ABOUT IT
What features of locomotion support the idea of development as a universal process? What features support the idea of development as a context-specific process?

The effect of these experiences tends to be specific to particular muscle groups. You wouldn't expect daily practice kicking a soccer ball to do much to improve your golf game. By the same token, infants who receive concentrated practice on one motor skill usually don't improve on other skills. This is shown by experiments in which scientists train infants in one skill, then test them on that skill plus another in which they have had no special training. Research by Zelazo and her colleagues (1993) with 6-week-olds illustrates this phenomenon. Some infants had daily sessions in which, with parents' help, they practiced stepping. Other infants had daily sessions in which they practiced sitting. After 7 weeks of practice, these infants, as well as a control group of children who had received no practice, were tested on their ability to step and to sit. The graphs tell the whole story. For both stepping and sitting, infants improved the skill they had practiced. When infants were tested on the skill that they had not practiced, they did no better than infants in the control group. Clearly, the impact of motor skill practice is specific, not general.

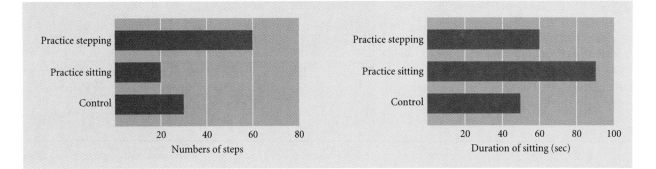

Experience becomes even more important in complex actions, in which discrete skills must be connected in the correct sequence and timed properly. Many of the games that older babies enjoy, like pat-a-cake and peek-a-boo, involve such complex actions. Mastering these games depends on a number of critical experiences, such as observing others play the game, practicing the game with a skilled partner, and receiving feedback when errors are made (Ferrari, 1996). Experiences of this sort build on maturational changes to allow youngsters to enjoy a wide range of motor behaviors: kicking a soccer ball, playing a violin, signing to communicate with people who do not hear, or, as in the You May Be Wondering feature, toilet training.

YOU MAY BE WONDERING **TOILET TRAINING**

Learning to walk and to eat with a spoon are surely important milestones of infancy, but many parents just as eagerly look forward to the day when the last diaper is changed! (They should—an average of 5 diapers a day for 2½ years makes more than 4,500 diaper changes!) Parents and children alike take pride when children learn to control their bladder and bowels. Training pants are worn proudly, as a sign that the child is a "big" girl or boy.

Today, control of the bladder during the day is achieved by about 50% of American 2-year-olds but by nearly 90% of 4-year-olds. Bladder control during the night is typically achieved a few months later (Erickson, 1987).

Controlling the bladder and bowels involves regulating the muscles that surround the openings to these organs. How do infants learn this all-important motor skill? Most do so through a combination of observing others, direct instruction from parents, and, unfortunately, trial and error. One popular approach, devised by Nathan Azrin and Richard Foxx, is described in their book, *Toilet Training in Less than a Day* (1974). Azrin and Foxx based their approach on learning theories, which we described in Chapter 1. They reasoned that the key principles of learning, including imitation, feedback, and reward, could be used to toilet train children. In this program, youngsters must first show their readiness for toilet training. Among the necessary signs are

1. *Bladder control:* The child stays dry for several hours, then urinates in large quantities.
2. *Physical maturation:* The child picks up objects easily and walks easily (requires no parental support, seldom falls).
3. *Instructional readiness:* The child readily responds to simple requests and commands (e.g., to sit down, to imitate, to bring an object).

A child who passes all of these tests is probably ready for toilet training, which involves several steps:

1. Parents use a doll that wets to teach the sequence involved in using the toilet (e.g., lowering pants, sitting on the potty seat, urinating).
2. Children are taught the difference between dry and wet pants; they are praised for the former and rewarded with a drink of a sweet beverage (thereby giving the child more opportunities to urinate).
3. About every 15 minutes, children are led to the potty, where they are encouraged to sit quietly so that they may urinate. When they are successful, parents show their approval verbally and nonverbally (e.g., hugging, smiling, clapping) and provide rewards.

This is just a quick sketch of the program. The basic idea is that youngsters learn to make a particular motor response in the presence of a distinctive stimulus. Imitation is used to illustrate what is desired; reward, feedback, and practice allow children to master the response. As the name suggests, most children taught this way master the essentials of toilet training in 24 hours or less. ●

1. When 4-month-olds tumble from a sitting position, they usually try to keep their head upright. This happens even when they are blindfolded, which means that the important cues to balance come from _____ .
2. When many 6- and 7-month-olds are held upright by an adult and placed on a treadmill, they _____ .
3. Akira uses both hands simultaneously, but not in a coordinated manner; each hand seems to be "doing its own thing." Akira is probably _____ months old.
4. Before the age of _____ , children show no signs of handedness; they use their left and right hands interchangeably.
5. Compared to infants reared in less restrictive environments, infants reared on cradle boards learn to walk _____ .
6. Describe how the mastery of a fine-motor skill such as learning to use a spoon or a crayon illustrates the integration of biological, psychological, and sociocultural forces in the biopsychosocial framework.

Answers: (1) the inner ear, (2) show the mature pattern of moving the legs alternately, (3) 4, (4) 1 year, (5) at about the same age

COMING TO KNOW THE WORLD: PERCEPTION

Coming to Know the World: Perception

Smell and Taste

Touch and Pain

Hearing

Seeing

Integrating Sensory Information

Learning Objectives

- **Are infants able to smell, to taste, and to experience pain?**

- **Can infants hear? How do they use sound to locate objects?**

- **How well can infants see? Can they see color and depth?**

- **How do infants coordinate information between different sensory modalities, such as between vision and hearing?**

*D*ARLA *is mesmerized by her newborn daughter, Olivia. Darla loves holding Olivia, talking to her, and simply watching her. Darla is certain that Olivia is already getting to know her, coming to recognize her face and the sound of her voice. Darla's husband, Steve, thinks she is crazy: "Everyone knows that babies are born blind, and they probably can't hear much either." Darla doubts Steve and wishes someone could tell her the truth about Olivia's vision and hearing.*

To answer Darla's questions, we need to define what it means for an infant to experience or sense the world. Humans have several kinds of sense organs, each of which is receptive to a different kind of physical energy. For example, the retina at the back of the eye is sensitive to some types of electromagnetic energy, and sight is the result. The eardrum detects changes in air pressure, and hearing is the result. Cells at the top of the nasal passage detect the passage of airborne molecules, and smell is the result. In each case, the sense organ translates the physical stimulus into nerve impulses that are sent to the brain. *The processes by which the brain receives, selects, modifies, and organizes these impulses is known as* perception. This is simply the first step in the complex process of accumulating information that eventually results in "knowing."

Darla's questions are really about her newborn daughter's perceptual skills. By the end of this section, you'll be able to answer her questions, because we're going to look at how infants use different senses to experience the world. We begin with smell and taste, which are often known as the chemical senses, because they are among the most mature senses at birth.

SMELL AND TASTE

Newborns have a keen sense of smell. Infants respond positively to pleasant smells but negatively to unpleasant smells. They have a relaxed, contented-looking facial expression when they smell honey or chocolate but frown, grimace, or turn away when they smell rotten eggs or ammonia (Maurer & Maurer, 1988). Young babies also use odor to identify their mothers. For example, 2-week-old infants will look in the direction of a pad that is saturated with the odor of their mother's breast. They will also look in the direction of a pad that is saturated with their mother's perfume (Porter et al., 1991; Schleidt & Genzel, 1990).

Infants also have a highly developed sense of taste. They readily differentiate salty, sour, bitter, and sweet tastes (Crook, 1987). Most infants seem to have a "sweet tooth"—they react to sweet substances by smiling, sucking, and licking their lips. In contrast, you can probably guess what the infant in the photograph has tasted! This grimace is typical when infants are fed bitter- or sour-tasting substances (Kaijura, Copwart, & Beauchamp, 1992). Infants are also sensitive to the changes in the taste of breast milk that reflect a mother's diet. Infants will nurse more after their mother has consumed a sweet-tasting substance such as vanilla (Mennella & Beauchamp, 1996).

This early sensitivity to odor and taste is valuable to an infant. Feeding is simplified, because infants favor odors and tastes associated with feeding, and sensitivity to odor and taste allows babies to recognize their mothers.

TOUCH AND PAIN

Newborns are sensitive to touch. As you'll remember from the first section of this chapter, many areas of the newborn's body respond reflexively when touched. Touching an infant's cheek, mouth, hand, or foot produces reflexive movements, documenting that infants perceive touch.

If babies react to touch, does this mean they experience pain? This is difficult to answer because pain has such a subjective element to it. The same pain-eliciting stimulus that leads some adults to complain of mild discomfort causes others to report they are in agony. Infants cannot express their pain to us directly, of course, so our conclusions about their experience of pain are based on indirect evidence.

The infant's nervous system definitely is capable of transmitting pain: Receptors for pain in the skin are just as plentiful in infants as they are in adults (Anand & Hickey, 1987). Furthermore, babies' behavior in response to apparent pain-provoking stimuli also suggests they experience pain. Look, for example, at the baby in the photograph who is receiving an inoculation. She lowers her eyebrows, purses her lips, and, of course, opens her mouth to cry. Although we can't hear her, the sound of her cry is probably the unique pattern associated with pain: The cry occurs rapidly, is high-pitched, and is not easily soothed. Also, she is agitated, moving her hands, arms, and legs (Craig & colleagues, 1993). Altogether, these signs strongly suggest that babies are definitely capable of experiencing pain.

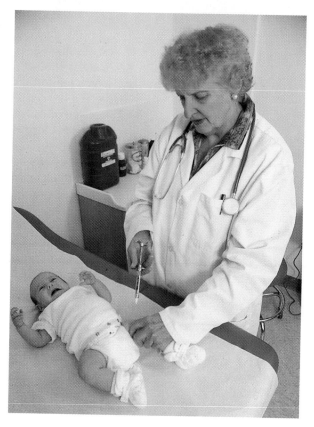

Such sensitivity to touch and pain is useful in maintaining contact with a caregiver, especially the mother, and in helping the infant avoid dangerous stimuli.

HEARING

Do you remember, from Chapter 2, the study in which mothers read aloud *The Cat in the Hat* late in pregnancy? This research showed that the fetus can hear at 7 or 8 months after conception. As you would expect from these results, newborns typically respond to sounds in their surroundings. If a parent is quiet but then coughs, an infant may startle, blink his eyes, and move his arms or legs. These responses may seem natural, but they do indeed indicate that infants are sensitive to sound.

Overall, adults can hear better than infants. Adults can hear some very quiet sounds that infants can't. More interestingly, infants best hear sounds that have pitches in the range of human speech—neither very high- nor very low-pitched. Infants can differentiate speech sounds, such as vowels from consonant sounds and by $4\frac{1}{2}$ months, they can recognize their own names (Mandel, Jusczyk, & Pisoni, 1995; Jusczyk, 1995).

In addition to carrying a message through words or music, sound can reveal much about its source. When we hear a person speak, the pitch of the speech can be used to judge the age and sex of the speaker; if the speech contains many relatively lower-pitched sounds, then the speaker is probably a man. The loudness of the speech tells us about the speaker's distance; if it can barely be heard, the speaker is far away. Also, differences in the time it takes sound to travel to the left and right ears tells us about the speaker's location; if the sounds arrive at exactly the same time, the speaker must be directly ahead or directly behind us.

Even infants can extract much of this information in sound. Young babies can distinguish sounds of different pitches; 6-month-olds do so nearly as accurately as adults (Spetner & Olsho, 1990). They are also able to differentiate speech sounds, such as different vowel and consonant sounds (a topic we examine in more detail in Chapter 4).

Like adults, infants use sound to locate objects, looking toward the source of sound (Morrongiello, Fenwick, & Chance, 1990). Infants also use sound to decide whether objects are near or far. In one study (Clifton, Perris, & Bullinger, 1991), 7-month-olds were shown a rattle. Next, the experimenters darkened the room and shook the rattle, either 6 inches away from the infant or about 2 feet away. Infants would often reach for the rattle in the dark when it was 6 inches away but not when it was 2 feet away. These 7-month-olds were quite capable of using sound to estimate distance—in this case, distinguishing a toy they could reach from one they could not.

Thus, by the middle of the first year, infants are responding to much of the information that is provided by sound. In Chapter 4, we will reach the same conclusion when we examine the perception of language-related sounds.

SEEING

If you've ever watched infants, you've probably noticed that they spend much of their waking time looking around. Sometimes they seem to be generally scanning their environment, and sometimes they seem to be focusing on nearby objects. What do they see as a result? Perhaps their visual world is a sea of confusing gray blobs. Or maybe they see the world essentially as adults do. Actually, neither of these descriptions is entirely accurate, but the second is closer to the truth.

The various elements of the visual system—the eye, the optic nerve, and the brain—are relatively well developed at birth. Newborns respond to light and can track moving objects with their eyes. How well do infants see? *The clarity of vision, called* visual acuity, *is defined as the smallest pattern that can be distinguished dependably.* You've undoubtedly had your acuity measured, probably by being asked to read rows of progressively smaller letters or numbers from a chart. The same approach is used to assess newborns' acuity, adjusted to compensate for the fact that we can't use words to explain to infants what we'd like them to do. Most infants will look at patterned stimuli instead of plain, patternless stimuli (Snow, 1998). For example, if we were to show these two stimuli to an infant, most babies would look longer at the striped pattern than at the gray pattern. As we make the lines narrower (along with the spaces between them), there comes a point at which the black and white stripes become so fine that they simply blend together and appear gray—just like the other pattern.

To estimate an infant's acuity, we pair the gray square with squares in which the widths of the stripes differ, like these: When infants look at the two stimuli equally, this indicates that they are no longer able to distinguish the stripes of the patterned stimulus. By measuring the width of the stripes and their distance from an infant's eye, we can estimate acuity, with detection of thinner stripes indicating better acuity. Measurements of this sort indicate that newborns and 1-month-olds see at 20 feet what normal adults would see at 200–400 feet. By the first birthday, infants' acuity is essentially the same as that of an adult with normal vision (Banks & Dannemiller, 1987).

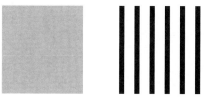

Now that we know that infants can see, an obvious next question is "What do they look at?" Videotapes of babies' eyes as they scan objects reveal that newborns and 1-month-olds often gaze at some conspicuous feature of an object, such as an edge (Bronson, 1991). Beginning at about 2 or 3 months, infants start to inspect the interior of objects, too (Aslin, 1987).

This general sequence also applies to how infants look at faces. Newborns and 1-month-olds typically gaze at the outer edges of faces and at the eyes, perhaps because they are attracted to objects that move (the eyes) and objects with light and dark contrast (the edge of the face). By age 3 months, infants recognize facial features as a unique configuration of elements (Aslin, 1987). As you can see in the diagram, when 3-month-olds look at a face, they focus on the eyes and the mouth.

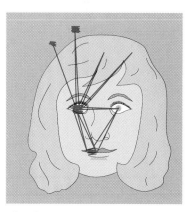

Salapatek, 1975.

Thus, long before the first birthday, infants are scanning objects thoroughly. Their skill allows them to recognize some features that coincide consistently, forming familiar objects.

Color

By today's standards, the first color televisions were primitive. Balancing the colors correctly, so that people didn't look green, for example, was extraordinarily difficult. Nevertheless, these televisions were immensely popular (as were the people who owned them), because adding color makes objects more engrossing, more enjoyable, and more beautiful. But color is more than pleasing; it is functional, too. Color helps us recognize objects and people, and it alerts us to danger.

How do we perceive color? The wavelength of light is the basis of color perception. In the diagram, light that we see as red has a relatively long wavelength, whereas violet, at the other end of the color spectrum, has a much shorter wavelength. *Concentrated in the back of the eye, along the retina, are specialized neurons called* cones. Some cones are particularly sensitive to short-wavelength light (blues and violets). Others are sensitive to medium-wavelength light (greens and yellows); still others are sensitive to long-wavelength

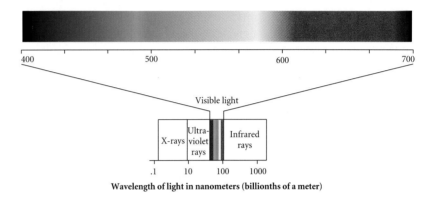

Wavelength of light in nanometers (billionths of a meter)

light (reds and oranges). These different kinds of cones are linked by complex circuits of neurons, and this circuitry is responsible for our ability to see the world in colors.

These circuits begin to function gradually in the first few months after birth (Adams, 1995). Apparently, newborns perceive few colors. However, 1-month-olds can differentiate blue from gray, which means that the short-wavelength circuit is functioning (Maurer & Adams, 1987). At this age, babies can also differentiate red from green, but not yellow from green or yellow from red. Apparently, the medium- and short-wavelength circuits are functioning (because infants discriminate red and green) but not with complete fidelity (because they cannot distinguish yellow). However, 3- and 4-month-olds perceive colors in much the same way that adults do, despite the fact that their visual acuity is not yet fully developed (Adams & Courage, 1995).

Depth

People see objects as having three dimensions: height, width, and depth. The retina of the eye is flat, so height and width can be represented directly on its two-dimensional surface. But the third dimension, depth, cannot be represented directly on this flat surface, so how do we perceive depth? We use perceptual processing to *infer* depth.

Depth perception tells us whether objects are near or far, which was the basis for some classic research by Eleanor Gibson and Richard Walk (1960) on the origins of depth perception. *In their work, babies were placed on the glass-covered platform shown in the photograph on page 111, a device known as the* visual cliff. On one side of the platform, a checkerboard pattern appeared directly under the glass; on the other side, the pattern appeared several feet below the glass. The result was that the first side looked shallow but the other looked deep, like a cliff.

Mothers stood on each side of the visual cliff and tried to coax their infants across the deep or the shallow side. Most babies willingly crawled to their mothers when they stood on the shallow side. In contrast, almost every baby refused to cross the deep side, even when the mothers called them by name and tried to lure them with an attractive toy. Clearly, infants can perceive depth by the time they are old enough to crawl.

What about younger babies who cannot yet crawl? When babies as young as 1½ months are simply placed on the visual cliff, their hearts beat more slowly when they are placed on the deep side of the cliff. Heart rate often decelerates when people notice something interesting, so this would suggest that 1½-month-olds notice that the deep side is different. At 7 months, infants' heart rate accelerates, a sign of fear. Thus, although young babies can detect a difference between the shallow and the deep sides of the visual cliff, only older, crawling babies are actually afraid of the deep side (Campos et al., 1978).

How do infants infer depth? They rely upon many sources of information. *One is* retinal disparity: *When a person views an object, the retinal images in the left and the right eyes differ.* When objects are distant, the retinal images are nearly identical; when they are nearby, the images differ. Thus, greater disparity in retinal images signifies that an object is close. By 4–6 months of age, infants use retinal disparity as a depth cue, correctly inferring that objects are nearby when disparity is great (Yonas & Owsley, 1987).

Motion can also provide information about depth. When an object such as a person or vehicle moves away, it looks smaller. Knowing that the object is not really getting smaller, we interpret the change to mean that the object is becoming more distant. Also, moving objects often pass in front of or behind other objects. When one object is partially obscured by another, we infer that the obscured object is farther away than the unobscured object. By 5 months of age, infants use both of these motion cues to deduce depth (Craton & Yonas, 1988).

Not only do infants use visual cues to judge depth, they also use sound. Remember that infants correctly judge quieter objects to be more distant than louder objects. Given such an assortment of cues, it is not surprising that infants gauge depth so accurately.

We've seen that infants use both auditory and visual information to estimate distance. This represents an important process in perception—integrating information from different senses. Let's look at this more carefully.

INTEGRATING SENSORY INFORMATION

We have described infants' sensory systems separately, but their experiences are usually "multimedia events." A nursing mother provides visual and taste cues to her baby. A rattle may stimulate vision, hearing, and touch. From

? THINK ABOUT IT
Psychologists often refer to "perceptual-motor skills," which implies that the two are closely related. Based on what you've learned in this chapter, how might motor skills influence perception? How could perception influence motor skills?

experiences like these, infants learn to coordinate information provided by different senses. Infants can integrate information from vision and touch. For example, if 6-month-olds are allowed to feel unfamiliar toys that they cannot see, they later look at these toys longer than unfamiliar toys that they have not felt previously. Infants come to know objects through touch and later recognize them visually (Rose, 1994).

Infants also coordinate sights and sounds. For example, by the first birthday, infants have linked the characteristic sounds of male and female voices with the characteristic appearances of male and female faces (Poulin-Dubois et al., 1994). Another example of integration from vision and hearing, judging distance, is the topic of the Spotlight on Research feature.

INTEGRATING SIGHT AND SOUND

Who was the investigator and what was the aim of the study? We already know that older infants use sight and sound independently to judge distance (pages 108, 110–111) but can infants integrate these different sensory systems? Do infants know that an approaching object looks larger *and* sounds louder whereas a departing object looks smaller *and* sounds quieter? Jeffrey Pickens (1994) conducted his study to answer these questions.

How did the investigator measure the topic of interest? Pickens created the setup shown in the diagram. He presented pairs of 25-second videotapes on two video monitors placed side by side. In one pair, the first monitor showed a toy train that appeared to

be coming toward the viewer; the second monitor showed a train going away from the viewer. These videos were shown eight times simultaneously. On four of the presentations, the soundtrack consisted of an engine getting louder; on the other four presentations, the engine was getting quieter. Research assistants wearing headphones (so that they couldn't hear the soundtrack) recorded which video the infant was watching.

What should 5-month-old infants do when they see these videos? If infants know the rules

getting closer = larger and louder
going farther away = smaller and quieter

then they may look at the video that matches the sound: They'll watch the video of the arriving train when the engine gets louder and the video of the departing train when the engine gets quieter. Infants might also do just the opposite—look at the mismatching sounds—because they're novel. In either case, there should be a strong link between what they hear and where they look. If, in contrast, infants don't know these rules, then the soundtrack should not influence what they watch: They should watch the videos equally.

Pickens also included another condition with a different pair of videos. One video showed a train moving from the top of the video monitor to the bottom; the other showed a train moving from the bottom to the top. The soundtracks were the same as in the first condition—the sound of an engine getting louder on some trials and getting quieter on others. Neither video corresponded to the soundtrack because the train remained a constant distance from the viewer. Consequently, if infants understand rules for integrating sight and sound to distance, they should look equally at the two videos.

Who were the children in the study? Pickens tested 64 5-month-olds.

What was the design of the study? This study was experimental. The independent variable was the type of video the infants saw. The dependent variable was the amount of time the infants spent watching each video monitor. The study focused on a single age, so it was not developmental (neither longitudinal nor cross-sectional).

Were there ethical concerns with the study? No. Most infants seemed to enjoy watching the videos. All parents agreed to allow their infants to participate.

What were the results? The top bar of the graph, labeled approach/retreat, shows the results for the videos in which the trains got nearer and farther. The variable shown in the graphs is the percentage of time these 5-month-olds looked at the video that corresponded to the soundtrack. You can see that infants spent nearly two-thirds of the time watching the video that matched the soundtrack; evidently infants knew the rules for integrating visual and auditory cues to distance. The second bar in the graph is from the control condition in which the two videos showed trains moving from top-to-bottom and from bottom-to-top. In this condition, the babies looked at the two videos equally, the expected result since neither video matched the soundtrack.

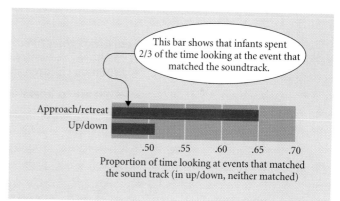

This bar shows that infants spent 2/3 of the time looking at the event that matched the soundtrack.

Proportion of time looking at events that matched the sound track (in up/down, neither matched)

What did the investigator conclude? By 5 months, infants coordinate sight and sound to determine an object's distance and direction of motion. That is, infants know that as objects get near, they look larger and sound louder; as objects move away, they look smaller and sound softer. •

Skillful integration of sight and sound is yet another indication that babies have extraordinary perceptual skill. Young infants perceive the world with impressive precision in each of the sensory systems that we have examined. Darla's daughter can smell, taste, and feel pain; she can distinguish sounds; and, in a few months, she will use sounds to locate objects. Her vision is blurry now but will improve rapidly; in a few months, she'll see the full range of colors and perceive depth. In short, Darla's daughter, like most infants, is exceptionally well prepared to begin to make sense out of her environment.

TEST YOURSELF

1. Taste and _____ are the chemical senses.

2. Infants respond negatively to substances that taste sour or _____ .

3. Infants respond to _____ with a high-pitched cry that is hard to soothe.

4. If an infant seated in a completely darkened room hears the sound of her favorite rattle nearby, she will reach for it; this demonstrates _____ .

5. At age _____ , infants' acuity is like that of an adult with normal vision.

6. _____ are specialized neurons in the retina that are sensitive to color.

7. The term _____ refers to the fact that the images of an object in the left and right eyes differ for nearby objects.

8. Infants integrate information between sight and touch and between sight and _____ .

9. What features of infants' perceptual skill show the influence of nature? What features show the influence of nurture?

Answers: (1) smell, (2) bitter, (3) pain, (4) the use of sound to judge distance, (5) 1 year, (6) Cones, (7) retinal disparity, (8) sound

BECOMING SELF-AWARE

Becoming Self-Aware

Origins of Self-Concept

Theory of Mind

Learning Objectives

- **When do children begin to realize that they exist?**

- **What are toddlers' and preschoolers' self-concepts like?**

- **When do preschool children begin to acquire a theory of mind?**

W HEN XIMENA *brushes her teeth, she puts her 20-month-old son, Christof, in an infant seat facing the bathroom mirror. She's been doing this for months and Christof always seems to enjoy looking at the images in the mirror. Lately, he seems to pay special attention to his own reflection. Ximena thinks that sometimes Christof deliberately frowns or laughs just to see what he looks like. Is this possible, Ximena wonders, or is her imagination simply running wild?*

As infants' physical, motor, and perceptual skills grow, they learn more and more of the world around them. As part of this learning, infants and toddlers begin to realize that they exist independently of other people and objects in the environment and that their existence continues over time. In this last section of Chapter 3, you'll see how children become self-aware and learn what Christof knows about himself.

ORIGINS OF SELF-CONCEPT

When do children begin to understand that they exist? Measuring the onset of this awareness is not easy. Obviously, we can't simply ask a 3-year-old, "So, tell me, when did you first realize you existed and weren't just part of the furniture?" A less direct approach is needed and the photograph shows one route

that many investigators have taken. Like Christof, the 9-month-old in the photograph is smiling at the face he sees in the mirror. Babies at this age sometimes touch the face in the mirror or wave at it, but none of their behaviors indicates that they recognize themselves in the mirror. Instead, babies act as if the face in the mirror is simply a very interesting stimulus.

How would we know that infants recognize themselves in a mirror? One clever approach is to have mothers place a red mark on their infant's nose; they do this surreptitiously, while wiping the baby's face. Then the infant is returned to the mirror. Many 1-year-olds touch the red mark on the mirror, showing that they notice the mark on the face in the mirror. By 15 months, however, an important change occurs: Babies see the red mark in the mirror, then reach up and touch their own noses. By age 2, virtually all children do this (Bullock & Lütkenhaus, 1990; Lewis & Brooks-Gunn, 1979). When these older children notice the red mark in the mirror, they understand that the funny looking nose in the mirror is their own!

We don't need to rely solely on the mirror task to know that self-awareness emerges between 18 and 24 months. During this same period, toddlers look more at photographs of themselves than at photos of other children. They also refer to themselves by name or with a personal pronoun, such as "I" or "me," and sometimes they know their age and their gender. These changes suggest that self-awareness is well established in most children by age 2 (Lewis, 1987).

As children's understanding of the mind becomes more elaborate, children begin to acquire a self-concept. That is, once children fully understand that they exist, they begin to wonder who they are. They want to define themselves.

Some insights into the first phases of self-concept come from Levine (1983), who studied 20- to 28-month-olds. This is an age when children are just beginning to become self-aware. Children were tested on several measures of self-awareness, including the mirror recognition task described earlier. They were also observed as they interacted with an unfamiliar peer in a playroom filled with toys. The key finding was that children who are self-aware are much more likely to say, "Mine!" while playing with toys than children who are not yet self-aware. Maybe you're thinking that these self-aware children were being confrontational in saying, "Mine" as in, "This car is mine and don't even think about taking it." But they weren't. Actually, self-aware children are more likely to say positive things during their interactions with peers. Levine argued that "[C]laiming toys was not simply a negative or aggressive behavior, but appeared

to be an important part of the child's definition of himself within his social world" (1983, p. 547). In other words, the girl on the left in the photograph saying, "Mine!" is not trying to deny the doll to the other girl; she is simply saying that playing with toy dolls is part of who she is.

Throughout the preschool years, possessions continue to be one of the ways in which children define themselves. Preschoolers are also likely to mention physical characteristics ("I have blue eyes"), their preferences ("I like spaghetti"), and their competencies ("I can count to 50"). What these features have in common is a focus on a child's characteristics that are observable and concrete (Damon & Hart, 1988).

As children enter school, their self-concepts become even more elaborate (Harter, 1994), changes that we'll explore in Chapter 8.

THEORY OF MIND

As youngsters gain more insights into themselves as thinking beings, they begin to realize that people have thoughts, beliefs, and intentions. They also understand that thoughts, beliefs, and intentions often cause people to behave as they do. *Collectively, ideas about connections between thoughts, beliefs, intentions, and behavior form a* theory of mind, *an intuitive understanding of the link between mind and behavior.*

One of the leading researchers on theory of mind, Henry Wellman (1992, 1993), believes that children's theory of mind moves through three phases during the preschool years. In the earliest phase, 2-year-olds are aware of desires and often speak of their wants and likes, as in "Lemme see" or "I wanna sit." And they often link their desires to their behavior, such as "I happy there more cookies" (Wellman, 1990). Thus, by age 2, children understand that people have desires and that desires can cause behavior.

By about age 3, children clearly distinguish the mental world from the physical world. For example, if told about a girl who has a cookie and another who is thinking about a cookie, 3-year-olds know that only the first girl can see, touch, and eat her cookie (Harris et al., 1991). And, most 3-year-olds use "mental verbs" like "think," "believe," "remember," and "forget," which suggests that they have a beginning understanding of different mental states (Bartsch & Wellman, 1995). Although 3-year-olds talk about thoughts and beliefs, they nevertheless emphasize desires when trying to explain why people act as they do.

Not until 4 years do mental states really take center stage in children's understanding of their and others' actions. That is, by age 4, children understand that behavior is often based on a person's beliefs about events and situations, even when those beliefs are wrong. This developmental transformation is particularly evident when children are tested on false-belief tasks like the one shown in the figure. In all false-belief tasks, a situation is set up so that the child being tested has accurate information but someone else does not. For example,

This is Sally. Sally has a basket.

This is Anne. Anne has a box.

Sally has a ball.

She puts the ball in her basket.

Sally goes out for a walk.

Anne takes the ball from the basket and puts it into the box.

Now Sally comes back. She wants to play with her ball. Where will she look for her ball?

in the story in the figure, the child being tested knows the ball is really in the box, but Sally, the girl in the story, believes that the ball is still in the basket. Remarkably, although 4-year-olds correctly say that Sally will look for the ball in the basket (acting on her false belief), most 3-year-olds claim that she will look for the ball in the box. The 4-year-olds understand that Sally's behavior is based on her beliefs, despite the fact that her beliefs are incorrect (Frye, 1993). As Bartsch and Wellman (1995) phrase it, 4-year-olds ". . . realize that people not only have thoughts and beliefs, but also that thoughts and beliefs are crucial to explaining why people do things; that is, actors' pursuits of their desires are inevitably shaped by their beliefs about the world" (p. 144).

Preschoolers understand false belief at a younger age if they have older siblings (Ruffman et al., 1998). During play, older brothers and sisters often talk with their younger siblings about internal states—who is happy or sad and why—and these conversations may help youngsters to see the link between beliefs and behavior.

You can see preschool children's growing understanding of false belief in the Real People feature.

THINK ABOUT IT
Suppose you believe that a theory of mind develops faster when preschoolers spend much time with other young children. What sort of correlational study would you devise to test this hypothesis? How could you do an experimental study to test the same hypothesis?

REAL PEOPLE

"SEEING IS BELIEVING . . ." FOR 3-YEAR-OLDS

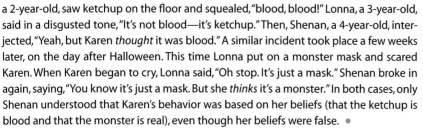

Preschoolers gradually recognize that people's behavior is sometimes guided by mistaken beliefs. We once witnessed an episode at a day care center that documented this growing understanding. After lunch, Karen, a 2-year-old, saw ketchup on the floor and squealed, "blood, blood!" Lonna, a 3-year-old, said in a disgusted tone, "It's not blood—it's ketchup." Then, Shenan, a 4-year-old, interjected, "Yeah, but Karen *thought* it was blood." A similar incident took place a few weeks later, on the day after Halloween. This time Lonna put on a monster mask and scared Karen. When Karen began to cry, Lonna said, "Oh stop. It's just a mask." Shenan broke in again, saying, "You know it's just a mask. But she *thinks* it's a monster." In both cases, only Shenan understood that Karen's behavior was based on her beliefs (that the ketchup is blood and that the monster is real), even though her beliefs were false. ●

Preschool children's growing knowledge of the mind is not an isolated accomplishment. This understanding is simply part of profound cognitive growth that occurs during the preschool years. We'll examine this cognitive growth next, in Chapter 4.

TEST YOURSELF

1. Apparently children are first self-aware at age 2 because this is when they first recognize themselves in the mirror and in photographs and when they first use _____ .

2. Unlike 4-year-olds, most 3-year-olds don't understand that other people's behavior is sometimes based on _____ .

3. During the preschool years, preschool children's self-concepts emphasize _____ , physical characteristics, preferences, and competencies.

4. During the preschool years, children acquire more sophisticated understanding of the mind. Do you think that this change occurs in much the same way in all cultures or does it vary from one culture to another?

Answers: (1) personal pronouns such as "I" and "we," (2) false beliefs, (3) possessions

---

PUTTING IT ALL TOGETHER

The first years of life are remarkable. We saw that newborn babies are endowed with reflexes that prepare them well for life outside of the uterus and that their behavior is already well organized into a number of distinct states. We learned that physical growth is extraordinarily rapid but can be slowed when children are malnourished. Different regions of the infant's brain are already regulating distinct functions, such as goal-directed behavior. This pattern of specialization helps to explain the impact of Martin's injury on his language.

We also looked at improvements in motor skill. Infants gradually become more mobile during the first year. Most begin to walk soon after their first birthday, reflecting biological maturation and integration of the different component skills involved in walking. Paralleling changes in locomotion are changes in fine-motor skills: During the first year, infants become more skilled at grasping and manipulating objects.

We saw that infants are endowed with powerful perceptual skills. Even newborn babies can smell, taste, feel, hear, and see—in some cases with remarkable accuracy. Finally, we discovered that children gradually become self-aware and understand that others think, too.

SUMMARY

The Newborn

The Newborn's Reflexes

• Babies are born with a number of different reflexes. Some help them adjust to life outside of the uterus, some help protect them from danger, and some serve as the basis for later voluntary motor behavior.

Assessing the Newborn

• The Apgar measures five vital signs to determine a newborn baby's physical well-being. The Neonatal Behavioral Assessment Scale provides a comprehensive evaluation of a baby's behavioral and physical status.

The Newborn's States

• Newborns spend their day in one of four states: alert inactivity, waking activity, crying, and sleeping. A newborn's crying includes a basic cry, a mad cry, and a pain cry. The best way to calm a crying baby is by putting it on the shoulder and rocking.

• Newborns spend approximately two-thirds of every day asleep and go through a complete sleep-wake cycle once every 4 hours. By 3 or 4 months, babies sleep through the night. Newborns spend about half of their time asleep in REM sleep, an active form of sleep that may stimulate growth in the nervous system.

• Some healthy babies die from sudden infant death syndrome. Factors that contribute to SIDS are prematurity, low birth weight, and smoking. Also, babies are vulnerable to SIDS when they sleep on their stomach and when they are overheated.

Temperament

• Temperament refers to a consistent style or pattern to an infant's behavior. Dimensions of temperament include emotionality, activity, and sociability. Temperament is a reasonably stable characteristic of infants and young children.

Physical Development

Growth of the Body

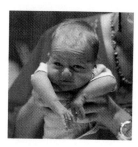

• Physical growth is particularly rapid during infancy, but babies of the same age differ considerably in their heights and weights. Size at maturity is largely determined by heredity.

• Growth follows the cephalocaudal principle, in which the head and trunk develop before the legs. Consequently, infants and young children have disproportionately large heads and trunks.

• Infants must consume a large number of calories, relative to their body weight, primarily because of the energy that is required for growth. Breast-feeding and bottle-feeding both provide babies with adequate nutrition.

• Malnutrition is a worldwide problem that is particularly harmful during infancy, when growth is so rapid. Treating malnutrition adequately requires improving children's diet and training their parents to provide stimulating environments.

The Emerging Nervous System

• A nerve cell, called a *neuron*, includes a cell body, a dendrite, and an axon. The mature brain consists of billions of neurons, organized into nearly identical left and right hemispheres connected by the corpus callosum. The cerebral cortex regulates most of the functions we think of as distinctively human. The frontal cortex is associated with personality and goal-directed behavior; the left hemisphere of the cortex with language; and the right hemisphere of the cortex with nonverbal processes such as perceiving music and regulating emotions.

• Case studies of children with brain injury and EEG records suggest that the left hemisphere specializes in language processing early in life, probably by birth.

• The right hemisphere controls some nonverbal functions, such as perception of music, very early in infancy; control of other functions, such as understanding spatial relations, is achieved by the preschool years. The frontal cortex has begun to regulate goal-directed behavior and emotional responding by the first birthday.

Moving and Grasping— Early Motor Skills

Locomotion

• Infants acquire a series of locomotor skills during their first year, culminating in walking a few months after the first birthday. Like most motor skills, learning to walk involves differentiation of individual skills, such as maintaining balance and using the legs alternately, and then integrating these skills into a coherent whole.

Fine-Motor Skills

• Infants first use only one hand at a time, then both hands independently, then both hands in common actions, and, finally, at about 5 months of age, both hands in different actions with a common purpose.

• Most people are right-handed, a preference that emerges after the first birthday and becomes well established during the preschool years. Handedness is determined by heredity but can also be influenced by cultural values.

Maturation and Experience Both Influence Motor Skills

• Biology and experience both shape the mastery of motor skills. On the one hand, the basic developmental timetable for motor skills is similar around the world, which emphasizes underlying biological causes. On the other hand, specific experience can accelerate motor development, particular for complex motor skills.

Coming to Know the World: Perception

Smell and Taste

• Newborns are able to smell, and some can recognize their mother's odor; they also taste, preferring sweet substances and responding negatively to bitter and sour tastes.

Touch and Pain

• Infants respond to touch. They probably experience pain, because their responses to painful stimuli are similar to those of older children.

Hearing

• Babies can hear. More importantly, they can distinguish different sounds and use sound to locate objects in space.

Seeing

• A newborn's visual acuity is relatively poor, but 1-year-olds can see as well as an adult with normal vision. Color vision develops as different sets of cones begin to function, a process that seems to be complete by 3 or 4 months of age. Infants perceive depth, based on retinal disparity and cues from motion.

Integrating Sensory Information

• Infants coordinate information from different senses. They can recognize, by sight, an object they've felt previously. They look at a woman's face when they hear a woman's voice or look at an object that is becoming more distant when a sound becomes softer.

Becoming Self-Aware

Origins of Self-Concept

• Beginning at about 15 months, infants begin to recognize themselves in the mirror, which is one of the first signs of self-recognition. They also begin to prefer to look at pictures of themselves, begin to refer to themselves by name (or use personal pronouns), and sometimes know their age and gender. Evidently, by 2 years, most children are self-aware.

• Preschoolers often define themselves in terms of observable characteristics, such as possessions, physical characteristics, preferences, and competencies. During the elementary school years, self-concept begins to include observable characteristics, such as a child's possessions and preferences.

Theory of Mind

• Theory of mind, which refers to a person's ideas about connections between thoughts, beliefs, intentions, and behavior, develops rapidly during the preschool years. Most 2-year-olds know that people have desires and that desires can cause behavior. By age 3, children distinguish the mental world from the physical world, but still emphasize desire in explaining others' actions. By age 4, however, children understand that behavior is based on beliefs about the world, even when those beliefs are wrong.

KEY TERMS

reflexes (85)
alert inactivity (86)
waking activity (86)
crying (86)
sleeping (86)
basic cry (87)
mad cry (87)
pain cry (87)
irregular (REM) sleep (88)
regular (nonREM) sleep (88)

sudden infant death syndrome (SIDS) (88)
temperament (89)
emotionality (89)
activity (89)
sociability (89)
neuron (94)
cell body (94)
dendrite (94)
axon (94)

terminal button (94)
neurotransmitter (94)
cerebral cortex (95)
hemispheres (95)
corpus callosum (95)
frontal cortex (95)
neural plate (95)
myelin (96)
electroencephalogram (EEG) (96)

positron emission tomography (PET scan) (96)
motor skills (98)
locomote (98)
fine-motor skills (99)

toddling (100)
toddler (100)
differentiation (100)
integration (100)
perception (106)

visual acuity (109)
cones (110)
visual cliff (110)
retinal disparity (111)
theory of mind (116)

IF YOU'D LIKE TO LEARN MORE

Readings

ASLIN, R. N. (1987). Visual and auditory discrimination in infancy. In J. D. Osofsky (Ed.), *Handbook of infant development* (2nd ed.). New York: Wiley. This text is a comprehensive but technical account of research on infant perception.

BARTSCH, K., & WELLMAN, H. M. (1995). *Children talk about the mind.* New York: Oxford. Wellman is one of the leading investigators of theory of mind and Bartsch is his student. In this book, they use actual samples of children's talk to show growth in children's understanding of the mind.

BRAZELTON, T. B. (1983). *Infants and mothers: Differences in development.* New York: Delta/Seymour Lawrence. In this classic book the author, a well-known pediatrician and creator of the Neonatal Behavioral Assessment Scale (NBAS), illustrates striking differences among babies by examining a few case studies in detail.

KOPP, C. (1993). *Baby steps: The "whys" of your child's behavior in the first two years.* New York: Freeman. As the title indicates, this book is not only about newborns. However, we recommend the book because the author begins with newborn babies and traces the changes that occur in physical, motor, mental, and social-emotional development.

TANNER, J. M. (1990). *Fetus into man: Physical growth from conception to maturity* (2nd ed.). Cambridge, MA: Harvard University Press. Tanner is a leading authority and presents a straightforward account of human growth.

For additional readings, explore Infotrac College Edition, your online library. Go to http://www.infotrac-college.com/wadsworth.

Web Sites

For more information about different aspects of temperament, visit

http://www.temperament.com/

the Web site of a publisher of a questionnaire used to measure temperament.

The Nemours Foundation maintains "Kidshealth"

http://kidshealth.org/

a site that has information about children's growth and nutrition.

Pampers (the diaper company) maintains a site

http://www.totalbabycare.com/

with information about infant and toddler development.

Web site addresses are subject to change. The Wadsworth Study Center Web site listed below can be accessed for updated links.

The Wadsworth Psychology Study Center Web Site

See http://psychology.wadsworth.com/ for practice quiz questions, internet links, updates, critical thinking exercises, discussion forums and more! The Wadsworth Psychology Study Center provides a wealth of information fully organized and integrated by chapter.

CHAPTER 4

THE EMERGENCE OF THOUGHT AND LANGUAGE

The Onset of Thinking: Piaget's Account
Basic Principles of Cognitive Development
Sensorimotor Thinking
Preoperational Thinking
Christine, Egocentrism, and Animism
Preoperational Thinking in Action
Evaluating Piaget's Theory

Information Processing During Infancy and Early Childhood
General Principles of Information Processing
Attention
Memory
Preschoolers on the Witness Stand
Quantitative Knowledge

Mind and Culture: Vygotsky's Theory
The Zone of Proximal Development
Scaffolding
How Do Mothers in Different Cultures Scaffold Children's Learning?
Private Speech

Language
The Road to Speech
First Words and Many More
Speaking in Sentences: Grammatical Development
How Children Learn Grammar
Communicating with Others

Putting It All Together

Summary

If You'd Like to Learn More

In the movie *Look Who's Talking,* we are privy to an infant's adult-like thoughts about his birth, diaper changes, and his mother's boyfriends. Of course, few of us believe that babies are capable of this sophisticated thinking. But what thoughts occupy the mind of an infant who is not yet speaking? How does cognition develop during infancy and early childhood? What makes these changes possible?

These questions provide the focus of this chapter. We begin with what has long been considered the definitive account of cognitive development, Jean Piaget's theory. In this theory, thinking progresses through four distinct stages between infancy and adulthood.

The next two sections of the chapter concern alternative accounts of cognitive development. One account, the information-processing perspective, traces children's emerging cognitive skills in many specific domains, among them memory skills. The other, Lev Vygotsky's theory, emphasizes the cultural origins of cognitive development and explains why children sometimes talk to themselves as they play or work.

Throughout development, children express their thoughts in oral and written language. In the last section of this chapter, you'll see how children master the sounds, words, and grammar of their native language.

THE ONSET OF THINKING: PIAGET'S ACCOUNT

The Onset of Thinking: Piaget's Account

Basic Principles of Cognitive Development

Sensorimotor Thinking

Preoperational Thinking

Evaluating Piaget's Theory

Learning Objectives

- According to Piaget, how do assimilation, accommodation, and organization provide the foundation for cognitive development throughout the life span?
- How do schemes become more advanced as infants progress through the six stages of sensorimotor thinking?
- What are the distinguishing characteristics of thinking during the preoperational stage?
- What are some of the shortcomings of Piaget's account of cognitive development?

HREE-YEAR-OLD JAMILA loves talking to her grandmother ("Gram") on the telephone. Sometimes these conversations are not very successful because Gram asks questions and Jamila replies by nodding her head "yes" or "no." Jamila's dad has explained that Gram (and others on the phone) can't see her nodding—that she needs to say "yes" or "no." But Jamila invariably returns to head-nodding. Her dad can't see why such a bright and talkative child doesn't realize that nodding is meaningless over the phone.

Why does Jamila insist on nodding her head when she's talking on the phone? This behavior is quite typical according to the famous Swiss psychologist, Jean Piaget (1896–1980). In Piaget's theory, children's thinking progresses through four qualitatively different stages. In this section, we'll begin by describing some of the general features of Piaget's theory, then examine Piaget's account of thinking during infancy and during the preschool years, and, finally, consider some of the strengths and weaknesses of the theory.

BASIC PRINCIPLES OF COGNITIVE DEVELOPMENT

Piaget believed that children are naturally curious. They constantly want to make sense of their experience and, in the process, construct their understanding of the world. For Piaget, children at all ages are like scientists in that they create theories about how the world works. Of course, children's theories are often incomplete. Nevertheless, children's theories are valuable to them because they make the world seem more predictable.

According to Piaget, children understand the world with schemes, *psychological structures that organize experience.* Schemes are mental categories of related events, objects, and knowledge. During infancy, most schemes are based on actions. That is, infants group objects based on the actions they can perform on them. For example, infants suck and grasp and they use these actions to create categories of objects that can be sucked and objects that can be grasped.

Schemes are just as important after infancy, but they are now based primarily on functional or conceptual relationships, not action. For example, preschoolers learn that forks, knives, and spoons form a functional category of "things I use to eat." Or they learn that dogs, cats, and goldfish form a conceptual category of "pets."

Like preschoolers, older children and adolescents have schemes based on functional and conceptual schemes. But they also have schemes that are based on increasingly abstract properties. For example, an adolescent might put fascism, racism, and sexism in a category of "ideologies I despise."

Thus, schemes of related objects, events, and ideas are present throughout development. But as children develop, their rules for creating schemes shift from physical activity to functional, conceptual, and, later, abstract properties of objects, events, and ideas.

Assimilation and Accommodation

Schemes change constantly, adapting to children's experiences. In fact, intellectual adaptation involves two processes working together: assimilation and accommodation. Assimilation *occurs when new experiences are readily incorporated into existing schemes.* Imagine a baby who has the familiar grasping scheme. Like the baby in the photograph, she will soon discover that the grasping scheme also works well on blocks, toy cars, and other small objects. Extending the existing grasping scheme to new objects illustrates assimilation. Accommodation *occurs when schemes are modified based on experience.* Soon the infant learns that some objects can only be lifted with two hands and that some can't be lifted at all. Changing the scheme so that it works for new objects (e.g., using two hands to grasp heavy objects) illustrates accommodation.

Assimilation and accommodation are often easier to understand when you remember Piaget's belief that infants, children, and adolescents create theories to try to understand events and objects around them. The infant whose theory is that objects can be lifted with one hand finds that her theory is confirmed when she tries to pick up small objects, but she's in for a surprise when she tries to pick up a heavy book. The unexpected result forces the infant, like a good scientist, to revise her theory to include this new finding.

Equilibration and Stages of Cognitive Development

Assimilation and accommodation are usually in balance, or equilibrium. Children find that many experiences are readily assimilated into their existing schemes but that they sometimes need to accommodate their schemes to adjust to new experiences. This balance between assimilation and accommodation is illustrated by the baby with the theory about lifting objects. Periodically, however, this balance is upset and a state of disequilibrium results. That is, children discover that their current schemes are not adequate because they are spending much time accommodating and much less time assimilating. *When disequilibrium occurs, children reorganize their schemes to return to a state of equilibrium, a process that Piaget called* equilibration. To restore the balance, current but now-outmoded ways of thinking are replaced by a qualitatively different, more advanced set of schemes.

One way to understand equilibration is to return to the metaphor of the child as a scientist. As we discussed in Chapter 1, good scientific theories readily explain some phenomena but usually must be revised to explain others.

Children's theories allow them to understand many experiences by predicting—for example, what will happen ("It's morning, so it's time for breakfast") or who will do what ("Mom's gone to work, so Dad will take me to school")—but the theories must be modified when predictions go awry ("Dad thinks I'm old enough to walk to school, so he won't take me").

Sometimes scientists find that their theories contain critical flaws that can't be fixed simply by revising; instead, they must create a new theory that draws upon the older theory but is fundamentally different. For example, when the astronomer Copernicus realized that the earth-centered theory of the solar system was fundamentally wrong, his new theory built on the assumption that the sun is the center of the solar system. In much the same way, periodically children reach states in which their current theories seem to be wrong much of the time, so they abandon these theories in favor of more advanced ways of thinking about their physical and social worlds.

According to Piaget, these revolutionary changes in thought occur three times over the life span, at approximately 2, 7, and 11 years of age. This divides cognitive development into the following four stages:

Period of Development	Age Range
Sensorimotor period	Infancy (0–2 years)
Preoperational period	Preschool and early elementary school years (2–7 years)
Concrete operational period	Middle and late elementary school years (7–11 years)
Formal operational period	Adolescence and adulthood (11 years and up)

The ages listed are only approximate. Some youngsters move through the periods more rapidly than others, depending on their ability and their experience. However, the only route to formal operations—the most sophisticated type of thought—is through the first three periods, in sequence. Sensorimotor thinking always gives rise to preoperational thinking; a child cannot "skip" preoperational thinking and move directly from the sensorimotor to the concrete operational period.

In the next few pages of this chapter, we consider Piaget's account of sensorimotor and preoperational thinking, the periods from birth to approximately 7 years of age. In Chapter 6, we will return to Piaget's theory to examine his account of concrete and formal operational thinking in older children and adolescents.

SENSORIMOTOR THINKING

Before examining Piaget's description of infancy, let's review some of the facts of infancy we've already learned. In Chapter 3, we saw that infants' locomotor skills improve rapidly during the first year, culminating in walking at 14 or 15 months of age; fine-motor skills develop rapidly during this same period; and perceptual skills, already powerful in early infancy, improve quickly.

Piaget (1951, 1952, 1954) proposed that this period of rapidly changing perceptual and motor skills forms a distinct phase in human development. *The sensorimotor period, from birth to roughly 2 years of age, is the first of Piaget's four periods of cognitive development.* Piaget divided this period into six stages. All infants progress through the six stages in the same order, but they do so at different rates, so the ages we list here are only approximations.

1. *Exercising reflexes (roughly 0–1 month).* We know from Chapter 3 that newborns respond reflexively to many stimuli. As infants use these reflexes during the first month, they become much more coordinated. For example, just as major-league players swing a bat with greater power and strength than do Little Leaguers, 1-month-olds suck more strongly and steadily than do newborns. Reflexes like this one provide the foundation for much cognitive growth during infancy.

2. *Learning to adapt: Primary circular reactions (roughly 1–4 months).* During these months, reflexes become modified by experience. *The chief mechanism for change is the* primary circular reaction, *in which infants accidentally produce a pleasing event involving their own body and then try to re-create the event.* For example, an infant may inadvertently touch his lips with his thumb, thereby initiating sucking and the pleasing sensations associated with sucking. Later, the infant tries to re-create these sensations by guiding his thumb to his mouth. Sucking no longer occurs only when the mother places a nipple at the infant's mouth; instead, the infant has found a way to initiate sucking himself.

3. *Making interesting events (roughly 4–8 months).* Initially, primary circular reactions involve such reflexes as sucking or grasping. However, beginning in Stage 3, the infant begins to show greater interest in the world. Now objects are more often the focus of circular reactions. For example, the infant shown in the photo accidentally shook a new toy. Hearing the interesting noise, she grasped the toy anew, tried to shake it, and expressed great pleasure when the noise resumed. This sequence was repeated several times.

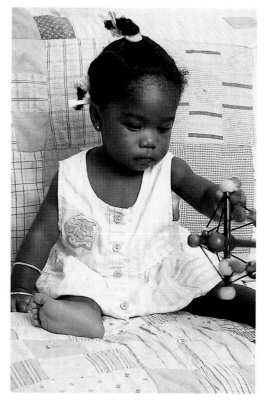

Novel actions that are repeated with objects characterize the secondary circular reaction. They are significant because they represent an infant's first efforts to learn about objects in the environment, to explore their properties. No longer are infants grasping objects "mindlessly," simply because something is in contact with their hands. Instead, they are learning about the sights and sounds associated with the objects.

4. *Behaving intentionally: Separating means from ends (roughly 8–12 months).* This stage marks the onset of deliberate, intentional behavior. For the first time, the means and the ends of activities are distinct. For example, if a father places his hand in front of a toy, an infant will move the father's hand to be able to play with the toy. The "move the hand" scheme is the means to achieve the end of activating the "grasp the toy" scheme. Combining schemes in this way is the first solid evidence of deliberate, purposeful behavior during infancy.

5. *Experimenting (roughly 12–18 months).* The infant at this stage is an active experimentalist. *An infant will repeat old schemes with novel objects—which Piaget called a* tertiary circular reaction—*as if trying to understand why different objects yield different outcomes.* A Stage 5 infant may deliberately shake a number of different objects, trying to discover which produce sounds and which do not. Or an infant may decide to drop different objects to see what happens. An infant in a crib discovers that stuffed animals land quietly, whereas harder toys often make a more satisfying "clunk" when they hit the ground.

Tertiary circular reactions represent a significant extension of the intentional behavior that emerged in Stage 4. Now babies repeat actions with different objects *solely* for the purpose of seeing what will happen.

? THINK ABOUT IT
Children with low birth weight often have delayed intellectual development (pp. 75–76). According to Piaget, what form might the delay take?

6. *Using symbols (roughly 18–24 months).* By 18 months, most infants have begun to talk and gesture (the subject of the last section of this chapter). These actions are significant because they illustrate toddlers' emerging capacity to use symbols. Words and gestures are symbols that stand for something else: Waving and saying "bye-bye" are both ways to indicate that you're leaving. Pretend play, which we'll examine in more detail in Chapter 5, also shows a youngster's use of symbols. For example, a 20-month-old may move her hand back and forth in front of her mouth, pretending to brush her teeth.

Once infants can use symbols, they can begin to anticipate the consequences of actions mentally, instead of having to perform them. Imagine that an infant and parent have constructed a tower of blocks next to an open door. Leaving the room, a Stage 5 infant might well close the door, knocking over the tower. This infant is unable to foresee the predictable outcome of closing the door. In contrast, a Stage 6 child can anticipate the consequence of closing the door and might well move the tower beforehand.

Using symbols is the crowning achievement of the sensorimotor period. In just two years, the infant has progressed from reflexive responding to symbolic processing. A summary of these changes is shown in the table.

Substages during the Sensorimotor Stage of Development

Substage	Age (months)	Accomplishment	Example	
1	0–1	Reflexes become coordinated.	Sucking a nipple	
2	1–4	Primary circular reactions appear —an infant's first learned reactions to the world.	Thumb sucking	
3	4–8	Secondary circular reactions emerge, allowing infants to explore the world of objects.	Shaking a toy to hear a rattle	
4	8–12	Means–end sequencing of schemes is seen, marking the onset of intentional behavior.	Moving an obstacle to reach a toy	
5	12–18	Tertiary circular reactions develop, allowing children to experiment.	Shaking different toys to hear the sounds they make	
6	18–24	Symbolic processing is revealed in language, gestures, and pretend play.	Eating pretend food with a pretend fork	

The ability to use mental symbols marks the end of sensorimotor thinking and the beginning of preoperational thought, which we'll examine next.

PREOPERATIONAL THINKING

Once they have crossed into preoperational thinking, the magical power of symbols is available to young children. Of course, mastering this power is a lifelong process; the preschool child's efforts are tentative and sometimes incorrect (DeLoache, 1995). Piaget identified a number of characteristic shortcomings in preschoolers' fledgling symbolic skills. Let's look at three.

Egocentrism

Preoperational children typically believe that others see the world—both literally and figuratively—exactly as they do. Egocentrism *is difficulty in seeing the world from another's outlook.* When youngsters stubbornly cling to their own way, they are not simply being contrary. Preoperational children simply do not comprehend that other people differ in their ideas, convictions, and emotions.

One of Piaget's famous experiments, the three-mountains problem, demonstrates preoperational children's egocentrism (Piaget & Inhelder, 1956, Chapter 8). Youngsters were seated at a table like the one shown in the drawing. When preoperational children were asked to choose the photograph that corresponded to another person's view of the mountains, they usually picked the photograph that showed their own view of the mountains, not the other person's. Preoperational youngsters evidently suppose that the mountains are seen the same way by all; they presume that theirs is the only view, not one of many conceivable views. According to Piaget, only concrete operational children fully understand that all people do not experience an event in exactly the same way.

Recall that in the vignette, 3-year-old Jamila nods her head during phone conversations with her grandmother. This, too, reflects preoperational egocentrism. Jamila assumes that because she is aware that her head is moving up and down (or side-to-side), her grandmother must be aware of it, too. In the Real People feature, we see yet another manifestation of this egocentrism.

REAL PEOPLE

CHRISTINE, EGOCENTRISM, AND ANIMISM

Because of their egocentrism, preoperational youngsters often attribute their own thoughts and feelings to others. *They may even credit inanimate objects with life and lifelike properties, a phenomenon known as* animism (Piaget, 1929). A 3½-year-old we know, Christine, illustrated this in a conversation we had with her recently on a dreary, rainy day when she was forced to stay indoors.

CHRISTINE: Mr. Sun is very sad today.

US: Why?

CHRISTINE: Because it's cloudy. He can't shine. And he can't see me!

US: That's too bad.

CHRISTINE: Trike [tricycle] is sad, too.

US: Why is that?

CHRISTINE: Because I can't ride him. And because he's all alone in the garage, where it's dark.

Caught up in her egocentrism, preoperational Christine believes that objects like the sun and her tricycle think and feel as she does. That is, because she has thoughts and feelings, she believes that other people and inanimate objects have them, too. •

Irreversibility

Logical and mathematical operations usually have inverses—operations that "undo" or reverse the effect of an operation. If you start with 5 and add 3, you obtain 8; by subtracting 3 from 8, you can reverse your steps and return to 5. For Piaget, reversibility of this sort also applies to psychological operations. Mature individuals can reverse their thinking if necessary. However, an inability to reverse thinking is one characteristic of preoperational youngsters.

Piaget demonstrated such irreversibility in another famous experiment, involving conservation of liquid quantity. Children were shown two identical beakers filled with exactly the same amount of juice, like those in the photograph. After the children had agreed that the juice in the two beakers was the same, juice was poured from one of the beakers into a third beaker. This beaker was thinner than the original two, which meant that the juice rose higher in the beaker. Children were then asked if the two beakers still contained the same amount of juice. "No," preoperational children said. They argued that the thinner beaker contains more juice; unable to reverse their mental operations to return to the original equality, they responded on the basis of level of the juice. In contrast, older, concrete-operational children often said, "yes." Commonly, they justified their answer by explaining that the juice can always be poured back into the original container and that the amounts will be the same.

Appearance as Reality

Many a 3-year-old has watched an older brother or sister slip on a ghoulish Halloween costume and become frightened when the sibling's face is hidden by a dreadful mask. For the youngster in the photo, the scary costume is reality, not just something that looks frightening but isn't real.

You shouldn't conclude that confusion between appearance and reality is specific to costumes and masks. It is a general characteristic of preoperational thinking. To see how, think about some common instances where appearances and reality may conflict:

• A boy is angry because a friend is being mean. Nevertheless, he smiles because he's afraid the friend will leave if he reveals his anger.

- A glass of milk looks brown when viewed through sunglasses with brown lenses.
- A piece of hard rubber looks like food (e.g., like a piece of pizza).

Older children and adults know that the boy *looks* happy, the milk *looks* brown, and the object *looks* like food—but that the boy is *really* angry, the milk is *really* white, and the object is *really* rubber. Preoperational children, however, readily confuse appearance and reality.

You can see evidence of this confusion in the results of a study by Friend and Davis (1993). Stories were presented in which a person's outward appearance conflicted with his or her underlying feelings. For example, children were told about Sally, a school-age child who was sad because her uncle gave her a baby rattle for her birthday. Sally didn't want to hurt her uncle's feelings, so she smiled as she took the gift out of the box. A photograph showed Sally smiling at her uncle. Children in the study were asked if Sally *looks* happy or sad and if she *really* is happy or sad.

The graph shows how accurately children answered the questions. Questions about Sally's appearance were easy for all children; 4- and 7-year-olds readily judged that Sally looked happy. Questions about her real feelings were much more difficult; most 4-year-olds answered the questions incorrectly, and even some 7-year-olds did. Thus, when presented stories about people who feel sad but look happy, preoperational youngsters claim not only that the people look happy but that they are really and truly happy! In contrast, 7-year-olds are more likely to have progressed to concrete-operational thinking. Consequently, they respond much more accurately.

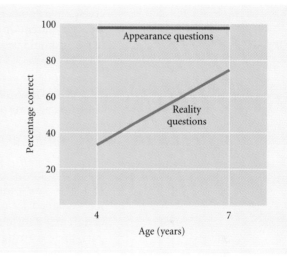

Based on Friend & Davis, 1993.

Are you skeptical of these findings? Do you doubt that young children are confused so easily? When these findings were first reported, many researchers shared your skepticism. They went to great lengths to show that the children were somehow being misled by some minor aspects of the experiment. Surprisingly enough, they were unable to disprove the original results. Rewording the instructions, using different materials, and even training children all had relatively little impact (Siegler, 1998). Confusion about appearance and reality is simply a deep-seated characteristic of preoperational thinking, especially in the early years of this period.

The See for Yourself feature shows how you can see some of these characteristics of preoperational thought firsthand.

PREOPERATIONAL THINKING IN ACTION

SEE FOR YOURSELF

The best way to see some of the developmental changes that Piaget described is to test some children with the same tasks that Piaget used. The conservation task shown on page 130 is good because it's simple to set up and children usually enjoy it. First ask a 3- or 4-year-old to confirm that the containers have the same amount of liquid. Then, pour the liquid from one container into a third, different-shaped container. Now ask the child if the quantities are still the same and have the child explain his or her answer.

You should also try to test the child on some appearance-reality tasks. Find rubber "play food" and ask children what the objects "look like" and what they "really and truly are." Have them look at a glass of water through the sunglasses and ask them what the water looks like and what it really and truly is. Just like the youngsters that Piaget tested, your 3-year-old will probably claim that the amount of liquid changes when you pour it into a different container and will say that the rubber is really and truly food and that the water is really and truly brown. See for yourself! ●

EVALUATING PIAGET'S THEORY

Because Piaget's theory is so comprehensive, it has stimulated much research. Much of this work supports Piaget's view that children actively try to understand the world around them and organize their knowledge and that cognitive development includes major qualitative changes (Brainerd, 1996; Flavell, 1996).

One important contribution of Piaget's theory is that many teachers and parents have found it a rich source of ideas about ways to foster children's development. For example, Piaget argued that cognitive growth occurs as children construct their *own* understanding of the world, so the teacher's role is to create environments where children can discover *for themselves* how the world works. A parent or teacher shouldn't simply tell children how to solve a problem but should provide children with materials so they can discover the solution themselves.

Although many general features of Piaget's theory have been supported, on specific issues some elements of the theory have held up better than others. Let's look at some of the criticisms that have been raised.

Alternative Explanations of Performance

As we have seen, Piaget explained cognitive development by using constructs like accommodation, assimilation, and schemes. However, subsequent researchers have found that children's performance on Piaget's tasks is often better explained by other theoretical constructs. For example, preoperational children's performance on the conservation task appears to reflect, at least in part, their growing sensitivity to the nuances of language, rather than purely their lack of reversibility. The phrasing of the questions concerning the amount of water turns out to be critical (Winer, Craig, & Weinbaum, 1992). Remember that in this procedure, youngsters are twice asked if the amount of water in the two beakers is the same—once before the water is poured and once after. In everyday conversation, a question is usually repeated like this because the answer was wrong the first time. Or it may be repeated because the answer was correct at first but something has changed so that it is now wrong. Both of these rules about questions would lead young children who had answered "yes" to the first question to wonder whether they were wrong and perhaps say "no" the second time. In fact, when the procedure is changed (e.g., by asking the question only once) preschoolers are more likely to answer correctly. Thus, children's performance on conservation problems is based partly on language development, not just the concepts that Piaget included in his theory.

Researchers have also questioned Piaget's studies of infants' understanding of objects (Goubet & Clifton, 1998; Munakata et al., 1997). According to Piaget, one of the milestones of infancy is the understanding that objects exist independently of oneself and one's actions. He claimed that 1- to 4-month-olds—who are in Stage 2 of the sensorimotor period—believe that objects no longer exist when they disappear from view (out of sight, out of mind). As astounding as this may seem, if you take a favorite toy from a 3-month-old and hide it under a cloth directly in front of her, she will not look for it. This

? THINK ABOUT IT
Erik Erikson and Sigmund Freud also proposed stages of development during infancy and early childhood. How do their stages compare to Piaget's?

is true even though the shape of the toy is clearly visible under the cloth and within reach!

Beginning at about 4 or 5 months, Piaget found that infants will search for objects. Understanding of objects is far from complete, because even older infants are sometimes unable to find hidden objects. If 9-month-olds see an object hidden under one container, then see it hidden under a second container, most of them routinely look for the toy under the first container. Piaget claimed that this showed 9-month-olds' fragmentary understanding of objects. Infants do not distinguish the object per se from the actions they used to locate it, such as lifting a particular container. Not until approximately 18 months of age do infants apparently have full understanding of the permanence of objects.

Other scientists, however, doubted that younger infants are so limited in their understanding of objects. Renée Baillargeon (1987, 1994) devised a clever method, shown in the diagram, to study young babies' understanding of

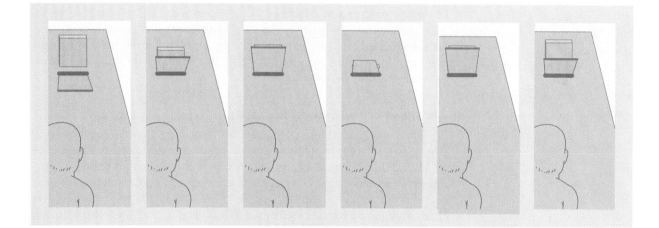

objects. Infants first saw a silver screen that appeared to be rotating back and forth. When they were familiar with this display, one of two new displays was shown. In the *possible event,* a yellow box appeared in a position behind the screen, making it impossible for the screen to rotate as far back as it had previously. Instead, the screen rotated until it made contact with the box, then rotated forward. In the *impossible event,* the yellow box appeared, but the screen continued to rotate as before. The screen rotated back until it was flat, then rotated forward, again revealing the yellow box. The illusion was possible because the box was mounted on a movable platform that allowed it to drop out of the way of the moving screen. However, from the infant's perspective, it appeared as if the box vanished behind the screen, only to reappear.

The disappearance and reappearance of the box violates the idea that objects exist permanently. Consequently, an infant who understands the permanence of objects should find the impossible event a truly novel stimulus and look at it longer than the possible event. Baillargeon found that 4½-month-olds consistently looked longer at the impossible event than the possible event. Infants apparently thought that the impossible event was novel, just as we are surprised when an object vanishes from a magician's scarf.

Evidently, infants have some understanding of the permanence of objects at a much younger age than Piaget's theory would predict. Why the difference? Remember that Piaget usually based his assessments on tasks in which infants had to search for missing objects. Search requires locomotor skills—reaching and grasping, for example—and apparently it is these skills that are limited in younger infants, not their understanding that objects are permanent.

The contrary findings regarding infants' understanding of object permanence and conservation do not mean that Piaget's theory is fundamentally wrong. In some cases, the theory needs to be revised to include important constructs that Piaget overlooked.

Consistency in Performance

In Piaget's view, each stage of intellectual development consists of a unified set of mental structures that pervades children's thinking. For example, preoperational thinking should leave its mark on all of a child's activities. On conservation and three-mountains tasks, a 4-year-old should always respond in a preoperational way: He should claim that the water is not the same after pouring and believe that the other person sees the mountains as he does. In fact, research reveals some consistency in performance on various tasks, but exceptions are common, too (Siegler, 1981). A youngster may be advanced on the conservation task, perfectly average on the three-mountains task, and somewhat delayed on other Piagetian tasks. This variability is not readily incorporated into Piaget's view of uniform stages that should leave the same characteristic imprint in all domains.

The Impact of Culture on Cognition

Piaget believed that children, through accommodation and assimilation, construct their own image of the world. This construction of reality is said to be largely the child's own doing, uninfluenced by others. The four periods of cognitive development are said to apply to children and adolescents everywhere, regardless of the culture in which they live. Although Piaget recognized that children's thinking is influenced by parents, siblings, school, and other elements of their culture, he insisted that these elements had relatively little impact on children's progression through his four periods. As we'll see in the next section of the chapter, not all theorists share Piaget's view that culture has little impact on cognitive development.

These criticisms do not mean that Piaget's theory is invalid or should be ignored. As noted earlier, it remains the most complete account of cognitive development. However, in recent years, researchers have attempted to round out our understanding of cognitive development, using other theoretical perspectives such as the information-processing approach that is examined in the next section.

TEST YOURSELF

1. The term _____ means modification of schemes based on experience.

2. According to Piaget, _____ are psychological structures that organize experience.

3. A _____ is an event that infants try to repeat because it produces interesting outcomes with objects.

4. The climax of the sensorimotor period occurs in Stage 6 when infants _____ .

5. Preschoolers are often _____ , meaning that they are unable to take another person's viewpoint.

6. Preoperational children sometimes attribute thoughts and feeling to inanimate objects. This is called _____ .

7. In contrast to the prediction of Piaget's theory, when children are tested on different Piagetian tasks, their performance _____ .

8. What forces in the biopsychosocial framework can you see in an infant's progression through the six stages of the sensorimotor period?

Answers: (1) accommodation, (2) schemes, (3) secondary circular reaction, (4) begin to use symbols, (5) egocentric, (6) animism, (7) is not always consistent from one task to the next

---

INFORMATION PROCESSING DURING INFANCY AND EARLY CHILDHOOD

Learning Objectives

- **What is the basis of the information-processing approach?**

- **How well do young children pay attention?**

- **Do infants and preschool children remember?**

- **What are the shortcomings of preschoolers' eyewitness testimony? What can we do to make it more reliable?**

- **Can infants discriminate different quantities?**

- **How do preschoolers count?**

Information Processing During Infancy and Early Childhood

General Principles of Information Processing

Attention

Memory

Quantitative Knowledge

FEW DAYS AGO, 4-year-old Cheryl told her mother a disturbing story. Several months ago, she said, Mr. Johnson, a neighbor and long-time family friend, had taken down her pants and touched her "private parts." Her mother was shocked. She had always believed Mr. Johnson to be an honest, decent man, which made her wonder if Cheryl's imagination had simply run wild. Yet Mr. Johnson had sometimes seemed a bit peculiar, so her daughter's claim did have a ring of truth.

Today, many developmentalists borrow from computer science to formulate their ideas about human thinking and how it develops (Kail & Bisanz, 1992; Plunkett, 1996). As you recall from Chapter 1, this approach is called information processing. In this section, we'll see what information processing has revealed about young children's thinking, and, along the way, see whether we should believe Cheryl.

GENERAL PRINCIPLES OF INFORMATION PROCESSING

In Chapter 1, we explained that, in the information-processing view, human thinking is based on both mental hardware and mental software. *The term* mental hardware *refers to mental and neural structures that are built-in and that allow the mind to operate. The term* mental software *refers to mental programs that are the basis for performing particular tasks.* According to information-processing psychologists, it is the combination of mental hardware and mental software that allows children to accomplish a specific task. Information-processing psychologists claim that as children develop, their mental software becomes more complex, more powerful, and more efficient.

Information-processing psychologists believe that solving tasks successfully usually requires some general processes. Attention and memory, for example, are essential for most tasks, because they allow children to store information and retrieve it later. Of course, successful performance often requires processes and knowledge that are specific to particular domains. For example, to subtract 37 from 58, to learn to play a new video game, and to decide what time it is, attention and memory are not enough; you need specialized procedures and knowledge.

In the next few pages, we'll look at the development of both general and specific processes, beginning with the general processes of attention and memory.

ATTENTION

? **THINK ABOUT IT**
How do attentional processes resemble the perceptual processes described on pages 106–114?

Have you ever been in a class where you knew you should be listening and taking notes, but the lecture was just so boring that you started to notice other things—the smell of popcorn cooking, the sound of construction outside, or an attractive person seated two rows ahead of you? After a while, maybe you had to tell yourself, "Pay attention!" Attentional processes *determine which information will be processed further.* In a class, the key is to direct attention to the lecture or discussion, not to other stimuli that are irrelevant to the task at hand.

As you might suspect, young children do not direct their attention very effectively, particularly when compared to older children and adults (Enns, 1990). Like the little boy on the left in the photo, preschoolers are more easily distracted by extraneous information. However, we can help children to pay attention better. One straightforward approach is to make relevant information stand out. For example, closing a classroom door may not eliminate competing sounds and smells entirely, but it does make them less noticeable. When preschoolers are working at a table or desk, we can remove other objects that are not necessary for the task. Another useful tack, particularly for young children, is to remind them to pay attention to relevant information and ignore the rest.

In Chapter 6, we'll see that some children experience a disorder in which they have particular difficulty paying attention. Now let's look at another process central to most cognitive tasks: memory.

MEMORY

Nearly six months have passed since 2½-year-old Clark last visited this playground, where he had fallen off a teeter-totter and badly scraped his chin. Nevertheless, as soon as he sees the teeter-totter, his face clouds and he remarks soberly, "Clark had big owie over der." Parents of preschoolers are often astounded by cases like this one, in which their youngsters obviously remember events that the parents themselves may have forgotten.

The roots of memory are laid down in the first few months after birth. Young babies remember events for days or even weeks at a time. Some of the studies that revealed the infant's ability to remember were based on a method devised by Carolyn Rovee-Collier (1987; Bhatt & Rovee-Collier, 1996) that is shown in this photograph. A ribbon from the mobile is attached to a baby's leg; within a few minutes after the ribbon is attached, the mobile is moving constantly, because the baby has learned to kick to produce motion in the mobile. Rovee-Collier found that when she returned to the infant's home several days or a few weeks later, the baby remembered to kick to make the mobile move. Of course, babies eventually forgot that kicking made the mobile move. However, if Rovee-Collier gave them a reminder—showing them the mobile without attaching the ribbon to their foot—the next day they would kick. Thus, in a 3-month-old's kicking to move a mobile, we see three important features of memory: (1) An event from the past is remembered successfully; (2) over time, the event can no longer be recalled; and (3) a cue can serve to recover a memory that seemed to have been forgotten (Rovee-Collier, 1997; Fagan et al., 1997).

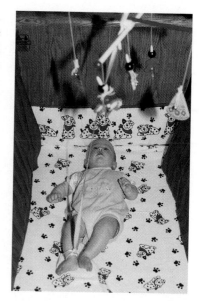

By the preschool years, children's memories of events can be surprisingly strong (Howe & Courage, 1997). In one study (Hamond & Fivush, 1991), 4-year-olds were asked about a trip they had taken to Disney World nearly 18 months previously, when they were only 2½ years old. These youngsters spontaneously recalled an average of about ten features of the trip, such as "Minnie Mouse liked my brother," or "My sister saw Captain Hook."

A trip to Disney World is special. More common are events that infants and toddlers experience repeatedly, such as going to bed, taking a bath, and going to a fast-food restaurant. These experiences include many elements that occur in a predictable sequence. At a fast-food restaurant, the sequence of events would include ordering the food, paying, getting the food, sitting down, eating, throwing away the trash, and leaving. *Typically, after a few experiences with these events, preschool children have abstracted the common, essential elements, which are stored in memory as a* script.

Preschoolers can use scripts to help them remember the individual elements in an activity. However, scripts can also distort children's recall. Sometimes children confuse what actually happened with what is specified in the script (Powell & Thomson, 1996). For example, when the little boy in the photo gets home, he may remember throwing trash in the receptacle because this is part of the after-dinner script for fast-food restaurants, not because he actually did so (Hudson, 1988). Inaccurate memory may not be critical in a situation like this, but it can be pivotal in court cases, as we see in the Current Controversies feature.

CURRENT CONTROVERSIES

PRESCHOOLERS ON THE WITNESS STAND

Remember Cheryl, the 4-year-old who claimed that a neighbor had touched her "private parts"? Regrettably, episodes like this one are all too common in America today. When abuse is suspected, the victim is usually the sole eyewitness. To prosecute the alleged abuser, the child's testimony is needed. Can preschool children like Cheryl be trusted on the witness stand?

Answering this question is not as easy as it might seem. In legal proceedings, children are often interviewed repeatedly, sometimes as many as 10 or 15 times. Over the

INFOTRAC
COLLEGE EDITION

To learn more, enter the following search term: children as witnesses.

course of repeated questioning, people of all ages sometimes confuse what actually happened, what they think might have happened, and what others have suggested may have happened. Preschoolers are particularly prone to confusion of this sort (Brainerd & Reyna, 1996; Bruck & Ceci, 1997). Their actual memory for the event may be more fragile than older children's and adults' memories. Also, preschoolers are less able to distinguish the source of memories and thoughts. Finally, if a youngster like the boy in the photo has begun to doubt his or her memory of an event, and a person in authority suggests another version, the preschool child often decides that the adult's account is correct simply because the adult is an authority figure (Kail, 1990).

Do you doubt that skilled professionals would be misled by a preschooler's fabrications? After all, TV lawyers usually have a cold, penetrating stare that seems to bore right through a witness who might try to violate the oath "to tell the truth, the whole truth, and nothing but the truth." Surely it must be a simple matter to tell when a young child is unintentionally describing events that never happened? Law enforcement officials and child protection workers *believe* that they can usually tell if children are telling the truth (Brigham & Spier, 1992), but research points to a different conclusion. Leichtman and Ceci (1995) had experts watch videotapes of preschoolers who were telling the truth, as well as other preschoolers who were telling imaginary stories. Law enforcement officials, caseworkers, and developmental psychologists could not distinguish the truthful children from the fabricators.

Preschool children *can* provide reliable testimony, but many commonly used legal procedures tend to undermine the credibility of that testimony. What can we do to improve the reliability of child witnesses? Here are some guidelines:

- Warn children that interviewers may sometimes try to trick them or suggest things that didn't happen.

- Use questions that evaluate alternative hypotheses instead of questions that imply a single correct answer.

- Avoid questioning children repeatedly on a single issue.

? THINK ABOUT IT
What does research on Piaget's theory (page 132) tell us about the dangers of questioning children repeatedly?

Following these guidelines can foster the conditions under which preschoolers (and older children, too) are more likely to provide accurate testimony. More importantly, with greater understanding of the circumstances that give rise to abuse—a topic of Chapter 7—we should be able to prevent its occurrence altogether. •

One of the benefits of youngsters' improving attention and memory is that they are better able to acquire knowledge in particular domains. Information-processing psychologists have traced these changes in a number of areas, including learning to read, learning to find one's way, learning to solve problems, and learning about numbers. We'll look at the last of these—quantitative skill—in some detail. It effectively illustrates the information-processing approach, and it also helps set the stage for Chapter 6, where we evaluate the level of American students' mathematical skill.

QUANTITATIVE KNOWLEDGE

At 2 years of age, when Laura Kail was asked how old she would be on her next birthday, she usually held up five fingers and proudly said, "Three!" At about this same time, she would count, saying, "1, 2, 3, 4, 5, 5, 8, 10." These anecdotes illustrate her emerging, if imperfect, understanding that a number name corresponds to a certain number of objects and that counting involves a sequence of number names in a specific order.

The origins of these basic number skills can be traced to infancy. Many babies and toddlers experience daily variation in quantity. They play with two blocks and see that another baby has three; they watch as a father sorts laundry and finds two black socks but only one blue sock, and they eat one hot dog for lunch while an older brother eats three.

From these experiences, babies apparently come to appreciate that quantity or amount is one of the ways in which objects in the world can differ. This conclusion is based on research in which babies are shown pictures like these.

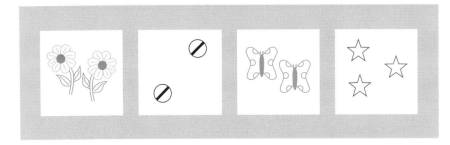

The objects in the pictures differ, as do their size, color, and position in the picture. The only common element is that each of the first three pictures depicts two of something. When the first of these pictures is shown, an infant looks at it for several seconds; after several such pairs have been shown, an infant glances at the picture briefly, then looks away, as if to say, "Enough of these pictures of two things—let's move on to something else." In fact, if a picture of a single object or of three objects is shown next, infants will again look for several seconds, their interest apparently renewed. Because the only systematic change is the number of objects in the picture, it is clear that babies can distinguish stimuli on the basis of number. Typically, 5-month-olds can distinguish two objects from three and, less often, three objects from four (Canfield & Smith, 1996; Wynn, 1996).

Several months later, babies say their first words. Names of numbers are not among the first words, but by 2 years of age, youngsters will know some number words and will have begun to count. Usually, their counting is full of mistakes. In Laura Kail's counting sequence that we mentioned earlier—"1, 2, 3, 4, 5, 5, 8, 10"—she repeats 5 and skips 6, 7, and 9. But if we ignore her mistakes momentarily, the counting sequence also reveals that she understands a great deal.

Understanding preschoolers' knowledge of numbers has been the aim of research by Rochel Gelman and her colleagues (e.g., Gelman & Meck, 1986). They simply placed various numbers of objects in front of a child and then asked, "How many?" By analyzing children's answers to many of these questions, Gelman and her co-workers discovered that by age 3, most children have mastered three basic principles of counting, at least when it comes to counting up to five objects.

- One-to-one principle: *There must be one and only one number name for each object that is counted.* A child who counts three objects as "1, 2, A" understands this principle, because the number of number words matches the number of objects to be counted.

- Stable-order principle: *Number names must be counted in the same order.* A child who counts in the same sequence most of the time—for example, consistently counting four objects as "1, 2, 4, 5"—shows understanding of this principle.

- Cardinality principle: *The last number name differs from the previous ones in a counting sequence in denoting the total number of objects.* Typically, 3-year-olds reveal their understanding of this principle by repeating the last number name, often with emphasis: "1, 2, 4, 8, . . . EIGHT!"

During the preschool years, youngsters like the girl in the photo master these basic principles and apply them to ever larger sets of objects. By age 5, most youngsters apply them consistently when counting as many as nine objects.

Learning to count beyond 9 is somewhat easier, because the counting words can be generated based on rules for combining decade number names (20, 30, 40) with unit names (1, 2, 3, 4). Later, similar rules are used for hundreds, thousands, and so on. By 4 years of age, most youngsters can count as high as 20 and sometimes as high as 99. Usually, they stop counting at a number ending in 9 (such as 29 or 59), apparently because they don't know the next decade name (Siegler & Robinson, 1982).

Learning to count this high is quite complicated in English. For example, *eleven* and *twelve* are completely irregular names, following no rules. Also, the remaining "teen" number names differ from the 20s, 30s, and the rest in that the decade number name comes after the unit (thir-*teen*, four-*teen*) rather than before (*twenty*-three, *thirty*-four). Also, except for the teens, the decade names only loosely correspond to the unit names on which they are based: *twenty* and *thirty* resemble two and three but are not the same. In contrast, the Chinese, Japanese, and Korean number systems are almost perfectly regular: *Eleven* and *twelve* are expressed as *ten-one* and *ten-two*. There are no special names for the decades: *Two-ten* and *two-ten-one* are the names for 20 and 21. These simplified number names help explain why youngsters growing up in Asian countries count more accurately than U.S. preschool children of the same age (Miller et al., 1995). Furthermore, the direct correspondence between the number names and the base-ten system makes it easier for Asian youngsters to learn base-ten concepts (Miura et al., 1988).

In Chapter 6, we will return to the development of quantitative skill, and we'll find more evidence of cultural differences in mathematics. Let's turn now to a theory developed by Vygotsky, who believed that cognitive development has its roots in social interactions.

TEST YOURSELF

1. One way to improve preschool children's attention is to make irrelevant stimuli _____ .

2. Four-month-old Tanya has forgotten that kicking moves a mobile. To remind her of the link between kicking and the mobile's movement, we could _____ .

3. The term _____ denotes the sequence in which routine activities occur.

4. Preschoolers' testimony is more likely to be reliable if interviewers test alternative hypotheses and avoid repeated questioning, and if we warn the children that _____ .

5. When a child who is counting a set of objects repeats the last number, usually with emphasis, this indicates the child's understanding of the _____ principle of counting.

6. Think back to the changes in attention and memory that we've described in this section. Were the changes all quantitative in nature, or were some qualitative, like those emphasized by Piaget?

Answers: (1) less noticeable, (2) let her view a stationary mobile, (3) script, (4) interviewers may try to trick them, (5) cardinality

MIND AND CULTURE: VYGOTSKY'S THEORY

Learning Objectives

- **What is the zone of proximal development? How does it help explain how children accomplish more when they collaborate with others?**

- **What is a particularly effective way of teaching youngsters new tasks?**

- **When and why do children talk to themselves as they solve problems?**

**Mind and Culture:
Vygotsky's Theory**

The Zone of Proximal Development

Scaffolding

Private Speech

ICTORIA, a 4-year-old, enjoys solving jigsaw puzzles, coloring, and building towers with blocks. While busy with these activities, she often talks to herself. For example, once as she was coloring a picture, she said, "Where's the red crayon? Stay inside the lines. Color the blocks blue." These remarks were not directed at anyone else; after all, Victoria was alone. Why did she say these things? What purpose did they serve?

Human development is often referred to as a journey that takes people along many different paths. For Piaget and for information-processing psychologists, children make the journey alone. Other people (and culture in general) certainly influence the direction that children take, but fundamentally the child is a solitary adventurer-explorer, boldly forging ahead. Lev Vygotsky (1896–1934), a Russian psychologist, proposed a very different account: Development is an apprenticeship, in which children advance when they collaborate with others who are more skilled. According to Vygotsky (1934/1986), children rarely make much headway on the developmental path when they walk alone; they progress when they walk hand in hand with an expert partner.

Vygotsky died of tuberculosis at the age of 37, so he never had the opportunity to develop his theory fully. He did not provide a complete theory of cognitive development throughout childhood and adolescence (as Piaget did), nor did he give definitive accounts of cognitive change in specific domains (as information-processing theorists do). However, many of his ideas are influential, largely because they fill in some gaps in the Piagetian and information-processing accounts. In the next few pages, we'll look at three of Vygotsky's most important contributions—the zone of proximal development, scaffolding, and private speech—and discover why Victoria talks to herself.

THE ZONE OF PROXIMAL DEVELOPMENT

Four-year-old Ian and his father, shown in the photo, often solve puzzles together. Although Ian does most of the work, his father encourages him, sometimes finds a piece that he needs, or shows Ian how to put parts together. When Ian tries to assemble the same puzzles by himself, he can rarely complete them. *The difference between what Ian can do with assistance and what he does alone defines his* zone of proximal development. That is, the zone is the area between the level of performance a child can achieve when working independently and a higher level of performance that is possible when working under the guidance or direction of more skilled adults or peers (Wertsch & Tulviste, 1992). For example, elementary school children are often asked to solve arithmetic story problems. Many youngsters have trouble with these problems, often because they simply don't know where to begin. By structuring the task for them—"first decide what you're supposed to figure out, then decide what information you're told in the problem . . ."—teachers can help children accomplish what they cannot do by themselves. Thus, just as training wheels help children learn to ride a bike by allowing them to concentrate on certain aspects of bicycling, collaborators help children perform more effectively by providing structure, hints, and reminders.

The idea of a zone of proximal development follows naturally from Vygotsky's basic premise: Cognition develops first in a social setting and only gradually comes under the child's independent control. What factors aid this shift? This leads us to the second of Vygotsky's key contributions.

SCAFFOLDING

Have you ever had the good fortune to work with a master teacher, one who seemed to know exactly when to say something to help you over an obstacle but otherwise let you work uninterrupted? Scaffolding *is a style in which teachers gauge the amount of assistance they offer to match the learner's needs.* Early in learning a new task, children know little, so teachers give much direct instruction about how to do all the different elements of a task. As the children catch on, teachers need to provide much less direct instruction; they are more likely to be giving reminders.

The Spotlight on Research feature shows how mothers in four different cultures scaffolded their children's learning.

HOW DO MOTHERS IN DIFFERENT CULTURES SCAFFOLD CHILDREN'S LEARNING?

Who were the investigators and what was the aim of the study? Do parents worldwide attempt to scaffold their children's learning? If so, do they use similar methods? Barbara Rogoff and her colleagues (1993) attempted to answer these questions by studying toddlers and mothers from four different cultures.

How did the investigators measure the topic of interest? The experimenter showed mothers eight novel toys. One was a wooden doll that danced when a string was pulled, another was a pencil box with a sliding lid. The mothers were asked to get their toddlers to operate each toy. No ground rules or guidelines concerning teaching were given; mothers were as free to be as direct or uninvolved as they cared. The interactions were videotaped so they could be analyzed in detail later.

Who were the participants in the study? The researchers studied 1- to 2-year-olds and their mothers living in four different settings: a medium-sized U.S. city, a small tribal village in India, a large city in Turkey, and a town in the highlands of Guatemala. In each setting, 14 children and mothers were studied.

What was the design of the study? The study was correlational because Rogoff and her colleagues were interested in the relation that existed naturally between cultural setting and behaviors that illustrate scaffolding. The study focused on a single age—1 to 2 years—so it was neither longitudinal nor cross-sectional.

Were there ethical concerns with the study? No. The task—teaching young children how to use a new toy—was one that mothers often did with their youngsters.

What were the results? In all four cultural settings, most of the mothers attempted to scaffold their children's learning, either by dividing a difficult task into easier subtasks or by doing parts of the task themselves, particularly the more complicated parts. However, as the graph shows, mothers in different cultures accomplish scaffolding in different ways. Turkish mothers give the most verbal instruction and use some gestures (pointing, nodding, shrugging). U.S. mothers also use these methods but to slightly lesser degrees.

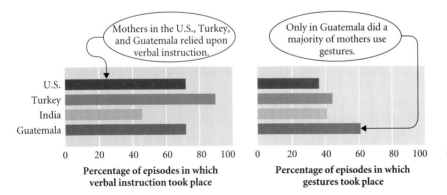

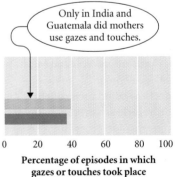

Turkish and U.S. mothers almost never touch (such as nudging a child's elbow) or gaze (eye contact, such as winking or staring). Indian mothers seem to use roughly equal amounts of speech, gesture, touch, and gaze to scaffold. Guatemalan mothers also use all three techniques and, overall, Guatemalan mothers give the most scaffolding of the four cultures.

What did the investigators conclude? Evidently, parents worldwide try to simplify learning tasks for their children but they use different methods. Rogoff et al. wrote, "Along with the universal processes that . . . characterized guided participation, there are also very important cultural variations, especially in the . . . nature of involvement between children and adults" (p. 150). ●

The sensitive adjustments that characterize scaffolding clearly promote learning. Youngsters do not learn readily when they are constantly told what to do or when they are simply left to struggle through a problem unaided. When parents and teachers scaffold a task for them, allowing them to take on more and more of a task as they master its different elements—children learn more effectively (Pacifici & Bearison, 1991; Plumert & Nichols-Whitehead, 1996). And, effective scaffolding shows the zone of proximal development—children can do much more with skilled guidance than when left to their own devices. Thus, scaffolding is an important element in transferring the control of cognitive skills from others to the child.

PRIVATE SPEECH

Remember Victoria, the 4-year-old in the vignette who talked to herself as she colored? *Her behavior demonstrates* private speech: *comments that are not intended for others but are designed to help children regulate their own behavior* (Vygotsky, 1934/1986). Thus, Victoria's remarks are simply an effort to help herself color the picture.

Vygotsky viewed private speech as an intermediate step toward self-regulation of cognitive skills. At first, children's behavior is regulated by speech from other people that is directed toward them. When youngsters like the girl in the photo first try to control their own behavior and thoughts, without others present, they instruct themselves by speaking aloud. Private speech seems to be children's way of guiding themselves, of making sure that they do all the required steps in solving a problem. Finally, as children gain ever greater skill, private speech becomes *inner speech,* which was Vygotsky's term for thought (Behrend, Rosengran, & Perlmutter, 1992).

If private speech functions in this way, can you imagine when a child would be most likely to use it? We should see children using private speech more often on difficult tasks than on easy tasks, because children are most likely to need extra guidance on harder tasks. Also, children should be more likely to use private speech after a mistake than after a correct response. These predictions are generally supported by research (Berk, 1992), which suggests the power of language in helping children learn to control their own behavior and thinking.

Thus, Vygotsky's work has characterized cognitive development not as a solitary undertaking but as a collaboration between expert and novice. His work reminds us of the importance of language, which we'll examine in detail in the last section of this chapter.

? THINK ABOUT IT
Vygotsky emphasized cognitive development as collaboration. How could such collaboration be included in Piaget's theory? In information processing?

TEST YOURSELF

1. The _____ is the difference between the level of performance that youngsters can achieve with assistance and the level they can achieve alone.

2. The term _____ refers to a style in which teachers adjust their assistance to match a child's needs.

3. According to Vygotsky, _____ is an intermediate step between speech from others and inner speech.

4. Compare the role of sociocultural influences in Piaget's theory, the information-processing approach, and Vygotsky's theory.

Answers: (1) zone of proximal development, (2) scaffolding, (3) private speech

LANGUAGE

Learning Objectives

- **When do infants first hear and make speech sounds?**

- **When do children start to talk? Why?**

- **How do youngsters learn the meanings of words?**

- **How do young children progress from two-word speech to more complex sentences?**

- **How well do youngsters communicate?**

Language

The Road to Speech

First Words and Many More

Speaking in Sentences: Grammatical
  Development

Communicating with Others

N ABINA *is just a few weeks away from her first birthday. For the past month, she has seemed to understand much of her mother's speech. If her mom asks, "Where's Garfield?" (the family cat), Nabina scans the room and points toward Garfield. Yet Nabina's own speech is still gibberish: she "talks" constantly, but her mom can't understand a word of it. If Nabina apparently understands others' speech, why can't she speak herself?*

An extraordinary human achievement occurs soon after the first birthday: Most children speak their first word, which is followed in the ensuing months by several hundred more. This marks the beginning of a child's ability to communicate orally with others. Through speech, youngsters impart their ideas, beliefs, and feelings to family, friends, and others.

Actually, the first spoken words represent the climax of a year's worth of language growth. To tell the story of language acquisition properly and explain Nabina's seemingly strange behavior, we must begin with the months preceding the first words.

THE ROAD TO SPEECH

The photograph depicts a common situation: A baby is upset and a concerned mother is trying to console it. The scene is overflowing with language-related information. The infant, not yet able to talk, is conveying its displeasure by one of the few means of communication available to it—crying. The mother, for her part, is using both verbal and nonverbal measures to cheer her baby, to send the message that the world is really not as bad as it may seem now.

The scene raises two questions about infants as nonspeaking creatures. First, can babies who are unable to speak understand any of the speech that is directed at them? Second, how do infants progress from crying to more effective methods of oral communication, such as speech? Let's start by answering the first question.

Perceiving Speech

Even newborn infants hear remarkably well (page 108). But can babies distinguish speech sounds? To answer this question, we first need to know more about the elements of speech. *The basic building blocks of language are phonemes, which are unique sounds that can be joined to create words.* Phonemes include consonant sounds, such as the sound of "t" in *toe* and *tap,* along with vowel sounds such as the sound of "e" in *get* and *bed.* Infants can distinguish many of these sounds, some of them as early as 1 month after birth.

How do we know that infants can distinguish different vowels and consonants? A number of clever techniques have provided hints; most involve determining whether babies respond differently to distinct sounds. In one approach, a rubber nipple is connected to a tape recorder in such a way that sucking turns on the tape and sound comes out a loudspeaker. In just a few minutes, 1-month-olds learn the relation between their sucking and the sound: They suck rapidly to hear a tape that consists of nothing more than the consonant sound "p" (as in *pin, pet,* and *pat*), pronounced "puh." *After a few more minutes, infants seemingly tire of this repetitive sound and suck less often, a phenomenon known as* habituation. But if the tape is changed to a different sound—such as the sound of "b" (as in *bed, bat,* or *bird*), pronounced "buh"—babies begin sucking rapidly again. Evidently, they recognize that the sound of "b" is different from "p," because they suck more often to hear this new sound (Jusczyk, 1981).

Surprisingly, young infants can discriminate speech sounds they have never heard! Not all languages use the same set of phonemes; a distinction important in one language may be ignored in another. For example, unlike English, the French and Polish languages differentiate between nasal and nonnasal vowels. To hear the difference, say the word *rod.* Now repeat it, but holding your nose. The subtle difference between the two sounds illustrates a nonnasal vowel (the first version of *rod*) and a nasal one (the second). Babies growing up in homes where English is spoken have no systematic experience with nasal and non-nasal vowels. Nevertheless, they can hear differences like this one. Interestingly, toward their first birthday, infants apparently lose this competence and no longer readily distinguish sounds that are not part of their own language environment (Werker & Desjardins, 1995).

Findings like these suggest that newborns are biologically capable of hearing the entire range of phonemes that are used in all languages worldwide. But as babies grow and are more exposed to a particular language, they only notice the linguistic distinctions that are meaningful in that environment. For example, the Japanese youngster in the photo will learn language sounds used in Japanese but will have difficulty hearing sounds used in other languages, such as English, that are not used in Japanese. Greater specialization in one language apparently comes at a cost; the potential to hear other language sounds easily is lost (Kuhl, 1993).

Of course, hearing individual phonemes is only the first step in perceiving speech. One of the biggest challenges for infants is identifying recurring patterns of sounds—words. Imagine, for example, an infant overhearing this conversation between a parent and an older sibling:

SIBLING: Jerry got a new *bike.*

PARENT: Was his old *bike* broken?

SIBLING: No. He'd saved his allowance to buy a new mountain *bike.*

An infant listening to this conversation hears *bike* three times. Can the infant learn from this experience? Yes. When 7- to 8-month-olds hear a word repeatedly in different sentences, they later pay more attention to this word than to words that they haven't heard. Evidently, 7- and 8-month-olds can listen to sentences and recognize the sound patterns that they hear repeatedly (Juscyzk & Aslin, 1995; Saffran, Aslin, & Newport, 1996). (Of course, they don't yet understand the meanings of these words; they just recognize a word as a distinct configuration of sounds.)

Parents (and other adults) often help infants master language sounds by talking in a distinctive style. *In* infant-directed speech, *adults speak slowly and with exaggerated changes in pitch and loudness.* If you could hear the mother in the photo talking to her baby, you would notice that she alternates between speaking softly and loudly and between high and low pitches. (Infant-directed speech was once known as *motherese* until it became clear that most caregivers, not just mothers, talk this way to infants.) Infant-directed speech attracts infants' attention more than adult-directed speech (Cooper & Aslin, 1994; Kaplan et al., 1996), perhaps because its slower pace and accentuated changes provide them with more and more salient language clues, just as understanding a person speaking in a foreign language is easier when that person talks slowly and carefully.

Infant-directed speech, then, helps infants perceive the sounds that are fundamental to their language. But how do infants accomplish the next step, producing speech? We answer this question next.

Steps to Speech

As new parents know all too well, newborns and young babies are experts when it comes to crying. For young infants, the cry is usually a distress signal of some sort. As you remember from Chapter 3, the type of cry varies somewhat with the nature of the distress. The high pitch of the pain cry, for example, distinguishes it from the cry of a baby who is hungry or tired.

The first sounds that are clearly linked to language come at about 3 months of age. *Babies begin to produce vowel-like sounds, such as "ooooooo" or "ahhhhhh," a phenomenon known as* cooing. Sometimes infants become quite excited as they coo, perhaps reflecting the joy of simply playing with sounds.

After cooing comes babbling, *which is speechlike sound that has no meaning.* A typical 4- or 5-month-old might say "dah" or "bah," utterances that sound like a single syllable consisting of a consonant and a vowel. Over the next several months, babbling becomes more elaborate. Apparently this is a form of experimentation with ever more complex speech sounds. Older infants sometimes repeat a sound, as in "bahbahbah," or combine different sounds, "dahmahbah" (Oller, 1986; Oller & Lynch, 1992).

Beginning at roughly 7 months of age, infants' babbling includes intonation, *a pattern of rising or falling pitch.* In English declarative sentences, for example, pitch first rises, then falls toward the end of the sentence. In questions, however, the pitch is level, then rises toward the end. Older babies' babbling reflects these patterns: Babies who are brought up by English-speaking parents have both the declarative and question patterns of intonation in their babbling.

? THINK ABOUT IT
Compare and contrast the steps in learning to make speech sounds with the stages of Piaget's sensorimotor period.

Babies who are brought up by parents who speak other languages with different patterns of intonation, such as Japanese or French, usually babble in ways that mimic their parents' use of intonation (Levitt & Utman, 1992).

The appearance of intonation in babbling clearly indicates a strong link between perception and production of speech: Infants' babbling is influenced by the characteristics of the speech that they hear. If perception of speech is indeed crucial for the development of babbling, then deaf children should learn to babble much more slowly than hearing children. This is the case. One-year-old deaf infants rarely babble repetitively (e.g., "bababa") in the manner that is common among hearing 7- to 10-month-olds (Oller & Eilers, 1988). Because of deaf children's limited exposure to human speech, their babbling emerges very slowly. However, the fact that deaf children babble at all shows that babbling also reflects maturational change.

For infants with normal hearing, the way in which babbling becomes progressively more complex suggests that it represents an infant's efforts to master the sounds of language, if not its meaning. Hearing *dog*, an infant may first say "dod," then "gog," before finally saying "dog" correctly. Just as beginning typists gradually link movements of their fingers with particular keys, through babbling infants learn how to use their lips, tongue, and teeth to produce specific sounds, gradually making sounds that approximate real words (Poulson et al., 1991). Fortunately, the task is easier for most babies than in the cartoon!

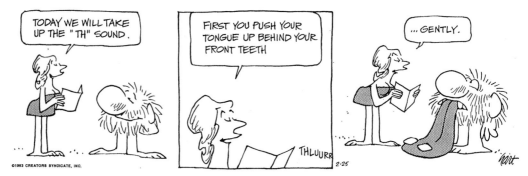

B.C. © 1993. Reprinted by permission of Johnny Hart and Creators Syndicate, Inc.

These developments in production of sound, coupled with the 1-year-old's advanced ability to perceive speech sounds, clearly set the stage for the infant's first true words.

FIRST WORDS AND MANY MORE

Remember that Nabina, the 1-year-old in the vignette, looks at the family cat when she hears its name. This phenomenon is common in 10- to 14-month-olds. They appear to understand what others say, despite the fact that they have yet to speak. In response to "Where is the book?" children will go find the book. They grasp the question, even though their own speech is limited to advanced babbling (Fenson et al., 1994; Hoff-Ginsberg, 1997). Evidently, children have made the link between speech sounds and particular objects, even though they cannot yet manufacture the sounds themselves. As fluent adult speakers, we forget that speech is a motor skill requiring perfect timing and tremendous coordination.

A few months later, most youngsters utter their first words. Typically, these words have a structure borrowed from their advanced babbling, consisting of a consonant-vowel pair that may be repeated. *Mama* and *dada* are common examples of this type of construction. Other common words in early vocabularies denote animals, food, and toys (Caselli et al., 1995; Nelson, 1973). Also common are words that denote actions (e.g., *go*). By the age of 2, youngsters have a vocabulary of a few hundred words; by 6, a typical child's vocabulary includes more than 10,000 words (Anglin, 1993). However, children differ markedly in the size of their vocabulary (Fenson et al., 1994). At 16 months, vocabularies typically range from as few as 10 words to as many as 150; at 2½ years, from 375 words to 650.

As youngsters expand their vocabulary, some adopt a distinctive style of learning language (Bates, Bretherton, & Snyder, 1988). *Some children adhere to a* referential *style; their vocabularies tend to be dominated by words that are the names of objects, persons, or actions. Other children use an* expressive *style; their vocabularies include some names but also many social phrases that are used like a single word, such as "Go away," "What'd you want?" and "I want it."*

For children with the referential style, language seems to be primarily an intellectual tool—a means of talking about objects (Pine, 1994). For children with an expressive style, in contrast, language is more of a social tool—a way of enhancing interactions with others. Of course, both of these functions—intellectual and social—are important ingredients of language; as you might expect, most children adopt a blend of the referential and expressive styles of learning language.

The Grand Insight: Words as Symbols

To make the transition from babbling to real speech, infants need to learn that speech is more than just entertaining sound. They need to know that particular sounds form words that can refer to objects, actions, and properties. Put another way, infants must recognize that words are symbols, entities that stand for other entities.

A vivid account of this insight came from Helen Keller, an American essayist shown here in middle age. Born in 1880 and left blind and deaf from an illness during infancy, she had no means to communicate with other people. When Helen was 7 years old, a tutor attempted to teach her words by spelling them in her hands. For Helen, the hurdle was to link the finger spelling with concepts she already knew; in her case, awareness came suddenly (Keller, 1965, p. 21):

> Someone was drawing water and my teacher placed my hand under the spout. As the cool stream gushed over one hand she spelled into the other the word *water*, first slowly, then rapidly. I stood still, my whole attention fixed upon the motions of her fingers. Suddenly I felt a misty consciousness as of something forgotten— a thrill of returning thought; and somehow the mystery of language was revealed to me. I knew then that "w-a-t-e-r" meant the wonderful and cool something that was flowing over my hand. That living word awakened my soul, gave it light, hope, joy, set it free!

When do youngsters who can hear and see have this insight? Piaget believed that it occurs roughly at 18 months of age and that it marks the transition into the sixth (and final) stage of sensorimotor thought (see pages 126–128). However, a glimmer of understanding of symbols occurs earlier, soon after the first birthday. By this age, children have already formed concepts such as "round, bouncy things" or "furry things that bark," based on their own experiences. With the insight that speech sounds can denote these concepts, infants begin to identify a word that goes with each concept (Reich, 1986).

What's What? Fast Mapping of Words

Having the insight that a word can symbolize an object or action, the young talker now faces a formidable task. Matching a word with its exact referent is challenging, because most words have many plausible but incorrect referents.

To illustrate, imagine what's going through the mind of the child in the photo. The mother has just pointed to the flower and said: "Flower. This is a flower. See the flower." This all seems crystal clear to you and incredibly straightforward. But what might the child learn from this episode? Perhaps the correct referent for "flower." But a youngster could, just as reasonably, conclude that "flower" refers to a petal, to the color of the flower, or to your actions in demonstrating the flower.

Surprisingly, most youngsters learn the proper meanings of simple words in just a few presentations. *By* fast mapping, *children make connections between new words and referents so rapidly that they cannot be considering all possible meanings for the new word.* Children must be using rules to link words with their meanings (Merriman & Stevenson, 1997; Samuelson & Smith, 1998).

What are the rules that guide children to discover a word's meaning? One of them is suggested in a study by Au and Glusman (1990). These investigators first taught preschoolers that a *mido* was a stuffed animal with pink horns that otherwise resembled a monkey. *Mido* was then repeated several times, always referring to the monkeylike stuffed animal with pink horns. Later, these same youngsters were asked to find a "theri" in a set of stuffed animals that included several mido. Never having heard the word *theri* before, what did the children do? They never picked a mido; instead, they selected other stuffed animals. Knowing that *mido* referred to monkeylike animals with pink horns, they evidently decided that *theri* had to refer to one of the other stuffed animals.

Apparently, the children were following this simple but effective rule for learning new words:

- If an unfamiliar word is heard in the presence of objects that already have names and those that don't, the word refers to one of the objects that doesn't have a name.

Can you think of other simple rules that might help children match words with the correct referent? Here are three more that scientists have discovered (Hall, 1996; Waxman & Markow, 1995):

- A name refers to a whole object, not its parts or its relation to other objects, and it refers not just to this particular object but to all objects of the same type.

- If an object already has a name and another name is presented, the new name denotes a subcategory of the original name.

- Given many similar category members (e.g., dogs), a word applied consistently to only one of them (e.g., "Spot") is a proper noun.

Rules like these are invaluable, for they help children substantially reduce the number of possible meanings for a word. Of course, the rules are not foolproof. *A common mistake, known as* overextension, *is defining a word too broadly.* Young children may use *car* to refer to buses and trucks or *doggie* to denote all four-legged animals. *Sometimes children make the opposite error,* underextension, *by defining a word too narrowly.* For instance, a child might use *car* to refer only to the family car or *ball* to a favorite toy ball. These errors disappear gradually as youngsters refine their meanings for words, broadening and narrowing them based on feedback they receive from parents and others.

Encouraging Language Growth

For children to expand their vocabularies, they need to hear others speak. Not surprisingly, children learn words more rapidly if their parents speak to them frequently, particularly when the parents' speech responds to and encourages the child's own speech (Pine, Lieven, & Rowland, 1997; Sénéchal, Thomas, & Monker, 1995).

Watching television can help word learning, under some circumstances. For example, preschool children who frequently view *Sesame Street* often have larger vocabularies by the time they enter kindergarten than do preschoolers who watch *Sesame Street* less often (Rice et al., 1990). Other kinds of television programs—notably cartoons—do not have this positive influence.

What accounts for the difference? The key to success is encouraging children to become actively involved in language-related activities. Video segments like the one shown in the photo encourage youngsters to name objects, to sing, and to count. Apparently, the fundamental principle is much the same for television and parents: Children expand their vocabularies when they have experiences that engage and challenge their emerging language talents.

SPEAKING IN SENTENCES: GRAMMATICAL DEVELOPMENT

Within months after children say their first words, they begin to form simple two-word sentences. Such sentences are based on "formulas" that children figure out from their own experiences (Braine, 1976; Radford, 1995). Armed with a few formulas, children can express an enormous variety of ideas:

Formula	Example
actor + action	Mommy sleep, Timmy run
action + object	gimme cookie, throw ball
possessor + possession	Kimmy pail, Maya shovel

Each child develops a unique repertoire of formulas, reflecting his or her own experiences. However, the formulas listed here are commonly used by many children growing up in different countries around the world.

From Two Words to Complex Sentences

Children rapidly move beyond two-word sentences, first doing so by linking two-word statements together: "Rachel kick" and "Kick ball" become "Rachel kick ball." Even longer sentences soon follow; sentences with ten or more words are common in 3-year-olds' speech. For example, at 1½ years, Laura Kail would say, "Gimme juice" or "Bye-bye Ben." As a 2½-year-old, she had progressed to "When I finish my ice cream, I'll take a shower, okay?" and "Don't turn the light out—I can't see better!"

Children's two- and three-word sentences often fall short of adults' standards of grammar. Youngsters will say, "He eating" rather than "He is eating," or "two cat" rather than "two cats." *This sort of speech is called* telegraphic *because, like telegrams of days gone by, children's speech includes only words directly relevant to meaning, and nothing more. The missing elements,* grammatical morphemes, *are words or endings of words (such as* -ing, -ed, *or* -s) *that make a sentence grammatical.* During the preschool years, children gradually acquire the grammatical morphemes, first mastering those that express simple relations like -*ing,* which is used to denote that the action expressed by the verb is ongoing. More complex forms, such as appropriate use of the various forms of the verb *to be,* are mastered later (Peters, 1995).

Children's use of grammatical morphemes is based on their growing knowledge of grammatical rules, not simply memory for individual words. This was first demonstrated in a landmark study by Berko (1958), in which preschoolers were shown pictures of nonsense objects like the one in the figure. The experimenter labeled it, saying, "This is a wug." Then youngsters were shown pictures of two of the objects, and the experimenter said, "These are two _____ ." Most children spontaneously said, "wugs." Because both the singular and plural forms of this word were novel for these youngsters, they could have generated the correct plural form only by applying the familiar rule of adding -*s.*

This is a wug.

Now there is another one.
There are two of them.
There are two _____ .

Berko, 1958.

Children growing up in homes where English is spoken face the problem that their native tongue is highly irregular, with many exceptions to the rules. *Sometimes children apply rules to words that are exceptions to the rule, errors called* overregularizations. With plurals, for example, youngsters may incorrectly add an -*s* instead of using an irregular plural—two "mans" instead of two "men." With the past tense, children may add -*ed* instead of using an irregular past tense: "I goed home" instead of "I went home" (Marcus et al., 1992; Mervis & Johnson, 1991).

These examples give some insight into the complexities of mastering the grammatical rules of one's language. Not only must children learn an extensive set of specific rules, but they must also absorb, on a case-by-case basis, all of the exceptions. Despite the enormity of this task, most children have mastered the basics of their native tongue by the time they enter school. How do they do it? As we see in the Forces in Action feature, biological, psychological, and sociocultural forces all contribute.

Mastery of grammar depends on biological, sociocultural, and psychological forces. On the biological side, the linguist Noam Chomsky claimed that the brain is "prewired" for learning grammar. That is, children are born with neural circuits to help them infer grammatical rules (Atkinson, 1992).

Sociocultural influences are important, too. Parents fine-tune their speech to include examples of the forms their children are learning (Hoff-Ginsberg, 1990). For example, when preschoolers first experiment with pronouns like *you, I,* and *they,* parents use many examples of these pronouns in their own speech. Thus, parents make it easier for children to unearth new grammatical rules by providing additional relevant speech.

Psychological forces are also fundamental. Children actively try to make sense out of language (Bloom, 1991; Braine, 1992). They formulate tentative grammatical rules, then look for feedback to evaluate them. For example, when a child's speech is incorrect or incomplete, parents rephrase or elaborate it. If a child says, "Sara eat cookie," a parent may reply, "Yes, Sara is eating a cookie." The parent's reply captures the meaning of the child's remark but demonstrates correct grammatical forms (Bohannon et al., 1996). When a child's remark is well formed, parents simply continue the conversation. By rephrasing their child's speech or continuing the conversation, parents give children feedback about their tentative rules.

The key players in grammatical development are thus a specialized brain (biological force), a rich language environment (sociocultural force), and a child actively seeking to identify rules in speech (psychological force). Combined, they direct children down the trail that leads to the mastery of grammar. ●

COMMUNICATING WITH OTHERS

Imagining these two preschoolers arguing is an excellent way to learn what is needed for effective communication. Both youngsters probably try to speak at the same time; their remarks may be rambling or incoherent; and they neglect to listen to each other altogether. These actions reveal three key elements in effective oral communication with others (Grice, 1975):

- People should take turns, alternating as speaker and listener.

- When speaking, remarks should be clear to the listener, from his or her own perspective.

- When listening, pay attention and let the speaker know if his or her remarks don't make sense.

Complete mastery of these elements is a lifelong pursuit. After all, even adults often miscommunicate with one another, violating each of these prescriptions in the process. However, youngsters grasp many of the basics of communication early in life.

Taking Turns

Many parents begin to encourage turn-taking long before infants have said their first words (Field & Widmayer, 1982):

PARENT: Can you see the bird?

INFANT: (cooing) ooooh.

PARENT: It *is* a pretty bird.

INFANT: ooooh.

PARENT: You're right, it's a cardinal.

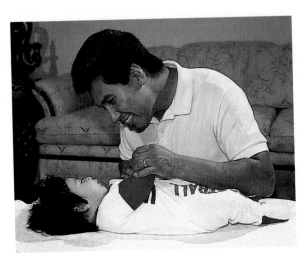

Soon after 1-year-olds begin to speak, parents like the father in the photo encourage their youngsters to participate in conversational turn-taking. To help their children along, parents often carry both sides of conversation to show how the roles of speaker and listener are alternated (Ervin-Tripp, 1970):

PARENT: (initiating conversation) What's Kendra eating?

PARENT: (illustrating reply for child) She's eating a cookie.

Help of this sort is needed less often by age 2, when spontaneous turn-taking is common in conversations between youngsters and adults (Barton & Tomasello, 1991). By 3 years of age, children have progressed to the point that if a listener fails to reply promptly, the child will often repeat his or her remarks to elicit a response and keep the conversation moving (Garvey & Berninger, 1981).

Speaking Effectively

The meaning of a message should be clear. However, clarity can only be judged with regard to the listener's age, the topic of conversation, and the setting of the conversation. For example, think about the simple request, "Please hand me the Phillips screwdriver." This message may be clear to older listeners who are familiar with variants of screwdrivers, but it is vague to younger listeners, to whom all screwdrivers come from the same mold. Of course, if the toolbox is filled with Phillips screwdrivers of assorted sizes, the message is ambiguous even to a knowledgeable listener.

Consistently constructing clear messages is a fine art, which we would hardly expect young children to have mastered. By the preschool years, however, youngsters have made their initial attempts to calibrate messages, adjusting them to match the listener and the context. For example, 4-year-olds use simpler grammar and avoid complex topics when talking to 2-year-olds (Shatz & Gelman, 1977). And, if listeners appear to misunderstand, 2- and 3-year-olds will clarify their messages (Shwe & Markman, 1997). These findings show that preschoolers are already sensitive to the importance of the listener's skill and understanding in formulating a clear message.

Listening Well

Sometimes, messages are vague or confusing; in such situations, a listener needs to ask the speaker to clarify the message. Preschoolers do not always realize when a message is ambiguous. Told to find "the red toy," they may promptly select the red ball from a pile that includes a red toy car, a red block, and a red toy hammer. Instead of asking the speaker to refer to a specific red toy, preschool listeners often assume they know which toy the speaker had in mind (Beal & Belgrad, 1990). During the elementary school years, youngsters gradually master the many elements involved in determining whether another person's message is consistent and clear (Ackerman, 1993).

Improvement in communication skill is yet another astonishing accomplishment in language during the first five years of life; changes are summarized in the table. By the time children are ready to enter kindergarten, they use language with remarkable proficiency and are able to communicate with growing skill.

? THINK ABOUT IT
Compare Piaget's, Vygotsky's, and the information-processing approaches in their emphasis on the role of language in cognitive development.

MAJOR MILESTONES OF LANGUAGE DEVELOPMENT

Age	Milestones
Birth to 1 year	Babies hear phonemes; they begin to coo and then babble.
About the 1st birthday	Babies begin to talk and to gesture, showing they have begun to use symbols.
1–2 years	Vocabulary expands rapidly (due to fast mapping); reflective and expressive language learning styles appear; two-word sentences emerge in telegraphic speech; turn-taking evident in communication.
3–5 years	Vocabulary continues to expand; grammatical morphemes added; children begin to adjust speech to listener but as listeners often ignore problems in messages they receive.

TEST YOURSELF

1. _____ are fundamental sounds used to create words.

2. Infants' mastery of language sounds may be fostered by _____ , in which adults speak slowly and exaggerate changes in pitch and loudness.

3. Older infants' babbling often includes _____ , a pattern of rising and falling pitch that distinguishes statements from questions.

4. Youngsters whose early vocabularies are dominated by words that are names, and for whom language is primarily an intellectual tool, use a _____ style.

5. In _____ , a young child's meaning of a word is broader than an adult's meaning.

6. Noam Chomsky, a noted linguist, emphasized the role of _____ in children's acquisition of grammar.

7. When talking to 2-year-olds, 4-year-olds _____ .

8. According to Piaget's theory, preschoolers are egocentric. How should this egocentrism influence their ability to communicate? Are the findings we have described on children's communication skills consistent with Piaget's view?

Answers: (1) Phonemes, (2) infant-directed speech, (3) intonation, (4) referential, (5) overextension, (6) biological mechanisms, (7) use simpler grammar and avoid complex topics

PUTTING IT ALL TOGETHER

The preschool years mark the transition from an infant who routinely depends on others to an independent 5-year-old ready to begin the long process of schooling. Piaget explained this transition in terms of a progression through qualitatively different stages. The first two years form the sensorimotor period, which has as its climax the ability to use symbols. The years 2–7 form the preoperational period, when children begin to explore the power of symbolic thought. Their thinking has limits, however, including the egocentrism that explains Jamila's head-nodding during phone conversations.

We also looked at the information-processing approach, in which cognitive development is described in terms of both general and task-specific processes. We saw that the basic skills of attention and memory improve considerably during the preschool years. However, there are imperfections in children's memory, so preschoolers like Cheryl (the child involved in an alleged case of abuse) do not always provide reliable testimony.

Next, we examined Vygotsky's view of cognitive development—that is, an apprenticeship in which children progress when collaborating with others who are more knowledgeable than they. We learned that children like Victoria talk to themselves during a transition period in which the control of cognitive processes is transferred from others to self.

In the last section, we saw that infants and preschoolers master the sounds, meanings, and grammar of their native language early in life. For example, infants like Nabina often understand words long before they have spoken. However, effective use of language to communicate is much slower to develop, continuing throughout the life span.

As a result of this growing intellectual and linguistic power, children are able to have more elaborate interactions and relationships with others, as we'll see in Chapter 5.

SUMMARY

The Onset of Thinking: Piaget's Account

Basic Principles of Cognitive Development

• In Piaget's view, children construct their own understanding of the world by creating schemes, categories of related events, objects, and knowledge. Infants' schemes are based on actions, but older children's and adolescents' schemes are based on functional, conceptual, and abstract properties.

• Schemes change constantly. In assimilation, experiences are readily incorporated into existing schemes. In accommodation, experiences cause schemes to be modified.

• When accommodation becomes much more common than assimilation, this is a sign that children's schemes are inadequate, so children reorganize them. This reorganization produces four different phases of mental development from infancy through adulthood.

Sensorimotor Thinking

• The first two years of life constitute Piaget's sensorimotor period, which is divided into six stages. As infants progress through the stages, schemes become more sophisticated. By 8–12 months, one scheme is used in the service of another; by 12–18 months, infants experiment with schemes; and by 18–24 months, infants engage in symbolic processing.

Preoperational Thinking

• From 2 to 7 years of age, children are in Piaget's preoperational period. Although now capable of using symbols, their thinking is limited by egocentrism, the inability to see the world from another's point of view. Preoperational children are also unable to reverse mental operations and sometimes confuse appearance with reality.

Evaluating Piaget's Theory

• One important contribution of Piaget's theory is the view that children actively try to understand their world. Another contribution is specifying conditions that foster cognitive development. However, the theory has been criticized because children's performance on tasks is sometimes better explained by ideas that are not part of his theory. Another shortcoming is that children's performance from one task to the next is not as consistent as the theory predicts it to be. Yet another criticism is that Piaget's account of thinking under-emphasizes sociocultural influences.

Information Processing During Infancy and Early Childhood

General Principles of Information Processing

• According to the information-processing view, cognitive development involves changes in mental hardware and in mental software.

Attention

• Compared to older children, preschoolers are less able to pay attention to task-relevant information. Their attention can be improved by making irrelevant stimuli less noticeable.

Memory

• Infants can remember and can be reminded of events they seem to have forgotten. Preschool children can remember events they experienced more than one year previously. Common activities consisting of a sequence of events are stored in memory as a script. However, scripts may distort children's recall when the actual events do not conform exactly to the script.

• Preschoolers sometimes testify in cases of child abuse. When they are questioned repeatedly, preschoolers often have difficulty distinguishing what they experienced from what others may suggest they have experienced. Inaccuracies of this sort can be minimized by following certain guidelines when interviewing children, such as warning them that interviewers may try to trick them.

Quantitative Knowledge

• Infants are able to distinguish small quantities, such as "twoness" from "threeness." By 3 years of age, children can count small sets of objects and in so doing adhere to the one-to-one, stable-order, and cardinality principles.

• Learning to count to larger numbers involves learning rules about unit and decade names. This learning is more difficult for English-speaking children compared to children from Asian countries, because names for numbers are irregular in English.

Mind and Culture: Vygotsky's Theory

The Zone of Proximal Development

• Vygotsky believed that cognition develops first in a social setting and only gradually comes under the child's independent control. The difference between what children can do with assistance and what they can do alone constitutes the zone of proximal development.

Scaffolding

• Control of cognitive skills is most readily transferred to the child through scaffolding, a teaching style in which teachers let children take on more and more of a task as they master its different components. Scaffolding is common worldwide, but the specific techniques for scaffolding children's learning vary from one cultural setting to the next.

Private Speech

• Children often talk to themselves, particularly when the task is difficult or after they have made a mistake. Such private speech is one way that children regulate their behavior, and it represents an intermediate step in the transfer of control of thinking from others to the self.

Language

The Road to Speech

• Phonemes are the basic units of sound from which words are constructed. Infants can hear phonemes soon after birth. They can even hear phonemes that are not used in their native language, but this ability diminishes after the first birthday.

• Infant-directed speech is adults' speech to infants that is slower and has greater variation in pitch and loudness. Infants prefer infant-directed speech, perhaps because it gives them additional language clues.

• Newborns' communication is limited to crying, but at about 3 months of age, babies coo. Babbling soon follows, consisting of a single syllable; over several months, infants' babbling comes to include longer syllables and intonation.

First Words and Many More

• After a brief period in which children appear to understand others' speech but do not speak themselves, most infants begin to speak around the first birthday. The first use of words is triggered by the realization that words are symbols. Soon after, the child's vocabulary expands rapidly. Some youngsters use a referential style that emphasizes words as names and that views language as an intellectual tool. Other children use an expressive style that emphasizes phrases and that views language as a social tool.

• Most children learn the meanings of words much too rapidly for them to consider all plausible meanings systematically. Instead, children use certain rules to determine the probable meanings of new words. The rules do not always yield the correct meaning. An underextension is a child's meaning that is narrower than an adult's meaning; an overextension is a child's meaning that is broader.

• Children's vocabulary is stimulated by experience. Both parents and television can foster the growth of vocabulary. The key ingredient is to actively involve children in language-related activities.

Speaking in Sentences: Grammatical Development

• Soon after children begin to speak, they create two-word sentences that are derived from their own experiences. Moving from two-word to more complex sentences involves adding grammatical morphemes. Children first master grammatical morphemes that express simple relations, then those that denote complex relations. Mastery of grammatical morphemes involves learning rules as well as exceptions to the rules.

• Some linguists claim that grammar is too complex for children to learn solely from their experience; instead, the brain must be prewired for the task. However, language experience is important. Parents' speech is a model for their children. Children try to infer grammatical rules from speech that they hear; parents give children feedback concerning these tentative rules.

Communicating with Others

• Parents encourage turn-taking even before infants begin to talk and, later, demonstrate both the speaker and listener roles for their children. By 3 years of age, children spontaneously take turns and prompt one another to take their turn.

• Preschool children adjust their speech in a rudimentary fashion to fit the listener's needs. However, preschoolers are unlikely to identify ambiguities in another's speech; instead, they are likely to assume they knew what the speaker meant.

KEY TERMS

scheme (124)
assimilation (125)
accommodation (125)
equilibration (125)
sensorimotor period (126)
primary circular reaction (127)
secondary circular reaction (127)
tertiary circular reaction (127)
egocentrism (129)
animism (129)
mental hardware (135)
mental software (135)

attentional processes (136)
script (137)
one-to-one principle (140)
stable-order principle (140)
cardinality principle (140)
zone of proximal development (142)
scaffolding (142)
private speech (144)
phonemes (146)
habituation (146)
infant-directed speech (147)

cooing (147)
babbling (147)
intonation (147)
referential style (149)
expressive style (149)
fast mapping (150)
overextension (151)
underextension (151)
telegraphic speech (152)
grammatical morpheme (152)
overregularization (152)

IF YOU'D LIKE TO LEARN MORE

Readings

CECI, S. J., & BRUCK, M. (1995). *Jeopardy in the courtroom: A scientific analysis of children's testimony.* Washington, D.C. American Psychological Association. Written by leading experts on the proper use of children as witnesses, the authors describe how best to ensure that interviews with child witnesses are conducted sensitively and professionally.

FLAVELL, J. H., MILLER, P. H., & MILLER, S. A. (1993). *Cognitive development* (3rd ed.). Englewood Cliffs, NJ: Prentice-Hall. This book, written by a trio of leading researchers, describes cognitive development during infancy and the preschool years. Piaget's and Vygotsky's theories are presented, as is the information-processing perspective. This is probably the best general-purpose reference book on cognitive development for undergraduates.

GARVEY, C. (1984). *Children's talk.* Cambridge, MA: Harvard University Press. This engaging book shows how children use language socially and also as an intellectual tool. It is filled with many entertaining examples of children's talk.

KAIL, R. (1990). *The development of memory in children* (3rd ed.). New York: Freeman. This book describes memory in infants and toddlers, as well as in older children and adolescents. Much research is discussed, but in a straightforward, easy-to-read style.

SIEGLER, R. S. (1998). *Children's thinking* (3rd ed.). Englewood Cliffs, NJ: Prentice-Hall. The author is a leading proponent of the information-processing approach to cognitive development, and this book reflects that orientation. He discusses Piaget's theory and language, but the best coverage is given to information-processing topics such as memory, problem solving, and academic skills.

For additional readings, explore Infotrac College Edition, your online library. Go to http://www.infotrac-college.com/wadsworth.

Web Sites

The Jean Piaget Society maintains a Web site

http://www.piaget.org

that includes biographical information about Piaget, suggested readings on Piaget's life and theory, and articles about cognitive development that appear in the Society's newsletter, *The Genetic Epistemologist.*

The Learning Disabilities Association of America maintains a site

http://www.kidsource.com/LDA/speech_language.html

that provides activities to foster language development.

The Animated American Sign Language Dictionary site

http://www.bconnex.net/~randys

is a good source of information about American Sign Language.

Web site addresses are subject to change. The Wadsworth Study Center Web site listed below can be accessed for updated links.

The Wadsworth Psychology Study Center Web Site

See http://psychology.wadsworth.com/ for practice quiz questions, internet links, updates, critical thinking exercises, discussion forums and more! The Wadsworth Psychology Study Center provides a wealth of information fully organized and integrated by chapter.

BEGINNINGS: TRUST AND ATTACHMENT

Beginnings: Trust and Attachment

Erikson's Stages of Early Psychosocial Development

The Growth of Attachment

Attachment, Work, and Alternative Caregiving

Learning Objectives

- **What are Erikson's first three stages of psychosocial development?**
- **How do infants form emotional attachments to mother, father, and other significant people in their lives?**
- **What are the different varieties of attachment relationships, how do they arise, and what are their consequences?**
- **Is attachment jeopardized when parents of infants and young children are employed outside of the home?**

KENDRA'S *son Roosevelt is a happy, affectionate 18-month-old. Kendra so loves spending time with him that she is avoiding an important decision. She wants to return to her job as a loan officer at the local bank. Kendra knows a woman in the neighborhood who has cared for some of her friends' children, and they all think she is a fantastic baby-sitter. But Kendra still has a nagging feeling that going back to work isn't a "motherly" thing to do— that being away during the day may hamper Roosevelt's development.*

Both developmental theorists and parents alike think the social-emotional relationship that develops between an infant and a parent (usually, but not necessarily the mother) is special. This is a baby's first social-emotional relationship, so theorists and parents believe it should be satisfying and trouble-free to set the stage for later relationships. In this section, we'll look at the steps involved in creating the baby's first emotional relationship. Along the way, you'll see how this relationship is affected by the separation that sometimes comes when a parent like Kendra works full-time.

ERIKSON'S STAGES OF EARLY PSYCHOSOCIAL DEVELOPMENT

Some of our keenest insights into the nature of psychosocial development come from a theory proposed by Erik Erikson (1982). We first encountered Erikson's theory in Chapter 1; recall that he describes development as a series of eight stages, each with a unique crisis for psychosocial growth. When a crisis is resolved successfully, an area of psychosocial strength is established. When the crisis is not resolved, that aspect of psychosocial development is stunted, which may limit the individual's ability to resolve future crises.

In Erikson's theory, infancy and the preschool years are represented by three stages, shown in the chart. Let's take a closer look at each stage.

ERIKSON'S FIRST THREE STAGES		
Age	**Crisis**	**Strength**
Infancy	Basic trust vs. mistrust	Hope
1–3 years	Autonomy vs. shame and doubt	Will
3–5 years	Initiative vs. guilt	Purpose

Basic Trust Versus Mistrust

Erikson argues that a sense of trust in oneself and others is the foundation of human development. Newborns leave the warmth and security of the uterus for an unfamiliar world. If parents respond to their infant's needs consistently, the infant comes to trust and feel secure in the world. Of course, the world is not always pleasant and can sometimes be dangerous. Parents may not always reach a falling baby in time, or they may accidentally feed an infant food that is too hot. Erikson sees value in these experiences, because infants learn mistrust. *With a proper balance of trust and mistrust, infants can acquire* hope, *which is an openness to new experience tempered by wariness that discomfort or danger may arise.*

Autonomy Versus Shame and Doubt

Between 1 and 3 years of age, children gradually come to understand that they can control their own actions. With this understanding, children strive for autonomy, for independence from others. However, autonomy is counteracted by doubt that the child can handle demanding situations and by shame that may result from failure. *A blend of autonomy, shame, and doubt gives rise to* will, *the knowledge that, within limits, youngsters can act on their world intentionally.*

Initiative Versus Guilt

Most parents have their 3- and 4-year-olds take some responsibility for themselves (by dressing themselves, for example). Youngsters also begin to identify with adults and their parents; they begin to understand the opportunities that are available in their culture. Play begins to have purpose as children explore adult roles, such as mother, father, teacher, athlete, or writer. Youngsters start to explore the environment on their own, ask innumerable questions about the world, and imagine possibilities for themselves.

This initiative is moderated by guilt as children realize that their initiative may place them in conflict with others; they cannot pursue their ambitions with abandon. Purpose *is achieved with a balance between individual initiative and a willingness to cooperate with others.*

One of the strengths of Erikson's theory is its ability to tie together important psychosocial developments across the entire life span. We will return to the remaining stages in later chapters. For now, let's concentrate on the first of Erikson's crises—the establishment of trust in the world—and look at the formation of bonds between infants and parents.

THE GROWTH OF ATTACHMENT

Sigmund Freud was the first modern theorist to emphasize the importance of the infant's emotional ties to the mother. Today, however, the dominant view of early human relationships is that of John Bowlby (1969). *His work originated in* ethology, *a branch of biology concerned with the adaptive behaviors of different species. Bowlby believed that children who form an* attachment *to an adult— that is, an enduring social-emotional relationship—are more likely to survive.* This person is usually the mother but need not be; the key is a strong emotional relationship with a responsive, caring person. Attachments also form with fathers, grandparents, or others.

Bowlby argued that evolutionary pressure favors behaviors likely to elicit caregiving from an adult, such as clinging, sucking, crying, and smiling. That is, over the course of human evolution, these behaviors have become a standard part of the human infant's biological heritage. Together with adults' responses, they create an interactive system that leads to the formation of attachment relationships.

Let's look at some of the steps in the formation of such attachments.

Steps Toward Attachment

The attachment relationship develops gradually over the first several months after birth, reflecting the baby's growing cognitive skill (described in Chapter 4). The first step is for the infant to learn the difference between people and other objects. Typically, in the first few months, babies begin to respond differently to people and to objects—for example, smiling more and vocalizing more to people. This suggests that they have begun to identify members of the social world.

During these months, mother and infant begin to synchronize their interactions (Nwokah & Fogel, 1993). Remember from Chapter 2 that young babies' behavior goes through cycles. Infants move from a state in which they are alert and attentive to a state in which they are distressed and inattentive. Caregivers begin to recognize these states of behavior and adjust their own behavior accordingly. A mother who notices that her baby is awake and alert begins to smile at her baby and talk to it. These interactions often continue until the baby's state changes, which prompts the mother to stop. By 3 months of age, if the baby is alert and the mother does not interact but just stares silently, the baby becomes at least moderately distressed, looking away from her and sometimes crying (Toda & Fogel, 1993).

Thus, mothers and infants gradually calibrate their behaviors so that they are both "on" at the same time (Gable & Isabella, 1992). These interactions provide the foundation for more sophisticated communication and foster the infant's trust that the mother will respond predictably and reassuringly.

By approximately 6 or 7 months, most infants have singled out the attachment figure—usually the mother—as a special individual (Thompson, 1998). An infant smiles at the mother and clings to her more than to other people. The attachment figure has emerged as the infant's stable social-emotional base. For example, a 7-month-old like the one in the photograph may explore a novel environment but periodically look toward the mother, as if seeking reassurance that all is well. Such behavior suggests that the infant trusts and has confidence in the mother, and it indicates that the attachment relationship has been established.

After infants become attached to their mothers, they rapidly develop attachment relationships with other people, including fathers, siblings, and grandparents (Schaffer & Emerson, 1964). Let's look at the nature of infants' relationships with their fathers.

Father-Infant Relationships

In North America, attachment typically first develops between infants and their mothers, because mothers are still the primary caregivers.

? THINK ABOUT IT
Based on Piaget's description of infancy (pages 126–128), what cognitive skills might be important prerequisites for the formation of an attachment relationship?

However, most babies soon become attached to their fathers, too (Belsky, 1996; Parke, 1995).

Although infants usually become attached to both parents, they interact with them differently. Fathers spend much more time playing with their babies than they do taking care of them. In countries around the world—Australia, India, Israel, Italy, Japan, and the United States—"playmate" is the customary role for fathers (Roopnarine, 1992). Fathers even play with infants differently than mothers do. Rough-and-tumble, physical play is the norm for fathers, whereas mothers spend more time reading and talking to babies, showing them toys, and playing games like pat-a-cake (Parke, 1990). These differences in interactional style remain even when fathers care for their infants full-time while mothers are employed full-time outside of the home (Lamb & Oppenheim, 1989).

Given the opportunity to play with mothers or fathers, infants more often choose their fathers. However, when the infants are distressed, mothers are preferred (Field, 1990). Thus, although most infants become attached to both parents, mothers and fathers typically have distinctive roles in their children's early social development.

Forms of Attachment

Thanks to biology, virtually all infants behave in ways that elicit caregiving from adults, and, because of this behavior, attachment almost always develops between infant and caregiver, by 8 or 9 months of age. However, attachment can take on many forms, and environmental factors help determine the quality of attachment between infants and caregivers. Mary Ainsworth (1978, 1993) pioneered the study of attachment relationships using a procedure that has come to be known as the Strange Situation. You can see in the chart that the Strange Situation involves a series of episodes, each about 3 minutes long. The mother and infant enter an unfamiliar room filled with interesting toys. The mother leaves briefly, then mother and baby are reunited. Meanwhile, the experimenter observes the baby, recording its response to both separation and reunion.

SEQUENCE OF EVENTS IN THE STRANGE SITUATION

1. Observer shows the experimental room to mother and infant, then leaves the room.

2. Infant is allowed to explore the playroom for 3 minutes; mother watches but does not participate.

3. A stranger enters the room and remains silent for 1 minute, then talks to the baby for a minute, and then approaches the baby. Mother leaves unobtrusively.

4. The stranger does not play with the baby but attempts to comfort it if necessary.

5. After 3 minutes, the mother returns, greets, and consoles the baby.

6. When the baby has returned to play, the mother leaves again, this time saying "bye-bye" as she leaves.

7. Stranger attempts to calm and play with the baby.

8. After 3 minutes, the mother returns, and the stranger leaves.

Based on how the infant reacts to separation from, and reunion with, the mother, Ainsworth and other researchers have discovered four primary types of attachment relationships (Ainsworth, 1993; Main & Cassidy, 1988). One is a secure attachment and three are different types of insecure attachment (avoidant, resistant, disorganized):

- Secure attachment: *The baby may or may not cry when the mother leaves, but when she returns, the baby wants to be with her and if the baby is crying, it stops.* Babies in this group seem to be saying, "I missed you terribly, I'm delighted to see you, but now that all is well, I'll get back to what I was doing." Approximately 60–65% of American babies have secure attachment relationships.

- Avoidant attachment: *The baby is not upset when the mother leaves and, when she returns, may ignore her by looking or turning away.* Infants with an avoidant attachment look as if they're saying, "You left me *again*. I always have to take care of myself!" About 20% of American infants have avoidant attachment relationships, which is one of the three forms of insecure attachment.

- Resistant attachment: *The baby is upset when the mother leaves and remains upset or even angry when she returns, and is difficult to console.* Like the baby in the photo, these babies seem to be telling the mother, "Why do you do this? I need you desperately and yet you just leave me without warning. I get so angry when you're like this." About 10–15% of American babies have this resistant attachment relationship, which is another form of insecure attachment.

- Disorganized (disoriented) attachment: *The baby seems confused when the mother leaves and when she returns, as if not really understanding what's happening.* The baby often behaves in contradictory ways, such as nearing the mother when she returns but not looking at her, as if wondering, "What's happening? I want you to be here, but you left and now you're back. I don't get what's going on!" About 5–10% of American babies have this disorganized attachment relationship, the last of the three kinds of insecure attachment.

The different forms of attachment seen in the Strange Situation also emerge when babies are studied in more natural situations (Vaughn et al., 1992). In one approach, an observer first watches babies in their homes. Then, the observer goes through a list of 90 descriptions of infant behaviors, such as "If held in the mother's arms, child stops crying and quickly recovers after being frightned or upset" and "Child quickly greets his mother with a big smile when she enters the room." The observer decides how well each statement describes the baby's behavior, and these judgments are used to characterize the nature of the baby's attachment to the mother (Posada et al., 1995).

Regardless of the method used to measure the attachment relationship, secure attachments and the different forms of insecure attachments are observed worldwide. As you can see in the graph on page 167, secure attachments are the most common throughout the world (van IJzendoorn & Kroonenberg, 1988). This is fortunate because, as you'll see, a secure attachment provides a solid basis for subsequent social development.

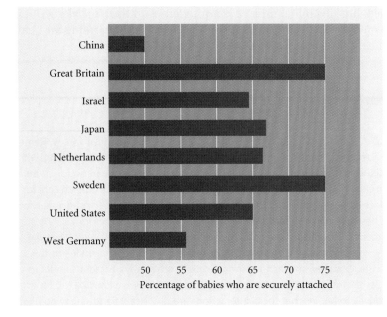

Percentage of babies who are securely attached

Consequences of Attachment

Erikson and other theorists (e.g., Sroufe & Fleeson, 1986) believe that infant-parent attachment, the first social relationship, lays the foundation for all of the infant's later social relationships. In this view, infants who experience the trust and compassion of a secure attachment should develop into preschool children who interact confidently and successfully with their peers. In contrast, infants who do not experience a successful, satisfying first relationship should be more prone to problems in their social interactions as preschoolers.

Both of these predictions are supported by research, as the following findings demonstrate:

• Among 11-year-olds, best friends were more responsive to one another (paying attention to each other, not interrupting), less critical, and more often did things together when both children were securely attached to their mother than when one child was securely attached but the other was not (Kerns, Klepac, & Cole, 1996).

• Preschool children were much more likely to behave in ways marked by abnormal levels of hostility if they had a disorganized attachment as an infant (Lyons-Ruth, Alpern, & Repacholi, 1993).

• At a summer camp, 11-year-olds who had secure attachment relationships as infants interacted more skillfully with their peers and had more close friends than did 11-year-olds who had insecure attachment relationships (Elicker, Englund, & Sroufe, 1992).

The conclusion seems inescapable: Secure attachment serves as the prototype for later successful social interactions. That is, a secure attachment evidently promotes trust and confidence in other humans, which leads to more skilled social interactions later in childhood (Thompson, 1998).

Of course, attachment is only the first of many steps along the long road of social development. Infants with insecure attachments are not forever damned, but this initial misstep *can* interfere with their social development. Consequently, we need to look at the conditions that determine the quality of attachment, which is the topic of the Forces in Action feature.

  **WHAT DETERMINES QUALITY OF ATTACHMENT?**

The answer to this question begins with biological forces. Remember, infants' biological heritage includes behaviors such as clinging and smiling, which are designed to elicit caregiving from adults. Along with their appearance, such behaviors make it clear that babies are dependent on others, which prods adults to care for them.

Once caregiving is under way, the quality of attachment reflects the quality of interaction between parents and their babies (De Wolff & van IJzendoorn, 1997). A secure attachment is most likely when parents respond to their infants predictably and appropriately. For example, Fabio always notices when his son Sasha smiles or talks. When Sasha cries, gestures, or tries to communicate in other ways, Fabio attempts to understand Sasha's intent and tries to respond appropriately. Behaviors like Fabio's evidently help convey to babies that social interactions are predictable and satisfying (Pederson et al., 1998). Apparently, they instill in infants the trust and confidence that is the hallmark of secure attachment.

Of course, not all caregivers react to babies in a reliable and proper manner. Some respond intermittently or only after the infant has cried long and hard. When these caregivers finally do respond, they are sometimes annoyed by the infant's demands and may misinterpret the baby's intent. Over time, these babies tend to see social relationships as erratic and often frustrating. Such conditions do little to foster trust and confidence.

Why does predictable and responsive parenting promote secure attachment relationships? To answer this question, think about your own friendships and romantic relationships. These relationships are usually most satisfying when we believe we can trust the other person and depend on them in times of need. The same formula seems to hold for infants. *Infants develop an* internal working model, *a set of expectations about parents' availability and responsivity.* When parents are dependable and caring, babies come to trust them, knowing they can be relied upon for comfort in times of stress. That is, babies develop an internal working model in which they believe that the parent is concerned about their needs and will try to meet them (Bretherton, 1992, 1995).

Many research findings attest to the importance of a caregiver's sensitivity for quality of attachment. For example, in a study conducted in Israel, infants were less likely to develop secure attachment when they slept in dormitories with other children under 12, where they received inconsistent (if any) attention when they became upset overnight (Sagi et al., 1994). And, in a study conducted in The Netherlands, infants were more likely to form a secure attachment when their mother had 3 months of training that emphasized monitoring an infant's signals and responding appropriately and promptly (van den Boom, 1994, 1995). Thus, secure attachment is most likely when parents are sensitive and responsive.

Another factor contributing to the quality of attachment is temperament. Babies with difficult temperaments are somewhat less likely to form secure attachment relationships (Goldsmith & Harman, 1994; Seifer et al., 1996). That is, babies who fuss often and are difficult to console are more prone to insecure attachment. This may be particularly likely when a difficult, emotional infant has a mother whose personality is rigid and traditional than when the mother is accepting and flexible (Mangelsdorf et al., 1990). Rigid mothers do not adjust well to the often erratic demands of their difficult babies;

instead, they want the baby to adjust to them. This means that rigid mothers less often provide the responsive, sensitive care that leads to secure attachment.

The formation of attachment illustrates well the combined influence of the different components of the biopsychosocial framework. Many infant behaviors that elicit caregiving in adults—smiling and crying, for example—are biological in origin. When the caregiver is responsive to the infant (a sociocultural force), then a secure attachment forms in which the infant trusts caregivers and knows that they can be relied upon in stressful situations (psychological force).

ATTACHMENT, WORK, AND ALTERNATIVE CAREGIVING

Each day, approximately 10 million U.S. children age 5 and under are cared for by someone other than their mother, a phenomenon linked to more dual-earner couples and to more single-parent households in the United States in the 1990s. Who is caring for America's children? The pie charts have the answer and reveal similar patterns for European American, African American, and Hispanic American infants and preschoolers (U.S. Bureau of the Census, 1995). About one third are cared for in the home, typically by the father or a grandparent. Another one third receive care in the provider's home. The provider is often but not always a relative. Finally, another one third attend day care or nursery school programs.

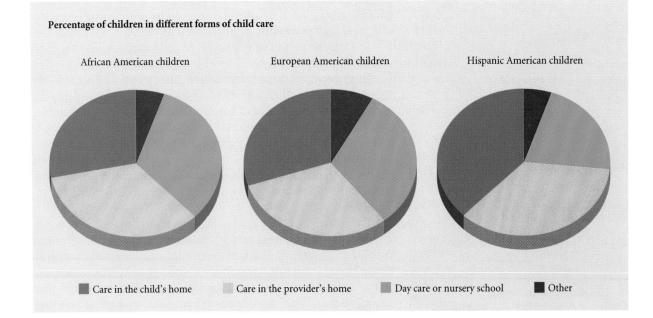

Percentage of children in different forms of child care

African American children   European American children   Hispanic American children

■ Care in the child's home   ■ Care in the provider's home   ■ Day care or nursery school   ■ Other

Many parents, particularly women who have traditionally been the primary caregivers, have misgivings about their children spending so much time in the care of others. Should parents worry? Can this care disrupt the development of parent-child relationships? The best answers to these questions come from a comprehensive study of early child care conducted by the National Institute of

? THINK ABOUT IT
Imagine that your best friend is the mother of a 3-month-old. Your friend is about to return to her job as a social worker, but she's afraid that she'll harm her baby by going back to work. What could you say to reassure her?

Child Health and Human Development. In 1991, the research team recruited 1,364 mothers and their newborns from 12 different U.S. cities. Both mothers and children have been tested repeatedly (and the testing continues, as the study is ongoing).

One of the first reports from this project concerned the impact of early child care on 15-month-olds' attachment to their mothers (NICHD Early Child Care Research Network, 1997). The results indicated no overall effects of child care experience on mother-infant attachment, which was measured with the Strange Situation. A secure mother-infant attachment was just as likely, regardless of the quality of child care, the amount of time the child spent in care, the age when the child began care, how frequently the parents changed child care arrangements, and the type of child care (e.g., child care center, in the home with a nonrelative). However, when the effects of child care were considered along with characteristics of mothers, an important trend emerged: When mothers who are less sensitive and less responsive place their infants in low-quality child care, insecure attachments are more common. As the investigators put it, ". . . poor quality, unstable, or more than minimal amounts of [outside] child care apparently added to the risks already inherent in poor mothering, so that the combined effects were worse than those of low maternal sensitivity and responsiveness alone" (p. 877).

Of course, the effects of day care need not be limited to attachment; other aspects of children's development might be affected, too. A second report from this project looked at links between early child care and behavioral problems at 2 and 3 years of age (NICHD Early Child Care Research Network, 1998). These results reveal that children who have extensive experience in child care beginning at any early age are *not* more likely to have behavioral problems than children who have limited experience in child care. Here, too, quality of care is a factor—children who receive poor-quality child care are slightly more likely to have behavioral problems.

In general, working parents like Kendra, the mother in the vignette, can enroll their infants and preschoolers in high-quality day care programs with no fear of harmful consequences. Some factors to look for in a first-rate program include (a) a low ratio of children to caregivers, (b) a well-trained staff, (c) ample opportunities for educational and social stimulation, and (d) effective communication between parents and day care workers concerning the general aims and routine functioning of the day care program (Rosenthal & Vandell, 1996).

Fortunately, employers, too, have begun to do their part, realizing that convenient, high-quality child care makes for better, more satisfied employees. In Flint, Michigan, for example, child care is an element of the contract between the United Auto Workers and General Motors. Many cities, such as Pittsburgh, have modified their zoning codes so that new shopping complexes and office buildings must include child care facilities, like those in the photograph. Businesses are realizing that the availability of excellent child care helps attract and retain a skilled labor force. Mayor Sophie Masloff, when Pittsburgh revised its zoning code, said, "With more women in the work force, more so than ever before, we just knew [providing workers with adequate child care] was a necessity."

With effort, organization, and help from the community and business, full-time employment and high-quality caregiving *can* be compatible. We will return to this issue in Chapter 11, from the perspective of the parents. For now, the Real People feature provides one example of a father who stays at home to care for his daughter while the mother works full-time.

REAL PEOPLE

LOIS, BILL, AND SARAH

Lois, 46, and Bill, 61, had been married nearly 4 years when Lois gave birth to Sarah. Lois, a kindergarten teacher, returned to work full-time 4 months after Sarah was born. Bill, who had been half-heartedly pursuing a Ph.D. in education, became a full-time househusband. Bill does the cooking and takes care of Sarah during the day. Lois comes home from school at noon so that the family can eat lunch together, and she is home from work by 4. Once a week, Bill takes Sarah to a parent-infant play program. The other parents, all mothers in their 20s or 30s, first assumed that Bill was Sarah's grandfather and had trouble relating to him as an older father. Soon, however, he was an accepted member of the group. On the weekends, Lois's and Bill's grown children from previous marriages often visit and enjoy caring for and playing with Sarah. By all accounts, Sarah looks to be a healthy, happy, outgoing 9-month-old. Is this arrangement nontraditional? Clearly. Is it effective for Sarah, Lois, and Bill? Definitely. Sarah receives the nurturing care that she needs, Lois goes to work assured that Sarah is in Bill's knowing and caring hands, and Bill relishes being the primary caregiver. ◉

TEST YOURSELF

1. _____ proposes that maturational and social factors come together to pose eight unique challenges for psychosocial growth during the life span.

2. Infants must balance trust and mistrust to achieve _____ , an openness to new experience that is coupled with awareness of possible danger.

3. By approximately _____ months of age, most infants have identified a special individual—usually but not always the mother—as the attachment figure.

4. Joan, a 12-month-old, was separated from her mother for about 15 minutes. When they were reunited, Joan would not let her mother pick her up. When her mother approached, Joan would look the other way or toddle to another part of the room. This behavior suggests that Joan has a(n) _____ attachment relationship.

5. The single most important factor in fostering a secure attachment relationship is _____ .

6. Tim and Douglas, both 3-year-olds, rarely argue; when they disagree, one goes along with the other's ideas. The odds are good that both boys have _____ attachment relationships with their parents.

7. An insecure attachment is likely when an infant receives poor-quality child care and _____ .

8. Most research on attachment has relied upon Ainsworth's Strange Situation. What are some assets of this method? What are some potential problems?

Answers: (1) Erik Erikson, (2) hope, (3) 6 or 7, (4) avoidant insecure, (5) responding consistently and appropriately, (6) secure, (7) insensitive, unresponsive mothering.

EMERGING EMOTIONS

Emerging Emotions

Basic Emotions

Complex Emotions

Recognizing and Using Others'
Emotions

Learning Objectives

- **At what ages do children begin to express basic emotions?**
- **What are complex emotions and when do they develop?**
- **When do children begin to understand other people's emotions? How do they use this information to guide their own behavior?**

𝕹ICOLE *is ecstatic that she is finally going to see her 7-month-old nephew, Claude. She rushes into the house, and seeing Claude playing on the floor with blocks, sweeps him up in a big hug. After a brief, puzzled look, Claude bursts into angry tears and begins thrashing his arms and legs, as if saying to Nicole, "Who are you? What do you want? Put me down! Now!" Nicole quickly hands Claude to his mother, who is surprised by her baby's outburst and even more surprised that he continues to sob while she rocks him.*

Nicole's initial happiness, Claude's anger, and his mother's surprise illustrate three common human emotions. These, along with joy, satisfaction, guilt, and humiliation, are just a few of the feelings that help give life meaning.

In this section, we look at when children first express emotions, then discover how children come to understand emotions in others.

BASIC EMOTIONS

Happiness, anger, and surprise, along with fear, disgust, and sadness are considered basic emotions *because people worldwide experience them and because each consists of three elements: a subjective feeling, a physiological change, and an overt behavior* (Izard, 1991). For example, suppose you wake to the sound of a thunderstorm, then discover that your roommate has left for class with your umbrella. Subjectively, you might feel ready to explode with anger; physiologically, your heart would beat faster; and behaviorally, you would be scowling.

Basic emotions are with us from the first few months of life. To see for yourself, look at these photographs of young babies. Which one is angry? Which are the sad and happy babies? The facial expressions are so revealing that

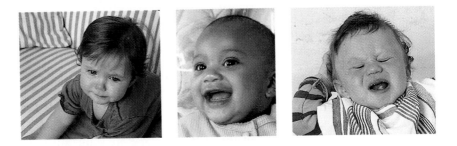

you've probably guessed that the babies are, in order, sad, happy, and angry. But, do these distinctive facial expressions mean that infants are actually experiencing these emotions? Not necessarily. Remember that facial expressions are only one component of emotion—the behavioral manifestation. Emotion also involves physiological responses and subjective feelings. Of course, infants can't express their feelings to us verbally, so we don't know much about their subjective experiences. We're on firmer ground with the physiological element. At least some of the physiological responses that accompany facial expressions are the same in infants and adults. For example, when infants and adults smile—which suggests they're happy—the left frontal cortex of the brain tends to have more electrical activity than the right frontal cortex (Fox et al., 1991).

Many scientists use this and similar findings to argue that facial expressions are reliable clues to an infant's emotional state. For example, research also shows that infants and adults worldwide express basic emotions in much the same way (Izard, 1991). The child in the photograph shows the universal signs of fear. Her eyes are open wide, her eyebrows are raised, and her mouth is relaxed but slightly open. The universality of emotional expression suggests that humans are biologically programmed to express emotions in specific ways; it's simply in our genes to smile when we're happy and scowl when we're unhappy.

Another finding linking infants' facial expressions to emotions is that, by 5–6 months, infants' facial expressions change predictably and meaningfully in response to events. When a happy mother greets her baby, the baby will probably smile in return; when a tired, distracted mother picks up her baby roughly, the baby will probably scowl at her. These findings suggest that by the middle of the first year (and maybe earlier), facial expressions are fairly reliable indicators of an infant's emotional state (Weinberg & Tronick, 1994) .

If facial expressions are a window on a baby's emotions, what do they tell us about the early phases of emotional development? Let's start with happiness. During the first few weeks after birth, infants begin to smile but this seems to be related to internal physiological states. An infant may smile after feeding or while asleep, for example. *At about 2 months of age,* social smiles *first appear: Infants smile when they see another human face.* Sometimes social smiling is accompanied by cooing, the early form of vocalization described in Chapter 4 (Sroufe & Waters, 1976). Smiling and cooing seem to be the infant's way of expressing pleasure at seeing another person.

At about 4 months, smiling is joined by laughter, which usually occurs when a baby experiences vigorous physical stimulation (Sroufe & Wunsch, 1972). Tickling 4-month-olds or bouncing them on your knee are good ways to prompt a laugh. Toward the end of the first year, infants often laugh when familiar events take a novel turn. For example, a 1-year-old will laugh when her mother pretends to drink from her bottle or her father drapes a diaper around his waist. Laughter is now a response to psychological stimulation as well as physical stimulation.

The early stages of positive feelings, like happiness, are fairly clear: An infant's experience of happiness is first linked primarily to physical states, such as feeling full after a meal or being tickled. Later, feelings of happiness are linked to the pleasure of recognizing familiar people, and, still later, they are linked to psychological states, such as the pleasure of seeing another person or an unusual event.

? THINK ABOUT IT
How might an infant's ability to express emotions relate to the formation of attachment? To the temperamental characteristics described on pages 88–90?

We know much less about the development of negative emotions such as fear, anger, and sadness. Certainly, newborns express distress, but specific negative emotions are hard to spot at this age. Anger emerges gradually, with distinct displays appearing between 4 and 6 months of age. Infants will become angry, for example, if a favorite food or favorite toy is taken away (Stenberg & Campos, 1990). Reflecting their growing understanding of goal-directed behavior, infants also become angry when they are frustrated because obstacles prevent them from achieving a goal. For example, if a parent restrains an infant from trying to pick up a toy, the guaranteed result is a very angry baby.

Like anger, fear seems to be rare in newborns and young infants. *The first distinct signs of fear emerge at about 6 months of age when infants become wary in the presence of an unfamiliar adult, termed* stranger anxiety. When a stranger approaches, a 6-month-old typically looks away and begins to fuss (Mangelsdorf, Shapiro, & Marzolf, 1995). The baby in the photo is showing the signs of stranger anxiety. The grandmother has picked him up without giving him a chance to warm up to her, and the outcome is as predictable here as it was with Claude, the baby boy in the vignette who was frightened by his aunt: He cries, looks frightened, and reaches with arms outstretched in the direction of someone familiar.

How anxious an infant feels around strangers depends on a number of factors (Thompson & Limber, 1991). First, infants tend to be less fearful of strangers when the environment is familiar and more fearful when it is not. Many parents know this firsthand from traveling with their infants: Enter a friend's house for the first time and the baby clings tightly to its mother. Second, the amount of anxiety depends on the stranger's behavior. Instead of rushing to greet or pick up the baby, as Nicole did in the vignette, a stranger should talk with other adults and in a while, perhaps offer the baby a toy (Mangelsdorf, 1992). Handled this way, many infants will soon seem to be curious about the stranger instead of afraid.

Fear of strangers is adaptive because it emerges at the same time that children begin to master creeping and crawling (described in Chapter 3). Like Curious George, the monkey in a famous series of children's books, babies are inquisitive and want to use their new locomotor skills to explore their worlds. Fear of strangers provides a natural restraint against the tendency to wander away from familiar caregivers (Thompson & Limber, 1990).

Fear of strangers declines gradually as infants learn to interpret facial expressions that indicate a stranger is friendly and not hostile, but then other fears develop. Many preschoolers are afraid of the dark and of imaginary creatures. These fears typically diminish during the elementary school years as children grow cognitively and better understand the difference between appearances and reality (Wicks-Nelson & Israel, 1991). Fears of specific objects or events, such as snakes or storms, often arise in childhood. Such fears are considered to be normal unless they become so extreme that children are overwhelmed by them (Rutter & Garmezy, 1983). For example, a 4-year-old girl's fear of spiders would not be unusual unless her fear grew to the point that she refused to go outside at all.

COMPLEX EMOTIONS

Basic emotions emerge early in infancy, but complex emotions such as feelings of guilt, embarrassment, and pride don't surface until 18–24 months of age (Lewis, 1992). *Unlike basic emotions,* complex emotions *have a self-evaluative component to them.* For example, a 2-year-old who has spilled juice all over the floor may hang his head in shame; another 2-year-old who has, for the first time, finished a difficult puzzle by herself will smile in a way that radiates pride. Also, in contrast to basic emotions, complex emotions are not necessarily experienced similarly in different cultures and are not always accompanied by obvious physiological states.

Complex emotions depend on the child having some understanding of the self, which typically surfaces between 15 and 18 months (see Chapter 4). Children feel guilty or embarrassed, for example, when they've done something that they know they shouldn't have done: A child who breaks a toy is thinking, "You told me to be careful. But I wasn't!" Similarly, children feel pride when they've done something that was challenging: A little girl who catches a ball for the first time thinks, "This was hard but I did it, all by myself!" For children to experience complex emotions, they need to be more advanced cognitively, which explains why complex emotions don't appear until the very end of infancy (Lewis et al., 1992).

Complex emotions also depend upon the cultural setting. Situations that evoke pride in one culture may evoke embarrassment or shame in another (Zahn-Waxler et al., 1996). For example, American children often show pride at personal achievement, such as getting the highest grade on a test or, as shown in the photograph, coming in first place in a contest. In contrast, Asian children would be embarrassed by such a public display of individual achievement but would show great pride when their entire class was honored for its achievement (Stevenson & Stigler, 1992). Thus, the conditions that trigger complex emotions such as pride, envy, and shame depend upon the culture, and children have to learn when these emotions are appropriate.

? THINK ABOUT IT
Explain how the different forces in the biopsychosocial framework contribute to the development of basic and complex emotions.

In sum, complex emotions like guilt and pride require more sophisticated understanding and are more culturally specific than basic emotions like happiness and fear, which are more biologically based and culturally universal. By age 2, however, children express both basic and complex emotions. Of course, expressing emotions is only part of the developmental story. Children must also learn to recognize others' emotions, which is our next topic.

RECOGNIZING AND USING OTHERS' EMOTIONS

Imagine you are broke (only temporarily, of course) and plan to borrow $20 from your roommate when she returns from class. Shortly, she storms into your apartment, slams the door, and throws her backpack on the floor. Immediately, you change your plans, realizing that now is hardly a good time to ask your roommate for a loan. This example reminds us that we often need to recognize others' emotions and sometimes change our behavior as a consequence.

When can infants first identify emotions in others? By 6 months, infants begin to distinguish facial expressions associated with different emotions. A

6-month-old can, for example, distinguish the features of a happy, smiling face from those of a sad, frowning face (Ludemann & Nelson, 1988; Ludemann, 1991). Strictly speaking, these studies tell us only that infants can discriminate the facial expressions, not the emotions per se. However, other research indicates that infants have indeed begun to recognize the emotions themselves. The best evidence is that infants often match their own emotions to other people's emotions. When happy mothers smile and talk in a pleasant voice, infants express happiness themselves. When mothers are angry or sad, infants become distressed, too (Izard et al., 1995).

Also like adults, infants use others' emotions to direct their behavior (Mumme, Fernald, & Herrera, 1996; Repacholi, 1998). *Infants in an unfamiliar or ambiguous environment often look at their mother or father, as if searching for cues to help them interpret the situation, a phenomenon known as* social referencing. For example, in a study by Hirshberg and Svejda (1990), 12-month-olds were shown novel toys that made sounds, such as a stuffed alligator that hissed. For some toys, parents were told to look happy; for others, parents were to look afraid. When, as in the figure, parents looked afraid, their infants, too, appeared distressed and moved further away from the toys. Thus, social referencing shows that infants rely on their parents' emotions to help them regulate their own behavior.

As children's cognitive skills continue to grow in childhood, they become more adept at identifying others' emotions and more adept at modifying their behavior accordingly (Boone & Cunningham, 1998; Dunn et al., 1995). Children learn that sometimes they should conceal their emotions (Jones, Abbey, & Cumberland, 1998). And, they begin to understand why people feel as they do and how emotions can influence a person's behavior. Preschool children, for example, understand that an angry child is more likely to hurt someone than a happy child (Russell & Paris, 1994).

TEST YOURSELF

1. The first detectable form of fear is _____ , which emerges at about 6 months.

2. Complex emotions, such as guilt and shame, emerge later than basic emotions because _____ .

3. In social referencing, infants use a parent's facial expression _____ .

4. How does the emergence of complex emotions at 18–24 months of age fit with Piaget's account of cognitive growth at this age, which we described in Chapter 4?

Answers: (1) stranger anxiety, (2) complex emotions require more advanced cognitive skills, (3) to direct their own behavior (e.g., deciding if an unfamiliar situation is safe or frightening)

INTERACTING WITH OTHERS

Learning Objectives

Interacting with Others

The Joys of Play

Learning to Cooperate

Helping Others

- **When do youngsters first begin to play with each other? How does play change during infancy and the preschool years?**

- **What determines whether preschool children cooperate with one another?**

- **What determines whether children help one another? What experiences make children more inclined to help?**

SIX-YEAR-OLD JUAN *got his finger trapped in the VCR when he tried to remove a tape. While he cried and cried, his 3-year-old brother, Antonio, and his 2-year-old sister, Carla, watched but did not help. Later, when their mother had soothed Juan and concluded that his finger was not injured, she worried about her younger children's reactions. In the face of their brother's obvious distress, why did Antonio and Carla do nothing?*

Infants' initial interactions are with parents, but soon they begin to interact with other people, notably their peers. In this section, we'll trace the development of these interactions and learn why children like Antonio and Carla don't always help others.

THE JOYS OF PLAY

If you watch two 5-month-olds together, hoping to see some social interaction, you'll be disappointed. The infants will look at each other, but you won't observe anything that qualifies as an interaction. However, at about 6 months, the first signs of peer interactions appear: Now an infant may point to or smile at another infant (Hartup, 1983).

Soon after the first birthday, children begin parallel play, *in which each youngster plays alone but maintains a keen interest in what another is doing.* For example, each of the toddlers in the photograph has his own toys, but each is watching the other play, too. Exchanges between youngsters become more common. When one toddler talks or smiles, the other usually responds (Howes, Unger, & Seidner, 1990).

Beginning at roughly 15–18 months, toddlers no longer simply watch one another at play. *Instead, they engage in similar activities and talk or smile at one another, illustrating* simple social play. Play has now become truly interactive. For example, youngsters now offer toys to one another (Howes & Matheson, 1992).

Toward the second birthday, cooperative play *is observed: Now a distinct theme organizes children's play, and they take on special roles based on the theme.* Like the children in the photograph, they may play "hide-and-seek" and alternate the roles of hider and finder, or they may have a tea party and take turns being the host and the guest (Parten, 1932).

The nature of young children's play changes dramatically in a few years (Howes & Matheson, 1992). In a typical day care center, 1- and 2-year-olds spend most of their time in parallel play; other forms of play are relatively rare. In contrast, among 3- and 4-year-olds, parallel play is much less common, and cooperative play is the norm.

Make-Believe

During the preschool years, cooperative play often takes the form of make-believe. Preschoolers have telephone conversations with imaginary partners or pretend to drink imaginary juice. In the early phases of make-believe, children rely on realistic props to support their play. While pretending to drink, younger preschoolers use a real cup; while pretending to drive a car, they use a toy steer-

ing wheel. In the later phases of make-believe, children no longer need realistic props; instead, they can imagine that a block is the cup, or, like the boys in the photo, that a paper plate is the steering wheel. Of course, this gradual movement toward more abstract make-believe is possible because of cognitive growth that occurs during the preschool years (Harris & Kavanaugh, 1993).

As you might suspect, make-believe reflects the values important in a child's culture. This influence is apparent in the results of research by Farver and Shin (1997), who studied European American and Korean American preschoolers. The Korean American children came from families who had recently immigrated to the United States and who still stressed the importance of traditional Korean values such as emphasis on the family and favoring harmony over conflict. The two groups of children differed in the themes common during make-believe. Adventure and fantasy were common themes for European American youngsters, but family roles and everyday activities were common for the Korean American youngsters. In addition, the groups differed in their style of play during make-believe. European American children were more assertive in their make-believe and more likely to disagree with their play partner's ideas about pretending ("*I* want to be the the king; *you* be the mom!"). In contrast, Korean American children were more polite and more likely to strive for harmony in their play ("Could I *please* be king?"). Thus, cultural values influence both the form and the content of make-believe.

Make-believe play is not only entertaining for children, it seems to promote children's cognitive development (Berk, 1994). Children who spend much time in make-believe play tend to be more advanced in their language, memory, and reasoning. They also tend to be more sophisticated in their understanding of other people's thoughts, beliefs, and feelings (Howe, Petrakos, & Rinaldi, 1998; Youngblade & Dunn, 1995).

Another benefit of make-believe is that it allows children to explore topics that frighten them. Children who are afraid of the dark may reassure a doll who is also afraid of the dark. By explaining to the doll why she need not be afraid, children come to understand and regulate their own fear of darkness. Or children may pretend that a doll has misbehaved and must be punished, which allows them to experience the parent's anger and the doll's guilt. With make-believe, children explore other emotions as well, including joy and affection (Gottman, 1986).

For many preschool children, make-believe play involves imaginary companions. These children can easily describe their imaginary playmates, mentioning their sex and age as well as the color of their hair and eyes. Imaginary companions were once thought to be fairly rare and a sign of possible developmental problems. But more recent research shows that nearly two-thirds of all preschoolers report imaginary companions (Taylor, Cartwright, & Carlson, 1993). Moroever, the presence of an imaginary companion is actually associated with many *positive* social characteristics: Preschoolers with imaginary companions tend to be more sociable and have more real friends than preschoolers without imaginary companions. Furthermore, vivid fantasy play with imaginary companions does *not* mean that the distinction between fantasy and reality is blurred: Children with imaginary companions can distinguish fantasy from reality just as readily as youngsters who do not have imaginary companions (Taylor et al., 1993).

? **THINK ABOUT IT**
How might Jean Piaget have explained the emergence of make-believe during the pre-school years? How would Erik Erikson explain it?

Gender Differences in Play

Between 2 and 3 years of age, the situation shown in the photo becomes more and more common: Most youngsters begin to prefer playing with peers of their own sex. This preference increases gradually during the preschool years and, by the elementary school years, children interact primarily with same-sex peers (Powlishta, 1995).

Is this pairing of boy with boy and girl with girl unique to Western cultures at the end of the 20th century? Apparently not. Whenever children around the world choose playmates, girls prefer playing with girls and boys with boys. Parental encouragement is not necessary for youngsters to segregate by sex. Should parents push their children into playing with peers of the other sex, most youngsters resist (Maccoby, 1990). Why? Boys and girls differ in how they play. When girls interact, their actions and remarks tend to support one another; conflicts that arise are resolved through discussion and compromise (McCloskey & Coleman, 1992). In contrast, boys' play is rougher. When boys interact, intimidation, threats, and exaggeration are common as one boy tries to dominate the others. When boys and girls are together, girls find that their supportive, compromising style has no impact on boys, who are more likely to respond to assertive overtures (Smith & Inder, 1993).

Whatever the exact cause, the preference to play with same-sex peers that emerges in the preschool years is a constant throughout the life span (Moller, Hymel, & Rubin, 1992). As we shall see in Chapters 7, 10, and 11, time spent at leisure (and later, at work) is commonly segregated by sex during adolescence and adulthood.

Parental Influence

Parents enjoy playing with toddlers and preschoolers and often use this as an opportunity to teach their young children. Mothers often adjust the level of their play so that it matches the child's level or is slightly more advanced (Damast, Tamis-LeMonda, & Bornstein, 1996). For example, if a toddler is stacking toy plates, a mom might help the child stack the plates (play at the same level) or might pretend to wash each plate (play at a more advanced level). When mothers demonstrate more advanced forms of play, their children often play at these more advanced levels later (Bornstein et al., 1996).

Parents also influence their children's play with peers. Preschoolers often disagree, argue, and sometimes fight. Children play more cooperatively and longer when parents are present to iron out conflicts (Mize, Pettit, & Brown, 1995; Parke & Bhavnagri, 1989). When young children can't agree on what to play, a parent can negotiate a mutually acceptable topic. When both youngsters want to play with the same toy, a parent can arrange for them to share. In other words, to use Vygotsky's ideas (described on pages 141–144), parents scaffold their preschoolers' play, smoothing the interaction by providing some additional social skills that preschoolers lack.

? THINK ABOUT IT
Suppose friends of yours ask you how their preschool daughter can get along well with peers. What advice would you give them?

Parents sometimes influence the success of their children's peer interactions in a less direct manner. As we described earlier (page 166), children's relationships with peers are most successful when, as infants, children had a secure attachment relationship with their mother (Ladd & LeSieur, 1995). Why does quality of attachment predict the success of children's peer relationships? One view is that a child's relationship with his or her parents is the internal working model for all future social relationships. When the parent-child relationship is high quality and emotionally satisfying, children are encouraged to form relationships with other people. Another possibility is that a secure attachment relationship with the mother makes an infant feel more confident about exploring the environment, which typically provides more opportunities to interact with peers. These two views are not mutually exclusive; both may contribute to the relative ease with which securely attached children interact with their peers (Hartup, 1992a).

LEARNING TO COOPERATE

Play is built on the implicit and sometimes explicit agreement that all players will adhere to certain rules for the common benefit. Hide-and-seek, for example, is no fun when one child only wants to hide and refuses to take a turn as the seeker. Of course, although cooperation may be the ideal, children do not always play together well: Conflicts and arguments are common.

What are some factors that determine whether children cooperate? Age is one. Older children are less egocentric and knowing that others view things differently helps reduce conflicts. Also, preschoolers' growing communicative and social skills make it easier for them to cooperate (Lourenco, 1993).

Cooperation is also influenced by other factors. Children are more likely to cooperate if they see peers who are cooperative and can observe, firsthand, that cooperation works. Children who observe successful cooperation more often cooperate when given the opportunity (Liebert, Sprafkin, & Poulos, 1975).

Children's eagerness to cooperate is strongly influenced by the response to their cooperative overtures (Brady, Newcomb, & Hartup, 1983). When children try to cooperate but their peers do not go along, the incentive to cooperate vanishes rapidly; instead, youngsters look after their own interests. In contrast, when one child's cooperative gesture leads to another youngster's cooperative response, children see for themselves the beauty of working together, and as shown in the photo, cooperation flourishes.

Piecing these findings together, we see why long-lasting cooperation is so fragile. Cooperation only works when all participants agree to cooperate; a few people—or perhaps even just one person— who fails to go along can undermine all the benefits of cooperation. Young children in particular need to be directed by their parents into practical cooperative relationships so that they can directly experience the benefits associated with greater cooperation (Parke & Bahvnagri, 1989).

Some cultures go to greater lengths than others to encourage cooperation. In the United States, the rights of the individual are emphasized, and self-reliance is encouraged. Other cultures, such as China, place a premium on what is good for all; people are seen as being strongly interdependent. Reflecting these cultural differences, Chinese children tend to be substantially more cooperative than North American children (Domino, 1992). For example, in one study (Orlick, Zhou, & Partington, 1990), investigators recorded the frequency of cooperation among kindergartners in Beijing, China, and in Ottawa, Canada. In the Canadian kindergartens, 22% of the interactions were cooperative, which meant that children supported or helped a peer. In the Chinese kindergartens, 85% of the interactions were cooperative.

What should we make of this difference? Evidently, young children *can* be cooperative if they view such behavior as mutually beneficial and if their culture expects them to cooperate. The See for Yourself feature describes how you can determine whether youngsters living near you are cooperative.

CHILDREN COOPERATING AND COMPETING

SEE FOR YOURSELF

You may not be convinced that youngsters growing up in the United States and Canada are especially uncooperative. To see for yourself, arrange to spend an hour observing young children. You could go to a neighborhood playground, but parents are often present to regulate youngsters' behavior. A better choice would be a nursery school or day care center. Your college may have a facility where you could, with permission, observe children from behind a one-way mirror. You should record all occurrences of cooperative behavior, defined as sharing, helping, or being physically affectionate with another child. Also record each instance of conflict behavior, defined as inconsiderate, aggressive, or destructive behavior.

If the facility where you make your observations is typical of those in North America, you can expect to see about 5–7 instances of cooperative behavior in 1 hour, but

15–30 cases of conflict behavior! If you should have the good fortune to travel to China and repeat your observations, you would observe 35–40 instances of cooperative behavior in that same hour, compared to perhaps 5–10 cases of conflict behavior. At least compared to their Chinese counterparts, North American preschoolers are much less considerate of their peers! •

HELPING OTHERS

Prosocial behavior *is any behavior that benefits another person.* Cooperation is one form of prosocial behavior. Of course, cooperation often "works" because individuals gain more than they would by not cooperating. *In contrast,* altruism *is behavior that is driven by feelings of responsibility toward other people, such as helping and sharing, in which individuals do not benefit directly from their actions.* If two youngsters pool their funds to buy a candy bar to share, this is cooperative behavior. If one youngster gives half of her lunch to a peer who forgot his own, this is altruism.

Rudimentary acts of altruism can be seen by 18 months of age. When toddlers see other people who are obviously hurt or upset, they will, like the toddler in the photograph, appear concerned, try to comfort the person who is in pain (by hugging or patting), and try to determine why the person is upset (Zahn-Waxler et al., 1992). Apparently, at this early age, they recognize some of the qualities of states of distress. During the preschool years, children gradually begin to understand others' needs and learn appropriate altruistic responses (Farver & Branstetter, 1994). Let's look at some specific skills that set the stage for altruistic behaviors.

Skills Underlying Altruistic Behavior

Remember from Chapter 4 that preschool children are often egocentric, so they may not see the need for altruistic behavior. For example, young children might not share candy with a younger sibling, because they cannot imagine how unhappy the sibling is without the candy. In contrast, school-age children, who can more easily take another person's perspective, would perceive the unhappiness and would be more inclined to share. In fact, research consistently indicates that altruistic behavior is related to perspective-taking skill. Youngsters who understand others' thoughts and feelings share better with others and help them more often (Roberts & Strayer, 1996).

Related to perspective-taking is empathy, *which is the actual experiencing of another's feelings.* Children who deeply feel another individual's fear, disappointment, sorrow, or loneliness are more inclined to help that person than children who do not feel those emotions (Carlo et al., 1996). In other words, youngsters like the little boy in the photo, who is obviously distressed by what he is seeing, are most likely to help if they can. The Spotlight on Research feature describes a study that investigated this link between empathy and prosocial behavior.

ARE EMPATHIC CHILDREN MORE LIKELY TO HELP?

What was the aim of the study and who were the investigators? A common idea in many theories of helping is that children (and adults) who "feel" another person's discomfort or distress should be more likely to help that person. That is, children and adults who are more empathic are thought to be more likely to help. Paul Miller and his colleagues, Nancy Eisenberg, Richard Fabes, and Rita Shell, tested this claim by measuring children's emotional responding and their tendency to help.

How did the investigators measure the topic of interest? Miller and his colleagues prepared brief films in which children appeared to hurt themselves when they fell. After watching the films, the children in the study were asked how they felt. Children responded by pointing to a happy, sad, sorry, or neutral face. Next, they were asked if they felt a little bit this way, kind of, or very much this way. Next, children were told that the child in the film was in the hospital and that the experimenter wanted to send that child some crayons. However, the crayons were loose in a large box and needed to be put into smaller boxes before they could be sent to the hospitalized child. The children were shown some toys and told that they could help sort the crayons or they could play with the toys. Thus, the measures were the type and intensity of the child's emotional response to the films and the number of crayons that they sorted.

Who were the children in the study? The researchers tested 74 5- and 6-year-old boys and girls.

What was the design of the study? This study was correlational because the investigators looked at the relations that existed naturally between helping (as measured by the number of crayons sorted) and the emotions that children experienced while watching the film. The study included only 5- and 6-year-olds, so it was neither longitudinal nor cross-sectional.

Were there ethical concerns with the study? No. The emotional episodes depicted in the films were fairly mild and similar to what children might experience in their own lives.

What were the results? The graph shows the correlations between children's emotions and their helping. Helping was greatest when children said they were sad after watching the film and least when they said they were happy after the film. Neutral or sorry emotional responses were unrelated to helping.

What did the investigators conclude? As predicted, children who are saddened by another person's discomfort are most likely to help that person. Children who are happy (perhaps because they think it is funny to see others make mistakes, such as falling down) are unlikely to help. •

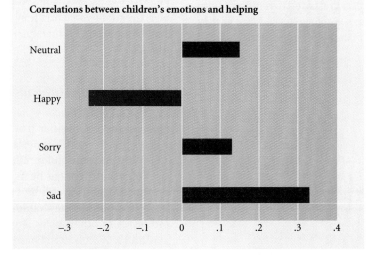

Correlations between children's emotions and helping

Of course, responding empathically does not guarantee that children will act altruistically. Some caring children who would like to help others may not be able to do so. An older brother might want to share candy with a younger sibling but will not because a parent forbids it. Sometimes children may not help because they lack the time or believe that others will help. It is necessary to consider the context in which behavior occurs, as this helps determine whether a child will act altruistically. A number of contextual features are known to influence children's altruism.

- *Feelings of responsibility.* Children act altruistically when they feel responsible for the person in need. Children may help siblings and friends, for example, more often than strangers, simply because they feel a direct responsibility for people they know well (Costin & Jones, 1992).

- *Feelings of competence.* Children act altruistically when they feel they have the skills to help the person in need. Suppose, for example, that a preschooler is growing more and more upset because she can't figure out how to work a computer game; a peer who knows little about computer games is not likely to come to the young girl's aid because the peer doesn't know what to do to help. If the peer tries to help, he or she could end up looking foolish (Peterson, 1983).

- *Mood.* Children act altruistically when they are happy or feeling successful but not when they are sad or feeling as if they have failed. A preschool child who has just spent an exciting morning as the "leader" in nursery school is more inclined to share treats with siblings than is a preschooler who was punished by the teacher (Moore, Underwood, & Rosenhan, 1973).

- *Costs of altruism.* Children act altruistically when such actions entail few or modest sacrifices. A preschool child who was given a snack that she doesn't particularly like is more inclined to share it with others than one who was given her very favorite food (Eisenberg & Shell, 1986).

So when are children most likely to help? When they feel responsible for the person in need, have the needed skills, are happy, and believe they will give up little by helping. When are children least likely to help? When they feel neither responsible nor capable of helping, are in a bad mood, and believe that helping will entail a large personal sacrifice.

With these guidelines in mind, can you explain why Antonio and Carla, the children in the opening vignette, watched idly as their older brother cried? The last two factors—mood and costs—are not likely to be involved. However, the first two factors may explain the failure of Antonio and Carla to help their older brother. Our explanation appears on pages 185–186, just before Test Yourself.

Socialization of Altruism

Contextual factors clearly play an important role in children's altruism. However, children also differ from one another in their feelings of obligation to other humans. Some youngsters are more inclined to help regardless of the setting. Why do some children feel a stronger obligation to help than others?

One factor that has been linked to children's altruism is parents' disciplinary style. Altruistic children typically have parents who emphasize reasoning when disciplining their children. This approach often emphasizes the rights and needs of others as well as the impact of a child's misbehavior on others (Hoffman, 1988, 1994). For example, in the following dialogue, the father tries to make his daughter see how her actions upset her friend.

FATHER: Why did you take the crayons away from Annie?

DAUGHTER: Because I wanted them.

FATHER: How do you think that made her feel? Do you think she was happy or sad?

DAUGHTER: I dunno.

FATHER: I think you know.

? THINK ABOUT IT
Suppose some kindergarten children want to raise money for a gift for one of their classmates who is ill. Based on the information presented here, what advice can you give the children as they plan their fund-raising?

DAUGHTER: Okay. She was sad.

FATHER: Would you like it if I took the crayons away from you? How would *you* feel?

DAUGHTER: I'd be mad. And sad, too.

FATHER: Well, that's how Annie felt, and that's why you shouldn't just grab things away from someone. It makes them angry and unhappy. Ask first, and if they say "no," then you mustn't take them.

Repeated exposure to reasoning during discipline apparently strengthens children's general feelings of responsibility toward other people (Krevans & Gibbs, 1996).

Parents also influence their children's altruism by their own altruistic behavior. When parents express warmth and concern for other people, this increases their children's feelings of empathy (Eisenberg et al., 1991). Parents who behave altruistically—by being helpful to others and being responsive to them—have children who help, share, and are less critical of others (Bryant & Crockenberg, 1980). Thus, by serving as good models of altruistic behavior, parents foster their children's altruism.

A third way to influence children's altruism is by praising them for it. By frequently making remarks such as, "It really makes me happy that you helped Matt tie his shoes," parents encourage their children's altruism. *Particularly effective is* dispositional praise, *in which parents link the child's altruistic behavior to an underlying altruistic disposition.* For example, a parent might say "Thanks for helping me make breakfast; I knew I could count on you because you are such a helpful person." When chil-

dren like the one in the photo hear remarks like this repeatedly, their self-concept apparently changes to include these characteristics. Children begin to believe that they really are helpful (or nice or friendly). With these characteristics as important elements of their self-concept, children are more likely to behave altruistically when others are in need (Mills & Grusec, 1989).

Thus, parents can foster altruism in their youngsters by using reasoning to discipline them, behaving altruistically themselves, and praising the children's altruistic acts. Also, contextual factors play a role, and altruism requires perspective-taking and empathy. Combining these ingredients, we can give a general account of children's altruistic behavior. As children get older, their perspective-taking and empathic skills develop, which enables them to see and feel another's needs. Nonetheless, children are never invariably altruistic (or, fortunately, invariably nonaltruistic), because particular contexts affect altruistic behavior, too.

Postscript: Why Didn't Antonio and Carla Help?

Here are our explanations. First, neither Antonio nor Carla may have felt sufficiently responsible to help, because (a) with two children who could help, each child's feeling of individual responsibility is reduced, and (b) younger children are less likely to feel responsible for an older sibling. Second, it's our guess that neither child has had many opportunities to use the VCR. In fact, it's likely that they both have been strongly discouraged from venturing near it. Consequently, they don't feel very competent to help, because neither knows how it works or what they should do to help Juan remove his finger.

TEST YOURSELF

1. Toddlers who are 12–15 months old often engage in _____ play, in which they play separately but look at one another and sometimes communicate verbally.

2. One of the advantages of _____ play is that children can explore topics that frighten them.

3. When girls interact, conflicts are typically resolved through _____ ; boys more often resort to intimidation.

4. Compared to young children in North America, youngsters in China are _____ cooperative.

5. _____ is the ability to understand and feel another person's emotions.

6. Contextual influences on prosocial behavior include feelings of responsibility, feelings of competence, _____ , and the costs associated with behaving prosocially.

7. Parents can foster altruism in their children by using reasoning to discipline them, behaving altruistically themselves, and _____ .

8. How might children's temperament, which we discussed in Chapter 2, influence the development of their play with peers?

Answers: (1) parallel, (2) make-believe, (3) discussion and compromise, (4) more, (5) Empathy, (6) mood, (7) praising their children for altruistic behavior

GENDER ROLES AND GENDER IDENTITY

Gender Roles and Gender Identity

Images of Men and Women: Facts and Fantasy

Gender Typing

Evolving Gender Roles

Learning Objectives

- **What are our stereotypes about males and females? How well do they correspond to actual differences between boys and girls?**

- **When do young children understand that gender is fixed? How does this understanding influence their learning about roles for girls and boys?**

- **How are gender roles changing? What further changes might the future hold?**

*M*EDA AND FRANK *are in their early 50s. Though not married, they have lived together since the early 1970s, when both were active in protests against the war in Vietnam. Their daughter Hope is now 6 years old. True to their countercultural roots, both Meda and Frank want their daughter to pick activities, friends, and, ultimately, a career based on her interests and abilities, not on her gender. Both are now astonished that Hope seems to be totally indistinguishable from other 6-year-olds reared by parents with conven-*

tional outlooks. Hope's close friends are all girls, and they often play "house" or play with dolls. What seems to be going wrong with Meda and Frank's plans for a "gender-neutral" girl?

Family and well-wishers are always eager to know the sex of a newborn. Why are people so interested in a baby's sex? The answer is that being a "boy" or "girl" is not simply a biological distinction. Instead, these terms are associated with distinct social roles. *Like a role in a play, a* social role *is a set of cultural guidelines as to how a person should behave, particularly with other people.* The roles associated with gender are among the first that children learn, starting in infancy. Youngsters rapidly learn about the behaviors that are assigned to males and females in their culture. At the same time, they begin to identify with one of these groups. As they do, they take on an identity as a boy or girl.

In this section, you'll learn about the "female role" and the "male role" in North America today, and you'll also discover why Meda and Frank are having so much trouble rearing a gender-neutral girl.

IMAGES OF MEN AND WOMEN: FACTS AND FANTASY

All cultures have gender stereotypes—*beliefs and images about males and females that may or may not be true.* For example, many men and women believe that males are rational, active, independent, competitive, and aggressive. At the same time, many men and women claim that females are emotional, passive, dependent, sensitive, and gentle (Williams & Best, 1990).

Based on gender stereotypes, we expect males and females to act and feel in particular ways, and we respond to their behavior differently, depending on their gender (Bigler, 1995). For example, if you saw the toddler in the photo, you would probably assume that she was a girl, based on her taste in toys. Furthermore, your assumption would lead you to believe (a) that she plays more quietly, and (b) that she is more readily frightened than if you had assumed the child to be a boy (Stern & Karraker, 1989). Once we assume the child is a girl, our gender stereotypes lead to a whole host of inferences about behavior and personality.

By the time children are ready to enter elementary school, they are well on their way to learning gender stereotypes. For example, 5-year-olds believe that boys are strong and dominant and that girls are emotional and gentle (Best et al., 1977; Etaugh & Liss, 1992).

Beyond the preschool years, children learn more about stereotypes but they also have greater flexibility when it comes to gender stereotypes (Serbin, Powlishta, & Gulko, 1993). They understand that it is often acceptable for children to deviate from gender stereotypes—a girl can be ambitious and a boy can be gentle (Levy, Taylor, & Gelman, 1995).

Of course, these are only people's *beliefs* about differences between males and females, and many of them are false. Research reveals that males and females often *do not* differ in the ways specified by cultural stereotypes. What are the bona fide differences between males and females? Of course, in addition to the obvious anatomical differences, males are typically larger and stronger than females throughout most of the life span. Beginning in infancy, boys are more active than girls (Eaton & Enns, 1986). In contrast, girls have a lower mortality rate and are less susceptible to stress and disease (Zaslow & Hayes, 1986).

When it comes to social roles, activities for males tend to be more strenuous, involve more cooperation with others, and often require travel. Activities for females are usually less demanding physically, more solitary, and take place closer to home. This division of roles is much the same worldwide (Whiting & Edwards, 1988).

The extent of gender differences in the intellectual and psychosocial arenas remains uncertain. Research suggests differences between males and females in several areas:

• *Verbal ability.* Females typically excel on standardized tests of general language development, in the quality of their speech production, and in reading (Hyde & Linn, 1988; Hedges & Nowell, 1995). Furthermore, girls are less likely to have language-related problems such as reading disability or stuttering (Halpern, 1986).

• *Mathematics.* Males tend to get higher grades on math achievement tests, but girls often get better grades in math courses (Beller & Gafni, 1996; Kimball, 1989).

• *Spatial ability.* On problems like those in the diagram, which measure the ability to manipulate visual information mentally, you must decide which figures are rotated variants of the standard shown at the left. Males typically respond more rapidly and accurately than females (Voyer, Voyer, & Bryden, 1995).

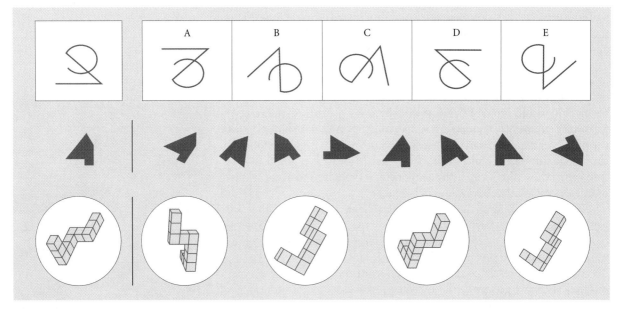

Pellegrino & Kail, 1982.

• *Social influence.* Girls are more likely than boys to comply with the directions of adults (Maccoby & Jacklin, 1974). Girls and women are also more readily influenced by others in a variety of situations, particularly when they are under group pressure (Becker, 1986; Eagly, Karau, & Makhijani, 1995).

• *Aggression.* In virtually all cultures that have been studied, males are more aggressive, particularly when aggression is not provoked by others (Bettencourt & Miller, 1996; Knight, Fabes, & Higgins, 1996). This difference begins as early as the preschool years and remains throughout the life span (Sanson et al., 1993).

In most other intellectual and social domains, boys and girls are similar. When thinking about areas in which sex differences have been found, keep in mind that gender differences often depend on a person's experiences and social class (Casey, 1996; Serbin, Powlishta, & Gulko, 1993). Also, gender differences may fluctuate over time, reflecting historical change in the contexts of childhood for boys and girls. Finally, each result just described refers to a difference in the *average* performance of boys and girls. These differences tend to be small, which means that they do not apply to all boys and girls. Many girls have greater spatial ability than many boys; many boys are more susceptible to social influence than are some girls.

GENDER TYPING

Folklore holds that parents and other adults—teachers and television characters, for example—directly shape children's behavior toward the roles associated with their sex. Boys are rewarded for boyish behavior and punished for girlish behavior. The folklore even has a theoretical basis: According to social learning theorists like Albert Bandura (1977, 1986) and Walter Mischel (1970), children learn gender roles in much the same way they learn other social behaviors, through reinforcement and observational learning. Parents and others thus shape appropriate gender roles in children, and children learn what their culture considers appropriate behavior for males and females by simply watching how adults and peers act.

How well does research support social learning theory? The best answer to this question comes from an extensive analysis of 172 studies involving 27,836 children showing that parents tend to treat sons and daughters similarly (Lytton & Romney, 1991). Parents interact equally with sons and daughters, are equally warm to both, and encourage both sons and daughters to achieve and be independent. The primary exception is in behavior related to gender roles, where parents respond differently to sons and daughters. Activities such as playing with dolls, dressing up, or helping an adult are encouraged more often in daughters than in sons; rough-and-tumble play and playing with blocks is encouraged more in sons than in daughters. Parents also assign sons and daughters different household chores. Daughters tend to be assigned stereotypically female chores such as washing dishes or housecleaning, whereas sons are assigned stereotypically male chores such as taking out the garbage or mowing the lawn (McHale et al., 1990).

Fathers are more likely than mothers to treat sons and daughters differently. More than mothers, fathers like the one in the photograph often encourage gender-related play. Fathers punish their sons more, but they accept dependence in their daughters (Snow, Maccoby, & Jacklin, 1983). A father, for example, may urge his frightened young son to jump off the diving board ("Be a man!") but not insist that his daughter do so ("That's okay, honey"). Apparently mothers are more likely to respond based on their knowledge of the needs of individual children, but fathers respond based on gender stereotypes. A mother responds to her son knowing that he's smart but unsure of himself; a father may respond based on what he thinks boys generally should be like.

THINK ABOUT IT
The women's liberation movement became a powerful social force in North America during the 1960s. Describe how you might do research to determine whether the movement has changed the gender roles that children learn.

Peers also contribute to sex typing. During the preschool years, most children's play becomes gender-appropriate—boys prefer blocks and trucks while girls prefer tea sets and dolls. Youngsters are critical of peers who engage in cross-gender play (Langlois & Downs, 1980). This is particularly true of boys who like feminine toys or play feminine activities. A boy who plays with dolls

or a girl like the one in the photo who plays with trucks will both be ignored, teased, or ridiculed by their peers, but the boy more harshly than the girl (Levy, Taylor, & Gelman, 1995). Once children learn rules about gender-typical play, they severely punish peers who violate those rules.

Thus, through encouraging words, critical looks, and other forms of praise and punishment, other people influence boys and girls to behave differently (Jacobs & Eccles, 1992). However, children learn more than simply the specific behaviors associated with their gender. *A child gradually begins to identify with one group and to develop a* gender identity—*a sense of the self as a male or a female.*

Gender Identity

If you were to listen to a typical conversation between two preschoolers, you might hear something like this:

MARIA: When I grow up, I'm going to be a singer.

JUANITA: When I grow up, I'm going to be a papa.

MARIA: No, you can't be a papa—you'll be a mama.

JUANITA: No, I wanna be a papa.

MARIA: You can't be a papa. Only boys can be papas and you're a girl!

Obviously, Maria's understanding of gender is more developed than Juanita's. How can we explain these differences? According to Lawrence Kohlberg (1966; Kohlberg & Ullian, 1974), children gradually develop a basic understanding that they are of either the female or the male sex. Gender then serves to organize many perceptions, attitudes, values, and behaviors. Full understanding of gender is said to develop gradually in three steps:

- Gender labeling: *By age 2 or 3, children understand that they are either boys or girls, and label themselves accordingly.*

- Gender stability: *During the preschool years, children begin to understand that gender is stable: Boys become men and girls become women.* However, children in this stage believe that a girl who wears her hair like a boy will become a boy and a boy who plays with dolls will become a girl (Fagot, 1985).

- Gender constancy: *Between 4 and 7 years, most children understand that maleness and femaleness do not change over situations or according to per-*

sonal wishes. They understand that a child's sex is unaffected by the cloth-ing a child wears or the toys a child likes.

Juanita and Maria both know that they're girls, but Maria has developed a greater sense of gender stability and gender constancy.

In Kohlberg's theory, only children who understand gender stability should have extensive knowledge of sex-stereotyped activities (Newman, Cooper, & Ruble, 1995). That is, not until children understand that gender is stable do they begin to learn about activities that are appropriate for their gender and those that are not. This pattern is found in research. For example, Martin and Little (1990) measured preschool children's understanding of gender and their knowledge of gender-typed activities (e.g., that girls play with dolls and that boys play with airplanes). The youngest children in their study—3½- to 4-year-olds—did not understand gender stability, and they knew little of gender-stereotyped activities. By age 4, children understood gender stability but still knew little of gender-stereotyped activities. By 4½ years, many children under-stood gender stability *and* knew gender-typical and gender-atypical activities. Importantly, there were no children who lacked gender stability but knew about gender-stereotyped activities, a combination that is impossible accord-ing Kohlberg's theory.

Kohlberg's theory specifies when children should begin to learn about gender-appropriate behavior and activities (once they understand gender sta-bility) but not *how* such learning takes place. A theory proposed by Martin and Halverson (1987) addresses how children learn about gender. *In* gender-schema theory, *children first decide if an object, activity, or behavior is female or male, then use this information to decide whether they should learn more about the object, activity, or behavior.* That is, as you can see in the diagram, once chil-dren know their gender, they now pay attention primarily to experiences and

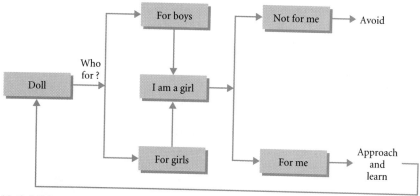

Martin & Halverson, 1981.

events that are gender-appropriate (Martin & Halverson, 1987). According to gender-schema theory, a preschool boy who sees a group of girls playing in sand will decide that playing in sand is for girls and because he is a boy, play-ing in sand is not for him. Seeing a group of older boys playing football, he will decide that football is for boys and, because he is a boy, that football is accept-able and that he should learn more about it. Thus, after children understand gender, it's as if they see the world through special glasses that allow only gender-typical activities to be in focus (Liben & Signorella, 1993; Martin, Eisenbud, & Rose, 1995).

EVOLVING GENDER ROLES

Gender roles are not etched in stone; they change with the times. In the United States, the range of acceptable roles for girls and boys and women and men has never been greater than today. For example, some fathers like the man in the photo stay home to be primary caregivers for children, and some mothers work full-time as sole support for the family.

What is the impact of these changes on gender roles? Some insights come from the results of the Family Lifestyles Project (Weisner & Wilson-Mitchell, 1990). This research has examined families in which the adults were members of the counterculture of the 1960s and 1970s. Some of the families are deeply committed to living their own lives and to rearing their children without traditional gender stereotypes. In these families, men and women share the household, financial, and child care tasks.

The results of this project show that parents like Meda and Frank, from the opening vignette, can influence some aspects of gender stereotyping more readily than others. On the one hand, children in these families tend to have same-sex friends and to like sex-typed activities: The boys enjoy physical play, and the girls enjoy drawing and reading. On the other hand, the children have few stereotypes concerning occupations: They agree that girls can be president of the United States and drive trucks and that boys can be nurses and secretaries. They also have fewer sex-typed attitudes about the use of objects. They claim that boys and girls are equally likely to use an iron, a shovel, a hammer and nails, and a needle and thread.

Apparently, some features of gender roles and identities are more readily influenced by experience than others. This is as it should be. For most of our history as a species, Homo sapiens have existed in small groups of families, hunting animals and gathering vegetation. Women have given birth to the children and cared for them. Over the course of human history, it has been adaptive for women to be caring and nurturing because this increases the odds of a secure attachment and, ultimately, the survival of the infant. Men's responsibilities have included protecting the family unit from predators and hunting with other males, roles for which physical strength and aggressiveness are crucial.

Circumstances of life at the start of the 21st century are, of course, substantially different. Men can rear children, and women can generate income to purchase food for the family. The range of acceptable roles for girls and boys and women and men has never been wider. At the same time, the cultural changes of the past few decades cannot erase hundreds of thousands of years of evolutionary history (Kenrick, 1987). Consequently, we should not be surprised to find that boys and girls often differ in their styles of play, that girls tend to be more supportive of one another in their interactions, and that boys are usually more aggressive. As indicated in the You May Be Wondering feature, children whose parents are lesbian or gay also tend to grow up with conventional gender-role identity and interests.

CHILDREN OF GAY AND LESBIAN PARENTS

More than a million youngsters in the United States have a gay or lesbian parent. In most of these situations, the children were born in a heterosexual marriage that ended in divorce when one parent revealed his or her homosexuality. Rarer, but becoming more common, are children born to single lesbians or to lesbian couples.

You may be wondering what happens to these youngsters. Is their development like that of children whose parents are heterosexual? Or does it differ, particularly when it comes to gender-related issues? Our answers to these questions must be tentative, because research on this topic is scarce. The number of studies is small, and almost all have examined children who were born to a heterosexual marriage that ended in divorce when the mother came out as a lesbian. Most of the lesbian mothers have been European American and well educated.

Bearing these limits in mind, the general pattern is one of normal psychosocial development in children of lesbian mothers (Patterson, 1992). Preschool boys and girls apparently identify with their own gender and acquire the usual gender-based preferences, interests, activities, and friends. As adolescents and young adults, the vast majority are heterosexual (Bailey et al., 1995). In other dimensions, such as self-concept, social skill, moral reasoning, and intelligence, the development of children of lesbian mothers resembles that of children of heterosexual parents. For example, in one study of 15 lesbian couples and 15 heterosexual couples, the children were comparably intelligent and comparably well adjusted psychologically (Flaks et al., 1995).

These conclusions, if substantiated by further research, have important implications. First, psychological theories have traditionally considered that the two-parent family, with both mother and father present, provides the best circumstances for development. Findings like these challenge the conventional wisdom in suggesting that it is what a parent provides for children that matters, not the parent's sexual orientation. Second, in many U.S. states, gay and lesbian adults are automatically deemed unfit as parents, a judgment that is totally unsupported by the research. ●

---

1. _____ are beliefs and images about males and females that may or may not be true.

2. Research on intellectual functioning and social behavior has revealed sex differences in verbal ability, mathematics, _____ , social influence, and aggression.

3. _____ may be particularly influential in teaching gender roles, because they more often treat sons and daughters differently.

4. According to Kohlberg's theory, understanding of gender includes gender labeling, gender stability, and _____ .

5. Children studied in the Family Lifestyles Project, whose parents were members of the counterculture of the 1960s and 1970s, had traditional gender-related views toward friends and _____ .

6. How do the different forces in the biopsychosocial framework contribute to the development of gender roles?

Answers: (1) Gender stereotypes, (2) spatial ability, (3) Fathers, (4) gender constancy, (5) preferred activities

PUTTING IT ALL TOGETHER

Though the cartoon is funny, you probably wouldn't care to consider the alternative—living alone—because interactions with other people are so important throughout life. Having completed this chapter, you now know that these interactions start early in life. In the first part of this chapter, we saw that responsive caregiving often leads to the formation of a secure attachment between infant and parent. When infants who have had secure attachments grow up, they tend to interact more successfully with other people. Infants who spend much time in early alternative child care also form secure attachments unless the child care is low quality and the mother is unresponsive. Children like Roosevelt, Kendra's 18-month-old, are not harmed by time spent in early alternative child care, as long as the care is high quality and mothers remain responsive and sensitive.

We showed that infants like Claude can express basic emotions like happiness and anger. By age 2, children experience complex emotions like guilt. Babies use others' emotions to guide their behavior, and this skill improves as children grow cognitively.

We traced how children's social relations expand from parents to peers. Even babies play with others, and play rapidly becomes more complex over the preschool years. Toddlers also show concern for others. However, as children grow older, whether they actually help others depends upon perspective-taking and empathic skills, the context in which help is required, and styles of parental discipline. For example, in the vignette, Antonio and Carla did not help their older brother because they did not feel great responsibility to help and because they did not feel capable of helping.

As children's social horizons continue to expand, they soon learn that they are expected to play certain roles in society, based on their gender. By the end of the preschool years, most children know that gender is fixed, and they begin to use this knowledge to select activities and objects that are appropriate for them. These choices are influenced by parents' values and expectations, but some aspects of gender roles are easier to change than others. For example, Meda and Frank, the parents in the vignette, will probably find it easier to modify their daughter's career goals than to modify her style of play.

Of course, despite the rapid and sometimes dramatic change we've witnessed in this chapter, social and interpersonal development is far from complete by the end of the preschool years. Much additional change takes place in school-age children and adolescents, as we'll see in Chapter 7.

SUMMARY

Beginnings: Trust and Attachment

Erikson's Stages of Early Psychosocial Development

• In Erikson's theory of psychosocial development, individuals face certain psychosocial crises at different phases in development. The crisis of infancy is to establish a balance between trust and mistrust of the world, producing hope; between 1 and 3 years of age, youngsters must blend autonomy and shame to produce will; and between 3 and 5 years of age, initiative and guilt must be balanced to achieve purpose.

The Growth of Attachment

• Attachment is an enduring social-emotional relationship between infant and parent. For both adults and infants, many of the behaviors that contribute to the formation of attachment are biologically programmed. Attachment develops gradually over the first year of life; by about 6 or 7 months, infants have identified an attachment figure, typically the mother. In the ensuing months, infants often become attached to other family members.

• Research with the Strange Situation, in which infant and mother are separated briefly, reveals four primary forms of attachment. Most common is a secure attachment, in which infants have complete trust in the mother. Less common are three types of attachment relationships in which this trust is lacking. In avoidant relationships, infants deal with the lack of trust by ignoring the mother; in resistant relationships, infants often seem angry with her; in disorganized relationships, infants do not appear to understand the mother's absence.

• Children who have had secure attachment relationships during infancy often interact with their peers more readily and more skillfully. Secure attachment is most likely to occur when mothers respond sensitively and consistently to their infant's needs.

Attachment, Work, and Alternative Caregiving

• Many U.S. children are cared for at home by a father or other relative, in a day care provider's home, or in a day care center. Infants and young children are not harmed by such care as long as the care is high quality and parents remain responsive to their children.

Emerging Emotions

Basic Emotions

• Scientists often use infants' facial expressions to judge when different emotional states emerge in development. The earliest indicator of happiness is the social smile, which emerges at about 2 months. Laughter appears at 4 months. Anger and fear are both evident by about 6 months of age. Fear first appears in infancy as stranger anxiety; fears of specific objects develop later in childhood.

Complex Emotions

• Complex emotions, which usually appear between 18 and 24 months, have a self-evaluative component and include guilt, embarrassment, and pride. These require more sophisticated cognitive skills than basic emotions like happiness and fear.

Recognizing and Using Others' Emotions

• By 6 months of age, infants have begun to recognize the emotions associated with different facial expressions. They use this information to evaluate unfamiliar situations. Beyond infancy, children understand the causes and consequences of different emotions.

Interacting with Others

The Joys of Play

• Even infants notice and respond to one another, but the first real interactions, at about 12 to 15 months, take the form of parallel play, in which toddlers play alone while watching each other. A few months later, simple social play emerges, in which toddlers engage in similar activities and interact with one another. At about 2 years of age, cooperative play organized around a theme becomes common. Make-believe play is also common; in addition to being fun, it allows children to examine frightening topics.

Learning to Cooperate

• Cooperation becomes more common as children get older. Children cooperate more readily if they are shown that cooperation is effective and if peers respond to their cooperation with further cooperation. Cooperation is also influenced by societal values; it is more common in cultures that prize cooperation more highly than competition.

Helping Others

• Prosocial behaviors, such as helping or sharing, are more common in children who understand (perspective-taking) and experience (empathy) another's feelings.

• Prosocial behavior is more likely when children feel responsible for the person in distress. Also, children help more often when they believe they have the skills needed, when they are feeling happy or successful, and when the perceived costs of helping are small.

• Parents can foster prosocial behavior in their children by using reasoning during discipline, by serving as good models of prosocial behavior, and by praising their children for prosocial acts.

Gender Roles and Gender Identity

Images of Men and Women: Facts and Fantasy

• Gender stereotypes are beliefs about males and females that are often used to make inferences about a person, simply based on his or her gender. Studies of gender differences reveal that girls have greater verbal skill and get better grades in math courses but boys have greater spatial skill and get higher scores on math achievement tests. Girls are more prone to social influence, but boys are more aggressive. These differences vary based on a number of factors, including the historical period.

Gender Typing

• Parents treat sons and daughters similarly, except in sex-typed activities. Fathers may be particularly important in sex typing, because they are more likely to treat sons and daughters differently.

• In Kohlberg's theory, children gradually learn that gender is stable over time and cannot be changed according to personal wishes. After children understand gender stability, they begin to learn gender-typical behavior. According to gender-schema theory, children learn about gender by paying attention to behaviors of members of their own sex and ignoring behaviors of members of the other sex.

Evolving Gender Roles

• Gender roles are changing. However, studies of nontraditional families indicate that some components of gender stereotypes are more readily changed than others.

KEY TERMS

hope (163)
will (163)
purpose (163)
ethology (163)
attachment (163)
secure attachment (166)
avoidant attachment (166)
resistant attachment (166)
disorganized (disoriented)
   attachment (166)

internal working model (168)
basic emotions (172)
social smiles (173)
stranger anxiety (174)
complex emotions (174)
social referencing (176)
parallel play (177)
simple social play (178)
cooperative play (178)
prosocial behavior (182)

altruism (182)
empathy (182)
dispositional praise (185)
social role (187)
gender stereotypes (187)
gender identity (190)
gender labeling (190)
gender stability (190)
gender constancy (190)
gender-schema theory (191)

IF YOU'D LIKE TO LEARN MORE

Readings

BRAZELTON, T. B., & CRAMER, R. (1990). *The earliest relationship.* Reading, MA: Addison-Wesley. This book, written by a well-known pediatrician and his colleague, illustrates the drama of attachment through lively case studies.

ERIKSON, E. H. (1982). *The life cycle completed: A review.* New York: Norton. Erikson summarizes his theory.

GOLOMBOK, S., & FIVUSH, R. (1994). *Gender development.* New York: Cambridge University Press. The authors provide a comprehensive overview of how and why boys and girls develop differently. Their approach is balanced and emphasizes the interactive influence of biological, psychological, and sociocultural forces on gender development.

SCARR, S. (1984). *Mother care, other care.* New York: Basic Books. A leading investigator of the effects of day care on children reviews the research, describes the elements of high-quality care, and tells how to obtain such care. Written in a straightforward style.

• For additional readings, explore Infotrac College Edition, your online library. Go to http://www.infotrac-college.com/wadsworth.

Web Sites

A site at the State University of New York at Stony Brook

http://www.psy.sunysb.edu/ewaters/

provides information about attachment theory and describes observational methods used to assess quality of attachment.

The American Psychological Association includes information on its Web site

http://www.apa.org/pubinfo/altruism.html

about why children care for others and includes tips for parents who want to encourage their children to be more altruistic.

The Web site of the Advocates of Women in Science, Engineering, and Mathematics (AWSEM)

http://www.awsem.com

describes ways to encourage girls and young women to pursue interests in science, math, and technology.

Web site addresses are subject to change. The Wadsworth Study Center Web site listed below can be accessed for updated links.

The Wadsworth Psychology Study Center Web Site

See http://psychology.wadsworth.com/ for practice quiz questions, internet links, updates, critical thinking exercises, discussion forums and more! The Wadsworth Psychology Study Center provides a wealth of information fully organized and integrated by chapter.

SNAPSHOTS OF DEVELOPMENT
A VISUAL SUMMARY

Prenatal Development, Infancy, and Early Childhood

BIOLOGICAL FORCES

The impact of biology is profound throughout this period. Biological forces are seen in the growth of the body before and after birth, in reflexes that protect newborns and help them adjust to life outside the uterus, in temperamental differences between children, and in the emergence early in infancy of basic emotions.

PSYCHOLOGICAL FORCES

Psychological forces become more important throughout this period as infants' and toddlers' thinking skills become more powerful. Piaget emphasized that even young infants create simple theories of the world. As children develop, these theories become more elaborate and include models of relationships with others, a self-concept, and a theory of mind.

SOCIOCULTURAL FORCES

Beginning with the impact of teratogens on prenatal development and continuing with the formation of mother-infant attachment, with the benefits of practice on toddlers' mastery of motor skills, and with the collaboration between novice and expert that marks Vygotsky's theory, sociocultural forces continuously shape children's development.

At about 2 weeks after conception, the fertilized egg becomes implanted in the wall of the uterus. This marks the beginning of the period of the embryo, a time when major body parts are created.

Despite much encouragement from their mother, most babies refuse to cross the "deep side" of the visual cliff. Their refusal shows that babies are able to perceive depth.

Make-believe is common throughout the preschool years and, in addition to being fun, promotes cognitive development and allows children to explore emotionally-laden topics.

Once children begin to speak, they learn new words very rapidly because they use simple rules to match names and objects.

PART TWO

SCHOOL-AGE CHILDREN AND ADOLESCENTS

- **CHAPTER 6**

  Off to School

- **CHAPTER 7**

  Expanding
  Social Horizons

- **CHAPTER 8**

  Rites of Passage to
  Young Adulthood

A CLOSER LOOK

Janet Jackson was the ninth and last child born to Joe and Katherine Jackson. By the time Janet was a preschooler, her older brothers, the Jackson Five, already had a number one hit song. Janet first gained fame herself as a TV actress. As a 9-year-old, she joined the cast of *Good Times*, and, a few years later, the cast of *Different Strokes*. As a teenager, Janet was called to music and recorded three albums. The first were not very successful, but the third, *Control*, topped the charts and had several top-10 songs. Her singing career skyrocketed and today she is one of the world's most successful and popular vocalists.

Janet's childhood and adolescence *are* extraordinary, yet childhood and adolescence are times of profound change for all children. At the beginning of childhood, children are still largely dependent on parents, rarely venture far from home, and their futures are uncertain; by the end of adolescence, they are largely independent, often travel widely, and have goals for their adult years. You'll learn more about this remarkable phase of development in Chapters 6–8. You'll see how biological, psychological, and social forces guide the transition from naive child to mature adolescent.

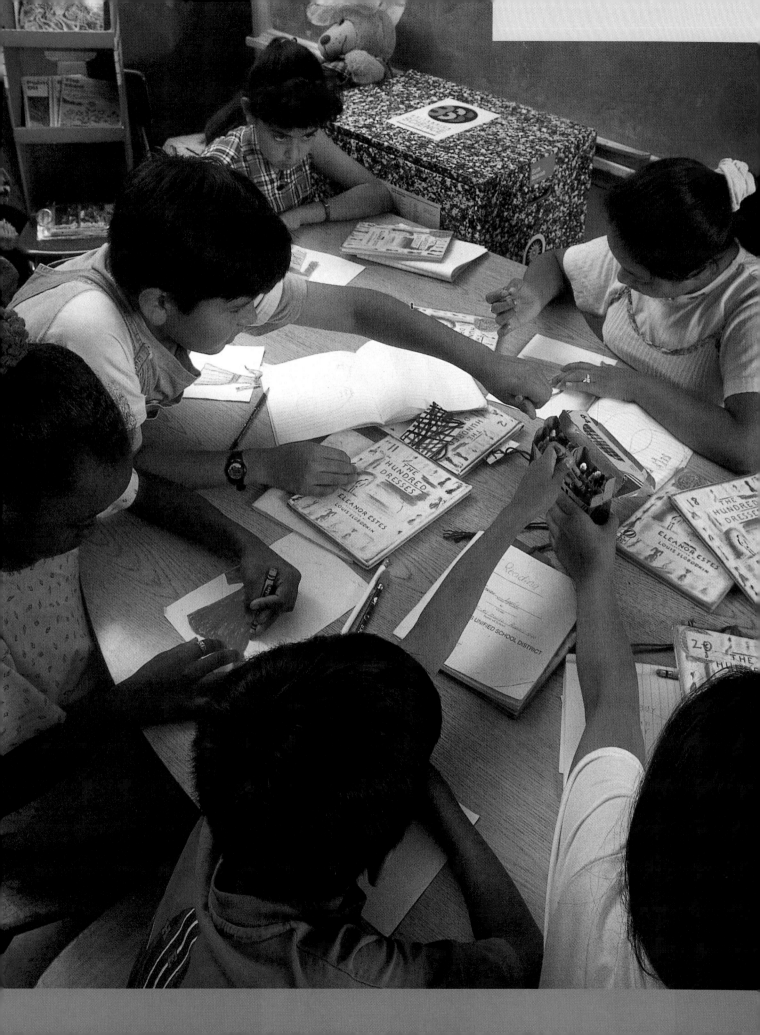

CHAPTER 6

OFF TO SCHOOL

Cognitive Development
More Sophisticated Thinking:
Piaget's Version
Combinatorial Reasoning
Goes to the Races
Information-Processing Strategies
for Learning and Remembering

Aptitudes for School
Binet and the Development of
Intelligence Testing
Do Tests Work?
The Elements of Intelligence
The Impact of Race, Ethnicity,
and Social Class
Hereditary and Environmental Factors
The Carolina Abecedarian Project

Special Children, Special Needs
Gifted and Creative Children
Children with Mental Retardation
Little David—the Rest of the Story
Children with Learning Disability
Attention-Deficit Hyperactivity Disorder
Treating ADHD

Learning in School
Grading U.S. Schools
Effective Schools, Effective Teachers
Computers in the Classroom
Recognizing Good Teaching

Putting It All Together

Summary

If You'd Like to Learn More

*E*very fall, American 5- and 6-year-olds trot off to kindergarten, starting an educational journey that lasts 13 or more years. As the journey begins, many children can read only a few words and know little math; by the end, most can read complete books and many have learned algebra and geometry. This mastery of complex academic skills is possible because of profound changes in children's thinking, changes described in the first section of this chapter.

For most American schoolchildren, intelligence and aptitude tests are a common part of their educational travels. In the second section of this chapter, you'll see what tests measure and why some children get lower scores on tests. In the third section, you'll discover how tests are often used to identify schoolchildren with atypical or special needs.

We conclude with a look at the smorgasbord of educational experiences available in the United States. In this section, you'll discover some of the educational practices that seem to foster students' learning.

COGNITIVE DEVELOPMENT

Cognitive Development

More Sophisticated Thinking:
  Piaget's Version

Information-Processing Strategies
  for Learning and Remembering

Learning Objectives

- **What are the distinguishing characteristics of thought during Piaget's concrete-operational and formal-operational stages?**
- **What are some of the limitations of Piaget's account of thinking during the formal-operational stage?**
- **How do children use strategies to improve learning and remembering?**
- **What is the role of monitoring in successful learning and remembering?**

*A*DRIAN, *a sixth-grader who is starting middle school, just took his first social studies test—and failed. He is shocked because he'd always gotten A's and B's in elementary school. Adrian realizes that glancing through the textbook chapter once before a test is probably not going to work in middle school, but he's not sure what else he should be doing.*

You're about one-third of the way through the book and deserve a break. Try this joke.

> Mr. Jones went into a restaurant and ordered a whole pizza for dinner. When the waiter asked if he wanted it cut into six or eight pieces, Mr. Jones said: "Oh, you'd better make it six! I could never eat eight!" (McGhee, 1976, p. 422)

Okay, this is not such a great joke (to put it mildly). However, many 6- to 8-year-olds think it's hilarious. To understand why children find this joke so funny and to learn more about the skills that will save Adrian's social studies grade, we need to learn more about cognitive development. Let's start with Piaget's theory, then look at information-processing accounts.

MORE SOPHISTICATED THINKING: PIAGET'S VERSION

You probably remember Jean Piaget, from Chapters 1 and 4. Piaget believed that thought develops in a sequence of stages. The first two stages, sensorimotor and preoperational thinking, characterize infancy and the preschool years. In the next few pages, we describe the remaining two stages, the concrete-operational and formal-operational, which apply to school-age children and adolescents.

The Concrete-Operational Period

Let's start by reviewing three important limits of preoperational thinking described in Chapter 4:

- Preschoolers are egocentric, believing that others see the world as they do.
- Preschoolers sometimes confuse appearances with reality.
- Preschoolers are unable to reverse their thinking.

None of these limits applies to children in the concrete-operational stage, which extends from approximately 7 to 11 years. Egocentrism wanes gradually. Why? As youngsters have more experiences with friends and siblings who assert their own perspectives on the world, children realize that theirs is not the only view (LeMare & Rubin, 1987). The understanding that events can be interpreted in different ways leads to the realization that appearances can be deceiving. *Also, thought can be reversed, because school-age children have acquired* mental operations, *which are actions that can be performed on objects or ideas and that consistently yield a result.* Recall from Chapter 4 that on the conservation task, concrete-operational children realize that the amount of liquid is the same after it has been poured into a different beaker, pointing out that the pouring can always be reversed.

Now you can understand why 7-year-olds laugh at the joke about cutting a pizza into six pieces instead of eight. Think of a joke as a puzzle in which the aim is to determine why a particular remark is funny or incongruous. Generally, people like jokes that are neither too simple nor too complex to figure out. Jokes are best when understanding the punch line involves an intermediate level of difficulty (Brodzinsky & Rightmyer, 1980). For children just entering the concrete-operational stage, knowing that the amount of pizza is the same whether it is cut into six or eight pieces taps their newly acquired understanding of conservation, so they laugh (McGhee, 1976).

In discussing the concrete-operational period, we have emphasized the advantages to children of mental operations. At the same time, as the name implies, concrete-operational thinking is limited to the tangible and real, to the here and now. The concrete-operational youngster takes "an earthbound, concrete, practical-minded sort of problem-solving approach . . ." (Flavell, 1985, p. 98). Thinking abstractly and hypothetically is beyond the ability of concrete-operational children; these skills are acquired in the formal-operational period, as you'll see in the next section.

? **THINK ABOUT IT**
Piaget, Freud, and Erikson each propose unique stages for ages 7–11 years. How similar are the stages they propose? How do they differ?

The Formal-Operational Period

With the onset of the formal-operational period, which extends from roughly age 11 into adulthood, children and adolescents expand beyond thinking about only the concrete and the real. Instead, they apply psychological operations to abstract entities, too; they are able to think hypothetically and reason abstractly (Bond, 1995).

To illustrate these differences, let's look at problem solving, where formal-operational adolescents often take a very different approach from concrete-operational children. In one of Piaget's experiments (Inhelder & Piaget, 1958), children and adolescents were presented with several flasks, each containing what appeared to be the same clear liquid. They were told that one combination of the clear liquids would produce a blue liquid; they were asked to determine the necessary combination. A typical concrete-operational youngster, like the one in the photograph, plunges

right in, mixing liquids from different flasks in a haphazard way. In contrast, formal-operational adolescents understand that setting up the problem in abstract terms is the key. The problem is not really about pouring liquids but about combining different elements until all possible combinations have been tested. So a teenager might mix liquid from the first flask with liquids from each of the other flasks. If none of those combinations produces a blue liquid, the teenager would conclude that the liquid in the first flask is not an essential part of the mixture. The next step would be to mix the liquid in the second flask with each of the remaining liquids. A formal-operational thinker would continue in this manner until he or she finds the critical pair that produces the blue liquid. For adolescents, the problem is not one of concrete acts of pouring and mixing. Instead, they understand that it involves identifying possible combinations and then evaluating each one. This sort of adolescent combinatorial reasoning is illustrated in the Real People feature.

REAL PEOPLE

COMBINATORIAL REASONING GOES TO THE RACES

As a 15-year-old, one of the authors (RK) delivered the *Indianapolis Star.* In the spring of 1965, the newspaper announced a contest for all newspaper carriers. The task was to list the most words that could be created from the letters contained in the words "SAFE RACE." Whoever listed the most words would win two tickets to the Indianapolis 500 auto race.

Kail realized that this was a problem in combinatorial reasoning. All he needed to do was create all possible combinations of letters, then look them up. Following this procedure, he had to win (or, at worst, tie). So he created exhaustive lists of possible words, beginning with each of the letters individually, then all possible combinations of two letters, and working his way up to all possible combinations of all eight letters (e.g., SCAREEFA, SCAREEAF). This was monotonous enough, but no more so than the next step: looking up all those possible words in a dictionary. (Remember, this was in the days before computerized spell-checkers.) Weeks later, he had generated a list of 126 words. As predicted, a few months later, he learned that he had won the contest. Combinatorial reasoning has its payoffs! ●

Adolescents' more sophisticated thinking is also shown in their ability to make appropriate conclusions from facts, what is known as deductive reasoning. Suppose we tell a person the following two statements:

1. If you hit a glass with a hammer, the glass will break.
2. You hit the glass with a hammer.

The correct conclusion, of course, is "The glass will break,"—a conclusion that formal-operational adolescents do reach. Concrete-operational youngsters sometimes reach this conclusion, too—but based on their experience, not because the conclusion is logically necessary. To see the difference, imagine that the two statements are now

1. If you hit a glass with a feather, the glass will break.
2. You hit the glass with a feather.

The conclusion "the glass will break" follows from these two statements just as logically as it did from the first pair. In this instance, however, the conclusion is contrary to fact—it goes against what experience tells us is really true. Concrete-operational 10-year-olds resist reaching conclusions that are contrary to known facts, whereas formal-operational 15-year-olds reach them much of the time (Markovits & Vachon, 1989). Formal-operational teenagers understand that these problems are about abstractions that need not correspond to real-world relations. In contrast, concrete-operational youngsters reach conclusions based on their knowledge of the world.

Comments on Piaget's View

As mentioned in Chapter 4, although Piaget provides our single most comprehensive theory of cognitive development, his account of mental development during the early years has some shortcomings. The same is true of his description of formal-operational thinking. Let's look at two questionable aspects.

1. *Formal-operational thinking as a capability.* Simply because adolescents have attained the formal-operational stage does not mean that they always reason at this level. Adolescents (and adults) often fail to reason logically, even when they are capable of doing so and when it would be beneficial to them (Klaczynski & Narasimham, 1998). For example, adolescents typically show more sophisticated reasoning when the problems are relevant to them personally than when they are not (Ward & Overton, 1990). And, as you'll see in Chapter 8, adolescents' thinking is sometimes egocentric and irrational. Consequently, Piaget's account of formal operations is really a description of how adolescents can think, not how they always or even usually think.

2. *Formal operations as an end point.* Cognitive development is complete by age 12 or 13 in Piaget's theory. After adolescents have attained the formal-operational level, their thinking is said to remain the same qualitatively. Of course, people continue to acquire more knowledge and skills, but the fundamental processes of thinking do not change, according to Piaget. Many theorists have criticized this aspect of the theory and have proposed further developmental changes in thinking during late adolescence and adulthood (Moshman, 1998), which we'll discuss in Chapter 9.

Because of these limits to Piaget's theory, we need to look at other approaches to complete our account of mental development during childhood and adolescence. In the next few pages, we'll focus on the information-processing approach we examined in Chapter 4.

INFORMATION-PROCESSING STRATEGIES FOR LEARNING AND REMEMBERING

Once one of us had just written four pages for this book that would have made Hemingway green with envy, when the unthinkable happened: A power failure knocked out the computer, and all those wonderful words were lost. If only the text had been saved to the hard drive . . . but it hadn't.

This tale of woe sets the stage for a main issue of the information-processing approach. As you'll remember from Chapter 4, information-processing psychologists believe that cognitive development proceeds by increases in the efficiency with which children process information.

One of the key issues in this approach is the means by which children store information in permanent memory and retrieve it when needed later. *That is, according to information-processing psychologists, most human thought takes place in* working memory, *where a relatively small number of thoughts and ideas can be stored briefly.* As you read these sentences, for example, the information is stored in working memory. However, as you read additional sentences, they displace the contents of sentences you read earlier. *For you to learn this information, it must be transferred to* long-term memory, *a permanent storehouse of knowledge that has unlimited capacity.* If information you read is not transferred to long-term memory, it is lost, just as our words vanished from the computer's memory when the power failed.

Memory Strategies

How do you try to learn the information in this or your other textbooks? If you're like the college student in the photo, you probably use some combination of highlighting key sentences, outlining chapters, taking notes, writing summaries, and testing yourself. These are all effective learning strategies that make it easier for you to store text information in long-term memory.

Children begin to use simple strategies fairly early. For example, 7- or 8-year-olds use rehearsal, a strategy of repetitively naming information that is to be remembered. As they get older, children learn other memory strategies, and they also learn when it is best to use them. That is, children and adolescents begin to identify the unique characteristics of different memory problems and figure out which memory strategies are most appropriate. For example, when reading a textbook or watching a television newscast, the aim is to remember the main points, not the individual words or sentences. Rehearsal is ineffective here. However, outlining or writing a summary works well in these instances, because such strategies identify the main points *and* group them (Kail, 1990).

Thus, successful learning and remembering involves identifying the goals of memory problems and choosing suitable strategies. As you might expect, younger children sometimes misjudge the objectives of a memory task and therefore choose an inappropriate strategy (Lovett & Pillow, 1996; McGilly & Siegler, 1990). Or they may understand the memory task but not pick the best strategy. These skills improve gradually during childhood and adolescence, but even high school students do not always use effective learning strategies when they should (Slate, Jones, & Dawson, 1993).

These developmental changes can be seen in research in which children and adolescents are taught two memory strategies. One is effective for the material to be learned, but the other is not. The children then have an opportunity to use each strategy. Later, when asked to learn more of the same material, 11- and 12-year-olds usually opt for the more effective strategy. Younger children, in contrast, use either strategy indiscriminately, apparently not understanding that only one is well suited for the material (McGivern et al., 1990).

Monitoring

Learning is most likely to occur when students evaluate their progress toward the goal of the memory task. That is, they need to monitor the effectiveness of the strategy they have chosen. Is the strategy working? If not, students should begin anew, reanalyzing the memory task to select a better approach. If the strategy *is* working, they should determine the portion of the material that they have not yet mastered and concentrate their efforts there.

? THINK ABOUT IT
Which elements of the bio-psychosocial framework are emphasized in the information-processing approach to cognitive development?

Monitoring skills improve gradually with age. For example, elementary school children can accurately identify material that they have not yet learned, but they do not consistently focus their study efforts on this material (Kail, 1990).

The diagram summarizes all these events and the sequence in which they should occur. Beginning by analyzing a task to determine the goals, people select an appropriate strategy, then monitor its usefulness until the task is completed. Throughout childhood and adolescence, individuals gradually become more competent in each of these skills, as well as more adept at coordinating them.

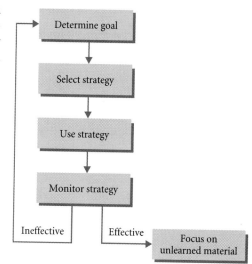

Perhaps this has a familiar ring to it. It should, for the chart simply summarizes an important set of study skills. Analyzing, strategizing, and monitoring are key elements of productive studying. The study goals change when you move from this book to your math text to a novel that you are reading for English, but the basic sequence still holds. Studying should always begin with a clear understanding of what goal you are trying to achieve, because this sets the stage for all the events that follow. Too often, we see students like Adrian—the student in the vignette—who just read text material, without any clear idea of what they should be getting out of it. Instead, students should be active readers (Adams, Treiman, & Pressley, 1998). Always study with a plan. Start by skimming the text to become familiar with the material. Before you read more carefully, try to anticipate some of the topics that the author will cover in detail. When you reach natural breaks in the material, try to summarize what you've read and think of questions that a teacher might ask about the material. Finally, when you don't understand something in the text, stop and determine the source of your confusion. Perhaps you don't know a word's meaning. Maybe you skipped or misunderstood an earlier section of the material. By reading actively, using strategies like these, you'll be much more likely to understand and remember what you've read (Adams et al., 1998; Brown et al., 1996).

1. During Piaget's _____ stage, children are first able to represent objects mentally in different ways and to perform mental operations.

2. Hypothetical and deductive reasoning are characteristic of children in Piaget's _____ stage.

3. Piaget's account of formal operations has been criticized because adolescents' reasoning is often less sophisticated than the theory predicts and because _____ .

4. Children and adolescents often select a memory strategy after they have _____ .

5. The term _____ refers to periodic evaluation of a strategy to determine whether it is working.

6. Formal-operational adolescents are able to reason abstractly. How might this ability help them use the study skills in the chart at the top of this page more effectively?

Answers: (1) concrete-operational, (2) formal-operational, (3) the formal-operational stage is portrayed as the final stage of intellectual development, (4) determined the goal of the memory task, (5) monitoring

APTITUDES FOR SCHOOL

Aptitudes for School

Binet and the Development of Testing

Do Tests Work?

The Elements of Intelligence

The Impact of Race, Ethnicity, and
Social Class

Hereditary and Environmental Factors

Learning Objectives

- **Why were intelligence tests first developed? What are their features?**
- **How well do intelligence tests work?**
- **What is the nature of intelligence?**
- **How and why do test scores vary for different racial and ethnic groups?**
- **How do heredity and environment influence intelligence?**

*C*HARLENE, *an African American third-grader, received a score of 75 on an intelligence test administered by a school psychologist. Based on the test score, the psychologist believes that Charlene is mildly mentally retarded and should receive special education. Charlene's parents are indignant; they believe that the tests are biased against African Americans, so the score is meaningless.*

American schools faced a crisis at the beginning of the 20th century. Between 1890 and 1915, school enrollment nearly doubled nationally, because of an influx of immigrants and because reforms restricted child labor and emphasized education (Chapman, 1988). With the increased enrollment, teachers were confronted by ever greater numbers of students who did not learn as readily as the "select few" students who had populated their classes previously. How to deal with "feebleminded" children was one of the pressing issues of the day for U.S. educators.

BINET AND THE DEVELOPMENT OF INTELLIGENCE TESTING

These problems were not unique to the United States. In 1904, the Minister of Public Instruction in France asked two noted psychologists of the day, Alfred Binet and Theophile Simon, to formulate a way to recognize children who would be unable to learn in school without special instruction. Binet and Simon's approach was to select simple tasks that French children of different ages ought to be able to do, such as naming colors, counting backward, and remembering numbers in order. Based on preliminary testing, Binet and Simon identified problems that normal 3-year-olds could solve, that normal 4-year-olds could solve, and so on. *Children's* mental age *or* MA *referred to the difficulty of the problems they could solve correctly.* A child who solved problems that the average 7-year-old could solve would have an MA of 7.

Binet and Simon used mental age to distinguish "bright" from "dull" children. A "bright" child would have the MA of an older child—for example, a 6-year-old with an MA of 9. A "dull" child would have the MA of a younger child—for example, a 6-year-old with an MA of 4. Binet and Simon confirmed that "bright" children identified using their test did better in school than "dull" children. Voilà—the first objective measure of intelligence!

The Stanford-Binet

Lewis Terman, of Stanford University, revised Binet and Simon's test substantially and published a version known as the Stanford-Binet in 1916. *Terman described performance as an* intelligence quotient, *or* IQ, *which was simply the ratio of mental age to chronological age, multiplied by 100:*

$$IQ = MA/CA \times 100$$

At any age, children who are perfectly average have an IQ of 100, because their mental age equals their chronological age. Furthermore, roughly two-thirds of children taking a test will have IQ scores between 85 and 115. The IQ score can also be used to compare intelligence in children of different ages. A 4-year-old girl with an MA of 5 has an IQ of 125 (5/4 × 100), just like that of an 8-year-old boy with an MA of 10 (10/8 × 100).

IQ scores are no longer computed in this manner. Instead, children's IQ scores are determined by comparing their test performance to that of others their age. When children perform at the average for their age, their IQ is 100. Children who perform above the average have IQs greater than 100; children who perform below the average have IQs less than 100. Nevertheless, the concept of IQ as the ratio of MA to CA helped to popularize the Stanford-Binet test.

By the 1920s, the Stanford-Binet had been joined by many other intelligence tests. Educators greeted these new devices enthusiastically, for they seemed to offer an efficient and objective way to assess a student's chances of succeeding in school (Chapman, 1988).

At this point, you're probably wondering why we've spent so much time discussing a test that is more than 75 years old. The reason is that the Stanford-Binet has more than historical value; it remains a popular test. The Stanford-Binet, last revised in 1986, along with the Wechsler Intelligence Scale for Children-III (WISC-III) and the Kaufman Assessment Battery for Children (K-ABC), are the primary individualized tests of intelligence in use today.

DO TESTS WORK?

To answer this question, two separate issues are important. First, we need to know whether a test is reliable, which means that it yields scores that are consistent. Reliability is often measured by administering similar forms of a test on two occasions. On a reliable test, a person will have similar scores on both occasions. In fact, modern intelligence tests are quite reliable. If a child takes an intelligence test and then retakes it days or a few weeks later, the two scores are usually quite similar (Wechsler, 1991).

What do these scores *mean?* Are they really measuring intelligence? These questions raise the issue of validity, which refers to the extent to which a test really measures what it claims to measure. Validity is usually assessed by determining the relation between test scores and other, independent measures of the construct that the test is thought to measure. For example, to measure the validity of a test of extroversion, we would first have children take the test. Then we would observe these same youngsters in some social setting, such as during a school recess, and record who is outgoing and who is shy. The test would be valid if scores correlated highly with our independent observations of extroverted behavior.

How can this approach be extended to intelligence tests? Ideally, we would administer the intelligence tests and then correlate the scores with other, independent estimates of intelligence. Therein lies the problem. There are no other

? THINK ABOUT IT

If Jean Piaget were to create an intelligence test, how would it differ from the type of test that Binet created?

independent ways to estimate intelligence; the only way to measure intelligence is with tests. Consequently, many follow Binet's lead and obtain measures of performance in school, such as grades or teachers' ratings of their students. The correlations between these measures and scores on intelligence tests typically fall somewhere between .4 and .6 (Neisser et al., 1996). For example, the correlation between scores on the WISC-III and grade-point average is .47 (Wechsler, 1991). That is, children with high scores on the WISC-III tend to get better grades. However, the correlation is far from perfect, which means that some youngsters with high test scores do not excel in school, whereas others with low scores get good grades. In general, however, tests do a reasonable job of predicting school success.

Does this mean that intelligence tests are synonymous with intelligence? Probably not. Tests measure intellectual skills, like verbal ability and abstract reasoning, that are important for success in school. However, tests are less effective in predicting success outside of school (Sternberg et al., 1995). Why? They were not designed to assess skills important for on-the-job success, such as practical problem-solving ability and interpersonal skills. Consequently, it is fair to conclude that current intelligence tests are reasonably valid primarily for measuring those components of intelligence that are required for achievement in school.

Can you think of other elements of intelligence that are not included in traditional tests? Let's see whether they're included in newer theories of intelligence.

THE ELEMENTS OF INTELLIGENCE

If verbal ability and abstract reasoning are only some of the elements of intelligence, what are the others? According to Howard Gardner's (1993, 1995) *theory of multiple intelligences,* intelligence includes seven distinct components:

- *Linguistic intelligence* includes knowing the meaning of words, the ability to use words to understand new ideas, and using language to convey ideas to others.
- *Logical-mathematical intelligence* includes understanding relations that exist among objects, actions, or ideas and the logical or mathematical operations that can be performed on these.
- *Spatial intelligence* is the ability to imagine the appearance of an object (e.g., a poodle) and to transform the appearance of an object mentally (the poodle acquires pink polka dots and stands on its nose).
- *Musical intelligence* is the ability to comprehend or produce sounds varying in pitch, rhythm, and emotional tone.
- *Bodily-kinesthetic intelligence* is the ability to use one's body (or parts of it) in highly differentiated ways, as do dancers, craftspeople, and athletes.
- *Interpersonal intelligence* involves identifying different feelings, moods, motivations, and intentions in others.
- *Intrapersonal intelligence* involves understanding one's emotions and knowing one's strengths and weaknesses.

The first three elements are familiar because they are similar to intelligence as it has been assessed on tests for nearly a century. But the last four elements are unique to Gardner's theory and stretch traditional, school-based definitions of intelligence. According to Gardner, a talented musician is showing intelligence as is the skilled athlete, the sensitive, caring child, and the high school sophomore who writes well.

Gardner (1993) argues that his theory has important implications for education. He believes that schools should foster all intelligences, not just the linguistic and logical-mathematical intelligences that have been important traditionally. Most children are particularly strong in some intelligences and teachers should capitalize on these strengths. Some students may best understand unfamiliar cultures, for example, by studying their music while other students, like those in the photo, may understand these cultures by studying their dance.

Some American schools use Gardner's ideas enthusiastically (Gardner, 1993). Are these schools better? We don't really know because school performance is usually evaluated with tests and there aren't acceptable tests to evaluate progress in the areas covered by Gardner's theory. At this point, researchers are still evaluating the theory and the educational reforms it has inspired. However, there is no doubt that Gardner's work *has* helped liberate researchers from narrow views of intelligence.

Another groundbreaking view of intelligence is Robert Sternberg's (1985) *triarchic theory,* which includes three subtheories:

- According to the *contextual* subtheory, intelligent behavior must always be considered in the context of the individual's culture. Intelligence involves adapting to that culture in order to achieve one's goals.

- According to the *experiential* subtheory, intelligence is revealed in different ways, depending on the familiarity of the task. For a novel task, intelligence is associated with the ability to apply one's existing knowledge to a new situation; for familiar tasks, intelligence is associated with being able to finish the task with little mental effort.

- According to the *componential* subtheory, intelligent behavior involves organizing basic cognitive processes into an efficient strategy for completing a task.

In contrast to most approaches to intelligence, Sternberg's does not concentrate on identifying specific domains of intelligence. Instead, the triarchic theory emphasizes that intelligence depends on the strategies that people use to complete tasks (the componential subtheory), the familiarity of those tasks (the experiential subtheory), and the relevance of the tasks to personal and cultural goals (the contextual subtheory).

The triarchic theory also pinpoints a profound problem. Look around you. Do you share the same experiences and cultural background with every one of your classmates? If you don't, should you compare your score on an intelligence test with others' scores? Comparing test scores for different cultural groups is a controversial practice, as we see in the next section.

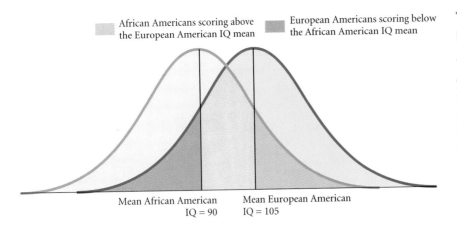

African Americans scoring above the European American IQ mean

European Americans scoring below the African American IQ mean

Mean African American IQ = 90

Mean European American IQ = 105

THE IMPACT OF RACE, ETHNICITY, AND SOCIAL CLASS

The results in this graph have been the source of controversy for decades. On many intelligence tests, the average score of African Americans is about 15 points lower than that of European Americans (Neisser et al., 1996). Why? Some of the difference is due to social class. Typically, children from lower social classes have lower scores on intelligence tests, and African American children are more likely than European American children to live in lower-class homes. When European and African American children of comparable social class are compared, the difference in IQ test scores is reduced but not eliminated (Brooks-Gunn, Klebanov & Duncan, 1996). So, social class explains some but not all of the difference between European and African American children's IQ scores.

Some critics contend that the difference in test scores reflects bias in the tests themselves (Neisser et al., 1996). They argue that test items reflect the cultural heritage of the test creators—most of whom are middle-class European Americans—and so tests are biased against lower-class and African American children. They point to test items like this one:

A conductor is to an orchestra as a teacher is to what?
book   school   class   eraser

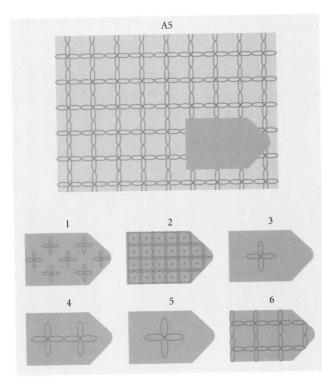

Children whose background includes exposure to orchestras are more likely to answer this question correctly than children who lack this exposure.

The problem of bias has led to the development of culture-fair *intelligence tests, which include test items that are based on experiences common to many cultures.* An example is Raven's Progressive Matrices, which consists solely of items like the one shown here. Examinees are asked to select the piece that would complete the design correctly (6, in this case). Culture-fair tests do predict achievement in school, but do not eliminate group differences in test scores: European and African Americans still differ (Anastasi, 1988; Herrnstein & Murray, 1994). Why? Culture can influence a child's familiarity with the entire testing situation, not simply familiarity with particular items. A culture-fair test will underestimate a child's intelligence if, for example, the child's culture encourages children to solve problems in collaboration with others and discourages them from excelling as individuals.

Moreover, because of their wariness of questions posed by unfamiliar adults, some children—

especially African American and economically disadvantaged children—often answer many test questions by saying, "I don't know." Obviously, this strategy guarantees an artificially low test score. When these children are given extra time to become at ease with the examiner, they often abandon the "I don't know" approach and their test scores increase (Boykin, 1994; Zigler & Finn-Stevenson, 1992).

If all test scores reflect cultural influences, at least to some degree, how should we interpret test scores? Remember that tests assess successful adaptation to a particular cultural context; they are less valid in other contexts. Most intelligence tests predict success in a school environment that often encompasses middle-class values. Tests do so for African American, Asian American, Hispanic American, and Native American students as well as for European American students. Regardless of their racial or ethnic group, children with low test scores are usually not destined for success in school. The low score reported for Charlene, the African American third-grader in the vignette, means that at this time she probably lacks the skills to succeed in school—nothing more and nothing less.

Outside of school, test scores are less useful; intelligence tests measure "school smarts," not "street smarts" (Sternberg et al., 1995). Consequently, when one group has higher average scores than another, this means that one group has more of the specific skills that are critical for success in the middle-class school environment, not that they have more of some pervasive general-purpose ability called intelligence.

By focusing, as we have, on groups of people, it's easy to lose sight of the fact that individuals *within* these groups differ in intelligence. Look again at the graph on page 214; you'll see that the average difference in IQ scores between European Americans and African Americans is small compared to the entire range of scores for these groups. What causes individuals within groups to differ? We'll see in the next section.

HEREDITARY AND ENVIRONMENTAL FACTORS

Joanna, a 5-year-old girl, was administered the WISC-III and obtained a score of 112. Ted, a 5-year-old boy, took the same test and received a score of 92. What can account for the 20-point difference in scores? Heredity and experience both matter (Ferrari & Sternberg, 1998). Some of the evidence for hereditary factors is shown in the graph. If genes influence intelligence, then

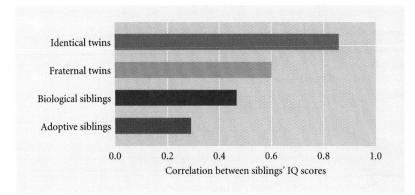

Based on data in Bouchard and McGue, 1981.

siblings' test scores should become more alike as siblings become more similar genetically. Identical twins are identical genetically, and they typically have virtually identical test scores, which would be a correlation of 1.0. Fraternal twins have about 50% of their genes in common, just like nontwins who have the same biological parents. Consequently, their test scores should be (a) less similar than scores for identical twins, (b) as similar as other siblings who have the same biological parents, and (c) more similar than those of children and their adopted siblings. You can see in the graph that each of these predictions is supported (Bouchard et al., 1990).

Studies of adopted children also show the impact of heredity. If heredity helps determine IQ, then children's IQs should be more like their biological parents' IQs than their adoptive parents' IQs. In fact, as adopted children like

the ones in the photograph grow, their test scores are more like their biological parents' scores and less like their adoptive parents' scores (Plomin et al., 1997). That is, adopted youngsters with high test scores have biological parents with high test scores but not necessarily adoptive parents with high test scores.

Environment does, however, contribute to intelligence. Children with high test scores typically have parents who are stimulating, responsive, and involved (Bradley, Caldwell, & Rock, 1988). In addition, among European American children, an environment that includes plenty of variety and appropriate play materials is linked to high test scores; among African American children, a well-organized home environment is associated with higher scores (Bradley et al., 1989).

The importance of a stimulating environment for intelligence is also demonstrated by intervention projects designed to prepare economically disadvantaged children for school (Neisser et al., 1996). When children grow up in never-ending poverty, the cycle is predictable and tragic: Youngsters have few of the intellectual skills to succeed in school, so they fail; lacking an education, they find minimal jobs (if they can work at all), guaranteeing that their children, too, are destined to grow up in poverty. Since Project Head Start was begun in 1965 by President Lyndon Johnson as part of his War on Poverty, massive educational intervention has been an important tool in the effort to break this repeated cycle of poverty. Intervention programs for preschool youngsters typically include an elaborate, structured curriculum for both children and their parents (Ramey & Ramey, 1990). When children participate in these enrichment programs, their test scores increase by about 10 points (Clarke & Clarke, 1989). In the Spotlight on Research feature, we look at one of these success stories in detail.

SPOTLIGHT ON RESEARCH   THE CAROLINA ABECEDARIAN PROJECT

What was the aim of the study and who were the investigators? Since the 1960s, many intervention programs have demonstrated that young children's intelligence test scores can be raised with enrichment, but the improvement is often short-lived. That is, within a few years after completing the intervention program, children's test scores are at the same level as before they participated in the program. Campbell and Ramey (Campbell & Ramey, 1994; Ramey & Campbell, 1991) designed their project, the Carolina Abecedarian Project, to see whether massive and sustained intervention could produce more long-lasting changes.

How did the investigators measure the topic of interest? Some children did not participate in any intervention program. Other children attended a special day care facility daily from 4 months until 5 years of age. The curriculum emphasized mental, linguistic, and social development for infants and prereading skills for preschoolers. Some children also participated in another intervention program during their first three years of elementary school. During this phase, a teacher visited the home a few times each month, bringing materials for improving reading and math. The teachers taught parents how to use the materials with their child and also acted as a facilitator between home and school.

Campbell and Ramey measured the impact of intervention in several ways, including scores on intelligence tests, scores on achievement tests, and children's need for special services in school.

Who were the children in the study? At the start, the project included 111 children; most were born to African American mothers who had less than a high school education, an average IQ score of 85, and on average, no income. Over the course of the study, 21 children dropped out of the project, leaving 90 children at the end.

What was the design of the study? This study was experimental because children were randomly assigned to an intervention condition (preschool intervention, elementary school intervention, both, or no intervention). The independent variable was the intervention condition. The dependent variables included performance on intelligence and achievement tests. The study was longitudinal because children were tested repeatedly over an 8-year period.

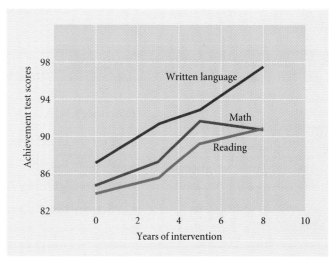

Based on data from Campbell and Ramey, 1994.

Were there ethical concerns with the study? No. The nature of the study was explained fully to parents, including the assignment of their child to a specific intervention condition.

What were the results? The graph shows performance on three achievement tests that children took as 12-year-olds, 4 years after the school-age intervention had ended. In all three areas tested—written language, math, and reading—performance clearly reflects the amount of intervention. Youngsters who had a full 8 years of intervention generally have the highest scores; children with no intervention have the lowest scores.

What did the investigators conclude? Massive, continued intervention works. An improvement of 7–10 points may not strike you as very much, but it *is* a substantial improvement from a practical standpoint. For example, the Written Language scores of the youngsters with 8 years of intervention place them near the 50th percentile, meaning that their scores are greater than about half of the children taking the test. In contrast, children with no intervention have scores at the 20th percentile, making their scores greater than only 20% of the children taking the test. Thus, with intervention, children were able to move from being substantially below average to average, quite an accomplishment. ●

Of course, massive intervention over 8 years is expensive. But so are the economic consequences of poverty, unemployment, and their by-products. Programs like the Abecedarian Project show that the repetitive cycle of school failure and education can be broken. And, in the process, they show that intelligence is fostered by an environment that is stimulating and responsive.

TEST YOURSELF

1. Binet devised his tests to identify children _____ .

2. IQ was first defined as the ratio of _____ × 100.

3. A test is _____ if it yields consistent scores.

4. The validity of intelligence tests is often documented by showing that test scores are correlated with _____ .

5. Sternberg's triarchic theory includes contextual, _____ , and componential subtheories.

6. Children from various racial and ethnic groups sometimes receive lower scores on intelligence tests because items on the test _____ .

7. When children participate in intervention programs, their scores on intelligence tests _____ .

8. How do the subtheories of Sternberg's triarchic theory illustrate the different forces in the biopsychosocial framework?

Answers: (1) who would have difficulty learning in school, (2) mental age to chronological age (MA/CA), (3) reliable, (4) success in school, (5) experiential, (6) assess experiences that are not part of their culture, (7) often increase, by about 10 points

---

SPECIAL CHILDREN, SPECIAL NEEDS

Special Children, Special Needs

Gifted and Creative Children

Children with Mental Retardation

Children with Learning Disability

Attention-Deficit Hyperactivity Disorder

Learning Objectives

- **What are the characteristics of gifted and creative children?**
- **What are the different forms of mental retardation?**
- **What is a learning disability?**
- **What are the distinguishing features of hyperactivity?**

SANJIT, *a second-grader, has taken two separate intelligence tests, and both times he had above-average scores. His parents took him to an ophthalmologist, who determined that his vision is 20-30—nothing wrong with his eyes. Nevertheless, Sanjit absolutely cannot read. Letters and words are as mysterious to him as Metallica's music would be to Mozart. What is wrong?*

Throughout history, societies have recognized children with unusual abilities and talents. Today, we know much about the extremes of human skill. Let's begin with a glimpse at gifted and creative children.

GIFTED AND CREATIVE CHILDREN

In many respects the boy in the photo, Bernie, is an ordinary middle-class 12-year-old: He is the goalie on his soccer team, takes piano lessons on Saturday mornings, sings in his church youth choir, and likes to go roller-blading. However, when it comes to intelligence and academic prowess, Bernie leaves the ranks of the ordinary—he's gifted. He received a score of 175 on an intelligence test and is taking a college calculus course.

Traditionally, giftedness was defined by scores on intelligence tests: a score of 130 or greater was the criterion for being gifted. Today, however, definitions of giftedness are broader and include exceptional talent in an assortment of areas, such as art, music, creative writing, and dance (Reis & Renzulli, 1995).

Exceptional talent—whether defined solely by IQ scores or more broadly—seems to have several prerequisites (Feldman & Goldsmith, 1991; Rathunde & Csikszentmihalyi, 1993):

- the child's love for the subject and overwhelming desire to master it
- instruction, beginning at an early age, with inspiring and talented teachers
- support and help from parents, who are committed to promoting their child's talent

The message here is that exceptional talent must be nurtured. Without encouragement and support from stimulating and challenging mentors, a youngster's talents will wither, not flourish. Talented children need a curriculum that is challenging and complex; they need teachers who know how to foster talent; and they need like-minded peers who stimulate their interests (Feldhusen, 1996).

What of the stereotype that gifted children are emotionally troubled and unable to get along with their peers? Bernie doesn't seem to fit this stereotype and, in fact, research discredits the stereotype of gifted people as distressed and socially inept. Actually, gifted youngsters tend to be more mature than their peers and to have fewer emotional problems (Luthar, Zigler, & Goldstein, 1992).

Creativity

If you've seen the movie *Amadeus,* you know the difference between being talented and being creative. Mozart and Salieri were rival composers in Europe during the 18th century. Both were talented, ambitious musicians. Yet, more than 200 years later, Mozart's work is revered but Salieri's is all but forgotten. Why? Then and now, Mozart's work was recognized as creative, but Salieri's was not.

What is creativity and how does it differ from intelligence? *Intelligence is often associated with* convergent thinking, *which means using the information provided to determine a standard, correct answer. In contrast, creativity is often linked to* divergent thinking, *in which the aim is not a single correct answer (often there isn't one) but instead to think in novel and unusual directions* (Guilford, 1967).

Divergent thinking is often measured by asking children to produce a large number of ideas in response to some specific stimulus (Kogan, 1983). Children might be asked to name different uses for a common object, such as a coat hanger. Or they might be shown a page filled with circles and asked to draw as many different pictures as they can, as shown in the figure. Both the number of responses and their originality are used to measure creativity.

Creativity, like giftedness, must be cultivated. Youngsters are more likely to be creative when their home and school environments value nonconformity and encourage children to be curious. When schools, for example, emphasize mastery of factual material and discourage self-expression and exploration, creativity usually suffers (Thomas & Berk, 1981). In contrast, creativity can be enhanced by experiences that stimulate children to be flexible in their thinking and to explore alternatives (Starko, 1988).

Gifted and creative children represent one extreme of human ability. Who are at the other extreme? Youngsters with mental retardation, the topic of the next section.

CHILDREN WITH MENTAL RETARDATION

"Little David" was the oldest of four children. He learned to sit days before his first birthday, he began to walk at 2, and said his first words as a 3-year-old. At 5 years of age, David's development was far behind that of his age-mates. A century ago, David would have been called "feebleminded" or "mentally defective." In fact, David had Down syndrome, which we first described in Chapter 2 (see pages 51–52). David had an extra 21st chromosome; as a consequence of this extra gene, David experienced retarded mental development.

Mental retardation *refers to substantially below-average intelligence and problems adapting to an environment that emerge before the age of 18.* Below-average intelligence is defined as a score of 70 or less on an intelligence test such as the Stanford-Binet. Adaptive behavior is usually evaluated from interviews with a parent or other caregiver and refers to those daily living skills needed to live, work, and play in the community, such as skills for caring for oneself and social skills. Only individuals who are under 18 and have problems in these areas *and* IQ scores of 70 or less are considered mentally retarded (Baumeister & Baumeister, 1995).

? THINK ABOUT IT
How might our definitions of giftedness and mental retardation differ if they were based on Robert Sternberg's triarchic theory?

Types of Mental Retardation

Your image of a child with mental retardation may be someone with Down syndrome, like the child shown on page 52. In reality, individuals with mental retardation are just as varied as are people without retardation. How should we describe this variety? One approach is to distinguish the causes of mental retardation (Baumeister & Baumeister, 1995). *Some cases of mental retardation—no more than 25%—can be traced to a specific biological or physical problem and are known as* organic mental retardation. Down syndrome is the most common organic form of mental retardation. Other forms of organic mental retardation can be linked to the teratogens described in Chapter 2. Other types of mental retardation apparently do not involve biological damage. Familial mental retardation *simply represents the lower end of the normal distribution of intelligence.*

Varieties of mental retardation are also distinguished based on the person's level of functioning. The American Association on Mental Retardation identifies four levels of retardation. The levels, along with the range of IQ scores associated with each level, are shown in the chart. Also shown are the three levels of retardation typically used by educators in the United States (Cipani, 1991). The more extreme forms of mental

AAMR	Profound	Severe	Moderate	Mild	
IQ level	10 20 30	40 50	60	70	
Educators	Custodial	Trainable		Educable	

retardation—for example, profound, severe, and moderate in the AAMR system—are usually organic in origin; the less extreme forms are usually familial.

The most severe forms of mental retardation are, fortunately, relatively uncommon. Profound, severe, and moderate retardation together make up only 10% of all cases. Individuals with profound and severe retardation usually have so few skills that they must be supervised constantly. Consequently, they usually live in institutions where they can sometimes be taught self-help skills such as dressing, feeding, and toileting (Reid, Wilson, & Faw, 1991).

Persons with moderate retardation may develop the intellectual skills of a nonretarded 7- or 8-year-old. With this level of functioning, they sometimes find employment working on simple tasks under close supervision. They do not live independently, but receive care from relatives or in institutions (Editorial Board, 1996).

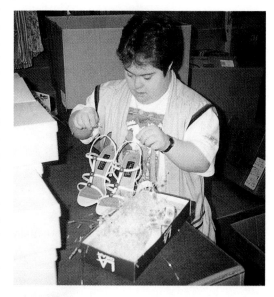

The remaining 90% of individuals with mental retardation are classified as mildly or educably mentally retarded. These individuals go to school and can master many academic skills, but at an older age than a nonretarded child. Individuals with mild mental retardation can lead independent lives. Like the man in the photograph, many mildly retarded people work. Some marry. Comprehensive training programs that focus on vocational and social skills help individuals with mild mental retardation be productive citizens and satisfied human beings (Baumeister & Baumeister, 1995).

The Real People feature describes the life of one person with mental retardation.

LITTLE DAVID—THE REST OF THE STORY

REAL PEOPLE

Little David—so named because his father was also David—was the oldest of four children; none of his siblings was mentally retarded. As the children grew up, they interacted the way most siblings do; they'd laugh and play together and sometimes fight and argue. Every day, beginning as a teenager and continuing into adulthood, David rode a city bus from home to his job at a sheltered workshop. He worked six hours daily, performing tasks such as making bows for packages and stuffing envelopes. He saved his earnings regularly and used them to buy what became his prized possessions—a camera, a color TV, and a VCR. As David's siblings entered adulthood, they began their own families. David relished his new role as "Uncle David" and looked forward to frequent visits from his nieces and nephews. As David entered his 40s, he began to suffer memory loss and was often confused. (These symptoms are common to Down syndrome adults during middle age; we'll discuss them in more detail in Chapter 13.) When he died, at age 47, family and friends grieved over their loss. Yet they all marveled at the richness of David's life; by any standards, he had led a full and satisfying life. •

Little David's mental retardation represents one end of the intelligence spectrum; Bernie's precocity represents the other. Falling between these two extremes are other special children: those who have learning disability.

CHILDREN WITH LEARNING DISABILITY

For some children with normal intelligence, learning is a struggle. *These youngsters suffer from* learning disability, *a term that refers to a child who (a) has difficulty mastering one or more academic subjects, (b) has normal intelligence, and*

(c) is not suffering from other conditions that could explain poor performance, such as sensory impairment or inadequate instruction (Lyon, 1996).

In the United States, about 5% of school-age children are classified as learning disabled, which translates into roughly 2 million affected youngsters (Moats & Lyon, 1993). The number of distinct disabilities and the degree of overlap among them is still hotly contested (Stanovich, 1993). However, one common classification scheme distinguishes disability in language (including listening, speaking, and writing), in reading, and in arithmetic (Dockrell & McShane, 1993).

The great number of learning disabilities complicates the task for teachers and researchers. It suggests that each type of learning disability may have its own cause and treatment (Lyon, 1996). Take reading as an example. *Many children with reading disability have problems in* phonological processing—*understanding and using the sounds in written and oral language.* For a reading-disabled child like Sanjit (in the vignette) or the boy in the photograph, all vowels sound alike. These youngsters benefit from explicit, extensive instruction on the connections between letters and their sounds (Lovett et al., 1994). In the case of arithmetic disability, children often have difficulty performing arithmetic operations correctly and reasoning through math problems (Fleishner, 1994; Lyon, 1996). Here, instruction emphasizes determining the goal of arithmetic problems, using the goals to select correct arithmetic operations, and using the operations accurately (Goldman, 1989).

The key to helping these children is to move beyond the generic label *learning disability* to pinpoint the specific cognitive and academic deficits that hamper an individual child's performance in school. With a precise account of these deficits, instruction can be planned to improve the child's skills (Moats & Lyon, 1993).

This is much easier said than done, because diagnosing learning disability remains so difficult. Some children have both reading and language disabilities; others have reading and arithmetic disabilities; still others have a learning disability and another problem, attention-deficit hyperactivity disorder, which we discuss next.

ATTENTION-DEFICIT HYPERACTIVITY DISORDER

Let's begin with a case study of Stuart, an 8-year-old.

> [His] mother reported that Stuart was overly active as an infant and toddler. His teachers found him difficult to control once he started school. He is described as extremely impulsive and distractible, moving tirelessly from one activity to the next. . . . His teacher reports that he is immature and restless, responds best in a structured, one-on-one situation, but is considered the class pest because he is continually annoying the other children and is disobedient. (Rapaport & Ismond, 1990, p. 120)

For many years, children like Stuart, who were restless and impulsive, were said to have "hyperactive child syndrome" (Barkley, 1996). In the 1960s and 1970s, researchers realized that these children often also had difficulty paying attention. By the 1980s, the disorder had been renamed, attention-deficit hyperactivity disorder (ADHD).

Roughly 3–5% of all school-age children are diagnosed with ADHD (Rapport, 1995); boys outnumber girls by a 3:1 ratio (Wicks-Nelson & Israel, 1991).

Three symptoms are at the heart of ADHD (Rapport, 1995):

- *Overactivity.* Children with ADHD are unusually energetic, fidgety, and unable to keep still, especially in situations where they need to limit their activity, such as school classrooms.

- *Inattention.* Youngsters with ADHD do not pay attention in class and seem unable to concentrate on schoolwork; instead, they skip from one task to another.

- *Impulsivity.* Children with ADHD often act before thinking; they may run into a street before looking for traffic or interrupt others who are already speaking.

Not all children with ADHD show all of these symptoms to the same degree. Some, like the boy in the photograph, may be primarily hyperactive. Others may be primarily impulsive and show no signs of hyperactivity; their disorder is often described simply as attention-deficit disorder (Barkley, 1990). Furthermore, symptoms are often not stable across settings. Some youngsters who are unable to maintain attention in school may sit still for hours playing a video game at home (Barkley, 1996).

In light of these inconsistencies, it probably won't surprise you that researchers disagree about the number of different subtypes of ADHD and the factors that give rise to ADHD (Barkley, 1996). However, it *is* clear that children with ADHD often have problems in conduct and in their academic performance. Like Stuart, many hyperactive children are aggressive and therefore are not liked by their peers (Barkley, 1990; McGee, Williams, & Feehan, 1992). Although youngsters with ADHD usually have normal intelligence, their scores on reading, spelling, and arithmetic achievement tests are often below average (Pennington, Groisser, & Welsh, 1993).

One myth about ADHD is that most children "grow out of it" in adolescence or young adulthood. More than half the children who are diagnosed with ADHD will have, as adolescents and young adults, problems related to overactivity, inattention, and impulsivity. Few of these young adults complete college and some will have work- and family-related problems (Fischer et al., 1993; Rapport, 1995).

Causes

Many parents believe that too much sugar or food additives cause their children to become "hyper." In fact, except for a few children who are allergic to food dyes or overly sensitive to sugar, research provides no support for a connection between children's diet and ADHD (Wolraich et al., 1994). Others have linked ADHD to lead poisoning. Although lead poisoning does put a child at somewhat greater risk for ADHD, most children with lead poisoning do not have ADHD, and most children with ADHD do not have lead poisoning (Barkley, 1996).

The primary causes of ADHD lie elsewhere. Heredity contributes; identical twins both have ADHD more often than do fraternal twins (Edelbrock et al., 1995). In addition, the overactive, inattentive, impulsive behaviors characteristic of children with ADHD force some parents to resort to less effective child-rearing techniques. That is, children with ADHD are often more defiant and less compliant; over time, their parents (particularly their mothers) become more directive, less responsive, and less rewarding (Danforth et al., 1991; Gomez & Sanson, 1994).

The Forces in Action feature shows how all of these factors must be considered in treating ADHD.

FORCES IN ACTION   **TREATING ADHD**

ADHD has its roots in the biological, psychological, and social forces of the biopsychosocial framework. Some children seemingly inherit a predisposition for the disorder (biological force). Their inattentive and impulsive thinking style (psychological factor) makes parents and teachers treat children with ADHD differently (sociocultural force).

Responding to the biological bases, many physicians prescribe stimulant drugs, such as Ritalin, for children with ADHD. Are you surprised that stimulants are given to children who are already overactive? Paradoxically, stimulants actually calm many of these youngsters, allowing them to focus their attention (Rapport, 1995).

Medication does not, by itself, improve children's performance in school, because it doesn't affect psychological and social influences. Consequently, children with ADHD need to learn to regulate their behavior and attention more effectively, so they can complete schoolwork. And people in their support network—their parents and teachers—need to learn techniques that facilitate their child's learning these behaviors. Teachers can reward children for staying "on task" and not behaving impulsively (Rapport, 1995), and parents can encourage attention and goal-oriented behavior at home (Anastopoulos et al., 1993). When parents reinforce children for paying attention and punish them for being inattentive, children show fewer symptoms of ADHD.

Thus, effective treatment of ADHD addresses the biological, psychological, and sociocultural contributions to the disorder. Such comprehensive treatment enables children with ADHD to become more attentive and to improve their schoolwork (Carlson et al., 1992). •

TEST YOURSELF

1. A problem with defining giftedness solely in terms of IQ scores is that _____ .

2. Creativity is associated with _____ thinking, in which the goal is to think in novel and unusual directions.

3. Cases of _____ mental retardation can be linked to specific biological or physical problems.

4. Individuals who are _____ mentally retarded often go to school, have jobs, and marry.

5. The most common forms of learning disability are _____ .

6. Key symptoms of attention-deficit hyperactivity disorder are overactivity, _____ , and impulsivity.

7. ADHD can be treated effectively by administering stimulant drugs, teaching children how to regulate their attention, and _____ .

8. How might Jean Piaget have explained differences between retarded and nonretarded children's intellectual functioning? How might an information-processing psychologist explain these differences?

LEARNING IN SCHOOL

Learning Objectives

- **How effectively do U.S. schools educate their students?**
- **What are the hallmarks of effective schools and effective teachers?**

Learning in School

Grading U.S. Schools

Effective Schools, Effective Teachers

WALLY *picked up the morning paper and saw the front-page headline, "U.S. students trail industrial world in math skills." Wally has seen many similar headlines and he wonders whether the situation is really as bad as newspapers make it seem. His 10-year-old son can read okay and can add and subtract, so what's the big deal? In his more cynical moments, Wally suspects that this is just a bunch of hype so that educators can take more of his hard-earned wages for schools.*

You, too, have probably read headlines like the one that caught Wally's attention. They're hard to miss—seemingly, they appear almost weekly. And maybe your response was like his—doubting that American schools and American students are really in such bad shape.

In this section, we evaluate U.S. schools and the students who attend them. As we do, you'll learn whether American schools are as ineffective as the headlines seem to imply. Next, we'll look at some of the characteristics that make some schools and some teachers better than others.

GRADING U.S. SCHOOLS

How would you decide whether U.S. schools are doing well or poorly? One approach is to compare students in the United States to students in other countries. Many studies of this sort have been done in recent years; one of the most comprehensive is the Third International Math and Science Study (1997), which compared math and science achievement of students in 41 different countries. The results for math, shown in the figure, reveal that U.S. fourth- and eighth-graders score substantially lower than students in the leading nations. Phrased another way, the very best U.S. students only perform at the level of average students in Asian countries like Singapore and Korea.

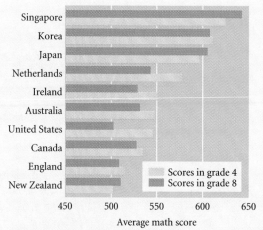

Based on data from the Third International Math and Science Study, 1997.

Many critics doubt these results. They contend that U.S. schools educate students with a wide range of abilities, not just the elite as in some other countries. Consequently, the critics say, U.S. scores just *look* lower because they are based on all students, not just the very best.

If this criticism were valid, differences should be small in elementary school, because these schools are not selective. (In industrialized countries, nearly all young children attend elementary school.) However, the results are the same: U.S. students trail students in other countries, beginning as early as first grade (Geary, 1996; Stevenson & Lee, 1990).

But, international comparisons are not the only way to evaluate U.S. students. Another approach is to ask, "How well educated are the products of U.S. schools?" That is, how literate are today's high school graduates? To answer these questions, we need to define what it means to be literate. During the 19th century, you were literate if you could print your own name. By World War II, you were literate if you had a fourth-grade education. *Today*, literacy is *"using printed and written information to function in society, to achieve one's goals, and to develop one's knowledge and potential"* (Kirsch et al., 1993, p. 2). Literacy includes understanding newspapers and magazines as well as comprehending documents such as tables, schedules, and applications, and quantitative material such as bank statements and pay stubs.

Using this modern definition, how do North American students fare? The best answer comes from the *National Adult Literacy Survey* (Kirsch et al., 1993), which included a nationally representative sample of 13,000 U.S. adults. Each was administered a series of problems designed to assess prose, document, and quantitative literacy. Performance was scored on a scale that ranged from 0 to 500, with larger numbers indicating greater literacy.

The graph shows average literacy levels for African American, Hispanic American, and European American high school graduates. European Americans tend to score about 15% higher than African Americans and Hispanic Americans, and all groups have average scores in the middle 200s. To understand the approximate level of skill represented by this number, let's look at specific items from the different scales.

? THINK ABOUT IT
How would a definition of literacy differ if it were based on Howard Gardner's theory of multiple intelligences? On Jean Piaget's theory?

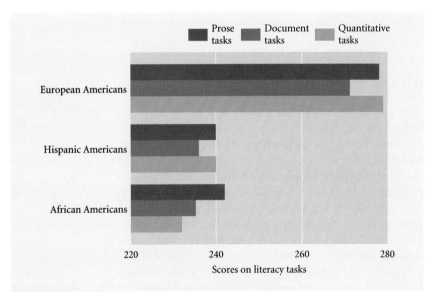

Based on data from the National Adult Literacy Survey (Kirsch et al., 1993).

- On the *prose* tasks, the average high school graduate can underline a sentence that explains the action in a short article but cannot write a brief letter that adequately explains an error on a credit-card statement.

- On the *document* tasks, the average high school graduate can locate an intersection on a map but cannot look at a bar graph to determine relative quantities.

- On the *quantitative* tasks, the average high school graduate can complete a bank deposit statement but cannot use a bus schedule to calculate the time to travel from one stop to another.

By traditional standards, the vast majority of all three groups *are* literate. Yet many critics contend that by modern standards, although high school graduates in the United States are not illiterate, they need to be more literate. Clerical workers like the woman in the photo must know much more than how to type: They must work with a variety of software—word processing and spreadsheets, for example—that continuously becomes more complex. Too often, today's workers fall short. For example, U.S. businesses report spending more than $25 billion annually in remedial training for new employees (Kearns, 1989). More direct evidence comes from analyses of the literacy requirements of specific jobs. Some analyses suggest that literacy scores of 300 or greater are needed for professional, technical, managerial, clerical, and sales positions (Barton & Kirsch, 1990). Jobs of this sort are vital to the economy—and will probably become more so—yet only about one-third of U.S. high school graduates achieve this level of literacy (Kirsch et al., 1993).

When international studies are combined with studies of literacy in U.S. high school graduates, the message is clear: American schools are not as successful as they need to be. Contrary to Wally's suspicions, there are solid reasons to be concerned.

How can U.S. students achieve greater literacy? Studies of effective schools and effective teachers suggest several answers, as you'll see in the next section.

EFFECTIVE SCHOOLS, EFFECTIVE TEACHERS

Because education is run locally in the United States, American education is a smorgasbord. Schools differ on many dimensions, including their emphasis on academic goals and the involvement of parents. Teachers, too, differ in many ways, such as how they run their classrooms and how they teach. These and other variables do affect student achievement, as you'll see in the next few pages. Let's begin with school-based influences.

School-Based Influences on Student Achievement

Roosevelt High School, in the center of Detroit, has an enrollment of 3,500 students in grades 9–12. Opened in 1936, the building shows its age. The rooms are drafty, the desks are decorated with generations of graffiti, and new technology means an overhead projector. Nevertheless, attendance at Roosevelt is good. Most students graduate and many continue their education at community colleges and state universities. Southport High School, in Newark, has about the same enrollment as Roosevelt High and the building is about the same age. Yet, truancy is commonplace at Southport, where fewer than half the students graduate and almost none go to college.

Although these schools are hypothetical, they accurately depict a common outcome in America. Some schools are much more successful than others, whether success is defined in terms of the percentage of students who are literate, graduate, or go to college. Why? Researchers (Good & Brophy, 1994; Stevenson & Stigler, 1992; Walberg, 1995) have identified a number of characteristics of schools where students typically succeed rather than fail:

- *Staff and students alike understand that academic excellence is the primary goal of the school and of every student in the school.* The school day emphasizes instruction (not simply filling time from 8:30 to 3:30 with nonacademic activities), and students are recognized publicly for their academic accomplishments.

- *The school climate is safe and nurturant.* Students know that they can devote their energy to learning (instead of worrying about being harmed in school) and that the staff truly cares that they succeed.

- *Parents are involved.* In some cases, this may be through formal arrangements, such as parent-teacher organizations. Or it may be informal. Parents may spend some time each week in school grading papers or, like the dad in the photo, tutoring a child. Such involvement signals both teachers and students that parents are committed to students' success.

- *Progress of students, teachers, and programs is monitored.* The only way to know whether schools are succeeding is by measuring performance. Students, teachers, and programs need to be evaluated regularly, using objective measures that reflect academic goals.

In schools where these guidelines are followed regularly, students usually succeed. In schools where the guidelines are ignored, students more often fail.

Some educators argue that schools should take greater advantage of technology—primarily computers—to improve instruction. Opponents believe that computers remove the all-important human factor from learning. The Current Controversies feature examines this issue.

CURRENT CONTROVERSIES

INFOTRAC
COLLEGE EDITION

To learn more, enter the following search term: technology in the classroom.

COMPUTERS IN THE CLASSROOM

New technologies—whether TV, videotape, or pocket calculator—soon find their way into the classroom. Personal computers are no exception; virtually all American public schools now use personal computers to aid instruction. A primary function of computers in the schools is as a tutor (Lepper & Gurtner, 1989). Children use computers to learn reading, spelling, arithmetic, science, and social studies. Computers allow instruction to be individualized and interactive. Students proceed at their own pace, receiving feedback and help when necessary.

Computers are also valuable as a medium for experiential learning (Lepper & Gurtner, 1989). Simulation programs allow students to explore the world in ways that would be impossible or dangerous otherwise. Students can change the law of gravity or see what happens to a city when no taxes are imposed.

Finally, the computer is a multipurpose tool that can help students achieve traditional academic goals (Steelman, 1994). A graphics program enables artistically untalented students to produce beautiful illustrations. A word-processing program relieves much of the drudgery associated with revising, thereby encouraging better writing.

Not all parents and teachers are enthusiastic about computers in classrooms. Some critics fear that computers eliminate an important human element in learning. To some, ". . . a classroom in which children spend the day plugged into their own individual desktop computers seems a chilling spectacle" (Lepper & Gurtner, 1989, p. 172). Many worry that computers isolate students from each other and from the teacher and make learning a solitary activity. In reality, students interact with each other more when computers are introduced into the classroom, not less (Pozzi, Healy, & Hoyles, 1993). As the photo shows, students often cluster around one student as he or she works and they often consult the class "expert" on a particular program. Teachers, freed from many of the drill-type tasks that now occupy the school day, can turn their attention to other aspects of instruction. •

Of course, on a daily basis, individual teachers have the most potential for impact. Let's see how teachers can influence their students' achievement.

Teacher-Based Influences

Take a moment to recall your teachers in elementary school, junior high, and high school. Some you probably remember fondly, for they were enthusiastic and innovative, and they made learning fun. You may remember others with bitterness. They seemed to have lost their love of teaching and children, making class a living hell. Your experiences tell you that some teachers are better than others, but what is it that makes an effective teacher? Personality and enthusiasm are *not* the key elements. Although you may enjoy warm and eager teachers, research (Good & Brophy, 1994; Stevenson & Stigler, 1992; Walberg, 1995) has revealed that several other factors are critical when it comes to students' achievement. Students tend to learn the most when teachers

- *Manage the classroom effectively so they can devote most of their time to instruction.* When teachers like the man in the photo spend a lot of time disciplining students, or when students do not move smoothly from one class activity to the next, instructional time is wasted, and students are apt to learn less.

- *Believe they are responsible for their students' learning and that their students will learn when taught well.* When students don't understand a new topic, these teachers may repeat the original instruction (in case the student missed something) or create

? THINK ABOUT IT
Would some of these ways in which teachers can foster students' learning be more appropriate for students in Piaget's concrete-operational stage? Would some be better for students in the formal-operational stage?

new instruction (in case the student heard everything but just didn't "get it"). These teachers keep plugging away because they feel at fault if students don't learn.

- *Emphasize mastery of topics.* Teachers should introduce a topic, then give students many opportunities to understand, practice, and apply the topic. Just as you'd find it hard to go directly from driver's ed to driving a race car, students more often achieve when they grasp a new topic thoroughly, then gradually move on to other, more advanced topics.

- *Teach actively.* They don't just talk or give students an endless stream of worksheets. Instead, they demonstrate topics concretely or have hands-on demonstrations for students. They also have students participate in class activities, and encourage students to interact, generating ideas and solving problems together.

- *Pay careful attention to pacing.* They present material slowly enough so that students can understand a new concept, but not so slowly that students get bored.

- *Value tutoring.* They work with students individually or in small groups, so they can gear their instruction to each student's level and check each student's understanding. They also encourage peer tutoring, in which, as

shown in the photo, more capable students tutor less capable students. Children who are tutored by peers *do* learn, and so do the tutors, evidently because teaching helps tutors to organize their knowledge.

- *Teach children techniques for monitoring and managing their own learning.* Students are more likely to achieve when they are taught how to recognize the aims of school tasks and know effective strategies for achieving those aims (like those described on pages 208–209).

When teachers rely on most of the guidelines for effective teaching most of the time, their students generally learn the material and enjoy doing so. When teachers rely on few of them, their students often fail, or, at the very least, find learning difficult and school tedious (Good & Brophy, 1994; Stevenson & Stigler, 1992; Walberg, 1995).

Of course, following each of these guidelines consistently can be quite a challenge in today's classroom, as you will discover in the See for Yourself feature.

SEE FOR YOURSELF RECOGNIZING GOOD TEACHING

The best way to understand the differences between good and bad teaching is to visit some actual school classrooms. Try to visit three or four rooms in at least two different schools. (You can usually arrange this by speaking with the school's principal.) Take along the principles of good teaching that are listed on pages 229–230. Start by watching how the teachers and children interact. Then, decide how much the teacher relies upon each of the principles. If possible, ask the teacher about teaching philosophies and practices, including his or her opinions about the teaching principles. You'll probably see that most teachers use some but not all of these principles. And you'll also see that, in today's classroom, consistently following all the principles is very challenging. See for yourself! •

TEST YOURSELF

1. Compared to students in other countries, U.S. students have _____ scores in math and science.

2. Today, literacy is defined as _____ .

3. Approximately _____ of U.S. high school graduates have the literacy skills needed for managerial, clerical, and sales positions.

4. In schools where students usually succeed, academic excellence is a priority, the school is safe and nurturant, progress of students and teachers is monitored, and _____ .

5. Effective teachers manage classrooms well, believe they are responsible for their students' learning, _____ , teach actively, pay attention to pacing, value tutoring, and show children how to monitor their own learning.

6. Many schools use computers to help students learn to read and to learn math facts. What characteristics of "effective teachers" would apply to computers?

Answers: (1) lower, (2) being able to use printed and quantitative information effectively, (3) one-third, (4) parents are involved, (5) emphasize mastery of topics

---

PUTTING IT ALL TOGETHER

We began the chapter by examining children's cognitive development. At about the same time that children begin school, they enter Piaget's period of concrete operations. As they grow, their thinking moves beyond the concrete to the abstract. Like Adrian, they gradually pick up the study strategies that are essential for school achievement.

Next, we traced the origins of intelligence testing and examined how tests are used today. Test scores predict school achievement because they tap the knowledge and skills that are prerequisites for school success. Low test scores, like the one reported for Charlene, indicate that the student probably lacks the skills needed for school success.

We also examined one of the reasons why educating U.S. children is such a challenge: Contemporary schools serve a wide range of youngsters, including gifted children, children with mental retardation, and children with learning disabilities like Sanjit. The aim is for all children to be educated to their fullest potential, but we still don't know how best to accommodate all students in today's schools.

We ended the chapter with a look at U.S. schools. By historical standards, today's students are extraordinarily capable. Nevertheless, for the needs of a technologically sophisticated society, American students are undereducated. Contrary to Wally's skepticism, U.S. students do lag behind students in other industrialized countries. However, there is reason for optimism. Research has revealed several school- and teacher-related factors that enhance students' achievement.

SUMMARY

Cognitive Development

More Sophisticated Thinking: Piaget's Version

• In progressing to Piaget's stage of concrete operations, children become less egocentric, rarely confuse appearances with reality, and are able to reverse their thinking. They now solve perspective-taking, conservation, and class-inclusion problems correctly. Thinking at this stage is limited to the concrete and the real.

• With the onset of formal-operational thinking, adolescents can think hypothetically and reason abstractly. In deductive reasoning, they understand that conclusions are based on logic, not on experience.

• Critics of Piaget's account of formal-operational thinking point to two shortcomings. First, in everyday thinking, adolescents' reasoning is often less sophisticated than would be expected of formal-operational thinkers. Second, Piaget assumed that after the formal-operational stage is reached, thinking never again changes qualitatively.

Information-Processing Strategies for Learning and Remembering

• Rehearsal and other memory strategies are used to transfer information from working memory, a temporary store of information, to long-term memory, a permanent store of knowledge. Children begin to rehearse at about 7 or 8 and take up other strategies as they get older.

• Effective use of strategies for learning and remembering begins with an analysis of the goals of any learning task. It also includes monitoring one's performance to determine whether the strategy is working. Collectively, these processes make up an important group of study skills.

Aptitudes for School

Binet and the Development of Intelligence Testing

• Binet created the first intelligence test in order to identify students who would have difficulty in school. Using this work, Terman created the Stanford-Binet in 1916; it remains an important intelligence test. The Stanford-Binet introduced the concept of the intelligence quotient (IQ): MA/CA × 100.

Do Tests Work?

• Intelligence tests are reliable, which means that people usually get consistent scores on the tests. Intelligence tests are reasonably valid measures of achievement in school, but they probably do not measure aspects of intelligence that are important outside of school.

The Elements of Intelligence

• Modern theories of intelligence include a number of discrete components of intelligence. Gardner's theory includes linguistic, logical-mathematical, spatial, musical, bodily-kinesthetic, interpersonal, and intrapersonal intelligences. Sternberg's triarchic theory includes contextual, experiential, and componential subtheories.

Impact of Race, Ethnicity, and Social Class

• The average IQ score for African Americans is about 15 points lower than the average score for European Americans. This difference has been attributed to the facts that more African American children live in poverty and that most intelligence tests assess knowledge based on middle-class experiences. IQ scores are valid predictors of school success, however, because middle-class experience is often a prerequisite for success in U.S. schools.

Hereditary and Environmental Factors

• Evidence for the impact of heredity on IQ comes from the finding that siblings' IQ scores become more alike as siblings become more similar genetically. Evidence for the impact of the environment comes from the finding that children who live in responsive, well-organized home environments tend to have higher IQ scores, as do children who participate in intervention projects.

Special Children, Special Needs

Gifted and Creative Children

• Traditionally, gifted children have been those with high scores on IQ tests. Modern definitions of giftedness have been broadened to include exceptional talent in, for example, the arts. However defined, giftedness must be nurtured by parents and teachers alike. Contrary to folklore, gifted children are socially mature and emotionally stable.

• Creativity is associated with divergent thinking, in which the aim is to think in novel and unusual directions. Tests of divergent thinking can predict which children are most likely to be creative. Creativity can be fostered by experiences that encourage children to think flexibly and to explore alternatives.

Children with Mental Retardation

• Individuals with mental retardation have IQ scores of 70 or lower and deficits in adaptive behavior. Organic mental retardation, which is severe but relatively infrequent, can be linked to specific biological or physical causes; familial mental retardation, which is less severe but more common, reflects the lower end of the normal distribution of intelligence. Most retarded persons are classified as mildly or educably retarded; they attend school, work, and have families.

Children with Learning Disability

• Children with a learning disability have normal intelligence but have difficulty mastering specific academic subjects. The most common is reading disability, which often can be traced to inadequate understanding and use of language sounds.

Attention-Deficit Hyperactivity Disorder

• Children with ADHD are distinguished by being overactive, inattentive, and impulsive. They often have conduct problems and do poorly in school. ADHD is due to heredity and ineffective parenting brought on by children's impulsive behavior. Children with ADHD are often administered stimulants, which calm them. They can also be taught more effective ways of regulating their behavior and attention.

Learning in School

Grading U.S. Schools

• Elementary and high school students in the United States do poorly in comparison with students from other industrialized countries. Furthermore, although U.S. citizens are literate by traditional standards, when literacy is defined in terms of understanding prose, documents, and quantitative information, only a minority of U.S. high school graduates have the skills necessary for success in today's increasingly sophisticated workplace.

Effective Schools, Effective Teachers

• Schools influence students' achievement in many ways. Students are most likely to achieve when their school emphasizes academic excellence, has a safe and nurturing environment, monitors pupils' and teachers' progress, and encourages parents to be involved.

• Students achieve at higher levels when their teachers manage classrooms effectively, take responsibility for their students' learning, teach mastery of material, pace material well, value tutoring, and show children how to monitor their own learning.

KEY TERMS

mental operations (205)	intelligence quotient (IQ) (211)	organic mental retardation (220)
deductive reasoning (206)	culture-fair intelligence tests (214)	familial mental retardation (220)
working memory (208)	convergent thinking (219)	learning disability (221)
long-term memory (208)	divergent thinking (219)	phonological processing (222)
mental age (MA) (210)	mental retardation (220)	literacy (226)

IF YOU'D LIKE TO LEARN MORE

Readings

BARKLEY, R. A. (1995). *Taking charge of ADHD: The complete, authoritative guide for parents.* New York: Guilford. Written by one of the leading experts on ADHD, this book clearly describes what research has revealed about the nature of ADHD. The book also provides a wealth of practical information for parents and teachers on many topics, such as the effects of medications and how to improve children's performance in the classroom.

FISKE, E. B. (1992). *Smart schools, smart kids.* New York: Touchstone. The author examines some exceptional U.S. schools in order to discover the key ingredients of a successful school.

FLAVELL, J. H., MILLER, P. H., & MILLER, S. A. (1993). *Cognitive development* (3rd ed.). Englewood Cliffs, NJ: Prentice-Hall. We recommended this book in Chapter 4 as a good source of information about cognitive development in young children, but it also covers the development of thinking in school-age children and adolescents.

GARDNER, H. (1993). *Creating minds.* New York: Basic Books. The author describes the lives of extraordinarily creative persons such as Einstein and Picasso in order to understand the conditions that foster creativity.

STEVENSON, H. W., & STIGLER, J. W. (1992). *The learning gap.* New York: Summit. The authors, who have done some of the most extensive cross-cultural research on schools, explore why U.S. schoolchildren do so poorly in comparison to Japanese students and suggest what we could learn from Japanese schools.

For additional readings, explore Infotrac College Edition, your online library. Go to http://www.infotrac-college.com/wadsworth.

Web Sites

Twenty-First Century Teachers, a nationwide volunteer initiative to encourage teachers to use technology in their teaching, has a Web site

http://www.21ct.org/

with information on the use of computers and other technology in schools.

The Web site of *Skeptic* magazine

http://www.skeptic.com/03.3.fm-sternberg-interview.html

includes an interview with Robert Sternberg, in which Sternberg talks about his triarchic theory, the influence of heredity and environment on intelligence, and Gardner's model of multiple intelligences.

This Web site of the library of the Psychology Department at Macquarie University

http://www.bhs.mq.edu.au/lib/testref.html

has information on different psychological tests, including those that measure intelligence and creativity.

The Web site of the National Association for Gifted Children

http://www.nagc.org/

contains information for parents of gifted children and links to related sites.

Web site addresses are subject to change. The Wadsworth Study Center Web site listed below can be accessed for updated links.

The Wadsworth Psychology Study Center Web Site

See http://psychology.wadsworth.com/ for practice quiz questions, internet links, updates, critical thinking exercises, discussion forums and more! The Wadsworth Psychology Study Center provides a wealth of information fully organized and integrated by chapter.

CHAPTER 7

EXPANDING SOCIAL HORIZONS

Family Relationships
Dimensions and Styles of Parenting
Siblings
  When Do Siblings Get Along?
Divorce and Remarriage
Parent-Child Relationships Gone Awry:
  Child Abuse

Peers
Friendships
Groups
  Identifying School Crowds
Popularity and Rejection
  *Long-Term Consequences of Popularity
    and Rejection*

**Television: Boob Tube or
Window on the World?**
Influence on Attitudes and Social
  Behavior
  No More Child Couch Potatoes!
Influences on Cognition

Understanding Others
Describing Others
  Tell Me About a Girl That You Like a Lot
Understanding What Others Think
Prejudice

Putting It All Together

Summary

If You'd Like to Learn More

lthough you've never had a course called "Culture 101," your knowledge of your culture is deep. Like all human beings, you have been learning, since birth, to live in your culture. *Teaching children the values, roles, and behaviors of their culture—socialization—is a major goal of all peoples.* In most cultures, the task of socialization falls initially to parents. In the first section of this chapter, we see how parents set and try to enforce standards of behavior for their children.

Soon other powerful forces contribute to socialization. In the second section, you'll discover how peers become influential, through both individual friendships and social groups. Next, you'll learn how the media—particularly television—contribute to socialization as well.

As children become socialized, they begin to understand more about other people. We'll examine this growing understanding in the last section of the chapter.

FAMILY RELATIONSHIPS

Family Relationships

Dimensions and Styles of Parenting

Siblings

Divorce and Remarriage

Parent-Child Relationships Gone Awry:
  Child Abuse

Learning Objectives

- **What are the primary dimensions of parenting? How do they affect children's development?**

- **What determines how siblings get along? How do first-born, later-born, and only children differ?**

- **How do divorce and remarriage affect children?**

- **What factors contribute to child abuse?**

*T*ANYA AND SHEILA, *both sixth-graders, wanted to go to a Smashing Pumpkins concert with two boys from their school. When Tanya asked if she could go, her mom said, "No way!" Tanya replied defiantly, "Why not?" Her mother blew up: "Because I say so. That's why. Stop bugging me." Sheila wasn't allowed to go either. When she asked why, her mom said, "I just think that you're still too young to be dating. I don't mind your going to the concert. If you want to go just with Tanya, that would be fine. What do you think of that?"*

Family. The term is as sacred to most Americans as baseball, apple pie, and Chevrolet. But what comes to mind when you think of family? Television has given us one answer. From *Leave It to Beaver* to *Family Ties* to *Home Improvement,* television says that the family in the United States consists of a mother, a father, and two or three children. In reality, of course, families are as diverse as the people in them. Some families consist of a single parent and an only child. Others include two parents, many children, and grandparents or other relatives.

All these family configurations have a common goal: the care and socialization of children. Our study of family functioning begins by looking at parent-child relationships and describing the different approaches to parenting illustrated by the two mothers in the vignette.

DIMENSIONS AND STYLES OF PARENTING

Were your parents like Tanya's, strict and controlling? Or did they encourage discussion, like Sheila's? Did your parents hug and kiss you often? Or were they more reserved? Did your parents often tell you exactly what to do? Or did they let you do what you wanted to do?

These questions focus on two key dimensions of parent-child relationships that emerge consistently in research. One dimension is the degree of warmth and responsiveness that parents show to their children. At one extreme, some parents are openly warm and affectionate with their children; they are involved with them emotionally and readily spend time and effort with them. At the other extreme are parents who are relatively uninvolved with their children and sometimes even hostile toward them. Such parents often seem more focused on their own wishes than their children's (Parke & Buriel, 1998).

As you might expect, children benefit from warm and responsive parenting. When parents are warm toward them, children typically feel secure, happy, and are better behaved. In contrast, when parents are uninvolved or hostile, their children are often anxious, less controlled, and, as the cartoon indicates, low in self-esteem (Pettit, Bates, & Dodge, 1997).

A second dimension of parental behavior has to do with the control that parents exercise over their children's behavior. At one extreme are controlling, demanding parents. Such parents sometimes seem to be running their children's lives. At the other extreme are parents who make few demands and rarely exert control; their children are free to do almost anything without fear of parental reproach.

B.C. © 1994. Reprinted by permission of Johnny Hart and Creators Syndicate, Inc.

Neither of these extremes is desirable. Overcontrol is unsatisfactory because it deprives children of the opportunity to meet behavioral standards on their own, which is the ultimate goal of socialization. Teenagers who constantly "report in" never learn to make decisions for themselves (e.g., "Should I go to this party with people that I don't know really well?"). Parenting without any control fails because children aren't shown the behavioral standards that their culture has for them. Teenagers who never "report in" believe that they need not account for their behavior, which is definitely not true in the long run.

Parents need to strike a balance, maintaining adequate control while still allowing children freedom to make some decisions for themselves. This is easier said than done, but a good starting point is setting standards that are appropriate for the child's age, then showing the child how to meet them, and, finally, rewarding him or her for doing so (Powers & Roberts, 1995; Rotto & Kratochwill, 1994). Suppose a mother wants her preschooler to fold and put away her socks. This is a reasonable request because the child is physically capable of this simple task and she knows where the socks should be stored. Like the woman in the photograph, the mother should show her daughter how to complete the task, and then praise her when she does.

Once standards are set, they should be enforced consistently. Time and time again, research has shown that children and adolescents are more compliant when parents enforce rules regularly. A mother, for example, should insist that her son pick up his toys every night, not just occasionally. When parents enforce rules erratically, children come to see rules as optional instead of obligatory and they try to avoid complying with them (Conger, Patterson, & Ge, 1995).

Another element of effective control is communication. Parents should explain why they've set standards and why they reward or punish as they do. A mother should explain to her son that a messy room is unsafe, makes it difficult to find objects that he wants, and makes it difficult for her to clean. Parents can also encourage children to ask questions if they don't understand or disagree with standards. If the son feels that his mother's standards for cleanliness are so high that it's impossible to play in his room, he should feel free to raise the issue with his mother without fear of making her angry.

? THINK ABOUT IT

How would a social learning theorist explain the importance of consistency and communication in effective parental control? Would an information-processing theorist's explanation be similar?

The balanced approach to control—based on age-appropriate standards, consistency, and communication—avoids the problems associated with over-control because the expectations should reflect the child's level of maturity and they're open to discussion. The balanced approach also avoids the problems of undercontrol because there are standards and parents expect children to meet those standards consistently.

What about punishment? Most parents use some form of punishment as a means of controlling their children. As we explained in Chapter 1, punishment consists of the application of an aversive stimulus or the removal of attractive stimuli. Take a moment to think of some common methods that parents use to punish. Perhaps your list includes spanking or making critical comments such as "No wonder you didn't clean up your room—you never do anything around here to help!" *These illustrate* power-assertion *methods of punishment, all of which rely upon a parent's greater power.* Power assertion includes physical punishment, threats, or humiliation. In the short term, power assertion "works," in the limited sense that children usually perform the desired behavior or stop the offending behavior. In the long term, however, power assertion is ineffective because (1) children become fearful of their parents, (2) they are less likely to internalize social rules, and (3) as social learning theory reminds

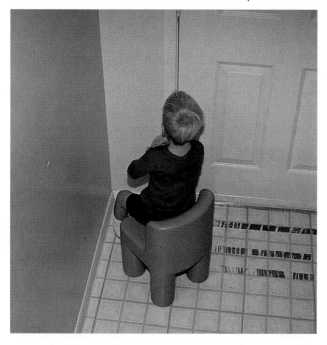

us, children often imitate their parents' aggressive behavior (Hoffman, 1970; Parke & Slaby, 1983).

Other methods of punishment are much more effective. *In* time-out, *when children misbehave, they briefly sit alone in a quiet, unstimulating location.* Some parents have children sit alone in a bathroom; others put them in an isolated corner of a room, as shown in the photograph. Time-out is punishing because it interrupts the child's ongoing activity and isolates him or her from other family members, toys, books, and generally, all forms of rewarding stimulation. The period is sufficiently brief—usually just a few minutes—for a parent to use the method consistently. During time-out, both parent and child typically calm down. Then, when time-out is over, the parent can talk with the child, making clear why the punished behavior was objectionable and explaining what the child should do instead. "Reasoning" like this—even with preschool children—is useful because it emphasizes why the parent punished and how punishment can be avoided in the future.

Cultural Differences in Dimensions of Parental Behavior

Views about the "proper" amount of control and the "proper" amount of warmth reflect parents' cultural heritage (Parke & Buriel, 1998). European Americans want their children to be happy and self-reliant individuals, and they believe that these goals can best be achieved when parents are warm and exert moderate control (Goodnow, 1992; Spence, 1985). In contrast, in many countries in Asia and Latin America, individualism is less important than cooperation and collaboration (Okagaki & Sternberg, 1993). In China, for example, Confucian principles dictate that parents are always right and that emotional restraint is the key to family harmony (Chao, 1983). Based on these principles, we would expect to find that Chinese parents are not as warm toward their children but are more controlling than their North American counterparts. Lin and Fu (1990) found exactly this pattern, as shown in the charts. Compared to mothers and fathers in the United States, mothers and fathers in Taiwan were more likely to emphasize parental control and less likely to express affection.

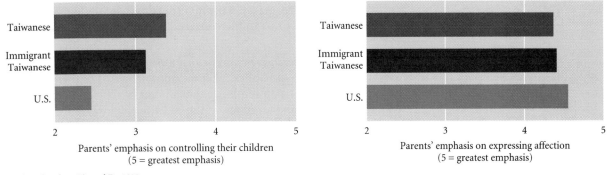

Parents' emphasis on controlling their children
(5 = greatest emphasis)

Parents' emphasis on expressing affection
(5 = greatest emphasis)

Based on data from Lin and Fu, 1990.

Also shown in the charts are the results for a third group studied by Lin and Fu. Parents in this group emigrated from Taiwan and were living in the United States, where their children were born. The findings for this group were between the other groups in terms of both warmth and control. That is, immigrant Taiwanese parents were less controlling than Taiwanese parents but more controlling than U.S. parents. Likewise, they were warmer toward their children than Taiwanese parents, but not as warm as U.S. parents. Both results suggest that the immigrant group was gradually becoming assimilated into U.S. culture.

The results of the Lin and Fu study show that parents' behavior reflects cultural values. The Taiwanese parents' behavior is consistent with the Confucian principles that are central to traditional Chinese culture. Among European Americans, parents' behavior often reflects longstanding cultural beliefs in the importance of individualism and self-reliance. The immigrant Taiwanese parents' behavior is a mix of traditional Chinese culture and Western values. In these and all societies, cultural values help specify appropriate ways for parents to interact with their offspring (Harwood et al., 1996; Patel, Power, & Bhavnagri, 1996).

Parental Styles

When the dimensions of warmth and control are combined, four prototypic styles of parenting emerge (Baumrind, 1975, 1991b).

- Authoritarian parenting *combines high control with little warmth.* These parents lay down the rules and expect them to be followed without discussion or argument. Hard work, respect, and obedience are what authoritarian parents wish to cultivate in their children. There is little give-and-take between parent and child, because authoritarian parents do not balance their demands with consideration for children's needs or wishes. This style was illustrated by Tanya's mother in the vignette. The mother felt no obligation whatsoever to explain why she would not allow Tanya to attend the concert.

- Authoritative parenting *combines a fair degree of parental control with warmth and responsiveness to the children.* Authoritative parents favor giving explanations for rules and encouraging discussion. This style is exemplified by Sheila's mother in the vignette. She explained why she did not want Sheila going to the concert with the boys and encouraged her daughter to discuss the issue with her.

- Indulgent-permissive parents *are warm and caring but exert little control over their children.* They tend to accept much of their children's behavior and punish them infrequently. A parent using this style would readily agree to the girls' request to go to the concert, simply because it is something that they want to do.

- Indifferent-uninvolved parents *are neither warm nor controlling.* These parents provide for the basic physical and emotional needs of their children but little else. They try to minimize the amount of time and effort spent with their children and avoid becoming emotionally involved with them. Had Tanya and Sheila had mothers who used this style, they might have simply gone to the concert without asking, knowing that their parents didn't care and would rather not be bothered.

Parental style is fairly stable over time. Parents who are authoritative with their school-age children tend to be authoritative when their children are adolescents (McNally, Eisenberg, & Harris, 1991). Given this stability, you shouldn't be surprised to learn that parental style influences children's development (Baumrind, 1991a; Hinshaw et al., 1997; Parke & Buriel, 1998).

- Children with authoritarian parents typically have lower grades in school, have lower self-esteem, and are less skilled socially.

- Children with authoritative parents tend to have higher grades and are often responsible, self-reliant, and friendly.

- Children with indulgent-permissive parents have lower grades and are often impulsive and easily frustrated.

- Children with indifferent-uninvolved parents usually have low self-esteem and are impulsive, aggressive, and moody.

Many of these outcomes can be seen in a study by Lamborn and her colleagues (1991), examining the influence of parental style on high school students' psychosocial development and performance in school. The results depicted in the graphs are complex but show a very consistent pattern. Adolescents with authoritative parents have the best scores on all measures: They are the most self-reliant, have the best grades, and misbehave the least in school.

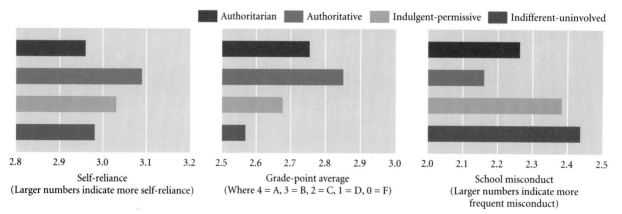

Based on data from Lamborn et al., 1991.

Adolescents with indifferent-uninvolved parents tend to be at the other extreme: They are lower in self-reliance, have lower grades, and are the most likely to be involved in school misconduct.

Adolescents with either authoritarian or indulgent-permissive parents are in between the other groups on most measures. Adolescents with authoritarian parents were the least self-reliant of all four groups, but in grades and school misconduct they ranked behind adolescents with authoritative parents. Adolescents with indulgent-permissive parents were nearly as self-reliant as those with authoritative parents, but their grades were lower, and they were more likely to misbehave in school.

The benefits of authoritative parenting are not restricted to European American children but apply to children and parents from several different ethnic groups in the United States, including people of African, Asian, and Hispanic descent (Steinberg et al., 1992). However, some researchers find that authoritarian parenting can benefit children growing up in poverty (Furstenberg, 1993). Why? When youngsters grow up in neighborhoods where violence and crime are common, strict obedience to parents can protect children (Kelley, Power, & Wimbush, 1993).

Thus, a parental style that combines control, warmth, and affection is often best for children. However, other factors, such as a dangerous or violent neighborhood, may make other parenting styles more appropriate for some children.

Children's Contributions: Reciprocal Influence

From what we've said thus far, it may seem that parent-child relations are a one-way street: Parents influence their children's behavior but not vice versa. Actually, nothing could be further from the truth. Beginning at birth and throughout the life span, children influence the way parents treat them. The family is really a dynamic, interactive system in which parents and children influence each other (Parke & Buriel, 1998).

One way to see the influence of children on parents is by looking at how parental behavior changes as children grow. The same parenting that is marvelously effective with infants and toddlers is inappropriate for adolescents. Let's consider the two dimensions of parental behavior—warmth and control. Warmth is beneficial throughout development—toddlers and teens alike enjoy knowing that others care about them. But the manifestation of parental affection changes, becoming more restrained as children develop (McNally, Eisenberg, & Harris, 1991). The enthusiastic hugging and kissing that delight toddlers embarrass adolescents.

Parental control also changes gradually as children develop (McNally et al., 1991). As children develop cognitively and are better able to make their own decisions, parents gradually relinquish control and expect children to be responsible for themselves. For instance, parents of school-age children often keep track of their children's progress on school assignments but parents of adolescents don't, expecting their children to do this themselves. Of course, throughout childhood and adolescence, authoritarian parents are more controlling than authoritative parents; however, both types of parents tend to be less controlling with older children and adolescents than with younger children.

Not only do parents change their expressions of warmth and control as children develop, parents behave differently depending upon a child's specific behavior. To illustrate the reciprocal influence of parents and children, imagine two children responding to a parent's authoritative style. Both parents are warm and try to use modest control, emphasizing consistent expectations and good communication. The first child readily complies with parental requests

and responds well to family discussions about parental expectations. These parent-child relations are a textbook example of successful authoritative parenting. In contrast, the second child, like the girl in the photo, often complies reluctantly and sometimes defies requests altogether. This parent becomes more controlling and less affectionate. This leads the child to become even less likely to comply in the future, producing even more authoritarian parental behavior. This case represents the exception to the general rule that parental style is stable: The child's behavior causes parents to abandon an authoritative style in favor of a more authoritarian style.

These two examples illustrate that parental behaviors often evolve as a consequence of children's behavior in general. With a young child who is eager to please adults and who is less active, a parent may discover a modest amount of control is adequate. But for a child who is not as sociable and who is more active, a parent may need to be more controlling and directive (Dumas, LaFreniere, & Serketich, 1995). Thus, influence is reciprocal. Children's behavior helps determine how parents treat them and the resulting parental behavior can influence children's behavior, which, in turn, causes parents to again change their behavior (Stice & Barrea, 1995).

A reciprocal parent-child relationship is central to human development, but other relationships within the family are also influential. For many children, relationships with siblings are very important, as we'll see in the next few pages.

SIBLINGS

Every first-born child starts life as an only child. Some remain "onlies" forever, but most children have brothers and sisters. Some first-borns are joined by many siblings in rapid succession. Others have a single younger brother or sister. As the family gains new members, parent-child relationships become more complex. Parents can no longer focus on a single child but must adjust to the needs of multiple children. Just as important, siblings also influence each other's development. By the preschool years, siblings spend more time together than with parents, which suggests just how influential sibling relationships can be (Dunn, 1993; Larson & Richards, 1994). In addition, interactions between siblings are often more emotionally intense than interactions in other relationships (Katz, Kramer, & Gottman, 1992).

The birth of a sibling is often distressing for older children. They may become withdrawn or return to more childish behavior. Distress of this sort is more common in first-born youngsters who are less than 3 years old when a sibling is born. Their distress can be linked to the many changes that occur in their lives with a sibling's birth, particularly the need to share parental attention and affection (Gottlieb & Mendelson, 1990). However, distress can be avoided if parents remain responsive to their older children's needs (Howe & Ross, 1990). In fact, one benefit of a sibling's birth is that fathers become more involved with their older children (Stewart et al., 1987).

With newborns, many older siblings are like the one in the photograph, taking on parental tasks such as feeding or changing diapers (Wagner, Schubert, & Schubert,

1985). As the infant grows, interactions between siblings become more common and more complicated. For example, toddlers tend to talk more to parents than to older siblings. However, by the time preschoolers are 4 years old, the situation is reversed: Now younger siblings talk more to older siblings than to their mother (Brown & Dunn, 1992). Older siblings also become a source of care and comfort for younger siblings when they are distressed or upset (Garner, Jones, & Palmer, 1994).

As time goes by, some siblings grow close, becoming best friends in ways that nonsiblings can never be. Other siblings constantly argue, compete, and, overall, simply do not get along with each other. These patterns of sibling interaction seem to be established early in development and remain fairly stable. Dunn, Slomkowski, and Beardsall (1994), for example, interviewed mothers twice about their children's interaction. The first time was when the children were 3- and 5-year-olds; the second time was 7 years later, when the children were 10- and 12-year-olds. Dunn and her colleagues found that siblings who got along as preschoolers often continued to do so as young adolescents, whereas siblings who quarreled as preschoolers often quarreled as young adolescents.

What factors contribute to the quality of sibling relationships? The Forces in Action feature has the answer.

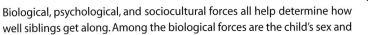

WHEN DO SIBLINGS GET ALONG?   FORCES IN ACTION

Biological, psychological, and sociocultural forces all help determine how well siblings get along. Among the biological forces are the child's sex and temperament. Sibling relations are more likely to be warm and harmonious between siblings of the same sex than between siblings of the opposite sex (Dunn & Kendrick, 1981). Also, relations are smoother when neither sibling is temperamentally emotional (Brody, Stoneman, & Gauger, 1996). Psychological forces contribute, too. Siblings' perceptions of each other and their parents' treatment of them is important. Siblings more often get along when they believe that parents have no "favorites" but treat all siblings similarly (McHale et al., 1995). Also, relationships generally improve as the younger sibling approaches adolescence, because siblings begin to perceive one another as equals (Buhrmester & Furman, 1990). Finally, sociocultural forces also come into play. When parents get along well, so do siblings; when parents argue, so do sibs (Volling & Belsky, 1992).

A biopsychosocial perspective on sibling relationships makes it clear that, in their pursuit of family harmony (otherwise known as peace and quiet), parents can influence some of the factors affecting sibling relationships but not others. Parents *can* help reduce friction between siblings by being equally affectionate, responsive, and caring to all of their children, and by caring for one another. At the same time, parents (and prospective parents!) must realize that some dissension is natural in families, especially those with young boys and girls. Children's different interests lead to conflicts that youngsters cannot resolve because their social skills are limited.

Impact of Birth Order

First-born children are often "guinea pigs" for most parents, who have lots of enthusiasm but little practical experience rearing children. Parents typically have high expectations for their first-borns (Furman, 1995). They are both more affectionate and more punitive toward them. As more children arrive, most parents become more adept at their roles, having learned "the tricks of the trade" from earlier children. With later-born children, parents have more realistic expectations and are more relaxed in their discipline (Baskett, 1985).

The different approaches that parents use with their first- and later-born children help explain differences that are commonly observed between these children. First-born children generally have higher scores on intelligence tests and are more likely to go to college. They are also more willing to conform to parents' and adults' requests. In contrast, perhaps because later-born children are less concerned about pleasing parents and adults, they are more popular with their peers and more innovative (Eaton, Chipperfield, & Singbeil, 1989).

What about only children? According to conventional wisdom, parents like the ones in the photograph dote on "onlies," who therefore become selfish and egotistical. Is the folklore correct? In a comprehensive analysis of more than 100 studies, only children were not worse off than other children on any measure. In fact, only children were found to succeed more in school and to have higher levels of intelligence, leadership, autonomy, and maturity (Falbo & Polit, 1986).

This general pattern is not limited to only children in North America. In China, only children are common because of governmental efforts to limit population growth. There, too, comparisons between only and non-only children often find no differences; when differences are found, the advantage usually goes to the only child (Jiao, Ji, & Jing, 1996; Yang et al., 1995). Thus, contrary to the popular stereotype, only children are not "spoiled brats" (nor, in China, are they "little emperors" who boss around parents, peers, and teachers). Instead, only children are, for the most part, much like children who grow up with siblings.

Whether U.S. children grow up with siblings or as onlies, they are more likely than children in other countries to have their family relationships disrupted by divorce. What is the impact of divorce on children and adolescents?

DIVORCE AND REMARRIAGE

In the 1990s, nearly half of all North American children experienced their parents' divorce (Goodman, Emery, & Haugaard, 1998). According to all theories of child development, divorce is distressing for children because it involves conflict between parents and, usually, separation from one of them. (Of course, divorce is also distressing to parents, as we'll describe in Chapter 10.) But what aspects of children's development are most affected by divorce? Are these effects long-lasting or are at least some of them temporary? To begin to answer these questions, let's start with a profile of life after divorce.

Family Life After Divorce

After divorce, children usually live with their mothers. Fathers are more likely to get custody today than in previous generations, but this arrangement is still rare. Only about 15% of children live with their fathers after divorce (Meyer & Garasky, 1993). Not much is known about family life in homes headed by single fathers, so the description on the next few pages is based entirely on research done on children living with their mothers.

The best portrait of family life after divorce comes from the Virginia Longitudinal Study of Divorce and Remarriage conducted by Mavis Hetherington and her colleagues (1988, 1989; Hetherington, Cox & Cox, 1982). The Virginia Study traced the lives of families for several years after divorce along with a comparison sample of families with parents who had not divorced. In the first few months after divorce, mothers were often less affectionate toward their children. They also accepted less mature behavior from their children than they would have before the divorce but at the same time, had a harder time controlling their children than before. Apparently, mothers and children showed the distress of a major change in life circumstances: Children regressed to less mature forms of behavior and mothers were less able to parent effectively. Fathers, too, were less able to control their children, but this was probably because they were often extremely indulgent with them.

Two years after the divorce, mother-child relationships had improved, particularly for daughters. Mothers were more affectionate. They were more likely to expect age-appropriate behavior from their children and to discipline their children effectively. Fathers also demanded more mature behavior of their children, but fathers had often become relatively uninvolved with their children.

Six years after divorce, the children in the study were entering adolescence. Family life continued to improve for mothers with daughters; many mothers and daughters grew extremely close. In contrast, family life was often problematic for mothers with sons. Mothers and sons were frequently in conflict. Neither was very happy with the other or with the overall quality of family life. Of course, conflict between mothers and adolescent sons is common when parents are married but it is more intense with single moms, perhaps because adolescent sons are more willing to confront their mothers concerning standards for their behavior.

Results like these from the Virginia Study underscore that divorce changes family life for parents and children alike (Parke & Buriel, 1998). Next, we'll look at the effects of these changes on children's development.

Impact of Divorce on Children

Do the disruptions, conflict, and stress associated with divorce affect children? Of course they do. Having answered this easy question, however, many more difficult questions remain: Are all aspects of children's lives affected equally by divorce? Are there factors that make divorce more stressful for some children and less so for others? Finally, how does divorce influence development? Many scholars have tried to answer these questions and, by 1990, there were nearly 100 studies of the impact of divorce, involving more than 13,000 preschool through college-age children. Amato and Keith (1991) integrated the results of these studies; their analysis revealed several areas in which children whose parents had divorced fare poorly compared to children from intact families. When parents divorce, their children are less successful in school and more often have problems linked to conduct and to self-concept. In addition, the parent-child relationship often deteriorates.

Amato and Keith (1991) discovered three other important results about divorce. First, overall, the impact of divorce is the same for boys and girls. Second, divorce is more harmful for school-age children and adolescents than for preschoolers or college-age adults. Third, as divorce became more frequent (and thus more familiar) in the 1980s, the consequences associated with divorce have become smaller. School achievement, conduct, adjustment, and the like, are still affected by divorce, but not as much as before the 1980s.

? THINK ABOUT IT
Based on the description provided here, what kinds of parental styles did mothers and fathers tend to use following divorce?

When children of divorced parents become adults, the effects of divorce persist. As adults, children of divorce are more likely to have their own children as teenagers and to divorce themselves. Also, they report less satisfaction with life and are more likely to become depressed (Furstenberg & Teitler, 1994; Kiernan, 1992). For example, in one study (Chase-Lansdale, Cherlin, & Kiernan, 1995), 11% of children of divorce had serious emotional problems as adults compared to only 8% of children from intact families. The differences between children of divorced parents and children from intact families are small, and most children of divorce do not suffer serious emotional disorders as adults. Nevertheless, divorce does increase the risk that adults will experience emotional disorders.

How does divorce influence development? Several factors have been identified (Amato & Keith, 1991). First, the absence of one parent means that children lose a role model, a source of parental help and emotional support, and a supervisor. For instance, a school-age child who is upset because classmates teased him may stay upset at home for several hours, waiting for his single parent to get home from work.

Second, single-parent families experience economic hardship, which creates stress and often means that opportunities once taken for granted are no longer available. When a single parent worries about having enough money for food and rent, she has less energy and effort to devote to parenting. And the drop in income often means that a family can no longer afford books for pleasure reading, music lessons, and other activities that promote child development.

Third, conflict between parents is extremely distressing to children. In fact, many of the problems ascribed to divorce are really caused by marital conflict occurring before the divorce (Cherlin et al., 1991; Erel & Burman, 1995). When parents are married but fight constantly, their children often show many of the same effects associated with divorce (Davies & Cummings, 1998; Harold et al., 1997).

Life for children after divorce is *not* all gloom and doom. Children can and do adjust to their new life circumstances (Chase-Lansdale & Hetherington, 1991). However, certain factors ease the transition. Children adjust to divorce more readily if their divorced parents get along, especially on disciplinary matters (Hetherington, 1989). *In* joint custody, *both parents retain legal custody of the children.* Children benefit from joint custody, if their parents get along (Goodman et al., 1998; Maccoby et al., 1993).

Of course, many parents do not get along after a divorce, which eliminates joint custody as an option. Traditionally, mothers have been awarded custody. This remains true but today fathers are more likely than before to be given custody, especially for sons. This practice coincides with findings that children often adjust better when they live with same-sex parents: Boys often fare better with fathers and girls fare better with mothers (Camara & Resnick, 1988). One reason why boys are often better off with their fathers is that teenage boys are more likely to become involved in conflict with their mothers than with their fathers. Another explanation is that both boys and girls may forge stronger emotional relationships with same-sex parents than with other-sex parents (Zimiles & Lee, 1991).

Blended Families

Following divorce, most children live in a single-parent household for about five years. However, like the adults in the photo at the top of page 249, more than two-thirds of divorced men and women eventually remarry (Glick, 1989; Glick & Lin, 1986). *The resulting unit, consisting of a biological parent, a step-*

parent, and children of one or both, is known as a blended family. Because mothers are more often granted custody, the most common form of blended family is a mother, her children, and a stepfather. Preadolescent boys typically benefit from the presence of a stepfather, particularly when he is warm and involved. In contrast, preadolescent girls do not adjust readily to their mother's remarriage, apparently because it disrupts the intimate relationship they have established with her. However, as boys and girls enter adolescence, both benefit from the presence of a caring stepfather (Hetherington, 1993).

The best strategy for stepfathers is to become interested in their new stepchildren but to avoid encroaching on established relationships. Newly remarried single mothers must be certain that their enthusiasm for their new spouse does not come at the expense of time and affection for their children. Both parents and children need to have realistic expectations about the blended family. They *can* be successful, but much effort is required, because of the many complicated relationships, conflicting loyalties, and jealousies that usually exist.

Sometimes blended families include children from both parents' previous marriages. Parents in these families need to make special efforts to treat their biological children and their stepchildren comparably. When they don't, conflicts and problem behaviors are common (Mekos, Hetherington, & Reiss, 1996).

Much less is known about blended families consisting of a father, his children, and a stepmother. Several factors converge to make a father's remarriage difficult for his children (Brand, Clingempeel, & Bowen-Woodward, 1988). First, one reason fathers are awarded custody may be that judges believe the children are unruly and will profit from a father's "firm hand." Consequently, many children in this type of family do not adjust well to many of life's challenges, such as a father's remarriage. Second, fathers are sometimes granted custody because they have a particularly close relationship with their children, especially their sons. As is the case with a mother's remarriage, the children sometimes fear that their father's remarriage will disturb this relationship. Finally, noncustodial mothers are more likely than noncustodial fathers to maintain close and frequent contact with their children (Maccoby et al., 1993). The constant presence of the noncustodial mother may interfere with a stepmother's efforts to establish close relationships with her stepchildren, particularly with her stepdaughters.

Over time, children adjust to the blended family. If the marriage is happy, most children clearly profit from the presence of two caring adults. Unfortunately, second marriages are slightly more likely than first marriages to end in divorce, so many children relive the trauma of divorce. As you can imagine, such recurring episodes of conflict severely disrupt children's development, accentuating the problems observed in youngsters following an initial divorce (Capaldi & Patterson, 1991).

Regrettably, divorce is not the only way that parents can disturb their children's development. As you'll see in the next few pages, some parents harm their children more directly, by abusing them.

PARENT-CHILD RELATIONSHIPS GONE AWRY: CHILD ABUSE

The first time that 7-year-old Max came to school with bruises on his face, he explained to his teacher that he had fallen down the basement steps. When Max had similar bruises a few weeks later, his teacher spoke with the school principal, who contacted local authorities. It turned out that Max's mother thrashed him with a paddle for even minor misconduct; for serious transgressions, she beat Max and made him sleep alone in a dark, unheated basement.

Unfortunately, cases like Max's occur far too often. Maltreatment comes in many forms (Goodman et al., 1998):

- *Physical abuse,* involving assault that leads to injuries including cuts, welts, bruises, and broken bones
- *Sexual abuse,* involving fondling, intercourse, or other sexual behaviors
- *Psychological abuse,* involving ridicule, rejection, or humiliation
- *Neglect,* in which children do not receive adequate food, clothing, or medical care

The frequency of child maltreatment is difficult to estimate, because so many cases go unreported. According to the National Center on Child Abuse and Neglect (1997), approximately 1 million children annually suffer maltreatment or neglect. About 50% are neglected, about 25% are abused physically, and 15% are abused sexually (National Center on Child Abuse and Neglect, 1997).

Who Are the Abusing Parents?

Parents who abuse their children were once thought to be severely disturbed or deranged. Today, we know that the vast majority of abusing parents cannot

be distinguished from other parents in terms of standard psychiatric criteria (Wolfe, 1985). In fact, modern accounts of child abuse no longer look to a single or even a small number of causes. Instead, a host of factors combine to place some children at risk for abuse and to protect others; the number and combination of factors determine whether the child is a likely target for abuse (Rogosch et al., 1995). Let's look at three of the most important factors: those associated with the cultural context, those associated with parents, and those associated with children themselves.

The most general category of contributing factors are those dealing with cultural values and the social conditions in which parents rear their children. For example, a culture's view of physical punishment contributes to child maltreatment. The scene in the photograph, a father spanking his child, is common in the United States. In contrast, many countries in Europe and Asia have strong cultural prohibitions against physical punishment, including spanking. It simply isn't done and would be viewed in much the same way we would view an American parent who punished by not feeding the child for a few days. Countries that do not condone physical punishment tend to have lower rates of child maltreatment than the United States (Zigler & Hall, 1989).

What social conditions seem to foster maltreatment? Poverty is one: Maltreatment is more common among children living in poverty, in part because lack of money increases the stress of daily life (Coulton et al., 1995). When parents are worrying about whether they can buy groceries or pay rent, they are more likely to punish their children physically instead of making the extra effort to reason with them.

Social isolation is a second force. Abuse is more likely when families are socially isolated from other relatives or neighbors. When a family like the one in the photo lives in relative isolation, it deprives the child of adults who could protect them and deprives parents of social support that would help them better deal with life's stresses (Garbarino & Kostelny, 1992).

Cultural factors clearly contribute to child abuse, but they are only part of the puzzle. Although maltreatment *is* more common among families living in poverty, it does not occur in a majority of these families and it does occur in middle- and upper-class families, too. Consequently, we need to look for additional factors to explain why abuse occurs in some families but not others.

Today, we know that parents who abuse their children

- were, as children, sometimes maltreated themselves (Simons et al., 1991)
- have high expectations for their children but do little to help them achieve these goals (Trickett et al., 1991)
- rely upon physical punishment to control their children (Trickett & Kuczynski, 1986)

Overall, then, the typical abusing parent often had an unhappy childhood and has limited understanding of effective techniques of parenting.

To place the last few pieces in the puzzle, we must look at the abused children themselves. The discussion on pages 243–244 of reciprocal influence between parents and children should remind you that children may inadvertently, through their behavior, contribute to their own abuse. In fact, infants and preschoolers are more often abused than older ones, probably because they are less able to regulate aversive behaviors that may elicit abuse (Belsky, 1993). You've probably heard stories about a parent who shakes a baby to death because the baby wouldn't stop crying. Because younger children are more likely to cry or whine excessively—behaviors that irritate all parents sooner or later—they are more likely to be the targets of abuse.

For much the same reason, children who are frequently ill are more often abused. When children are sick, they're more likely to cry and whine, annoying parents. Also, when children are sick, they need medical care (which means additional expense) and they can't go to school (which often means that parents must arrange alternative child care). Because sick children increase the level of stress in a family, they can inadvertently become the targets of abuse. By behaving immaturely or being ill, children unintentionally place themselves at risk for maltreatment (Rogosch et al., 1995).

Thus, cultural, parental, and child factors all contribute to child maltreatment. Any single factor will usually not result in abuse. For instance, a sick infant who cries constantly would not be maltreated in countries where physical punishment is not tolerated. Maltreatment becomes a possibility only when cultures condone physical punishment, parents lack effective skills for dealing with children, and a child's behavior is frequently aversive.

Effects of Abuse on Children

You probably aren't surprised to learn that the prognosis for youngsters like Max is not very good. Some, of course, suffer permanent physical damage. Even when there is no lasting physical damage, their social and emotional development is often disrupted. They tend to have poor relationships with peers, often because they are too aggressive (Parker & Herrera, 1996). Their cognitive development and academic performance is also disturbed. Abused youngsters tend to get lower grades in school, have lower scores on standardized achievement tests, and are often retained in a grade rather than promoted. Also, school-related behavior problems are common, such as being disruptive in class (Trickett & McBride-Chang, 1995). Adults who were abused as children often experience emotional problems such as depression or anxiety, are more prone to think about or to attempt suicide, and are more likely to be violent to spouses and to their own children (Malinosky-Rummell & Hansen, 1993). In short, when children are maltreated, many aspects of their development are affected and these effects do not vanish with time (Goodman et al., 1998).

Eliminating Child Abuse

Changing many of the sociocultural forces that contribute to abuse is a daunting task. However, by focusing on some of the more manageable factors, the risk of maltreatment can be reduced, if not eliminated entirely. For example, families can be taught more effective ways of coping with situations that might otherwise trigger abuse (Wicks-Nelson & Israel, 1991). Parents can learn the benefits of authoritative parenting and effective ways of using feedback and modeling to regulate children's behavior. In role-playing sessions in which problems from home are recreated, child development professionals can demonstrate more effective means of solving problems and parents can practice them.

Social supports also help. When parents know they can turn to other helpful adults for advice and reassurance, they can more readily manage the stresses of child rearing, stresses that might otherwise lead to abuse. Finally, we need to remember that most parents who mistreat their children deserve care and compassion, not censure. In most families in which maltreatment takes place, parents and children *are* attached to each other; maltreatment is a consequence of ignorance and burden, not malice.

TEST YOURSELF

1. A(n) _____ parental style combines high control with low involvement.

2. Children who have low self-esteem and are impulsive, aggressive, and moody often have parents who rely on a(n) _____ style.

3. Typically, the birth of a sibling is less traumatic when children are older and when parents _____ .

4. With later-born children, parents often have more realistic expectations and are _____ .

5. Among the effects of divorce on children are inadequate supervision of children, conflict between parents, and _____ .

6. When mothers remarry, daughters do not adjust as readily as sons because _____ .

7. Child abuse is more common in countries that _____ .

8. Children are more likely to be abused when they are younger and when they are _____ .

9. How can child abuse be explained in terms of the biological, psychological, and sociocultural forces in the biopsychosocial framework?

Answers: (1) authoritarian, (2) indifferent-uninvolved, (3) remain responsive to the older child's needs, (4) more relaxed in their discipline, (5) economic hardship, (6) the remarriage disrupts an intimate mother-daughter relationship, (7) condone physical punishment, (8) unhealthy

PEERS

Learning Objectives

- **What are the benefits of friendship?**
- **What are the important features of groups of children and adolescents? How do these groups influence individuals?**
- **Why are some children more popular than others? What are the causes and consequences of being rejected?**

Peers

Friendships

Groups

Popularity and Rejection

ONLY 36 hours had passed since the campers arrived at Crab Orchard Summer Camp. Nevertheless, groups had already formed spontaneously, based on the campers' main interests: arts and crafts, hiking, and swimming. Within each group, leaders and followers had already emerged. This happens every year, but the staff is always astonished at how quickly a "social network" emerges at camp.

The groups that form at summer camps—as well as in schools and neighborhoods—represent one of the more complex forms of peer relationships: Many children are involved and there are multiple relationships. We'll examine these kinds of interactions later in this section. Let's start by looking at a simpler social relationship, friendship.

FRIENDSHIPS

As you saw in Chapter 4, peer interactions begin in late infancy and become more frequent and more influential as children grow. How do peer interactions lead to friendships? According to an influential early theory proposed by Harry Stack Sullivan (1953), the development of interpersonal relationships follows a stagelike sequence. Between 4 and 8 years, children single out specific peers as playmates and companions. However, the relationships are usually short-lived and the interactions often superficial. At about 8 or 9, Sullivan proposed, more advanced cognitive development means that children begin to have their first real friendships, which are characterized by intimacy and reciprocity. Friends care for each other, and the relationship has mutual give-and-take.

More recent research provides support for some of Sullivan's ideas. By 4 or 5 years, many youngsters will claim to have a "best friend." If you ask them how they can tell that a child is their best friend, their comments will probably resemble those of 5-year-old Kara.

INTERVIEWER: *Why* is Heidi your best friend?

KARA: Because she plays with me. And she's nice to me.

INTERVIEWER: Are there any other reasons?

KARA: Yeah, she lets me play with her dolls.

Of course, older children and adolescents also have best friends, but they describe them differently. Comments by 12-year-old Shauna are typical:

INTERVIEWER: Why is Leah your best friend?

SHAUNA: She helps me. And we think alike. My mom says we're like twins!

INTERVIEWER: What else tells you that she's your best friend?

SHAUNA: Because I can tell her stuff—special stuff, like secrets—and I know she won't tell anybody else.

INTERVIEWER: Anything else?

SHAUNA: Yeah. If we fight, later we always tell each other we're sorry.

As Sullivan proposed, Kara's description of her friendship emphasizes Heidi's role as a playmate. In contrast, Shauna's account of her friendship with Leah emphasizes trust and intimacy.

Older children and adolescents also emphasize loyalty in their friendships. They believe that friends should defend one another and that friends should not deceive or abandon one another (Newcomb & Bagwell, 1995). The emphasis on loyalty in adolescent friendships apparently goes hand in hand with the emphasis on intimacy: If a friend is disloyal, adolescents are afraid they may be humiliated because their intimate thoughts and feelings will become known to a much broader circle of people (Berndt & Perry, 1990).

Intimacy is more common in friendships among girls, who are more likely than boys to have one exclusive "best friend." Because intimacy is at the core of their friendships, girls are also more likely to be concerned about the faithfulness of their friends and to worry about possible rejection by them (Buhrmester & Furman, 1987).

The emergence of intimacy in adolescent friendships means that friends also come to be seen as sources of social and emotional support. Levitt and her colleagues (1993) asked African American, European American, and Hispanic American 7-, 10-, and 14-year-olds to whom they would turn when they need help or are bothered by something. For all ethnic groups, 7- and 10- year-olds relied upon close family members—parents, siblings, and grandparents—as primary sources of support, but not friends. However, 14-year-olds relied upon close family members less often and said they would turn to friends instead. Because adolescent friends share intimate thoughts and feelings, they can provide support during emotional or stressful periods (Denton & Zarbatany, 1996).

Who Are Friends?

Like the children shown in the photograph, most friends are alike in age, sex, and race (Hartup, 1992b). Because friends are supposed to treat each other as equals, friendships are rare between an older, more experienced child and a younger, less experienced child. Because children typically play with same-sex peers, boys and girls rarely become friends. In fact, the relatively small percentage of children whose primary friends are members of the opposite sex tend to have poorer social skills (Kovacs, Parker, & Hoffman, 1996).

Friendships are more common between children from the same race or ethnic group than between children from different groups. This reflects the racial segregation of U.S. society. Friendships among children of different groups are more common in schools where classes are smaller (Hallinan & Teixeira, 1987). Evidently, when classes are large, children select friends from the large number of available same-race peers. In contrast, fewer same-race peers are available in smaller classes, so children more often become friends with children of other races. Interracial friendships are usually confined to school, unless children come from integrated neighborhoods. That is, when children live in different, segregated neighborhoods, their friendship does not extend to out-of-school settings (DuBois & Hirsch, 1990).

Of course, friends are not only alike in age, sex, and race. Children and adolescents are usually drawn together because they have similar attitudes toward school, recreation, and the future (Hartup, 1992b; Tolson & Urberg, 1993). Tom, who enjoys school, likes to read books, and plans to go to Harvard, will probably not befriend Barry, who thinks that school is stupid, listens to his CD player constantly, and plans to quit high school to become a rock star. As time passes, friends becomes more similar in their attitudes and values (Kandel, 1978).

Consequences of Friendships

Friends are good for you. Researchers consistently find that children benefit from having a friend (Hartup & Stevens, 1997). For example, children with friends more often act prosocially—sharing and cooperating with others (Hartup, 1996). Children with friends tend to be better adjusted as well. For example, kindergarten children with good friendships get along better with peers and have more positive attitudes toward peers (Ladd, Kochenderfer, & Coleman, 1997). Similarly, adolescents with high-quality friendships adjust more readily to new schools and become more involved in school (Berndt & Keefe, 1995). Furthermore, friendships enhance self-esteem in children whose families are not very supportive (Gauze et al., 1996).

Thus, friends are not simply special playmates and companions; instead, they are important resources. Children learn from their friends and can turn to them for support in times of stress. Friendships are one important way in which peers influence children's development. Peers also influence development through groups, the topic of the next section.

GROUPS

At the summer camp in the vignette, new campers always form groups based on common interests. Groups are just as prevalent in American schools. "Jocks," "preps," "burnouts," "druggies," "nerds," and "brains"—you may remember these or similar terms referring to groups of older children and adolescents. During late childhood and early adolescence, the peer group becomes the focal point of social relationships for youth (Rubin, Bukowski, & Parker, 1998). *The starting point is often a* clique—*a small group of children or adolescents who are friends and tend to be similar in age, sex, race, and attitudes.* Members of a clique spend time together and often dress, talk, and act alike. *Several cliques that have similar values and attitudes sometimes become part of a larger group called a* crowd, *known by a label such as "jocks" or "nerds."*

Some crowds have more status than others. For example, students in many junior and senior high schools say that the "jocks" are the most prestigious crowd, whereas the "burnouts" are among the least prestigious. Self-esteem in older children and adolescents often reflects the status of their crowd. During the school years, young people from high-status crowds tend to have greater self-esteem than those from low-status crowds (Brown & Lohr, 1987).

SEE FOR YOURSELF

IDENTIFYING SCHOOL CROWDS

Most junior high and high school students know the different crowds in their school and the status of each. The number of crowds varies, as do their names, but the existence of crowds seems to be a basic fact of social life in late childhood and early adolescence.

To learn more about crowds, try to talk individually to four or five students from the same junior high or high school. You could begin by describing one of the crowds from your own high school days. Then ask each student to name the different crowds in his or her school. Ask each student to describe the defining characteristics of people in each crowd. Finally, ask each student which crowd has the highest status in school and which has the lowest.

When you've interviewed all of the students, compare their answers. Do the students agree about the number and types of crowds in their school? Do they agree on the status of each? Next, compare your results with those of other students in your class. Are the results similar in different schools? Can you find any relation between the types of crowds and characteristics of the school (e.g., rural versus urban)? See for yourself! •

Why do some students become nerds but others join the burnouts? Parenting style is part of the answer. A study by Brown and his colleagues (1993) examined the impact of three parental practices on students' membership in particular crowds. The investigators measured the extent to which parents emphasized academic achievement, monitored their children's out-of-school activities, and involved their children in joint decision making. When parents emphasized achievement, their children were more likely to be in the popular, jock, and normal crowds and less likely to be in the druggie crowd. When parents monitored their children's out-of-school behavior, their children were more likely to be in the brain crowd and less likely to be in the druggie crowd. Finally, when parents included their children in joint decision making, their children were more likely to be in the brain and normal crowds and less likely to be in the druggie crowd. These relations were true for African American, Asian American, European American, and Hispanic American children and their parents.

What seems to happen is that when parents use the practices associated with authoritative parenting—control coupled with warmth—their children become involved with crowds that endorse adult standards of behavior (e.g., normals, jocks, brains). However, when parents' style is uninvolved or indulgent, their children are less likely to identify with adult standards of behavior. In fact, they become involved with crowds like druggies, who disavow these standards.

Group Structure

Groups—be they in school, at a summer camp as in the vignette, or elsewhere—typically have a well-defined structure. *Often groups have a* dominance hierarchy, *headed by a leader to whom all other members of the group defer.* Other members know their position in the hierarchy. They yield to members who are above them in the hierarchy and assert themselves over members who are below them. A dominance hierarchy is useful in reducing conflict within groups, because every member knows his or her place.

What determines where members stand in the hierarchy? In children, especially boys, physical power is often the basis for the dominance hierarchy. The leader is usually the member who is the most intimidating physically (Pettit et al., 1990). Among girls and older boys, hierarchies are often based on individual traits that relate to the group's main function. At Crab Orchard Summer Camp, for example, the leaders are most often the children with the greatest camping experience. Among Girl Scouts like those in the photo, girls chosen to be patrol leaders tend to be bright and goal-oriented and to have new ideas (Edwards, 1994). These characteristics are appropriate, because the primary function of patrols is to help plan activities for an entire troop of Girl Scouts. Thus, this type of group structure is effective; the people with the most useful skills have the greatest influence (Rubin et al., 1998).

THINK ABOUT IT
Chapter 5 described important differences in the ways that boys and girls interact with same-sex peers. How might these differences help explain why boys' and girls' dominance hierarchies often differ?

Peer Pressure

Groups establish norms—standards of behavior that apply to all group members. Groups may pressure members to conform to these norms. Such "peer pressure" is often characterized as an irresistible, harmful force. The stereotype is that teenagers exert enormous pressure on each other to behave antisocially. In reality, peer pressure is neither all-powerful nor always evil. For example, most junior and senior high students *resist* peer pressure to behave in ways that are clearly antisocial, such as stealing (Brown, Lohr, & McClenahan, 1986). Peer pressure can be positive, too, such as urging peers to participate in school activities, such as trying out for a play or working on the yearbook, or becoming involved in community-action projects, such as Habitat for Humanity.

Peer pressure is most powerful when the standards for appropriate behavior are not clear-cut. Tastes in music and clothing, for example, are completely subjective; consequently, youth conform to peer group guidelines, as you can see in the all-too-familiar sight shown in the photo— girls wearing very similar "in" clothing.

Similarly, standards concerning smoking, drinking, and using drugs are often fuzzy. Drinking is a good case in point. Parents and groups like SADD (Students Against Driving Drunk) may discourage teens from drinking, yet American culture is filled with youthful models who drink, seem to enjoy it, and suffer no apparent ill effects. To the contrary, they seem to enjoy life even more. With such contradictory messages, it is not surprising that youth look to their peers for answers (Urberg, Değirmencioğlu,

& Pilgrim, 1997). Consequently, some youth *will* drink (or smoke, use drugs, have sex) to conform to *their* group's norms; others will abstain, again, reflecting their group's norms.

Even when standards are fuzzy, not all teenagers are equally susceptible to peer influence (Vitaro et al., 1997). Adolescents are less likely to be influenced by peer pressure when their parents use an authoritative style and more likely to be influenced when their parents are not authoritative (Mounts & Steinberg, 1995).

POPULARITY AND REJECTION

Eileen is, without question, the most popular child in her fourth-grade class. Most of the other youngsters like to play with her and want to sit near her at lunch or on the school bus. Whenever the class must vote to pick a child for something special—to be class representative to the student council, to recite the class poem on Martin Luther King Day, or to lead the classroom to the lunchroom—Eileen invariably wins.

Jay is not as fortunate as Eileen. In fact, he is the least popular child in the class. His presence is obviously unwanted in any situation. When he sits down at the lunch table, other kids move away. When he tries to join a game of four-square, the others quit. Students in the class detest Jay as much as they like Eileen.

Popular and rejected children like Eileen and Jay are common. In fact, studies of popularity (Rubin et al., 1998) reveal that most children in elementary school classrooms can be placed, fairly consistently, in one of five categories:

- Popular children *are liked by many classmates.*
- Rejected children *are disliked by many classmates.*
- Controversial children *are both liked and disliked by classmates.*
- Average children *are liked and disliked by some classmates, but without the intensity found for popular, rejected, or controversial children.*
- Neglected children *are ignored by classmates.*

What determines who's hot and who's not? Why is a child popular, rejected, controversial, or neglected? Smarter and physically attractive children are more often popular (Johnstone, Frame, & Bouman, 1992). However, the most important ingredient in popularity is social skill. Popular children are better at initiating social interactions with other children (Rubin et al., 1998). They are more skillful at communicating and better at integrating themselves into an ongoing conversation or play session. Popular children also seem relatively gifted in assessing and monitoring their own social impact in various situations and in tailoring their responses to the requirements of each new social situation (Crick & Dodge, 1994; Wentzel & Asher, 1995). For example, Wentzel and Erdley (1993) asked sixth- and seventh-grade children to evaluate their peers' prosocial behavior, antisocial behavior, and popularity. Popular youngsters were more likely than unpopular children to share, cooperate, and help; popular children were also less likely to start fights and break rules.

Why do some children fail in their efforts to be popular and end up in one of the other categories—rejected, controversial, average, or neglected? We know the most about rejected children, who tend to be socially unskilled

(Harrist et al., 1997). Many rejected children are aggressive. When children are too bossy or tease others too much, their peers quickly shun them (Rubin, Chen, & Hymel, 1993). Other rejected children are withdrawn and timid (Volling et al., 1993). When children act "like babies," their peers start to avoid them.

Being well liked seems straightforward: Be pleasant and friendly, not obnoxious. Share, cooperate, and help instead of being disruptive. These results don't apply just to American children; they hold for children in many areas of the world, including Canada, Europe, Israel, and China. Sometimes, however, popular children have other characteristics unique to their cultural setting. In Israel, for example, popular children are more likely to be assertive and direct than in other countries (Krispin, Sternberg, & Lamb, 1992). In China, popular children are more likely to be shy than in other countries (Chen, Rubin, & Li, 1995). Evidently, good social skills are at the core of popularity in most countries, but other features are important, reflecting culturally specific values.

Consequences of Rejection

No one enjoys being rejected. For children, repeated peer rejection in childhood can have serious long-term consequences including dropping out of school, committing juvenile offenses, and suffering from psychopathology (Bagwell, Newcomb, & Bukowski, 1998; Rubin et al., 1998).

The Spotlight on Research describes one study that shows some of the long-term effects of popularity and rejection.

THINK ABOUT IT

Effective parents and popular children have many characteristics in common. What are they?

SPOTLIGHT ON RESEARCH

LONG-TERM CONSEQUENCES OF POPULARITY AND REJECTION

Who were the investigators and what was the aim of the study? Is the outcome of development the same for popular and unpopular children? Or do popularity and rejection steer children down different developmental paths? Patricia Morison and Ann Masten (1991) wanted to answer these questions.

How did the investigators measure the topic of interest? Morison and Masten identified popular and rejected children by asking students in grades 3 – 6 to nominate classmates for roles in an imaginary class play. Popular children were identified as those who were frequently nominated for roles like "a good leader," "everyone likes to be with," and "has many friends." Rejected children were those frequently nominated for roles like "picks on other kids," "too bossy," and "teases other children too much." Seven years later, children and their parents completed questionnaires measuring academic achievement, social skill, and self-worth.

Who were the children in the study? Initially, 207 children in grades 3 – 6 were tested, and 183 of them completed the questionnaires 7 years later.

What was the design of the study? This study was correlational because Morison and Masten were interested in the relation that existed naturally between two sets of variables: popularity and rejection at the first testing and academic achievement, social skill, and self-worth at the second. The study was longitudinal because children were tested twice, once in grades 3 – 6 and again 7 years later.

Were there ethical concerns with the study? No. The general purpose of the study was explained and then parents and children consented to participate.

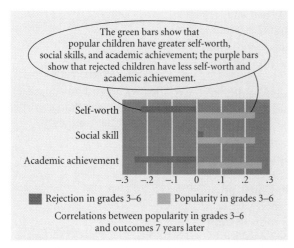

The green bars show that popular children have greater self-worth, social skills, and academic achievement; the purple bars show that rejected children have less self-worth and academic achievement.

Self-worth

Social skill

Academic achievement

−.3   −.2   −.1   0   .1   .2   .3

■ Rejection in grades 3–6   ■ Popularity in grades 3–6

Correlations between popularity in grades 3–6
and outcomes 7 years later

Based on data from Morison and Masten, 1991.

What were the results? The graph shows correlations between popularity and rejection in grades 3–6 and academic achievement, social skill, and self-worth measured 7 years later. Children popular in grades 3–6 were doing well in school, were socially skilled, and had high self-esteem. In contrast, children who were most rejected in grades 3–6 were not doing well in school and had low self-esteem.

What did the investigators conclude? Popular children fit in with groups instead of making groups adjust to them. When conflicts arise, popular children try to understand the problem and provide solutions. Over time, popular children's prosocial skill pays dividends; unfortunately, rejected children's lack of skill has a price as well. ●

Causes of Rejection

Peer rejection can be traced, at least in part, to the influences of parents (Ladd & LeSieur, 1995; Pettit & Mize, 1993). As expected from Bandura's social cognitive theory, children see how their parents respond in different social situations and often imitate these responses later. Parents who are friendly and cooperative with others demonstrate effective social skills for their youngsters. Parents who are belligerent and combative demonstrate tactics that are much less effective. In particular, when parents typically respond to interpersonal conflict like the father in the photo—with intimidation or aggression—their children may imitate them, hampering the development of their social skills and making them less popular in the long run (Keane, Brown, & Crenshaw, 1990).

Parents also contribute to their children's social skill and popularity through their disciplinary practices. Inconsistent discipline—punishing a child for misbehaving one day and ignoring the same behavior the next—is associated with antisocial, aggressive behavior, paving the way for rejection. Consistent punishment that does not rely upon power assertion but is tied to parental love and affection is more likely to promote social skill and, in the process, popularity (Dekovic & Janssens, 1992; Rubin, Stewart, & Chen, 1995).

Thus, the origins of rejection are clear: Socially awkward, aggressive children are often rejected because they rely upon an aggressive interpersonal style, which can be traced to parenting. The implication is that by teaching youngsters (and their parents) more effective ways of interacting with others, we can make rejection less likely. With improved social skills, rejected children would not need to resort to antisocial behaviors that peers deplore. Training of this sort *does* work. Rejected children can learn skills that lead to peer acceptance and thereby avoid the long-term harm associated with being rejected (LaGreca, 1993; Mize & Ladd, 1990).

TEST YOURSELF

1. Friends are usually similar in age, sex, race, and _____ .

2. Children with friends more often act prosocially and are _____ than children without friends.

3. As a group forms, a _____ typically emerges, with the leader at the top.

4. Peer pressure is most powerful when _____ .

5. Popular children often share, cooperate, and _____ .

6. Rejected youngsters are more likely to drop out of school, to commit juvenile offenses, and _____ .

7. How could developmental change in the nature of friendship be explained in terms of Piaget's stages of intellectual development, discussed in Chapters 4 and 6?

Answers: (1) attitudes, (2) better adjusted, (3) dominance hierarchy, (4) standards for appropriate behavior are vague, (5) help others, (6) to suffer psychopathology

---

TELEVISION: BOOB TUBE OR WINDOW ON THE WORLD?

Learning Objectives

- **What is the impact of watching television on children's attitudes and behavior?**

- **How does TV viewing influence children's cognitive development?**

> **Television: Boob Tube or Window on the World?**
>
> Influence on Attitudes and Social Behavior
>
> Influences on Cognition

EVERY *day, 7-year-old Roberto follows the same routine when he gets home from school: He watches one action-adventure cartoon after another until it's time for dinner. Roberto's mother is disturbed by her son's constant TV viewing, particularly because of the amount of violence in the shows he likes. Her husband tells her to stop worrying: "Let him watch what he wants to. It won't hurt him and, besides, it keeps him out of your hair."*

The cartoon exaggerates TV's impact on North American children, but only somewhat. After all, think about how much time you spent in front of a TV while you were growing up. If you were a typical U.S. child and adolescent, you spent much more time watching TV than you did interacting with your parents or in school. The numbers tell an incredible story. School-age children spend about 25 hours each week watching TV (Nielson, 1990). Extrapolated through adolescence, the typical U.S. high school graduate has watched 20,000 hours of TV—the equivalent of 2 full years of watching TV 24 hours daily! No wonder social scientists and laypeople alike have come to see TV as an important contributor to the socialization of North American children.

Of course, not all children watch the same amount of TV. For most youngsters, however, viewing time increases gradually during the preschool and elementary school years, reaching a peak at about 11 or 12 years of age. Boys watch more TV than girls. Also, children with lower IQs watch more than those with higher IQs; children from lower-income families watch more TV than children from higher-income families (Huston & Wright, 1998).

It is hard to imagine that such massive viewing of TV would have no effect on children's behavior. After all, 30-second TV ads are designed to influence children's preferences in toys, cereals, and hamburgers, so the programs themselves ought to have even more impact.

"MRS. HORTON, COULD YOU STOP BY SCHOOL TODAY?"

©1995 Martha F. Campbell. Reprinted with permission.

INFLUENCE ON ATTITUDES
AND SOCIAL BEHAVIOR

Back in 1954, the chairman of the U.S. Senate Subcommittee on Juvenile Delinquency, Estes Kefauver, was concerned about the amount of violence in television programming. At that time, only about half of the households in the United States had television sets, yet the public was already aware of the frequent portrayal of violence in TV programs and worried about its effects on viewers, especially young ones. Anecdotes suggesting a link were common: A 6-year-old fan of Hopalong Cassidy (a TV cowboy of the 1950s) asked his father for real bullets for his toy gun, because his toy bullets didn't kill people the way Hopalong's did (Schramm, Lyle, & Parker, 1961).

More than 45 years later, citizens remain concerned about violence on TV—with good reason. Children's cartoons, like the one shown in this photograph, typically have one violent act every three minutes. (The term *violence*

here refers to use of physical force against another person.) The average North American youngster will see several thousand murders on TV before reaching adolescence (Waters, 1993).

What is the impact of this steady diet of televised mayhem and violence? According to Bandura's (1986) social-cognitive theory, which we first described in Chapter 1, children learn by observing others; they watch others and often imitate what they see. Applied to TV, this theory predicts more aggressive behavior from children who watch violent TV. This prediction was supported by laboratory studies conducted in the 1960s (Bandura, Ross, & Ross, 1963). Children watched specially created TV programs in which an adult behaved violently toward a plastic "Bobo" doll; the adult kicked and hit the doll with a plastic hammer. When children were given the opportunity to play with the doll, those who had seen the TV program were much more likely to behave aggressively toward the doll than were children who had not seen the program.

Critics noted many limitations in this and other early studies and doubted that viewing TV violence in more realistic settings would have such pronounced effects on children (Klapper, 1968). Consequently, scientists began to study the impact of viewing actual TV violence on children's behavior. The results of this research showed a consistent result: Frequent exposure to TV violence causes children to be more aggressive (Huston & Wright, 1998).

One of the most compelling studies examined the impact of children's TV viewing at age 8 on criminal activity at age 30 (Huesmann & Miller, 1994). The graph shows quite clearly that 8-year-olds exposed to large doses of TV vio-

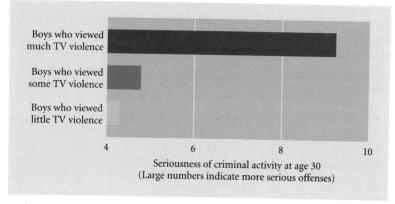

Based on data in Huesmann and Miller, 1994.

lence had the most extensive criminal records as 30-year-olds. The link was found for both males and females, although females' level of criminal activity was much lower overall.

Thus, children like Roberto who are frequent viewers of TV violence learn to resort to aggression in their interactions with others. For many, their aggression eventually puts them behind bars. Of course, violence is only one part of what children see on TV. Let's examine other ways in which TV is an important influence on children as they develop.

Stereotypes

TV is said to provide a "window on the world." Unfortunately, the view on prime-time TV is distorted, particularly when it comes to minorities, women, and the elderly. In the early days of TV, African Americans almost never appeared in programs. When they did appear, they were limited to minor roles such as the gentle buffoon. Today, African American actors account for 10–15% of TV casts, which approximates the percentage of African Americans in the U.S. population, and they are not relegated to buffoon roles. However, other minorities—including Asian Americans, Hispanic Americans, and Native Americans—appear very infrequently in prime time (Huston & Wright, 1998). In contrast, educational programs for children often include minority characters and often depict them in positions of authority (Neapolitan & Huston, 1994; Williams & Cox, 1995).

The situation is much the same for women and the elderly. Their portrayal on prime-time TV bears little resemblance to reality. No more than one-third of all TV roles are for women. When women are shown on TV, they are often passive and emotional. Most are not employed; those who have jobs are often in stereotypical female careers such as teachers or secretaries (Huston & Wright, 1998). Also, the land of television evidently has a fountain of youth,

? THINK ABOUT IT
Some skeptics remark that TV programming is simply a reflection of society at large, so children learn nothing—good or bad—that they wouldn't learn from their culture sooner or later. Do you agree?

because older Americans are grossly underrepresented. Although nearly 20% of the U.S. population is 60 or older, less than 5% of the characters in prime-time TV are that age. Ironically, older adults on TV are usually men, despite the fact that women far outnumber men at this point in the life span (Gerbner, 1993).

Surprisingly, we know relatively little about the effects of these stereotyped portrayals on children's attitudes toward minorities or the elderly. However, the impact of the stereotyped presentation of males and females is clear. As you can imagine, children who watch TV frequently end up with more stereotyped views of males and females. For example, Kimball (1986) studied sex-role stereotypes in a small Canadian town that was located in a valley and could not receive TV programs until a transmitter was installed nearby in 1974. Two years later, views of personality traits, behaviors, occupations, and peer relations were measured in the town's children. The graphs show that boys' and girls' views on these issues became more stereotyped after TV was introduced.

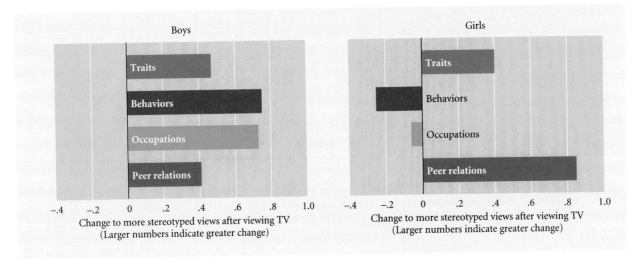

Based on data in Kimball, 1986.

For example, after the introduction of TV, girls had more stereotyped views of peer relations. They believed that boasting and swearing were characteristic of boys but that sharing and helping were characteristic of girls. The boys in the town acquired more stereotyped views of occupations, believing that girls could be teachers and cooks, whereas boys could be physicians and judges.

Findings like these indicate that TV viewing causes children to adopt many of the stereotypes that dominate television programming (Signorielli & Lears, 1992). For many children and adolescents, TV's slanted depiction of the world *becomes* reality.

Consumer Behavior

Sugary cereals, hamburgers and french fries, snack foods, expensive toys. . . . These products are the focus of a phenomenal amount of TV advertising that is directed toward children. A typical youngster may see more than 50 commercials a day! As early as 3 years of age, children distinguish commercials from programs. However, preschool children often believe that commercials are simply a different form of entertainment—one designed to inform viewers. Not until 8 or 9 years of age do most children understand the persuasive intent of commercials. At the same time that children grasp the aim of commercials, they begin to realize that commercials are not always truthful (Liebert & Sprafkin, 1988).

Commercials are effective sales tools with children. Children grow to like many of the products advertised on TV. Like the youngster in the photograph, they may urge parents to buy products they have seen on television. In one study (Greenberg, Fazel, & Weber, 1986), more than 75% of the children reported that they had asked their parents to buy a product they had seen advertised on TV. More often than not, parents purchased the product for them!

This selling power of TV commercials has long concerned advocates for children, because so many ads focus on children's foods that have little nutritional value and that are associated with problems such as obesity and tooth decay. The U.S. government once regulated the amount and type of advertising on children's TV programs (Huston, Watkins, & Kunkel, 1989), but today the responsibility falls largely to parents. In the You May Be Wondering Feature, we recommend some ways for parents to regulate their children's TV viewing.

YOU MAY BE WONDERING

NO MORE CHILD COUCH POTATOES!

If you know a child who sits glued to the TV screen from after school until bedtime, has his or her own remote control, and reads *TV Guide* from cover to cover, it's time to take action. Here are some suggestions:

1. Children need absolute rules concerning the amount of TV and the types of programs they can watch. These rules must be enforced consistently!

2. Children shouldn't fall into the trap of "I'm bored, so I'll watch TV." Children should be encouraged to know what they want to watch *before* they turn on the TV set.

3. Adults should watch TV with children and discuss the programs. Parents can, for example, express their disapproval of a character's use of aggression and suggest other means of resolving conflicts. Parents can also point to the stereotypes that are depicted. The aim is for children to learn that TV's account of the world is often inaccurate and to encourage the children to watch TV critically. (What may happen, of course, is that they can't stand the parent's constant chatter and stop watching altogether!)

4. Parents need to be good TV viewers themselves. The first two tips listed here apply to viewers of all ages! When a child is present, parents shouldn't watch violent programs or others that are inappropriate for the young. And parents should throw away the remote control so that they, too, will watch TV deliberately and selectively, not mindlessly flip between channels. ●

Prosocial Behavior

TV is clearly a potent influence on children's aggression and on the stereotypes they form. Can this power be put to more prosocial goals? Can TV viewing help children learn to be more generous, to be more cooperative, and to have greater self-control? Yes, according to early laboratory studies. In these experiments, children were more likely to act prosocially after they watched brief films in which a peer acted prosocially. For example, children were more likely to share or more likely to resist the temptation to take from others when they had seen a filmed peer sharing or resisting temptation (Liebert & Sprafkin, 1988).

An early study by Bryan and Walbek (1970) typifies this sort of experimentation. Third- and fourth-grade children received a prize for playing a game, then watched a film about another child who had received the same prize and was asked to donate some of the prize to charity. In one version of the film, the child donated part of the prize; in another version, the child did not. The children in the study were then given the opportunity to donate a portion of their winnings to the same charity shown in the film. Children were much more likely to donate when they had seen the film about the generous child than when they had seen the film about the stingy one. Thus, from watching others who were generous, children acted more generously themselves.

Research with actual TV programs leads to the same conclusion. Youngsters who watch TV shows that emphasize prosocial behavior, such as *Mister Rogers' Neighborhood,* are more likely to behave prosocially (Huston & Wright, 1998). In fact, a comprehensive analysis revealed that the impact of viewing prosocial TV programs is much greater than the impact of viewing televised violence (Hearold, 1986). Boys, in particular, benefit from viewing prosocial TV, perhaps because they are usually much less skilled prosocially than girls are.

Although research indicates that prosocial behavior *can* be influenced by TV watching, two important factors restrict the actual prosocial impact of TV viewing. First, prosocial behaviors are portrayed on TV programs far less frequently than aggressive behaviors; opportunities to learn prosocial behaviors from television are limited. Second, in the real world of TV watching, the relatively small number of prosocial programs must compete with other kinds of television programs, as well as other activities, for children's time. Children simply may not watch the few prosocial programs that are televised. Clearly, we are far from harnessing the power of television for prosocial uses.

> ? **THINK ABOUT IT**
> Would all developmental theories predict that *merely* watching prosocial behavior on TV is enough to lead children to behave prosocially themselves?

INFLUENCES ON COGNITION

You undoubtedly know Big Bird, Kermit the Frog, Cookie Monster, Oscar the Grouch, and their friends, for they are the cast of *Sesame Street,* one of the longest-running shows in TV history. First appearing in 1969, *Sesame Street* has helped educate generations of preschoolers. Today, mothers and fathers who watched *Sesame Street* as preschoolers are watching with their own youngsters.

Produced by Children's Television Workshop, the goal of *Sesame Street* was to use the power of video and animation to fosters skills like recognizing letters and numbers, counting, and vocabulary in preschool children. Evaluations conducted in the early years of *Sesame Street* showed that the program achieved its goals—preschoolers who watched *Sesame Street* regularly were more proficient at the targeted academic skills than were children who watched less often. And frequent viewers adjusted to school more readily, according to teachers' ratings (Bogatz & Ball, 1972).

More recent studies have confirmed these benefits. Wright and Huston (1995), for example, found that preschoolers who watch *Sesame Street* frequently have larger vocabularies, better math and prereading skills, and are better prepared for school than preschoolers who watch infrequently. Importantly, these gains were the same for European American and Hispanic American children and the same for children from lower-class and middle-class homes.

Building on the success of *Sesame Street,* Children's Television Workshop developed a number of other successful programs. *Electric Company* was designed to teach reading skills, *3-2-1 Contact* has a science and technology focus, and *Square One TV* aims at mathematics (Liebert & Sprafkin, 1988). More recent programs have included *Reading Rainbow, Ghostwriter, Where in the World Is Carmen Sandiego?,* and *Bill Nye Science Guy.* These programs have not been evaluated to the same extent as *Sesame Street.* However, the typical finding is that children who watch these sorts of programs frequently improve their academic skills and develop more positive attitudes as well (Huston & Wright, 1998).

Programs like these leave little doubt that TV's socializing influence need not be limited to the learning of aggression and stereotypes. Children *can* learn academic skills and useful social skills, if parents insist that their youngsters be good viewers, and if they insist that TV improve the quality and variety of programs available for children and adolescents.

---

1. When children watch a lot of TV violence, they often become _____ .

2. Preschool children believe that commercials _____ .

3. Youngsters who watch *Sesame Street* frequently improve their academic skills and, according to their teachers, _____ .

4. Use the difference between divergent and convergent thinking, explained in Chapter 6, to describe the impact of TV viewing on children.

Answers: (1) more aggressive, (2) represent a different, informative type of program but do not understand the intent to persuade, (3) adjust to school more readily.

UNDERSTANDING OTHERS

Learning Objectives

- **As children develop, how do they describe others differently?**

- **How does understanding of others' thinking change as children develop?**

- **When do children develop prejudice toward others?**

Understanding Others

Describing Others

Understanding What Others Think

Prejudice

HEN *12-year-old Ian agreed to babysit his 5-year-old brother, Kyle, their mother reminded Ian to keep Kyle out of the basement because Kyle's birthday presents were there, unwrapped. But as soon as their mother left, Kyle wanted to go to the basement to ride his tricycle. When Ian told him no, Kyle burst into angry tears and shouted, "I'm gonna tell Mom that you were mean to me!" Ian wished he could explain to Kyle but he knew that would just cause more trouble!*

As children spend more time with other people (either directly or vicariously, through television), they begin to understand other people better. In this vignette, for example, Ian realizes why Kyle is angry and he knows that if he gives in to Kyle now, his mother will be angry when she returns. Children's growing understanding of others is the focus of this section. We begin by looking at how children describe others, then examine their understanding of how others think. Finally, we'll also see how children's recognition of different social groups can lead to prejudices.

Later that day, Holly and her friends meet Sean. Sean's kitten is caught up in a tree and cannot get down. Something has to be done right away or the kitten may fall. Holly is the only one who climbs well enough to reach the kitten and get it down, but she remembers her promise to her father. (Selman & Byrne, 1974, p. 805)

This dilemma is typical in that it includes several people who don't share the same knowledge about the events taking place. After hearing the story, children and adolescents were asked questions to investigate their ability to take on each character's view and predict what would happen to Holly.

Selman found that answers to dilemmas like this became more sophisticated as children developed. In fact, he proposed the five different stages of perspective-taking that are shown in the table.

SELMAN'S STAGES OF PERSPECTIVE TAKING

Stage	Approximate Ages	Description
Undifferentiated	3–6 years	Children know that self and others can have different thoughts and feelings, but often confuse the two.
Social-informational	4–9 years	Children know that perspectives differ because people have access to different information.
Self-reflective	7–12 years	Children can step into another's shoes and view themselves as others do. They know that others can do the same.
Third-person	10–15 years	Children can step outside of the immediate situation to see how they and another person are viewed by a third person.
Societal	14 years to adult	Adolescents realize that a third person's perspective is influenced by broader personal, social, and cultural contexts.

? THINK ABOUT IT
How do Selman's stages of perspective-taking correspond to Piaget's and Erikson's stages?

The first stage is called undifferentiated, because children in this stage get confused about "who thinks what." A child in this stage might reply, "Holly's father will be happy because he likes kittens." This answer confuses Holly's feelings with her father's and ignores Holly's promise. Children in the social-informational stage might say, "If Holly's father knew why she climbed the tree, he probably wouldn't be angry." This answer indicates that the child understands that the father's response depends upon whether or not he knows the reason for Holly's behavior.

In the self-reflective stage, a child might say, "Holly's father would understand that she thought saving the kitten's life was really important, so he wouldn't be mad. He'd probably be proud." This comment shows Holly's father stepping into Holly's shoes, the defining characteristic of the self-reflective stage.

At the next level, the third-person stage, a child might respond, "Holly remembers the promise, but she doesn't think her father will be angry when she explains that she wouldn't have climbed the tree except to save the kitten's life. Her father might wish that Holly had asked an adult for help, but he'd also understand why it was important to Holly to save the kitten." This child simultaneously considers both Holly's and her father's perspectives on the dilemma. That is, in answering, the child has stepped outside the immediate situation to take the perspective of a neutral third party who can look at both Holly's and her father's views.

At the most advanced level, the societal stage, an adolescent might reply, "Holly and her father both know that she almost always obeys him. So, they'd both know that if she disobeyed him to climb the tree, there would have to be an awfully good reason. So, they'd talk about it." This child's answer, like the previous one, considers Holly's and her father's perspectives simultaneously. The difference is that this comment puts the issue in the broader context of the history of their father-daughter relationship.

As predicted by Selman's theory, research shows that as children develop, their reasoning moves through each stage, in sequence. In addition, regardless of age, children at more advanced cognitive levels tend to be at more advanced stages in perspective-taking (Gurucharri & Selman, 1982; Krebs & Gillmore, 1982).

Other support for Selman's theory comes from studies of the connections between perspective-taking and social behavior. In the photo, the children with the soccer ball apparently recognized that the girl on the sidelines wanted to play, so they're inviting her to join the game. Children who can anticipate what others are thinking should get along better with their peers, and research indicates that they do. For example, children with good perspective-taking skills are typically well liked by their peers (LeMare & Rubin, 1987). Of course, mere understanding does not guarantee good social behavior; sometimes children who understand what another child is thinking take advantage of that child. But, in general, greater understanding of others seems to promote positive interactions with others.

PREJUDICE

As children learn more about others, they discover that people belong to different social groups, based on variables such as gender, ethnicity, and social class. By the preschool years, most children can distinguish males from females and can identify people from different ethnic groups (Aboud, 1993). Once children learn their membership in a specific group—"I'm a Vietnamese American boy"—they typically show prejudice. That is, they view their own group more favorably than others. Preschool and kindergarten children more often attribute positive traits (being friendly and smart) to their own group and attribute negative traits (being mean and fighting a lot) to other groups (Black-Gutman & Hickson, 1996).

As children move into the elementary school years, prejudice typically declines somewhat (Powlishta et al., 1994). Why? Cognitive development holds the answer. Preschool and kindergarten children usually believe all people from other groups are very different from their own group, and, typically, not as good. Older children understand that social groups are heterogeneous—they know that individual European Americans, girls, and obese children, for example—are not all alike. And they have learned that people from different groups may be more alike than people from the same group. Gary, an African American whose passion is computers finds that he enjoys being with Vic, an Italian American who shares his love of computers, but not Curtis, another

African American whose passion is music. As children realize that social groups consist of all kinds of different people, prejudice lessens.

Prejudice may be less pronounced in older children, but it does not vanish. Older children and adolescents remain biased positively toward their

own group and negatively toward others (Powlishta et al., 1994). Of course, many adults have this same bias toward their own group; children and adolescents are simply reflecting the attitudes of those around them.

What can parents, teachers, and other adults do to rid children of prejudice? One way is to encourage friendly and constructive contacts between children from different groups (Ramsey, 1995). Adults can create situations in which children from different groups work together toward common goals. In school, this might be a class project, as shown in the photo. In sports, it might be mastering a new skill. By working together, Gary starts to realize that Vic acts, thinks, and feels as he does simply because he's Vic, not because he's an Italian American.

Another useful approach is to ask children to play different roles (Davidson & Davidson, 1994). They can be asked to imagine that, because of their race, ethnic background, or gender, they have been insulted verbally or not allowed to participate in special activities. A child might be asked to imagine that she can't go to a private swimming club because she's African American or that she wasn't invited to a party because she's Hispanic American. Afterward, children reflect on how they felt when prejudice and discrimination was directed at them. And they're asked to think about what would be fair—what should be done in situations like these.

From experiences like these, children and adolescents discover for themselves that a person's membership in a social group tells us very little about that person. They learn, instead, that all children are different, each a unique mix of experiences, skills, and values.

TEST YOURSELF

Answers: (1) try to provide a cohesive, integrated account, (2) provide a third person's perspective on situations and recognize the influence of context on this perspective, (3) with cognitive development, children realize that social groups are not homogeneous

1. When adolescents describe others, they usually _____ .

2. In the most advanced stage of Selman's theory, adolescents _____ .

3. Prejudice declines somewhat as children get older because _____ .

4. How might an information-processing theorist describe the stages of Selman's perspective-taking theory?

PUTTING IT ALL TOGETHER

In this chapter, we've examined some of the many forces that contribute to socialization. Parents, peers, and TV emerged as mighty shapers of children's development.

We learned that parental style influences both cognitive and social development. Children reared by parents with the authoritarian style favored by Tanya's mother often have low self-esteem and low social skill; children reared by parents with the authoritative style used by Sheila's mother tend to be self-reliant and friendly and to do well in school. We saw that groups like those at Crab Orchard Summer Camp are an important element of social life among older children and adolescents and that their impact is greatest when behavioral standards are not clear. We saw that TV's influence is tremendous. It can cause children like Roberto to rely on aggression to resolve interpersonal conflict, and it can give them a stereotyped view of the world. Finally, we learned that children's descriptions and understanding of others become more complex with age, so that

young adolescents like Ian are often fully aware of what others are thinking. And, we saw that prejudice declines with age, especially when children interact with peers from other groups.

Thus, parents, siblings, peers, and television define much of the sociocultural context of development for American children, and their impact is considerable. Through the combined power of parents, siblings, peers, and television, children acquire the beliefs and behaviors of their culture. Full, adult membership in their culture is not far away. Only adolescence remains, and that topic will be examined in Chapter 8.

SUMMARY

Family Relationships

Dimensions and Styles of Parenting

• One key factor in parent-child relationships is the degree of warmth that parents express: Children clearly benefit from warm, caring parents. A second factor is control, which is complicated because neither too much nor too little control is desirable. Effective parental control involves setting appropriate standards, enforcing them, and trying to anticipate conflicts.

• Power assertion is an ineffective and sometimes harmful form of punishment. Time-out, in which children are isolated briefly, is a much more effective way of punishing children.

• Taking into account both warmth and control, four prototypic parental styles emerge. (a) Authoritarian parents are controlling but uninvolved. (b) Authoritative parents are fairly controlling but are also responsive to their children. (c) Indulgent-permissive parents are loving but exert little control. (d) Indifferent-uninvolved parents are neither warm nor controlling. Authoritative parenting seems best for children, in terms of both cognitive and social development.

• Parenting is influenced by characteristics of children themselves. A child's age and temperament will influence how a parent tries to exert control over the child.

Siblings

• The birth of a sibling can be stressful for children, particularly when the children are still young and when parents ignore their needs. Siblings get along better

when they are of the same sex, believe that parents treat them similarly, enter adolescence, and have parents who get along well.

• Parents have higher expectations for first-born children, which explains why such children are more intelligent and more likely to go to college. Later-born children are more popular and more innovative. Contradicting the folklore, only children are almost never worse off than children with siblings. In some respects (such as intelligence, achievement, and autonomy), they are often better off.

Divorce and Remarriage

• In the months after a divorce, a mother's parenting is often less effective and her children behave immaturely. By 2 years after the divorce, family life is much improved. At 6 years after the divorce, mother-daughter relationships are often very positive but mother-son relationships are often conflict-filled.

• Divorce can harm children in a number of areas, ranging from school achievement to adjustment. The impact of divorce stems from less supervision of children following divorce, economic hardship, and conflict between parents. Children often benefit when parents have joint custody following divorce, or when they live with the same-sex parent.

• When a mother remarries, daughters sometimes have difficulty adjusting because the new stepfather encroaches on an intimate mother-daughter relationship. A father's remarriage can cause problems because children fear that the stepmother will disturb intimate father-child relationships and because of tension between the stepmother and the noncustodial mother.

Parent-Child Relationships Gone Awry: Child Abuse

• Cultural factors contributing to child abuse include a culture's views on violence, poverty, and social isolation. Parents who abuse their children were often neglected or abused themselves and tend to be unhappy, socially unskilled individuals. Younger or unhealthy children are more likely to be targets of abuse. Children who are abused often lag behind in cognitive and social development.

Peers

Friendships

• Friendships among preschoolers are based on common interests and getting along well. As children grow, loyalty, trust, and intimacy become more important features in their friendships. Friends are usually similar in age, sex, race, and attitudes. Children with friends are more skilled socially and better adjusted.

Groups

• Older children and adolescents often form cliques—small groups of like-minded individuals—that become part of a crowd. Some crowds have higher status than others, and members of higher-status crowds often have higher self-esteem than members of lower-status crowds.

• Common to most groups is a dominance hierarchy, a well-defined structure with a leader at the top. Physical power often determines the dominance hierarchy, particularly among boys. However, with older children and adolescents, dominance hierarchies are more often based on skills that are important to the group.

• Peer pressure is neither totally powerful nor totally evil. In fact, groups influence individuals primarily in areas where standards of behavior are unclear, such as tastes in music or clothing, or concerning drinking, drug use, and sex.

Popularity and Rejection

• Popular children are socially skilled. They often share, cooperate, and help others. They are unlikely to behave in antisocial ways, such as starting a fight.

• Some children are rejected by their peers, typically because they are too aggressive or withdrawn. Such children are often unsuccessful in school and have behavioral problems. The aggressive style of some rejected children can be linked to parents who are bel-ligerent or combative and who are inconsistent in their discipline.

Television: Boob Tube or Window on the World?

Influence on Attitudes and Social Behavior

• Children's social behaviors and attitudes are influenced by what they see on TV. Youngsters who frequently watch televised violence become more aggressive, whereas those who watch prosocial TV become more socially skilled. Children who watch TV frequently may adopt TV's distorted view of women, minorities, and older people.

Influences on Cognition

• TV programs designed to foster children's cognitive skills, such as *Sesame Street* and *Ghostwriter,* are effective. Children frequently improve their academic skills and often adjust more readily to school.

Understanding Others

Describing Others

• Children's descriptions of others change in much the same way that children's descriptions of themselves change. During the early elementary school years, descriptions emphasize concrete characteristics. In the late elementary school years, they emphasize personality traits. In adolescence, they emphasize providing an integrated picture of others.

Understanding What Others Think

• According to Selman's theory, children's understanding of how others think progresses through five stages. In the first, the undifferentiated stage, children often confuse their own and another's view. In the last, the societal stage, adolescents can take a third person's perspective and know that this perspective is influenced by context.

Prejudice

• Prejudice emerges in the preschool years, soon after children recognize different social groups. Prejudice declines during childhood, as children's cognitive growth helps them understand that social groups are heterogeneous, not homogeneous. However, older children and adolescents still show prejudice, which is best reduced by additional exposure to individuals from other social groups.

KEY TERMS

socialization (237)
power assertion (240)
time-out (240)
authoritarian parenting (241)
authoritative parenting (241)
indulgent-permissive parents (242)

indifferent-uninvolved parents
 (242)
joint custody (248)
blended family (249)
clique (256)
crowd (256)

dominance hierarchy (257)
popular children (258)
rejected children (258)
controversial children (258)
average children (258)
neglected children (258)

IF YOU'D LIKE TO LEARN MORE

Readings

CANTOR, J. (1998). *Mommy, I'm scared: How TV and movies frighten children and what we can do to protect them.* New York: Harvest Books. The author shows some of the consequences of violent programs and movies on children, gives some age-related guidelines for what kind of material is likely to scare children, and describes ways to comfort frightened children. An excellent resource for parents.

DUNN, J. (1993). *Young children's close relationships.* Newbury Park, CA: Sage. A leading expert provides a straightforward and entertaining account of children's social relationships.

MATHIAS, B., & FRENCH, M. A. (1996). *40 ways to raise a nonracist child.* New York: HarperCollins. The authors provide age-appropriate ways to teach children that color does not indicate a person's worth, and dis-

cuss such practical topics as how to pick toys for youngsters and how to talk with older children and adolescents about what they see about race in the media.

McCLANAHAN, S., & SANDEFUR, G. (1996). *Growing up with a single parent: What hurts, what helps.* Cambridge, MA: Harvard University Press. The authors describe many disadvantages for children of growing up in a single-parent family. Then they recommend changes in government policies for assisting single-parent families. A penetrating analysis of an important problem for many U.S. children.

For additional readings, explore Infotrac College Edition, your online library. Go to http://www. infotrac-college.com/wadsworth.

Web Sites

The Web site of *Today's Parent*

http://www.todaysparent.com/

offers tips on how to deal with the different problems—large and small—that come up in rearing children.

The Web site of the National Committee to Prevent Child Abuse

http://www.childabuse.org

provides information on how to prevent child abuse, with parenting tips, statistics on child abuse, a directory of state chapters, and a variety of related material.

The Educational Resources Information Center (ERIC) maintains a Web site that allows access to documents related to education. Part of the site

http://ericps.ed.uiuc.edu/npin/respar/texts/fampeer.html

is devoted to family and peer relationships in childhood.

A Web site maintained by the National Coalition Building Institute

http://www.ncbi.org

describes methods like those described on page 272 to eliminate prejudice and discrimination.

Web site addresses are subject to change. The Wadsworth Study Center Web site listed below can be accessed for updated links.

The Wadsworth Psychology Study Center Web Site

See http://psychology.wadsworth.com/ for practice quiz questions, internet links, updates, critical thinking exercises, discussion forums and more! The Wadsworth Psychology Study Center provides a wealth of information fully organized and integrated by chapter.

CHAPTER 8

RITES OF PASSAGE TO YOUNG ADULTHOOD

Farewell to Childhood: Puberty
Physical Growth
Eating Disorders
  What Causes Anorexia and Bulimia?

Who Am I? The Search for Identity
Identity Versus Role Confusion
Resolving the Identity Crisis
Ethnic Identity
  *Identity in Children of Transracial
    Adoptions*
The Myth of Storm and Stress

**Flipping Burgers and Waiting Tables:
Entering the World of Work**
Part-Time Work
Career Development
  *"The Life of Lynne," A Drama
    in Three Acts*

**"How Do I Love Thee?"—
Romantic Relationships**
Dating
Awakening of Sexual Interests
  *Promoting Greater Awareness on
    Campus About Sexual Assault*

**A Look at the Dark Side: Problems
of Adolescent Development**
Use of Drugs
Depression
  Preventing Teen Suicides
Delinquency
  *When Juveniles Commit Serious Crimes,
    Should They Be Tried as Adults?*

Putting It All Together

Summary

If You'd Like to Learn More

You probably have vivid memories of your teenage years. Remember the exhilarating moments—high school graduation, your first paycheck from a part-time job, and your first feelings of love and sexuality? There were, of course, painful times—your first day on the job when you couldn't do anything right, not knowing what to say on a date with a person you desperately wanted to impress, and countless arguments with your parents. Feelings of pride and accomplishment accompanied by feelings of embarrassment and bewilderment are common to individuals who are on the threshold of adulthood.

You may be surprised to know that adolescence is a recent cultural invention. For much of history, children moved directly into adulthood; when they attained puberty, they were considered to be young adults. In today's industrialized societies, the transition from childhood to adulthood is more gradual, spanning the teenage years that we know as adolescence. During these years, individuals try to adjust to the changes taking place in their bodies; they grapple with their identities; some first enter the world of work; and many have their first experiences with love and sex. In the first four sections, we investigate these challenging developmental issues. Then, we look at the special obstacles adolescents sometimes encounter that make adolescence difficult to handle.

FAREWELL TO CHILDHOOD: PUBERTY

Farewell to Childhood: Puberty

Physical Growth

Eating Disorders

Learning Objectives

- **What changes define puberty? When do they occur?**

- **What are the effects of maturing early or late? Are they the same for boys and girls?**

- **What are some causes of eating-related disorders, such as obesity and anorexia nervosa?**

ETE just had his fifteenth birthday, but, as far as he is concerned, there is no reason to celebrate. Although most of his friends have grown about 6 inches in the past year or so, have a much larger penis and larger testicles, and mounds of pubic hair, Pete looks just as he did when he was 10 years old. He is embarrassed by his appearance, particularly in the locker room, where he looks like a little boy among men. "Won't I ever change?" he wonders.

The appearance of body hair, the emergence of breasts, and the enlargement of the penis and testicles are all signs that the child is gone, and the adolescent is here. Many adolescents take great satisfaction in these signs of maturity. Others, like Pete, worry through their teenage years as they wait for the physical signs of adolescence.

In this section, we'll study the biological signs of adolescence and see why some children mature early and others (like Pete) mature later. We'll also examine disorders of physical development that affect some adolescents.

PHYSICAL GROWTH

For physical growth, the elementary school years represent the calm before the adolescent storm. In an average year, a typical 6- to 10-year-old girl or boy gains about 5–7 pounds and grows 2–3 inches. In contrast, during the peak of the growth spurt, a girl may gain 20 pounds in a year and a boy, 25 (Tanner, 1970). This adolescent growth spurt lasts a few years, so that girls have typically achieved most of their mature stature by age 15 and boys by age 17.

The growth spurt is but one of a collection of physical changes occurring in early adolescence known as puberty. These changes and when they usually occur are shown in the chart. In girls, puberty begins with growth of the breasts and the start of the growth spurt. *Later, pubic hair emerges, followed by the onset of menstruation,* menarche, *typically at about age 13.* Early menstrual cycles can be irregular and often happen without ovulation.

For boys, puberty usually commences with the growth of the testes and scrotum, followed by the appearance of pubic hair, the start of the growth spurt, and growth of the penis. Approximately 1 year later, at about age 13, most boys have their first spontaneous ejaculation, a discharge of fluid containing sperm. Ini-

Average timing of pubertal changes in North American youth
(The beginning of the bar marks the start of change, and the end of the bar marks its completion.)

Malina & Bouchard, 1991.

tial ejaculations often contain relatively few sperm; only months or sometimes years later are there sufficient sperm to fertilize an egg. Finally, at about age 14, the largynx enlarges and the vocal cords lengthen, causing boys' voices to deepen.

These physical signs of maturation are initiated by changing levels of hormones in children's bodies. Growth of the bones and muscles, which leads to overall increases in stature, is stimulated by two hormones: thyroxine and growth hormone. Both are secreted throughout childhood, but in much greater amounts prior to and during puberty. In addition, as puberty approaches, sex hormones are secreted that trigger the many events leading to sexual maturation. In girls, the ovaries secrete more estrogen, which leads to menarche and growth of the breasts and pubic hair. In boys, the testes secrete more androgen, which causes the testes to enlarge and leads to growth of muscles, bones, and pubic hair (Tanner, 1990).

Today's children enter puberty earlier and are, as adults, taller and heavier than previous generations. *These changes in physical development from one generation to the next are known as* secular growth trends, *and they have been quite large.* For example, the average height of a U.S. sailor in the War of 1812 was 5 feet, 2 inches. The graph shows that the age at which American girls experience menarche has dropped more than 1½ years since the start of the 20th century.

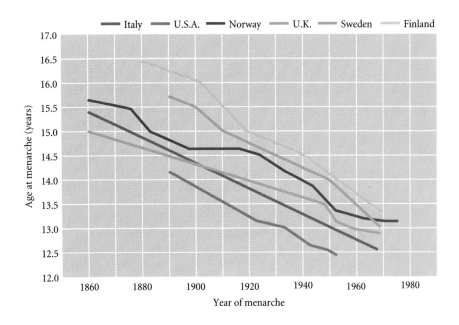

This accelerated development has occurred primarily in industrialized societies where health care and diet have improved substantially. In many Third World countries, where children's living conditions have not improved, adult stature has remained the same (Martorell, Mendoza, & Castillo, 1988). Also, there is a limit to the impact of improved living conditions on growth. In countries that provide adequate nutrition and health care for most of their young, children of recent generations are no longer growing bigger than previous generations (Roche, 1979; Tanner, 1990).

These findings seem to demonstrate the combined power of heredity and experience on physical growth. Genetics apparently determines a target stature. Historically, few people received enough nutrition and health care throughout childhood to reach this target. Only in the past century have industrialized nations provided adequate food and health care, which explains why adult stature has increased so much and is now leveling off in those countries (Tanner, 1990).

Rate of Maturation

Of course, puberty does not always begin at age 11 for girls and age 13 for boys. For many children, puberty begins months or years before or after these norms. An early-maturing boy might begin puberty at age 11 or 12, whereas a late-maturing boy might start at 15 or 16. An early-maturing girl might start puberty at 9 or 10, a late-maturing girl, at 14 or 15. For example, the girls shown in the photographs are the same age, but only one has reached puberty.

The timing of maturity is regulated, in part, by genetics. For example, a mother's age at menarche is related to her daughter's age at menarche (Graber, Brooks-Gunn, & Warren, 1995). However, experience also influences the onset of puberty, at least for girls. Menarche occurs at younger ages in girls who experience much family conflict (Belsky, Steinberg, & Draper, 1991; Moffit et al., 1992). Furthermore, girls who are depressed begin to menstruate at a younger age than girls who are not depressed (Graber et al., 1995). Family conflict and depression may lead to early menarche by affecting the levels of hormones that trigger menstruation (Graber et al., 1995).

The psychological consequences of maturing early or late differ for boys and girls. In several longitudinal studies, the general pattern is that early maturation has benefits for boys and, more often than not, costs for girls. Boys who mature early tend to be more independent and self-confident. They're also more popular with peers. In contrast, girls who mature early often lack self-confidence, are less popular, are more likely to be depressed, and more often have behavior problems (Ge, Conger, & Elder, 1996; Simmons & Blyth, 1987; Swarr & Richards, 1996).

Why does rate of maturation have these consequences? Early maturation may benefit boys because others perceive them as more mature and may be more willing to give them adultlike responsibilities. In contrast, late-maturing boys, such as Pete in the vignette, are often frustrated because others treat them like little boys instead of like young men. Early maturation may hamper girls' development by leading them to associate with older adolescents who apparently encourage them to engage in age-inappropriate activities, such as drinking, smoking, and sex, for which they are ill-prepared (Ge et al., 1996).

By young adulthood, many of the effects associated with rate of maturation vanish. When Pete, for example, finally matures, others will treat him like an adult and the few extra years of being treated like a child will not have lasting effects. For some adolescents, however, particularly early-maturing girls, rate of maturation can have long-lasting effects. A girl who matures early, is pressured into sex, and becomes pregnant ends up with a vastly different life course than a girl who matures later and is better prepared to resist pressures for sex. Thus, rate of maturation sometimes leads to events that determine the path of the rest of one's life.

EATING DISORDERS

Growth requires enormous reserves of energy, and many parents worry that their children may not be getting enough to eat. At the same time, however, some youngsters *do* become fat, and some adolescents become irrationally preoccupied with their weight. Let's look at each of these problems.

Obesity

In the United States, about 5–10% of children and adolescents are obese, which means they are at least 20% over the ideal body weight for their age and height. Like the boy in the photo, obese children are often unpopular and have low self-esteem (Braet, Mervielde, & Vandereycken, 1997). These children and adolescents often dislike the physical games that entertain their classmates after school, have relatively few friends, and are not particularly happy with their lot in life. Furthermore, they are at risk for many medical problems, including high blood pressure and diabetes, which are made all the more likely because the vast majority of overweight children and adolescents become overweight adults (Serdula et al., 1993).

Heredity plays an important role in juvenile obesity. For example, adopted children's and adolescents' weight is related to the weight of their biological parents, not to the weight of their adoptive parents (Stunkard et al., 1990). Genes may influence obesity by helping determine a person's activity level. Some young people may be genetically more prone to be inactive, making it more difficult for them to burn off calories and easier for them to gain weight. *Heredity may also help set a youth's* basal metabolic rate, *which is the speed with which the body consumes calories.* Children and adolescents with a slower basal metabolic rate burn off calories less rapidly, making it easier for them to gain weight (Epstein & Cluss, 1986).

The environment is also influential. Television advertising, for example, encourages people to eat tasty but fattening goods. Parents play a role, too. They may inadvertently encourage obesity by shifting control of eating from internal to external signals. Infants eat primarily because of internal signals: They eat when they experience hunger and stop eating as they begin to feel full. During the preschool years, this internal control of eating is replaced gradually by a reliance on external signals. After school or while watching television, children and adolescents may have a candy bar out of habit, not because they are hungry. Parents who urge their children to "clean their plates" even when they are no longer hungry are encouraging them to ignore internal cues to eating. Obese children and adolescents may overeat because they rely on such external cues, disregarding internal cues to stop (Birch, 1991).

Obese youth *can* lose weight. The most effective programs have several features in common (Epstein et al., 1995; Foreyt & Goodrick, 1995; Israel et al., 1994):

- The focus of the program is to change obese children's eating habits, encourage them to become more active, and discourage sedentary behavior.

- As part of the treatment, children learn to monitor their eating, exercise, and sedentary behavior. Goals are established in each area and rewards are earned when the goals are met.

- Parents are trained to help children set realistic goals and to use behavioral principles to assist children in meeting these goals. Parents are also encouraged to monitor their own life-styles to be sure that they aren't inadvertently contributing to their child's obesity.

When programs incorporate these different features, obese children do lose weight. However, even after losing weight, many of these children remain overweight. It is best to establish good eating and exercise habits in order to avoid obesity in the first place.

Anorexia and Bulimia

Tracey Gold, an actress on the TV program *Growing Pains*, left the show in the early 1990s. After dieting compulsively, she withered away to a mere 90 pounds and had to be hospitalized (Sporkin, Wagner, & Tomashoff, 1992). Tracey suffers from an eating disorder. Anorexia nervosa *is a disorder marked by a persistent refusal to eat and an irrational fear of being overweight.* Individuals with anorexia nervosa have a grossly distorted image of their own body. Like the girl in the photo, they claim to be overweight despite being painfully thin (Wilson, Heffernan, & Black, 1996).

A related eating disorder is bulimia nervosa. *Individuals with* bulimia nervosa *alternate between binge eating—periods when they eat uncontrollably—and purging through self-induced vomiting or with laxatives.* The frequency of binge eating varies remarkably among people with bulimia nervosa. Some will binge a few times a week; others, more than 30 times! What's common to all is the feeling that they cannot stop eating (Mizes, 1995).

Anorexia and bulimia are alike in many respects. Tracey Gold, who eventually returned to her acting career but still battles anorexia, is typical in that eating disorders primarily affect females. Girls are 10 times more likely than boys to be affected (Wilson et al., 1996). Both disorders emerge in adolescence, typically in girls who are well-behaved and conscientious students (Attie, Brooks-Gunn, & Petersen, 1990). Left untreated, both disorders can lead to death. Why should adolescents who—on the surface at least—seem to be ideal teens resort to drastic dieting or binging and purging? The Forces in Action feature has the answer.

? THINK ABOUT IT
Describe how obesity, anorexia, and bulimia represent nonnormative influences on development, as defined in Chapter 1. Can you make a case that anorexia and bulimia also illustrate history-graded influences on development?

FORCES IN ACTION **WHAT CAUSES ANOREXIA AND BULIMIA?**

Biological, psychological, and sociocultural influences all contribute to eating disorders. In many industrialized cultures, the ideal female body is tall and slender. These cultural norms become particularly salient during adolescence, when girls typically experience a "fat spurt" in which they gain about 25 pounds. Although this pattern is normal, some girls see themselves as overweight and begin to diet. Faced with a culture that values being thin (sociocultural influence) and a change in her body (biological influence), the adolescent girl believes she is fat (psychological force) and tries to lose weight.

The elements of the biopsychosocial framework foster eating disorders in other ways. Family dynamics—including psychological and sociocultural forces—are important. Eating disorders are more likely with autocratic parents who give daughters little freedom. As girls enter adolescence and seek greater autonomy, they discover that their weight is something they can control. In dieting or binging, they can assert their autonomy (Swarr & Richards, 1996).

Cultural emphasis on thinness and a regimented home life contribute to eating disorders, but there is also a biological factor. Twin and family studies point to an inherited predisposition for anorexia and bulimia, perhaps in the form of personality that tends to be rigid and anxious (Strober, 1995).

Summarizing all of these influences, who is most susceptible to eating disorders? The disorder is most likely to develop in girls who inherit the predisposition (biological force), who internalize cultural ideals of thinness (psychological force), and whose parents grant them little independence (sociocultural force). ●

The desire to achieve independence and autonomy from parents is not unique to adolescents with eating disorders. All adolescents struggle with these issues, as you'll see in the next section.

---

1. The adolescent growth spurt typically begins at about 11 years of age in girls and at _____ years of age in boys.

2. The onset of puberty in girls is marked by the growth of the breasts and in boys by _____ .

3. In countries where children receive _____ , children of recent generations are no longer growing bigger than children of previous generations.

4. Maturing early tends to be beneficial, at least temporarily, for _____ .

5. Parents may inadvertently contribute to obesity by _____ .

6. Girls are more likely to have eating disorders such as anorexia and bulimia when their parents _____ .

7. Compare the effects of early maturation on boys and on girls.

Answers: (1) 13, (2) the growth of testes and scrotum, (3) adequate nutrition and health care, (4) boys, (5) encouraging children to ignore internal cues for hunger and to rely upon external cues, (6) are autocratic and give their daughters little freedom

---

WHO AM I? THE SEARCH FOR IDENTITY

Learning Objectives

- **How do adolescents achieve a unique identity?**

- **How do adolescents achieve an ethnic identity?**

- **Is adolescence always a time of storm and stress?**

Who Am I? The Search for Identity

Identity Versus Role Confusion

Resolving the Identity Crisis

Ethnic Identity

The Myth of Storm and Stress

*B*ORN *in Seoul of Korean parents, Dea was adopted by a Dutch couple in Michigan when she was 3 months old. Growing up, she considered herself a "red-blooded American." In college, however, Dea realized that* *others saw her as an Asian American, an identity she had never given much thought. She began to wonder, "Who am I really? American? Dutch American? Asian American?"*

Like Dea, do you sometimes wonder who you are? *Answers to "Who am I?" reflect a person's* self-concept, *which refers to the attitudes, behaviors, and values that a person believes make him or her a unique individual.* As we learned in Chapter 6, when children enter the teenage years, their thinking is no longer limited to the concrete, the here-and-now. Instead, formal operations afford them the power of abstract and hypothetical reasoning. Because of these advances, young adolescents describe themselves in increasingly abstract psychological and social terms. The complexity of the typical adolescent's emerging sense of self or identity is evident in one teenage girl's answer to "Who am I?"

> I'm sensitive, friendly, outgoing, popular, and tolerant, though I can also be shy, self-conscious, and even obnoxious! I'd like to be friendly and tolerant all of the time. That's the kind of person I want to be, and I'm disappointed when I'm not. I'm responsible, even studious now and then, but on the other hand, I'm a goof-off, too, because if you're too studious, you won't be popular. (Harter, 1990, p. 352)

This sort of self-reflection is common as adolescents look for an identity that integrates the many different and sometimes conflicting elements of the self (Marcia, 1991). In this section, we'll see how adolescents acquire an identity and how some adolescents, like Dea, also acquire an ethnic identity.

IDENTITY VERSUS ROLE CONFUSION

Erik Erikson's (1968) account of identity formation has been particularly influential in our understanding of adolescence. By now, Erikson's theory should have a familiar ring to it, because we've discussed it in Chapters 1 and 5. Erikson proposed eight stages of development, each constituting a unique developmental challenge. For adolescents, the crisis is between identity and role confusion. As adolescents near adulthood, they struggle to achieve an identity that will allow them to become a part of the adult world. This crisis involves balancing the desire to try out many possible selves and the need to select a single self.

Adolescents who achieve a sense of identity are well prepared to face the next developmental challenge—establishing intimate, sharing relationships with others. However, Erikson believed that teenagers who are confused about their identity can never experience intimacy in any human relationship. Instead, throughout their lives, they remain isolated and respond to others stereotypically.

How do adolescents achieve an identity? They deliberately experiment with different selves to learn more about possible identities (Nurmi, Poole, & Kalakoski, 1996). Much of this testing is career-oriented. Some adolescents imagine being professional athletes, Peace Corps workers, or best-selling novelists. Other teenagers, like the ones in the photo, envision themselves as rock stars. Other testing is romantically oriented. Some teens fall in love and imagine living independently with the loved one. Still other exploration involves religious and political beliefs (King, Elder, & Whitbeck, 1997; Yates & Youniss, 1996).

We'll concentrate on the career and romantic aspects of identity later in this chapter. For now the important point is that teens commonly give different identities a trial run, just as you might test-drive different cars before selecting one. By fantasizing about their future, adolescents begin to discover who they will be.

The self-absorption that marks the teenage search for identity is often called adolescent egocentrism (Elkind, 1978). Unlike preschoolers, adolescents know that others have different perspectives on the world. However, many adolescents believe, wrongly, that they are the usual focus of others' attention. A teen who spills catsup on herself while eating lunch may imagine that her friends are thinking only about the stain on her blouse. *The feeling of many adolescents is that they are, in effect, actors whose performance is watched constantly by their peers—a phenomenon called the* imaginary audience.

A related feature of adolescent self-absorption is the personal fable, *which is the tendency for teenagers to believe that their experiences and feelings are unique, that no one has ever felt or thought as they do.* Whether it is the excitement of first love, the despair of broken relationships, or the confusion of planning for the future, adolescents often believe that they are the first to experience these feelings and that no one else could possibly understand the power of their emotions (Elkind & Bowen, 1979).

For most youth, adolescent egocentrism, imaginary audiences, and personal fables become less important as they move through adolescence, reflecting their progress toward achieving their identity. Let's look at this progress more carefully.

? THINK ABOUT IT
Although Piaget's theory is not concerned with identity formation, how might his theory explain why identity is central in adolescence?

RESOLVING THE IDENTITY CRISIS

As adolescents strive to achieve an identity, they progress through different phases or statuses. Four different identity statuses are common (Marcia, 1980, 1991):

- Achievement—*individuals who have explored alternatives and have deliberately chosen a specific identity*
- Moratorium—*individuals who are still examining different alternatives and have yet to find a satisfactory identity*
- Foreclosure—*individuals whose identity is determined largely by adults, rather than from personal exploration of alternatives*
- Diffusion—*individuals who are confused or often overwhelmed by the task of achieving an identity and are doing little to achieve one*

In early adolescence, diffusion and foreclosure are the most common statuses. The common element in these statuses is that teens are not exploring alternative identities. They are avoiding the crisis altogether or have resolved it by taking on an identity based on suggestions from parents or other adults. However, as individuals move further into adolescence and into young adulthood, they have more opportunities to explore alternative identities, so diffusion and foreclosure become less common. At the same time, the pie charts show that achievement and moratorium become more common (Meilman, 1979).

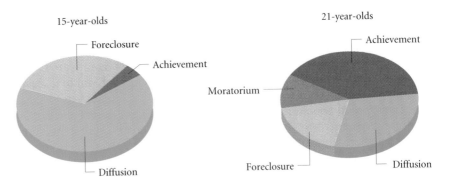

As we mentioned earlier, identity has different facets, including occupation, religion, and politics. Typically, young people do not reach the achievement status for all aspects of identity at the same time (Dellas & Jernigan, 1990; Kroger & Green, 1996). Some adolescents reach the achievement status for occupations before achieving it for religion and politics. Others reach the achievement status for religion before other domains. Evidently, few youth achieve a sense of identity all at once; instead, the crisis of identity is first resolved in some areas and then in others.

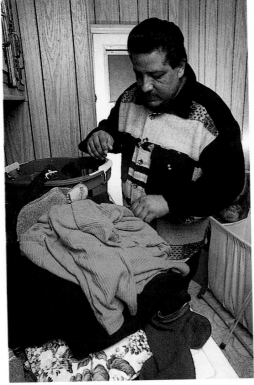

When the achievement status is attained, the period of active experimentation ends, and individuals have a well-defined sense of self. However, over a lifetime, an individual's identity is sometimes reworked, in response to new life challenges and circumstances. Consequently, individuals may return to the moratorium status for a period, only to reemerge later with a changed identity. In fact, individuals may go through these changes several times, creating "MAMA" cycles in which they alternate between the *moratorium* and *achievement* statuses as they explore new alternatives in response to personal and family crises (Marcia, 1991). For example, a man like the one in the photo who has placed career above all else but finds himself unemployed may reorganize his life around his family and become the primary caregiver of his children.

What circumstances help adolescents achieve identity? The parenting styles described in Chapter 7 play an important role (Marcia, 1980). Authoritative parenting, in which parents encourage discussion and recognize their children's autonomy, is associated with the achievement status. This style of parenting apparently encourages adolescents to undertake the personal experimentation that leads to the attainment of an identity. In contrast, authoritarian parenting, in which parents set rules with little justification and enforce them without explanation, is associated with the foreclosure status. These teens are discouraged from personal experimentation; instead, their parents simply tell them what identity to adopt. Finally, an indulgent-permissive parental style, in which parents make few demands on their children, is associated with the diffuse status. This result fits the general pattern: Children of indulgent-permissive parents tend to be less mature socially than their peers. Overall, adolescents are most likely to establish a well-defined identity in a family atmosphere where the parents encourage the children to explore alternatives on their own but do not pressure or provide explicit direction (Harter, 1990).

ETHNIC IDENTITY

Roughly one-third of the adolescents and young adults living in the United States are members of ethnic minority groups, including African Americans, Asian Americans, Hispanic Americans, and Native Americans. These individuals typically develop an ethnic identity: They feel a part of their ethnic group and learn the unique elements of their group's culture and heritage (Phinney, 1990).

Achieving an ethnic identity seems to occur in three phases. Initially, adolescents do not examine their ethnic roots. A teenage African American girl in this phase remarked, "Why do I need to learn about who was the first Black woman to do this or that? I'm just not too interested" (Phinney, 1989, p. 44). For this girl, ethnic identity is not yet an important personal issue. In the second phase, adolescents begin to explore the personal impact of their ethnic heritage. The curiosity and questioning characteristic of this stage is captured in the comments of a teenage Mexican American girl who said, "I want to know what we do and how our culture is different from others. Going to festivals and cultural events helps me to learn more about my own culture and about myself" (Phinney, 1989, p. 44). Part of this phase involves learning cultural traditions; for example, like the girl in the photo, many adolescents learn to prepare ethnic food.

In the third phase, individuals achieve a distinct ethnic self-concept. One Asian American adolescent explained his ethnic identification like this: "I have been born Filipino and am born to be Filipino . . . I'm here in America, and people of many different cultures are here, too. So I don't consider myself only Filipino, but also American" (Phinney, 1989, p. 44).

To see whether you understand the differences between these stages of ethnic identity, reread the vignette about Dea, the Dutch-Asian-American college student. Then decide which stage applies to her. Our answer appears on pages 290–291, before Test Yourself.

Older adolescents are more likely than younger ones to have achieved an ethnic identity, because they are more likely to have had opportunities to explore their cultural heritage (Phinney & Chavira, 1992). As is the case with overall identity, adolescents are most likely to achieve an ethnic self-concept when their parents encourage them to explore alternatives instead of pressuring them to adopt a particular ethnic identity (Rosenthal & Feldman, 1992).

Do adolescents benefit from a strong ethnic identity? Yes. Adolescents who have achieved an ethnic identity tend to have higher self-esteem and find that their interactions with family and friends are more satisfying (Phinney, Cantu, & Kurtz, 1997). In addition, many investigators have found that adolescents with a strong ethnic identity do better in school than adolescents whose ethnic identities are weaker (Stalikas & Gavaki, 1995). Finally, adolescents with a strong ethnic identity tend to have more positive views of their own groups and of other ethnic groups, too (Phinney, Ferguson, & Tate, 1997).

Some individuals achieve a well-defined ethnic self-concept and, at the same time, identify strongly with the mainstream culture. In the United States, for example, many Chinese Americans embrace both Chinese and American culture; in England, many Indians identify with both Indian and British cultures. For other individuals, the cost of strong ethnic identification is a weakened tie to mainstream culture. Some investigators report that, for Hispanic Americans, strong identification with Hispanic culture is associated with a weakened identification with mainstream American culture (Phinney, 1990).

We shouldn't be too surprised that identifying with mainstream culture weakens ethnic identity in some groups but not in others (Berry, 1993). Racial and ethnic groups living in the United States are diverse. African American, Asian American, Hispanic American, and Native American cultures and heritages differ, and so we should expect that the nature and consequences of a strong ethnic self-concept will differ across these and other ethnic groups. Some ethnic cultures share more elements with mainstream culture; individuals growing up in these ethnic groups should find it easier to identify with both ethnic and mainstream cultures.

Even within any particular group, the nature and consequences of ethnic identity may change over successive generations (Cuellar et al., 1997). As successive generations become more acculturated to mainstream culture, they may identify less strongly with ethnic culture. Thus, parents may maintain strong feelings of ethnic identity that their children don't share.

Ethnic identity is a particularly salient issue for children like Dea, who are members of minority groups and are adopted by European American parents. The Spotlight on Research feature shows how identity develops in these children.

? **THINK ABOUT IT**
What factors in the biopsychosocial framework are shown by adolescents who develop an ethnic identity?

SPOTLIGHT ON RESEARCH

IDENTITY IN CHILDREN OF TRANSRACIAL ADOPTIONS

What was the aim of the study and who were the investigators? For many years, the policy of many adoption agencies stipulated that children could be adopted only by adults of their own race. However, in the 1960s, transracial adoption became more common. Why? Children from minority groups needing adoption far outnumbered the adults from minority groups who wanted to adopt, yet many European American adults were eager to adopt these children. When African American children are reared by European American parents, what racial identity do the children acquire? How does this identity affect their development? Kimberly DeBerry, Sandra Scarr, and Richard Weinberg (1996) wanted to answer these questions.

How did the investigators measure the topic of interest? The investigators created a structured interview that included 83 different items. Some items measured the children's orientation toward African Americans, including the number of African American friends they had, their knowledge of people of African descent, and whether they referred to themselves as African American. Other, comparable items measured children's orientation toward European Americans. Finally, general psychological adjustment was measured with questions addressing behavioral, emotional, interpersonal, and academic problems. Children and parents were interviewed separately.

Who were the children in the study? Scarr and Weinberg began the Minnesota Transracial Adoption Project in the 1970s. Their original sample included 131 families with 176 adopted children and 145 biological children. DeBerry and her colleagues focused on a subsample that included 88 African American children, 29 boys and 59 girls.

What was the design of the study? This study was correlational because DeBerry and her colleagues were interested in the relations that existed naturally between children's identity as African or European Americans and their adjustment. The study was longitudinal because testing took place when the children were approximately 4, 7, and 17 years old. However, we are describing only the results that were obtained when the children were 17.

Were there ethical concerns with the study? No. The investigators obtained permission from the parents for the children to participate.

What were the results? Parents' and children's responses to the interview were similar, so we'll just describe the children's responses. Two results are key. First, most of the children in this sample identified more strongly as European American than as African American. Second, having a strong cultural identity was associated with better psychological adjustment. The correlation with adjustment was .45 for identifying with African Americans and .50 for identifying with European Americans. In other words, adolescents who identified strongly with *either* African or European Americans tended to be better adjusted than adolescents who identified with neither African nor European Americans.

What did the investigators conclude? The investigators caution that their results, which are based on African American children reared by European Americans in Minnesota, may not apply to all transracial adoptions. Nevertheless, the results underscore the importance of being able to identify with a cultural group. Being able to think of oneself as a member of some larger, recognized cultural group is an important part of being psychologically healthy. Adolescents who do not feel a part of any group are at risk for psychological problems. •

THE MYTH OF STORM AND STRESS

Does the search for identity always make adolescence a time of storm and stress? For many early theorists, personal tumult was an essential and often positive component of development during the adolescent years. For example, G. Stanley Hall, an influential American developmental psychologist at the beginning of the 20th century, wrote that adolescence was ". . . strewn with wreckage of mind, body, and morals" (1904, p. xiv). Of course, the combative teen has been a favorite character of U.S. novelists and filmmakers for the past 50 years.

Today, we know that the rebellious teen is largely a myth. Consider the following conclusions derived from research findings (Steinberg, 1990). Most adolescents

- admire and love their parents
- rely upon their parents for advice
- embrace many of their parents' values
- feel loved by their parents

Not exactly the image of the rebel, is it? These results undermine the view that adolescence is necessarily a time of turmoil and conflict. Some particularly convincing evidence comes from a study (Offer et al., 1988) of adolescents from 10 different countries: the United States, Australia, Germany, Italy, Israel, Hungary, Turkey, Japan, Taiwan, and Bangladesh. Repeatedly, these investigators found most adolescents moving confidently and happily toward adulthood. For example, as the graphs show, most adolescents around the world report that they are usually happy, and few avoid their homes.

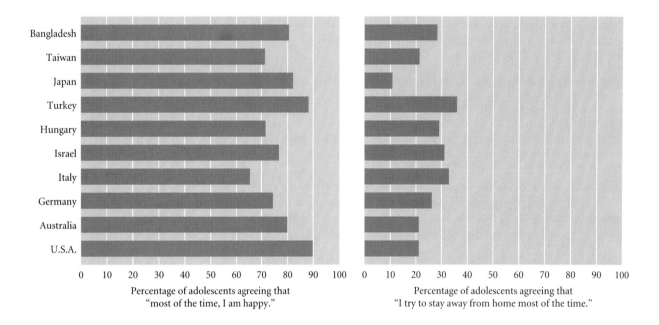

Percentage of adolescents agreeing that "most of the time, I am happy."

Percentage of adolescents agreeing that "I try to stay away from home most of the time."

Of course, parent-child relations do change during adolescence. As teens become more independent, their relationships with their parents become more egalitarian. Parents must adjust to their children's growing sense of autonomy by beginning to treat them more like equals (Laursen & Collins, 1994). As a consequence, teens tend to spend less time with their parents, to be less affectionate toward them, and to argue more often with them about matters of style, taste, and freedom. And, teenagers are more moody and more likely to enjoy spending some time alone (Larson, 1997; Wolfson & Carskadon, 1998). However, these changes are not a matter of storm and stress; they are natural by-products of a changing parent-child relationship, in which the "child" is nearly a fully independent young adult (Steinberg, 1990). Adolescence is an interesting and challenging time for youth and their parents, but not inherently tempestuous as the myth would lead us to believe.

Dea's Ethnic Identity

Dea, the Dutch-Asian-American college student, doesn't know how to integrate the Korean heritage of her biological parents with the Dutch American culture in which she was reared. This would put her in the second stage: On the one hand, she has begun to examine her ethnic roots, which means that she's progressed beyond the first stage. On the other hand, she has not yet integrated her Asian and European roots, as would be characteristic of adolescents in the third stage.

1. For Erikson, the crisis of adolescence is between identity and _____ .

2. The _____ status describes an adolescent who has attained an identity largely based on her parents' advice and urging.

3. Adolescents are more likely to achieve an ethnic identity when their parents use a(n) _____ style of parenting.

4. When teenagers identify strongly with their own ethnic group, this means that their identification with mainstream American culture is _____ .

5. In 10 countries around the world, most adolescents report that they are happy and that _____ .

6. Children's relations with their parents change in adolescence, reflecting adolescents' growing independence and a _____ parent-child relationship.

7. Your local newspaper has just printed a feature article describing all of the "storm and stress" that typifies adolescence. Write a letter to the editor in which you set the record straight.

Answers: (1) role confusion, (2) fore-closure, (3) authoritative, (4) sometimes strong and sometimes weak, depending on the individual circumstances, (5) they do not avoid being home, (6) more egalitarian

FLIPPING BURGERS AND WAITING TABLES: ENTERING THE WORLD OF WORK

Learning Objectives

- **What is the impact of part-time employment on adolescent development?**

- **How do adolescents choose a specific career?**

Flipping Burgers and Waiting Tables: Entering the World of Work

Part-Time Work

Career Development

*W*HEN *15-year-old Aaron announced that he wanted an after-school job at the local supermarket, his mother was delighted, believing that he would learn much from the experience. Five months later, she has her doubts. Aaron has lost interest in school, and they argue constantly about how he spends his money.*

"What do you want to be when you grow up?" Children are often asked this question in fun. Beginning in adolescence, however, it takes on special significance because work is such an important component of a person's identity. A job—be it as bricklayer, reporter, or child care worker—helps define who we are.

Like Aaron, many U.S. teens have their first exposure to the world of work in part-time employment after school or on weekends, so let's begin with this topic.

PART-TIME WORK

The teen in the photo is engaged in an American adolescent ritual—the part-time job. Today, a substantial majority of high school seniors work part-time.

Of every five adolescent part-time workers, one works at a fast-food restaurant like McDonald's or Burger King, and another works in a retail store as a cashier or salesperson. Boys are more likely to be manual laborers, busboys, or newspaper carriers. Girls are more often baby-sitters, maids, or restaurant workers, and they are usually paid less than boys (Call, 1996; Mortimer, 1991).

Part-time work is a new aspect of adolescence. In the 1970s, only 25% of high school students worked part-time compared to 75% in the 1980s and 1990s. This development is unique to the United States. In other industrialized countries in Western Europe and Asia, high school students who also hold part-time jobs are a clear minority. Compared to high-school students in these countries, U.S. students have a shorter school day and much less homework, which means they have time to work (Reubens, Harrison, & Kupp, 1981).

Adults often praise these emerging work habits, believing that through early exposure to the workplace, adolescents will learn self-discipline, become self-confident, and acquire important job skills (Snedeker, 1982). For most adolescents, however, the reality is quite different. Indeed, part-time work can actually be harmful. Several problems are common.

1. *School performance suffers.* When students work more than approximately 15 hours per week, they devote less time to homework and are more apt to cut classes. Not surprisingly, their grades are lower than those of their peers who work less or not at all (Steinberg, Fegley, & Dornbusch, 1993). Why should 15 hours of work be so detrimental to school performance? A 15-hour work schedule might involve four 3-hour shifts after school and another 3-hour shift on the weekend. This would seem to leave ample opportunity to study, but only if students use their time effectively. In fact, many high school students apparently do not have the foresight and discipline necessary to consistently meet the combined demands of work and school. Like the girl in the photo, many teens have great difficulty balancing work, study, and sleep.

2. *Mental health and behavioral problems.* Adolescents who work long hours—more than 15 or 20 hours a week—are more likely to experience anxiety and depression, and their self-esteem often suffers. Many adolescents find themselves in jobs that are repetitive and boring but stressful. Conditions like these undermine self-esteem and breed anxiety.

Extensive part-time work also leads to more frequent substance abuse, including cigarettes, alcohol, marijuana, and cocaine (Bachman & Schulenberg, 1993; Mortimer et al., 1996). Extensive work is also associated with more frequent problem behavior, including violence toward others, trouble with police, and arguments with parents (Bachman & Schulenberg, 1993).

Why employment is associated with all of these problems is not clear. Perhaps employed adolescents turn to drugs to help them cope with the anxiety and depression brought on by work. Arguments with parents may become more common because anxious, depressed adolescents are more prone to argue or because wage-earning adolescents may believe that their freedom should match their income. Regardless of the exact mechanism involved, extensive part-time work is clearly detrimental to the mental health of most adolescents.

3. *Misleading affluence.* Adults sometimes argue that work is good for teenagers because it teaches them "the value of a dollar." Here, too, reality is at odds with the adage. The typical teenage pattern is to "earn and spend." Working adolescents spend most of their earnings on themselves—to buy clothing, snack food, or cosmetics and to pay for entertainment. Few working teens set aside much of their income for future goals, such as a college education, or use it to contribute to their family's expenses (Shanahan et al., 1996a). Because parents customarily pay for many of the essential expenses associated with truly independent living—rent, utilities, and groceries, for example—working adolescents often have a vastly higher percentage of their income available for discretionary spending than do working adults. Thus, for many teens, the part-time work experience provides unrealistic expectations about how income can be allocated (Bachman, 1983).

The message that emerges repeatedly from research on part-time employment is hardly encouraging. Like Aaron in the vignette, adolescents who work long hours at part-time jobs do not benefit from the experience. To the contrary, they do worse in school, are more likely to have behavioral problems, and learn how to spend money rather than how to manage it. These effects are similar for adolescents from different ethnic groups (Steinberg & Dornbusch, 1991) and are comparable for boys and girls (Bachman & Schulenberg, 1993).

Does this mean that teenagers who are still in school should never work part-time? Not necessarily. Part-time employment can be successful, depending on the circumstances. One key is the number of hours of work. Although the exact number of hours varies, of course, from one student to the next, most students could easily work 5 hours weekly without harm, and many could work 10 hours weekly. Another key is the type of job (Barling, Rogers, & Kelloway, 1995). When adolescents have jobs that allow them to use their skills (e.g., bookkeeping, computing, or typing) and to acquire new ones, self-esteem can be enhanced, and they can learn from their experiences. Yet another factor is how teens spend their earnings. When they save their money or use it to pay for clothes and school expenses, their relationships with their parents often improve (Shanahan et al., 1996b).

By these criteria, who is likely to show harmful effects from part-time work? A teen who spends 30 hours each week bagging groceries and spends most of it on CDs or videos. Who may show some benefits of part-time work? A teen who likes to tinker with cars and spends Saturdays working in a repair shop and who sets aside some of his earnings for community college.

Finally, summer jobs typically do not involve conflict between work and school. Consequently, many of the harmful effects associated with part-time employment during the school year do not hold for summer employment. In fact, such employment sometimes enhances adolescents' self-esteem, especially when they save part of their income for future plans (Marsh, 1991).

? THINK ABOUT IT
Think back to your own high school years and those of your friends. Can you think of students (including yourself!) who showed harmful effects from part-time work? Can you think of people who benefited from part-time work?

CAREER DEVELOPMENT

Faced with the challenge of selecting a career, many adolescents may be attracted to the approach taken by the teenage boy in the cartoon. Choosing a career *is* difficult, in part because it involves determining the kinds of jobs that will be available in the future. Predicting the future is risky, but the U.S. Bureau of Labor Statistics projects that by the year 2006, about 75% of all jobs will be in service industries, such as education, health care, and banking. The remaining 25% of jobs will be associated with the production of goods. In the future, there will be fewer jobs in agriculture, forestry, and manufacturing (Franklin, 1997).

"Your son has made a career choice, Mildred. He's going to win the lottery and travel a lot."

LAUGH PARADE, © 1985. Reprinted courtesy of Bunny Hoest and *Parade Magazine.*

Knowing the types of jobs that experts predict will be plentiful, how do adolescents begin the long process of selecting a career that will bring them happiness and fortune? Theories of vocational choice describe this process. According to the theory proposed by Donald Super (1976, 1980), identity is a primary force in an adolescent's choice of a career. *Beginning at the age of 13 or 14, adolescents use their emerging identities as an initial source of ideas about careers, a process called* crystallization. During those years, teenagers start to use their ideas about their own talents and interests to narrow down potential career prospects. A teenage boy who is extroverted and sociable may decide that working with people should be part of his career. Such initial decisions are provisional; many adolescents experiment with different hypothetical careers and try to envision what each might be like.

The next phase often begins at about 18 years of age; it is an extension of the activities associated with crystallization. *During* specification, *adolescents further limit their career possibilities by learning more about specific lines of work and starting to obtain the training required for a specific job.* Our hypothetical extroverted teenage boy who wants to work with people may decide that a career in sales would be a good match for his abilities and interests. Some, like the teen shown in the photo, may begin an apprenticeship as a way to learn a trade.

The end of the teenage years or the early 20s marks the beginning of the third phase. *During* implementation, *individuals enter the work force and learn about jobs firsthand.* This is a time of learning about responsibility and productivity, learning to get along with co-workers, and altering one's life-style to accommodate work. This period is often unstable. Individuals sometimes change positions frequently, as they adjust to the reality of life in the workplace.

In the Real People feature, you can see these three phases in one person's career development.

"THE LIFE OF LYNNE,"
A DRAMA IN THREE ACTS

Act 1: Crystallization—Throughout high school, Lynne was active in a number of organizations. She enjoyed being busy and liked the constant contact with people. Lynne was often nominated for office, and more often than not, she asked to be treasurer. Not that she was greedy or had her hand in the till; she simply found it satisfying to keep the financial records in order. By the end of her junior year, Lynne decided that she wanted to study business in college, a decision that fit with her good grades in English and math.

Act 2: Specification—Lynne was accepted into the business school of a large state university. She decided that accounting fit her skills and temperament, so this became her major. During the summers, she worked as a cashier at J. C. Penney's. This helped pay for college and gave her experience in the world of retail sales.

Act 3: Implementation—A few months after graduation, Lynne was offered a junior accounting position with Wal-Mart. Her job required that she work Tuesday through Friday, auditing Wal-Mart stores in several nearby cities. Lynne liked the pay, the company car, the pay, the feeling of independence, and the pay. However, having to hit the road every morning by 7:30 A.M. was a jolt to someone used to rising casually at 10 A.M. Also, Lynne often found it awkward to deal with store managers, many of whom were twice her age and very intimidating. She was coming to the conclusion that there was much more to a successful career as an accountant than simply making the numbers add up correctly. ●

The "Life of Lynne" illustrates the continuous give-and-take between an individual's self-concept and his or her career development. A person's self-concept makes some careers more attractive than others; occupational experiences further refine and shape a person's self-concept.

One other aspect of Lynne's life sheds more light on Super's theory. After 18 months on the job, Lynne's accounting group was merged with another; this would have required Lynne to move to another state, so she quit. After six months looking for another accounting job, Lynne gave up and began to study to become a real estate agent. The moral? Economic conditions and opportunities also shape career development. Changing times can force individuals to take new, often unexpected career paths.

Personality-Type Theory

Super's (1976, 1980) work helps explain how self-concept and career aspirations develop hand in hand, but it does not explain why particular individuals are attracted to one line of work rather than another. Explaining the match between people and occupations has been the aim of a theory devised by John Holland (1985, 1987, 1996). *According to Holland's* personality-type theory, *people find work fulfilling when the important features of a job or profession fit the worker's personality.* Holland identified six prototypic personalities that are relevant to the world of work. Each one is best suited to a specific set of occupations, as indicated in the right-hand column of the table on page 296. Remember, these are merely prototypes. Most people do not match any one personality type exactly. Instead, their work-related personalities are a blend of the six.

This model is useful in describing the career preferences of African, Asian, European, Native, and Mexican American adolescents; it is also useful for both males and females (Day, Rounds, & Swaney, 1998). And, research shows that when people have jobs that match their personality type, in the short run they are more productive employees, and, in the long run they have more stable

GENERAL OCCUPATIONAL THEMES IN HOLLAND'S THEORY

Theme	Description	Careers
Realistic	Individuals enjoy physical labor and working with their hands, and they like to solve concrete problems.	mechanic, truck driver, construction worker
Investigative	Individuals are task-oriented and enjoy thinking about abstract relations.	scientist, technical writer
Social	Individuals are skilled verbally and interpersonally, and they enjoy solving problems using these skills.	teacher, counselor, social worker
Conventional	Individuals have verbal and quantitative skills that they like to apply to structured, well-defined tasks assigned to them by others.	bank teller, payroll clerk, traffic manager
Enterprising	Individuals enjoy using their verbal skills in positions of power, status, and leadership.	business executive, television producer, real estate agent
Artistic	Individuals enjoy expressing themselves through unstructured tasks.	poet, musician, actor

career paths (Holland, 1996). For example, an enterprising youth like the one in the photo is likely to be successful in business because he will enjoy positions of power in which he can use his verbal skills.

Combining Holland's general occupational themes with Super's theory of career development gives us a comprehensive picture of vocational growth. On the one hand, Super's theory explains the developmental progression by which individuals translate general interests into a specific career; on the other hand, Holland's theory explains what makes a good match between specific interests and specific careers.

Of course, trying to match interests to occupations can be difficult. Fortunately, several assessments can be used to describe a person's work-related personality and the jobs for which he or she is best suited. In the Strong Interest Inventory® (SII®), for example, people express their liking of different occupations, school subjects, activities, and types of people (e.g., very old people, people who live dangerously). These answers are compared to the responses obtained from a normative sample of individuals from different occupations. The result is a profile, a portion of which is shown on page 297.

You can see that each of Holland's types—called "General Occupational Themes" on the SII®—is listed. Under each heading are black and shaded bars that show typical responses of women and men. The dot shows where the person's responses fall compared to other people of the person's own gender. Looking in the left column, you can see that this woman has less interest than the average female on the Realistic and Investigative Themes but has more interest than the average female on the Artistic Theme. In the right column, this woman has average interest on the Social and Conventional Themes, but less-than-average interest on the Enterprising Theme. Of the six General Occupational Themes, this person's interests seem to correspond best with the artistic personality in Holland's theory.

By looking at the Basic Interest Scales that are listed under the Artistic Occupational Theme, we can get an even more precise idea of this woman's interests. Compared to the average female, this woman shows high interest in Art, Writing, and Culinary Arts (cooking). Her interest in Music and Applied Arts is only average. Evidently, her ideal job would be as a writer for either an art magazine or a cooking magazine!

Looking at the remaining Occupational Themes serves as a reminder that the match between interests and occupations is often far from perfect. Although this woman's interest in the Realistic and Social Occupational Themes is only average overall, she has high interest in Agriculture and in Religious Activities.

If you are still undecided about a career, we encourage you to visit your college's counseling center and arrange to take an assessment like the SII®. The results will help you focus on careers that match your interests and help you choose a college major that would lead to those careers.

Even if you are fairly certain of your vocational plans, you might take one of these assessments anyway. As we saw with Lynne (and will discuss more in Chapters 11 and 14), career development does not end with the first job. People continuously refine their career aspirations over the life span, and these results might be useful later in your life.

Consulting Psychologists Press, Inc., 1994. Strong Interest Inventory and SII are registered trademarks of Stanford University Press.

? THINK ABOUT IT
How do the different personality types in Holland's theory relate to the different types of intelligence proposed by Howard Gardner (described in Chapter 6)?

TEST YOURSELF

1. Adolescents who work extensively at part-time jobs during the school year often get lower grades, have behavior problems, and _____ .

2. Part-time employment during the school year can be beneficial if adolescents limit the number of hours they work and _____ .

3. During the _____ phase of vocational choice, adolescents learn more about specific lines of work and begin training.

4. Individuals with a(n) _____ personality type are best suited for a career as a teacher or counselor.

5. Using the six personality types in Holland's theory, think of a person you know well who fits one of these types. (The chart on page 296 will be helpful as you do this.) Do you think the person's occupation represents a good match for his or her personality type?

Answers: (1) experience misleading affluence, (2) hold jobs that allow them to use and develop skills, (3) specification, (4) social

"HOW DO I LOVE THEE?"—ROMANTIC RELATIONSHIPS

"How Do I Love Thee?"—Romantic Relationships

Dating

Awakening of Sexual Interests

Learning Objectives

- **What are the functions of dating?**
- **What determines an adolescent's sexual orientation?**
- **At what age do adolescents become sexually active? What factors influence them to do so?**
- **Why do sexually active adolescents use contraceptives so infrequently?**
- **What are some of the behaviors that make adolescents particularly vulnerable to AIDS?**
- **What circumstances can make date rape especially likely?**

*F*OR 6 *months, 15-year-old Rebecca has been dating Michael, a 17-year-old. She thinks she is truly in love for the first time and she often imagines being married to Michael. They have had sex a few times, each time without contraception. It sometimes crosses Rebecca's mind that if she gets pregnant, she could move into her own apartment and begin a family.*

The fires of romantic relationships have long warmed the hearts of American adolescents. Often, as with Rebecca and Michael, romance leads to sex. In this section, we'll explore adolescent dating and sex. As we do, you'll better understand Rebecca's reasons for having unprotected sex with Michael.

DATING

American boys and girls typically begin to date at about age 15 (Miller et al., 1997). The first experiences with dating often occur when same-sex groups go places knowing that a mixed-sex crowd will be attending. Examples include going to a mall with friends or going to a school dance. A somewhat more advanced form of dating involves several boys and several girls going out together as a group. Ultimately, dates involve well-defined couples. By the high school years, most students will have had at least one steady girlfriend or boyfriend.

As you might suspect, cultural factors strongly influence dating patterns. For example, European American parents tend to encourage independence in their teenagers more than traditional Hispanic American and Asian American parents, who emphasize family ties and loyalty to parents. Dating is a sign of independence and usually results in less time spent with family, which explains why Hispanic American and Asian American adolescents often begin to date at an older age and date less frequently (Xiaohe & Whyte, 1990).

Originally, the primary function of dating was to select a mate, but today dating serves a variety of functions for adolescents (Padgham & Blyth, 1991; Sanderson & Cantor, 1995). Dating

- is a pleasant form of recreation and entertainment
- helps teach adult standards of interpersonal behavior
- is a means to establish status among peers
- provides an outlet for sexual experimentation
- provides companionship like that experienced between best friends
- leads to intimacy, in which teens share innermost feelings with their partners

The functions of dating change during adolescence. As adolescents mature, companionship and intimacy become more important while recreation and status seeking become less important (Roscoe, Diana, & Brooks, 1987; Sanderson & Cantor, 1995).

Sexual Orientation

For most adolescents, dating and romance involve members of the opposite sex. However, as part of the search to establish an identity, many adolescents wonder, at least in passing, if they are homosexual. In fact, roughly 15% of adolescent boys and girls report emotional and sexual attractions to a member of their own sex (D'Augelli, 1996). For most adolescents, these experiences are simply a part of the larger process of role experimentation common to adolescence. However, the adolescent search for self-definition leads roughly 5% of teenage boys and girls to identify themselves as gay in their sexual orientation. This identification usually occurs in mid-adolescence, but not until young adulthood do most gay individuals express their sexual orientation publicly (D'Augelli, 1996).

Why do gay adolescents wait so long—3–5 years—before declaring their sexual orientation? Many believe, correctly, that their peers are not likely to support them (Newman & Muzzonigro, 1993). For example, in one national survey, only 40% of 15- to 19-year-old boys agreed that they could befriend a gay person (Marsiglio, 1993). Adolescents who said that they could not befriend a gay peer were most often younger, identified themselves as religious fundamentalists, and had parents who were less educated.

The roots of sexual orientation remain poorly understood. However, scientists have discredited several ideas concerning the roots of sexual orientation. Research (Bell, Weinberg, & Hammersmith, 1981; Golombok & Tasker, 1996; Patterson, 1992) has shown each of the following to be *false:*

- Sons become gay when raised by a domineering mother and a weak father.
- Girls become lesbians when their father is their primary role model.
- Children raised by gay and lesbian parents usually end up adopting their parents' sexual orientation.
- Gay and lesbian adults were, as children, seduced by an older person of their sex.

What, then, determines a person's sexual orientation? The exact factors probably differ from one person to the next, but many scientists today share the view that biology plays an important role. Some evidence suggests that heredity and hormones influence sexual orientation (Hamer et al., 1993; Meyer-Bahlberg et al., 1995). One intriguing idea (Bem, 1996) is that genes and hormones don't prompt sexual orientation per se but lead to temperaments that affect children's preference for same- and opposite-sex activities. Children who do not enjoy gender-typical activities come to see themselves as different, ultimately leading to a different gender identity.

Though the origins of sexual orientation may not be obvious, it is clear that gay and lesbian individuals face many special challenges. Their family and peer relationships are often disrupted. They endure both verbal and physical attacks. Given these problems, it's not surprising that gay and lesbian youth often experience mental health problems such as anxiety and depression (D'Augelli, 1996; Hershberger & D'Augelli, 1995; Rotheram-Borus et al., 1995).

In recent years, social changes have helped gay and lesbian youth respond more effectively to these unique challenges. The "official" stigma associated with being gay or lesbian was removed in 1973 when the American Psychological Association and the American Psychiatric Association declared that homosexuality was not a psychological disorder. Other helpful changes include more (and more visible) gay role models like the couple in the photo, and more numerous centers in cities for gay and lesbian youth. These resources are making it easier for gay and lesbian youth to understand their sexual orientation and to cope with the many other demands of adolescence.

AWAKENING OF SEXUAL INTERESTS

Part of the experimentation and exploration associated with adolescence involves sex. Sexuality is a central issue for adolescents because of their growing involvement in romantic relationships. Sex is also a prominent issue because television and movies continually emphasize it and because teens see it as a way to establish adult status.

Many adolescents first experience sexuality in masturbation, *self-stimulation of the genitals.* Teenage boys are more likely than girls to masturbate and to begin masturbating at a younger age (Oliver & Hyde, 1993). From masturbation, sex progresses to kissing, to petting above the waist, to petting below the waist, and to intercourse. By the end of adolescence, most American boys and girls have had intercourse at least once (Jakobsen, 1997; Miller et al., 1997; Rodgers & Rowe, 1993).

Why are some adolescents sexually active while others are not? A number of factors contribute (Capaldi, Crosby, & Stoolmiller, 1996; DiBlasio & Benda, 1990; Windle & Windle, 1996). Adolescents are more likely to have sex when they

- think their parents have positive attitudes generally toward sexuality
- believe that their friends are also sexually active
- judge the rewards of sex (e.g., emotional and physical closeness) to outweigh the costs (guilt and fear of pregnancy or disease)

- are lower in their religious commitment
- mature early and begin to date at a relatively young age
- have peer and conduct problems as children

Thus, sexual activity reflects the influence of parents and peers as well as the individual's own beliefs, values, and experiences.

Adolescents' sexual behavior is a cause for concern because it can have life-long consequences. In the next few pages, let's ponder some of these problems.

? THINK ABOUT IT
According to the "storm and stress" view of adolescence, sexual behavior would be one way for adolescents to rebel against their parents. Does research on adolescent sexuality support this prediction?

Teenage Pregnancy

Roughly 1 in 10 adolescent girls in the United States becomes pregnant. About 60% of pregnant teenagers give birth; the remaining 40% abort the pregnancy (Henshaw, 1993). As you can see in the graph, African American and Hispanic

Percentage of 15- to 19-year-olds giving birth

American adolescents are the most likely to become teenage moms; Asian American adolescents are the least likely (Ventura et al., 1997).

For teenage moms and their children like the ones in the photo, the future is not promising. The babies face medical problems, largely because most teenage mothers receive little or no prenatal care. As they grow, babies of teenage mothers generally do less well in school and more often have behavioral problems (Dryfoos, 1990). For the mothers, incomplete education, poverty, and marital problems are common (Allen et al., 1997; Furstenberg, Brooks-Gunn, & Morgan, 1987). Of course, not all teenage mothers and their infants follow this dismal life course. Some teenage mothers finish school, find good jobs, and have happy marriages; their children do well in school, academically and socially. However, we need to emphasize that teenage pregnancies with "happy endings" are clearly the exception; for most teenage mothers and their children, life is a struggle.

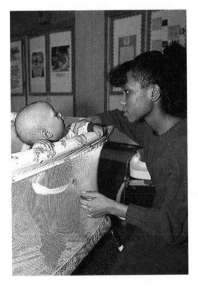

The solution to teen pregnancies seems simple enough—abstinence from sex, or contraception—but as you'll see in a few pages, the problem is more complicated. First, let's look at another problem associated with adolescent sex.

Sexually Transmitted Diseases

A number of diseases are transmitted from one person to another through sexual intercourse. For example, herpes and genital warts are two common viral infections. Other diseases, like chlamydia, syphilis, and gonorrhea, are caused by bacteria. Although these diseases can have serious complications if left untreated, they are usually cured readily with penicillin. In contrast, the prognosis is bleak for individuals who contract the human immunodeficiency virus (HIV), which typically leads to acquired immunodeficiency syndrome (AIDS). In persons with AIDS, the immune system is no longer able to protect the body from infections, and they often die from one of these infections.

Young adults—those in their 20s—account for roughly 15% of all AIDS cases in the United States (National Center for Health Statistics, 1997). Most of these people contracted the disease during adolescence. Many factors make adolescents especially susceptible to AIDS. Teenagers and young adults are more likely than older adults to engage in unprotected sex and to use intravenous drugs—common pathways for the transmission of AIDS. Also, adolescents often have sex with many partners, increasing their risk of exposure to the disease.

Safe Sex? No Sex?

Teens could reduce the risk of becoming pregnant and contracting sexually transmitted diseases if they used contraceptives or avoided sexual intercourse altogether. Let's talk first about contraception. Only a minority of sexually active teenagers use birth control. Those who do often use ineffective methods, such as withdrawal, or use them inconsistently (Besharov & Gardiner, 1997; National Research Council, 1987).

Adolescents' infrequent and ineffective use of contraceptives can be traced to several factors (Adler, 1994; Gordon, 1996):

- *Ignorance.* Many adolescents are seriously misinformed about the facts of conception. For example, many do not know when during the menstrual cycle conception is most likely to occur.

- *Illusion of invulnerability.* Too many adolescents deny reality. They believe they are invincible—"It couldn't happen to me"—only others become pregnant or contract AIDS.

- *Lack of motivation.* For some adolescent girls, becoming pregnant is appealing. Like Rebecca in the vignette, they picture having a child as a way to break away from their parents, to gain status as independent-living adults, and to have "someone to love them."

- *Access to contraceptives.* Some teenagers do not know where to obtain contraceptives. Others may find it awkward to do so. Still others don't know how to use contraceptives.

One strategy to reduce teen pregnancy and teen cases of AIDS involves making contraceptives more readily available. In many middle schools and high schools throughout the United States, students can obtain contraceptives, usually by visiting a health clinic located in the school. Many programs require parents' permission for students to obtain contraceptives, but some do not.

Providing contraceptives in schools is not the only solution to teenage pregnancy. Broader educational programs that present the truth about sex, teenage pregnancy, AIDS, and contraception can be effective for adolescents, who too often rely on peers for information about health and sexuality (Boyer & Hein, 1991). Such programs not only teach the relevant biology but also include a focus on responsible sexual behavior or abstention from premarital sex altogether (Dryfoos, 1990).

One effective program is called "Postponing Sexual Involvement" (Howard & McCabe, 1990). Under the direction of trained, older adolescents, students

? THINK ABOUT IT
Suppose you were asked to write a brochure for high school students about the potential hazards of sex. What would you say?

discuss the pressures to become involved sexually, common "lines" that teens use to induce others to have sex, and strategies for responding to those lines. Accompanying the discussions are opportunities for students to practice the strategies in role-playing sessions. Students who participate in these programs are less likely to have intercourse; when they do have intercourse, they are more likely to use contraceptives (Howard & McCabe, 1990).

The conclusion is that adolescents need more than catchy aphorisms like "True love waits." Love and sex are enormously complicated and emotionally charged issues, even for adults; effective programs recognize this complexity and try to provide adolescents with useful skills for dealing with the many issues involved in their emerging sexuality.

These interpersonal skills are also critical in understanding another problem associated with sexual behavior among adolescents and young adults.

Sexual Coercion

Cindy reported that her date "lifted up my skirt and took off my panties when I was drunk. Then he laid down on top of me and went to work." *Like Cindy, many adolescent and young women are forced to have sexual intercourse by males they know, a situation known as* date rape *or* acquaintance rape (Ogletree, 1993). Traditional gender-role socialization helps set the stage for sexual coercion. Males learn that an intense sexual drive is a sign of masculinity. Females learn that being sexually attractive is one way to gain a male's attention. However, "good girls" are expected to be uninterested in sex and to resist attempts for sex. Both males and females learn these expectations; consequently, males often assume that a female says "no" because she is supposed to say "no," not because she really means it (Muehlenhard, 1988). Unless, and sometimes even if, a woman's communications are crystal clear— "*STOP!!* I *don't* want to do this!"—an adolescent or young adult male will often assume, incorrectly and egocentrically, that her interest in sex matches his own (Kowalski, 1992).

A number of circumstances increase the possibility that adolescent and young adult males will misinterpret or ignore a female's verbal or nonverbal communications regarding sexual intent. For example, heavy drinking usually impairs a female's ability to send a clear message and makes males less able and less inclined to interpret such messages (Abbey, 1991). Similarly, when a female dresses provocatively, males assume that she is interested in sex and may ignore what she says (Cassidy & Hurrell, 1995). Yet another factor is a couple's sexual history. If a couple has had sex previously, the male may tend to dismiss his partner's protests, interpreting them as fleeting feelings that can be overcome easily (Shotland & Goodstein, 1992).

Most programs dealing with date rape emphasize the importance of communication. In one program, ads like the one shown here are used to encourage males and females to communicate about sex. Date-rape workshops represent another approach (Feltey, Ainslie, & Geib, 1991). Most programs emphasize the need for females to be clear and consistent in expressing their

If you don't take no for an answer, these could be your new roommates.

If she says, "No, stop!" and you don't listen, you're committing rape. A felony. And you could go to jail. Where it may take you a while to get used to the guys in your new dorm.

Against her will is against the law.
This tagline is used with permission from Pi Kappa Phi.

©1992 Rape Treatment Center, Santa Monica Hospital.

intent. Before engaging in sex, males need to understand a female's intentions, not simply assume that they know. Here are some guidelines that are often presented at such workshops; you may find them useful (Allgeier & Allgeier, 1995):

1. Know your own sexual policies. Decide when sexual intimacy is acceptable for *you*.

2. Communicate these policies openly and clearly.

3. Avoid being alone with a person until you have communicated these policies and believe you can trust the person.

4. Avoid using alcohol or other drugs when you are with a person with whom you do not wish to become sexually intimate.

5. If someone tries to force you to have sex, make your objections known: Talk first, but struggle and scream if necessary.

The See for Yourself feature suggests ways for you to get more information about sexual coercion.

SEE FOR YOURSELF

PROMOTING GREATER AWARENESS ON CAMPUS ABOUT SEXUAL ASSAULT

In recent years, colleges and universities in the United States have taken a much more visible and vigorous stance against sexual assault and date rape. Many now offer a range of activities and services designed to prevent sexual assault and to assist those who are victims of it. Most universities have an office—usually associated with student services—dealing with women's issues. These offices offer educational programs as well as counseling and confidential advice to women with problems. Some campuses sponsor sexual assault awareness days that include workshops, films, and plays designed to promote greater understanding of the issues associated with sexual assault. On some campuses, female self-defense programs are offered. In these programs, which are often run by campus police, women are taught ways to reduce the risk of sexual assault and ways to defend themselves if they are attacked.

Find out which of these services and activities are available to women on your campus. If it's difficult to learn how your college or university deals with issues related to sexual assault and date rape, think about how you could make this information more available to other women. And, if some of these services and activities are not available, think about how you could urge your college to provide them. See for yourself! ●

TEST YOURSELF

1. For college students, three primary functions of dating are learning adult standards of behavior, intimacy, and _____ .

2. Not until _____ do most gay individuals express their sexual orientation publicly.

3. _____ apparently plays a key role in determining sexual orientation.

4. When parents approve of sex, their adolescent children are _____ .

5. Babies born to teenage mothers usually face medical problems, do less well in school, and often have _____ .

6. Adolescents are particularly vulnerable to AIDS because they often engage in unprotected sex and because they _____ .

7. Adolescents often fail to use contraception, due to ignorance, the illusion of invulnerability, lack of access to contraception, and _____ .

8. Date rape is more likely if either partner has been drinking and if the couple _____ .

9. First look at the functions of dating, listed on page 299, then review Chapter 5, where we discussed differences in boys' and girls' ways of interacting with peers. How well do these styles of interaction prepare boys and girls for romantic relationships?

Answers: (1) companionship, (2) young adulthood, (3) Biology, (4) more likely to be sexually active, (5) behavioral problems, (6) sometimes experiment with intravenous drugs, (7) because the girl may see becoming pregnant as a sign of adult independence, (8) has had sex previously.

A LOOK AT THE DARK SIDE: PROBLEMS OF ADOLESCENT DEVELOPMENT

Learning Objectives

- **Why do teenagers drink?**
- **What leads some adolescents to become depressed? How can depression be treated?**
- **What are the causes of juvenile delinquency?**

A Look at the Dark Side: Problems of Adolescent Development

Use of Drugs

Depression

Delinquency

ROD *is an excellent student and a starter on his high school basketball team. He was looking forward to going to the senior prom with Peggy, his long-time girlfriend, and going to the state college with her in the fall. Then, out of the blue, Peggy dropped Rod and moved in with the drummer of a local rock band. Rod is stunned and miserable. Without Peggy, life means little. Basketball and college seem pointless. Some days Rod wonders whether he should just kill himself to make the pain go away.*

Some young people do not adapt well to the new demands and responsibilities of adolescence and respond in ways that are unhealthy. In this final section, we look at three problems, often interrelated, that spell out the three D's of adolescent development: drugs, depression, and delinquency. As we look at these problems, you'll understand why Rod feels so miserable without Peggy.

USE OF DRUGS

Throughout history, people have used substances that alter their behavior, thoughts, and emotions. Today, drugs used commonly in America include alcohol, marijuana, hallucinogens (like LSD), heroin, cocaine, barbiturates, and amphetamines. The graph paints a surprising picture of U.S. teenage drug use (Monitoring the Future Study, 1997). In fact, most adolescents avoid drugs, with one glaring exception—alcohol. A majority of high school seniors have drunk alcohol within the past month (Monitoring the Future Study, 1997).

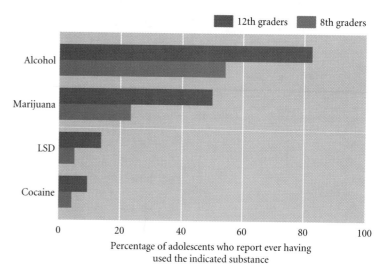

Percentage of adolescents who report ever having used the indicated substance

Teenage Drinking

Why do so many adolescents drink alcohol? There are a number of reasons (Fields, 1992):

- *Experimentation*—something new to try

- *Relaxation*—a means to reduce tension

- *Escape*—to avoid a harsh or unpleasant real world

- *Feelings of exhilaration*—to increase one's self-confidence, usually by reducing one's inhibitions

Of course, these reasons don't apply to all teenagers. Some never drink. Others experiment briefly with drinking, then decide it is not for them. Still others, however, drink heavily: Nearly one-third of high school seniors report having had five or more drinks within the previous two weeks (Johnston et al., 1993).

What determines whether an adolescent joins the majority who drink? Many factors contribute (Petraitis, Flay, & Miller, 1995). Parents are instrumental in determining adolescents' drinking. When drinking is an important part of parents' social lives—for example, stopping at a bar after work or inviting friends over for a drink—adolescents apparently learn that drinking is a pleasant activity and are more likely themselves to drink. In contrast, when parents don't drink at all or limit their drinking to small quantities of alcohol to complement meals, their adolescent children are less likely to drink (Andrews, Hops, & Duncan, 1997; Kline, Canter, & Robin, 1987).

Not surprisingly, peers are influential. As the photo shows, many adolescents drink because their peers do so and exert pressure on them to join the group (Dielman et al., 1992).

Finally, like adults, many adolescents drink to cope with stress. Teens who report frequent life stresses—problems with parents, with interpersonal relationships, or at school—are more likely to drink and to drink more often (Rhodes & Jason, 1990; Windle & Windle, 1996).

Because teenage drinking has so many causes, no single approach is likely to eliminate alcohol abuse. Adolescents who drink to reduce their tension can profit from therapy designed to teach them more effective means of coping with stress. School-based programs that are interactive—featuring student-led discussion—can be effective in teaching the facts about drinking and strategies for resisting peer pressure to drink (Baker, 1988; Tobler & Stratton, 1997).

DEPRESSION

Sometime in your life, you have probably had the blues—days when you had little energy or enthusiasm for activities that you usually enjoy. You wanted to be alone, and you may have doubted your abilities. These feelings are perfectly normal, can usually be explained as reactions to specific events, and vanish in a matter of hours or days. For example, after an exciting vacation with family and friends, you may be depressed at the thought of returning to school to start new and difficult courses. Yet your mood improves as you renew friendships and become involved in activities on campus.

Now imagine experiencing these same symptoms continuously for weeks or months. Also suppose that you have lost your appetite, sleep poorly, and are unable to concentrate. *Pervasive feelings of sadness, irritability, and low self-esteem characterize an individual with* depression. About 3–10% of adolescents are depressed; adolescent girls are more often affected than boys (Nolen-Hoeksema & Girgus, 1994).

Research reveals that unhappiness, anger, and irritation often dominate the lives of depressed adolescents. They believe that family members, friends, and classmates are not friendly to them (Cole & Jordan, 1995). Depressed adolescents wish to be left alone much more often than do nondepressed adolescents (Larson et al., 1990). Rather than being satisfying and rewarding, life is empty and joyless for depressed adolescents.

For some adolescents, depression is triggered by a life event that results in fewer positive reinforcements. The loss of a friend, for example, may deprive a teenager of many rewarding experiences and interactions, making the teen feel sad. Feeling lethargic and melancholy like the girl in the photo, the adolescent withdraws from social interaction and thereby misses further opportunities for rewarding experiences. This situation can degenerate rapidly into a vicious circle in which the depressed adolescent becomes progressively more depressed and more likely to avoid interactions that could draw them out of the depression (Lewinsohn & Gotlib, 1995).

Depression often begins with a situation in which an adolescent feels helpless to control the outcome. Remember Rod, the adolescent in the vignette? His girlfriend had been the center of his life. After she left him unexpectedly, he felt helpless to control his own destiny. Similarly, an athlete may play poorly in the championship game because of illness; or, a high school senior may get a lower score on the SAT exam due to a family crisis the night before taking the test. In each case, the adolescent could do nothing to avoid an undesirable result. Most teens recognize that such feelings of helplessness are specific to the particular situation. *In* learned helplessness, *however, adolescents and adults generalize these feelings of helplessness and believe that they are always at the mercy of external events, with no ability to control their own destinies.* Such feelings of learned helplessness often give rise to depression (Peterson, Maier, & Seligman, 1993).

Experiences like these do not lead all adolescents to become depressed. Some adolescents seem more vulnerable to depression than others, which has led scientists to look for biological factors. Studies of twins and adopted children indicate that heredity definitely plays a part in depression. The exact biochemical mechanism seems to involve neurotransmitters (Sevy, Mendlewicz, & Mendelbaum, 1995). *Some depressed adolescents have reduced levels of* norepinephrine *and* serotonin, *neurotransmitters that regulate brain centers that allow people to experience pleasure.* Some adolescents feel depressed because lower levels of neurotransmitters make it difficult for them to experience happiness, joy, and other pleasurable emotions (Peterson, 1996).

THINK ABOUT IT
How does depression illustrate the interaction of biological, psychological, and sociocultural forces on development?

Treating Depression

It is essential to treat depression; otherwise, depressed adolescents are prone to more serious problems (including suicide, which is examined in the You May Be Wondering feature). Two general approaches are commonly used in treating depression (Kazdin, 1990). One is to administer antidepressant drugs designed to correct the imbalance in neurotransmitters. The well-known drug Prozac, for example, reduces depression by increasing levels of serotonin (Peterson, 1996). The other approach is psychotherapy. Many different forms are available (Lewinsohn & Gotlib, 1995; Sacco & Beck, 1995), but the most effective teach social skills—so that teens can have rewarding social interactions—and to restructure their interpretation of events—so that teens can recognize situations where they can exert control over their lives.

YOU MAY BE WONDERING

PREVENTING TEEN SUICIDES

Suicide is the third most frequent cause of death (after accidents and homicide) among U.S. adolescents (National Center for Health Statistics, 1993). Roughly 10 adolescents in 100 report having attempted suicide at least once, but only 1 in 10,000 actually commits suicide. Suicide is more common among boys than girls and more common among European American adolescents than among African American adolescents. However, Native American adolescents have the highest rate of suicide of any ethnic group in the United States (Garland & Zigler, 1993).

Depression is one frequent precursor of suicide; substance abuse is another (Rich, Sherman, & Fowler, 1990; Summerville, Kaslow, & Doepke, 1996). Few suicides are truly spontaneous; in most cases, there are warning signals (Atwater, 1992). Here are some common signs:

- threats of suicide
- preoccupation with death
- change in eating or sleeping habits
- loss of interest in activities that were once important
- marked changes in personality
- persistent feelings of gloom and helplessness
- giving away valued possessions

If someone you know shows these signs, *don't ignore them,* hoping they aren't for real. Instead, ask the person if he or she is planning on hurting himself or herself. Be calm and supportive and, if the person appears to have made preparations to commit suicide, don't leave him or her alone. Stay with the person until other friends or relatives can come. More important: *Insist* that the adolescent seek professional help. Therapy is essential for treating the feelings of depression and hopelessness that give rise to thoughts of suicide (Garland & Zigler, 1993). •

DELINQUENCY

Skipping school. Shoplifting. Selling cocaine. Murder. *When adolescents commit acts like these, which are illegal and destructive toward themselves or others, this represents* juvenile delinquency. Because delinquency applies to such a broad range of activities, it is useful to identify different forms of delinquent behavior. Status offenses *are acts that are not crimes if committed by an adult, such as truancy, sexual promiscuity, and running away from home. (An adult is someone older than 16, 17, 18, or 19, depending on the state.)* Index offenses *are acts such as robbery, rape, and arson, which are crimes regardless of the age of the perpetrator.*

Adolescents are responsible for many of the index offenses committed in the United States. The graph, based on information presented in the FBI's *Uniform Crime Reports* (1996), shows the percentage of cases of motor vehicle theft, burglary, robbery, murder, arson, rape, and assault that were committed by 15- to 20-year-olds. Adolescents are responsible for nearly one-half of the cars stolen in the United States and for more than one-fourth of the murders.

Causes of Delinquency

Why is delinquent behavior so common among adolescents? To answer this question, Moffitt (1993) notes that it's important to distinguish two kinds of delinquent behavior. The first, life-course persistent antisocial behavior, refers to antisocial behavior that emerges at an early age and continues throughout life. These individuals may start with hitting peers at 3 years, then progress to shoplifting at age 12, and then to car theft at 16. Perhaps only 5% of youth fit this pattern of antisocial behavior, but they account for most of the criminal activity shown in the graph.

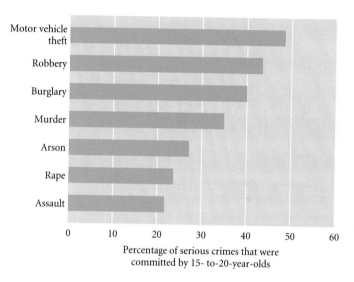

Percentage of serious crimes that were committed by 15- to-20-year-olds

The second form of delinquent behavior described by Moffitt (1993), adolescent-limited antisocial behavior, is far more common. As the name implies, this type of antisocial behavior is limited to adolescence. During the teenage years, many youth engage in relatively minor criminal acts, such as shoplifting or using drugs. Yet they aren't consistently antisocial; they may follow school rules, for example. And, their antisocial behavior vanishes in late adolescence or early adulthood.

Why do so many teens have this brief bout of delinquent activity? Remember, part of the struggle of adolescence is to acquire adult status. Youth with life-course persistent antisocial behavior often acquire high status and, therefore, unfortunately become role models. These youth often appear to be relatively independent (free of parental influence), they often have desirable possessions like cars and expensive clothes, and they're often sexually experienced. These are attractive features, so many youth apparently imitate the criminal activity that supports this adultlike life-style. However, as adolescence ends, the same desirable outcomes can be reached through more prosocial means and the potential costs of antisocial behavior increase, so most youth rapidly abandon antisocial behavior. Thus, adolescence-limited antisocial behavior can be understood as one way for adolescents to achieve adultlike status and privileges (Moffitt, 1993).

Explaining life-course persistent antisocial behavior is more complex. Researchers have identified several forces that contribute to this type of delinquent behavior.

1. *Social class.* Adolescent crime occurs in all social strata but is more frequent among adolescents from lower social classes. This relationship may reflect a number of factors. First, crime is more common in lower-class neighborhoods, so adult criminal models are readily available to children. Second, lower-class adolescents often experience little success in school and usually have little invested in the outcome of their academic efforts; criminal activity

is an arena in which they can excel and gain the recognition of their peers. According to Katie Buckland, a prosecutor in Los Angeles, youth who join gangs are "the ambitious kids . . . trying to climb up their own corporate ladder. And the only corporate ladder they see has to do with gangs and drugs" (Kantrowitz, 1993, p. 44). Third, the constant stress of life on the brink of economic disaster can reduce the effectiveness of parenting in lower-class homes (Patterson, DeVaryshe, & Ramsey, 1989).

2. *Family processes.* Delinquent behavior is often related to inadequate parental supervision. Adolescents who are unsupervised (because, for example, their parents are at work) are much more likely to become involved in delinquent acts. Parents may also contribute to delinquent behavior if their discipline is inconsistent and if their marital relationship is marked by constant conflict (Patterson, 1995). When family life is riddled with arguments, threats, and the like, the gang represents an appealing makeshift family for some adolescents.

3. *Self-control.* As most children develop, they become more capable of regulating their own behavior. They are better able to inhibit impulsive tendencies, to delay gratification, and to consider the impact of their behavior on others (Rotenberg & Mayer, 1990). That is, they learn to rise above the immediate pressures of a situation, to avoid giving in to impulses, and to think about the consequences of their actions. Delinquent youth do not follow the usual developmental pattern. Instead, they often act impulsively, and they seem unable or unwilling to postpone pleasure (Patterson, 1995). Seeing a fancy new CD player or a car, delinquent youth are tempted to steal it, simply so that they can have it *right now.* When others inadvertently get in their way, delinquent adolescents often respond without regard to the nature of the other person's acts or intentions.

4. *Biological forces.* The aggressive and impulsive behaviors that are a common part of antisocial behavior have biological roots. Some antisocial youth apparently inherit a predisposition to behave aggressively and impulsively (Carey, 1996). This is not an "antisocial gene." Instead, individuals who are genetically predisposed to aggression and impulsivity will be more sensitive to experiences that foster antisocial behavior than will individuals who are not genetically predisposed in this way.

Treatment and Prevention

Given the wide-ranging causes of delinquency, it is naive of us to expect a single or simple cure. Instead, delinquency must be attacked along several fronts simultaneously:

- Delinquent adolescents can be taught effective techniques for self-control.
- Parents of delinquent youth can be taught the importance of supervising and monitoring their children's behavior and the necessity for consistent discipline.
- Families of delinquents can learn to function more effectively as a unit, with special emphasis on better means of resolving conflict.
- Schools can develop programs that motivate delinquent youth to become invested in their school performance.
- Communities can improve economic conditions in neighborhoods where delinquency reigns.

Programs that use these strategies have met with success; adolescents who participate in these programs are less likely to be arrested again. The programs

? THINK ABOUT IT
A letter to the editor of your local paper claims that "juvenile delinquents should be thrown in jail because they're born as 'bad apples' and will always be that way." Write a reply that states the facts correctly.

thereby address a major problem affecting not only adolescent development but all of North American society (Alexander et al., 1989; Dryfoos, 1990).

We conclude this chapter with a Current Controversies feature that describes another approach to dealing with adolescent crime.

WHEN JUVENILES COMMIT SERIOUS CRIMES,

CURRENT CONTROVERSIES

INFOTRAC
COLLEGE EDITION

To learn more, enter the following search term: juvenile delinquency.

Traditionally, when adolescents under 18 commit crimes, the case is handled in the juvenile justice system. Although procedures vary from state to state, most adolescents who are arrested do not go to court; instead, law enforcement and legal authorities have considerable discretionary power. They may, for example, release arrested adolescents into the custody of their parents. However, when adolescents commit serious or violent crimes, there will be a hearing with a judge. This hearing is closed to the press and public; no jury is involved. Instead, the judge receives reports from police, probation officers, school officials, medical authorities, and other interested parties. Adolescents judged guilty can be placed on probation at home, in foster care outside the home, or in a facility for youth offenders.

Because of the increasing number of serious crimes committed by juveniles, many law enforcement and legal authorities believe that juveniles should be tried as adults. Advocates of this position argue for lowering the minimum age for mandatory transfer of a case to adult courts, increasing the range of offenses that must be tried in adult court, and giving prosecutors more authority to file cases with juveniles in adult criminal court. Critics argue that treating juvenile offenders as adults ignores the fact that juveniles are less able than adults to understand the nature and consequences of commiting a crime. Also, they argue, punishments appropriate for adults are inappropriate for juveniles.

What do you think? Should we lower the age at which juveniles are tried as adults? Based on the theories of development we have discussed, what guidelines would you propose in deciding when a juvenile should be tried as an adult? •

TEST YOURSELF

1. The reasons that teenagers drink include relaxation, escape, a desire for feelings of exhilaration, and _____ .

2. Teens are less likely to drink when their parents drink _____ .

3. Depression has been linked to life events that produce fewer positive reinforcements, situations in which teenagers feel helpless, and _____ .

4. Treatments for depression include drugs that correct imbalances in neurotransmitters and therapy that emphasizes _____ .

5. Acts like truancy and running away from home, which are not crimes when committed by adults, are _____ .

6. The factors that contribute to juvenile delinquency include social class, _____ , and inadequate self-control.

7. Are the causes of teenage drinking, depression, and delinquency much the same, or is each problem of adolescent development caused by a unique set of factors?

Answers: (1) experimentation, (2) in small amounts, to complement meals, (3) an imbalance in neurotransmitters, (4) the development of social skills, (5) status offenses, (6) disrupted family processes

PUTTING IT ALL TOGETHER

In the voyage from the land of childhood to the land of adulthood, the choppy waters of adolescence must be navigated. Most teens complete the journey successfully, becoming adults who will someday watch their own children make the same trip. As one writer noted:

> It is easy to forget that a personality unfurling itself can be glorious as well as inconvenient. No doubt Jesus was considered a pain by his elders, as was Gandhi. The young need to check out their wingspreads, and adults need to be adult enough to withstand the onslaught of beautiful hair, terrible noise and challenge to every sensible norm. . . . (Pacy, 1993, p. 35)

The spreading of wings that characterizes adolescence is evident in all its splendor and aggravation in this chapter.

We began with the physical changes associated with puberty. These outward signs of looming adulthood come early in adolescence for some youth but much later for others like Pete.

Next, we looked at the struggle to achieve an identity. Adolescents and young adults often experiment with different roles in their efforts to realize an identity.

When parents support this experimentation, the search for identity is more likely to succeed. For example, Dea came to realize that she is uniquely blessed with roots in three different cultures; she loves elements of each, and she is forging a novel Dutch-Asian-American identity.

Our next stop was the world of work. Aaron's experiences in part-time work are typical. Adolescents rarely balance school and heavy part-time work effectively. We also saw that selecting a career involves matching interests and aptitudes with specific occupations, then determining the skills and education needed for the chosen line of work.

From work we moved to romance and sex. Interest in sex mounts in the teenage years, and many adolescents become sexually active. Like Rebecca, many teenagers have unprotected sex, which can lead to pregnancy and sexually transmitted diseases.

We ended the chapter by looking at the dark side of adolescence. Some young people do not handle adolescent difficulties well, leading to use of illegal drugs, depression (like Rod, the basketball player in the throes of first love), and delinquency.

SUMMARY

Farewell to Childhood: Puberty

Physical Growth

• Puberty consists of a series of bodily changes occurring in early adolescence, including a period of rapid growth. Today, children enter puberty earlier and are bigger at maturity than in previous generations.

• Early maturation tends to be beneficial to boys, apparently because others perceive them to be more mature and are more likely to treat them as adults. Early maturation is sometimes harmful to girls, both in terms of their success in school and their interactions with other girls and boys.

Eating Disorders

• Many obese children and adolescents are unpopular, have low self-esteem, and are at risk for medical disorders. Obesity reflects both heredity and acquired eating habits. The most effective programs for treating obesity in adolescents are those in which children and their parents set eating and exercise goals, and both parents and children are rewarded for their performance.

• Anorexia and bulimia nervosa are disorders that primarily affect adolescent girls. Anorexia is characterized by an irrational fear of being overweight. Bulimia is marked by binge eating followed by purging. Several factors contribute to anorexia and bulimia, including cultural standards for thinness, a need for independence within autocratic families, and heredity.

Who Am I? The Search for Identity

Identity Versus Role Confusion

• Erikson claimed that the main crisis of adolescence is to achieve an identity. Experimentation with different possible selves is an integral part of the quest for identity.

Resolving the Identity Crisis

• Associated with the search for identity are four statuses: Diffusion and foreclosure are more common in early adolescence; moratorium and achievement tend to emerge in late adolescence and young adulthood.

• Authoritative parenting is most conducive to the achievement of identity. Authoritarian parenting is associated with foreclosure, whereas indulgent-permissive parenting is associated with diffusion.

Ethnic Identity

• Adolescents from ethnic groups often progress through three phases in acquiring an ethnic identity: initial disinterest, exploration, and identity achievement. Achieving an ethnic identity usually results in higher self-esteem. It is more likely with authoritative parents, and it is not consistently related to the strength of the child's identification with mainstream culture.

The Myth of Storm and Stress

• Contrary to myth, adolescence is not usually a period of storm and stress. Most adolescents love their parents, rely on them for advice, and adopt their values. The parent-child relationship becomes more egalitarian during the adolescent years, reflecting adolescents' growing independence.

Flipping Burgers and Waiting Tables: Entering the World of Work

Part-Time Work

• Most U.S. adolescents have part-time jobs. This phenomenon, which gathered steam in the 1980s, is unique to the United States (among industrialized countries). Adolescents who are employed more than 15 hours per week during the school year typically do poorly in school, often have lowered self-esteem and increased anxiety, and have problems interacting with others. Employed adolescents save relatively little of their income. Instead, they spend most of it on clothing, food, and entertainment for themselves, which can give misleading expectations about how to allocate income.

• Part-time employment can be beneficial if adolescents work relatively few hours, if the work allows them to use existing skills or to acquire new ones, and if teens save some of their earnings. Summer employment, because it does not conflict with the demands of school, can also be beneficial.

Career Development

• Super's theory of vocational choice proposes that an adolescent's identity and career aspirations develop in parallel. He proposes three phases of vocational development during adolescence and young adulthood: crystallization, in which basic interests are identified; specification, in which jobs associated with interests are identified; and implementation, which marks entry into the work force.

• Holland proposed six different work-related personality types: realistic, investigative, social, conventional, enterprising, and artistic. Each is uniquely suited to certain jobs. People are happier when their personality fits their job and less happy when it does not.

"How Do I Love Thee?"— Romantic Relationships

Dating

• Boys and girls begin to date in mid-adolescence. Dating often begins with the meeting of same-sex groups and progresses to well-defined couples. For high school students, dating is for both recreation and status; for college students, it is a source of intimacy and companionship.

• Adolescents often wonder about their sexual orientation, but only a small percentage report engaging in homosexual experiences. Research has discredited many explanations of the origins of a homosexual orientation. Current theorizing emphasizes the contributions of biology.

Awakening of Sexual Interests

• By age 18, most North American adolescents have had sexual intercourse. Adolescents are more likely to be sexually active if they believe that their parents and peers approve of sex. Pregnancy and sexually transmitted diseases are two common consequences of adolescent sexual behavior, because sexually active adolescents use contraceptives infrequently.

• Another common problem is that adolescent and young adult females are forced into sex against their will, typically because males misinterpret or disregard females' intentions. Sexual coercion is particularly likely when either partner has been drinking or when the couple has had sex previously. Date-rape workshops strive to improve communication between males and females.

A Look at the Dark Side: Problems of Adolescent Development

Use of Drugs

• Today, many adolescents drink alcohol regularly. Adolescents are attracted to alcohol and other drugs by their need for experimentation, for relaxation, for escape, and for feelings of exhilaration. The primary factors that influence whether adolescents drink are encouragement from others (parents and peers) and stress.

Depression

• Depressed adolescents have little enthusiasm for life, believe that others are unfriendly, and wish to be left alone. Depression can be triggered by an event that deprives them of rewarding experiences, by an event in which they feel unable to control their own destiny, or by an imbalance in neurotransmitters.

• Treatment of depression relies on medications that correct the levels of neurotransmitters and on therapy designed to improve social skills and restructure adolescents' interpretation of events.

Delinquency

• Many youth engage in antisocial behavior briefly during adolescence. In contrast, the small percentage of adolescents who engage in life-course persistent antisocial behavior are involved in one-fourth to one-half of the serious crimes committed in the United States. Life-course persistent antisocial behavior has been linked to social class, family processes, lack of self-control, and heredity. Efforts to reduce adolescent criminal activity must address all of these variables.

KEY TERMS

puberty (278)
menarche (278)
secular growth trends (279)
basal metabolic rate (281)
anorexia nervosa (282)
bulimia nervosa (282)
self-concept (284)
adolescent egocentrism (285)
imaginary audience (285)

personal fable (285)
achievement status (285)
moratorium status (285)
foreclosure status (285)
diffusion status (285)
crystallization (294)
specification (294)
implementation (294)
personality-type theory (295)

masturbation (300)
date (acquaintance) rape (303)
depression (307)
learned helplessness (307)
norepinephrine (307)
serotonin (307)
juvenile delinquency (308)
status offense (308)
index offense (308)

IF YOU'D LIKE TO LEARN MORE

Readings

GALLO, D. R. (Ed.) (1997). *No easy answers: Short stories about teenagers making tough choices.* New York: Basic Books. This readable collection of short stories shows youth dealing with common problems of adolescence, including peer pressure, substance abuse, and teen pregnancy.

HECHINGER, F. (1992). *Fateful choices.* New York: Hill & Wang. The author discusses many of the problems that adolescents face—teen pregnancy and drug abuse—and recommends how we can improve the well-being of adolescents.

OSTER, G. D., & MONTGOMERY, S. S. (1994). *Helping your depressed teenager: A guide for parents and* caregivers. New York: Wiley. The authors use many case studies to describe depression, its causes, and its treatment.

STEINBERG, L. D., & LEVINE, A. (1990). *You and your adolescent.* New York: Harper Perennial. This outstanding book has a number of useful guidelines that help parents recognize when their teenager has a problem that may require professional help.

For additional readings, explore Infotrac College Edition, your online library. Go to http://www.infotrac-college.com/wadsworth.

Web Sites

The New York Online Access to Health has a Web site

http://www.noah.cuny.edu/pregnancy/march_of_dimes/stds/stdsbro.html

that discusses many STDs, including how they are harmful, how they can be prevented, and how they can be treated.

A young adult Korean American adoptee created this site

http://www.medill.nwu.edu/people/chappell/kor.am.adoptees.html

to address ethnic identity, interracial dating, and related issues.

The Web site of the Center for Effective Collaboration and Practice

http://www.air-dc.org/cecp/resources/schfail/prevsch.html

has a wealth of information on the causes of antisocial behavior and different ways to prevent it.

Anorexia Nervosa and Related Eating Disorders, Inc. maintains a Web site

http://www.anred.com

that describes different eating disorders, their causes, and treatments.

Web site addresses are subject to change. The Wadsworth Study Center Web site listed below can be accessed for updated links.

The Wadsworth Psychology Study Center Web Site

See http://psychology.wadsworth.com/ for practice quiz questions, internet links, updates, critical thinking exercises, discussion forums and more! The Wadsworth Psychology Study Center provides a wealth of information fully organized and integrated by chapter.

SNAPSHOTS OF DEVELOPMENT
A VISUAL SUMMARY

School-Age Children and Adolescents

BIOLOGICAL FORCES

Biological forces are particularly obvious with the start of puberty, but this is not their only influence on school-age children and adolescents. Intelligence, depression, and teenage sexuality all reflect the impact of biology.

PSYCHOLOGICAL FORCES

Psychological forces become very influential during these years as children's and adolescents' thinking becomes ever more mature. Children and adolescents use their greater cognitive power to understand more complicated concepts, to learn about other people, and to interpret their own experiences.

SOCIOCULTURAL FORCES

Parents are usually the first means by which sociocultural influences are transmitted to children, but they are soon joined by a host of other forces. Peers, schools, and television are all potent sociocultural forces that combine to create unique developmental pathways that children follow during the school-age years and adolescence.

In terms of intelligence, adopted children resemble their biological parents more than their adoptive parents, which shows the influence of heredity on human intelligence.

Many social factors can place children at risk for child abuse, including cultural acceptance of physical punishment, poverty, and living in social isolation.

Adolescence is a time when all youth search for an identity. For youth from ethnic groups, it is also a time to acquire an ethnic identity, which often involves learning the traditions of one's culture.

Although the folklore says that teenagers benefit from part-time jobs, the reality is they often do worse in school, have mental health and behavioral problems, and get a distorted sense of their own affluence.

PART THREE

YOUNG AND MIDDLE ADULTHOOD

- **CHAPTER 9**

  Becoming an Adult

- **CHAPTER 10**

  Relationships
  in Adulthood

- **CHAPTER 11**

  Work and Leisure

- **CHAPTER 12**

  Experiencing
  Middle Age

A CLOSER LOOK

Debbi Fields has always believed in herself—especially in her ability to make delicious cookies. Although she had little formal background in business, she went to banks with a plan and a plate of cookies until someone decided to take a chance on her. So as a young mother barely in her 20s, she opened her first cookie store in Palo Alto, California, in 1977. No one thought she could make it. Her husband even bet that she would not make $50 on the first day. When Debbi had no sales by 3 P.M. she decided to take a chance. With a plate of cookies in her hand, she walked up and down the street giving free samples, telling people if they liked them to go to her

store to buy more. She ended the day making $75, winning the bet. Through a combination of risk taking and self-determination, Debbi Fields became the mastermind behind Mrs. Fields' Cookies. By 1999, there were over 700 Mrs. Fields' Cookies franchises located around the world.

Debbi Fields exemplifies the major themes of young adulthood and middle age discussed in Chapters 9–12: striking out on one's own, experiencing personal growth, choosing and developing in an occupation, continuing to learn new skills, and balancing work and family.

CHAPTER 9

BECOMING AN ADULT

When Does Adulthood Begin?
Role Transitions Marking Adulthood
Going to College
*Individuals with Disabilities
    and the Transition to College*
Psychological Views
So When Do People Become Adults?

Physical Development and Health
Growth, Strength, and
    Physical Functioning
Health Status
Life-Style Factors
Binge Drinking on College Campuses
Social, Gender, and Ethnic Issues
    in Health
Healthy Adulthood

Cognitive Development
How Should We View Intelligence
    in Adults?
What Happens to Intelligence
    in Adulthood?
The Seattle Longitudinal Study
Going Beyond Formal Operations:
    Thinking in Adulthood

Moral Reasoning
Kohlberg's Theory
Schindler's List
Alternatives to Justice
Cultural Differences in Moral Reasoning

Who Do You Want to Be?
Personality in Young Adulthood
Creating Scenarios and Life Stories
When I Was 35, It Was a Very Good Year
Possible Selves
Self-Concept
Personal Control Beliefs

Putting It All Together

Summary

If You'd Like to Learn More

There comes a time in life when we turn away from our childhood and we aspire to being adults. In some societies, the transition to adulthood is abrupt and dramatic, marked by clear rites of passage. In Western society, it is fuzzier; the only apparent marker may be a birthday ritual. We may even ask "real" adults what it's like to be one. Adulthood is marked in numerous ways, some of which we explore in the first section.

Without question, young adulthood is the peak of physical processes and health. It is also a time when people who acquired unhealthy habits earlier in life may decide to adopt a better life-style. Young adulthood also marks the peak of some cognitive abilities, and the continued development of others.

On a more personal level, young adulthood is a time when we make plans and dream of what lies ahead. It is a time when we think about what life as an adult will be like. These different elements help define young adulthood, which will be examined in this chapter.

WHEN DOES ADULTHOOD BEGIN?

When Does Adulthood Begin?

Role Transitions Marking Adulthood

Going to College

Psychological Views

So When Do People Become Adults?

Learning Objectives

- **What role transitions mark entry into adulthood in Western societies? How do non-Western cultures mark the transition to adulthood?**
- **How does going to college fit in the transition to adulthood?**
- **What psychological criteria mark the transition to adulthood?**

𝕸**ARCUS** *woke up with the worst headache he ever remembered having. "If this is adulthood, they can keep it," he muttered to himself. Like many young adults in the United States, Marcus spent his 21st birthday celebrating at a nightclub. But the phone call from his mother that woke him in the first place reminds him that he isn't an adult in every way; she called to see if he needs money.*

Imagine that you are Marcus. Think for a minute about the first time you felt like an adult. When was it? What was the context? Who were you with? How did you feel? Now think about yourself between the ages of 18 and 22. Is this the period when you completed transition to adulthood? Why or why not?

Even though becoming an adult is one of our most important life transitions, it is difficult to pin down exactly when it occurs in Western societies. Celebrations like the one in the photograph marking the achievement of a certain age such as 21 are helpful, but do not signal a clean break with youth and full acceptance as an adult. Certainly, Marcus may feel like an adult because he can purchase alcohol legally, but he may not feel that way in other respects, such as supporting himself financially.

In this section, we examine some of the ways in which societies mark the transition to adulthood, and we'll see that the criteria vary widely from culture to culture.

ROLE TRANSITIONS MARKING ADULTHOOD

One cool spring evening, a group of former high school classmates got together to catch up on what had been going on in their lives. The conversation eventually turned to the topic of growing up and becoming adults, as each of them would be turning 21 in the next few months. Joyce looked older than her 20 years. Her 5-year-old son was playing quietly on the floor. Next to Joyce sat

Sheree, an art major. She wore extremely cool clothes, purchased at the store where she works part-time. The third young woman, Marcia, looked a bit tired from her long day as an intern at Arthur Andersen, one of the major accounting firms. Joyce spoke first. "I had Jimmy when I was 15. I thought it would make me grown up and give me someone who would love me. But it gave me grownup bills and no job. I still can't afford my own place, so I live with my mom." Sheree declared, "It's like, sure I'm an adult. I can do whatever I want, whenever I want. It's like, I don't have to answer to anybody, OK?" Marcia had a different view: "As for me, I don't think I'll *really* be an adult until I complete my education, can support myself, and get married."

Are these young people adults? Yes and no. As we will see, it depends on how you define adulthood.

Role Transitions in Western Cultures

The most widely used criteria for deciding whether a person has reached adult-hood are role transitions, *which involve assuming new responsibilities and duties.* Certain role transitions serve as key markers for attaining adulthood: completing education, beginning full-time employment, establishing an independent household, marriage, and becoming a parent (Hogan & Astone, 1986).

Interestingly, the age at which people tend to experience these marker events varies over time. Such changes are examples of cohort effects, described in Chapter 1 (page 35). For example, the average age for completing school rose steadily during the 20th century as the proportion of people going to college increased from roughly 10% in the early part of the century to over 50% today. In contrast, the average age of first marriage and parenthood dropped steadily from 1900 to around 1960, before rising sharply from 1960 to the late 1980s (U.S. Bureau of the Census, 1998). Such complexities make it difficult to use any one event as the marker for becoming an adult. Like the three women we encountered earlier, people experience some marker events but not others, further complicating the issue. Such is not the case in all cultures, however.

> **? THINK ABOUT IT**
> **Why are there no clear-cut transitions to adulthood in Western cultures?**

Cross-Cultural Evidence of Role Transitions

Non-Western cultures tend to be clearer about when a person becomes an adult. In these cultures, marriage is the most important determinant of adult status (Schlegel & Barry, 1991). The Indian family in the photograph is representative of this view.

Many non-Western cultures also have a well-defined set of requirements that boys must meet in order to become men (Gilmore, 1990). These requirements typically focus on three key features: One must be able to provide, protect, and impregnate. In contrast, most cultures rely on menarche as the primary, and usually the only, marker of adulthood for girls (Gilmore, 1990).

Rituals marking initiation into adulthood, often among the most important ones in a culture, are termed rites of passage. Rites of passage may involve highly elaborate steps that take days or weeks, or they may be compressed into a few minutes. Initiates are usually dressed in apparel reserved for the ritual, to denote their special position. Traces of these rites remain in Western culture; consider, for example, the ritual attire for graduations or weddings. Because rites change little over the years, they provide continuity through the life span (Keith, 1990). Older adults lead young people through the same rites they themselves experienced years earlier. Western counterparts are much less formalized and diffuse; indeed, you may be hard pressed to think of any. However, a father buying his son his first razor or a mother helping her daughter with her first menstrual period may be as close as we get in the larger society. Certain ethnic groups maintain more formal rites, like bar and bat mitzvahs. Through rites of passage, cultures the world over maintain contact and social continuity across the generations.

GOING TO COLLEGE

One of the most common markers of adulthood in the United States is completing one's education. For more than half of the people 18–22 years of age, this means going to college (National Center for Educational Statistics, 1993), which serves as a catalyst for intellectual and personal growth (Kitchener & King, 1989; Perry, 1970). We examine some of these cognitive changes later in this chapter.

We commonly think of people between the ages of 18 and 25 as college students. However, the face of college campuses is changing rapidly, as you can probably tell by looking around your own; the average age of college students in the United States is roughly 29 (Milford, 1998).

Colleges usually refer to students over 25 as returning adult students, *which implies that these individuals have already reached adulthood.* Overall, returning adult students like the woman in the photograph tend to be problem solvers, self-directed, and pragmatic, and to have relevant life experiences that they can integrate with their coursework (Harringer, 1994). Compared to younger college students, returning adult students are more highly motivated, more involved in studying and learning, more likely to use critical thinking in their learning, and more likely to interact with faculty (Ross, 1989). Why these differences exist is related to the kinds of changes in thinking that occur in adulthood, which we explore in detail on pages 335–345.

One group of Americans who are experiencing the going-to-college-as-passage-into-adulthood in greater numbers are people with disabilities. With the enactment of the Americans with Disabilities Act in 1990, colleges and universities became more accessible for these adults, and supportive services now exist on every campus. In part, these services serve an educational function, to correct misinformation and stereotypes about people with disabilities. For example, people with disabilities have long faced barriers in college and in the workplace (Rusch, Szymanski, & Chadsey-Rusch, 1992). These issues and programs designed to address them are discussed in more detail in the You May Be Wondering feature.

INDIVIDUALS WITH DISABILITIES AND THE TRANSITION TO COLLEGE

The number of college students with disabilities has increased tenfold since the late 1970s (McGuire, Norlander, & Shaw, 1990); officials estimate that over 160,000 U.S. college students have some type of learning disability, representing 18% of students with a disability of any kind (Madaus, 1997). Numerous programs have been established at two- and four-year colleges to assist students with disabilities (Bursuck & Rose, 1992; Gajar, 1992). These programs range from providing training and outreach services to making course materials available in alternative formats such as Braille. Entrance ramps to buildings provide access to learning resources and opportunities. In all cases, the goals of such efforts are to help students succeed in college to the best of their abilities and deal with their subsequent transition to the world of work.

Many students with disabilities first enroll in a community college after high school (Bursuck & Rose, 1992). Providing support services in the academic environment appears to work; most students with disabilities have successful experiences in college (Bursuck & Rose, 1992; Gajar, 1992). Support services that provide help with other aspects of the transition to adulthood, such as becoming financially independent, also increase the likelihood of success. •

PSYCHOLOGICAL VIEWS

From a psychological perspective, becoming an adult means interacting with the world in a fundamentally different way. Cognitively, young adults think in different ways than adolescents (King & Kitchener, 1994). Behaviorally, a major difference between adolescence and adulthood is the significant drop in the frequency of reckless behavior such as driving at high speed, having sex without contraception, or committing antisocial acts like vandalism (Arnett & Taber, 1994). From this perspective, young adults like the one in the photograph maintain a higher degree of self-control and compliance with social conventions (Hart, 1992).

On the psychosocial front, young adulthood marks the transition from concern with identity (see pages 284–290) to concern with autonomy and intimacy, which we explore here and in Chapter 10 (Erikson, 1982). Becoming independent from one's parents entails being able to fend for oneself, but it does not imply a complete severing of the relationship. On the contrary, adult children usually establish a rewarding relationship with their parents, as we will see in Chapter 12.

Establishing Intimacy

According to Erikson, the major task for young adults is dealing with the psychosocial conflict of intimacy versus isolation. This is the sixth step in Erikson's theory of psychosocial development, the basic tenets of which are summarized in Chapter 1. Erikson believed that once a person's identity has been established, he or she is ready to create a shared identity with another, the key ingredient for intimacy (Erikson, 1982). Without a clear sense of identity, Erikson argued, the woman in the photograph would be afraid of committing to a long-term relationship or might become overly dependent on the partner for her identity.

Several studies support this view (Matula et al., 1992). For example, Whitbourne and Tesch (1985) interviewed college seniors and 24- to 27-year-old alumni to ascertain their levels of identity formation and intimacy. Interestingly, the researchers found that identity formation continues into young adulthood; more alumni than seniors were classified as being in the moratorium or achievement stages of identity formation (see pages 285–287 for discussions of these levels). Additionally, more alumni than seniors had begun developing intimate relationships. Most important, those alumni who had well-formed identities were more likely than those who did not to be capable of true intimacy, which is exactly what Erikson predicted.

It looks as if Erikson's theory is strongly supported, but investigators began wondering whether the same patterns hold for men and women. The results of this research are more complicated. Apparently, most men and career-oriented women resolve identity issues before intimacy issues (Dyk & Adams, 1990; Patterson, Sochting, & Marcia, 1992). These individuals complete their educations and make initial career choices before becoming involved in a committed relationship.

In contrast, some women resolve intimacy issues before identity issues. They marry and rear children, and only after their children have grown and moved away do they deal with the question of their own identity (Schiedel & Marcia, 1985; Whitbourne & Tesch, 1985). Still other women deal with both identity and intimacy issues simultaneously—for example, by entering into relationships that allow them to develop identities based on caring for others (Dyk & Adams, 1990).

Thus, this part of Erikson's theory is most applicable in the cases of men and career-oriented women. But many women confront and resolve the issues of identity and intimacy in young adulthood in reverse order or even simultaneously.

SO WHEN DO PEOPLE BECOME ADULTS?

The perspectives considered in this section do not give any definitive answers to the question of when people become adults. All we can say is that the transition depends on culture and a number of psychological factors. In cultures without clearly defined rites of passage, defining oneself as an adult rests on one's perception of whether personally relevant key criteria have been met.

? THINK ABOUT IT
What are the sources of gender differences in resolving intimacy?

TEST YOURSELF

1. The most widely used criteria for deciding whether a person has reached adulthood are _____ .

2. Rituals marking initiation into adulthood are called _____ .

3. Students over 25 are referred to as _____ .

4. Behaviorally, a major difference between adolescence and adulthood is a significant drop in the frequency of _____ .

5. Research indicates that Erikson's idea of resolving identity followed by intimacy best describes men and _____ .

6. Why are formal rites of passage important? What has Western society lost by eliminating them? What have they gained?

Answers: (1) role transitions, (2) rites of passage, (3) returning adult students, (4) reckless behavior, (5) career-oriented women

PHYSICAL DEVELOPMENT AND HEALTH

Learning Objectives

- **In what respects are young adults at their physical peak?**
- **How healthy are young adults in general?**
- **How do smoking, drinking alcohol, and nutrition affect young adults' health?**
- **How does young adults' health differ as a function of socioeconomic status, gender, and ethnicity?**

Physical Development and Health

Growth, Strength, and Physical
 Functioning

Health Status

Life-Style Factors

Social, Gender, and Ethnic Issues
 in Health

J **UAN** *is a 25-year-old who started smoking cigarettes in high school in order to be popular. Juan wants to quit, but he knows that it will be difficult. He has also heard that it doesn't really matter if he quits or not, because his health will never recover. Juan wonders whether it is worthwhile to try.*

Juan is at the peak of his physical functioning. Most young adults are in the best physical shape of their lives. Indeed, the early 20s are the best years for strenuous work, trouble-free reproduction, and peak athletic performance. These achievements reflect a physical system at its peak. But people's physical functioning is affected by several health-related behaviors, like smoking.

GROWTH, STRENGTH, AND PHYSICAL FUNCTIONING

As a young adult, you're as tall as you will ever be (Tanner, 1978). Height remains stable through middle adulthood, declining somewhat in old age (as described in Chapter 13). Although men have more muscle mass and tend to be stronger than women, physical strength in both sexes peaks during the late 20s and early 30s, declining slowly throughout the rest of life (Whitbourne, 1996). Coordination and dexterity peak around the same time (Whitbourne, 1996). Because of these trends, few professional athletes remain at the top of their sport in their mid-30s. Indeed, individuals such as Warren Moon, who played quarterback for the NFL in his early 40s, and Nolan Ryan, who pitched for the Texas Rangers until his mid-40s, are famous partly because they are exceptions. Most sports superstars, like Eric Lindros shown in the photograph, are in their 20s.

Sensory acuity is also at its peak in the early 20s (Whitbourne, 1985). Visual acuity remains high until middle age, when people tend to become farsighted and require glasses for reading. Hearing begins to decline somewhat by the late 20s, especially for high-pitched tones. By old age, this hearing loss may affect one's ability to understand speech. People's ability to smell, taste, feel pain and changes in temperature, and maintain balance largely remain unchanged until late life.

HEALTH STATUS

How is your overall health? If you are a young adult, chances are better than 90% that you will say that your health is good or better (USDHHS, 1998). Relatively speaking, young adults get many fewer colds and respiratory infections than they did when they were children. Indeed, only about 1% of young adults are limited in their ability to function because of a health-related condition.

Because of the overall healthy status of American young adults, death from disease, especially during the early 20s, is relatively rare until late middle age (U.S. Bureau of the Census, 1998). For example, the death rate due to cancer for people aged 15–24 is less than 5 people per 100,000 population, compared with 261 per 100,000 for people aged 45–61, and 1,135 per 100,000 for people over 65 (U.S. Bureau of the Census, 1997). So what are the leading causes of death among young adults in the United States? Between the ages of 25 and 44, accidents are the leading cause, followed by AIDS and cancer.

There are important gender and ethnic differences in these statistics (USDHHS, 1997). Young adult men are twice as likely to die as women of the same age; men are most likely to die in auto accidents and women from cancer. African American young adults are more than twice as likely to die as their European American counterparts, and Hispanic Americans have more health problems than any other ethnic group, largely due to poverty, which reduces access to health care (Otten et al., 1990; USDHHS, 1998).

LIFE-STYLE FACTORS

The man in the photograph illustrates something you should *not* do if you are trying to maintain good health. Life-style factors such as smoking, drinking, and eating poorly negatively affect health. We return to this theme in Chapter 12, when we examine additional aspects of health promotion, especially concerning cardiovascular disease and exercise.

Smoking

Smoking is the single biggest contributor to health problems, a fact known for decades. In the United States alone, roughly 430,000 people die each year and medical treatment of smoking-related ailments costs over $100 billion annually (Centers for Disease Control and Prevention, 1998).

The risks of smoking are many. The American Cancer Society estimates that over half of all cancers (including cancer of the lung, larynx, mouth, esophagus, bladder, kidney, pancreas, and cervix) are related to smoking. Emphysema, a disease that destroys the air sacs in the lungs, is primarily caused by smoking, and the carbon monoxide and nicotine inhaled in cigarette smoke foster the development of cardiovascular disease (Wantz & Gay, 1981). As noted in Chapter 2, nicotine in cigarettes is a potent teratogen; smoking during pregnancy can cause stillbirth, low birth weight, or perinatal death.

Nonsmokers like those in the photograph who breathe environmental smoke are also at considerably higher risk for smoking-related diseases; 3,000 nonsmokers die from lung cancer and 300,000 children suffer from lung problems annually in the United States due to environmental smoke (Centers for Disease Control and Prevention, 1998; Nachtigall & Nachtigall, 1990). For these reasons, many states and communities have passed stricter legislation banning smoking in public buildings, and smoking is banned entirely on airline flights within the United States and on many international flights.

Juan, the young man in the vignette, is typical of people who want to stop smoking. Most people who try to stop smoking begin the process in young adulthood. Although some smokers who want to quit find formal programs helpful, over 90% of those who stop do so on their own. But as Juan suspects, quitting is not easy; 70 – 80% of those who try to quit relapse at least once (Cohen et al., 1989). For most people, success is attained only after a long period of stopping and relapsing.

Regardless of how it happens, quitting smoking has enormous health benefits, despite what you may have heard. For example, women who have stopped smoking for 3 years have a risk of heart attack equivalent to women who have never smoked (Rosenberg, Palmer, & Shapiro, 1990). The risk of lung cancer returns to normal after a period of 10 –15 years. Even people who do not quit until late life (even after age 70) show marked improvements in health (LaCroix et al., 1991). In sum, the evidence is clear: If you don't smoke, don't start. If you do, you're never too old to stop.

Drinking Alcohol

If you are over 21, chances are you drink occasionally; over half of the people in the United States have consumed alcohol in the past month (National Center for Health Statistics, 1997). Total consumption of alcohol in industrialized countries has declined for the past few decades (Wattis & Seymour, 1994), partly in response to tougher laws regarding underage drinking and drinking and driving.

For the majority of people, drinking alcohol poses no serious health problems, as long as they do not drink and drive. In fact, numerous studies show that for people like those in the photograph who drink no more than two glasses of beer per day, alcohol consumption may be beneficial. For example, light drinkers (one glass of beer or wine per day) have a lower risk of stroke than either abstainers or heavy drinkers, even after controlling for hypertension, smoking, and medication (Gill et al., 1986).

One type of drinking that is particularly troublesome among young adults, especially college students, is binge drinking, *defined for men as consuming five or more drinks in a row and for women as consuming four or more drinks in a row within the past two weeks.* Binge drinking has been identified as a major national health problem (Wechsler et al., 1994; Gfroerer, Greenblatt, & Wright, 1997) and is the focus of several efforts to reduce the number of college students who binge. As discussed in the Current Controversies feature, these efforts come at a time when national attention is directed at the problem, unfortunately as the result of an epidemic of accidental deaths due to binge drinking.

CURRENT CONTROVERSIES

INFOTRAC
COLLEGE EDITION

To learn more, enter the following search term: binge drinking.

BINGE DRINKING ON COLLEGE CAMPUSES

A widely held notion about college life is that it is a time when young adults "cut loose" and enjoy all available social activities. For many students, this involves drinking alcohol. Indeed, to many students, college parties and drinking alcohol are virtually synonymous.

Unfortunately, drinking among college students often goes beyond moderate intake. Binge drinking is on the upswing in U.S. colleges. In one representative national survey of over 17,500 undergraduate students, 44% reported that they were binge drinkers (Wechsler et al., 1994). Although students between the ages of 17 and 23 are more likely to binge drink than older students, there is no relation between year in school and binge-drinking rates.

Binge drinking is extremely dangerous. But comatose youth and death are only two of its numerous ill effects. As you can see in the graph, the rate of drinking-related

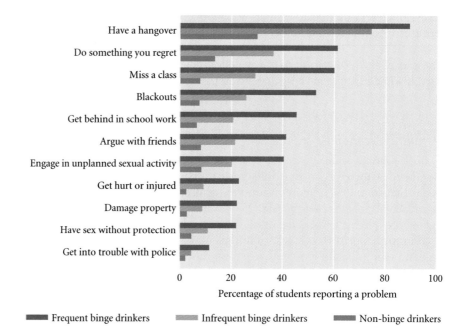

Percentage of students reporting a problem

■ Frequent binge drinkers   ■ Infrequent binge drinkers   ■ Non-binge drinkers

problems, including missing class and engaging in unwanted sexual behavior, is much higher in binge drinkers, especially those who binge three or more times within a 2-week period ("frequent binge drinkers"). These problems have important long-lasting consequences, from poorer grades and unplanned pregnancies to contracting sexually transmitted diseases.

Equally important, but often overlooked are secondhand drinking effects, those negative drinking-related consequences experienced by others. For example, a nondrinker may be insulted, assaulted, or have to care for an ill binge drinker, which may in turn have important academic consequences for these students.

Many colleges and universities are developing programs to respond to this growing problem. Because students who participate in extracurricular activities, work at part-time jobs, or study more than 4 hours a day are less likely to binge drink (Wechsler et al., 1995), programs to get students involved in such activities may have some success. And because binge-drinking college students are more likely to have been binge drinkers in high school, strategies that focus on younger students are also important.

The key is to change the culture of college from one strongly supportive of binge drinking to one in which binge drinking is something popular people do not do. Whether programs now in place actually lower the rate of binge drinking remains to be seen. However, one thing is for certain—binge drinking must be dealt with. •

? THINK ABOUT IT
: **What would be some successful strategies to reduce binge drinking?**

For roughly 1 in 10 drinkers and their family members, alcohol consumption does considerable harm. Around 18 million North Americans are heavy drinkers; roughly 11 million of them are alcoholics. The incidence of heavy drinking remains fairly constant at around 10% through the adult life span (Post, 1987; Wattis & Seymour, 1994). However, identification of individuals as alcoholics tends to peak by middle age (Scott & Mitchell, 1988).

Alcoholism is viewed by most experts as a form of addiction, *which means that alcoholics demonstrate physical dependence on alcohol and experience withdrawal symptoms when they do not drink.* Dependence occurs when a drug, such as alcohol, becomes so incorporated into the functioning of the body's cells that the drug becomes necessary for normal functioning (Berkow, 1987). Alcoholism results when the person becomes so dependent on the drug that it interferes with his or her personal relationships, health, occupation, and social functioning.

Because the identification of alcoholism peaks by middle age, most people seeking treatment are young adults (Scott & Mitchell, 1988). The most widely known treatment option is Alcoholics Anonymous, founded in Akron, Ohio, in 1935 by two recovering alcoholics. Other treatment approaches include inpatient and outpatient programs at treatment centers, behavior modification, and group therapy (Zimberg, 1985). Typically, the goal of these programs is abstinence. Unfortunately, we know very little about the long-term success of the various programs.

Nutrition

How many times did your parents tell you to eat your vegetables? Or perhaps they said, "You are what you eat." Most people have disagreements with parents about food while growing up, but as adults like those in the photograph they later realize that those lima beans and other despised foods really are healthful.

Experts agree that nutrition directly affects one's mental, emotional, and physical functioning (McDonald & Sapone, 1993; Steen, 1987). Nutritional requirements and eating habits change across the life span. *This change is due mainly to*

differences in metabolism, *or how much energy the body needs.* Body metabolism and the digestive process slow down with age (McDonald & Sapone, 1993).

Requirements for some specific nutrients also change, but others remain constant (McDonald & Sapone, 1993; Steen, 1987). Younger adults require more carbohydrates than older adults, because they need more energy to run their higher metabolism. However, the needs for protein, vitamins, and minerals show little change during adulthood.

Did you ever worry as you were eating a triple-dip cone of premium ice cream that you really should be eating fat-free frozen yogurt instead? If so, you are one of the people who have taken to heart (literally) the link between diet and cardiovascular disease. The American Heart Association (1990) makes clear that foods high in saturated fat (such as our beloved ice cream) should be replaced with foods low in fat (such as fat-free frozen yogurt).

The main goal of these recommendations is to lower your level of cholesterol. High cholesterol is one risk factor for cardiovascular disease. *There is an important difference between two different types of cholesterol:* low-density lipoproteins (LDLs) *and* high-density lipoproteins (HDLs). Lipoproteins are fatty chemicals attached to proteins carried in the blood. LDLs cause fatty deposits to accumulate in arteries, impeding blood flow, whereas HDLs help keep arteries clear and break down LDLs. It is not so much the overall cholesterol number, but the ratio of LDLs to HDLs that matters most in cholesterol screening. High levels of LDLs are a risk factor in cardiovascular disease, and high levels of HDLs are considered a protective factor. Reducing LDL levels is effective in diminishing the risk of cardiovascular disease in adults of all ages (Löwik et al., 1991). HDL levels can be raised through exercise and a high-fiber diet. Weight control is also an important component.

Some researchers believe that diet plays a role in roughly one-third of all cancers. For example, high levels of fat in the diet increase the risk of breast, pancreatic, prostate, ovarian, and colon cancers. Eating a high-fiber, low-fat, low-sodium diet lowers the risk of cancer (Petrus & Vetrosky, 1990). Evidence supporting the diet-cancer link comes from a cross-cultural study of Japanese and Japanese American women. Japanese women were more likely to get stomach and esophageal cancers, associated with high levels of dietary nitrates, whereas Japanese American women were more likely to get breast cancer, associated with higher levels of dietary fat. These findings clearly demonstrate that diet and health have important connections.

SOCIAL, GENDER, AND ETHNIC ISSUES IN HEALTH

Which of the two individuals shown in the photographs on page 333 is likely to be healthier? Why? We have indicated that although most young adults are very healthy, there are important individual differences. Let's see what they are.

Social Factors

The two most important social influences on health are socioeconomic status and education. In the United States, income level is a major determinant of how healthy a person is likely to be, mainly because income is linked to having access to adequate health care. Regardless of ethnic group, people who live in poverty are more likely to be in poor health than people who do not.

? **THINK ABOUT IT**
What are some key psychological and social factors related to eating a low-fat diet?

Related to income is education. College graduates are less likely to develop chronic diseases such as hypertension and cardiovascular disease than people who do not go to college. In fact, people who have less education are not only more likely to contract a chronic disease, they are more likely to die from it. In a large, representative sample of 5,652 working adults between 18 and 64, educational level was associated with good health even when the effects of age, gender, ethnicity, and smoking were accounted for (Pincus, Callahan, & Burkhauser, 1987).

Does education *cause* good health? Not exactly. Higher educational level is associated with higher income, as well as more awareness of dietary and lifestyle influences on health. Thus, more highly educated people are in a better position to afford health care and to know about the kinds of foods and lifestyle that affect health.

Gender

Are men or women healthier? This question is difficult to answer, primarily because women were not routinely included in many major studies of health until the 1990s (Kolata, 1990b). For example, most of the longitudinal data about risk factors for cardiovascular disease comes from studies of men. We do know that women live longer than men, for reasons discussed in Chapter 13. Women also use health services more often, because they tend to pay more attention to changes in their bodies (Nathanson & Lorenz, 1982).

Ethnic Group Differences

In the United States, the poorest health conditions exist in inner-city slums. For example, African American men in New York's Harlem have a lower life expectancy than men in some Third World countries (McCord & Freeman, 1990). Like the people in the photograph, many inner-city residents rely on overcrowded clinics. Why is this the case?

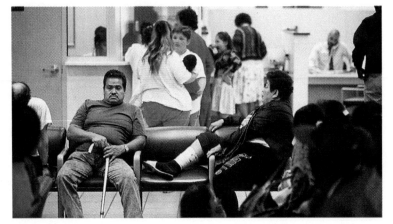

The main reasons are poverty and racism. As noted earlier, poverty is associated with poor nutrition and inadequate health care throughout life (Otten et al., 1990). Even when they have access to health care, African Americans are less likely than European Americans to receive coronary bypass surgery, kidney transplants, and other treatments (Council on Ethical and Judicial Affairs, 1990).

But there is another factor: stress related to racism. Unlike men in most Third World countries, African American men are the targets of racism. Research demonstrates that people who suppress their anger are at increased risk of hypertension. People who are subjected to racism may not feel they can show their anger and therefore keep it bottled up. Coupled with a physiological predisposition of many African Americans to retain sodium in their kidneys while under stress, which can result in kidney disease, this combined reaction can be fatal (Goleman, 1990).

To the extent that other ethnic groups suffer from poverty and cannot obtain adequate health care, they also have poorer health. Thus, until poverty and access to health care and racism are addressed, inner-city minority groups will be at a serious disadvantage in terms of health.

FORCES IN ACTION   HEALTHY ADULTHOOD

In this section we have seen that physical development in young adulthood involves a complex set of interacting influences. On the biological front, genetics plays a key role. We may have inherited superb athletic ability (or not), and we may have predispositions for or protection against such things as cardiovascular disease or alcoholism. Psychologically, we may have learned about the influence of life-style on physical health. As we see next, we have cognitive abilities to think about what we eat and do to our bodies. The sociocultural influence of poverty is powerful, reducing the quality of health care to which poor people have access. The importance of life-cycle forces is also critical, though they are less apparent. As we see in Chapters 12 and 13, health and life-style decisions we make as young adults have profound effects later in life; for example, failure to maintain sufficient calcium intake can cause osteoporosis in later life, and eating a high-fat diet can cause cardiovascular disease years later.

It is important that we recognize how the basic forces of development interact. For example, intervention programs will not work if they fail to consider the interrelated effects of individual differences in genetics, cognitive developmental level, and access to care. Moreover, money spent on prevention at one point in the life span can yield great savings on treatment of disease later. One way to understand how the biopsychosocial model works is to think of a major health problem, identify an existing program aimed at addressing it, and analyze it to see whether all of the forces on development are being addressed. The results of your analysis may surprise you. ●

TEST YOURSELF

1. In young adulthood, most people reach their maximum _____ .

2. Sensory acuity peaks during the _____ .

3. During the early 20s, death from disease is _____ .

4. Young adult _____ are the most likely to die.

5. _____ is the biggest contributor to health problems.

6. Alcoholism is viewed by most experts as a form of _____ .

7. The two most important social influences on health are education and
   _____ .

8. In the United States, the poorest health conditions exist for African Americans living in _____ .

9. How could you design a health care system that provides strong incentives
   for healthy life-styles during young adulthood?

COGNITIVE DEVELOPMENT

Learning Objectives

- **What is intelligence in adulthood?**

- **What types of abilities have been identified? How do they change?**

- **What is postformal thought? How does it differ from formal operations?**

Cognitive Development

How Should We View Intelligence
  in Adulthood?

What Happens to Intelligence
  in Adulthood?

Going Beyond Formal Operations:
  Thinking in Adulthood

S USAN, *a 33-year-old woman recently laid off from her job as a secretary, slides into her seat on her first day of college classes. She is clearly nervous. "I'm worried that I won't be able to compete with these younger students, that I may not be smart enough," she sighs. "Guess we'll find out soon enough, though, huh?"*

Many returning adult students like Susan worry that they may not be "smart enough" to keep up with 18- or 19-year-olds. Are these fears realistic? In this section, we examine the evidence concerning intellectual performance in adulthood. We will see how the answer to this question depends on the types of intellectual skills being used.

HOW SHOULD WE VIEW INTELLIGENCE IN ADULTS?

We interrupt this section for a brief exercise. Take a sheet of paper and write down all the abilities that you think reflect intelligence in adults like the woman in the photograph. When you have finished, read further to see how your perceptions match research results.

It's a safe bet that you listed more than one ability as reflecting intelligence in adults. You are not alone. *Most theories of intelligence are* multidimensional—*that is, they identify several types of intellectual abilities.* As discussed in Chapter 6 (pages 212–213), there is disagreement about the number and types of abilities, but virtually everyone agrees that no single generic type of intelligence is responsible for all the different kinds of mental activities we perform.

Sternberg (1985) emphasized multidimensionality in his triarchic theory of intelligence (discussed on page 213). Baltes and colleagues introduced

three other concepts as vital to intellectual development in adults: multi-directionality, interindividual variability, and plasticity (Baltes, 1993; Baltes, Dittmann-Kohli, & Dixon, 1984; Dittmann-Kohli & Baltes, 1990; Schaie, 1995). Let's look at each of these concepts in turn.

Over time, the various abilities underlying adults' intelligence show multi-directionality: *Some aspects of intelligence improve whereas other aspects decline during adulthood. Closely related to this is* interindividual variability: *These patterns of change also vary from one person to another.* In the next two sections, we will see evidence for both multidirectionality and interindividual variability when we examine developmental trends for specific sets of intellectual abilities.

Finally, people's abilities reflect plasticity: *They are not fixed, but can be modified under the right conditions at just about any point in adulthood.* Because most research on plasticity has focused on older adults, we return to this topic in Chapter 13.

Baltes and colleagues emphasize that intelligence has many components and these components show varying development in different abilities and different people. Their view is closely related to Riley's (1979) theory that development occurs because of the integration of biological, psychological, sociocultural, and life-cycle forces (see pages 25–26). Let's turn our attention to the evidence that supports this theoretical view.

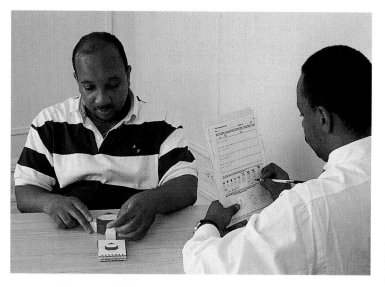

WHAT HAPPENS TO INTELLIGENCE IN ADULTHOOD?

Given that intelligence in adults is a complex, multifaceted construct, how might we study adult intelligence? Two common ways involve formal testing and assessing practical problem-solving skills. Formal testing such as the session shown in the photograph typically assesses primary or secondary abilities and involves tests from which we can compute overall IQ scores like those discussed in Chapter 6. Tests involving practical problems assess people's ability to use intelligence in everyday situations. So what happens in each type of ability?

Primary Abilities

From our previous discussion, we know that intelligence consists of many different skills and abilities. *Since the 1930s, researchers have agreed that intellectual abilities can be studied as groups of related skills (such as memory or spatial ability) organized into hypothetical constructs called* primary mental abilities. Roughly 25 primary mental abilities have been identified (Horn, 1982). Because it is difficult to study all of the primary mental abilities, researchers have focused on five representative ones:

- *Number*—the basic skills underlying our mathematical reasoning
- *Word fluency*—how easily we produce verbal descriptions of things

- *Verbal meaning*—our vocabulary ability
- *Inductive reasoning*—our ability to extrapolate from particular facts to general concepts
- *Spatial orientation*—our ability to reason in the three-dimensional world in which we live

Do these primary abilities show change in adulthood? One answer is examined in the Spotlight on Research feature.

THE SEATTLE LONGITUDINAL STUDY

SPOTLIGHT ON RESEARCH

Who was the investigator and what was the aim of the study? In the 1950s, little information was available concerning longitudinal changes in adults' intellectual abilities. What little there was showed a developmental pattern quite different from the picture of across-the-board decline obtained in cross-sectional studies. To provide a more thorough picture of intellectual change, K. Warner Schaie began the Seattle Longitudinal Study in 1956.

How did the investigator measure the topic of interest? Schaie used standardized tests of primary mental abilities to assess a wide range of abilities such as logical reasoning and spatial ability.

Who were the participants in the study? Over the course of the study, more than 5,000 individuals were tested at six testing cycles (1956, 1963, 1970, 1977, 1984, and 1991). The participants were representative of the upper 75% of the socioeconomic spectrum and were recruited through a very large health maintenance organization in Seattle.

What was the design of the study? To provide a thorough view of intellectual change over time, Schaie invented a new type of research design—the sequential design (see page 36). Participants were tested every 7 years. Like most longitudinal studies, Schaie's sequential study encountered selectivity effects—that is, people who return over the years for retesting tend to do better initially than those who fail to return. However, an advantage of Schaie's sequential design is that by bringing in new groups of participants, he was able to estimate the importance of selection effects, a major improvement over previous research.

Were there ethical concerns with the study? The most serious issue in any study in which participants are followed over time is confidentiality. Because people's names must be retained for future contact, the researchers were very careful about keeping personal information secure.

What were the results? Among the many important findings from the study are differential changes in abilities over time and cohort effects. As you can see in the graph, scores on tests of primary mental abilities improve gradually until the late 30s or early 40s. Small declines begin in the 50s, increase as people age into their 60s, and become increasingly large in the 70s (Schaie, 1994).

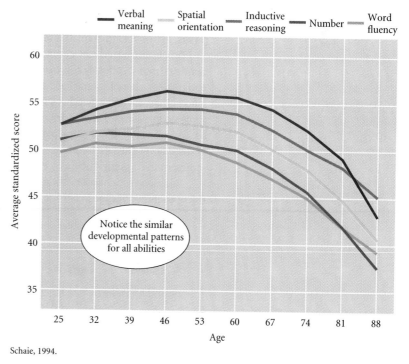

Schaie, 1994.

Cohort differences were also found. The graph shows that on some skills, such as inductive reasoning ability, but not others, more recently born younger and middle-

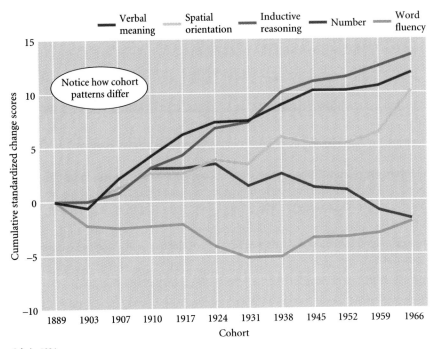

Schaie, 1994.

aged cohorts performed better than cohorts born earlier. An example of the latter is that older cohorts outperformed younger ones on number skills (Schaie, 1994). These cohort effects probably reflect differences in educational experiences; younger groups' education emphasized figuring things out on one's own, whereas older groups' education emphasized rote learning. Additionally, older groups did not have calculators or computers, so they had to do mathematical problems by hand.

Schaie uncovered many individual differences as well; some people showed developmental patterns closely approximating the overall trends, but others showed unusual patterns. For example, some individuals showed steady declines in most abilities beginning in their 40s and 50s, others showed declines in some abilities but not others, but some people showed little change in most abilities over a 14-year period. Such individual variation in developmental patterns means that average trends, like those depicted in the graphs, must be interpreted cautiously; they reflect group averages and do not represent the patterns shown by each person in the group.

Additionally, Schaie (1994) identified several variables that appear to reduce the risk of cognitive decline in old age:

- Absence of cardiovascular and other chronic diseases

- Living in favorable environmental conditions (such as good housing)

- Remaining cognitively active through reading and lifelong learning

- Having a flexible personality style in middle age

- Being married to a person with high cognitive status

- Being satisfied with one's life achievements in middle age

What did the investigator conclude? Three points are clear. First, intellectual development during adulthood is marked by a gradual leveling off of gains, followed by a period of relative stability, and then a time of gradual decline in most abilities. Second, these trends vary from one cohort to another. Third, individual patterns of change vary considerably from person to person.

Overall, Schaie's findings indicate that intellectual development in adulthood is influenced by a wide variety of health, environmental, personality, and relationship factors. By attending to these influences throughout adulthood, we can at least stack the deck in favor of maintaining good intellectual functioning in late life. ●

Secondary Mental Abilities

Rather than focusing separately on specific primary abilities, some researchers argue that it makes more sense to study a half dozen or so broader skills, termed secondary mental abilities, *that subsume and organize the primary abilities.* The figure below shows how performance data, primary mental abilities, and secondary mental abilities relate to each other. Notice that as you move up to secondary mental abilities you are moving away from the data. Two secondary mental abilities have received a great deal of attention in adult developmental research: fluid intelligence and crystallized intelligence (Horn, 1982).

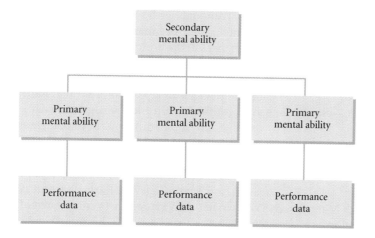

Fluid intelligence *consists of the abilities that make you a flexible and adaptive thinker, that allow you to make inferences, and that enable you to understand the relations among concepts.* It includes the abilities you need to understand and respond to any situation, but especially new ones: inductive reasoning, integration, abstract thinking, and the like (Horn, 1982). An example of a question that taps fluid abilities is the following:

What letter comes next in the series *d f i m r x e* ?*

*The next letter is *m*. The rule is to increase the difference between adjacent letters in the series by one each time *and* use a continuous circle of the alphabet for counting. Thus, *f* is two letters from *d*, *i* is three letters from *f*, and *e* is seven letters from *x*.

Other typical ways of testing fluid intelligence include mazes, puzzles, and relations among shapes. Most of the time, these tests are timed, and higher scores are associated with faster solutions.

Crystallized intelligence *is the knowledge you have acquired through life experience and education in a particular culture.* Crystallized intelligence includes your breadth of knowledge, comprehension of communication, judgment, and sophistication with information (Horn, 1982). Your ability to remember historical facts, definitions of words, knowledge of literature, and sports trivia information are some examples. Many popular television game shows (such as *Jeopardy* and *Wheel of Fortune*) are based on contestants' accumulated crystallized intelligence.

Even though crystallized intelligence involves cultural knowledge, it is based partly on the quality of a person's underlying fluid intelligence (Horn, 1982; Horn & Hofer, 1992). For example, the breadth of your vocabulary depends to some extent on how quickly you are able to make connections between new words you read and information already known, which is a component of fluid intelligence.

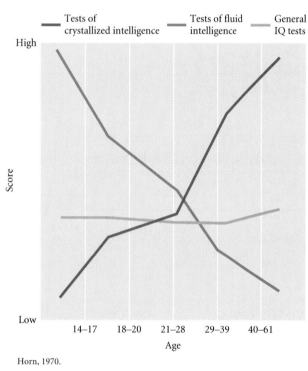

Horn, 1970.

Developmentally, fluid and crystallized intelligence follow two very different paths, as you can see in the graph. Notice that fluid intelligence declines throughout adulthood, whereas crystallized intelligence improves. Although we do not yet fully understand why fluid intelligence declines, it may be related to underlying changes in the brain from the accumulated effects of disease, injury, and aging or from lack of practice (Horn & Hofer, 1992). In contrast, the increase in crystallized intelligence (at least until late life) indicates that people continue adding knowledge every day.

What do these different developmental trends imply? First, they indicate that although learning continues through adulthood, it becomes more difficult the older one gets. Consider what happens when Michael, age 17, and Marge, age 50, learn a second language. Although Marge's verbal skills in her native language (a component of crystallized intelligence) are probably better than Michael's, his probable superiority in the fluid abilities necessary to learn another language will usually make it easier for him to do so.

Second, these developmental trends point out once again that intellectual development varies a great deal from one set of skills to another. Beyond the differences in overall trends, differences in individuals' fluid and crystallized intelligence also vary. Whereas individual differences in fluid intelligence remain relatively uniform over time, individual differences in crystallized intelligence increase with age, largely because maintaining crystallized intelligence depends on being in situations that require its use (Horn, 1982; Horn & Hofer, 1992). For example, few adults get much practice in solving complex letter series tasks like the one on page 339. But because people can improve their vocabulary skills by reading, and because people differ considerably in how much they read, differences are likely to emerge. In short, crystallized intelligence provides a rich knowledge base to draw upon when material is somewhat

THINK ABOUT IT
What are the primary biological and sociocultural forces affecting fluid and crystallized intelligence?

familiar, whereas fluid intelligence provides the power to deal with learning in novel situations.

GOING BEYOND FORMAL OPERATIONS: THINKING IN ADULTHOOD

Suppose you are given the following problem to solve (Labouvie-Vief et al., 1985):

> John is known to be a heavy drinker, especially when he goes to parties. Mary, John's wife, warns him that if he gets drunk one more time, she will leave him and take the children. Tonight John is out late at an office party. John comes home drunk. Does Mary leave John? How certain are you of your answer? (p. 13)

When this and similar problems are presented to adolescents and adults, interesting differences emerge. Adolescents tend to point out that Mary gave John a clear ultimatum, which he ignored, and conclude that Mary will leave him. Adolescents thus tend to approach the problem in formal-operational terms, as discussed in Chapter 6. They reason deductively from the information given to come to a single solution grounded in their own experience. Formal-operational thinkers are certain that such solutions are right because they are based on their own experience and are logically driven.

But many adults like the couple in the photo are reluctant to draw any conclusions based on the limited information in the problem, especially when the problem can be interpreted in different ways (Sinnott, 1998). They point out that there is much about John and Mary we don't know: How long have they been married? Did Mary know about John's drinking before she married him? Can Mary support herself financially if she leaves? How old are the children? From this perspective, the problem is much more ambiguous. Adults may eventually decide that Mary leaves (or stays), but they do so only after considering aspects of the situation that go well beyond the information given in the problem. Such thinking shows a recognition that other people's experiences may be quite different from one's own.

Clearly, the thought process these adults use is different from formal operations (Cavanaugh et al., 1985; Labouvie-Vief et al., 1985; Sinnott, 1998). Unlike formal-operational thinking, this approach involves considering situational constraints and circumstances, realizing that reality sometimes constrains solutions, and knowing that feelings matter.

Perry (1970) first uncovered adults' different thinking and traced its development. He found that 18-year-old first-year students tend to rely heavily on the expertise of authority figures to determine which ways of thinking are right and which are wrong. For these students, thinking is tightly tied to logic, as

Piaget had argued, and the only legitimate answers are ones that are logically derived.

Perceptions change over the next few years. Students go through a phase in which they are much less sure of which answers are right—or whether there are any right answers at all. However, by the time they are ready to graduate, students are fairly adept at examining different sides of an issue and have developed commitments to particular viewpoints. They recognize that they are the source of their own authority, that they must take a position on an issue, and that other people may hold different positions from theirs but be equally committed. During the college years, then, individuals become able to understand many perspectives on an issue, choose one, and still allow others the right to hold differing views. Perry concluded that this kind of thinking is very different from formal operations and represents another level of cognitive development.

Based on several additional longitudinal studies and numerous cross-sectional investigations, researchers have concluded that this type of thinking represents a qualitative change beyond formal operations (King & Kitchener, 1994; Kitchener & King, 1989; Kramer et al., 1991; Sinnott, 1998). Postformal thought *is characterized by a recognition that truth (the correct answer) may vary from situation to situation, that solutions must be realistic in order to be reasonable, that ambiguity and contradiction are the rule rather than the exception, and that emotion and subjective factors usually play a role in thinking.* In general, the research evidence indicates that postformal thinking has its origins in young adulthood (Sinnott, 1998).

Several research-based descriptions of the development of thinking in adulthood have been offered. *One of the best is the description of the development of* reflective judgment, *a way in which adults reason through dilemmas involving current affairs, religion, science, personal relationships, and the like.* Based on more than a decade of longitudinal and cross-sectional research, Kitchener and King (1989; King & Kitchener, 1994) refined descriptions and identified a systematic progression of reflective judgment in young adulthood.

In Kitchener and King's theory, young adults like those in the photograph begin with the assumption that knowledge is absolute and there is a correct answer to every question. For example, Martina's pressuring of her instructor for the "right" theory to explain human development reflects this stage. She is also likely to hold firm positions on controversial issues, but does so without acknowledging other people's ability to reach a different, but nevertheless equally logical, position.

About halfway through the developmental progression, Martina thinks very differently. Now she is likely to say that nothing can be known for certain, and to change her conclusions based on the situation and the evidence. At this point, she argues that knowledge is quite subjective. She is also less persuasive with her positions on controversial issues: "Each person is entitled to his or her own view; I cannot force my opinions on anyone else."

As Martina continues her development of the stages through reflective judgment, she begins to realize that people construct knowledge using evidence and argument after very careful analysis of the problem or situation. She once again holds very firm convictions, but reaches them only after careful consideration of several points of view. Martina also realizes that she has to continually reevaluate her beliefs in view of new evidence.

As you can see from these descriptions, adults move from a firm belief in an absolute correspondence between personal perception and reality to the recognition that the search for truth is an ongoing, never-ending process. Other researchers describe similar trends. For example, Kramer (1989; Kramer et al., 1991) reported a developmental process involving three stages: absolutist, relativistic, and dialectical. Absolutist thinking involves firmly believing that there is only one correct solution to a problem and that personal experience is the basis for all truth. People aged 18–22 like those in the photo tend to think this way. Relativistic thinking involves realizing that there are many sides to an issue and that correct actions or solutions depend on circumstances. Adults in their late 20s through early middle age use this style most. One potential danger with relativistic thinking is that it can lead to a cynical approach to life: "I'll do my thing and you do yours."

Because relativistic thinkers tend to reason things out on a case-by-case basis, they are unlikely to be committed to any one position for long. The final stage, dialectical thinking, solves this problem. Dialectical thinkers see the merits in different viewpoints, but are able to synthesize them into a workable solution to which they are strongly committed (Kramer & Kahlbaugh, 1994; Sinnott, 1994a, 1994b; Sinnott, 1998).

Although the various approaches to postformal thinking differ in some details, they all agree that adults progress from believing in one and only one right way of thinking and acting to accepting the fact that there are multiple solutions, each potentially equally acceptable (or equally flawed). This progression is important; it allows for the integration of emotion with thought in dealing with practical, everyday problems, as we will see next.

Integrating Emotion and Logic in Life Problems

One theme in descriptions of postformal thinking is the movement from thinking "I'm right because I've experienced it" to thinking "I'm not so sure who's right because your experience is different from mine." Problem situations that used to seem pretty straightforward now appear much more complicated; the "right thing to do" is much tougher to figure out.

Differences in thinking styles have major implications for dealing with life problems. For example, couples who are able to understand and synthesize each other's point of view are much more likely to resolve conflicts; couples not able to do so are more likely to feel resentful, drift apart, or even break up (Kramer, 1989; Kramer et al., 1991).

Besides an increasing understanding that there is more than one "right" answer, adult thinking is characterized by the integration of emotion with logic (Labouvie-Vief, 1985). Adults tend to make decisions and analyze problems not so much on logical grounds, but rather on pragmatic and emotional grounds. Mature thinkers realize that thinking is an inherently social enterprise that demands making compromises with other people and tolerating contradiction and ambiguity.

A good example of the difference between formal and postformal thought from this perspective can be seen in decisions regarding sexual behavior. As we saw on pages 302–303, sexually active adolescents rarely use condoms; in contrast, condom use increases in adulthood. Labouvie-Vief might argue that this is because sexuality is too emotionally charged for adolescents to deal with intellectually, whereas adults are better able to incorporate emotion into their thinking. But is this interpretation reasonable?

It appears to be. In one study, high school students, college students, and middle-aged adults were given three dilemmas to resolve (Blanchard-Fields, 1986). One dilemma had low emotional involvement, involving conflicting accounts of a war between two fictitious countries, North and South Livia, written by a partisan from each country. The other two dilemmas had high emotional involvement. In one, parents and their adolescent son disagreed about going to visit the grandparents (the son did not want to go). In the other, a man and a woman had to resolve an unintentional pregnancy (the man was antiabortion, the woman was pro-choice).

The results are shown in the graph. You should note two important findings. First, there were clear developmental trends in reasoning level, with the middle-aged adults best able to integrate emotion into thinking. Second, the high school and college students were equivalent on the fictitious war dilemma, but the young adult students more readily integrated emotion and thought on the visit and pregnancy dilemmas. These results support the kinds of developmental shifts suggested by Labouvie-Vief. Thus, practicing safe sex may require the integration of thought and emotion, which is done better by young adults.

The mounting evidence of continued cognitive development in adulthood paints a more positive view of adulthood than that of Piaget, who focused only on logical thinking. The integration of emotion with logic that happens in adulthood provides the basis for decision making in the very personal and sometimes difficult arenas of love and work, which we examine in detail in Chapters 10 and 11, respectively. In the present context, it sets the stage for envisioning one's future life, a topic we take up later in this chapter.

? THINK ABOUT IT
Why are formal operations inadequate for integrating emotion and thought?

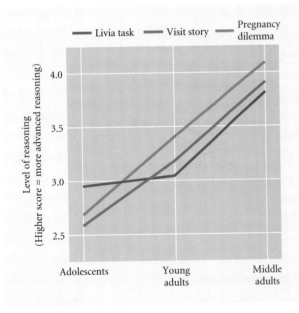

Blanchard-Fields, 1986.

TEST YOURSELF

1. Most modern theories of intelligence are _____ because they identify many domains of intellectual abilities.

2. Number, verbal fluency, and spatial orientation are some of the _____ mental abilities.

3. _____ reflects knowledge that you have acquired through life experience and education in a particular culture.

4. Kitchener and King describe a kind of postformal thinking called _____ .

5. Adult thinking is marked by the integration of _____ and logic.

6. Many young adult college students seemingly get more confused about what they want to major in and less certain about what they know as they progress through college. From a cognitive-developmental approach, why does this happen?

Answers: (1) multidimensional, (2) primary, (3) Crystallized intelligence, (4) reflective judgment, (5) emotion

MORAL REASONING

Learning Objectives

- **How does reasoning about moral issues change through the life span?**
- **How does concern for justice and caring for other people contribute to moral reasoning?**
- **Is moral reasoning similar in all cultures?**

Moral Reasoning

Kohlberg's Theory

Alternatives to Justice

Cultural Differences in Moral Reasoning

N Europe, a woman was near death from cancer. One drug might save her, a form of radium that a druggist in the same town had recently discovered. The druggist was charging $2,000, ten times what the drug cost him to make. The sick woman's husband, Heinz, went to everyone he knew to borrow the money, but he could only get together about half of what it cost. He told the druggist that his wife was dying and asked him to sell it cheaper or let him pay later. But the druggist said, "No." The husband got desperate and broke into the man's store to steal the drug for his wife. Should the husband have done that? Why? (Kohlberg, 1969, p. 379)

This is a difficult moral dilemma. In fact, some of the world's great stories, such as *Les Misérables*, are based on elaborate moral dilemmas: Should Jean Valjean, shown in the photo, have stolen bread for his sister's starving child? One can think of many reasons why Heinz should or should not steal the drug or why Valjean should or should not have stolen the bread. Lawrence Kohlberg created several such stories to study how people reason about moral dilemmas. These stories present deliberately complicated decision making; choosing the "correct"

thing to do is hard, because every choice involves undesirable consequences. Such dilemmas abound in real life; think of the choices people who cannot afford to pay their medical bills must make every day.

Kohlberg analyzed children's, adolescents', and adults' responses to a large number of difficult dilemmas. He was not interested in an individual's decision but in the reasoning that the individual used to justify the decision. *Moral reasoning involves the rules of ethical conduct that people bring to bear on a problem to justify their solution to the problem.* Of course, reasoning about hypothetical situations, such as whether or not Heinz should steal the drug, may not correspond to what a person would actually do if faced with a real situation. Indeed, the connection between moral reasoning and moral behavior is far from perfect.

KOHLBERG'S THEORY

Kohlberg (1984, 1987) believed very strongly that moral reasoning develops over the life span in a sequence of discrete stages. Using Piaget's theory as a starting point, Kohlberg describes a universal, invariable sequence of stages that show qualitative changes in reasoning.

How would you determine this woman's stage of moral reasoning? You could do so by focusing on "why she chose the answer she chose" instead of classifying "what she says the person in the story should do." Thus, Kohlberg examined the rules that people use to make moral decisions rather than the decisions themselves. At the earliest stages, moral reasoning is based on external forces, such as the promise of reward or the threat of punishment. However, at the most advanced levels, a personal, internal moral code emerges that is unaffected by others' views or society's expectations. Let's take a closer look.

Kohlberg identified three levels of moral reasoning: preconventional, conventional, and postconventional. Each level is further subdivided into two substages. *At the preconventional level, moral reasoning is based on external forces.* For most children, many adolescents, and some adults, moral reasoning is controlled almost exclusively by rewards and punishments. *Individuals in Stage 1 moral reasoning assume an obedience orientation, which means believing that authority figures know what is right and wrong.* Consequently, Stage 1 individuals do what authorities say is right to avoid being punished. At this stage, one might argue that Heinz shouldn't steal the drug because an authority figure (e.g., parent or police officer) said he shouldn't do it. Alternatively, one might argue that he should steal the drug because he would get into trouble if he let his wife die.

In Stage 2 of the preconventional level, people adopt an instrumental orientation, in which they look out for their own needs. Stage 2 individuals are nice to others because they expect the favor to be returned in the future. Someone at this stage could justify stealing the drug because Heinz's wife might do something nice for Heinz in return. Or, they might argue that Heinz shouldn't steal the drug because it will create more problems for him if his wife remains bedridden and he is burdened with caring for her.

At the conventional level, *adolescents and adults look to society's norms for moral guidance.* In other words, people's moral reasoning is largely determined by others' expectations of them. *In Stage 3, adolescents' and adults' moral reasoning is based on* interpersonal norms. The aim is to win the approval of other people by behaving as "good boys" and "good girls" would. Stage 3 individuals might argue that Heinz shouldn't steal the drug because he must keep his reputation as an honest man, or that no one would think negatively of him for trying to save his wife's life.

Stage 4 of the conventional level focuses on social system morality. Here, adolescents and adults believe that social roles, expectations, and laws exist to maintain order within society and to promote the good of all people. Stage 4 individuals might reason that Heinz shouldn't steal the drug, even though his wife might die, because it is illegal and no one is above the law. Alternatively, they might claim that he should steal it to live up to his marriage vow of protecting his wife, even though he will face negative consequences for his theft. Politicians like those in the photograph who emphasize "law and order" appeal to people who reason at this stage.

At the postconventional level, *moral reasoning is based on a personal moral code.* The emphasis is no longer on external forces like punishment, reward, or social roles. *In Stage 5, people base their moral reasoning on a* social contract. Adults agree that members of social groups adhere to a social contract because a common set of expectations and laws benefits all group members. However, if these expectations and laws no longer promote the welfare of individuals, they become invalid. Consequently, Stage 5 individuals might reason that Heinz should steal the drug because social rules about property rights no longer benefit individuals' welfare. (Indeed, the Declaration of Independence, written by Thomas Jefferson in 1776, made a similar argument about the laws of England.) They could alternatively argue that he shouldn't steal it because it would create social anarchy.

Finally, in Stage 6 of the postconventional level, universal ethical principles *dominate moral reasoning.* Abstract principles such as justice, compassion, and equality form the basis of a personal code that may sometimes conflict with society's expectations and laws. Stage 6 individuals might argue that Heinz should steal the drug because saving a life takes precedence over everything, including the law. Or, they might claim that Heinz's wife has a right to die and that he should not force his views on her by stealing and administering the drug.

Putting the stages together, the entire sequence of moral development looks like this:

Preconventional Level: Punishment and Reward
Stage 1: Obedience to authority
Stage 2: Nice behavior in exchange for future favors

Conventional Level: Social Norms
Stage 3: Live up to others' expectations
Stage 4: Follow rules to maintain social order

Postconventional Level: Moral Codes
Stage 5: Adhere to a social contract when it is valid
Stage 6: Personal moral system based on abstract principles

Evidence for the Theory

Kohlberg proposed that his stages form an invariant sequence. That is, individuals move through the six stages in the order listed and only in that order. In reality, however, most individuals do not progress to the final stages; adults' reasoning usually remains at the conventional level.

In this theory, then, the level of moral reasoning should be strongly associated with a person's age and level of cognitive development. Older and more advanced thinkers should, on average, be more advanced in their moral development, and indeed they usually are (Stewart & Pascual-Leone, 1992).

Support for Kohlberg's sequence of stages also comes from longitudinal studies in which participants' reasoning levels are traced over several years. According to the theory, individuals should progress through each stage in sequence, never skipping stages. In fact, virtually no individuals skip any of the stages in Kohlberg's sequence (Colby et al., 1983). A related prediction is that, over time, individuals should either become more advanced in their level of moral reasoning or remain at the same level. They should *not* regress to a lower level of moral reasoning. Longitudinal studies find that only a small percentage of individuals regress to a lower stage. As predicted, the vast majority remain at the same level or progress to a more advanced level, even through age 80 (Pratt et al., 1996; Walker & Taylor, 1991).

The developmental sequence described by Kohlberg usually takes many years to unfold. But on occasion, we may see the process occur much more dramatically, such as when individuals undergo a major transformation in their moral motivation. One noteworthy example of such a transformation was depicted in Steven Spielberg's Oscar-winning movie *Schindler's List,* as described in the Real People feature.

? THINK ABOUT IT
How might cognitive-developmental level and stage of moral reasoning be raised?

REAL PEOPLE

SCHINDLER'S LIST

The outbreak of war typically provides numerous opportunities for shrewd business people to profit from the increased demand for manufactured goods. The outbreak of World War II in Europe in 1939 was no exception. Oskar Schindler, shown in the photograph, was one such entrepreneur who made a great deal of money working for the Germans after they conquered Poland. His flamboyant demeanor brought him to the attention of the local German commanders, for whom Schindler did favors. Motivated at first strictly by the potential for personal profit, he opened a factory in which he employed Jews as slave labor with few, if any, qualms.

Schindler's company was quite successful. But as the war continued, official German policy toward Jews changed to one of extermination. Jewish citizens in Poland and other countries were rounded up and shipped to concentration camps, or summarily executed. Schindler was deeply disturbed by this, and his attitudes began to change. His employees suggested that he give the Germans a list of workers essential to the factory's continued operation. The list provided protection, as the plant's products were used in the war effort. This, of course, also kept the profits rolling in. But Schindler's motivation gradually underwent a profound transformation as well. No longer driven by profit, he went to great lengths to preserve life, at no small danger to himself. He created cover stories to support his claims that certain employees were essential, and he went to Auschwitz to rescue employees who were sent there by mistake.

Oskar Schindler's list saved many lives. Profits were made (and helped provide the perfect cover), but he employed Jews in his factory primarily to save them from the gas chamber. Schindler may have begun the war at Kohlberg's preconventional level—where he was motivated solely by personal profit—but he ultimately moved to the post-conventional level—where he was motivated by the higher principle of saving lives. And it is at the postconventional level that heroes are made. •

A final and particularly controversial aspect of the theory is Kohlberg's claim that the sequence of stages is universal—that all people in all cultures should progress through the six-stage sequence. Here, the evidence is mixed. When children and adolescents from various cultures think about moral dilemmas, their responses typically fall in Stages 2 or 3, just like answers from North American children and adolescents. In contrast, moral reasoning by adults in other cultures is not always described well by Kohlberg's stages (Snarey, 1985). For example, Taiwanese adults reason according to moral principles but do not emphasize justice as Kohlberg does in Stages 5 and 6 (Lei, 1994). This suggests that Kohlberg's theory may be most applicable to moral reasoning in cultures with philosophical and religious traditions like those of Western nations. However, we'll see in

the next section that even within Western cultures, justice is not the sole basis for moral thinking. We return to the issue of cultural differences in moral reasoning a bit later.

ALTERNATIVES TO JUSTICE

Carol Gilligan (1982, 1985) has sharply criticized Kohlberg's theory. She claims that care and responsibility in interpersonal relationships also play a critical role in moral development, especially for women:

> The moral imperative that emerges repeatedly in interviews with women is an injunction to care, a responsibility to discern and alleviate the "real and recognizable trouble" of this world. For men, the moral imperative appears rather as an injunction to respect the rights of others and thus to protect from interference the rights to life and self-fulfillment. (1982, p. 100)

In place of Kohlberg's preconventional, conventional, and postconventional levels, Gilligan identifies a developmental progression in which individuals gain greater understanding of caring and responsibility. In the first stage, children are preoccupied with their own needs. In the second stage, people care for others, particularly those who are less able to care for themselves, like infants and the aged. The third stage unites caring for others and for oneself in an emphasis on caring in all human relationships.

Notice that Gilligan shares Kohlberg's view that moral reasoning becomes qualitatively more sophisticated as individuals develop, progressing through a number of distinct stages. However, Gilligan emphasizes care instead of justice—that is, helping people in need and treating people fairly.

What does research tell us about the importance of justice and care in moral reasoning? Gilligan's claim that females and males differ in the bases of their moral reasoning might be wrong. The common outcome is that girls and boys as well as men and women reason about moral issues similarly (Walker, 1995; Wilson, 1995). However, females are somewhat more likely than males to recognize issues of an ethic of care in their responses (Garmon et al., 1996). Additionally, the exact characteristics of the moral problem at hand determine whether justice, care, or both will be the basis for moral reasoning (Wark & Krebs, 1997).

CULTURAL DIFFERENCES IN MORAL REASONING

We have seen that U.S. children, adolescents, and adults include both justice and care in their moral reasoning, weighing them differently depending on the situation. Overall, North American children and adults use justice-based reasoning more often than care-based reasoning, but this is not true of all cultures.

Indeed, many critics have noted that Kohlberg's emphasis on the rights of individuals and on justice reflects both Western culture and Judeo-Christian theology. But not all cultures and religions share this emphasis, so moral reasoning might be based on different values in other cultures. The Hindu religion, for example, emphasizes duties and responsibilities to others as the starting point for society (Simpson, 1974). Accordingly, the children and adults in the photograph, who have been reared with traditional Hindu beliefs, will more likely emphasize care in their moral reasoning than will individuals brought up in the Judeo-Christian tradition.

Miller and Bersoff (1992) tested this hypothesis by constructing moral dilemmas that included two solutions: one based on justice and one based on care. For example, in one dilemma,

Ben planned to travel to San Francisco in order to attend the wedding of his best friend. He needed to catch the very next train if he was to be on time for the ceremony, as he had to deliver the wedding rings. However, Ben's wallet was stolen in the train station. He lost all of his money as well as his ticket to San Francisco.

Ben approached several officials as well as passengers . . . and asked them to loan him money to buy a new ticket. But, because he was a stranger, no one was willing to lend him the money he needed.

While Ben . . . was trying to decide what to do next, a well-dressed man sitting next to him walked away for a minute. . . . Ben noticed that the man had left his coat unattended. Sticking out of the man's coat pocket was a train ticket to San

Francisco. . . . He also saw that the man had more than enough money in his coat pocket to buy another train ticket. (p. 545)

One course of action emphasizes individual rights and justice:

Ben should not take the ticket from the man's coat pocket—even though it means not getting to San Francisco in time to deliver the wedding rings to his best friend. (p. 545)

Another course of action places a priority on caring for others:

Ben should go to San Francisco to deliver the wedding rings to his best friend—even if it means taking the train ticket from the other man's coat pocket. (p. 545)

Children and adults living in India and in the United States read dilemmas like these and indicated the alternative they preferred. The results revealed substantial cultural differences. The graph shows that a slight majority of U.S. children and adults selected the justice-based alternative. In contrast, the overwhelming majority of Indian children and adults selected the care-based alternative.

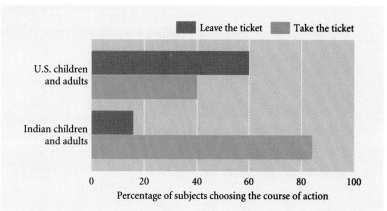

Clearly, our moral reasoning reflects the paradigms of the culture in which we are reared. Consistent with the predictions of Kohlberg's theory, judgments by U.S. children and adults mirror their culture's priority on individual rights and justice. In contrast, judgments by Indian children and adults mirror their culture's priority on caring for other people. Research in Taiwan (Lei, 1994) documented that children, adolescents, and young adults also respond in a developmental sequence based more on care.

The net result of this and other work is a broader view of moral reasoning. As Kohlberg claimed, moral reasoning becomes progressively more sophisticated as children develop, shifting from external rewards and punishments to social norms and personal moral codes. However, contrary to Kohlberg's original claims, those codes are not always based on justice and rights. Instead, caring for others sometimes serves the basis for moral reasoning, depending on the exact nature of the moral dilemma and the cultural context in which a person develops.

TEST YOURSELF

1. For children at the preconventional level, moral reasoning is strongly influenced by the presence of _____ .

2. Gilligan criticized Kohlberg's theory on the grounds that it is based exclusively on using _____ as the basis for moral reasoning.

3. In India, moral judgments are often based on _____ , whereas in the United States, they tend to be based on justice.

4. What parallels can you draw between cognitive development and Kohlberg's theory of moral reasoning?

Answers: (1) reward or punishment, (2) justice, (3) care for others

WHO DO YOU WANT TO BE? PERSONALITY IN YOUNG ADULTHOOD

Who Do You Want to Be? Personality in Young Adulthood

Creating Scenarios and Life Stories

Possible Selves

Self-Concept

Personal Control Beliefs

Learning Objectives

- **What is the life-span construct? How do adults create scenarios and life stories?**

- **What are possible selves? Do they show differences during adulthood?**

- **How does self-concept come to take adult form? What is its developmental course through adulthood?**

- **What are personal control beliefs?**

*F*ELICIA *is a 19-year-old sophomore at a community college. She expects her study of early childhood education to be difficult but rewarding. She figures that along the way she will meet a great guy, whom she will marry soon after graduation. They will have two children before she turns 30. Felicia sees herself getting a good job teaching preschool children and some day owning her own day care center.*

In Chapter 8, we saw how children and adolescents deal with the question "What do you want to be when you grow up?" As a young adult, Felicia has arrived at the "grown up" part, and is experimenting with some idealistic answers to the question. Are Felicia's answers typical of most young adults?

In this section, we examine how the search for identity in adolescence meets the cognitive, social, and personal reality of adulthood. In particular, we will see how people create life scenarios and life stories, possible selves, self-concept, and personal control beliefs. Let's begin by considering how Felicia, and the rest of us, construct images of our adult lives.

CREATING SCENARIOS AND LIFE STORIES

Figuring out what (and who) you want to be as an adult takes lots of thought, hard work, and time. *Based on personal experience and input from other people, young adults create a* life-span construct *that represents a unified sense of the past, present, and future.* Several factors influence the development of a life-span construct; identity, values, and society are only a few. Together, they not only shape the creation of the life-span construct, they influence the way it is played out (Whitbourne, 1987). The life-span construct represents a link between Erikson's notion of identity, which is a major focus during adolescence, and our adult view of ourselves.

The first way in which the life-span construct is manifested is through the scenario, *which consists of expectations about the future.* The scenario takes aspects of a person's identity that are particularly important now and projects them into a plan for the future. For example, you may find yourself thinking

? THINK ABOUT IT
What biopsychosocial forces most influence people's scenarios?

about the day you will graduate and be able to apply all of the knowledge and skills you have learned. In short, a scenario is a game plan for how your life will play out in the future.

Felicia, the sophomore human development student, has a fairly typical scenario. She plans on completing a degree in early childhood education, marrying after graduation, and having two children by age 30. *Tagging future events with a particular time or age by which they are to be completed creates a* social clock. This personal timetable gives people like those in the photograph a way to track progress through adulthood. They use biological markers of time (such as menopause), social aspects of time (such as getting married), and historical time (such as the turn of the century) (Hagestad & Neugarten, 1985).

Felicia will use her scenario to evaluate her progress toward her personal goals. With each new event, she will check where she is against where her scenario says she should be. If she is ahead of her plan, she may be proud of having made it. If she is lagging behind, she may chastise herself for being slow. But if she criticizes herself too much, she may change her scenario altogether. For example, if she does not go to college, she may decide to change her career goals entirely: Instead of owning her own day care center, she may aim to be a manager in a department store.

As a way to understand how people create scenarios, and to appreciate the similarities and differences among them, take the time to complete the exercises in the See for Yourself feature.

WHEN I WAS 35, IT WAS A VERY GOOD YEAR

How do people think through the future and create scenarios? Here's an exercise for you. First, over the next few days write your own scenario. Imagine what your future will be like (or what you thought it would be like). Will you get married? When? To what kind of person? Will you have children? A career? How far will you advance? What will you be known for? Will you coach your child's sports team? Run for the school board?

When you've finished your scenario, talk to your friends and ask them the same kinds of questions. Are there similarities and differences between their responses and yours? Ask them where they got their ideas about the future. Bring the results of your explorations into class for discussion and comparison. Have you and your classmates identified common themes that people see in their future? See for yourself. •

As people begin to achieve some of the goals in their scenarios, they create the second aspect of the life-span construct, the life story, *which is a personal narrative that organizes past events into a coherent sequence.* Our life story becomes our autobiography as we move through adulthood.

According to research, what we remember about the events that make up our life story changes over time (Neisser & Winograd, 1988). These distortions occur in part because subsequent events change the meaning of earlier events, and in part because we want to present ourselves in a positive and favorable light. Such distortions may enable us to believe that we accomplished something on time (when we were actually late) and to feel better about our current, changed plans than about achievements that did not materialize.

As shown in the figure, scenarios and life stories provide the bases for the continuing process of identity formation during adulthood (Whitbourne, 1986). Whitbourne believes that, using assimilation and accommodation, we create our own identities in much the same way that Piaget said we create our knowledge. As the figure shows, there is continuous feedback between identity and experience; this explains why we may evaluate ourselves positively at

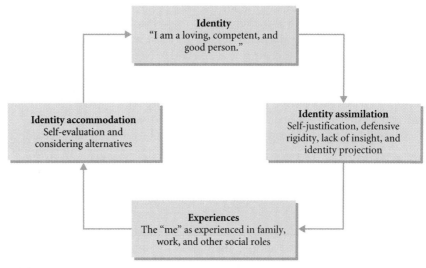

Whitbourne, 1986.

one point in time, yet appear defensive and self-protective at another. This assimilation-accommodation process results in a developmental progression in which people show increasingly mature identity with age (Whitbourne & VanManen, 1996). Chapter 12 discusses how this process results in changes in middle age, and Chapter 14 examines how it relates to integrity in late life.

POSSIBLE SELVES

Creating a scenario presupposes that adults have the ability to project themselves into the future and to speculate about what they might be like (Markus & Nurius, 1986). How do we do this? *Projecting ourselves into the future involves creating* possible selves *that represent what we could become, what we would like to become, and what we are afraid of becoming.*

What you could or would like to become reflects personal goals or values; you may envision yourself as a good parent, as rich and famous with thousands of adoring fans, or as in good physical condition. What you are afraid of becoming is usually reflected in specific fears—of being alone, of having little meaning in your life, or of being a certifiable couch potato. Possible selves are powerful motivators. In fact, much adult behavior can be interpreted as efforts to achieve or avoid these possible selves and to protect the current view of the self (Markus & Nurius, 1986).

Whether age differences appear in possible selves is a complicated issue, depending on how the investigators examine the data. In one approach, researchers asked people to describe their hoped-for and feared possible selves (Cross & Markus, 1991). The subjects were mostly middle-class men and women, ranging in age from 18 to 86. Their responses were grouped into categories (such as family, personal, material). Age differences depended on the type of possible self examined. In terms of hoped-for selves, 18- to 24-year-olds list family concerns most often (such as marrying the right person). In contrast, 25- to 39-year-olds list family concerns last; their main concerns are personal issues such as being a more caring or loving person. By age 40–59, family issues reemerge as primary, but the focus is on different issues (such as being the kind of parent who can "let go" of their children). For 60- to 86-year-olds, personal issues are again the most important, involving such things as remaining active and healthy.

All age groups list physical issues as part of their most feared selves. For the younger groups, the fears most often involve being overweight and, for women, getting wrinkles and becoming unattractive. Middle-aged and older subjects often fear contracting Alzheimer's disease or being unable to care for themselves.

Overall, young adults are far more likely to have multiple possible selves and to believe that they can actually become the hoped-for self and successfully avoid the feared self. By old age, both the number of possible selves and strength of belief has decreased. Older adults are more likely to believe that neither the hoped-for nor the feared self is under their personal control.

Other researchers have examined possible selves in a different way by asking adults to describe their present, past, future, and ideal self (Ryff, 1991). Instead of examining categories of possible selves, this approach focuses on people's perceptions of change over time. The data indicate that young and middle-aged adults see themselves as improving with age (like Linus in the cartoon) and expecting to continue getting better in the future. In contrast, older

? **THINK ABOUT IT**
Why are there age differences in the ordering of concerns about possible selves?

PEANUTS reprinted by permission of United Features Syndicate, Inc.

adults see themselves as having remained stable over time, but they foresee decline in their future. These findings may indicate that the older group has internalized negative stereotypes about aging, especially in view of the fact that they are currently healthy and well educated.

Taken together, the research on possible selves enables us to examine the creation of scenarios and life stories systematically. It also helps us understand how adults organize their self-perceptions into a coherent whole.

SELF-CONCEPT

In addition to looking into the future, adulthood brings with it a reexamination of the self-perceptions first formed in adolescence (see Chapter 8). The changes that occur in self-concept during young adulthood can best be understood as the outcome of a developmental process integrating self-concept with thinking (Kegan, 1982). Does the self-concept created through this interactive process undergo further change with age? The answer is, apparently not. In one of the few longitudinal studies of self-concept, researchers first surveyed a group of men about their self-concept when they were first-year college students, and then followed them for 14 years (Mortimer, Finch, & Kumka, 1982). The results raise important issues concerning the stability of self-concept and the importance of self-perceptions and life events.

Over the 14-year period, the men showed little change in self-concept as a group. The basic components of self-concept remained stable, despite some fluctuations in specific variables. For example, well-being and competence declined during college but increased after graduation.

The data also reveal intriguing relations between perceptions of competence and life events. The course of a man's career, his satisfaction with his marriage, his relationship with his parents, and his overall life satisfaction can be predicted by his perceived level of competence. For example, an

employee like the man in the photo—whose competence scores remained above the group average—will report fewer job problems and higher marital and life satisfaction than men whose competence scores are below the group average.

Even more interesting is that a man's degree of confidence as a college senior is related to his later evaluation of life events—this may even be a self-fulfilling prophecy. The researchers suggest that these men may actively seek and create experiences that fit their perceptions of competence. This explanation is supported by longitudinal research on gifted women, whose high self-confidence in early adulthood is mirrored as high life satisfaction during their 60s (Sears & Barbee, 1978). These findings also provide additional support for Whitbourne's (1986) model (see page 354), as they demonstrate that identity colors the way people interpret and experience events, which in turn shapes the future directions of their identity.

PERSONAL CONTROL BELIEFS

At several points in this section, we have encountered the notion of personal control. Personal control beliefs *reflect the degree to which you believe that your performance in a situation depends on something you do.* For example, suppose you don't get a job you think you should have gotten. Was it your fault? Or was it because the company was too shortsighted to recognize your true talent? Which of these options you select provides insight into a general tendency. Do you generally believe that outcomes depend on the things you do? Or are they due to factors outside of yourself, such as luck or the power of others?

Personal control is a very important concept that can be applied broadly (Baltes & Baltes, 1986). For example, personal control beliefs are not only important in personality development, but also (as we will see in Chapter 13) in memory performance in late life. Research indicates that people experience four types of personal control (Tiffany & Tiffany, 1996): control from within oneself; control over oneself; control over the environment; and control from the environment.

Despite its importance, we do not have a clear picture of the developmental course of personal control beliefs. Evidence from both cross-sectional studies (Gatz & Siegler, 1981) and longitudinal studies (Lachman, 1985) is contradictory. Some data indicate that younger adults are less likely to hold internal control beliefs (i.e., believe that they are in control of outcomes) than are older adults. Other research finds the opposite.

The contradiction may derive from the complex nature of personal control beliefs (Lachman, 1985). These beliefs vary depending on which domain, such as intelligence or health, is being assessed. Indeed, other research shows that perceived control over one's development declines with age, whereas perceived control over marital happiness increases (Brandtstädter, 1989). Additionally, younger adults are less likely than older adults to acknowledge the effect of outside influences on their behavior.

Brandstädter and Greve (1994) propose that control beliefs in later life involve three interdependent processes. First, people engage in activities that prevent or alleviate losses in domains that are important for self-esteem and identity. Second, people readjust their goals as a way to lessen negative self-evaluations in key domains. Third, people guard against the effects of self-discrepant evidence through denial or by looking for another explanation. This approach, though, has been criticized on the grounds that the losses people experience may not actually threaten the self, and that changes in goals could simply represent normative developmental processes (Carstensen & Freund, 1994).

Clearly, the sense of personal control is a complex, multidimensional aspect of personality that has broad implications for other aspects of adult development. Thus, it is possible that no overall age trends can be identified. Instead, changes in personal control beliefs may well depend on our experiences in different domains, may differ widely from one domain to another, and may involve complex, interdependent processes.

TEST YOURSELF

1. A _____ is a unified sense of a person's past, present, and future.

2. A personal narrative that organizes past events into a coherent sequence is a _____ .

3. Representations of what we could become, what we would like to be, and what we are afraid of becoming are our _____ .

4. The organized, coherent, integrated pattern of self-perceptions that includes the notions of self-esteem and self-image is called the _____ .

5. _____ reflect the degree to which a person's performance in a situation is believed to be under his or her control.

6. How might people's scenarios, life stories, and other aspects of personality vary as a function of cognitive-developmental level and self-definition as an adult?

Answers: (1) life-span construct, (2) life story, (3) possible selves, (4) self-concept, (5) Personal control beliefs

PUTTING IT ALL TOGETHER

In this chapter, we have seen how people make the transition from adolescence to adulthood. For many people like Marcus, the transition is fuzzy, having more to do with arbitrary legal issues than anything else. In some cultures, though, there are clear, formalized rites of passage that make it much easier to pinpoint the beginning of adulthood. Young adults are fine physical specimens, reaching their peak in most areas of functioning. It is a time when people like Juan think about abandoning unhealthy habits acquired earlier in life, in favor of healthier life-styles. People like Susan decide to return to college to further their education. Indeed, young adulthood is a time when intellectual growth continues in some areas but decline begins in others. Although people have been making moral decisions since early childhood, it becomes harder for young adults to know what is right when faced with the dilemmas of real-world pressures exemplified by Heinz's dilemma. Young adults also tend to dream about their future like Felicia does, mapping out their lives in detail.

All in all, young adulthood is an exciting time of life. In many respects, life will never be this good, at least physically, ever again. New avenues are opened, and adult responsibilities are undertaken. The most important of these responsibilities are the topics for the next two chapters: love and work.

SUMMARY

When Does Adulthood Begin?

Role Transitions Marking Adulthood

• The most widely used criteria for deciding whether a person has reached adulthood are role transitions, which involve assuming new responsibilities and duties.

• Some societies use rituals, called rites of passage, to mark this transition clearly. These rituals tend to focus mainly on men. However, such rituals are largely absent in Western culture.

Going to College

• Over half of all college students are over 25. These students tend to be more motivated and have many other positive characteristics. College also serves as a catalyst for cognitive development.

Psychological View

• Adolescents and adults differ in their abilities to acquire knowledge and to apply knowledge and skills. A second major difference is a drop in the rate of participation in reckless behavior.

So When Do People Become Adults?

• In cultures without clearly defined rites of passage, people become adults when they fully feel like adults.

Physical Development and Health

Growth, Strength, and Physical Functioning

• Young adulthood is the time when certain physical abilities peak: strength, muscle development, coordination, dexterity, and sensory acuity. Most of these abilities begin to decline in middle age.

Health Status

• Young adults are also at the peak of health. Death from disease is relatively rare, especially during the 20s. Accidents are the leading cause of death. However, homicide and violence are major factors in some groups, and AIDS is an important cause of death. Poor ethnic minorities have less access to good health care, and poverty is also a major barrier to good health.

Life-Style Factors

• Smoking is the single biggest contributor to health problems. It is related to half of all cancers and is a primary cause of respiratory and cardiovascular disease. Although it is difficult, quitting smoking has many health benefits.

• For most people, drinking alcohol poses few health risks. Several treatment approaches are available for alcoholics.

- Nutritional needs change somewhat during adulthood, mostly due to changes in metabolism. Some nutrient needs, such as carbohydrates, change. The ratio of LDLs to HDLs in serum cholesterol, which can be controlled through diet in most people, is an important risk factor in cardiovascular disease.

Social, Gender, and Ethnic Issues in Health

- The two most important social factors in health are socioeconomic status and education. The poorest health conditions exist for African Americans living in poor, inner-city slums. Other ethnic groups who have limited access to health care also suffer.

- Whether women or men are healthier is difficult to answer, because women have been excluded from much health research.

- Higher education is associated with better health, due to better access to health care, and more knowledge about proper diet and life-style.

Cognitive Development

How Should We View Intelligence in Adults?

- Most modern theories of intelligence are multidimensional. For instance, Baltes' research shows that development varies among individuals and across different categories of abilities.

What Happens to Intelligence in Adulthood?

- Intellectual abilities can be studied as groups of related skills called *primary mental abilities*. These abilities develop differently and change in succeeding cohorts. More recent cohorts perform better on some skills, such as inductive reasoning, but older cohorts perform better on number skills.

- Fluid intelligence consists of abilities that make people flexible and adaptive thinkers. Fluid abilities generally decline during adulthood. Crystallized intelligence reflects knowledge that people acquire through life experience and education in a particular culture. Crystallized abilities improve until late life.

Going Beyond Formal Operations: Thinking in Adulthood

- Postformal thought is characterized by a recognition that truth may vary from one situation to another, that solutions must be realistic, that ambiguity and contradiction are the rule, and that emotion and sub-jectivity play a role in thinking. One example of postformal thought is reflective judgment.

Moral Reasoning

Kohlberg's Theory

- Kohlberg developed a theory of moral reasoning based on how people think about moral dilemmas. The theory proposes three levels (preconventional, conventional, postconventional), each containing two stages, resulting in a universal sequence. Stage 1 people obey authority; Stage 2 people behave nicely in exchange for future favors; Stage 3 people live up to others' expectations; Stage 4 people follow rules to maintain social order; Stage 5 people adhere to a social contract when it is valid; Stage 6 people develop personal morals based on abstract principles. There is strong evidence that the stages occur in sequence, but there is less evidence for the universality of the theory.

Alternatives to Justice

- Gilligan criticizes Kohlberg's theory on the grounds that it gives too much importance to justice in moral reasoning. Gilligan claims that women base their reasoning more on an ethic of care and responsibility in interpersonal relationships. Research evidence suggests that males and females use both the justice approach and the care/responsibility approach, depending on the circumstances.

Cultural Differences in Moral Reasoning

- Research evidence suggests that people in Western cultures tend to use a justice-based approach to moral reasoning more often than individuals in other cultures.

Who Do You Want to Be? Personality in Young Adulthood

Creating Scenarios and Life Stories

- Young adults create a life-span construct that represents a unified sense of the past, present, and future. This is manifested in two ways: through a scenario that maps the future based on a social clock, and in the life story, which creates an autobiography.

Possible Selves

• People create possible selves by projecting themselves into the future and thinking about what they would like to become, what they could become, and what they are afraid of becoming.

• Age differences in these projections depend on the dimension examined. In hoped-for selves, 18- to 24-year-olds and 40- to 59-year-olds report family issues as most important, whereas 25- to 39-year-olds and older adults consider personal issues to be most important. However, all groups include physical aspects as part of their most feared selves.

Self-Concept

• Self-concept in adulthood is believed to develop in stages that integrate Piagetian and postformal thinking with emotional development. Self-concept appears to be relatively stable during adulthood.

Personal Control Beliefs

• Personal control is an important concept with broad applicability. However, the developmental trends are complex, because personal control beliefs vary considerably from one domain to another.

KEY TERMS

role transitions (323)
rites of passage (323)
returning adult students (324)
intimacy versus isolation (325)
binge drinking (329)
addiction (331)
metabolism (332)
low-density lipoproteins (LDLs) (332)
high-density lipoproteins (HDLs) (332)
multidimensional (335)
multidirectionality (336)

interindividual variability (336)
plasticity (336)
primary mental abilities (336)
secondary mental abilities (339)
fluid intelligence (339)
crystallized intelligence (340)
postformal thought (342)
reflective judgment (342)
moral reasoning (346)
preconventional level (346)
obedience orientation (346)
instrumental orientation (346)
conventional level (347)

interpersonal norms (347)
social system morality (347)
postconventional level (347)
social contract (347)
universal ethical principles (347)
life-span construct (352)
scenario (352)
social clock (353)
life story (353)
possible selves (354)
personal control beliefs (356)

IF YOU'D LIKE TO LEARN MORE

Readings

KEGAN, R. (1982). *The evolving self: Problem and process in human development.* Cambridge, MA: Harvard University Press. This is a very intriguing, sometimes poetic, thought-provoking integration of cognitive and personality development.

SCHAIE, K. W. (1995). *Intellectual development in adulthood: The Seattle longitudinal study.* New York: Cambridge University Press. This is an excellent summary of the history and findings of the most extensive study of intellectual development across adulthood.

SINNOTT, J. D. (1998). *The development of logic in adulthood: Postformal thought and its applications.* New York: Plenum. This book provides both a history of research on postformal thinking and Sinnott's own ideas.

WHITBOURNE, S. K. (1986). *The me I know: A study of adult identity.* New York: Springer-Verlag. This is the definitive study on the search for identity. It is based on extensive interviews and shows how adults integrate personal, family, and work issues.

For additional readings, explore Infotrac College Edition, your online library. Go to http://www.infotrac-college.com/wadsworth.

Web Sites

The Centers for Disease Control and Prevention provides a well-organized collection of resources about tobacco. Included in the site are resources for people who want to quit smoking. The information can be obtained at

http://www.cdc.gov/tobacco/

The National Institute on Alcohol Abuse and Alcoholism provides a wide variety of information for consumers and researchers. The list of frequently asked questions on the home page is especially helpful. The site is at

http://www.niaaa.nih.gov/

The American Heart Association Web site offers a wealth of tips and research summaries about heart disease and ways to prevent it. Complete the interactive risk assessment to see how well you're doing. The home page is at

http://www.amhrt.org

Web site addresses are subject to change. The Wadsworth Study Center Web site listed below can be accessed for updated links.

The Wadsworth Psychology Study Center Web Site

See http://psychology.wadsworth.com/ for practice quiz questions, internet links, updates, critical thinking exercises, discussion forums and more! The Wadsworth Psychology Study Center provides a wealth of information fully organized and integrated by chapter.

CHAPTER 10

RELATIONSHIPS IN ADULTHOOD

Relationships
Friendships
Love Relationships
The Mating Game Around the World
The Dark Side of Relationships: Violence
Influences on Relationships in Adulthood

Life-Styles
Singlehood
Cohabitation
Gay and Lesbian Couples
Maggie O'Carroll's Story
Marriage

The Family Life Cycle
Family Life-Cycle Stages
Deciding Whether to Have Children
The Cost of Raising a Child
The Parental Role

Divorce and Remarriage
Divorce
"Covenant Marriage," A Way to Keep Couples Together?
The Effects of Divorce on Adult Children
Remarriage

Putting It All Together

Summary

If You'd Like to Learn More

Imagine yourself years from now. Your children are grown and have children and grandchildren of their own. In honor of your 80th birthday, they have all come together, along with your friends, to celebrate. Their present to you is an assemblage of hundreds of photographs and dozens of home videos. As you look at them, you realize how lucky you've been to have so many wonderful people in your life. Your relationships have made your adult life fun and worthwhile. As you watch the videos and look at the pictures, you wonder what it must be like to go through life totally alone. You think of all the wonderful experiences you would have missed in early and middle adulthood—never knowing what friendship is all about, never being in love, never dreaming about children and becoming a parent. That is what we'll explore in this chapter—the ways in which we share our lives with others. First, we consider what makes good friendships and love relationships. Because these relationships form the basis of our life-styles, we examine these next. In the third section, we consider what it is like to be a parent. Finally, we see what happens when marriages end. Throughout this chapter, the emphasis is on aspects of relationships that nearly everyone experiences during young adulthood and middle age. In Chapter 12, we examine aspects of relationships specific to middle-aged adults; in Chapter 14, we will do the same for relationships in later life.

RELATIONSHIPS

Relationships

Friendships

Love Relationships

The Dark Side of Relationships: Violence

Learning Objectives

- **What types of friendships do adults have? How do adult friendships develop?**

- **What is love? How does it begin? How does it develop through adulthood?**

- **What is the nature of violence in some relationships?**

*J*AMAL *and Deb, both 25, have been madly in love since they met at a party about a month ago. They spend as much time together as possible and pledge that they will stay together forever. Deb finds herself daydreaming about Jamal at work and can't wait to go over to his apartment. She wants to move in, but her co-workers tell her to slow down.*

You know what Jamal and Deb are going through. Each of us wants to be wanted by someone else. What would your life be like if you had no one to share it with? There would be no one to go shopping or cruising with, no one to talk to on the phone, no one to cuddle close to while watching the sunset at a mountain lake. Although there are times when being alone is desirable, for the most part we are social creatures. We need people. Without friends and lovers, life would be pretty lonely.

In the next sections, we explore both life-enhancing and life-diminishing relationships. We consider friendships, what happens when love enters the picture, and how people find mates. Unfortunately, some relationships turn violent; we'll also examine the factors underlying aggressive behaviors between partners.

FRIENDSHIPS

What is an adult friend? Someone who is there when you need to share? Someone not afraid to tell you the truth? Someone to have fun with? Friends, of course, are all of these and more.

Friends are very different from family, and represent a point of contrast (de Vries, 1996). Friendships are predominantly based on feelings, and grounded in reciprocity and choice. Our friends help us develop self-esteem, self-awareness, and self-respect. They also help us become socialized into new roles throughout adulthood.

The Meaning of Friendship

People seem to know what friendship is until they are asked to define it. At that point, everyone has a great deal of trouble verbalizing exactly what friendship means (Fehr, 1996). Compared with other close relationships, such as with family members or lovers, friendships are less regulated by social norms and are easier to dissolve, for example, than romantic relationships (Wright, 1985).

Friendships often involve emotional or companionship aspects, but their depth varies a great deal from person to person.

From a developmental perspective, adult friendships can be viewed as having identifiable stages (Levinger, 1980, 1983): Acquaintanceship, Buildup, Continuation, Deterioration, and Ending. This ABCDE model describes not only the stages of friendships, but also the processes by which they change. For example, whether the friendship between the two women in the photograph will develop from Acquaintanceship to Buildup depends on where the individuals fall on several dimensions, such as the basis of the attraction, what each person knows about the other, how good the communication is between the partners, the perceived importance of the friendship, and so on. Although many friendships reach the deterioration stage, whether a friendship ultimately ends depends importantly on the availability of alternative relationships. If new potential friends appear, old friendships end; if not, they may continue, although they may not be considered important by either person.

Friendships in Adulthood

People tend to have more friends and acquaintances during young adulthood than at any subsequent period (Antonucci, 1985). Friendships are important throughout adulthood, in part because a person's life satisfaction is strongly related to the quantity and quality of contacts with friends (Antonucci, 1985). The importance of maintaining contacts with friends cuts across ethnic lines as well. For example, African Americans who have many friends are happier than those with only a few friends (Ellison, 1990). Thus, regardless of one's background, friendships play a major role in determining how much we enjoy life.

Researchers have uncovered three broad themes that underlie adult friendships (de Vries, 1996):

1. The most frequently mentioned dimension represents the *affective* or emotional basis of friendship. This dimension refers to self-disclosure and expressions of intimacy, appreciation, affection, and support, all of which are based on trust, loyalty, and commitment.

2. A second theme reflects the *shared or communal* nature of friendship, in which friends participate in or support activities of mutual interest.

3. The third dimension represents *sociability and compatibility;* our friends keep us entertained and are sources of amusement, fun, and recreation.

These three dimensions are found in friendships among adults of all ages (de Vries, 1996).

Gender Differences in Friendships

Men's and women's friendships tend to differ in adulthood, continuing the patterns we first encountered in adolescence in Chapter 7 (Fehr, 1996; Rawlins, 1992; Tannen, 1990). Women tend to base their friendships on more intimate and emotional sharing and use friendship as a means to confide in others. For women, getting together with friends often involves discussing personal matters. Confiding in others, which is essential for intimacy as we will see later, is a common basis for female friendship. In contrast, men often base friendships

? THINK ABOUT IT
What experiences in childhood shape the development of friendships in adulthood?

on shared activities or interests. They are more likely to go bowling or fishing or to talk sports with their friends. For men, confiding in others is inconsistent with the need to compete; this may be one reason men are reluctant to do so (Huyck, 1982). Indeed, competition is often a part of men's friendships, as evidenced in basketball games with friends. However, the competition is usually set up so that the social interaction is the most important element, not who wins or who loses (Rawlins, 1992). Men's friendships are usually less intimate than women's, no matter how one defines intimacy (Fehr, 1996).

Why are women's friendships typically more intimate than men's? Compared to men, women have much more experience with such intimate sharing from early childhood, and they are more comfortable with vulnerability. Social pressure on men to be brave and strong may actually inhibit their ability to form close friendships (Rawlins, 1992).

Male-Female Friendships

Such differences in friendship formation create interesting opportunities and difficulties when men and women like those in the photograph want to

be friends with each other. Cross-gender friendships offer an opportunity to explore tasks or skills that are more commonly associated with the other gender. But women may not understand why men want to set up mini-competitions all the time, and men may be baffled at why women keep wanting to talk about their problems (Tannen, 1990). Men also have a tendency to sexualize cross-gender friendships more often than women, who may be offended at such overtures and would prefer to remain just friends (Rawlins, 1992). In general, other-sex friendships decline for men after marriage but increase with age for women, who typically form such friendships in the workplace. In fact, highly educated, employed women have the highest number of other-sex friendships (Swain, 1992).

LOVE RELATIONSHIPS

Love is one of those things everybody feels but nobody can define completely. (Test yourself: Can you explain fully what you mean when you look at someone special and say, "I love you"?) One way researchers have tried to understand love is to think about what components are essential. In an interesting series of studies, Sternberg (1986) found that love has three basic components: (1) *passion,* an intense physiological desire for someone; (2) *intimacy,* the feeling that one can share all one's thoughts and actions with another; and (3) *commitment,* the willingness to stay with a person through good and bad times. Based on different combinations of these three components, Sternberg identified seven forms of love:

1. *Liking.* Intimacy is present, as are closeness, understanding, support, and affection, but there is no commitment or passion. This form describes most of our friendships.

2. *Infatuation.* As with Jamal and Deb, the couple we met in the vignette, there is lots of passion here, based on strong physical attraction. This is what people call "love at first sight." But infatuation can end just as quickly as it starts, as there is no intimacy or commitment.

3. *Empty love.* Sometimes, relationships lose their passion and intimacy, and are based only on commitment. An example is couples who no longer "love" each other but do not divorce for some reason, such as children, religious beliefs, or fear of loneliness.

4. *Romantic love.* When couples connect both intimately and passionately, romance is born. But there is no commitment to complement their physical and emotional bonds.

5. *Fatuous love.* Once in a while, couples are "swept off their feet" into a rapid courtship and marriage. Their commitment is based on passion, because they have not given themselves time to let intimacy develop. Such relationships often fail as a result.

6. *Companionate love.* In this case, intimacy and commitment are both present. This type characterizes long-term friendships, as well as long-term marriages in which passion has diminished.

7. *Consummate love.* The best love relationships have commitment, intimacy, and passion all present. Such complete love is very difficult to maintain without devoting a great deal of energy to making it work.

Ideally, a true love relationship has all three components. As we will see next, the balance among these components often shifts as time passes.

Love Through Adulthood

The different combinations of love can be used to understand how relationships develop (Sternberg, 1986). Early in any relationship, passion is usually high, but intimacy and commitment tend to be low. This is infatuation: an intense, physically based relationship in which the two people have a high risk of misunderstanding and jealousy. The desire for physical intimacy is high; emotional intimacy and commitment are low.

But infatuation is short-lived. Whereas even the smallest touch is enough to drive each partner into wild, lustful ecstasy in the beginning, with time it takes more and more effort to get the same level of feeling. As passion fades, a relationship either acquires emotional intimacy or it is likely to end. Trust, honesty, openness, and acceptance must be a part of any strong relationship; when they are present, romantic love develops.

Given more time, people who work at their relationship may become committed to each other. They spend much of their time together, make decisions together, care for each other, share possessions, and develop ways to settle conflicts. Couples usually show outward signs of commitment, such as wearing a lover's ring, having children together, or simply sharing the mundane details of daily life, from making toast at breakfast to before-bed rituals.

Although the styles of love appear to differ with age, some important aspects of love relationships maintain their same relative importance over time. In one study, researchers examined communication, sexual intimacy, respect, help and play behaviors, emotional security, and loyalty. As can be

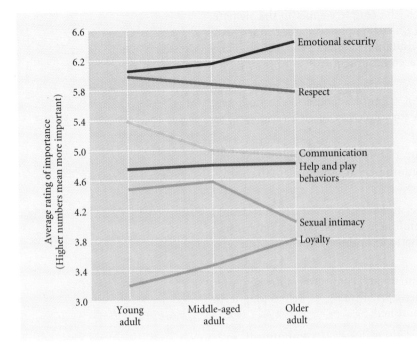

seen in the graph, the importance of some aspects of love differ as a function of age. But the relative rankings of the different components of love are the same for all age groups. Thus, although the particular weightings may vary, there are remarkable similarities across age groups in the nature of love relationships (Reedy, Birren, & Schaie, 1981). These results make intuitive sense. For example, young couples may focus more on communication, because they are still in the process of getting to know each other, but communication is important in any relationship.

Falling in Love

Everybody wants to be loved by somebody, but actually having it happen is fraught with difficulties. In his book *The Prophet,* Kahlil Gibran points out that love is two-sided: Just as it can give you great ecstasy, so can it cause you great pain. Yet, most of us are willing to take the risk.

As you may have experienced, taking the risk is fun (at times) and difficult (at other times). Making a connection can be ritualized, as when people use pickup lines in a bar, or it can happen almost by accident, as when two people literally run into each other in a crowded corridor. The question that confronts us is "How do people fall in love?"

The best explanation of the process is the theory of assortative mating, *which states that people find partners based on their similarity to each other.* Assortative mating occurs along many dimensions, including religious beliefs, physical traits, age, socioeconomic status, intelligence, and political ideology among others (Sher, 1996). Such nonrandom mating occurs most often in Western societies, which allow people to have more control over their own dating and pairing behaviors. The Far Side cartoon illustrates that common activities are one basis for identifying potential mates.

Some researchers believe that couples progress in stages. According to Murstein's (1987) classic theory, people apply three filters, representing discrete stages, when they meet someone: (a) *Stimulus:* Does the person's physical appearance, social class, and manners match your own? (b) *Values:* Does the person's values regarding sex, religion, politics, and so on match your own? (c) *Role:* Does the person's ideas about the relationship, communication style, gender roles, and so on match your own? If the answer to all three filters is "yes," then you are likely to form a couple.

"Say, honey ... didn't I meet you last night at the feeding-frenzy?"

THE FAR SIDE © 1980 Farworks, Inc.,/Dist. by UNIVERSAL PRESS SYNDICATE. Reprinted by permission. All rights reserved.

A much more important aspect in understanding how adults form couples relates to the attachments they made to adults in infancy and childhood as described in Chapter 5 (Hazan & Shaver, 1994). Researchers have shown that each of us tends to re-create in our partnership relationships the kind of attachments we had as children to key adults (e.g., Hazan & Shaver, 1994; Kobak, 1994; Main, 1996). For example, Hazan and Shaver (1987, 1990) found that adults who get close to people fairly easily (*secure style*) had the strongest relationships as children; those who are lonely had trouble forming close relationships (*avoidant style*) as children. Similarity in attachment styles is an important element for assortative mating (Collins & Read, 1990).

Once they come together, do men and women differ in how they behave? The answer is yes. Men tend to be more romantic: believing in love at first sight, feeling that there is only one true love destined for them, regarding love as magical and impossible to understand, and believing rather quickly that they are compatible with their partner. Women tend to be cautious pragmatists who believe that financial security is as important as passion in a relationship, that there are many people whom a person could learn to love, and that love does not conquer all differences (Peplau & Gordon, 1985). These differences even carry over into views about the best way to make up after a fight: Most men believe that the best way for a woman to apologize is through passionate sex, whereas most women believe the best way for a man to apologize is through a personal, heartfelt discussion (Peplau & Gordon, 1985). Finally, a man's dissatisfaction with a heterosexual relationship is a much better predictor of the relationship's demise than a woman's dissatisfaction, in part because women's approach to love includes a stronger desire to try to make the relationship work (Cowan & Cowan, 1992).

How do these behaviors compare cross-culturally? In an extraordinary study, Buss and a large team of researchers (1990) identified the effects of culture and gender on heterosexual mate preferences in 37 cultures worldwide, as described in the Spotlight on Research feature. What characteristics predict mate selection? Read on and find out.

? **THINK ABOUT IT**
What are the effects of increasing interaction among cultures on mate selection?

THE MATING GAME AROUND THE WORLD

SPOTLIGHT ON RESEARCH

Who were the investigators and what was the aim of the study? Culture and gender may play major roles in determining who is desirable as a mate in various locations around the world. To conduct the most thorough study of this topic ever, David Buss assembled a large international team of researchers.

How did the investigators measure the topic of interest? The researchers asked participants to complete questionnaires concerning important factors in choosing a mate, such as rating desired characteristics of potential mates, and preferences concerning potential mates, such as ranking characteristics of potential mates from highest to lowest.

Who were the participants in the study? A total of 9,474 adults from 33 countries, on 6 continents and 5 islands, took part in the study. Such large and diverse samples are unusual in developmental research.

What was the design of the study? Data for this cross-sectional, nonexperimental study were gathered by research teams in each country. In some cases, the survey items had to be modified to reflect the local culture. For example, many couples in Sweden, Finland, and Norway never get married, opting instead simply to live together. In Nigeria, items had to reflect the possibility of multiple wives due to the practice of polygyny. Data collection in South Africa was described as "a rather frightening experience," due to the difficulty in collecting data from both white and Zulu samples in the midst of civil unrest. Finally, in some cases data were never received, because of government interference or the lack of official approval to conduct the study. Such problems highlight the difficulty in doing cross-cultural research and the need to take local culture into account in designing research instruments.

Were there ethical concerns with the study? Because the study involved volunteers, there were no ethical concerns. However, ensuring that all participants' rights were protected was a challenge because of the number of countries and cultures involved.

What were the results? Men and women in each culture displayed unique orderings of their preferences concerning the ideal characteristics of a mate. When all of the orderings and preferences were compared, the two main dimensions shown in the figure below emerged. As you look at the figure, the closer that two or more countries are, the more similar men and women in them were in ranking desirable qualities in a mate.

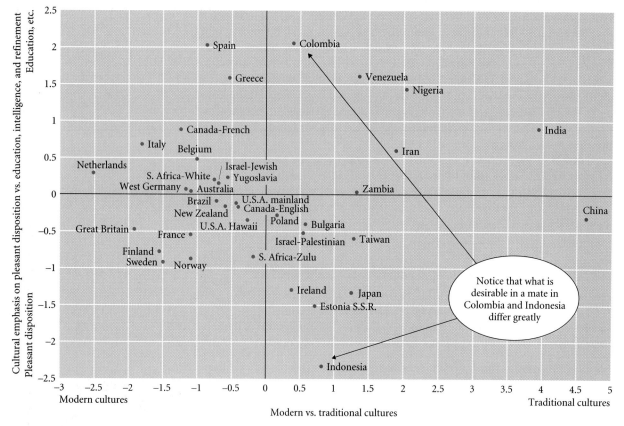

(Note: Numbers refer to the number of rating points away from average.)

In the first main dimension (represented in the figure by the horizontal axis), the characteristics of a desirable mate changed because of cultural values—that is, whether the respondents' country has more traditional values or Western-industrial values. In traditional cultures, men place a high value on a woman's chastity, desire for home and children, and being a good cook and housekeeper; women place a high value on a man's ambition and industry, being a good financial prospect, and holding favorable social status. Countries such as China, India, Iran, and Nigeria represent the traditional end of this dimension. In contrast, people in Western-industrial cultures value these qualities to a much lesser extent. Countries such as the Netherlands, Great Britain, Finland, and Sweden represent this end of the dimension.

The second main dimension (the vertical axis) reflects the relative importance of education, intelligence, and social refinement, as opposed to a pleasing disposition in choosing a mate. As you can see in the figure, people in Spain, Colombia, and Greece highly value education, intelligence, and social refinement; in contrast, people in Indonesia place a greater emphasis on having a pleasing disposition. Note that this dimension emphasizes the same traits for both men and women.

Chastity proved to be the characteristic showing the most variability across cultures, being highly desired in some cultures but mattering little in others. Interestingly, in their respective search for mates, men around the world value physical attractiveness in women, whereas women around the world look for men capable of being good providers. But men and women around the world agree that love and mutual attraction are most important, and nearly all cultures rate dependability, emotional stability, kindness, and understanding as important factors. Attraction, it seems, has some characteristics that transcend culture.

What have the investigators concluded? Overall, Buss and his colleagues concluded that mate selection is a complex process no matter where you live. However, each culture has a describable set of high-priority traits that men and women look for in the perfect mate. The study also shows that socialization within a culture plays a key role in being attractive to the opposite sex; characteristics that are highly desirable in one culture may not be so desirable in another. •

THE DARK SIDE OF RELATIONSHIPS: VIOLENCE

Fortunately, most friendships and love relationships are normal, in that the individuals involved usually treat each other with respect and kindness. Sadly, though, this is not always the case. *Sometimes relationships become violent; one person becomes aggressive toward the partner, creating an* abusive relationship. Such relationships have received increasing attention over the past few decades.

What kinds of aggressive behaviors occur in abusive relationships? What causes such abuse? Researchers are beginning to find answers to these and related questions. Based on a decade of research on abusive partners, O'Leary (1993) argues that there is a continuum of aggressive behaviors toward a spouse, which progresses as follows: verbally aggressive behaviors, physically aggressive behaviors, severe physically aggressive behaviors, and murder of the partner. Examples of each are listed in the chart below.

Verbal aggression $\longrightarrow$	*Physical aggression* $\longrightarrow$	*Severe aggression* $\longrightarrow$	*Murder*
Insults	Pushing	Beating	
Yelling	Slapping	Punching	
Name-calling	Shoving	Hitting with object	

Two points should be noted concerning this continuum. First, there may be fundamental differences in how the types of aggression play out, beyond the level of severity. Lower levels of physically aggressive behavior, such as pushing or slapping, are relatively common; 25–40% of men and women in committed relationships display such behaviors on occasion (Riggs & O'Leary, 1992; Straus, Gelles, & Steinmetz, 1980). In contrast, some men are extremely abusive from the outset of the relationship; they are thought to make up the subset of batterers who cause serious physical injury to their partners and exert coercive control over their lives (Stark, 1992).

Verbal aggression $\longrightarrow$	Physical aggression $\longrightarrow$	Severe aggression $\longrightarrow$	Murder
Insults	Pushing	Beating	
Yelling	Slapping	Punching	
Name-calling	Shoving	Hitting with object	

Causes
Need to control[a] $\longrightarrow$
Misuse of power[a] $\longrightarrow$
Jealousy[a] $\longrightarrow$
Marital discord $\longrightarrow$

Accept violence as a means of control $\longrightarrow$
Modeling of physical aggression $\longrightarrow$
Abused as a child $\longrightarrow$
Aggressive personality styles $\longrightarrow$
Alcohol abuse $\longrightarrow$

Personality disorders $\longrightarrow$
Emotional lability $\longrightarrow$
Poor self-esteem $\longrightarrow$

Contributing factors: job stressors and unemployment

Note: The need to control and the other variables on the left are associated with all forms of aggression; acceptance of violence and the variables in the middle are associated with physical aggression, severe aggression, and murder. Personality disorders and the variables on the right are associated with severe aggression and murder.

[a] More relevant for males than for females

The second point, depicted in this chart, is that the suspected underlying causes of aggressive behaviors differ as the type of aggressive behavior changes (O'Leary, 1993). As you can see, the number of suspected causes of aggressive behavior increases as the level of aggression increases. Thus, the causes become more complex as the level of aggression worsens.

Differences in the causes of abuse imply that the approaches to treating abusers should vary with the nature of the aggressive behavior (O'Leary, 1993). For example, feeling the need to control another may be amenable to psychotherapy; alcohol abuse may require additional steps.

The presence of situational factors that contribute to all levels of aggression, such as alcoholism, job stress, and unemployment, increases the likelihood that violence will occur in the relationship (O'Leary, 1993). Such factors may prove difficult to address.

Gender differences have been reported in some of the underlying causes of abusive behavior (O'Leary, 1993). Most important, the triad of the need to control, the misuse of power, and jealousy are more pertinent causes for men than for women. For example, men are more likely than women to act aggressively because they want to make sure their partner knows "who the boss is" and who makes the rules.

Two additional, and controversial, causes of aggressive or abusive behaviors have been widely discussed: attitudes held by a patriarchal society and having been abused as a child. Feminist critiques of the causes of family violence argue that male aggression toward the female partner results in part from the inequality of women in a patriarchal society (Dobash & Dobash, 1992; Yllö,

1993). From this perspective, abuse is considered to be a "normal" result of male socialization, in which domination of women is strongly reinforced in society. Indeed, the pattern of gender differences discussed above supports this view, in that men are more likely than women to act aggressively out of a need to exert control or power. Also, there is some cross-cultural evidence showing that when women and men are treated more equally, men are unlikely to abuse women (Levinson, 1988). Thus, male violence against women is thought to be one of the means for men to dominate women (Ylló, 1993).

The second controversy concerns the widely held belief that people who are abusers were probably abused themselves as children (O'Leary, 1993). But is there evidence to support this view? It certainly looks that way when people who are in therapy for abusing their partners are examined. In this case, 60% of men were victims of child abuse themselves, and 44% witnessed violence between parents (O'Leary, 1993). Because few women are in therapy as abusers, similar statistics for them are unavailable.

But if abusive individuals in the general population are examined, including those who are not in therapy, the picture changes dramatically. In the population at large, only 13% of men and 12% of women who are physically aggressive toward their partners have been exposed to violence in their families of origin, either by being abused themselves or by witnessing their parents be violent toward each other (O'Leary, 1993).

These statistics underscore the complexity of the causes of aggressive behaviors toward one's partner. At least in the population at large, the majority of aggressive partners were not victims of abuse themselves as children. Having experienced or witnessed violence as a child may be more predictive of which people end up in therapy for abusive behavior than of who is likely to become abusive in the first place.

Researchers are also beginning to document differences in how aggressive behaviors are viewed by the men and women who display them. For example, partners in a relatively new relationship who display lower levels of physical aggression (pushing, shoving), like the couple in the photograph, tend not to view them as abusive, and they claim not to have done them in self-defense (Cascardi, Vivian, & Meyer, 1991; O'Leary et al., 1989). However, women in longer-term relationships view their aggressive acts as self-defense; men still tend not to see them as either abusive or self-defense (Cascardi et al., 1991). And the reasons why men and women kill their partners also differ (Browne & Williams, 1993; Cascardi & O'Leary, 1992). Men tend to murder their partners on the basis of jealousy and the need for control. In contrast, women have usually contacted law enforcement agencies repeatedly to ask for protection prior to murdering their partners, indicating that women kill mainly in self-defense. Indeed, some authors believe, as does the U.S. criminal justice system under some circumstances, that abusive relationships may explain antisocial or criminal behavior (Walker, 1984). *In the case of* battered woman syndrome, *a woman believes that she cannot leave the abusive situation, and she may even go so far as to kill her abuser.*

Why do people stay in abusive relationships? The reasons—self-esteem, fear, and denial—are both simple and complex. Abused individuals with low self-esteem often do not believe they can do anything about their situation; indeed, many believe they deserve their abuse (Walker, 1984). Fear plays a major role, especially with abused women; all too frequently women who leave the relationship are tracked down and killed by (ex-)boyfriends and (ex-)husbands. Other victims minimize or deny the abuse—"it only happens when he's drunk" (or highly stressed) or "he really does love me." Surprisingly, some abused women who are beaten regularly do not consider their relationships unhappy (O'Leary et al., 1989).

Alarmed at the seriousness of abuse, many communities have established shelters for battered women and their children, and programs that treat abusive men. However, the legal system in many localities is still not set up to deal with domestic violence; women in some locations cannot sue their husbands for assault, and restraining orders all too often offer little real protection from additional violence. Much remains to be done to protect women and their children from the fear and the reality of continued abuse.

FORCES IN ACTION | **INFLUENCES ON RELATIONSHIPS IN ADULTHOOD**

As is clear from the ABCDE and Sternberg models, adult relationships are complex. Who chooses whom, and whether the feelings will be mutual, results from the interaction of developmental forces described in the biopsychosocial model presented in Chapter 1. Biologically, it turns out that there are two distinct stages, attraction and attachment (Liebowitz, 1983), which reflect fundamentally different neurochemical processes (Fisher, 1994). Attraction is associated with neurochemicals related to the amphetamines, which account for the exhilaration of falling in love. Attachment, which some people might call long-term commitment and tranquility, is reflected neurochemically in substances related to morphine, a powerful narcotic. (Love really does do a number on your brain!)

Psychologically, as we saw in Chapter 9, an important developmental issue is intimacy; according to Erikson, mature relationships are impossible without it. Additionally, the kinds of relationships you saw and experienced as a child (and whether they involved violence) affect how you define and act in relationships you develop as an adult. Sociocultural forces shape the characteristics you find desirable in a mate and determine whether you are likely to encounter resistance from your family when you have made your choice. Life-cycle forces matter, too; different aspects of love are more or less important, depending on your stage in life.

In short, to understand adult relationships, we must take the forces of the biopsychosocial model into account. Relying too heavily on one or two of the forces provides an incomplete description of why people are successful (or not) in finding a partner or a friend. •

TEST YOURSELF

1. Friendships based on intimacy and emotional sharing are more characteristic of _____ .

2. Competition is a major part of most friendships among _____ .

3. Love relationships in which intimacy and passion are present but commitment is not are termed _____ .

4. Chastity is an important quality that men look for in a potential female mate in _____ cultures.

5. Aggressive behavior that is based on abuse of power, jealousy, or the need to control is more likely to be displayed by _____ .

6. Why is intimacy (discussed in Chapter 9) a necessary prerequisite for adult relationships, according to Erikson? What aspects of relationships discussed here support (and refute) this view?

Answers: (1) women, (2) men, (3) romantic love, (4) traditional, (5) men

LIFE-STYLES

Learning Objectives

- **Why do some people decide not to marry, and what are these people like?**

- **What are the characteristics of cohabiting people?**

- **What are gay and lesbian relationships like?**

- **What is marriage like through the course of adulthood?**

Life-Styles

Singlehood

Cohabitation

Gay and Lesbian Couples

Marriage

KEVIN AND BETH *are on cloud nine. They got married one month ago and have recently returned from their honeymoon. Everyone who sees them can tell that they love each other a lot. They are highly compatible and have much in common, sharing most of their leisure activities. Kevin and Beth wonder what lies ahead in their marriage.*

Developing relationships is only part of the picture in understanding how adults live their lives with other people. Putting relationships like Kevin and Beth's in context is important for us to understand how relationships come into existence and how they change over time. In the following sections, we explore relationship life-styles: singlehood, cohabitation, gay and lesbian couples, and marriage.

SINGLEHOOD

When Susan graduated from college with a degree in accounting, she took a job at a consulting firm. For the first several years in her job, she spent more time traveling than she did at home. During this time, she had a series of love relationships, but none really resulted in commitment even though she had marriage as a goal. By the time she was in her mid-thirties, Susan had decided that she no longer wanted to get married. "I'm now a partner in my firm, I enjoy traveling, and I'm pretty flexible in terms of moving if something better comes along," she tells her friend Michele. "But I do miss not being with someone to share my day or to just hang around with."

During the early years of adulthood, most people like those in the photograph are single like Susan, defined as

not living with an intimate partner. Estimates are that approximately 75% of men and 60% of women between the ages of 20 and 25 are unmarried, with increasing numbers deciding to stay that way. These percentages have been rising over the past few decades, and they are fairly similar in all industrialized countries (Burns, 1992).

Susan's experience is common among women who ultimately decide not to marry (Dalton, 1992). Many women focus on career goals rather than on marriage or relationships. Others report that they simply did not meet "the right person" or prefer singlehood to the disappointment they experienced with men. However, the pressure to marry is especially strong for women; frequent questions like "Any good prospects yet?" may leave women feeling conspicuous or left out as many of their friends marry. Research indicates that single women have unresolved or unrecognized ambivalences about being single (Lewis & Moon, 1997). Such feelings result from being aware of the advantages and disadvantages of being single, and ambivalence over the reasons they are single.

Men like those in the photograph tend to remain single longer in young adulthood because they tend to marry at a later age than women (U.S. Bureau of the Census, 1998). Fewer men than women remain unmarried throughout adulthood, largely because men find partners more easily as they can select from a larger age range of unmarried women. Because men also tend to "marry down" in social status, women with higher levels of education are overrepresented among unmarried adults than are men with similar levels of education.

Ethnic differences in singlehood reflect both differences in age at marriage as well as social factors. For example, nearly twice as many African Americans are single during young adulthood compared to European Americans; however, the high unemployment rate among young adult African American males has a strong influence on marriage rates (Cherlin, 1992; U.S. Bureau of the Census, 1998). However, by the time both African and European Americans are in their 40s, marriage rates are comparable between the groups (U.S. Bureau of the Census, 1998).

In general, singles recognize the plusses and minuses in their life-styles. They enjoy the freedom and flexibility, but also feel the loneliness, hassles of dating, limited social life in a couple-oriented society, and a lesser sense of security (Chasteen, 1994). Interestingly, being single has negative health and longevity effects on men but not on women (Whitbourne, 1996). Never-married adults often develop a strong network of close friends. In the end, most singles come to terms with their life-styles, and may even become parents.

COHABITATION

? THINK ABOUT IT
Why are there such large differences in cohabitation rates among countries?

Being unmarried does not necessarily mean living alone. *People in committed, intimate, sexual relationships may decide that living together, or* cohabitation, *provides a way to share daily life.* Cohabitation is becoming an increasingly popular life-style choice in the United States as well as in Canada, Europe, Australia, and elsewhere. As you can see in the graph on page 377, cohabitation in the United States has increased eightfold over the past three decades (U.S. Bureau of the Census, 1998). Notice the change in the people who cohabit. In 1970, the majority of cohabiting couples were adults over age 45; by the late 1990s, the majority were adults between 25 and 44. This age change is related to a combination of increasing age of first marriage and the increased divorce rate since 1970.

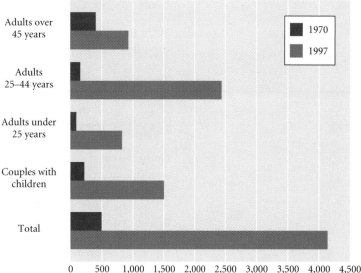

Although couples cohabit for various reasons, in the United States many young adults tend to view cohabitation more as a step toward marriage than as a permanent alternative to it (Bumpass, Sweet, & Cherlin, 1991). This is especially true of women, who are much more eager to marry their partners than are men (Blumstein & Schwartz, 1983). Cohabitation is acceptable to young adults in a strong, affectionate, monogamous relationship. Men are more open to cohabiting and do not feel the need for as strong an emotional commitment before living together. Women generally expect a deeper commitment and may feel exploited if it is absent (Macklin, 1988).

The picture is quite different in some European countries, where cohabitation is a much more common alternative to marriage. For example, cohabitation is extremely common in the Netherlands, Norway, and Sweden, where this life-style is part of the culture. Couples living together there are just as devoted to each other as are married couples, and believe that such relationships are grounded in love and commitment to each other (Kaslow, Hansson, & Lundblad, 1994). Decisions to marry in these countries are typically made to legalize the relationship after children are born, in contrast to Americans, who marry to confirm their love and commitment to each other.

Interestingly, having cohabitated does not seem to make American or Canadian marriages any better; in fact, it may do more harm than good, resulting in marriages that are less happy with a higher risk of divorce (Booth & Johnson, 1988; Hall & Zhao, 1995). Why is this the case? Part of the answer may be that cohabiting couples tend to be less conventional, less religious, and come from lower socioeconomic backgrounds, which may put them at higher risk for divorce (DeMaris & Rao, 1992). Part of the reason may also be that marrying after already having lived with someone represents much less of a change in the relationship than when a couple marries who have not been cohabiting; such couples lack the newly wedded bliss seen in couples who have not cohabited (Thomson & Colella, 1992).

More recent data indicate that the negative relation between cohabiting and marital stability may be weakening somewhat (McRae, 1997). Why would this be the case? Much of the previous data comes from a time when cohabitation was viewed as unconventional. As cohabitation becomes more common, and perhaps the majority pattern, this negative link is likely to grow progressively weaker (McCrae, 1997).

GAY AND LESBIAN COUPLES

What is it like to be in a gay or lesbian relationship? One woman shares her experience in the Real People feature.

REAL PEOPLE **MAGGIE O'CARROLL'S STORY**

I am a 35-year-old woman who believes that each person is here with a purpose to fulfill in his or her lifetime. "Add your light to the sum of light" are words I live by in my teaching career, my personal life with friends and family, and living in general. I do not believe that our creator makes mistakes, although at times I am very discouraged by the level of hatred that is evident in the world against many groups, but against homosexuals in particular.

For me, being a lesbian is the most natural state of being. I do not think of it as a mishap of genetics, a result of an unhappy or traumatic childhood, or an unnatural tendency. From the time I was a child I had a definite and strong sense of my sexual identity. However, I am aware of the homophobia that is present at all levels of my own life and in the community. That is where my sense of self and living in the world collide.

Society does not value diversity. We, as a people, do not look to people who are different and acknowledge the strength it takes to live in this society. Being gay in a homophobic, heterosexist society is a burden that manifests itself in many forms, such as through alcohol and drug abuse rates that are much higher than in the heterosexual community. The lack of acknowledgment of gay people's partners by family members, co-workers, and society at large is a stamp of nonexistence and invisibility. How can we build a life with a partner and then not share that person with society?

I consider myself a fortunate gay person in that I have a supportive family. Of the five children in my family, two of us are gay. My parents are supportive and love our partners. My siblings vary in their attitudes. One sister invited me and my partner to her wedding. Nine years later, my other sister refused to do that. Her discomfort over my sexual orientation meant that I spent a special event without my partner at my side. However, my straight brother was allowed to bring a date. It was very hurtful and hard to forgive.

In the larger community, I have been surprised by the blatant hatred I have experienced. I have demeaning comments aimed at me. The home I live in has been defaced with obscenities. But on a more positive note, I have never been more strongly certain of who I am. I am indebted to those who have supported me over the years with love and enlightenment, knowing that who I am is not a mistake. As I age, it becomes clearer to me that I am meant to share the message that our differences are to be appreciated and respected. •

Less is known about the developmental course of gay and lesbian relationships than heterosexual relationships, largely because they were almost never the focus of research. To date, two primary aspects of gay and lesbian relationships have been examined, usually in comparison to married heterosexual couples: sexual expression and interpersonal relations.

Sexual expression is one difference between heterosexual couples and gay or lesbian couples. On average, gay men have sex with each other earlier in the relationship than any other type of couple, but frequency declines rapidly as the relationship continues (Blumstein & Schwartz, 1983). In contrast, lesbian couples like the one in the photograph are more likely to have intense, intimate, monogamous relationships than are gay men, and they tend to have sex far less frequently than any other group (Blumstein & Schwartz, 1983). Lesbian couples are also more likely to stay together than are gay men.

Gay and lesbian relationships are similar to marriages in many ways; financial problems and decisions, household chores, and deciding who has the most decision-making power are issues for all couples. Moreover, gay and lesbian parents do not differ substantially from heterosexual parents in terms of style (Harris & Turner, 1986). Like all couples, decisions are made about the style of the relationship, whether the roles of nurturer and provider are clearly defined, and whether the relationship will be sexually open (Blumstein & Schwartz, 1983). Gay and lesbian couples overall are more egalitarian than heterosexual couples, with lesbian couples most egalitarian of all (Peplau, 1991). Overall, there appear to be few differences and many similarities between heterosexual, gay, and lesbian couples.

MARRIAGE

Most adults want their love relationships to result in marriage. However, U.S. residents are in less of a hurry to achieve this goal; the median age at first marriage for adults in the United States has been rising for several decades. As you can see in the graph, between 1970 and 1997, the median age for men rose

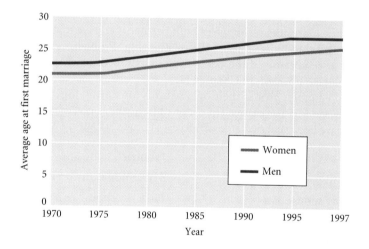

about 4 years, from roughly 23 to 27, and the age for women rose nearly 5 years, from roughly 20 to 25 (U.S. Bureau of the Census, 1997). This trend is not bad; women under age 20 at the time they are first married are three times more likely to end up divorced than women who first marry in their 20s, and six times more likely than first-time wives in their 30s (U.S. Bureau of the Census, 1997). Let's explore age and other factors that keep marriages going strong over time.

What Factors Help Marriages Succeed?

One reason that age is important has to do with the couple's level of psychosocial development. Erikson (1982) points out that intimacy, the task of young adulthood, is difficult to achieve unless one has developed a strong sense of identity, the task of adolescence (see Chapter 8). Because many adolescents are still trying to decide who they are, teenage newlyweds may initially find themselves compatible but soon grow apart as they mature. Additional complicating factors, such as pregnancy and unemployment, also stack the deck against successful teenage marriages.

A second important predictor of successful marriage is homogamy, *or similarity of values and interests.* To the extent that the partners like the couple in the photograph share similar values, goals, attitudes, socioeconomic status, and ethnic background, their relationship is more likely to succeed (Diamond, 1986). Homogamy is an important factor in a wide variety of cultures and societies, as diverse as suburbanites in Michigan and Africans in Chad (Diamond, 1986).

A third factor in predicting marital success is a feeling that the relationship is equal. *According to* exchange theory, *marriage is based on each partner contributing something to the relationship that the other would be hard-pressed to provide.* Satisfying and happy marriages result when both partners perceive that there is a fair exchange in all the dimensions of the relationship. Problems achieving such equity can arise because of the competing demands of work and family, an issue we will take up again in Chapter 11.

What do couples give as their own reasons for staying together? The lists below show the top 10 reasons (in order of frequency) given by women and men who have been married at least 15 years (Lauer & Lauer, 1985).

Men	Women
My spouse is my best friend.	My spouse is my best friend.
I like my spouse as a person.	I like my spouse as a person.
Marriage is a long-term commitment	Marriage is a long-term commitment.
Marriage is sacred.	Marriage is sacred.
We agree on aims and goals.	We agree on aims and goals.
My spouse has grown more interesting.	My spouse has grown more interesting.
I want the relationship to succeed.	I want the relationship to succeed.
An enduring marriage is important to social stability.	We laugh together.
We laugh together.	We agree on a philosophy of life.
I am proud of my spouse's achievements.	We agree on how and how often to show affection.

The lists are striking for their high degree of similarity in the reasons and their rankings. But does similarity in reasons for staying together translate inevitably into happy marriages?

Do Married Couples Stay Happy?

Few sights are happier than a couple on their wedding day. Newlyweds like Kevin and Beth, in the vignette, are at the peak of marital bliss. As you might suspect, though, couples' feelings do change over time. Like any relationship, marriage has its peaks and valleys. As shown in the graph, overall marital satisfaction tends to be highest at the beginning of the marriage, falls until the children begin leaving home, and rises again in later life (Berry & Williams, 1987).

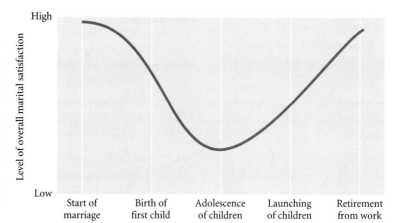

The Early Years

Marriages are most intense in their early days. When husbands and wives share many activities and are open to new experiences together, bliss results (Olson & McCubbin, 1983). When the marriage is troubled, the intensity of the early phase creates considerable unhappiness (Swenson, Eskew, & Kohlhepp, 1981).

Early in a marriage, the couple must learn to adjust to the different perceptions and expectations each person has for the other. Many wives tend to be more concerned than their husbands with keeping close ties with their friends. Women are also more likely to identify problems in the marriage and want to talk about them (Peplau & Gordon, 1985). The couple must also learn to handle confrontation. Indeed, learning effective strategies for resolving conflict is an essential component of a strong marriage, as these strategies provide ways for couples to discuss their problems maturely.

Less-educated couples experience greater dissatisfaction with their marriages, as do couples who do not pool their financial resources (Kurdek, 1991a). This occurs because less-educated couples face many additional stressors (e.g., higher rates of unemployment, lower financial security), and the failure to pool resources may reflect a lack of trust in the partner.

As couples settle into a routine, marital satisfaction tends to decline (Glenn & McLanahan, 1981, 1982). Research shows that the primary reason for this drop for most couples is the birth of children (Carstensen et al., 1996). Indeed, for most couples like the one in the photograph, having children means strong pressures to engage in traditional gender-role behaviors for mothers and fathers (Carstensen et al., 1996). Parenthood also means having substantially less time to devote to the marriage. Taking care of children is hard work, requiring energy that used to be spent on keeping the marriage alive and well (Glenn & Weaver, 1978). Most couples are ecstatic over having their first child, a tangible product of their love for each other. But soon the reality of child care sets in, with 2:00 A.M. feedings, diaper changing, and the like, not to mention the long-term financial obligations that will continue at least until the child becomes an adult.

However, using the birth of a child as the explanation of the drop in marital satisfaction is much too simplistic (Clements &

? THINK ABOUT IT
What types of interventions would help keep married couples happier?

Markman, 1996). In fact, child-free couples also experience a decline in marital satisfaction. It appears that a decline in overall marital satisfaction over time is a common developmental phenomenon, even for couples who choose to be child-free (Clements & Markman, 1996). Additionally, couples who are child-free because of infertility face the stress associated with the inability to have children, which lowers their marital satisfaction (Matthews & Matthews, 1986).

Marriage At Midlife

By midlife, marital satisfaction hits its lowest point, but there are differences in how husbands and wives view the relationship (Turner, 1982). Husbands at all stages of the marriage tend to describe it in positive terms, whereas middle-aged wives tend to be more critical. For example, one study found that 80% of

husbands but only 40% of wives rated their marriages favorably in midlife (Lowenthal, Thurnher, & Chiriboga, 1975). Wives' chief complaint about their husbands was that they were too dependent and clingy; interestingly, newlyweds also differ in this regard, but at that point husbands describe their wives as being too dependent.

For most couples like the one in the photograph, marital satisfaction improves after the children begin to leave (Rhyne, 1981). The upward shift is especially apparent in wives, and it stems from the increased financial security after children leave, the relief from the day-to-day duties of parenting, and the additional time that wives have with their husbands.

For some middle-aged couples, however, marital satisfaction continues to be low. They may have grown apart but continue to live together (exhibiting empty love in Sternberg's theory). In essence, they have become emotionally divorced; for these couples, spending more time together is not a welcome change (Fitzpatrick, 1984). Because the physical appearance of one's partner is a contributor to marital satisfaction, particularly for men, age-related changes in appearance may contribute to further deterioration of the relationship (Margolin & White, 1987).

Older Couples

Marital satisfaction is fairly high in older couples (Miller, Hemesath, & Nelson, 1997). However, satisfaction in long-term marriages—that is, marriages of 40 years or more—is a complex issue. One study found that 80% of couples married at least 50 years recollected their marriages as being happy from their wedding day to the present (Sporakowski & Axelson, 1984). In general, however, marital satisfaction among older couples increases shortly after retirement but then decreases with health problems and advancing age (Miller et al., 1997). The level of satisfaction in these marriages appears to be unrelated to the amount of past or present sexual interest or sexual activity, but it is positively related to the degree of interaction with friends (Bullock & Dunn, 1988). Surprisingly, though, only approximately 25% of these couples named their spouse as being one of their closest friends (Sporakowski & Axelson, 1984). Indeed, many older couples have simply developed detached, contented styles (Norton & Moorman, 1987).

Keeping Marriages Happy

Although no two marriages are exactly the same, couples must be flexible and adaptable. Couples like the one shown in the photograph who have been happily married for many years show an ability to roll with the punches and to adapt to changing circumstances in the relationship. For example, a serious problem of one spouse may not be detrimental to the relationship and may even make the bond stronger. Likewise, couples' expectations about marriage change over time, gradually becoming more congruent (Weishaus & Field, 1988). In contrast, the physical illness of one spouse almost invariably affects marital quality negatively, even after other factors such as work stress, education, and income are considered (Wickrama et al., 1997).

How well couples communicate their thoughts, actions, and feelings to each other largely determines the level of conflict couples experience, and, by extension, how happy they are likely to be over the long term (Notarius, 1996). And increasing demands from work and family put enormous pressures on a marriage (Rogers & Amato, 1997). It takes a great deal of love, humor, and perseverance to stay happily married a long time. But it *can* be done, providing couples work at seven key things (Donatelle & Davis, 1997; Enright, Gassin, & Wu, 1992; Knapp & Taylor, 1994):

- Make time for your relationship.
- Express your love to your spouse.
- Be there in times of need.
- Communicate constructively and positively about problems in the relationship.
- Be interested in your spouse's life.
- Confide in your spouse.
- Forgive minor offenses, and try to understand major ones.

TEST YOURSELF

1. A difficulty for many single people is that other people may expect them to _____ .

2. Young adults view cohabitation as a _____ marriage.

3. Gay and lesbian relationships are similar to _____ .

4. According to ________ , marriage is based on each partner contributing something to the relationship that the other would be hard-pressed to provide.
5. For most couples, marital satisfaction ________ after the birth of the first child.
6. What sociocultural forces affect decisions to marry rather than to cohabit indefinitely?

Answers: (1) marry, (2) step toward, (3) marriages, (4) exchange theory, (5) decreases

THE FAMILY LIFE CYCLE

The Family Life Cycle
Family Life-Cycle Stages
Deciding Whether to Have Children
The Parental Role

Learning Objectives

- **What are family life stages?**
- **Why do people have children?**
- **What is it like to be a parent? What differences are there in different types of parenting?**

Bob, 32, and Denise, 33, just had their first child, Matthew, after several years of trying. They've heard that having children in their 30s can have advantages, but Bob and Denise wonder whether people are just saying that to be nice to them. They are also concerned about the financial obligations they are likely to face.

"When are you going to start a family?" is a question young couples like Bob and Denise are asked frequently. Most couples want children because they believe they will bring great joy, which they often do. But once the child is born, adults may feel inadequate, because children don't come with instructions. Young adults may be surprised when the reality of being totally responsible for another person hits them. Experienced middle-aged parents often smile knowingly to themselves.

Frightening as it might be, the birth of a child transforms a couple (or a single parent) into a family. *Although the most common form of family in Western societies is the* nuclear family, *consisting only of parent(s) and child(ren), the most common form around the world is the* extended family, *in which grandparents and other relatives live with parents and children.* Because we have discussed families from the child's perspective in earlier chapters, here we focus on families from the parents' point of view.

FAMILY LIFE-CYCLE STAGES

From a developmental perspective, families experience a series of relatively predictable changes, which constitute the family life cycle. One example of the family life cycle is shown in the figure at the top of page 385. This model describes eight sequential stages, based on the age of the oldest child and the kinds of tasks families confront (Duvall, 1977). As described in Chapter 1, this theory is conceptually related to life-span and life-course theories.

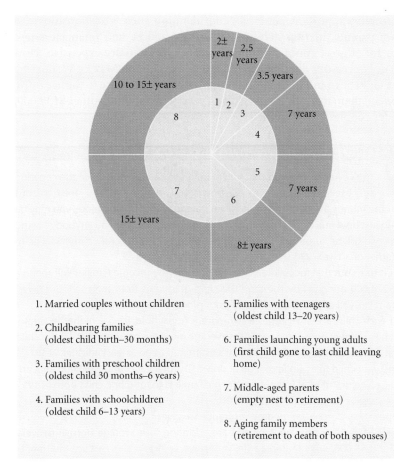

1. Married couples without children

2. Childbearing families
   (oldest child birth–30 months)

3. Families with preschool children
   (oldest child 30 months–6 years)

4. Families with schoolchildren
   (oldest child 6–13 years)

5. Families with teenagers
   (oldest child 13–20 years)

6. Families launching young adults
   (first child gone to last child leaving
   home)

7. Middle-aged parents
   (empty nest to retirement)

8. Aging family members
   (retirement to death of both spouses)

Durvall & Miller, 1985.

Family life-cycle models help us understand the changes families go through as children mature, but they also have limitations. They are based on traditional, first-time marriages with children; child-free relationships are ignored, as are the effects of occupational factors, friends, family, and spouse. Only the issues pertaining to raising the oldest child are used to define a family's current stage, and ethnic differences in parenting are overlooked (Vinovskis, 1988).

Despite their limitations, family life-cycle models provide a way to organize our discussion of couples' experience of parenting. In this section, we focus on the first six stages. The "empty nest" stage is discussed in Chapter 12, and the last stage is discussed in Chapter 14.

DECIDING WHETHER TO HAVE CHILDREN

One of the biggest decisions couples have to make is whether to have children. This decision is more complicated than most people think, because a couple must weigh the many benefits of child rearing, such as personal satisfaction, fulfilling personal needs, continuing the family line, and companionship, with the many drawbacks, including expense and life-style changes. What influences the decision process? Psychological and marital factors are always important, and career and life-style factors matter when the prospective mother works outside the home (Wilk, 1986). As you can see in the figure, these four factors are interconnected.

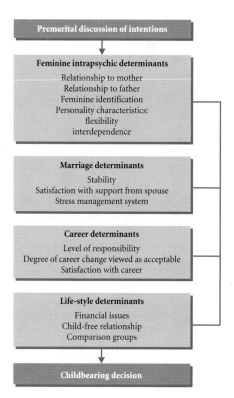

They raise many important matters for consideration, such as relationships with one's own parents, marital stability, career satisfaction, and financial issues. Finances are of great concern to most couples; children are expensive. How expensive? For reasons discussed in more detail in the You May Be Wondering feature, a child born in 1992 will cost roughly $225,000 to raise to the age of 18. Want to send them to a public college for 4 years? Add about another $130,000. No wonder couples are concerned.

YOU MAY BE WONDERING

THE COST OF RAISING A CHILD

You've just discovered that you're going to be a parent! Once the cheering and excitement begin to die down, you realize that you need to start putting some money aside for the child. Never having had children before, you may be wondering just how much will be enough. "I can almost guarantee you anybody having their first child will be surprised," says F. Stephen Wershing, Jr., a certified financial planner and father of a 1-year-old son (Johnston, 1993). Why, you ask?

Well, it turns out that for children born in 1992, middle-income families will spend a total of $224,800 per child by the time the child graduates from high school. Lower-income families will spend $161,620, and upper-income families will spend $314,550. That's for *each* child, and it assumes a two-parent household. It's 5% higher in single-parent families, where household expenses average more per person, especially for child care. What about college, you say? Well, that's estimated to be at least another $139,000 if you send your child to a public college or university for 4 years, and $293,000 for a private college. The grand total for middle-income families to raise one child born in 1992 through 4 years at a public college: $363,800.

Suppose you don't have medical insurance to cover the baby's delivery, or you're going through fertility treatment, or you are adopting. The average normal delivery costs around $5,000, with caesarean deliveries averaging $8,000. Fertility treatments typically cost $10,000 to $15,000 for each attempt at high-tech conception (e.g., *in vitro* fertilization); multiple attempts are usually necessary, and few expenses are covered by medical insurance. Adoptions range from $5,000 to $11,000 for domestic adoptions and $8,000 to $20,000 for international adoptions.

Now that you've experienced "sticker shock" of a sort, here's what the experts suggest about expenses and strategies to soften the blow:

1. Drastically limit expenses as soon as you find out you're going to have a baby. You need to save money and get used to a much tighter budget. Keep in mind that you may need a bigger apartment or house, putting additional strain on your already stretched resources.

2. It's essential to keep a budget in order to know where your money is going. Comparison shopping is a must. Teach these skills to your child.

3. Take advantage of payroll savings plans at work that let you set aside pretax earnings to pay child care expenses. If you hire someone to care for your child in your home, don't forget about withholding and Social Security taxes.

4. Make out a will, and acquire adequate disability and life insurance to provide for your children if something should happen to you.

In sum, having children is an extremely expensive proposition. But knowing what lies ahead, you can plan appropriately. •

For many reasons, such as personal choice, financial instability, and infertility, an increasing number of couples are remaining child-free. These couples have several advantages over those who choose to have children (Van Hoose & Worth, 1982): happier marriages, more freedom, and higher standards of living. But the larger society does not view being child-free as something positive, providing that being child-free is by choice and not due to infertility (Lampman & Dowling-Guyer, 1995). Child-free couples must also face social criticism from the larger child-oriented society and may run the risk of feeling more lonely in old age (Van Hoose & Worth, 1982).

THE PARENTAL ROLE

Today, couples have fewer children and have their first child later than in the past. Indeed, until 1993, couples in which mothers were over 30 when they had their first child were increasing. The slight decline since then is due mainly to smaller numbers of women of childbearing age in cohorts following the baby boomers. Delaying the first child like the couple in the photograph did has important benefits. Traditionally, the relationship with the mother has been thought to be crucial for the normal development of the child (Field & Widmayer, 1982). Older mothers, like Denise in the vignette, are more at ease being parents, spend more time with their babies, and are more affectionate and sensitive to them (Ragozin et al., 1982).

On the other hand, the trend for young, unmarried women to have children is still increasing. As we saw in Chapter 8, adolescent mothers are especially at risk for many problems and have none of the benefits older mothers do.

The age of the father also makes a difference in how fathers interact with their children. Remember Bob, the 32-year-old first-time father in the vignette? Compared to men who become fathers in their 20s, men like Bob who become fathers in their 30s are generally more invested in their paternal role and spend up to three times as much time in caring for their preschool children as younger fathers do (Cooney et al., 1993). However, men who become fathers in their 30s are also more likely to feel ambivalent and resentful about time lost to their careers (Cooney et al., 1993).

Parenting is full of rewards, but it also takes a great deal of work. Caring for young children is demanding. It may create disagreements over division of labor, especially if both parents are employed outside the home (see Chapters 4 and 11). Mothers appear equally divided among those who love taking care of their children and working, those who don't, and those who are neutral about it (Thompson & Walker, 1989). Fathers largely report that they like taking care of their children, but they are also less involved in direct child care (LaRossa, 1988).

Being a middle-aged parent with adolescent and adult children involves special issues. As we will see in Chapter 12, the nature of parent-child relationships changes during this period, going from clearly hierarchical to more egalitarian, as both children and parents mature. As you have experienced yourself, as well as studied in Chapter 8, adolescence is a particularly trying time for all.

In general, parents manage to deal with the many challenges of child rearing reasonably well. They learn how to compromise when necessary, and when to apply firm but fair discipline. Given the choice, most parents do not regret their decision to have children.

Single Parents

The number of single parents, most of whom are women, is increasing rapidly. Among the causes are high divorce rates, the decision to keep children born out of wedlock, and the desire of many single adults to have or adopt children. Being a single parent raises important questions. How are children affected when only one adult is responsible for child care? How do single parents meet their own needs for emotional support and intimacy?

Many divorced single parents report feelings of frustration, failure, guilt, and ambivalence toward the parent-child relationship (Van Hoose & Worth, 1982). Frustration usually results from a lack of companionship and from loneliness, as many social activities are typically reserved for couples. Feelings of guilt may lead to attempts to make up for the child's lack of a father or mother. The parent may experience ambivalence toward the children, who are sometimes seen as hindrances to developing new relationships. These feelings may also arise if the children serve as a reminder of a failed marriage.

Single parents, regardless of gender, face considerable obstacles. Financially, they are usually much less well-off than their married counterparts. Integrating the roles of work and parenthood are difficult enough for two persons; for the single parent, the hardships are compounded. Financially, single mothers are hardest hit. Emotionally, single fathers may have the worst of it; according to some research, their sleep, eating, play, work, and peer relations are badly affected, and they are more depressed than any other group of men (Pearlin & Johnson, 1977). Moreover, because most men are not socialized for child rearing, the lack of basic skills necessary to care for children may compound these problems.

One particular concern is dating (Phillis & Stein, 1983). Indeed, the three most popular questions asked by single parents involve dating: "How do I become available again?" "How will my children react?" "How do I cope with my own sexual needs?" Initiating a new relationship is difficult for many single parents, especially those with older children. They may be hesitant to express this side of themselves in front of their children. The children may ask discomforting questions about their dates or express resentment toward them.

? THINK ABOUT IT
How do the difficulties of single parenting relate to the development of young children?

Alternative Forms of Parenting

Not all parents raise their own biological children. In fact, roughly one-third of North American couples like the one in the photograph become stepparents or foster or adoptive parents sometime during their lives.

To be sure, the parenting issues we have discussed thus far are just as important in these situations as when people raise their own biological children. However, some special problems arise as well.

A big issue for foster parents, adoptive parents, and stepparents is how strongly the child will bond with them. Although infants less than 1 year old will probably bond well, children who are old enough to have formed attachments with their biological parents may have competing loyalties. For example, some stepchildren remain strongly attached to the noncustodial parent and actively resist attempts to integrate them into the new family ("My real mother wouldn't make me do that"). Or they may exhibit behavioral problems such as drinking or continually invading the stepparent's privacy (Pasley & Ihinger-Tallman, 1987). Children in blended families also tend not to have as good mental health as children in nondivorced families (Cherlin & Furstenberg, 1994). Stepparents must often deal with continued visitation by the noncustodial parent, which may exacerbate any difficulties. These problems are a major reason why second marriages are at high risk for dissolution, as discussed earlier in this chapter.

Still, many stepparents and stepchildren ultimately develop good relationships with each other. Stepparents must be sensitive to the relationship between the stepchild and his or her biological, noncustodial parent. Allowing stepchildren to develop the relationship with the stepparent at their own pace also helps. What style of stepparenting ultimately develops is influenced by the expectations of the stepparent, stepchild, spouse, and nonresidential parent (Erera-Weatherley, 1996).

Adoptive parents like those in the photograph also contend with attachment to birth parents, but in different ways. Even if they don't remember them, adopted children may wish to locate and meet their birth parents. Wanting to know one's origins is understandable, but such searches can strain the relationships between these children and their adoptive parents, who may interpret these actions as a form of rejection (Rosenberg, 1992). In general, though, research indicates that, compared to nonadopted children, adopted children are more confident, have a more positive view of the world, feel more in control of their lives, and view their adoptive parents as more nurturing (Marquis & Detweiler, 1985).

Foster parents tend to have the most tenuous relationship with their children, because the bond can be broken for any of a number of reasons having nothing to do with the quality of the care being provided. For example, a court may award custody back to the birth parents, or another couple may legally adopt the child. Dealing with attachment is difficult; foster parents want to provide secure homes, but they may not have the children long enough to establish continuity. Furthermore, because many children in foster care have been unable to form attachments at all, they are less likely to form ones that will inevitably be broken. Thus, foster parents must be willing to tolerate considerable ambiguity in the relationship and have few expectations about the future.

Finally, many gay and lesbian women also wish to be parents. Some have biological children themselves, whereas others choose adoption or foster parenting. Although gay men and lesbian women make good parents, they often experience resistance from other people to the idea of their having children, as well as religious and legal barriers. For example, some argue that it is unnatural and inherently deviant for gay men and lesbians to be parents (Marciano, 1985). According to this argument, gay men and lesbians are not fit parents and will raise their children to be just like them. Despite these and related claims, no credible scientific evidence exists to support them. On the contrary, substantial evidence exists that children raised by gay or lesbian parents do not develop problems of sexual identity or any other problems any more than children raised by heterosexual parents (Bozett, 1988; Parrot & Ellis, 1985). For example, research evidence indicates that roughly 90% of sons (aged 17 or older) of gay fathers are heterosexual (Bailey et al., 1995).

Additional evidence shows that children raised by gay men may even have some advantages over children raised by heterosexual men. Gay men are often especially concerned about being good and nurturing fathers, and they try hard to raise their children with nonsexist, egalitarian attitudes (Bozett, 1988). Children of lesbian couples and heterosexual couples are equally adjusted behaviorally, show equivalent cognitive development, and have similar behaviors in school. Indeed, one study found that the only difference between such couples was that lesbian couples exhibit more awareness of parenting skills than do heterosexual couples (Flaks et al., 1995).

These data will not make the controversy go away, as much of it is based on long-held beliefs and prejudices. Admittedly, the data comparing children raised by different types of parents are inadequate; for example, there is very little information about children raised by lesbian women. Only when societal attitudes toward gay men and lesbians become more accepting will there be greater acceptance of their right to be parents like anyone else.

TEST YOURSELF

1. The series of relatively predictable changes that families experience is called _____ .

2. Major influences on the decision to have children are marital factors, career factors, life-style factors, and _____ .

3. A new father who is invested in his parental role, but who may also feel ambivalent about time lost to his career is probably over age _____ .

4. A major issue for foster parents, adoptive parents, and stepparents is _____ .

5. What difference do you think it would make to view children as a financial asset (i.e., a source of income) as opposed to a financial burden (i.e., mainly an expense)? Which of these do you think characterizes most Western societies? Can you think of an example of the other type?

Answers: (1) the family life-cycle, (2) psychological factors, (3) 30, (4) how strongly the child will bond with them

DIVORCE AND REMARRIAGE

Divorce and Remarriage

Divorce

Remarriage

Learning Objectives

- **Who gets divorced? How does divorce affect parental relationships with children?**

- **What are remarriages like? How are they similar to and different from first marriages?**

*F*RANK AND MARILYN, *both in their late 40s, thought their marriage would last forever. They weren't so lucky; they just got divorced. Although two of their children are married, their youngest daughter is still in college. The financial pressures Marilyn feels now that she's on her own are beginning to take their toll. She wonders whether her financial situation is similar to that of other recently divorced women.*

Despite what Frank and Marilyn pledged on their wedding day, their marriage did not last until death parted them; they dissolved their marriage through divorce. But even though divorce is stressful and difficult, thousands of people each year also choose to try again. Most enter their second (or third or fourth) marriage with renewed expectations of success. Are these new dreams realistic? As we'll see, it depends on many things; among the most important is whether children are involved.

DIVORCE

Most couples enter marriage with the idea that their relationship will be permanent. Unfortunately, fewer and fewer couples experience this permanence. Rather than growing together, couples grow apart.

Who Gets Divorced and Why?

Compared to other countries, divorce in the United States is common; as you can see in the graph, couples have roughly a 50-50 chance of remaining married for life (Fisher, 1987). In contrast, the divorce rates in Canada, Great Britain, Australia, and Sweden are about 1 in 3, and only 1 in 10 in Japan, Italy, Israel, and Spain (U.S. Bureau of the Census, 1991). However, divorce rates in nearly every country have increased significantly over the past several decades (Lester, 1996). Statistics worldwide and from different historical periods also indicate that if marriages fail, they do so on average within 3 or 4 years (Fisher, 1987).

One factor consistently related to divorce rates in the United States is ethnicity. African Americans are more likely than European Americans to divorce or separate (U.S. Bureau of the Census, 1998). Hispanic groups show considerable variability; Mexican Americans and Cuban Americans have divorce rates similar to European Americans, whereas the rate for Puerto Ricans is much higher (Bean & Tienda, 1987). Ethnically mixed marriages are at greater risk of divorce than ethnically homogenous ones (Jones, 1996).

Another major factor is the change in laws and social norms, which is reflected in the reasons people give for divorcing. In 1948, divorced women cited cruelty, excessive drinking, and nonsupport as the most common reasons (Goode, 1956). With the advent of no-fault divorce and changing expectations about marriage, reasons for divorce shifted to communication problems, unhappiness, and incompatibility (Cleek & Pearson, 1985). Men and women typically agree on the reasons for divorce, listed below from most frequently cited to least (Cleek & Pearson, 1985):

Reasons Men Give	Reasons Women Give
Communication problems	Communication problems
Basic unhappiness	Basic unhappiness
Incompatibility	Incompatibility
Sexual problems	Emotional abuse
Financial problems	Financial problems
Emotional abuse	Sexual problems
Women's liberation	Alcohol abuse by spouse
In-laws	Infidelity by spouse
Infidelity by spouse	Physical abuse
Alcohol abuse by self	In-laws

Additionally, increases in the U.S. divorce rate reflect higher expectations of marriage. Couples now expect to find partners who will help them grow personally and provide much more than just financial support, a sexual partner, and children. Such expectations have paradoxically lowered the quality of marriages in recent generations (Rogers & Amato, 1997). In many other cultures, such expectations are rare or contrary to traditional values.

The high divorce rate in the United States and the reasons typically cited for getting divorced have sparked a controversial approach to keeping couples together. As described in the Current Controversies feature, *covenant marriage* is an option being tried in some states that makes divorce much harder to obtain. Will it work? Read the feature and draw your own conclusion.

CURRENT CONTROVERSIES

INFOTRAC
COLLEGE EDITION
To learn more, enter the following search term: marriage.

"COVENANT MARRIAGE," A WAY TO KEEP COUPLES TOGETHER?

The divorce rate in the United States, the highest in the world, has become a national concern. As our society strives to make marriage more successful, numerous approaches, such as mandatory premarital counseling, cooling-off periods, and the abolition of no-fault divorce, are being tried, with varying degrees of success.

In 1997, Louisiana adopted a different and controversial approach. When couples get married, they choose between a "no-fault marriage" and a "covenant marriage." Under a no-fault marriage, a couple may divorce after 6 months of separation without proof of adultery, abuse, neglect, or other basis. Under a covenant marriage, couples seeking divorce must undergo separation for 2 years or verify that one spouse is an adulterer, abuser, deserter, or felon. Couples opting for covenant marriage must also undergo mandatory premarital counseling. Couples already married may recast their vows and their marriage under terms of the covenant.

Proponents of covenant marriage point out that about 20% of couples who participate in premarital counseling decide not to marry their partners (Etzioni, 1997). Making divorce harder to obtain addresses lawmakers' concerns that divorce laws are too lenient. It is hoped that the provisions of covenant marriage will get couples to think more seriously about marriage and to make a deeper commitment to each other.

Opponents of covenant marriage argue that the option may force couples to stay together when it is in their and their children's best interest to end the marriage. Bad marriages are not supportive environments for children. Opponents also point out that covenant marriage is a backward step that reintroduces the idea that divorce has to be someone's fault. These opponents also question whether couples really have a choice; that is, peer pressure may force them into covenant marriage.

Will covenant marriage reduce divorce rates in Louisiana? It's too early to tell. Making sure couples who want to marry fully appreciate the emotional and financial realities is good. Whether making divorce more difficult to obtain is equally good for couples and children remains to be seen. •

Effects of Divorce on the Couple

Although the changes in attitudes toward divorce have eased the social trauma associated with it, divorce still takes a high toll on the psyche of the couple. A nationwide survey revealed that divorce impairs individuals' well-being for at least 5 years after the event, producing a greater variety of long-lasting negative effects than even the death of a spouse (Nock, 1981). A longitudinal study of divorced people showed that they are more depressed than they were when they were married (Menaghan & Lieberman, 1986). Indeed, divorced people of all ages are less likely than married, never-married, and widowed people to say that they are "very happy" with their lives (Kurdek, 1991b; Lee, Seccombe, & Shehan, 1991). Even 10 years afterward, many divorced people still report feeling angry, lonely, disappointed, abandoned, and betrayed (Wallerstein & Blakeslee, 1989).

Even though the psychological cost of divorce is high, divorced people generally do not wish they were still married. One longitudinal study found that 5 years after the divorce, only 20% of former partners think that the divorce was a mistake. However, most people say they underestimated the pain the divorce would cause (Wallerstein & Kelly, 1980).

The effects of divorce change over time. Shortly after the breakup, ex-partners often become even angrier and more bitter toward each other than they were beforehand. Like the people in the photograph, many also underestimate their attachment to each other and may be overly sensitive to criticism from the ex-spouse. Increased hostility is often accompanied by periods of depression and disequilibrium (Kelly, 1982). Indeed, ex-spouses who are preoccupied with thoughts of their former partner, and who have high feelings of hostility toward him or her have significantly poorer emotional well-being than ex-spouses who are not preoccupied or who have feelings of friendship toward the former partner (Masheter, 1997). It appears that low preoccupation is the key to healthy postdivorce relationships, and may be an indicator of the extent to which ex-spouses are able to move on with their lives.

Gender differences are also found. Men report being shocked by the breakup, especially if the wife filed for divorce (Kelly, 1982). Men are more likely to be blamed for the problems that led to the divorce, to accept the

> **? THINK ABOUT IT**
> Given the serious impact of divorce, what changes in mate selection might lower the divorce rate?

blame, to move out, and to thereby find their social life disrupted (Kitson & Sussman, 1982). Women are affected differently. Socially, they have fewer prospects for potential remarriage, and they find it more difficult to establish new relationships if they have custody of the children (Maccoby, Depner, & Mnookin, 1991; Masheter, 1991). Women are at a serious financial disadvantage, largely because they usually have custody of the children, are typically paid less than men, and are likely to have inadequate child support from their ex-husbands (Gallagher, 1996; Kurz, 1995). Marilyn, the recently divorced middle-aged woman we met in the vignette, probably has a difficult road ahead as she tries to meet her own expenses as well as help pay her daughter's college tuition.

Divorce in middle age or late life has some special characteristics. In general, the trauma is greater for these individuals, because of the long period of investment in each other's emotional and practical lives (Uhlenberg, Cooney, & Boyd, 1990). Longtime friends may turn away or take sides, causing additional disruption to the social network. Middle-aged and elderly women are at a significant disadvantage for remarriage—an especially traumatic situation for women who obtained much of their identity from their roles as wife and mother. Even if the divorce occurred many years earlier, children may still blame their parents for breaking the family apart (Hennon, 1983).

We must not overlook the financial problems faced by middle-aged divorced women (Gallagher, 1996; Kurz, 1995). These problems are especially keen for the middle-aged divorcee who may have spent years as a homemaker and has few marketable job skills. For her, divorce presents an especially difficult financial hardship.

Relationships with Young Children

The difficulty in adjusting to divorce often depends on whether young children are involved. Deciding who will have custody of the children often triggers the problems. Over 90% of the time, the mother receives custody, and the father becomes an occasional parent. Like the woman in the photograph, most divorced mothers of young children end up being the primary custodial parent. For many of them, the price they pay for custody is very high; at the same time as their parental responsibilities are increasing, their financial resources are decreasing significantly (Gallagher, 1996; Kurz, 1995). Child care is expensive, and most divorced fathers contribute less than before the separation. Furthermore, in the United States, many child support payments are not made; to address this problem, most states have passed laws to enforce child support payments (Gallagher, 1996).

Divorced fathers pay a psychological price (Furstenberg & Nord, 1985). Although many would like to remain active in their children's lives, few actually do. One reason is that children's needs change; anticipating these changes requires frequent contact, which is hard for many men. Additionally, even when child support payments are made, noncustodial fathers find it difficult to develop good relationships with their children, often because their ex-wives express their anger by limiting contact with the children. The fact that about one-fourth of divorced couples end up as bitter enemies only makes matters worse for all concerned (Ahrons & Wallisch, 1986). The unfortunate result is that many divorced fathers become peripheral in their children's lives, often through no fault of their own (Seltzer, 1991). As you can see in the graphs, within 3 years after the divorce, fewer than half of the fathers are involved in decisions regarding their child, and less than 60% of the children see their fathers even once a month.

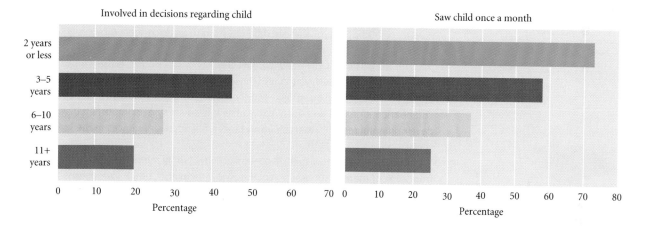

It is possible to overcome the problems between divorced people who have young children. Some former couples are able to get over their anger and cooperate with each other (Masheter, 1991). Adjustment is easier if both remarry or neither does. Interestingly, it is easier for a new husband to accept his wife's friendly relationship with her former husband than it is for a new wife to accept her husband's friendly relationship with his ex-wife (Masheter, 1991).

Relationships with Adult Children

We saw in Chapter 5 that young children can be seriously affected by their parents' divorce. But what happens when the parents of adult children divorce? Are adult children affected too? It certainly looks that way. Young adults whose parents divorce experience a great deal of emotional vulnerability and stress (Cooney, Smyer, Hagestad, & Klock, 1986; Cooney & Uhlenberg, 1990). One young man put it this way:

> . . . the difficult thing was that it was a time where, you know [you're] making the transition from high school to college . . . your high school friends are dispersed . . . they're all over the place. . . . It's normally a very difficult transition [college], new

? THINK ABOUT IT
What effect might parental divorce have on this person's view of marriage and committed relationships?

atmosphere, new work load, meeting new people. You've got to start deciding what you want to do, you've got to sort of start getting more independent, and so forth. And then, at the same time you find out about a divorce. You know, it's just that much more adjustment you have to make. (Cooney et al., 1986)

Anger, conflicting loyalties, and worry about the parents' future are common reactions. Relationships with parents may be irreparably harmed. Even many years later, divorced fathers are less likely than mothers to experience positive relationships with their adult children. Fathers also do not believe that they will be able to rely on their children for support in times of need (Cooney & Uhlenberg, 1990). In contrast, adult daughters' relationships with their mothers are much more resilient; they may even intensify after the divorce (Cooney et al., 1986).

SEE FOR YOURSELF

THE EFFECTS OF DIVORCE ON ADULT CHILDREN

One of the most overlooked effects of divorce is how it changes the relationships between parents and their adult children. Indeed, most of the research conducted on the effects of divorce on children focuses on school-age children and ignores those over the age of 18. This emphasis ignores the importance of life-cycle forces in the biopsychosocial model (see Chapter 1). Being an adult child of divorced parents creates problems that are different from those experienced by young children of divorce.

Adult children of divorced parents form two subgroups: those whose parents divorced when they were young, and those whose parents divorced when they were 18 or older. An interesting question is whether these subgroups differ in their experiences. You be the judge and find out. While you're at it, you may gain important insights into developmental research and the importance of life-cycle influences in the biopsychosocial model.

Ask your classmates, friends, co-workers, and family members. Locate one person from each of the two subgroups, and interview them about their experiences. Find out what they thought (and still think) about their parents' divorce, what their relationships with them are like now, and how having divorced parents influences their own love relationships. Collate and tabulate your results, then compare them to those in this section. Do they agree? See for yourself. •

REMARRIAGE

The trauma of divorce does not deter people from beginning new relationships, which often lead to another marriage. Nearly 80% of divorced people remarry within the first 3 years (Glick & Lin, 1986). However, rates vary somewhat across ethnic groups. African Americans remarry a bit more slowly than European Americans, and Hispanics remarry more slowly than either of these other two groups (Coleman & Ganong, 1990). Remarriage is much more likely if the divorced people are young, mainly because more partners are available. Partner availability favors men at all ages, because men tend to marry women younger than themselves. For this reason, the probability that a divorced woman will remarry declines with increasing age.

Remarried people report that they experience their second marriage differently from their first. They claim to enjoy much better communication, to resolve disagreements with greater goodwill, to arrive at decisions more equitably, and to divide chores more fairly (Furstenberg, 1982). Indeed, most couples believe that they will be more likely to succeed the second time around (Furstenberg, 1982). For African Americans, this appears to be true; divorce rates for remarriages are lower than for first marriages (Teachman, 1986). However, second marriages for most other groups have about a 25% higher risk of dissolution than first marriages, and the divorce rate for remarriages involving stepchildren is about three times higher than the rate for first marriages (Glenn, 1991).

Although women are more likely to initiate a divorce, they are less likely to remarry (Buckle, Gallup, & Rodd, 1996). Divorced men without children tend to marry women who have never been married; divorced men with children tend to marry divorced women (Buckle et al., 1996).

For the couples in the photograph, adapting to new relationships in remarriage is different for men and women (Hobart, 1988). For remarried men, the preeminent relationship is with his new wife; other relationships, especially those with his children from his first marriage, take a backseat. For remarried women, the relationship with a new husband remains more marginal than the relationship with the children from the first marriage.

---

1. Following divorce, most women suffer disproportionately in the _____ domain compared to most men.

2. On average, within 2 years after a divorce, _____ fathers remain central in their children's lives.

3. Even many years later, divorced _____ may not experience positive relationships with their adult children.

4. For African American couples, divorce rates for remarried couples are _____ than for first marriages.

5. Despite greatly increased divorce rates over the past few decades, the rate of marriage has not changed very much. Why do you think this is?

Answers: (1) financial, (2) few, (3) fathers, (4) lower

PUTTING IT ALL TOGETHER

In this chapter, we have seen how people find and develop adult relationships. We considered the important role that friendships play in adulthood. Some relationships, like Jamal and Deb's, turn into love. Although the romantic love they feel won't last forever, their love may evolve so that the relationship can last. Although young love like Jamal and Deb's gets played out the world over, what people look for in a mate varies in different cultures. Turning a love relationship into newly wedded bliss, as Kevin and Beth did, is very common;

it's still true that the vast majority of people get married at some point in their lives. If Kevin and Beth have children, their newfound happiness is likely to fade a bit, but as long as they maintain their commitment to each other, their marriage will probably last. Frank and Marilyn's divorce has had fairly typical results: Marilyn is having trouble making the financial ends meet. Because Bob and Denise were in their 30s when their first child was born, they will likely be better suited and better

prepared for parenthood than many younger parents.

Throughout the chapter, we saw that human relationships are complex. Although there are similarities around the world in how people find mates, culture plays a large part in helping people find the person who will say, "I am for you." Maintaining a strong relationship takes a great deal of work, and there are many pressures that can divert partners' attention from each other.

SUMMARY

Relationships

Friendships

• People tend to have more friendships during young adulthood than during any other period. Friendships are especially important for maintaining life satisfaction throughout adulthood.

• Men tend to have fewer close friendships and to base them on shared activities, such as sports. Women tend to have more close friendships, and to base them on intimate and emotional sharing. Gender differences in same-gender friendship patterns may explain the difficulties men and women have forming cross-gender friendships.

Love Relationships

• Passion, intimacy, and commitment are the key components of love. These combine to form seven types of love relationships: liking, infatuation, empty love, romantic love, fatuous love, companionate love, and consummate love.

• Although styles of love change with age, the priorities within relationships do not. Men tend to be more romantic earlier in relationships than women, who tend to be cautious pragmatists.

• Selecting a mate works best when there are shared values, goals, and interests. There are cross-cultural differences with regard to the specific aspects of these that are considered most important.

The Dark Side of Relationships: Violence

• Levels of aggressive behavior range from verbal aggression, to physical aggression, to murdering one's

partner. The causes of aggressive behaviors become more complex as the level of aggression increases. People remain in abusive relationships for many reasons, including low self-esteem and the belief that they cannot leave.

Life-Styles

Singlehood

• Most adults decide by age 30 whether they plan on getting married. Never-married adults often develop a strong network of close friends. Dealing with other people's expectations that they should marry is often difficult for single people.

Cohabitation

• Young adults usually cohabit as a step toward marriage, and adults of all ages may also cohabit for financial reasons. Cohabitation is only rarely seen as an alternative to marriage. Overall, more similarities than differences exist between cohabiting and married couples.

Gay and Lesbian Couples

• Gay and lesbian relationships are similar to marriages in terms of relationship issues. Lesbian couples tend to be more egalitarian and are more likely to remain together than gay couples. Frequency of sexual expression differs in gay, lesbian, and heterosexual couples.

Marriage

• The most important factors in creating stable marriages are creating a stable sense of identity as a foundation for intimacy, similarity of values and interests, and the contribution of unique skills by each partner.

• For couples with children, marital satisfaction tends to decline until the children leave home, although individual differences are apparent, especially in long-term marriages. Most long-term marriages are happy.

The Family Life Cycle

Family Life-Cycle Stages

• Although the nuclear family is the most common form of family in Western societies, the most common form around the world is the extended family. Families experience a series of relatively predictable changes called the *family life cycle*. This cycle provides a framework for understanding the changes families go through as children mature.

Deciding Whether to Have Children

• Although having children is stressful and very expensive, most people do it anyway. However, the number of child-free couples is increasing.

The Parental Role

• The timing of parenthood is important in how involved parents are in their families as opposed to their careers.

• Single parents are faced with many problems, especially if they are women and are divorced. The main problem is significantly reduced financial resources.

• A major issue for adoptive parents, foster parents, and stepparents is how strongly the child will bond with them. Each of these relationships has some special characteristics.

• Gay and lesbian parents also face numerous obstacles, but they usually prove to be good parents.

Divorce and Remarriage

Divorce

• Currently, odds are about 50-50 that a new marriage will end in divorce. Recovery from divorce is different for men and women. Men tend to have a tougher time in the short run, but women clearly have a harder time in the long run, often for financial reasons. Difficulties between divorced partners usually involve visitation and child support. Disruptions also occur in divorced parents' relationships with their children, whether the children are young or are adults themselves.

Remarriage

• Most divorced couples remarry. Second marriages are especially vulnerable to stress if spouses must adjust to having stepchildren. Remarriage in middle age and beyond tends to be happy.

KEY TERMS

assortative mating (368)
abusive relationship (371)
battered woman syndrome (373)

cohabitation (376)
homogamy (380)
exchange theory (380)

nuclear family (384)
extended family (384)
family life cycle (384)

IF YOU'D LIKE TO LEARN MORE

Readings

BOSS, P. G., DOHERTY, W. J., LAROSSA, R., SCHUMM, W. R., & STEINMETZ, S. K. (Eds.). (1993). *Sourcebook of family theories and methods.* New York: Plenum. This superb resource book covers all major theories and methods used in family and relationship research.

PRATHER, H., & PRATHER, G. (1990). *Notes to each other.* New York: Bantam. This collection of reflections on making relationships work, staying happy, and parenting makes easy reading.

SETTLES, B. H., HANKS, R. S., & SUSSMAN, M. B. (1993). *American families and the future: Analyses of possible destinies.* New York: Haworth Press. This highly readable yet scholarly discussion of the future of the North American family takes a life-span and interdisciplinary perspective.

TANNEN, D. (1990). *You just don't understand.* New York: Morrow. This highly readable and intriguing book discusses the different communication styles men and women use.

Web Sites

Research findings and professional materials about all aspects of families can be obtained through the National Council on Family Relations at

http://www.ncfr.com

The Family Violence Prevention Fund is a national nonprofit organization that focuses on domestic violence education, prevention, and public policy reform. Information on all these topics can be obtained at

http://www.igc.org/fund/

The National Parent Information Network is a clearinghouse of information for and about parents that is sponsored by Teachers College, Columbia University

VANZETTI, N., & DUCK, S. (1996). *A life time of relationships.* Pacific Grove: Brooks/Cole. A very readable summary of the research literature on different types of relationships across the life span.

For additional readings, explore Infotrac College Edition, your online library. Go to http://www. infotrac-college.com/wadsworth.

and the University of Illinois at Urbana-Champaign. The Network can be found at

http://ericps.ed.uiuc.edu/npin/

Web site addresses are subject to change. The Wadsworth Study Center Web site listed below can be accessed for updated links.

The Wadsworth Psychology Study Center Web Site

See http://psychology.wadsworth.com/ for practice quiz questions, internet links, updates, critical thinking exercises, discussion forums and more! The Wadsworth Psychology Study Center provides a wealth of information fully organized and integrated by chapter.

CHAPTER 11

WORK AND LEISURE

Occupational Selection and Development
The Meaning of Work
Holland's Theory of Occupational
    Choice Revisited
Occupational Development
Job Satisfaction
    Periodicity and Job Satisfaction

Gender, Ethnicity, and Discrimination Issues
Gender Differences in Occupational
    Selection
Women and Occupational Development
Ethnicity and Occupational
    Development
Bias and Discrimination
    Sexual Harassment in the Workplace
    Occupational Success Is More
       Than Just Hard Work

Occupational Transitions
    Changing Occupations to
       Find Satisfying Work
Retraining Workers
Occupational Insecurity
Coping with Unemployment

Work and Family
The Dependent Care Dilemma
Juggling Multiple Roles
    How Do Dual-Earner Couples Handle
       Division of Labor and Work-Family
       Conflict?

Time to Relax: Leisure Activities
    Varieties of Leisure Activity in Adulthood
Types of Leisure Activities
Developmental Changes in Leisure
Consequences of Leisure Activities

Putting It All Together

Summary

If You'd Like to Learn More

Work—it seems as though that's all we do sometimes. From the small chores children do to putting in 12-hour days at the office, we are taught that working is a natural part of life. For some, work *is* life. In this chapter, we explore the world of work first by considering how people choose occupations and develop in them. After that, we examine how women and minorities contend with barriers to their occupational selection and development. Dealing with occupational transitions is considered in the third section. How to balance work and family obligations is a difficult issue for many people; this is discussed in the fourth section. Finally, we will see how people spend their time away from work in leisure activities.

As in Chapter 10, our focus in this chapter is on issues faced by both young and middle-aged adults. No longer is it the case that only young adults have to deal with occupational selection issues. It is increasingly common for middle-aged people to have to confront the issues of occupational selection all over again, as their industry changes or their company downsizes. Similarly, the other topics we consider apply to both younger and middle-aged adults.

OCCUPATIONAL SELECTION AND DEVELOPMENT

Occupational Selection and Development

The Meaning of Work

Holland's Theory of Occupational Choice Revisited

Occupational Development

Job Satisfaction

Learning Objectives

- **How do people view work? How do occupational priorities vary with age?**
- **How do people choose their occupations?**
- **What factors influence occupational development?**
- **What is the relation between job satisfaction and age?**

ONIQUE, *a 28-year-old senior communications major, wonders about careers. Should she enter the broadcast field as a behind-the-scenes producer, or would she be better suited as a public relations spokesperson? She thinks that her outgoing personality is a factor she should consider. Should she become a broadcast producer?*

Choosing one's work is serious business. Like Monique, we try to select a field in which we are trained, and that is also appealing. Work colors much of what we do in life. You may be taking this course as part of your preparation for work. People make friends at work and arrange personal activities around work schedules. Parents often choose child care centers on the basis of their proximity to their place of employment.

In this section, we explore what work means to adults. We also revisit issues pertaining to occupational selection, first introduced in Chapter 8, as well as examine occupational development. Finally, we will see how satisfaction with one's job changes during adulthood.

THE MEANING OF WORK

Did you ever stop to think about why we fight the commuting crowds like the people in the photograph are doing? Studs Terkel, the author of the fascinating book *Working* (1974), writes that work is "a search for daily meaning as

well as daily bread, for recognition as well as cash, for astonishment rather than torpor; in short, for a sort of life rather than a Monday through Friday sort of dying" (p. xiii). Kahlil Gibran (1923), in his mystical book *The Prophet,* put it this way: "Work is love made visible."

For some of us, work is a source of prestige, social recognition, and a sense of worth. For others, the excitement of creativity and the opportunity to give something of themselves make work meaningful. But for most, the main purpose of work is to earn a living. This is not to imply, of course, that money is the only reward in a job; friendships, the chance to exercise power, and feeling useful are also important. The meaning most of us derive from working includes both the money that can be exchanged for life's necessities (and maybe a few luxuries, too) and the possibility of personal growth. *These* occupational priorities, *or what people want from their employment, reflect the culture and the times in which people live.*

Occupational priorities change over time because cultural values change. An excellent example of these influences is the longitudinal study conducted by American Telephone and Telegraph (AT&T), begun in the mid-1950s (Howard & Bray, 1980). Look carefully at the graph. Three key things are depicted. First, the vertical axis represents the rating of the importance of work in employees' lives. The horizontal axis reflects two things: length of time in the study at AT&T (which gives an idea of the length of employment), and relative age (in general, the less time in the study, the younger the employee).

Notice how the importance of work changed dramatically over time. The longer employees were in the study, the more differentiated the various levels of managers became in terms of the importance of work. Underlying these changes are key differences in motivation for upward mobility, leadership, and desire for emotional support, depending on the age of the managers. For higher management levels, those who had been in the AT&T study briefly had expectations of rewards from work that were much lower than those who had been in the study

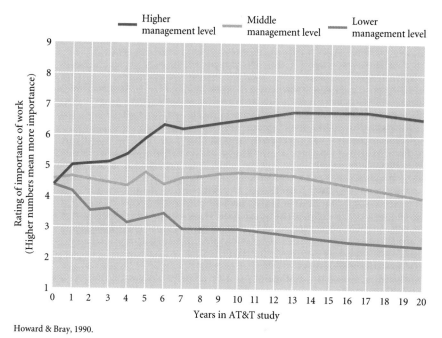

Howard & Bray, 1990.

ten years or more; they did not see most of their major rewards or life satisfaction coming from work. Interestingly, the picture was reversed for lower-level managers; those who had been in the study longer gave a lower rating of the importance of work.

The findings at AT&T are not unique. Other research has also documented that younger workers in upper management are less interested in materialism, power seeking, upward mobility, and competition; instead, they consistently emphasize individual freedom, personal growth, and cooperation (Jones, 1980; Yankelovich, 1981).

Regardless of what occupational priorities people have, they view their occupation as a key element in their sense of identity (Whitbourne, 1996). This can be readily observed when adults introduce themselves socially. You've probably noticed that when asked to tell something about themselves, people usually provide information about what they do for a living. Occupation affects your life in a host of ways, often influencing where you live, what friends you make, and even what clothes you wear. In short, the impact of work cuts across all aspects of life. Work, then, is a major social role and influence on adult life. Occupation is an important anchor that complements the other major role of adulthood—love relationships.

As we will see, occupation is part of human development. Young children, in their pretend play, are in the midst of the social preparation for work. Adults are always asking them, "What do you want to be when you grow up?" School curricula, especially in high school and college, are geared toward preparing people for particular occupations. People develop interests in various occupations over time, and changes in occupation are among the most important events in the life cycle. Let's turn our attention to one of the theories explaining how and why people choose the occupations they do.

HOLLAND'S THEORY OF OCCUPATIONAL CHOICE REVISITED

In Chapter 8, we saw that early decisions about what people want to do in the world of work are related to their personalities. Holland's (1973, 1985) theory makes explicit an intuitively appealing idea: that people choose occupations to optimize the fit between their individual traits (such as personality, intelligence, skills, and abilities) and their occupational interests. Recall from the table in Chapter 8 (page 296) that Holland categorizes occupations in two ways: by the interpersonal settings in which people must function and by their associate life-styles. From this perspective, he identifies six personality types that combine these factors: investigative, social, realistic, artistic, conventional, and enterprising.

How does Holland's theory help us understand the continued development of occupational interests in adulthood? Monique's situation helps illustrate this point. Monique, the college senior in the vignette, found a good match between her outgoing nature and her major, communications. Indeed, most college students, regardless of age, tend to like courses and majors best when they provide a good fit with their personalities. Thus, the early occupational choices in adolescence continue to be modified and fine-tuned in adulthood.

Although the relations between personality and occupational choice are important, we must also recognize the limits of the theory as it relates to adults' occupational choices. If we simply consider the gender distribution of Holland's personality types, adult men and women are represented differently (Costa, McCrae, & Holland, 1984). Regardless of age, women are more likely than men to have the social, artistic, and conventional personality types. In part, gender differences reflect different experiences in growing up (e.g., hearing that girls grow up to be nurses whereas boys grow up to be firefighters), differences in personality (e.g., gender-role identity), and differences in socialization (e.g., women being expected to be more outgoing and people-oriented than men). However, if we look within a specific occupational type, women and men are very similar to each other, and closely correspond to the interests Holland describes (Betz, Harmon, & Borgen, 1996).

We know very little about how Holland's personality types vary in different ethnic groups, mostly because such groups have not been included in the studies investigating the links between personality and occupation. Additionally, Holland's theory ignores the context in which occupational decisions are made. For example, he overlooks the fact that many people have little choice in the kind of job they can get, because of external factors such as family, financial pressures, or ethnicity.

Holland's theory also ignores evidence that the match between personality type and occupation changes during adulthood (Adler & Aranya, 1984). Hol-

? THINK ABOUT IT

How do the cognitive developmental changes in adulthood affect the ability to choose an occupation?

land takes a static view of both personality and occupations, but it must be recognized that what occupation we choose is not dictated solely by what we are like. Equally important is the dynamic interplay between us and the sociocultural context we find ourselves in—just as one would suspect, given the biopsychosocial model presented in Chapter 1. Occupational selection is a complex developmental process involving interactions among personal, ethnic, gender, and economic factors.

OCCUPATIONAL DEVELOPMENT

For most of us, getting a job is not enough; we would also like to move up the ladder. Promotion is a measure of how well one is doing in one's career. How quickly occupational advancement occurs (or does not) may lead to such labels as "fast-tracker" or "dead-ender" (Kanter, 1976). Bill Clinton, shown here being inaugurated as the president of the United States at age 46, is an example of a fast-tracker. People who want to advance learn quickly how long to stay at one level and how to seize opportunities as they occur, while others experience the frustration of remaining in the same job, with no chance for promotion.

How a person advances in a career seems to depend on professional socialization, which includes several factors besides those that are important in choosing an occupation. Among these are expectations, support from co-workers, priorities, and job satisfaction. Before we consider these aspects, let's look at a general scheme of occupational development.

Super's Theory

Over four decades, Super (1957, 1980) developed a theory of occupational development based on self-concept, first introduced in Chapter 8. He proposed a progression through five distinct stages during adulthood, resulting from changes in individuals' self-concept and adaptation to an occupational role: implementation, establishment, maintenance, deceleration, and retirement. *People are located along a continuum of* vocational maturity *through their*

Implementation ⟶ Establishment ⟶ Maintenance ⟶ Deceleration ⟶ Retirement

working years; the more congruent their occupational behaviors are with what is expected of them at different ages, the more vocationally mature they are. We saw in Chapter 8 that the initial two phases of Super's theory, crystallization and specification, occur primarily during adolescence, and that the first adulthood phase has its origins then as well. Each of the stages in adulthood has distinctive characteristics:

- The *implementation* stage begins in late adolescence or the early 20s, when people take a series of temporary jobs to learn firsthand about work roles and to try out some possible career choices.

- The *establishment* stage begins with selecting a specific occupation during young adulthood. It continues as the person advances up the career ladder in the same occupation.

- The *maintenance* stage is a transition phase during middle age, as workers begin to reduce the amount of time they spend fulfilling work roles.

- The *deceleration* stage begins as workers begin planning in earnest for their upcoming retirement and separating themselves from their work.

- The *retirement* stage begins when people stop working full-time.

In Super's framework, people's occupations evolve in response to changes in their self-concept (Salomone, 1996). Consequently, this is a developmental process that reflects and explains important life changes. This developmental process complements Holland's ideas. Investigative and enterprising types are likely to come from more affluent families, in which the parents tend not to be in investigative or enterprising occupations. Interestingly, initial occupational goals are not as important for social types as for the other two; social types appeared more flexible in eventual occupational choice.

However, a shortcoming of Super's theory is that the progression assumes that once people choose an occupation, they stay in it for the rest of their working lives. Although this may have been true for many employees in the past, it is not the case for most North American workers today (Cascio, 1995). The downsizing of public and private organizations since the late 1980s has all but eliminated the notion of lifetime job security with a particular employer. It remains to be seen whether new developmental stages will be found to underlie the new occupational reality.

Occupational Expectations

As we saw in Chapter 8, individuals form opinions about what work in a particular occupation will be like based on what they learn in school and from their parents, peers, other adults, and the media. People have expectations regarding what they want to become and when they hope to get there. Levinson and his colleagues (1978) built these expectations into their theory of adult male development, which was later extended to women (Levinson & Levinson, 1996). Based on findings from the original longitudinal study begun in the 1940s on men attending an elite private college, Levinson and his colleagues (1978) found considerable similarity among the participants in terms of major life tasks during adulthood. *Forming a dream, with one's career playing a prominent role, is one of the young adult's chief tasks.*

Throughout adulthood, people continue to refine and update their occupational expectations. This usually involves trying to achieve the dream, monitoring progress toward it, and changing or even abandoning it as necessary. For some, modifying the dream comes as a result of realizing that interests have changed or that the dream was not a good fit. In other cases, failure leads to changing the dream—for example, dropping a business major because one is failing economics courses. Other causes are age, racial, or sexual discrimination, lack of opportunity, obsolescence of skills, and changing interests. In some cases, one's initial occupational choice may simply have been unrealistic.

? THINK ABOUT IT
What biological, psychological, and sociocultural forces influence the progression of one's career?

For example, nearly half of all young adults would like to become professionals (such as lawyers or physicians), but only one person in seven actually makes it (Cosby, 1974). Some goal modification is essential from time to time, but it usually surprises us to realize that we could have been wrong about what seemed to be a logical choice in the past. As Marie, a 38-year-old advertising manager, put it, "I really thought I wanted to be a pilot; the travel sounded really interesting. But it just wasn't what I expected."

Perhaps the rudest jolt for most of us first comes during the transition from school to the real world. Reality shock sets in, and things never seem to happen the way we expect. Reality shock befalls everyone, from the young worker in the photograph to the accountant who learns that the financial forecast that took days to prepare may simply end up in a file cabinet (or, worse yet, in the wastebasket) (Van Maanen & Schein, 1977). The visionary aspects of the dream may not disappear altogether, but a good dose of reality goes a long way toward bringing a person down to earth. Such feedback comes to play an increasingly important role in a person's occupational development and self-concept. For example, the woman

who thought that she would receive the same rewards as her male counterparts for comparable work is likely to become increasingly angry and disillusioned when her successes result in smaller raises and fewer promotions.

The Role of Mentors

Imagine how hard it would be to figure out everything you needed to know in a new job with no support from the people around you. Entering an occupation involves more than the relatively short formal training a person receives. Indeed, much of the most critical information is not taught in training seminars. Instead, most people are shown the ropes by co-workers. In many cases, an older, more experienced person makes a specific effort to do this, taking on the role of a *mentor*. Although mentors by no means provide the only source of guidance in the workplace, they have been studied fairly closely.

A mentor is part teacher, part sponsor, part model, and part counselor (Heimann & Pittenger, 1996). The mentor helps a young worker avoid trouble ("Be careful what you say around Harry"). He or she also provides invaluable information about the unwritten rules that govern day-to-day activities in the workplace (not working too fast on the assembly line, wearing the right clothes, and so on) (Levinson et al., 1978; Levinson & Levinson, 1996). As part of the relationship, a mentor makes sure that his or her protégé is noticed and receives credit for good work from supervisors. Thus, occupational success often depends on the quality of the mentor-protégé relationship. The mentor fulfills two main functions: improving the protégé's chances for advancement and promoting his or her psychological and social well-being (Kram, 1980, 1985).

Kram (1985) also theorized that the mentor relationship develops through four phases: initiation (mentors and protégés begin the relationship), cultivation (mentors work with protégés), separation (protégés and mentors spend less time together), and redefinition (the mentor-protégé relationship either ends or is transformed into a different type of relationship). Research supports this developmental process, as well as the benefits of having a mentor (Chao, 1997). Clearly, protégés get tangible benefits from having a mentor.

What do mentors get from the relationship? In Chapter 1, we saw that the ideas in Erikson's theory (1982) included important aspects of adulthood related to work. Helping a younger employee learn the job is one way to fulfill aspects of Erikson's phase of generativity. As we will see in more detail in Chapter 12, generativity reflects middle-aged adults' need to ensure the continuity of society through activities such as socialization or having children. In work settings, generativity is most often expressed through mentoring. In particular, the mentor ensures that there is some continuity in the corporation or profession by passing on the knowledge and experience he or she has gained over the years. Being a mentor helps middle-aged people fulfill their need to ensure the continuity of society and accomplish or produce something worthwhile (Erikson, 1982).

Some authors suggest that women have a greater need for mentors than men because they receive less socialization in the skills necessary to do

well in the workplace (Busch, 1985). Women with mentors also have higher expectations about career advancement opportunities (Baugh, Lankau, & Scandura, 1996). However, women seem to have a more difficult time finding adequate mentors; some evidence suggests that only one-third of professional women find mentors as young adults (Kittrell, 1998). One reason is that there are few female role models, such as the woman in the photo, who could serve a mentoring function, especially in upper-level management. This is unfortunate, especially in view of evidence that women who have female mentors are significantly more productive than women with male mentors (Goldstein, 1979). Although many young women report that they would feel comfortable with a male mentor (Olian et al., 1988), researchers note that male mentor–female protégé relationships may involve conflict and tension resulting from possible sexual overtones, even when there has been no overtly sexual behavior on anyone's part (Kram, 1985).

JOB SATISFACTION

Job satisfaction is the positive feeling that results from an appraisal of one's work. In general, job satisfaction tends to increase gradually with age (James & Jones, 1980). The increased satisfaction has been linked to several factors:

- As workers get older, they have had more time to find a job in which they are reasonably happy.

- As workers get older, they are more satisfied with the intrinsic, personal aspects of their jobs than they are with the extrinsic aspects, such as pay (Morrow & McElroy, 1987).

- As workers get older, they may have resigned themselves to the fact that things are unlikely to improve, resulting in a better congruence between worker desires and job attributes (White & Spector, 1987).

- As workers get older, they make work less of a focus in their lives partly because they have achieved occupational success (Bray & Howard, 1983), so that it takes less to keep them satisfied.

However, job satisfaction does not simply increase over a lifetime, but rather follows a cyclical pattern. Shirom and Mazeh (1988) found that satisfaction may fluctuate periodically based on changes that people intentionally make in their occupations. Job satisfaction increases over time because people change jobs or responsibilities on a regular basis, thereby keeping their occupation interesting and challenging. How did Shirom and Mazeh figure out that job satisfaction can be cyclical? For the answer, read the Spotlight on Research feature.

PERIODICITY AND JOB SATISFACTION

SPOTLIGHT ON RESEARCH

Who were the investigators and what was the aim of the study? Why does job satisfaction tend to increase with age? One hypothesis is that job satisfaction has a complex relationship to the length of time one has been in a job, and not to age per se. Satisfaction might be high in the beginning of a job, stabilize or drop during the middle phase, and rise again later. Each time a person changes jobs, the cycle might repeat. Arie Shirom and Tsevi Mazeh (1988) decided to test this hypothesis and see whether this cycle happens.

How did the investigators measure the topic of interest? Shirom and Mazeh administered questionnaires containing items measuring teachers' satisfaction with salary, working hours, social status, contacts with pupils, autonomy, opportunities for professional growth, and opportunities for carrying out educational goals.

Who were the participants in the study? A representative sample of 900 Israeli junior high school teachers with varying seniority participated.

What was the design of the study? Shirom and Mazeh studied the cyclical nature of job satisfaction using a cross-sectional research design. By using sophisticated data analysis techniques, they were able to identify year-to-year changes in job satisfaction.

Were there ethical concerns with the study? There were no concerns in this study; the topics were not controversial nor were they likely to cause strongly negative feelings.

What were the results? Shirom and Mazeh found that teachers' job satisfaction followed systematic 5-year cycles that were strongly related to seniority but unrelated to age. That is, the cycles begin when the person starts a job, and the level of satisfaction is then linked to how long the person has been on the job. Because the age at which people start new teaching jobs can vary a great deal, Shirom and Mazeh were able to show that the cycles had nothing to do with how old the teachers were; all ages showed the same basic pattern.

Most interesting, Shirom and Mazeh noted that a major work-related change, a sabbatical leave, or a change in school assignment seemed to occur approximately every 5 years. They concluded that such changes reinitiated the cycle with high job satisfaction. When tracked over long periods, the cycle appears to show a steady increase in overall job satisfaction. This long-term gradual increase in job satisfaction is consistent with the general finding of gradual increases in job satisfaction with age, even though the fundamental cyclic nature of job satisfaction is unrelated to age.

What did the investigators conclude? An important implication of Shirom and Mazeh's data is that change may be necessary for long-term job satisfaction. Although the teaching profession has change built into it (such as sabbatical leaves), many occupations do not (Latack, 1984). Based on Shirom and Mazeh's data, the option of periodic changes in job structure would probably benefit other occupations as well. ●

Alienation and Burnout

No job is perfect; there is always something about it that is not as good as it could be. Perhaps the hours are not optimal, the pay is lower than one would

like, or the boss does not have a pleasant personality. For most workers, such negatives are merely annoyances. But for others, like the air traffic controller in the photograph, extremely stressful situations on the job may result in deeply rooted unhappiness with work: alienation and burnout.

When workers feel that what they are doing is meaningless and that their efforts are devalued, or when they do not see the connection between what they do and the final product, a sense of alienation *is likely to result.* Studs Terkel (1974) interviewed several alienated workers and found that all of them expressed the feeling that they were nameless, faceless cogs in a large machine.

Employees are most likely to feel alienated when they perform routine, repetitive actions such as those on an assembly line (Terkel, 1974). (Interestingly, many of these functions are being automated and performed by robots.) But other workers can become alienated, too. Especially since the beginning of corporate downsizing in the 1980s, many middle-level managers do not have the same level of job security that they once had. Consequently, their feelings toward their employers have become more negative in many cases (Roth, 1991).

How can employers avoid alienating workers? Research indicates that it is helpful to involve employees in the decision-making process, create flexible work schedules, and institute employee development and enhancement programs (Roth, 1991). Indeed, many organizations have instituted new practices such as total quality management (TQM), partly as a way to address worker alienation. TQM and related approaches make a concerted effort to get employees involved in the operation and administration of their plant or office. Such programs work; absenteeism drops and the quality of work improves in organizations that implement them (Offermann & Growing, 1990).

Sometimes the pace and pressure of the occupation becomes more than a person can bear, resulting in burnout, *a depletion of a person's energy and motivation, the loss of occupational idealism, and the feeling that one is being exploited.* Burnout is a stress syndrome, characterized by emotional exhaustion, depersonalization, and diminished personal accomplishment (Cordes & Dougherty, 1993). Burnout is most common among people in the helping professions, such as teaching, social work, and health care (Cordes & Dougherty, 1993). For example, nurses in intensive care units like the one in the photograph have high levels of burnout from stress (Iskra et al., 1996). People in these professions must constantly deal with other people's complex problems, usually under difficult time constraints. Dealing with these pressures every day, along with bureaucratic paperwork, may become too much for the worker to bear. Ideals are abandoned, frustration builds, and disillusionment and exhaustion set in. In short, the worker is burned out. The situation is exacerbated when people must work long shifts in stressful jobs (Iskra et al., 1996).

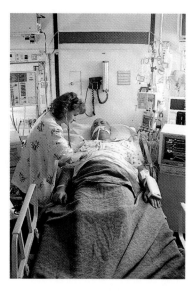

The best defenses against burnout appear to be practicing stress-reduction techniques, lowering people's expectations of themselves, and enhancing communication within organizations. Providing longer rest periods between shifts in highly stressful jobs may help (Iskra et al., 1996). No one in the helping professions can resolve all problems perfectly; lowering expectations of what can be realistically accomplished will help workers deal with real-world constraints. Similarly, improving communication among different sections of organizations, to keep workers informed of the outcome of their efforts, gives them a sense that what they do matters in the long run. Finally, research also suggests that lack of support from one's co-workers may cause depersonalization; improving such support through teamwork can be an effective intervention (Corrigan et al., 1994).

In short, making workers feel that they are important to the organization by involving them in decisions, keeping expectations realistic, ensuring good communication, and promoting teamwork helps employees avoid alienation and burnout. As organizations adopt different management styles, perhaps these goals can be achieved.

TEST YOURSELF

1. Compared with workers a few decades ago, workers today are more concerned with individual freedom, personal growth, and _____ .

2. Holland's theory deals with the relationship between occupation and _____ .

3. Super believes that through their working years, people are located along a continuum of _____ .

4. The role of a mentor is part teacher, part sponsor, part model, and part _____ .

5. Recent research has shown that job satisfaction does not increase consistently as a person ages; rather, satisfaction may be _____ .

6. Two negative aspects of job satisfaction are alienation and _____ .

7. What is the relation between Holland's theory, occupational development, and job satisfaction? Would these relations be different in the case of a person with a good match between personality and occupation rather than a poor match?

Answers: (1) cooperation, (2) personality, (3) vocational maturity, (4) counselor, (5) cyclical, (6) burnout

GENDER, ETHNICITY, AND DISCRIMINATION ISSUES

Gender, Ethnicity, and Discrimination Issues

Gender Differences in Occupational Selection

Women and Occupational Development

Ethnicity and Occupational Development

Bias and Discrimination

Learning Objectives

- **How do women's and men's occupational expectations differ? How are people viewed when they enter occupations that are not traditional for their gender?**
- **What factors are related to women's occupational development?**
- **What factors affect ethnic minority workers' occupational experiences and occupational development?**
- **What types of bias and discrimination hinder the occupational development of women and ethnic minority workers?**

*J*ANICE, *a 35-year-old African American manager at a business consulting firm, is concerned because her career is not progressing as rapidly as she had hoped. Janice works hard and has received excellent performance ratings every year. But she has noticed that there are very few women in upper management positions in her company. Janice wonders whether she will ever be promoted.*

Occupational choice and development are not equally available to all, as Janice is experiencing. Gender, ethnicity, and age may create barriers to achieving one's occupational goals. Although they're in similar occupations, the men and women depicted in the photograph on page 415 come from different backgrounds. Each received somewhat different socialization as children and adolescents, which made it easier or harder for them to set their sights on a career in the health professions. Bias and discrimination also create barriers to occupational success. In this section, we'll get a better appreciation for the personal and structural barriers that exist for many people.

GENDER DIFFERENCES IN OCCUPATIONAL SELECTION

Traditionally, men have been groomed from childhood for future employment. Boys learn at an early age that men are known by the work they do, and they are strongly encouraged to think about what occupation they would like

to have. Occupational achievement is stressed as a core element of masculinity. Important social skills are taught through team games, in which they learn how to play by the rules, to accept setbacks without taking defeat personally, to follow the guidance of a leader, and to move up the leadership hierarchy by demonstrating qualities that are valued by others.

Traditionally, women have not been trained in this manner. The skills that they have learned have been quite different: how to be accommodating, deferential, quiet, and supportive (Shainess, 1984). However, an increasing emphasis has been placed on the importance of providing girls with the necessary skills for occupations outside the home. The growth of women's athletic programs is giving more women the opportunity to learn key skills as well.

Given that over 63% of women are employed outside the home (U.S. Department of Labor, 1996), and that this number will probably continue to increase, it is especially important that women be exposed to the same occupational socialization opportunities as men. However, major structural barriers to women's occupational selection remain (Schwartz, 1992; Shaiko, 1996; Yamagata et al., 1997). It is still the case that many occupational opportunities are more available to men than to women (Lyness & Thompson, 1997).

? **THINK ABOUT IT**
What changes in children's school and other socialization experiences will allow girls to acquire different skills?

Traditional and Nontraditional Occupations

In the past, women employed outside the home tended to enter traditional, female-dominated occupations such as secretarial, teaching, and social work jobs. This was due mainly to their socialization into these occupational tracks. However, as more women enter the work force and as new opportunities are opened for women, a growing number of them work in occupations that have traditionally been male-dominated, such as construction and engineering. Research in this area has focused on three issues (Swanson, 1992): selection of nontraditional occupations, characteristics of women in nontraditional occupations, and perceptions of nontraditional occupations.

Why some women end up in nontraditional occupations appears to be related to personal feelings and experiences as well as expectations about the occupation (Brooks & Betz, 1990). Concerning personal experiences, women who attend single-sex high schools and who have both brothers and sisters end up in the least traditional occupations, apparently because they have been exposed to more options and fewer gender-role stereotypes (Rubenfeld & Gilroy, 1991). Personal feelings are important; a study of Japanese students found that women had significantly lower confidence in their ability to perform in male-dominated occupations than in female-dominated occupations (Matsui, Ikeda, & Ohnishi, 1989).

The characteristics of women in nontraditional occupations have been studied as well. Betz, Heesacker, and Shuttleworth (1990) found that women who scored high on femininity, as defined by endorsing traditional feminine gender roles, and those in female-dominated occupations had the poorest match between their abilities and their occupational choices. These findings mean that women who score high on traditional measures of femininity have difficulty finding occupations that allow them to take advantage of their abilities. Additionally, women in female-dominated occupations generally find that their jobs do not allow them to use their abilities to the fullest. In sum, it appears that many women have difficulty finding occupations that match their skills.

Despite the efforts to counteract gender stereotyping of occupations, women who choose nontraditional occupations are still viewed with disapproval by their peers of either sex, even though they have high job satisfaction themselves (Brabeck & Weisgerber, 1989; Pfost & Fiore, 1990). This finding holds up in cross-cultural research as well. In a study conducted in India, both women and men gave higher "respectability" ratings to males than to females in the same occupation (Kanekar, Kolsawalla, & Nazareth, 1989). People even make inferences about working conditions based on their perception of an occupation as traditionally masculine or feminine. Scozzaro and Subich (1990) report that occupations such as the secretarial job depicted are perceived as offering nice working conditions, whereas male-dominated occupations are perceived as offering good pay and promotion potential. Worst of all, people are less likely to perceive incidents of sexual coercion as harassing when a woman is in a nontraditional occupation (Burgess & Borgida, 1997).

Taken together, these studies show that we still have a long way to go before people can choose any occupation they want without having to contend with gender-related stereotypes. Although differences in opportunities for women in traditional and nontraditional occupations are narrowing, key differences remain. Finally, virtually no research has examined differences between males in traditional and nontraditional occupations (Swanson, 1992). This lack of data is troubling, for it prevents our answering important questions such as why men choose traditional or nontraditional occupations, and why some men still perpetuate gender stereotypes about particular occupations.

WOMEN AND OCCUPATIONAL DEVELOPMENT

If you were to guess what the young woman in the photograph who has just graduated from college will be doing occupationally 10 years from now, what would you say? Would you guess that she will be strongly committed to her occupation? Will she have abandoned it for other things? Betz (1984) wanted to know the answers to these questions, so she examined the occupational histories of 500 college women 10 years after graduation. Two-thirds of these women were highly committed to their occupations, which for 70% were traditionally female ones. Most had worked continuously since graduation. Only 1% had been full-time homemakers during the entire 10-year period; 79% reported that they had successfully combined occupations with homemaking. Women in traditional female occupations changed jobs less often. If they did change, the move was more likely to be to a job with a lower rank and pay compared to the changes made by women in nontraditional occupations.

An intriguing question is why highly educated women leave what appear to be well-paid occupations. Studies of women MBAs with children have identified a number of family and workplace issues (Rosin & Korabik, 1990, 1991). Family obligations, such as child care, appear to be most important for mothers working part-time. For these women, adequate child care arrangements or having the flexibility to be at home when children get out of school often make the difference between being able to accept a job or remaining at home. In contrast, mothers who have made the decision to work full-time have resolved the problem of child care. The most important workplace issues for these women are gender-related. Unsupportive or insensitive work environments, organizational politics, and the lack of occupational development opportunities appear most important for women working full-time (Schwartz, 1992). In this case, women are focusing on issues that create barriers to their occupational development and are looking for ways around the barriers.

Such barriers are a major reason why women's work force participation is discontinuous. Because they cannot find affordable and dependable child care, or freely choose to take on this responsibility, many women stay home while their children are young. Discontinuous participation makes it difficult to maintain an upward trajectory in one's career through promotion, and in terms of maintaining skills. Some women make this choice willingly; however, many find themselves forced into it.

ETHNICITY AND OCCUPATIONAL DEVELOPMENT

What factors are related to occupational selection and development for people from ethnic minorities? Unfortunately, not much research has been conducted from a developmental perspective. Rather, most researchers have focused on the limited opportunities ethnic minorities have and the structural barriers, such as discrimination, that they face. Most of the developmental research to date focuses on occupational selection issues and variables that foster occupational development. Three topics have received the most focus: nontraditional occupations, vocational identity, and issues pertaining to occupational aspirations.

African American women and European American women do not differ in terms of plans to enter nontraditional occupations (Murrell, Frieze, & Frost, 1991). However, African American women who choose nontraditional occupations tend to plan for more formal education than necessary to achieve their goal. This may actually make them overqualified for the jobs they get; for example, a woman with a college degree may be working in a job that does not require that level of education.

Vocational identity is the degree to which one views one's occupation as a key element of identity. Research shows that vocational identity varies with both ethnicity and gender. Compared to European American women and Hispanic American men, African American and European American men have higher vocational identity when they graduate from college (Steward & Krieshok, 1991). Lower vocational identity means that people define themselves primarily in terms of aspects of their lives other than work.

A person's occupational aspiration is the kind of occupation he or she would like to have. In contrast, occupational expectation is the occupation the person believes he or she will actually get. Hispanic Americans differ from European Americans in several ways with regard to these variables. They have high occupational aspirations but low expectations, and they differ in their educational attainment as a function of national origin, generational status, and social class (Arbona, 1990). However, Hispanic Americans are similar to European Americans in occupational development and work values.

Research on occupational development of ethnic minority workers is clear on one point: Whether an organization is responsive to the needs of ethnic minorities like the African American woman in the photograph makes a big difference for employees. Both European American and ethnic minority managers who perceive their organizations as responsive and positive for ethnic minority employees are more satisfied with and committed to the organizations (Burke, 1991a, 1991b). But much still remains to be accomplished. African American managers report less choice of jobs, less acceptance, more career dissatisfaction, lower performance evaluations and promotability ratings, and more rapid attainment of plateaus in their careers than European American managers (Greenhaus, Parasuraman, & Wormley, 1990). Over 60% of African American protégés have European American mentors, which is problematic because same-ethnicity mentors provide more psychosocial support than cross-ethnicity mentors (Thomas, 1990). Nevertheless, having any mentor is more beneficial than having none (Bridges, 1996).

BIAS AND DISCRIMINATION

Since the 1960s, organizations in the United States have been sensitized to the issues of bias and discrimination in the workplace. Hiring, promotion, and termination procedures have come under close scrutiny in numerous court cases, resulting in judicial rulings governing these processes.

Gender Bias and the Glass Ceiling

Even though the majority of women work outside the home, women in high-status jobs are unusual (Morrison et al., 1992). Not until 1981 was a woman, Sandra Day O'Connor, appointed to the U.S. Supreme Court; it took another 12 years before a second woman, Ruth Bader Ginsburg, was appointed. As Janice noticed in the vignette, few women serve in the highest ranks of major corporations, and women are substantially outnumbered at the senior faculty level of most universities and colleges.

Why are there so few women? *The most important reason is* sex discrimination, *denying a job to someone solely on the basis of whether the person is a man or a woman.* Baron and Bielby (1985) pull no punches in discussing sex discrimination. "Our analyses portray [sex] discrimination as pervasive, almost omnipresent, sustained by diverse organizational structures and processes. Moreover, this segregation drastically restricts women's career opportunities, by blocking access to internal labor markets and their benefits" (Baron & Bielby, 1985, p. 245). Despite some progress over the past two decades, sex discrimination is still common; women are being kept out of high-status jobs by the men at the top (Lyness & Thompson, 1997; Shaiko, 1996; Yamagata et al., 1997).

Women themselves refer to a glass ceiling, *the level to which they may rise in a company but beyond which they may not go.* This problem is most obvious in companies that classify jobs at various levels (as does the Civil Service). The greatest barrier facing women is at the boundary between lower-tier and upper-tier job grades (Morrison et al., 1992). Women like Janice tend to move to the top of the lower tier and remain there, whereas men are more readily promoted to the upper tier, even when other factors, such as personal attributes and qualifications, are controlled (DiPrete & Soule, 1988). Indeed, a longitudinal study of women in the high school class of 1972 showed that despite better academic records, women's achievement in the workplace is limited by structural barriers (Adelman, 1991). The U.S. Department of Labor (1991) admitted that the glass ceiling pervades the workplace. Some surveys indicate that over 90% of women believe that there is a glass ceiling in the workplace. Clear evidence of the glass ceiling has been found in private corporations (Lyness & Thompson, 1997), government agencies (Yamagata et al., 1997), and nonprofit organizations (Shaiko, 1996). Indeed, estimates are that if the present rate of advancement continues, it will take until the late 25th century for women to achieve equality with men in the executive suite (Feminist Majority Foundation, 1991).

Besides discrimination in hiring and promotion, women are also subject to pay discrimination. According to the U.S. Department of Labor, in many occupations men are paid substantially more than women in the same positions; indeed, on average, women are paid less than three-fourths of what men are paid on an annual basis (U.S. Department of Labor, 1997). The situation is

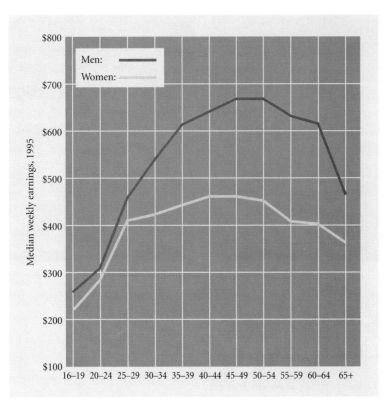

much worse for women of color; African American women only earn roughly 63% and Hispanic American women earn roughly 57% as much as white men (Castro, 1997). Even more distressing, the gender wage gap remains substantial even when educational backgrounds are equivalent (Castro, 1997).

Such averages conceal important developmental aspects of the gender difference: The wage gap widens over women's working years (Castro, 1997). As you can see in the graph, the wage gap begins widening rapidly in the 30s, and remains substantial through age 65. These broadening differences reflect several factors: sex discrimination, the discontinuous participation of women in the work force, and the disproportionate number of women in low-paying jobs (Castro, 1997).

Several solutions to this problem have been promoted. *One of these is* comparable worth: *equalizing pay in occupations that are determined to be equivalent in importance but differ in the gender distribution of the people doing the jobs.* Determining which male-dominated occupations should be considered equivalent to which female-dominated occupations for pay purposes can be difficult and controversial. One way to do this is with gender-neutral job evaluations, which examine all positions within an organization in order to establish fair-pay policies (Castro, 1997).

Sexual Harassment

Although sexual harassment of women has been documented for centuries, only recently has it received much attention from researchers (Fitzgerald & Shullman, 1993). Interest among U.S. researchers increased dramatically after the 1991 Senate hearings involving Supreme Court nominee Clarence Thomas and Anita Hill, who accused him of sexual harassment, the scandals involving military personnel, and charges against President Bill Clinton. By no means is sexual harassment a U.S.-only phenomenon; sad to say, it occurs around the world (Luo, 1996).

Research on sexual harassment focuses on situations in which there is a power differential between two people, most often involving men with more power over women (Berdahl, Magley, & Waldo, 1996). Such situations exist in the workplace and in academic settings (Zappert, 1996). However, peer-to-peer harassment also occurs, such as among classmates in academic settings (Ivy & Hamlet, 1996).

How many people have been sexually harassed? Evidence suggests that about 70% of women report they "had experienced or heard offensive slurs or jokes or remarks about women" (Piotrkowski, 1998). Interestingly, men report a similar level of such behavior. Reliable statistics on more serious forms of harassment, such as touching and sexual activity, are more difficult to obtain, in part due to the unwillingness of many victims to report harassment and to differences in reporting procedures. Indeed, estimates are that less than 5% of victims ever report their experiences to anyone in authority (Fitzgerald et al., 1988). Even given these difficulties, several studies document that over 40% of women report having been sexually harassed in the workplace at least once (Fitzgerald & Shullman, 1993). Victims are most often single or divorced women under age 35 (Tang & McCollum, 1996).

What effects does being sexually harassed have? Research evidence shows clear, negative emotional, mental health, and job-related outcomes (Schneider, Swan, & Fitzgerald, 1997). Establishing the degree of problems is difficult, though, because many women try to minimize or hide their reactions or feelings (Tang & McCollum, 1996). It is becoming evident, though, that one does not have to experience the worst kinds of sexual harassment in order to be affected. Even low-level but frequent experience of sexual harassment can have significant negative consequences for women (Schneider et al., 1997).

Sexual harassment also has numerous ripple effects throughout a company (Piotrkowski, in progress, cited in Murray, 1998). For example, men in all ethnic backgrounds who work in companies that have cases of sexual harassment, but who are not harassers themselves, report less satisfaction with their jobs. Productivity at such companies also declines, as does general worker morale.

Of course, the crux of the matter is what constitutes harassment. What would have to be going on in the situation depicted in the photograph for you to say that it is harassment? Using ambiguous situations like this is a technique that many researchers use. In fact, research on perceptions of what constitutes harassing behavior usually requires people to read vignettes of hypothetical incidents involving sexually suggestive touching, sexual remarks, and the like, and then decide whether it was harassment. In general, women are more likely to view such behaviors as offensive than are men (Berdahl, Magley, & Waldo, 1996; Fitzgerald & Ormerod, 1991). *Because of this gender gap in perceptions, a federal court, in the case of* Ellison v. Brady, *instituted the* "reasonable woman" standard *as the appropriate legal criterion for determining whether sexual harassment has occurred.* If a rea-

sonable woman would view a behavior as offensive, the court held, then it is offensive even if the man did not consider it to be so. Even this standard, though, is more likely to be understood by women than by men (Wiener et al., 1997).

? THINK ABOUT IT
What are the key biological, psychological, and sociocultural factors that should inform training programs concerning sexual harassment?

Besides the gender of the perceiver, several other factors influence whether a behavior is considered offensive (Fitzgerald & Ormerod, 1991). These include the degree to which the behavior is explicit or extreme (e.g., rape as against a friendly kiss), victim behavior (whether the victim was at all responsible for what happened), supervisory status (whether the perpetrator was a direct supervisor of the victim), harasser's intentions (whether the perpetrator knew that the victim found the behavior offensive), and frequency of occurrence (e.g., a one-time occurrence as opposed to a regular event). Cultural differences are also important. For example, one study found that U.S. women judged specific interactions as more harassing than U.S. men, but women and men from Australia, Brazil, and Germany did not differ in their judgments (Pryor et al., 1997). Unfortunately, little research has been done to identify what aspects of organizations foster harassment or to determine the impact of educational programs aimed at addressing the problem.

In 1998, the U.S. Supreme Court (*Oncale v. Sundowner Offshore Services*) ruled that sexual harassment is not limited to female victims, but that the relevant laws also protect men. This case is also important for establishing that same-sex harassment is barred by the same laws that ban heterosexual harassment. Thus, the standard by which sexual harassment is judged could now be said to be a "reasonable person" standard.

What can be done to provide people with safe work and learning environments, free from sexual harassment? Training in gender awareness is a common approach that often works (Tang & McCollum, 1996). Clearly differentiating between workplace romance and sexual harassment is another essential element (Pierce & Aguinis, 1997). The Current Controversies feature discusses the complexities involved in solving the problem. Take a minute to read it, and ask yourself what you would do.

CURRENT CONTROVERSIES

INFOTRAC
COLLEGE EDITION

To learn more, enter the following search term: sexual harrassment.

SEXUAL HARASSMENT IN THE WORKPLACE

No policy topic captured the public's attention faster in the 1990s than sexual harassment. The watershed event was the 1991 Senate Judiciary Committee confirmation hearings concerning Clarence Thomas's nomination as an Associate Justice of the U.S. Supreme Court. Thomas was accused of sexual harassment by a former employee, Anita Hill. In dramatic testimony, broadcast live, charges and countercharges were debated for days. Even though Thomas was eventually confirmed, the event sparked a widespread political and social consciousness raising. The topic received further attention when various branches of the U.S. military investigated a series of serious sexual harassment charges in training and in field settings, and President Bill Clinton was accused of sexual harassment for actions while he was governor of Arkansas.

The main problem confronting society in the wake of these events is how to define sexual harassment. As noted in the text, the courts adopted the "reasonable woman" standard. But how does this standard get translated into specific behavioral guidelines that both men and women interpret in the same way? How do people know ahead of time whether what they plan to do or say is or is not harassment?

Of course, it is relatively easy to define what is clearly not harassment (such as normal social interactions, polite compliments, or friendly conversation) and what clearly is (such as rape, asking for sex in return for a good job evaluation or a grade, or sending hate mail of a sexual nature). What is extraordinarily difficult to articulate is the in-between area, the "gray zone," of all the behaviors between the two extremes. Is telling someone that they look "great" in a particular outfit harassment? How about yelling "babe" or "hunk" at someone? What about asking someone out on a date?

Answers to these questions are complicated because they depend on where they occur (at work/school or at home) and whether or not one person has a supervisory position over the other. Increasingly, behaviors that used to be written off as "boys will be boys" are now being ruled as harassing, because the victims interpret them as such. For example, several cases of name-calling in high schools (such as "slut") have been ruled to constitute harassment; the victims have successfully argued that they suffered psychological harm.

You should take a minute or two and think about what your definition of sexual harassment is. Have you ever experienced harassment? How did you feel? How has that experience affected your views? You might then talk it over with other people of both sexes to see how your definition and experiences are similar or different. One thing is certain. It is likely that the issue of sexual harassment will remain controversial for years to come. •

Age Discrimination

Another structural barrier to occupational development is age discrimination, *which involves denying a job or promotion to someone solely on the basis of age.* The U.S. Age Discrimination in Employment Act of 1986 protects workers over age 40. This law stipulates that people must be hired based on their ability, not their age. Under this law, employers are banned from refusing to hire and from discharging workers like the man in the photograph solely on the basis of age. Additionally, employers cannot segregate or classify workers or otherwise denote their status on the basis of age.

Employment prospects for middle-aged people around the world are lower than for their younger counterparts. For example, age discrimination toward those over age 45 is common in Germany (Frerichs & Naegele, 1997) and Britain (Ginn & Arber, 1996), resulting in long periods of unemployment and early retirement. Such practices may save companies money in the short run, but the loss of expertise and knowledge comes at a high price. Indeed, global corporations are beginning to realize that retraining and integrating middle-aged workers is a better strategy (Frerichs & Naegele, 1997).

Age discrimination occurs in several ways (Snyder & Barrett, 1988). For example, employers can make certain types of physical or mental performance a job requirement and argue that older workers cannot meet the standard. Or they can attempt to get rid of older workers by using retirement. Supervisors sometimes use age as a factor in performance evaluations for raises or promotions or in decisions about which employees are eligible for additional training.

Perceptions of age discrimination are widespread; nearly 1,600 suits were filed in 1993 alone, up from roughly 1,100 in 1990 (Cornish, 1994). Many of these cases stem from the corporate downsizing that began in the late 1980s. Winning an age discrimination case is difficult, however (Snyder & Barrett, 1988). Job performance information is crucial.

However, most companies tend to report this information in terms of general differences between younger and older adults (such as differences in recent memory ability) rather than in specific terms of older and younger workers in a particular occupation (which rarely show any differences in productivity or performance). Surprisingly, many courts do not question inaccurate information or stereotypic views of aging presented by employers, despite the lack of scientific data documenting age differences in actual job performance.

FORCES IN ACTION

OCCUPATIONAL SUCCESS IS MORE THAN JUST HARD WORK

At some point in your life, you probably were told (and maybe believed) that choosing an occupation and enjoying occupational success were both simply a matter of working hard and performing well. As you've gotten older and experienced the world of work, you have probably seen firsthand (or you will) that there is more to it than that. The biopsychosocial model provides a good framework for understanding how people choose their occupations and develop in them.

Biological forces help shape job-related abilities and skills to the extent that the skills have a genetic component (some people are clearly "natural" athletes or chemists; others are not). Whether a person actually develops these innate abilities depends in part on psychological forces such as personality and behavior. These forces find expression in what people "like" to do, the choices they make about which courses to take, or the kinds of extracurricular activities they try. Holland's theory stresses the importance of psychological forces. But whether people actually have the opportunity to make these choices reflects the social forces that either create or limit options. The powerful social forces of socioeconomic class, prejudice, and discrimination, among others, opens doors for some and closes doors for others. These social forces are a major factor in antidiscrimination, affirmative action, and related legislation in the United States. But reality also tells us that a person's position in the life cycle confers a relative advantage (or disadvantage) in a competitive job market. Two individuals with identical skills and experience may not be viewed as equivalent by an organization if one is 25 and the other 55. So it matters a great deal *when* in our lives opportunity comes knocking. •

TEST YOURSELF

1. Women who choose nontraditional occupations are viewed _____ by their peers.

2. Among reasons why women in well-paid occupations leave, _____ are most important for part-time workers.

3. Ethnic minority workers are more satisfied with and committed to organizations that are responsive and provide _____ .

4. Three barriers to women's occupational development are sex discrimination, the glass ceiling, and _____ .

5. What steps need to be taken in order to eliminate gender, ethnic, and age bias in the workplace?

Answers: (1) negatively, (2) family obligations, (3) positive work environments, (4) pay discrimination

OCCUPATIONAL TRANSITIONS

Learning Objectives

- **Why do people change occupations?**

- **Is worrying about potential job loss a major source of stress?**

- **How does the timing of job loss affect the amount of stress experienced?**

Occupational Transitions

Retraining Workers

Occupational Insecurity

Coping with Unemployment

*F*RED *has 32 years of service for an automobile manufacturer. Over the years, more and more assembly-line jobs have been eliminated by robots and other technology, and the export of manufacturing jobs to other countries. Although Fred has been assured by his boss that his job is safe, he isn't so sure. He worries that he could be laid off at any time.*

In the past, people like Fred commonly chose an occupation during young adulthood and stayed in it throughout their working years. Today, however, not many people take a job with the expectation that it will last a lifetime. Changing jobs is almost taken for granted; the average North American will change jobs between five and ten times during adulthood (Toffler, 1970). Some authors view occupational changes as positive; Havighurst (1982), for example, strongly advocates such flexibility. According to his view, building change into the occupational life cycle may help to avoid disillusionment with one's initial choice. Changing occupations may be one way to guarantee challenging and satisfying work, and it may be the best option for those in a position to exercise it (Shirom & Mazeh, 1988). The case of Kevin, told in the Real People feature, exemplifies many of these aspects of occupational change.

REAL PEOPLE

CHANGING OCCUPATIONS TO FIND SATISFYING WORK

From the time he was in college, Kevin knew he wanted to be an accountant. His only question was whether it would be in a large public accounting firm or in a private corporation. After much consideration (and several job offers), he chose to work for a major global corporation. Kevin rose through the ranks, and all seemed well. He eventually was in charge of the Far East division of the international tax unit, which allowed him to travel to fun and exotic places.

However, Kevin's company, like many others, went through several rounds of downsizing. Although his job was extremely secure, Kevin saw his staff reduced considerably. These cuts led to many long hours and much more job stress. So, after 17 years with the company, Kevin decided that even though the pay was good, the hours and the stress were not worth it. He left, and began working for a start-up biotechnology firm. At first, conditions were much better. But soon the long hours and stress started in again. This time, he quit with no new job. He needed time to think and re-set his priorities.

After much careful thought, he decided that what he really wanted was to work in a nonprofit organization. Eventually, he ended up with a large foundation that funds minority businesses and other community-based companies.

The change for Kevin has been very successful. Although he makes less money than he did in the private sector, he is much happier and less stressed. And for him, this is worth it all. ●

Several factors have been identified as important in determining who will remain in an occupation and who will change. Some factors—such as whether the person likes the occupation—lead to self-initiated occupation changes like Kevin experienced. For example, people who really like their occupation may seek additional training like those in the photograph or accept overtime assignments in hopes of acquiring new skills that will enable them to get better jobs. Others will use the training to become more marketable. However, other factors, such as obsolete skills and economic trends, cause forced occupational changes. For example, continued improvement of robots has caused some auto industry workers to lose their jobs; corporations send jobs overseas in order to increase profits; and economic recessions usually result in large-scale layoffs. But even forced occupational changes can have benefits. As we will see in Chapter 12, for instance, many adults go to college. Some are taking advantage of educational benefits offered as part of a separation package. Others are pursuing educational opportunities in order to obtain new skills; still others are looking to advance in their careers.

In this section, we explore the positive and negative aspects of occupational transitions. First we examine the retraining of mid-career and older workers. The increased use of technology, corporate downsizing, and an aging work force have focused attention on the need to keep older workers' skills current. Later, we will examine occupational insecurity and the effects of job loss.

RETRAINING WORKERS

When you are hired into a specific job, you are selected because your employer believes you offer the best fit between abilities you already have and those needed to perform the job. As most people can attest, though, the skills needed to perform a job usually change over time. Such changes may be due to the introduction of new technology, additional responsibilities, or promotion.

Unless a person's skills are kept up-to-date, the outcome is likely to be either job loss or career plateauing (Froman, 1994). Career plateauing *occurs when there is a lack of promotional opportunity in the organization or when a person decides not to seek advancement.* In cases of job loss or career plateauing, retraining may be an appropriate response. Nearly one-third of the U.S. work force participates each year in courses aimed at improving job skills (American

Council on Education, 1997). One objective of these courses is to improve technical skills, such as new computer skills. For mid-career or older employees, who make up the largest percentage of those who take courses (American Council on Education, 1997), retraining might focus on how to advance in one's occupation or how to find new career opportunities—for example, through résumé preparation and career counseling.

Many corporations, as well as community and technical colleges, offer retraining programs in a variety of fields. Organizations that promote employee development typically promote in-house courses to improve employee skills. Or they may offer tuition reimbursement programs for individuals who successfully complete courses at colleges or universities.

The retraining of mid-career and older workers highlights the need for lifelong learning (Sinnott, 1994). If corporations are to meet the challenges of a global economy, it is imperative that they include retraining in their employee development programs. Such programs will help improve people's chances of advancement in their chosen occupations, and they will also assist people in making successful transitions from one occupation to another.

OCCUPATIONAL INSECURITY

Changing economic conditions in the United States over the past few decades (such as the move toward a global economy), as well as changing demographics, have forced many people out of their jobs. Heavy manufacturing and support businesses (such as the steel, oil, and automotive industries) and farming were the hardest hit during the 1970s and 1980s. But no one is immune. Indeed, the corporate takeover frenzy of the 1980s and the recession of the early 1990s put many middle- and upper-level corporate executives out of work in all kinds of businesses.

As a result of these trends, many people feel insecure about their jobs. Like Fred, the auto worker in the vignette, many worried workers have numerous years of dedicated service to a corporation. Unfortunately, people who worry about their jobs tend to have poorer mental health (Roskies & Louis-Guerin, 1990). For example, anxiety about one's job may result in negative attitudes about one's employer or even work in general, which in turn may result in diminished desire to be successful. Whether there is any actual basis for people's feelings of job insecurity may not matter; sometimes what people think is true about their work situation is more important than what is actually the case. If people believe that they are at risk of losing their jobs, their mental health and behavior are often affected negatively even when the actual risk of losing their jobs is very low (Roskies & Louis-Guerin, 1990).

? THINK ABOUT IT
How do recent changes in job security affect the occupational socialization that children and adolescents receive?

COPING WITH UNEMPLOYMENT

What does it feel like to lose one's job after many years of dedicated service? One man put it this way.

> After becoming used to living like a human being, then losing your job, working six days a week just to make the house payment for two years before selling it at a loss, then losing your wife because of all the hardships that were not your fault,

then looking endlessly for a decent job only to find jobs for [minimum wage so that I] can't afford an apartment or any place to live so having to live out of a van for the past two-and-one-half years, *how should one feel?* Please, I'm a hard worker and did a good job. I always go to work—check my record! I want to be normal again, like a real human being with a house instead of a van. (Leana & Feldman, 1992, p. 51)

As this man states so poignantly, losing one's job can have enormous personal impact (DeFrank & Ivancevich, 1986). Unemployed people like those in the photograph commonly experience declines in physical health and self-esteem, alcohol abuse, depression, anxiety, and suicide (Lajer, 1982; Viinamaki, Koskela, & Niskanen, 1996). Men and women generally experience similar levels of distress following the loss of a job (Leana & Feldman, 1991; Vosler & Page-Adams, 1996). However, these effects vary with age. Middle-aged men are more vulnerable to negative effects than older or younger men, largely because they have greater financial responsibilities than the other two groups (DeFrank & Ivancevich, 1986).

Besides the degree of financial strain, the extent of the distress from losing a job is related to the timing of the loss in the adult life cycle (Estes & Wilensky, 1978). Lajer (1982) reports that admission to a psychiatric unit following job loss is more likely for people who are over age 45 or have been unemployed for a long period. However, Leana and Feldman (1992) write that workers in their 50s who lose their jobs are not always highly distressed. Some may have been planning to retire in the near future, others may be hired back as consultants, and still others see it as an opportunity to try something new.

Because unemployment rates for many ethnic minority groups are substantially higher than for European Americans (U.S. Department of Labor, 1997), the effects of unemployment are experienced by a greater proportion of people in these groups. As far as is known, however, the nature of the distress resulting from job loss is the same regardless of ethnicity. Compared to European Americans, however, it usually takes minority workers longer to find another job.

? THINK ABOUT IT
What are some of the broader effects of unemployment on an individual's personal and family life?

TEST YOURSELF

1. One response to the pressures of a global economy and an aging work force is to provide _____ .

2. Two factors that could cause involuntary occupational change are economic trends and _____ .

3. Fear of job loss is often a more important determinant of stress than _____ .

4. The age group that is most at risk for negative effects of job loss is _____ .

5. It is likely that the trend toward multiple careers will continue and become the norm. What implications will this have for theories of career development in the future?

WORK AND FAMILY

Learning Objectives

- **What are the issues faced by employed people who care for dependents?**

- **How do partners view the division of household chores? What is work-family conflict? How does it affect couples' lives?**

Work and Family

The Dependent Care Dilemma

Juggling Multiple Roles

ENNIFER, a 38-year-old sales clerk at a department store, feels that her husband, Bill, doesn't do his share of the housework or child care. Bill says that real men don't do housework, and that he's really tired when he comes home from work. Jennifer thinks that this isn't fair, especially because she works as many hours as her husband.

One of the most difficult challenges facing adults like Jennifer is trying to balance the demands of occupation with the demands of family. Over the past few decades, the rapid increase in the number of families in which both parents are employed has fundamentally changed how we view the relation between work and family. As the photograph shows, this can even mean taking a young child to work as a way to deal with the pushes and pulls of being an employed parent. In nearly two-thirds of two-parent households today, both adults work outside the home (U.S. Department of Labor, 1997). The main reason? Families need the dual income in order to pay the bills and maintain a moderate standard of living.

As we will see, dual-earner couples with children experience both benefits and costs from this arrangement. The stresses of living in this arrangement are substantial—and gender differences are clear, especially in the division of household chores.

THE DEPENDENT CARE DILEMMA

Many employed adults must also provide care for dependent children or parents. As we will see, the issues they face are complex.

Employed Caregivers Revisited

Many mothers have no option but to return to work after the birth of a child. In fact, 56% of married mothers and nearly half of unmarried mothers with children under the age of 1 year are in the work force (U.S. Department of Labor, 1997). The number of mothers in the work force with children of any age is even higher. As you can see in the graph, the overall number of women in the work force with children under age 18 has increased dramatically since the mid-1970s (U.S. Department of Labor, 1997).

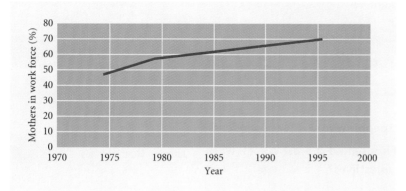

Some women, though, grapple with the decision of whether they want to return. Surveys of mothers with preschool children reveal that the motivation for returning to work tends to be related to how attached mothers are to their work. For example, in one survey of Australian mothers, those with high work attachment were more likely to cite intrinsic personal achievement reasons for returning. Those with low work attachment cited pressing financial needs. Those with moderate work attachment were divided between intrinsic and financial reasons (Cotton, Anthill, & Cunningham, 1989). Those who can afford to give up careers and stay home also must deal with changes in identity (Milford, 1997). Giving up a career means that those aspects of one's identity that came from work must be redefined to come from being a stay-at-home mother.

An increasing and often overlooked group of employed caregivers are those caring for a parent or partner. Of women in this situation, 60% work at least 35 hours per week (Jenkins, 1997). Because most of these women are middle aged, we will consider their situation in more detail in Chapter 12.

Whether assistance is needed for one's children or parent, key factors in selecting an appropriate care site are quality of care, price, and hours of availability (Metropolitan Area Agency on Aging, 1998; Vandell, Pierce, & Stright, 1997). Depending on one's economic situation, it may not be possible to find affordable and quality care that is available when needed. In such cases, there may be no option but to drop out of the work force or enlist the help of friends and family.

Dependent Care and Effects on Workers

Workers who care for dependents face tough choices. Especially when both partners are employed, dependent care is the central organizing aspect of the couple's lives (Hertz, 1997).

Being responsible for dependent care has significant negative effects, especially for women. For example, when they are responsible for caring for an older parent, women report missing more meetings and being absent from work more often (Gignac, Kelloway, & Gottlieb, 1996). Such women also report higher levels of stress (Jenkins, 1997). Likewise, parents often exhibit poor quality of life, and report higher stress and trouble coping with it (Galinsky, Bond, & Friedman, 1996).

How can these negative effects be lessened? For example, when women's partners provide good support and women have average or high control over their jobs, employed mothers are significantly less distressed than employed nonmothers (Roxburgh, 1997). When support and job control are lacking, though, employed mothers are significantly more distressed than employed nonmothers. Clearly, having partner support and being in a job that allows one to have control over such things as one's schedule is key. What employers provide is also important, as we see next.

? THINK ABOUT IT
How do the effects of dependent care on mothers relate to the debate on whether children should be placed in day care?

Dependent Care and Employer Responses

Employed parents with small children are confronted with the difficult act of leaving their children in the care of others. In response to pressure from parents, most industrialized countries (but not the United States) provide government-supported child care centers for employees as one way to help ease this burden. Does providing a center make a difference in terms of an employee's feelings about work, absenteeism, and productivity?

The answer is that there is no simple answer. Just making a child care center like the one in the photograph available to employees does not necessarily reduce parents' work-family conflict or their absenteeism (Goff, Mount, & Jamison, 1990). A "family-friendly" company must also pay attention to the attitudes of their employees and make sure that the company provides broad-based support. The key is how supervisors act. Irrespective of where the child care center is located, when supervisors are sympathetic and supportive regarding family issues and child care, parents report less work-family conflict and have lower absenteeism.

Research on specific working conditions and benefits that help caregivers perform optimally on the job points to several consistent conclusions. To the extent that employers provide better job security, autonomy, lower productivity demands, supervisor support, and flexible schedules, caregivers fare better (Aryee & Luk, 1996; Frone & Yardley, 1996; Galinsky et al., 1996).

It will be interesting to watch how these issues, especially flexible schedules, play out in the United States over the next several years. With the passage of the Family and Medical Leave Act in 1993, for the first time people will be able to take unpaid time off to care for their dependents, having the right to return to their jobs. Experience from other countries indicates that parental leave affects each parent differently. For example, a large-scale study in Sweden showed that fathers who take parental leave are more likely to continue their involvement in child care and to reduce their work involvement. Regardless of fathers' participation, however, mothers still retain primary responsibility for child care and stay less involved in and receive fewer rewards in the labor market (Haas, 1990; Schwartz, 1992).

JUGGLING MULTIPLE ROLES

When both members of a heterosexual couple with dependents are employed, who cleans the house, cooks the meals, and takes care of the children when they are ill? This question gets to the heart of the core dilemma of modern, dual-earner couples: How are household chores divided? How are work and family role conflicts handled?

Dividing Household Chores

Despite much media attention and claims of increased sharing in the duties, women still perform the lion's share of housework, regardless of employment status. Working mothers spend about twice as many hours per week as men in family work and bear the greatest responsibility for household and child care tasks (Benin & Agostinelli, 1988). This unequal division of labor causes the most arguments and the most unhappiness for dual-earner couples. This is the case with Jennifer and Bill, the couple in the vignette; Jennifer does most of the housework.

A great deal of evidence indicates that since the 1970s women have reduced the amount of time they spend on housework, especially when they are employed, and that men have increased the amount of time they spend on

such tasks (Swanson, 1992). The increased participation of men in these tasks is not all that it seems, however. Most of the increase is on weekends, with specific tasks that they agree to perform, and it is largely unrelated to women's employment status (Zick & McCullough, 1991). In short, the increase in men's participation has not done much to lower women's burdens around the house, as the photograph shows.

Men and women view the division of labor in very different terms. Men are often most satisfied with an equitable division of labor based on the number of hours spent, especially if the amount of time needed to perform household tasks is relatively small. Women are often most satisfied when men are willing to perform women's traditional chores (Benin & Agostinelli, 1988). When ethnic minorities are studied, much the same is true concerning satisfaction. For example, in African American dual-earner couples, women were twice as likely as men to feel overburdened with housework and to be dissatisfied with their family life (Broman, 1988).

Ethnic differences in the division of household labor are also apparent. In a study of European American, African American, and Hispanic American men, several interesting patterns emerged (Shelton & John, 1993). African American and Hispanic American men tend to spend more time doing household tasks than do European American men. In the case of African American men, this finding supports the view that such households are more egalitarian than European American households. Moreover, the increased participation of African American men was primarily true of employed (as opposed to unemployed) men. There was greater participation in traditionally female tasks, such as washing dishes and cooking. Similarly, Hispanic American men also tended to participate more in these tasks. Overall, European American men spent the least time helping with traditionally female tasks. Clearly, the degree to which men and women divide household tasks varies not only with gender, but with ethnicity as well.

In sum, the available evidence from heterosexual couples indicates that women still perform more household tasks than men, but that the difference varies with ethnic groups. The discrepancy is greatest when the male endorses traditional masculine gender roles and is less when the male endorses more feminine or androgynous gender roles (Gunter & Gunter, 1990).

Work-Family Conflict

When people have both occupations and children, they must figure out how to balance the demands of each. People agonize over how to be at their daughter's ball game at the same time they have to be at an important business meeting. *These competing demands cause* work-family conflict, *which is the feeling of being pulled in multiple directions by incompatible demands from one's job and one's family.*

Work-family conflict regarding parenting issues is a problem expressed by many single adults and dual-earner couples alike. Figuring out how to balance time at work and time with family is difficult. One major arena in which this conflict regularly erupts is in the division of household chores, as described in the You May Be Wondering feature.

HOW DO DUAL-EARNER COUPLES HANDLE DIVISION OF LABOR AND WORK-FAMILY CONFLICT?

YOU MAY BE WONDERING

Dual-earner couples must find a balance between their occupational and family roles. With roughly 64% of married couples with children comprising dual-earner households (U.S. Department of Labor, 1997), how to divide the household chores and how to care for the children have become increasingly important.

Many people believe that work and family roles influence each other in such families: When things go badly at work, family suffers, and when there are troubles at home, work suffers. However, this appears not to be the case all the time (Aryee & Luk, 1996). Whether work influences family or vice versa is a complex function of support resources, type of job, and a host of other factors (Frone, Russell, & Barnes, 1996; Matthews, Conger, & Wickrama, 1996; Stephens & Sommer, 1996).

Of course, it is important that the partners negotiate agreeable arrangements of household and child care tasks, but (as noted earlier) truly equitable divisions of labor are clearly the exception. Most U.S. households with heterosexual dual-worker couples still operate under a gender-segregated system: There are traditional chores for men and women. All of these tasks are important and must be performed to keep homes safe, clean, and sanitary. These tasks also take time. The important point for women is not how much time is spent in performing household chores, but which tasks are performed. What bothers wives the most is not that their husbands are lazy but that they will not perform some "women's work." Men may mow the lawn, wash the car, and even cook, but they rarely vacuum, scrub the toilet, or change the baby's diaper.

The division of labor apparently occurs the way it does because that's how people saw their parents do it, and that's what they are comfortable with. John Cavanaugh had an interesting experience in this regard. While doing some volunteer maintenance work at a battered women's shelter in Appalachia, he had to use the vacuum cleaner. He soon became aware that several women were following him around, pointing at him and talking excitedly. A little later, he asked why they did that. He was told that it was the first time in these adult women's lives that they had ever seen a man use a vacuum cleaner.

So how and when will things change? An important step would be to talk about these issues with your partner. Keep communication lines open all the time, and let your partner know if something is bothering you. Teaching your children that men and women are equally responsible for household chores will also help end the problem. Only by creating true gender equality, without differentiating among household tasks, will the unfair division of labor be ended. •

? THINK ABOUT IT
How does the issue of dependent care relate to the level of work-family stress felt by women?

Research provides some evidence of how to deal with work-family conflict successfully. Women in one study were clear in their commitment to their careers, marriage, and children, and they successfully combined them without high levels of distress (Guelzow, Bird, & Koball, 1991). How did they do it? Contrary to popular belief, the age of the children was not a factor in stress level. However, the *number* of children was important, as stress increases greatly with each additional child, irrespective of their ages. Guilt was also not an issue for these women. In the same study, men reported sharing more of the child care tasks as a way of dealing with multiple role pressures. Additionally, stress is lower for men who have a flexible work schedule that allows them to care for sick children and other family matters. Together, these findings are encouraging; they indicate that more heterosexual dual-earner couples are learning how to balance work and family.

Dual-earner couples often have difficulty finding time for each other, especially if both work long hours. The amount of time together is not necessarily the most important issue; as long as the time is spent in shared activities such as eating, playing, and conversing, couples tend to be happy (Kingston & Nock, 1987). Unfortunately, many couples find themselves in the same position as Hi and Lois; by the time they have an opportunity to be alone together, they are too tired to make the most of it.

Cross-cultural data show that burnout from work and parenting is more likely to affect women. A study of dual-earner married couples in Singapore

HI AND LOIS, © 1993. Reprinted with special permission of King Features Syndicate.

showed that wives are more likely to suffer from burnout than husbands; wives' burnout resulted from both work and nonwork stress, whereas husbands' burnout resulted only from work stress (Aryee, 1993).

So exactly what effects do family matters have on work performance and vice versa? Evidence suggests that our work-family conflict is a major source of stress in couples' lives. In general, women feel the work-to-family spillover to a greater extent than men, but both men and women feel the pressure (Gutek, Searle, & Klepa, 1991). Single mothers have an especially hard time if they have more than one child (Polit, 1984).

TEST YOURSELF

1. Parents report lower work-family conflict and have lower absenteeism when supervisors are sympathetic and supportive regarding _____ .

2. Men are satisfied with an equitable division of labor based on _____ , whereas women are satisfied _____ .

3. What should organizations do to help ease work-family conflict?

Answers: (1) family issues and child care; (2) the number of hours spent; when men perform traditionally female chores

---

TIME TO RELAX: LEISURE ACTIVITIES

Learning Objectives

- **What activities are leisure activities? How do people choose among them?**
- **What changes in leisure activities occur with age?**
- **What do people derive from leisure activities?**

Time to Relax: Leisure Activities
Types of Leisure Activities
Developmental Changes in Leisure
Consequences of Leisure Activities

CLAUDE *is a 55-year-old electrician who has enjoyed outdoor activities his whole life. From the time he was a boy, he has fished and water-skied in the calm inlets of coastal Florida. Although he doesn't compete in slalom races any more, Claude still skis regularly, and he participates in fishing competitions every chance he gets.*

Adults do not work every waking moment of their lives. As each of us knows, we need to relax sometimes and engage in leisure activities. Intuitively, leisure consists of activities not associated with work. *More formally, researchers define* leisure *as discretionary activity that includes simple relaxation, activities for enjoyment, creative pursuits, and sensual transcendence* (Gordon, Gaitz, & Scott, 1976). However, men and women differ in their views of leisure, as do people in different ethnic groups (Henderson, 1990). For example, one study of African American women revealed that they view leisure as both freedom from the constraint of needing to work and as a form of self-expression (Allen & Chin-Sang, 1990).

You can preview much of what we will learn about leisure activities by completing the exercise in the See for Yourself feature. How do your lists compare to the discussion in the text?

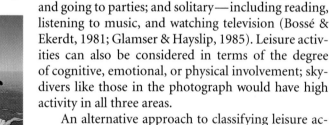
VARIETIES OF LEISURE ACTIVITY IN ADULTHOOD

Before reading about the research findings on the types of things people do for fun, try to find out as much about them as possible on your own. Here's an easy way. Ask several of your friends, as well as adults of different ages, what their current favorite leisure activities are. Ask your parents, their friends, your grandparents, your adult children if you have any, and so on, in order to get a good cross section of ages. Once you have a list of current favorites, ask them what their favorites were 10 years ago. Now compare the lists and see for yourself which activities changed and which did not. Compare your results to the research described in the text, and discuss the similarities and differences in class. •

TYPES OF LEISURE ACTIVITIES

Leisure can include virtually any activity. To organize the options, researchers have classified leisure activities into four categories: cultural—such as attending sporting events, concerts, church services, and meetings; physical—such as basketball, hiking, aerobics, and gardening; social—such as visiting friends

and going to parties; and solitary—including reading, listening to music, and watching television (Bossé & Ekerdt, 1981; Glamser & Hayslip, 1985). Leisure activities can also be considered in terms of the degree of cognitive, emotional, or physical involvement; skydivers like those in the photograph would have high activity in all three areas.

An alternative approach to classifying leisure activities involves the distinction between preoccupations and interests (Rapoport & Rapoport, 1975). Preoccupations are much like daydreaming. Sometimes, preoccupations become more focused and are converted to interests. Interests are ideas and feelings about things one would like to do, is curious about, or is attracted to. Jogging, surfing the Web, fishing, and painting are some examples of interests.

Rapoport and Rapoport's distinction draws attention to a key truth about leisure: Any specific activity has different meaning and value, depending on the individual involved. For example, cooking a gourmet meal is an interest, or a leisure activity, for many people. For professional chefs, however, it is work and thus is not leisure at all.

Given the wide range of options, how do people pick their leisure activities? Apparently, each of us has a leisure repertoire, a personal library of intrinsically motivated activities that we do regularly (Mobily, Lemke, & Gisin, 1991). The activities in our repertoire are determined by two things: perceived competence (how good we think we are at the activity compared to other people our age) and psychological comfort (how well we meet our personal goals for performance). Other factors are important as well: income, interest, health, abilities, transportation, education, and social characteristics. For example, some leisure activities, such as downhill skiing, are relatively expensive and require transportation and reasonably good health and physical coordination for maximum enjoyment. In contrast, reading requires minimal finances (if one uses a public library) and is far less physically demanding. It is probable that how these factors influence leisure activities changes through adulthood (e.g., physical prowess typically declines somewhat). However, exactly how these factors result in changes in leisure activities is currently unknown (Burrus-Bammel & Bammel, 1985).

DEVELOPMENTAL CHANGES IN LEISURE

Cross-sectional studies report age differences in leisure activities (Bray & Howard, 1983). Young adults participate in a greater range of activities than middle-aged adults. Furthermore, young adults tend to prefer intense leisure activities, such as scuba diving and hang gliding. In contrast, middle-aged adults focus more on home- and family-oriented activities. In later middle age, they spend less of their leisure time in strenuous physical activities and more in sedentary activities such as reading and watching television. Older adults narrow the range of activities and lower their intensity even further (Gordon et al., 1976). People of all ages report feelings of freedom during leisure activities (Larson, Gillman, & Richards, 1997).

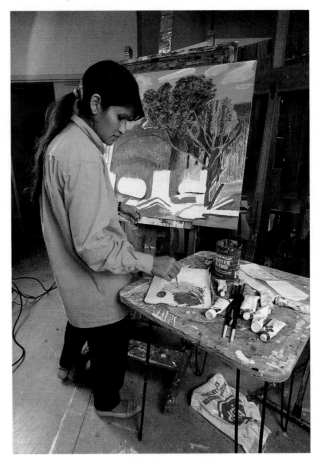

Longitudinal studies of changes in individuals' leisure activities over time show considerable stability over reasonably long periods (Cutler & Hendricks, 1990). Claude, the 55-year-old in the vignette who likes to fish and ski, is a good example of this overall trend. As Claude demonstrates, frequent participation in leisure activities during childhood tends to continue into adulthood. Similar findings hold for the pre- and post-retirement years. Apparently, one's preferences for certain types of leisure activities are established early in life; they tend to change over the life span primarily in terms of how physically intense they are.

CONSEQUENCES OF LEISURE ACTIVITIES

What do people like the woman in the photograph gain from participating in leisure activities? Researchers agree that involvement in leisure activities is related to well-being (Kelly, Steinkamp, & Kelly, 1987). The key aspect of this relation is not the level of participation. Instead, how much satisfaction you derive from your leisure activities is the important element in promoting well-being (Lawton, Moss, & Fulcomer, 1986–1987). Indeed, an Israeli study showed that satisfaction with leisure activities is the crucial variable (Lomranz et al., 1988). Whether leisure enhances one's well-being appears to depend on whether you like what you do for fun.

But what if leisure activities are pursued very seriously? In some cases, people create leisure-family conflict by engaging in leisure activities to extremes (Goff, Fick, & Opplinger, 1997). Only when there is support from others for such extreme involvement are problems avoided (Goff et al., 1997). As in most things, moderation in leisure activities is probably best.

TEST YOURSELF

1. Preoccupations are conscious mental absorptions, whereas interests are _____ .

2. Compared to younger adults, middle-aged and older adults prefer leisure activities that are more family- and home-centered and _____ .

3. Being involved in leisure activities is related to _____ .

4. How are choices of leisure activities related to physical, cognitive, and social development?

Answers: (1) focused preoccupations, (2) less physically intense, (3) well-being

PUTTING IT ALL TOGETHER

Sigmund Freud once said that the two most important aspects of adulthood are love and work. In this chapter, we have seen how pervasive work is in our lives, and how it is affected by many things. The occupation Monique ultimately chooses is partly influenced by talents or skills she may have inherited from her parents, the kind of environment in which she grew up, and the match between her personality style and her occupational skills.

We saw that occupational development is not an inevitable outcome of hard work. Unfortunately, the world of work also reflects the biases, prejudices, and discrimination people face in the world at large. Janice found that being a woman and a member of an ethnic minority may make it difficult to achieve the levels of advancement in her career that she truly deserves. Work spills over into our personal lives, too. Fred and others like him worry about job security, and this sometimes affects home life. Although retraining may be an option, it may not alleviate all the concerns. Dual-earner couples are forced to think about how to divide household tasks in order to maintain balance. Jennifer and her husband are struggling with this issue; too often, women perform most of the chores at home.

But a life that is all work and no play is dull. Just as children need a certain amount of play for their development, adults like Claude find playful outlets through leisure activities. Such activities may be as quiet as reading a book or as daring as skydiving, but being able to do something besides work gives these activities value.

SUMMARY

Occupational Selection and Development

The Meaning of Work

• Although most people work for money, other reasons are highly variable. Occupational priorities have changed over time; younger workers' expectations from their occupations are now lower, and their emphasis on personal growth potential is higher.

Holland's Theory of Occupational Choice Revisited

• Holland's theory is based on the idea that people choose occupations to optimize the fit between their individual traits and their occupational interests. Six personality types, representing different combinations of these, have been identified. Support for these types has been found in several studies.

Occupational Development

• Super's developmental view of occupations is based on self-concept and adaptation to an occupational role. Super describes five stages in adulthood: implementation, establishment, maintenance, deceleration, and retirement.

• Reality shock is the realization that one's expectations about an occupation are different from the reality one experiences. Reality shock is common among young workers.

• A mentor is a co-worker who teaches a new employee the unwritten rules and fosters occupational development. Mentor-protégé relationships develop over time, through stages, like other relationships.

Job Satisfaction

• Older workers report higher job satisfaction than younger workers, but this may be partly due to self-selection; unhappy workers may quit. Other reasons include intrinsic satisfaction, good fit, lower importance of work, finding nonwork diversions, and life-cycle factors.

• Alienation and burnout are important considerations in understanding job satisfaction. Both involve significant stress for workers.

Gender, Ethnicity, and Discrimination Issues

Gender Differences in Occupational Selection

• Boys and girls are socialized differently for work, and their occupational choices are affected as a result. Women choose nontraditional occupations for many reasons, including expectations and personal feelings. Women in such occupations are still viewed more negatively than men in the same occupations.

Women and Occupational Development

• Women leave well-paid occupations for many reasons, including family obligations and workplace environment. Women who continue to work full-time have adequate child care and look for ways to further their occupational development.

Ethnicity and Occupational Development

• Vocational identity and vocational goals vary in different ethnic groups. Whether an organization is sensitive to ethnicity issues is a strong predictor of satisfaction among ethnic minority employees.

Bias and Discrimination

• Sex discrimination remains the chief barrier to women's occupational development. In many cases, this operates as a glass ceiling. Pay inequity is also a problem; women are often paid less than what men in similar jobs earn.

• Sexual harassment is a problem in the workplace. Current criteria for judging harassment are based on the "reasonable woman" standard. Denying employment to anyone over 40 because of age is age discrimination.

Occupational Transitions

Retraining Workers

• To adapt to the effects of a global economy and an aging work force, many corporations are providing retraining opportunities for workers. Retraining is especially important in cases of outdated skills and career plateauing.

Occupational Insecurity

• Important reasons why people change occupations include personality, obsolescence, and economic trends. Occupational insecurity is a growing problem. Fear that one may lose one's job is a better predictor of anxiety than the actual likelihood of job loss.

Coping with Unemployment

• Job loss is a traumatic event that can affect every aspect of a person's life. Degree of financial distress and the extent of attachment to the job are the best predictors of distress.

Work and Family

The Dependent Care Dilemma

• Whether a woman returns to work after having a child depends largely on how attached she is to her work. Simply providing child care on-site does not always result in higher job satisfaction. The more important factor is the degree to which supervisors are sympathetic.

Juggling Multiple Roles

• Although women have reduced the amount of time they spend on household tasks over the past two decades, they still do most of the work. European American men are less likely than either African American or Hispanic American men to help with traditionally female household tasks.

• Flexible work schedules and number of children are important factors in role conflict. Recent evidence shows that work stress has a much bigger impact on family life than family stress has on work performance. Some women pay a high personal price for having careers.

Time to Relax: Leisure Activities

Types of Leisure Activities

• Preoccupations can become more focused as interests, which can lead to the selection of particular leisure activities. People develop a repertoire of preferred leisure activities.

Developmental Changes in Leisure

• As people grow older, they tend to engage in leisure activities that are less strenuous and more family-oriented. Leisure preferences in adulthood reflect those earlier in life.

Consequences of Leisure Activities

• Leisure activities enhance well-being and can benefit all aspects of people's lives.

KEY TERMS

occupational priorities (405)
vocational maturity (407)
dream (408)
job satisfaction (410)
alienation (412)

burnout (413)
sex discrimination (419)
glass ceiling (419)
comparable worth (420)
"reasonable woman" standard (421)

age discrimination (423)
career plateauing (426)
work-family conflict (433)
leisure (435)

IF YOU'D LIKE TO LEARN MORE

Readings

BOLLES, R. N. (1997). *The 1998 what color is your parachute: A practical manual for job-hunters and career changers.* Berkeley, CA: Ten Speed Press. This popular reference is a valuable resource for people in search of careers. It is regularly updated.

CROSBY, F. (1991). *Juggling: The unexpected advantages of balancing career and home for women, their families and society.* New York: Free Press. Although it is moderately difficult, this book makes for eye-opening reading on the topic of balancing work and family.

FEATHER, N. T. (1990). *The psychological impact of unemployment.* New York: Springer-Verlag. Feather presents a thorough, scholarly treatment of the topic, one of the best available. The reading level is moderately difficult.

GERSON, K. (1993). *No man's land: Men's changing commitments to family and work.* New York: Basic Books. This very readable book about modern men's roles is based on a series of life history interviews.

HOCHSCHILD, A. R. (1989). *Second shift: Working parents and the revolution at home.* New York: Viking Press. This classic provides an excellent discussion of the gender differences in child care and work-family conflict issues.

McDANIELS, C., & GYSBERS, N. C. (1992). *Counseling for career development.* San Francisco: Jossey-Bass. This is a good introduction to topics relating to career counseling and occupational development.

For additional readings, explore Infotrac College Edition, your online library. Go to http://www.infotrac-college.com/wadsworth.

Web Sites

The U.S. Department of Labor provides many reports on various aspects of work force participation. Check out the many agencies within the Department by clicking on the "DOL Agencies" button. The Women's Bureau on that list is especially good for statistics on women's employment status. The Department's homepage is at

http://www.dol.gov

A well-organized set of links to all aspects of employment, including career planning, law, unemployment, and women's issues can be found at

http://www.yahoo.com/Business/Employment/

Many Web sites are devoted to the issue of sexual harassment. The Feminist Majority Foundation Web site *911 for Women* has several topics, including a good list of places to report and to understand one's rights related to sexual harassment. The homepage can be found at

http://www.feminist.org/911/1_supprt.html

Web site addresses are subject to change. The Wadsworth Study Center Web site listed below can be accessed for updated links.

The Wadsworth Psychology Study Center Web Site

See http://psychology.wadsworth.com/ for practice quiz questions, internet links, updates, critical thinking exercises, discussion forums and more! The Wadsworth Psychology Study Center provides a wealth of information fully organized and integrated by chapter.

CHAPTER 12

EXPERIENCING MIDDLE AGE

Physical Changes and Health
Changes in Appearance
Dealing with Physical Aging
Reproductive Changes
Having Babies After Menopause
Stress and Health
Exercise

Cognitive Development
Practical Intelligence
Becoming an Expert
Lifelong Learning
College at Midlife

Personality
Stability Is the Rule: The Five-Factor
    Model
Change Is the Rule: Changing Priorities
    in Midlife
Does Everyone Have a Midlife Crisis?

Family Dynamics and Middle Age
Letting Go: Middle-Aged Adults and
    Their Children
*How Do You Think Your Children Turned
    Out?*
Giving Back: Middle-Aged Adults and
    Their Aging Parents
Caring for Parents
*The Complexities of Caring for
    Older Parents*
Grandparenthood

Putting It All Together

Summary

If You'd Like to Learn More

There's an old saying that life begins at 40. That's good news for middle-aged adults. As we will see, they face many stressful events, but they also leave many of the pressures of young adulthood behind. In many respects, middle age is the prime of life: A person's health is generally good and their earnings at their peak.

Of course, during middle age people typically get wrinkles, gray hair, and a bulging waistline. But middle-aged adults also achieve new heights in cognitive development, change their behavior if they choose, develop adult relationships with their children, and ease into grandparenthood. Along the way, they must deal with stress, changes in the way they learn, and the challenges of dealing with their aging parents.

Some of these issues are based more on stereotypes than on hard evidence. Which is which? You will know by the end of the chapter.

PHYSICAL CHANGES AND HEALTH

Physical Changes and Health

Changes in Appearance

Reproductive Changes

Stress and Health

Exercise

Learning Objectives

- **How does appearance change in middle age?**

- **What reproductive changes occur in men and women in middle age?**

- **What is stress? How does it affect physical and psychological health?**

- **What benefits are there to exercise?**

$\mathcal{B}$Y all accounts, Dean is extremely successful. Among other things, he became the head of a moderate-sized manufacturing firm by the time he was 43. Dean has always considered himself to be a rising young star in the company. Then one day he found more than the usual number of hairs in his brush. "Oh no!" he exclaimed. "I can't be going bald! What will people think?" What does Dean think about these changes?

The reality of middle age generally strikes early one morning in the bathroom mirror. Standing there, staring through half-awake eyes, you see *it*. One solitary gray hair, or one tiny wrinkle at the corner of your eye, or, like Dean, some excess hairs falling out, and you worry that your youth is gone, your life is over, and you will soon be acting the way your parents did when they totally embarrassed you in your younger days. Middle-aged people become concerned that they are over the hill, sometimes going to great lengths to prove that they are still vibrant.

Crossing the boundary to middle age in the United States is typically associated with turning 40 (or the big four-oh, as many people term it). This event is frequently marked with a special party as shown in the photograph. Often the party has an "over the hill" motif. Such events are society's attempt at creating a rite of passage between youth and maturity.

As people move into middle age, they begin experiencing some of the physical changes associated with aging. In this section, we focus on the ones most obvious in middle-aged adults: appearance, reproductive capacity, and stress and coping. In Chapter 13, we will consider changes that may begin in middle age but are usually not apparent until later in life, such as slower reaction time and sensory changes.

CHANGES IN APPEARANCE

On that fateful day when the hard truth stares at you in the bathroom mirror (as for the person in the photograph), it probably doesn't matter to you that getting wrinkles and gray hair are universal and inevitable. Wrinkles are caused by changes in the structure of the skin and its connective and supporting tissues, as well as the cumulative effects of damage from exposure to sunlight and smoking cigarettes (Whitbourne, 1996). It may not make you feel better to know that gray hair is perfectly natural and caused by a normal cessation of pigment production in hair follicles (Kenney, 1982). Male pattern baldness, a genetic trait in which hair is lost progressively beginning with the top of the head, often begins to appear in middle age (Whitbourne, 1996). No, the scientific evidence that these changes occur to many people isn't what matters most. What matters is that these changes are affecting *you*.

To make matters worse, you may have also noticed that your clothes aren't fitting properly, even though you watch what you eat. You remember a time not very long ago when you could eat whatever you wanted; now it seems that as soon as you look at food you put on weight. Your perceptions are correct; most people gain weight between their early 30s and mid-50s, producing the infamous "middle-aged bulge" as metabolism slows down (Whitbourne, 1996).

People's reactions to these changes in appearance vary. Dean wonders how people will react to him now that he's balding. Some people rush out to purchase hair coloring and wrinkle cream. Others just take it as another stage in life. You've probably experienced several different reactions yourself. To get a sense of the wide range of individual differences, especially those between men and women and across cultures, try the exercise in the See for Yourself feature.

DEALING WITH PHYSICAL AGING

SEE FOR YOURSELF

How do people deal with the signs of physical aging? Find out for yourself by doing the following exercises.

1. Look through popular fashion magazines such as *Vogue, Cosmopolitan, GQ,* and *Elle,* and watch television programs. Pay attention to advertisements and articles dealing with wrinkles, hair, and weight. How many telegraph the message that these natural signs of aging are acceptable? Do you detect a difference between messages aimed at men and women?

2. Talk to men and women you know who are over 40. Ask them how they feel about the physical changes they are experiencing. Do you detect any gender differences?

3. Talk to someone from a culture other than your own. Find out how people in other cultures view the physical changes associated with aging. Are the changes that accompany aging viewed the same way around the world?

These exercises should provide you with some insights into how people and corporations (through their advertisements) view the physical changes that occur in middle age. Compare your findings with other students' results and discuss any gender differences you have uncovered. Do people ignore these changes? See for yourself. •

Osteoporotic bone tissue

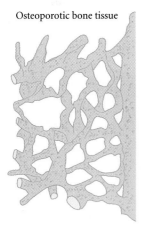

Normal bone tissue

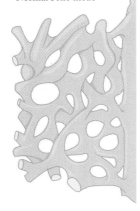

Another physical change is loss of bone mass, a potentially serious problem. Bone mass peaks in one's 20s, and then declines with age (Weldon, 1997). Loss of bone mass makes bones weaker and more brittle, thereby making them easier to break. Because there is less bone mass, bones also take longer to heal in middle-aged and older adults. *If the loss of bone mass is severe, the disease* osteoporosis *results; as you can see in the diagram, bones become porous like honeycombs and extremely easy to break.* In severe cases, osteoporosis can cause spinal vertebrae to collapse, causing the person to stoop and to become shorter (Masi & Bilezikian, 1997; Weldon, 1997). Although the severe effects of osteoporosis typically are not observed until later life, this disease can occur in people in their 50s.

Osteoporosis is more common in women than men, largely because women have less bone mass in general, because some girls and women do not consume enough calcium to build strong bones from childhood to young adulthood, and because the decrease in estrogen following menopause greatly accelerates bone loss (Masi & Bilezikian, 1997). To reduce the risk of osteoporosis, the National Institutes of Health and the Food and Drug Administration (Masi & Bilezikian, 1997) recommend dietary, drug, and activity approaches to prevent osteoporosis. People should eat foods high in calcium (such as milk and broccoli), reduce alcohol intake, and take calcium supplements if necessary. Estrogen replacement is clearly effective in preventing women's bone loss after menopause, but is controversial due to potential side effects (as discussed later). There is also some evidence that regular exercise is beneficial, but results vary depending on the type and intensity of the regimen. The best results come from a regular regimen of moderate aerobic exercise.

REPRODUCTIVE CHANGES

Besides changes in the way we look, middle age brings transitions in our reproductive systems. These changes differ dramatically for women and men. Some people, like the teenagers in the cartoon, view the changes in women as the flip side of puberty, and to some extent the analogy is appropriate. Even in the context of these changes, though, middle-aged adults continue to have active sex

FOR BETTER OR WORSE © Lynn Johnston Productions Inc./Dist. by United Features Syndicate, Inc.

lives. In fact, 73% of men and 69% of women between the ages of 40 and 49, and 67% of men and 48% of women between 50 and 59 have sex at least several times a month (Michael et al., 1994). The declines in frequency of sexual activity with age reflect complex biopsychosocial factors, including physiological changes, the stresses of everyday life, and negative social stereotypes about sex and growing older (Michael et al., 1994).

The Climacteric and Menopause

For women, middle age brings a major biological change: the loss of the ability to bear children through natural means (Rykken, 1987). *This process, termed the* climacteric, *usually begins in the 40s and is usually complete by the late 50s.* The length of time it takes for all of the reproductive changes to occur differs considerably from woman to woman; for some it takes only a year or two, but others may experience more gradual changes for a decade. The most important change during the climacteric is a dramatic drop in the production of estrogen, the primary female hormone (Mayo Clinic, 1992).

During the climacteric, menstruation becomes irregular and eventually stops; this specific change is termed menopause. Although some women stop menstruating around age 40, and others may still be having regular periods in their mid-50s, most women have their last period in their early 50s. However, ovulation may continue for a year or two after the last period; thus, women who do not want to risk pregnancy should continue to use contraceptives for this length of time.

Researchers have identified two primary sets of symptoms associated with the climacteric and menopause (DeAngelis, 1997). Estrogen-related symptoms *include hot flashes, night sweats, vaginal dryness, and urine leakage, which are due to the rapid drop in estrogen.* Somatic symptoms *include difficulties sleeping, headaches, rapid heartbeat, and stiffness or soreness in the joints, neck, or shoulders.* Ethnic differences in the symptoms women experience have been noted. In one study, for example, European American women report a decrease in somatic symptoms after the climacteric (Jackson, Taylor, & Pyngolil, 1991); in contrast, African American women report more estrogen-related symptoms and fewer somatic symptoms than any other ethnic group (DeAngelis, 1997). Hispanic American women report more rapid heartbeat and urinary leakage, whereas Asian American women report the fewest symptoms of any kind (DeAngelis, 1997).

The decline in estrogen that women experience is related to increased risk of osteoporosis, cardiovascular disease, and memory loss (Lichtman, 1996; Sherwin, 1997). In the case of cardiovascular disease, before they turn 50, women have three times less risk of heart attacks than men. Ten years after menopause, when women are about 60, their risks equal that of men. *Due to these increased risks, and the estrogen-related symptoms women experience, many physicians and researchers advocate the use of* hormone replacement therapy (HRT), *in which women take low doses of estrogen, which is often combined with progestin.* HRT is controversial, and has been the focus of many research studies (Brinton & Schairer, 1997; Lichtman, 1996; Mayeaux & Johnson, 1996). There appear to be both benefits and risks with HRT. It has been well documented for decades that HRT reduces the estrogen-related symptoms described earlier. More recent evidence indicates that HRT also reduces the risk of osteoporosis, and lowers blood lipids (Lichtman, 1996). Although there is a belief

? THINK ABOUT IT

Why does sexual desire remain largely unchanged despite the biological changes that are occurring?

that HRT reduces the risk of cardiovascular disease, evidence is mixed. It may be that the weight gain that often accompanies menopause, in conjunction with the fact that health-conscious women are more likely to be using HRT, are more important factors (DeAngelis, 1997). Results also indicate that HRT helps maintain short- and long-term memory (Sherwin, 1997). There are suggestive data that HRT may have a role in helping prevent Alzheimer's disease (Henderson, 1997; Simpkins et al., 1997).

Despite these benefits, HRT can have drawbacks. The primary concerns are increased risk of endometrial cancer (cancer in the lining of the uterus) and breast cancer, especially after being on HRT for 10 or more years (Lichtman, 1996). Fortunately, the risk of endometrial cancer is greatly reduced when HRT is based on a lower dosage of estrogen combined with progestin. The data concerning increased risk of breast cancer are quite complex and contradictory—some studies find increased risk, some do not; some find the risk only with long-term use of HRT, others find no clear relationship. For these reasons, the Women's Health Initiative and several other longitudinal studies funded by the National Institutes of Health are continuing to examine these risks.

Even without hormone replacement therapy, most women report that the symptoms accompanying the climacteric are not very severe (Matthews et al., 1990). In all the cultures studied, few women express regret at the loss of fertility; rather, they feel more powerful and free (Sheehy, 1992). Alternative approaches to addressing both estrogen-related and somatic symptoms are gaining in popularity (Soffa, 1996). Herbal remedies, especially those rich in phytosterols, used effectively in Asian cultures may be one reason why Asian American women report the fewest symptoms (DeAngelis, 1997). The use of a nonpetroleum-based lubricating jelly (such as K-Y Jelly) usually solves the problem of vaginal dryness, which often makes intercourse painful.

Recent advances in reproductive technology have enabled women who have undergone the climacteric to have children. As discussed in the Current Controversies segment, such births force us to rethink the meaning of the climacteric.

CURRENT CONTROVERSIES   **HAVING BABIES AFTER MENOPAUSE**

Reproductive technology such as fertility drugs and *in vitro* fertilization (see Chapter 2) has made it possible for postmenopausal women to have children. Indeed, in 1997 Rosanno Dalla Corta, the 63-year-old woman from Viterbo, Italy, shown in the photograph, gave birth to a baby conceived through *in vitro* fertilization. Scientists have thus fundamentally changed the rules of reproduction. Even though a woman has gone through the climacteric, she can still have children. Technology can make her pregnant, if she so chooses and if she has access to the proper medical centers.

What does this do to our understanding of human reproduction? It changes the whole notion of menopause representing an absolute end to childbearing. Some of the women who have given birth after menopause have done so because their daughters were unable to have children; they consider this act another way to show their parental love. Others view it as a way to equalize reproductive potential in middle age between men and women, as men remain fertile throughout adulthood.

Clearly, these are complicated issues that currently affect a very small number of women. But as reproductive technology continues to advance faster than our ability to think through the issues, we will be confronted with increasingly complex ethical questions (Lindlaw, 1997). Should children be born to older parents? Might not there be some advantage, considering the life experience such parents would have, compared to young parents? Are such births merely selfish acts? Are they a viable alternative way for younger adults to have a family? What dangers are there to older pregnant women? How do you feel about it? •

INFOTRAC
COLLEGE EDITION

To learn more, enter the following search terms: in vitro fertilization, menopause.

Reproductive Changes in Men

Reproductive changes in men are far less dramatic. Sperm production declines gradually by approximately 30% between the ages of 25 and 60 (Solnick & Corby, 1983). But even a man of 80 is still half as fertile as he was at age 25 and remains potentially capable of fathering a child. Sexual functioning does change as men age. Most men need more time to achieve an erection and orgasm, feel less need to ejaculate, and experience a longer resolution phase during which erection is impossible (Rykken, 1987). The introduction of the drug Viagra in 1998 offered a medical treatment for erectile difficulties for some men. An important point is that unlike women, men do not normally experience a loss of fertility in adulthood.

Many men experience problems due to changes in the prostate gland, which is located beneath the bladder and surrounds the urethra. The gland produces fluids in semen that help sperm survive in the acidic environment of the vagina (Mayo Clinic, 1992). With increasing age, a man's prostate gland enlarges and stiffens, which may make it more difficult to urinate. Unless there is an accompanying infection, an enlarged prostate is not serious. However, prostate cancer becomes a serious threat during middle age, with incidence peaking between the ages of 60 and 80 (Mayo Clinic, 1992). Although prostate cancer is not caused by enlargement (indeed, the cause is unknown), enlargement may be misdiagnosed as cancer unless more careful diagnostic tests are performed (Calciano et al., 1995).

STRESS AND HEALTH

There's no doubt about it—life is full of stress. Look at the man in the photograph and think for a moment about all the things that bother you, such as exams, jobs, relationships, and finances. For most people, this list lengthens quickly. But, you may wonder, isn't this true for people of all ages? Is stress more important in middle age?

Although stress affects people of all ages, it is during middle age that the effects of both short- and long-term stress become most apparent. In part, this is because it takes time for stress disorders to manifest themselves, and in part it is due to the gradual loss of physical capacity, as the normal changes accompanying aging begin to take their toll. As we will see, psychological factors play a major role as well.

You may think that stress affects health mainly in people who hold certain types of jobs, such as air traffic controllers, high-level business executives, and textbook authors. In fact, business executives actually have *fewer* stress-related health problems than waitresses, construction workers, secretaries, laboratory technicians, machine operators, farm workers, and painters (McEwen, 1998; Smith et al., 1978). What do all of these truly high-stress jobs have in common? These workers have little direct control over their jobs.

Although we understand some important workplace factors related to stress, our knowledge is largely based on research examining middle-aged men. Unfortunately, the relation of stress to age, gender, and ethnic status remains to be researched. For example, in all age groups, women are more likely than men to report that stress has a significant effect on their health (U.S. Department of Health and Human Services, 1988). Middle-aged people report the highest levels of stress, whereas people over age 65 report the lowest. Why? As we will see in the next section, part of the reason may be due to the number of pressures middle-aged people feel: Children may be in college, the job has high demands, the mortgage payment and other bills always need paying, the marriage needs some attention, the in-laws would like to visit, and on it goes.

What Is Stress?

Think about the last time you felt stressed. What was it about the situation that made you feel stressed? How did you feel? *The answers to questions like these provide a way to understand the dominant framework used to study stress, the* stress and coping paradigm. Because the stress and coping paradigm emphasizes the interaction between a person and the environment, it fits well with the biopsychosocial framework.

Physiologically, stress refers to a number of specific changes in the body (e.g., increased heart rate, sweaty palms, hormone secretion) (McEwen, 1998). In the short run, stress can be beneficial and may even allow you to perform at your peak. In the long run, though, if the woman in the photograph continues to be highly stressed, a high physical toll and even death may result (McEwen, 1998).

Whether you report feeling stressed depends on how you interpret a situation or event (Lazarus & Folkman, 1984). What the situation or event is, or what you do to deal with it, does not matter. *Stress results when you* appraise *a situation or event as taxing or exceeding your personal, social, or other resources and endangering your well-being. It is the day-to-day* hassles, *or the things that upset and annoy us, that prove to be particularly stressful.*

Coping *is any attempt to deal with stress.* People cope in several different ways (Ishler et al., 1998). Sometimes people cope by trying to solve the problem at hand; for example, you may cope with a messy roommate by moving out. At other times, people focus on how they feel about the situation and deal with things on an emotional level; feeling sad after breaking up with your partner would be one way of coping with the stress of being alone. Sometimes people cope by simply redefining the event as not stressful— saying that it was no big deal that you failed to get the job you wanted would be an example of this approach. Still others focus on religious or spiritual approaches, perhaps asking God for help.

People appraise different types of situations or events as stressful at different times during adulthood. For example, the pressures from work and raising a family are typically greater for younger and middle-aged adults than for older adults. However, stressors due to chronic disease are often more important to older adults than to their younger counterparts. Similarly, the same kind of event may be appraised differently at different ages. For example, uncertainty about one's job security may be less stressful in young adulthood, when one might get another job more easily, than in middle age, when alternative job prospects might diminish. From a biopsychosocial perspective, such life-cycle factors must be taken into account when considering what kinds of stress adults of different ages are experiencing.

? THINK ABOUT IT
How might life experience and cognitive developmental level influence the appraisal of and coping with stress?

How Does Stress Affect Physical Health?

A great deal of research has been conducted over the years examining links between stress and physical health. Several links have been discovered and some are relatively widely known. You may already know that stress has been linked to tension headaches (Holyroad, Appel, & Andrasik, 1983). Probably the most well-known connection between stress and health involves the link with cardiovascular disease. Due mostly to the pioneering work of Friedman and Rosenman (1974), we know that two behavior patterns differ dramatically in terms of risk of cardiovascular disease.

People who demonstrate Type A behavior pattern *tend to be intensely competitive, angry, hostile, restless, aggressive, and impatient. In contrast, people who show* Type B behavior pattern *tend to be just the opposite.* Type A individuals are at least twice as likely as Type B people to develop cardiovascular disease, even when other risk factors such as smoking and hypertension are taken into account. In fact, Type A behavior is a more important predictor than body weight, alcohol intake, or activity level (Zmuda et al., 1997).

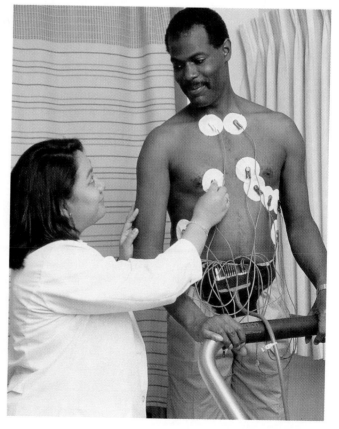

How do these behavior types relate to *recovery* from a heart attack? Although it is relatively rare, Type B people sometimes do have heart attacks. Who recovers better, Type A people or Type B people?

The answer may surprise you. Ragland and Brand (1988) conducted a 22-year longitudinal follow-up of the original Friedman and Rosenman study and discovered that Type A people recover from a heart attack better than Type B people. Why? Some of the characteristics of being Type A may help motivate people like the man shown in the photograph to stick to diet and exercise regimens after heart attacks and to have a more positive attitude toward recovery (Ivancevich & Matteson, 1988). Indeed, although the anger and hostility components of Type A behavior increase the risk for cardiovascular disease, the other components appear to aid the recovery process (Ivancevich & Matteson, 1988). In contrast, the laid-back approach to life of Type B people may actually work against them during recovery.

Being under stress also has effects on the immune system depending on the kind of event (Cohen & Herbert, 1996). Experiencing negative events results in lower immune function (Kiecolt-Glaser et al., 1984; Stone et al., 1994). Likewise, experiencing positive events seems to improve immune functioning (Stone et al., 1994). Although the links between stress and immune system functioning are becoming well established, it remains to be seen whether stress-reduction techniques can reverse the effects of negative events (Cohen & Hebert, 1996).

How Does Stress Affect Psychological Health?

Many people still believe that stress causes psychological disorders. Actually, researchers have known for decades that even an accumulation of stress does not directly cause depression, schizophrenia, or anxiety disorders (Dohrenwend, 1979). Although stress is not directly related to psychopathology, it is associated with other psychological processes. For example, chronic stress related to financial pressures and fear of crime promotes social isolation and distrust of others in some adults (Krause, 1991). Thus, although stress does not directly cause psychopathology, it does influence how people behave.

EXERCISE

Ever since the time of Hippocrates, physicians and researchers have known that exercise significantly slows the aging process. Indeed, evidence suggests that a program of regular exercise, in conjunction with the healthy life-styles we discussed in Chapter 9, can slow the physiological aging process by as much as a decade (Thomas & Rutledge, 1986). Being sedentary is hazardous to your health.

Adults benefit from aerobic exercise, *which places moderate stress on the heart by maintaining a pulse rate between 60% and 90% of the person's maximum heart rate.* You can calculate your maximum heart rate by subtracting your age from 220. Thus, if you are 40 years old, your target range would be 108–162 beats per minute. The minimum time necessary for aerobic exercise to be of benefit depends on its intensity; at low heart rates, sessions may need to last an hour, whereas at high heart rates, 15 minutes may suffice. Examples of aerobic exercise include jogging, step aerobics, swimming, and cross-country skiing.

What happens when a person exercises aerobically (besides becoming tired and sweaty)? Physiologically, adults of all ages show improved cardiovascular functioning and maximum oxygen consumption; lower blood pressure; and better strength, endurance, flexibility, and coordination (Surgeon General, 1996). Psychologically, people who exercise aerobically report lower levels of stress, better moods, and better cognitive functioning (Surgeon General, 1996).

The best way to gain the benefits of aerobic exercise is to maintain physical fitness through the life span, beginning at least in middle age like the people in the photograph. In planning an exercise program, three points should be remembered (Surgeon General, 1996). First, check with a physician before beginning an aerobic exercise program. Second, bear in mind that moderation is important. A study of nearly 17,000 middle-aged and older men found that those who exercised moderately (walked 9 miles per week or cycled for 6–8 hours per week) had a 21%–50% lower risk of dying than men who did not exercise, whereas men who exercised strenuously (walked 20 miles per week or cycled more than 15 hours per week) had a significantly higher risk of dying than men who exercised moderately. Third, the reasons why people exercise change during adulthood. Younger adults tend to exercise to improve their physical appearance, whereas middle-aged and older adults are more concerned with physical and psychological health (Trujillo, Walsh, & Brougham, 1991).

1. Severe bone loss may result in the disease _____ .

2. The cessation of menstruation is termed _____ .

3. Reduction of fertility in men occurs _____ .

4. The stress and _____ paradigm defines stress on the basis of the person's appraisal of a situation as taxing his or her well-being.

5. Research indicates that Type _____ individuals have a better chance of recovering from a heart attack than Type _____ individuals.

6. The media are full of advertisements for anti-aging creams, diets, and exercise plans. Based on what you have read in this section, how would you evaluate these ads?

Answers: (1) osteoporosis, (2) menopause, (3) gradually, (4) coping, (5) A, B

COGNITIVE DEVELOPMENT

Learning Objectives

- **How does practical intelligence develop in adulthood? What are the developmental trends of exercised and unexercised abilities?**

- **How does a person become an expert?**

- **What is meant by lifelong learning? What differences are there between adults and young people in how they learn?**

Cognitive Development
Practical Intelligence
Becoming an Expert
Lifelong Learning

KESHA, a 54-year-old social worker, is widely regarded as the resident expert when it comes to working the system of human services. Her co-workers look up to her for her ability to get several agencies to cooperate, which they do not do normally, and to keep clients coming in for routine matters and follow-up visits. Kesha claims there is nothing magical about it—it's just her experience that makes the difference.

Form **1040** Department of the Treasury–Internal Revenue Service
U.S. Individual Income Tax Return 1998 (99) IRS Use Only–Do not write or staple in this space.

For the year Jan. 1–Dec. 31, 1998, or other tax year beginning , 1998, ending , 19 OMB No. 1545-0074

Label
(See instructions on page 18.)
Use the IRS label. Otherwise, please print or type.

Your first name and initial | Last name | Your social security number

If a joint return, spouse's first name and initial | Last name | Spouse's social security number

Home address (number and street). If you have a P.O. box, see page 18. | Apt. no.

City, town or post office, state, and ZIP code. If you have a foreign address, see page 18.

▲ **IMPORTANT!** ▲
You **must** enter your SSN(s) above.

Presidential Election Campaign (See page 18.)
Do you want $3 to go to this fund? . . . .
If a joint return, does your spouse want $3 to go to this fund? . . . .
Yes No
Note: Checking "Yes" will not change your tax or reduce your refund.

Filing Status
Check only one box.
1 Single
2 Married filing joint return (even if only one had income)
3 Married filing separate return. Enter spouse's social security no. above and full name here. ▶
4 Head of household (with qualifying person). (See page 18.) If the qualifying person is a child but not your dependent, enter this child's name here. ▶
5 Qualifying widow(er) with dependent child (year spouse died ▶ 19). (See page 18.)

Exemptions
6a Yourself. If your parent (or someone else) can claim you as a dependent on his or her tax return, do not check box 6a.
b Spouse
c Dependents:
(1) First name Last name
(2) Dependent's social security number
(3) Dependent's relationship to you
(4) ✓ if qualifying child for child tax credit (see page 19)

If more than six dependents, see page 19.

d Total number of exemptions claimed

No. of boxes checked on 6a and 6b
No. of your children on 6c who:
• lived with you
• did not live with you due to divorce or separation (see page 19)
Dependents on 6c not entered above
Add numbers entered on lines above ▶

Income
Attach Copy B of your Forms W-2, W-2G, and 1099-R here.
If you did not get a W-2, see page 20.
Enclose, but do not staple, any payment. Also, please use Form 1040-V.

7 Wages, salaries, tips, etc. Attach Form(s) W-2 . . . . | 7
8a Taxable interest. Attach Schedule B if required . . . . | 8a
b Tax-exempt interest. DO NOT include on line 8a . | 8b
9 Ordinary dividends. Attach Schedule B if required . . . . . . | 9
10 Taxable refunds, credits, or offsets of state and local income taxes (see page 21) . | 10
11 Alimony received . . . . | 11
12 Business income or (loss). Attach Schedule C or C-EZ . . . . . | 12
13 Capital gain or (loss). Attach Schedule D . . . . | 13
14 Other gains or (losses). Attach Form 4797 . . . . | 14
15a Total IRA distributions . 15a b Taxable amount (see page 22) | 15b
16a Total pensions and annuities 16a b Taxable amount (see page 22) | 16b
17 Rental real estate, royalties, partnerships, S corporations, trusts, etc. Attach Schedule E | 17
18 Farm income or (loss). Attach Schedule F . . . . | 18
19 Unemployment compensation . . . . | 19
20a Social security benefits . 20a b Taxable amount (see page 24) | 20b
21 Other income. List type and amount—see page 24 . . . . . . | 21
22 Add the amounts in the far right column for lines 7 through 21. This is your **total income** ▶ | 22

Adjusted Gross Income
If line 33 is under $30,095 (under $10,030 if a child did not live with you), see EIC inst. on page 36.

23 IRA deduction (see page 25) . . . . . . | 23
24 Student loan interest deduction (see page 27) . . . . | 24
25 Medical savings account deduction. Attach Form 8853 . | 25
26 Moving expenses. Attach Form 3903 . . . . | 26
27 One-half of self-employment tax. Attach Schedule SE . | 27
28 Self-employed health insurance deduction (see page 28) | 28
29 Keogh and self-employed SEP and SIMPLE plans . . | 29
30 Penalty on early withdrawal of savings . . . . | 30
31a Alimony paid b Recipient's SSN ▶ | 31a
32 Add lines 23 through 31a . . . . | 32
33 Subtract line 32 from line 22. This is your **adjusted gross income** . . . . ▶ | 33

For Disclosure, Privacy Act, and Paperwork Reduction Act Notice, see page 51. Cat. No. 11320B Form **1040** (1998)

Compared to the rapid cognitive growth of childhood, or the controversies about postformal cognition in young adulthood, cognitive development in middle age is relatively quiet. For the most part, the trends in intellectual development discussed in Chapter 9 are continued and solidified. The hallmark of cognitive development in middle age involves developing higher levels of expertise like Kesha shows and flexibility in solving practical problems, such as dealing with complex forms like the tax form on the left. We will also see how important it is to continue learning throughout adulthood.

PRACTICAL INTELLIGENCE

Take a moment to think about the following problems (Denney, 1989, 1990; Denney, Pearce, & Palmer, 1982).

- A middle-aged woman is frying chicken in her home when, all of a sudden, a grease fire breaks out on top of the stove. Flames begin to shoot up. What should she do?

- A man finds that the heater in his apartment is not working. He asks his landlord to send someone out to fix it, and the landlord agrees. But, after a week of cold weather and several calls to the landlord, the heater is still not fixed. What should the man do?

These practical problems are different from the examples of measures of fluid and crystallized intelligence in Chapter 9. These problems are more realistic; they reflect real-world situations that people routinely face. One criticism of traditional measures of intelligence is that they do not assess the kinds of skills adults actually use in everyday life (Labouvie-Vief, 1985). Most people spend more time at tasks such as managing their personal finances, dealing with uncooperative people, and juggling busy schedules than they do solving esoteric mazes.

In reaction to the shortcomings of traditional approaches to testing adults' intelligence, different ways of viewing intelligence have emerged (Cavanaugh, 1991; Ceci, 1990; Dixon, 1992). *These alternative views focus on the skills and knowledge necessary for people to function in everyday life, termed* practical intelligence. The examples at the beginning of this section illustrate how practical intelligence is measured. Such real-life problems differ in three main ways from traditional tests (Wagner & Sternberg, 1986): People are more motivated to solve them; personal experience is more relevant; and they have more than one correct answer.

Denney's Theory

Denney (1982) postulated that performance on tests of practical intelligence depends on two different components, whose developmental trends are shown in the graph on page 455. *The bottom dashed line represents* unexercised ability, the level of performance a person exhibits with-out practice or training. Unexercised abilities are those that are not used very often, are not well developed, or are called upon to handle new situations. For example, when you are presented with a problem you have never seen before, the cognitive skills you bring to bear are your unexercised abilities. Unexercised abilities reflect the lower limit to your ability to perform cognitive problems. Notice that performance on traditional laboratory tasks, such as those included in many intelligence tests, closely approximates unexercised ability.

The dotted line represents optimally exercised ability, *the level of performance a normal, healthy adult demonstrates under the best conditions of training or practice.* Optimally exercised abilities are those you use the most, or ones you have practiced the most. Problems that tap these abilities are typically performed accurately and more quickly than those that test unexercised abilities, as you can see by

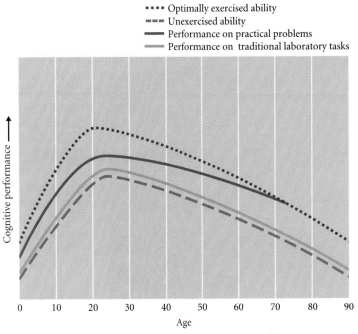

Denney, 1982.

comparing the solid line with the dotted line in the figure. Optimally exercised abilities, then, reflect areas in which you have greater expertise.

Whether a specific ability is unexercised or optimally exercised varies from individual to individual; for example, one person may have little training in computer programming, whereas the leader of a programming team at Microsoft would be highly skilled. Thus, how an ability is classified depends on the person's experience and expertise; it is not a property of the skill in question. This is an important distinction, as it means that interventions such as additional practice or education could shape the developmental trajectory of a particular ability.

The developmental course of unexercised and optimally exercised abilities is the same: They increase until young adulthood, plateau through middle age, and decline thereafter. As shown in the graph, the difference between performance on practical problems and optimally exercised ability is hypothesized to close rapidly during middle age. But do the data support Denney's speculations?

When people's answers to practical problems are evaluated in terms of how likely their answers are to be effective, practical intelligence does not appear to decline appreciably until late life (Denney, 1989, 1990). Successful solutions depend on prior experience, so it is not surprising that maturity brings effective approaches to problems. This pattern is similar to the one we encountered for crystallized intelligence on page 340 (Heidrich & Denney, 1994). However, the number of solutions generated tends to peak in middle age and decline somewhat thereafter (Denney & Pearce, 1989). This pattern is reminiscent of the one for fluid intelligence (see pages 339–340). Thus, whereas adults of all ages can figure out one effective way to deal with an uncooperative landlord, the *number* of solutions a person generates tends to decrease with age.

Practical Intelligence and Postformal Thinking

Additional links have been made between practical intelligence and postformal thinking across adulthood (Blanchard-Fields, Janke, & Camp, 1995). Specifically, the extent to which a practical problem evokes an emotional reaction, in

? THINK ABOUT IT
How are cognitive analysis, problem-focused action, passive-dependent behavior, and avoidant thinking and denial related to coping with stress?

conjunction with experience and one's preferred mode of thinking, determines whether one will use a cognitive analysis (thinking one's way through the problem), a problem-focused action (tackling the problem head-on by doing something about it), passive-dependent behavior (withdrawing from the situation), or avoidant thinking and denial (attempting to manage the meaning of the problem). For late middle-aged adults, highly emotional problems are associated most with passive-dependent and avoidant-denial approaches. Interestingly, though, problems that deal more with instrumental issues such as consumer issues and home management are dealt with differently (Blanchard-Fields, Chen, & Norris, 1997). Middle-aged adults use problem-focused strategies more frequently in dealing with instrumental problems than do adolescents or young adults. Clearly, we cannot characterize problem solving in middle age in any one way.

Practical intelligence has also emerged as an important approach in assessing adults' competence in performing everyday tasks. The Observed Tasks of Daily Living (ODTL) test assesses food preparation, medication intake, and telephone use, three key skills necessary for independent living (Diehl, Willis, & Schaie, 1995). The ODTL is a useful tool in determining whether adults are capable of living on their own. We will learn more about this issue in Chapter 14 when we consider the topic of frail older adults.

BECOMING AN EXPERT

One day, John Cavanaugh was driving along when his car suddenly began coughing and sputtering. As deftly as possible, he pulled over to the side of the road, turned off the engine, opened the hood, and proceeded to look inside. It

was hopeless; to him, it looked like a jumble of unknown parts. After the car was towed to a garage, a middle-aged mechanic like the man in the photograph set about fixing it. Within a few minutes, the car was running like new. How?

We saw in Chapter 9 that aspects of intelligence grounded in experience (crystallized intelligence) tend to improve throughout most of adulthood. Some developmentalists have gone so far as to claim that each of us becomes an expert at something that is important to us, such as our work, interpersonal relationships, cooking, sports, or auto repair (Dixon, Kramer, & Baltes, 1985). In this sense, an expert (like the mechanic or Kesha, the social worker in the vignette) is someone who is much better at a task than people who have not put much effort into it (such as John Cavanaugh, in terms of auto repair). We tend to become selective experts in some areas, while remaining rank amateurs or novices at others.

What makes experts better than novices? Most important, experts have built up a wealth of knowledge about alternative ways of solving problems or making decisions. These enable them to bypass steps needed by novices (Ericsson & Smith, 1991). Experts don't always follow the rules as novices do; are more flexible, creative, and curious; and have superior strategies for accomplishing a task (Charness & Bosman, 1990). Even though they may be slower in terms of raw speed because they spend more time planning, experts' ability to skip steps puts them at a decided advantage. In a way, this represents "the triumph of knowledge over reasoning" (Charness & Bosman, 1990).

Research evidence indicates that expert performance tends to peak in middle age and drop off slightly after that (Charness & Bosman, 1990). However, the declines in expert performance are not nearly as great as they are for the abilities of information processing, memory, and fluid intelligence that underlie expertise. Thus, it appears that knowledge based on experience is an important component of expertise.

But why are expertise and information processing, memory, and fluid intelligence not strongly related? After all, we saw in Chapter 9 that the latter abilities underlie good cognitive performance. Rybash, Hoyer, and Roodin (1986) proposed a process called *encapsulation* as the answer. *Their notion is that the* processes of thinking *(information processing, memory, fluid intelligence) become connected or* encapsulated *to the* products of thinking *(expertise).* This process of encapsulation allows expertise to compensate for declines in underlying abilities, perhaps by making thinking more efficient (Hoyer & Rybash, 1994).

Let's consider how encapsulation might work with auto mechanics. As a rule, people who become auto mechanics are taught to think as if they were playing a game of Twenty Questions, in which the optimal strategy is to ask a question such that the answer eliminates half of the remaining possibilities. In the beginning, the mechanic learns the thinking strategy and the content knowledge about automobiles separately. But as the person's experience with repairing automobiles increases, the thinking strategy and content knowledge merge; instead of having to go through a Twenty Questions approach, the expert mechanic just "knows" how to proceed. This cognitive-developmental pattern in adults is very different from the one that occurs in children (Hoyer & Rybash, 1994). In the adult's case, development is directed toward mastery and adaptive competency in specific domains, whereas during childhood it is more uniform across content domains.

One of the outcomes of encapsulation appears to be a decrease in the ability to explain how one arrives at a particular answer (Hoyer & Rybash, 1994). It appears that the increased efficiency that comes through merging the process with the product of thinking comes at the cost of being able to explain to others what one is doing. This could be why some instructors have a difficult time explaining the various steps involved in solving a problem to novice students, but an easier time explaining it to graduate students who have more background and experience.

We will return to the topic of expertise in Chapter 13 when we discuss wisdom, which some believe to be the outcome of becoming an expert in living.

THINK ABOUT IT
Can expertise be taught? Why or why not?

LIFELONG LEARNING

What do all of the people in the photographs at the top of page 458 have in common? They work in occupations in which information and technology change rapidly. To keep up with these changes, many organizations and professions now emphasize the importance of learning how to learn, rather than learning specific content that may become outdated in a couple of years. For most people, a college education will probably not be the last educational experience they have in their careers. Workers in many professions, such as medicine, nursing, social work, psychology, and teaching, are now required to obtain continuing education credits in order to stay current in their fields.

The need for lifelong learning is obvious on most college campuses. You have probably seen middle-aged adults in your classes (or you may be one yourself). The story of one middle-aged student is presented in the Real People feature. Many college instructors are including experiential elements in courses, as a response to the need for real-world connections.

REAL PEOPLE

COLLEGE AT MIDLIFE

Patrice worked for a savings and loan for 15 years, rising to the level of Vice President for Savings and Investment. Her achievement was even more remarkable because she had only a high school education. But when she wanted to change jobs, she ran into a cruel reality: Without a college degree, she had little chance of getting another executive-level position, even with her 15 years of experience. So, at age 37, Patrice decided to quit her job and get her degree.

Overcoming her fear that she couldn't compete with young adults was hard at first. Her reasons for being in school were much different from those of her younger classmates; Patrice was there for her self-esteem more than to please someone else. She found that her life experience was an advantage; many students eventually looked up to her for her insights. Her study skills were different. She found it hard to learn information by rote memorization; instead, she emphasized how information fit together. Although grades were somewhat important to her, learning was her primary goal. She enjoyed seeing how she could apply knowledge learned in one class to another one, and professors expressed delight at having her in class.

After 5½ years, Patrice graduated with a degree in accounting. She distinguished herself by being on the dean's list every semester she was in college, which really made her feel good about what she had accomplished. •

Lifelong learning takes place in settings other than college campuses, too. Many organizations offer workshops for their employees on a wide range of topics, from specific job-related topics to leisure-time activities. Additionally, many channels on cable television offer primarily educational programming, and computer networks and bulletin boards are available for educational exchanges. Only a few generations ago, a high school education was the ticket to a lifetime of secure employment. Today, lifelong learning is rapidly becoming the norm.

Lifelong learning is gaining acceptance as the best way to approach the need for continuing education and for retraining displaced workers. But should lifelong learning be approached as merely an extension of earlier educational experiences? Knowles (1984) argues that teaching aimed at children and youth differs from teaching aimed at adults. Adult learners differ from their younger counterparts in several ways:

- Adults have a higher need to know why they should learn something before undertaking it.

- Adults enter a learning situation with more and different experience on which to build.

- Adults are most willing to learn those things they believe are necessary to deal with real-world problems rather than abstract, hypothetical situations.

- Most adults are more motivated to learn by internal factors (such as self-esteem or personal satisfaction) than by external factors (such as a job promotion or pay raise).

Lifelong learning is becoming increasingly important, but educators need to keep in mind that learning styles change as people age.

---

1. The skills and knowledge necessary for people to function in everyday life make up _____ .

2. The difference between performance on practical problems and optimally exercised ability is hypothesized to _____ during middle age.

3. Even though they may be slower in terms of raw speed, experts are at a distinct advantage over novices because they _____ .

4. The way in which the process of thinking becomes connected to the products of thinking is termed _____ .

5. Due to rapidly changing technology and information, many educators now support the concept of _____ .

6. Based on the cognitive-developmental changes described in this section, what types of jobs would be done best by middle-aged adults?

Answers: (1) practical intelligence, (2) narrow, (3) can skip steps, (4) encapsulation, (5) lifelong learning

PERSONALITY

Personality

Stability Is the Rule: The Five-Factor Model

Change Is the Rule: Changing Priorities in Midlife

Learning Objectives

- **What is the five-factor model? What evidence is there for stability in personality traits?**

- **What changes occur in people's priorities and personal concerns? How does a person achieve generativity? How is midlife best described?**

$\mathcal{J}$**IM** *showed all the signs. He divorced his wife of nearly 20 years to enter into a relationship with a woman 15 years younger, sold his ordinary-looking mid-size sedan for a red sports car, and began working out regularly at the health club after years of being a couch potato. Jim claims he hasn't felt this good in years; he is happy to be making this change in middle age. All of Jim's friends agree: This is a clear case of midlife crisis. Or is it?*

The topic of personality development in middle age immerses us in one of the hottest debates in theory and research in adult development and aging. Take Jim's case. *Many people believe strongly that middle age brings with it a normative crisis called the* midlife crisis. There would appear to be lots of evidence to support this view, based on case studies like Jim's. But is everything as it seems? We'll find out in this section.

Unlike most of the other topics we have covered in this chapter, research on personality in middle-aged adults, like those in the photograph, is grounded in several competing theories, such as the psychoanalytic approach we encountered in Chapter 1. Another difference is that much of the research we will consider is longitudinal research, also discussed in Chapter 1.

First, we examine the evidence that personality traits remain fairly stable in adulthood. This position makes the claim that what you are like in young adulthood predicts pretty well what you will be like the rest of your life. Second, we consider the evidence that people's priorities and personal concerns change throughout adulthood, requiring adults to reassess themselves from time to time. This alternative position claims that change is the rule during adulthood.

At no other point in the life span is the debate about stability versus change as heated as it is concerning personality in middle age. In this section, we consider the evidence for both positions.

STABILITY IS THE RULE:
THE FIVE-FACTOR MODEL

One of the most important advances in research on adult development and aging in the past few decades has been the emergence of a personality theory aimed specifically at describing adults. Due mostly to the efforts of Paul Costa, Jr., and Robert McCrae, we are able to describe adults' personality traits using five dimensions (Costa & McCrae, 1990): neuroticism, extraversion, openness to experience, agreeableness, and conscientiousness. These dimensions are strongly grounded in cross-sectional, longitudinal, and sequential research. First, though, let's take a closer look at each dimension.

- Neuroticism. *People who are high on the* neuroticism *dimension tend to be anxious, hostile, self-conscious, depressed, impulsive, and vulnerable.* They may show violent or negative emotions that interfere with their ability to get along with others or to handle problems in everyday life. People who are low on this dimension tend to be calm, even-tempered, self-content, comfortable, unemotional, and hardy.

- Extraversion. *Individuals who are high on the* extraversion *dimension thrive on social interaction, like to talk, take charge easily, readily express their opinions and feelings, like to keep busy, have boundless energy, and prefer stimulating and challenging environments.* Such people tend to enjoy people-oriented jobs, such as social work and sales, and they often have humanitarian goals. People who are low tend to be reserved, quiet, passive, sober, and emotionally unreactive.

- Openness to experience. *Being high on the* openness to experience *dimension tends to mean a vivid imagination and dream life, appreciation of art, and a strong desire to try anything once.* These individuals tend to be naturally curious about things and to make decisions based on situational factors rather than absolute rules. People who are readily open to new experiences place a relatively low emphasis on personal economic gain. They tend to choose jobs such as the ministry or counseling, which offer diversity of experience rather than high pay. People who are low tend to be down-to-earth, uncreative, conventional, uncurious, and conservative.

- Agreeableness. *Scoring high on the* agreeableness *dimension is associated with being accepting, willingness to work with others, and caring.* Interestingly, people who score low on this dimension (i.e., demonstrate high levels of *antagonism*) show many of the characteristics of the Type A behavior pattern discussed earlier in this chapter. They tend to be ruthless, suspicious, stingy, antagonistic, critical, and irritable.

- Conscientiousness. *People who show high levels of* conscientiousness *tend to be hard-working, ambitious, energetic, scrupulous, and persevering.* Such people have a strong desire to make something of themselves. People at the opposite end of this scale tend to be negligent, lazy, disorganized, late, aimless, and nonpersistent.

What's the Evidence for Trait Stability?

Costa and McCrae, as well as other researchers, have examined whether their dimensions of personality remain stable through adulthood. In one study (Costa, McCrae, & Arenberg, 1980), more than 100 men were tested three times, with each of the follow-up testings about 6 years apart. Even over a 12-year span, the personality trait dimensions examined remained very stable.

Was this finding a fluke? Apparently not. Other researchers find similar stability over 8-year spans (Siegler, George, & Okun, 1979) and even 30-year spans (Leon et al., 1979). Even spouses' ratings of their partner's personality traits showed no systematic changes over a 6-year period (Costa & McCrae, 1988). Thus, it looks like people's personality traits change little over very long periods of time.

Although the five-factor model enjoys great popularity and appears to have much supporting evidence, it is not perfect. Some writers have argued that the findings of stability are due to statistical artifacts and that more carefully designed research is needed (Alwin, 1994; Block, 1995). Others point out that the five-factor model does not explain human behavior, ignores the sociocultural context in which development occurs, and reduces a person to scores on five dimensions anchored by terms that are assumed to be both meaningful and opposite (McAdams, 1992). There are also some data indicating that certain personality traits (self-confidence, cognitive commitment, outgoingness, and dependability) show some change over a 30- to 40-year period (Jones & Meredith, 1996).

Even acknowledging the problems, though, evidence for overall stability in personality traits across adulthood is a very important finding, especially considering the many life situations that do change (e.g., getting married, changing jobs, having children leave home). One way to view this evidence is that the traits described by Costa and McCrae only provide the building blocks of one's personality (McAdams, 1992). In this view, the raw material on which personality is built remains relatively constant. But, as we will see next and again in Chapter 14, what a person chooses to do with these building blocks, and the behaviors based on them, may not be as consistent.

CHANGE IS THE RULE: CHANGING PRIORITIES IN MIDLIFE

Joyce, a 52-year-old preschool teacher, thought carefully about what she thinks is important in life. "I definitely feel differently about what I want to accomplish. When I was younger, I wanted to advance and be a great teacher. Now, although I still want to be good, I'm more concerned now with providing help to the new teachers around here. I've got lots of on-the-job experience that I can pass along."

Joyce is not alone. Despite the evidence that personality traits remain stable during adulthood, many middle-aged people like the man in the photograph report that their personal priorities change during middle age. In general, they report that they are increasingly concerned with helping younger people achieve rather than with getting ahead themselves. *In his psychosocial theory, Erikson argued that this shift in priorities reflects gen*erativity, *or being productive by helping others in order to ensure the continuation of society by guiding the next generation.*

Achieving generativity can be very enriching. It is grounded in the successful resolution of the previous six phases of Erikson's theory (see Chapter 1). There are many avenues for generativity, such as through mentoring (see Chapter 11), volunteering, foster grandparent programs, and many other activities.

Some adults do not achieve generativity. Instead, they become bored, self-indulgent, and unable to contribute to the continuation of society. *Erikson referred to this state as* stagnation, *in which people are unable to deal with the needs of their children or to provide mentoring to younger adults.*

What Are Generative People Like?

In order to describe generativity so that we can recognize it in someone, several researchers have constructed a research-based description of it. One of the best is McAdams's model (McAdams, Hart, & Maruna, 1997), shown in the figure. This multidimensional model shows how generativity results from the complex interconnections among societal and inner forces, which create a concern for the next generation and a belief in the goodness of the human enterprise, leading to generative commitment, which produces generative actions. A person derives personal meaning from being generative by constructing a life story, or narration, which helps create the person's identity (Whitbourne, 1986, 1996; see Chapter 9).

The components of McAdams's model relate differently to personality traits. For example, generative *concern* relates to life satisfaction and overall happiness, whereas generative *action* does not (de St. Aubin & McAdams, 1995). New grandparents may derive much satisfaction from their grandchildren and are greatly concerned with their well-being, but have little desire to engage in the daily hassles of caring for them on a regular basis. Women who exhibit high generativity tend to have prosocial personality traits, are personally invested in being a parent, express generative attitudes at work, and exhibit caring behaviors toward others outside their immediate families (Peterson & Klohnen, 1995), as well as show high well-being in their role as a spouse (MacDermid, De Haan, & Heilbrun, 1996). These results have led to the creation of positive and negative generativity indices that reliably identify differences between generative and nongenerative individuals (Himsel et al., 1997).

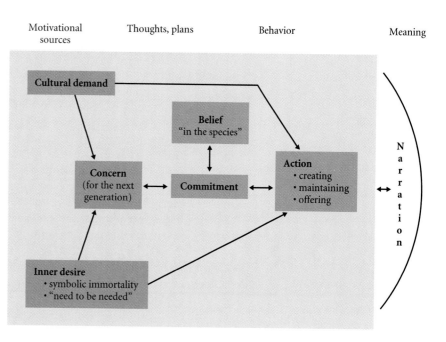

The growing evidence on generativity indicates that the personal concerns and priorities of middle-aged adults are different from those of younger adults. But is this view supported in other aspects of personality? Let's consider gender-role identity as an example.

Does Gender-Role Identity Converge?

People's beliefs about the appropriate characteristics for men and women reflect shared cultural beliefs and stereotypes of "masculinity" and "femininity" (Williams & Best, 1990). Across a wide age range in U.S. society, women are traditionally described as weaker, less active, more concerned with affiliation, and more nurturing and deferential. Men are regarded as stronger; more active; and higher in autonomy, achievement, and aggression (Huyck, 1990). Collectively, such descriptions help form one's gender-role identity.

As we know, the five-factor model makes a strong case for the stability of personality traits through adulthood. In contrast, we have seen that people's priorities and personal concerns change during adulthood. Does stability or change describe what happens to the gender-role identity of the man and woman in the photograph?

Beginning with Jung (1933), several researchers and theorists argue for a "crossover effect" of gender identity during middle age. Specifically, Jung (1933) proposed that certain aspects of personality are suppressed in adolescence and young adulthood, only to reemerge during middle age. For example, Jung believed that women initially suppress their masculine aspects and men initially suppress their feminine aspects; each discovers these suppressed aspects and develops them in midlife, with the goal of achieving a balance between one's masculine and feminine characteristics. For example, during midlife women may place increased emphasis on achievement and accomplishment, and men may place more emphasis on familial and nurturant concerns (Parker & Aldwin, 1997).

Overall, the data on actual changes in people's gender-role identity are mixed. Some studies find a tendency for middle-aged and older adults to endorse similar self-descriptions concerning gender-role identity. For example, some research indicates that both men and women describe themselves as more nurturing, intimate, and tender with increasing age (Gutmann, 1987; Sinnott, 1986), trends that are related to generativity. Other studies show decreasing endorsement of traditional feminine traits in both men and women, but stable endorsements of masculine traits (Parker & Aldwin, 1997). Collectively, the data indicate that men and women are most different in their gender-role identities in late adolescence and young adulthood but become increasingly similar in midlife and old age (Huyck, 1990).

Increasing similarity in self-descriptions does not guarantee increased similarity in the way men and women behave. For example, older men often indicate a willingness to develop close relationships, but few actually do, because they lack the necessary skills (Turner, 1982). Thus, the convergence may be happening more internally than behaviorally (Parker & Aldwin, 1997; Troll & Bengtson, 1982). Does gender-role identity converge? At this point, the statistical evidence appears to indicate that it does, but the behavioral evidence appears to indicate it does not.

Life Transition Theories and the Midlife Crisis

Erikson's notion that people experience fundamental changes in their priorities and personal concerns was grounded in the possibility that middle adulthood includes other important changes. Indeed, Carl Jung, one of the founders of psychoanalytic theory, believed that adults may experience a midlife crisis. This belief led to the development of several theories postulating that adulthood consists of alternating periods of stability and transition that people experience in a fixed sequence.

Levinson and colleagues (1978; Levinson & Levinson, 1996), Gould (1978), and Vaillant (1977) developed life transition theories based on longitudinal studies of fairly exclusive and nonrepresentative groups of adults (in some cases only men) over several decades. Data were gathered mainly through interviews and personal reflections of the participants.

Despite the popularity of these theories, some of which were turned into best-selling books, the evidence for universal age-related stages is based on far fewer and much more selective samples than are the data from the personality trait research or research on generativity. As the You May Be Wondering feature indicates, the bulk of the evidence does not support the view of a universal stage such as a midlife crisis that everyone experiences at the same point in life.

Nevertheless, as we saw in our consideration of generativity, there is substantial evidence that people do experience some sort of fundamental change in themselves at some point during adulthood. Thus, it may well be that most adults pass through transitions at some point; when those transitions will occur, though, is largely unpredictable. Perhaps a better way to view midlife is as a time that presents unique challenges and issues that must be negotiated (Bumpass & Aquilino, 1995).

DOES EVERYONE HAVE A MIDLIFE CRISIS?

Ask people to give an example of what they think a midlife crisis is, and chances are they will relate a story like that of Jim, the recently divorced guy with the red sports car in the vignette. Indeed, few people in the United States would have difficulty providing an example, as most people believe that a midlife crisis is inevitable. In part, this belief is fostered by descriptions of personality development in adulthood that have appeared in the popular press.

We have seen that theorists such as Erikson believe that adults face several important challenges and that by struggling with these issues people develop new aspects of themselves. But does this mean that everyone necessarily has a midlife crisis? Some researchers say it does; middle-aged men report intense inner struggles that are much like depression (Levinson et al., 1978).

However, by far the bulk of the research evidence fails to support the idea that most adults experience difficulty at the level of a crisis in midlife. Research involving women and men, using a variety of methods such as interviews and personality tests, shows that unexpected events (such as divorce or job transfers) are much more likely to create stress than are normative midlife events (such as menopause or becoming a grandparent) (Baruch, 1984; Haan, Milsap, & Hartka, 1986; Roberts & Newton, 1987). Reanalysis of Costa and McCrae's data, specifically looking for evidence of a midlife crisis, revealed only a handful of men who fit the classic profile, and even then the crisis came anywhere between the ages of 30 and 60 (Costa & McCrae, 1978; Farrell & Rosenberg, 1981). There may be universal stresses during midlife, but there is no set way of dealing with them (Farrell & Rosenberg, 1981).

Is there a midlife crisis? The evidence indicates that for most people, midlife is no more or no less traumatic than any other period. Even investigators who believed strongly in the existence of a midlife crisis when they began their research admitted that they could find no support for it despite extensive testing and interviewing (Farrell & Rosenberg, 1981). Thus, Jim's behavior may have an explanation, but it's not because he's going through a universal midlife crisis. ●

If midlife is not characterized by a crisis, but does present unique challenges and issues, how do people negotiate it successfully? *The secret seems to be* ego resilience, *a powerful personality resource that enables people to handle midlife changes.* Longitudinal data from two samples indicate that people who enter middle age with high ego resilience are more likely to experience it as an opportunity for change and growth, whereas people with low ego resilience are more likely to experience it as a time of stagnation or decline (Klohnen, Vandewater, & Young, 1996). Individual differences in the timing of such experiences and how people deal with midlife are very large, which probably accounts for the failure to find a universal midlife crisis (Klohnen et al., 1996). Ego resilience may also be the resource that could account for the two outcomes (generativity and stagnation) of Erikson's view of midlife.

In sum, perhaps the best way to view the life transitions associated with middle age is through the words of a 52-year-old woman (Klohnen et al., 1996):

> Middle age. . . . The time when you realize you've moved to the caretaker, senior responsibility role. . . . A time of discomfort because you watch the generation before you, whom you have loved and respected and counted on for emotional back-up, for advice . . . become more dependent on you and then die. Your children grow up, move out, try their wings . . . ; indeed, they attempt to teach you the "truths" they've discovered about life. . . . It's time to make some new choices—groups, friends, activities need not be so child related anymore.

TEST YOURSELF

1. The _____ dimension in the five-factor theory of personality includes anxiety, hostility, and impulsiveness.

2. According to Erikson, an increasing concern with helping younger people achieve is termed _____ .

3. According to McAdams, the meaning one derives from being generative happens through the process of _____ .

4. Statistical evidence indicates that gender-role identity _____ in middle age.

5. Research indicates that _____ is a key personality factor in predicting who will negotiate midlife successfully.

6. How can you reconcile the data from trait research, which indicates little change, with the data from other research, which shows substantial change in personality in adulthood?

Answers: (1) neuroticism, (2) generativity, (3) narration, (4) converges, (5) ego resilience

FAMILY DYNAMICS AND MIDDLE AGE

Learning Objectives

- **How does the relationship between middle-aged parents and their young adult children change?**

- **How do middle-aged adults deal with their aging parents?**

- **What styles of grandparenthood do middle-aged adults experience? How do grandchildren and grandparents interact?**

Family Dynamics and Middle Age

Letting Go: Middle-Aged Adults and Their Children

Going Back: Middle-Aged Adults and Their Aging Parents

Grandparenthood

Ɛ **STHER** *is facing a major milestone: Her youngest child, Megan, is about to head off to college. But instead of feeling depressed, as she thought she would, Esther feels almost elated at the prospect. She and Bill are finally free of the day-to-day parenting duties of the past 30 years. Esther is looking forward to getting to know her husband again. She wonders whether there is something wrong with her for being excited that her daughter is moving away.*

People like Esther connect generations. Family ties across the generations like those shown in the photograph provide the context for socialization and for continuity in the family's identity. At the center age-wise are members of the middle-aged generation, like Esther, who serve as the links between their aging parents and their own maturing children (Hareven & Adams, 1996). *Middle-aged mothers (more than fathers) tend to take on this role of* kinkeeper, *the person who gathers family members together for celebrations and keeps them in touch with each other.*

Think about the major issues confronting a typical middle-aged couple: maintaining a good marriage, parenting responsibilities, children who are becoming adults themselves, job pressures, and concern about aging parents, just to name a few. Middle-aged adults truly have quite a lot to deal with every day (Hamill & Goldberg, 1997). *Indeed, middle-aged adults are sometimes referred to as the* sandwich *generation; they are caught between the competing demands of two generations (their parents and their children).* Being in the sandwich generation means different things for women and men. When middle-aged women assess how well they are dealing with the midlife transition, their most pressing issues relate more to their adolescent children than to their aging parents; for middle-aged men, it is the other way around (Hamill & Goldberg, 1997).

In this section, we first examine the dynamics of middle-aged parents and their maturing children and discover whether Esther's feelings are typical. Next, we consider the issues facing middle-aged adults and their aging parents. Later, we consider what happens when people become grandparents.

LETTING GO: MIDDLE-AGED ADULTS AND THEIR CHILDREN

Being a parent has a rather strange side, when you think about it. After creating children out of love, parents spend considerable time, effort, and money preparing them to become independent and leave. For most parents, the leaving (and sometimes returning) occurs during midlife.

Becoming Friends and the Empty Nest

Sometime during middle age, most parents like those in the photograph experience two positive developments with regard to their children. Suddenly their

children see them in a new light, and the children leave home.

After the strain of raising adolescents, parents appreciate the transformation that occurs when their children head into young adulthood. In general, parent-child relationships improve when children become young adults (Troll & Fingerman, 1996). The difference can be dramatic, as in the case of Deb, a middle-aged mother. "When Sacha was 15, she acted as if I was the dumbest person on the planet. But now that she's 21, she acts as if I got smart all of a sudden. I like being around her. She's a great kid, and we're really becoming friends."

A key factor in making this transition as smoothly as possible is the extent to which parents foster and approve of their children's attempts at being independent. Most parents are like Esther, the mother in the vignette, and manage the transition to an empty nest successfully (Lewis & Lin, 1996). That's not to say that parents are heartless. When children leave home, emotional bonds are disrupted. Both mothers and fathers feel the change. It's just that only about 25% of mothers and fathers report being very sad and unhappy when the last child leaves home (Lewis & Lin, 1996).

Still, parents provide considerable financial help (such as paying college tuition) when possible. Most help in other ways ranging from the mundane (such as making the washer and dryer available to their college-age children) to the extraordinary (providing the down payment for their child's house). Young adults and their middle-aged parents generally believe that they have strong, positive relationships and that they can count on each other for help when necessary (Troll & Bengtson, 1982).

Of course, all this help doesn't mean that everything is perfect. Conflicts still arise. One study found that about one-third of middle-class fathers surveyed complained about their sons' lack of achievement or about their daughters' poor choice of husbands (Nydegger, 1986). This study highlights the importance parents place on how their children turned out. As discussed in the Spotlight on Research feature, this issue is rather complex.

HOW DO YOU THINK YOUR CHILDREN TURNED OUT?

Who was the investigator and what was the aim of the study? Carol Ryff and colleagues (1994) believed that parents' assessment of their children's accomplishments is an important part of the parents' midlife evaluation of themselves. Moreover, because parents are the major influence on children (see Chapters 4 and 7), the stakes for this self-evaluation are high; how one's child turns out is a powerful statement about one's success or failure as a parent (Ryff et al., 1994). Ryff and colleagues decided to see how these issues actually play out in parents' and children's lives.

How did the investigators measure the topic of interest? Ryff and colleagues asked parents to rate their child's adjustment and educational and occupational attainment, to compare the child to others of that age, and to rate their psychological well-being.

Who were the participants in the study? Ryff and colleagues selected a random sample of 114 middle-aged mothers and 101 middle-aged fathers, all from different middle-class families in the Midwest, who had at least one child aged 21 or over. With these characteristics, the sample was not representative of the population at large.

What was the design of the study? The study was a cross-sectional examination of parents' ratings of their children's achievements.

Were there ethical concerns with the study? Because the study used volunteers who completed surveys containing no questions about sensitive topics, there were no ethical concerns.

What were the results? As you can see in the graph, mothers and fathers have many hopes and dreams for their children. Happiness and educational success were the most common responses, followed by career success. There were no statistically significant differences between mothers' and fathers' responses.

The data also showed that the parents' views of their children's personal and social adjustment correlated closely with measures of the parents' own well-being. Parents' sense of self-acceptance, purpose in life, and environmental mastery were strongly related to how well they thought their children were adjusted. Similar, but somewhat weaker, relations were found between children's accomplishments and

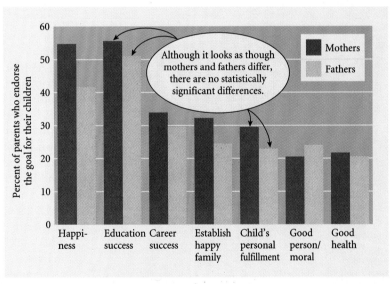

parental well-being. Again, no differences between mothers and fathers were found.

Parents were also asked how well they thought their children were doing compared to themselves when they were the same age. These data were intriguing. Parents who thought their children were better adjusted (i.e., more self-confident, happy, and interpersonally skilled) than they themselves were in early adulthood reported low levels of well-being. Why? Shouldn't parents be pleased that their children are well adjusted? Ryff and colleagues suggest that this finding, though seemingly counterintuitive, is really understandable in terms of social comparison. That is, people suffer negative consequences (such as having lower self-esteem) when they perceive other people as doing better than they are (Suls & Wills, 1991). Even though parents by and large want their children to be happy, they may have difficulty accepting it if they turn out to be *too* happy.

In contrast, parents who rated their children as having attained better educational and occupational levels felt more positive about themselves compared to parents who rated their children lower on these dimensions. In this case, parents may feel that they have fulfilled the American dream, helping the next generation do better than they did.

What did the investigators conclude? Ryff and colleagues showed that midlife parents' self-evaluations of their own well-being are clearly related to their perceptions of how their children turned out. Thus, their supposition that how children turn out is strongly connected with middle-aged parents' sense of self was supported. •

When Children Come Back

Parents' satisfaction with the empty nest is sometimes short-lived. Like the father in the photograph, roughly half of all middle-aged parents who have adult children have at least one, typically unmarried, child living with them. Interestingly, this living arrangement is more common if the parents are in good health, and the parents continue to do most of the housework (Ward, Logan, & Spitze, 1992). Moreover, adult children do not move back home primarily to help their parents, but rather for financial reasons or help with child care, when the young adult is a single parent.

Although middle-aged parents rarely turn their backs on their children, most had not planned on children returning home to live once they had moved out. Neither generation is thrilled with living together again. Both tend to handle the situation better if the returning children are in their early 20s and if the situation is clearly temporary (Clemons & Axelson, 1985). Still, conflict can arise. About 4 in 10 parents report serious conflicts, and arguments over lifestyle, friends, and personal care habits are common (Clemons & Axelson, 1985). Unless parents and adult children both choose to live together, parents' marriages are negatively affected when such conflicts arise. When times are hard, though, adult children may not have much choice but to live with their parents.

GIVING BACK: MIDDLE-AGED ADULTS AND THEIR AGING PARENTS

No matter how old you may be, being someone's child is a role that people still play well into adulthood and, sometimes, into their 60s and 70s. How do middle-aged adults relate to their parents?

Middle-aged children and their parents contact each other fairly frequently. Roughly 80% of older parents have seen one of their children in the past two weeks, a rate that does not differ between urban and rural dwellers (Krout, 1988). Some middle-aged children use these visits to reevaluate the meaning of the relationship as their parents approach death (Helson & Moane, 1987).

What happens when their parents become frail? How do middle-aged adults like the man in the photograph deal with the need to care for their parents?

Caring for Aging Parents

Most middle-aged adults have parents who are in reasonably good health. For a growing number of people, however, being a middle-aged child of aging parents involves providing some level of care. The job of caring for older parents usually falls to a daughter or a daughter-in-law (Stephens & Franks, 1999). Even after ruling out all other demographic characteristics of adult child caregivers and their care recipients, daughters are more than three times as likely to provide care as sons (Dwyer & Coward, 1991). This gender difference is also found in other cultures. For example, in Japan, even though the oldest son is responsible for parental care, it is his wife who actually does the day-to-day caregiving (Morioka, 1998).

In some situations, older parents must move in with one of their children. Such moves usually occur after decades of both generations living independently. This history of independent living sets the stage for adjustment difficulties following the move; both life-styles must be accommodated. Most of the time, adult children provide care for their mothers, who may in turn have provided care for their husbands before they died. (Spousal caregiving is discussed in Chapter 14.) In other situations, adult daughters must try to manage care from a distance, as depicted in the cartoon *For Better or Worse*. As we will see later, irrespective of the location of care, women are under considerable stress from the pressures of caregiving.

© Lynn Johnston Productions Inc./Dist. by United Features Syndicate, Inc.

Caring for one's parent presents a dilemma (Wolfson et al., 1993). *Most adult children feel a sense of responsibility, termed* filial obligation, *to care for their parent if necessary.* For example, adult child caregivers sometimes express the feeling that they "owe it to Mom or Dad" to care for them; after all, their parent provided for them for many years, and now the shoe is on the other foot (Myers & Cavanaugh, 1995). This appears to be universal: Adult children provide care when needed to their parents in all Western and non-Western cultures studied (Hareven & Adams, 1996). Viewed from a global perspective, all but a small percentage of care to older adults is provided by adult children and other family members (Hareven & Adams, 1996; Pavalko & Artis, 1997).

Research indicates that middle-aged adults expend a great deal of energy, time, and money helping their older parents (Brody, 1990). In fact, nearly 90% of the daily help older people receive comes from adult children and other relatives (Morris & Sherwood, 1984). These efforts pay off. Family care helps prevent or at least delay institutionalization (Brody, 1981).

Caring for an older parent is not easy. It usually doesn't happen by choice; each party would just as soon live apart. The potential for conflict over daily routines and life-styles is high. Indeed, one major source of conflict between middle-aged daughters and their older mothers is differences in perceived need for care, with middle-aged daughters believing that their mothers needed care more than the mothers believed they did (Fingerman, 1996).

Caregiving Stress

Caregiving is also a major source of stress. Adult children and other family caregivers are especially vulnerable to stress from two main sources (Pearlin et al., 1990):

- Adult children may have trouble coping with declines in their parents' functioning, especially those involving cognitive abilities and problematic behavior, and with the work overload, burnout, and loss of the previous relationship with a parent.

- When the caregiving situation is perceived as confining, or seriously infringes on the adult child's other responsibilities (spouse, parent, employee, etc.), the situation is likely to be perceived negatively, which may lead to family or job conflicts, economic problems, loss of self-identity, and decreased competence.

? **THINK ABOUT IT**
Why does parental caregiving fall mainly to women?

Caring for a parent entails psychological costs. Even the most devoted adult child caregiver feels depressed, resentful, angry, and guilty at times (Halpern, 1987). Many middle-aged caregivers are pressed financially, as they may still be paying child care or college tuition expenses, and trying to save adequately for their own retirement. Financial pressures are especially serious for those caring for parents with chronic conditions, such as Alzheimer's disease, that require services that are not covered by medical insurance. In some cases, adult children may even need to quit their jobs in order to provide care if adequate alternatives, such as adult day care, are unavailable or unaffordable.

The stresses of caring for one's parent are especially difficult for women, as is likely true for the woman in the photograph on page 473. In terms of its timing in the life course, caring for a parent is typically something that coincides with women's peak employment years of 35–64 (Moen, Robinson, & Fields, 1994). Longitudinal research clearly shows that employment status has no effect on women's decisions to become caregivers (many have little choice), but that becoming a caregiver makes it likely that women will reduce employment hours or stop working (Pavalko & Artis, 1997). When you consider that most women caring for parents are also mothers, wives, and employees, it should come as no surprise that stress from these other roles exacerbates the effects of stress due to caregiving (Stephens & Townsend, 1997).

What aspects of women's roles reduce the stress of caregiving? Having a secure attachment style to one's parent appears to buffer some aspects of stress (Crispi, Schiaffino, & Berman, 1997). Additionally, the rewards one gains as an employee, but not those from being a wife or mother, also seem to buffer the experience of caregiving stress (Stephens & Townsend, 1997).

Ethnic differences in adult children's experiences of caregiving stress are becoming better documented. Compared to European Americans, Hispanic American family members are likely to be caring for people who are at higher risk of chronic disease and are more disabled (Aranda & Knight, 1997). Hispanic American and African American caregivers, compared to European Americans, are more likely to be an adult child, friend, or other relative; report lower levels of caregiver stress, burden, and depression; believe more strongly in filial obligation; and are more likely to use prayer, faith, or religion as a coping strategy (Connell & Gibson, 1997). Such differences show that the relation between caregiving and stress is mediated by beliefs in family cohesiveness versus individual independence, as well as one's socialization.

From the parent's perspective, things aren't always rosy either. Independence and autonomy are important traditional values in some ethnic groups, and their loss is not taken lightly. Older adults in these groups are more likely to express the desire to pay a professional for assistance rather than ask a family member for help; they may find it demeaning to live with their children (Hamon & Blieszner, 1990). Most move in only as a last resort. Frank, a 79-year-old retired steelworker, put it more bluntly: "Getting help from my kid and living in her house were the *last* things I wanted to do. I don't need her telling me what to do and messing up my life. I'm her *father*. I'd rather have help from a stranger. I just don't have the money."

THE COMPLEXITIES OF CARING FOR OLDER PARENTS

FORCES IN ACTION

Caring for older parents is not something for which most people are prepared, but which many of us will experience. As anyone in the situation can attest, providing care to parents is a complex and demanding aspect of one's life, making it an excellent example of the biopsychosocial model.

Biologically, caregiving can place high levels of physiological stress on caregivers. Long-term stress takes a serious toll on health; indeed, it is too often the case that caregivers develop serious health problems as a direct result of the stress of caregiving. Psychologically, caring for our parent forces us to reevaluate our relationship with the parent, and engage in a type of "role reversal" from being the one cared for to the person providing the care. Trying to balance our responsibilities between our children and parents is especially tough. Additionally, we as the caregiver are confronted and must come to terms with the negative consequences of aging, a difficult task when it involves our parent. Socioculturally, how we assume the caregiving role is influenced very heavily by cultural and socioeconomic factors. In most cultures, daughters and daughters-in-law are expected to take care of parents far more often than sons and sons-in-law. The financial aspects of caregiving, such as health care costs, can be enormous, and create serious financial hardships and stresses for middle- and lower-income families.

Clearly, caring for parents involves a complex interaction among biological, psychological, and sociocultural forces. Maintaining a balance among them in order to be a successful caregiver is difficult, but can be achieved. •

GRANDPARENTHOOD

Becoming a grandparent takes some help. Being a parent yourself, of course, is a prerequisite. But it is your children's decisions and actions that determine whether you will experience the transition to grandparenthood, making this role different from most others we experience throughout life (Stephens & Clark, 1996). Most people become grandparents in their 40s and 50s (Thomas, 1992), though some are older or perhaps as young as their late 20s or early 30s (Kivnick, 1982). In most cases, grandparents are quite likely to still be employed and to have living parents themselves. Thus, although being a grandparent may be an exciting time, it is often only one part of their busy lives (Stephens & Clark, 1996).

How Do Grandparents Interact with Grandchildren?

Keisha, an 8-year-old girl, smiled brightly when asked to describe her grandparents. "Nana Mary gives me chocolate ice cream, and that's my favorite! Poppy Bill sometimes takes care of me when Momma and Daddy go out, and plays ball with me." Kyle, a 14-year-old, had a different view. "My grandparents generally tell me stories of what life was like back when they were young."

As Keisha's and Kyle's experiences show, grandparents have many different ways of interacting with their grandchildren. Categorizing these styles has been attempted over the years (e.g., Neugarten & Weinstein, 1964), but none has been overly successful because grandparents use different styles with different grandchildren and styles change as grandparents and grandchildren age (Stephens & Clark, 1996).

Many of the functions grandparents serve can be understood as reflecting different levels of the social and personal dimensions (Cherlin & Furstenberg, 1986). The social dimension includes societal needs and expectations of what grandparents are to do, such as passing on family history to grandchildren. The personal dimension includes the personal satisfaction and individual needs that are fulfilled by being a grandparent. Like the grandfather in the photograph, many grandparents pass on skills, as well as religious, social, and vocational values (social dimension) through storytelling and advice, and they may feel great pride and satisfaction (personal dimension) from working with grandchildren on joint projects.

Grandchildren give grandparents a great deal in return. For example, grandchildren keep grandparents in touch with youth and the latest trends. Sharing the excitement of surfing the Web in school may be one way in which grandchildren keep grandparents on the technological forefront.

Being a Grandparent Is Meaningful

Does being a grandparent matter to people? You bet it does, at least to the vast majority of grandparents. Kivnick (1982, 1985) identified five dimensions of meaning that grandparents often assign to their roles. *For some, grandparenting is the most important thing in their lives, termed* centrality. *For others, meaning comes from being seen as wise* (valued elder), *from spoiling grandchildren* (indulgence), *from recalling the relationship they had with their own grandparents* (reinvolvement with personal past), *or from taking pride in the fact that they will be followed by not one but two generations* (immortality through clan).

Most grandparents derive several different meanings, regardless of the style of their relationship with the grandchildren (Miller & Cavanaugh, 1990). Similar findings are reported when overall satisfaction with being a grandparent is examined; no matter what their style is, grandparents find their role meaningful (Thomas, Bence, & Meyer, 1988).

Grandchildren also highly value their relationships with grandparents (Kennedy, 1991). Grandparents are valued as role models, and for their personalities, the activities they share, and the attention they show to grandchildren. Grandchildren also note that when their grandparents are frail, helping their grandparents is a way for them to act on their altruistic beliefs (Kennedy, 1991).

Ethnic Differences

How grandparents and grandchildren interact varies in different ethnic groups. For example, African American grandmothers under age 40 report feeling pressured to provide care for grandchildren they were not eager to have; in contrast, those over age 60 tend to feel that they are fulfilling an important role (Kivett, 1991). African American grandparents tend to be more involved in teaching their grandchildren and more willing to take a grandparent education course than are European American grandparents (Watson & Koblinsky, 1997). African American grandfathers tend to perceive grandparenthood as a central role to a greater degree than European American grandfathers (Kivett, 1991).

Grandparenting style also varies with ethnicity, which may sometimes create tension within families. Kornhaber (1985) relates the case of an 18-month-old girl who had one pair of Latino grandparents and one pair of Nordic grandparents. Her Latino grandparents tickled her, frolicked with her, and doted over her. Her Nordic grandparents loved her just as much but tended to just let her be. Her Latina mother thought that the Nordic grandparents were "cold and hard," and her Nordic father accused the Latino grandparents of "driving him crazy" with their displays of affection. The child, though, was flexible enough to adapt to both styles.

Native American grandparents like those in the photograph appear to have some interactive styles

? **THINK ABOUT IT**
How is being a grandparent related to generativity?

different from those of other groups (Weibel-Orlando, 1990). Fictive grand-parenting *is a style that allows adults to fill in for missing or deceased biological grandparents, functionally creating the role of surrogate grandparent.* These adults provide a connection to the older generation that otherwise would be absent for these children. *In the* cultural conservator *style, grandparents request that their grandchildren be allowed to live with them in order to ensure that the grandchildren learn the native ways.* These grandparents provide grandchildren a way to connect with their cultural heritage. In general, Native American grand-mothers take a more active role in these styles than grandfathers.

The Changing Role of Grandparents

Grandparenthood today is tougher than it used to be. For many reasons, detachment rather than close involvement characterizes an increasing number of grandparent-grandchild relationships, in contrast to the more involved styles of a few decades ago (Rodeheaver & Thomas, 1986). Families are more mobile, which means that grandparents are more often separated from their grandchildren by geographical distance. Grandparents are more likely to have independent lives, apart from their children and grandchildren. What being a grandparent entails as we move into the 21st century is more ambiguous than it once was (Stephens & Clark, 1996).

In addition to mobility and life-style factors, divorce is a key factor in deter-mining how grandparents and grandchildren interact, if at all. We noted in Chapter 10 that the divorce rate in the United States is roughly 50% for recent marriages. Many grandparents face the possibility that contact with their grand-children will be limited as a result of divorce (Johnson, 1988). Both grandpar-ents and grandchildren express strong desires for continued contact (Schutter, Scherman, & Carroll, 1997). Unfortunately, many states do not have specific protections for grandparents' rights following their child's divorce (Edelstein, 1990). In general, contact is highest for maternal grandmothers whose daugh-ters have custody of the grandchildren. In contrast, paternal grandfathers are least likely to maintain contact if their sons do not have custody of the grand-children (Cherlin & Furstenberg, 1986). Because grandparenthood is an impor-tant and meaningful role, diminished contact with grandchildren due to divorce is an especially difficult ordeal for everyone concerned.

Another major change is the increasing number of grandparents who serve as surrogate parents for their grandchildren (Burton, 1992; Minkler & Roe, 1993). These situations result most often when parents are addicted, incarcer-ated, or unable to raise their children for some other reason. Such grand-parents face difficult challenges, as the stresses of parenting have changed over the possibly several decades since they last faced them. Lack of legal recogni-tion due to the lack of legal guardianship also poses problems and challenges, for example, in dealing with schools and obtaining records.

Despite the obstacles, most grandparents are comfortable with their role. Most report that they have little desire (and no responsibility) to rear their grandchildren. In fact, grandparents who feel responsible for advising their grandchildren tend to be less satisfied with their role than those who feel that their role is mainly to enjoy their grandchildren (Thomas, 1986). Thus, for maximum satisfaction, the role should be grandparental rather than parental.

TEST YOURSELF

1. The term _____ refers to middle-aged adults who have both living parents and children of their own.

2. The people who gather the family together for celebrations and keep family members in touch are called _____ .

3. Most caregiving for aging parents is provided by _____ .

4. The sense of personal responsibility to care for one's parents is called _____ .

5. The _____ meaning of grandparenthood refers to the desire to be an esteemed and wise resource to grandchildren.

6. _____ grandparents have a style called cultural conservator.

7. If you were to create a guide to families for middle-aged adults, what would your most important pieces of advice be? Why did you select these?

Answers: (1) sandwich generation, (2) kin-keepers, (3) daughters and daughters-in-law, (4) filial obligation, (5) valued elder, (6) Native American

PUTTING IT ALL TOGETHER

Is it any wonder why middle age gets bad press? There's a lot to face: signs of biological aging, children leaving, cognitive abilities changing, and parents dying. But middle age also has much going for it, from many people's perspective: generally good relationships with children, grandparenthood, and accumulated experience. We saw how middle age is partly a continuation of previous developmental trends (e.g., in aspects of cognitive development and personality) and partly a time of new challenges (such as getting used to physical changes and dealing with different generations in the family).

We learned that Dean, the man who reacted negatively to losing his hair, is pretty typical of many middle-aged people confronting the first signs of aging. Kesha's expertise in social work is also typical of middle-aged adults, many of whom become experts in one area or another. We saw that Jim's behavior is not a reflection of a universal midlife crisis. Esther's joy and relief when her youngest daughter moved out is the reaction of most middle-aged parents who acquire an empty nest (at least until their adult children decide to move back).

Judging from the information in this chapter and in Chapters 10 and 11, middle age has many positive aspects—relatively good health, the best financial security most people ever have, stable relationships with partners, good relations with children, expertise in some area, and the prospect of rewarding relationships with grandchildren. It has its challenges, too. Getting used to physical aging can be hard, as is caring for an aging parent. But for many people, on balance these are the best years of their lives.

SUMMARY

Physical Changes and Health

Changes in Appearance

• Some of the signs of aging appearing in middle age include wrinkles, gray hair, and weight gain. An important change, especially in women, is loss of bone mass, which in severe form may result in the disease osteoporosis.

Reproductive Changes

• The climacteric (loss of the ability to bear children by natural means) and menopause (cessation of menstruation) occur in the 40s and 50s and constitute a major change in reproductive ability in women. Most women do not have severe physical symptoms associated with the hormonal changes.

• Reproductive changes in men are much less dramatic; even older men are usually still fertile. Physical changes do affect sexual response.

Stress and Health

• In the stress and coping paradigm, stress results from a person's appraisal of an event as taxing his or her resources. Daily hassles are viewed as the primary source of stress.

• The types of situations people appraise as stressful change through adulthood. Family and career issues are more important for young and middle-aged adults; health issues are more important for older adults.

• Type A behavior pattern is characterized by intense competitiveness, anger, hostility, restlessness, aggression, and impatience. It is linked with a person's first heart attack and with cardiovascular disease. Type B behavior pattern is the opposite of Type A; it is associated with lower risk of first heart attack, but the prognosis after an attack is poorer. Following an initial heart attack, Type A behavior pattern individuals have a higher recovery rate.

• Whereas stress is unrelated to serious psychopathology, it is related to social isolation and distrust.

Exercise

• Aerobic exercise has numerous benefits, especially to cardiovascular health and fitness. The best results are obtained through a moderate exercise program maintained throughout adulthood.

Cognitive Development

Practical Intelligence

• Research on practical intelligence reveals differences between optimally exercised ability and unexercised ability. This gap closes during middle adulthood. Practical intelligence appears not to decline appreciably until late life.

Becoming an Expert

• People tend to become experts in some areas and not in others. Experts tend to think in more flexible ways than novices and are able to skip steps in solving problems. Expert performance tends to peak in middle age.

Lifelong Learning

• Adults learn differently than children and youth. Older students need practical connections and rationale for learning, and are more motivated by internal factors.

Personality

Stability Is the Rule: The Five-Factor Model

• The five-factor model postulates five dimensions of personality: neuroticism, extraversion, openness to experience, agreeableness, and conscientiousness. Several longitudinal studies indicate that personality traits show long-term stability.

Change Is the Rule: Changing Priorities at Midlife

• Erikson believed that middle-aged adults become more concerned with doing for others and passing social values and skills to the next generation—a set of behaviors and beliefs he labeled *generativity.* Those who do not achieve generativity are thought to experience stagnation.

• For the most part, there is little support for theories based on the premise that all adults go through predictable life stages at specific points in time. Individuals may face similar stresses, but transitions may occur at any time in adulthood. Research indicates that not everyone experiences a crisis at midlife.

• There is some evidence that gender-role identity converges in middle age, to the extent that men and women are more likely to endorse similar self-descriptions. However, these similar descriptions do not necessarily translate into similar behavior.

Family Dynamics and Middle Age

• Middle-aged mothers tend to adopt the role of kinkeepers in order to keep family traditions alive and as a way to link generations.

• Middle age is sometimes referred to as the sandwich generation.

Letting Go: Middle-Aged Adults and Their Children

• Parent-child relations improve dramatically when children emerge from adolescence. Most parents look forward to having an empty nest. Difficulties emerge to the extent that raising children has been a primary source of personal identity for parents. However, once children have left home, parents still provide considerable support.

• Children move back home primarily for financial or child-rearing reasons. Neither parents nor children generally choose this arrangement.

Giving Back: Middle-Aged Adults and Their Aging Parents

• Middle-aged children contact their parents fairly frequently and use the visits to strengthen the relationship.

• Caring for aging parents usually falls to a daughter or daughter-in-law. Caregiving creates a stressful situation due to conflicting feelings and roles. The potential for conflict is high, as is financial pressure.

• Caregiving stress is usually greater in women, who must deal with multiple roles. Older parents are often dissatisfied with the situation as well.

Grandparenthood

• Becoming a grandparent means assuming new roles. Styles of interaction vary across grandchildren and with the age of the grandchild. Also relevant are the social and personal dimensions of grandparenting.

• Grandparents derive several different types of meaning regardless of style: centrality, valued elder, indulgence, reinvolvement with personal past, and immortality through clan. Most children and young adults report positive relationships with grandparents, and young adults feel a responsibility to care for them if necessary.

• Ethnic differences are found in the extent to which grandparents take an active role in their grandchildren's lives.

• In an increasingly mobile society, grandparents are more frequently assuming a distant relationship with their grandchildren. An important concern for some grandparents is their ability to maintain contact with grandchildren following the divorce of the grandchildren's parents. Some grandparents must also serve as surrogate parents for grandchildren.

KEY TERMS

osteoporosis (446)
climacteric (446)
menopause (447)
estrogen-related symptoms (447)
somatic symptoms (447)
hormone replacement therapy (HRT) (447)
stress and coping paradigm (450)
appraise (450)
hassles (450)
coping (450)
Type A behavior pattern (451)
Type B behavior pattern (451)
aerobic exercise (452)

practical intelligence (454)
unexercised ability (454)
optimally exercised ability (455)
processes of thinking (457)
encapsulated (457)
products of thinking (457)
midlife crisis (460)
neuroticism (461)
extraversion (461)
openness to experience (461)
agreeableness (461)
conscientiousness (461)
generativity (462)
stagnation (463)

ego resilience (466)
kinkeeper (467)
sandwich generation (467)
filial obligation (472)
centrality (475)
valued elder (475)
indulgence (475)
reinvolvement with personal past (475)
immortality through clan (475)
fictive grandparenting (476)
cultural conservator (476)

IF YOU'D LIKE TO LEARN MORE

Readings

BRODY, E. M. (1990). *Women in the middle: Their parent-care years.* New York: Springer. This description of the experiences of women who provide care for their parents is research-based and contains many good examples.

CHERLIN, A. J., & FURSTENBERG, F. F. (1986). *The new American grandparent.* New York: Basic Books. This is a very readable overview of research on the meanings and styles of grandparenthood.

ESTES, C. P. (1992). *Women who run with the wolves.* New York: Ballantine Books. Femininity is discussed from a Jungian point of view, as revealed through story and myth.

KEEN, S. (1991). *Fire in the belly: On being a man.* New York: Bantam Books. This very readable book presents a new model of masculinity in contemporary society.

Web Sites

An excellent general site for information on health, including stress, is the Mayo Health O@sis sponsored by the Mayo Clinic. This site is also worthwhile for general medical information on most other conditions. It is located at

http://www.mayohealth.org

A comprehensive summary of the physical changes and therapeutic approaches, as well as life-style guidelines, to menopause is under the topic of Women's Health in the Planned Parenthood site at

http://www.plannedparenthood.org

The Family Caregiver Alliance provides a wealth of information about medical, policy, and resource issues concerning caregiving. It is aimed at people caring for adults with Alzheimer's disease, stroke, brain injury, and related brain disorders. It can be found at

http://www.caregiver.org

TAN, A. (1989). *The Joy Luck Club.* New York: Putnam. This novel explores the bond among four Chinese American women and their adult daughters.

WHITBOURNE, S. K. (1996). *The aging individual.* New York: Springer. This excellent resource covers the biological and physiological changes that occur in adulthood, with the psychological implications of these changes discussed in detail.

 For additional readings, explore Infotrac College Edition, your online library. Go to http://www. infotrac-college.com/wadsworth.

A good source of information about grandparenting resources on the World Wide Web is maintained by Third Age. Among its many useful features is a section on legal aspects of grandparenting. It can be found at

http://www.thirdage.com/grand/

Web site addresses are subject to change. The Wadsworth Study Center Web site listed below can be accessed for updated links.

The Wadsworth Psychology Study Center Web Site

See http://psychology.wadsworth.com/ for practice quiz questions, internet links, updates, critical thinking exercises, discussion forums and more! The Wadsworth Psychology Study Center provides a wealth of information fully organized and integrated by chapter.

SNAPSHOTS OF DEVELOPMENT
A VISUAL SUMMARY
Young and Middle Adulthood

Physical prowess peaks. Life-style factors such as smoking, drinking alcohol, and nutrition are key to quality of health. Reducing stress is also important. Changes in appearance during middle age affect self-image. Menopause is a major change for women due to changes in estrogen levels.

Healthy life-styles can slow some normative age-related physiological changes.

PSYCHOLOGICAL FORCES

The achievement of postformal thought is a major advance. Young adulthood and middle age are times of deepening personal insights, and the shift from intimacy to generativity is a major psychosocial issue. Friendships, the relationship with one's partner, and career play major roles in self-identity.

SOCIOCULTURAL FORCES

Societal views on relationships help explain why people get (and stay) married. Laws regarding discrimination and bias have changed the workplace. Social expectations about providing care for elderly parents leaves middle-aged people feeling sandwiched between two generations.

Most adults derive great psychological satisfaction from being grandparents.

Genetic potential, good cognitive skills, and the opportunity to obtain advanced education jointly affect one's career path.

Equitable division of household tasks is a predictor of successful marriages.

PART FOUR

LATE LIFE

- **CHAPTER 13**

  The Personal Context
  of Later Life

- **CHAPTER 14**

  Social Aspects
  of Later Life

- **CHAPTER 15**

  Dying and Bereavement

A CLOSER LOOK

On October 29, 1998, John Glenn became the oldest human to travel in space, spending 9 days in the space shuttle Discovery conducting experiments focused on understanding the connections between aging and space flight. Glenn's 1998 flight was his second history-making trip; he was also the first United States astronaut to orbit the earth on February 20, 1962. Between his trips to space, Glenn served 24 years as a senator from Ohio, and distinguished himself as a strong supporter of older adults and as a lay expert on the biology of aging. Glenn noticed similarities between some of the physiological changes measured in astronauts (such as sleep problems

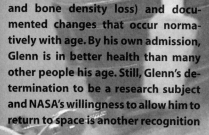

and bone density loss) and documented changes that occur normatively with age. By his own admission, Glenn is in better health than many other people his age. Still, Glenn's determination to be a research subject and NASA's willingness to allow him to return to space is another recognition that chronological age alone is a very poor index of people's capabilities.

John Glenn illustrates many of the points made in Chapters 13–14: the normal changes people experience with age, the variability of change across people, and the need to rethink stereotypes about older adults.

CHAPTER 13

THE PERSONAL CONTEXT OF LATER LIFE

What Are Older Adults Like?
The Demographics of Aging
How Long Will You Live?

Physical Changes and Health
Biological Theories of Aging
Physiological Changes
Preventing Accidents Involving Older Adults
Health Issues

Cognitive Processes
Information Processing
Information Processing in Everyday Life: Older Drivers
Memory
Helping People Remember
Training Intellectual Abilities
Creativity and Wisdom
Cognitive Changes in Later Life

Mental Health and Intervention
Depression
Anxiety Disorders
Dementia: Alzheimer's Disease
What's the Matter with Mary?
What's Her Name? Memory Training in Alzheimer's Disease

Putting It All Together

Summary

If You'd Like to Learn More

STOP! Before you read this chapter, do the following exercise. Take out a piece of paper and write down all the adjectives you can think of that describe aging and older adults, as well as all of the "facts" about aging that you know.

Now that you have your list, look over it carefully. Are most of your descriptors positive or negative? Do you have lots of "facts" written down, or just a few? Most people's lists contain at least some words and phrases that reflect images of older adults as portrayed by the media. Many of the media's images are stereotypes of aging that are only loosely based on reality. For example, people over age 60 are almost never pictured in ads for perfume (Elizabeth Taylor is a notable exception), but they are shown in ads for wrinkle removers.

In this chapter, our journey through old age begins. Our emphasis in this chapter is on physical and cognitive changes. To begin, we consider the key physical changes and health issues confronting older adults. Changes in cognitive abilities, as well as interventions to help remediate the changes are discussed next. Finally, some of the most well-known mental health issues are considered, including depression, anxiety disorders, and Alzheimer's disease.

WHAT ARE OLDER ADULTS LIKE?

What Are Older Adults Like?

The Demographics of Aging

How Long Will You Live?

Learning Objectives

- **What are the characteristics of older adults in the population?**
- **How long will most people live? What factors influence this?**

*S*ARAH *is an 87-year-old African American woman who comes from a family of long-lived individuals. She has never been to a physician in her entire life, and she has never really been seriously ill. Sarah figures it's just as well that she has never needed a physician, because for most of her life she had no health insurance. Because she feels healthy and has more living that she wants to do, Sarah figures that she'll live for several more years.*

What is it like to be old? Do you want your own late life to be described by the words and phrases you wrote at the beginning of the chapter? Do you look forward to becoming old, or are you afraid of what may lie ahead?

Most of us probably want to be like Sarah and enjoy a long healthy life. Growing old is not something we think about very much until we have to. Most of us experience the coming of old age the way Jim does in the *Far Side* cartoon. It's as if we go to bed one night middle-aged and wake up the next day feeling old. But we can take comfort in knowing that when that day comes, we will have plenty of company.

You never see it coming

THE DEMOGRAPHICS OF AGING

Did you ever stop to think about how many older adults you see in your daily life? Did you ever wonder whether your great-grandparents had the same experience? There have never been as many older adults alive as there are now. The proportion of older adults in the population of industrialized countries has increased tremendously in this century, due mainly to better health care and to lowering women's mortality rate during childbirth.

People who study population trends, called demographers, use a graphic technique called a population pyramid *to illustrate these changes.* Notice the shape of the population pyramid in 1900, shown in the first panel of the figure on page 489. At the turn of the century, there were so many more people under the age of 20 than there were people over age 60 that the figure is indeed shaped like a pyramid. Projections for 2030 (when the last of the baby boomers have reached 65) indicate that a dramatic change will have occurred; the 1900 pyramid will have turned upside down! The number of people over 65 will outnumber those in any other age group.

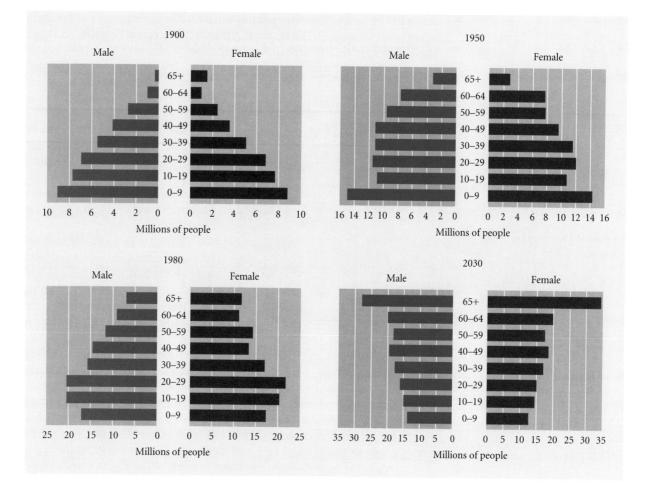

The rapid increase in the number of older adults (individuals over age 60) will bring profound changes to everyone's lives. In the first half of the 21st century, older adults will be a major marketing target, and they will wield considerable political and economic power. The sheer number of older adults will place enormous pressure on pension systems (especially Social Security), health care (including long-term care), and other human services. The costs will be borne by a relatively small number of taxpaying workers in the cohorts behind them.

The growing strain on social service systems will be intensified because the most rapidly growing segment of the U.S. population is the group of people over age 85. In fact, the number of such people will increase 400% between 1995 and 2050 (Administration on Aging, 1997). As we will see in this chapter and in Chapter 14, individuals over age 85 generally need more assistance with daily living than do people under 85, placing increasing strain on the health care system.

? THINK ABOUT IT
How will the demographic changes in the first 30 years of the 21st century affect the need for retraining workers?

The Diversity of Older Adults

Older adults are not all alike, any more than people at other ages. Older women outnumber older men in all ethnic groups in the United States, for reasons we will explore later. The number of older adults among ethnic minority groups is increasing faster than among European Americans. For example, the number of Native American elderly has increased 65% in recent decades; Asian and Pacific Islander elderly have quadrupled; older adults are the fastest-growing segment of the African American population; and the number of Hispanic American elderly is also increasing rapidly (U.S. Bureau of the Census, 1997). Projections for the future diversity of the U.S. population are shown in the graph. You should note the very large increases in the number of Asian, Native, and Hispanic American older adults relative to European and African American older adults.

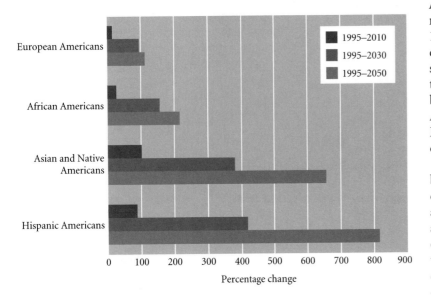

Older adults in the future will be better educated, too. At present, only about half of the people over age 65 have a high school diploma, and 10% have four or more years of college. By 2030, it is estimated that 85% will have a high school diploma and 75% will have a college degree (U.S. Bureau of the Census, 1997). These dramatic changes will be due mainly to better educational opportunities for more students and greater need for formal schooling (especially college) in order to find a good job. Also, better-educated people tend to live longer, mostly because they have higher incomes—which give them better access to good health care and a chance to follow healthier life-styles.

Internationally, the number of older adults is also growing rapidly, especially among developing countries. To a large extent, these rapid increases are due to improved health care in these countries. Such increases will literally change the face of the population, as more people live to old age.

Economically powerful countries around the world such as Japan are trying to cope with increased numbers of older adults that strain the country's resources. Indeed, the rate of growth of older adults in Japan is the highest in the industrialized world; by 2025 there will be twice as many adults over age 65 as there will be children (WuDunn, 1997). The economic impact will include much higher pension costs and very substantial increases in health care costs, which will have to be borne by far fewer workers (WuDunn, 1997).

Even though the financial implications of an aging population are predictable, we have done surprisingly little to prepare. For example, there are little research data on the characteristics of older workers (even though mandatory retirement has been virtually eliminated for several years), on differences between the young-old (ages 65–80) and the old-old (over age 80), or on specific health care needs of older adults with regard to chronic illness (American Psychological Society, 1993). As of 1998, the U.S. Congress had yet to adopt long-term plans for funding Social Security and Medicare, even though the first baby boomers will turn 60 in 2006. These issues will need to be addressed in the very near future, so that the appropriate policies can be implemented (Binstock, 1999).

HOW LONG WILL YOU LIVE?

The number of years a person can expect to live, termed longevity, *is jointly determined by genetic and environmental factors.* Researchers distinguish between three types of longevity: average life expectancy, useful life expectancy, and maximum life expectancy.

Average life expectancy *(or median life expectancy) is the age at which half of the people born in a particular year will have died.* As you can see in the graph, average life expectancy for people in the United States has increased steadily during this century. This increase is due mainly to significant declines in infant mortality and in the number of women dying during childbirth, the elimination of major diseases such as smallpox and polio, and improvements in medical technology that prolong the lives of people with chronic disease.

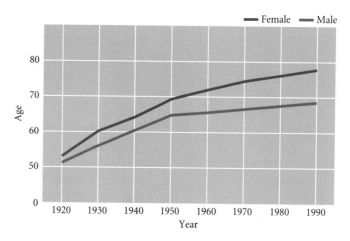

Useful life expectancy *is the number of years that a person is free from debilitating chronic disease and impairment.* Ideally, useful life expectancy exactly matches the actual length of a person's life. However, medical technology sometimes enables people to live for years even though they may be unable to perform routine daily tasks. Accordingly, people are placing greater emphasis on useful life expectancy, rather than just the sheer number of years they may live, in making medical treatment decisions.

Maximum life expectancy *is the oldest age to which any person lives.* Currently, scientists estimate that the maximum limit for humans is around 120 years, mostly because the heart and other key organ systems are limited in how long they can last without replacement (Hayflick, 1994).

Genetic and Environmental Factors in Life Expectancy

Probably the best predictor of a long life is coming from a family of long-lived individuals. For example, roughly 4 years are added to your average life expectancy for each parent who lives to age 80 (Woodruff-Pak, 1988). Some chronic diseases also have genetic links that shorten life expectancy, including cardiovascular disease, several forms of cancer, cystic fibrosis, and Alzheimer's disease. For example, for each parent, grandparent, or sibling who dies of cardiovascular disease before age 50, you lose 4 years from your average life expectancy (Woodruff-Pak, 1988).

Many aspects of the environment affect how long you will live: acquired diseases (e.g., AIDS), toxins, and pollutants. Additionally, life-style factors such as stress, smoking, diet, drugs, alcohol, and exercise influence life expectancy. Being married helps extend life, but more so for men than for women (Woodruff-Pak, 1988). Environmental influences are even more important for poor people. People living in poor neighborhoods are more likely to have little money for good diets, to be more exposed to toxins such as lead, and to live in more polluted areas. Each of these factors can significantly reduce life expectancy (American Association of Retired Persons, 1991). The combined effects of environmental factors can be shocking: The American

Cancer Society estimates that an unmarried smoker living alone in a large city may lose up to 22 years.

Perhaps the most controversial of environmental influences on longevity are technological improvements in health care. We now have the ability to extend life significantly, as we can keep people alive longer through medical interventions. Even when a disease is incurable, many of its victims may live longer because medical technology, such as life-support systems, keeps them alive. But many people are asking a tough question: Is extending life always beneficial? This question forces people to separate the quality of life from the quantity of life. We will also revisit this issue in more detail in Chapter 15, in connection with euthanasia.

Ethnic and Gender Differences in Life Expectancy

? THINK ABOUT IT
How do ethnic and gender differences in life expectancy relate to biological, psychological, and sociocultural forces?

Ethnic differences in average life expectancy are complex (Go et al., 1995). For example, African Americans' average life expectancy at birth in 1995 was roughly 9 years lower for men and 5.5 years lower for women than that of European Americans. At age 65, the average life expectancy for African Americans was 2 years less for both men and women than it was for European Americans, but by age 85 African Americans tend to live longer (National Center for Health Statistics, 1997). Perhaps because they do not typically have access to the same quality of care that European Americans usually do, and are at greater risk for disease and accidents, African Americans who survive to age 85 tend to be healthier than their European American counterparts. Like Sarah, the 87-year-old woman in the vignette, they may well have needed little medical care throughout their lives. The complexity of ethnic group differences is evident in the fact that Hispanic Americans' average life expectancy exceeds European Americans' at all ages, despite access problems to health care for many (National Center for Health Statistics, 1997).

A visit to a senior center or to a nursing home can easily lead to the question, "Where are all the very old men?" Women's average longevity is about 7 years more on average than men at birth, narrowing to roughly 1 year by age 85 (National Center for Health Statistics, 1997). Why? The brief, but accurate, answer is that we do not know for sure (Hayflick, 1994). Increased vulnerability of males to disease and accidents, coupled with lower rates of death during childbirth for women are all factors. Some researchers also believe that other keys for women are having two X chromosomes (compared to only one in men), lower metabolic rates, higher brain-to-body weight ratios, and lower levels of testosterone (Hayflick, 1994). To date, though, none of these factors has been shown to adequately explain why women live longer on average than men.

International Differences in Life Expectancy

Countries around the world differ dramatically in how long their populations live on average. As you can see on the map on page 493, the current range extends from 38 years in Sierra Leone in Africa to 80 years in Japan. Such a wide divergence in life expectancy reflects vast discrepancies in social and economic conditions, health care, disease, and the like across industrialized and developing nations.

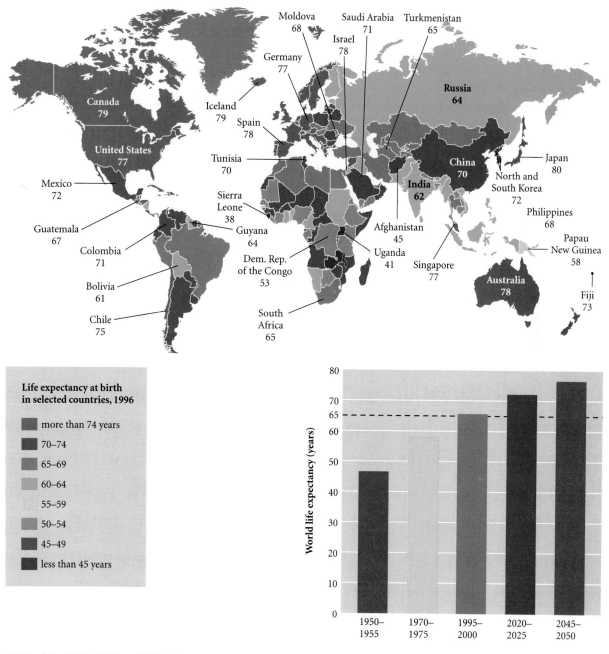

Life expectancy at birth in selected countries, 1996

- more than 74 years
- 70–74
- 65–69
- 60–64
- 55–59
- 50–54
- 45–49
- less than 45 years

U.N. Population Division Database, 1996 Revision.

1. The fastest-growing segment of the population in the United States is people over age _____ .

2. The age at which half of the people born in a particular year have died is called _____ .

3. Think back to the life-style influences on health discussed in Chapter 12. If most people actually followed very healthy life-styles, what do you think would happen to average life expectancy?

Answers: (1) 85, (2) average life expectancy

PHYSICAL CHANGES AND HEALTH

Physical Changes and Health

Biological Theories of Aging

Physiological Changes

Health Issues

Learning Objectives

- **What are the major biological theories of aging?**
- **What physiological changes normally occur in later life?**
- **What are the principal health issues for older adults?**

*F*RANK *is an 80-year-old man who has been physically active his whole life. He still enjoys sailing, long-distance biking, and cross-country skiing. Although he considers himself to be in excellent shape, he has noticed that his endurance has decreased, and his hearing isn't quite as sharp as it used to be. Frank wonders: Can he do something to stop these declines, or are they an inevitable part of growing older?*

If your family has kept photograph albums over many years, you are able to see how your grandparents or great-grandparents changed over the years. Some of the more visible differences are changes in the color and amount of hair and the addition of wrinkles, but many other physical changes are harder to see. In this section, we consider some of these, as well as a few things that adults can do to improve their health. As noted in Chapter 12, many aging changes begin during middle age but typically do not affect people in their daily lives until later in life, as Frank is discovering. But first, we will ask a basic question: Why do people grow old in the first place?

BIOLOGICAL THEORIES OF AGING

Why does everyone who lives long enough grow old and eventually die? To date, there is no one definitive answer, but several complementary biological theories, taken together, provide some insights (Hayflick, 1994).

There are four major groups of biological theories of aging. Wear-and-tear theory *suggests that the body, much like any machine, gradually deteriorates and finally wears out.* This theory explains some diseases, such as osteoarthritis, rather well. Years of use of the joints causes the protective cartilage lining to deteriorate, resulting in pain and stiffness. However, wear-and-tear theory does not explain most other aspects of aging very well (Hayflick, 1994).

Cellular theories *explain aging by focusing on processes that occur within individual cells, leading to the buildup of harmful substances over a lifetime.* Most of these theories stress the destructive effects that certain substances have on cellular functioning. *For example, some theorists believe that* free radicals— *chemicals produced randomly during normal cell metabolism, which bond easily to other substances inside cells—cause cellular damage that impairs functioning.* Aging is caused by the cumulative effects of free radicals over the life span. Free radicals may play a role in some diseases, such as atherosclerosis and cancer. *Another cellular theory focuses on* cross-linking, *in which some proteins interact randomly with certain body tissues, such as muscles and arteries.* The result of cross-linking is that normal, elastic tissue becomes stiffer, so that muscles and arteries are less flexible over time. The results in some cases can be serious; for example, stiffening in the heart muscle forces the heart to work harder, which may increase the risk of heart attacks. Although we know that these substances accumulate, we do not fully understand how they may cause aging.

Metabolic theories *focus on aspects of the body's metabolism to explain why people age.* Two important processes in this approach are caloric intake and stress. There is some evidence that people like the man in the photograph who limit the number of calories they eat in an otherwise well-balanced diet can expect longer life expectancy and lower rates of disease (Monczunski, 1991). It remains to be seen whether the type of diet (e.g., low-fat) or the number of calories per se is the secret. How readily one adapts to physical stress is also significant; younger adults can tolerate higher levels of physical exertion than can older adults (Whitbourne, 1996). It is possible that death occurs because the body can no longer adapt to stress (Hayflick, 1994).

Finally, programmed cell death theories *suggest that aging is genetically programmed.* Although there may not be a single aging gene as such, there is growing evidence that there may be a genetic code, yet to be discovered, that controls cell life. We know that there is a genetic component involved in many age-related chronic diseases such as Alzheimer's disease, cardiovascular disease, and some forms of cancer. We also know that cells eventually stop dividing, perhaps because the long spirals of DNA called telomeres, which protect the ends of every chromosome, get shorter after every cell division and may reach a point where they are not sufficient to support further divisions. However, these encouraging leads have not yet answered the question of how such programming gets activated or how it causes aging.

Despite the variety of biological theories, none is adequate by itself to explain aging fully. Indeed, much about the aging process remains to be discovered, especially in sorting out the differences between normal aging (the disease-free changes that happen to everyone) and disease-related aging. Moreover, we also need to learn how these various factors in biological aging may interact.

> **? THINK ABOUT IT**
> What would be the psychological and sociocultural effects of discovering a single, comprehensive biological theory of aging?

PHYSIOLOGICAL CHANGES

Growing older brings with it several inevitable physiological changes. Like Frank, whom we met in the vignette, older adults find that their endurance has declined, relative to what it was 20 or 30 years earlier, and that their hearing has declined. In this section, we consider some of the most important physiological changes that occur in neurons, the cardiovascular and respiratory systems, the motor system, and the sensory systems. We also consider general health issues such as sleep, nutrition, and cancer. Throughout this discussion, you should keep in mind that although the changes we will consider happen to everyone, the rate and the amount of change varies a great deal across people.

Changes in the Neurons

The most important normative changes with age involve structural changes in the neurons, the basic cells in the brain, and in communication among neurons (Whitbourne, 1996). Recall the basic structures of the neuron we encountered in Chapter 3 (pages 94–95), shown again here. Two structures in neurons are most important in understanding aging: the dendrites, which pick up information from other neurons, and the axon, which transmits information inside a neuron from the dendrites to the terminal branches. Each of the changes we consider impairs the neurons' ability to transmit information, which ultimately affects how well the person functions (Whitbourne, 1996). Three structural changes are most important in normal aging: neurofibrillary tangles, dendritic changes, and neuritic plaques.

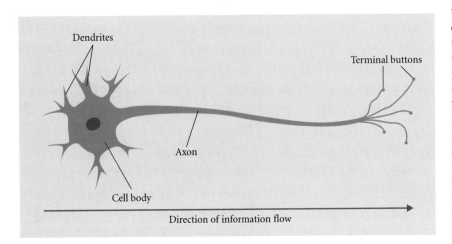

Dendrites

Terminal buttons

Axon

Cell body

Direction of information flow

For reasons that are not understood, fibers that compose the axon sometimes become twisted together to form spiral-shaped masses called neurofibrillary tangles. These tangles interfere with the neuron's ability to transmit information down the axon. Some degree of tangling occurs normally with age, but large numbers of neurofibrillary tangles are associated with Alzheimer's disease (Scheibel, 1996).

Changes in the dendrites are more complicated. Some dendrites shrivel up and die, making it more difficult for neurons to communicate with each other. However, some dendrites continue to grow (Curcio, Buell, & Coleman, 1982). This may help explain why older adults continue to improve in some areas, as we will discover later in this chapter. Why some dendrites degenerate and others do not is poorly understood; it may reflect the existence of two different families of neurons.

Damaged and dying neurons sometimes collect around a core of protein and produce neuritic plaques. It is likely that plaques interfere with normal functioning of healthy neurons. Although large numbers of plaques are associated with dementia (e.g., Alzheimer's disease), researchers have not established an "allowable number" of plaques that indicate a healthy aging brain (Scheibel, 1996).

Because neurons do not physically touch each other, they must communicate via chemicals called neurotransmitters. With age, the levels of these neurotransmitters decline (Whitbourne, 1999). These declines are believed to be responsible for numerous age-related behavioral changes, including those in memory and sleep, and perhaps in afflictions such as Parkinson's disease.

These changes in neurons are a normal part of aging. However, when these changes occur at a much greater rate, they cause considerable problems and are associated with Alzheimer's or related diseases, conditions we discuss in more detail on pages 517–522. This point is important, as it means that serious behavioral changes such as very severe memory impairment are not a result of normative changes in the brain; rather, they are indicators of disease.

Unfortunately, we know much more about the kinds of changes that occur with age than we do about the links between neuronal changes and behavior. The evidence is often indirect, obtained by careful observation of individuals who have suffered brain damage, or by mapping known behavioral patterns with findings from autopsies on people's brains. We know the links must be there; discovering most of them will take time and creativity.

Cardiovascular and Respiratory Systems

The incidence of cardiovascular diseases such as heart attack, irregular heartbeat, stroke, and hypertension increase dramatically with age (National Center for Health Statistics, 1997). However, the overall death rates from these diseases have been declining over recent decades, mainly because fewer adults smoke cigarettes and many people have reduced the amount of fat in their diets. However, the death rate for some ethnic groups, such as African Americans, remains much higher because of poorer preventive health care and less healthy life-styles due to lack of financial resources (National Center for Health Statistics, 1997).

Normative changes in the cardiovascular system that contribute to disease begin by young adulthood. Fat deposits are found in and around the heart and in the arteries (Whitbourne, 1996). Eventually, the amount of blood that the heart can pump per minute will decline roughly 30%. The amount of muscle tissue in the heart also declines, due to its replacement by connective tissue. There is also a general stiffening of the arteries, due to calcification. These changes appear irrespective of life-style, but they occur more slowly in people who exercise, eat low-fat diets, and manage to lower stress effectively (see Chapter 12). In persons who do not have hypertension, blood pressure changes little over adulthood (Pearson et al., 1997).

As people grow older, their chances of having a stroke increase. *Strokes, or cerebral vascular accidents, are caused by interruptions in the blood flow in the brain due to a blockage or to a hemorrhage in a cerebral artery.* Blockages of arteries may be caused by clots or by deposits of fatty substances due to the disease atherosclerosis. Hemorrhages are caused by ruptures of the artery. *Older adults often experience transient ischemic attacks (TIAs), which involve an interruption in blood flow to the brain, and are often early warning signs of stroke.* A single, large cerebral vascular accident may produce serious cognitive impairment, such as the loss of the ability to speak, or physical problems, such as the inability to move an arm. The nature and severity of the impairment in functioning a person experiences are usually determined by which specific area of the brain is affected. Recovery from a single stroke depends on many factors, including the extent and type of the loss, the ability of other areas in the brain to assume the functions that were lost, and personal motivation.

Numerous small cerebral vascular accidents can result in a disease termed vascular dementia. Unlike Alzheimer's disease, another form of dementia discussed later in this chapter, vascular dementia can have a sudden onset and may or may not progress gradually. Moreover, individuals' symptom patterns vary a great deal, depending on which specific areas of the brain are damaged. In some cases, vascular dementia has a much faster course than Alzheimer's disease, resulting in death an average of two to three years after onset; in others, the disease may progress much more slowly, with idiosyncratic symptom patterns (Qualls, 1999).

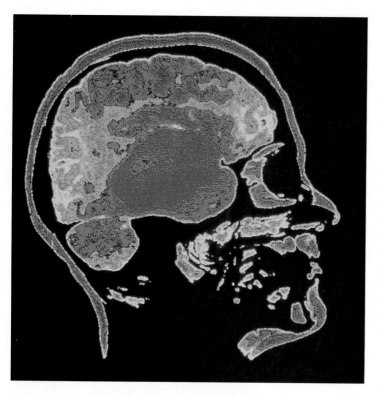

Single cerebral vascular accidents and vascular dementia are diagnosed similarly. Evidence of damage may be obtained from diagnostic imaging (e.g., computed tomography, or CT scans; magnetic resonance imaging, or MRI), which provides pictures like the one shown here, which is then confirmed by neuropsychological tests. Known risk factors for both conditions include hypertension and a family history of the disorders.

The maximum amount of air in one breath drops 40% from age 25 to age 85, due mostly to stiffening of the rib cage and air passages with age, and destruction of the air sacs in the lungs from pollution and smoking (Whitbourne, 1996). This decline is the main cause of shortness of breath after physical exertion in later life. Because of the cumulative effects of breathing polluted air over a lifetime, it is hard to say how much of these changes are strictly age-related. *The most common form of incapacitating respiratory disease among older adults is* chronic obstructive pulmonary disease (COPD). COPD can be an extremely debilitating condition, resulting in depression, anxiety, and the need to be continually connected to oxygen (Frazer, Leicht, & Baker, 1996). Emphysema is the most common form of COPD; although most cases of emphysema are due to smoking, some forms are genetic. Asthma is another common type of COPD.

Parkinson's Disease

Parkinson's disease *is known primarily for its characteristic motor symptoms: very slow walking, difficulty getting into and out of chairs, and a slow hand tremor.* These problems are caused by a deterioration of neurons in the midbrain that produce the neurotransmitter dopamine. Symptoms are treated effectively with the drug L-dopa, which raises the functional level of dopamine in the brain (Youngjohn & Crook, 1996). Recent research indicates that a device that acts like a brain pacemaker by regulating brain activity may prove effective in eliminating the tremors and shaking (Neergaard, 1997).

For reasons we do not yet understand, roughly 30–50% of the time Parkinson's disease also involves severe cognitive impairment, with additional brain changes similar to Alzheimer's disease (Youngjohn et al., 1992). It remains to be seen whether this form of Parkinson's disease actually represents a separate disease.

Sensory Changes

Many changes occurring in the sensory system are noticeable by late life. In the eye, the lens becomes thicker and takes on a yellowish cast. Because of these structural changes, older adults are much more susceptible to glare, take longer to adapt to changes in illumination, experience trouble reading things close to them, and generally require more light to see (Kline & Schieber, 1985). As people age, it takes longer for their eyes to adapt when going from bright light to darkness, or vice versa (Whitbourne, 1996). This is relevant in many situations, such as while driving at night and having to adjust between bright oncoming headlights and the darkness of the road.

Declines in hearing are among the best-known sensory changes. *There is substantial loss in the ability to hear high-pitched tones, a condition called* presbycusis. Although this condition is most severe in older adults, individuals at any age can severely damage their hearing through continued exposure to loud noise, including loud music (Whitbourne, 1996). For example, listening to loud music through headphones while exercising like the woman in the photograph is doing is particularly harmful, because blood flow to the receptor cells for hearing is increased, making them particularly vulnerable to damage. Loud music and other environmental noise may be some of the reasons why at age 51 President Bill Clinton needed hearing aids in both ears. Although using a hearing aid reduces one's self-perceived hearing handicap, it does not by itself improve one's social interactions (Tesch-Römer, 1997). One's level of social skills is equally as important as hearing in improving interactions.

The sense of taste remains largely intact in older adults, as do touch, temperature, and pain sensitivity (Whitbourne, 1999). However, substantial age declines in smell occur after age 70 in many people (Murphy, 1986), and large declines are characteristic of Alzheimer's disease (Youngjohn & Crook, 1996). These changes can be dangerous; for example, very old adults often have difficulty detecting the substance added to natural gas to make leaks noticeable, which can prove fatal.

Changes in balance make older people increasingly likely to fall (Ochs et al., 1985). Indeed, the fear of falling and getting injured is a real concern for many older adults, and can affect their willingness to engage in certain types of activities (Lachman et al., 1998).

The sensory changes people experience have important implications for their everyday lives (Whitbourne, 1996). Some, such as difficulty reading things close up, are minor annoyances that are easily corrected (by wearing reading glasses). Others are more serious and less easily addressed. For example, the ability to drive a car is affected by changes in vision and in hearing. Because sensory changes may also lead to accidents around the home, it is important to design a safer environment that takes these changes into account. The You May Be Wondering feature summarizes some of these interventions.

? THINK ABOUT IT
How might fear of falling and osteoporosis (see Chapter 12, page 446) be linked?

PREVENTING ACCIDENTS INVOLVING OLDER ADULTS

Accidental injuries become more frequent and serious in later life. Changes in physical and information-processing abilities contribute to increases in accident frequency. For example, the awareness of hazards is dimmed by poor eyesight and hearing. Arthritis and impaired coordination can make older adults unsteady. Medications for many chronic diseases can cause drowsiness or distractibility. How can these problems be avoided?

Many accidents can be prevented by maintaining health through prevention and conditioning. But making some relatively simple environmental changes also helps. For example, falls are the most common cause of accidental serious injury and death among older adults. Here are some steps that can help reduce the potential for falls:

- Illuminate stairways and provide light switches at both the top and the bottom of the stairs.

- Avoid high-gloss floor finishes, due to glare and their tendency to be slippery when wet.

- Provide nightlights or bedside remote-control light switches.

- Be sure that both sides of stairways have sturdy handrails.

- Tack down carpeting on stairs, or use nonskid treads.

- Remove throw or area rugs that tend to slide on the floor.

- Arrange furniture and other objects so that they are not obstacles.

- Use grab bars on bathroom walls and nonskid mats or strips in bathtubs.

- Keep outdoor steps and walkways in good repair. •

HEALTH ISSUES

In Chapter 12, we examined how life-style factors can lower the risk of many chronic diseases. The importance of health promotion does not diminish with increasing age. As we will see, life-style factors influence sleep, nutrition, and cancer.

Sleep

Older adults have more trouble sleeping than do younger adults (Bootzin et al., 1996). Compared to younger adults, older adults report that it takes roughly twice as long to fall asleep, that they get less sleep on an average night, and that they feel more negative effects following a night with little sleep. Some of these problems are due to physical disorders, medication side effects, and the effects of caffeine, nicotine, and stress (Bootzin et al., 1996). *Sleep problems can disrupt a person's* circadian rhythm, *or sleep-wake cycle.* Circadian rhythm disruptions can cause problems with attention and memory. Research shows that interventions such as properly timed exposure to bright light is effective in correcting circadian rhythm sleep disorders (Terman, 1994).

Nutrition

Under normal circumstances, older adults do not need any vitamin or mineral supplements, as long as they are eating a well-balanced diet (Bortz & Bortz, 1996). Even though body metabolism declines with age, older adults need to consume the same amounts of proteins and carbohydrates as young adults, because of changes in how readily the body extracts the nutrients from these substances. Because they are typically in poor health, residents of nursing homes are prone to weight loss and may have various nutritional deficiencies, such as vitamin B_{12} and folic acid, unless closely monitored (Wallace & Schwartz, 1994).

Cancer

One of the most important health promotion steps people can take is cancer screening. In many cases, screening procedures involve little more than tests performed in a physician's office (e.g., screening for colon cancer), at home (breast self-exams), blood tests (screening for prostate cancer), or X-rays (mammograms).

Why is cancer screening so important? As you can see in the graph, the risk of getting cancer increases markedly with age (Frazer et al., 1996). Why this happens is not fully understood. Unhealthy life-styles (smoking and poor diet), genetics, and exposure to cancer-causing chemicals certainly are important, but they do not fully explain the age-related increase in risk (Frazer et al., 1996). Early detection of cancer even in older adults is essential in order to maximize the odds of surviving (Segal, 1996). However, some physicians are reluctant to use aggressive screening and prevention measures with older adults (List, 1988), perhaps due to the mistaken belief that older patients have lower survival rates. For their part, older adults may be reluctant to request the necessary tests, because they tend not to question their physician's judgment (List, 1988). More attention needs to be paid to such screening programs among older adults.

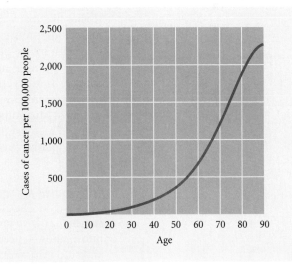

---

1. The biological theory of aging that includes the factors of free radicals and cross-linking is _____ .

2. Damaged and dying neurons that collect around a core of protein produce _____ .

3. The risk of getting cancer _____ markedly with age.

4. In this section, we have concentrated on the biological forces in development. Think about the other forces (psychological, social, and life-cycle), and list some reasons why scientists have yet to propose a purely biological theory that accounts for all aspects of aging.

TEST YOURSELF

Answers: (1) cellular theory, (2) neuritic plaques, (3) increases

COGNITIVE PROCESSES

Cognitive Processes

Information Processing

Memory

Training Intellectual Abilities

Creativity and Wisdom

Learning Objectives

- **What changes occur in attention and reaction time as people age? How do these changes relate to everyday life?**

- **What changes occur in memory with age? What can be done to remediate these changes?**

- **What is wisdom, and how is it related to age?**

*R*OCIO *is a 75-year-old widow who feels that she does not remember recent events, such as whether she took her medicine, as well as she used to, but has no trouble remembering things from her 20s. Rocio wonders if this is normal, or whether she should be worried.*

Rocio, like many older people, takes medications for arthritis, allergies, and high blood pressure. However, each drug has its own pattern; some are taken only with meals, others are taken every eight hours, and still others are taken twice daily. Keeping these regimens straight is important to avoid potentially dangerous interactions and side effects, and older people thus face the problem of remembering to take each medication at the proper time.

Such situations place a heavy demand on cognitive resources, such as attention and memory. In this section, we examine age-related changes in these and other cognitive processes, such as reaction time, intelligence, and wisdom.

INFORMATION PROCESSING

In Chapter 1 we saw that one theoretical framework for studying cognition is information-processing theory. This framework provides a way to identify and study the basic mechanisms by which people take in, store, and remember information. We have already seen in Chapters 4 and 6 that information-processing theory has guided much research on cognition in childhood and adolescence. This approach has also been important to investigators examining age-related differences in basic processes such as attention and reaction time (Stine-Morrow & Soederberg Miller, 1999).

Attention

Imagine yourself sitting at a computer terminal. You are told to press a key as fast as you can every time you see a red X, the target. To make things more difficult, you will also see other letters and colors (green X's, green O's, red O's), which you are to ignore. You will also have no idea where on the screen the target will appear, so you must search for it. *This task is aimed at assessing individuals' attentional* selectivity, *or the ability to pick out important from irrelevant information in the environment.* Adults over age 60 are much slower than adults under age 25 at finding targets in visual arrays like computer screens, especially when the arrays are complex (e.g., when nontargets are similar to targets). However, if a signal is given indicating where on the display the target will appear, these age differences disappear (Plude & Doussard-Roosevelt, 1989). Thus, older adults have trouble locating targets but, once they are found, can identify them as well as younger adults.

A second way that attention has been studied is a familiar one. You have probably encountered many situations in which you had to do two things at once: writing notes while listening to a lecture; talking on the phone while driving, like the man in the photo; or listening to a CD while reading a book. *These situations demand* divided attention, *or performing more than one task at a time.* As long as the two competing tasks are relatively easy, older and younger adults are equally able to perform both fairly well. However, as task difficulty increases, older adults are less able to perform both equally well; younger adults usually do better (Stine-Morrow & Soederberg Miller, 1999). For example, age differences are unlikely if the tasks are folding laundry and conversing with a friend, as both tasks are well rehearsed. However, age differences are likely if the tasks are listening to the news while assembling furniture, as these tasks are not well rehearsed.

The research on attention shows that older adults are slower than younger adults at finding targets; they are especially at a disadvantage as tasks become more complicated. However, providing signals or other types of support helps their performance.

Psychomotor Speed

You are driving home from a friend's house when all of a sudden, a car pulls out of a driveway right into your path. You must hit the brakes as fast as possible or you will have an accident. How quickly can you move your foot from the accelerator to the brake?

This real-life situation is an example of psychomotor speed, *the speed with which a person can make a specific response.* Psychomotor speed (also called reaction time) is one of the most studied phenomena of aging, and hundreds of studies all point to the same conclusion: People slow down as they get older. In fact, the slowing-with-age finding is so well documented that many researchers accept it as the only universal behavioral change in aging yet discovered (Kail & Salthouse, 1994). As the cartoon shows, even Garfield feels the effects.

GARFIELD © 1994 Paws, Inc. Reprinted with permission of UNIVERSAL PRESS SYNDICATE. All rights reserved.

Data suggest, however, that the rate at which cognitive processes slow down from young adulthood to late life varies a great deal depending on the task (Stine-Morrow & Soederberg Miller, 1999).

The most important reason reaction times slow down is that older adults take longer to decide that they need to respond. This is especially true when the situation involves ambiguous information (Stelmach, Goggin, & Garcia-Colera, 1988). Even when the information presented indicates that a response will definitely be needed, there is an orderly slowing of responding with age. As the uncertainty of whether a response is needed increases, older adults get differentially slower; the difference between them and middle-aged adults increases as the uncertainty level increases.

Although response slowing is inevitable, the amount of the decline can be reduced if older adults are allowed to practice making quick responses or if they are experienced in the task. In a classic study, Salthouse (1984) showed that although older secretaries' reaction times (measured by how fast they could tap their finger) were slower than those of younger secretaries, their computed typing speed was no slower than that of their younger counterparts. Why? Typing speed is calculated on the basis of words typed corrected for errors; because older typists are more accurate, their final speeds were just as good as those of younger secretaries, whose work tended to include more errors. Also, older secretaries are better at anticipating what letters come next (Kail & Salthouse, 1994).

Because psychomotor slowing is a universal phenomenon, many researchers have argued that it may explain a great deal of the age differences in cognition (e.g., Salthouse, 1996). Indeed, psychomotor slowing is a very good predictor of cognitive performance, but there's a catch. The prediction is best when the task requires little effort (Park et al., 1996). When the task requires more effort and is more difficult, then working memory (which we consider later) is a better predictor of performance (Park et al., 1996). Psychomotor slowing with age has also sparked considerable controversy concerning whether older adults should be allowed to drive. As discussed in the Current Controversies feature, knowledge about sensory and cognitive changes have resulted in research on this issue, and the development of screening tests.

THINK ABOUT IT

? What are some of the practical consequences of psychomotor slowing?

CURRENT CONTROVERSIES

To learn more, enter the following search term: aged automobile drivers.

INFORMATION PROCESSING IN EVERYDAY LIFE: OLDER DRIVERS

Several bits of information we have considered so far coalesce around a controversial issue: whether older drivers should be screened more closely before their driver's licenses are renewed. This is a sensitive topic. For many people, the automobile is their only reliable means of transportation, and a means of remaining independent. However, age-related changes in vision, hearing, attention, and reaction time do affect people's competence as drivers. Moreover, the number of older adults is rapidly increasing.

Experts agree that decisions about whether "at risk" drivers should be allowed to continue driving must be based on performance measures rather than age or medical diagnosis alone (Borlange Consensus Group, 1997). Since the mid-1980s, researchers such as Karlene Ball and others have been working to develop these measures. Their work resulted in the *Useful Field of View (UFOV)* measure, which is the area from which one can extract visual information in a single glance without turning one's head or moving one's eyes (Ball & Owsley, 1993). The UFOV test simulates driving in that it demands quick processing of information, simultaneous monitoring of central and peripheral stimuli, and the extraction of relevant target stimuli from irrelevant background information while performing a task. A reduction in the UFOV is directly related to the odds of being in automobile accidents (Ball et al., 1993). Indeed, in an analysis of 364 crashes involving older adults, 220 occurred at intersections and were caused by inattention (e.g., not seeing an on-coming car), exactly as would be predicted by a decline in UFOV (Ball et al., 1993). Importantly, driving performance improves after training in how to expand one's UFOV; for example, people reduce the number of dangerous maneuvers made while driving (Ball, 1997).

Should there be mandatory testing of older drivers? The data clearly indicate that the answer should be "yes." What form this testing should take, however, will spark increasing debate over the next few decades. •

Working Memory

One evening while you are watching television, you suddenly remember that your lover's birthday is a week from tomorrow. You decide that a nice romantic dinner would be just the thing, so you open the phone book, look up the number for a special restaurant, go over to the phone, and make the call. *Remembering the number long enough to dial it successfully requires* working memory, *the processes and structures involved in holding information in mind and simultaneously using it.*

Working memory has a relatively small capacity (Craik & Jennings, 1992). Because working memory deals with information that is being used right at the moment, it acts as a kind of mental scratchpad or blackboard. Unless we take some action to keep the information active (perhaps by rehearsal), or pass it along to long-term storage, the page we are using will get filled up quickly; in order to handle more information, some of the old information must be discarded.

Working memory declines with age (Smith, 1996). As noted earlier, working memory is increasingly invoked to explain age-related differences in cognitive performance on tasks that are difficult and demand considerable effort and resources (Park et al., 1996). Taken together, working memory and psychomotor speed provide a powerful set of explanatory constructs in predicting cognitive performance (Earles et al., 1997; Park et al., 1996; Salthouse, 1996).

MEMORY

"Memory is power" (Johnson-Laird, 1988, p. 41). Indeed it is, when you think of the importance of remembering tasks, faces, lists, instructions, and our personal past and identity. Perhaps that is why people put such a premium on maintaining a good memory in old age; like Dagwood in the cartoon, many

BLONDIE, © 1993. Reprinted with special permission of King Features Syndicate.

older adults use it to judge whether their mind is intact. But as depicted in the cartoon, poor memory is often viewed as an inevitable part of aging. Many people like Rocio, the woman in the vignette, believe that forgetting a loaf of bread at the store when one is 25 is not a big deal, but forgetting it when one is 65 is cause for alarm—a sign of Alzheimer's disease or some other malady. In this section, we sort out the myth and the reality of memory changes with age.

What Changes?

In order to understand age differences in memory, we need to distinguish between different types of memory tests, different settings for testing memory, and different types of memory. Two main ways are used to test memory. *In a* free recall *test, people are simply asked to report everything they can remember about the material they learned. In a* recognition *test, people are asked to choose the correct item from a list of correct and incorrect choices.*

The typical pattern of results is that older adults do much worse than younger adults on free recall tests, but age differences are minimal on recognition tests. Because older adults have shorter memory spans, they recall substantially fewer items from lists and text passages (Verhaeghen, Marcoen & Goosens, 1993). These age differences are large; for example, more than 80% of a sample of adults in their 20s do better than adults in their 70s. These differences are not reliably lowered by slower presentation, giving cues or reminders during recall, or providing specific strategies (such as imagery) during study.

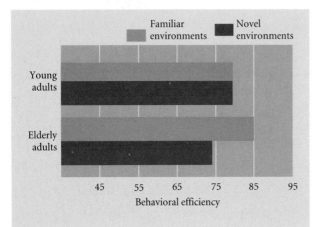

A second important distinction is where memory testing occurs. In general, we know the most about testing memory in laboratory settings; age differences usually occur here, especially on free recall tests. However, age differences are sometimes not found when memory is tested in the real world. One of the best examples of this is seen in research by Kirasic and Allen (1985), who examined younger and older adults' ability to find items in familiar and unfamiliar grocery stores. As you can see in the graph, older adults were actually better than younger adults in familiar stores, while the opposite was true for novel stores. Interestingly, though, the ability to learn one's way around in the environment is predicted by basic cognitive processes independent of the location of the test (Allen et al., 1996).

A third distinction relates to different types of memory. Age differences are largest when secondary memory is tested (Kausler, 1994). Secondary memory *refers to the ability to remember relatively large amounts of information from a few seconds to a few minutes.* Remembering to buy bread at the grocery store, the main aspects of a movie you just saw, or what you had for breakfast this morning are examples. Declines in secondary memory are normative (Kausler, 1994). Another type of memory, called tertiary memory, shows a different pattern. Tertiary memory *refers to the ability to remember information for a very long time, from a few hours to many years.* This information could be personal events from one's youth and the definition of words, for example. Tertiary memory does not typically decline with age (Kausler, 1994).

The Impact of Beliefs About Memory Aging

Regardless of the results from research, there is widespread belief that memory inevitably declines. This is significant, because research shows that what adults like the woman in the photograph believe about their memory ability is related to how well they perform (Cavanaugh, 1996). This relation is seen in how much effort people exert trying to remember, how well people predict they will perform, and what strategies people use. For example, people who believe that their memory is good work harder at remembering than people who believe their memory is poor. Moreover, these beliefs are also related to the assumptions people make about the degree to which memory (or other cognitive abilities) is "supposed" to change (Cavanaugh, Feldman, & Hertzog, 1998). For example, if you think that memory is supposed to get much worse as you get older, then your estimate of how much your memory has declined will be much greater than an estimate by someone who thinks memory should decline only a little with age.

Overall, research on memory beliefs shows that although some changes in memory are normal, people can essentially convince themselves that these changes are much worse and more pervasive than they really are (Cavanaugh et al., 1998). It may even be the case that altering your central beliefs about memory aging may help you develop compensatory strategies that lower the magnitude of these changes, or at least help compensate for them (Cavanaugh, 1996).

Still, one's beliefs about memory are influenced by changes in basic information processing, such as working memory (Hultsch, 1998). Although beliefs are important, they must also be realistic about normative change.

When Is Memory Change Abnormal?

Because people are concerned that memory failures may reflect disease, identifying true cases of memory-impairing disease is extremely important. Differentiating normal and abnormal memory changes is usually accomplished through a wide array of tests that are grounded in the various developmental patterns discussed earlier. Such testing focuses on measuring performance and identifying declines in aspects of memory that typically do not change, such as tertiary memory (Edelstein & Kalish, 1999).

Even if a decline is identified in an aspect of memory that is cause for concern, it does not automatically follow that there is a serious problem. A first step is to find out whether the memory problem is interfering with everyday functioning. When the memory problem does interfere with functioning, such as not remembering how to get home or your spouse's name, it is appropriate to suspect a serious, abnormal underlying reason.

Once a serious problem is suspected, the next step is to obtain a thorough examination (Edelstein & Kalish, 1999). This should include a complete physical and neurological examination and a complete battery of neuropsychological tests. These may help identify the nature and extent of the underlying problem and provide information about what steps, if any, can be taken to alleviate the difficulties.

The most important point to keep in mind is that there is no magic number of times that a person must forget something before it becomes a matter for concern. Indeed, many memory-impairing diseases progress slowly, and poor memory performance may only be noticed gradually over an extended period of time. The best course is to have the person examined; only with complete and thorough testing can these concerns be checked appropriately.

Remediating Memory Problems

Remember Rocio, the person in the vignette who had to remember when to take several different medications? In the face of normal age-related declines, how can her problem be solved?

Support programs can be designed for people to help them remember. Sometimes, people like Rocio who are experiencing normal age-related memory changes need extra help because of the high memory demands they face. At other times, people need help because the memory changes they are experiencing are greater than normal.

Camp and colleagues (1993) developed the E-I-E-I-O framework to handle both situations. The E-I-E-I-O framework combines two types of memory: explicit and implicit. Explicit memory *involves the conscious and intentional recollection of information; remembering this definition on an exam is one example.* Implicit memory *involves effortless and unconscious recollection of information; knowing that stop signs are red octagons is usually not something that people need to exert effort to remember when encountering one on the road.* The framework also includes two types of memory aids. External aids *are memory aids that rely on environmental resources, such as notebooks or calendars.* Internal aids *are memory aids that rely on mental processes, such as imagery.* The aha experience that comes with suddenly remembering something (as in, "Oh, I remember!) is the O that follows these E's and I's. As you can see in the table, the E-I-E-I-O framework allows different types of memory to be combined with different types of memory aids to provide a broad range of intervention options to help people remember.

? **THINK ABOUT IT**
How might people's beliefs about memory be important elements of memory training programs?

Type of Memory	Type of Memory Aid	
	External	**Internal**
Explicit	Appointment book	Mental imagery
	Grocery list	Rote rehearsal
Implicit	Color-coded maps	Spaced retrieval
	Sandpaper letters	Conditioning

You are probably most familiar with the explicit-external and explicit-internal types of memory aids. Explicit-internal aids like rehearsal help people remember phone numbers. Explicit-external aids are used when information needs to be better organized and remembered, such as taking notes during a visit to the physician (McGuire & Codding, 1998). Implicit-internal aids represent nearly effortless learning, such as the association between the color of the particular wing of the apartment building one lives in and the fact that one's residence is there. Implicit-external aids such as icons representing time of day and the number of pills to take help older adults remember their medication (Morrow et al., 1998).

In general, explicit-external interventions are the most frequently used to remediate the kinds of memory problems older adults face, probably because they are easy to use and widely available (Cavanaugh, Grady, & Perlmutter, 1983). For example, virtually everyone owns an address book, and small notepads are sold in hundreds of stores. Explicit-external interventions have other important applications, too. The medication problem is best solved with an explicit-external intervention: a pillbox that is divided into compartments corresponding to days of the week and different times of the day. Research shows that this type of pillbox is the easiest to load and results in the fewest errors (Park et al., 1991; Park, Morrell, & Shifren, 1999). Memory interventions like this can help older adults maintain their independence. Nursing homes also use explicit-external interventions, such as bulletin boards with the date and weather conditions, or activities charts like the one shown in the photograph, to help residents keep in touch with current events.

The E-I-E-I-O framework can be used to design remediation strategies for any kind of memory problem, including those due to disease or abnormal patterns of aging. Later, we will see how the E-I-E-I-O framework provides insight into how people with Alzheimer's disease can be helped to improve their memory. In the meantime, see how many different categories of memory interventions you can discover. Check the See for Yourself feature for details.

HELPING PEOPLE REMEMBER

SEE FOR YOURSELF

The text lists several different ways in which people's memory can be helped. Perhaps you never thought about how many memory aids you use in your everyday life, such as notebooks, calendars, lists, setting things by the door, asking your friends, rereading things, and so forth.

This real-world exercise has two parts. First, using the E-I-E-I-O framework, analyze your own daily routine and list all of the ways you help yourself remember. (You may be surprised at how many different ways you do this!) Next, do the same for a few of your friends and relatives. Try to talk with people of different ages. Tabulate your results and share them with your classmates. Which category in the table contains the aids that people use the most? See for yourself. •

TRAINING INTELLECTUAL ABILITIES

In Chapter 12, we saw that intelligence reaches its overall peak in middle age, then begins to decline. Are these declines an inevitable part of aging, or can they be slowed or even eliminated?

This question provided the basis for Willis's important series of studies in the 1980s and early 1990s examining how much older adults' performance could be boosted through direct intervention and training (e.g., Baltes & Willis, 1982; Willis & Schaie, 1992). Because her participants came from the Seattle Longitudinal Study, described in Chapter 9 (pages 337–339), Willis had longitudinal data on each person's past performance. To see how well training worked, two groups of people were identified. One group included people who had shown significant declines in inductive reasoning (figuring out the general concept from a list of specific examples) or spatial ability (being able to create three-dimensional images from two-dimensional representations) over a span of 14 years. The other group included people whose performance on these abilities had remained roughly constant over the same period.

Willis and her colleagues provided training in both abilities. Their results were impressive: Roughly two-thirds of the people showed significant improvements in performance. About 40% of the people who had previously declined improved so much that, after training, they performed as well as they had 14 years earlier! These training effects were maintained over time; 7 years after their initial training, people were still performing well. This was especially true for people who had previously shown declining performance.

These results provide strong evidence that declines in performance on intelligence tests are reversible in at least some areas. However, much research remains; we do not know whether these impressive gains would also be found for other abilities. Still, Willis's findings provide reason for hope that, for some abilities in some people, intellectual decline may not be inevitable.

CREATIVITY AND WISDOM

Creativity

What makes a person creative? Is it exceptional productivity? Duke Ellington wrote numerous musical pieces, Diego Rivera painted hundreds of pictures, and Thomas Edison had 1,093 patents (still the record for one person). But Gregor Mendel had only 7 scientific papers, yet endures as a major figure in the history of genetics. Lao Tzu is remembered mostly for the enduring *Tao Te Ching*. Does creativity mean having a career marked by precocity and longevity? Wolfgang Goethe wrote poetry as a teenager, a best-selling novel in his 20s, popular plays in his 30s and 40s, Part I of *Faust* at 59 and Part II at 83. But others are "early bloomers" and decline thereafter, whereas still others are relatively unproductive early and are "late bloomers."

Creative output, in terms of the number of creative ideas a person has or the major contributions a person makes, varies across adult life span and across disciplines (Simonton, 1997). When considered as a function of age, the overall number of creative ideas a person has tends to increase through one's 20s, plateaus in one's 30s, and declines thereafter, as shown in the graph. However, the decline does *not* mean that people stop being creative at all; rather, it means that creative people keep producing creative ideas, but fewer of them than they did when they were younger (Dixon & Hultsch, 1999). When translated into a mathematical equation, the graph can be used to predict the creative output of a specific individual (e.g., Duke Ellington) or a group of similar people (e.g., jazz composers). In both

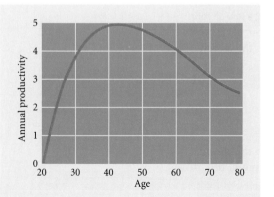

cases, the graph accurately describes the level of creative output. Thus, creative output peaks in early to middle adulthood, and declines thereafter.

What does the trend look like if one compares different disciplines, such as mathematics, biology, and earth science? One way to examine this is to compare three points in a career: the age at the time of the first major contribution, most important contribution, and the last important contribution (Simonton, 1997). As you can see in the graph, the overall shape of the graphs in several scientific disciplines is the same as in the first graph, with a rise, a peak, and a decline with increasing age. The average age at which the people studied died is shown by small crosses. Notice that the specific ages for the three contributions depends on the discipline. For example, mathematics has the youngest age of first major contribution, and earth sciences tends to have the oldest age at last important contribution.

Taken together, Simonton's (1997) analysis provides the most powerful model available to explain individual differences in creative output across adulthood. The trend is clear: Across a variety of disciplines, creative output tends to peak during late young adulthood to early middle age and decline thereafter. This pattern may help explain why senior researchers include many younger scholars in their work. The senior scholar can provide the overall context, while the younger researchers may provide a continuous flow of innovative ideas (Dixon & Hultsch, 1999).

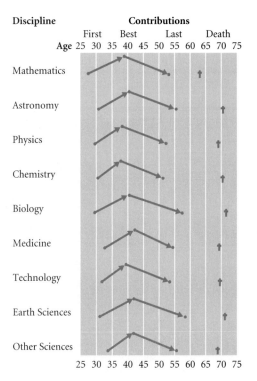

Wisdom

For thousands of years, cultures around the world have greatly admired people who were wise. Tales of wise people, usually older adults, have been passed down from generation to generation to teach lessons about important matters of life and love (Chinen, 1989). What is it about these truths that makes someone who knows them wise?

From a psychological perspective, wisdom has been viewed as involving three cognitive processes (Kramer, 1990): practical and social intelligence, such as the ability to solve difficult real-world problems; insight or knowledge into the deeper meanings underlying a given situation; and awareness of the relative, uncertain, and paradoxical nature of human problems, reflected in postformal thinking (see Chapter 9, pages 341–344). A growing body of research has been examining these aspects.

Based on years of research using in-depth think-aloud interviews with young, middle-aged, and older adults about normal and unusual problems that people face, Baltes and Staudinger (1993) describe four characteristics of wisdom:

- Wisdom deals with important and/or difficult matters of life and the human condition.
- Wisdom is truly "superior" knowledge, judgment, and advice.
- Wisdom is knowledge with extraordinary scope, depth, and balance, applicable to specific situations.
- Wisdom, when used, is well intended and combines mind and virtue (character).

The researchers used this framework to discover that people who are wise are experts in the basic issues in life (Baltes & Staudinger, 1993). Wise people know a great deal about how to conduct life, how to interpret life events, and what life means.

Research shows that wisdom is not the same thing as creativity. Wisdom is the growth of expertise and insight, whereas creativity is the generation of a new

solution to a problem (Simonton, 1990). Baltes and Staudinger (1993) have shown that wisdom may not be the province of older adults exclusively. For example, one study had people respond to life planning problems like the following. A 15-year-old girl wants to get married right away. What should she consider and do? Answers were then analyzed in terms of the degree to which they reflect wisdom. Contrary to what many people expect, there is no association between age and wise answers; any of the people in the photograph could show wisdom. Whether a person is wise depends on whether he or she has extensive life experience with the type of problem given (Smith & Baltes, 1990).

Research based on cognitive developmental changes in adulthood, such as those discussed in Chapter 9, has uncovered other aspects in the growth of wisdom. According to several investigators, a wise person is one who is able to integrate thinking, feeling, and acting into a coherent approach to a problem (Kramer, 1990; Orwoll & Perlmutter, 1990). This research implies that empathy and compassion are important characteristics of wise people (Wink & Helson, 1997). They are able to overcome automatic responses so as to show concern for core human experiences and values (Pascual-Leone, 1990). Thus, wise people are able to see through situations and get to the heart of the matter, rather than being caught in the superficial aspects (Wink & Helson, 1997). Indeed, there is some evidence that, compared to young and middle-aged adults, older adults are more generous in donating their time and money to charity and express greater social concern (Haan, Milsap, & Hartka, 1986).

So what specific factors help one become wise? Baltes (1993) identified three factors: (a) *general personal conditions,* such as mental ability; (b) *specific expertise conditions,* such as mentoring or practice; and (c) *facilitative life contexts,* such as education or leadership experience. Other researchers point to additional criteria. For example, Kramer (1990) argues that the *integration of affect and cognition* that occurs during adulthood results in the ability to act wisely. Personal growth during adulthood, reflecting Erikson's concepts of generativity and integrity, helps foster the process as well. All of these factors take time. Thus, although growing old is no guarantee of wisdom, it does provide the time that, if used well, creates a supportive context for it.

FORCES IN ACTION   COGNITIVE CHANGES IN LATER LIFE

Normal aging brings decline in several abilities, whereas others remain largely intact or even improve. Why is there such variation in developmental trends?

Biological forces operate to reduce the efficiency of basic information-processing abilities, primarily through both normal and disease-related changes in some areas of the brain. Additionally, psychological forces from the differential use of cognitive abilities and the sociocultural forces from lower cognitive demands in certain situations can help account for declines in some areas. Similar explanations of abilities that remain constant or improve can be made. Physiological changes in the brain do not affect all areas equally; psychological forces create greater practice with some skills; and sociocultural pressures to maintain contact with the world mean that some skills, such as in areas of expertise, continue to operate well.

Life-cycle forces are also important in understanding cognitive changes in later life. The same cognitive event often has very different meanings, depending on where in life people are. For example, not being efficient at remembering grocery items without a list may be only mildly annoying and easily dismissed in young adulthood, but may be viewed as a sign of cognitive slippage by an older adult. Such changes in interpretation even of apparently universal events, such as forgetting something at the grocery store, become even more common as people reach late life and worry about whether they may be getting Alzheimer's disease, a topic we will explore next. •

---

1. As long as the competing tasks in a test of divided attention are easy, older adults perform _____ younger adults.

2. Compared to age differences in free recall performance, age differences in recognition memory performance are _____ .

3. When older adults received training in inductive reasoning and spatial ability, most _____ .

4. Three factors that help a person become wise are _____ .

5. How would the view that wisdom involves life experience fit into the discussion of expertise in Chapter 12?

Answers: (1) as well as, (2) smaller, (3) showed significant improvements in performance, (4) general personal conditions, special expertise conditions, and facilitative life contexts

---

MENTAL HEALTH AND INTERVENTION

Learning Objectives

- **How does depression in older adults differ from depression in younger adults? How is it diagnosed and treated?**

- **How are anxiety disorders treated in older adults?**

- **What is Alzheimer's disease? How is it diagnosed and managed? What causes it?**

Mental Health and Intervention

Depression

Anxiety Disorders

Dementia: Alzheimer's Disease

ARY lived by herself for 30 years after her husband died. For all but the last 5 years or so, she managed very well. Little by little, family members and friends began noticing that Mary wasn't behaving quite right. For example, her memory slipped, she sounded confused sometimes, and her moods changed without warning. Her appearance deteriorated. Some of her friends attribute these changes to the fact that Mary is in her 80s. But others wonder whether this is something more than normal aging.

Suppose Mary is a relative of yours. How would you deal with the situation? How would you decide whether her behavior is normal? What would you do to try to improve Mary's life?

Every day, families turn to mental health professionals for help in dealing with psychological problems their aging relatives are having. Unfortunately, myths interfere with appropriate mental health diagnoses and interventions for older adults. For example, many people mistakenly believe that nearly all older adults are either depressed, demented, or both. When they observe older adults behaving in these ways, they take no action because they believe that nothing can be done.

In this section, we will see that such beliefs are wrong. Only a minority of older adults have mental health problems, and most such problems respond to therapy. Sometimes these problems manifest themselves differently in younger and older adults, so we need to know what to look for. Accurate diagnosis is essential. Let's examine some of the most commonly occurring and widely known disorders: depression, anxiety disorders, and Alzheimer's disease.

DEPRESSION

Most people feel down or sad from time to time, perhaps in reaction to a problem at work or in one's relationships. But does this mean that most people are depressed? How is depression diagnosed? Are there age differences in the symptoms examined in diagnosis? How is depression treated?

First of all, let's dispense with a myth. Contrary to popular belief that most older adults are depressed, the rate of severe depression *declines* from young adulthood to old age (Qualls, 1999). For those people who do experience depression, let's examine its diagnosis and treatment.

How Is Depression Diagnosed in Older Adults?

Depression in later life is usually diagnosed on the basis of two clusters of symptoms that must be present for at least two weeks: feelings and physical changes. *As with younger people, the most prominent symptom of depression in older adults is feeling sad or down, termed* dysphoria. But whereas younger people are likely to label these feelings directly as "feeling depressed," older adults like the man in the photograph may refer to them as "feeling helpless," or in terms of physical health such as "feeling tired" (Wolfe, Morrow, & Fredrickson, 1996). Older adults are also more likely than younger people to appear apathetic and expressionless, to confine themselves to bed, to neglect themselves, and to make derogatory statements about themselves.

The second cluster of symptoms includes physical changes such as loss of appetite, insomnia, and trouble breathing (Wolfe et al., 1996). In young people, these symptoms usually indicate an underlying psychological problem. But in older adults, they may simply reflect normal, age-related changes. Thus, older adults' physical symptoms of depression must be evaluated very carefully (Qualls, 1999).

An important step in diagnosis is ruling out other possible causes of the symptoms. For example, other physical health problems, neurological disorders, medication side effects, metabolic conditions, and substance abuse can all cause behaviors that resemble depression (Qualls, 1999). For many minorities, immigration status and degree of acculturation and assimilation are key factors to consider (Black, Markides, & Miller, 1998). An important criterion to be established is that the symptoms interfere with daily life; clinical depression involves significant impairment of daily living (Edelstein & Kalish, 1999; Qualls, 1999).

What Causes Depression?

There are two main schools of thought about the causes of depression. One focuses on biological and physiological processes, particularly on imbalances in specific neurotransmitters (see Chapter 8, pages 307–308). Because most neurotransmitter levels decline with age, some researchers believe that depression in later life is likely to be a biochemical problem (Thompson & Gallagher, 1986). The general view that depression has a biochemical basis underlies current approaches to drug therapies, discussed a bit later.

The second view focuses on psychosocial factors, such as loss and internal belief systems. Although several types of loss have been associated with depression, including loss of a spouse, a job, or good health, it is how a person interprets a loss, rather than the event itself, that causes depression (Gaylord & Zung, 1987). *In this approach,* internal belief systems, *or what one tells oneself about why certain things are happening, are emphasized as the cause of depression.* For example, experiencing an unpredictable and uncontrollable event such as the death of a spouse may cause depression because you believe the event happened to you because you are a bad person (Beck, 1967). People who are depressed tend to believe that they are personally responsible for all the bad things that happen to them, that things are unlikely to get better, and that their whole life is a shambles.

How Is Depression Treated in Older Adults?

Regardless how severe depression is, people benefit from treatment, often through a combination of medication and psychotherapy (Qualls, 1999; Wolfe et al., 1996). Medications work by altering the balance of specific neurotransmitters in the brain. *For very severe cases of depression, medications such as* heterocyclic antidepressants (HCAs), monoamine oxidase (MAO) inhibitors, *or* selective serotonin reuptake inhibitors (SSRIs) *can be administered.* For many years, HCAs were known as *tricyclic antidepressants,* because this was the only form available, but the introduction of monocyclic, bicyclic, and tetracyclic drugs led to the change in name (Berkow, 1987). Although they are widely prescribed, HCAs cannot be used if the person is also taking medications to control hypertension or has certain metabolic conditions. MAO inhibitors cause very dangerous and potentially fatal interactions with foods containing tyramine or dopamine, such as cheddar cheese, wine, and chicken liver. Consequently, MAO inhibitors are usually used only as a last resort. Selective serotonin reuptake inhibitors (SSRIs) gained wide popularity beginning in the late 1980s, because they have the lowest overall side effects of any antidepressant. SSRIs work by boosting the level of serotonin, which is a neurotransmitter involved in regulating moods. One of the SSRIs, Prozac, has been the subject of controversy, as it has been linked in a small number of cases with the serious side effect of high levels of agitation. Other SSRIs, such as Zoloft and Serzone, appear to have fewer adverse reactions.

Psychotherapy is a popular approach to treating depression, based on the idea that focusing on the psychological aspects of depression is helpful. Two forms of psychotherapy have been shown to be effective with older adults. *The basic idea in* behavior therapy *is that depressed people experience too few rewards or reinforcements from their environment.* Thus, the goal of behavior therapy is to increase the good things that happen and minimize the negative things (Lewinsohn, 1975). Often, this is accomplished by having people increase their activities; simply by doing more, the likelihood that something nice will happen is increased. Additionally, behavior therapy seeks to get people to reduce the negative things that happen by learning how to avoid them. The net increase in positive events and net decrease in negative events comes about through practice and homework assignments during the course of therapy, such as going out more or joining a club to meet new people.

A second effective approach is cognitive therapy, *which is based on the idea that maladaptive beliefs or cognitions about oneself are responsible for depression.* From this perspective, a depressed person views oneself as unworthy and inadequate, the world as insensitive and ungratifying, and the future as bleak and unpromising (Beck et al., 1979). In a cognitive therapy session like the one shown here, a person is taught how to recognize these thoughts and to reevaluate the self, the world, and the future more realistically, resulting in a change in the underlying beliefs.

The most important fact to keep in mind about depression is that it *is* treatable. Thus, if an older person behaves in ways that indicate depression, it is a good idea to have him or her examined by a mental health professional. Even if it turns out not to be depression, another underlying and possibly treatable condition may be uncovered.

ANXIETY DISORDERS

Imagine you are about to give a speech to an audience of several hundred people. During the last few minutes before you begin, you start to feel nervous, your heart begins to pound, your mouth gets very dry, and your palms get sweaty. These feelings, common even to veteran speakers, are similar to those experienced more frequently by people with anxiety disorders.

Anxiety disorders *include problems such as feelings of severe anxiety for no apparent reason, phobias with regard to specific things or places, and obsessive-compulsive disorders, in which thoughts or actions are repeatedly performed* (Fisher & Noll, 1996; Qualls, 1999). Although anxiety disorders occur in adults of all ages, they are particularly common in older adults due to loss of health, relocation stress, isolation, fear of losing independence, and many other reasons. Anxiety disorders are diagnosed in as many as 10% of older women and 5% of older men (Cohen, 1990). The reasons for this gender difference are unknown.

Anxiety disorders can be treated with medication and psychotherapy (Fisher & Noll, 1996). The most commonly used medications are benzodiazepine (e.g.,Valium and Librium), SSRIs (Paxil, among others), buspirone, and beta-blockers. Though moderately effective, these drugs must be monitored very carefully in older adults, because the amount needed to treat the disorder is very low and the potential for side effects is great. For older adults, the clear treatment of choice is psychotherapy, especially relaxation therapy (Fisher & Noll, 1996). Relaxation therapy is highly effective, is easily learned, and presents a technique that is useful in many situations (e.g., falling asleep at night).

To this point, we have focused on psychopathologies that can be treated effectively. In the next section, we consider Alzheimer's disease, which at present cannot be treated effectively over the long run, progressively worsening until the person dies.

DEMENTIA: ALZHEIMER'S DISEASE

Arguably the most serious condition associated with aging is dementia, *a family of diseases involving serious impairment of behavioral and cognitive functioning.* Of these disorders, Alzheimer's disease is the most common. The Real People feature shows how Alzheimer's disease progressed in one person.

REAL PEOPLE

WHAT'S THE MATTER WITH MARY?

Remember Mary, the 80-year-old woman in the vignette who had become forgetful, confused, and moody? Her friends and family soon discovered that she occasionally forgot where she lived, and began to think differently about Mary's problem. Her family ultimately realized that she could no longer care for herself; help had to be found. She moved to a group home but continued to deteriorate. She started having trouble remembering things from even a few minutes before. Names of family members became mixed up at first and later forgotten entirely. She began to wander. Finally, Mary had to be placed in a nursing home. The times when she was living in the present became fewer. Her physical abilities continued to decline, until she eventually could not feed herself. Toward the end of her life, she could not eat solid food and had to be force-fed. Mary died from Alzheimer's disease after 15 years of slow, agonizing decline. •

As the Real People feature demonstrates, Alzheimer's disease causes people to change from thinking, communicative human beings to confused, bedridden victims unable to recognize their family members and close friends. As a result, the *fear* of Alzheimer's disease among healthy older adults is a significant problem beyond the actual disease (Youngjohn & Crook, 1996).

Millions of people are afflicted with Alzheimer's disease, including such notable individuals as former U.S. President Ronald Reagan; the disease cuts across ethnic, racial, and socioeconomic groups. The incidence of Alzheimer's disease increases with age, rising from extremely low rates in the 50s to nearly half of the people aged 85 and older (Youngjohn & Crook, 1996). Women tend to have a higher risk (Henderson, 1997). As the number of older adults increases rapidly over the next several decades, the number of cases is expected to increase substantially.

What Are the Symptoms of Alzheimer's Disease?

Mary, the woman in the Real People feature, showed several of the key symptoms of Alzheimer's disease: *gradual declines in memory, learning, attention, and judgment; confusion as to time and place; difficulties in communicating and finding the right words; decline in personal hygiene and self-care skills; inappropriate social behavior; and changes in personality.* These classic symptoms may be vague and only occur occasionally in the beginning, but as the disease progresses, they become much more pronounced and are exhibited much more regularly (Youngjohn & Crook, 1996). Wandering away from home and not being able to remember how to return increases. Paranoid and other accusatory behaviors develop. Spouses become strangers. Patients may not even recognize

themselves in a mirror; they wonder who is looking back at them. *In its advanced stages, Alzheimer's disease often causes* incontinence *(the loss of bladder or bowel control) and total loss of mobility.* Like the man in the photo, victims eventually become completely dependent on others for care. At this point many caregivers seek facilities such as adult day care centers, and other sources of help, such as family and friends, in order to provide a safe environment for the Alzheimer's patient while the primary caregiver is at work or needs to do basic errands.

Although progression is usually faster the earlier in adulthood it is diagnosed, the rate of deterioration in Alzheimer's disease is highly variable (Bondareff, 1983). Thus, it is difficult to generalize about the level of a person's impairment based solely on how long ago the diagnosis was made. Likewise, it is very difficult to predict how long a specific patient will survive, which only adds to the stress experienced by the caregiver (Cavanaugh & Nocera, 1994).

How Is Alzheimer's Disease Diagnosed?

Given that the behavioral symptoms of Alzheimer's disease eventually become quite obvious, one would assume that diagnosis would be straightforward. Quite the contrary. In fact, absolute certainty that a person has Alzheimer's disease cannot even be achieved while the individual is still alive. Definitive diagnosis must be based on an autopsy of the brain after death, because the defining criteria for diagnosing Alzheimer's disease involve documenting large numbers of structural changes in neurons that can only be observed under a microscope after brain tissue has been removed and specially prepared (Youngjohn & Crook, 1996; Qualls, 1999).

Of course, one is still left with the issue of figuring out whether a person probably has Alzheimer's disease while he or she is still alive. Although not definitive, the number and severity of behavioral changes lead clinicians to make fairly accurate diagnoses of *probable* Alzheimer's disease (Qualls, 1999). But accuracy depends on a broad-based and thorough series of medical and psychological tests, including complete blood tests, metabolic and neurological tests, and neuropsychological tests (Youngjohn & Crook, 1996). A great deal of diagnostic work goes into ruling out virtually all other possible causes of the observed symptoms. This effort is essential. Because Alzheimer's disease is an incurable and fatal disease, every treatable cause of the symptoms must be explored first. In essence, Alzheimer's disease is diagnosed by excluding all other possible explanations.

Differential diagnosis (recognizing the difference between one disease and another) of Alzheimer's disease is extremely important (Youngjohn & Crook, 1996; Qualls, 1999). *For example, severe depression and some types of vitamin deficiencies can cause serious memory impairments, sometimes called* pseudo-dementia. Other medical conditions, such as thyroid deficiency, some brain tumors in the temporal lobe, strokes in certain areas of the brain, and normal pressure hydrocephalus, can cause memory problems or behavioral outbursts. Other types of dementia, such as vascular dementia (caused by cerebrovascular disease) and Parkinson's disease, also can cause severe memory and other problems. Without a complete battery of medical and neuropsychological tests, these conditions may be misdiagnosed as Alzheimer's disease and left untreated.

In an attempt to be as thorough as possible, clinicians usually interview family members about their perceptions of the observed behavioral symptoms. Most clinicians view this information as essential to understanding the history of the difficulties the person is experiencing. However, research indicates that spouses are often inaccurate in their assessments of the level of their partner's impairment (McGuire & Cavanaugh, 1992). In part, this inaccuracy is due to lack of knowledge about the disease. Also, spouses wish to portray themselves as in control, either by denying that the symptoms are in fact severe or by exaggerating the severity in order to give the appearance that they are coping well in a very difficult situation. Some spouses describe their partner's symptoms accurately, but family reports should not be the only source of information about the person's ability to function.

A great deal of attention has been given to the development of more definitive tests for Alzheimer's disease while the person is still alive. *Much of this work has focused on* amyloid, *a protein that is produced in abnormally high levels in Alzheimer's patients, perhaps causing the neurofibrillary tangles and neuritic plaques described earlier.* Research is progressing toward developing a way to measure amyloid concentrations in cerebrospinal fluid and blood. Additional work focuses on testing for the presence or absence of specific genes, a topic to which we now turn.

What Causes Alzheimer's Disease?

We do not know for sure what causes Alzheimer's disease (Youngjohn & Crook, 1996). Over the years, several hypotheses have been offered, such as aluminum deposits in the brain and a slow-acting virus, but none have explained more than a few cases.

Currently, most research is concentrating on identifying genetic links (Clark & Goate, 1993). The evidence is growing that at least some forms of Alzheimer's disease are inherited, based on studies of family trees, relatives, and identical twins. Indeed, several sites on various chromosomes have been tentatively identified as being involved in the transmission of Alzheimer's disease,

including chromosomes 12, 14, 19, and 21. If researchers can identify the gene(s) responsible for Alzheimer's disease, it would be possible to develop a test to see whether people had the inheritance pattern. Tests already exist for Huntington's disease, another type of dementia that shows an autosomal pattern. Persons at risk can find out whether they have the gene responsible for the disease through a blood test. Persons testing positive will get the disease, which usually strikes during young adulthood or middle age and is fatal. Thus, the development of genetic tests for Alzheimer's disease will provide not only a potential way to diagnose it, but also some difficult personal choices for people like the woman in the photograph. For example, individuals who know they have the genes responsible for the disease may be faced with difficult decisions about having children. Genetic counseling programs, which currently focus mostly on diseases of childhood, would need to be expanded to help individuals face decisions about diseases occurring later in life.

More recently, estrogen level is being examined as a factor in women's increased risk of Alzheimer's disease (Henderson, 1997; Simpkins et al., 1997). It is known that loss of estrogen after menopause is related to memory loss (see Chapter 12), and that this loss may be a source of the increased risk for Alzheimer's disease. There is some evidence that estrogen replacement therapy may lower this risk.

What Can Be Done for Victims of Alzheimer's Disease?

Even though Alzheimer's disease is incurable, much can be done to alleviate its symptoms. Most of the research has been focused on drugs aimed at improving memory. Despite much research with numerous types of drugs, none currently available reverses the memory symptoms permanently (Abrams & Berkow, 1990; Brioni & Decker, 1997).

In addition to memory drugs, medications to combat hostile behavior symptoms are widely used. These drugs, such as *thioridazine* and *haloperidol,* are the same ones used to treat severe psychotic disorders in adults. Additionally, antidepressants are effective in alleviating the depression that often accompanies Alzheimer's disease during its early stages. All of these medications must be used carefully, as older adults have a high risk of side effects such as severe motor impairment and increased cognitive impairment (Brioni & Decker, 1997).

Numerous effective behavioral and educational interventions have also been developed. *One behavioral intervention, based on the E-I-E-I-O approach to memory intervention discussed earlier in this chapter, involves using the implicit-internal memory intervention called* spaced retrieval. Adapted by Camp and colleagues (Camp & McKitrick, 1991), spaced retrieval involves teaching persons with Alzheimer's disease to remember new information by gradually increasing the time between retrieval attempts. How this is done is explained in the Spotlight on Research feature. This easy, almost magical technique has been used to teach names of staff members and other information; it holds considerable potential for broad application.

WHAT'S HER NAME? MEMORY TRAINING IN ALZHEIMER'S DISEASE

Who were the investigators and what was the aim of the study? Alzheimer's disease is marked by progressive and severe memory loss. But can memory problems be remediated using implicit-internal memory strategies? Cameron Camp and Leslie McKitrick decided to find out by training a technique called *spaced retrieval*.

How did the investigators measure the topic of interest? The secret to spaced retrieval is progressively increasing the amount of time between the recall of the target information (e.g., a person's name). For example, the instructor shows the client a picture of a person and says the person's name. After an initial recall interval of 5 seconds, the instructor asks the client to remember the name. As long as the client remembers correctly, recall intervals are increased to 10, 20, 40, 60, 90, 120, 150 seconds, and so on. If the client forgets the target information, the correct answer is provided, and the next recall interval is decreased to the length of the last correct trial. During the interval, the instructor engages the client in conversation to prevent active rehearsal of the information.

Who were the participants in the study? Camp and McKitrick tested people who had been diagnosed as probably having Alzheimer's disease who were also in an adult day care center.

What was the design of the study? The study used a longitudinal design so that Camp and McKitrick could track participants' performance over several weeks.

Were there ethical concerns with the study? Having persons with Alzheimer's disease as research participants raises important issues with informed consent. Because of their serious cognitive impairments, these individuals may not fully understand the procedures. Thus, family members such as a spouse or adult child caregiver are also asked to give informed consent. Additionally, researchers must pay careful attention to participants' emotions; if participants become agitated or frustrated, the training or testing session must be stopped. Camp and McKitrick took all these precautions.

What were the results? Spaced retrieval worked like magic, because even people who earlier could not retain information for more than 60 seconds could remember names taught through this technique for very long periods (e.g., 5 weeks or more). Learning the staff names usually involved a few failures, but with additional practice success occurred. For example, one participant looked sternly at the researchers who had come to her day care center. "I know you're going to ask me for Jane's name." Yet only a month before, Iris could not remember Jane's name; in fact, she seemed incapable of learning it at all using rote rehearsal. Most important, the new learning did not interfere with other information in long-term memory.

What did the investigators conclude? It appears that many types of information can be taught, making spaced retrieval a flexible intervention. Spaced retrieval can be used in virtually any setting, such as playing games or normal conversation, making it comfortable and nonthreatening to the client.

Although more work is needed to continue refining the technique, spaced retrieval is one of the most promising nondrug memory interventions for people with cognitive impairments. ●

? THINK ABOUT IT
Could spaced retrieval be used to address the normative changes in recall discussed earlier in the chapter? Why or why not?

In designing interventions for persons with Alzheimer's disease, the guiding principle should be optimizing the person's functioning. Regardless of the level of impairment, attempts should be made to help the person cope as well as possible with the symptoms. The key is helping all persons maintain their dignity as human beings. This can be achieved in some very creative ways, such as adapting the principles of Montessori methods of education to bring older adults with Alzheimer's disease together with preschool children so that they can perform tasks together (Camp et al., 1997).

One of the best ways to find out about the latest medical and behavioral research, as well as about the educational and support programs available in your area, is to call the Alzheimer's Association number listed in the advertisement. The chapter in your area will be happy to supply a range of educational material and information about local programs.

TEST YOURSELF

1. Compared to younger adults, older adults are less likely to label their feelings of sadness as _____ .

2. A form of psychotherapy that focuses on people's beliefs about the self, the world, and the future is called _____ .

3. Relaxation techniques are an effective therapy for _____ .

4. The only way to definitively diagnose Alzheimer's disease is through a _____ .

5. Twisted fibers called _____ occur in the axon of neurons in persons with Alzheimer's disease.

6. After reading about the symptoms of Alzheimer's disease, what do you think would be the most stressful aspects of caring for a parent who has the disease? (You may want to refer back to the section on caring for aging parents in Chapter 12.)

Answers: (1) depression, (2) cognitive therapy, (3) anxiety disorders, (4) brain autopsy, (5) neurofibrillary tangles

PUTTING IT ALL TOGETHER

Someone once observed that, all things considered, growing old is much better than the alternative. Based on what we have seen concerning the personal contexts of aging, it is indeed much better in many respects (though not totally rosy, to be sure) than what our cultural conditioning expects it to be. We began by wondering why people like Sarah live a long time and others do not, and we learned that many factors influence longevity. We saw how genetic and environmental factors interact (the biopsychosocial model strikes again!). We encountered Frank, the active 80-year-old, who exemplifies how maintaining fitness throughout life has an important influence on health in the later years. We also discovered how physical changes that began in midlife continue to affect functioning as a person keeps growing older.

Rocio experiences the kinds of changes in recent memory ability common in older adults. Some older people gain wisdom through their experience in living. Thus, cognitive changes in later life are not all a matter of decline. Finally, we saw that psychopathologies can exact a terrible toll among older adults; they must be properly diagnosed in order to separate treatable from untreatable conditions. People like Mary, who had Alz-

heimer's disease, must be examined carefully to identify the most likely cause of the problems.

Many of the stereotypes society holds about older adults are simply untrue. For one thing, only a minority of people over age 65 ever get Alzheimer's disease, whereas the clear majority continue to demonstrate improvement in some cognitive functions such as wisdom. Old age does not imply the across-the-board decline that is often portrayed. Indeed, some segments of society are beginning to understand the beauty and importance of older adults.

Our initial foray into later life reveals the complexity of older adults. Just as it is impossible to characterize all children, adolescents, or young adults as being all alike, older adults are also a very diverse group of people. This diversity will continue to be in evidence in the next chapter.

SUMMARY

What Are Older Adults Like?

The Demographics of Aging

• The number of older adults is growing rapidly, especially the number of people over age 85. In the future, older adults will be more ethnically diverse and better educated than they are now.

How Long Will You Live?

• *Average life expectancy* has increased dramatically in this century, due mainly to improvements in health care. *Useful life expectancy* refers to the number of years that a person is free from debilitating disease. *Maximum life expectancy* is the longest time any human can live.

• Genetic factors that can influence longevity include familial longevity and a family history of certain diseases. Environmental factors include acquired diseases, toxins, pollutants, and life-style.

• Due to technological advances, there is controversy regarding the quantity of life as against the quality. Women have a longer average life expectancy at birth than men. Ethnic group differences are complex; depending on how old people are, the patterns of differences change.

Physical Changes and Health

Biological Theories of Aging

• There are four main biological theories of aging. Wear-and-tear theory postulates that aging is caused by body systems simply wearing out. Cellular theories focus on reactions within cells, involving free radicals and cross-linking. Metabolic theories focus on changes in cell metabolism. Programmed cell death theories propose that aging is genetically programmed. No single theory is sufficient to explain aging.

Physiological Changes

• Three important structural changes in the neurons are neurofibrillary tangles, dendritic changes, and neuritic plaques. These have important consequences for functioning, because they reduce the effectiveness with which neurons transmit information.

• The risk of cardiovascular disease increases with age. Normal changes in the cardiovascular system include buildup of fat deposits in the heart and arteries, a decrease in the amount of blood the heart can pump, a decline in heart muscle tissue, and stiffening of the arteries. Most of these changes are affected by life-style.

Stroke and vascular dementia cause significant cognitive impairment, depending on the location of the brain damage.

• Strictly age-related changes in the respiratory system are hard to identify, due to the lifetime effects of pollution. However, older adults suffer shortness of breath, and the risk of chronic obstructive pulmonary disorder increases.

• Parkinson's disease is caused by insufficient levels of dopamine, and it can be effectively managed with L-dopa. In a minority of cases, dementia develops.

• Age-related declines in vision and hearing are well documented. However, similar changes in taste, smell, touch, pain, and temperature are not as clear.

Health Issues

• Older adults have more sleep disturbances than younger adults. Nutritionally, most older adults do not need vitamin or mineral supplements. Cancer risk increases sharply with age.

Cognitive Processes

Information Processing

• Older adults are much slower than younger adults at visual search, unless there is an advance signal.

• Age differences in divided-attention tasks depend on the level of difficulty; on easy tasks, there are no differences, but on hard tasks, younger adults do better.

• Older adults' psychomotor speed is slower than younger adults'. However, the amount of slowing is lessened if older adults have practice or expertise in the task.

• Sensory and information-processing changes create problems for older drivers. Working memory is another powerful explanatory concept for changes in information processing with age.

Memory

• On memory tasks requiring free recall, older adults almost always do worse than younger adults. The difference is less on recognition memory tasks and on some real-world memory tasks.

• What people believe to be true about their memory is related to their performance. Beliefs about whether cognitive abilities are supposed to change may be most important.

• Differentiating memory changes associated with aging from memory changes due to disease should be accomplished through comprehensive evaluations.

• Memory training can be achieved in many ways. A useful framework is to combine explicit-implicit memory distinctions with external-internal types of memory aids.

Training Intellectual Abilities

• Evidence from training studies indicates that performance on at least some intellectual abilities (e.g., inductive reasoning and spatial orientation) can be significantly improved.

Creativity and Wisdom

• Research indicates that creative output peaks in late young adulthood or early middle age and declines thereafter, but that the point of peak activity varies across disciplines and occupations.

• Wisdom has more to do with being an expert in living than with age per se. Three factors that help people become wise are general personal conditions, specific expertise conditions, and facilitative life contexts.

Mental Health and Intervention

Depression

• The key symptom of depression is persistent sadness. Other psychological and physical symptoms also occur, but the importance of these depends on the age of the person reporting them.

• Major causes of depression include imbalances in neurotransmitters and psychosocial forces such as loss and internal belief systems.

• Depression can be treated with medications, such as heterocyclic antidepressants, MAO inhibitors, and selective serotonin reuptake inhibitors, and through psychotherapy, such as behavioral or cognitive therapy.

Anxiety Disorders

• A variety of anxiety disorders afflict many older adults. All of them can be effectively treated with either medications or psychotherapy.

Dementia: Alzheimer's Disease

• Dementia is a family of diseases that cause severe cognitive impairment. Alzheimer's disease is the most common form of irreversible dementia.

• Symptoms of Alzheimer's disease include memory impairment, personality changes, and behavioral changes. These symptoms usually worsen gradually, with rates varying considerably among individuals.

• Definitive diagnosis of Alzheimer's disease can only be made following a brain autopsy. Diagnosis of probable Alzheimer's disease in a living person involves a thorough process through which other potential causes are eliminated.

• Most researchers are focusing on a probable genetic cause of Alzheimer's disease.

• Although Alzheimer's disease is incurable, various therapeutic interventions can improve the quality of the patient's life.

KEY TERMS

demographers (488)
population pyramid (488)
longevity (491)
average life expectancy (491)
useful life expectancy (491)
maximum life expectancy (491)
wear-and-tear theory (494)
cellular theories (494)
free radicals (494)
cross-linking (495)
metabolic theories (495)
programmed cell death theories (495)
neurofibrillary tangles (496)
neuritic plaques (496)
neurotransmitters (496)
strokes (497)
cerebral vascular accidents (497)
hemorrhage (497)

transient ischemic attacks (TIAs) (497)
vascular dementia (497)
chronic obstructive pulmonary disease (COPD) (498)
Parkinson's disease (498)
presbycusis (499)
circadian rhythm (500)
selectivity (502)
divided attention (503)
psychomotor speed (503)
working memory (505)
free recall (506)
recognition (506)
secondary memory (506)
tertiary memory (506)
explicit memory (508)
implicit memory (508)
external aids (508)

internal aids (508)
dysphoria (514)
internal belief systems (515)
heterocyclic antidepressants (HCAs) (515)
monoamine oxidase (MAO) inhibitors (515)
selective serotonin reuptake inhibitors (SSRIs) (515)
behavior therapy (516)
cognitive therapy (516)
anxiety disorders (516)
dementia (517)
Alzheimer's disease (518)
incontinence (518)
pseudodementia (519)
amyloid (519)
spaced retrieval (520)

IF YOU'D LIKE TO LEARN MORE

Readings

CARSTENSEN, L. L., EDELSTEIN, B. A., & DORNBRAND, L. (Eds.). (1996). *The practical handbook of clinical gerontology.* Thousand Oaks, CA: Sage. This book provides an overview of a wide range of issues, including assessment, psychological disorders, behavior problems, and medical problems of older adults.

HAYFLICK, L. (1994). *How and why we age.* New York: Ballantine. This summary of the biology of aging is presented in a very readable and easy-to-understand format. It is probably the best comprehensive summary available at the introductory level.

KAUSLER, D. H. (1994). *Learning and memory in normal aging.* San Diego, CA: Academic Press. This is one of the very best one-volume summaries of age-related differences in information processing and memory.

KOTRE, J. (1996). *White gloves: How we create ourselves through memory.* New York: Norton. This is the autobiographical story of a man who explores the meaning of memory after he finds his grandfather's white gloves. Interesting weaving of basic research on memory with everyday experience.

MARTZ, S. H. (Ed.). (1987). *When I am an old woman, I shall wear purple*; and (1992). *If I had my life to live over, I would pick more daisies*. Watsonville, CA: Papier-Mache Press. Both of these books are anthologies of poems and short stories about the personal meanings of aging to women.

Web Sites

Two of the very best sites on the Web for starting a search for information about any aspect of aging are ones kept and organized by the University of Utah and the Adult Development and Aging Division (Division 20) of the American Psychological Association, respectively. Any topic you need to research can be found from here. The addresses are

http://www.nurs.utah.edu/gerontology/web.html

http://www.iog.wayne.edu/apadiv20/apadiv20.htm

Statistical information about older adults on a variety of topics is collected annually by the U.S. government. In addition, there are several reports available on such things as demographic projections and health. One good source is the Administration on Aging's statistical site, which can be found at

http://www.aoa.dhhs.gov/aoa/stats/statpage.html

 For additional readings, explore Infotrac College Edition, your online library. Go to http://www. infotrac-college.com/wadsworth.

Research findings concerning Alzheimer's disease are reported nearly daily. Trying to sort through them is challenging, so the Alzheimer's disease research site is especially useful. The site provides links to all major research centers, and gives brief summaries of the work occurring there. It is at

http://www.aoa.dhhs.gov/aoa/webres/alz-acad.htm

Web site addresses are subject to change. The Wadsworth Study Center Web site listed below can be accessed for updated links.

The Wadsworth Psychology Study Center Web Site

See http://psychology.wadsworth.com/ for practice quiz questions, internet links, updates, critical thinking exercises, discussion forums and more! The Wadsworth Psychology Study Center provides a wealth of information fully organized and integrated by chapter.

SOCIAL ASPECTS OF LATER LIFE

Theories of Psychosocial Aging
Continuity Theory
Competence and Environmental Press
Finding Where You Fit

Personality Development in Later Life
Integrity Versus Despair
Well-Being and Possible Selves
    in Later Life
Views of a Life: Well-Being and Aging
Religiosity and Spiritual Support

I Used to Work at . . . :
Living in Retirement
What Does Being Retired Mean?
Are You Retired?
Why Do People Retire?
Adjustment to Retirement
Interpersonal Ties

Friends and Family in Late Life
Friends and Siblings
Marriage
Caring for a Partner
'Til Death Do Us Part: Spousal Caregiving
Widowhood
Great-Grandparenthood

Social Issues and Aging
Frail Older Adults
Living in Nursing Homes
How Do You Respond to a Nursing Home
    Resident?
Elder Abuse and Neglect
Which Older People Are Abused and Why?
Public Policy Issues and Older Adults

Putting It All Together
Summary
If You'd Like to Learn More

What's it really like to be an older adult? As we saw in Chapter 13, aging brings with it both physical limits (such as declines in vision and hearing) and psychological gains (such as increased expertise). Old age also brings social challenges. Older adults are sometimes stereotyped as marginal and powerless in society, much like children. Psychosocial issues confront older adults as well. How do people think about their lives and bring meaning and closure to them as they approach death? What constitutes well-being for older people? How do they use their time once they are no longer working full-time? Do they like being retired? What roles do relationships with friends and family play in their lives? How do older people cope if their partners are ill and require care? What if their partner should die? Where do older people live who need assistance?

These are a few of the issues we will examine in this chapter. As in Chapter 13, our main focus will be on the majority of older adults who are healthy and live in the community. The distinction made in Chapter 1 between young-old (60- to 80-year-olds) and old-old (80-year-olds and up) adults is important. We know the most about young-old people, even though the old-old reflect the majority of frail elderly and those who live in nursing homes.

Just as at other times in life, getting along in the environment is a complicated issue. We begin by considering a few ideas about how to optimize our fit with the environment. Next, we examine how we bring the story of our lives to a culmination. After that, we will consider how interpersonal relationships and retirement provide contexts for life satisfaction. We conclude with an examination of the social contexts of aging.

THEORIES OF PSYCHOSOCIAL AGING

Theories of Psychosocial Aging

Continuity Theory

Competence and Environmental Press

Learning Objectives

- **What is continuity theory?**
- **What is the competence and environmental press model, and how do docility and proactivity relate to the model?**

S INCE SANDY *retired from her job as secretary at the local African Methodist Episcopal Church, she has hardly slowed down. She sings in the gospel choir, is involved in the Black Women's Community Action Committee, and volunteers one day per week at a local Head Start school. Sandy's friends say that she has to stay involved, as that's the only way she's ever known. They claim that you'd never know Sandy is 71 years old.*

"WE HAVE A LOT IN COMMON, DON'T WE? I'M TOO YOUNG TO DO MOST EVERYTHING AND YOU'RE TOO OLD TO DO MOST EVERYTHING."

DENNIS THE MENACE® used by permission of Hank Ketcham and © by North America Syndicate.

Understanding how people grow old is not as simple as asking someone how old he or she is, as Sandy shows. As we saw in Chapter 13, aging is an individual process involving many variations in physical changes, cognitive functioning, and mental health. As Dennis the Menace notes, older adults are often marginalized in society. Psychosocial approaches to aging recognize these issues.

Sandy's life reflects several key points. Her level of activity has remained constant across her adult life. This consistency fits well in continuity theory, the first framework considered in this section. Her ability to maintain this level of commitment indicates that the match between her abilities and her environment is just about right, as discussed in competence–environmental press theory a bit later in this section.

CONTINUITY THEORY

People tend to keep doing whatever works for them (Atchley, 1989). *According to* continuity theory, *people tend to cope with daily life in later adulthood by applying familiar strategies based on past experience to maintain and preserve both internal and external structures.* By building upon and linking to one's past life, change becomes part of continuity. Thus, Sandy's new activities represent both change (because they are new) and continuity (because she has always been engaged in her community). In this sense, continuity represents an evolution, not a complete break with the past (Atchley, 1989).

The degree of continuity in life falls into one of three general categories: too little, too much, and optimal (Atchley, 1989). Too little continuity results in feeling that life is too unpredictable. Too much continuity can create utter boredom or a rut of predictability; there is simply not enough change to make life interesting. Optimal continuity provides just enough change to be challenging and provide interest, but not so much as to overly tax one's resources.

Continuity can be either internal or external (Atchley, 1989). Internal continuity refers to a remembered inner past, such as temperament, experiences, emotions, and skills; in brief, it is one's personal identity. Internal continuity allows you to see that how you are now is connected with your past, even if your current behavior looks different. Internal continuity provides feelings of competence, mastery, ego integrity (discussed later in the chapter), and self-esteem. External continuity concerns remembered physical and social environments, role relationships, and activities. A person feels external continuity from being in familiar environments or with familiar people, for example. External continuity provides social support, accurate feedback, coping, and redefined goals for later life.

Maintaining both internal and external continuity is very important for adaptation in later life (Atchley, 1989). For example, internal discontinuity, if severe enough, can seriously affect mental health (Atchley, 1989). Indeed, one of the most pernicious aspects of Alzheimer's disease is that it destroys internal continuity as it strips away one's identity. Similarly, external discontinuity can have serious consequences for adaptation (Atchley, 1989). For example, if your physical environment becomes much more difficult to negotiate, the resulting problems can eat away at your identity as well.

Clearly, monitoring whether a person is maintaining internal and external continuity matters. Exactly how changes in either affect adaptation is the focus of the competence–environmental press framework, to which we now turn.

? THINK ABOUT IT
How does the five-factor theory of personality fit with continuity theory?

COMPETENCE AND ENVIRONMENTAL PRESS

Understanding psychosocial aging thus requires attention to individuals' needs, rather than treating all older adults alike. One way of doing this is to focus on the relation between competence and environmental press. As discussed in Chapter 1 (pages 25–26), this approach is a good example of a theory that incorporates elements of the biopsychosocial model (Lawton, 1982; Lawton & Nahemow, 1973).

Competence *is defined as the upper limit of a person's ability to function in five domains: physical health, sensory-perceptual skills, motor skills, cognitive skills, and ego strength.* We discussed most of these domains in Chapter 13; ego strength, which is related to Erikson's concept of integrity, is discussed later in this chapter. These domains are viewed as underlying all other abilities and reflecting the biological and psychological forces. Environmental press *refers to the physical, interpersonal, or social demands that environments put on people.* Physical demands might include having to walk up three flights of stairs to your apartment. Interpersonal demands include having to adjust your behavior patterns to different types of people. Social demands include dealing with laws or customs that place certain expectations on people. These aspects of the theory reflect biological, psychological, and social forces. Both competence and environmental press change as people move through the life span; what you are capable of doing as a 5-year-old differs from what you are capable of doing as a 25-, 45-, 65-, or 85-year-old. Similarly, the demands put on you by the environment change as you age. Thus, the competence–environmental press framework reflects life-cycle factors as well.

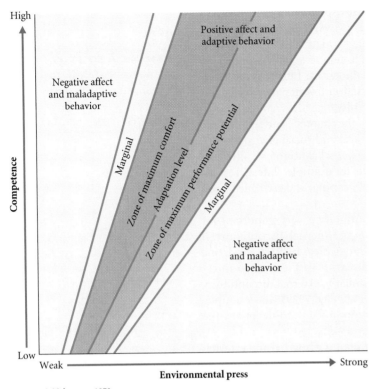

Lawton & Nahemow, 1973.

The competence and environmental press model, depicted in the figure, shows how the two are related. Low to high competence is represented on the vertical axis, and weak to strong environmental press is represented on the horizontal axis. Points in the figure represent various combinations of the two. Most important, the shaded areas show that adaptive behavior and positive affect can result from many different combinations of competence and press levels. Adaptation level *is the area where press level is average for a particular level of competence; this is where behavior and affect are normal. Slight increases in press tend to improve performance; this area on the figure is labeled the* zone of maximum performance potential. *Slight decreases in press create the* zone of maximum comfort, *in which people are able to live happily without worrying about environmental demands.* Combinations of competence and environmental press that fall within either of these two zones result in adaptive behavior and positive affect, which translate into a high quality of life.

As one moves away from these areas, behavior becomes increasingly maladaptive and affect becomes negative. Notice that these outcomes, too, can result from several different combinations, and for different reasons. For example, too many environmental demands on a person with low competence and too few demands on a person with high competence both result in maladaptive behaviors and negative affect.

What does this graph mean with regard to late life? Is aging merely an equation relating certain variables? The important thing to realize about the competence–environmental press model is that each person has the potential of being happily adapted to some living situations, but not to all. Whether people are functioning well depends on whether what they are able to do fits what the environment forces them to do. When the abilities match the demands, then people adapt; when there is a mismatch, they don't. In this view, aging is more than an equation, as the best fit must be determined on an individual basis.

How do people deal with changes in their particular combinations of environmental press (such as adjusting to a new living situation) and competence (perhaps due to illness)? People respond in two basic ways (Lawton, 1989). *When people choose new behaviors to meet new desires or needs, they exhibit* proactivity *and exert control over their lives.* In contrast, *when people allow the situation to dictate the options they have, they demonstrate* docility *and have little control.* Lawton (1989) argues that proactivity is more likely to occur in people with relatively high competence, and docility in people with relatively low competence.

The model has considerable research support. For example, the model accounts for why people choose the activities they do (Lawton, 1982), move to particular kinds of housing (Lawton, 1982), and need to exert some degree of

THINK ABOUT IT
How does the competence–environmental press approach help explain which coping strategies might work best in a particular situation?

control over their lives (Langer & Rodin, 1976). In short, there is considerable merit to the view that aging is a complex interaction between a person's competence level and environmental press, mediated by choice. This model can be applied in many different settings.

FINDING WHERE YOU FIT   FORCES IN ACTION

Lawton and Nahemow's competence–environmental press model is an excellent example of the biopsychosocial framework in action. Competence can be viewed as the result of the dual influence of biological and psychological forces. As we have seen, competence is reflected in physical capacity and in the breadth of a person's behavioral repertoire. For example, as a person's health deteriorates (and biological forces increase in importance), competence decreases accordingly. Or, as a person learns new coping strategies (and psychological forces increase in magnitude), competence improves. Similarly, environmental press reflects the influence of social forces. As we have seen, the demands of other people, the neighborhood, or society at large tax a person's physical and psychological abilities.

A person's position in the life span makes a difference in how relative increases and decreases in competence and environmental press are interpreted. Young children might be expected to have little competence, so we try to protect them from high levels of environmental demands. Young adults might be expected to be able to deal with much higher demands, because we expect them to have greater competence. Older adults may be experiencing declines in competence, so we may need to find ways to reduce the demands put on them.

In general, the competence–environmental press framework can be useful in helping people find the best fit that balances their abilities and the demands put on them. We could also view Lawton and Nahemow's framework as a way to help people balance the forces in the biopsychosocial framework. ●

---

1. A central premise of _____ theory is that people make adaptive choices to maintain and preserve existing internal and external structures.

2. A person's ability to function in several key domains is termed _____, whereas demands put on a person from external sources are termed _____ .

3. How does continuity theory incorporate aspects of the biopsychosocial model?

TEST YOURSELF

Answers: (1) continuity, (2) competence, environmental press.

PERSONALITY DEVELOPMENT IN LATER LIFE

Learning Objectives

- **What is integrity in late life? How do people achieve it?**

- **How is well-being defined in adulthood? How do people view themselves differently as they age?**

- **What role does religion play in late life?**

Personality Development in Later Life

Integrity Versus Despair

Well-Being and Possible Selves in Later Life

Religiosity and Spiritual Support

O LIVE *is a spry 88-year-old who spends more time thinking and reflecting about her past than she used to. She also tends to be much less critical now of decisions made years ago than she was at the time. Olive remembers her visions of the woman she wanted to become and concludes that she's come pretty close. Olive wonders if this process of reflection is something that most older adults go through.*

Think for a minute about the older adults you know well. Perhaps they are your grandparents, co-workers, or neighborhood acquaintances. What are they really like? How do they see themselves today? How do they visualize their lives a few years from now? How do they see themselves in the past?

These questions have intrigued authors for many years. A century ago, William James (1890), one of the early pioneers in psychology, wrote that a person's personality traits are set by young adulthood. Some researchers agree; as we saw in Chapter 12, some aspects of personality remain relatively stable through adulthood. But people also change in important ways, as Carl Jung (1960/1931) argued, by integrating opposite tendencies, such as masculine and feminine traits. Erik Erikson (1982) was convinced that personality development takes a lifetime, unfolding over a series of stages.

In this section, we explore how people like Olive assemble the final pieces in the personality puzzle, to see how important aspects of personality continue to evolve in later life. The issue of integrity, the process by which people try to make sense of their lives, we consider first. Next, we see how well-being is achieved, and how personal aspirations play themselves out. Finally, we will examine how religiosity is an important aspect of many older adults' lives.

INTEGRITY VERSUS DESPAIR

As people enter late life, they begin the struggle of integrity versus despair, *which involves the process by which people try to make sense of their lives.* According to Erikson (1982), this struggle comes about as older adults like Olive try to understand their lives in terms of the future of their family and community. Thoughts of a person's own death are balanced by the realization that they will live on through children, grandchildren, great-grandchildren, and the community as a whole. This realization produces what Erikson calls a "life-affirming involvement" in the present.

The struggle of integrity versus despair requires people to engage in a life review, *the process by which people reflect on the events and experiences they have had over their lifetimes.* To achieve integrity, a person must come to terms with the choices and events that have made his or her life unique. There must also be an acceptance of the fact that one's life is drawing to a close. Looking back on one's life may resolve some of the second-guessing of decisions that may have occurred earlier in adulthood (Erikson, Erikson, & Kivnick, 1986). People who were unsure whether they made the right choices concerning their children, for example, now feel satisfied that things eventually worked out well. In contrast, others feel bitter about their choices, blame themselves or others for their misfortunes, see their lives as meaningless, and greatly fear death. These people end up in despair rather than integrity.

Research shows a connection between engaging in a life review and achieving integrity. In one study, homebound older adults who were part of a program that assisted people in remembering and reviewing their lives showed significant improvements in life satisfaction, positive feelings, and depressive symptoms, compared to homebound older adults who did not participate (Haight, 1992). These improvements were still evident 2 months after the program ended.

Who reaches integrity? Erikson (1982) emphasizes that there is no one path. Like the people in the photograph, they come from many backgrounds and cultures. Such people have made many different choices and follow many different life-styles; everyone has this opportunity. Those who reach integrity become self-affirming and self-accepting; they judge their lives to have been worthwhile and good. They are glad to have lived the lives they did.

WELL-BEING AND POSSIBLE SELVES IN LATER LIFE

How do older adults view themselves? Traditionally, researchers addressed this question by having older adults tell them how they saw themselves at the moment (Lawton, 1984). From a life-span perspective, however, a better way to answer this question would be to have older adults report how they see themselves right now in comparison to how they remember themselves in the past and where they see themselves headed in the future.

The aspects of people's self-concept representing what they could become, what they would like to become, and what they are afraid of becoming are called possible selves. Possible selves provide insights into our self-concept (Markus & Nurius, 1986). What we could or would like to become often reflects personal goals; we may see ourselves becoming a wise grandparent in late life. What we are afraid of becoming reflects our fears; we may be afraid of becoming a burden on our families when we grow old.

Age differences are apparent in possible selves. For example, Cross and Markus (1991) asked people 18–86 to describe their hoped-for and feared possible selves. Young adults (18- to 24-year-olds) listed family concerns most often, especially marrying the "right" person. Interestingly, 25- to 39-year-olds listed family concerns last; their biggest goals were personal, such as becoming a more loving and caring person. The 40- to 59-year-olds returned to family issues for their possible selves, with a major concern of being able to "let go" of children. Finally, the 60- to 86-year-olds had personal issues as most important for their possible selves, such as staying healthy and active.

This general look at the issues that most influence possible selves indicates that the most important ones differ with age. But how are these issues reflected in aspects of personal well-being? Do the age differences in possible selves

? THINK ABOUT IT
What do you think are some common hoped-for and feared selves for older adults?

depend on whether one is projecting to the future or to the past? Such questions require a more complex approach.

This is exactly what Ryff (1991) did. In a fascinating series of studies, she redefined the meaning of well-being in adulthood and showed how adults' views of themselves are different at various points in adulthood. Based on the responses of hundreds of adults, Ryff (1989b, 1991) identified six dimensions of psychological well-being for adults and discovered that there are many important age and gender differences in well-being based on these components.

- *Self-acceptance:* having a positive view of oneself; acknowledging and accepting the multiple parts of oneself; and feeling positive about one's past.

- *Positive relation with others:* having warm, satisfying relationships with people; being concerned with their welfare; being empathic, affectionate, and intimate with them; and understanding the reciprocity of relationships.

- *Autonomy:* being independent and determining one's own life; being able to resist social pressures to think or behave in a particular way; evaluating one's life by internal standards.

- *Environmental mastery:* being able to manipulate, control, and effectively use resources and opportunities.

- *Purpose in life:* having goals and a sense of direction in one's life; feeling that one's present and past life have meaning; having a reason for living.

- *Personal growth:* feeling a need for continued personal improvement; seeing oneself as getting better and being open to new experiences; growing in self-knowledge and personal effectiveness.

How do these aspects of well-being change in adulthood? The Spotlight on Research feature has one answer.

SPOTLIGHT ON RESEARCH

VIEWS OF A LIFE: WELL-BEING AND AGING

Who was the investigator and what was the aim of the study? How people see themselves is an important part of their sense of well-being. However, previous research on well-being in late life had been conducted without theoretical guidance (Ryff, 1989a). Consequently, many researchers approached well-being from the perspective of loss; that is, researchers assumed that well-being, like physical prowess, was something that declined as people age. Carol Ryff (1989a) disagreed with this loss perspective and set out to demonstrate her point. She thought that well-being is a more complex issue and that it can improve in late life.

How did the investigator measure the topic of interest? In preliminary studies, Ryff administered numerous self-report scales that measured many aspects of personality and well-being. Her method in this investigation represented a new approach, one aimed at describing the complex developmental patterns she wanted to uncover. This new approach drew from life-span developmental theories (such as those presented in this text), clinical theories of personal growth adapted from successful techniques in psychotherapy, and various definitions of mental health, yielding the most complete description yet of well-being in adulthood. On the basis of her research and thinking, Ryff (1989b) developed a new measure of well-being that reflects the six-dimension model discussed above. This new measure allowed her to obtain people's ratings of how they view themselves right now, what they were like in the past, what they think they might be like in the future, and what they would most like to be like.

Who were the participants in the study? A total of 308 young, middle-aged, and older men and women participated. The middle-aged and older adults were contacted through community and civic organizations. All participants were relatively well educated.

What was the design of the study? Ryff used a cross-sectional design that compared young adult, middle-aged, and older adult groups.

Were there ethical concerns with the study? There were no serious concerns; each participant was informed about the purpose of the study, and participation was voluntary.

What were the results? The most important discovery from Ryff's research is that young, middle-aged, and older adults have very different views of themselves, depending on whether they are describing their present, past, future, or ideal self-perceptions. The left graph shows that young and middle-aged adults are much more accepting of their ideal and future selves than they are of their present and past selves. For older adults, differences are much smaller. The right graph shows a similar pattern for autonomy, the feelings of being independent and determining one's own life.

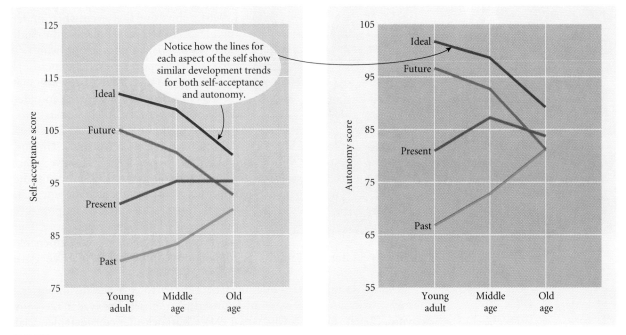

Ryff, 1991.

Perhaps the most interesting findings of Ryff's research concern the difference between people's ideal vision of themselves and what they think they are really like. If you look carefully at the graphs, you will notice that the differences between the "ideal self" ratings and the "present self" ratings diminish with age. When combined with similar findings in other aspects of well-being, this implies that older adults see themselves as closer to really being the person they wanted to become than does any other age group. Ryff's data fit well with Erikson's (1982) idea of integrity. As people achieve integrity, they view their past less critically and become content with how they have lived their lives.

What did the investigator conclude? As Ryff (1991) notes, only by including all of these self-ratings will we understand people's sense of personal progress or decline over time from their goal of ideal functioning. Clearly, people judge themselves by many standards, and these differ with age. ●

RELIGIOSITY AND SPIRITUAL SUPPORT

When faced with the daily problems of living, what do most older adults do to help themselves cope? According to research, older adults use their religious faith more than anything else, including family or friends (McFadden, 1996). When asked to describe their most frequent ways of dealing with problems in life, nearly half of the people surveyed in one study listed coping strategies associated with religion (Koenig, George, & Siegler, 1988). Of these, the most frequently used were placing trust in God, praying, and getting strength and help from God. These strategies can also be used to augment other ways of coping. Spouses caring for partners with Alzheimer's disease also report using religion as a primary coping mechanism (Ishler et al., 1998).

Researchers are increasingly focusing on spiritual support, *which includes seeking pastoral care, participation in organized and nonorganized religious ac-*

tivities, and expressing faith in a God who cares for people as a key factor in understanding how older adults cope. McFadden (1996) points out that even when under high levels of stress, people like the Buddhist monks in the photograph who rely on spiritual support report better personal well-being. Krause (1995) reports that feelings of self-worth are lowest in older adults who have very little religious commitment, a finding supported by cross-cultural research with Muslims, Hindus, and Sikhs (Mehta, 1997). However, Pargament and colleagues (1995) also note the importance of individual differences in the effectiveness of spiritual support, because some people are helped more than others, some problems are more amenable to religious coping, and certain types of religious coping may be more effective than others.

Reliance on religion in times of stress appears to be especially important for many African Americans, who as a group are intensely involved in religious activities (Levin, Taylor, & Chatters, 1994). Churches offer considerable social support for the African American community, as well as serving an important function for the advocacy of social justice (Roberts, 1980). For example, the civil rights movement in the 1950s and 1960s was led by Dr. Martin Luther King, Jr., a Baptist minister, and contemporary congregations often champion equal rights. The role of the church in African Americans' lives is central; indeed, one of the key predictors of life satisfaction among African Americans is regular church attendance (Coke, 1992).

Within the African American community, religion is especially important to many women. The greater importance of the church in the lives of these older African American women is supported by results from four national surveys of African American adults (Levin, Taylor, & Chatters, 1994). The women participants reported that they are more active in church groups and attend services more frequently than African American men or either European American men or women. However, the gender differences diminish in people over age 70; among the participants, religion becomes equally important for older African American men. Religion and spiritual support also serve as more

? THINK ABOUT IT
What psychological and sociocultural factors make religion and spiritual support important for minority groups?

important resources for many African American caregivers than for European American caregivers (Picot et al., 1997).

Many older persons of Mexican heritage adopt a different approach. Research indicates that they use *la fé de la gente* ("the faith of the people") as a coping strategy (Villa & Jaime, 1993). The notion of *fé* incorporates varying degrees of faith, spirituality, hope, cultural values, and beliefs. *Fé* does not necessarily imply that people identify with a specific religious community. Rather, they identify with a cultural value or ideology.

Among many Native Americans, the spiritual elders are the wisdom-keepers, the repositories of the sacred ways and philosophies that extend indefinitely back in time (Wall & Arden, 1990). The wisdom-keepers also share dreams and visions, perform healing ceremonies, and may make apocalyptic prophecies. The place of the wisdom-keepers in the tribe is much more central than that of religious leaders in Western society.

Service providers would be well advised to keep in mind the self-reported importance of religion in the lives of many older adults when designing interventions to help them adapt to life stressors. For example, older adults may be more willing to talk with their minister about a personal problem than they would be to talk with a psychotherapist. However, when working with people of Mexican heritage, providers should realize that a major source of distress for this group is lack of familial interaction and support. Overall, many churches offer a wide range of programs to assist poor or homebound older adults in the community. Such programs may be more palatable to the people served than programs based in social service agencies. To be successful, service providers should try to view life as their clients see it.

TEST YOURSELF

1. The Eriksonian struggle that older adults face is termed _____ .

2. According to Ryff, the six major aspects of well-being are self-acceptance, positive relations with others, autonomy, environmental mastery, purpose in life, and _____ .

3. The most commonly reported method for coping with life stress among older adults is _____ .

4. Based on Ryff's research, discussed in this section, what do you think would be good areas to target for interventions designed to improve older adults' well-being?

Answers: (1) integrity versus despair, (2) personal growth, (3) religion or spiritual support.

I USED TO WORK AT . . . : LIVING IN RETIREMENT

Learning Objectives

- **What does being retired mean?**

- **Why do people retire?**

- **How satisfied are retired people?**

- **What specific effects does retirement have on maintaining family and community ties?**

I Used to Work at . . .:
Living in Retirement

What Does Being Retired Mean?

Why Do People Retire?

Adjustment to Retirement

Interpersonal Ties

$\mathcal{M}$ ARCUS *is a 77-year-old retired construction worker who labored hard all of his life. He managed to save a little money, but he and his wife live primarily off of his monthly Social Security checks. Though not rich, they have enough to pay the bills. Marcus is largely happy with retirement, and he stays in touch with his friends. He thinks maybe he's a little strange, though — he has heard that retirees are supposed to be isolated and lonely.*

You probably take it for granted that some day, after working for many productive years, you will retire. But did you know that until 1934, when a railroad union sponsored a bill promoting mandatory retirement, and 1935, when Social Security was inaugurated, retirement was not considered by most Americans like Marcus (Sterns & Gray, 1999)? Only since World War II has there been a substantial number of retired people in the United States (Elder & Pavalko, 1993). Today, the number is increasing rapidly, and the notion that people work a specified time and then retire is built into our expectations about work. As we noted in Chapter 11, an increasing number of middle-aged workers either retire prior to age 65 or are planning for retirement.

In this section, we consider what retirement is like for older adults. We consider people like Marcus as we examine how retirement is defined, why people retire, how people adjust to being retired, and how retirement affects interpersonal relationships.

WHAT DOES BEING RETIRED MEAN?

Take a moment to look at the photograph to the left and those on the next page. Can you pick out which of the people would claim that he or she is "retired"? It turns out that retirement is more difficult to define than just guessing from someone's age (Ekerdt & DeViney, 1990; Henretta, 1997). One way is to equate retirement with complete withdrawal from the work force. But this definition is inadequate; many retired people continue to work part-time (Mutchler et al., 1997; Ruhm, 1990). Another possibility would be to define retirement as a self-described state. However, this definition does not work either, because some African Americans define themselves with labels other than "retired" in order to qualify for certain social service programs (Gibson, 1991).

Part of the reason it is difficult to define retirement precisely is that the decision to retire involves the loss of occupational identity (see Chapter 11). What people do for a living is a major part of their identity; we introduce ourselves as postal workers, teachers, builders, or nurses as a way to tell people something about ourselves. Not doing those jobs anymore means that we either put that aspect of our lives in the past tense—"I used to work as a manager at the Hilton"—or say nothing at all. Loss of this aspect of ourselves can be difficult to face, so some look for a label other than "retired" to describe themselves.

A useful way to view retirement is as a complex process by which people withdraw from full-time participation in an occupation (Henretta, 1997; Mutchler et al., 1997; Sterns & Gray, 1999). This withdrawal process can be described as either "crisp" (making a clean break from employment by stopping work entirely) or "blurred" (repeatedly leaving and returning to work, with some unemployment periods) (Mutchler et al., 1997). Bob is a good example of a "crisp" retirement. He retired from TWA at age 65; now in his late eighties, he has done nothing work-related in the interim.

Whereas many people think of retirement as a crisp transition, the evidence shows that less than half of older men who retire fit this pattern (Mutchler et al., 1997). Most men adopt a more gradual or "blurred" process involving part-time work in an effort to maintain economic status. Jack is one of these men. When he retired from DuPont at age 62, he and a friend began a small consulting company. For about five years, Jack worked when he wanted, gradually cutting back over time.

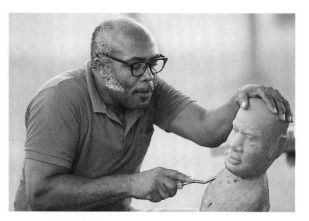

The lack of crisp retirement creates another complicating factor—the idea of a "normal" retirement age such as age 65 may no longer be appropriate (Cornman & Kingson, 1996; Mutchler et al., 1997). Instead, the notion of a typical retirement age changes to a range of ages, further blurring the meaning of "early" or "late" retirement (Cornman & Kingson, 1996).

The complexity of the retirement process must be acknowledged in order to understand what retirement means to people in different ethnic groups. For example, whereas middle-class European Americans often use a criterion of full-time employment to define themselves as retired or not, Mexican Americans use any of several different criteria, depending on how the question is asked (Zsembik & Singer, 1990). For example, Mexican Americans are most likely to claim that they are retired when asked directly ("Are you retired?") than when asked indirectly ("What are you doing these days?"). It may be that people want to appear active, so they choose some other descriptor. In contrast, European Americans are just as likely to call themselves retired no matter how they are asked. To learn how self-definitions vary from one group to another, complete the exercise in the See for Yourself feature.

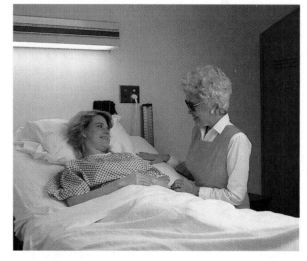

ARE YOU RETIRED?   SEE FOR YOURSELF

As mentioned in the text, people who no longer work full-time may or may not label themselves as retired. To find out firsthand how people label themselves and how they occupy their time, try the following exercise. Interview several older adults who you believe do not work full-time anymore. Don't interview only your relatives; make sure that you have a diverse sample of older adults.

Begin your interview by asking them about the kinds of work (for pay or as a volunteer) they do now and the kinds they did in the past. Ask them if they call themselves retired. If so, why do they? If not, why not? How much do they miss not working in their old jobs? Ask also about how they keep themselves occupied now.

Gather the results of your interviews and see whether you can draw any general conclusions. Are there certain characteristics common to people who call themselves retired? Or to those who do not? Are there similarities in how people keep themselves occupied? Bring the data to class and compare your results with other students' findings. See for yourself how people view retirement. •

WHY DO PEOPLE RETIRE?

? THINK ABOUT IT
In the absence of mandatory retirement, what does the term "early retirement" really mean?

More workers retire by choice than for any other reason (Hayward, Friedman, & Chen, 1998; Henretta, Chan, & O'Rand, 1992). Individuals usually retire when they feel financially secure, considering projected income from Social Security, pensions, and personal savings. Of course, some people are forced to retire because they lose their jobs (Henretta et al., 1992). As corporations downsized in the early and mid-1990s, some older workers were offered buyout packages involving supplemental payments if they retired. Others were permanently furloughed, laid off, or dismissed.

The decision to retire is complex, and is influenced by one's occupational history (Hayward et al., 1998). The longest occupation held in the middle of one's career combines with occupational roles held in the last stages of the career to influence the decision to retire and the connection with health and disability. For example, self-employed people have few retirement options, often retiring only when health problems intervene. Additionally, health problems that cause functional impairment, such as serious cardiovascular disease or cancer, are the main reason European Americans, African Americans, and Hispanic Americans retire early (Stanford et al., 1991). Feeling that retirement is a choice rather than a requirement is associated with an earlier planned retirement age, as well as adjustment to retirement (Sterns & Gray, 1999).

Gender Differences

Most of what we know about retirement decisions is based on research on men (Sterns & Gray, 1999). However, women may enter the work force later, have more discontinuous work histories, spend less time in the work force, and their financial resources may differ from men's, which may affect women's decisions to retire (Calasanti, 1996; Sterns & Gray, 1999). In fact, research indicates that men's and women's decisions to retire may be based on different factors. Talaga and Beehr (1995) found that women whose husbands were in poor health or who had more dependents were more likely to retire; the opposite was true for men. However, there were some similarities; having a retired spouse increased the likelihood that spouses would also retire.

As more women remain in the work force for much of their adult lives, more research will be necessary in order to understand the extent to which gender differences matter in the decision to retire. At this point, though, it appears that the male model of retirement is insufficient to account for women's experiences (Sterns & Gray, 1999).

Ethnic Differences

Very little research has been conducted on retirement decisions as a function of ethnicity. A few investigators have examined the characteristics of retired African Americans like the couple in the photograph (e.g., Gibson, 1986, 1987; Jackson & Gibson, 1985). These studies show that African Americans tend to label themselves as retired or not based on subjective disability, work history, and source of income, rather than simply on whether or not they are currently employed. An important finding is that gender differences appear to be absent among African Americans; men and women base their self-labels on the same variables. Thus, findings based on European American samples must not be generalized to African Americans, and separate theoretical models for African Americans may be needed (Gibson, 1987). The same may be true for other ethnic groups as well.

ADJUSTMENT TO RETIREMENT

Researchers agree on one point: Retirement is an important life transition. New patterns of involvement must be developed in the context of changing roles and life-styles (Antonovsky & Sagy, 1990). Until the early 1990s, research focused on what was thought to be a sequence of predictable phases of retirement, such as honeymoon, disenchantment, reorientation, acceptance, and termination (Atchley, 1982). Because retirement is now viewed as a process, the "typical" age of retirement has lost its meaning, and gender differences are evident in the decision to retire, the idea that retirement proceeds in an orderly stagelike sequence has been abandoned (Sterns & Gray, 1999). Instead, researchers support the idea that people's adjustment to retirement evolves over time as a result of complex interrelations with physical health, financial status, voluntary retirement status, and feelings of personal control (Gall, Evans, & Howard, 1997).

How do most people fare? As long as people like those in the photograph have financial security, health, and a supportive network of relatives and friends, they report feeling very good about being retired (Gall et al., 1997; Matthews & Brown, 1987). For men, being in good health, having enough income, and having retired voluntarily is associated with relatively high satisfaction early in retirement; having an internal sense of personal control is correlated with well-being over the long run (Gall et al., 1997). For men, personal priorities are also important. Men who place more emphasis on family roles (e.g., as husband or grandfather) report being happier retirees. Interestingly, women's morale in retirement does not appear to be related to an emphasis on any specific roles (Matthews & Brown, 1987). For both men and women, high personal competence is associated with higher retirement satisfaction, probably because competent people are able to optimize their level of environmental press (as described on pages 531–533).

One stereotype of retirement is that health begins to decline as soon as people stop working. Research findings do not support this belief; in fact, there is no evidence that retirement has any immediate negative effects on health (Ekerdt, 1987). Moreover, well-being typically increases for men during the first year of retirement (Gall et al., 1997).

A second stereotype is that retirement dramatically reduces the number and quality of personal friendships. Again, there is no research support for this belief. In fact, several studies have shown that men like Marcus, from the vignette, are typical; neither the number nor the quality of friendships declines as a result of retiring (Bossé et al., 1993). When friendships change during retirement, it is usually due to other factors, such as very serious health problems, that interfere with people's ability to maintain friendships.

Finally, some people believe that retired people become much less active overall. This stereotype is also not supported by research. Although the number of hours in paid work decreases on average with age, older adults are still engaged for hundreds of hours per year in productive activities such as unpaid volunteer work and helping others (Herzog et al., 1989). We will specifically consider volunteer activities in the next section.

INTERPERSONAL TIES

Retirement rarely affects only a single individual. No matter how personal the joys and sorrows of retirement may be, retirees' reactions are shaped by the interpersonal relationships they have. Social ties help people deal with the stresses of retirement, as they do in other life transitions. In many cases, these ties involve friendships and other relationships formed earlier in adulthood.

Social relationships help cushion the effects of any life stress throughout adulthood. This support takes many forms: letting people know that they are loved, offering help if needed, providing advice, taking care of others' needs, and just being there to listen. As we noted earlier, retirees who have close and strong social ties tend to have an advantage in adjusting to the life changes that retirement brings.

We will consider general issues regarding social relationships in more detail later in this chapter. At this point, we focus on two: what specific adjustments couples must make and how retirees maintain connections with their communities.

Intimate Relationships

Much attention was focused in the past on the role of intimate relationships in adjusting to retirement. Marriage has provided the framework for almost all of this research. Marital status by itself has little effect on older women's satisfaction with retirement (Fox, 1979). Never-married people are as satisfied as married retirees. In contrast, divorced, separated, or widowed retired men are much less happy (Barfield & Morgan, 1978), which points to the stabilizing effects of marriage for men.

What about the impact of retirement on the marital relationship itself? Retirement has profound effects on intimate relationships, often disrupting long-established patterns of family interaction, forcing both partners (and others living in the house) to adjust (Pearson, 1996). Simply being together more may put strain on the relationship. The daily routines of couples like the one shown in the photograph may need rearrangement, which may be stressful. However, because marital satisfaction among older couples tends to be quite high, most couples are able to resolve these stresses.

One change that confronts most retired married couples (in traditional households in which only the husband was employed) is the division of household chores (Pearson, 1996). Although retired men tend to do more work around the home than they did before retirement, this does not always lead to desirable outcomes (Ingraham, 1974). For example, an employed husband may compliment his wife on her domestic skills, but after retirement he may suddenly want to teach her how to do things "correctly." Part of the problem may be that such men are not used to taking orders. One retired executive remarked that before he retired, when he said, "Jump," highly paid employees wanted to know how high. "Now, I go home, I walk in the door and my wife says, 'Milton, take out the garbage.' I never saw so much garbage" (Quigley, 1979, p. 9). Finally, part of the problem may be in the perception of one's turf; after retirement men feel that they are thrust into doing things that they, and their partners, may have traditionally thought of as "women's work" (Troll, 1971). As more dual-earner couples retire, it will be interesting to see how these issues are handled.

Community Ties

Throughout adulthood, most people become and remain connected with their communities. Thus, an important consideration is whether the social environment aids retirees' ability to continue old ties and form new ones. The past few decades have witnessed the rapid growth of organizations devoted to providing such opportunities to retirees. National groups such as the American Association of Retired Persons (AARP) provide the chance to learn, through magazines and pamphlets, about other retirees' activities and about services such as insurance and discounts. Many smaller groups exist at the community level, including senior centers and clubs. Several trade unions also have programs for their retired members. These activities promote the notion of lifelong learning and help keep older adults cognitively active.

A common way for retired adults to maintain community ties is by volunteering. Older adults report that they volunteer to help themselves deal with life transitions (Adlersberg & Thorne, 1990), to provide service to others (Hudson, 1996), and to maintain social interactions and improve their communities (Morrow-Howell & Mui, 1989). There are many opportunities for retirees to help others. One federal agency, ACTION, administers four programs that have hundreds of local chapters: Foster Grandparents, Senior Companions, the Retired Senior Volunteer Program (RSVP), and the Service Corps of Retired Executives (SCORE). Nearly half of adults aged 65–74 volunteer their services in some way, with substantial participation rates even among people over age

? THINK ABOUT IT
What might the opportunity for more older adults to volunteer for organizations mean politically? Check your answer with research data later in the chapter.

80 (Chambré, 1993). These rates represent a more than 400% increase since the mid-1960s, when only about 1 in 10 older adults did volunteer work. What accounts for this tremendous increase?

Several factors are responsible (Chambré, 1993): improved public perception of the skills and wisdom older adults have to offer, a redefinition of the nature and merits of volunteer work, a more highly educated population of older adults, and greatly expanded opportunities for people to become involved in volunteer work that they enjoy. Given the demographic trends of increased numbers and educational levels of older adults (discussed in Chapter 13), even higher rates of voluntarism are expected during the next few decades (Chambré, 1993). This is a way for society to tap into the vast resources that older adults offer.

TEST YOURSELF

1. One useful way to view retirement is as a _____ .

2. The most common reason people retire is _____ .

3. Overall, most retirees are _____ with retirement.

4. Many retirees keep contacts in their communities by _____ .

5. Using the information from Chapter 11 on occupational development, create a developmental description of occupations that incorporates retirement.

Answers: (1) complex process by which people gradually withdraw from employment, (2) by choice, (3) satisfied, (4) volunteering

FRIENDS AND FAMILY IN LATE LIFE

Learning Objectives

Friends and Family in Late Life

Friends and Siblings

Marriage

Caring for a Partner

Widowhood

Great-Grandparenthood

- **What role do friends and family play in late life?**

- **What are older adults' marriages like?**

- **What is it like to provide basic care for one's partner?**

- **How do people cope with widowhood? How do men and women differ?**

- **What special issues are involved in being a great-grandparent?**

LMA was married to Charles for 46 years. Even though he died 20 years ago, Alma still speaks about him as if he had only recently passed away. Alma still gets sad on special dates, such as their anniversary, or Charles's birthday, or the date on which he died. Alma tells everyone that she and Chuck, as she called him, had a wonderful marriage and that she still misses him terribly even after all these years.

To older adults like Alma, the most important thing in life is relationships. In this section, we consider many of the relationships older adults have. Whether it is friendship or family ties, having relationships with others is what keeps us connected. Thus, when one's spouse is in need of care, it is not surprising to find wives and husbands devoting themselves to caregiving. Widows like Alma also feel close to departed spouses. For a growing number of older adults, becoming a great-grandparent is an exciting time.

We have seen throughout this text how our lives are shaped and shared by the company of others. *The term* social convoy *is used to suggest how a group of people journeys with us throughout our lives, providing us support in good and bad times.* Especially for older adults, the social convoy also provides a source of affirmation of who they are and what they mean to others (Antonucci, 1985).

Several studies have shown that the size of the social convoy and the amount of support it provides do not differ across generations, a result that generalizes to Hispanic American adults as well (Levitt, Weber, & Guacci, 1993b). The lack of differences by age strongly supports the conclusion that friends and family are essential aspects of all adults' lives.

FRIENDS AND SIBLINGS

By late life, some members of a person's social network have been friends for several decades. Research consistently finds that older adults' life satisfaction is hardly related at all to the number or quality of relationships with younger family members, but it is strongly correlated with the number and quality of their friendships (Essex & Nam, 1987; Fehr, 1996). Why? As will become clear, friends serve as confidants and sources of support in ways that children and nieces and nephews, for example, typically do not. Both of Charlie Brown's grandmothers in the cartoon are examples of active older adults who like to be with friends.

PEANUTS reprinted by permission of United Feature Syndicate, Inc.

Friendships

The quality of late-life friendships is particularly important (Matthews, 1996). Having at least one very close friend or confidant provides a buffer against the losses of roles and status that accompany old age, such as retirement or the death of a loved one (Antonucci, 1985; Matthews, 1996). Patterns of friendship among older adults tend to mirror those in young adulthood described in Chapter 10 (Fehr, 1996). That is, women have more numerous and more intimate friendships than men do. As noted previously, these differences help explain why women are in a better position to deal with the stresses of life. Widows, especially, take advantage of their friendship networks; they are more involved with their friends than are married women, never-married women, or men (Hatch & Bulcroft, 1992).

In general, older adults have fewer relationships with people in general and develop fewer new relationships than younger or middle-aged adults (Carstensen, 1995). This decline in numbers does not merely reflect the loss of relationships to death or other means. Rather, the changes reflect a more complicated process (Carstensen, 1993, 1995). *This process, termed* socioemotional selectivity, *implies that social contact is motivated by many goals, including information seeking, self-concept, and emotional regulation.* Each of these goals is differentially relevant at different times, and results in different social behaviors. For example, information seeking tends to lead to meeting more people, whereas emotional regulation results in being very picky in the choice of social partners, with a strong preference for people who are familiar.

This latter tendency may help explain why older adults tend to prefer the friends they have had for many years, tending not to want to make new ones (Antonucci, 1985). Old friends can share aspects of the past that may be unknown to younger adults. Sadly, cherished friends may become incapacitated, making it difficult to maintain contact (Rawlins, 1992). To keep the friendships going, many older adults turn to phone calls or letters, and increasingly to e-mail.

Sibling Relationships

For many older adults like those in the photo, the preference for long-term friendships may explain older adults' desire to keep in touch with their siblings. Among people over age 60, 83% report that they feel close to at least one brother or sister (Dunn, 1984). Besides closeness, other dimensions of sibling friendships include involvement with each other, frequency of contact, envy, and resentment. Five types of relationships among older adult siblings have been identified (Gold, Woodbury, & George, 1990):

- *Intimate sibling relationships,* characterized by high levels of closeness and involvement but low levels of envy and resentment.

- *Congenial sibling relationships,* characterized by high levels of closeness and involvement, average levels of contact, and relatively low levels of envy and resentment.

- *Loyal sibling relationships,* characterized by average levels of closeness, involvement, and contact and relatively low levels of envy and resentment.

- *Apathetic sibling relationships,* characterized by low levels on all dimensions.

- *Hostile sibling relationships,* characterized by relatively high levels of involvement and resentment and relatively low levels on all other dimensions.

The relative frequencies of these five types of sibling relationships are shown in the figure. As you can see, loyal and congenial relationships characterize nearly two-thirds of all older sibling pairs. Additionally, it appears that older African American siblings have apathetic or hostile relationships with their siblings nearly five times less often than older European Americans do (4.5% for African Americans versus 22% for European Americans; Gold, 1990). Sometimes, hostile sibling relationships in late life date back to sibling rivalries in childhood (Greer, 1992).

When different combinations of siblings are considered separately, ties between sisters are typically the strongest, most frequent, and most intimate (Cicirelli, 1980; Lee, Mancini, & Maxwell, 1990). In contrast, brothers tend to maintain less frequent contact (Connidis, 1988). Little is known about brother-sister relationships. Even though many older adults end up providing care for or living with one of their siblings, we know virtually nothing about how well this works.

Clearly, there are major gaps in our understanding of sibling relationships. This is truly unfortunate, as brothers and sisters play an important and meaningful role throughout life.

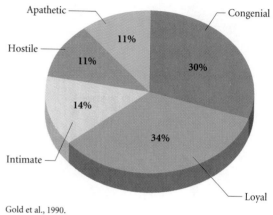

Gold et al., 1990.

MARRIAGE

"It's great to be 72 and still married," said Lucia. "Yeah, it's great to have Juan around to share old times with and have him know how I feel even before I tell him." Lucia and Juan are typical of most older married couples. Marital satisfaction improves once the children leave home and remains fairly high in older couples (Lee, 1988; Pearson, 1996). One study found that 80% of couples married at least 50 years recollected their marriages as being happy from their wedding day to the present (Sporakowski & Axelson, 1984).

Older married couples show several specific differences from their middle-aged counterparts (Levenson, Carstensen, & Gottman, 1993). Older couples have a reduced potential for marital conflict and greater potential for pleasure, are more likely to be similar in terms of mental and physical health, and show fewer gender differences in sources of pleasure. In short, most older married couples have developed adaptive ways to avoid conflict and have grown more alike. In general, marital satisfaction among older couples remains high until health problems begin to interfere with the relationship (Gilford, 1984; Pearson, 1996).

? THINK ABOUT IT
What specific strategies do you think older married couples use to reduce the potential for conflict?

CARING FOR A PARTNER

When most couples pledge their love to each other "in sickness and in health," most envision the sickness part to be no worse than an illness lasting a few weeks. That may be the case for many couples, but for some the illness they experience severely tests their pledge. Almost certainly, Nancy Reagan did not think that she would need to care for her husband, former U.S. President Ronald Reagan, who developed Alzheimer's disease.

Francine and Ron are another such couple. After 42 years of mainly good times together, Ron was diagnosed as having Alzheimer's disease. When first contacted by researchers, Francine had been caring for Ron for six years. "At times it's very hard, especially when he looks at me and doesn't have any idea who I am. Imagine, after all these years, not to recognize me. But I love him, and I know that he would do the same for me. But, to be perfectly honest, we're not the same couple we once were. We're just not as close; I guess we really can't be."

Francine and Ron are typical of couples like the one in the photograph in which one spouse cares for the other. Caring for a chronically ill partner presents different challenges than caring for a chronically ill parent (see Chapter 12). The partner caregiver assumes the new role after decades of shared responsibilities. Often without warning, the division of labor that had worked for years must be readjusted. Such change inevitably puts stress on the relationship (Cavanaugh & Kinney, 1994). This is especially true in cases involving Alzheimer's disease or other dementias, because of the cognitive and behavioral consequences of the disease (see Chapter 13), but is also the case in diseases such as AIDS. Caregiving challenges are felt by partner caregivers in any type of long-term, committed relationship.

Studies of people like those in the Real People feature, who are spousal caregivers of persons with Alzheimer's disease, show that marital satisfaction is much lower than for healthy couples (Cavanaugh & Kinney, 1994; Kinney et al., 1993). Spousal caregivers report a loss of companionship and intimacy over the course of caregiving (Williamson & Schulz, 1990; Wright, 1991). Marital satisfaction is also an important predictor of spousal caregivers' reports of depressive symptoms; the better the perceived quality of the marriage, the fewer symptoms caregivers report (Kinney et al., 1993). Sadly, caring for a spouse often leads the caregiver to question the meaningfulness of life (Wells & Kendig, 1997).

REAL PEOPLE 'TIL DEATH DO US PART: SPOUSAL CAREGIVING

"To be perfectly honest, I never in a million years thought I would be in the position I'm in now. When I married Mike, I thought we would be happy and live out our lives with our families and friends. But now ..."

Harriet's voice trailed off as her eyes filled with tears. Mike, 68 years old, had been diagnosed with Alzheimer's disease about six years earlier. Harriet, 2 years younger, dried her eyes and continued. "The worst part is when he gets aggressive with me. Sometimes he doesn't remember who I am and thinks I'm going to steal all of his clothes. All I want to do is the laundry. It's just so hard to keep telling myself that it's the disease. After 44 years of marriage, it's hard to accept that his mind is going and he just can't remember.

"Me, I just try to focus on all the good years we had. We've got three great kids, who help out as much as they can. But they have their own families, and jobs, and pressures. I know that. But sometimes I could really use a break; they're the best thing I have left.

"Why do I do what I'm doing? I promised Mike that I'd love him no matter what, and I've always kept my promises to him. It may sound strange, but I truly believe that somewhere inside he loves me as much as ever. I know I do. And that's what keeps me going. Besides, I couldn't afford to pay what it costs in a nursing home, and I don't think they would do as good a job as I'm doing. I'm biased, I guess, but he's my husband. To them, he'd only be another patient." •

Most partner caregivers are forced to respond to an environmental challenge that they did not choose—their partner's illness. They adopt the caregiver role out of necessity. Once they adopt the role, caregivers assess their ability to carry out the duties required. Longitudinal research indicates that how caregivers perceive their ability to provide care at the outset of caregiving may be all-important (Kinney & Cavanaugh, 1993). Caregivers who perceive themselves as competent try to rise to the occasion. For example, data indicate that spousal caregivers who perceive themselves as highly competent report fewer and less intense caregiving hassles than spousal caregivers who see themselves as less competent (Kinney & Cavanaugh, 1993). However, spousal caregivers do not always remember their major hassles accurately over time; in one study, caregivers only remembered about two-thirds of their major hassles after a one-month delay (Cavanaugh & Kinney, 1998). This finding points out that health care professionals should not rely exclusively on partner caregivers' reports about the caregiving situation in making diagnostic judgments.

The importance of feeling competent as a partner caregiver fits with the docility component of the competence–environmental press model presented earlier in this chapter. Caregivers attempt to balance their perceived competence with the environmental demands of caregiving. Perceived competence allows them to be proactive rather than merely reactive (and docile), which gives them a better chance to optimize their situation.

Even in the best of committed relationships, providing full-time care for a partner is very stressful (Kinney & Cavanaugh, 1993). Coping with a wife, for example, who may not remember her husband's name, who may act strangely, and who has a chronic and fatal disease presents serious challenges even to the happiest of couples, as depicted in the Doonesbury cartoon.

DOONESBURY © 1997 by Gary Trudeau. Reprinted by UNIVERSAL PRESS SYNDICATE. All rights reserved.

WIDOWHOOD

Alma, the woman we met in the vignette, still feels the loss of her husband Chuck. "There are lots of times when I feel him around. We were together for so long that you take it for granted that your husband is just there. And there are times when I just don't want to go on without him. But I suppose I'll get through it."

Traditional marriage vows proclaim that the union will last "'til death do us part." Like Alma and Chuck, virtually all older married couples will see their marriages end because one partner dies. For most people, the death of a spouse is one of the most traumatic events they will ever experience (Pearson, 1996). Although widowhood may occur at any age, it is much more likely to occur in old age—and to women (Matthews, 1996). More than half of all women over age 65 are widows, but only 15% of men the same age are widowers. The reasons for this discrepancy are related to biological and social forces: As we saw in Chapter 13, women have longer life expectancies. Also, women typically marry men older than themselves, as discussed in Chapter 10. Consequently, the average married woman can expect to live 10–12 years as a widow.

The impact of widowhood goes well beyond the ending of a long-term partnership (Matthews, 1996; Pearson, 1996). Widowed people like the man in the photograph may be left alone by family and friends who do not know how to deal with a bereaved person (see Chapter 15). As a result, widows and widowers often lose not only a spouse but also those friends and family who feel uncomfortable including a single person rather than a couple in social functions (Matthews, 1996). Additionally, widowed individuals may feel awkward as the third party or may even view themselves as a threat to married friends (Field & Minkler, 1988). Because going to a movie or a restaurant alone may be unpleasant or unsatisfying to older widows or widowers, they may just stay home. Unfortunately, others may assume that they simply wish or need to be alone.

For both widows and widowers, the first few months alone can be very difficult. Newly widowed people are at risk for increased physical illness and report more symptoms of depression, lost status, economic hardship, and lower social support (Stroebe & Stroebe, 1983). But feelings of loss do not dissipate quickly, as the case of Alma shows clearly. As we will see in Chapter 15, feeling sad on important dates is a common experience, even many years after a loved one has died.

Men and women react differently to widowhood. Widowers are at higher risk of dying themselves soon after their spouse, either by suicide or natural causes (Osgood, 1992; Smith & Zick, 1996). Some people believe that the loss of a wife presents a more serious problem for a man than the loss of a husband for a woman. Perhaps this is because a wife is often a man's only close friend and confidant, or because men are usually unprepared to live out their lives alone (Glick, Weiss, & Parkes, 1974; see Chapter 10). Older men are often ill equipped to handle such routine and necessary tasks as cooking, shopping, and keeping house, and they become emotionally isolated from family members.

? THINK ABOUT IT
What effects might cohort differences in men's participation in household chores have on future generations of widowers?

Although both widows and widowers suffer financial loss, widows often suffer more because survivor's benefits are usually only half of their husband's pensions (Smith & Zick, 1986, 1996). For many women, widowhood results in poverty (Pearson, 1996).

An important factor to keep in mind about gender differences in widowhood is that men are usually older than women when they are widowed. To some extent, the difficulties reported by widowers may be partly due to this age difference. Indeed, if age is held constant, data over many years indicate that widows actually report higher anxiety than widowers (Atchley, 1975). Regardless of age, men have a clear advantage over women in the opportunity to form new heterosexual relationships, as there are fewer social restrictions on relationships between older men and younger women (Matthews, 1996). However, older widowers are actually less likely to form new, close friendships than are widows. Perhaps this is simply a continuation of men's lifelong tendency to have few close friendships (see Chapter 10). Also, widows are more likely to join support groups, which foster the formation of new friendships (Vachon et al., 1980).

For many reasons, including the need for companionship and financial security, some widowed people remarry. One study examined remarriage as a coping response by older widows by interviewing 39 widows who had remarried, 192 who had considered remarriage, and 420 who had not considered it (Gentry & Schulman, 1988). Women who had remarried reported significantly fewer concerns than either of the other groups. Interestingly, the remarried widows were also the ones who recalled the most concerns about being alone and reported higher levels of emotional distress immediately after the death of their spouses. Apparently, remarriage helped these widows deal with the loss of their husbands by providing companionship and comfort.

GREAT-GRANDPARENTHOOD

As discussed in Chapter 12, grandparenting is an important and enjoyable role for many adults. With increasing numbers of people, especially women, living to very old age, more people are experiencing great-grandparenthood. Age at first marriage and age at parenthood also play a critical role; people who reach these milestones at relatively younger ages are more likely to become great-grandparents. Most current great-grandparents, like the woman in the photograph, are women who married relatively young and had children and grandchildren who also married and had children relatively early in adulthood.

Although little research has been conducted on great-grandparents, their sources of satisfaction and meaning apparently differ from those of grandparents (Doka & Mertz, 1988; Wentkowski, 1985). Compared to grandparents, great-grandparents are much more similar as a group in what they derive from the role, largely because they are less involved with the children than grandparents are. Three aspects of great-grandparenthood appear to be most important (Doka & Mertz, 1988).

First, being a great-grandparent provides a sense of personal and family renewal—important components for achieving integrity. Their grandchildren have produced new life, renewing their own excitement for life and reaffirming the continuance of their lineage. Seeing their families stretch across four generations may also provide psychological support, through feelings of symbolic immortality, to help them face death. Like the woman in the photograph on page 553, they take pride and comfort in knowing that their families will live many years beyond their own lifetime.

Second, great-grandchildren provide new diversions in great-grandparents' lives. There are now new people with whom they can share their experiences. Third, becoming a great-grandparent is a major milestone, a mark of longevity that most people never achieve. The sense that one has lived long enough to see the fourth generation is perceived very positively.

As you might expect, people with at least one living grandparent and great-grandparent interact more with their grandparent, who is also perceived as more influential (Roberto & Skoglund, 1996). Unfortunately, some great-grandparents must assume the role of primary caregiver to their great-grandchildren, a role that few great-grandparents are prepared to assume (Bengtson, Mills, & Parrott, 1995; Burton, 1992). As more people live longer, it will be interesting to see whether the role of great-grandparents changes and becomes more prominent.

TEST YOURSELF

1. The two most common forms of sibling relationships in old age are loyal and _____ .

2. In general, marital satisfaction in older couples is high until _____ .

3. A key predictor of stress among spousal caregivers is _____ .

4. _____ are at a higher risk of dying themselves soon after they lose their spouses.

5. Three aspects of being a great-grandparent that are especially important are personal and family renewal, diversion, and _____ .

6. How do the descriptions of marital satisfaction and spousal caregiving presented here fit with the descriptions of marital satisfaction in Chapter 10 and caring for aging parents in Chapter 12? What similarities and differences are there?

Answers: (1) congenial, (2) health problems arise, (3) marital satisfaction, (4) Widowers, (5) the fact that it is a milestone

---

SOCIAL ISSUES AND AGING

Social Issues and Aging

Frail Older Adults

Living in Nursing Homes

Elder Abuse and Neglect

Public Policy Issues and Older Adults

Learning Objectives

- **Who are frail older adults? How common is frailty?**

- **Where do older adults live in the community?**

- **Who are the most likely people to live in nursing homes? What are the characteristics of good nursing homes?**

- **How do you know whether an older adult is abused or neglected? Which people are most likely to be abused and to be abusers?**

- **What are the key social policy issues affecting older adults?**

*R*OSA *is an 82-year-old woman who still lives in the same neighborhood where she grew up. She has been in relatively good health for most of her life, but in the last year she has needed help with tasks, such as preparing meals and shopping for personal items. Rosa wants very much to continue living in her own home. She dreads being placed in a nursing home, but her family wonders whether that might be the best option.*

Our consideration of late life thus far has focused on the experiences of most people. In this final section, we consider people like Rosa, who represent a substantial number, but still a minority of all older adults. Like Rosa, some older adults experience problems completing such common tasks as taking care of themselves. We consider the prevalence and kinds of problems such people face. Although most older adults live in the community, some reside in nursing homes; we consider the kinds of people most likely to live in institutional settings. Unfortunately, some older adults are the victims of abuse or neglect; we will examine some of the key issues relating to how elder abuse happens. Finally, we conclude with an overview of the most important emerging social policy issues.

FRAIL OLDER ADULTS

In our discussion about aging to this point, we have focused on the majority of older adults who are healthy, cognitively competent, financially secure, and have secure family relationships. Some older adults, like the woman in the photograph, are not as fortunate. *They are* frail older adults *who have physical disabilities, are very ill, and may have cognitive or psychological disorders.* These frail older adults constitute a minority of the population over age 65, but a proportion that increases with age.

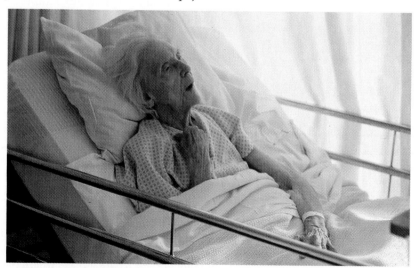

Frail older adults are people whose competence (in terms of the competence–environmental press model presented earlier) is declining. However, they do not have one specific problem that differentiates them from their active, healthy counterparts (Guralnick & Simonsick, 1993; Strawbridge et al., 1998). *In general, they are unable to perform one or more basic self-care tasks such as eating, bathing, toileting, walking, or dressing; collectively, these tasks are called* activities of daily living *or* ADLs. A person could be considered frail if he or she needs help with one of these tasks.

Other tasks are also considered important for living independently. *These instrumental activities of daily living (IADLs) are actions that require some intellectual competence and planning.* Which actions constitute IADLs vary considerably from one culture to another (Katz, 1983). For example, for most older adults in Western culture IADLs would include shopping for personal items, paying bills, making telephone calls, taking medications appropriately, and keeping appointments. In other cultures, IADLs might include caring for animal herds, making bread, threshing grain, and tending crops.

Prevalence of Frailty

How common are people like Rosa, the 82-year-old woman in the vignette who still lives in the same neighborhood in which she grew up? As you can see in the graph, the number of older people needing help with ADLs increases

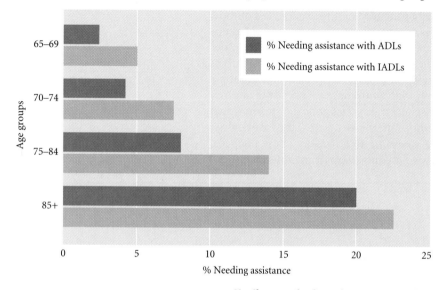

dramatically with age (Crimmins, Saito, & Reynolds, 1997; Guralnick & Wallace, 1991). Less than 5% of adults aged 65–74 need assistance, whereas 20% of those over age 85 may need help (National Aging Information Center, 1997). Poor health exacerbates the problem. One extensive study of people's functioning in the year prior to their death showed that over 70% of all older adults need help with ADLs; indeed, virtually everyone over age 85 needs some assistance, and half require help with all ADLs (Lentzner et al., 1992).

Similar results have been reported for IADLs. As you can also see in the graph, the number of adults requiring assistance with IADLs also increases drastically after age 85 (National Aging Information Center, 1997). However, there is some evidence that the number of people who need assistance with IADLs has decreased slightly between the early 1980s and the mid-1990s (Crimmins et al., 1997). This decrease may be due to improved support systems available to those in need.

Although frailty becomes more likely with increasing age, especially during the last year of life, there are many ways to provide a supportive environment for frail older adults. We have already seen how many family members provide care. Later, we will consider the role that nursing homes play. The key to providing a supportive context for frail older adults is to create an optimal match between the person's competence and the environmental demands.

LIVING IN NURSING HOMES

The last place that Bessie thought she would ever end up was in a bed in a local nursing home. "That's a place where old people go to die," she would tell her friends. "It's not gonna be for me." But here she is. Bessie fell a few weeks ago and broke her hip. Because she lives alone, she needs to stay in the nursing home until she recovers. She detests the food; "tasteless" she calls it. Her room-mate, Doris, refers to her room as "jail" to her daughter. Doris, age 78, has dementia.

Bessie and Doris represent many of the people who live in nursing homes, some temporarily, some permanently. If given the choice, the vast majority of older adults do not want to live in nursing homes; their families would also prefer some other solution. Sometimes, though, placement in a nursing home is necessary because of the older person's needs or the family's circumstances.

Misconceptions about nursing homes are common. Contrary to what some people believe, only about 5% of older adults live in nursing homes on any given day. However, about 50% of people who live past age 85 will spend at least some time in a long-term care facility (National Academy on Aging, 1997). Thus, over the adult life span, the numbers of people who spend time in a nursing home is rather large.

Governmental regulations in the United States define two primary levels of care in nursing homes (Johnson & Grant, 1985). Intermediate care *consists of 24-hour care necessitating nursing supervision, but usually not at an intense level.* Skilled nursing care *consists of 24-hour care requiring fairly constant monitoring and provision of medical and other health services, usually by nurses.* Each state has specific regulations concerning each type of care.

Who Lives in Nursing Homes?

In 1997, over 1.5 million older adults lived in nursing homes; by 2018 this number is expected to rise to 3.6 million (National Academy on Aging, 1997). Overall, women are much more likely to enter nursing homes than are men. Why is this the case? Usually, older men who need health or living assistance get help from their wives, whereas older women with similar needs are more likely to be like the woman in the photograph: widows or women living alone for other reasons who have fewer caregiving options. Thus, these women are at higher risk for nursing home placement (National Academy on Aging, 1997; Wolinsky et al., 1992).

In general, ethnic minority older adults are less likely to live in nursing homes than European Americans (Wolinsky et al., 1992). The reasons for these differences are not entirely clear. They may be due in part to different norms for caregiving: African Americans, for example, tend to prefer to rely on family caregivers rather than institutions (Johnson & Barer, 1990). Also, for financial reasons, poor people in all ethnic groups have less access to health care providers, including nursing homes (Belgrave, Wykle, & Choi, 1993). Furthermore, a lack of knowledge about nursing homes as an option is also a factor for minority groups (Segall & Wykle, 1988–89).

What Characterizes a Good Nursing Home?

Nursing homes vary a great deal in the amount and quality of care they provide. One useful way of evaluating them is by applying the competence–environmental press model. When applied to nursing homes, the goal is to find the optimal level of environmental support for people who have relatively low levels of competence.

Selecting a nursing home should be done carefully. The Health Care Financing Administration of the U.S. Department of Health and Human Services provides a detailed guide for choosing a nursing home (see the Web site at the end of the chapter for details). Among the most important things to consider are quality of life for residents (e.g., whether residents are well groomed, the food is tasty, and rooms contain comfortable furniture); quality of care (whether staff respond quickly to calls, whether staff and family are involved in care decisions); safety (whether there are enough staff, whether hallways are free of clutter); and other issues (whether there are outdoor areas for residents to use). These aspects of nursing homes reflect those dimensions considered by states in their inspections and licensing process.

Some researchers point out that congruence between the resident's needs and the ability of the nursing home to meet them is the crucial element for optimizing well-being (Kahana, 1982). An important part of meeting residents' needs is fostering family visitation. Research has shown that residents who are visited often by their families have significantly higher levels of psychosocial functioning (Greene & Monahan, 1982). Some tips on visiting people in nursing homes are presented in the You May Be Wondering feature.

YOU MAY BE WONDERING

HOW DO YOU RESPOND TO A NURSING HOME RESIDENT?

The first time most people visit a nursing home, they are ill-prepared for what they experience: trying to talk to family members who are frail, have trouble remembering, and cannot get around very well. The hardest part is trying to figure out what to say.

However, visiting residents of nursing homes like those in the photograph is a way to maintain social contacts and provide a meaningful activity. Even if the person you are visiting is frail or has a sensory impairment or some other type of disability, visits can be uplifting. As noted earlier in the chapter, high-quality social contacts help older adults maintain their life satisfaction. Listed below are several suggestions for making visits more pleasant (Papalia & Olds, 1995; adapted from Davis, 1985).

- Concentrate on the older adult's expertise and wisdom, as discussed in Chapter 13, by asking for advice on a life problem that he or she knows a lot about, such as dealing with friends, cooking, or crafts.

- Allow the older person to exert control over the visit: where to go (even inside the facility), what to wear, what to eat (if choices are possible).

- Listen attentively, even if the older person is repetitive. Avoid being judgmental, be sympathetic to complaints, and acknowledge feelings.

- Talk about things the person likes to remember, such as raising children, military service, growing up, work, courtship, and so on.

- Do a joint activity, such as putting a jigsaw puzzle together, arranging a photograph album, or doing arts and crafts.

- Record your visit on audiotape or videotape. This is valuable for creating a family history that you will be able to keep. The activity may facilitate a life review, as well as provide an opportunity for the older person to leave something of value for future generations by describing important personal events and philosophies.

- Bring children when you visit, if possible. Grandchildren are especially important, as most older adults are very happy to include them in conversations. Such visits also give children the opportunity to see their grandparents and learn about the diversity of older adults.

- Stimulate as many senses as possible. Wearing bright clothes, singing songs, reading books, and sharing foods (as long as they have been checked with the staff) help keep residents involved with their environment. Above all, though, hold the resident's hands. There's nothing like a friendly touch.

Always remember that your visits may be the only way that the residents have of maintaining social contacts with friends and family. By following these guidelines, you will be able to avoid difficulties and make your visits more pleasurable. ●

How nursing home residents are treated by staff is also key to well-being. Most important, residents need to perceive that they have some degree of control in their lives (Langer, 1985). To demonstrate this point, Langer and Rodin (1976) conducted an ingenious experiment. One group of nursing home residents was told that staff members were there to care for them and to make decisions for them about their daily lives. In contrast, a second group of residents like the man in the photograph were encouraged to make their own decisions about meals, recreational activities, and so forth. Results showed that more than 90% of the second group showed significant improvement in well-being and activity level. But more than 70% of the passive group became weaker and more disabled, and they were more likely to have died 18 months later (Rodin & Langer, 1977). Subsequent research showed that it is feelings of self-efficacy that are crucial in this process (Johnson et al., 1998).

An implication of these findings is that staff should provide help only when necessary, and repetitive routines should be avoided (Langer, 1985). These characteristics are most likely to be found in larger nonprofit facilities that have a high ratio of nurses to nurse's aides (Pillemer & Moore, 1989).

Equally important, people interacting with nursing home residents must avoid patronizing speech, *which is marked by slower speech, exaggerated intonation, higher pitch, increased volume, repetitions, closed-ended questions, and simplified vocabulary and grammar. A related form of demeaning speech, called* infantilization, *involves the use of a person's first name when it is not appropriate, terms of endearment, simplified expressions, short imperatives, assumptions that the resident has no memory, and manipulation to get compliance.* Several studies document that the use of patronizing speech and infantilization result in negative feelings on the part of residents, and may lower self-esteem among those who perceive such speech negatively (O'Connor & Rigby, 1996; Ryan, Hamilton, & See, 1994; Whitbourne, Culgin, & Cassidy, 1995; Whitmer & Whitbourne, 1997). As with people of any age, nursing home residents should be treated with dignity and respect.

ELDER ABUSE AND NEGLECT

Arletta, an 82-year-old woman in relatively poor health, has been living with her 60-year-old daughter Sally for the past two years. Recently, neighbors became concerned because they had not seen Arletta very much for several months. When they did, she looked rather worn and extremely thin, and as if she had not bathed in weeks. Finally, the neighbors decided that they should do something, so they called the local office of the department of human services. Upon

hearing the details of the situation, a caseworker immediately investigated. The caseworker found that Arletta was severely malnourished, had not bathed in weeks, and appeared disoriented. Based on these findings, the agency concluded that Arletta was a victim of neglect. She was moved to a county nursing home temporarily.

Unfortunately, some older adults like the woman in the photograph who need quality caregiving by family members or in nursing homes do not receive it. In some cases, older adults, like Arletta, are treated inappropriately. Arletta's case is representative of this sad but increasing problem: elder abuse and neglect. In this section, we consider what elder abuse and neglect are, how often they happen, and what victims and abusers are like.

Defining Elder Abuse and Neglect

Like child abuse (see Chapter 7, pages 250–252) and partner abuse (see Chapter 10, pages 371–374), elder abuse is difficult to define precisely in practice. In general, researchers and public policy advocates describe several different categories of elder abuse (National Center on Elder Abuse [NCEA], 1997): physical (such as beating or withholding care); psychological/emotional (such as verbal assaults and social isolation); sexual; material or financial exploitation (such as illegal or improper use of funds); and abandonment (desertion of an older adult by a person who has physical custody of the older person or who has assumed responsibility for providing care).

In addition to abuse, neglect of older adults is also a growing problem (NCEA, 1997). Neglecting older adults can be either intended, such as refusing to fulfill basic caregiving obligations with the intention of inflicting harm, or unintended, such as not providing adequate medical care because of a lack of knowledge on the caregiver's part (Wolf, Godkin, & Pillemer, 1986).

Part of the problem in agreeing on a common definition of elder abuse and neglect is that perceptions differ among ethnic groups. For example, African American, Korean American, and European American older females used different criteria in deciding whether scenarios they read represented abuse (Moon & Williams, 1993). Specifically, older Korean American women were much less likely to judge a particular scenario as abusive and to indicate that help should be sought than women in either of the other two groups. Such ethnic differences may result in conflicts between social service workers using one set of definitions and clients using another, in deciding who should receive protective services (Williams & Griffin, 1996).

Prevalence

Official estimates suggest that 3–4% of older adults in the United States are the victims of abuse or neglect. However, as is the case with child and spousal abuse, most researchers believe these estimates to be low, and that the true numbers are not known (NCEA, 1997). The most common forms are neglect (roughly 60%), physical abuse (16%), and financial or material exploitation (12%). Thus, Arletta's case of neglect would be one of the most common types.

Abuse and neglect are not limited to older adults living in the community. In a study of 577 randomly selected nurses and nurse's aides who worked in intermediate care and skilled nursing facilities, Pillemer and Moore (1989) asked respondents about actions they had either performed themselves or had witnessed other staff commit. They reported that 10% of the respondents admitted to physically abusing a resident, and 40% admitted to psychologically abusing a resident at least once during the previous year. Additionally, 36% reported seeing acts of physical abuse, and 81% reported observing acts of psychological abuse over the same time period.

Victim and Abuser Profiles

Relatively little research has focused on the characteristics of victims of elder abuse or neglect. Moreover, there is considerable controversy about the characteristics of abuse victims and perpetrators. One view is that victims tend to be overly dependent on others, and abuse is caused by the extreme stress associated with providing care (Steinmetz, 1993). An alternative view is that the victim is not dependent; rather, it is the perpetrator who is dependent on the victim (Pillemer, 1993). That is, abuse is thought to be caused by the deviance and dependence of caregivers. These differing views of who gets abused and why are discussed more thoroughly in the Current Controversies feature.

WHICH OLDER PEOPLE ARE ABUSED AND WHY?

CURRENT CONTROVERSIES

INFOTRAC
COLLEGE EDITION

To learn more, enter the following search terms: abuse of aged.

One of the most controversial issues in aging is which older adults are at greatest risk for abuse and neglect. Sorting out this issue is important, in order to provide the most appropriate services to victims and to develop effective prevention strategies. As noted, there are two competing views of who is at risk. At the heart of the debate is a deceptively simple question: Are abuse victims dependent on perpetrators, or are perpetrators dependent on abuse victims?

Most researchers and policymakers assume that abuse victims are dependent. Indeed, the typical picture is one of a victim who has been abused by his or her caregiver, who in turn is under considerable stress from having to provide care (Steinmetz, 1993). Such victims are usually over age 80, female, excessively loyal to their caregiver, involved in frequent intergenerational conflict, burdened with a history of past abuse, socially isolated, and characterized by the abusers as unpleasant or demanding. The stress, frustration, and burden caregivers experience are too much for some to take; they lash out and turn their emotions into abusive behavior. For example, there is evidence that the onset of new cognitive impairments in a care recipient increases the likelihood of abuse (Lachs et al., 1997). In this view, abuse and neglect of older adults have much in common with child abuse and neglect; both involve victims who are highly dependent on their perpetrators for basic care. This view is easy for people to understand, which is probably the reason why most prevention programs are based on a dependent-victim model.

Other researchers strongly disagree. Rather than the victims being dependent on caregiver-perpetrators, they see the perpetrators as being dependent on the victims (Pillemer, 1993). These perpetrators are not merely acting out their frustration; they are seen as deviant and suffering from mental disorders. In this approach, perpetrators depend on their victims in four areas: housing, financial assistance, household repair, and transportation. Perpetrators also tend to be more violent in general, to have been arrested for other crimes, and to have been hospitalized for psychiatric disorders (Pillemer, 1993).

Which of these views is correct? Based on the research to date, both positions have support. This has profound implications for prevention and treatment. If victims are dependent, then programs are needed to provide basic services to caregivers to lower their stress. If perpetrators are deviant and have mental disorders, then programs need to identify individuals who are at risk for abusing older adults. Clearly, additional research is needed to provide the appropriate direction for policymakers and to settle the controversy. •

Much more attention has been paid to identifying characteristics of abusers. Adult children are generally more likely to abuse older adults than are other people (NCEA, 1997). In general, people who abuse or neglect older adults show higher rates of substance abuse and mental health problems, are inexperienced caregivers, have more economic problems, receive little help from other family members for caregiving, are hypercritical and insensitive to others, and are more likely to have been abused themselves (NCEA, 1997; Pillemer, 1993).

An important exception to these general patterns is abuse of persons with dementia. Research has shown that in this case, the spouse is much more likely to actually become violent with the care-recipient, especially when the spousal caregiver has previously experienced violent or aggressive behavior from the care-recipient (Pillemer & Suitor, 1992), or cognitive impairment increases (Lachs et al., 1997). There is some reason for hope, however. Additional data suggest that spousal caregivers who have violent feelings report a greater likelihood that they will place the care-recipient in a nursing home in the near future (Pillemer & Suitor, 1992).

These characteristics fit with the family violence model as an explanation of abuse in general (see Chapter 10). Some authors argue that elder abuse and neglect can be likened to cases of spousal abuse when the perpetrator is a partner, and likened to child abuse when the perpetrator is a family caregiver (Steinmetz, 1993). Other writers (Pillemer, 1993) deny any similarity between abuse of older adults and that of children, except in cases where mental disorders are present in both types of abusers. Although more research is needed to sort out these possible connections, abuse and neglect of older adults clearly could have aspects in common with other types of family violence. More research could lead to a general theoretical model of partner and intergenerational abuse, which would allow us to know the circumstances most likely to give rise to abuse and neglect.

PUBLIC POLICY ISSUES AND OLDER ADULTS

Without doubt, the 20th century saw a dramatic improvement in the everyday lives of older adults in industrialized countries. The advent of the "Old Age Welfare State" (Myles, 1983) due to the creation of Social Security and Medicare, among other benefits, greatly changed the social and political landscape of the United States. The economic well-being of the majority of older adults has never been better than it is currently; for example, in the 1950s, roughly 35% of older adults were below the federal poverty line compared to about 11% in the mid-1990s (Baugher & Lamison-White, 1996). But times have changed. Many younger and middle-aged adults are quite skeptical of the long-term viability of these governmental programs, especially in view of the enormous increase in costs associated with the aging of the baby boom generation (Binstock, 1999). The political climate has also changed, though the seeds were planted two decades earlier.

The Political Landscape

Beginning in the 1970s, older adults began to be portrayed as scapegoats in the political debates concerning government resources. Part of the reason was due to the tremendous growth in the amount and proportion of federal dollars expended on benefits to them. Additionally, older adults were portrayed as highly politically active and fiscally conservative and selfish; people like those in the photograph reinforced this view (Fairlie, 1988; Gibbs, 1988; Smith, 1992). The health care reform debate of the early 1990s focused attention on the spiraling costs of care for older adults that were projected to bankrupt the federal budget if left uncontrolled (Binstock, 1999). Consequently, older adults emerged as the source of all the United States' fiscal problems.

It was in this context that the U.S. Congress began making substantive changes in the benefits for older adults on the grounds of intergenerational fairness. The argument was that the United States must treat all generations fairly, and cannot provide differential benefits to any one generation (Binstock, 1994). Beginning in 1983, Congress has made several changes in Social Security, Medicare, the Older Americans Act, and other programs and policies. Some of these changes reduced benefits to wealthy older adults, whereas others provided targeted benefits for poor older adults (Binstock, 1999).

Pressure to balance the U.S. federal budget resulted in 1995 in the Bipartisan Commission on Entitlement and Tax Reform, which issued a report on the financial consequences of the baby boom for Social Security and Medicare in the 21st century. The picture was gloomy—if something was not done, the financial health of both benefits was in serious doubt. The Balanced Budget Act of 1997 (Public Law No. 105-33, 1997) included measures to reduce the growth of Medicare spending by $115 billion by 2002 in order to prevent a crisis in the Hospital Insurance part of Medicare (covered by FICA payroll taxes, which would have been inadequate to pay the anticipated expenses).

The aging of the baby boom generation presents very difficult and expensive problems (Congressional Budget Office, 1997). In fiscal year 1996, federal spending on Social Security, Medicare, and Medicaid for older adults was $630 billion, representing 8.4% of the nation's gross domestic product (GDP). If spending patterns do not change, by 2030 (when most of the baby boom will have reached old age) these expenditures are projected to consume 16% of GDP, nearly double the current amount.

Clearly, the political and social issues concerning benefits to older adults are quite complex. The next decade will see increased urgency and action in confronting the issues. There are no easy solutions, and it will be essential to discuss all aspects of the problem. Let's look more closely at three key issues: political activity, Social Security, and Medicare.

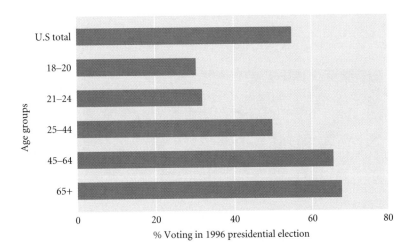

% Voting in 1996 presidential election

Political Activity

By most measures, adults over age 65 are the most politically active of all age groups. They write more letters to elected representatives, belong to more organizations that lobby for their positions, and are better informed about local and national issues (Binstock & Day, 1996; Torres-Gil, 1992). Perhaps most important, they vote at a higher rate than any other age group, as you can see in the graph depicting voting rates in the presidential election of 1996 (Federal Election Commission, 1998). Although people over age 65 represent roughly 16% of all registered voters, they constituted about 20% of all voters in the 1996 presidential election—meaning that proportionately, older adults had a bigger voice in Bill Clinton's victory than other age groups. Similar voting patterns are found for congressional, state, and local elections.

These activities have created a very powerful and active constituency, one that has increasing influence on legislation. The primary organization representing the interests of older adults is the American Association of Retired Persons (AARP), which is also the largest interest group in the United States. In 1999, membership in AARP exceeded 33 million. Anyone over age 50 is eligible to join; one need not be retired. It is largely due to the political influence of AARP that Social Security and Medicare have become very difficult issues for politicians to confront.

AARP is not alone in mobilizing older adults in the political arena (Binstock & Day, 1996). Organizations such as the National Committee to Preserve Social Security and Medicare (over 5.5 million members) and the National Council of Senior Citizens (over 500,000 members) also help shape public policy. Together, these and over 100 other national organizations in the United States work to further the interests and concerns of older adults.

Social Security

Social Security had its beginnings in 1935 as an initiative by President Franklin Roosevelt to "frame a law which will give some measure of protection to the average citizen and to his family against the loss of a job and against poverty-ridden old age." Thus, Social Security was originally intended to provide a supplement to savings and other means of financial support.

Over the years, revisions to the original law have changed Social Security so that it now represents the primary source of financial support after retirement for most U.S. citizens, and the only source for many (Binstock, 1999). Since the 1970s, however, increasing numbers of workers are included in employer-sponsored pension plans such as mutual funds, as well as various types of Individual Retirement Accounts (IRAs) (Schulz, 1996). This inclusion of various retirement plans, especially savings options, may permit more future retirees to use Social Security as the supplemental financial source it was intended to be.

The primary challenge facing Social Security is the aging of the very large baby boom generation and the much smaller generation that follows them. Because Social Security is funded by payroll taxes, the amount of money each worker must pay depends to a large extent on the ratio of the number of people paying Social Security taxes to the number of people collecting benefits. By 2030, this ratio will drop nearly in half; that is, by the time baby boomers have largely retired, there will be nearly twice as many people collecting Social Security per worker paying into the system as there is today (U.S. Bureau of the Census, 1998). Actions taken by the U.S. Congress in the 1990s may keep Social Security solvent for the next few decades; whether the actions are successful and affordable remains to be seen.

Medicare

Over 37 million U.S. citizens depend on Medicare for their medical insurance. To be eligible, a person must meet one of the following criteria: be over age 65, be disabled, or have permanent kidney failure. Medicare consists of two parts (Health Care Financing Administration, 1998): Part A, which covers inpatient hospital services, skilled nursing facilities, home health services, and hospice care, and Part B, which covers the cost of physician services, outpatient hospital services, medical equipment and supplies, and other health services and supplies. Expenses relating to most long-term care needs are funded by Medicaid, another major health care program funded by the U.S. government aimed at people who are poor. Out-of-pocket expenses associated with co-payments and other charges are often paid by supplemental insurance policies sometimes referred to as "Medigap" policies (Wiener & Illston, 1996).

Like Social Security, Medicare is funded by a payroll tax. So, the funding problems facing Medicare are very similar to those facing Social Security, and are grounded in the aging of the baby boom generation. Additionally, Medicare costs have increased dramatically due to more general rapid cost increases in health care; by the mid-1990s, the rate of increase was still more than twice that of inflation (Health Care Financing Administration, 1998).

Due to these rapid increases and the specter of the baby boom generation, cost containment was a major concern in the 1990s. Indeed, two major policy trends emerged. First, a growing emphasis was placed on managed care through health maintenance organizations (HMOs). To date, HMOs have been only partially successful due to the reluctance of many older adults to join them and give up their free choice of health providers (Wiener & Illston, 1996).

Second, home health care has been championed by some as a means to minimize the need for more expensive hospital and long-term care (Hudson, 1996). By enabling people to be cared for in their homes, policymakers and service providers hope to reserve hospitals and nursing homes for those in most need. At this point, it is still too early to tell whether this strategy will be successful.

Taken together, the challenges facing society concerning older adults' financial security and health will likely be major political issues throughout the first few decades of the 21st century. There are no easy answers, but open discussion of the various arguments will be essential for creating the optimal solution.

TEST YOURSELF

1. Activities of daily living (ADLs) include functioning in the areas of bathing, toileting, walking, dressing, and _____ .

2. Most people who live in nursing homes are _____ .

3. The group that most often abuses older adults is _____ .

4. The two important public policy issues in the United States that are being affected by the aging baby boom generation are Social Security and _____ .

5. How would the competence–environmental press framework, presented earlier in this chapter, apply specifically to the various types of housing and nursing homes discussed in this section?

Answers: (1) eating, (2) older European American women who are very ill, (3) their adult children, (4) Medicare

---

PUTTING IT ALL TOGETHER

We are involved in human relationships throughout our lives. In a very real sense, people grow old within the broader social context of their environment and social network.

The match between people's competence and the environmental demands they face sets the stage for how well they adapt. How older people cope with daily life is typically a continuation of the ways they coped throughout their lives. We encountered people who, like Olive, spend time reflecting on their past in order to determine whether their lives have been well spent. We saw that the view of retirement as detrimental to health and as a cause of isolation is wrong; most people are like Marcus, who greatly enjoys retirement. Many older women, like Alma, are widows; such women are especially vulnerable to financial pressures. Also, like Rosa, many people over 80 need assistance with their daily activities.

The general picture of older adults is characterized by continued activity for most. Still, we need to recognize that, especially among the oldest old, physical limitations are an important aspect of living. Although only a very small proportion of older adults are in nurs-

ing homes, many people over 80 need varying degrees of help to continue living independently. The rapid increase in the number of older people that the United States will experience over the next few decades will seriously strain traditional public policies toward older adults.

Combined with Chapter 13, this chapter provides insight into the complexities of old age. So what is known about a person if we know she is 85 years old? Not much more than the fact that she has celebrated 85 birthdays. That's not bad, either—it means that if you want to know something more than that, you'll need to get to know her.

We can now take a broader view of the biopsychosocial model as it relates to aging. In this chapter, we focused mainly on how sociocultural forces shape people's lives by setting the context for retirement and interpersonal relationships, as well as setting the agenda for social and public policy issues. How well people are able to face sociocultural forces (as exemplified by environmental press) is a function of their biological and psychological competence. Of course, this function is a dynamic one that changes as people grow older.

SUMMARY

Theories of Psychosocial Aging

Continuity Theory

• Continuity theory is based on the view that people tend to cope with daily life in later adulthood by applying familiar strategies based on past experience to maintain and preserve both internal and external structures.

Competence and Environmental Press

• According to competence–environmental press theory, people's optimal adaptation occurs when there is a balance between their ability to cope and the level of environmental demands placed on them. When balance is not achieved, behavior becomes maladaptive. Several studies indicate that competence–environmental press theory can be applied to a variety of real-world situations.

Personality Development in Later Life

Integrity Versus Despair

• Older adults face the Eriksonian struggle of integrity versus despair, primarily through a life review. Integrity involves accepting one's life for what it is; despair involves bitterness about one's past. People who reach integrity become self-affirming and self-accepting, and they judge their lives to have been worthwhile and good.

Well-Being and Possible Selves in Later Life

• Ryff has identified six aspects to well-being: self-acceptance, positive relation with others, autonomy, environmental mastery, purpose in life, and personal growth. Older adults view their past more positively than younger or middle-aged adults, and they see themselves as closer to their ideal selves.

Religiosity and Spiritual Support

• Older adults use religion and spiritual support more often than any other strategy to help them cope with problems of life. This is especially true for African American women, who are more active in their church groups and attend services more frequently.

I Used to Work at . . . : Living in Retirement

What Does Being Retired Mean?

• Retirement is a complex process by which people withdraw from full-time employment. No single definition is adequate for all ethnic groups; self-definition involves several factors, including eligibility for certain social programs.

Why Do People Retire?

• People generally retire because they choose to, although some people are forced to retire or do so because of serious health problems, such as cardiovascular disease or cancer. However, there are important gender and ethnic differences in why people retire and how they label themselves after retirement. Most of the research is based on European American men from traditional marriages.

Adjustment to Retirement

• Retirement is an important life transition. Most people are satisfied with retirement. Most retired people maintain their health, friendship networks, and activity levels, at least in the years immediately following retirement. For men, personal life priorities are all-important; little is known about women's retirement satisfaction. Most retired people stay busy in activities such as volunteer work and helping others.

Interpersonal Ties

• Retiring can disrupt long-held behavior patterns in marriages. Social relationships help buffer the stress of retirement. Readjusting to being home rather than at work is difficult for men in traditional marriages. Marriages are sometimes disrupted, but married men are generally happier in retirement than men who are not married. Participation in community organizations helps raise satisfaction. In particular, volunteer work can fill the void. Improved attitudes toward older adults in society also help.

Friends and Family in Late Life

Friends and Siblings

• A person's social convoy is an important source of satisfaction in late life. Patterns of friendships among older adults are very similar to those among young adults, but older adults are more selective. Sibling relationships are especially important in old age. Five types of sibling relationships have been identified: intimate, congenial, loyal, apathetic, and hostile. The loyal and congenial types are the most common. Ties between sisters are the strongest.

Marriage

• Long-term marriages tend to be happy until one partner develops serious health problems. Older married couples show a lower potential for marital conflict and greater potential for pleasure. Overall, older married couples are more alike than younger married couples.

Caring for a Spouse

• Caring for a spouse puts considerable strain on the relationship. The degree of marital satisfaction strongly affects how spousal caregivers perceive stress. Although caught off guard initially, most spousal caregivers are able to provide adequate care. Perceptions of competence among spousal caregivers at the outset of caregiving may be especially important.

Widowhood

• Widowhood is a difficult transition for most people. Feelings of loneliness are hard to cope with, especially during the first few months following bereavement. Men generally have problems in social relationships and in household tasks; women tend to have more severe financial problems. Some widowed people remarry, partly to solve loneliness and financial problems.

Great-Grandparenthood

• Becoming a great-grandparent is an important source of personal satisfaction for many older adults. Great-grandparents as a group are more similar to each other than grandparents are. Three aspects of great-grandparenthood are most important: sense of personal and family renewal; new diversions in life; and a major life milestone.

Social Issues and Aging

Frail Older Adults

• The number of frail older adults is growing. Frailty is defined in terms of impairment in activities of daily living (basic self-care skills) and instrumental activities of daily living (actions that require intellectual competence or planning). As many as half of the women over age 85 may need assistance with ADLs or IADLs. Supportive environments are useful in optimizing the balance between competence and environmental press.

Living in Nursing Homes

• Two levels of care are provided in nursing homes: intermediate care and skilled nursing care. Most residents of nursing homes are European American women who are in poor health. Ethnic minority older adults have a lower rate of placement in nursing homes than European Americans. Maintaining a resident's sense of control is an important component of good nursing homes. Communications with residents must avoid patronizing speech and infantilization.

Elder Abuse and Neglect

• Abuse and neglect of older adults is an increasing problem, both in people living in the community and in nursing home residents. However, abuse and neglect are difficult to define precisely. Several categories are used, including physical, psychological/emotional, sexual, material or financial, and violation of rights. Most perpetrators are adult children of the victims. Research indicates that abuse may result when older adult victims are dependent on their caregivers or the caregivers are dependent on the victims; which situation is more prevalent is unknown.

Public Policy Issues and Older Adults

• Treating all generations fairly in terms of government programs is a difficult public policy challenge. The U.S. Congress has enacted several changes in social program benefits to older adults to address the changing demographics of the U.S. population.

• Older adults are the most politically active age group. Numerous organizations are dedicated to furthering issues and positions pertaining to older adults.

• Although designed as an income supplement, Social Security has become the primary source of retirement income for most U.S. citizens. The aging of the baby boom generation will place considerable stress on the financing of the system.

• Medicare is the principle health insurance program for adults in the United States over age 65. Cost containment is a major concern, resulting in emphases on health maintenance organizations and home health care.

KEY TERMS

continuity theory (530)
competence (531)
environmental press (531)
adaptation level (532)
zone of maximum performance potential (532)
zone of maximum comfort (532)
proactivity (532)

docility (532)
integrity versus despair (534)
life review (534)
possible selves (535)
spiritual support (538)
social convoy (547)
socioemotional selectivity (548)
frail older adults (555)

activities of daily living (ADLs) (555)
instrumental activities of daily living (IADLs) (556)
intermediate care (557)
skilled nursing care (557)
patronizing speech (559)
infantilization (559)

IF YOU'D LIKE TO LEARN MORE

Books

ERIKSON, E. H. (1982). *The life cycle completed: Review.* New York: Norton. By Erikson's own account, this short book represents a summary of his theory. It is moderately difficult reading.

GUBRIUM, J. F. (1994). *Speaking of life: Horizons of meaning for nursing home residents.* Hawthorne, NY: Aldine de Gruyter. This easy-to-read book provides a wealth of information about what life is like in nursing homes.

HARGRAVE, T. D., & HANNA, S. M. (1997). *The aging family.* New York: Brunner/Mazel. This easy to moderately difficult book gives a comprehensive overview of many family issues, including marriage, caregiving, and therapy.

MACE, N. L., & RABINS, P. V. (1991). *The 36-hour day* (2nd ed.). Baltimore: Johns Hopkins University Press. This is still the best available overall guide to family caregiving for dementia patients.

MACNAB, F. (1994). *The 30 vital years.* New York: Wiley. This easy-to-read book discusses psychosocial aging and includes many anecdotes and case studies.

For additional readings, explore Infotrac College Edition, your online library. Go to http://www.infotrac-college.com/wadsworth.

Web Sites

Information on all aspects of caring for older persons who are frail or who have dementia can be found at Eldercare Web. The site includes such topics as health care, living arrangements, spiritual support, financial and legal information, and regional resources. The site is at

http://www.elderweb.com

The U.S. government's Health Care Financing Administration provides a superb site describing in detail the key factors one should use in choosing a nursing home. The site gives step-by-step guides for what type of facility to consider, information to collect, visiting, and so forth. The site is at

http://www.hcfa.gov/medicare/nurshm1.htm

The official Web site of the Social Security Administration provides information about Social Security including its history, funding sources, statistics on recipients, and plans for the future. It can be found at

http://www.ssa.gov/

The official Web site for information about Medicare is sponsored by the Health Care Financing Administration of the U.S. government. The site contains much information both for the general public and for those interested in more technical background and data. The consumer information section provides a wealth of basic information about how Medicare works and its basic guidelines. The main site can be found at

http://www.hcfa.gov/medicare/medicare.htm

Consumer information about Medicare is available directly at

http://www.medicare.gov/

Web site addresses are subject to change. The Wadsworth Study Center Web site listed below can be accessed for updated links.

The Wadsworth Psychology Study Center Web Site

See http://psychology.wadsworth.com/ for practice quiz questions, internet links, updates, critical thinking exercises, discussion forums and more! The Wadsworth Psychology Study Center provides a wealth of information fully organized and integrated by chapter.

CHAPTER 15

DYING AND BEREAVEMENT

Definitions and Ethical Issues
Sociocultural Definitions of Death
Funerals
Legal and Medical Definitions
Ethical Issues
Physician-Assisted Suicide

Ideas About Death
Through the Life Span
Childhood
Adolescence
Young Adulthood
Middle Age
Late Adulthood
Understanding Death

The Process of Dying
Death Anxiety
The Stage Theory of Dying
Alternative Views
Dying with Dignity: Hospice
The Hospice Alternative
A Life-Span Developmental
    Perspective on Dying

Surviving the Loss:
The Grieving Process
The Grief Process
Normal Grief Reactions
Family Stress and Adaptation Before and
    After Bereavement
Abnormal Grief Reactions

Dealing with Different Types of Loss
Death of One's Parent
Death of One's Child
The Grief of Miscarriage
Death of One's Partner
Comparisons of Types of Loss

Putting It All Together

Summary

If You'd Like to Learn More

We have a paradoxical relationship with death. Sometimes, we are fascinated by it. As tourists, we visit places where famous people died or are buried. We watch as television newscasts show people who have been killed in war. But when it comes to pondering our own death or that of people close to us, we have many problems. As La Rochefoucauld, a French writer and reformer, wrote over 300 years ago, looking into the sun is easier than contemplating our death. When death is personal, we become uneasy. Looking at the sun is hard indeed.

In this chapter, we first consider definitional and ethical issues surrounding death. Next, we examine how people view death at different points in the life span. Third, we look specifically at the process of dying. Dealing with grief is important for survivors, so we will consider this topic in the fourth section. In the fifth section, we see how people cope with different types of loss.

DEFINITIONS AND ETHICAL ISSUES

Definitions and Ethical Issues

Sociocultural Definitions of Death

Legal and Medical Definitions

Ethical Issues

Learning Objectives

- **How is death defined?**
- **What legal and medical criteria are used to determine when death occurs?**
- **What are the ethical dilemmas surrounding euthanasia?**

*G*RETA, *a college sophomore, was very upset when she learned that her room-mate's mother had died suddenly. Her roommate is Jewish, and Greta had no idea what customs would be followed during the funeral. When Greta arrived at her roommate's house, she was surprised to find all of the mirrors in the house covered. Greta realized for the first time that death rituals vary in different religious traditions.*

Take a look at the deceased person in the photograph. When one first thinks about it, death seems a very simple concept to define: It is the point at which a person is no longer alive. Similarly, dying is simply the process of making the transition from being alive to being dead. It all seems clear enough, doesn't it? But death and dying are actually far more complicated concepts that are very hard to define.

As we will see, Greta's experience reflects the many cultural and religious differences in the definition of death and the customs surrounding it. The meaning of death depends on the observer's perspective, as well as the specific medical and biological criteria one uses.

SOCIOCULTURAL DEFINITIONS OF DEATH

What comes to mind when you hear the word *death*? A driver killed in a traffic accident? A transition to an eternal reward? Flags at half-staff? A cemetery? A car battery that doesn't work anymore? Each of these possibilities represents a way in which death can be considered in Western culture (Kalish, 1987; Kastenbaum, 1999). All cultures have their own views. Among the Melanesians, the term *mate* includes the very sick, the very old, and the dead; the term *toa* refers to all other living people (Counts & Counts, 1985). Other South Pacific cultures believe that the life force leaves the body during sleep or illness; sleep, illness, and death are considered together. Thus, people "die" several times before experiencing "final death" (Counts & Counts, 1985).

Mourning rituals and states of bereavement also vary in different cultures (Simmons, 1945). Some cultures have formalized periods of time during which certain prayers or rituals are performed. For example, after the death of a close relative, Orthodox Jews recite ritual prayers and cover all the mirrors in the house. The men slash their ties as a symbol of loss. These are the customs that Greta, the college student in the vignette, experienced. Ancestor worship, a deep respectful feeling toward individuals from whom a family is descended or who are important to them, is an important part of Japanese culture and of Buddhism in Japan (Klass, 1996a). Thus, we must keep in mind that the experiences of our culture or particular group may not generalize to other cultures or groups.

Death can be a truly cross-cultural experience. The international outpouring of grief over the death of Princess Diana in 1997, whose funeral procession is shown in the photograph, drew much attention to the ways in which the deaths of people we do not know personally can still affect us. It is at these times we realize that death happens to us all, and that death can simultaneously be personal and public.

Altogether, death can be viewed in at least 10 ways (Kalish, 1987; Kastenbaum, 1985). Look at the list that follows and think about the examples given for these definitions. Then take another moment to think up additional examples of your own.

Death as an Image or Object

A flag at half-staff

Sympathy cards

Tombstone

Black crepe paper

Hearse

Monument or memorial

Death as a Statistic

Mortality rates

Number of AIDS patients
who die

Murder and suicide rates

Life expectancy tables

Death as an Event

Funeral

Cemetery service

Family gathering

Memorial service

Viewing or wake

Death as a State of Being

Time of waiting

Nothingness

Transformation

Being happy with God all the time

State of being; pure energy

Death as an Analogy

Dead as a doornail

Dead-letter box

Dead-end street

You're dead meat

In the dead of winter

Death as a Mystery

What is it like to die?

Will we meet family?

What happens after death?

Will I learn everything when I die?

Death as a Boundary

How many years do I have left?

What happens to my family?

What do I do now?

You can't come back

Death as a Thief of Meaning

I feel so cheated

Why should I go on living?

Life doesn't mean much anymore

I have much left to do

Death as Fear and Anxiety	Death as Reward or Punishment
Will dying be painful?	Live long and prosper
I worry about my family	The wicked go to hell
I'm afraid to die	Heaven awaits the just
Who will care for the kids?	Purgatory prepares you for heaven

The many ways of viewing death can be seen in various customs involving funerals. Perhaps you have experienced a range of different types of funeral customs, from very small, private services to very elaborate rituals. Variations in the customs surrounding death are reflected in some of the oldest monuments on earth, such as the pyramids in Egypt, and some of the most beautiful, such as the Taj Mahal in India. Your experience in completing the exercise in the See for Yourself feature will give you an idea of how variations in customs involve everything from the cost of the casket to the type of funeral service, if any, people choose.

THINK ABOUT IT
Funeral customs vary around the world. How do they reflect differences in how death is viewed?

SEE FOR YOURSELF

FUNERALS

To gain firsthand knowledge of how the rituals and customs surrounding death vary across cultures, gather the following information from your local community. Visit a funeral home and learn about the different options for burial or cremation. Find out the costs associated with each option, and the range of prices and services that are available. Talk with members of various religious groups about the different types of funeral services that each uses. Bring your information to class and discuss the wide variations you have discovered. •

LEGAL AND MEDICAL DEFINITIONS

Sociocultural approaches help us understand the different ways in which people view death. But they do not address a very fundamental question: How do we determine that someone has died? The medical and legal communities have grappled with this question for centuries and continue to do so today. Let's see what the current answers are.

Determining when death occurs has always been subjective. *For hundreds of years, people accepted and applied the criteria that now define* **clinical death**: *lack of heartbeat and respiration. Today, however, the most widely accepted criteria are those that characterize* **brain death**. In 1981, the President's Commission for the Ethical Study of Problems in Medicine and Biomedical and Behavioral Research established several criteria that must be met for the determination of brain death:

1.   no spontaneous movement in response to any stimuli
2.   no spontaneous respirations for at least one hour
3.   total lack of responsiveness to even the most painful stimuli
4.   no eye movements, blinking, or pupil responses
5.   no postural activity, swallowing, yawning, or vocalizing
6.   no motor reflexes
7.   a flat electroencephalogram (EEG) for at least 10 minutes
8.   no change in any of these criteria when they are tested again 24 hours later

For a person to be declared brain dead, all eight criteria must be met. More-over, other conditions that might mimic death—such as deep coma, hypother-mia, or drug overdose—must be ruled out. Finally, according to most hospi-tals, the lack of brain activity must occur both in the brainstem, which involves vegetative functions such as heartbeat and respiration, and in the cortex, which involves higher processes such as thinking. *It is possible for a person's cortical functioning to cease while brainstem activity continues; this is a* **persistent vege-tative state,** *from which the person does not recover.* This condition can occur following a severe head injury or a drug overdose.

Because of conditions like persistent vegetative state, family members sometimes face difficult ethical decisions concerning care for the individual. These issues are the focus of the next section.

ETHICAL ISSUES

An ambulance screeches to a halt, and emergency personnel rush a woman into the emergency room. As a result of an accident at a swimming pool, she has no pulse and no respiration. Working rapidly, the trauma team reestablishes a heartbeat through electric shock. A respirator is connected. An EEG and other tests reveal extensive and irreversible brain damage. What should be done?

This is an example of the kinds of problems faced in the field of **bioethics,** *the study of the interface between human values and technological advances in health and life sciences.* Bioethics grew from two bases: respect for individual freedom and the impossibility of establishing any single version of morality by rational argument or common sense (Cole & Holstein, 1996). In practice, bioethics emphasizes the minimization of harm over the maximization of good, and the importance of individual choice.

In the arena of death and dying, the most important bioethical issue is **euthanasia**—*the practice of ending life for reasons of mercy.* The moral dilemma posed by euthanasia becomes apparent when we try to decide the circumstances under which a person's life should be ended. In our society this dilemma occurs most often when a person is being kept alive by machines or when someone is suffering from a terminal illness.

Active Euthanasia

Euthanasia can be carried out in two different ways: active and passive. **Active euthanasia** *involves the deliberate ending of someone's life, which may be based on a clear statement of the person's wishes or a decision made by someone else who has the legal authority to do so.* Usually, this involves situations in which people are in a persistent vegetative state or suffer from the end stages of a terminal disease. Examples of active euthanasia would be administering a drug overdose, disconnecting a life-support system, or ending a person's life through so-called mercy killing.

The most controversial version of active euthanasia involves physi-cian-assisted suicide. Dr. Jack Kevorkian, a physician in Michigan shown in the photo, is a strong proponent of the right to die, and he has created a suicide machine to help people end their lives. In an equally controver-sial move, voters in Oregon passed the "Death with Dignity" Act in 1994, the United State's first physician-assisted suicide law. This law makes it legal for individuals to request a lethal dose of medication providing that they have a terminal disease and make the request voluntarily. Although the U.S. Supreme Court ruled in two cases in 1997 (*Vacco v. Quill, Washington v. Glucksberg*) that there is no right to assisted suicide, the Court decided in 1998 not to overturn the Oregon law. As discussed in the Current Controversies feature, the issues concerning physician-assisted suicides will continue to be debated both publicly and in the courts.

CURRENT CONTROVERSIES

INFOTRAC
COLLEGE EDITION

To learn more, enter the following search terms: assisted suicide.

PHYSICIAN-ASSISTED SUICIDE

Should individuals have the right to obtain information that will help them end their lives soon, before enduring horrible pain that will ultimately end in death anyway? Should physicians be permitted to give that information and provide assistance if the patient asks? What do you think?

Taking one's own life has never been popular in the United States due to religious and other prohibitions. In other cultures, such as Japan, suicide is viewed as an honorable way to die under certain circumstances. Some countries, like the Netherlands, allow physicians to assist people who want to commit suicide (Cutter, 1991). In 1984, the Dutch Supreme Court eliminated prosecution of physicians who assist in suicide if five criteria are met:

1. The patient's condition is intolerable with no hope for improvement.
2. No relief is available.
3. The patient is competent.
4. The patient makes a request repeatedly over time.
5. Two physicians agree with the patient's request.

As noted, voters in Oregon passed the first physician-assisted suicide law in the United States so that a terminally ill person may obtain a prescription for medication for the purpose of ending his or her life. The Oregon law is similar to the situation in the Netherlands. The law requires that physicians inform the person that he or she is terminally ill, and of alternative options (e.g., hospice care, pain control); the person must be mentally competent and make two oral requests and a written one, with at least 15 days between each oral request. Such provisions are included to ensure that people making the request fully understand the issues, and that the request is not made hastily.

Although many people support a person's right to decide when to die, many people do not. The differences of opinions have resulted in several court challenges to the right to die. Bioethicists must make the dilemmas clear, and we must make ourselves aware of the issues. What is at stake is literally a matter of life and death. What do you think? •

? THINK ABOUT IT
What kinds of safeguards are needed to ensure that Oregon's physician-assisted suicide law is not misused?

Passive Euthanasia

A second form of euthanasia, **passive euthanasia,** *involves allowing a person to die by withholding available treatment.* For example, chemotherapy might be withheld from a cancer patient; a surgical procedure might not be performed; or food could be withdrawn. Again, these approaches are controversial. On the one hand, few would argue with a decision not to treat a newly discovered cancer in a person in the late stages of Alzheimer's disease, if treatment would do nothing but prolong and make even more agonizing an already certain death. On the other hand, many people might argue against withholding nourishment from a terminally ill person; indeed, such cases often end up in court. For example, in 1990 the U.S. Supreme Court took up the case of Nancy Cruzan, whose family wanted to end her forced feeding. The court ruled that unless clear and incontrovertible evidence is presented that an individual desires to have nourishment stopped, such as through a durable power of attorney or living will, a third party, such as a parent or partner, cannot decide to end it.

Euthanasia is a complex legal and ethical issue. In most jurisdictions, euthanasia is legal only when a person has made known his or her wishes concerning medical intervention. Unfortunately, many people fail to take this step, perhaps because it is difficult to think about such situations or because they do not know the options available to them. But without clear directions, medical personnel may be unable to take a patient's preferences into account.

There are two ways to make one's intentions known: living wills, in which a person simply states his or her wishes about life support and other treatments, and durable power of attorney, like the one shown below. The purpose of both is to make known people's wishes about the use of life support, in the event they are unconscious or otherwise incapable of expressing them (Freer & Clark, 1994). A durable power of attorney has an additional advantage: It names an individual who has the legal authority to speak for the person if necessary. Although there is considerable support for both mechanisms, there are several problems as well. Many people fail to inform their relatives and physicians about their health care decisions. Others do not tell the person named in a durable power of attorney where the document is kept. Obviously, this puts relatives at a serious disadvantage if decisions concerning the use of life-support systems need to be made.

A living will or a durable power of attorney can be the basis for a "Do Not Resuscitate" (DNR) medical order. A DNR order applies only to cardiopulmonary resuscitation should one's heart and breathing stop. In the normal

California Medical Association
DURABLE POWER OF ATTORNEY FOR HEALTH CARE DECISIONS
(California Probate Code Sections 4600-4753)

WARNING TO PERSON EXECUTING THIS DOCUMENT

This is an important legal document. Before executing this document, you should know these important facts:

This document gives the person you designate as your agent (the attorney-in-fact) the power to make health care decisions for you. Your agent must act consistently with your desires as stated in this document or otherwise made known.

Except as you otherwise specify in this document, this document gives your agent power to consent to your doctor not giving treatment or stopping treatment necessary to keep you alive.

Notwithstanding this document, you have the right to make medical and other health care decisions for yourself so long as you can give informed consent with respect to the particular decision. In addition, no treatment may be given to you over your objection, and health care necessary to keep you alive may not be stopped or withheld if you object at the time.

This document gives your agent authority to consent, to refuse to consent, or to withdraw consent to any care, treatment, service, or procedure to maintain, diagnose, or treat a physical or mental condition. This power is subject to any statement of your desires and any limitations that you include in this document. You may

state in this document any types of treatment that you do not desire. In addition, a court can take away the power of your agent to make health care decisions for you if your agent (1) authorizes anything that is illegal, (2) acts contrary to your known desires or (3) where your desires are not known, does anything that is clearly contrary to your best interests.

This power will exist for an indefinite period of time unless you limit its duration in this document.

You have the right to revoke the authority of your agent by notifying your agent or your treating doctor, hospital, or other health care provider orally or in writing of the revocation.

Your agent has the right to examine your medical records and to consent to their disclosure unless you limit this right in this document.

Unless you otherwise specify in this document, this document gives your agent the power after you die to (1) authorize an autopsy, (2) donate your body or parts thereof for transplant or therapeutic or educational or scientific purposes, and (3) direct the disposition of your remains.

If there is anything in this document that you do not understand, you should ask a lawyer to explain it to you.

1. CREATION OF DURABLE POWER OF ATTORNEY FOR HEALTH CARE

By this document I intend to create a durable power of attorney by appointing the person designated below to make health care decisions for me as allowed by Sections 4600 to 4753, inclusive, of the California Probate Code. This power of attorney shall not be affected by my subsequent incapacity. I hereby revoke any prior durable power of attorney for health care. I am a California resident who is at least 18 years old, of sound mind, and acting of my own free will.

2. APPOINTMENT OF HEALTH CARE AGENT

(Fill in below the name, address and telephone number of the person you wish to make health care decisions for you if you become incapacitated. You should make sure that this person agrees to accept this responsibility. The following may not serve as your agent: (1) your treating health care provider; (2) an operator of a community care facility or residential care facility for the elderly; or (3) an employee of your treating health care provider, a community care facility, or a residential care facility for the elderly, unless that employee is related to you by blood, marriage or adoption, or unless you are also an employee of the same treating provider or facility. If you are a conservatee under the Lanterman-Petris-Short Act (the law governing involuntary commitment to a mental health facility) and you wish to appoint your conservator as your agent, you must consult a lawyer, who must sign and attach a special declaration for this document to be valid.)

I, _____, hereby appoint:
               (insert your name)

Name _____

Address _____

Work Telephone (_____) _____   Home Telephone (_____) _____

as my agent (attorney-in-fact) to make health care decisions for me as authorized in this document. I understand that this power of attorney will be effective for an indefinite period of time unless I revoke it or limit its duration below.

(Optional) This power of attorney shall expire on the following date: _____.

© California Medical Association 1996 (revised)

course of events, a medical team will immediately try to restore normal heart-beat and respiration. With a DNR order, this treatment is not done. As with living wills and durable powers of attorney, it is very important to let all appropriate medical personnel know that a DNR order is desired.

TEST YOURSELF

1. The phrase "dead as a doornail" is an example of the sociocultural definition of death as _____ .

2. The difference between brain death and a persistent vegetative state is _____ .

3. Withholding an antibiotic from a person who dies as a result is an example of _____ .

4. Describe how people at each level of Kohlberg's theory of moral reasoning (described in Chapter 9) would deal with the issue of euthanasia.

Answers: (1) an analogy, (2) the brainstem still functions in a persistent vegetative state, (3) passive euthanasia

IDEAS ABOUT DEATH THROUGH THE LIFE SPAN

Ideas About Death Through the Life Span

Childhood

Adolescence

Young Adulthood

Middle Age

Late Adulthood

Learning Objectives

- **What do children understand about death? How should adults help them deal with it?**
- **What concerns do adolescents have about death?**
- **How do young adults view death?**
- **What issues about death are most important for middle-aged adults?**
- **How do older adults view death?**

*D*ONNA AND CARL *have a 6-year-old daughter, Jennie, whose grandmother just died. Jennie and her grandmother were very close, as the two saw each other almost every day. Other adults have told her parents not to take Jennie to the funeral. Donna and Carl aren't sure what to do. They wonder whether Jennie will understand what happened to her grandmother, and they worry about how she will react.*

Coming to grips with the reality of death is probably one of the hardest things we have to do in life. American society does not help much either, as it tends to distance itself from death through euphemisms, such as "passed away" or "dearly departed," and by relocating many rituals from the home or church to the funeral parlor.

These trends make it difficult for people like Donna, Carl, and Jennie to learn about death in its natural context. Dying itself has been moved from the home to hospitals and other institutions such as nursing homes. The closest most people get to death is a quick glance inside a nicely lined casket at a corpse that has been made to look as if the person were still alive.

What do people, especially children like Jennie, understand about death? How do Donna and Carl feel? In this section, we consider how our understanding of death changes through the life span.

CHILDHOOD

Parents often take their children to funerals of relatives and close friends. But many adults, like Donna and Carl in the vignette, wonder whether young children really know what death means. Young preschool-age children tend to believe that death is temporary and magical. They think it is something dramatic that comes to get you in the middle of the night like a burglar or a ghost (Dickinson, 1992). Not until 5–7 years of age do children like those in the photograph realize that death is permanent, that it eventually happens to everyone, and that dead people no longer have any biological functions (Silverman & Nickman, 1996).

Why does this shift occur? Think back to Chapters 4 and 6, especially to the discussion of Piaget's theory of cognitive development. Take Jennie, the 6-year-old daughter of Donna and Carl in the vignette. Where would she be in Piaget's terms? In this perspective, the ages 5–7 include the transition from preoperational to concrete-operational thinking. Concrete-operational thinking permits children to know that death is final and permanent. Therefore, Jennie is likely to understand what happened to her grandmother.

First Experiences

The first time a child experiences the death of a relative or a pet, they are very vulnerable (Attig, 1996). Children have no prior experience to help them come to terms with the event. Research indicates that children show a range of responses (Normand, Silverman, & Nickman, 1996). Some find it highly traumatic, whereas others appear less affected. Many children feel afraid, alone, and upset. Some children try to cry and find they cannot. They are likely to ask adults many questions about death rituals. Like the boy in the cartoon, children feel the loss of relatives and miss them during special family times.

"I wish Granddad could've been at the reunion, too."

FAMILY CIRCUS, ©1993. Reprinted with special permission of King Features Syndicate.

Many children first experience death when a pet dies (Dickinson, 1992). There seems to be little difference in children's reactions to the death of a relative and the death of a pet, as the following example shows.

> I had a cute little hamster. I think we had been talking about hibernation in school because when I came home and found the hamster lying there, I thought he was hibernating! My next door neighbor, Sharon, came over and said that if we warmed him up then he would come back to life. So I put him in my electric blanket to see if he would wake up. He never did and by that time my mom realized what had happened, so we had to bury him. My brother and I put him in the shoebox, put a blanket in there to keep him warm and a picture of us to keep him company. Then we buried him in the backyard. (Dickinson, 1992, p. 177)

Adults must be sensitive to children's needs at the time of a death, even that of a pet. How adults handle such situations could later help the child deal with the death of a relative (Attig, 1996; Dickinson, 1992).

Children often react to and understand death much more like adults than adults might think. Young adults, looking back on their first encounter with death as children, report having many of the feelings adults have: They're angry, confused, disbelieving, fearful, relieved, guilty, sad, and empty (Buchsbaum, 1996; Dickinson, 1992). One male college student recalled how, when he was 9, his father helped him deal with his feelings after his grandfather's death:

> The day of my grandfather's death my dad came over to my aunt and uncle's house where my brother and I were staying. He took us into one of the bedrooms and sat us down. He told us Grandaddy Doc had died. He explained to us that it was okay if we needed to cry. He told us that he had cried, and that if we did cry we wouldn't be babies, but would just be men showing our emotions. (Dickinson, 1992, pp. 175–176)

It is important for children to know that it is okay for them to feel sad, to cry, or to show their feelings in whatever way they want. Such reassurance helps children deal with their confusion at adults' explanations of death. Young adults remember feeling uncomfortable as children around dead bodies, often fearing that the deceased person would come after them. Still, researchers believe it is very important for children to attend the funeral of a relative. Even though they tend to remember few details immediately, their overall recovery is enhanced (Silverman & Worden, 1992).

Understanding death can be particularly difficult for children when adults are not open and honest with them, especially about the meaning of death (Buchsbaum, 1996). The use of euphemisms, such as "Grandma has gone away" or "Mommy is only sleeping," is unwise. Young children do not understand the deeper level of meaning in such statements; they are likely to take them literally (Attig, 1996; Silverman & Nickman, 1996).

When explaining death to children, it is best to deal with them on their terms. Keep explanations simple, at a level they can understand. Try to allay their fears and reassure them that whatever reaction they have is okay. Providing loving support for the child will maximize the potential for a successful (albeit painful) introduction to one of life's realities.

? THINK ABOUT IT
How would your explanation of death differ when talking to 4-year-olds vs. 8-year-olds?

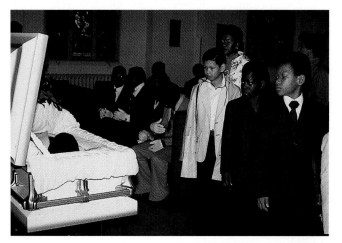

ADOLESCENCE

Adolescence is a time of personal and physical change, when one is trying to develop a theory of self. When teenagers experience the death of someone close to them, they may have considerable trouble making sense of the event (Hogan & DeSantis, 1996).

In general, adolescents are reluctant to discuss death and dying. As we saw in Chapter 8, adolescents have a sense that they are immortal, that nothing bad will happen to them. Even though they may come in contact with death through the loss of a friend or a friend's sibling or parent, adolescents like those in the photograph tend to believe that nothing similar will happen to them. Therefore, they are unlikely to come forward to discuss their feelings and fears (Kastenbaum, 1985).

In contrast to common belief, adolescents often do not demonstrate a clear end point to their grief, especially when the loss involves a parent or sibling (Hogan & DeSantis, 1996). For example, bereaved adolescent siblings continue to miss and to love their dead siblings and to anticipate their eventual reunion in the afterlife. However, grief does not interfere with normative developmental processes. Bereaved adolescent siblings experience continued personal growth following the death of a person to whom they were attached, in much the same way as adolescents who did not experience the loss of such a person (Hogan & DeSantis, 1996).

YOUNG ADULTHOOD

Because young adults are just beginning to pursue the family, career, and personal goals they have set, they tend to be more intense in their feelings toward death. When asked how they feel about death, young adults report a strong sense that those who die at this point in their lives would be cheated out of their future (Attig, 1996; Pattison, 1977).

Understanding how young adults deal with death is best understood from the perspective of attachment theory (Balk, 1996; Jacobs, 1993). In this view, a person's reactions are a natural consequence of forming attachments and then losing them. We will consider adult grief a bit later in the chapter.

Although not specifically addressed in research, the shift from formal-operational to postformal thinking could be an important one in young adults' contemplation of death. Presumably, this shift in cognitive development is accompanied by a lessening of the feeling of immortality, as young adults begin to integrate personal feelings and emotions with their thinking.

> **? THINK ABOUT IT**
> What specific characteristics of postformal thinking would be most helpful in dealing with death?

MIDDLE AGE

Midlife is the time when most people confront the death of their parents. Until that point, people tend not to think much about their own death (see Chapter 12); the fact that their parents are still alive buffers them from this issue. After all, in the normal course of events, our parents are supposed to die before we do.

Once their parents have died, people realize that they are now the oldest generation of their family—the next in line to die. Reading the obituary pages, they are reminded of this, as the ages of many of the people who have died get closer and closer to their own.

Probably as a result of this growing realization of their own mortality, middle-aged adults' sense of time undergoes a subtle yet profound change. It changes from an emphasis on how long they have already lived to how long they have left to live (Attig, 1996; Neugarten, 1969). This may lead to occupational change or other redirection such as improving relationships that had deteriorated over the years (see Chapter 12).

LATE ADULTHOOD

In general, older adults are less anxious about death and more accepting of it than any other age group (Kastenbaum, 1999; Keller, Sherry, & Piotrkowski, 1984). In part, this is due to the achievement of ego integrity, as described in

Chapter 14 (pages 534–535). For many older adults, the joy of living is diminishing (Kalish, 1987). More than any other group, they have experienced loss of family and friends and have come to terms with their own mortality. Older adults have more chronic diseases, which are not likely to just go away. They may feel that their most important life tasks have been completed (Kastenbaum, 1999).

Learning about and dealing with death is clearly a developmental process across the life span. As noted in the Forces in Action feature, it reflects the integration of biological, psychological, and sociocultural forces.

FORCES IN ACTION | **UNDERSTANDING DEATH**

Understanding death is not a topic in which you expect to see the biopsychosocial framework in action. Actually, the framework provides an excellent way to tie together several different threads. Most apparent is that biological forces are essential to understanding death. The very definition of death is based on whether certain biological functions are present; these same definitions create numerous ethical dilemmas that must be dealt with psychologically and socioculturally. Life-cycle forces also play a key role. We have seen that the same concept—death—has varied meanings beyond the mere cessation of life depending on people's age.

How a person's understanding of death develops is also the result of psychological forces. As the ability to think and reflect undergoes fundamental change, the view of death changes from a mostly magical approach to one that can be transcendent and transforming. As we see in the next section, people who are facing their own imminent death experience certain stages based on their feelings at the time. Having gained experience through the deaths of friends and relatives, a person's level of comfort with his or her own death may increase. Such personal experience may also come about by sharing rituals, defined through sociocultural forces. People observe how others deal with death and how the culture sets the tone and prescribes behavior for survivors. The combined action of forces also determines how they cope with the grief that accompanies the loss of someone close. Psychologically, confronting grief depends on many things, including the quality of the support system we have. We examine grief later in this chapter. •

TEST YOURSELF

1. In general, adults should avoid _____ when discussing death with children.

2. Adolescents are usually more concerned with the quality of their lives than _____ .

3. Young adults faced with death feel _____ .

4. An important concern of middle-aged adults is _____ .

5. In general, older adults are _____ about death.

6. How do the different ways that adults view death relate to the stages of Erikson's theory discussed in Chapters 9, 11, 12, and 14?

Answers: (1) euphemisms, (2) how long they will live, (3) cheated out of their lives, (4) their growing realization of their own mortality, (5) less anxious

THE PROCESS OF DYING

Learning Objectives

- **What is death anxiety?**
- **What are the stages of dying?**
- **How does the phase theory of dying differ from the stage theory?**
- **How does dying differ through the life span?**

The Process of Dying

Death Anxiety

The Stage Theory of Dying

Alternative Views

Dying with Dignity: Hospice

A Life-Span Developmental Perspective
  on Dying

BETTY, *48 years old, was recently diagnosed with terminal ovarian cancer. She is having trouble dealing with the news. Betty wonders why she ended up with the disease rather than someone else, and she is very angry about it. Betty wonders whether her feelings are normal.*

Like Betty, most people are uncomfortable thinking about their own death. Completing the short exercise below might provide you with some interesting insights into your own anxieties about death.

A Self-Reflective Exercise on Death

1. In 200 words or less, write your own obituary. Be sure to include your age and cause of death. List your lifetime accomplishments. Don't forget to list your survivors.
2. Think about all the things you will have done that are not listed in your obituary. List some of them.
3. Think of all the friends you will have made and how you will have affected them.
4. Would you make any changes in your obituary now?

Well, how was it to think about your own death? Most people report feeling a little uncomfortable at first, but then getting more comfortable as they allow themselves through this process to reflect on their life and its meaning.

These exercises are preparation for asking the really tough questions that, like Betty, we all must eventually address: Why are we so anxious about dying? What is it like to die? How do terminally ill people feel about dying? Are people more concerned about dying as they grow older? To answer these questions, scholars have developed theories of dying, based on interviews and other methods. The theories show that dying is complex and that our thoughts, concerns, and feelings change as we move closer to death. We examine two ways of conceptualizing the dying process: a stage approach and a phase approach. We will also consider how the feelings of dying people vary as a function of age.

DEATH ANXIETY

At some point during our lives, most of us have at least one moment in which we experience **death anxiety,** *the fear over the reality of our eventual death.* Perhaps it is for this reason that the earliest research on dying focused on death anxiety. Since the 1970s, for example, we have known that death anxiety includes concerns over pain, bodily malfunctioning, humiliation, rejection, nonbeing, punishment, interruption of personal goals, and negative effects on survivors (Schulz, 1978). Research also shows that trying to identify which variables predict higher (or lower) death anxiety is difficult; for example, contrary to popular belief, religious beliefs are not directly related to death anxiety (Kalish, 1985).

Developmentally, the level of death anxiety one feels varies by age (Gesser, Wong, & Reker, 1987–88). Middle-aged adults are typically the most anxious, older adults the least anxious, and younger adults are in between. Higher anxiety in middle-aged adults makes sense, given that psychologically they are trying to deal with their own mortality and their parents' failing health (see Chapter 12). Older adults have experienced death as part of their lives in many ways for a long time (Kastenbaum, 1999). It may also be the case that older adults have successfully resolved Erikson's issues of intimacy, generativity, and ego integrity, which in turn may help them accept the inevitability of their own death.

THE STAGE THEORY OF DYING

Imagine interacting with dying people every day in your job and being actively discouraged from talking to them about their feelings. This seems strange to us, but that was the accepted practice in the medical profession even in the 1960s.

Such was the situation confronting one of the most influential people in the history of research and theory on dying, Elisabeth Kübler-Ross (shown in the photo), a physician in Chicago who wanted to help four seminary students conduct research on how people cope with impending death. In 1965, such research was quite controversial; her physician colleagues were initially outraged, and some even denied that their patients were terminally ill. Still, Kübler-Ross persisted and obtained permission to do the study. Eventually, she conducted over 200 interviews with terminally ill people. Kübler-Ross became convinced that most dying people follow a sequence of emotional reactions. Using her observations, she developed a sequence of five stages to describe the process of an appropriate death: denial, anger, bargaining, depression, and acceptance (Kübler-Ross, 1969).

When people like Betty, the woman in the vignette, are told that they have a terminal illness, their first reaction is likely to be shock and disbelief. *Denial* is a normal part of getting ready to die. Some people shop around for a more favorable diagnosis, and most feel that a mistake has been made. Others try to find reassurance in religion. Eventually, though, most people accept the diagnosis and begin to feel angry.

In the *anger* stage, people express hostility, resentment, and envy toward health care workers, family, and friends. Like Betty, they ask, "Why me?" and express a great deal of frustration. It seems so unfair that they are going to die when so many others will live. As the person deals with these feelings, they begin to diminish, and the person enters the bargaining stage.

In the *bargaining* stage, people look for a way out. Maybe a deal can be struck with someone (perhaps God) to allow survival. For example, a woman might promise to be a better mother if only she could live. Eventually, the individual becomes aware that such deals aren't going to happen.

When the illness can no longer be denied, perhaps due to surgery or pain, feelings of *depression* are very common. People report feeling deep loss, sorrow, guilt, and shame over their illness and its consequences. Kübler-Ross believes that discussing their feelings with others helps move them to an acceptance of death.

In the *acceptance* stage, the person accepts the inevitability of death. He or she often seems detached from the world and at complete peace. "It is as if the pain is gone, the struggle is over, and there comes a time for the 'final rest before the journey'" (Kübler-Ross, 1969, p. 100).

Although Kübler-Ross (1974) believes that these five stages represent the typical course of emotional development in the dying, she cautions that not everyone goes through all of them or progresses through them at the same rate or in the same order. Progression through the stages depends on people's physical health, their view of death, and many other factors. If we recognize that these individual differences are normal, Kübler-Ross's stages help people understand that feelings about dying change over time.

Subsequent research supports the idea that Kübler-Ross's stages are better viewed as reflecting the range of feelings people have rather than a rigid sequence. Cross-cultural research shows that the stages reflect a particular set of cultural expectations that are not true universally. Of her stages, only depression appears to be a universal experience in Western cultures (Shneidman, 1980). Some Plains Indian tribes compose a death song to describe an individual's life and complete the cycle, and Mexicans believe that the way you die is a reflection of the kind of person you have been, so open discussion of death occurs frequently (DeSpelder & Strickland, 1983).

ALTERNATIVE VIEWS

Kübler-Ross conceptualized dying as a series of discrete stages. The decades since her landmark research have produced several alternative views that capture the essence of the major criticisms of her approach. Two of the most important regard dying as consisting of phases or as a series of tasks that people need to address. Both approaches agree with Kübler-Ross in considering dying as a process.

The Phase Theory of Dying

Pattison (1977) argued that dying people do not traverse a sequence of stages in a fixed order. Rather, they experience a complex set of emotions that mix knowledge of their imminent death with anxiety and eventual acceptance. These phases are represented in the diagram at the top of page 588.

The *acute phase* begins when the individual becomes aware that his or her condition is terminal. This phase is marked by a high level of anxiety, denial, anger, and even bargaining. In time, the person adjusts to the idea of being terminally ill, and anxiety gradually declines. During this *chronic living-dying*

? THINK ABOUT IT
How could the stages of dying be used to help people deal with death?

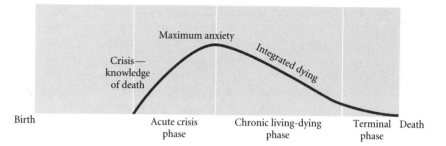

phase, a person generally has many contradictory feelings that must be integrated. These include fear of loneliness, fear of the unknown, and anticipatory grief over the loss of friends, of body, of self-control, and of identity (Pattison, 1977). These feelings of fear and grief exist simultaneously or alternate with feelings of hope, determination, and acceptance (Shneidman, 1973). Finally, the *terminal phase* begins, and the individual starts to withdraw from the world. This last phase is the shortest, and it ends with death.

Task-Based Approach to Dying

Although the phase approach to dying has several proponents, others argue that *any* attempt to put people's feelings into any kind of order is inappropriate (e.g., Shneidman, 1980). Rather, the notion is that dying is really a process in which people deal with certain themes, such as fear, uncertainty, denial, feelings of unfairness, battling pain, and so forth.

In this context, Corr (1991–92) proposed a task-based approach for understanding and describing how people cope with dying. He proposed four primary dimensions of coping:

1. satisfying physical needs and minimizing physical stress
2. maximizing psychological security, autonomy, and living life to the fullest
3. sustaining and enhancing important interpersonal attachments
4. identifying, developing, or reaffirming sources of spiritual energy to foster hope

Corr argued that these tasks incorporate the various themes discussed by other researchers and theorists, but do so in a way that is very helpful to health care workers and other helpers. By emphasizing the tasks that dying people have to perform, everyone who interacts with a dying person can do so in a positive way, and may offer assistance with a specific task to the dying person.

DYING WITH DIGNITY: HOSPICE

Theories of dying agree that how people deal with their own death is a complicated process. The range of emotions people experience take many forms and often occur simultaneously. In the same time frame, people may take a last vacation and update their will, feel sad and resigned about the fact they will die. Clearly, the task of care providers is to understand the unique responses and needs of terminally ill individuals. People must stay in touch with the dying person's (and their own) feelings and be available for support. In this way, people can be helped to die with dignity.

Dying with dignity is an important right of every individual; ensuring this right is one of the goals of hospice. **Hospice** *is a holistic approach to care that emphasizes quality of life and personal comfort.* As described in the You May Be

Wondering feature, hospice is a movement that began out of concern for terminally ill people. Hospice represents a key aspect of end-of-life care because it focuses on pain management and control (Zuckerman, 1997). Hospice seeks to provide a supportive environment for dying people by keeping families engaged in caregiving and by providing professional assistance during this very stressful time (Kastenbaum, 1999). Hospice care is an important option for people of all ages (Corr & Corr, 1992a, 1992b).

THE HOSPICE ALTERNATIVE

Consider how dying people should be treated and how they themselves face death. Clearly, the right to die with dignity is important. For many people, death with dignity means being with family and friends when they die, preferably at home. Hospice offers hope in this regard (Holstein, 1997; Koff, 1981). The emphasis in a hospice is on the quality of life. The concern is to make the person as peaceful and comfortable as possible, not to delay an inevitable death. Although medical care is available at a hospice, it is aimed primarily at controlling pain and restoring normal functioning, whereas medical care at a hospital usually attempts to cure the disease (Holstein, 1997; Saunders, 1997).

Modern hospices are modeled after St. Christopher's Hospice in England, founded in 1967 by Dr. Cicely Saunders. The services offered by a hospice are requested only after the person or physician believes that no treatment or cure is possible. Thus, the hospice program is markedly different from hospital care or home care. The differences are evident in the principles that underlie hospice care: Clients and their families are viewed as a unit; clients should be kept free of pain; emotional and social impoverishment must be minimal; clients must be encouraged to maintain competencies; conflict resolution and fulfillment of realistic desires must be assisted; clients must be free to begin or end relationships; and staff members must seek to alleviate pain and fear (Saunders, 1977, 1997).

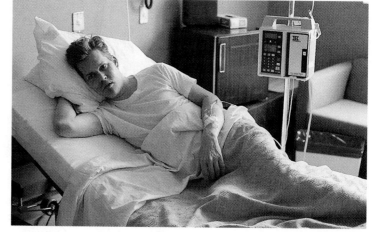

Two types of hospices exist: inpatient and outpatient. Inpatient hospices provide all care for clients; AIDS patients, like the man in the photograph, are often cared for in these facilities. Outpatient hospices provide services to clients who remain in their own homes. The latter variation is becoming increasingly popular, largely because more clients can be served at a lower cost.

Researchers have documented important differences between inpatient hospices and hospitals (Saunders & Kastenbaum, 1997; VandenBos, DeLeon, & Pallack, 1982). In contrast to hospitals, the primary aim of the hospice is comfort care; hospitals usually use more aggressive treatment approaches. A person is admitted to a hospice only after the diagnosis of a terminal disease, which usually means that the person is given less than six months to live by two physicians. Hospice clients are more mobile, less anxious, and less depressed; spouses visit hospice clients more often and participate more actively in their care; and hospice staff members are perceived as more accessible. In addition, most hospice clients who have been in hospitals before coming to a hospice strongly prefer the care at the hospice (Walsh & Cavanaugh, 1984).

Although hospice is a valuable alternative for many people, it may not be appropriate for everyone (Holstein, 1997). Some disorders require treatments or equipment not available at inpatient hospices, and some people may find that a hospice does not meet their needs or fit with their personal beliefs. The perceived needs of hospice clients, their families, and the staff do not always coincide. Often, the staff and family members emphasize pain management, whereas many of the clients want more attention paid to personal issues, such as talking directly about death or about their religious beliefs (Walsh & Cavanaugh, 1984). Staff and family members should ask clients what they need, rather than making assumptions about what they need.

Although a hospice offers an important alternative to a hospital or other institution as a place to die, it is not always available. For example, older adults who are slowly dying but whose time of death is uncertain may not be eligible, as many hospices are only able to take in clients who have six months or less to live. Meeting the needs of these other dying individuals will be a challenge for future health care providers. •

A LIFE-SPAN DEVELOPMENTAL PERSPECTIVE ON DYING

The feelings associated with death and dying are personal and powerful. Yet we know from Chapter 1 that life-cycle forces are important ingredients in understanding the richness of any developmental issue. So it is with feelings associated with dying.

Take a look at the four people in the photographs. Think for a minute how you would react to the news that each of these people had died in a plane crash. How would you feel? Would your feelings be different for the different individuals? In this section, we briefly examine how the age of a dying person changes the way death is viewed and experienced.

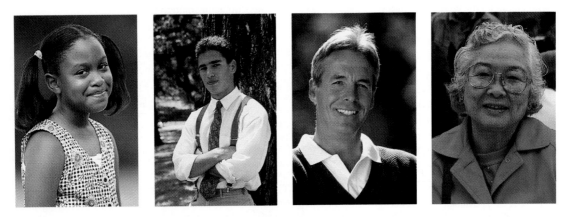

Intellectually, we realize that dying is not something that happens only to one age group. But most of us tend not to think about it, because we prefer to associate dying with old age. Death knows no age limits, yet one person's death often seems more acceptable than another's (Kastenbaum, 1985, 1999). The death of a 95-year-old woman is considered natural; she has lived a long, full life. But the death of an infant is considered to be a tragedy. Whether or not such feelings are justified, they point to the fact that death is viewed and experienced differently depending on age.

Children die from acute diseases and accidents, young adults die mainly from accidents, and the old die mainly from chronic diseases such as heart disease and cancer (National Center for Health Statistics, 1997). Because people of different ages die in different ways, their dying processes differ (Kalish, 1985), a point not usually made by theorists. Most notably, older adults' dying trajectory is longer, and they are more likely to die in isolation than any other age group (Kastenbaum, 1999). From the perspective of Corr's theory, older adults have a more difficult time successfully completing the tasks of dying.

Many of the concerns of dying individuals have to do with their age (Kalish, 1987). The most obvious difference comes in the extent to which people feel cheated, or possibly angry in Kübler-Ross's approach. Younger people feel cheated in that they are losing what they might attain; older adults feel cheated that they are losing what they have. Beyond these general differences, not much is known about how people of various ages differ in how they face death.

One important factor that affects dying older adults is that their deaths are viewed by the community as less tragic than the deaths of younger people (Kalish & Reynolds, 1976; Kastenbaum, 1985). Consequently, older adults receive less intense life-saving treatment and are perceived as less valuable and not as worthy of a large investment of time, money, or energy. "The terminally ill aged may be as helpless as a child, but they seldom arouse tenderness" (Weisman, 1972, p. 144). Many dying older adults reside in long-term care facilities, where contacts with family and friends are fewer. Older adults, especially the ill and the frail, offer less to their communities. Consequently, when their death occurs, the emotional pain is not as great, because the resulting losses are viewed as less significant and meaningful (Kalish, 1987; Kastenbaum, 1999).

This does not mean that the deaths of older adults are not felt deeply by family and friends. On the contrary. The loss is felt across the generations (Anderson, 1997). It is simply that society at large puts less emotional "value" on the death of older people than on children and young adults. In the next section, we will see how individuals deal with the loss of someone close to them.

? THINK ABOUT IT
One argument against physician-assisted suicide is that it will lead to wholesale euthanasia. How does the view of older adults' deaths relate to this concern?

TEST YOURSELF

1. Feeling uncomfortable thinking about your own death is a manifestation of _____ .

2. The five stages of dying are denial, anger, _____ , depression, and acceptance.

3. When an individual begins withdrawing from the world, he or she has entered the _____ phase of dying.

4. A _____ is a place that focuses on pain management for the terminally ill rather than treatment.

5. Older adults mainly die from _____ .

6. How would being in a hospice facilitate people's coming to terms with their death?

Answers: (1) death anxiety, (2) bargaining, (3) terminal, (4) hospice, (5) chronic diseases

SURVIVING THE LOSS: THE GRIEVING PROCESS

Learning Objectives

- **How do people experience the grief process?**
- **What feelings do grieving people have?**
- **What is the difference between normal and abnormal grief?**

Surviving the Loss:
The Grieving Process
The Grief Process
Normal Grief Reactions
Abnormal Grief Reactions

FTER 67 years of marriage, Bertha recently lost her husband. At 90, Bertha knew that neither she nor her husband was likely to live much longer, but the death was a shock just the same. Bertha thinks about him much of the time and often finds herself making decisions on the basis of "what John would have done" in the same situation.

Each of us suffers many losses over a lifetime. Whenever we lose someone close to us through death or other separation, like Bertha we experience bereavement, grief, and mourning. **Bereavement** *is the state or condition caused by loss through death.* **Grief** *is the sorrow, hurt, anger, guilt, confusion, and other feelings that arise after suffering a loss.* **Mourning** *concerns the ways in which we express our grief.* For example, you can tell that the woman in the photograph is bereaved and in mourning because of her black dress and the veil covering her face. Mourning is highly influenced by culture. For some, mourning may involve wearing black, attending funerals, and observing an official period of grief; for others, it means drinking, wearing white, and marrying the deceased spouse's sibling. Grief corresponds to the emotional reactions following loss, whereas mourning is the culturally approved behavioral manifestations of those feelings. Even though mourning rituals may be fairly standard within a culture, how people grieve varies, as we see next. We will also see how Bertha's reactions are fairly typical of most people.

THE GRIEF PROCESS

How do people grieve? What do they experience? Perhaps you already have a good idea about the answers to these questions from your own experience. If so, you already know that the process of grieving is a complicated and personal one. Just as there is no right way to die, there is no right way to grieve. Recognizing that there are plenty of individual differences, we consider these patterns in this section.

The grieving process is often described as reflecting many themes and issues that people confront (Attig, 1996; Stroebe et al., 1996). Like the process of dying, grieving does not have clearly demarcated stages through which we pass in a neat sequence. When someone close to us dies, we must reorganize our lives, establish new patterns of behavior, and redefine relationships with family and friends. Indeed, Attig (1996) considers grief to be the process by which we relearn the world.

Unlike bereavement, over which we have no control, grief is a process that involves choices in coping (Attig, 1996). From this perspective, grief is an active process in which a person must do several things (Worden, 1991):

- *Acknowledge the reality of the loss.* We must overcome the temptation to deny the reality of our loss, fully and openly acknowledge it, and realize that it affects every aspect of our life.

- *Work through the emotional turmoil.* We must find effective ways to confront and express the complete range of emotions we feel after the loss, and must not avoid or repress them.

- *Adjust to the environment where the deceased is absent.* We must define new patterns of living that adjust appropriately and meaningfully to the fact that the deceased is not present.

- *Loosen ties to the deceased.* We must free ourselves from the bonds of the deceased in order to re-engage with our social network. This means finding effective ways to say goodbye.

The notion that grief is an active coping process emphasizes that survivors must come to terms with the physical world of things, places, and events, as well as our spiritual place in the world; the interpersonal world of interactions with family and friends, the dead, and, in some cases, God; and aspects of our inner selves and our personal experiences (Attig, 1996). Bertha, the woman in the vignette, is in the middle of this process. Like the woman in the photograph, even the matter of deciding what to do with the deceased's personal effects can be part of this active coping process (Attig, 1996).

In considering the grief process, we must avoid making several mistakes. First, grieving is a highly individual experience. The process that works well for one person may not be the best for someone else. Second, we must not underestimate the amount of time people need to deal with the various issues. To a casual observer, it may appear that a survivor is "back to normal" after a few weeks. Actually, it takes much longer to resolve the complex emotional issues that are faced during bereavement (Attig, 1996; Stroebe et al., 1996). Researchers and therapists alike agree that a person needs at least 1 year following the loss to begin recovery, and 2 years is not uncommon. Finally, *recovery* may be a misleading term. It is probably more accurate to say that we learn to live with our loss rather than that we recover from it (Attig, 1996). The impact of the loss of a loved one lasts a very long time, perhaps for the rest of one's life. Recognizing these aspects of grief make it easier to know what to say and do for bereaved people. Among the most useful things are to simply let the person know that you are sorry for his or her loss, that you are there for support, and mean what you say.

Expected Versus Unexpected Death

When the death of a loved one is expected, people respond differently than when the death is unexpected. When death is anticipated, people go through a period of anticipatory grief before the death (Attig, 1996). This supposedly serves to buffer the impact of the loss when it does come, as well as facilitating recovery. The opportunity for anticipatory grieving results in a lower likelihood of psychological problems such as depression 1 year after the death of a spouse (Ball, 1976–77), greater acceptance by parents following the death of a child (Binger et al., 1969), and more rapid recovery of effective functioning and subsequent happiness (Glick, Weiss, & Parkes, 1974). However, anticipating the death of someone close does produce considerable stress in itself (Attig, 1996; Norris & Murrell, 1987). Caregivers of Alzheimer's patients, for example, show a decline in feelings of anticipatory grief during the middle stages of caregiving, only to have these feelings increase in intensity later (Ponder & Pomeroy, 1996).

The reasons why recovery from anticipated deaths is sometimes quicker and sometimes not are not yet fully understood. We know that the long-term effects of stressful events are generally less problematic if they are expected, so the same principle probably holds for death. Perhaps it is helpful that there is an opportunity to envision life without the dying person and a chance to make appropriate adjustments. During this "practice" period, we may realize that we need support, may feel lonely and scared, and may take steps to get ourselves ready. Moreover, if we recognize that we are likely to have certain feelings, they may be easier to understand and deal with when they come.

Also an anticipated death is often less mysterious (Attig, 1996). Most of the time, we understand why (e.g., from what disease) the person died. An unexpected death leaves us with many questions: Why *my* loved one? Why now? Survivors may feel vulnerable; what happened to their loved one could just as easily happen to them. Understanding the real reason why someone dies makes adjustment easier.

These findings do not mean that people who experience the anticipated death of a loved one fail to grieve. Indeed, one study revealed that widows whose husbands had been ill for at least 1 month prior to their deaths grieved just as intensely as did widows whose husbands died unexpectedly, as the graph below shows (Hill, Thompson, & Gallagher, 1988). In fact, widows who anticipated the deaths of their husbands had greater levels of grief 6 months after the death than did widows whose husbands died unexpectedly. The knowledge that one's spouse will die soon does not necessarily make the feelings of loss any easier to handle in the long run. It may be that the key to understanding anticipatory grief is that the advance warning of a loss per se is not as important as reconstructing meaning in one's life after the loss occurs (Fulton, Madden, & Minichiello, 1996).

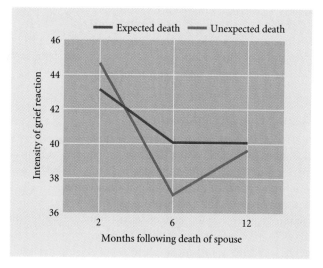

NORMAL GRIEF REACTIONS

The feelings experienced during grieving are intense, which not only makes it difficult to cope but can also make a person question her or his own reactions. The feelings involved usually include sadness, denial, anger, loneliness, and guilt. A summary of these feelings is presented in the following list (Vickio,

Cavanaugh, & Attig, 1990). Take a minute to read through them to see whether they agree with what you expected.

Disbelief	Denial	Shock
Sadness	Anger	Hatred
Guilt	Fear	Anxiety
Confusion	Helplessness	Emptiness
Loneliness	Acceptance	Relief
Happiness	Lack of enthusiasm	Absence of emotion

Many authors refer to the psychological side of coming to terms with bereavement as **grief work**. This notion fits well with the earlier discussion of grief as active coping (Attig, 1996). Even without personal experience of the death of close family members, people recognize the need to give survivors time to deal with their many feelings. One study asked college students to describe the feelings they thought were typically experienced by a person who had lost particular loved ones (such as a parent, child, sibling, friend). The students were well aware of the need for grief work, recognized the need for at least a year to do it, and were very sensitive to the range of emotions and behaviors demonstrated by the bereaved (Vickio, Cavanaugh, & Attig, 1990).

In the time following the death of a loved one, dates that have personal significance may reintroduce feelings of grief. For example, holidays such as Thanksgiving or birthdays that were spent with the deceased person may be difficult times. The actual anniversary of the death can be especially troublesome. *The term* **anniversary reaction** *refers to changes in behavior related to feelings of sadness on this date.* Personal experience and research show that recurring feelings of sadness or other examples of the anniversary reaction are very common in normal grief (Attig, 1996; Rosenblatt, 1996).

? THINK ABOUT IT
How are the theories of dying and grief reactions similar?

Grief over Time

Most research on how people react to the death of a loved one is cross-sectional. However, some work has been done to examine how people continue grieving many years after the loss. Rosenblatt (1996) reported that people still felt the effects of the deaths of family members 50 years after the event. The depth of the emotions over the loss of loved ones never totally went away, as people still cried and felt sad when discussing the loss despite the length of time that had passed.

Norris and Murrell (1987) conducted a longitudinal study of older adults' grief work; three interviews were conducted before the death and one after. The fascinating results of their research are described in more detail in the Spotlight on Research feature. The results of this study fit nicely with the earlier discussion on expected versus unexpected death. They also have important implications for interventions. That is, interventions aimed at reducing stress or promoting health may be more effective if performed before the death. Additionally, because health problems increased only among those in the bereaved group who felt no stress before the death, it may be that the stress felt before the death is a product of anticipating it. Lundin (1984) also found it to be the case that health problems increased only for those experiencing sudden death.

FAMILY STRESS AND ADAPTATION BEFORE AND AFTER BEREAVEMENT

Who were the investigators and what was the aim of the study? What happens to a family that experiences the death of a loved one? Fran Norris and Stanley Murrell (1987) sought to answer this question by tracking families before and after bereavement.

How did the investigators measure the topic of interest? As part of a very large normative longitudinal study, they conducted detailed interviews approximately every 6 months. The researchers used a variety of instruments to obtain extensive information on physical health, including functional abilities and specific ailments, psychological distress, and family stress. The psychological distress measure tapped symptoms of depression. The family stress measure assessed such things as new serious illness of a family member, having a family member move in, additional family responsibilities, new family conflict, or new marital conflict.

Who were the participants in the study? In all, 63 older adults in families experiencing the death of an immediate family member were compared to 387 older adults in families who had not experienced such a death in order to document the extra stress people feel due to grief.

What was the design of the study? Norris and Murrell used a longitudinal design and assessed people every 6 months from 18 months before bereavement to 12 months after bereavement.

Were there ethical concerns in the study? Like all researchers who study bereavement, Norris and Murrell needed to be sensitive to people's feelings and monitor their participants for signs of abnormal reactions.

What were the results? Among bereaved families, overall family stress increased before the death and then decreased. The level of stress experienced by these families was highest in the period right around the death. Moreover, bereavement was the only significant predictor of family stress, meaning that the anticipation and experience of bereavement caused stress.

Even more interesting were the findings concerning the relationship between health and stress. As shown in the graph below, bereaved individuals who reported stress before the death were in poorer health before the death than were bereaved persons

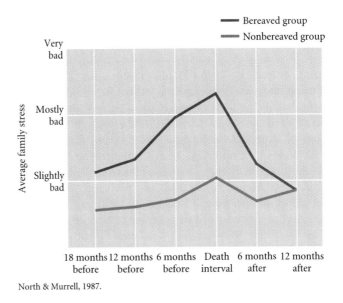

North & Murrell, 1987.

who were not experiencing stress. However, as shown in the second graph, bereaved individuals reporting prior stress showed a significant drop in physical symptoms 6 months after the death; bereaved persons reporting no prior stress reported a slight increase. The net result was that both groups ended up with about the same level of physical symptoms 6 months after bereavement.

What did the investigators conclude? Norris and Murrell described two major implications. First, bereavement does not appear to cause poor health; the bereaved groups were not much different from the group of nonbereaved people in nonstressful families. Second, bereavement appears to increase psychological distress substantially. In sum, marked changes in psychological distress following bereavement are normal, but marked changes in physical health are not. •

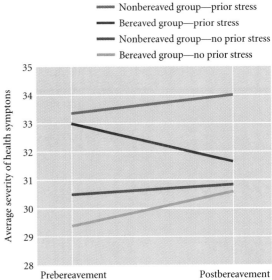

North & Murrell, 1987.

Effects of Normal Grief on Adults' Health

Many people have assumed that losing a close loved one must have obvious negative effects on the health of the survivor, especially if the survivor is elderly. As the Norris and Murrell study showed, however, such health effects are not inevitable.

Additional research supports this point (Perkins & Harris, 1990). Middle-aged adults are most likely to report physical health problems following bereavement; younger and older adults report few health problems. Younger adults may be able to deal with their losses because they are better equipped overall to handle stress. Older adults have more experience with such losses and anticipate them, and they may draw on their background in order to cope physically. In contrast, middle-aged adults have less experience, and they are also in the midst of dealing with their own mortality. As a result, the loss of a close family member is an emotionally unsettling reminder of their own fate (Perkins & Harris, 1990).

ABNORMAL GRIEF REACTIONS

Not everyone is able to cope with grief well and begin rebuilding a life. Sometimes the feelings of hurt, loneliness, and guilt are so overwhelming that they become the focus of the survivor's life, to such an extent that there is never any closure and the grief continues to interfere indefinitely with one's ability to function. Thus, what distinguishes normal from abnormal grief is not the kind of reaction but rather its intensity and duration (Schulz, 1985).

Overall, the most common manifestation of abnormal grief is excessive guilt and self-blame (Anderson, 1997). In some people, guilt results in a disruption of everyday routines and a diminished ability to function. People begin to make judgment errors, may reach a state of agitated depression, may experience problems sleeping or eating, and may have intense recurring thoughts about the deceased person. Many of these individuals either seek professional help voluntarily or are referred by concerned family members or friends. Unfortunately, the long-term prognosis for people suffering abnormal grief responses is not good unless they obtain professional help (Schulz, 1985). The most common problem is depression, which can become severe and chronic. Other problems include social withdrawal, with a resulting loss of the person's social network.

? THINK ABOUT IT
How can clinicians be sensitive to cultural differences in expressing grief in determining abnormal reactions?

How long intense grief needs to continue before it is considered abnormal is a matter of judgment. As we have seen, several research studies indicate that it takes at least 1 year for survivors to begin to move forward with their lives and may in many cases take longer. There are cultural variations in the process of grief that must be respected (Anderson, 1997). Consequently, clinicians tend to suspect that the person's grief is interfering with his or her daily life if intense grief reactions are still present more than 2 years after the loss. However, such judgments must be made on a case-by-case basis; no set period of time is used as a firm criterion.

TEST YOURSELF

1. Grief is best conceptualized as a form of _____ .

2. Feeling sad on the date when your grandmother died the previous year is an example of an _____ .

3. Compared to other age groups, _____ show the most negative effects following bereavement.

4. The most common manifestations of abnormal grief are guilt and _____ .

5. If you were to create a brochure listing the five most important things to do and not to do in connection with losing a close family member or friend through death, what would you include? Why?

Answers: (1) active coping, (2) anniversary reaction, (3) middle-aged adults, (4) self-blame

---

DEALING WITH DIFFERENT TYPES OF LOSS

Dealing with Different Types of Loss

Death of One's Parent

Death of One's Child

Death of One's Partner

Comparisons of Types of Loss

Learning Objectives

- **Why does the death of a parent cause surviving children to redefine their role as parents?**

- **How do people deal with the death of a child?**

- **Why is the death of a partner usually so traumatic?**

- **How do people deal with different types of losses?**

CLARE, *37, and her brother Alex, 41, lost their parents in an accident a few months ago. Since then, they feel a tremendous sense of loss, and have been thinking a lot about becoming the oldest generation in their family. Their experience has given both of them a new perspective on life and made them aware of their own mortality.*

The loss of any loved one is traumatic. Yet, there are important differences in how adults react to different types of loss—for example, between the loss of their parents and the loss of their children. As Clare and Alex indicate, the loss of our parents has implications for where we are in terms of generation within our family. The loss of a child is deeply troubling for most, as it reverses the way we tend to think things are supposed to happen. Although we know intellectually that the odds of losing our partner to death are high, the effects of actually experiencing it are often devastating. In this concluding section, let's see how adults confront and cope with their grief in the context of different types of loss.

DEATH OF ONE'S PARENT

Most parents die after their children are grown. But whenever parental death occurs, it hurts. We lose not only a key relationship but also an important psychological buffer between ourselves and death (Anderson, 1997; Attig, 1996). We, the children, are now next in line. Indeed, the death of a parent often leads the surviving children to redefine the meaning of parenthood and the importance of time together (Malinak, Hoyt, & Patterson, 1979). Clare and Alex, the surviving adult children in the vignette, are examples of this redefinition.

As it did for the woman in the photo, the death of a parent deprives people of many important things: a source of guidance and advice, a source of love, and a model for their own parenting style (Buchsbaum, 1996). It also cuts off the opportunity to improve aspects of their relationship with the parent. Expressing feelings toward a parent before he or she dies is important. The loss of a parent is perceived as a very significant one; no matter how old we are, society allows us to grieve for a reasonable length of time.

DEATH OF ONE'S CHILD

The couple in the photo are experiencing what many people believe is the worst type of loss: the death of a child (Klass, 1996b). Because children are not supposed to die before their parents, it is as if the natural order of things has been violated. Unexpected loss is especially traumatic, as in sudden infant death syndrome or automobile accidents. But parents of terminally ill children still suffer a great deal, even with the benefit of anticipatory grieving. Mourning is always intense, and some parents never recover or reconcile themselves to the death of their child (Klass, 1996).

Some of the most overlooked losses are those that happen through stillbirth, miscarriage, abortion, or neonatal death (Borg & Lasker, 1981; Klass, 1996). Attachment to the child begins before birth, so the loss hurts deeply. Yet parents who experience this type of loss are expected to recover very quickly. The experience of parents in support groups, such as Compassionate Friends, tells a very different story, though (Klass, 1996). These parents report a deep sense of loss and hurt, especially when others do not understand their feelings. Worst of all, if societal expectations for quick recovery are not met, the parents may be subjected to unfeeling comments. As one mother notes, parents often just wish somebody would acknowledge the loss (Okonski, 1996). The Real People feature tells the personal story of one couple's experience of miscarriage.

THE GRIEF OF MISCARRIAGE

As noted in the text, one of the most overlooked types of loss is through miscarriage. Unfortunately, many people react to miscarriages by telling the grieving couple that they "can have more children," "It's not that bad, because you really didn't know the baby," "It probably would have been deformed anyway, so it's good that it happened this way," and similar insensitive statements.

One of the authors personally experienced this type of loss. He and his wife had undergone extensive treatment for infertility, and they were elated at the news of the pregnancy. When they lost their baby, they were devastated. All the statements noted above were actually said to them. Their grief was worse because they knew that it would be difficult to get pregnant again. The poem below was written the night the miscarriage happened, and serves as testimony to the grief couples in this situation experience.

> *Last night*
> *as I sat holding your hand*
> *in the emergency room,*
> *watching helplessly as the life we had created*
> *came to an end,*
> *I felt more alone and powerless*
> *than in my whole life.*
> *Your look of fear, your trembling, the*
> *lack of control over events, my own*
> *ocean of grief*
> *All swept over me like a tidal wave.*
> *I became too intimately familiar with*
> *the deepest pit of my stomach,*
> *too closely acquainted with utter helplessness.*
> *Intellectually, the event is over now.*
> *Gone. In the past. Life goes on.*
> *But I know that from time to time*
> *for the rest of my life*
> *I'll see him or her in every child I'll*
> *ever meet.*
> *I'll never really forget.*
> *How could I?* •

? THINK ABOUT IT

How does the death of a child or grandchild relate to Erikson's notion of generativity?

Finally, grandparents' feelings can easily be overlooked. They, too, feel pain and loss when their grandchild dies. Moreover, they grieve not only for their grandchild but also for their own child's loss (Hamilton, 1978). Grandparents must also be included in whatever rituals or support groups the family chooses.

DEATH OF ONE'S PARTNER

The death of a partner differs from other losses. It clearly represents a deep personal loss, especially when the couple has had a long and close relationship. In a very real way, when our partner dies, a part of ourselves dies, too. Bertha, the widow in the vignette, is a good case in point. She and her husband had a strong partnership, and the loss of her longtime companion hurt deeply.

There is pressure from society to mourn the loss of one's partner for a period of time (Lopata, 1996; Moss & Moss, 1996). Typically, this pressure is manifested if the survivor begins to show interest in finding another partner before an "acceptable" period of mourning has passed. Although Americans no longer specify the length of the period, many feel that about a year is appropriate. The fact that such pressure and negative commentary usually do not accompany other losses is another indication of the seriousness with which most people take the death of a partner.

Research on the responses to the loss of a spouse shows that they vary with the age of the survivor. Young adult spouses, like the woman in the photograph, tend to grieve more intensely immediately following the death than do older spouses. However, the situation 18 months later is reversed. At that time, older spouses report more grief than do younger spouses (Sanders, 1980–81). Indeed, older bereaved spouses may grieve for at least 30 months (Thompson et al., 1991). The differences seem to be related to four factors. The death of a young spouse is often unexpected; there are fewer same-age role models for young widows and widowers; older widows feel the loss of their long-term companion keenly, while younger widows grieve over the future they won't get to experience; and the opportunities for remarriage are greater for younger survivors. Older widows anticipate fewer

years of life and prefer to cherish the memory of their deceased spouse rather than attempting a new marriage (Raphael, 1983).

Social support plays a significant role in the outcome of the grieving process during the first 2 years after the death of a partner. Particularly important is the quality of the support system for the grieving partner, rather than simply the number of friends. Survivors who have a few friends or relatives with whom they have strong, close relationships are better off than survivors who have many acquaintances (Dimond, Lund, & Caserta, 1987).

One study of spousal bereavement measured how the surviving spouse rated the marriage. Bereaved older adults rated their relationships at 2, 12, and 30 months after the death of their spouses. Nonbereaved older adults served as a comparison group. The results are summarized in the graphs on page 602. Bereaved widows and widowers gave their marriages more positive ratings than nonbereaved older adults. A marriage lost through death left a positive bias in memory. However, bereaved spouses' ratings were related to depression in an interesting way. The more depressed the bereaved spouse, the more positive the marriage's rating. In contrast, depressed nonbereaved spouses gave their marriages negative ratings. This result suggests that depression following bereavement signifies positive aspects of a relationship; whereas depression not connected with bereavement indicates a troubled relationship (Futterman et al., 1990).

Several studies of widows document a tendency for some women to "sanctify" their husbands (Lopata, 1996). Sanctification involves describing deceased

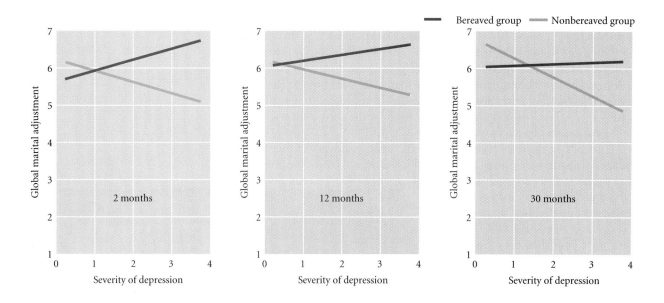

husbands in idealized terms, and serves several functions: validating that the widow had a strong marriage, is a good and worthy person, and is capable of rebuilding her life. European American women who view being a wife as above all other roles a woman can perform are somewhat more likely to sanctify their husbands (Lopata, 1996).

Unmarried heterosexual couples and gay and lesbian couples may experience other feelings and reactions on top of typical feelings of grief. For example, family members of the deceased may not make the partner feel welcome at the funeral, making it hard for the partner to bring closure to the relationship. Gays whose partner died of AIDS may experience increased personal concern and have difficulty dealing with feelings (Goodkin et al., 1997).

COMPARISONS OF TYPES OF LOSS

There has been little research comparing people's grief reactions from different types of loss. Much of the writing has focused instead on similarities in the process of grief rather than on the differences in dealing with different types of loss (Attig, 1996). In the available studies, bereaved parents typically show higher levels of depression and other grief reactions than bereaved spouses or adult children (Owen, Fulton, & Markusen, 1982). Other research reveals that the intensity of depression following loss is related specifically to how important the survivor considers the relationship with the deceased person (Murphy, 1988). Survivors are more often depressed (and more seriously so) following the deaths of people who were particularly important to them.

One study compared the grief reactions of 255 middle-aged women who had experienced the loss of a spouse, a parent, or a child within the preceding 2 years. Bereaved mothers reported significantly higher levels of depression than widows, who in turn reported significantly greater depression than adult children. In fact, over 60% of the bereaved mothers had depression scores in the moderate to severe depression range (Leahy, 1993).

We must be careful in our interpretation of these data. As noted earlier, there are many aspects of grief other than depression. Until researchers pro-

? THINK ABOUT IT
Given the earlier discussion on life-span differences in dealing with death, how might the age of the person who experiences the loss make a difference in these results?

vide evidence on the other aspects, it is premature to conclude that some types of loss result in greater grief than others. All we can say at this point is that following some types of loss, some people tend to report more depressive symptoms, at more serious levels.

TEST YOURSELF

1. The death of a parent deprives people of _____ .

2. Some of the most overlooked losses are the loss of a child through _____ .

3. Shortly after the death of a spouse, _____ widows grieve more intensely than _____ widows.

4. In a study comparing different types of loss, _____ reported the highest level of depression.

5. What insights into the quality of relationships can we get by observing grief following loss?

Answers: (1) a key relationship and a psychological buffer against death, (2) stillbirth, miscarriage, abortion, and neonatal death, (3) younger; older, (4) grieving mothers

PUTTING IT ALL TOGETHER

As we've discovered in this chapter, thinking about death isn't easy. We aren't taught how to deal with it very well. Like Greta, we encounter different rituals and customs concerning funerals and mourning and we do not fully understand them. You may have been in a situation like that of Donna and Carl, facing the dilemma of whether to bring young children to a funeral. You may know someone like Betty who has just been diagnosed with a terminal disease, or someone like Bertha who just lost a spouse. Like Clare and Alex, you may have experienced the loss of a close relative or friend.

Death is not as pleasant a topic as children's play or occupational development. It's not something we can go to college to master. What it represents to many people is the end of their existence, and that is a very scary prospect. But because we all share in this fear at some level, each of us is equipped to provide support and comfort for grieving survivors.

Death is the last life-cycle force we encounter, the ultimate triumph of biological forces that limit the length of life. Yet the same psychological and social forces that are so influential throughout life help us deal with death, either our own or someone else's. As we come to the end of our life journey, we understand death through an interaction of psychological forces, such as coping skills and intellectual and emotional understanding of death, and the sociocultural forces expressed in a particular society's traditions and rituals.

SUMMARY

Definitions and Ethical Issues

Sociocultural Definitions of Death

• Death is a difficult concept to define precisely. Different cultures have different meanings for death. Among the meanings in Western culture are images, statistics, events, state of being, analogy, mystery, boundary, thief of meaning, basis for anxiety, and reward or punishment.

Legal and Medical Definitions

• For many centuries, a clinical definition of death was used: the absence of a heartbeat and respiration. Currently, brain death is the most widely used definition.

It is based on several highly specific criteria, including brain activity and responses to specific stimuli.

Ethical Issues

• Two types of euthanasia are distinguished. Active euthanasia consists of deliberately ending someone's life, such as turning off a life-support system. Physician-assisted suicide is a controversial issue and form of active euthanasia. Passive euthanasia is ending someone's life by withholding some type of intervention or treatment (e.g., by stopping nutrition). It is essential that people make their wishes known, either through a durable power of attorney or a living will.

Ideas About Death Through the Life Span

Childhood

• Children do not fully understand the permanence, universality, and lack of functioning in death until around the ages of 5–7. Their first experiences are likely to be with pets. Adults must exercise patience and avoid the use of euphemisms when discussing death with children. Given proper support, children are capable of attending funerals and other rituals.

Adolescence

• Adolescents tend to not talk about death, although their understanding approaches that of adults. However, they have feelings of immortality—a tendency to believe that death affects other people but not themselves.

Young Adulthood

• Young adults tend to believe that their peers who die are cheated out of their future. Cognitive developmental changes involving postformal thought may help integrate feelings and thoughts about death.

Middle Age

• Middle-aged adults come to realize that they are next in line to die, usually at the point when they experience the loss of their parents. It is common for middle-aged adults to change their perception of time from the amount of time they have lived to the amount of time they have left.

Late Adulthood

• Older adults are least concerned about dying. They may even look forward to it, for a variety of reasons.

This is due in part to the achievement of integrity in Erikson's framework.

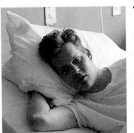

The Process of Dying

Death Anxiety

• Death anxiety is a universal concern. Death anxiety tends to be highest in middle-aged adults and lowest in older adults.

The Stage Theory of Dying

• Kübler-Ross's theory includes five stages: denial, anger, bargaining, depression, and acceptance. People do not necessarily go through all of them or go through them in this order. Cross-cultural differences have been found.

Alternative Views

• A second view states that dying occurs in three phases: an acute phase, a chronic living-dying phase, and a terminal phase. Feelings and emotions vary according to the specific phase an individual is in.

• Some view the process of dying as involving four important tasks that a person must complete, involving physical, psychological, social, and spiritual issues.

Dying with Dignity: Hospice

• Hospice involves an approach to caring for terminally ill people that focuses on relieving pain and the person's feelings. Hospice care differs from hospital care on several dimensions. The goal of hospice is to maintain the quality of life and to manage the pain of terminal patients. Hospice clients are typically better off psychologically than hospital patients.

A Life-Span Developmental Perspective on Dying

• Older adults take longer to die and are more likely to die alone than any other group. Age differences in the dying experience and in the social definition of loss help put the meaning of dying into perspective.

Surviving the Loss: The Grieving Process

The Grief Process

• Grief is an active process of coping with loss. Four aspects of grieving must be confronted: the reality of the loss, the emotional turmoil, adjusting to the environment, and loosening the ties with the deceased. When death is expected, survivors go through anticipatory grief; unexpected death is usually more difficult for people to handle.

Normal Grief Reactions

• Dealing with grief, called *grief work,* usually takes at least 1–2 years. Grief is equally intense for both expected and unexpected death, but it may begin before the actual death when the patient has a terminal illness. Normal grief reactions include sorrow, sadness, denial, disbelief, guilt, and anniversary reactions.

• In terms of dealing with normal grief, middle-aged adults have the most difficult time. Poor copers tend to have low self-esteem before losing a loved one.

Abnormal Grief Reactions

• Excessive guilt and self-blame are common signs of abnormal grief. Intense grief reactions that impair normal functioning more than 2 years after the loss are often viewed as abnormal.

Dealing with Different Types of Loss

Death of One's Parent

• The death of a parent reminds people of their own mortality and deprives them of a very important person in their lives. The transition to being the oldest generation in one's family is sometimes a difficult one.

Death of One's Child

• The death of a child is thought to be the most tragic type of loss. Miscarriage, abortion, stillbirth, and neonatal death are also highly traumatic. For most people, losing a child violates the natural order of things; children are not supposed to die before their parents.

Death of One's Partner

• The death of a partner is the loss of a lover and companion. Bereaved spouses tend to view their marriages in a positive light. The loss of a spouse does not significantly impair a person's physical health, although it does increase psychological stress.

Comparisons of Types of Loss

• Little research has been done comparing different types of loss. What we know reveals that bereaved mothers report more depressive symptoms than widows, who report more symptoms than bereaved adult daughters.

KEY TERMS

clinical death (576)
brain death (576)
persistent vegetative state (577)
bioethics (577)
euthanasia (577)

active euthanasia (577)
passive euthanasia (578)
death anxiety (585)
hospice (588)
bereavement (592)

grief (592)
mourning (592)
grief work (595)
anniversary reaction (595)

IF YOU'D LIKE TO LEARN MORE

Books

ATTIG, T. (1996). *How we grieve: Relearning the world.* New York: Oxford University Press. An easy-to-read book that offers a refreshingly new view of the grief process told through personal accounts.

KASTENBAUM, R. (1985). Death and dying: A life-span approach. In J. E. Birren and K. W. Schaie (Eds.), *Handbook of the psychology of aging* (2nd ed., pp. 619–643). New York: Van Nostrand Reinhold. Moderately difficult reading, this chapter presents a summary of the research literature. Some familiarity with the issues and terminology is assumed.

KÜNG, H., & JENS, W. (1995). *Dying with dignity: A plea for personal responsibility.* New York: Continuum. A superb, easy-to-read book that discusses death with dignity. This book will make you think.

KUSHNER, H. S. (1981). *When bad things happen to good people.* New York: Schocken. This is easy reading but contains very thought-provoking material. The book was written by a rabbi after the death of his son.

NULAND, S. B. (1994). *How we die: Reflections on life's final chapter.* New York: Knopf. This is a good discussion of the actual things that happen when people die. It is excellent for countering myths about death.

TAYLOR, N. (1993). *A necessary end.* New York: Nan A. Talese. The author tells how he dealt with the death of his parents and found meaning in it.

For additional readings, explore Infotrac College Edition, your online library. Go to http://www.infotrac-college.com/wadsworth.

Web Sites

A general site that provides information about several topics related to death, including euthanasia, living wills, and approaches to terminal illnesses is Death Net, which can be found at

http://www.rights.org/deathnet/open.html

A resource for detailed information about hospice is the National Hospice Organization. The site includes general information, conference and educational opportunities, and information for members and about the National Hospice Foundation. Their Web site can be found at

http://www.nho.org/

The Compassionate Friends is a national organization dedicated to helping parents deal with the grief of the loss of a child. They have chapters throughout the United States and Canada. A list of chapters and extensive information can be found at

http://www.compassionatefriends.org/

One of the most extensive collections of resources on all facets of grief, including historical and cross-cultural information, is Kathi Webster's Death, Dying, and Grief Guide. It is very well organized, and contains links to numerous other sites. It can be found at

http://www.katsden.com/death/index.html

Web site addresses are subject to change. The Wadsworth Study Center Web site listed below can be accessed for updated links.

The Wadsworth Psychology Study Center Web Site

See http://psychology.wadsworth.com/ for practice quiz questions, internet links, updates, critical thinking exercises, discussion forums and more! The Wadsworth Psychology Study Center provides a wealth of information fully organized and integrated by chapter.

SNAPSHOTS OF DEVELOPMENT
A VISUAL SUMMARY

Late Life

BIOLOGICAL FORCES

With old age comes many physiological changes, mostly involving decline of function. Older adults have a much higher risk of chronic diseases. Alzheimer's disease, depression, and anxiety disorders are important problems. Impairment of daily living activities are especially common in the very old.

PSYCHOLOGICAL FORCES

Several aspects of cognitive functioning decline, but some involving tertiary memory do not decline until late life. Older adults benefit from interventions when they are targeted to specific problems. Issues of ego integrity and life review color older adults' personality development. Most retired individuals are content with their lives.

SOCIOCULTURAL FORCES

Societal views on aging in industrialized countries are often negative. Stereotypes about aging can become incorporated and result in self-fulfilling prophecies. Elder abuse and neglect is a major social problem. Health care and retirement financing are key political issues.

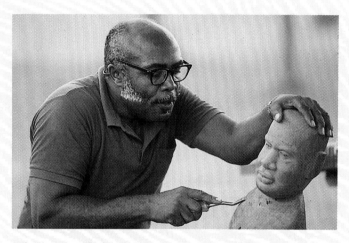

Whether people label themselves as "retired" varies across ethnic groups.

Even people with Alzheimer's disease can benefit from carefully designed psychological interventions.

Some deaths, like Princess Diana's in 1997, bring grieving people together across many cultures.

Whether people are healthy in late life is influenced by the life-style choices they made earlier in adulthood.

GLOSSARY

abusive relationship when one partner in a relationship becomes violent or aggressive toward the other.

accommodation according to Piaget, changing existing knowledge based on new knowledge.

achievement status identity status in Marcia's theory in which adolescents have explored alternative identities and are now secure in their chosen identities.

active euthanasia deliberate ending of someone's life.

activities of daily living (ADLs) self-care tasks such as eating, bathing, toileting, walking, or dressing.

activity dimension of temperament defined by the tempo and vigor of a child's activity.

adaptation level area where environmental press is average for a particular level of competence.

addiction physical dependence on a particular substance, such as alcohol.

adolescent egocentrism self-absorption that is characteristic of teenagers as they search for identity.

aerobic exercise exercise that places a moderate stress on the heart by maintaining a pulse rate between 60% and 90% of the maximum heart rate.

age discrimination denying a job or promotion to someone solely on the basis of age.

age-integrated housing where people of all ages live together and interact.

age of viability age at which a fetus can survive because most of its bodily systems function adequately; typically at 7 months after conception.

age-segregated housing where all residents are of the same age.

agreeableness dimension of personality associated with being accepting, willing to work with others, and caring.

alert inactivity state in which a baby is calm with eyes open and attentive, and the baby seems to be deliberately inspecting the environment.

alienation when workers feel that what they are doing is meaningless, that their efforts are devalued, or when they do not see the connection between what they do and the final product.

alleles variations of genes.

altruism prosocial behavior such as helping and sharing in which the individual does not benefit directly from his or her behavior.

Alzheimer's disease disease associated with aging characterized by gradual declines in memory, learning, attention, and judgment; confusion as to time and where one is; difficulties in communicating and finding the words one wants to use; declines in personal hygiene and self-care skills; inappropriate social behavior; and changes in personality.

amniocentesis prenatal diagnostic technique that involves withdrawing a sample of amniotic fluid through the abdomen using a syringe.

amnion inner sac in which the developing child rests.

amniotic fluid fluid that surrounds the fetus.

amyloid protein that is produced in abnormally high levels in Alzheimer's disease and that may be responsible for the neurofibrillary tangles and neuritic plaques.

animism crediting inanimate objects with life and lifelike properties such as feelings.

anniversary reaction changes in behavior related to feelings of sadness on the actual anniversary of a death.

anorexia nervosa persistent refusal to eat, accompanied by an irrational fear of being overweight.

anoxia lack of oxygen during delivery, typically because the umbilical cord becomes pinched or tangled during delivery.

anxiety disorders problems such as feelings of severe anxiety for no apparent reason, phobias to specific things or places, and obsessive-compulsive disorders in which thoughts or actions are repeatedly performed.

appraise to evaluate a situation to determine whether it exceeds a person's resources and is, therefore, stressful.

assimilation according to Piaget, taking in information that is compatible with what one already knows.

assortative mating theory of mating that states that people find partners based on their similarity to each other.

attachment   enduring social-emotional relationship between infants and their caregivers.

attentional processes   processes that determine which information will be processed further by an individual.

authoritarian parents   parents who show high levels of control and low levels of warmth toward their children.

authoritative parents   parents who use a moderate amount of control and who are warm and responsive to their children.

autosomes   first 22 pairs of chromosomes.

average life expectancy   age at which half of the people born in a particular year will have died.

avoidant attachment   relationship in which infants turn away from their mothers when they are reunited following a brief separation.

axon   tubelike structure that emerges from the cell body and transmits information to other neurons.

babbling   speechlike sounds that consist of vowel-consonant combinations.

basal metabolic rate   speed with which the body consumes calories.

basic cry   cry that starts softly and gradually becomes more intense; often heard when babies are hungry or tired.

basic emotions   emotions experienced by humankind and that consist of three elements: a subjective feeling, a physiological change, and an overt behavior.

battered woman syndrome   situation in which a woman believes that she cannot leave an abusive situation.

behavior therapy   approach to treating depression based on increasing the number of rewards or reinforcements in the environment.

bioethics   study of the interface between human values and technological advances in health and life sciences.

biological forces   all genetic and health-related factors that affect development.

biopsychosocial framework   view that integrates biological, psychological, sociocultural, and life-cycle forces on development.

blended family   family consisting of a biological parent, a stepparent, and children.

brain death   most widely accepted definition of death, including no heartbeat, respiration, responsiveness, reflexes, and brain activity.

bulimia nervosa   disease in which people alternate between binge eating—periods when they eat uncontrollably—and purging through self-induced vomiting or with laxatives.

burnout   depletion of a person's energy and motivation.

cardinality principle   counting principle that the last number name denotes the number of objects being counted.

career plateauing   either a lack of promotional opportunity from the organization or a person's decision not to seek advancement.

cell body   center of the neuron that keeps the neuron alive.

cellular theories   theories of aging that focus on processes that occur within individual cells, which cause the buildup of harmful substances over one's lifetime.

centrality   meaning derived when grandparenting is the most important thing in grandparents' lives.

cephalocaudal principle   principle that growth occurs from the head first and then down the spine.

cerebral cortex   wrinkled surface of the brain that regulates many functions that are distinctly human.

cerebral vascular accidents   see strokes.

chorionic villus sampling   prenatal diagnostic technique that involves taking a sample of tissue from the chorion.

chromosomes   threadlike structures in the nuclei of the sperm and egg that contain genetic material.

chronic obstructive pulmonary disease (COPD)   most common form of incapacitating respiratory disease among older adults; examples are asthma and emphysema.

circadian rhythm   sleep-wake cycle.

climacteric   loss of ability to bear children, which usually begins in the 40s and is complete by age 50 or 55.

clinical death   death defined by a lack of heartbeat and respiration.

clique   small group of friends who are similar in age, sex, and race.

codominance   situation in which one allele does not dominate another completely.

cognitive therapy   approach to depression based on the idea that maladaptive beliefs or cognitions about oneself are responsible for depression.

cohabitation   two or more unrelated adults living together.

cohort effects   differences between individuals that result from experiences and circumstances unique to a person's particular generation.

comparable worth   equating pay in occupations that are determined to be equivalent in importance but differ in terms of the gender distribution of the people in them.

competence   upper limit of a person's ability to function in five domains: physical health, sensory-perceptual skills, motor skills, cognitive skills, and ego strength.

complex emotions   emotions that have a self-evaluative component.

cones   specialized neurons in the back of the eye that sense color.

conscientiousness   dimension of personality associated with being hard-working, ambitious, energetic, scrupulous, and persevering.

continuity theory   view that people tend to cope with daily life in late adulthood in essentially the same ways they coped in earlier periods of life.

continuity-discontinuity issue   issue concerned with whether a developmental phenomenon follows a smooth progression throughout the life span or a series of abrupt shifts.

conventional level   second level of reasoning in Kohlberg's theory, where moral reasoning is based on society's norms.

convergent thinking   using information to arrive at one standard and correct answer.

cooing   early vowel-like sounds that babies produce.

cooperative play   play that is organized around a theme, with each child taking on a different role; begins at about 2 years of age.

coping   attempts to deal with stress.

corpus callosum   thick bundle of neurons that connects the two hemispheres.

correlation coefficient   statistic that reveals the strength and direction of the relation between two variables.

correlational study   investigation looking at relations between variables as they exist naturally in the world.

cross-linking   theory of aging in which some proteins interact randomly with certain body tissues, such as muscles and arteries.

cross-sectional study   research design in which people of different ages are compared at one point in time.

crowd   large group including many cliques that have similar attitudes and values.

crowning   appearance of the top of the baby's head during labor.

crying   state in which a baby cries vigorously, usually accompanied by agitated but uncoordinated movement.

crystallization   first phase in Super's theory of career development, in which adolescents use their emerging identities for ideas about careers.

crystallized intelligence   knowledge acquired through experience and education in a particular culture.

cultural conservator   status of grandparents whose grandchildren live with them to learn the native ways.

culture-fair intelligence tests   intelligence tests devised using items common to many cultures.

date (acquaintance) rape   when someone is forced to have sexual intercourse with someone they know.

death anxiety   refers to the fact that people are uncomfortable thinking about their own death.

deductive reasoning   drawing conclusions from facts; characteristic of formal operational thought.

dementia   family of diseases involving serious impairment of behavioral and cognitive functioning.

demographers   people who study population trends.

dendrite   end of the neuron that receives information; it looks like a tree with many branches.

deoxyribonucleic acid (DNA)   molecule composed of four nucleotide bases that is the biochemical basis of heredity.

dependent variable   behavior that is observed after other variables are manipulated.

depression   disorder characterized by pervasive feelings of sadness, irritability, and low self-esteem.

differentiation   distinguishing and mastering individual motions.

diffusion status   identity status in Marcia's theory in which adolescents do not have an identity and are doing nothing to achieve one.

disorganized (disoriented) attachment   relationship in which infants don't seem to understand what's happening when they are separated and later reunited with their mothers.

dispositional praise   praise that links a child's altruistic behavior to an underlying altruistic disposition.

divergent thinking   thinking in novel and unusual directions.

divided attention   performing more than one task at a time.

dizygotic twins   result of the fertilization of two separate eggs by two sperm; also called fraternal twins.

docility   when people allow the situation to dictate the options they have.

dominance hierarchy   ordering of individuals within a group in which group members with lower status defer to those with greater status.

dominant   form of an allele whose chemical instructions are followed.

dream   as related to vocational development, a vision of one's career.

dysphoria   feeling sad or down; the most prominent symptom of depression.

ecological theory   view that human development cannot be separated from the environmental contexts in which development occurs.

ectoderm   outer layer of the embryo that will become the hair, outer layer of skin, and the nervous system.

ego   according to Freud, the rational component of the personality; develops during the first few years of life.

egocentrism   difficulty in seeing the world from another's point of view; typical of children in the preoperational period.

ego resilience   powerful personality resource that enables people to handle midlife.

electroencephalogram (EEG)   pattern of brain waves recorded from electrodes that are placed on the scalp.

embryo   term given to the zygote once it is completely embedded in the uterine wall.

emotionality   aspect of temperament that refers to the strength of the infant's emotional response to a situation, the ease with which that response is triggered, and the ease with which the infant can be returned to a nonemotional state.

empathy   experiencing another person's feelings.

encapsulated   result of the processes of thinking becoming connected with the products of thinking.

endoderm   inner layer of the embryo, which will become the lungs and the digestive system.

environmental press   number and type of physical, interpersonal, or social demands that environments make on people.

epigenetic principle   view in Erikson's theory that each psychosocial stage has its own period of importance.

equilibration   according to Piaget, a process by which children reorganize their schemes to return to a state of equilibrium when disequilibrium occurs.

estrogen-related symptoms   symptoms associated with the climacteric and menopause, including hot flashes, night sweats, vaginal dryness, and urine leakage that are due to the drop in estrogen.

ethology branch of biology concerned with adaptive behaviors that are characteristic of different species.

eugenics effort to improve the human species by letting only people whose characteristics are valued by a society mate and pass along their genes.

euthanasia practice of ending a life for reasons of mercy.

exchange theory view that marriage is based on each partner contributing something to the relationship that the other would be hard-pressed to provide.

exosystem according to Bronfenbrenner, social settings that influence one's development even though one does not experience them firsthand.

experiment systematic way of manipulating factors that a researcher thinks cause a particular behavior.

explicit memory conscious and intentional recollection of information.

expressive style language-learning style that describes children whose vocabularies include many social phrases that are used like one word.

extended family family in which grandparents and other relatives live with parents and children.

external aids memory aids that rely on environmental resources, such as notebooks or calendars.

extraversion dimension of personality in which an individual thrives on social interaction, likes to talk, takes charge easily, readily expresses opinions and feelings, likes to keep busy, has seemingly unending energy, and prefers stimulating and challenging environments.

extremely low birth weight newborns who weigh less than 1,000 grams (2 pounds).

familial mental retardation form of mental retardation that does not involve biological damage but represents the low end of the normal distribution of intelligence.

family life cycle a series of relatively predictable changes that families experience.

fast mapping fact that children make connections between new words and ref-

erents so quickly that they can't be considering all possible meanings.

fetal alcohol syndrome disorder affecting babies whose mothers consumed large amounts of alcohol while they were pregnant.

fetal medicine field of medicine concerned with treating prenatal problems before birth.

fictive grandparenting style that allows adults to fill in for missing or deceased biological grandparents, functionally creating the role of surrogate grandparent.

filial obligation sense of responsibility to care for a parent if necessary.

fine-motor skills motor skills associated with grasping, holding, and manipulating objects.

fluid intelligence abilities such as thinking in a flexible, adaptive manner, drawing inferences, and understanding relations between concepts.

foreclosure status identity status in Marcia's theory in which adolescents have an identity that was chosen based on advice from adults, rather than one that resulted from personal exploration of alternatives.

frail older adults older adults who have physical disabilities, are very ill, and may have cognitive or psychological disorders.

free radicals chemicals produced randomly during normal cell metabolism that bond easily to other substances inside cells; may cause cellular damage associated with aging.

free recall memory task in which people report everything they can remember about the material they learned.

frontal cortex brain region that regulates personality and goal-directed behavior.

gender constancy understanding that maleness and femaleness do not change over situations or personal wishes.

gender identity sense of oneself as male or female.

gender labeling young children's understanding that they are either boys or girls and naming themselves accordingly.

gender-schema theory theory that states that children first decide whether

an object, activity, or behavior is female or male, then use this information to decide whether they should learn more about the object, activity, or behavior.

gender stability understanding in preschool children that boys become men and girls become women.

gender stereotype beliefs and images about males and females that are not necessarily true.

gene group of nucleotide bases that provide a specific set of biochemical instructions.

generativity according to Erikson, being productive by helping others to ensure the continuation of society by guiding the next generation.

genotype person's hereditary makeup.

germ disc small cluster of cells near the center of the zygote that will eventually develop into a baby.

glass ceiling level to which women and minorities may rise in a company but beyond which they may not go.

grammatical morphemes words or endings of words that make a sentence grammatical.

grief sorrow, hurt, anger, guilt, confusion, and other feelings that arise after suffering a loss.

grief work psychological side of coming to terms with bereavement.

habituation becoming unresponsive to a stimulus that is presented repeatedly.

hassles day-to-day events that upset and annoy people.

hemispheres right and left halves of the cortex.

hemorrhage break in any blood vessel that leads to loss of blood.

heterocyclic antidepressants (HCAs) type of medication used to treat depression.

heterozygous when the alleles differ from each other.

high-density lipoproteins (HDLs) lipoproteins that help clear arteries.

homogamy similarity of values and interests.

homozygous when the chromosomes in a pair are the same.

hope according to Erikson, an openness to new experience tempered by wariness that occurs when trust and mistrust are in balance.

hormone replacement theory treatment for symptoms accompanying the climacteric in which women take low doses of estrogen and progesterone.

hospice movement that provides a supportive environment for dying people by keeping families engaged in caregiving and by providing professional assistance during this very stressful time.

human development multidisciplinary scientific study of how people change and how they stay the same.

Huntington's disease progressive and fatal type of dementia.

id according to Freud, the element of personality that wants immediate gratification of bodily wants and needs; present at birth.

imaginary audience adolescents' feeling that their behavior is constantly being watched by their peers.

imitation (observational learning) learning that happens by watching those around us.

immortality through clan meaning derived from grandparenting when grandparents take pride in the fact that they will be followed by not one but two generations.

implantation step in which the zygote burrows into the uterine wall and establishes connections with a woman's blood vessels.

implementation third phase in Super's theory of career development, in which individuals now enter the work force.

implicit memory effortless recollection of information.

incontinence loss of bladder or bowel control.

independent variable factor that researchers manipulate in an experiment.

index offense acts that are illegal regardless of the age of the perpetrator.

indifferent-uninvolved parents parents who are neither warm nor controlling and who try to minimize the amount of time spent with their children.

indulgence meaning derived when grandparents spoil their grandchildren.

indulgent-permissive parents parents who are warm and caring but exert little control over their children.

infant-directed speech way of speaking in which adults speak slowly and with exaggerated changes in pitch and loudness.

infantilization way of speaking to a nursing home resident based on using a person's first name when it is not appropriate, terms of endearment, simplified expressions, short imperatives, assumptions that a nursing home resident has no memory, and manipulation to get compliance.

information-processing theory view that human cognition consists of mental hardware and software.

insecure attachment relationship in which infants act as if they do not perceive the mother to be dependable.

instrumental activities of daily living (IADLs) acts that require some intellectual competence and planning, such as cooking and doing the laundry.

instrumental orientation characteristic of Kohlberg's Stage 2, in which moral reasoning is based on the aim of looking out for one's own needs.

integration linking individual motions into a coherent, coordinated whole.

integrity versus despair according to Erikson, a struggle that comes about as older adults try to integrate their lives with a view of their family's and community's futures.

intelligence quotient mathematical representation of how a person scores on an intelligence test in relation to how other people of the same age score.

interindividual variability patterns of change in a domain (e.g., intelligence) are different for different people.

intermediate care facility that provides 24-hour care, but does not involve intensive skilled nursing.

internal aids memory aids that rely on mental processes, such as imagery.

internal belief systems what one tells oneself about why certain things are happening.

internal working model infant's understanding of how responsive and dependable the mother is; thought to influence close relationships throughout the child's life.

interpersonal norms characteristic of Kohlberg's Stage 3, in which moral reasoning is based on winning the approval of others.

intimacy versus isolation according to Erikson, the psychosocial conflict of young adulthood.

intonation pattern of rising and falling pitch that appears around the age of 7 months in infants' babbling.

in vitro fertilization process by which sperm and an egg are mixed in a petri dish in order to create a zygote, which is then placed in a woman's uterus.

job satisfaction good feeling that results from a positive appraisal of one's work.

joint custody when, following divorce, both parents retain legal custody of their children.

juvenile delinquency when adolescents commit illegal acts that are destructive toward themselves or others.

kinkeepers people who gather their family together for celebrations and keep family members in touch with each other.

learned helplessness feeling that one is always at the mercy of external events and that one does not have any control over one's own destiny.

learning disability when a child with normal intelligence has difficulty mastering at least one academic subject.

leisure discretionary activity that includes simple relaxation, activities for enjoyment, creative pursuits, and sensual transcendance.

life-cycle forces differences in how the same event may affect people of different ages.

life review process of reviewing one's life.

life-span construct unified sense of the past, present, and future that is based on one's experiences and input from others.

life-span perspective view that development is determined by many biological, psychological, and social factors and that all parts of the life span are interrelated.

life story second manifestation of the life-span construct, a personal narrative that organizes past events into a coherent sequence.

locomotion ability to move around in the world.

long-term memory permanent storehouse for memories that has unlimited capacity.

longevity number of years a person will live.

longitudinal study research design in which a single cohort is studied over multiple measurements.

low birth weight newborns who weigh less than 2,500 grams (5 pounds).

low density lipoproteins (LDLs) lipoproteins that cause fatty acids to accumulate in arteries, which impedes the flow of blood.

macrosystem according to Bronfenbrenner, the cultural and subcultural settings in which the microsystems, mesosystems, and exosystems are embedded.

mad cry more intense version of a basic cry.

masturbation self-stimulation of the genitals, which is the way many adolescents first experience sexuality.

maximum life expectancy oldest age to which any person lives.

menarche onset of menstruation.

menopause cessation of menstruation.

mental age in intelligence testing, a measure of children's performance corresponding to the chronological age of those whose performance equals the child's.

mental hardware mental and neural structures that are built-in and that allow the mind to operate.

mental software mental "programs" that are the basis for performing particular tasks.

mental operations cognitive actions that can be performed on objects or ideas.

mesoderm middle layer of the embryo; becomes the muscles, bones, and circulatory system.

mesosystem according to Bronfenbrenner, the interrelations between different microsystems.

metabolic theories theories of aging that focus on aspects of the body's metabolism as a reason why people age.

metabolism energy required for bodily functions.

microsystem according to Bronfenbrenner, the people and objects that are present in one's immediate environment.

midlife crisis time of psychological questioning during which people reevaluate their lives.

monoamine oxidase (MAO) inhibitors type of medication used to treat depression.

monozygotic twins result when a single fertilized egg splits to form two new individuals; also called identical twins.

moral reasoning ethical rules that people use to explain what they think is right or wrong behavior in a particular situation.

moratorium status identity status in Marcia's theory in which adolescents are still examining different alternatives and have yet to find a satisfactory identity.

motor skills coordinated movements of the muscles and limbs.

mourning culturally approved ways in which people express their grief.

multidimensional approaches to intelligence that identify different areas of intellectual abilities.

multidirectionality refers to the fact that some aspects of intelligence improve and other aspects decline across adulthood.

myelin fatty sheath that wraps around neurons to permit them to transmit information more rapidly.

naturalistic observation form of systematic observation in which people are observed as they behave spontaneously in some real-life situation.

nature-nurture issue issue concerning the manner in which genetic and environmental factors influence development.

neural plate flat group of cells present in prenatal development that becomes the brain and spinal cord.

neuritic plaques damaged and dying neurons that collect around a core of protein.

neurofibrillary tangles abnormal filaments found in large numbers of neurons in persons with Alzheimer's disease.

neuron basic cellular unit of the brain and nervous system that specializes in receiving and transmitting information.

neuroticism dimension of personality that refers to the extent that individuals tend to be anxious, hostile, self-conscious, depressed, impulsive, and vulnerable.

neurotransmitters chemicals released by the terminal buttons that allow neurons to communicate with each other.

niche-picking process of deliberately seeking environments that are compatible with one's genetic makeup.

nonnormative influences forces that affect only a few people.

norepinephrine neurotransmitter that helps control arousal; low levels are related to depression.

normative age-graded influences forces that affect all people at certain points in the life span.

normative history-graded influences forces that affect people in a certain generation at a particular point in history.

nuclear family family consisting of parent(s) and child(ren).

obedience orientation characteristic of Kohlberg's Stage 1, in which moral reasoning is based on the belief that adults know what is right and wrong.

occupational priorities what people want from their employment.

one-to-one principle counting principle that states that there must be one and only one number name for each object counted.

openness to experience dimension of personality that displays a vivid imagination and dream life, appreciation of art, and a strong desire to try anything once.

operant conditioning   view of learning, proposed by B. F. Skinner, that emphasizes reward and punishment.

optimally exercised ability   level of performance a normal, healthy adult demonstrates under the best conditions of training or practice.

organic mental retardation   mental retardation that can be traced to a specific biological or physical problem.

osteoporosis   disease in which bones become porous like honeycombs and extremely easy to break.

overextension   when children define words more broadly than adults do.

overregularization   grammatical usage that results from applying rules to words that are exceptions to the rule.

pain cry   cry that begins with a sudden, long burst, followed by a long pause and gasping.

parallel play   when children play alone but are aware of and interested in what another child is doing.

Parkinson's disease   common disease among older adults that results in motor problems, including slow walking, difficulty getting into and out of chairs, and hand tremors.

passive euthanasia   allowing a person to die by withholding an available treatment.

patronizing speech   way of speaking to older adults that is marked by slower rate, exaggerated intonation, higher pitch, increased volume, repetitions, closed-end questions, and simplified vocabulary and grammar.

perception   processes by which the brain receives, selects, modifies, and organizes incoming nerve impulses that are the result of physical stimulation.

period of the fetus   longest period of prenatal development, extending from the 9th until the 38th week after conception.

persistent vegetative state   state in which a person's cortical functioning ceases while brainstem activity continues.

personal control beliefs   beliefs about the degree to which one's performance in a situation is within one's control.

personal fable   attitude of many adolescents that their feelings and experiences are unique and have never been experienced by anyone else before.

personality-type theory   view proposed by Holland that people find their work fulfilling when the important features of a job or profession fit the workers' personalities.

phenotype   physical, behavioral, and psychological features that result from the interaction between one's genes and the environment.

phenylketonuria (PKU)   inherited disorder in which the infant lacks a liver enzyme.

phonemes   unique speech sounds that can be used to create words.

phonological processing   understanding and using sounds in written and oral language.

placenta   structure through which nutrients and wastes are exchanged between the mother and the developing child.

plasticity   the fact that abilities can be modified by certain conditions or experiences.

polygenic inheritance   when phenotypes are the result of the combined activity of many separate genes.

population   broad group of people that is the focus of research.

population pyramid   graphic technique used by demographers to illustrate population trends.

positron emission tomography   procedure that shows the amount of activity in various regions of the brain by monitoring levels of radioactive glucose.

possible selves   representation of what one could become, what one would like to become, and what one is afraid of becoming.

postconventional level   third level of reasoning in Kohlberg's theory, in which morality is based on a personal moral code.

postformal thought   thought characterized by the realization that the correct answer may vary from situation to situation, that problem solutions must be realistic, that most situations are ambiguous, and that emotion and other subjective factors are an important part of thought.

power assertion   punishment that relies upon parents having greater power than their children.

practical intelligence   skills and knowledge necessary for people to function in everyday life.

preconventional level   first level of reasoning in Kohlberg's theory, where moral reasoning is based on external forces.

prenatal development   the many changes that turn a fertilized egg into a newborn human.

presbycusis   loss in the ability to hear high-pitched tones.

preterm (premature)   babies born before the 36th week after conception.

primary circular reaction   according to Piaget, when infants accidentally produce pleasant events that are centered on the body and then try to re-create the events.

primary mental abilities   groups of related intellectual skills, such as spatial skill and mathematical skill.

private speech   comments that are not intended for others but serve the purpose of helping children regulate their behavior.

proactivity   when people choose new behaviors to meet new desires or needs.

processes of thinking   information processing, memory, fluid intelligence.

products of thinking   products applied to thinking, expertise.

programmed cell death theories   theories that suggest that aging is genetically programmed.

prosocial behavior   any behavior that benefits another person.

proximodistal principle   principle that growth occurs first from the center of the body and then out to the extremities.

pseudodementia   treatable diseases that mimic the symptoms of early Alzheimer's disease or related disorders.

psychodynamic theories   theories in which human behavior is said to be guided by motives and drives that are internal and often unconscious.

psychological forces all internal perceptual, cognitive, emotional, and personality factors that affect development.

psychomotor speed speed with which a person makes a particular response.

psychosocial theory theory proposed by Erik Erikson in which personality development results from the interaction of maturation and societal demands.

puberty collection of physical changes that marks the onset of adolescence, such as growth of breasts or testes and the growth spurt.

punishment applying an aversive stimulus (e.g., a spanking) or removing an attractive stimulus (e.g., TV viewing).

purpose according to Erikson, balance between individual initiative and the willingness to cooperate with others.

rapid eye movement (REM) sleep sleep in which an infant's eyes dart rapidly beneath the eyelids.

reasonable woman standard appropriate legal criterion for determining whether sexual harassment has occurred; based on whether a reasonable woman would view a behavior as harassing.

recessive allele whose instructions are ignored when it is combined with a dominant allele.

recognition memory task requiring the selection of the correct item from a list of correct and incorrect choices; an example is a multiple-choice test.

referential style language-learning style that describes children whose vocabularies are dominated by names of objects, persons, or actions.

reflective judgment reasoning about dilemmas that is characterized by the realization that the search for truth is an ongoing, never-ending journey.

reflexes unlearned responses triggered by specific stimulation.

regular (nonREM) sleep sleep in which heart rate, breathing, and brain activity are steady.

reinforcement consequence that increases the likelihood that a behavior will be repeated in the future.

reinvolvement with personal past meaning grandparents derive from recalling the relationship they had with their own grandparents.

reliability as applied to tests, when test scores are consistent from one testing time to another.

resistant attachment relationship in which, after a brief separation, infants want to be held but are difficult to console.

retinal disparity way to infer depth based on differences in the retinal images in the left and right eyes.

returning adult students college students over the age of 25 years.

rites of passage initiation rituals that mark the onset of a new phase of development, such as adulthood.

role transitions assuming new responsibilities and duties when a person moves from one phase of development (e.g., adolescence) to another (e.g., adulthood).

sample subset of a population.

sandwich generation middle-aged adults between two generations (their parents and children) that put demands and pressures on them.

scaffolding teaching style in which adults adjust the amount of assistance that they offer, based on the learner's needs.

scenario life-span construct that consists of expectations about the future.

scheme according to Piaget, a mental structure that organizes information and regulates behavior.

scripts means by which people remember common events consisting of sequences of activities.

secondary circular reaction according to Piaget, when infants accidentally produce interesting events with objects and then try to repeat those events.

secondary memory ability to remember relatively large amounts of information from a few seconds to a few minutes.

secondary mental abilities broad categories of related primary mental abilities.

secular growth trends fact that people in industrialized societies are larger and are maturing earlier than in previous generations.

secure attachment relationship in which infants have come to trust and depend on their mothers.

selective serotonin reuptake inhibitors (SSRIs) type of medication used to treat depression that alters the balance of serotonin in the brain.

selectivity as applied to attention, the ability to pick out important from irrelevant information in the environment.

self-efficacy belief that one is capable of performing a certain task.

self reports people's answers to questions about the topic of interest.

sensorimotor period first of Piaget's four stages of cognitive development, which lasts from birth to approximately 2 years.

sequential design complex research design consisting of multiple cross-sectional or longitudinal designs.

serotonin neurotransmitter that regulates brain centers to allow people to experience pleasure.

sex chromosomes 23rd pair of chromosomes; these determine the sex of the child.

sex discrimination denying a job to someone solely on the basis of whether the person is a man or woman.

sickle-cell trait disorder in which individuals only show signs of mild anemia when they are seriously deprived of oxygen; occurs in individuals who have one dominant allele for normal blood cells and one recessive sickle-cell allele.

simple social play play that begins at about 15–18 months; toddlers engage in similar activities as well as talk and smile at each other.

skilled nursing care 24-hour care requiring fairly constant monitoring and provision of medical and other health services, usually by nurses.

sleeping state in which a baby alternates from being still and breathing regularly to moving gently and breathing irregularly and in which the eyes are closed throughout.

sociability dimension of temperament defined by preference for being with other people.

social clock when adults associate future events with a time or age by which they expect to complete them.

social contract characteristic of Kohlberg's Stage 5, in which moral reasoning is based on the belief that laws are for the good of all members of society.

social convoy group of people who journey together throughout their lives and provide each other support in good and bad times.

social cognitive theory view that thinking, as well as direct reinforcement and punishment, plays an important part in shaping behavior.

social referencing behavior in which infants in unfamiliar or ambiguous environments often look at their mother or father, as if searching for cues to help them interpret the situation.

social role set of cultural guidelines about how one should behave, especially with other people.

social smiles smile that infants produce when they see a human face.

social systems morality characteristic of Kohlberg's Stage 4, in which moral reasoning is based on maintenance of order in society.

sociocultural forces all interpersonal, societal, cultural, and ethnic factors that influence development.

socioemotional selectivity way of maintaining social contact that is motivated by many goals, including information seeking, self-concept, and emotional regulation.

somatic symptoms changes related to the climacteric and menopause unrelated to changes in estrogen, such as difficulties sleeping, headaches, rapid heartbeat, and stiffness or soreness in the joints, neck, or shoulders.

spaced retrieval memory intervention that involves teaching persons with Alzheimer's disease to remember new information by gradually increasing the time between retrieval attempts.

specification second phase in Super's theory of career development, in which adolescents learn more about specific lines of work and begin training.

spiritual support type of coping in which people seek pastoral care, participate in organized and nonorganized religious activities, and express faith in a God who cares for people.

stable-order principle counting principle that states that number names must always be counted in the same order.

stagnation according to Erikson, a state in which people are not able to deal with the needs of their children or are unable to provide mentoring to younger adults.

status offense an act that is not a crime if it is committed by an adult, such as truancy and running away from home.

stranger anxiety first distinct signs of fear that emerge around 6 months of age when infants become wary in the presence of unfamiliar adults.

stress and coping paradigm dominant framework used to study stress.

strokes interruption in the flow of blood in the brain due to a blockage in a cerebral artery.

structured observations setting created by a researcher that is particularly likely to elicit the behavior of interest so that it can be observed.

sudden infant death syndrome (SIDS) situation in which a healthy baby dies suddenly, for no apparent reason.

superego according to Freud, the moral component of the personality that has incorporated adult standards of right and wrong.

systematic observation involves watching people and carefully recording what they say or do.

telegraphic speech speech used by young children that contains only the words that are necessary to get a message across.

temperament consistent style or pattern of behavior.

terminal buttons small knobs at the end of the axon that release neurotransmitters.

teratogen agent that causes abnormal prenatal development.

tertiary circular reaction according to Piaget, repeating old schemes with new objects.

tertiary memory ability to remember information for a very long time, from a few hours to many years.

theory organized set of ideas that explains development.

theory of mind ideas about connections between thoughts, beliefs, intentions, and behavior that create an intuitive understanding of the link between mind and behavior.

time-out punishment that involves removing children who are misbehaving from a situation to a quiet, unstimulating environment.

toddlers young children who have learned to walk.

toddling early, unsteady form of walking done by infants.

type A behavior pattern ongoing displays of intense competitiveness, anger, hostility, restlessness, aggression, and impatience.

type B behavior pattern ongoing displays of noncompetitiveness, calm, lack of aggression, and patience.

ultrasound prenatal diagnostic technique that bounces sound waves off the fetus to generate an image of the fetus.

umbilical cord structure containing veins and arteries that connects the developing child to the placenta.

underextension when children define words more narrowly than adults do.

unexercised ability level of performance a person exhibits without practice or training.

universal ethical principles characteristic of Kohlberg's Stage 6, in which moral reasoning is based on moral principles that apply to all.

universal–context-specific development issue issue of whether there is one path of development or several.

useful life expectancy number of years a person has that are free from debilitating chronic disease and impairment.

validity as applied to tests, the extent to which the test measures what it is supposed to measure.

valued elder status grandparents derive from being seen as wise.

vascular dementia disease caused by numerous small cerebrovascular accidents.

very low birth weight newborns who weigh less than 1,500 grams (3 pounds).

visual acuity smallest pattern that one can distinguish reliably.

visual cliff glass-covered platform that appears to have a "shallow" side and "deep" side; used to study infants' depth perception.

vocational maturity degree of congruity between a person's age and the person's occupational behaviors.

waking activity state in which a baby's eyes are open but seem unfocused and the arms or legs move in bursts of uncoordinated motion.

wear-and-tear theory theory of aging that suggests that the body, much like a machine, gradually deteriorates over time and finally wears out.

will according to Erikson, a young child's understanding that he or she can act on the world intentionally, which occurs when autonomy, shame, and doubt are in balance.

work-family conflict feeling of being pulled in multiple directions by incompatible demands from one's job and one's family.

working memory type of memory in which a small number of items can be stored briefly.

zone of maximum performance potential in environmental press theory, the area in which slight increases in press tend to improve performance.

zone of maximum comfort in environmental press theory, the area where slight decreases in press allow people to live happily without worrying about environmental demands.

zone of proximal development difference between what children can do with assistance and what they can do alone.

zygote fertilized egg.

REFERENCES

Abbey, A. (1991). Acquaintance rape and alcohol consumption on college campuses: How are they linked? *Journal of American College Health, 39,* 165–169.

Aboud, F. E. (1993). The developmental psychology of racial prejudice. *Transcultural Psychiatric Research Review, 30,* 229–242.

Abrams, W. B., & Berkow, R. (1990). *The Merck manual for geriatrics.* Rahway, NJ: Merck, Sharp, & Dohme Research Laboratories.

Ackerman, B. P. (1993). Children's understanding of the speaker's meaning in referential communication. *Journal of Experimental Child Psychology, 55,* 56–86.

Adams, M. J., Treiman, R., & Pressley, M. (1998). Reading, writing, and literacy. In W. Damon (Series Ed.) & I. E. Siegel & K. A. Renninger (Vol. Eds.), *Handbook of child psychology,* (Vol. 4) (5th ed). New York: Wiley.

Adams, R. J. (1995). Further exploration of human neonatal chromatic-achromatic discrimination. *Journal of Experimental Child Psychology, 60,* 344–360.

Adams, R. J., & Courage, M. L. (1995). Development of chromatic discrimination in early infancy. *Behavioural Brain Research, 67,* 99–101.

Adelman, C. (1991). *Women at thirtysomething: Paradoxes of attainment.* Washington, DC: U.S. Department of Education, Office of Educational Research, Office of Research.

Adler, N. (1994). *Adolescent sexual behavior looks irrational—But looks are deceiving.* Washington, DC: Federation of Behavioral, Psychological, and Cognitive Sciences.

Adler, S., & Aranya, N. (1984). A comparison of the work needs, attitudes, and preferences of professional accountants at different career stages. *Journal of Vocational Behavior, 25,* 574–580.

Adlersberg, M., & Thorne, S. (1990). Emerging from the chrysalis: Older women in transition. *Journal of Gerontological Social Work, 16,* 4–8.

Administration on Aging. (1997). Aging into the 21st century. Online document available at http://www.aoa.dhhs.gov/aoa/stats/aging21/

Ahrons, C., & Wallisch, L. (1986). The relationship between former spouses. In D. Perlman & S. Duck (Eds.), *Intimate relationships: Development, dynamics, and deterioration* (pp. 269–296). Newbury Park, CA: Sage.

Ainsworth, M. D. S. (1978). The development of infant-mother attachment. In B. M. Caldwell & H. N. Ricciuti (Eds.), *Review of child development research* (Vol. 3). Chicago: University of Chicago Press.

Ainsworth, M. S. (1993). Attachment as related to mother-infant interaction. *Advances in Infancy Research, 8,* 1–50.

Ales, K. L., Druzin, M. L., & Santini, D. L. (1990). Impact of advanced maternal age on the outcome of pregnancy. *Surgery, Gynecology & Obstetrics, 171,* 209–216.

Alexander, J. F., Waldron, H. B., Barton, C., & Mas, C. H. (1989). The minimizing of blaming attributes and behaviors in delinquent families. *Journal of Consulting and Clinical Psychology, 57,* 19–24.

Allen, G. L., Kirasic, K. C., Dobson, S. H., Long, R. G., & Beck, S. (1996). Predicting environmental learning from spatial abilities: An indirect route. *Intelligence, 22,* 327–355.

Allen, J. P., Philliber, S., Herrling, S., & Kuperminc, G. P. (1997). Preventing teen pregnancy and academic failure: Experimental evaluation of a developmentally based approach. *Child Development, 68,* 729–742.

Allen, K. R., & Chin-sang, V. (1990). A lifetime of work: The context and meanings of leisure for aging black women. *The Gerontologist, 30,* 734–740.

Allen, M. C. (1984). Developmental outcome and follow-up of the small for gestational age infant. *Seminars in Perinatology, 8,* 123–156.

Allgeier, A. R., & Allgeier, E. R. (1995). *Sexual interactions* (4th ed.). Lexington, MA: Heath.

Alwin, D. F. (1994). Aging, personality, and social change: The stability of individual differences over the adult life span. In D. L. Featherman, R. M. Lerner, & M. Perlmutter (Eds.), *Life-span development and behavior* (Vol. 12, pp. 135–185). Hillsdale, NJ: Erlbaum.

Amato, P. R., & Keith, B. (1991). Parental divorce and the well-being of children: A meta-analysis. *Psychological Bulletin, 110,* 26–46.

American Council on Education. (1997). Many college graduates participate in training courses to improve their job skills. *Higher Education and National Affairs, 46(19),* 3.

American Heart Association. (1990). *The healthy American diet.* Dallas, TX: Author.

American Psychological Society (1993, December). Vitality for life. *APS Observer.*

Anand, K. J., & Hickey, P. R. (1987). Pain and its effect in the human neonate and fetus. *New England Journal of Medicine, 31,* 1321–1329.

Anastasi, A. (1988). *Psychological testing* (6th ed.). New York: Macmillan.

Anastopoulos, A. D., Guevremont, D. C., Shelton, T. L., & Dupaul, G. J. (1992). Parenting stress among families of children with attention deficit hyperactivity disorder. *Journal of Abnormal Child Psychology, 20,* 503–520.

Anastopoulos, A. D., Shelton, T. L., Dupaul, G. J., & Guevremont, D. C. (1993). Parent training for attention-deficit hyperactivity disorder: Its impact on parent functioning. *Journal of Abnormal Child Psychology, 21,* 581–596.

Anderson, W. T. (1997). Dying and death in aging intergenerational families. In T. D. Hargrave & S. M. Hanna (Eds.), *The aging family* (pp. 270–291). New York: Brunner/Mazel.

Andrews, J. A., Hops, H., & Duncan, S. C. (1997). Adolescent modeling of parent substance abuse: The moderating effect of the relationship with the parent. *Journal of Family Psychology, 11,* 259–270.

Aneshensel, C. S., Pearlin, L. I., Mullan, J. T., Zarit, S. H., & Whitlach, C. J. (1995). *Profiles in caregiving: The unexpected career.* San Diego, CA: Academic Press.

Anglin, J. M. (1993). Vocabulary development: A morphological analysis. *Monographs of the Society for Research in Child Development, 58*(10, Serial No. 238).

Antonarakis, S. E., & The Down Syndrome Collaborative Group. (1991). Parental origin of the extra chromosome in trisomy 21 as indicated by analysis of DNA polymorphisms. *New England Journal of Medicine, 324,* 872–876.

Antonovsky, A., & Sagy, S. (1990). Confronting developmental tasks in the retirement transition. *The Gerontologist, 30,* 362–368.

Antonucci, T. C. (1985). Personal characteristics, social support, and social behavior. In R. H. Binstock & E. Shanas (Eds.), *Handbook of aging and the social sciences* (2nd ed., pp. 94–128). New York: Van Nostrand Reinhold.

Antonucci, T. C. (1990). Attachment, social support, and coping with negative life events. In E. M. Cummings, A. L. Greene, & E. H. Karraker (Eds.), *Life-span developmental psychology: Vol. 11. Stress and coping across the life-span.* Hillsdale, NJ: Erlbaum.

Apgar, V. (1953). A proposal for a new method of evaluation of the newborn infant. *Current Researches in Anesthesia and Analgesia, 32,* 260–267.

Apgar, V., & Beck, J. (1974). *Is my baby all right?* New York: Pocket Books.

Aranda, M. P., & Knight, B. G. (1997). The influence of ethnicity and culture on the caregiver stress and coping process: A sociocultural review and analysis. *The Gerontologist, 37,* 342–354.

Arbona, C. (1990). Career counseling research and Hispanics: A review of the literature. *Counseling Psychologist, 18,* 300–323.

Arnett, J., & Taber, S. (1994). Adolescence terminable and interminable: When does adolescence end? *Journal of Youth and Adolescence, 23,* 517–537.

Aryee, S. (1993). Dual-earner couples in Singapore: An examination of work and nonwork sources of their experienced burnout. *Human Relations, 46,* 1441–1468.

Aryee, S., & Luk, V. (1996). Work and nonwork influences on the career satisfaction of dual-earner couples. *Journal of Vocational Behavior, 49,* 38–52.

Aslin, R. N. (1987). Visual and auditory discrimination in infancy. In J. D. Osofsky (Ed.), *Handbook of infant development* (2nd ed.). New York: Wiley.

Atchley, R. C. (1975). The life course, age grading, and age-linked demands for decision making. In N. Datan & L. H. Ginsberg (Eds.), *Life-span developmental psychology: Normative life crises* (pp. 261–278). New York: Academic Press.

Atchley, R. C. (1982). Retirement as a social institution. *American Review of Sociology, 8,* 263–287.

Atchley, R. C. (1989). A continuity theory of normal aging. *The Gerontologist, 29,* 183–190.

Atkinson, M. (1992). *Children's syntax.* Cambridge, MA: Blackwell.

Attie, J., Brooks-Gunn, J., & Petersen, A. C. (1990). A developmental perspective on eating disorders and eating problems. In M. Lewis and S. M. Miller, (Eds.), *Handbook of developmental psychopathology.* New York: Plenum.

Attig, T. (1996). *How we grieve: Relearning the world.* New York: Oxford University Press.

Atwater, E. (1992). *Adolescence.* Englewood Cliffs, NJ: Prentice-Hall.

Au, T. K., & Glusman, M. (1990). The principle of mutual exclusivity in word learning: To honor or not to honor? *Child Development, 61,* 1474–1490.

Azrin, N. H., & Foxx, R. M. (1974). *Toilet training in less than a day.* New York: Simon & Schuster.

Bachman, J. (1983, Summer). Premature affluence: Do high school students earn too much? *Economic Outlook USA,* 64–67.

Bachman, J. G., & Schulenberg, J. (1993). How part-time work intensity relates to drug use, problem behavior, time use, and satisfaction among high school seniors: Are these consequences or merely correlates? *Developmental Psychology, 29,* 220–235.

Baer, D. M., & Wolf, M. M. (1968). The reinforcement contingency in preschool and remedial education. In R. D. Hess & R. M Baer (Eds.), *Early education.* Chicago: Aldine.

Bagwell, C. L., Newcomb, A. F., & Bukowski, W. M. (1998). Preadolescent friendship and peer rejection as predictors of adult adjustment. *Child Development, 69,* 140–153.

Bailey, J. M., Bobrow, D., Wolfe, M., & Mikach, S. (1995). Sexual orientation of adult sons of gay fathers. *Developmental Psychology, 31,* 124–129.

Baillargeon, R. (1987). Object permanence in 32- and 42-month-old infants. *Developmental Psychology, 23,* 655–664.

Baillargeon, R. (1994). How do infants learn about the physical world? *Current Directions in Psychological Science, 3,* 133–140.

Baker, T. B. (1988). Models of addiction. *Journal of Abnormal Psychology, 97,* 115–117.

Balk, D. E. (1996). Attachment and the reactions of bereaved college students: A longitudinal study. In D. Klass, P. R. Silverman, & S. L. Nickman (Eds.), *Continuing bonds: New understandings of grief* (pp. 311–328). Washington, DC: Taylor & Francis.

Ball, J. F. (1976/1977). Widow's grief: The impact of age and mode of death. *Omega: Journal of Death and Dying, 7,* 307–333.

Ball, K. (1997). Enhancing mobility in the elderly: Attentional interventions for driving. In S. M. C. Dollinger & L. F. Dilalla (Eds.), *Assessment and intervention issues across in the lifespan* (pp. 267–292). Mahwah, NJ: Erlbaum.

Ball, K., & Owsley, C. (1993). The Useful Field of View Test: A new technique for evaluating age-related declines in visual function. *Journal of the American Optometric Association, 64,* 71–79.

Baltes, M. M., & Baltes, P. B. (Eds.). (1986). *The psychology of control and aging.* Hillsdale, NJ: Erlbaum.

Baltes, P. B. (1993). The aging mind: Potential and limits. *The Gerontologist, 33,* 580–594.

Baltes, P. B., & Staudinger, U. M. (1993). The search for a psychology of wisdom. *Current Directions in Psychological Science, 2,* 75–80.

Baltes, P. B., & Willis, S. L. (1982). Enhancement (plasticity) of intellectual functioning: Penn State's Adult Development and Enrichment Project (ADEPT). In F. I. M. Craik & S. Trehub (Eds.), *Aging and cognitive processes* (pp. 353–389). New York: Plenum.

Baltes, P. B., Dittmann-Kohli, F., & Dixon, R. A. (1984). New perspectives on the development of intelligence in adulthood: Toward a dual-process conception and a model of selective optimization with compensation. In P. B. Baltes & O. G. Brim, Jr. (Eds.), *Life-span development and behavior* (Vol. 6, pp. 33–76). New York: Academic Press.

Baltimore School Clinics to Offer Birth Control by Surgical Implant (1992, December 4). *New York Times,* pp. A1, A28.

Bancroft, J., Axworthy, D., & Ratcliffe, S. (1982). The personality and psychosexual development of boys with 47-XXY chromosome constitution. *Journal of Child Psychology and Psychiatry, 23,* 169–180.

Bandura, A. (1977). *Social learning theory.* Englewood Cliffs, NJ: Prentice-Hall.

Bandura, A. (1986). *Social foundations of thought and action: A social-cognitive theory.* Englewood Cliffs, NJ: Prentice-Hall.

Bandura, A., Ross, D., & Ross, S. A. (1963). Imitation of film-mediated aggressive models. *Journal of Abnormal and Social Psychology, 66,* 3–11.

Banks, M. D., & Dannemiller, J. L. (1987). Infant visual psychophysics. In P. Salapatek & L. Cohen (Eds.), *Handbook of infant perception* (Vol. 1). Orlando, FL: Academic Press.

Barenboim, C. (1981). The development of person perception in childhood and adolescence: From behavioral comparisons to psychological constructs to psychological comparisons. *Child Development, 52,* 129–144.

Barfield, R. E., & Morgan, J. N. (1978). Trends in satisfaction with retirement. *The Gerontologist, 18,* 19–23.

Barkley, R. A. (1990). Attention deficit disorders: History, definition, and diagnosis. In M. Lewis & S. M. Miller (Eds.), *Handbook of developmental psychopathology.* New York: Plenum.

Barkley, R. A. (1996). Attention-deficit hyperactivity disorder. In E. J. Mash & R. A. Barkley (Eds.), *Child psychopathology.* New York: Guilford Press.

Barling, J., Rogers, K., & Kelloway, E. K. (1995). Some effects of teenagers' part-time employment: The quantity and quality of work make the difference. *Journal of Organizational Behavior, 16,* 143–154.

Baron, J. N., & Bielby, W. T. (1985). Organizational barriers to gender equality: Sex segregation of jobs and opportunities. In A. S. Rossi (Ed.), *Gender and the life course* (pp. 233–251). New York: Aldine.

Barr, H. M., Streissguth, A. P., Darby, B. L., & Sampson, P. D. (1990). Prenatal exposure to alcohol, caffeine, tobacco, and aspirin: Effects on fine and gross motor performance in 4-year-old children. *Developmental Psychology, 26,* 339–348.

Barton, M. E., & Tomasello, M. (1991). Joint attention and conversation in mother-infant-sibling triads. *Child Development, 62,* 517–529.

Barton, P. E., & Kirsch, I. S. (1990). *Workplace competencies: The need to improve literacy and employment readiness.* Washington, DC: U.S. Government Printing Office.

Bartsch, K., & Wellman, H. M. (1995). *Children talk about the mind.* New York: Oxford University Press.

Baruch, G. K. (1984). The psychological well-being of women in the middle years. In G. K. Baruch & J. Brooks-Gunn (Eds.), *Women in midlife* (pp. 161–180). New York: Plenum.

Baskett, L. M. (1985). Sibling status effects: Adult expectations. *Developmental Psychology, 21,* 441–445.

Bates, E., Bretherton, I., & Snyder, L. (1988). *From first words to grammar: Individual differences and dissociable mechanisms.* New York: Cambridge University Press.

Baugh, S. G., Lankau, M. J., & Scandura, T. A. (1996). An investigation of the effects of protégé gender on responses to mentoring. *Journal of Vocational Behavior, 49,* 309–323.

Baugher, E., & Lamison-White, L. (1996). *Poverty in the United States: 1995.* Washington, DC: U.S. Government Printing Office.

Baumeister, A. A., & Baumeister, A. A. (1995). Mental retardation. In M. Hersen & R. T. Ammerman (Eds.), *Advanced abnormal child psychology.* Hillsdale, NJ: Erlbaum.

Baumrind, D. (1975). *Early socialization and the discipline controversy.* Morristown, NJ: General Learning Press.

Baumrind, D. (1991a). Effective parenting during the early adolescent transition. In P. A. Cowan & E. M. Hetherington (Eds.), *Family transitions.* Hillsdale, NJ: Erlbaum.

Baumrind, D. (1991b). Parenting styles and adolescent development. In R. M. Lerner, A. C. Petersen, & J. Brooks-Gunn (Eds.), *Encyclopedia of adolescence.* New York: Garland.

Bayley, N. (1969). *Bayley scales of infant development: Manual.* New York: The Psychological Corporation.

Beal, C. R., & Belgrad, S. L. (1990). The development of message evaluation skills in young children. *Child Development, 61,* 705–712.

Bean, F., & Tienda, M. (1987). *The Hispanic population in the United States.* New York: Russell Sage Foundation.

Beck, A. T. (1967). *Depression: Clinical, experimental, and theoretical aspects.* New York: Harper & Row.

Beck, A. T., Rush, J., Shaw, B., & Emery, G. (1979). *Cognitive therapy of depression.* New York: Guilford Press.

Beck, M. (1994). How far should we push Mother Nature? *Newsweek* (January 17), 54–57.

Becker, B. J. (1986). Influence again: An examination of reviews and studies of gender differences in social influence. In J. S. Hyde & M. C. Linn (Eds.), *The psychology of gender differences. Advances through meta-analysis.* Baltimore, MD: Johns Hopkins University Press.

Behnke, M., & Eyler, F. D. (1993). The consequences of prenatal substance use for the developing fetus, newborn, and young child. *International Journal of the Addictions, 28,* 1341–1391.

Behrend, D. A., Rosengren, K. S., & Perlmutter, M. S. (1992). The relation between private speech and parental interactive style. In R. M. Diaz & L. E. Berk (Eds.), *Private speech: From social interaction to self-regulation* (pp. 85–100). Hillsdale, NJ: Erlbaum.

Belgrave, L. L., Wykle, M. L., & Choi, J. M. (1993). Health, double jeopardy, and culture: The use of institutionalization by African-Americans. *The Gerontologist, 33,* 379–385.

Bell, A. P., Weinberg, M. S., & Hammersmith, S. K. (1981). *Sexual preference: Its development in men and women.* New York: Simon & Schuster.

Beller, M., & Gafni, N. (1996). 1991 International Assessment of Educational Progress in Mathematics and Sciences: The gender differences perspective. *Journal of Educational Psychology, 88,* 365–377.

Belsky, J. (1993). Etiology of child maltreatment: A developmental-ecological analysis. *Psychological Bulletin, 114,* 413–434.

Belsky, J. (1996). Parent, infant, and social-contextual antecedents of father-son attachment security. *Developmental Psychology, 32,* 905–913.

Belsky, J., Hsieh, K., & Crnic, K. (1996). Infant positive and negative emotionality: One dimension or two? *Developmental Psychology, 32,* 289–298.

Belsky, J., Steinberg, L., & Draper, P. (1991). Childhood experience, interpersonal development, and reproductive strategy: An evolutionary theory of socialization. *Child Development, 62,* 647–670.

Bem, D. J. (1996). Exotic becomes erotic: A developmental theory of sexual orientation. *Psychological Review, 103,* 320–335.

Bengtson, V. L. (1985). Diversity and symbolism in grandparental roles. In V. L. Bengtson & J. F. Robertson (Eds.), *Grandparenthood* (pp. 11–25). Newbury Park, CA: Sage.

Bengtson, V. L., Mills, T. L., & Parrott, T. M. (1995). Ageing in the United States at the end of the century. *Korea Journal of Population and Development, 24,* 215–244.

Benin, M. H., & Agostinelli, J. (1988). Husbands' and wives' satisfaction with the division of labor. *Journal of Marriage and the Family, 50,* 349–361.

Berdahl, J. L., Magley, V. J., & Waldo, C. R. (1996). The sexual harassment of men? *Psychology of Women Quarterly, 20,* 527–547.

Berk, L. E. (1992). Children's private speech: An overview of theory and the status of research. In R. M. Diaz & L. E. Berk (Eds.), *Private speech: From social interaction to selfregulation.* Hillsdale, NJ: Erlbaum.

Berk, L. E. (1992). Children's private speech: An overview of theory and the status of research. In R. M. Diaz & L. E. Berk (Eds.), *Private speech: From social interaction to self-regulation.* Hillsdale, NJ: Erlbaum.

Berk, L. E. (1994). *Child development* (3rd ed.). Needham Heights, MA: Allyn & Bacon.

Berk, L. E. (1994). Vygotsky's theory: The importance of make believe play. *Young Children, 50,* 30–38.

Berko, J. (1958). The child's learning of English morphology. *Word, 14,* 150–177.

Berkow, R. (Ed.). (1987). *The Merck manual of diagnosis and therapy* (15th ed.). Rahway, NJ: Merck, Sharp, & Dohme Research Laboratories.

Berndt, T. J., & Keefe, K. (1995). Friends' influence on adolescents' adjustment to school. *Child Development, 66,* 1312–1329.

Berndt, T. J., & Perry, T. B. (1990). Distinctive features and effects of adolescent friendships. In R. Montemeyer, G. R. Adams, &

T. P. Gullotta (Eds.), *From childhood to adolescence: A transition period?* London: Sage.

Berry, J. W. (1993). Ethnic identities in plural societies. In M. E. Bernal & G. P. Knight (Eds.), *Ethnic identity: Formation and transmission among Hispanics and other minorities.* New York: State University of New York Press.

Berry, R. E., & Williams, F. L. (1987). Assessing the relationship between quality of life and marital and income satisfaction: A path analytical approach. *Journal of Marriage and the Family, 49,* 107–116.

Besharov, D. J., & Gardiner, K. N. (1997). Trends in teen sexual behavior. *Children and Youth Services Review, 19,* 341–367.

Best, D. L., Williams, J. E., Cloud, J. M., Davis, S. W., Robertson, L. S., Edwards, J. R., Giles, H., & Fowles, J. (1977). Development of sex-trait stereotypes among young children in the United States, England, and Ireland. *Child Development, 48,* 1375–1384.

Bettencourt, B. A., & Miller, N. (1996). Gender differences in aggression as a function of provocation: A meta-analysis. *Psychological Bulletin, 119,* 422–447.

Betz, E. L. (1984). A study of career patterns of women college graduates. *Journal of Vocational Behavior, 24,* 249–263.

Betz, N. E., Harmon, L. W., & Borgen, F. H. (1996). The relationships of self-efficacy for the Holland themes to gender, occupational group membership, and vocational interests. *Journal of Counseling Psychology, 43,* 90–98.

Betz, N. E., Heesacker, R. S., & Shuttleworth, C. (1990). Moderators of the congruence and realism of major and occupational plans in college students: A replication and extension. *Journal of Counseling Psychology, 37,* 269–276.

Bhatt, R. S., & Rovee-Collier, C. (1996). Infants' forgetting of correlated attributes and object recognition. *Child Development, 67,* 172–187.

Bigler, R. S. (1995). The role of classification skill in moderating environmental influences on children's gender stereotyping: A study of the functional use of gender in the classroom. *Child Development, 66,* 1072–1087.

Binger, C. M., Ablin, A. R., Feuerstein, R. C., Kushner, J. H., Zoger, S., & Mikkelson, C. (1969). Childhood leukemia—Emotional impact on patient and family. *New England Journal of Medicine, 280,* 414.

Binstock, R. H. (1994). Changing criteria in old-age programs: The introduction of economic status and need for services. *The Gerontologist, 34,* 726–730.

Binstock, R. H. (1999). Public policy issues. In J. C. Cavanaugh & S. K. Whitbourne (Eds.), *Gerontology: Interdisciplinary perspectives* (pp. 414–447). New York: Oxford University Press.

Binstock, R. H., & Day, C. L. (1996). Aging and politics. In R. H. Binstock & L. K. George (Eds.), *Handbook of aging and the social sciences* (4th ed., pp. 362–387). San Diego, CA: Academic Press.

Birch, L. L. (1991). Obesity and eating disorders: A developmental perspective. *Bulletin of the Psychonomic Society, 29,* 265–272.

Biringen, Z., Emde, R. N., Campos, J. J., & Appelbaum, M. I. (1995). Affective reorganization in the infant, the mother, and the dyad: The role of upright locomotion and its timing. *Child Development, 66,* 499–514.

Black, S. A., Markides, K. S., & Miller, T. Q. (1998). Correlates of depressive symptomatology among older community-dwelling Mexican Americans: The Hispanic EPESE. *Journal of Gerontology: Social Sciences, 53B,* S198–S208.

Black-Gutman, D., & Hickson, F. (1996). The relationship between racial attitudes and social-cognitive development in children: An Australian study. *Developmental Psychology, 32,* 448–456.

Blanchard-Fields, F. (1986). Reasoning on social dilemmas varying in emotional saliency: An adult developmental study. *Psychology and Aging, 1,* 325–333.

Blanchard-Fields, F., Chen, Y., & Norris, L. (1997). Everyday problem solving across the adult life span: Influence of domain specificity and cognitive appraisal. *Psychology and Aging, 12,* 684–693.

Blanchard-Fields, F., Janke, H. C., & Camp, C. J. (1995). Age differences in problem-solving style: The role of emotional salience. *Psychology and Aging, 10,* 173–180.

Block, J. (1995). A contrarian view of the five-factor approach to personality description. *Psychological Bulletin, 117,* 187–215.

Bloom L. (1991). *Language development from two to three.* Cambridge, UK: Cambridge University Press.

Blumenthal, J. A., Emery, C. F., Cox, D. R., Walsh, M. A., Kuhn, C. M., Williams, R. B., & Williams, R. S. (1988). Exercise training in healthy Type A middle-aged men: Effects on behavioral and cardiovascular responses. *Psychosomatic Medicine, 50,* 418–433.

Blumstein, P., & Schwartz, P. (1983). *American couples.* New York: Morrow.

Bogatz, G. A., & Ball, S. (1972). *The second year of "Sesame Street": A continuing evaluation.* Princeton, NJ: Educational Testing Service.

Bohannon, J. N., Padgett, R. J., Nelson, K. E., & Mark, M. (1996). Useful evidence on negative evidence. *Developmental Psychology, 32,* 551–555.

Bond, T. G. (1995). Piaget and measurement II: Empirical validation of the Piagetian model. *Archives de Psychologie, 63,* 155–185.

Bondareff, W. (1983). Age and Alzheimer's disease. *Lancet, 1,* 1447.

Boone, R. T., & Cunningham, J. G. (1998). Children's decoding of emotion in expressive body movement: The development of cue attention. *Developmental Psychology, 34,* 1007–1016.

Booth, A., & Johnson, E. (1988). Premarital cohabitation and marital success. *Journal of Family Issues, 9,* 387–394.

Bootzin, R. R., Epstein, D., Engle-Friedman, M., & Salvio, M. A. (1996). Sleep disturbances. In L. L. Carstensen, B. A. Edelstein, & L. Dornbrand (Eds.), *The practical handbook of clinical gerontology* (pp. 398–420). Thousand Oaks, CA: Sage.

Borg, S., & Lasker, J. (1981). *When pregnancy fails.* Boston: Beacon Press.

Bornstein, M. H., Haynes, O. M., O'Reilly, A. W., & Painter, K. M. (1996). Solitary and collaborative pretense play in early childhood: Sources of individual variation in the development of representational competence. *Child Development, 67,* 2910–2929.

Bortz, W. M., II, & Bortz, S. S. (1996). Prevention, nutrition, and exercise in the aged. In L. L. Carstensen, B. A. Edelstein, & L. Dornbrand (Eds.), *The practical handbook of clinical gerontology* (pp. 36–53). Thousand Oaks, CA: Sage.

Bossé, R., & Ekerdt, D. J. (1981). Change in self-perception of leisure activities with retirement. *The Gerontologist, 21,* 650–653.

Bossé, R., Aldwin, C. M., Levenson, M. R., Spiro, A., III, & Mroczek, D. K. (1993). Change in social support after retirement: Longitudinal findings from the Normative Aging Study. *Journal of Gerontology: Psychological Sciences, 48,* P210–P217.

Bouchard, T. J., Lykken, D. T., McGue, M., Segal, N. L., et al. (1990). Sources of human psychological differences: The Minnesota Study of Twins Reared Apart. *Science, 250,* 223–228.

Bouza, A. V. (1990). *The police mystique: An insider's look at cops, crime, and the criminal justice system.* New York: Plenum.

Bowlby, J. (1969). *Attachment and loss* (Vol. 1). New York: Basic Books.

Boyer, C. B., & Hein, K. (1991). AIDS and HIV infection in adolescents: The role of education and antibody testing. In R. M. Lerner, A. C. Petersen, & J. Brooks-Gunn (Eds.), *Encyclopedia of adolescence* (Vol. 1). New York: Garland.

Boykin, A. W. (1994). Harvesting talent and culture: African-American children and educational reform. In R. Rossi (Ed.), *Schools and students at risk* (pp. 116–138). New York: Teachers College Press.

Bozett, F. W. (1988). Gay fatherhood. In P. Bronstein & C. P. Cowan (Eds.), *Fatherhood today: Men's changing role in the family* (pp. 214–235). New York: Wiley.

Brabeck, M. M., & Weisgerber, K. (1989). College students' perceptions of men and women choosing teaching and management: The effects of gender and sex role egalitarianism. *Sex Roles, 21,* 841.

Bradley, R. H., Caldwell, B. M., & Rock, S. L. (1988). Home environment and school performance: A ten-year follow-up and examination of three models of environmental action. *Child Development, 59,* 852–867.

Bradley, R. H., Caldwell, B. M., Rock, S. L., Ramey, C. T., Barnard, K. E., Gray, C., Hammond, M. A., Mitchell, S., Gottfried, A. W., Siegel, L., & Johnson, D. L. (1989). Home environment and cognitive development in the first 3 years of life: A collaborative study involving six sites and three ethnic groups in North America. *Developmental Psychology, 25,* 217–235.

Brady, J. E., Newcomb, A. F., & Hartup, W. W. (1983). Context and companion's behavior as determinants of cooperation and competition in school-age children. *Journal of Experimental Child Psychology, 36,* 396–412.

Braet, C., Mervielde, I., & Vandereycken, W. (1997). Psychological aspects of childhood obesity: A controlled study in a clinical and nonclinical sample. *Journal of Pediatric Psychology, 22,* 59–71.

Braine, M. D. S. (1976). Children's first word combinations. *Monographs of the Society for Research in Child Development, 41* (Serial No. 164).

Braine, M. D. S. (1992). What sort of innate structure is needed to "bootstrap" into syntax? *Cognition, 45,* 77–100.

Brainerd, C. J. (1996). Piaget: A centennial celebration. *Psychological Science, 7,* 191–203.

Brainerd, C. J., & Reyna, V. F. (1996). Mere memory testing creates false memories in children. *Developmental Psychology, 32,* 467–478.

Brand, E., Clingempeel, W. G., & Bowen-Woodward, D. (1988). Family relationships and children's psychological adjustment in stepmother and stepfather families. In E. M. Hetherington & J. D. Arasten (Eds.), *Impact of divorce, single parenting, and step parenting on children* (pp. 299–324). Hillsdale, NJ: Erlbaum.

Brandtstädter, J. (1989). Personal self-regulation of development: Cross-sequential analyses of development-related control beliefs and emotions. *Developmental Psychology, 25,* 96–108.

Brandtstädter, J., & Greve, W. (1994). The aging self: Stabilizing and protective processes. *Developmental Review, 14,* 52–80.

Braungart, J. M., Plomin, R., DeFries, J. C., & Fulker, D. W. (1992). Genetic influence on tester-rated infant temperament as assessed by Bayley's Infant Behavior Record: Nonadoptive and adoptive siblings and twins. *Developmental Psychology, 28,* 40–47.

Bray, D. W., & Howard, A. (1983). The AT&T longitudinal studies of managers. In K. W. Schaie (Ed.), *Longitudinal studies on adult psychological development* (pp. 266–312). New York: Guilford Press.

Brazelton, T. B. (1984). *Brazelton Behavior Assessment Scale* (rev. ed.). Philadelphia: Lippincott.

Brazelton, T. B., Nugent, J. K., & Lester, B. M. (1987). Neonatal behavioral assessment scale. In J. D. Osofsky (Ed.), *Handbook of infant development* (2nd ed). New York: Wiley.

Bretherton, I. (1992). The origins of attachment theory: John Bowlby & Mary Ainsworth. *Developmental Psychology, 28,* 759–775.

Bretherton, I. (1995). A communication perspective on attachment relationships and internal working models. *Monographs of the Society for Research in Child Development, 60,* 310–329.

Bridges, C. R. (1996). The characteristics of career achievement perceived by African American college administrators. *Journal of Black Studies, 26,* 748–767.

Brigham, J. C., & Spier, S. A. (1992). Opinions held by professionals who work with child witnesses. In H. Dent & R. Flin (Eds.), *Children as witnesses.* New York: Wiley.

Brim, O. G., Jr., & Kagan, J. (1980). Constancy and change: A view of the issues. In O. G. Brim, Jr., & J. Kagan (Eds.), *Constancy and change in human development* (pp. 1–25). Cambridge, MA: Harvard University Press.

Brinton, L. A., & Schairer, C. (1997). Postmenopausal hormone-replacement therapy: Time for reappraisal? *New England Journal of Medicine, 336,* 1821–1822.

Brioni, J. D., & Decker, M. W. (Eds.). (1997). *Pharmacological treatment of Alzheimer's disease.* New York: Wiley.

Brody, E. M. (1981). Women in the middle and family help to older people. *The Gerontologist, 21,* 471–480.

Brody, E. M. (1990). *Women in the middle: Their parent-care years.* New York: Springer.

Brody, G. H., Stoneman, Z., & Gauger, K. (1996). Parent-child relationships, family problem-solving behavior, and sibling relationship quality: The moderating role of sibling temperaments. *Child Development, 67,* 1289–1300.

Brodzinsky, D. M., & Rightmyer, J. (1980). Individual differences in children's humor development. In P. McGhee & A. Chapman (Eds.), *Children's humour.* Chichester, UK: Wiley.

Broman, C. L. (1988). Household work and family life satisfaction of blacks. *Journal of Marriage and the Family, 50,* 743–748.

Bronfenbrenner, U. (1979). Contexts of child rearing: Problems and prospects. *American Psychologist, 34,* 844–850.

Bronfenbrenner, U. (1989). Ecological systems theory. In R. Vasta (Ed.), *Annals of child development: Vol. 6. Theories of child development: Revised formulations and current issues.* Greenwich, CT: JAI Press.

Bronfenbrenner, U. (1995). Developmental ecology through space and time: A future perspective. In P. Moen, G. H. Elder, Jr., & K. Luscher (Eds.), *Examining lives in context: Perspectives on the ecology of human development.* Washington, DC: American Psychological Associaton.

Bronson, G. W. (1991). Infant differences in rate of visual encoding. *Child Development, 62,* 44–54.

Brooks, L., & Betz, N. E. (1990). Utility of expectancy theory in predicting occupational choices in college students. *Journal of Counseling Psychology, 37,* 57–64.

Brooks-Gunn, J. (1991). How stressful is the transition to adolescence for girls? In M. E. Colten & S. Gore (Eds.), *Adolescent stress: Causes and consequences. Social institutions and social change* (pp. 131–149). New York: Aldine de Gruyter.

Brooks-Gunn, J., Klebanov, P. K., & Duncan, G. J. (1996). Ethnic differences in children's intelligence test scores: Role of economic deprivation, home environment, and maternal characteristics. *Child Development, 67,* 396–408.

Brown, B. B., & Lohr, M. J. (1987). Peer-group affiliation and adolescent self-esteem: An integration of ego-identity and symbolic-interaction theories. *Journal of Personality and Social Psychology, 52,* 47–55.

Brown, B. B., Lohr, M. J., & McClenahan, E. L. (1986). Early adolescents' perceptions of peer pressure. *Journal of Early Adolescence, 6,* 139–154.

Brown, B. B., Mounts, N., Lamborn, S. D., & Steinberg, L. (1993). Parenting practices and peer group affiliation in adolescence. *Developmental Psychology, 64,* 467–482.

Brown, J. R., & Dunn, J. (1992). Talk with your mother or your sibling? Developmental changes in early family conversations about feelings. *Child Development, 63,* 336–349.

Brown, R., Pressley, M., Van Meter, P., & Schuder, T. (1996). A quasi-experimental validation of transactional strategies instruction with low-achieving second-grade readers. *Journal of Educational Psychology, 88,* 18–37.

Browne, A., & Williams, K. R. (1993). Gender, intimacy, and lethal violence: Trends from 1976 to 1987. *Gender and Society, 7,* 78–98.

Bruck, M., & Ceci, S. J. (1997). The suggestibility of young children. *Current Directions in Psychological Science, 6,* 75–79.

Bryan, J. H., & Walbek, N. B. (1970). Preaching and practicing generosity: Children's actions and reactions. *Child Development, 41,* 329–353.

Bryant, B. K., & Crockenberg, S. B. (1980). Correlates and dimensions of prosocial behavior: A study of female siblings with their mothers. *Child Development, 51,* 529–554.

Buchsbaum, B. C. (1996). Remembering a parent who has died: A developmental perspective. In D. Klass, P. R. Silverman, & S. L. Nickman (Eds.), *Continuing bonds: New understandings of grief* (pp. 113–124). Washington, DC: Taylor & Francis.

Buckle, L., Gallup, G. G., Jr., & Rodd, Z. A. (1996). Marriage as a reproductive contract: Patterns of marriage, divorce, and remarriage. *Ethology and Sociobiology, 17,* 363–377.

Buhrmester, D., & Furman, W. (1987). The development of companionship and intimacy. *Child Development, 58,* 1101–1113.

Buhrmester, D., & Furman, W. (1990). Perceptions of sibling relationships during middle childhood and adolescence. *Child Development, 61,* 1387–1398.

Bullock, M., & Lutkenhaus, P. (1990). Who am I? The development of self-understanding in toddlers. *Merrill-Palmer Quarterly, 36,* 217–238.

Bullock, W. A., & Dunn, N. J. (1988, August). *Aging, sex, and marital satisfaction.* Paper presented at the meeting of the American Psychological Association, Atlanta.

Bumpass, L. L., & Aquilino, W. S. (1995). *A social map of midlife: Family and work over the middle years.* University of Wisconsin-Madison, Center for Demography and Ecology.

Bumpass, L. L., Sweet, J. A., & Cherlin, A. (1991). The role of cohabitation in declining rates of marriage. *Journal of Marriage and the Family, 53,* 913–927.

Burgess, D., & Borgida, E. (1997). Sexual harassment: An experimental test of sex-role spillover theory. *Personality and Social Psychology Bulletin, 23,* 63–75.

Burke, R. J. (1991a). Organizational treatment of minority managers and professionals: Costs to the majority? *Psychological Reports, 68,* 439–449.

Burke, R. J. (1991b). Work experiences of minority managers and professionals: Individual and organizational costs of perceived bias. *Psychological Reports, 69,* 1011–1023.

Burns, A. (1992). Mother-headed families: An international perspective and the case of Australia. *Society for Research in Child Development: Social Policy Report, 6,* 1–22.

Burrus-Bammel, L. L., & Bammel, G. (1985). Leisure and recreation. In J. E. Birren & K. W. Schaie (Eds.), *Handbook of the psychology of aging* (2nd ed., pp. 848–889). New York: Van Nostrand Reinhold.

Bursuck, W. D., & Rose, E. (1992). Community college options for students with mild disabilities. In F. R. Rusch, L. DeStefano, J. Chadsey-Rusch, L. A. Phelps, & E. Szymanski (Eds.), *Transition from school to life* (pp. 71–91). Sycamore, IL: Sycamore.

Burton, L. M. (1992). Black grandparents rearing children of drug-addicted parents: Stressors, outcomes, and social service needs. *The Gerontologist, 32,* 744–751.

Busch, J. W. (1985). Mentoring in graduate schools of education: Mentors' perceptions. *American Educational Research Journal, 22,* 257–265.

Buss, A. H., & Plomin, R. (1984). *Temperament: Early developing personality traits.* Hillsdale, NJ: Erlbaum.

Buss, D. M. (1994). *The evolution of desire.* New York: Basic Books.

Buss, D. M., et al. (1990). International preferences in selecting mates: A study of 37 cultures. *Journal of Cross-Cultural Psychology, 21,* 5–47.

Calasanti, T. M. (1996). Gender and life satisfaction in retirement: An assessment of the male model. *Journal of Gerontology: Social Sciences, 51B,* S18–S29.

Calciano, R., Chodak, G. W., Garnick, M. B., Kuban, D. A., & Resnick, M. I. (1995, April 15). The prostate cancer conundrum. *Patient Care, 29,* 84–88, 91–95, 99–102, 104.

Call, K. T. (1996). Adolescent work as an "arena of comfort" under conditions of family discomfort. In J. T. Mortimer & M. D. Finch (Eds.), *Adolescents, work, and family: An intergenerational developmental analysis.* Thousand Oaks, CA: Sage.

Camara, K. A., & Resnick, G. (1988). Interparental conflict and cooperation. Factors moderating children's post-divorce adjustment. In E. M. Hetherington & J. D. Arasten (Eds.), *Impact of divorce, single parenting and step parenting on children.* Hillsdale, NJ: Erlbaum.

Camp, C. J., & McKitrick, L. A. (1991). Memory interventions in Alzheimer's-type dementia populations: Methodological and theoretical issues. In R. L. West & J. D. Sinnott (Eds.), *Everyday memory and aging: Current research and methodology* (pp. 155–172). New York: Springer-Verlag.

Camp, C. J., Foss, J. W., Stevens, A. B., Reichard, C. C., McKitrick, L. A., & O'Hanlon, A. M. (1993). Memory training in normal and demented elderly populations: The E-I-E-I-O model. *Experimental Aging Research, 19,* 277–290.

Camp, C. J., Judge, K. S., Bye, C. A., Fox, K. M., Bowden, J., Bell, M., Valencic, K., & Mattern, J. M. (1997). An intergenerational program for persons with dementia using Montessori methods. *The Gerontologist, 37,* 688–692.

Campbell, A. (1981). *The sense of well-being in America: Recent patterns and trends.* New York: McGraw-Hill.

Campbell, F. A., & Ramey, C. T. (1994). Effects of early intervention on intellectual and academic achievement: A follow-up study of children from low-income families. *Child Development, 65,* 684–698.

Campos, J. J., Hiatt, S., Ramsay, D., Henderson, C., & Svejda, M. (1978). The emergence of fear on the visual cliff. In M. Lewis & L. Rosenblum (Eds.), *The origins of affect.* New York: Plenum.

Campos, R. G. (1989). Soothing pain-elicited distress in infants with swaddling and pacifiers. *Child Development, 60,* 781–792.

Canfield, R. L., & Smith, E. G. (1996). Number-based expectations and sequential enumeration by 5-month-old infants. *Developmental Psychology, 32,* 269–279.

Capaldi, D. M., & Patterson, G. R. (1991). Relation of parental transitions to boys' adjustment problems: I. A linear hypothesis. II. Mothers at risk for transitions and unskilled parenting. *Developmental Psychology, 27,* 489–504.

Capaldi, D. M., Crosby, L., & Stoolmiller, M. (1996). Predicting the timing of first sexual intercourse for at-risk adolescent males. *Child Development, 67,* 344–359.

Carey, G. (1996). Family and genetic epidemiology of aggressive and antisocial behavior. In D. M. Stoff & R. B. Cairns (Eds.), *Aggression and violence: Genetic, neurobiological, and biosocial perspecives.* Mahwah, NJ: Erlbaum.

Carlo, G., Koller, S. H., Eisenberg, N., Da Silva, M. S., & Frohlich, C. B. (1996). A cross-national study on the relations among prosocial moral reasoning, gender role orientations, and prosocial behaviors. *Developmental Psychology, 32,* 231–240.

Carlson, C. L., Pelham, W. E., Milich, R., & Dixon, J. (1992). Single and combined effects of methylphenidate and behavior therapy on the classroom performance of children with attention-deficit hyperactivity disorder. *Journal of Abnormal Child Psychology, 20,* 213–232.

Carroll, J. L., & Loughlin, G. M. (1994). Sudden infant death syndrome. In F. A. Oski, C. D. DeAngelis, R. D. Feigin, J. A. McMillan, & J. B. Warshaw (Eds.), *Principals and practice of pediatrics.* Philadelphia: Lippincott.

Carstensen, L. L. (1987). Age-related changes in social activity. In L. L. Carstensen & B. A. Edelstein (Eds.), *Handbook of clinical gerontology* (pp. 222–237). New York: Pergamon.

Carstensen, L. L. (1993). Motivation for social contact across the life span: A theory of socioemotional selectivity. In J. E. Jacobs (Ed.), *Nebraska symposium on motivation: Vol. 40. Developmental perspectives on motivation* (pp. 209–254). Lincoln: University of Nebraska Press.

Carstensen, L. L. (1995). Evidence for a life-span theory of socioemotional selectivity. *Current Directions in Psychological Science, 4,* 151–156.

Carstensen, L. L., & Freund, A. M. (1994). The resilience of the aging self. *Developmental Review, 14,* 81–92.

Carstensen, L. L., Graff, J., Levenson, R. W., & Gottmann, J. M. (1996). Affect in intimate relationships: The developmental course of marriage. In C. Magai & S. H. McFadden (Eds.), *Handbook of emotion, adult development, and aging* (pp. 227–247). San Diego, CA: Academic Press.

Casaer, P. (1993). Old and new facts about perinatal brain development. *Journal of Child Psychology and Psychiatry, 34,* 101–109.

Cascardi, M., & O'Leary, K. D. (1992). *Gender specific trends in spousal homicide across a decade.* Unpublished manuscript, State University of New York, Stony Brook.

Cascardi, M., Vivian, D., & Meyer, S. (1991). *Context and attributions for marital violence in discordant couples.* Paper presented at the annual meeting of the Association for the Advancement of Behavior Therapy, New York.

Cascio, W. F. (1995). Whither industrial and organizational psychology in a changing world of work? *American Psychologist, 50,* 928–939.

Caselli, M. C., Bates. E., Casadio, P., Fenson, J., Fenson, L., Sanderl, L., & Weir, J. (1995). Cross-linguistic lexical development. *Cognitive Development, 10,* 159–199.

Casey, M. B. (1996). Understanding individual differences in spatial ability within females: A nature/nurture interactionist framework. *Developmental Review, 16,* 241–260.

Caspi, A., & Silva, P. A. (1995). Temperamental qualities at age three predict personality traits in young adulthood: Longitudinal evidence from a birth cohort. *Child Development, 66,* 485–498.

Cassidy, L., & Hurrell, R. M. (1995). The influence of victim's attire on adolescents' judgments of date rape. *Adolescence, 30,* 319–323.

Castro, I. L. (1997). Worth more than we earn: Fair pay as a step toward gender equity. *National Forum, 77(2),* 17–21.

Cavanaugh, J. C. (1981). Early developmental theories: A brief review of attempts to organize developmental data prior to 1925. *Journal of the History of the Behavioral Sciences, 17,* 38–47.

Cavanaugh, J. C. (1991). On the concept of development: Contextualism, relative time, and the role of dialectics. In P. van Geert & L. Mohs (Eds.), *Annals of theoretical psychology: Vol. 6. Developmental psychology* (pp. 325–333). New York: Plenum.

Cavanaugh, J. C. (1996). Memory self-efficacy as a key to understanding cognitive aging. In F. Blanchard-Fields & T. M. Hess (Eds.), *Perspectives on cognitive changes in adulthood and aging* (pp. 488–507) New York: McGraw-Hill.

Cavanaugh, J. C., & Kinney, J. M. (1994, July). *Marital satisfaction as an important contextual factor in spousal caregiving.* Paper presented at the 7th International Conference on Personal Relationships, Groningen, The Netherlands.

Cavanaugh, J. C., & Kinney, J. M. (1998). Accuracy of caregivers' recollections of caregiving hassles. *Journal of Gerontology: Psychological Sciences, 53B,* P40–P42.

Cavanaugh, J. C., & Nocera, R. (1994). Cognitive aspects and interventions in Alzheimer's disease. In J. D. Sinnott (Ed.), *Interdisciplinary handbook of adult lifespan learning* (pp. 389–407). New York: Greenwood Press.

Cavanaugh, J. C., Feldman, J. M., & Hertzog, C. (1998). Metamemory as social cognition: A reconceptualization of what memory questionnaires assess. *Review of General Psychology, 2,* 48–65.

Cavanaugh, J. C., Grady, J. G., & Perlmutter, M. (1983). Forgetting and use of memory aids in 20 to 70 year olds' everyday life. *International Journal of Aging and Human Development, 17,* 113–122.

Cavanaugh, J. C., Kinney, J. M., Dunn, N. J., McGuire, L. C., & Nocera, R. (1994). Caregiver-patient dyads: Documenting the verbal instructions caregivers provide in joint cognitive tasks. *Journal of Adult Development, 1,* 27–36.

Cavanaugh, J. C., Kramer, D. A., Sinnott, J. D., Camp, C. J., & Markley, R. J. (1985). On missing links and such: Interfaces between cognitive research and everyday problem solving. *Human Development, 28,* 146–168.

Ceci, S. J. (1990). *On intelligence . . . more or less: A bioecological treatise on intellectual development.* Hillsdale, NJ: Erlbaum.

Centers for Disease Control and Prevention. (1998). *Targeting tobacco use: The nation's leading cause of death.* Available at the Web site http://www.cdc.gov/nccdphp/osh/oshaag.htm

Chambré, S. M. (1993). Voluntarism by elders: Past trends and future prospects. *The Gerontologist, 33,* 221–228.

Chao, G. T. (1997). Mentoring phases and outcomes. *Journal of Vocational Behavior, 51,* 15–28.

Chao, P. (1983). *Chinese kinship.* London, UK: Kegan Paul International.

Chapman, P. D. (1988). *Schools as sorters: Lewis M. Terman, applied psychology, and the intelligence testing movement, 1890–1930.* New York: New York University Press.

Charness, N., & Bosman, E. A. (1990). Expertise and aging: Life in the lab. In T. M. Hess (Ed.), *Aging and cognition: Knowledge organization and utilization* (pp. 343–385). Amsterdam, The Netherlands: North-Holland.

Chase-Lansdale, P. L., & Hetherington, E. M. (1990). The impact of divorce on life-span development: Short and long term effects. In P. B. Baltes, B. L. Featherman, & R. M. Lerner (Eds.), *Life-span development and behavior* (Vol. 10). Hillsdale, NJ: Erlbaum.

Chase-Lansdale, P. L., Cherlin, A. J., & Kiernan, K. E. (1995). The long-term effects of parental divorce on the mental health of young adults: A developmental perspective. *Child Development, 66,* 1614–1634.

Chasteen, A. L. (1994). "The world around me": The environment and single women. *Sex Roles, 31,* 309–328.

Chen, S., & Miyake, K. (1986). Japanese studies of infant development. In H. Stevenson, H. Azuma, & K. Hakuta (Eds.), *Child development and education in Japan.* New York: Freeman.

Chen, X., Rubin, K. H., & Li, Z. (1995). Social functioning and adjustment in Chinese children. *Developmental Psychology, 31,* 531–539.

Cherlin, A. J. (1992). *Marriage, divorce, remarriage* (rev. ed.). Cambridge, MA: Harvard University Press.

Cherlin, A. J., & Furstenberg, F. F., Jr. (1986). *The new American grandparent: A place in the family, a life apart.* New York: Basic Books.

Cherlin, A. J., & Furstenberg, F. F., Jr. (1994). Stepfamilies in the United States: A reconsideration. *Annual Review of Sociology, 20,* 359–381.

Cherlin, A. J., Furstenberg, F. F., Jr., Chase-Lansdale, P. L., Kiernan, D. E., Robins, P. K., Morrison, D. R., & Teitler, J. O. (1991). Longitudinal studies of effects of divorce on children in Great Britain and the United States. *Science, 252,* 1386–1389.

Chinen, A. B. (1989). *In the ever after.* Willmette, IL: Chiron.

Chisholm, J. S. (1983). *Navajo infancy: An ethological study of child development.* New York: Aldine.

Chugani, H. T., & Phelps, M. E. (1986). Maturational changes in cerebral function in infants determined by 18FDG positron emission tomography. *Science, 231,* 840–843.

Church, M. W., Eldis, F., Blakley, B. W., & Bawle, E. V. (1997). Hearing, language, speech, vestibular, and dentofacial disorders in fetal alcohol syndrome. *Alcoholism: Clinical and Experimental Research, 21,* 227–237.

Cicirelli, V. G. (1980). Sibling relationships in adulthood: A life-span perspective. In L. W. Poon (Ed.), *Aging in the 1980s* (pp. 455–474). Washington, DC: American Psychological Association.

Cielinski, K. L., Vaughan, B. E., Seifer, R., & Contreras, J. (1995). Relations among sustained engagement during play, quality of play, and mother-child interaction in samples of children with Down syndrome and normally developing toddlers. *Infant Behavior and Development, 18,* 163–176.

Cipani, E. (1991). Educational classification and placement. In J. L. Matson & J. A. Mulick (Eds.), *Handbook of mental retardation* (2nd ed.). New York: Pergamon Press.

Clark, R. F., & Goate, A. M. (1993). Molecular genetics of Alzheimer's disease. *Archives of Neurology, 50,* 1164–1167.

Clarke, A. M., & Clarke, A. D. (1989). The later cognitive effects of early intervention. *Intelligence, 13,* 289–297.

Cleek, M. B., & Pearson, T. A. (1985). Perceived causes of divorce: An analysis of interrelationships. *Journal of Marriage and the Family, 47,* 179–191.

Clements, M., & Markman, H. J. (1996). The transition to parenthood: Is having children hazardous to marriage? In N. Vanzetti & S. Duck (Eds.), *A lifetime of relationships* (pp. 290–310). Pacific Grove, CA: Brooks/Cole.

Clemons, A. W., & Axelson, L. J. (1985). The not-so-empty nest: The return of the fledgling adult. *Family Relations, 34,* 259–264.

Clifton, R. K. (1992). The development of spatial hearing in human infants. In L. A. Werner & E. W. Rubel (Eds.), *Developmental psychoacoustics* (pp. 135–157). Washington, DC: American Psychological Association.

Clifton, R., Perris, E., & Bullinger, A. (1991). Infants' perception of auditory space. *Developmental Psychology, 27,* 187–197.

Cohen, C., Teresi, J., Holmes, D., & Roth, E. (1988). Survival strategies of older homeless men. *The Gerontologist, 28,* 58–65.

Cohen, G. D. (1990). Psychopathology and mental health in the mature and elderly adult. In J. E. Birren & K. W. Schaie (Eds.), *Handbook of the psychology of aging* (3rd ed., pp. 359–371). San Diego, CA: Academic Press.

Cohen, S., & Hebert, T. B. (1996). Psychological factors and physical disease from the perspective of human psychoneuroimmunology. *Annual Review of Psychology, 47,* 113–142.

Cohen, S., Lichtenstein, E., Prochaska, J. O., Rossi, J. S., Gutz, E. R., Carr, C. R., et al. (1989). Debunking myths about self-quitting: Evidence from 10 prospective studies of persons who attempt to quit smoking by themselves. *American Psychologist, 44,* 1355–1365.

Coke, M. M. (1992). Correlates of life satisfaction among elderly African Americans. *Journal of Gerontology: Psychological Sciences, 47,* P316–P320.

Colby, A., Kohlberg, L., Gibbs, J. C., & Lieberman, M. (1983). A longitudinal study of moral development. *Monographs of the Society for Research in Child Development, 48* (Whole #200).

Cole, D. A., & Jordan, A. E. (1995). Competence and memory: Integrating psychosocial and cognitive correlates of child depression. *Child Development, 66,* 459–473.

Cole, T. R., & Holstein, M. (1996). Ethics and aging. In R. H. Binstock & L. K. George (Eds.), *Handbook of aging and the social sciences* (4th ed., pp. 480–497). San Diego, CA: Academic Press.

Coleman, M., & Ganong, L. H. (1990). Remarriage and stepfamily research in the 1980s: Increased interest in an old family form. *Journal of Marriage and the Family, 52,* 925–940.

Collins, N. L., & Read, S. J. (1990). Adult attachment, working models, and relationship quality in dating couples. *Journal of Personality and Social Psychology, 58,* 644–663.

Conger, R. D., Patterson, G. R., & Ge, X. (1995). It takes two to replicate: A mediational model for the impact of parents' stress on adolescent adjustment. *Child Development, 66,* 80–97.

Congressional Budget Office. (1997). *Long-term budgetary pressures and policy options.* Washington, DC: U.S. Government Printing Office.

Connell, C. M., & Gibson, G. D. (1997). Racial, ethnic, and cultural differences in dementia caregiving: Review and analysis. *The Gerontologist, 37,* 355–364.

Connidis, I. (1988, November). *Sibling ties and aging.* Paper presented at the Gerontological Society of America, San Francisco.

Consulting Psychologists Press, Inc. (1994). *Strong Interest Inventory of the Strong Vocational Interest Blanks, Form T317.* Palo Alto, CA: Stanford University Press.

Cooney, T. M., & Uhlenberg, P. (1990). The role of divorce in men's relations with their adult children after mid-life. *Journal of Marriage and the Family, 52,* 677–688.

Cooney, T. M., Pedersen, F. A., Indelicato, S., & Palkovitz, R. (1993). Timing of fatherhood: Is "on time" optimal? *Journal of Marriage and the Family, 55,* 205–215.

Cooney, T. M., Smyer, M. A., Hagestad, G. O., & Klock, R. (1986). Parental divorce in young adulthood: Some preliminary findings. *American Journal of Orthopsychiatry, 56,* 470–477.

Cooper, R. P., & Aslin, R. N. (1994). Developmental differences in infant attention to the spectral properties of infant-directed speech. *Child Development, 65,* 1663–1677.

Corballis, M. C. (1997). The genetics and evolution of handedness. *Psychological Review, 104,* 714–727.

Cordes, C. L., & Dougherty, T. W. (1993). A review and integration of research on job burnout. *Academy of Management Review, 18,* 621–656.

Cornish, N. (1994, Sept. 12). Over the hill? *News Journal* (Wilmington, DE), pp. D10–D11.

Cornman, J. M., & Kingson, E. R. (1996). Trends, issues, perspectives, and values for the aging of the baby boom cohorts. *The Gerontologist, 36,* 15–26.

Cornwell, K. S., Harris, L. J., & Fitzgerald, H. E. (1991). Task effects in the development of hand preference in 9-, 13-, and 20-month-old infant girls. *Developmental Neuropsychology, 7,* 19–34.

Corr, C. A. (1991–92). A task-based approach to coping with dying. *Omega: Journal of Death and Dying, 24,* 81–94.

Corr, C. A., & Corr, D. M. (1992a). Adult hospice day care. *Death Studies, 16,* 155–171.

Corr, C. A., & Corr, D. M. (1992b). Children's hospice care. *Death Studies, 16,* 431–449.

Corrigan, P. W., Holmes, E. P., Luchins, D., Buichan, B., et al. (1994). Staff burnout in a psychiatric hospital: A cross-lagged panel design. *Journal of Organizational Behavior, 15,* 65–74.

Cosby, A. (1974). Occupational expectations and the hypothesis of increasing realism of choice. *Journal of Vocational Behavior, 5,* 53–65.

Costa, P. T., Jr., & McCrae, R. R. (1978). Objective personality assessment. In M. Storandt, I. C. Siegler, & M. F. Elias (Eds.), *The clinical psychology of aging* (pp. 119–143). New York: Plenum.

Costa, P. T., Jr., & McCrae, R. R. (1988). Personality in adulthood: A six-year longitudinal study of self-reports and spouse ratings on the NEO Personality Inventory. *Journal of Personality and Social Psychology, 54,* 853–863.

Costa, P. T., Jr., McCrae, R. R., & Arenberg, D. (1980). Enduring dispositions in adult males. *Journal of Personality and Social Psychology, 38,* 793–800.

Costa, P. T., Jr., McCrae, R. R., & Holland, J. L. (1984). Personality and vocational interests in an adult sample. *Journal of Applied Psychology, 42,* 390–400.

Costin, S. E., & Jones, D. C. (1992). Friendship as a facilitator of emotional responsiveness and prosocial interventions among young children. *Developmental Psychology, 28,* 941–947.

Cotton, S., Anthill, J. K., & Cunningham, J. D. (1989). The work motivations of mothers with preschool children. *Journal of Family Issues, 10,* 189–210.

Coulton, C. J., Korbin, J. E., Su, M., & Chow, J. (1995). Community level factors and child maltreatment rates. *Child Development, 66,* 1262–1276.

Council on Ethical and Judicial Affairs. (1990). Black-white disparities in health care. *Journal of the American Medical Association, 263,* 2344–2346.

Counts, D., & Counts, D. (Eds.). (1985). *Aging and its transformations: Moving toward death in Pacific societies.* Lanham, MD: University Press of America.

Cowan, C. P., & Cowan, P. A. (1992). *When partners become parents.* New York: Basic Books.

Craig, K. D., Whitfield, M. F., Grunau, R. V. E., Linton, J., & Hadjistavropoulos, H. D. (1993). Pain in the preterm neonate: Behavioural and physiological indices. *Pain, 52,* 238–299.

Craik, F. I. M., & Jennings, J. M. (1992). Human memory. In F. I. M. Craik, & T. A. Salthouse (Eds.) *The handbook of aging and cognition* (pp. 51–110). Hillsdale, NJ: Erlbaum.

Craton, L. G., & Yonas, A. (1988). Infants' sensitivity to boundary flow information for depth at an edge. *Child Development, 59,* 1522–1529.

Crick, N. R., & Dodge, K. A. (1994). A review and reformulation of social information-processing mechanisms in children's social adjustment. *Psychological Bulletin, 115,* 74–101.

Crimmins, E. M., Saito, Y., & Reynolds, S. L. (1997). Further evidence on recent trends in the prevalence and incidence of disability among older Americans from two sources: The LSOA and the NHIS. *Journal of Gerontology: Social Sciences, 52B,* S59–S71.

Crispi, E. L., Schiaffino, K., & Berman, W. H. (1997). The contribution of attachment to burden in adult children of institutionalized parents with dementia. *The Gerontologist, 37,* 52–60.

Crook, C. (1987). Taste and olfaction. In P. Salapatek & L. Cohen (Eds.), *Handbook of infant perception* (Vol. 1). Orlando, FL: Academic Press.

Cross, S., & Markus, H. (1991). Possible selves across the life span. *Human Development, 34,* 230–255.

Cuellar, I., Nyberg, B., Maldonado, R. E., & Roberts, R. E. (1997). Ethnic identity and acculturation in a young adult Mexican-origin population. *Journal of Community Psychology, 25,* 535–549.

Cumming, E., & Henry, W. H. (1961). *Growing old: The process of disengagement.* New York: Basic Books.

Cunningham, F. G., Macdonald, P. C., & Gant, N. F. (1989). *Williams obstetrics* (18th ed.). London, UK: Appleton & Lange.

Curcio, C. A., Buell, S. J., & Coleman, P. D. (1982). Morphology of the aging central nervous system: Not all downhill. In J. A. Mortimer, F. J. Pirozzola, & G. I. Maletta (Eds.), *Advances in neurogerontology: Vol. 3. The aging motor system* (pp. 7–35). New York: Praeger.

Cutler, S. J., & Hendricks, J. (1990). Leisure and time use across the life course. In R. H. Binstock & L. K. George (Eds.), *Handbook of aging and the social sciences* (3rd ed., pp. 169–185). San Diego, CA: Academic Press.

Cutter, M. A. G. (1991). Euthanasia: Reassessing the boundaries. *Journal of NIH Research, 3(5),* 59–61.

Dalton, S. T. (1992). Lived experience of never-married women. *Issues in Mental Health Nursing, 13,* 69–80.

Damast, A. M., Tamis-Lemonda, C. S., & Bornstein, M. H. (1996). Mother-child play: Sequential interactions and the relation between maternal beliefs and behaviors. *Child Development, 67,* 1752–1766.

Damon, W., & Hart, D. (1988). *Self-understanding in childhood and adolescence.* New York: Cambridge University Press.

Danforth, J. S., Barkley, R. A., & Stokes, T. F. (1991). Observations of parent-child interactions with hyperactive children. Research and clinical implications. *Clinical Psychology Review, 11,* 703–727.

D'Augelli, A. R. (1996). Lesbian, gay, and bisexual development during adolescence and young adulthood. In R. P. Cabaj & T. S. Stein (Eds.), *Textbook of homosexuality and mental health.* Washington DC: American Psychiatric Press.

Davidson, F. H., & Davidson, M. M. (1994). *Changing childhood prejudice: The caring work of the schools.* Westport CT: Bergin & Garvey/Greenwood.

Davidson, K. M., Richards, D. S., Schatz, D. A., & Fisher, D. A. (1991). Successful in utero treatment of fetal goiter and hypothyroidism. *New England Journal of Medicine, 324,* 543–546.

Davies, P. T., & Cummings, E. M. (1998). Exploring children's emotional security as a mediator of the link between marital relations and child adjustment. *Child Development, 69,* 124–139.

Davis, B. W. (1985). *Visits to remember: A handbook for visitors of nursing home residents.* University Park: Pennsylvania State University Cooperative Extension Service.

Day, S. X., Rounds, J., & Swaney, K. (1998). The structure of vocational interests for diverse racial-ethnic groups. *Psychological Science, 9,* 40–44.

De St. Aubin, E., & McAdams, D. P. (1995). The relations of generative concern and generative action to personality traits, satisfaction/happiness with life, and ego development. *Journal of Adult Development, 2,* 99–112.

De Vries, B. (1996). The understanding of friendship: An adult life course prespective. In C. Magai & S. H. McFadden (Eds.), *Handbook of emotion, adult development, and aging.* San Diego, CA: Academic Press.

De Wolff, M. S., & van IJzendoorn, M. H. (1997). Sensitivity and attachment: A meta-analysis on parental antecedents of infant attachment. *Child Development, 68,* 571–591.

DeAngelis, T. (1997). Menopause symptoms vary among ethnic groups. *APA Monitor, 28(11),* 16–17.

DeBerry, K. M., Scarr, S., & Weinberg, R. (1996). Family racial socialization and ecological competence: Longitudinal assessments of African-American transracial adoptees. *Child Development, 67,* 2375–2399.

Decasper, A. J., & Spence M. J. (1986). Prenatal maternal speech influences newborn's perception of speech sounds. *Infant Behavior and Development, 9,* 133–150.

Defrank, R., & Ivancevich, J. M. (1986). Job loss: An individual level review and model. *Journal of Vocational Behavior, 19,* 1–20.

Dekovic, M., & Janssens, J. M. (1992). Parents' child-rearing style and child's sociometric status. *Developmental Psychology, 28,* 925–932.

Dellas, M., & Jernigan, L. P. (1990). Affective personality characteristics associated with undergraduate ego identity formation. *Journal of Adolescent Research, 5,* 306–324.

DeLoache, J. S. (1995). Early understanding and use of models: The model model. *Current Directions in Psychological Science, 4,* 109–113.

DeMaris, A., & Rao, K. V. (1992). Premarital cohabitation and subsequent marital stability in the United States: A reassessment. *Journal of Marriage and the Family, 54,* 178–190.

Denney, N. W. (1982). Aging and cognitive changes. In B. B. Wolman (Ed.), *Handbook of developmental psychology* (pp. 807–827). Englewood Cliffs, NJ: Prentice-Hall.

Denney, N. W. (1989). Everyday problem solving: Methodological issues, research findings, and a model. In L. W. Poon, D. C. Rubin, & B. A. Wilson (Eds.), *Everyday cognition in adulthood and late life* (pp. 330–351). Cambridge, UK: Cambridge University Press.

Denney, N. W. (1990). Adult age differences in traditional and practical problem solving. In E. A. Lovelace (Ed.), *Aging and cognition: Mental processes, self-awareness, and interventions* (pp. 329–349). Amsterdam, The Netherlands: North-Holland.

Denney, N. W., & Pearce, K. A. (1989). A developmental study of practical problem solving in adults. *Developmental Psychology, 11,* 521–522.

Denney, N. W., Pearce, K. A., & Palmer, A. M. (1982). A developmental study of adults' performance on traditional and practical problem-solving tasks. *Experimental Aging Research, 8,* 115–118.

Dennis, W., & Dennis, M. G. (1940). The effects of cradling practices upon the onset of walking in Hopi children. *Journal of Genetic Psychology, 56*, 77–86.

Denton, K., & Zarbatany, L. (1996). Age differences in support processes in conversations between friends. *Child Development, 67*, 1360–1373.

DeSpelder, L. A., & Strickland, A. L. (1983). *The last dance: Encountering death and dying.* Palo Alto, CA: Mayfield.

Diamond, A., Prevor, M. B., Callender, G., & Druin, D. P. (1997). Prefontal cortex deficits in children treated early and continuously for PKU. *Monographs of the Society for Research in Child Development, 62* (4, Serial No. 252).

Diamond, J. (1986). I want a girl just like the girl . . . *Discover, 7(11)*, 65–68.

DiBlasio, F. A., & Benda, B. B. (1990). Adolescent sexual behavior: Multivariate analysis of a social learning model. *Journal of Adolescent Research, 5*, 449–466.

Dickinson, G. E. (1992). First childhood death experiences. *Omega, 25*, 169–182.

Diehl, M., Willis, S. L., & Schaie, K. W. (1995). Everyday problem solving in older adults: Observational assessment and cognitive correlates. *Psychology and Aging, 10*, 478–491.

Dielman, T., Schulenberg, J., Leech, S., & Shope, J. T. (1992, March). *Reduction of susceptibility to peer pressure and alcohol use/misuse through a school-based prevention program.* Paper presented at the meeting of the Society for Research on Adolescence, Washington, DC.

Dimond, M., Lund, D. A., & Caserta, M. S. (1987). The role of social support in the first two years of bereavement in an elderly sample. *The Gerontologist, 27*, 599–604.

Diprete, T. A., & Soule, W. T. (1988). Gender and promotion in segmented job ladder systems. *American Sociological Review, 53*, 26–40.

Dittmann-Kohli, F., & Baltes, P. B. (1990). Toward a neofunctionalist conception of adult intellectual development: Wisdom as a prototypical case of intellectual growth. In C. Alexander & E. Langer (Eds.), *Higher stages of human development: Perspectives on adult growth* (pp. 54–78). New York: Oxford University Press.

Dixon, R. A. (1992). Contextual approaches to adult intellectual development. In R. J. Sternberg & C. A. Berg (Eds.), *Intellectual development* (pp. 350–380). New York: Cambridge University Press.

Dixon, R. A., & Hultsch, D. F. (1999). Intelligence and cognitive potential in late life. In J. C. Cavanaugh & S. K. Whitbourne (Eds.), *Gerontology: An interdisciplinary perspective.* New York: Oxford University Press.

Dixon, R. A., Kramer, D. A., & Baltes, P. B. (1985). Intelligence: A life-span developmental perspective. In B. B. Wolman (Ed.), *Handbook of intelligence: Theories, measurements, and application* (pp. 301–350). New York: Wiley.

Dobash, R. P., & Dobash, R. E. (1992). *Women, violence, and social change.* New York: Routledge.

Dockrell, J., & McShane, J. (1993). *Children's learning difficulties: A cognitive approach.* Cambridge, UK: Blackwell.

Dohrenwend, B. P. (1979). Stressful life events and psychopathology: Some issues of theory and method. In J. E. Barrett, B. M. Rose, & G. L. Klerman (Eds.), *Stress and mental disorder* (pp. 1–15). New York: Raven Press.

Doka, K. J., & Mertz, M. E. (1988). The meaning and significance of great-grandparenthood. *The Gerontologist, 28*, 192–197.

Domino, G. (1992). Cooperation and competition in Chinese and American children. *Journal of Cross Cultural Psychology, 23*, 456–467.

Donatelle, R. J., & Davis, L. G. (1997). *Health: The basics* (2nd ed.). Englewood Cliffs, NJ: Prentice-Hall.

Downey, J., Elkin, E. J., Ehrhardt, A. A., Meyer-Bahlburg, H. F. L., Bell, J. J., & Morishima, A. (1991). Cognitive ability and everyday functioning in women with Turner's syndrome. *Journal of Learning Disabilities, 24*, 32–39.

Dryfoos, J. G. (1990). *Adolescents at risk: Prevalence and prevention.* New York: Oxford University Press.

Dubois, D. L., & Hirsch, B. J. (1990). School and neighborhood friendship patterns of black and whites in early adolescence. *Child Development, 61*, 524–536.

Dumas, J. E., LaFreniere, P. J., & Serketich, W. J. (1995). "Balance of power": A transactional analysis of control in mother-child dyads involving socially competent, aggressive, and anxious children. *Journal of Abnormal Psychology, 104*, 104–113.

Dunn, J. (1984). Sibling studies and the developmental impact of critical incidents. In P. B. Baltes & O. G. Brim, Jr. (Eds.), *Life-span development and behavior* (Vol. 6). New York: Academic Press.

Dunn, J. (1993). *Young children's close relationships.* Newbury Park, CA: Sage.

Dunn, J., & Kendrick, C. (1981). Social behavior of young siblings in the family context: Differences between same-sex and different-sex dyads. *Child Development, 52*, 1265–1273.

Dunn, J., Brown, J. R., & Maguire, M. (1995). The development of children's moral sensibility: Individual differences and emotion understanding. *Developmental Psychology, 31*, 649–659.

Dunn, J., Slomkowski, C., & Beardsall, L. (1994). Sibling relationships from the preschool period through middle childhood and early adolescence. *Developmental Psychology, 30*, 315–324.

Duvall, E. M. (1977). *Marriage and family development* (5th ed.). Philadelphia: Lippincott.

Duvall, E. M., & Miller, B. C. (1985). *Marriage and family development* (6th ed.). New York: Harper & Row.

Dwyer, J. W., & Coward, R. T. (1991). A multivariate comparison of the involvement of adult sons versus daughters in the care of impaired parents. *Journal of Gerontology: Social Sciences, 46*, S259–S269.

Dyk, P. H., & Adams, G. R. (1990). Identity and intimacy: An initial investigation of three theoretical models using cross-lag panel correlations. *Journal of Youth and Adolescence, 19,* 91–110.

Eagly, A. H., Karau, S. J., & Makhijani, M. G. (1995). Gender and the effectiveness of leaders: A meta-analysis. *Psychological Bulletin, 117,* 125–145.

Earles, J. L. K., Connor, L. T., Smith, A. D., & Park, D. C. (1997). Interrelations of age, self-reported health, speed, and memory. *Psychology and Aging, 12,* 675–683.

Earnshaw, A. R., Amundson, N. E., & Borgen, W. A. (1990). The experience of job insecurity for professional women. *Journal of Employment Counseling, 27,* 2–18.

Eaton, W. O., & Enns, L. R. (1986). Sex differences in human motor activity level. *Psychological Bulletin, 100,* 19–28.

Eaton, W. O., Chipperfield, J. G., & Singbeil, C. E. (1989). Birth order and activity level in children. *Developmental Psychology, 25,* 668–672.

Edelbrock, C., Rende, R., Plomin, R., & Thompson, L. A. (1995). A twin study of competence and problem behavior in childhood and early adolescence. *Journal of Child Psychology & Psychiatry & Allied Principles, 36,* 775–785.

Edelstein, B., & Kalish, K. (1999). Clinical assessment of older adults. In J. C. Cavanaugh & S. K. Whitbourne (Eds.), *Gerontolgy: An interdisciplinary perspective* (pp. 269–304). New York: Oxford University Press.

Edelstein, S. (December 1990–January 1991). Do grandparents have rights? *Modern Maturity,* pp. 40–42.

Editorial Board. (1996). Definition of mental retardation. In J. W. Jacobson & J. A. Mulick (Eds.), *Manual of diagnosis and professional practice in mental retardation.* Washington, DC: American Psychological Association.

Edwards, C. A. (1994). Leadership in groups of school-age girls. *Developmental Psychology, 30,* 920–927.

Eisenberg, N. (1988). The development of prosocial and aggressive behavior. In M. H. Bornstein & M. E. Lamb (Eds.), *Developmental psychology: An advanced textbook* (2nd ed., pp. 461–495). Hillsdale, NJ: Erlbaum.

Eisenberg, N., & Miller, P. A. (1987). The relation of empathy to prosocial and related behaviors. *Psychological Bulletin, 101,* 91–119.

Eisenberg, N., & Shell, R. (1986). Prosocial moral judgement and behavior in children: The mediating role of cost. *Personality and Social Psychology Bulletin, 12,* 426–433.

Eisenberg, N., Fabes, R. A., Schaller, M., Carlo, G., & Miller, P. A. (1991). The relations of parental characteristics and practices to children's vicarious emotional responding. *Child Development, 62,* 1393–1408.

Ekerdt, D. J. (1987). Why the notion persists that retirement harms health. *The Gerontologist, 27,* 454–457.

Ekerdt, D. J., & DeViney, S. (1990). On defining persons as retired. *Journal of Aging Studies, 4,* 211–229.

Elder, G. H., Jr., & Pavalko, E. K. (1993). Work careers in men's later years: Transitions, trajectories, and historical change. *Journal of Gerontology: Social Sciences, 48,* S180–S191.

Elicker, J., Englund, M., & Sroufe, L. A. (1992). Predicting peer competence and peer relationships in childhood from early parent-child relationships. In R. D. Parke & G. W. Ladd (Eds.), *Family-peer relationships: Modes of linkage.* Hillsdale, NJ: Erlbaum.

Elkind, D. (1978). *The child's reality: Three developmental themes.* Hillsdale, NJ: Erlbaum.

Elkind, D., & Bowen, R. (1979). Imaginary audience behavior in children and adolescents. *Developmental Psychology, 15,* 38–44.

Ellison v. Brady, 924 F.2d 871 (9th Circuit 1991).

Ellison, C. G. (1990). Family ties, friendships, and subjective well-being among black Americans. *Journal of Marriage and the Family, 52,* 298–310.

Elmer-DeWitt, P. (1994). The genetic revolution. *Time* (January 17), 46–53.

Emory, E. K., Schlackman, L. J., & Fiano, K. (1996). Drug-hormone interactions on neuorbehavioral responses in human neonates. *Infant Behavior and Development, 19,* 213–220.

Enns, J. T. (1990). Relations between components of visual attention. In J. T. Enns (Ed.), *The development of attention: Research and theory.* Amsterdam: Elsevier.

Enright, R. D., Gassin, E. A., & Wu, C. (1992). Forgiveness: A developmental view. *Journal of Moral Education, 21,* 99–114.

Eppler, M. A. (1995). Development of manipulative skills and the deployment of attention. *Infant Behavior and Development, 18,* 391–405.

Epstein, L. H., & Cluss, P. A. (1986). Behavioral genetics of childhood obesity. *Behavior Therapy, 17,* 324–334.

Epstein, L. H., Valoski, A. M., Vara, L. S., McCurley, J., et al. (1995). Effects of decreasing sedentary behavior and increasing activity on weight change in obese children. *Health Psychology, 14,* 109–108.

Erel, O., & Burman, B. (1995). Interrelatedness of marital relations and parent-child relations: A meta-analytic review. *Psychological Bulletin, 118,* 108–132.

Erera-Weatherley, P. I. (1996). On becoming a stepparent: Factors associated with the adoption of alternative stepparenting styles. *Journal of Divorce and Remarriage, 25,* 155–174.

Erickson, M. T. (1987). *Behavior disorders of children and adolescents.* Englewood, Cliffs, NJ: Prentice-Hall.

Ericsson, K. A., & Smith, J. (Eds.). (1991). *Toward a general theory of expertise: Prospects and limits.* New York: Cambridge University Press.

Erikson, E. H. (1968). *Identity: Youth and crisis.* New York: Norton.

Erikson, E. H. (1982). *The life cycle completed: Review.* New York: Norton.

Erikson, E. H., Erikson, J. M., & Kivnick, H. Q. (1986). *Vital involvement in old age.* New York: Norton.

Ervin-Tripp, S. (1970). Discourse agreement: How children answer questions. In J. R. Hayes (Ed.), *Cognition and the development of language.* New York: Wiley.

Essex, M. J., & Nam, S. (1987). Marital status and loneliness among older women. *Journal of Marriage and the Family, 49,* 93–106.

Estes, R. J., & Wilensky, H. L. (1978). Life cycle squeeze and the morale curve. *Social Problems, 25,* 277–292.

Etaugh, C., & Liss, M. B. (1992). Home, school, and playroom: Training grounds for adult gender roles. *Sex Roles, 26,* 129–147.

Etzioni, A. (1997, August 13). Marriage with no easy outs. *New York Times on the Web.* http://www.nytimes.com

Fagen, J., Prigot, J., Carroll, M., Pioli, L., Stein, A., & Franco, A. (1997). Auditory context and memory retrieval in young infants. *Child Development, 68,* 1057–1066.

Fagot, B. I. (1985). Changes in thinking about early sex role development. *Developmental Review, 5,* 83–98.

Fairlie, H. (1988). Talkin' bout my generation. *New Republic, 198,* 19–22.

Falbo, T., & Polit, E. F. (1986). Quantitative review of the only child literature: Research evidence and theory development. *Psychological Bulletin, 100,* 176–186.

Falkner, J., & Tanner, J. M. (Eds.). (1962). *Human growth: A comprehensive treatise: Vol. 2. Postnatal growth, neurobiology* (2nd ed.). New York: Plenum.

Farrell, M. P., & Rosenberg, S. D. (1981). *Men at midlife.* Boston: Auburn House.

Farver, J. M., & Branstetter, W. H. (1994). Preschoolers' prosocial responses to their peers' distress. *Developmental Psychology, 30,* 334–341.

Farver, J. M., & Shin, Y. L. (1997). Social pretend play in Korean- and Anglo-American preschoolers. *Child Development, 68,* 544–556.

Federal Election Commission. (1998). Voter registration and turnout in federal elections by age—1972–1996. Available at the Web site http://www.fec.gov/pages/agedemog.htm

Fehr, B. (1996). *Friendship processes.* Thousand Oaks, CA: Sage.

Feldhusen, J. F. (1996). Motivating academically able youth with enriched and accelerated learning experiences. In C. P. Benbow & D. J. Lubinski (Eds.), *Intellectual talent: Psychometric and social issues.* Baltimore, MD: Johns Hopkins Press.

Feldman, D. H., & Goldsmith, L. T. (1991). *Nature's gambit.* New York: Teachers College Press.

Feltey, K. M., Ainslie, J. J., & Geib, A. (1991). Sexual coercion attitudes among high school students: The influence of gender and rape education. *Youth and Society, 23,* 229–250.

Feminist Majority Foundation. (1991). *Empowering women in business.* Washington, DC: Author.

Fenson, L., Dale, P. S., Reznick, J. S., Bates, E., Thal, D. J., & Pethick, S. J. (1994). Variability in early communicative development. *Monographs of the Society for Research in Child Development, 59* (5, Serial No. 242).

Ferrari, M. (1996). Observing the observer: Self-regulation in the observational learning of motor skills. *Developmental Review, 16,* 203–240.

Field, D., & Minkler, M. (1988). Continuity and change in social support between young-old and old-old or very-old age. *Journal of Gerontology: Psychological Sciences, 43,* P100–P106.

Field, T. M. (1990). *Infancy.* Cambridge, MA: Harvard University Press.

Field, T. M., & Widmayer, S. M. (1982). Motherhood. In B. J. Wolman (Ed.), *Handbook of developmental psychology* (pp. 681–701). Englewood Cliffs, NJ: Prentice-Hall.

Field, T., Fox, N. A., Pickens, J., & Nawrocki, T. (1995). Relative right front EEG activation in 3- to 6-month-old infants of "depressed" mothers. *Developmental Psychology, 31,* 358–363.

Fields, R. (1992). *Drugs and alcohol in perspective.* Dubuque, IA: William C. Brown.

Fingerman, K. L. (1996). Sources of tension in the aging mother and adult daughter relationship. *Psychology and Aging, 11,* 591–606.

Fischer, M., Barkley, R. A., Fletcher, K. E., & Smallish, L. (1993). The adolescent outcome of hyperactive children: Predictors of psychiatric, academic, social, and emotional adjustment. *Journal of the American Academy of Child and Adolescent Psychiatry, 32,* 324–332.

Fisher, H. E. (1987). The four-year itch. *Natural History, 96(10),* 22–33.

Fisher, H. E. (1994). The nature of romantic love. *Journal of NIH Research, 6(4),* 59–64.

Fisher, J. E., & Noll, J. P. (1996). Anxiety disorders. In L. L. Carstensen, B. A. Edelstein, & L. Dornbrand (Eds.), *The practical handbook of clinical gerontology* (pp. 304–323). Thousand Oaks, CA: Sage.

Fitzgerald, L. F., & Ormerod, A. J. (1991). Perceptions of sexual harassment: The influence of gender and academic context. *Psychology of Women Quarterly, 15,* 281–294.

Fitzgerald, L. F., & Shullman, S. L. (1993). Sexual harassment: A research analysis and agenda for the 1990s. *Journal of Vocational Behavior, 42,* 5–27.

Fitzgerald, L. F., Shullman, S. L., Bailey, N., Richards, M., Swecker, J., Gold, Y., et al. (1988). The incidence and dimensions of sexual harassment in academia and the workplace. *Journal of Vocational Behavior, 32,* 152–175.

Fitzpatrick, M. A. (1984). A topological approach to marital interaction—Recent theory and research. *Advances in Experimental Sociology, 18,* 1–47.

Flaks, D. K., Filcher, I., Masterpasqua, F., & Joseph, G. (1995). Lesbians choosing motherhood: A comparative study of lesbian and heterosexual parents and their children. *Developmental Psychology, 31,* 105–114.

Flavell, J. H. (1985). *Cognitive development* (2nd ed.). Englewood Cliffs, NJ: Prentice-Hall.

Flavell, J. H. (1996). Piaget's legacy. *Psychological Science, 7,* 200–203.

Fleishner, J. E. (1994). Diagnosis and assessment of mathematics learning disabilities. In G. R. Lyon (Ed.), *Frames of reference for the assessment of learning disabilities: New views on measurement issues.* Baltimore, MD: Brookes.

Foreyt, J. P., & Goodrick, G. K. (1995). Obesity. In R. T. Ammerman & M. Hersen (Eds.), *Handbook of child behavior therapy in the psychiatric setting.* New York: Wiley.

Fox, A. (1979, January). Earnings replacement rates of retired couples: Findings from the Retirement History Study. *Social Security Bulletin, 42,* 17–39.

Fox, N. A. (1991). If it's not left, it's right. *American Psychologist, 46,* 863–872.

Fox, N. A., Kimmerly, N. L., & Schaffer, W. D. (1991). Attachment to mother/attachment to father: A meta-analysis. *Child Development, 62,* 210–225.

Frankenburg, W. K., & Dobbs, J. B. (1969). The Denver Developmental Screening Test. *Journal of Pediatrics, 71,* 181–191.

Franklin, J. C. (1997, November). Industry output and employment projections to 2006. *Monthly Labor Review.*

Frazer, D. W., Leicht, M. L., & Baker, M. D. (1996). Psychological manifestations of physical disease in the elderly. In L. L. Carstensen, B. Edelstein, & L. Dornbrand (Eds.), *The practical handbook of clinical gerontology* (pp. 217–235). Thousand Oaks, CA: Sage.

Freer, J. P., & Clark, E. G. (1994). *The living will: A guide to health care decision making.* Available at the Web site http://freenet.buffalo.edu/%7Ebioethic/lwill.html

Frerichs, F., & Naegele, G. (1997). Discrimination of older workers in Germany: Obstacles and options for the integration into employment. *Journal of Aging and Social Policy, 9,* 89–101.

Friedman, M., & Rosenman, R. H. (1974). *Type A behavior and your heart.* New York: Random House.

Friend, M., & Davis, T. L. (1993). Appearance-reality distinction: Children's understanding of the physical and affective domains. *Developmental Psychology, 29,* 907–914.

Froman, L. (1994). Adult learning in the workplace. In J. D. Sinnott (Ed.), *Interdisciplinary handbook of adult lifespan learning* (pp. 203–217). Westport, CT: Greenwood Press.

Frone, M. R., & Yardley, J. K. (1996). Workplace family-supportive programmes: Predictors of employed parents' importance ratings. *Journal of Occupational and Organzational Psychology, 69,* 351–366.

Frone, M. R., Russell, M., & Barnes, G. M. (1996). Work-family conflict, gender, and health-related outcomes: A study of employed parents in two community samples. *Journal of Occupational Health Psychology, 1,* 57–69.

Fry, P. S. (1986). *Depression, stress, and adaptation in the elderly.* Rockville, MD: Aspen.

Frye, D. (1993). Causes and precursors of children's theories of mind. In D. F. Hay & A. Angold (Eds.), *Precursors and causes in development and psychopathology.* Chichester, UK: Wiley.

Fulton, G., Madden, C., & Minichiello, V. (1996). The social construction of anticipatory grief. *Social Science and Medicine, 43,* 1349–1358.

Furman, W. (1995). Parenting siblings. In M. H. Bornstein (Ed.), *Handbook of parenting* (Vol. 1). Mahwah, NJ: Erlbaum.

Furstenberg, F. F. (1993). How families manage risk and opportunity in dangerous neighborhoods. In W. J. Wilson (Ed.), *Sociology and the public agenda.* Newbury Park, CA: Sage.

Furstenberg, F. F., & Teitler, J. O. (1994). Reconsidering the effects of marital disruption: What happens to children of divorce in early adulthood? *Journal of Family Issues, 15,* 173–190.

Furstenberg, F. F., Brooks-Gunn, J., & Morgan, S. P. (1987). *Adolescent mothers in later life.* New York: Cambridge University Press.

Furstenberg, F. F., Jr. (1982). Conjugal succession: Reentering marriage after divorce. In P. B. Baltes & O. G. Brim, Jr. (Eds.), *Life-span development and behavior* (Vol. 5, pp. 108–146). New York: Academic Press.

Furstenberg, F. F., Jr., & Nord, C. W. (1985). Parenting apart: Patterns of childbearing after marital disruption. *Journal of Marriage and the Family, 47,* 893–912.

Futterman, A., Gallagher, D., Thompson, L. W., Lovett, S., & Gilewski, M. (1990). Retrospective assessment of marital adjustment and depression during the first two years of spousal bereavement. *Psychology and Aging, 5,* 277–283.

Gable, S., & Isabella, R. A. (1992). Maternal contributions to infant regulation of arousal. *Infant Behavior and Development, 15,* 95–107.

Gage, N. (1978). The yield of research on teaching. *Phi Delta Kappan, 59,* 229–235.

Gajar, A. H. (1992). University-based models for students with learning disabilities: The Pennsylvania State University model. In F. R. Rusch, L. DeStefano, J. Chadsey-Rusch, L. A. Phelps, & E. Szymanski (Eds.), *Transition from school to life* (pp. 51–70). Sycamore, IL: Sycamore.

Galinsky, E., Bond, J. T., & Friedman, D. E. (1996). The role of employers in addressing the needs of employed parents. *Journal of Social Issues, 52,* 111–136.

Gall, T. L., Evans, D. R., & Howard, J. (1997). The retirement adjustment process: Changes in the well-being of male retirees across time. *Journal of Gerontology: Psychological Sciences, 52B,* P110–P117.

Gallagher, M. (1996). Re-creating marriage. In D. Popenoe, J. B. Elshtain, & D. Blankenhorn (Eds.), *Promises to keep: Decline and renewal of marriage in America* (pp. 233–246). Lanham, MD: Rowman & Littlefield.

Galler, J. R., & Ramsey, F. (1989). A follow-up study of the influence of early malnutrition on development: Behavior at home and at school. *Journal of the American Academy of Child and Adolescent Psychiatry, 28,* 254–261.

Galler, J. R., Ramsey, F., & Forde, V. (1986). A follow-up study of the influence of early malnutrition on subsequent development: IV. Intellectual performance during adolescence. *Nutrition and Behavior, 3,* 211–222.

Garbarino, J., & Kostelny, K. (1992). Child maltreatment as a community problem. *Child Abuse and Neglect, 16,* 455–464.

Gardner, H. (1993). *Multiple intelligences: The theory in practice.* New York: Basic Books.

Gardner, H. (1995). Reflections on multiple intelligences: Myths and messages. *Phi Delta Kappan, 77(2).*

Garland, A. F., & Zigler, E. (1993). Adolescent suicide prevention: Current research and social policy implications. *American Psychologist, 48,* 169–182.

Garmon, L. C., Basinger, K. S., Gregg, V. R., & Gibbs, J. C. (1996). Gender differences in stage and expression of moral judgment. *Merrill-Palmer Quarterly, 42,* 418–437.

Garn, S. M. (1975). Bone loss and aging. In R. Goldman & M. Rockstein (Eds.), *The physiology and pathology of aging.* New York: Academic Press.

Garner, P. W., Jones, D. C., & Palmer, D. J. (1994). Social cognitive correlates of preschool children's sibling caregiving behavior. *Developmental Psychology, 30,* 905–911.

Garvey, C., & Berninger, G. (1981). Timing and turn taking in children's conversations. *Discourse Processes, 4,* 27–59.

Gatz, M., & Siegler, I. C. (1981, August). *Locus of control: A retrospective.* Paper presented at the meeting of the American Psychological Association, Los Angeles.

Gauze, C., Bukowski, W. M., Aquan-Assee, J., & Sippola, L. K. (1996). Interactions between family environment and friendship and associations with self-perceived well-being during early adolescence. *Child Development, 67,* 2201–2216.

Gaylord, S. A., & Zung, W. W. K. (1987). Affective disorders among the aging. In L. L. Carstensen & B. A. Edelstein (Eds.), *Handbook of clinical gerontology* (pp. 76–95). New York: Pergamon Press.

Ge, X., Conger, R. D., & Elder, G. H. (1996). Coming of age too early: Pubertal influences on girls' vulnerability to psychological distress. *Child Development, 67,* 3386–3400.

Geary, D. C. (1996). International differences in mathematical achievement: Their nature, causes, and consequences. *Current Directions in Psychological Science, 5,* 133–137.

Gelman, R., & Meck, E. (1986). The notion of principle: The case of counting. In J. Hiebert (Ed.), *Conceptual and procedural knowledge: The case of mathematics.* Hillside, NJ: Erlbaum.

Gentry, M., & Schulman, A. D. (1988). Remarriage as a coping response for widowhood. *Psychology and Aging, 3,* 191–196.

Gerbner, G. (1993). *Women and minorities on television (a report to the Screen Actors Guild).* Philadelphia: University of Pennsylvania, Annenberg School for Communication.

Gesser, G., Wong, P. T. P., & Reker, G. T. (1987–88). Death attitudes across the life-span: The development and validation of the death attitude profile (DAP). *Omega, 18,* 113–128.

Gfroerer, J. C., Greenblatt, J. C., & Wright, D. A. (1997). Substance use in the U.S. college-age population: Differences according to educational status and living arrangement. *American Journal of Public Health, 87,* 62–65.

Gibbs, N. R. (1988). Grays on the go. *Time, 131(8),* 66–75.

Giberson, P. K., & Weinberg, J. (1992). Fetal alcohol syndrome and functioning of the immune system. *Alcohol Health and Research World, 16,* 29–38.

Gibran, K. (1923). *The prophet.* New York: Knopf.

Gibson, E. J. (1969). *Principles of perceptual learning and development.* New York: Appleton-Century-Crofts.

Gibson, E. J., & Walk, R. D. (1960). The visual cliff. *Scientific American, 202,* 64–71.

Gibson, R. C. (1986). *Blacks in an aging society.* New York: Carnegie.

Gibson, R. C. (1987). Reconceptualizing retirement for black Americans. *The Gerontologist, 27,* 691–698.

Gibson, R. C. (1991). The subjective retirement of black Americans. *Journal of Gerontology: Social Sciences, 46,* S204–S209.

Gignac, M. A. M., Kelloway, E. K., & Gottlieb, B. H. (1996). The impact of caregiving on employment: A mediational model of work-family conflict. *Canadian Journal on Aging, 15,* 525–542.

Gilford, R. (1984). Contrasts in marital satisfaction throughout old age: An exchange theory analysis. *Journal of Gerontology, 39,* 325–333.

Gill, J. S., Zezulka, A. V., Shipley, M. J., Gill, S. K., & Beevers, D. G. (1986). Stroke and alcohol consumption. *New England Journal of Medicine, 315,* 1041–1046.

Gilligan, C. (1982). *In a different voice: Psychological theory and women's development.* Cambridge, MA: Harvard University Press.

Gilligan, C. (1985, March). *Remapping development.* Paper presented at the biennial meeting of the Society for Research in Child Development, Toronto.

Gilmore, D. (1990). *Manhood in the making: Cultural components of masculinity.* New Haven, CT: Yale University Press.

Ginn, J., & Arber, S. (1996). Gender, age, and attitudes toward retirement in mid-life. *Ageing and Society, 16,* 27–55.

Glamser, F., & Hayslip, B., Jr. (1985). The impact of retirement on participation in leisure activities. *Therapeutic Recreation Journal, 19,* 28–38.

Glenn, N. D. (1991). The recent trend in marital success in the United States. *Journal of Marriage and the Family, 53,* 261–270.

Glenn, N. D., & McLanahan, S. (1981). The effects of offspring on the psychological well-being of older adults. *Journal of Marriage and the Family, 43,* 409–421.

Glenn, N. D., & McLanahan, S. (1982). Children and marital happiness: A further specification of the relationship. *Journal of Marriage and the Family, 44,* 63–72.

Glenn, N. D., & Weaver, C. N. (1978). The marital happiness of remarried divorced persons. *Journal of Marriage and the Family, 40,* 269–282.

Glick, I. O., Weiss, R. S., & Parkes, C. M. (1974). *The first year of bereavement.* New York: Wiley.

Glick, P. C. (1989). The family life cycle and social change. *Family Relations, 38,* 123–129.

Glick, P. C., & Lin, S. (1986). Recent changes in divorce and remarriage. *Journal of Marriage and the Family, 48,* 737–747.

Glick, P. C., & Norton, A. J. (1979). Marrying, divorcing, and living together in the U.S. today. *Population Bulletin, 32,* 1–41.

Go, C. G., Brustrom, J. E., Lynch, M. F., & Aldwin, C. M. (1995). Ethnic trends in survival curves and mortality. *The Gerontologist, 35,* 318–326.

Goff, S. J., Fick, D. S., & Opplinger, R. A. (1997). The moderating effect of spouse support on the relation between serious leisure and spouses' perceived leisure-family conflict. *Journal of Leisure Research, 29,* 47–60.

Goff, S. J., Mount, M. K., & Jamison, R. L. (1990). Employer supported child care, work/family conflict, and absenteeism: A field study. *Personnel Psychology, 43,* 793–809.

Gold, D. T. (1990). Late-life sibling relationships: Does race affect typological distribution? *The Gerontologist, 30,* 741–748.

Gold, D. T., Woodbury, M. A., & George, L. K. (1990). Relationship classification using grade of membership analysis: A typology of sibling relationships in later life. *Journal of Gerontology: Social Sciences, 45,* S43–S51.

Goldenberg, R. L., & Klerman, L. V. (1995). Adolescent pregnancy—another look. *New England Journal of Medicine, 332,* 1161–1162.

Goldman, S. R. (1989). Strategy instruction in mathematics. *Learning Disability Quarterly, 12,* 43–55.

Goldsmith, H. H., & Harman, C. (1994). Temperament and attachment: Individuals and relationships. *Current Directions in Psychological Science, 3,* 53–57.

Goldsmith, H. H., Buss, A. H., Plomin, R., & Rothbart, M. K. (1987). What is temperament? Four approaches. *Child Development, 58,* 505–529.

Goldstein, E. (1979). Effect of same-sex and cross-sex role models on the subsequent academic productivity of scholars. *American Psychologist, 34,* 407–410.

Goleman, D. (1990, April 24). Anger over racism is seen as a cause of blacks' high blood pressure. *New York Times,* p. C3.

Golombok, S., & Tasker, F. (1996). Do parents influence the sexual orientation of their children? Findings from a longitudinal study of lesbian families. *Developmental Psychology, 32,* 3–11.

Gomez, R. & Sanson, A. V. (1994). Effects of experimenter and mother presence on attentional performance and activity of hyperactive boys. *Journal of Abnormal Child Psychology, 22,* 517–529.

Good, T. L., & Brophy, J. E. (1994). *Looking in classrooms* (6th ed.). New York: HarperCollins.

Goode, W. J. (1956). *After divorce.* Glencoe, IL: Free Press.

Goodkin, K., Burkhalter, J. E., Blaney, N. T., Leeds, B., Tuttle, R. S., & Feaster, D. J. (1997). A research derived bereavement support group technique for the HIV-1 infected. *Omega: Journal of Death and Dying, 34,* 279–300.

Goodman, G. S., Emery, R. E., & Haugaard, J. J. (1998). Developmental psychology and law: Divorce, child maltreatment, foster care, and adoption. In W. Damon (Ed.), *Handbook of child psychology* (5th ed.), Vol. 4. New York: Wiley.

Goodnow, J. J. (1992). *Parental belief systems: The psychological consequences for children.* Hillsdale, NJ: Erlbaum.

Gordon, C. P. (1996). Adolescent decision making: A broadly based theory and its application to the prevention of early pregnancy. *Adolescence, 31,* 561–584.

Gordon, C., Gaitz, C. M., & Scott, J. (1976). Leisure and lives: Personal expressivity across the life span. In R. H. Binstock & E. Shanas (Eds.), *Handbook of aging and the social sciences* (2nd ed., pp. 310–341). New York: Van Nostrand Reinhold.

Gottesman, I. I. (1963). Genetic aspects of intelligent behavior. In N. R. Ellis (Ed.), *Handbook of mental deficiency.* New York: McGraw-Hill.

Gottlieb, L. N., & Mendelson, M. J. (1990). Parental support and firstborn girls' adaptation to the birth of a sibling. *Journal of Applied Developmental Psychology, 11,* 29–48.

Gottman, J. M. (1986). The world of coordinated play: Same- and cross-sex friendships in children. In J. M. Gottman and Jeffrey G. Parker (Eds.), *Conversations of friends.* New York: Cambridge University Press.

Goubet, N., & Clifton, R. K. (1998). Object and event representation in 6½-month-old infants. *Developmental Psychology, 34,* 63–76.

Gould, R. L. (1978). *Transformation: Growth and change in adult life.* New York: Simon & Schuster.

Graber, J. A., Brooks-Gunn, J., Paikoff, R. L., & Warren, M. P. (1994). Prediction of eating problems: An 8-year study of adolescent girls. *Developmental Psychology, 30,* 823–834.

Graber, J. A., Brooks-Gunn, J., & Warren, M. P. (1995). The antecedents of menarcheal age: Heredity, family environment, and stressful life events. *Child Development, 66,* 346–359.

Greenberg, B. S., Fazel, S., & Weber, M. (1986). *Children's view on advertising.* New York: Independent Broadcasting Authority Research Report.

Greenberg, M. T., & Crnic, K. A. (1988). Longitudinal predictors of developmental status and social interaction in premature and full-term infants at age two. *Child Development, 59,* 554–570.

Greene, V. L., & Monahan, D. J. (1982). The impact of visitation on patient well-being in nursing homes. *The Gerontologist, 22,* 418–423.

Greenhaus, J. H., Parasuraman, S., & Wormley, W. M. (1990). Effects of race on organizational experiences, job performance evaluations, and career outcomes. *Academy of Management Journal, 33,* 64–86.

Greenough, W. T., & Black, J. E. (1992). Induction of brain structure by experience: Substrates for cognitive development. In

M. R. Gunnar & C. A. Nelson (Eds.), *Minnesota symposia on child psychology.* Hillsdale, NJ: Erlbaum.

Greer, J. (1992). *Adult sibling rivalries.* New York: Crown.

Grice, H. P. (1975). Logic and conversation. In P. Cole & J. Morgan (Eds.), *Speech acts: Syntax and semantics.* (Vol. 3, pp. 41–58). New York: Academic Press.

Groome, L. J., Swiber, M. J., Atterbury, J. L., Bentz, L. S., & Holland, S. B. (1997). Similarities and differences in behavioral state organization during sleep periods in the perinatal infant before and after birth. *Child Development, 68,* 1–11.

Guelzow, M. G., Bird, G. W., & Koball, E. H. (1991). An exploratory path analysis of the stress process for dual-career men and women. *Journal of Marriage and the Family, 53,* 151–164.

Guilford, J. P. (1967). *The nature of human intelligence.* New York: McGraw-Hill.

Gunter, N. C., & Gunter, B. G. (1990). Domestic division of labor among working couples: Does androgyny make a difference? *Psychology of Women Quarterly, 14,* 355–370.

Guralnick, J. M., & Simonsick, E. M. (1993). Physical disability in older Americans. *The Journals of Gerontology, 48* (Special Issue), 3–10.

Guralnick, J. M., & Wallace, R. B. (1991). The conceptualization and design of intervention studies on frailty in the older population: Insights from observational epidemiologic studies. In R. Weindruch, E. C. Hadley, & M. G. Ory (Eds.), *Reducing frailty and falls in older persons* (pp. 29–43). Springfield, IL: Charles C. Thomas.

Gurucharri, C., & Selman, F. L. (1982). The development of interpersonal understanding during childhood, preadolescence, and adolescence: A longitudinal follow-up study. *Child Development, 53,* 924–927.

Gutek, B. A., Searle, S., & Klepa, L. (1991). Rational versus gender role explanations for work-family conflict. *Journal of Applied Psychology, 76,* 560–568.

Gutmann, D. L. (1987). *Reclaimed powers: Toward a new psychology of men and women in later life.* New York: Basic Books.

Guttmacher, A. F., & Kaiser, I. H. (1986). *Pregnancy, birth, and family planning.* New York: New American Library.

Haan, N., Milsap, R., & Hartka, E. (1986). As time goes by: Change and stability in personality over fifty years. *Psychology and Aging, 1,* 220–232.

Haas, L. (1990). Gender equality and social policy: Implications of a study of parental leave in Sweden. *Journal of Family Issues, 11,* 401–423.

Hagestad, G. O., & Neugarten, B. L. (1985). Age and the life course. In R. H. Binstock & E. Shanas (Eds.), *Handbook of aging and the social sciences* (2nd ed., pp. 35–61). New York: Van Nostrand Reinhold.

Hahn, W. (1987). Cerebral lateralization of function: From infancy through childhood. *Psychological Bulletin, 101,* 376–392.

Haight, B. K. (1992). Long-term effects of a structured life review process. *Journal of Gerontology: Psychological Sciences, 47,* P312–P315.

Hall, D. G. (1996). Preschoolers' default assumptions about word meaning: Proper names designate unique individuals. *Developmental Psychology, 32,* 177–186.

Hall, D. R., & Zhao, J. Z. (1995). Cohabitation and divorce in Canada: Testing the selectivity hypothesis. *Journal of Marriage and the Family, 57,* 421–427.

Hall, G. S. (1904). *Adolescence.* New York: Appleton.

Hallinan, M. T., & Teixeira, R. A. (1987). Opportunities and constraints: Black-white differences in the formation of interracial friendships. *Child Development, 58,* 1358–1371.

Halpern L. F., MacLean, W. E., & Baumeister, A. A. (1995). Infant sleep-wake characteristics: Relation to neurological status and the prediction of developmental outcome. *Developmental Review, 15,* 255–291.

Halpern, D. F. (1986). *Sex differences in cognitive abilities.* Hillsdale, NJ: Erlbaum.

Halpern, J. (1987). *Helping your aging parents.* New York: McGraw-Hill.

Hamer, D. H., Hu, S., Magnuson, V. L., Hu, N., & Pattatucci, A. M. (1993). A linkage between DNA markers on the X chromosome and male sexual orientation. *Science, 261,* 321–327.

Hamill, S. B., & Goldberg, W. A. (1997). Between adolescents and aging grandparents: Midlife concerns of adults in the sandwich generation. *Journal of Adult Development, 4,* 135–147.

Hamilton, J. (1978). Grandparents as grievers. In J. O. Sahler (Ed.), *The child and death.* St. Louis: C. V. Mosby.

Hamon, R. R., & Blieszner, R. (1990). Filial responsibility expectations among adult child–older parent pairs. *Journal of Gerontology: Psychological Sciences, 45,* P110–P112.

Hamond, N. R., & Fivush, R. (1991). Memories of Mickey Mouse: Young children recount their trip to Disney World. *Cognitive Development, 6,* 433–448.

Hareven, T. K., & Adams, K. (1996). The generation in the middle: Cohort comparisons in assistance to aging parents in an American community. In T. K. Hareven (Ed.), *Aging and generational relations: Life course and cross-cultural perspectives* (pp. 3–29). New York: Aldine de Gruyter.

Harold, G. T., Fincham, F. D., Osborne, L. N., & Conger, R. D. (1997). Mom and Dad are at it again: Adolescent perceptions of marital conflict and adolescent psychological distress. *Developmental Psychology, 33,* 335–350.

Harringer, C. (1994). Adults in college. In J. D. Sinnott (Ed.), *Interdisciplinary handbook of adult lifespan learning* (pp. 171–185). Westport, CT: Greenwood Press.

Harris, L. J. (1983). Laterality of function in the infant: Historical and contemporary trends in theory and research. In G. Young, S. J. Segalowitz, C. M. Corter, & S. E. Trehub (Eds.), *Manual specialization and the developing brain.* New York: Academic Press.

Harris, M. B., & Turner, P. H. (1986). Gay and lesbian parents. *Journal of Homosexuality, 12,* 101–113.

Harris, P. L., & Kavanaugh, R. D. (1993). Young children's understanding of pretense. *Monographs of the Society for Research in Child Development, 58* (Serial No. 231).

Harris, P. L., Brown, E., Marriot, C., Whithall, S., & Harmer, S. (1991). Monsters, ghosts, and witches: Testing the limits of the fantasy-reality distinction in young children. *British Journal of Developmental Psychology, 9,* 105–123.

Harrist, A. W., Zaia, A. F., Bates, J. E., Dodge, K. A., & Pettit, G. S. (1997). Subtypes of social withdrawal in early childhood: Sociometric status and social-cognitive differences across four years. *Child Development, 68,* 278–294.

Hart, D. A. (1992). *Becoming men: The development of aspirations, values, and adaptational styles.* New York: Plenum.

Harter, S. (1990). Self and identity development. In S. S. Feldman & G. R. Elliott (Eds.), *At the threshold: The developing adolescent.* Cambridge, MA: Harvard University Press.

Harter, S. (1994). Developmental changes in self-understanding across the 5 to 7 shift. In A. Sameroff & M. M. Haith (Eds.), *Reason and responsibility: The passage through childhood.* Chicago: University of Chicago Press.

Hartup, W. W. (1983). Peer relations. In P. H. Mussen (Ed.), *Handbook of child psychology* (Vol. 4). New York: Wiley.

Hartup, W. W. (1992a). Friendships and their developmental significance. In H. McGurk (Ed.), *Contemporary issues in childhood social development.* London, UK: Routledge.

Hartup, W. W. (1992b). Peer relations in early and middle childhood. In V. B. Van Hasselt & M. Hersen (Eds.), *Handbook of social development: A lifespan perspective* (pp. 257–281). New York: Plenum.

Hartup, W. W. (1996). The company they keep: Friendships and their developmental significance. *Child Development, 67,* 1–13.

Hartup, W. W., & Stevens, N. (1997). Friendships and adaptation in the life course. *Psychological Bulletin, 121,* 355–370.

Harwood, R. L., Schoelmerich, A., Ventura-Cook, E., Schulze, P. A., & Wilson, S. P. (1996). Culture and class influences on Anglo and Puerto Rican mothers' beliefs regarding long-term socialization goals and child behavior. *Child Development, 67,* 2446–2461.

Hatch, L. R., & Bulcroft, C. (1992). Contact with friends in later life: Disentangling the effects of gender and marital stability. *Journal of Marriage and the Family, 54,* 222–232.

Havighurst, R. J. (1982). The world of work. In B. B. Wolman (Ed.), *Handbook of developmental psychology* (pp. 771–787). Englewood Cliffs, NJ: Prentice-Hall.

Hayflick, L. (1994). *How and why we age.* New York: Ballantine.

Hayward, M. D., Friedman, S., & Chen, H. (1998). Career trajectories and older men's retirement. *Journal of Gerontology: Social Sciences, 53B,* S91–S103.

Hazan, C., & Shaver, P. (1987). Romantic love conceptualized as an attachment process. *Journal of Personality and Social Psychology, 52,* 511–524.

Hazan, C., & Shaver, P. (1990). Love and work: An attachment-theoretical perspective. *Journal of Personality and Social Psychology, 59,* 270–280.

Hazan, C., & Shaver, P. (1994). Attachment as an organizational framework for research on close relationships. *Psychological Inquiry, 5,* 1–22.

Health Care Financing Administration. (1998). Medicare. Available at the Web site http://www.hcfa.gov/medicare/medicare.htm.

Hearold, S. (1986). A synthesis of 1,043 effects of television on social behavior. In G. Comstock (Ed.), *Public communications and behavior* (Vol. 1, pp. 65–133). New York: Academic Press.

Hedges, L. V., & Nowell, A. (1995). Sex differences in mental test scores, variability, and numbers of high-scoring individuals. *Science, 269,* 41–45.

Hedges, L. V., & Stock, W. (1983, Spring). The effects of class size: An examination of rival hypotheses. *American Education Research Journal,* 63–85.

Heidrich, S. M., & Denney, N. W. (1994). Does social problem solving differ from other types of problem solving during the adult years? *Experimental Aging Research, 20,* 105–126.

Heimann, B., & Pittenger, K. K. S. (1996). The impact of formal mentorship on socialization and commitment of newcomers. *Journal of Managerial Issues, 8,* 108–117.

Helson, R., & Moane, G. (1987). Personality change in women from college to midlife. *Journal of Personality and Social Psychology, 52,* 1176–1186.

Henderson, K. A. (1990). The meaning of leisure for women: An integrative review of the research. *Journal of Leisure Research, 22,* 228–243.

Henderson, V. W. (1997). Estrogen, cognition, and a woman's risk of Alzheimer's disease. *American Journal of Medicine, 103(3A),* 11S-18S.

Hennon, C. B. (1983). Divorce and the elderly: A neglected area of research. In T. H. Brubaker (Ed.), *Family relationships in later life* (pp. 149–172). Newbury Park, CA: Sage.

Henretta, J. C. (1997). Changing perspectives on retirement. *Journal of Gerontology: Social Sciences, 52B,* S1–S3.

Henretta, J. C., Chan, C. G., & O'Rand, A. M. (1992). Retirement reason versus retirement process: Examining the reasons for retirement typology. *Journal of Gerontology: Social Sciences, 47,* S1–S7.

Henshaw, S. K. (1993). Teenage abortion, birth and pregnancy statistics by state, 1988. *Family Planning Perspectives, 25,* 122–126.

Herrnstein, R. J., & Murray, C. (1994). *The bell curve: Intelligence and class structure in American life.* New York: Free Press.

Hershberger, S. L., & D'Augelli, A. R. (1995). The impact of victimization on the mental health and suicidality of lesbian, gay, and bisexual youths. *Developmental Psychology, 31,* 65–74.

Hertz, R. (1997). A typology of approaches to child care: The centerpiece of organizing family life for dual-earner couples. *Journal of Family Issues, 18,* 355–385.

Herzog, A. R., Kahn, R. L., Morgan, J. N., Jackson, J. S., & Antonucci, T. C. (1989). Age differences in productive activities. *Journal of Gerontology: Social Sciences, 44,* S129–S138.

Hetherington, E. M. (1988). Family relations six years after divorce. In K. Pasley & M. Ihinger-Tallman (Eds.), *Remarriage and stepparenting: Current research and theory* (pp. 185–205). New York: Guilford Press.

Hetherington, E. M. (1989). Coping with family transitions: Winners, losers and survivors. *Child Development, 60,* 1–14.

Hetherington, E. M. (1993). An overview of the Virginia Longitudinal Study of Divorce and Remarriage with a focus on early adolescence. *Journal of Family Psychology, 7,* 39–56.

Hetherington, E. M., & Arasten, J. D. (Eds.), *Impact of divorce, single parenting and step parenting on children* (pp. 299–324). Hillsdale, NJ: Erlbaum.

Hetherington, E. M., Cox, M., & Cox, R. (1982). Effects of divorce on parents and children. In M. E. Lamb (Ed.), *Nontraditional families* (pp. 233–288). Hillsdale, NJ: Erlbaum.

Hetherington, S. E. (1990). A controlled study of the effect of prepared childbirth classes on obstetric outcomes. *Birth, 17,* 86–90.

Hill, C. D., Thompson, L. W., & Gallagher, D. (1988). The role of anticipatory bereavement in older women's adjustment to widowhood. *The Gerontologist, 28,* 792–796.

Himsel, A. J., Hart, H., Diamond, A., & McAdams, D. P. (1997). Personality characteristics of highly generative adults as assessed in Q-sort ratings of life stories. *Journal of Adult Development, 4,* 149–161.

Hinshaw, S. P., Zupan, B. A., Simmel, C., Nigg, J. T., & Melnick, S. (1997). Peer status in boys with and without attention-deficit hyperactivity disorder: Predictions from overt and covert antisocial behavior, social isolation, and authoritative parenting beliefs. *Child Development, 68,* 880–896.

Hirshberg, L. M., & Svejda, M. (1990). When infants look to their parents: I. Infants' social referencing of mothers compared to fathers. *Child Development, 61,* 1175–1186.

Hobart, C. (1988). The family system in remarriage: An exploratory study. *Journal of Marriage and the Family, 50,* 649–661.

Hoff-Ginsberg, E. (1990). Maternal speech and the child's development of syntax: A further look. *Journal of Child Language, 17,* 85–99.

Hoff-Ginsberg, E. (1997). *Language development.* Pacific Grove, CA: Brooks/Cole.

Hoffman, M. L. (1970). Moral development. In P. H. Mussen (Ed.), *Carmichael's manual of child psychology* (3rd ed.) (Vol. 2). New York: Wiley.

Hoffman, M. L. (1988). Moral development. In M. H. Bornstein & M. E. Lamb (Eds.), *Developmental psychology: An advanced textbook* (2nd ed.). Hillsdale, NJ: Erlbaum.

Hoffman, M. L. (1994). Discipline and internalization. *Developmental Psychology, 30,* 26–28.

Hogan, D. P., & Astone, N. M. (1986). The transition to adulthood. *Annual Review of Sociology, 12,* 109–130.

Hogan, N., & DeSantis, L. (1996). Basic constructs of a theory of adolescent sibling bereavement. In D. Klass, P. R. Silverman, & S. L. Nickman (Eds.), *Continuing bonds: New understandings of grief* (pp. 235–254). Washington, DC: Taylor & Francis.

Hogge, W. A. (1990). Teratology. In I. R. Merkatz & J. E. Thompson (Eds.), *New perspectives on prenatal care.* New York: Elsevier.

Holden, G. W. (1988). Adults' thinking about a child-rearing problem: Effects of experience, parental status and gender. *Child Development, 59,* 1623–1632.

Holland, J. L. (1973). *Making vocational choices: A theory of careers.* Englewood Cliffs, NJ: Prentice-Hall.

Holland, J. L. (1985) *Self-directed search professional manual.* Lutz, FL: Psychological Assessment Resources.

Holland, J. L. (1985). *Making vocational choices: A theory of vocational personalities and work environments* (2nd ed.). Englewood Cliffs, NJ: Prentice-Hall.

Holland, J. L. (1987). Current status of Holland's theory of careers: Another perspective. *Career Development Quarterly, 36,* 24–30.

Holland, J. L. (1996). Exploring careers with a typology: What we have learned and some new directions. *American Psychologist, 51,* 397–406.

Holstein, M. (1997). Reflections on death and dying. *Academic Medicine, 72,* 848–855.

Holyroad, K. A., Appel, M. A., & Andrasik, F. (1983). A cognitive-behavioral approach to psychophysiological disorders. In D. Meichenbaum & M. E. Jarenko (Eds.), *Stress reduction and prevention.* New York: Plenum.

Horn, J. L. (1970). Organization of data on life-span development of human abilities. In L. R. Goulet & P. B. Baltes (Eds.), *Lifespan developmental psychology: Research and theory.* New York: Academic Press.

Horn, J. L. (1982). The aging of human abilities. In B. B. Wolman (Ed.), *Handbook of developmental psychology* (pp. 847–870). Englewood Cliffs, NJ: Prentice-Hall.

Horn, J. L., & Hofer, S. M. (1992). Major abilities and development in the adult period. In R. J. Sternberg & C. A. Berg (Eds.), *Intellectual development* (pp. 44–99). Cambridge, UK: Cambridge University Press.

Howard, A. (1992). Work and family crossroads along the career. In S. Zedeck (Ed.), *Work, families, and organizations* (p. 375). San Francisco: Jossey-Bass.

Howard, A., & Bray, D. W. (1980, August). *Career motivation in mid-life managers.* Paper presented at the meeting of the American Psychological Association, Montreal.

Howard, M., & McCabe, J. B. (1990). Helping teenagers postpone sexual involvement. *Family Planning Perspectives, 22,* 21–26.

Howe, M. L., & Courage, M. L. (1997). The emergence and early development of autobiographical memory. *Psychological Review, 104,* 499–523.

Howe, N., Petrakos, H., & Rinaldi, C. M. (1998). "All the sheeps are dead. He murdered them": Sibling pretense, negotiation, internal state language, and relationship quality. *Child Development, 69,* 182–191.

Howe, N., & Ross, H. S. (1990). Socialization, perspective taking and the sibling relationship. *Developmental Psychology, 26,* 160–165.

Howes, C., & Matheson, C. C. (1992). Sequences in the development of competent play with peers: Social and social pretend play. *Developmental Psychology, 28,* 961–974.

Howes, C., Unger, O., & Seidner, L. B. (1990). Social pretend play in toddlers: Parallels with social play and with solitary pretend. *Child Development, 60,* 77–84.

Hoyer, W. J., & Rybash, J. M. (1994). Characterizing adult cognitive development. *Journal of Adult Development, 1,* 7–12.

Hudson, J. (1988). Children's memory for atypical actions in script-based stories: Evidence for a disruption effect. *Journal of Experimental Child Psychology, 46,* 159–173.

Hudson, R. B. (1996). Social protection and services. In R. H. Binstock & L. K. George (Eds.), *Handbook of aging and the social sciences* (4th ed., pp. 446–466). San Diego, CA: Academic Press.

Huesmann, L. R., & Miller, L. S. (1994). Long-term effects of repeated exposure to media violence in childhood. In L. R. Huesmann (Ed.), *Aggressive behavior: Current perspectives.* New York: Plenum.

Huston, A. C., & Wright, J. C. (1994). Educating children with television: The forms of the medium. In D. Zillmann, J. Bryant, & A. C. Huston (Eds.), *Media, children, and the family: Social scientific, psychodynamic, and clinical perspectives* (pp. 73–84). Hillsdale, NJ: Erlbaum.

Huston, A. C., & Wright, J. C. (1998). Mass media and children's development. In W. Damon (Series Ed.), *Handbook of child psychology* (Vol. 4). New York: Wiley.

Huston, A. C., Watkins, B. A., & Kunkel, D. (1989). Public policy and children's television. *American Psychologist, 44,* 424–433.

Huttenlocher, P. R. (1990). Morphometric study of human cerebral cortex development. *Neuropsychologia, 28,* 517–527.

Huyck, M. H. (1982). From gregariousness to intimacy: Marriage and friendship over the adult years. In T. M. Field, A. Huston, H. C. Quay, L. Troll, & G. E. Finley (Eds.), *Review of human development* (pp. 471–484). New York: Wiley.

Huyck, M. H. (1990). Gender differences in aging. In J. E. Birren & K. W. Schaie (Eds.), *Handbook of the psychology of aging* (3rd ed., pp. 124–132). San Diego, CA: Academic Press.

Hyde, J. S., & Linn, M. C. (1988). Gender differences in verbal ability. *Psychological Bulletin, 104,* 53–69.

Ingraham, M. (1974). *My purpose holds: Reactions and experiences in retirement of TIAA/CREF annuitants.* New York: Educational Research Division, Teachers Insurance and Annuity Association-College Retirement Equities Fund.

Inhelder, B., & Piaget, J. (1958). *The growth of logical thinking from childhood to adolescence.* New York: Basic Books.

Ishler, K., Pargament, K. I., Kinney, J. M., & Cavanaugh, J. C. (1998). *Religious coping, general coping, and controllability: Testing the hypothesis of fit.* Unpublished manuscript, Bowling Green State University.

Iskra, G., I., Folkard, S., Marek, T., & Noworol, C. (1996). Health, well-being and burnout of ICU nurses on 12- and 8-h shifts. *Work and Stress, 10,* 251–256.

Israel, A. C., Guile, C. A., Baker, J. E., & Silverman, W. K. (1994). An evaluation of enhanced self-regulation training in the treatment of childhood obesity. *Journal of Pediatric Psychology, 19,* 737–749.

Ivancevich, J. M., & Matteson, M. T. (1988). Type A behavior and the healthy individual. *British Journal of Medical Psychology, 61,* 37–56.

Ivy, D. K., & Hamlet, S. (1996). College students and sexual dynamics: Two studies of peer sexual harassment. *Communication Education, 45,* 149–166.

Izard, C. E. (1991). *The psychology of emotions.* New York: Plenum.

Izard, C. E., Fantauzzo, C. A., Castle, J. M., Haynes, O. M., Rayias, M. F., & Putnam, P. H. (1995). The ontogeny and significance of infants' facial expressions in the first 9 months of life. *Developmental Psychology, 31,* 997–1013.

Jackson, B., Taylor, J., & Pyngolil, M. (1991). How age conditions the relationship between climacteric status and health symptoms in African American women. *Research in Nursing and Health, 14,* 1–9.

Jackson, J. S., & Gibson, R. C. (1985). Work and retirement among the black elderly. In Z. Blau (Ed.), *Current perspectives on aging and the life cycle* (pp. 193–222). Greenwich, CT: JAI.

Jacobs, J. (1975). *Older persons and retirement communities.* Springfield, IL: Charles C. Thomas.

Jacobs, J. E., & Eccles, J. S. (1992). The impact of mothers' gender-role stereotypic beliefs on mothers' and children's ability perceptions. *Journal of Personality and Social Psychology, 63,* 932–944.

Jacobs, S. (1993). *Pathologic grief: Maladaptation to loss.* Washington, DC: American Psychological Association.

Jacobson, J. L., Jacobson, S. W., & Humphrey, H. E. B. (1990). Effects of in utero exposure to polychlorinated biphenyls and related contaminants on cognitive functioning in young children. *Journal of Pediatrics, 116,* 38–45.

Jakobsen, R. (1997). Stages of progression in noncoital sexual interactions among young adolescents: An application of the Mokken scale analysis. *International Journal of Behavioral Development, 21,* 537–553.

James, L. R., & Jones, A. P. (1980). Perceived job characteristics and job satisfaction: An examination of reciprocal causation. *Personnel Psychology, 33,* 97–135.

James, W. (1890). *The principles of psychology.* New York: Holt.

Jenkins, C. L. (1997). Women, work, and caregiving: How do these roles affect women's well-being? *Journal of Women and Aging, 9,* 27–45.

Jensen, M. D., Benson, R. C., & Bobak, I. M. (1981). *Maternity care.* St. Louis, MO: C. V. Mosby.

Jiao, S., Ji, G., & Jing, Q. (1996). Cognitive development of Chinese urban only children and children with siblings. *Child Development, 67,* 387–395.

Johanson, R. B., Rice, C., Coyle, M., Arthur, J., Anyanwu, L., Ibrahim, J., Warwick, A., Redman, C. W. E., & O'Brien, P. M. S. (1993). A randomized prospective study comparing the new vacuum extractor policy with forceps delivery. *British Journal of Obstetrics and Gynecology, 100,* 524–530.

Johnson, B. D., Stone, G. L., Altmaier, E. M., & Berdahl, L. D. (1998). The relationship of demographic factors, locus of control and self-efficacy to successful nursing home adjustment. *The Gerontologist, 38,* 209–216.

Johnson, C. L. (1988). Active and latent functions of grandparenting during the divorce process. *The Gerontologist, 28,* 185–191.

Johnson, C. L., & Barer, B. M. (1990). Family and networks among inner city blacks. *The Gerontologist, 30,* 726–733.

Johnson, C. L., & Grant, L. (1985). *The nursing home in American society.* Baltimore, MD: Johns Hopkins University Press.

Johnson-Laird, P. N. (1988). *The computer and the mind: An introduction to cognitive science.* London, UK: Fontana.

Johnston, J. A. (1993, July 4). The cost of kids. *Sunday News Journal* (Wilmington, DE), p. E1.

Johnston, L. D., O'Malley, P. M., & Bachman, J. G. (1993). *National survey results on drug use from Monitoring the Future Study, 1975–1992* (Vol. 1). Rockville, MD: National Institute on Drug Abuse.

Johnstone, B., Frame, C. L., & Bouman, D. (1992). Physical attractiveness and athletic and academic ability in controversial-aggressive and rejected-aggressive children. *Journal of Social and Clinical Psychology, 11,* 71–79.

Jones, C. J., & Meredith, W. (1996). Patterns of personality change across the life span. *Psychology and Aging, 11,* 57–65.

Jones, D. C., Abbey, B. B., & Cumberland, A. (1998). The development of display rule knowledge: Linkages with family expressiveness and social competence. *Child Development, 69,* 1209–1222.

Jones, F. L. (1996). Convergence and divergence in ethnic divorce patterns: A research note. *Journal of Marriage and the Family, 58,* 213–218.

Jones, L. Y. (1980). *Great expectations: America and the baby boom generation.* New York: Coward, McCann, & Geoghegan.

Jung, C. G. (1960/1933). The stages of life. In G. Adler, M. Fordham, & H. Read (Eds.), *The collected works of C. J. Jung: Vol. 8. The structure and dynamics of the psyche.* London, UK: Routledge & Kegan Paul.

Jusczyk, P. W. (1981). The processing of speech and nonspeech sounds by infants: Some implications. In R. N. Aslin, J. R. Alberts, & M. R. Peterson (Eds.), *Development of perception* (Vol. 1). New York: Academic Press.

Jusczyk, P. W. (1995). Language acquisition: Speech sounds and phonological development. In J. L. Miller & P. D. Eimas (Eds.), *Handbook of perception and cognition: Vol. 11. Speech, language, and communication.* Orlando, FL: Academic Press.

Jusczyk, P. W., & Aslin, R. N. (1995). Infants' detection of the sound patterns of words in fluent speech. *Cognitive Psychology, 29,* 1–23.

Kagan, J., Arcus, D., Snidman, N., Feng, W. Y., Hendler, J., & Greene, S. (1994). Reactivity in infants: A cross-national comparison. *Developmental Psychology, 30,* 342–345.

Kahana, E. (1982). A congruence model of person-environment interaction. In M. P. Lawton, P. G. Windley, & T. O. Byerts (Eds.), *Aging and the environment: Theoretical approaches* (pp. 97–121). New York: Springer.

Kaijura, H., Cowart B. J., & Beauchamp, G. K. (1992). Early developmental change in bitter taste responses in human infants. *Developmental Psychobiology, 25,* 375–386.

Kail, R. (1990). *The development of memory in children* (3rd ed.). New York: Freeman.

Kail, R., & Bisanz, J. (1992). The information-processing perspective on cognitive development in childhood and adolescence. In R. J. Sternberg & C. A. Berg (Eds.), *Intellectual development.* New York: Cambridge University Press.

Kail, R. V., & Salthouse, T. A. (1994). Processing speed as a mental capacity. *Acta Psychologica, 86,* 199–225.

Kail, R. V., & Wicks-Nelson, R. (1993). *Developmental psychology* (5th ed.). Englewood Cliffs, NJ: Prentice-Hall.

Kalil, K. M., Gruber, J. E., Conley, J. G., & LaGrandeur, R. M. (1995). Relationships among stress, anxiety, Type A, and pregnancy-related complications. *Pre and Peri Natal Psychology Journal, 9,* 221–232.

Kalish, R. A. (1985). The social context of death and dying. In R. H. Binstock & E. Shanas (Eds.), *Handbook of aging and the social sciences* (2nd ed., pp. 149–170). New York: Van Nostrand Reinhold.

Kalish, R. A. (1987). Death and dying. In P. Silverman (Ed.), *The elderly as modern pioneers* (pp. 320–334). Bloomington: Indiana University Press.

Kalish, R. A., & Reynolds, D. (1976). *Death and ethnicity: A psychocultural study.* Los Angeles: University of Southern California Press.

Kamerman, S. B. (1993). International perspectives on child care policies and programs. *Pediatrics, 91,* 248–252.

Kandel, D. B. (1978). Homophily, selection, and socialization in adolescent friendships. *American Journal of Sociology, 84,* 427–436.

Kanekar, S., Kolsawalla, M. B., & Nazareth, T. (1989). Occupational prestige as a function of occupant's gender. *Journal of Applied Social Psychology, 19,* 681–688.

Kanter, R. M. (1976, May). Why bosses turn bitchy. *Psychology Today,* pp. 56–59.

Kantrowitz, B. (1993, August 2). Murder and mayhem, guns and gangs: A teenage generation grows up dangerous and scared. *Newsweek,* pp. 40–46.

Kaplan, P. S., Jung, P. C., Ryther, J. S., & Zarlengo-Strouse, P. (1996). Infant-directed versus adult-directed speech as signals for faces. *Developmental Psychology, 32,* 880–891.

Karniol, R. (1989). The role of manual manipulative states in the infant's acquisition of perceived control over objects. *Developmental Review, 9,* 205–233.

Kaslow, F. W., Hansson, K., & Lundblad, A. (1994). Long-term marriages in Sweden: And some comparisons with similar couples in the United States. *Contemporary Family Therapy, 16,* 521–537.

Kastenbaum, R. (1985). Dying and death: A life-span approach. In J. E. Birren & K. W. Schaie (Eds.), *Handbook of the psychology of aging* (2nd ed., pp. 619–643). New York: Van Nostrand Reinhold.

Kastenbaum, R. (1999). Dying and bereavement. In J. C. Cavanaugh & S. K. Whitbourne (Eds.), *Gerontology: An interdisciplinary perspective.* New York: Oxford University Press.

Katz, L. F., Kramer, L., & Gottman, J. M. (1992). Conflict and emotions in marital, sibling, and peer relationships. In C. U. Shantz & W. W. Hartup (Eds.), *Conflict in child and adolescent development.* Cambridge, UK: Cambridge University Press.

Katz, S. (1983). Assessing self-maintenance: Activities of daily living, mobility, and instrumental activities of daily living. *Journal of the American Geriatrics Society, 31,* 721–727.

Kausler, D. H. (1994). *Learning and memory in normal aging.* San Diego, CA: Academic Press.

Kazdin, A. E. (1982). Applying behavioral principles in the schools. In C. R. Reynolds & T. B. Gutkin (Eds.), *The handbook of school psychology.* New York: Wiley.

Kazdin, A. E. (1990). Childhood depression. *Journal of Child Psychology and Psychiatry and Allied Disciplines, 31,* 121–160.

Keane, S. P., Brown, K. P., & Crenshaw, T. M. (1990). Children's intention-cue detection as a function of maternal social behavior: Pathways to social rejection. *Developmental Psychology, 26,* 1004–1009.

Kearns, D. (1989, December 17). Improving the workforce: Competitiveness begins at school. *New York Times,* sec. 3, p. 2.

Kegan, R. (1982). *The evolving self.* Cambridge, MA: Harvard University Press.

Keith, J. (1990). Age in social and cultural context: Anthropological perspectives. In R. H. Binstock & L. K. George (Eds.), *Handbook of aging and the social sciences* (3rd ed., pp. 91–111). San Diego, CA: Academic Press.

Keith, J. (1994). Conclusion. In J. Keith et. al., *The aging experience: Diversity and commonality across cultures.* Newbury Park, CA: Sage.

Keller, H. (1965). *Helen Keller: The story of my life.* New York: Airmont.

Keller, J. W., Sherry, D., & Piotrowski, C. (1984). Perspectives on death: A developmental study. *Journal of Psychology, 116,* 137–142.

Kelley, M. L., Power, T. G., & Wimbush, D. D. (1992). Determinants of disciplinary practices in low-income Black mothers. *Child Development, 63,* 573–582.

Kelly, J. B. (1982). Divorce: The adult perspective. In B. B. Wolman (Ed.), *Handbook of developmental psychology* (pp. 734–750). Englewood Cliffs, NJ: Prentice-Hall.

Kelly, J. R., Steinkamp, M. W., & Kelly, J. R. (1987). Later-life satisfaction: Does leisure contribute? *Leisure Sciences, 9,* 189–200.

Kennedy, G. E. (1991). Grandchildren's reasons for closeness with grandparents. *Journal of Social Behavior and Personality, 6,* 697–712.

Kenney, R. A. (1982). *Physiology of aging: A synopsis.* Chicago: Yearbook Medical.

Kenrick, D. T. (1987). Gender, genes, and the social environment. In P. C. Shaver & C. Hendrick (Eds.), *Review of Personality and Social Psychology: Vol. 7. Sex and gender* (pp. 14–43). Newbury Park, CA: Sage.

Kerns, K. A., Klepac, L., & Cole, A. K. (1996). Peer relationships and preadolescents' perceptions of security in the child-mother relationship. *Developmental Psychology, 32,* 457–466.

Kiecolt-Glaser, J. K., Garner, W., Speicher, C. E., Penn, G. M., Holliday, J., & Glaser, R. (1984). Psychosocial modifiers of immunocompetence in medical students. *Psychosomatic Medicine, 46,* 7–14.

Kiernan, K. E. (1992). The impact of family disruption in childhood on transitions made in young adult life. *Population Studies, 46,* 213–234.

Kimball, M. M. (1986). Television and sex-role attitudes. In T. M. Williams (Ed.), *The impact of television* (pp. 265–301). New York: Academic Press.

Kimball, M. M. (1989). A new perspective on women's math achievement. *Psychological Bulletin, 105,* 198–214.

Kimmerle, M., Mick, L. A., & Michel, G. F. (1995). Bimanual role-differentiated toy play during infancy. *Infant Behavior and Development 18,* 299–307.

King, P. M., & Kitchener, K. S. (1994). *Developing reflective judgment: Understanding and promoting intellectual growth and critical thinking in adolescents and adults.* San Francisco: Jossey-Bass.

King, V., Elder, G. H., & Whitbeck, L. B. (1997). Religious involvement among rural youth: An ecological and life-course perspective. *Journal of Research on Adolescence, 7,* 431–456.

Kingston, P. W., & Nock, S. L. (1987). Time together among dual-earner couples. *American Sociological Review, 52,* 391–400.

Kinney, J. M. (1993, August). *Sense of coherence and mastery among spousal caregivers.* Paper presented at the meeting of the American Psychological Association, Toronto.

Kinney, J. M., & Cavanaugh, J. C. (1993, November). *Until death do us part: Striving to find meaning while caring for a spouse with dementia.* Paper presented at the annual meeting of the Gerontological Society of America, New Orleans.

Kinney, J. M., Haff, M., Isacson, A., Nocera, R., Cavanaugh, J. C., & Dunn, N. J. (1993, November). *Marital satisfaction and caregiving hassles among caregivers to spouses with dementia.* Paper presented at the annual meeting of the Gerontological Society of America, New Orleans.

Kinsbourne, M. (1989). Mechanisms and development of hemisphere specialization in children. In C. R. Reynolds & E. Fletcer-Janzen (Eds.), *Handbook of clinical child neuropsychology.* New York: Plenum.

Kirasic, K. C., & Allen, G. L. (1985). Aging, spatial performance, and spatial competence. In N. Charness (Ed.), *Aging and human performance* (pp. 191–223). Chichester, UK: Wiley.

Kirsch, I. S., Jungeblut, A., Jenkings, L., & Kolstad, A. (1993). *Adult literacy in America.* Washington, DC: U.S. Government Printing Office.

Kisilevsky, B. S., & Low, J. A. (1998). Human fetal behavior: 100 years of study. *Developmental Review, 18,* 1–29.

Kitchener, K. S., & King, P. M. (1989). The reflective judgment model: Ten years of research. In M. L. Commons, C. Armon, L. Kohlberg, F. A. Richards, T. A. Grotzer, & J. D. Sinnott (Eds.), *Adult development: Vol. 2. Models and methods in the study of adolescent and adult thought* (pp. 63–78). New York: Praeger.

Kitson, G. L., & Sussman, M. B. (1982). Marital complaints, demographic characteristics, and symptoms of mental distress in divorce. *Journal of Marriage and the Family, 44,* 87–101.

Kittrell, D. (1998). A comparison of the evolution of men's and women's dreams in Daniel Levinson's theory of adult development. *Journal of Adult Development, 5,* 105–115.

Kivett, V. R. (1991). Centrality of the grandfather role among older rural black and white men. *Journal of Gerontology: Social Sciences, 46,* S250–S258.

Kivnick, H. Q. (1982). *The meaning of grandparenthood.* Ann Arbor, MI: UMI Research.

Kivnick, H. Q. (1985). Grandparenthood and mental health: Meaning, behavior, and satisfaction. In V. L. Bengtson & J. F. Robertson (Eds.), *Grandparenthood* (pp. 151–158). Beverly Hills, CA: Sage.

Klaczynski, P. A., & Narasimham, G. (1998). Development of scientific reasoning biases: Cognitive versus ego-protective explanations. *Developmental Psychology, 34,* 175–187.

Klapper, J. T. (1968). The impact of viewing aggression: Studies and problems of extrapolation. In O. N. Larsen (Ed.), *Violence and the mass media.* New York: Harper & Row.

Klass, D. (1996a). Grief in Eastern culture: Japanese ancestor worship. In D. Klass, P. R. Silverman, & S. L. Nickman (Eds.), *Continuing bonds: New understandings of grief* (pp. 59–70). Washington, DC: Taylor & Francis.

Klass, D. (1996b). The deceased child in the psychic and social worlds of bereaved parents during the resolution of grief. In D. Klass, P. R. Silverman, & S. L. Nickman (Eds.), *Continuing bonds: New understandings of grief* (pp. 199–215). Washington, DC: Taylor & Francis.

Kline, D. W., & Schieber, F. (1985). Vision and aging. In J. E. Birren & K. W. Schaie (Eds.), *Handbook of the psychology of aging* (2nd ed., pp. 296–331). New York: Van Nostrand Reinhold.

Kline, R. B., Canter, W. A., & Robin, A. (1987). Parameters of teenage alcohol use: A path analytic conceptual model. *Journal of Consulting and Clinical Psychology, 55,* 521–528.

Klohnen, E. C., Vandewater, E. A., & Young, A. (1996). Negotiating the middle years: Ego-resiliency and successful midlife adjustment in women. *Psychology and Aging, 11,* 431–442.

Knapp, M. L., & Taylor, E. H. (1994). Commitment and its communication in romantic relationships. In A. L. Weber & J. H. Harvey (Eds.), *Perspectives on close relationships* (pp. 153–175). Boston: Allyn & Bacon.

Knight, G. P., Fabes, R. A., & Higgins, D. A. (1996). Concerns about drawing causal inferences from meta-analyses: An example in the study of gender differences in aggression. *Psychological Bulletin, 1996, 119,* 410–421.

Knowles, M. (1984). *The adult learner: A neglected species.* Houston, TX: Gulf.

Kobak, R. (1994). Adult attachment: A personality or relationship construct? *Psychological Inquiry, 5,* 42–44.

Koenig, H. G., George, L. K., & Siegler, I. C. (1988). The use of religion and other emotion-regulating coping strategies among older adults. *The Gerontologist, 28,* 303–310.

Koff, T. H. (1981). *Hospice: A caring community.* Cambridge, MA: Winthrop.

Kogan, N. (1983). Stylistic variation in childhood and adolescence: Creativity, metaphor, and cognitive style. In P. H. Mussen (Ed.), *Handbook of child psychology* (Vol. 3, pp. 630–706). New York: Wiley.

Kohlberg, L. (1966). A cognitive-developmental analysis of children's sex-role concepts and attitudes. In. E. E. Maccoby (Ed.), *The development of sex differences.* Palo Alto, CA: Stanford University Press.

Kohlberg, L. (1969). Stage and sequence: The cognitive-developmental approach to socialization. In D. Goslin (Ed.), *Handbook of socialization theory and research* (pp. 347–480). Chicago: Rand McNally.

Kohlberg, L. (1984). *Essays on moral development: Vol. II. The psychology of moral development.* San Francisco: Harper & Row.

Kohlberg, L. (1987). The development of moral judgment and moral action. In L. Kohlberg (Ed.), *Child psychology and childhood education: A cognitive-developmental view* (pp. 259–328). New York: Longman.

Kohlberg, L., & Ullian, D. Z. (1974). Stages in the development of psychosexual concepts and attitudes. In R. C. Friedman, R. M. Richart, & R. L. Van Wiele (Eds.), *Sex differences in behavior.* New York: John Wiley.

Kolata, G. (1990a). *The baby doctors.* New York: Delacorte.

Kolata, G. (1990b, February 6). Rush is on to capitalize on test for gene causing cystic fibrosis. *New York Times,* p. C3.

Kolb, B. (1989). Brain development, plasticity, and behavior. *American Psychologist, 44,* 1203–1212.

Kopp, C. B., & Krakow, J. B. (1982). *The child: Development in a social context.* Reading, MA: Addison-Wesley.

Kornhaber, A. (1985). Grandparenthood and the "new social contract." In V. L. Bengtson & J. F. Robertson (Eds.), *Grandparenthood* (pp. 159–172). Newbury Park, CA: Sage.

Kovacs, D. M., Parker, J. G., & Hoffman, L. W. (1996). Behavioral, affective, and social correlates of involvement in cross-sex friendship in elementary school. *Child Development, 67,* 2269–2286.

Kowalski, R. M. (1992). Nonverbal behaviors and perceptions of sexual intentions: Effects of sexual connotativeness, verbal response, and rape outcome. *Basic and Applied Social Psychology, 13,* 427–445.

Kram, K. E. (1980). *Mentoring processes at work: Developmental relationships in managerial careers.* Unpublished doctoral dissertation, Yale University, New Haven, CT.

Kram, K. E. (1985). *Mentoring at work: Developmental relationships in organizational life.* Glenview, IL: Scott, Foresman.

Kramer, D. A. (1989). A developmental framework for understanding conflict resolution processes. In J. D. Sinnott (Ed.), *Everyday problem solving: Theory and applications* (pp. 138–152). New York: Praeger.

Kramer, D. A. (1990). Conceptualizing wisdom: The primacy of affect-cognition relations. In R. J. Sternberg (Ed.), *Wisdom: Its nature, origins, and development* (pp. 279–313). Cambridge, UK: Cambridge University Press.

Kramer, D. A., Angiuld, N., Crisafi, L., & Levine, C. (1991, August). *Cognitive processes in real-life conflict resolution.* Paper presented at the annual meeting of the American Psychological Association, San Francisco.

Kramer, D. A., & Bacelar, W. T. (1994). The educated adult in today's world: Wisdom and the mature learner. In J. D. Sinnott (Ed.), *Interdisciplinary handbook of adult lifespan learning* (pp. 31–50). Westport, CT: Greenwood Press.

Kramer, D. A., & Kahlbaugh, P. E. (1994). Memory for a dialectical and nondialectical prose passage in younger and older adults. *Journal of Adult Development, 1,* 13–26.

Krause, N. (1991). Stress and inoculation from close ties in later life. *Journal of Gerontology: Social Sciences, 46,* S183–S194.

Krause, N. (1995). Religiosity and self-esteem among older adults. *Journal of Gerontology: Psychological Sciences, 50B,* P236–P246.

Krebs, D., & Gillmore, J. (1982). The relationship among the first stages of cognitive development, role-taking abilities, and moral development. *Child Development, 53,* 877–886.

Krevans, J., & Gibbs, J. C. (1996). Parents' use of inductive discipline: Relations to children's empathy and prosocial behavior. *Child Development, 67,* 3263–3277.

Krispin, O., Sternberg, K. J., & Lamb, M. E. (1992). The dimensions of peer evaluation in Israel: A cross-cultural perspective. *International Journal of Behavioral Development, 15,* 299–314.

Kroger, J., & Green, K. E. (1996). Events associated with identity status change. *Journal of Adolescence, 19,* 477–490.

Krout, J. A. (1988). Rural versus urban differences in elderly parents' contacts with their children. *The Gerontologist, 28,* 198–203.

Kübler-Ross, E. (1969). *On death and dying.* New York: Macmillan.

Kübler-Ross, E. (1974). *Questions and answers on death and dying.* New York: Macmillan.

Kuhl, P. K. (1993). Early linguistic experience and phonetic perception: Implications for theories of developmental speech perception. *Journal of Phonetics, 21,* 125–139.

Kurdek, L. A. (1991a). Predictors of increases in marital distress in newlywed couples: A 3-year prospective longitudinal study. *Developmental Psychology, 27,* 627–636.

Kurdek, L. A. (1991b). The relations between reported well-being and divorce history, availability of a proximate adult, and gender. *Journal of Marriage and the Family, 53,* 71–78.

Kurz, D. (1995). *For richer, for poorer: Mothers confront divorce.* Philadelphia: Women's Studies Program, University of Pennsylvania.

Labouvie-Vief, G. (1985). Intelligence and cognition. In J. E. Birren & K. W. Schaie (Eds.), *Handbook of the psychology of aging* (2nd ed., pp. 500–530). New York: Van Nostrand Reinhold.

Labouvie-Vief, G., Adams, C., Hakim-Larson, J., Hayden, M., & Devoe, M. (1985). *Logical problem solving and metalogical knowledge from preadolescence to adulthood.* Unpublished manuscript, Wayne State University, Detroit.

Lachman, M. E. (1985). Personal efficacy in middle and old age: Differential and normative patterns of change. In G. H. Elder, Jr. (Ed.), *Life-course dynamics: Trajectories and transitions, 1968–1980* (pp. 188–213). Ithaca, NY: Cornell University Press.

Lachman, M. E., Howland, J., Tennstedt, S., Jette, A., Assmann, S., & Peterson, E. W. (1998). Fear of falling and activity restriction: The survey of activities and fear of falling in the elderly (SAFE). *Journal of Gerontology, 53B,* P43–P50.

Lachs, M. S., Williams, C., O'Brien, S., Hurst, L., & Horwitz, R. (1997). Risk factors for reported elder abuse and neglect: A nine-year observational cohort study. *The Gerontologist, 37,* 469–474.

LaCroix, A. Z., Lang, J., Scherr, P., Wallace, R. B., Cornoni-Huntley, J., Berkman, L., et al. (1991). Smoking and mortality among older men and women in three communities. *New England Journal of Medicine, 324,* 1619–1625.

Ladd, G. W., & Le Sieur, K. D. (1995). Parents and children's peer relationships. In M. H. Bornstein (Ed.), *Handbook of parenting: Vol. 4. Applied and practical parenting* (pp. 377–410). Mahwah, NJ: Erlbaum.

Ladd, G. W., Kochenderfer, B. J., & Coleman, C. C. (1997). Classroom peer acceptance, friendship, and victimization: Distinct relational systems that contribute uniquely to children's school adjustment? *Child Development, 68,* 1181–1197.

LaGreca, A. M. (1993). Social skills training with children: Where do we go from here? *Journal of Clinical Child Psychology, 22,* 288–298.

Lajer, M. (1982). Unemployment and hospitalization among bricklayers. *Scandinavian Journal of Social Medicine, 10,* 3–10.

Lamb, M. E., & Oppenheim, D. (1989). Fatherhood and father-child relationships: Five years of research. In S. H. Cath, A. Gurwitt, & L. Gunsberg (Eds.), *Fathers and their families.* Hillsdale, NJ: Erlbaum.

Lamborn, S. D., Mounts, N. S., Steinberg, L., & Dornbusch, S. M. (1991). Patterns of competence and adjustment among adolescents from authoritative, authoritarian, indulgent, and neglectful families. *Child Development, 62,* 1049–1065.

Lampman, C., & Dowling-Guyer, S. (1995). Attitudes toward voluntary and involuntary childlessness. *Basic and Applied Social Psychology, 17,* 213–222.

Langer, E. J. (1985). Playing the middle against both ends: The usefulness of older adult cognitive activity as a model for cognitive activity in childhood and old age. In S. Yussen (Ed.), *The growth of reflection in children* (pp. 267–285). New York: Academic Press.

Langer, E. J., & Rodin, J. (1976). The effects of choice and enhanced personal responsibility for the aged: A field experiment in an institutional setting. *Journal of Personality and Social Psychology, 34,* 191–198.

Langlois, J. H., & Downs, A. C. (1980). Mothers, fathers, and peers as socialization agents of sex-typed play behaviors in young children. *Child Development, 51,* 1237–1247.

LaRossa, R. (1988). Fatherhood and social change. *Family Relations, 34,* 451–457.

Larson, R. W. (1997). The emergence of solitude as a constructive domain of experience in early adolescence. *Child Development, 68,* 80–93.

Larson, R. W., Gillman, S. A., & Richards, M. H. (1997). Divergent experiences of family leisure: Fathers, mothers, and young adolescents. *Journal of Leisure Research, 29,* 78–97.

Larson, R. W., Raffaelli, M., Richards, M. H., Ham, M., & Jewell, L. (1990). Ecology of depression in late childhood and early adolescence: A profile of daily states and activities. *Journal of Abnormal Psychology, 99,* 92–102.

Larson, R., & Richards, M. H. (1994). *Divergent realities: The emotional lives of mothers, fathers, and adolescents.* New York: Basic Books.

Larue, A., Dessonville, C., & Jarvik, L. F. (1985). Aging and mental disorders. In J. E. Birren & K. W. Schaie (Eds.), *Handbook of the psychology of aging* (2nd ed., pp. 664–702). New York: Van Nostrand Reinhold.

Latack, J. C. (1984). Career transitions within organizations: An exploratory study of work, nonwork, and coping strategies. *Organizational Behavior and Human Performance, 34,* 296–322.

Lauer, J., & Lauer, R. (1985). Marriages made to last. *Psychology Today, 19,* 22–26.

Laursen, B., & Collins, W. A. (1994). Interpersonal conflict during adolescence. *Psychological Bulletin, 115,* 197–209.

Lawton, M. P. (1982). Competence, environmental press, and the adaptation of old people. In M. P. Lawton, P. G. Windley, & T. O. Byerts (Eds.), *Aging and the environment: Theoretical approaches* (pp. 33–59). New York: Springer-Verlag.

Lawton, M. P. (1984). The varieties of well-being. In C. Z. Malatesta & C. E. Izard (Eds.), *Emotion in adult development* (pp. 67–84). Newbury Park, CA: Sage.

Lawton, M. P. (1989). Environmental proactivity in older people. In V. L. Bengtson & K. W. Schaie (Eds.), *The course of later life: Research and reflections* (pp. 15–23). New York: Springer.

Lawton, M. P., & Nahemow, L. (1973). Ecology of the aging process. In C. Eisdorfer & M. P. Lawton (Eds.), *The psychology of adult development and aging* (pp. 619–674). Washington, DC: American Psychological Association.

Lawton, M. P., Moss, M. S., & Fulcomer, M. (1986–1987). Objective and subjective uses of time by older people. *International Journal of Aging and Human Development, 24,* 171–188.

Lazarus, R. S., & Folkman, S. (1984). *Stress, appraisal, and coping.* New York: Springer.

Leahy, J. M. (1993). A comparison of depression in women bereaved of a spouse, a child, or a parent. *Omega, 26,* 207–217.

Leana, C. R., & Feldman, D. C. (1991). Gender differences in responses to unemployment. *Journal of Vocational Behavior, 38,* 65–77.

Leana, C. R., & Feldman, D. C. (1992). *Coping with job loss.* New York: Lexington Books.

Lee, D. J., & Markides, K. S. (1990). Activity and aging among persons over an eight year period. *Journal of Gerontology: Social Sciences, 45,* S39–S42.

Lee, G. R. (1988). Marital satisfaction in later life: The effects of nonmarital roles. *Journal of Marriage and the Family, 50,* 775–783.

Lee, G. R., Seccombe, K., & Shehan, C. L. (1991). Marital status and personal happiness: An analysis of trend data. *Journal of Marriage and the Family, 53,* 839–844.

Lee, T. R., Mancini, J. A., & Maxwell, J. W. (1990). Sibling relationships in adulthood: Contact patterns and motivation. *Journal of Marriage and the Family, 52,* 431–440.

Lei, T. (1994). Being and becoming moral in a Chinese culture: Unique or universal? *Cross Cultural Research: The Journal of Comparative Social Science, 28,* 59–91.

Leichtman, M. D., & Ceci, S. L. (1995). The effects of stereotypes and suggestions on preschoolers' reports. *Developmental Psychology, 31,* 568–578.

LeMare, L. J., & Rubin, K. H. (1987). Perspective taking and peer interaction: Structural and developmental analyses. *Child Development, 58,* 306–315.

Lemire, R. J., Loeser, J. D., Leech, R. W., & Alvord, E. C., Jr. (1975). *Normal and abnormal development of the nervous system.* Philadelphia: Lippincott.

Lentzner, H. R., Pamuk, E. R., Rhodenhiser, R. R., & Powell-Griner, E. (1992). The quality of life in the year before death. *American Journal of Public Health, 82,* 1093–1098.

Leon, G. R., & Dinklage, D. (1989). Obesity and anorexia nervosa. In T. H. Ollendick & M. Hersen (Eds.), *Handbook of child psychopathology* (2nd ed.). New York: Plenum.

Leon, G. R., Gillum, B., Gillum, R., & Gouze, M. (1979). Personality stability and change over a 30-year period: Middle to old age. *Journal of Consulting and Clinical Psychology, 47,* 517–524.

Lepper, M. R., & Gurtner, J. (1989). Children and computers. *American Psychologist, 44,* 170–178.

Lester, D. (1996). Trends in divorce and marriage around the world. *Journal of Divorce and Remarriage, 25,* 169–171.

Levenson, R. W., Carstensen, L. L., & Gottman, J. M. (1993). Long-term marriage: Age, gender, and satisfaction. *Psychology and Aging, 8,* 301–313.

Levin, J. S., Taylor, R. J., & Chatters, L. M. (1994). Race and gender differences in religiosity among older adults: Findings from four national surveys. *Journal of Gerontology: Social Sciences, 49,* S137–S145.

Levine, L. E. (1983). Mine: Self-definition in 2-year-old boys. *Developmental Psychology, 19,* 544–549.

Levinger, G. (1980). Toward the analysis of close relationships. *Journal of Experimental Social Psychology, 16,* 510–544.

Levinger, G. (1983). Development and change. In H. H. Kelley, E. Berscheid, A. Christensen, J. H. Harvey, T. L. Hutson, G. Levinger, E. McClintock, L. A. Peplau, & D. R. Peterson (Eds.), *Close relationships* (pp. 315–359). New York: Freeman.

Levinson, D. (1988). Family violence in cross cultural perspective. In V. B. Van Hasselt, R. L. Morrison, A. S. Bellack, & M. Hersen (Eds.), *Handbook of family violence* (pp. 435–456). New York: Plenum.

Levinson, D. J., Darrow, C., Kline, E., Levinson, M., & McKee, B. (1978). *The seasons of a man's life.* New York: Knopf.

Levinson, D., & Levinson, J. D. (1996). *The seasons of a woman's life.* New York: Knopf.

Levitt, A. G., & Utman, J. A. (1992). From babbling towards the sound systems of English and French: A longitudinal two-case study. *Journal of Child Language, 19,* 19–49.

Levitt, M. J., Guacci-franco, N., & Levitt, J. L. (1993a). Convoys of social support in childhood and early adolescence: Structure and function. *Developmental Psychology, 29,* 811–818.

Levitt, M. J., Weber, R. A., & Guacci, N. (1993b). Convoys of social support: An intergenerational analysis. *Psychology and Aging, 8,* 323–326.

Levy, G. D., Taylor, M. G., & Gelman, S. A. (1995). Traditional and evaluative aspects of flexibility in gender roles, social conventions, moral rules, and physical laws. *Child Development, 66,* 515–531.

Levy, J. (1976). A review of evidence for a genetic component in the determination of handedness. *Behavior Genetics, 6,* 429–453.

Lewin, T. (1992, Dec. 4). Baltimore school clinics to offer birth control by surgical implant. *New York Times,* pp. A1, A28.

Lewinsohn, P. M. & Gotlib, I. H. (1995). Behavioral theory and treatment of depression. In E. E. Beckham & W. R. Leber (Eds.), *Handbook of depression* (2nd ed.). New York: Guilford Press.

Lewinsohn, P. M. (1975). The behavioral study and treatment of depression. In M. Hersen, R. M. Eisler, & P. M. Miller (Eds.), *Progress in behavior modification* (Vol. 1, pp. 19–64). New York: Academic Press.

Lewis, K. G., & Moon, S. (1997). Always single and single again women: A qualitative study. *Journal of Marital and Family Therapy, 23,* 115–134.

Lewis, M. (1987). Social development in infancy and early childhood. In J. D. Osofsky (Ed.), *Handbook of infant development.* New York: Wiley.

Lewis, M. (1992). *Shame: The exposed self.* New York: Free Press.

Lewis, M., & Brooks-Gunn, J. (1979). *Social cognition and the acquisition of self.* New York: Plenum.

Lewis, M., Alessandri, S. M., & Sullivan, M. W. (1992). Differences in shame and pride as a function of children's gender and task difficulty. *Child Development, 63,* 630–638.

Lewis, M., Ramsay, D. S., & Kawakami, K. (1993). Differences between Japanese infants and Caucasian American infants in behavioral and cortisol response to inoculation. *Child Development, 64,* 1722–1731.

Lewis, R. A., & Lin, L-W. (1996). Adults and their midlife parents. In N. Vanzetti & S. Duck (Eds.), *A lifetime of relationships* (pp. 364–382). Pacific Grove, CA: Brooks/Cole.

Liben, L. S., & Signorella, M. L. (1993). Gender-schematic processing in children: The role of initial interpretations of stimuli. *Developmental Psychology, 29,* 141–149.

Lichtman, R. (1996). Perimenopausal and postmenopausal hormone replacement therapy. Part 1. An update of the literature on benefits and risks. *Journal of Nurse Midwifery, 41,* 3–28.

Liebert, R. M., & Sprafkin, J. (1988). *The early window: Effects of television on children and youth.* New York: Pergamon Press.

Liebert, R. M., Sprafkin, J. N., & Poulos, R. W. (1975). Selling cooperation to children. In W. S. Hale (Ed.), *Proceedings of the 20th annual conference of the Advertising Research Foundation* (pp. 54–57). New York: Advertising Research Foundation.

Liebowitz, M. (1983). *The chemistry of love.* Boston: Little, Brown.

Lin, C. C., & Fu, V. R. (1990). A comparison of childrearing practices among Chinese, immigrant Chinese, and Caucasian-American parents. *Child Development, 61,* 429–433.

Linden, M. G., Bender, B. G., Harmon, R. J., Mrazek, D. A., & Robinson, A. (1988). 47, XXX: What is the prognosis? *Pediatrics, 82,* 619–630.

Lindlaw, S. (1997, April 25). Ethical issues surround oldest new mom. *News Journal* (Wilmington, DE), p. A13.

Lindsay, P. (1984). High school size, participation in activities, and young adult social participation: Some enduring effects of schooling. *Educational Evaluation and Policy Analysis, 6,* 73–83.

List, N. D. (1988). Cancer screening in the elderly. In R. Chernoff & D. A. Lipschitz (Eds.), *Health promotion and disease prevention in the elderly* (pp. 113–129). New York: Raven Press.

Livesley, W. J., & Bromley, D. B. (1973). *Person perception in childhood and adolescence.* New York: Wiley.

Logan, R. D. (1986). A reconceptualization of Erikson's theory: The repetition of existential and instrumental themes. *Human Development, 29,* 125–136.

Lomranz, J., Bergman, S., Eyal, N., & Shmotkin, D. (1988). Indoor and outdoor activities of aged women and men as related to depression and well-being. *International Journal of Aging and Human Development, 26,* 303–314.

Longino, C. F. (1982). American retirement communities and residential relocation. In M. A. Warnes (Ed.), *Geographical perspectives on the elderly* (pp. 239–262). London, UK: Wiley.

Lopata, H. Z. (1996). Widowhood and husband sanctification. In D. Klass, P. R. Silverman, & S. L. Nickman (Eds.), *Continuing bonds: New understandings of grief* (pp. 149–162). Washington, DC: Taylor & Francis.

Lourenco, O. M. (1993). Toward a Piagetian explanation of the development of prosocial behaviour in children: The force of negational thinking. *British Journal of Developmental Psychology, 11,* 91–106.

Lovett, M. W., Borden, S. L., Deluca, T., Lacerenza, L., Benson, N. J., & Brackstone, D. (1994). Treating the core deficits of developmental dyslexia: Evidence of transfer of learning after phonologically and strategy-based reading programs. *Developmental Psychology, 30,* 805–822.

Lovett, S. B., & Pillow, B. H. (1996). Development of the ability to distinguish between comprehension and memory: Evidence from goal-state evaluation tasks. *Journal of Educational Psychology, 88,* 546–562.

Lowenthal, M., Thurnher, M., & Chiriboga, D. (1975). *Four stages of life.* San Francisco: Jossey-Bass.

Löwik, M. R. H., Wedel, M., Kok, F. J., Odink, J., Westenbrink, S., & Meulmeester, J. F. (1991). Nutrition and serum cholesterol levels among elderly men and women (Dutch nutrition surveillance system). *Journal of Gerontology: Medical Sciences, 46,* M23–M28.

Lozoff, B., Klein, N. K., Nelson, E. C., McClish, D. K., Manuel, M., & Chacon, M. E. (1998). Behavior of infants with iron-deficiency anemia. *Child Development, 69,* 24–36.

Ludemann, P. M. (1991). Generalized discrimination of positive facial expressions by seven- and ten-month-old infants. *Child Development, 62,* 55–67.

Ludemann, P. M., & Nelson, C. A. (1988). Categorical representation of facial expressions by 7-month-old infants. *Developmental Psychology, 24,* 492–501.

Lundgren, B. K., Steen, G. B., & Isaksson, B. (1987). Dietary habits in 70- and 75-year-old males and females: Longitudinal and cohort data from a population study. *Näringsforskning.*

Lundin, T. (1984). Morbidity following sudden and unexpected bereavement. *British Journal of Psychiatry, 144,* 84–88.

Luo, T. Y. (1996). Sexual harassment in the Chinese workplace: Attitudes toward and experiences of sexual harassment among workers in Taiwan. *Violence Against Women, 2,* 284–301.

Luthar, S. S., Zigler, E., & Goldstein, D. (1992). Psychosocial adjustment among intellectually gifted adolescents: The role of cognitive-developmental and experiential factors. *Journal of Child Psychology and Psychiatry and Allied Disciplines, 33,* 361–373.

Lyness, K. S., & Thompson, D. E. (1997). Above the glass ceiling? A comparison of matched samples of female and male executives. *Journal of Applied Psychology, 82,* 359–375.

Lyon, G. R. (1996). Learning disabilities. In E. J. Mash & R. A. Barkley (Eds.), *Child psychopathology.* New York: Guilford Press.

Lyons-Ruth, K., Alpern, L., & Repacholi, B. (1993). Disorganized infant attachment classification and maternal psychosocial problems as predictors of hostile-aggressive behavior in the preschool classroom. *Child Development, 64,* 572–585.

Lytton, H., & Romney, D. M. (1991). Parents' differential socialization of boys and girls: A meta-analysis. *Psychological Bulletin, 109,* 267–296.

Maccoby, E. E. (1990). Gender and relationships: A developmental account. *American Psychologist, 45,* 513–520.

Maccoby, E. E., & Jacklin, C. N. (1974). *The psychology of sex differences.* Palo Alto, CA: Stanford University Press.

Maccoby, E. E., Buchanon, C. M., Mnookin, R. H., & Dornbusch, S. M. (1993). Postdivorce roles of mothers and fathers in the lives of their children. *Journal of Family Psychology, 7,* 24–38.

Maccoby, E. E., Depner, C. E., & Mnookin, R. H. (1990). Coparenting in the second year after divorce. *Journal of Marriage and the Family, 52,* 141–155.

MacDermid, S. M., De Haan, L. G., & Heilbrun, G. (1996). Generativity in multiple roles. *Journal of Adult Development, 3,* 145–158.

Macklin, E. D. (1988). Heterosexual couples who cohabit nonmaritally: Some common problems and issues. In C. S. Chilman, E. W. Nunnally, & F. M. Cox (Eds.), *Variant family forms* (pp. 56–72). Newbury Park, CA: Sage.

Madaus, J. W. (1997). Accommodation, not privilege, for LD students. *AGB*, January/February, 25–29.

Main, M. (1996). Introduction to the special section on attachment and psychopathology: 2. Overview of the field of attachment. *Journal of Consulting and Clinical Psychology, 64,* 237–243.

Main, M., & Cassidy, J. (1988). Categories of response to reunion with the parent at age 6: Predictable from infant attachment classifications and stable over a 1-month period. *Developmental Psychology, 24,* 415–426.

Malina, R. M., & Bouchard, C. (1991). *Growth, maturation, and physical activity.* Champaign, IL: Human Kinetics Academic.

Malinak, D. P., Hoyt, M. F., & Patterson, V. (1979). Adults' reactions to the death of a parent: A preliminary study. *American Journal of Psychiatry, 136,* 1152–1156.

Malinosky-Rummell, R., & Hansen, D. J. (1993). Long-term consequences of childhood physical abuse. *Psychological Bulletin, 114,* 68–79.

Mandel, D. R., Jusczyk, P. W., & Pisoni, D. B. (1995). Infants' recognition of the sound patterns of their own names. *Psychological Science, 6,* 314–317.

Mange, A. P., & Mange, E. J. (1990). *Genetics: Human aspects* (2nd ed.). Sunderland, MA: Sinhauer Associates.

Mangelsdorf, S. C. (1992). Developmental changes in infant-stranger interaction. *Infant Behavior and Development, 15,* 191–208.

Mangelsdorf, S. C., Shapiro, J. R., & Marzolf, D. (1995). Developmental and temperamental differences in emotional regulation in infancy. *Child Development, 66,* 1817–1828.

Mangelsdorf, S., Gunnar, M., Kestenbaum, R., Lang, S., & Andreas, D. (1990). Infant proneness-to-distress temperament, maternal personality, and mother-infant attachment: Associations and goodness of fit. *Child Development, 61,* 820–831.

Marcia, J. E. (1980). Identity in adolescence. In J. Adelson (Ed.), *Handbook of adolescent psychology.* New York: Wiley.

Marcia, J. E. (1991). Identity and self-development. In R. M. Lerner, A. C. Petersen, & J. Brooks-Gunn (Eds.), *Encyclopedia of adolescence* (Vol. 1). New York: Garland.

Marciano, T. D. (1985). Homosexual marriage and parenthood should not be allowed. In H. Feldman & M. Feldman (Eds.), *Current controversies in marriage and family* (pp. 293–302). Newbury Park, CA: Sage.

Marcus, G. F., Pinker, S., Ullman, M., Hollander, M., Rosen, T. J., & Xu, F. (1992). Overregularization in language acquisition. *Monographs of the Society for Research in Child Development, 58* (4, Serial No. 228).

Margolin, L., & White, J. (1987). The continuing role of physical attractiveness in marriage. *Journal of Marriage and the Family, 49,* 21–27.

Markovits, H., & Vachon, R. (1989). Reasoning with contrary-to-fact propositions. *Journal of Experimental Child Psychology, 47,* 398–412.

Markus, H., & Nurius, P. (1986). Possible selves. *American Psychologist, 41,* 954–969.

Marquis, K. S., & Detweiler, R. A. (1985). Does adopted mean different? An attributional analysis. *Journal of Personality and Social Psychology, 48,* 1054–1066.

Marsh, H. W. (1991). Employment during high school: Character building or a subversion of academic goals? *Sociology of Education, 64,* 172–189.

Marshall, E. (1995). Gene therapy's growing pains. *Science, 269,* 1050–1052.

Marshall, V. W. (1994). Sociology, psychology, and the theoretical legacy of the Kansas City studies. *The Gerontologist, 34,* 768–774.

Marshall, W. A., & Tanner, J. M. (1962). Puberty. In J. Faulkner & J. M. Tanner (Eds.), *Human growth: A comprehensive treatise: Vol. 2. Postnatal growth, neurobiology* (2nd ed.). New York: Plenum.

Marshall, W. A., & Tanner, J. M. (1970). Variations in the pattern of pubertal changes in boys. *Archives of Disease in Childhood, 45,* 13–23.

Marsiglio, W. (1993). Attitudes toward homosexual activity and gay friends: A national survey of heterosexual 15- to 19-year-old males. *Journal of Sex Research, 30,* 12–17.

Martin, C. L., & Halverson, C. F. (1981). A schematic processing model of sex typing and stereotyping in children. *Child Development, 52,* 1119–1134.

Martin, C. L., & Halverson, C. F. (1987). The roles of cognition in sex roles and sex typing. In D. B. Carter (Ed.), *Current conceptions of sex roles and sex typing: Theory and research.* New York: Praeger.

Martin, C. L., & Little, J. K. (1990). The relation of gender understandings to children's sex-typed preferences and gender stereotypes. *Child Development, 61,* 1427–1439.

Martin, C. L., Eisenbud, L., & Rose, H. (1995). Children's gender-based reasoning about toys. *Child Development, 66,* 1453–1471.

Martin, M. A. (1990). The homeless elderly: No room at the end. In Z. Harel, P. Ehrlich, & R. Hubbard (Eds.), *The vulnerable aged* (pp. 149–166). New York: Springer.

Martorell, R. Mendoza, F., & Castillo, R. (1988). Poverty and stature in children. In J. C. Waterlow (Ed.), *Linear growth retardation in less developed countries.* New York: Raven Press.

Masheter, C. (1991). Postdivorce relationships between ex-spouses: The roles of attachment and interpersonal conflict. *Journal of Marriage and the Family, 53,* 103–110.

Masheter, C. (1997). Healthy and unhealthy friendship and hostility between ex-spouses. *Journal of Marriage and the Family, 59,* 463–475.

Masi, L., & Bilezikian, J. P. (1997). Osteoporosis: New hope for the future. *International Journal of Fertility and Women's Medicine, 42,* 245–254.

Matsui, T., Ikeda, H., & Ohnishi, R. (1989). Relation of sex-typed socializations to career self-efficacy expectations of college students. *Journal of Vocational Behavior, 35,* 1–16.

Matthews, A. M., & Brown, K. H. (1987). Retirement as a critical life event: The differential experiences of men and women. *Research on Aging, 9,* 548–571.

Matthews, K., Wing, R., Kuller, L., Meilahn, E., Kelsey, S., Costello, E., & Caggiula, A. (1990). Influences of natural menopause on psychological characteristics and symptoms of middle-aged healthy women. *Journal of Consulting and Clinical Psychology, 58,* 345–351.

Matthews, L. S., Conger, R. D., & Wickrama, K. A. S. (1996). Work-family conflict and marital quality: Mediating processes. *Social Psychology Quarterly, 59,* 62–79.

Matthews, R., & Matthews, A. M. (1986). Infertility and involuntary childlessness: The transition to nonparenthood. *Journal of Marriage and the Family, 48,* 641–649.

Matthews, S. H. (1996). Friendships in old age. In N. Vanzetti & S. Duck (Eds.), *A lifetime of relationships* (pp. 406–430). Pacific Grove, CA: Brooks/Cole.

Matula, K. E., Huston, T. L., Grotevant, H. D., & Zamutt, A. (1992). Identity and dating commitment among women and men in college. *Journal of Youth and Adolescence, 21,* 339–356.

Maurer, D., & Adams, R. J. (1987). Emergence of the ability to discriminate blue from gray at one month of age. *Journal of Experimental Child Psychology, 44,* 147–156.

Maurer, D., & Maurer, C. (1988). *The world of the newborn.* New York: Basic Books.

Mayeaux, E. J., & Johnson, C. (1996). Current concepts in post-menopausal hormone replacement therapy. *Journal of Family Practice, 43,* 69–75.

Mayer-Bahlburg, H. F. L., Ehrhardt, A. A., Rosen, L. R., Gruen, R. S., Veridiano, N. P., Vann, F. H., & Neuwalder, H. F. (1995). Prenatal estrogens and the development of sexual orientation. *Developmental Psychology, 31,* 12–21.

Mayo Clinic. (1992). *Mayo Clinic family health book* (Interactive edition). Rochester, MN: Mayo Foundation for Medical Education and Research. (CD-ROM published by Interactive Ventures, Inc.)

McAdams, D. P. (1992). The five-factor model in personality: A critical appraisal. *Journal of Personality, 60,* 329–361.

McAdams, D. P., Hart, H., & Maruna, S. (1997). The anatomy of generativity. In D. P. McAdams & E. de St. Aubin (Eds.), *Generativity and adult development* (pp. 7–43). Washington, DC: American Psychological Association.

McCall, R. B. (1979). *Infants.* Cambridge, MA: Harvard University Press.

McCloskey, L. A., & Coleman, L. M. (1992). Difference without dominance: Children's talk in mixed- and same-sex dyads. *Sex Roles, 27,* 241–257.

McCord, C., & Freeman, H. P. (1990). Excess mortality in Harlem. *New England Journal of Medicine, 322,* 173–177.

McCormick, C. M., & Maurer, D. M. (1988). Unimanual hand preferences in 6-month-olds: Consistency and relation to familial-handedness. *Infant Behavior and Development, 11,* 21–29.

McCrae, R. R., & Costa, P. T., Jr. (1990). *Personality in adulthood.* New York: Guilford Press.

McCrae, S. (1997). Cohabitation: A trial run for marriage? *Sexual and Marital Therapy, 12,* 259–273.

McDonald, H. J., & Sapone, F. M. (1993). *Nutrition for the prime of life.* New York: Plenum.

McEwen, B. S. (1998). Protective and damaging effects of stress mediators. *New England Journal of Medicine, 338,* 171–179.

McFadden, S. H. (1996). Religion, spirituality, and aging. In J. E. Birren & K. W. Schaie (Eds.), *Handbook of the psychology of aging* (4th ed., pp. 162–177). San Diego, CA: Academic Press.

McGee, R., Stanton, W. R., & Sears, M. R. (1993). Allergic disorders and attention deficit disorder in children. *Journal of Abnormal Child Psychology, 21,* 79–88.

McGee, R., Williams, S., & Feehan, M. (1992). Attention deficit disorder and age of onset of problem behaviors. *Journal of Abnormal Child Psychology, 20,* 487–502.

McGhee, P. E. (1976). Children's appreciation of humor: A test of the cognitive congruency principle. *Child Development, 47,* 420–426.

McGilly, K., & Siegler, R. S. (1990). The influence of encoding and strategic knowledge on children's choices among serial recall strategies. *Developmental Psychology, 26,* 931–941.

McGivern, J. E., Levin, J. R., Pressley, M., & Ghatala, E. S. (1990). A developmental study of memory monitoring and strategy selection. *Contemporary Educational Psychology, 15,* 103–115.

McGuire, J. M., Norlander, K. A., & Shaw, S. F. (1990). Postsecondary education for students with learning disabilities: Forecasting challenges for the future. *Learning Disabilities Focus, 5,* 69–74.

McGuire, L. C., & Cavanaugh, J. C. (1992, April). *Objective measures versus spouses' perceptions of cognitive status in dementia patients.* Paper presented at the biennial Cognitive Aging Conference, Atlanta.

McGuire, L. C., & Codding, R. (1998, August). *Improving older adults' memory for medical information: The efficacy of note taking and elderspeak.* Paper presented at the annual meeting of the American Psychological Association, San Francisco.

McHale, S. M., Bartko, W. T., Crouter, A. C., & Perry-Jenkins, M. (1990). Children's housework and psychosocial functioning: The mediating effects of parents' sex-role behaviors and attitudes. *Child Development, 61,* 1413–1426.

McHale, S. M., Crouter, A. C., McGuire, S. A., & Updegraff, K. A. (1995). Congruence between mothers' and fathers' differential treatment of siblings: Links with family relations and children's well being. *Child Development, 66,* 116–128.

McManus, I. C., Sik, G., Cole, D. R., Kloss, J., Mellon, A. F., & Wong, J. (1988). The development of handedness in children. *British Journal of Developmental Psychology, 6,* 257–273.

McNally, S., Eisenberg, N., & Harris, J. D. (1991). Consistency and change in maternal child-rearing practices and values: A longitudinal study. *Child Development, 62,* 190–198.

Mehta, K. K. (1997). The impact of religious beliefs and practices on aging: A cross-cultural comparison. *Journal of Aging Studies, 11,* 101–114.

Meilman, P. W. (1979). Cross-sectional age changes in ego identity status during adolescence. *Developmental Psychology, 15,* 230–231.

Mekos, D., Hetherington, E. M., & Reiss, D. (1996). Sibling differences in problem behavior and parental treatment in nondivorced and remarried families. *Child Development, 67,* 2148–2165.

Menaghan, E. G., & Lieberman, M. A. (1986). Changes in depression following divorce: A panel study. *Journal of Marriage and the Family, 48,* 319–328.

Mennella, J. A., & Beauchamp, G. K. (1996). The human infant's response to vanilla flavors in mother's milk and formula. *Infant Behavior and Development, 19,* 13–19.

Merriman, W. E., & Stevenson, C. M. (1997). Restricting a familiar name in response to learning a new one: Evidence for the mutual exclusivity bias in young two-year-olds. *Child Development, 68,* 211–228.

Mervis, C. B., & Johnson, K. E. (1991). Acquisition of the plural morpheme: A case study. *Developmental Psychology, 27,* 222–235.

Metropolitan Area Agency on Aging. (1998). Checklist on adult day care. Available at the Web site http://www.tcaging.org/com_adck.htm

Meyer, D. R., & Garasky, S. (1993). Custodial fathers: Myths, realities, and child support policy. *Journal of Marriage and the Family, 55,* 73–79.

Meyer-Bahlburg, H. F. L., Ehrhardt, A. A., Rosen, L. R., Gruen, R. S., et al. (1995). Prenatal estrogens and the development of homosexual orientation. *Developmental Psychology, 31.* 12–21.

Meyers, R. (1983). *D.E.S.: The bitter pill.* New York: Putnam.

Michael, R. T., Gagnon, J. H., Lauman, E. O., & Kolata, G. (1994). *Sex in America: A definitive survey.* Boston: Little, Brown.

Milford, M. (1997, November 9). Making a tough transition. *Sunday News Journal* (Wilmington, DE), pp. G1, G6.

Milford, M. (1998, November 1). Mired in the low wage pool. *Sunday News Journal* (Wilmington, DE), pp. A1, A8.

Miller, B. C., Norton, M. C., Curtis, T., Hill, E. J., Schvaneveldt, P., & Young, M. H. (1997). The timing of sexual intercourse among adolescents: Family, peer, and other antecedents. *Youth and Society, 29,* 54–83.

Miller, J. G., & Bersoff, D. M. (1992). Culture and moral judgment: How are conflicts between justice and interpersonal responsibilities resolved? *Journal of Personality and Social Psychology, 62,* 541–554.

Miller, K. F., Smith, C. M., Zhu, J., & Zhang, H. (1995). Preschool origins of cross-national differences in mathematical competence: The role of number-naming systems. *Psychological Science, 6,* 56–60.

Miller, P. A., Eisenberg, N., Fabes, R. A., & Shell, R. (1996). Relations of moral reasoning and vicarious emotion to young children's prosocial behavior toward peers and adults. *Developmental Psychology, 32,* 210–219.

Miller, R. B., Hemesath, K., & Nelson, B. (1997). Marriage in middle and later life. In T. D. Hargrave & S. M. Hanna (Eds.), *The aging family: New visions in theory, practice, and reality* (pp. 178–198). New York: Brunner/Mazel.

Miller, S. S., & Cavanaugh, J. C. (1990). The meaning of grandparenthood and its relationship to demographic, relationship, and social participation variables. *Journals of Gerontology: Psychological Sciences, 45,* 244–246.

Mills, R. S. L., & Grusec, J. E. (1989). Cognitive, affective, and behavioral consequences of praising altruism. *Merrill-Palmer Quarterly, 35,* 299–326.

Minkler, M., & Roe, K. M. (1993). *Grandmothers as caregivers: Raising children of the crack cocaine epidemic.* Newbury Park, CA: Sage.

Mischel, W. (1970) Sex-typing and socialization. In P. H. Mussen, (Ed.). *Carmichaels' manual of child psychology* (Vol. 2). New York: Wiley.

Miura, I. T., Kim, C. C., Chang, C. M., & Okamoto, Y. (1988). Effects of language characteristics on children's cognitive representation of number: Cross-national comparisons. *Child Development, 59,* 1445–1450.

Mize, J., & Ladd, G. W. (1990). A cognitive social-learning approach to social skill training with low-status preschool children. *Developmental Psychology, 26,* 388–397.

Mize, J., Pettit, G. S., & Brown, E. G. (1995). Mothers' supervision of their children's peer play: Relations with beliefs, perceptions, and knowledge. *Developmental Psychology, 31,* 311–321.

Mizes, J. S. (1995). Eating disorders. In M. Hersen, R. T. Ammerman, et al. (Eds.), *Advanced abnormal child psychology* (pp. 375–391). Hillsdale, NJ: Erlbaum.

Moats, L. C., & Lyon, G. R. (1993). Learning disabilities in the United States: Advocacy, science, and the future of the field. *Journal of Learning Disabilities, 26,* 282–294.

Mobily, K. E., Lemke, J. H., & Gisin, G. J. (1991). The idea of leisure repertoire. *Journal of Applied Gerontology, 10,* 208–223.

Moen, P. J., Robinson, J., & Fields, V. (1994). Women's work and caregiving roles: A life course approach. *Journal of Gerontology: Social Sciences, 49,* S176–S186.

Moffitt, T. E. (1993). Adolescence-limited and life-course-persistent antisocial behavior: A developmental taxonomy. *Psychological Review, 100,* 674–701.

Moffitt, T. E., Caspi, A., Belsky, J., & Silva, P. A. (1992). Childhood experience and the onset of menarche: A test of a sociobiological model. *Child Development, 63,* 47–58.

Molfese, D. L., & Burger-Judisch, L. M. (1991). Dynamic temporal-spatial allocation of resources in the human brain: An alternative to the static view of hemisphere differences. In F. L. Ketterle (Ed.), *Cerebral laterality: Theory and research. The Toledo symposium.* Hillsdale, NJ: Erlbaum.

Moller, L. C., Hymel, S., & Rubin, K. H. (1992). Sex typing in play and popularity in middle childhood. *Sex Roles, 26,* 331–353.

Monczunski, J. (1991). That incurable disease. *Notre Dame Magazine, 20(1),* 37.

Moody, R. A., Jr. (1975). *Life after life.* Atlanta, GA: Mockingbird.

Moody, R. A., Jr. (1977). *Reflections on life after life.* New York: Bantam Books.

Moody, R. A., Jr. (1988). *The light beyond.* New York: Bantam Books.

Moon, A., & Williams, O. (1993). Perceptions of elder abuse and help-seeking patterns among African-American, Caucasian American, and Korean-American elderly women. *The Gerontologist, 33,* 386–395.

Moore, B. S., Underwood, B., & Rosenhan, D. L. (1973). Affect and altruism. *Developmental Psychology, 8,* 99–104.

Moore, K. L., & Persaud, T. V. N. (1993). *Before we are born* (4th ed.). Philadelphia: Saunders.

Morgan, B., & Gibson, K. R. (1991). Nutritional and environmental interactions in brain development. In K. R. Gibson and A. C. Peterson (Eds.), *Brain maturation and cognitive development: Comparative and cross-cultural perspectives.* New York: Aldine de Gruyter.

Morgane, P. J., Austin-Lafrance, R., Bronzino, J. D., Tonkiss, J., Diaz-Cintra, S., Cintra, L., Kemper, T., & Galler, J. R. (1993). Prenatal malnutrition and development of the brain. *Neuroscience and Biobehavioral Reviews, 17,* 91–128.

Morioka, K. (1998). Comment 1: Toward a paradigm shift in family sociology. *Japanese Journal of Family Sociology, 10,* 139–144.

Morison, R., & Masten, A. S. (1991). Peer reputation in middle childhood as a predictor of adaptation in adolescence: A seven-year follow-up. *Child Development, 62,* 991–1007.

Morris, J. N., & Sherwood, S. (1984). Informal support resources for vulnerable elderly persons: Can they be counted on, why do they work? *International Journal of Aging and Human Development, 18,* 1–17.

Morrison, A. M., White, R. P., Van Velsor, E., & the Center for Creative Leadership. (1992). *Breaking the glass ceiling: Can women reach the top of America's largest corporations?* (Updated ed.). Reading, MA: Addison-Wesley.

Morrongiello, B. A., & Fenwick, K. D. (1991). Infants' coordination of auditory and visual depth information. *Journal of Experimental Child Psychology, 52,* 277–296.

Morrongiello, B. A., Fenwick, K. D., & Chance, G. (1990). Sound localization acuity in very young infants: An observer-based testing procedure. *Developmental Psychology, 26,* 75–84.

Morrow, D. G., Hier, C. M., Menard, W. E., & Leirer, V. O. (1998). Icons improve older and younger adults' comprehension of medication information. *Journal of Gerontology: Psychological Sciences, 53B,* P240–P254.

Morrow, P. C., & McElroy, J. C. (1987). Work commitment and job satisfaction over three career stages. *Journal of Vocational Behavior, 30,* 330–346.

Morrow-Howell, N., & Mui, A. (1989). Elderly volunteers: Reasons for initiating and terminating service. *Journal of Gerontological Social Work, 13,* 21–34.

Mortimer, J. T. (1991). Employment. In R. M. Lerner, A. C. Petersen, & J. Brooks-Gunn (Eds.), *Encyclopedia of adolescence* (Vol. 1). New York: Garland.

Mortimer, J. T., Finch, M. D., & Kumka, D. (1982). Persistence and change in development: The multidimensional self-concept. In P. B. Baltes & O. G. Brim, Jr. (Eds.), *Life-span development and behavior* (Vol. 4, pp. 263–313). New York: Academic Press.

Mortimer, J. T., Finch, M. D., Rye, S., Shanahan, M. J., & Call, K. T. (1996). The effects of work intensity on adolescent mental health, achievement, and behavioral adjustment: New evidence from a prospective study. *Child Development, 67,* 1243–1261.

Moshman, D. (1998). Cognitive development beyond childhood. In W. Damon (Series Ed.) & D. Kuhn & R. S. Siegler (Vol. Eds.), *Handbook of child psychology* (Vol. 2) (5th ed.). New York: Wiley.

Moss, M. S., & Moss, S. Z. (1996). Remarriage of widowed persons: A triadic relationship. In D. Klass, P. R. Silverman, & S. L. Nickman (Eds.), *Continuing bonds: New understandings of grief* (pp. 163–178). Washington, DC: Taylor & Francis.

Mounts, N. S., & Steinberg, L. (1995). An ecological analysis of peer influence on adolescent grade point average and drug use. *Developmental Psychology, 31,* 915–922.

Muehlenhard, C. L. (1988). "Nice women" don't say yes and "Real men" don't say no: How miscommunication and the double standard can cause sexual problems. *Women and Therapy, 7,* 95–108.

Mumme, D. L., Fernald, A., & Herrera, C. (1996). Infants' responses to facial and vocal emotional signals in a social referencing paradigm. *Child Development, 67,* 3219–3237.

Munakata, Y., McClelland, J. L., Johnson, M., H., & Siegler, R. S. (1997). Rethinking infant knowledge: Toward an adaptive process account of successes and failures in object permanence tasks. *Psychological Review, 104,* 686–713.

Murphy, C. (1986). Taste and smell in the elderly. In H. L. Meiselman & R. S. Rivlin (Eds.), *Clinical measurement of taste and smell* (pp. 343–371). New York: Macmillan.

Murphy, S. (1988). Mental distress and recovery in a high-risk bereavement sample three years after untimely death. *Nursing Research, 37,* 30–35.

Murray, B. (1998). Workplace harassment hurts everyone on the job. *APA Monitor, 29(7),* 36.

Murrell, A. J., Frieze, I. H., & Frost, J. L. (1991). Aspiring to careers in male- and female-dominated professions: A study of black and white college women. *Psychology of Women Quarterly, 15,* 103–126.

Murstein, B. I. (1987). A clarification and extension of the SVR theory of dyadic pairing. *Journal of Marriage and the Family, 49,* 929–933.

Mutchler, J. E., Burr, J. A., Pienta, A. M., & Massagli, M. P. (1997). Pathways to labor force exit: Work transitions and work instability. *Journal of Gerontology: Social Sciences, 52B,* S4–S12.

Myers, E. G., & Cavanaugh, J. C. (1995). Filial anxiety in mothers and daughters: Cross-validation of the Filial Anxiety Scale. *Journal of Adult Development, 2,* 137–145.

Myles, J. F. (1983). Conflict, crisis, and the future of old age security. *Milbank Memorial Fund Quarterly/Health and Society, 61,* 462–472.

Nachmias, M., Gunnar, M., Mangelsdorf, S., Parritz, R. H., & Buss, K. (1996). Behavioral inhibition and stress reactivity: The moderating role of attachment security. *Child Development, 67,* 508–522.

Nachtigall, L. E., & Nachtigall, L. B. (1990). Protecting older women from their growing risk of cardiac disease. *Geriatrics, 45(5),* 24–34.

Nathanson, C. A., & Lorenz, G. (1982). Women and health: The social dimension of biomedical data. In J. Z. Giele (Ed.), *Women in the middle years* (pp. 37–87). New York: Wiley.

National Academy on Aging. (1997). *Facts on . . . Long-term care.* Washington, DC: Author.

National Aging Information Center. (1997). *Profile of older Americans.* Available through the Web site http://www.aoa.dhhs.gov/aoa/stats/profile/

National Center for Education Statistics. (1991). *Preliminary data: Participation in adult education, 1991.* Washington, DC: U.S. Government Printing Office.

National Center for Education Statistics. (1993). *Preliminary data: Participation in adult education, 1993.* Washington, DC: U.S. Government Printing Office.

National Center for Health Statistics. (1997a). *Health, United States, 1996–1997.* Hyattesville, MD: Health and Human Services.

National Center for Health Statistics. (1997b). *Report of final mortality statistics, 1995.* Washington, DC: Public Health Service. (Also available through the Web site http://www.cdc.gov/nchswww/releases)

National Center for Health Statistics. (1997c). *Health, United States 1996–97 and injury chartbook.* Hyattsville, MD: Author. Available at the Web site http://www.cdc.gov/nchswww/data/hus96_97.pdf

National Center on Child Abuse and Neglect. (1997). *Child maltreatment 1995: Reports from the states to the National Center on Child Abuse and Neglect.* Washington DC: Department of Health and Human Services.

National Center on Elder Abuse. (1997). *Elder abuse in domestic settings.* Available at the Web site http://internic.com/NCEA/Statistics/

National Research Council. (1987). *Risking the future: Adolescent sexuality, pregnancy, and childbearing* (Vol. 1). Washington, DC: National Academy Press.

National Research Council. (1989). *Recommended dietary allowances* (10th ed.). Washington, DC: National Academy Press.

Neergaard, L. (1997, August 5). Implant may curb shaking. *News Journal* (Wilmington, DE), p. A1.

Neisser, U., Boodoo, G., Bouchard, T. J., Boykin, A W., Brody, N., Ceci, S. J., Halpern, D. F., Loehlin, J. C., Perloff, R., Sternberg, R. J., & Urbina, S. (1996). Intelligence: Knowns and unknowns. *American Psychologist, 51,* 77–101.

Neisser, U., & Winograd, E. (Eds.). (1988). *Remembering reconsidered.* New York: Cambridge University Press.

Nelson, K. (1973). Structure and strategy in learning to talk. *Monographs of the Society for Research in Child Development, 38* (Serial No. 149).

Neugarten, B. L. (1969). Continuities and discontinuities of psychological issues into adult life. *Human Development, 12,* 121–130.

Neugarten, B. L., & Weinstein, K. K. (1964). The changing American grandparent. *Journal of Marriage and the Family, 26,* 299–304.

Newcomb, A. F., & Bagwell, C. L. (1995). Children's friendship relations: A meta-analytic review. *Psychological Bulletin, 117,* 306–347.

Newman, B. S., & Muzzonigro, P. G. (1993). The effects of traditional family values on the coming out process of gay male adolescents. *Adolescence, 28,* 213–226.

Newman, L. S., Cooper, J., & Ruble, D. N. (1995). Gender and computers: II. Interactive effects of knowledge and constancy on gender-stereotyped attitudes. *Sex Roles, 33,* 325–351.

NICHD Early Child Care Research Network. (1997). The effects of infant child care on infant-mother attachment security: Results of the NICHD Study of Early Child Care. *Child Development, 68,* 860–879.

NICHD Early Child Care Research Network. (1998). Early child care and self-control, compliance, and problem behavior at twenty-four and thirty-six months. *Child Development, 69,* 1145–1170.

Nielson, A. C. (1990). *Annual Nielsen report on television: 1990.* New York: Nielson Media Research.

Nielson, G. H., Nordhus, I. H., & Kvale, G. (1998). Insomnia in older adults. In I. H. Nordhus, G. R. VandenBos, S. Berg, & P. Fromholt (Eds.), *Clinical gerospsychology* (pp. 167–175). Washington, DC: American Psychological Association.

Nock, S. L. (1981). Family life transitions: Longitudinal effects on family members. *Journal of Marriage and the Family, 43,* 703–714.

Nolen-Hoeksema, S. (1988). Life-span views on depression. In P. B. Baltes & R. M. Lerner (Eds.), *Life-span development and behavior* (Vol. 9, pp. 203–241). Hillsdale, NJ: Erlbaum.

Nolen-Hoeksema, S., & Girgus, J. S. (1994). The emergence of gender differences in depression during adolescence. *Psychological Bulletin, 115,* 424–443.

Normand, C. L., Silverman, P. R., & Nickman, S. L. (1996). Bereaved children's changing relationships with the deceased. In D. Klass, P. R. Silverman, & S. L. Nickman (Eds.), *Continuing bonds: New understandings of grief* (pp. 87–111). Washington, DC: Taylor & Francis.

Norris, F. N., & Murrell, S. A. (1987). Older adult family stress and adaptation before and after bereavement. *Journal of Gerontology, 42,* 606–612.

Norton, A. J., & Moorman, J. E. (1987). Current trends in marriage and divorce among American women. *Journal of Marriage and the Family, 49,* 3–14.

Notarius, C. I. (1996). Marriage: Will I be happy or will I be sad? In N. Vanzetti & S. Duck (Eds.), *A lifetime of relationships* (pp. 265–289). Pacific Grove, CA: Brooks/Cole.

Nurmi, J., Poole, M. E., & Kalakoski, V. (1996). Age differences in adolescent identity exploration and commitment in urban and rural environments. *Journal of Adolescence, 19,* 443–452.

Nwokah, E., & Fogel, A. (1993). Laughter in mother-infant emotional communication. *Humor: International Journal of Humor Research, 6,* 137–161.

Nydegger, C. N. (1986). Asymmetrical kin and the problematic son-in-law. In N. Datan, A. L. Greene, & H. W. Reese (Eds.), *Life-span developmental psychology: Intergenerational relations* (pp. 99–123). Hillsdale, NJ: Erlbaum.

O'Connor, B. P., & Rigby, H. (1996). Perceptions of baby talk, frequency of receiving baby talk, and self-esteem among community and nursing home residents. *Psychology and Aging, 11,* 147–154.

O'Leary, K. D. (1993). Through a psychological lens: Personality traits, personality disorders, and levels of violence. In R. J. Gelles & D. R. Loseke (Eds.), *Current controversies on family violence* (pp. 7–30). Newbury Park, CA: Sage.

O'Leary, K. D., Barling, J., Arias, I., Rosenbaum, A., Malone, J., & Tyree, A. (1989). Prevalence and stability of physical aggression between spouses: A longitudinal analysis. *Journal of Consulting and Clinical Psychology, 57,* 263–268.

Ochs, A. L., Newberry, J., Lenhardt, M. L., & Harkins, S. W. (1985). Neural and vestibular aging associated with falls. In J. E. Birren & K. W. Schaie (Eds.), *Handbook of the psychology of aging* (2nd ed., pp. 378–399). New York: Van Nostrand Reinhold.

Offer, D., Ostrov, E., Howard, K. I., & Atkinson, R. (1988). *The teenage world: Adolescents' self-image in ten countries.* New York: Plenum.

Offermann, L. R., & Growing, M. K. (1990). Organizations of the future: Changes and challenges. *American Psychologist, 45,* 95–108.

Ogletree, R. J. (1993). Sexual coercion experience and help-seeking behavior of college women. *Journal of American College Health, 41,* 149–153.

Ohlendorf-Moffat, P. (1991, February). Surgery before birth. *Discover,* 59–65.

Okagaki, L., & Sternberg, R. J. (1993). Parental beliefs and children's school performance. *Child Development, 64,* 36–56.

Okonski, B. (1996, May 6). Just say something. *Newsweek,* 14.

Okun, M. A., Stick, W. A., Haring, M. J., & Witter, R. A. (1984). The social activity/subjective well-being relation: A quantitative synthesis. *Research on Aging, 6,* 45–65.

Oldham, J. M., & Liebert, R. S. (Eds.). (1989). *The middle years.* New Haven, CT: Yale University Press.

Olian, J. D., Carroll, S. J., Giannantonia, C. M., & Feren, D. B. (1988). What do proteges look for in a mentor? Results from three experimental studies. *Journal of Vocational Behavior, 33,* 15–37.

Oliver, M. B., & Hyde, J. S. (1993). Gender differences in sexuality: A meta-analysis. *Psychological Bulletin, 114,* 29–51.

Oller, D. K. (1986). Metaphonology and infant vocalizations. In B. Lindblom & R. Zetterstrom (Eds.), *Precursors of early speech.* Basingstoke, UK: Macmillan.

Oller, D. K., & Eilers, R. E. (1988). The role of audition in infant babbling. *Child Development, 59,* 441–449.

Oller, D. K., & Lynch, M. P. (1992). Infant vocalizations and innovations in infraphonology: Toward a broader theory of development and disorders. In C. A. Ferguson, L. Menn, & C. Stoel-Gammon (Eds.), *Phonological development: Models, research, implications* (pp. 509–538). Timonium, MD: York Press.

Olson, D. H., & McCubbin, H. (1983). *Families: What makes them work.* Newbury Park, CA: Sage.

Orlick, T., Zhou, Q. Y., & Partington, J. (1990). Co-operation and conflict within Chinese and Canadian kindergarten settings. *Canadian Journal of Behavioural Science, 22,* 20–25.

Orwoll, L., & Perlmutter, M. (1990). The study of wise persons: Integrating a personality perspective. R. J. Sternberg (Ed.), *Wisdom: Its nature, origins, and development* (pp. 160–177). Cambridge, UK: Cambridge University Press.

Osgood, N. J. (1992). *Suicide in later life.* Lexington, MA: Lexington Books.

Otten, M. W., Teutsch, S. M., Williamson, D. F., & Marks, J. S. (1990). The effect of known risk factors on the excess mortality of black adults in the United States. *Journal of the American Medical Association, 263,* 845–850.

Oviatt, S. L. (1982). Inferring what words mean: Early development in infants' comprehension of common object names. *Child Development, 53,* 274–277.

Owen, G., Fulton, R., & Markusen, E. (1982). Death at a distance: A study of family survivors. *Omega, 13,* 191–225.

Pacifici, C., & Bearison, D. J. (1991). Development of children's self-regulations in idealized and mother-child interactions. *Cognitive Development, 6,* 261–277.

Pacy, B. (1993, Spring). Plunged into flux. *Notre Dame Magazine, 22,* 34–38.

Padgham, J. J., & Blyth, D. A. (1991). Dating during adolescence. In R. M. Lerner, A. C. Petersen, & J. Brooks-Gunn (Eds.), *Encyclopedia of adolescence* (Vol. 1). New York: Garland.

Palmore, E. B. (1990). *Ageism: Negative and positive.* New York: Springer.

Papalia, D. E., & Olds, S. W. (1995). *Human development* (6th ed.). New York: McGraw-Hill.

Parazzini, F., Luchini, L., La Vecchia, C., & Crosignani, P. G. (1993). Video display terminal use during pregnancy and reproductive outcome—a meta-analysis. *Journal of Epidemiology and Community Health, 47,* 265–268.

Pargament, K. I., Van Haitsma, K., & Ensing, D. S. (1995). When age meets adversity: Religion and coping in the later years. In M. A. Kimble, S. H. McFadden, J. W. Ellor, & J. J. Seeber (Eds.), *Aging, spirituality, and religion: A handbook* (pp. 47–67). Minneapolis: Fortress Press.

Park, D. C., Morrell, R. W., & Shifren, K. (Eds.). (In Press). *Processing of medical information in aging patients: Cognitive and human factors perspectives.* Mahwah, NJ: Erlbaum.

Park, D. C., Morrell, R. W., Frieske, D. A., Blackburn, A. B., & Birchmore, D. (1991). Cognitive factors and the use of over-the-counter medication organizers by arthritis patients. *Human Factors, 33,* 57–67.

Park, D. C., Smith, A. D., Lautenschlager, G., Earles, J. L., Frieski, D., Zwahr, M., & Gaines, C. L. (1996). Mediators of long-term memory performance across the life span. *Psychology and Aging, 11,* 621–637.

Parke, R. D. (1990). In search of fathers: A narrative of an empirical journey. In I. Sigel & G. Brody (Eds.), *Methods of family research.* Hillsdale, NJ: Erlbaum.

Parke, R. D. (1995). Fathers and families. In M. H. Bornstein (Ed.), *Handbook of parenting* (Vol. 3). Mahwah, NJ: Erlbaum.

Parke, R. D., & Bhavnagri, N. P. (1989). Parents as managers of children's peer relationships. In D. Belle (Ed.), *Children's social networks and social supports.* New York: Wiley.

Parke, R. D., & Buriel, R. (1998). Socialization in the family: Ethnic and ecological perspectives. In W. Damon (Ed.), *Handbook of child psychology* (Vol. 3). New York: Wiley.

Parke, R. D., & Slaby, R. G. (1983). The development of aggression. In E. M. Hetherington (Ed.), *Handbook of child psychology: Vol. 4. Socialization, personality, and social development* (4th ed.). New York: Wiley.

Parker, J. G., & Herrera, C. (1996). Interpersonal processes in friendship: A comparison of abused and nonabused children's experiences. *Developmental Psychology, 32,* 1025–1038.

Parker, R. A., & Aldwin, C. M. (1997). Do aspects of gender identity change from early to middle adulthood? Disentangling age, cohort, and period effects. In M. E. Lachman & J. B. James (Eds.), *Multiple paths of midlife development* (pp. 67–107). Chicago: University of Chicago Press.

Parrot, A., & Ellis, M. J. (1985). Homosexuals should be allowed to marry and adopt or rear children. In H. Feldman & M. Feldman (Eds.), *Current controversies in marriage and family* (pp. 303–312). Newbury Park, CA: Sage.

Parten, M. (1932). Social participation among preschool children. *Journal of Abnormal and Social Psychology, 27,* 243–269.

Pascual-Leone, J. (1990). An essay on wisdom: Toward organismic processes that make it possible. In R. J. Sternberg (Ed.), *Wisdom: Its nature, origins, and development* (pp. 244–278). Cambridge, UK: Cambridge University Press.

Pasley, K., & Ihinger-Tallman, M. (1987). *Remarriage and stepparenting.* New York: Guilford Press.

Patel, N., Power, T. G., & Bhavnagri, N. P. (1996). Socialization values and practices of Indian immigrant parents: Correlates of modernity and acculturation. *Child Development, 67,* 302–313.

Patterson, C. J. (1992). Children of lesbian and gay parents. *Child Development, 63,* 1025–1042.

Patterson, G. R. (1995). Coercion as a basis for early age of onset for arrest. In J. McCord (Ed.), *Coercion and punishment in long-term perspectives.* New York: Cambridge University Press.

Patterson, G. R., DeVaryshe, B. D., & Ramsey, E. (1989). A developmental perspective on antisocial behavior. *American Psychologist, 44,* 329–335.

Patterson, S. J., Sochting, I., & Marcia, J. E. (1992). The inner space and beyond: Women and identity. In G. R. Adams, T. P. Gullotta, & R. Montemayor (Eds.), *Adolescent identity formation: Vol. 4. Advances in adolescent development.* Newbury Park, CA: Sage.

Pattison, E. M. (Ed.). (1977). *The experience of dying.* Englewood Cliffs, NJ: Prentice-Hall.

Pavalko, E. K., & Artis, J. E. (1997). Women's caregiving and paid work: Causal relationships in late midlife. *Journals of Gerontology: Social Sciences, 52B,* S170–S179.

Pearlin, L. I., & Johnson, J. (1977). Marital status, life strains, and depression. *American Sociological Review, 42,* 704–715.

Pearlin, L. I., Mullan, J. T., Semple, S. J., & Skaff, M. M. (1990). Caregiving and the stress process: An overview of concepts and their measures. *The Gerontologist, 30,* 583–594.

Pearson, J. C. (1996). Forty-forever years? Primary relationships and senior citizens. In N. Vanzetti & S. Duck (Eds.), *A lifetime of relationships* (pp. 383–405). Pacific Grove, CA: Brooks/Cole.

Pearson, J. D., Morrell, C. H., Brant, L. J., Landis, P. K., & Fleg, J. L. (1997). Age-associated changes in blood pressure in a longitudinal study of healthy men and women. *Journal of Gerontology: Medical Sciences, 52A,* M177–M183.

Pederson, D. R., Gleason, K. E., Moran, G., & Bento, S. (1998). Maternal attachment representations, maternal sensitivity, and the infant-mother attachment relationship. *Developmental Psychology, 34,* 925–933.

Pellegrino, J. W., & Kail, R. V. (1982). Process analysis of spatial aptitude. In R. J. Sternberg (Ed.), *Advances in the psychology of human intelligence* (Vol. 1). Hillsdale, NJ: Erlbaum.

Pennington, B. F., Groisser, D., & Welsh, M. C. (1993). Contrasting cognitive deficits in attention deficit hyperactivity disorder versus reading disability. *Developmental Psychology, 29,* 511–523.

Peplau, L. A. (1991). Lesbian and gay relationships. In J. C. Gonsiorek & J. D. Weinrich (Eds.), *Homosexuality: Research implications for public policy* (pp. 177–196). Newbury Park, CA: Sage.

Peplau, L., & Gordon, S. L. (1985). Women and men in love: Sex differences in close heterosexual relationships. In V. O'Leary, R. K. Unger, & B. S. Wallston (Eds.), *Women, gender, and social psychology* (pp. 257–292). Hillsdale, NJ: Erlbaum.

Perkins, H. W., & Harris, L. B. (1990). Familial bereavement and health in adult life course perspective. *Journal of Marriage and the Family, 52,* 233–241.

Perry, W. I. (1970). *Forms of intellectual and ethical development in the college years.* New York: Holt, Rinehart and Winston.

Peters, A. M. (1995). Strategies in the acquisition of syntax. In P. Fletcher & B. MacWhinney (Eds.), *The handbook of child language* (pp. 462–483). Oxford, UK: Blackwell.

Peterson, B. E., & Klohnen, E. C. (1995). Realization of generativity in two samples of women at midlife. *Psychology and Aging, 10,* 20–29.

Peterson, C. (1996). *The psychology of abnormality.* Fort Worth TX: Harcourt Brace.

Peterson, C., Maier, S. F., & Seligman, M. E. P. (1993). *Learned helplessness: A theory for the age of personal control.* New York: Oxford University Press.

Peterson, L. (1983). Role of donor competence, donor age, and peer presence on helping in an emergency. *Developmental Psychology, 19,* 873–880.

Petraitis, J., Flay, B. R., & Miller, T. Q. (1995). Reviewing theories of adolescent substance use: Organizing pieces in the puzzle. *Psychological Bulletin, 117,* 67–86.

Petrus, J. J., & Vetrosky, D. T. (1990, April). Cancer: Risk factors, prevention, and screening. *Physician Assistant,* pp. 21–38.

Pettit, G. S., & Mize, J. (1993). Substance and style: Understanding the ways in which parents teach children about social relationships. In S. Duck (Ed.), *Learning about relationships.* Newbury Park, CA: Sage.

Pettit, G. S., Bakshi, A., Dodge, K. A., & Coie, J. D. (1990). The emergence of social dominance in young boys' play groups: Developmental differences and behavioral correlates. *Developmental Psychology, 26,* 1017–1025.

Pettit, G. S., Bates, J. E., & Dodge, K. A. (1997). Supportive parenting, ecological context, and children's adjustment: A seven-year longitudinal study. *Child Development, 68,* 908–923.

Pfost, K. S., & Fiore, M. (1990). Pursuit of nontraditional occupations: Fear of success or fear of not being chosen? *Sex Roles, 23,* 15–24.

Phelps, J. A., Davis, J. O., & Schartz, K. M. (1997). Nature, nurture, and twin research strategies. *Current Directions in Psychological Science, 6,* 117–121.

Phillis, D. E., & Stein, P. J. (1983). Sink or swing? The lifestyles of single adults. In E. R. Allgeier & N. B. McCormick (Eds.), *Changing boundaries: Gender roles and sexual behavior* (pp. 205–225). Palo Alto, CA: Mayfield.

Phinney, J. (1989). Stage of ethnic identity in minority group adolescents. *Journal of Early Adolescence, 9,* 34–49.

Phinney, J. (1990). Ethnic identity in adolescents and adults. *Psychological Bulletin, 108,* 499–514.

Phinney, J. S. (1993). Multiple group identities: Differentiation, conflict, and integration. In J. Kroger (Ed.), *Discussions on ego identity* (pp. 46–73). Hillsdale, NJ: Erlbaum.

Phinney, J. S., & Chavira, V. (1992). Ethnic identity and self-esteem: An exploratory longitudinal study. *Journal of Adolescence, 15,* 271–281.

Phinney, J. S., Cantu, C. L., & Kurtz, D. A. (1997). Ethnic and American identity as predictors of self-esteem among African American, Latino, and White adolescents. *Journal of Youth and Adolescence, 26,* 165–185.

Phinney, J. S., Ferguson, D. L., & Tate, J. D. (1997). Intergroup attitudes among ethnic minority adolescents: A causal model. *Child Development, 68,* 955–969.

Piaget, J. (1929). *The child's conception of the world.* New York: Harcourt, Brace.

Piaget, J. (1951). *Plays, dreams, and imitation in childhood.* New York: Norton.

Piaget, J. (1952). *The origins of intelligence in children.* New York: International Universities Press.

Piaget, J. (1954). *The construction of reality in the child.* New York: Basic Books.

Piaget, J., & Inhelder, B. (1956). *The child's conception of space.* Boston: Routledge & Kegan Paul.

Pickens, J. (1994). Perception of auditory-visual distance relations by 5-month-old infants. *Developmental Psychology, 30,* 537–544.

Picot, S. J., Debanne, S. M., Namazi, K. H., & Wykle, M. L. (1997). Religiosity and perceived rewards of black and white caregivers. *The Gerontologist, 37,* 89–101.

Pierce, C. A., & Aguinis, H. (1997). Bridging the gap between romantic relationships and sexual harassment in organizations. *Journal of Organizational Behavior, 18,* 197–200.

Pillemer, K. (1993). The abused offspring are dependent. In R. J. Gelles & D. R. Loseke (Eds.), *Current controversies on family violence* (pp. 237–249). Newbury Park, CA: Sage.

Pillemer, K., & Moore, D. W. (1989). Abuse of patients in nursing homes: Findings from a survey of staff. *The Gerontologist, 29,* 314–320.

Pillemer, K., & Suitor, J. J. (1992). Violence and violent feelings: What causes them among family caregivers? *Journal of Gerontology: Social Sciences, 47,* S165–S172.

Pincus, T., Callahan, L. F., & Burkhauser, R. V. (1987). Most chronic diseases are reported more frequently by individuals with fewer than 12 years of formal education in the age 18–64 United States population. *Journal of Chronic Diseases, 40,* 865–874.

Pine, J. M. (1995). Variation in vocabulary development as a function of birth order. *Child Development, 66,* 272–281.

Pine, J. M., Lieven, E. V. M., & Rowland, C. F. (1997). Stylistic variation at the "single-word" stage: Relations between maternal speech characteristics and children's vocabulary composition and usage. *Child Development, 68,* 807–819.

Piotrkowski, C. (1998). Gender harassment, job satisfaction, and distress among employed white and minority women. *Journal of Occupational Health Psychology, 3,* 33–43.

Plan for wider use of Norplant by girls dividing Baltimore (1993, Feb. 16). *New York Times,* p. B16.

Plomin, R. (1990). *Nature and nurture.* Pacific Grove, CA: Brooks/Cole.

Plomin, R., Defries, J. C., & McClearn, G. E. (1990). *Behavioral genetics: A primer* (2nd ed.). New York: Freeman.

Plomin, R., Fulker, D. W., Corley, R., & DeFries, J. C. (1997). Nature, nurture, and cognitive development from 1 to 16 years: A parent-offspring adoption study. *Psychological Science, 8,* 442–447.

Plomin, R., Owen, M. J., & McGuffin, P. (1994). The genetic basis of complex human behaviors. *Science, 264,* 1733–1739.

Plude, D. J., & Doussard-Roosevelt, J. A. (1989). Aging, selective attention, and feature integration. *Psychology and Aging, 4,* 98–105.

Plumert, J. M., & Nichols-Whitehead, P. (1996). Parental scaffolding of young children's spatial communication. *Developmental Psychology, 32,* 523–532.

Plunkett, K. (1996). *Connectionism and development: Neural networks and the study of change.* New York: Oxford University Press.

Polit, D. (1984). The only child in single-parent families. In T. Falbo (Ed.), *The single-child family* (pp. 178–210). New York: Guilford Press.

Ponder, R. J., & Pomeroy, E. C. (1996). The grief of caregivers: How pervasive is it? *Journal of Gerontological Social Work, 27,* 3–21.

Poon, L. W. (1992). *The Georgia centenarian study.* Amityville, NY: Baywood.

Porter, R. H., Makin, J. W., Davis, L. B., & Christensen, K. M. (1992). Breast-fed infants respond to olfactory cues from their own mother and unfamiliar lactating females. *Infant Behavior and Development, 15,* 85–93.

Posada, G., Waters, E., Crowell, J. A., & Lay, K. (1995). Is it easier to use a secure mother as a secure base? Attachment Q-sort correlates of the adult attachment interview. *Monographs of the Society for Research in Child Development, 60,* 133–145.

Post, F. (1987). Paranoid and schizophrenic disorders among the aging. In L. L. Carstensen & B. A. Edelstein (Eds.), *Handbook of clinical gerontology* (pp. 43–56). New York: Pergamon Press.

Poulin-Dubois, D., Serbin, L. A., Kenyon, B., & Derbyshire, A. (1994). Infants' intermodal knowledge about gender. *Developmental Psychology, 30,* 436–442.

Poulson, C. L., Kymissis, E., Reeve, K. F., Andreatos, M., & Reeve, L. (1991). Generalized vocal imitation in infants. *Journal of Experimental Child Psychology, 51,* 267–279.

Powell, M. B., & Thomson, D. M. (1996). Children's memory of an occurrence of a repeated event: Effects of age, repetition, and retention interval across three question types. *Child Development, 67,* 1988–2004.

Powers, S. W., & Roberts, M. W. (1995). Simulation training with parents of oppositional children: Preliminary findings. *Journal of Clinical Child Psychology, 24,* 89–97.

Powlishta, K. K. (1995). Intergroup processes in childhood: Social categorization and sex role development. *Developmental Psychology, 31,* 781–788.

Powlishta, K., Serbin, L. A., Doyle, A., & White, D. R. (1994). Gender, ethnic, and body type biases: The generality of prejudice in childhood. *Developmental Psychology, 30,* 526–536.

Pozzi, S., Healy, L., & Hoyles, C. (1993). Learning and interaction in groups with computers: When do ability and gender matter? *Social Development, 2,* 222–241.

Pratt, M. W., Diessner, R., Pratt, A., Hunsberger, B., & Pancer, S. M. (1996). Moral and social reasoning and perspective taking in later life: A longitudinal study. *Psychology and Aging, 11,* 66–73.

Pryor, J. B., Desouza, E. R., Fitness, J., Hutz, C. (1997). Gender differences in the interpretation of social-sexual behavior: A cross-cultural perspective on sexual harassment. *Journal of Cross Cultural Psychology, 28,* 509–534.

Qualls, S. H. (1999). Mental health and mental disorders in older adults. In J. C. Cavanaugh & S. K. Whitbourne (Eds.), *Gerontology: An interdisciplinary perspective* (pp. 305–328). New York: Oxford University Press.

Quigley, M. W. (1979, June 19). Executive corps: Free advice pays off for both sides. *Newsday,* p. 9.

Radford, A. (1995). Phrase structure and functional categories. In P. Fletcher & B. MacWhinney (Eds.), *The handbook of child language* (pp. 483–507). Oxford, UK: Blackwell.

Ragland, O. R., & Brand, R. J. (1988). Type A behavior and mortality from coronary heart disease. *New England Journal of Medicine, 318,* 65–69.

Ragozin, A. S., Basham, R. B., Crnic, K. A., Greenberg, M. T., & Robinson, N. M. (1982). Effects of maternal age on parenting role. *Developmental Psychology, 18,* 627–634.

Ramey, C. T., & Campbell, F. A. (1991). Poverty, early childhood education, and academic competence: The Abecedarian experiment. In A. Huston (Ed.), *Children reared in poverty.* New York: Cambridge University Press.

Ramey, C. T., & Ramey, S. L. (1990). Intensive educational intervention for children of poverty. *Intelligence, 14,* 1–9.

Ramsey, P. G. (1995). Growing up with the contradictions of race and class. *Young Children, 50,* 18–22.

Rapaport, J. L., & Ismond, D. R. (1990). *DSM-III-R training guide for diagnosis of childhood disorders.* New York: Brunner/Mazel.

Raphael, B. (1983). *The anatomy of bereavement.* New York: Basic Books.

Rapoport, R., & Rapoport, R. N. (1975). *Leisure and the family life cycle.* London, UK: Routledge & Kegan Paul.

Rapport, M. D. (1995). Attention-deficit hyperactivity disorder. In M. Hersen & R. T. Ammerman (Eds.), *Advanced abnormal child psychology.* Hillsdale, NJ: Erlbaum.

Rast, M., & Meltzoff, A. N. (1995). Memory and representation in young children with Down syndrome: Exploring deferred imitation and object permanence. *Development and Psychopathology, 7,* 393–407.

Rathunde, K. R., & Csikszentmihalyi, M. (1993). Undivided interest and the growth of talent: A longitudinal study of adolescents. *Journal of Youth and Adolescence, 22,* 385–405.

Rawlins, W. K. (1992). *Friendship matters.* Hawthorne, NY: Aldine de Gruyter.

Reedy, M. N., Birren, J. E., & Schaie, K. W. (1981). Age and sex differences in satisfying love relationships across the adult life span. *Human Development, 24,* 52–66.

Reich, P. A. (1986). *Language development.* Englewood Cliffs, NJ: Prentice-Hall.

Reid, D. H., Wilson, P. G., & Faw, G. D. (1991). Teaching self-help skills. In J. L. Matson & J. A. Mulick (Eds.), *Handbook of mental retardation* (2nd ed.). New York: Pergamon Press.

Reis, S. M., & Renzulli, J. S. (1995). Gifted and talented students. In M. C. Wang, M. C. Reynolds, & H. J. Walberg (Eds.), *Handbook of special and remedial education: Research and practice* (2nd ed.). Oxford, UK: Elsevier, Science.

Repacholi, B. M. (1998). Infants' use of attentional cues to identify the referent of another person's emotional expression. *Developmental Psychology, 34,* 1017–1025.

Reubens, B., Harrison, J., & Kupp, K. (1981). *The youth labor force, 1945–1995: A cross-national analysis.* Totowa, NJ: Allanheld, Osmun.

Rhodes, J. E., & Jason, L. A. (1990). A social stress model of substance abuse. *Journal of Consulting and Clinical Psychology, 58,* 395–401.

Rhyne, D. (1981). Basis of marital satisfaction among men and women. *Journal of Marriage and the Family, 43,* 941–955.

Ricciuti, H. N. (1993). Nutrition and mental development. *Current Directions in Psychological Science, 2,* 43–46.

Rice, M. L., Huston, A. C., Truglio, R., & Wright, J. (1990). Words from "Sesame Street": Learning vocabulary while viewing. *Developmental Psychology, 26,* 421–428.

Rich, C. L., Sherman, M., & Fowler, R. C. (1990, Winter). San Diego suicide study: The adolescents. *Adolescence,* pp. 855–865.

Riggs, D. S., & O'Leary, K. D. (1992). *Violence between dating partners: Background and situational correlates of courtship aggression.* Unpublished manuscript, State University of New York, Stony Brook.

Riley, M. W. (1979). Introduction. In M. W. Riley (Ed.), *Aging from birth to death: Interdisciplinary perspectives* (pp. 3–14). Boulder, CO: Westview Press.

Riley, V. (1981). Psychoneuroendocrine influence on immunocompetence and neoplasia. *Science, 212,* 1100–1109.

Roberto, K. A., & Skoglund, R. R. (1996). Interactions with grandparents and great-grandparents: A comparison of activities, influences, and relationships. *International Journal of Aging and Human Development, 43,* 107–117.

Roberts, J. D. (1980). *Roots of a black future: Family and church.* Philadelphia: Westminster.

Roberts, P., & Newton, P. M. (1987). Levinsonian studies of women's adult development. *Psychology and Aging, 2,* 154–163.

Roberts, W., & Strayer, J. (1996). Empathy, emotional expressiveness, and prosocial behavior. *Child Development, 67,* 449–470.

Roche, A. F. (1979). Secular trends in stature, weight, and maturation. *Monographs of the Society for Research in Child Development, 44* (Serial No. 179).

Rodeheaver, D., & Thomas, J. L. (1986). Family and community networks in Appalachia. In N. Datan, A. Greene, & H. W. Reese (Eds.), *Life-span developmental psychology: Intergenerational relations* (pp. 77–98). Hillsdale, NJ: Erlbaum.

Rodgers, J. L., & Rowe, D. C. (1993). Social contagion and adolescent sexual behavior: A developmental EMOSA model. *Psychological Review, 100,* 479–510.

Rodin, J., & Langer, E. J. (1977). Long-term effects of a control-relevant intervention with the institutionalized aged. *Journal of Personality and Social Psychology, 35,* 897–902.

Roffwarg, H. P., Muzio, J. N., & Dement, W. C. (1966). Ontogenetic development of the human sleep-dream cycle. *Science, 152,* 604–619.

Rogers, S. J., & Amato, P. R. (1997). Is marital quality declining? The evidence from two generations. *Social Forces, 75,* 1089–1100.

Rogoff, B., Mistry, J., Goncu, A., & Mosier, C. (1993). Guided participation in cultural activity by toddlers and caregivers. *Monographs of the Society for Research in Child Development, 58* (Serial No. 236).

Rogosch, F. A., Cicchetti, D., Shields, A., & Toth, S. L. (1995). Parenting dysfunction in child maltreatment. In M. H. Bornstein (Ed.), *Handbook of parenting* (Vol. 4). Mahwah NJ: Erlbaum.

Rooks, J. P., Weatherby, N. L., Ernst, E. K. M., Stapleton, S., Rosen, D., & Rosenfield, A. (1989). Outcomes of care in birth centers: The national birth center study. *New England Journal of Medicine, 321,* 1804–1811.

Roopnarine, J. (1992). Father-child play in India. In K. MacDonald (Ed.), *Parent-child play.* Albany: State University of New York Press.

Roscoe, B., Diana, M. S., & Brooks, R. H. (1987). Early, middle, and late adolescents' views on dating and factors influencing partner selection. *Adolescence, 22,* 59–68.

Rose, S. A. (1994). From hand to eye: Findings and issues in infant cross-modal transfer. In D. J. Lewkowicz and R. Lickliter (Eds.), *The development of intersensory perception.* Hillsdale, NJ: Erlbaum.

Rosenberg, E. B. (1992). *The adoption life cycle.* Lexington, MA: Lexington Books.

Rosenberg, L., Palmer, J. R., & Shapiro, S. (1990). Decline in the risk of myocardial infarction among women who stop smoking. *New England Journal of Medicine, 322,* 213–217.

Rosenblatt, P. C. (1996). Grief that does not end. In D. Klass, P. R. Silverman, & S. L. Nickman (Eds.), *Continuing bonds: New understandings of grief* (pp. 45–58). Washington, DC: Taylor & Francis.

Rosenthal, D. A., & Feldman, S. S. (1992). The relationship between parenting behaviour and ethnic identity in Chinese-American and Chinese-Australian adolescents. *International Journal of Psychology, 27,* 19–31.

Rosenthal, R., & Vandell, D. L. (1996). Quality of care at school-aged child-care programs: Regulatable features, observed experiences, child perspectives, and parent perspectives. *Child Development, 67,* 2434–2445.

Rosin, H. M., & Korabik, K. (1990). Marital and family correlates of women managers' attrition from organizations. *Journal of Vocational Behavior, 37,* 104–120.

Rosin, H. M., & Korabik, K. (1991). Workplace variables, affective responses, and intention to leave among women managers. *Journal of Occupational Psychology, 64,* 317–330.

Roskies, E., & Louis-Guerin, C. (1990). Job insecurity in managers: Antecedents and consequences. *Journal of Organizational Behavior, 11,* 345–359.

Ross, J. M. (1989). Recruiting and retaining adult students in higher education. *New Directions for Continuing Education* (Vol. 41, pp. 49–62). San Francisco: Jossey-Bass.

Rotenberg, K. J., & Mayer, E. V. (1990). Delay of gratification in native and white children: A cross-cultural comparison. *International Journal of Behavioral Development, 13,* 23–30.

Roth, W. F. (1991). *Work and rewards: Redefining our work-life reality.* New York: Praeger.

Rotheram-Borus, M. J., Rosario, M., Van Rossem, R., Reid, H., et al. (1995). Prevalence, course, and predictors of multiple problem behaviors among gay and bisexual male adolescents. *Developmental Psychology, 31,* 75–85.

Rotto, P. C., & Kratochwill, T. R. (1994). Behavioral consultation with parents: Using competency-based training to modify child noncompliance. *School Psychology Review, 23,* 669–693.

Rovee-Collier, C. (1987). Learning and memory in infancy. In J. D. Osofsky (Ed.), *Handbook of infant development* (2nd ed.). New York: Wiley.

Rovee-Collier, C. (1997). Dissociations in infant memory: Rethinking the development of implicit and explicit memory. *Psychological Review, 104,* 467–498.

Roxburgh, S. (1997). The effect of children on the mental health of women in the paid labor force. *Journal of Family Issues, 18,* 270–289.

Rubenfeld, M. I., & Gilroy, F. D. (1991). Relationship between college women's occupational interests and a single-sex environment. *Career Development Quarterly, 40,* 64–70.

Rubin, K. H., Bukowski, W., & Parker, J. G. (1998). Peer interactions, relationships, and groups. In W. Damon (Series Ed.) & N. Eisenberg (Vol. Ed.), *Handbook of child psychology* (Vol. 3). New York: Wiley.

Rubin, K. H., Chen, X., & Hymel, S. (1993). Socioemotional characteristics of withdrawn and aggressive children. *Merrill-Palmer Quarterly, 39,* 518–534.

Rubin, K. H., Stewart, S., & Chen, X. (1995). Parents of aggressive and withdrawn children. In M. Bornstein (Ed.), *Handbook of parenting* (Vol. 1). Hillsdale, NJ: Erlbaum.

Ruffman, T., Perner, J., Naito, M., Parkin, L., & Clements, W. A. (1998). Older (but not younger) siblings facilitate false belief understanding. *Developmental Psychology, 34,* 161–174.

Ruhm, C. J. (1990). Career jobs, bridge employment, and retirement. In P. Doeringer (Ed.), *Bridges to retirement: Older workers in a changing labor market* (pp. 92–107). Ithaca, NY: ILR Press.

Rusch, F. R., Szymanski, E. M., & Chadsey-Rusch, J. (1992). The emerging field of transition services. In F. R. Rusch, L. DeStefano, J. Chadsey-Rusch, L. A. Phelps, & E. Szymanski (Eds.), *Transition from school to life* (pp. 5–15). Sycamore, IL: Sycamore.

Russell, J. A., & Paris, F. A. (1994). Do children acquire concepts for complex emotions abruptly? *International Journal of Behavioral Development, 17,* 349–365.

Rutter, M., & Garmezy, N. Developmental psychopathology. (1983). In P. H. Mussen (Ed.), *Handbook of child psychology* (Vol. 4). New York: Wiley.

Ryan, E. B., Hamilton, J. M., & See, S. K. (1994). Patronizing the old: How do younger and older adults respond to baby talk in the nursing home? *International Journal of Aging and Human Development, 39,* 21–32.

Rybash, J. M., Hoyer, W. J., & Roodin, P. A. (1986). *Adult cognition and aging.* New York: Pergamon Press.

Ryff, C. D. (1989a). Beyond Ponce de Leon and life satisfaction: New directions in quest of successful aging. *International Journal of Behavioral Development, 12,* 35–55.

Ryff, C. D. (1989b). Happiness is everything, or is it? Explorations on the meaning of psychological well-being. *Journal of Personality and Social Psychology, 57,* 1069–1081.

Ryff, C. D. (1991). Possible selves in adulthood and old age: A tale of shifting horizons. *Psychology and Aging, 6,* 286–295.

Ryff, C. D., Lee, Y. H., Essex, M. J., & Schmutte, P. S. (1994). My children and me: Mid-life evaluations of grown children and of self. *Psychology and Aging, 9,* 195–205.

Rykken, D. E. (1987). Sex in the later years. In P. Silverman (Ed.), *The elderly as modern pioneers* (pp. 125–144). Bloomington: University of Indiana Press.

Sacco, W. P., & Beck, A. T. (1995). Cognitive theory and therapy. In E. E. Beckham & W. R. Leber (Eds.), *Handbook of depression* (2nd ed.). New York: Guilford Press.

Saffran, J. R., Aslin, R. N., & Newport, E. L. (1996). Statistical learning by 8-month-old infants. *Science, 274,* 1926–1928.

Sagi, A., van IJzendoorn, M. H., Aviezer, O., Donnell, F., & Mayseless, O. (1994). Sleeping out of home in a kibbutz communal arrangement: It makes a difference for infant-mother attachment. *Child Development, 65,* 992–1004.

Salapatek, P. (1975). Pattern perception in infancy. In L. B. Cohen & P. Salapatek (Eds.), *Infant cognition: From sensation to perception.* New York: Academic Press.

Salomone, P. R. (1996). Tracing Super's theory of vocational development: A 40-year retrospective. *Journal of Career Development, 22,* 167–184.

Salthouse, T. A. (1984). Effects of age and skill in typing. *Journal of Experimental Psychology: General, 113,* 345–371.

Salthouse, T. A. (1996). The processing-speed theory of adult age differences in cognition. *Psychological Review, 103,* 403–428.

Samuelson, L. K., & Smith, L. B. (1998). Memory and attention make smart word learning: An alternative account of Akhtar, Carpenter, and Tomasello. *Child Development, 69,* 94–104.

Sanders, C. M. (1980–1981). Comparison of younger and older spouses in bereavement outcome. *Omega: Journal of Death and Dying, 11,* 217–232.

Sanderson, C. A., & Cantor, N. (1995). Social dating goals in late adolescence: Implications for safer sexual activity. *Journal of Personality and Social Psychology, 68,* 1121–1134.

Sanson, A., Prior, M., Smart, D., & Oberklaid, F. (1993). Gender differences in aggression in childhood: Implications for a peaceful world. *Australian Psychologist, 28,* 86–92.

Saunders, C. (1977). Dying they live: St. Christopher's Hospice. In H. Feifel (Ed.), *New meanings of death* (pp. 153–179). New York: McGraw-Hill.

Saunders, C. (1997). Hospices worldwide: A mission statement. In C. Saunders & R. Kastenbaum (Eds.), *Hospice care on the international scene* (pp. 3–12). New York: Springer.

Saunders, C., & Kastenbaum, R. (Eds.), *Hospice care on the international scene* (pp. 3–12). New York: Springer.

Saxe, G. B. (1988). The mathematics of child street vendors. *Child Development, 59,* 1415–1425.

Scarr, S. (1992). Developmental theories for the 1990s: Development and individual differences. *Child Development, 63,* 1–19.

Scarr, S., & McCartney, K. (1983). How people make their own environments: A theory of genotype environment effects. *Child Development, 54,* 424–435.

Schaffer, H. R., & Emerson, P. E. (1964). The development of social attachments in infancy. *Monographs of the Society for Research in Child Development, 29* (Serial No. 3).

Schaie, K. W. (1994). The course of adult intellectual development. *American Psychologist, 49,* 304–313.

Schaie, K. W. (1995). *Intellectual development in adulthood: The Seattle longitudinal study.* New York: Cambridge University Press.

Scheibel, A. B. (1996). Structural and functional changes in the aging brain. In J. E. Birren & K. W. Schaie (Eds.), *Handbook of the psychology of aging* (4th ed., pp. 105–128). San Diego, CA: Academic Press.

Schiedel, D. G., & Marcia, J. E. (1985). Ego identity, intimacy, sex role orientation, and gender. *Developmental Psychology, 21,* 149–160.

Schlegel, A., & Barry, H. (1991). *Adolescence: An anthropological inquiry.* New York: Free Press.

Schleidt, M., & Genzel, C. (1990). The significance of mother's perfume for infants in the first weeks of their life. *Ethology and Sociobiology, 11,* 145–154.

Schneider, E. L., & Guralnick, J. M. (1990). The aging of America: Impact on health care costs. *Journal of the American Medical Association, 263,* 2335–2340.

Schneider, K. T., Swan, S., & Fitzgerald, L. F. (1997). Job-related and psychological effects of sexual harassment in the workplace: Empirical evidence from two organizations. *Journal of Applied Psychology, 82,* 401–415.

Schneider, M. L., Roughton, E. C., & Lubach, G. R. (1997). Moderate alcohol consumption and psychological stress during pregnancy induce attention and neuromotor impairments in primate infants. *Child Development, 68,* 747–759.

Schnorr, T. M., Grajewski, B. A., Hornung, R. W., Thun, M. J., Egeland, G. M., Murray, W. E., Conover, D. L., & Halperin, W. E. (1991). Video display terminals and the risk of spontaneous abortion. *The New England Journal of Medicine, 324,* 727–733.

Schramm, W., Lyle, J., & Parker, E. B. (1961). *Television in the lives of our children.* Palo Alto, CA: Stanford University Press.

Schulz, J. H. (1996). Economic security policies. In R. H. Binstock & L. K. George (Eds.), *Handbook of aging and the social sciences* (4th ed., pp. 410–426). San Diego, CA: Academic Press.

Schulz, R. (1978). *The psychology of death, dying and bereavement.* Reading, MA: Addison-Wesley.

Schulz, R. (1985). Emotion and affect. In J. E. Birren & K. W. Schaie (Eds.), *Handbook of the psychology of aging* (2nd ed., pp. 531–543). New York: Van Nostrand Reinhold.

Schutter, M. E., Scherman, A., & Carroll, R. S. (1997). Grandparents and children of divorce: Their contrasting perceptions and desires for the postdivorce relationship. *Educational Gerontology, 23,* 213–231.

Schwartz, F. (with J. Zimmerman). (1992). *Breaking with tradition: Women and work, the new facts of life.* New York: Warner Books.

Scott, R. B., & Mitchell, M. C. (1988). Aging, alcohol, and the liver. *Journal of the American Geriatrics Society, 36,* 255–265.

Scozarro, P. P., & Subich, L. M. (1990). Gender and occupational sex-type differences in job outcome factor perceptions. *Journal of Vocational Behavior, 36,* 109–119.

Sears, P. S., & Barbee, A. H. (1978). Career and life satisfaction among Terman's gifted women. In J. C. Stanley, W. C. George, & C. H. Solano (Eds.), *The gifted and the creative: Fifty year perspective* (pp. 28–66). Baltimore, MD: Johns Hopkins University Press.

Segal, E. S. (1996). Common medical problems in geriatric patients. In L. L. Carstensen, B. A. Edelstein, & L. Dornbrand (Eds.), *The practical handbook of clinical gerontology* (pp. 451–467). Thousand Oaks, CA: Sage.

Segall, M., & Wykle, M. L. (1988–1989). The black family's experience with dementia. *Journal of Applied Social Science, 13,* 170–191.

Seifer, R., Schiller, M., Sameroff, A. J., Resnick, S., & Riordan, K. (1996). Attachment, maternal sensitivity, and infant temperament during the first year of life. *Developmental Psychology, 32,* 12–25.

Selman, R. L. (1980). *The growth of interpersonal understanding: Developmental and clinical analyses.* New York: Academic Press.

Selman, R. L. (1981). The child as a friendship philosopher: A case study in the growth of interpersonal understanding. In S. R. Asher & J. M. Gottman (Eds.), *The development of children's friendships.* Cambridge, UK: Cambridge University Press.

Selman, R. L., & Byrne, D F. (1974). A structural-developmental analysis of levels of role-taking in middle childhood. *Child Development, 45,* 803–806.

Seltzer, J. A. (1991). Relationships between fathers and children who live apart: The father's role after separation. *Journal of Marriage and the Family, 53,* 79–102.

Sénéchal, M., Thomas, E., & Monker, J. (1995). Individual differences in 4-year-old children's acquisition of vocabulary during storybook reading. *Journal of Educational Psychology, 87,* 218–229.

Serbin, L. A., Powlishta, K. K., & Gulko, J. (1993). The development of sex typing in middle childhood. *Monographs of the Society for Research in Child Development, 58* (Serial No. 232).

Serdula, M. K., Ivery, D., Coates, R. J., Freedman, D. S., Williamson, D. F., & Byers, T. (1993). Do obese children become obese adults? A review of the literature. *Preventive Medicine, 22,* 167–177.

Sevy, S., Mendlewicz, J., & Mendelbaum, K. (1995). Genetic research in bipolar illness. In E. E. Beckham & W. R. Leber (Eds.), *Handbook of depression* (2nd ed.). New York: Guilford Press.

Shaiko, R. G. (1996.). Female participation in public interest nonprofit governance: Yet another glass ceiling? *Nonprofit and Voluntary Sector Quarterly, 25,* 302–320.

Shainess, N. (1984). *Sweet suffering: Woman as victim.* Indianapolis, IN: Bobbs-Merrill.

Shanahan, M. J., Elder, G. H., Burchinal, M., & Conger, R. D. (1996). Adolescent earnings and relationships with parents: The work-family nexus in urban and rural ecologies. In J. T. Mortimer & M. D. Finch (Eds.), *Adolescents, work, and family: An intergenerational developmental analysis.* Thousand Oaks, CA: Sage.

Shanahan, M. J., Elder, G. H., Burchinal, M., & Conger, R. D. (1996). Adolescent paid labor and relationships with parents: Early work-family linkages. *Child Development, 67,* 2183–2200.

Shatz, M., & Gelman, R. (1977). Beyond syntax: The influence of conversational constraints on speech modifications. In C. E. Snow & C. A. Ferguson (Eds.), *Talking to children: Language input and acquisition.* Cambridge, UK: Cambridge University Press.

Shaw, G. M., Schaffer, D., Velie, E. M., Morland, K., & Harris, J. A. (1995). Periconceptional vitamin use, dietary folate, and the occurrence of neural tube defects. *Epidemiology, 6,* 219–226.

Sheehy, G. (1992). *The silent passage: Menopause.* New York: Random House.

Shelov, S. P. (1993). *Caring for your baby and young child: Birth to age 5.* New York: Bantam Books.

Shelton, B. A., & John, D. (1993). Ethnicity, race, and difference: A comparison of white, black, and Hispanic men's household labor time. In J. C. Hood (Ed.), *Men, work, and family* (pp. 131–150). Newbury Park, CA: Sage.

Sher, T. G. (1996). Courtship and marriage: Choosing a primary relationship. In N. Vanzetti & S. Duck (Eds.), *A lifetime of relationships* (pp. 243–264). Pacific Grove, CA: Brooks/Cole.

Sherwin, B. B. (1997). Estrogen effects on cognition in menopausal women. *Neurology, 48(5 Suppl. 7),* S21–26.

Shirley, M. M. (1931). *The first two years: A study of twenty-five babies: Vol. 1. Postural and locomotor development.* Westport, CT: Greenwood Press.

Shirom, A., & Mazeh, T. (1988). Periodicity in seniority-job satisfaction relationship. *Journal of Vocational Behavior, 33,* 38–49.

Shiwach, R. (1994). Psychopathology in Huntington's disease patients. *Acta Psychiatrica Scandinavica, 90,* 241–246.

Shneidman, E. S. (1973). *Deaths of man.* New York: Quadrangle/New York Times.

Shneidman, E. S. (1980). *Voices of death.* New York: Harper & Row.

Shotland, R. L., & Goodstein, L. (1992). Sexual precedence reduces the perceived legitimacy of sexual refusal: An examination of attributions concerning date rape and consensual sex. *Personality and Social Psychology Bulletin, 18,* 756–764.

Shwe, H. I., & Markman, E. M. (1997). Young children's appreciation of the mental impact of their communicative signals. *Developmental Psychology, 33,* 630–636.

Siegel, R. K. (1980). The psychology of life after death. *American Psychologist, 35,* 911–931.

Siegler, I. C., George, L. K., & Okun, M. A. (1979). A cross-sequential analysis of adult personality. *Developmental Psychology, 15,* 350–351.

Siegler, R. S. (1981). Developmental sequences within and between concepts. *Monographs of the Society for Research in Child Development, 46* (Serial No. 189).

Siegler, R. S. (1998). *Children's thinking* (3rd ed). Upper Saddle River, NJ: Prentice-Hall.

Siegler, R. S., & Robinson, M. (1982). The development of numerical understandings. In H. W. Reese & L. P. Lipsitt (Eds.), *Advances in child development and behavior* (Vol. 16). New York: Academic Press.

Signorielli, N., & Lears, M. (1992). Children, television, and conceptions about chores: Attitudes and behaviors. *Sex Roles, 27,* 157–170.

Silverman, P. (1987). Community settings. In P. Silverman (Ed.), *The elderly as modern pioneers* (pp. 185–210). Bloomington: Indiana University Press.

Silverman, P. R., & Nickman, S. L. (1996). Children's construction of their dead parents. In D. Klass, P. R. Silverman, & S. L. Nickman (Eds.), *Continuing bonds: New understandings of grief* (pp. 73–86). Washington, DC: Taylor & Francis.

Silverman, P. R., & Worden, J. W. (1992). Children's understanding of funeral ritual. *Omega, 25,* 319–331.

Simmons, L. W. (1945). *Role of the aged in primitive society.* New Haven, CT: Yale University Press.

Simmons, R., & Blyth, D. (1987). *Moving into adolescence.* New York: Aldine de Gruyter.

Simons, R. L., Whitbeck, L. B., Conger, R. D., & Chyiin, W. (1991). Intergenerational transmission of harsh parenting. *Developmental Psychology, 27,* 159–171.

Simonton, D. K. (1990). Creativity and wisdom in aging. In J. E. Birren & K. W. Schaie (Eds.), *Handbook of the psychology of aging* (3rd ed., pp. 320–329). San Diego, CA: Academic Press.

Simonton, D. K. (1997). Creative productivity: A predictive and explanatory model of career trajectories and landmarks. *Psychological Review, 104,* 66–89.

Simpkins, J. W., Green, P. S., Gridley, K. E., Singh, M., De Fiebre, N. C., & Rajakumar, G. (1997). Role of estrogen replacement therapy in memory enhancement and the prevention of neu-ronal loss associated with Alzheimer's disease. *American Journal of Medicine, 103(3A),* 19S–25S.

Simpson, E. L. (1974). Moral development research: A case study of scientific cultural bias. *Human Development, 17,* 81–106.

Sinnott, J. D. (1986). Sex roles and aging: Theory and research from a systems perspective. *Contributions to human development* (Vol. 15). New York: Karger.

Sinnott, J. D. (1994a). New science models for teaching adults: Teaching as a dialogue with reality. In J. D. Sinnott (Ed.), *Interdisciplinary handbook of adult lifespan learning* (pp. 90–104). Westport, CT: Greenwood Press.

Sinnott, J. D. (1994b). The relationship of postformal thought, adult learning, and lifespan development. In J. D. Sinnott (Ed.), *Interdisciplinary handbook of adult lifespan learning* (pp. 105–119). Westport, CT: Greenwood Press.

Sinnott, J. D. (1994c). The future of adult lifespan learning: Learning institutions face change. In J. D. Sinnott (Ed.), *Interdisciplinary handbook of adult lifespan learning* (pp. 449–465). Westport, CT: Greenwood Press.

Sinnott, J. D. (Ed.). (1994d). *Interdisciplinary handbook of adult lifespan learning.* Westport, CT: Greenwood Press.

Sinnott, J. D. (1998). *The development of logic in adulthood: Postformal thought and its applications.* New York: Plenum.

Slate, J. R., Jones, C. H., & Dawson, P. (1993). Academic skills of high school students as a function of grade, gender, and academic track. *High School Journal, 76,* 245–251.

Smart, J. C. (1989). Life history influences on Holland vocational type development. *Journal of Vocational Behavior, 34,* 69–87.

Smith, A. B., & Inder, P. M. (1993). Social interaction in same and cross gender pre-school peer groups: A participant observation study. *Educational Psychology, 13,* 29–42.

Smith, A. D. (1996). Memory. In J. E. Birren & K. W. Schaie (Eds.), *Handbook of the psychology of aging* (4th ed., pp. 236–250). San Diego, CA: Academic Press.

Smith, J., & Baltes, P. B. (1990). Wisdom-related knowledge: Age/cohort differences in responses to life-planning problems. *Developmental Psychology, 26,* 494–505.

Smith, K. R., & Zick, C. D. (1986). The incidence of poverty among the recently widowed: Mediating factors in the life course. *Journal of Marriage and the Family, 48,* 619–630.

Smith, K. R., & Zick, C. D. (1996). Risk of mortality following widowhood: Age and sex differences by mode of death. *Social Biology, 43,* 59–71.

Smith, L. (1992). The tyranny of America's old. *Fortune, 125(1),* 68–72.

Smith, M., Colligan, M., Horning, R. W., & Hurrell, J. (1978). *Occupational comparisons of stress-related disease incidence.* Cincinnati, OH: National Institute for Occupational Safety and Health.

Snarey, J. R. (1985). Cross-cultural universality of social-moral development: A critical review of Kohlbergian research. *Psychological Bulletin, 97,* 202–232.

Snedeker, B. (1982) *Hard knocks: Preparing youth for work.* Baltimore, MD: Johns Hopkins University Press.

Snow, C. W. (1998). *Infant development* (2nd ed.). Upper Saddle River, NJ: Prentice-Hall.

Snow, M. E., Jacklin, C. N., & Maccoby, E. E. (1983). Sex-of-child differences in father-child interaction at one year of age. *Child Development, 54,* 227–232.

Snyder, C. J., & Barrett, G. V. (1988). The Age Discrimination in Employment Act: A review of court decisions. *Experimental Aging Research, 14,* 3–47.

Soffa, V. M. (1996). Alternatives to hormone replacement therapy. *Alternative Therapy, 2,* 34–39.

Solnick, R. L., & Corby, N. (1983). Human sexuality and aging. In D. S. Woodruff & J. E. Birren (Eds.), *Aging: Scientific perspectives and social issues* (2nd ed., pp. 202–224). Pacific Grove, CA: Brooks/Cole.

Spence, J. T. (1985). Achievement American style: The rewards and costs of individualism. *American Psychologist, 40,* 1285–1295.

Spetner, N. B., & Olsho, L. W. (1990). Auditory frequency resolution in human infancy. *Child Development, 61,* 632–652.

Sporakowski, M. J., & Axelson, L. J. (1984). Long-term marriages: A critical review. *Lifestyles: A Journal of Changing Patterns, 7(2),* 76–93.

Sporkin, E., Wagner, J., & Tomashoff, C. (1992, February). A terrible hunger. *People,* 92–98.

Sroufe, L. A., & Fleeson, J. (1986). Attachment and the construction of relationships. In W. W. Hartup & Z. Rubin (Eds.), *Relationships and development.* Hillsdale, NJ: Erlbaum.

Sroufe, L. A., & Waters, E. (1976). The ontogenesis of smiling and laughter: A perspective on the organization of development in infancy. *Psychological Review, 83,* 173–189.

Sroufe, L. A., & Wunsch, J. P. (1972). The development of laughter in the first year of life. *Child Development, 43,* 1324–1344.

St. James-Roberts, I., & Plewis, I. (1996). Individual differences, daily fluctuations, and developmental changes in amounts of infant waking, fussing, crying, feeding, and sleeping. *Child Development, 67,* 2527–2450.

Stalikas, A., & Gavaki, E. (1995). The importance of ethnic identity: Self-esteem and academic achievement of second-generation Greeks in secondary school. *Canadian Journal of School Psychology, 11,* 1–9.

Stanford, E. P., Happersett, C. J., Morton, D. J., Molgaard, C. A., & Peddecord, K. M. (1991). Early retirement and functional impairment from a multi-ethnic perspective. *Research on Aging, 13,* 5–38.

Stanovich, K. E. (1993). Dysrationalia: A new specific learning disability. *Journal of Learning Disabilities, 26,* 501–515.

Stark, E. (1992, May). *From dependency to empowerment: Framing and reframing the battered woman.* Paper presented at the Second Annual Conference: Domestic Violence: The Family/Community Connection, State University of New York Division of Nursing, Stony Brook.

Starko, A. J. (1988). Effects of the Revolving Door Identification Model on creative productivity and self-efficacy. *Gifted Child Quarterly, 32,* 291–297.

Steelman, J. D. (1994). Revision strategies employed by middle level students using computers. *Journal of Educational Computing Research, 11,* 141–152.

Steen, B. (1987). Nutrition and the elderly. In M. Bergener (Ed.), *Psychogeriatrics* (pp. 349–361). New York: Springer.

Steinberg, L. (1990). Autonomy, conflict, and harmony in the family relationship. In S. S. Feldman & G. R. Elliott (Eds.), *At the threshold: The developing adolescent.* Cambridge, MA: Harvard University Press.

Steinberg, L., & Dornbusch, S. M. (1991). Negative correlates of part-time employment during adolescence: Replication and elaboration. *Developmental Psychology, 27,* 304–313.

Steinberg, L., Fegley, S., & Dornbusch, S. M. (1993). Negative impact of part-time work on adolescent adjustment: Evidence from a longitudinal study. *Developmental Psychology, 29,* 171–180.

Steinberg, L., Lamborn, S. D., Dornbusch, S. M., & Darling, N. (1992). Impact of parenting practices on adolescent achievement: Authoritative parenting, school involvement, and encouragement to succeed. *Child Development, 63,* 1266–1281.

Steinmetz, S. K. (1993). The abused elderly are dependent. In R. J. Gelles & D. R. Loseke (Eds.), *Current controversies on family violence* (pp. 222–236). Newbury Park, CA: Sage.

Stelmach, G. E., Goggin, N. L., & Garcia-Colera, A. (1987). Movement specification time with age. *Experimental Aging Research, 13,* 39–46.

Stenberg, C., & Campos, J. (1990). The development of anger expressions in infancy. In N. Stein, B. Leventhal, & T. Trabasso (Eds.), *Psychological and biological approaches to emotion.* Hillsdale, NJ: Erlbaum.

Stephen, T. (1987). Taking communication seriously: A reply to Murstein. *Journal of Marriage and the Family, 49,* 937–938.

Stephens, G. K., & Sommer, S. M. (1996). The measurement of work to family conflict. *Educational and Psychological Measurement, 56,* 475–486.

Stephens, M. A. P., & Clark, S. L. (1996). Interpersonal relationships in multi-generational families. In N. Vanzetti & S. Duck (Eds.), *A lifetime of relationships* (pp. 431–454). Pacific Grove, CA: Brooks/Cole.

Stephens, M. A. P., & Franks, M. (1999). Intergenerational relationships in later-life families: Adult daughters and sons as caregivers to aging parents. In J. C. Cavanaugh & S. K. Whitbourne (Eds.), *Gerontology: An interdisciplinary perspective* (pp. 329–354). New York: Oxford University Press.

Stephens, M. A. P., & Townsend, A. L. (1997). Stress of parent care: Positive and negative effects of women's other roles. *Psychology and Aging, 12,* 376–386.

Stern, M., & Karraker, K. H. (1989). Sex stereotyping of infants: A review of gender labeling studies. *Sex Roles, 20,* 501–522.

Sternberg, R. J. (1985). *Beyond IQ: A triarchic theory of human intelligence.* Cambridge, UK: Cambridge University Press.

Sternberg, R. J. (1986). A triangular theory of love. *Psychological Review, 93,* 119–135.

Sternberg, R. J., Wagner, R. K., Williams, W. M., & Horvath, J. A. (1995). Testing common sense. *American Psychologist, 50,* 912–927.

Sterns, H. L., & Gray, J. H. (1999). Work, leisure, and retirement. In J. C. Cavanaugh & S. K. Whitbourne (Eds.), *Gerontology: Interdisciplinary perspectives.* New York: Oxford University Press.

Stevenson, H. W. (1988). Culture and schooling: Influences on cognitive development. In E. M. Hetherington, R. M. Lerner, & M. Perlmutter (Eds.), *Child development in life-span perspective* (pp. 241–258). Hillsdale, NJ: Erlbaum.

Stevenson, H. W., & Lee, S. (1990). Contexts of achievement. *Monographs of the Society for Research in Child Development, 55* (Serial No. 221).

Stevenson, H. W., & Stigler, J. W. (1992). *The learning gap.* New York: Summit Books.

Steward, R. J., & Krieshok, T. S. (1991). A cross-cultural study of vocational identity: Does a college education mean the same for all persisters? *Journal of College Student Development, 32,* 562–563.

Stewart, L., & Pascual-Leone, J. (1992). Mental capacity constraints and the development of moral reasoning. *Journal of Experimental Child Psychology, 54,* 251–287.

Stewart, R. B., Mobley, L. A., Van Tuyl, S. S., & Salvador, W. A. (1987). The firstborns' adjustment to the birth of a sibling: A longitudinal assessment. *Child Development, 58,* 341–355.

Stice, E., & Barrera, M., Jr. (1995). A longitudinal examination of the reciprocal relations between perceived parenting and adolescents' substance use and externalizing behaviors. *Developmental Psychology, 31,* 322–334.

Stifter, C. A., & Fox, N. A. (1990). Infant reactivity: Physiological correlates of newborn and 5-month temperament. *Developmental Psychology, 26,* 582–588.

Stine-Morrow, E. A. L., & Soederberg Miller, L. M. (1999). Basic cognitive processes. In J. C. Cavanaugh & S. K. Whitbourne (Eds.), *Gerontology: An interdisciplinary perspective.* New York: Oxford University Press.

Stone, A. A., Neale, J. M., Cox, D. S., Napoli, A., Valdimarsdottir, H., & Kennedy-Moore, E. (1994). Daily events are associated with a secretory immune response to an oral antigen in men. *Health Psychology, 13,* 440–446.

Straus, M. A., Gelles, R. J., & Steinmetz, S. K. (1980). *Behind closed doors: Violence in the American family.* Garden City, NY: Anchor/Doubleday.

Strawbridge, W. J., Shema, S. J., Balfour, J. L., Higby, H. R., & Kaplan, G. A. (1998). Antecedents of frailty over three decades in an older cohort. *Journal of Gerontology: Social Sciences, 53B,* S9–S16.

Streissguth, A. P., Barr, H. M., Sampson, P. D., & Bookstein, F. L. (1994). Prenatal alcohol and offspring development: The first fourteen years. *Drugs & Alcohol Dependence, 36,* 89–99.

Strober, M. (1995). Family-genetic perspectives on anorexia nervosa and bulimia nervosa. In K. Brownell & C. G. Fairburn (Eds.), *Eating disorders and obesity: A comprehensive handbook.* New York: Guilford Press.

Stroebe, M. S., & Stroebe, W. (1983). Who suffers more? Sex differences in health risks of the widowed. *Psychological Bulletin, 93,* 279–301.

Stroebe, M. S., Gergen, M., Gergen, K., & Stroebe, W. (1996). Broken hearts or broken bonds? In D. Klass, P. R. Silverman, & S. L. Nickman (Eds.), *Continuing bonds: New understandings of grief* (pp. 31–44). Washington, DC: Taylor & Francis.

Stunkard, A. J., Harris, J. R., Pedersen, N. L., & McClearn, G. E. (1990). The body-mass index of twins who have been reared apart. *New England Journal of Medicine, 322,* 1483–1487.

Stunkard, A. J., Sorensen, T. I. A., Hanis, C., Teasdale, T. W., Chakraborty, R., Schull, W. J., & Schulsinger, F. (1986). An adoption study of human obesity. *New England Journal of Medicine, 314,* 193–198.

Sullivan, H. S. (1953). *The interpersonal theory of psychiatry.* New York: Norton.

Sullivan, L. W. (1987). The risks of the sickle-cell trait: Caution and common sense. *New England Journal of Medicine, 317,* 830–831.

Sullivan, S. A., & Birch, L. L. (1990). Pass the sugar, pass the salt: Experience dictates preference. *Developmental Psychology, 26,* 546–551.

Suls, J., & Wills, T. A. (1991). *Social comparison: Contemporary theory and research.* Hillsdale, NJ: Erlbaum.

Summerville, M. B., Kaslow, N. J., & Doepke, K. J. (1996). Psychopathology and cognitive and family functioning in suicidal African-American adolescents. *Current Directions in Psychological Science, 5,* 7–11.

Super, C. M. (1981). Cross-cultural research on infancy. In H. C. Triandis & A. Heron (Eds.), *Handbook of cross-cultural psychology: Vol. 4. Developmental psychology.* Boston: Allyn & Bacon.

Super, C. M., Herrera, M. G., & Mora, J. O. (1990). Long-term effects of food supplementation and psychosocial intervention on the physical growth of Colombian infants at risk of malnutrition. *Child Development, 61,* 29–49.

Super, D. E. (1957). *The psychology of careers.* New York: Harper & Row.

Super, D. E. (1976). *Career education and the meanings of work.* Washington, DC: U.S. Offices of Education.

Super, D. E. (1980). A life span, life space approach to career development. *Journal of Vocational Behavior, 16,* 282–298.

Surgeon General. (1996). *Physical activity and health: A report of the Surgeon General.* Atlanta: Centers for Disease Control.

Swain, S. O. (1992). Men's friendships with women: Intimacy, sexual boundaries, and the informant role. In P. M. Nardi (Ed.), *Men's friendships* (pp. 153–171). Newbury Park, CA: Sage.

Swanson, J. L. (1992). Vocational behavior, 1989–1991: Life-span career development and reciprocal interaction of work and nonwork. *Journal of Vocational Behavior, 41,* 101–161.

Swarr, A. E., & Richards, M. H. (1996). Longitudinal effects of adolescent girls' pubertal development, perceptions of pubertal timing, and parental relations in eating problems. *Developmental Psychology, 32,* 636–646.

Swenson, C. H., Eskew, R. W., & Kohlhepp, K. A. (1981). Stages of the family life cycle, ego development, and the marriage relationship. *Journal of Gerontology, 43,* 841–853.

Sykes, D. H., Hoy, E. A., Bill, J. M., McClure, B. G., et al. (1997). Behavioral adjustment in school of very low birthweight children. *Journal of Child Psychology and Psychiatry and Allied Disciplines, 38,* 315–325.

Talaga, J. A., & Beehr, T. A. (1995). Are there gender differences in predicting retirement decisions? *Journal of Applied Psychology, 80,* 16–28.

Tang, T. L. P., & McCollum, S. L. (1996). Sexual harassment in the workplace. *Public Personnel Management, 25,* 53–58.

Tannen, D. (1990). *You just don't understand.* New York: Morrow.

Tanner, J. M. (1970). Physical growth. In P. H. Mussen (Ed.), *Carmichael's manual of child psychology* (3rd ed.). New York: Wiley.

Tanner, J. M. (1978). *Fetus into man: Physical growth from conception to maturity.* Cambridge, MA: Harvard University Press.

Tanner, J. M. (1990). *Fetus into man: Physical growth from conception to maturity* (2nd ed.). Cambridge, MA: Harvard University Press.

Taylor, M., & Gelman, S. A. (1989). Incorporating new words into the lexicon: Preliminary evidence for language hierarchies in two-year-old children. *Child Development, 60,* 625–636.

Taylor, M., Cartwright, B. S., & Carlson, S. M. (1993). A developmental investigation of children's imaginary companions. *Developmental Psychology, 29,* 276–285.

Teachman, J. (1986). First and second marital dissolution: A decomposition exercise for whites and blacks. *Sociological Quarterly, 27,* 571–590.

Terkel, S. (1974). *Working.* New York: Pantheon Books.

Terman, M. (1994). Light therapy. In M. H. Kryger, T. Roth, & W. C. Dement (Eds.), *Principles and practice of sleep medicine* (2nd ed., pp. 1012–1029). Philadelphia: Saunders.

Tesch-Römer, C. (1997). Psychological effects of hearing aid use in older adults. *Journal of Gerontology: Psychological Sciences, 52B,* P127–P138.

Thelen, E. (1996). The improvising infant: Learning about learning to move. In M. R. Merrens & G. G. Brannigan (Eds.), *The developmental psychologists: Research adventures across the life span.* New York: McGraw-Hill.

Thelen, E., & Ulrich, B. D. (1991). Hidden skills. *Monographs of the Society for Research in Child Development, 56* (Serial No. 223).

Thelen, E., Ulrich, B. D., & Jensen, J. L. (1989). The developmental origins of locomotion. In M. H. Woollacott & A. Shumway-Cook (Eds.), *Development of posture and gait across the life span.* Columbia: University of South Carolina Press.

Thomas, D. A. (1990). The impact of race on managers' experiences of developmental relationships (mentoring and sponsorship): An intra-organizational study. *Journal of Organizational Behavior, 11,* 479–492.

Thomas, G. S., & Rutledge, J. H. (1986). Fitness and exercise for the elderly. In K. Dychtwald (Ed.), *Wellness and health promotion for the elderly* (pp. 165–178). Rockville, MD: Aspen.

Thomas, J. L. (1986). Age and sex differences in perceptions of grandparenthood. *Journal of Gerontology, 41,* 417–423.

Thomas, J. L. (1992). *Adult development and aging.* Boston: Allyn & Bacon.

Thomas, J. L., Bence, S. L., & Meyer, S. M. (1988, August). *Grandparenting satisfaction: The roles of relationship meaning and perceived responsibility.* Paper presented at the meeting of the American Psychological Association, Atlanta.

Thomas, N. G., & Berk, L. E. (1981). Effects of school environments on the development of young children's creativity. *Child Development, 52,* 1152–1162.

Thompson, L. W., & Gallagher, D. (1986). Treatment of depression in elderly outpatients. In G. Maletta & F. J. Pirozzolo (Eds.), *Advances in neurogerontology: Vol. 4. Assessment and treatment of the elderly patient.* New York: Praeger.

Thompson, L. W., Gallagher-Thompson, D., Futterman, A., Gilewski, M. J., & Peterson, J. (1991). The effects of late-life spousal bereavement over a 30-month interval. *Psychology and Aging, 6,* 434–441.

Thompson, L., & Walker, A. J. (1989). Gender in families: Women and men in marriage, work, and parenthood. *Journal of Marriage and the Family, 51,* 845–871.

Thompson, R. A., & Limber, S. (1991). "Social anxiety" in infancy: Stranger wariness and separation distress. In H. Leitenberg (Ed.), *Handbook of social and evaluation anxiety.* New York: Plenum.

Thomson, E., & Colella, U. (1992). Cohabitation and marital stability: Quality or commitment? *Journal of Marriage and the Family, 54,* 259–267.

Tiffany, D. W., & Tiffany, P. G. (1996). Control across the life span: A model for understanding self-direction. *Journal of Adult Development, 3,* 93–108.

Tobler, N. S., & Stratton, H. H. (1997). Effectiveness of school-based drug prevention programs: A meta-analysis of the research. *Journal of Primary Prevention, 18,* 71–128.

Toda, S., & Fogel, A. (1993). Infant response to the still-face situation at 3 and 6 months. *Developmental Psychology, 29,* 532–538.

Toffler, A. (1970). *Future shock.* New York: Random House.

Tolson, J. M., & Urberg, K. A. (1993). Similarity between adolescent best friends. *Journal of Adolescent Research, 8,* 274–288.

Torres-Gil, F. M. (1992). *The new aging.* New York: Auburn House.

Trickett, P. K., & McBride-Chang, C. (1995). The developmental impact of different forms of child abuse and neglect. *Developmental Review, 15,* 311–337.

Trickett, P. K., & Kuczynski, L. (1986). Children's misbehaviors and parental discipline strategies in abusive and nonabusive families. *Developmental Psychology, 22,* 115–123.

Trickett, P. K., Aber, J. L., Carlson, V., & Cicchetti, D. (1991). Relationship of socioeconomic status to the etiology and developmental sequelae of physical child abuse. *Developmental Psychology, 27,* 148–158.

Troll, L. E. (1971). The family of later life: A decade review. *Journal of Marriage and the Family, 33,* 263–290.

Troll, L. E., & Bengtson, V. (1982). Intergenerational relations throughout the life span. In B. B. Wolman (Ed.), *Handbook of developmental psychology* (pp. 890–911). Englewood Cliffs, NJ: Prentice-Hall.

Troll, L. E., & Fingerman, K. L. (1996). Connections between parents and their adult children. In C. Magai & S. H. McFadden (Eds.), *Handbook of emotion, adult development, and aging* (pp. 185–205). San Diego, CA: Academic Press.

Trujillo, K. M., Walsh, D. M., & Brougham, R. R. (1991, June). *Age differences in exercise motivation.* Paper presented at the annual meeting of the American Psychological Society, Washington, DC.

Tubman, J. G., Windle, M., & Windle, R. C. (1996). The onset and cross-temporal patterning of sexual intercourse in middle adolescence: Prospective relations with behavioral and emotional problems. *Child Development, 67,* 327–343.

Turner, B. F. (1982). Sex-related differences in aging. In B. B. Wolman (Ed.), *Handbook of developmental psychology* (pp. 912–936). Englewood Cliffs, NJ: Prentice-Hall.

Uecker, A., & Nadel, L. (1996). Spatial locations gone awry: Object and spatial memory deficits in children with fetal alcohol syndrome. *Neuropsychologia, 34,* 209–223.

Uhlenberg, P., Cooney, T. M., & Boyd, R. (1990). Divorce for women after midlife. *Journal of Gerontology: Social Sciences, 45,* S3–S11.

Uniform Crime Reports for the United States (1996). Washington, DC: U.S. Government Printing Office.

U.S. Bureau of the Census. (1995). *Statistical abstract of the United States* (115th ed.). Washington, DC: U.S. Government Printing Office.

U.S. Bureau of the Census. (1997). *Statistical abstract of the United States.* Washington, DC: U.S. Government Printing Office.

U.S. Bureau of the Census. (1998). *Statistical abstract of the United States.* Washington, DC: U.S. Government Printing Office.

U.S. Department of Health and Human Services. (1993). *Mortality surveillance system.* Hyattsville, MD: U.S. Public Health Service.

U.S. Department of Health and Human Services. (1997). *Vital statistics of the United States, 1994: Vol. 2. Mortality* (Part A). Hyattsville, MD: U.S. Public Health Service.

U.S. Department of Health and Human Services. (1998). *Health United States 1997* (DHHS Publication No. PHS 90–1232). Washington, DC: U.S. Government Printing Office.

U.S. Department of Labor. (1991). *A report on the glass ceiling initiative.* Washington, DC: Author.

U.S. Department of Labor. (1997). *Current population survey.* Washington, DC: Author.

Urberg, K. A., Değirmencioğlu, S. M., & Pilgrim, C. (1997). Close friend and group influence on adolescent cigarette smoking and alcohol use. *Developmental Psychology, 33,* 834–844.

Vachon, M. L. S., Lyall, W. A. L., Rogers, J., Freedman-Letofsky, K., & Freeman, S. J. A. (1980). A controlled study of self-help intervention for widows. *American Journal of Psychiatry, 137,* 1380–1384.

Vaillant, G. E. (1977). *Adaptation to life.* Boston: Little, Brown.

Valenzuela, M. (1997). Maternal sensitivity in a developing society: The context of urban poverty and infant chronic undernutrition. *Developmental Psychology, 33,* 845–855.

van den Boom, D. C. (1994). The influence of temperament and mothering on attachment and exploration: An experimental manipulation of sensitive responsiveness among lower-class mothers with irritable infants. *Child Development, 65,* 1457–1477.

van den Boom, D. C. (1995). Do first-year intervention effects endure? Follow-up during toddlerhood of a sample of Dutch irritable infants. *Child Development, 66,* 1798–1816.

Van Gennep, A. (1909). *Les rites de passage.* Paris: E. Nourry. (Trans. as *The rites of passage* by M. B. Vizedom & G. L. Caffee (1960). Chicago: University of Chicago Press.)

Van Hoose, W. H., & Worth, M. R. (1982). *Adulthood in the life cycle.* Dubuque, IA: William C. Brown.

van IJzendoorn, M. H., & Kroonenberg, P. M. (1988). Cross-cultural patterns of attachment: A meta-analysis of the Strange Situation. *Child Development, 59,* 147–156.

Van Loosbroek, E., & Smitsman, A. W. (1990). Visual perception of numerosity in infancy. *Developmental Psychology, 26,* 916–922.

Van Maanen, J., & Schein, E. H. (1977). Career development. In R. J. Hackman & J. L. Suttle (Eds.), *Improving life at work* (pp. 30–95). New York: Goodyear.

Vandell, D. L., Pierce, K., & Stright, A. (1997). Child care. In G. Bear, K. Minke, & A. Thomas (Eds.), *Children's needs II: Development, problems and alternatives* (pp. 575–584). Washington, DC: National Association of School Psychologists.

VandenBos, G. R., DeLeon, P. H., & Pallack, M. S. (1982). An alternative to traditional medical care for the terminally ill. *American Psychologist, 37,* 1245–1248.

Vaughn, B. E., Stevenson-Hinde, J., Waters, E., Kotsaftis, A., et al. (1992). Attachment security and temperament in infancy and early childhood: Some conceptual clarifications. *Developmental Psychology, 28,* 463–473.

Ventura, S. J., Martin, J. A., Curtin, S. C., & Mathews, T. J. (1997). Report of final natality statistics, 1995. *Monthly Vital Statistics Report, 45,* June 1997.

Ventura, S. J., Martin, J. A., Hartin, A., Taffell, S. M., Mathews, T. J., & Clarke, S. C. (1994). Advance report of final natality statistics, 1992. *National Center for Health Statistics, Monthly Vital Statistics Report, 43.*

Verhaeghen, P., Marcoen, A., & Goosens, L. (1993). Facts and fiction about memory aging: A quantitative integration of research findings. *Journal of Gerontology: Psychological Sciences, 48,* P157–P171.

Verma, I. M. (1990). Gene therapy. *Scientific American, 263,* 68–84.

Vickio, C. J., Cavanaugh, J. C., & Attig, T. (1990). Perceptions of grief among university students. *Death Studies, 14,* 231–240.

Viinamaki, H., Koskela, K., & Niskanen, L. (1996). Rapidly declining mental well-being during unemployment. *European Journal of Psychiatry, 10,* 215–221.

Villa, R. F., & Jaime, A. (1993). *La fé de la gente.* In M. Sotomayor & A. Garcia (Eds.), *Elderly Latinos: Issues and solutions for the 21st century.* Washington, DC: National Hispanic Council on Aging.

Vinovskis, M. A. (1988). The historian and the life course: Reflections on recent approaches to the study of American family life in the past. In P. B. Baltes, D. L. Featherman, & R. M. Lerner (Eds.), *Life-span development and behavior* (Vol. 8, pp. 33–59). Hillsdale, NJ: Erlbaum.

Vitaro, F., Tremblay, R. E., Kerr, M., Pagani, L., & Bukowski, W. M. (1997). Disruptiveness, friends' characteristics, and delinquency in early adolescence: A test of two competing models of development. *Child Development, 68,* 676–689.

Volling, B. L., MacKinnon-Lewis, C., Rabiner, D., & Baradaran, L. P. (1993). Children's social competence and sociometric status: Further exploration of aggression, social withdrawal, and peer rejection. *Development and Psychopathology, 5,* 459–483.

Volling, B., & Belsky, J. (1992). The contribution of mother-child and father-child relationships to the quality of sibling interaction: A longitudinal study. *Child Development, 63,* 1209–1222.

Vorhees, C. V., & Mollnow, E. (1987). Behavior teratogenesis: Long-term influences on behavior. In J. D. Osofsky (Ed.). *Handbook of infant development* (2nd ed.). New York: Wiley.

Vosler, N. R., & Page-Adams, D. (1996). Predictors of depression among workers at the time of a plant closing. *Journal of Sociology and Social Welfare, 23(4),* 25–42.

Voyer, D., Voyer, S., & Bryden, M. P. (1995). Magnitude of sex differences in spatial abilities: A meta-analysis and consideration of critical variables. *Psychological Bulletin, 117,* 250–270.

Vygotsky, L. S. (1986). *Thought and language* (A. Kozulin, Trans.). Cambridge, MA: MIT Press. (Original work published in 1934.)

Wachs, T. D. (1983). The use and abuse of environment in behavior-genetic research. *Child Development, 54,* 396–407.

Wagner, N. E., Schubert, H. J. P., & Schubert, D. S. P. (1985). Family size effects: A revision. *Journal of Genetic Psychology, 146,* 65–78.

Wagner, R. K., & Sternberg, R. J. (1986). Tacit knowledge and intelligence in the everyday world. In R. J. Sternberg & R. K. Wagner (Eds.), *Practical intelligence* (pp. 51–83). Cambridge, UK: Cambridge University Press.

Walberg, H. J. (1995). General practices. In G. Cawelti (Ed.), *Handbook of research on improving student achievement.* Arlington, VA: Educational Research Service.

Walker, L. E. A. (1984). *The battered woman syndrome.* New York: Springer.

Walker, L. J. (1995). Sexism in Kohlberg's moral psychology? In W. M. Kurtines & J. L. Gewirtz (Eds.), *Moral development: An introduction* (pp. 83–107). Boston: Allyn & Bacon.

Walker, L. J., & Taylor, J. H. (1991). Family interactions and the development of moral reasoning. *Child Development, 62,* 264–283.

Wall, S., & Arden, H. (1990). *Wisdomkeepers: Meetings with Native American spiritual elders.* Hillsboro, OR: Beyond Words Publishing.

Wallace, J. I., & Schwartz, R. S. (1994). Involuntary weight loss in the elderly. In R. R. Watson (Ed.), *Handbook of nutrition in the aged* (pp. 99–111). Boca Raton, FL: CRC Press.

Wallerstein, J. S., & Blakeslee, S. (1989). *Second chances: Men, women, and children a decade after divorce.* New York: Ticknor & Fields.

Wallerstein, J. S., & Kelly, J. B. (1980). *Surviving the breakup: How children and parents cope with divorce.* New York: Basic Books.

Walsh, E. K., & Cavanaugh, J. C. (1984, November). *Does hospice meet the needs of dying clients?* Paper presented at the meeting of the Gerontological Society of America, San Antonio.

Wantz, M. S., & Gay, J. E. (1981). *The aging process: A health perspective.* Cambridge, MA: Winthrop.

Ward, R., Logan, J., & Spitze, G. (1992). The influence of parent and child needs on coresidence in middle and later life. *Journal of Marriage and the Family, 54,* 209–221.

Ward, S. L., & Overton, W. F. (1990). Semantic familiarity, relevance, and the development of deductive reasoning. *Developmental Psychology, 26,* 288–493.

Wark, G. R., & Krebs, D. L. (1997). Sources of variation in moral judgment: Toward a model of real-life morality. *Journal of Adult Development, 4,* 163–178.

Waters, H. F. (1993, July 12). Networks under the gun. *Newsweek,* pp. 64–66.

Watson, J. A., & Koblinsky, S. A. (1997). Strengths and needs of working-class African-American and Anglo-American grandparents. *International Journal of Aging and Human Development, 44,* 149–165.

Wattis, J. P., & Seymour, J. (1994). Alcohol abuse and elderly people: Medical and psychiatric consequences. In R. R. Watson (Ed.), *Handbook of nutrition in the aged* (2nd ed., pp. 317–329). Boca Raton, FL: CRC Press.

Waxman, S. R., & Markow, D. B. (1995). Words as invitations to form categories: Evidence from 12- to 13-month-old infants. *Cognitive Psychology, 29,* 257–303.

Wechsler, D. (1991). *Manual for the Wechsler Intelligence Test for Children-III.* New York: The Psychological Corporation.

Wechsler, H., Davenport, A., Dowdall, G., Moeykens, B., & Castillo, S. (1994). Health and behavioral consequences of binge drinking in college. *Journal of the American Medical Association, 272,* 1672–1677.

Wechsler, H., Dowdall, G. W., Davenport, A., & Castillo, S. (1995). Correlates of college student binge drinking. *American Journal of Public Health, 85,* 921–926.

Wegman, M. E. (1994). Annual summary of vital statistics—1993. *Pediatrics, 95,* 792–803.

Weibel-Orlando, J. (1990). Grandparenting styles: Native American perspectives. In J. Sokolovsky (Ed.), *The cultural context of aging* (pp. 109–125). New York: Bergin & Garvey.

Weinberg, M. K., & Tronick, E. Z. (1994). Beyond the face: An empirical study of infant affective configurations of facial, vocal, gestural, and regulatory behaviors. *Child Development, 65,* 1503–1515.

Weishaus, S., & Field, D. (1988). A half century of marriage: Continuity or change? *Journal of Marriage and the Family, 50,* 763–774.

Weisman, A. D. (1972). *On dying and denying.* New York: Behavioral Publications.

Weisner, T. S., & Wilson-Mitchell, J. E. (1990). Nonconventional family lifestyles and sex typing in six-year-olds. *Child Development, 61,* 1915–1933.

Weldon, B. (1997). *Arthritis and osteoporosis: Women's health seminar.* Online document available at http://www.nih.gov/niams/healthinfo/orwhseminar.htm (National Institute of Arthritis and Musculoskeletal and Skin Diseases).

Wellman, H. M. (1992). *The child's theory of mind.* Cambridge, MA: MIT Press.

Wellman, H. M. (1993). Early understanding of mind: The normal case. In S. Baron-Cohen, H. Tager-Flusberg, & D. J. Cohen (Eds.), *Understanding other minds: Perspectives from autism.* Oxford, UK: Oxford University Press.

Wells, Y. D., & Kendig, H. L. (1997). Health and well-being of spouse caregivers and the widowed. *The Gerontologist, 37,* 666–674.

Welsh, M. C., Pennington, B. F., & Groisser, D. B. (1991). A normative-developmental study of executive function: A window on prefrontal function in children. *Developmental Neuropsychology, 7,* 131–149.

Wentkowski, G. (1985). Older women's perceptions of great-grandparenthood: A research note. *The Gerontologist, 25,* 593–596.

Wentzel, K. R., & Asher, S. R. (1995). The academic lives of neglected, rejected, popular, and controversial children. *Child Development, 66,* 754–763.

Wentzel, K. R., & Erdley, C. A. (1993). Strategies for making friends: Relations to social behavior and peer acceptance. *Developmental Psychology, 29,* 819–826.

Werker, J. F., & Desjardins, R. N. (1995). Listening to speech in the 1st year of life: Experiential influences on phoneme perception. *Current Directions in Psychological Science, 4,* 76–81.

Werner, E. (1994). Overcoming the odds. *Journal of Developmental and Behavioral Pediatrics, 15,* 131–136.

Werner, E. E. (1989). Children of Garden Island. *Scientific American, 260,* 106–111.

Werner, E. E., & Smith, R. S. (1992). *Overcoming the odds: High risk children from birth to adulthood.* Ithaca, NY: Cornell University Press.

Werner, H. (1948). *Comparative psychology of mental development.* Chicago: Follet.

Wertsch, J. V. (1985). *Vygotsky and the social formation of mind.* Cambridge, MA: Harvard University Press.

Wertsch, J. V., & Tulviste, P. (1992). L. S. Vygotsky and contemporary developmental psychology. *Developmental Psychology, 28,* 548–557.

Whitall, J., & Getchell, N. (1995). From walking to running: Applying a dynamical systems approach to the development of locomotor skills. *Child Development, 66,* 1541–1553.

Whitbourne, S. K. (1986). *The me I know: A study of adult identity.* New York: Springer-Verlag.

Whitbourne, S. K. (1987). Personality development in adulthood and old age: Relationships among identity style, health, and well-being. In K. W. Schaie (Ed.), *Annual review of gerontology and geriatrics* (Vol. 7, pp. 189–216). New York: Springer.

Whitbourne, S. K. (1996). *The aging individual.* New York: Springer.

Whitbourne, S. K. (1999). Physiological changes. In J. C. Cavanaugh & S. K. Whitbourne (Eds.), *Gerontology: Interdisciplinary perspectives* (pp. 91–122). New York: Oxford University Press.

Whitbourne, S. K., & Tesch, S. A. (1985). A comparison of identity and intimacy statuses in college students and alumni. *Developmental Psychology, 21,* 1039–1044.

Whitbourne, S. K., & VanManen, K. W. (1996). Age differences in and correlates of identity status from college through middle adulthood. *Journal of Adult Development, 3,* 59–70.

Whitbourne, S. K., Culgin, S., & Cassidy, E. (1995). Evalutaion of infantilizing intonation and content of speech directed at the aged. *International Journal of Aging and Human Development, 41,* 109–116.

White, A. T., & Spector, P. E. (1987). An investigation of age-related factors in the age-job satisfaction relationship. *Psychology and Aging, 2,* 261–265.

Whiting, B. B., & Edwards, P. E. (1988). *Children of different worlds.* Cambridge, MA: Harvard University Press.

Whitmer, R. A., & Whitbourne, S. K. (1997). Evaluation of infantilizing speech in a rehabilitation setting: Relation to age. *International Journal of Aging and Human Development, 44,* 129–136.

Wickrama, K. A. S., Lorenz, F. O., Conger, R. D., & Elder, G. H., Jr. (1997). Marital quality and physical illness: A latent growth curve analysis. *Journal of Marriage and the Family, 59,* 143–155.

Wicks-Nelson, R., & Israel, A. C. (1991). *Behavior disorders of childhood* (2nd ed.). Englewood Cliffs, NJ: Prentice-Hall.

Wiener, J. M., & Illston, L. H. (1996). The financing and organization of health care for older Americans. In R. H. Binstock & L. K. George (Eds.), *Handbook of aging and the social sciences* (4th ed., pp. 427–445). San Diego, CA: Academic Press.

Wiener, R. L., Hurt, L., Russell, B., Mannen, K., & Gasper, C. (1997). Perceptions of sexual harassment: The effects of gender, legal standard, and ambivalent sexism. *Law and Human Behavior, 21,* 71–93.

Wilk, C. (1986). *Career, women, and childbearing: A psychological analysis of the decision process.* New York: Van Nostrand Reinhold.

Williams, J. E., & Best, D. L. (1990). *Measuring sex stereotypes: A thirty-nation study* (rev. ed.). Newbury Park: Sage.

Williams, O. J., & Griffin, L. W. (1996). Elderly maltreatment and cultural diversity: When laws are not enough. *Journal of Multicultural Social Work, 4,* 1–13.

Williams, T. M., & Cox, R. (1995, April). *Informative versus other children's TV programs: Portrayals of ethnic diversity, gender, and aggression.* Paper presented at the meeting of the Society for Research in Child Development, Indianapolis, IN.

Williamson, G. M., & Schulz, R. (1990). Relationship orientation, quality of prior relationship, and distress among caregivers of Alzheimer's patients. *Psychology and Aging, 5,* 502–509.

Willinger, M. (1995). Sleep position and sudden infant death syndrome. *Journal of the American Medical Association, 273,* 818–819.

Willis, S. L., & Schaie, K. W. (1992, November). *Maintaining and sustaining cognitive training effects in old age.* Paper presented at the annual meeting of the Gerontological Society of America, Washington, DC.

Wilson, G. T., Hefferman, K., & Black, C. M. D. (1996). Eating disorders. In E. J. Mash & R. A. Barkley (Eds.), *Child psychopathology.* New York: Guilford.

Windle, M., & Windle, R. C. (1996). Coping strategies, drinking motives, and stressful life events among middle adolescents: Assocations with emotional and behavioral problems and with academic functioning. *Journal of Abnormal Psychology, 105,* 551–560.

Winer, G. A., Craig, R. K., & Weinbaum, E. (1992). Adults' failure on misleading weight-conservation tests: A developmental analysis. *Developmental Psychology, 28,* 109–120.

Wink, P., & Helson, R. (1997). Practical and transcendent wisdom: Their nature and some longitudinal findings. *Journal of Adult Development, 4,* 1–15.

Witelson, S. F. (1987). Neurobiological aspects of language in children. *Child Development, 58,* 653–688.

Wolf, R. S., Godkin, M. A., & Pillemer, K. A. (1986). Treatment of the elderly: A comparative analysis. *Journal of Long Term Home Health Care, 5(4),* 10–17.

Wolfe, D. A. (1985). Child-abusive parents: An empirical review and analysis. *Psychological Bulletin, 97,* 462–482.

Wolfe, R., Morrow, J., & Fredrickson, B. L. (1996). Mood disorders in older adults. In L. L. Carstensen, B. A. Edelstein, & L. Dornbrand (Eds.), *The practical handbook of clinical gerontology* (pp. 274–303). Thousand Oaks, CA: Sage.

Wolff, P. H. (1987). *The development of behavioral states and the expression of emotions in early infancy.* Chicago: University of Chicago Press.

Wolfson, A. R., & Carskadon, M. A. (1998). Sleep schedules and daytime functioning in adolescents. *Child Development, 69,* 875–887.

Wolfson, C., Handfield-Jones, R., Glass, K. C., McClaran, J., & Keyserlingk, E. (1993). Adult children's perceptions of their responsibility to provide care for dependent elderly parents. *The Gerontologist, 33,* 315–323.

Wolinsky, F. D., Callahan, C. M., Fitzgerald, J. F., & Johnson, R. L. (1992). The risk of nursing home placement and subsequent death among older adults. *Journal of Gerontology: Social Sciences, 47,* S173–S182.

Wolraich, M. L., Lindgren, S. D., Stumbo, P. J., Stegink, L. D., Appelbaum, M. I., & Kiritsy, M. C. (1994). Effects of diets high in sucrose or aspartame on the behavior and cognitive performance of children. *New England Journal of Medicine, 330,* 301–307.

Woodruff-Pak, D. S. (1988). *Psychology and Aging.* Englewood Cliffs, NJ: Prentice-Hall.

Woollacott, M. H., Shumway-Cook, A., & Williams, H. (1989). The development of balance and locomotion in children. In M. H. Woollacott, & A. Shumway-Cook (Eds.), *Development of posture and gait across the life span.* Columbia: University of South Carolina Press.

Worden, W. (1991). *Grief counseling and grief therapy: A handbook for the mental health practitioner* (2nd ed.). New York: Springer.

Wright, L. K. (1991). The impact of Alzheimer's disease on the marital relationship. *The Gerontologist, 31,* 224–237.

Wright, P. H. (1985). The Acquaintance Description Form. In S. Duck & D. Perlman (Eds.), *Understanding personal relationships: An interdisciplinary approach* (pp. 39–62). London: Sage.

WuDunn, S. (1997, September 2). The face of the future in Japan. *New York Times,* D1, D14.

Wynn, K. (1996). Infants' individuation and enumeration of actions. *Psychological Science, 7,* 164–169.

Xiaohe, X., & Whyte, M. K. (1990). Love matches and arranged marriages. *Journal of Marriage and the Family, 52,* 709–722.

Yamagata, H., Yeh, K. S., Stewman, S., & Dodge, H. (1997, August). *Sex segregation and glass ceilings: A comparative statics model of women's career opportunities in the federal government over a quarter of a century.* Paper presented at the annual meeting of the American Sociological Association, Toronto.

Yang, B., Ollendick, T. H., Dong, Q., Xia, Y., & Lin, L. (1995). Only children and children with siblings in the People's Republic of China: Levels of fear, anxiety, and depression. *Child Development, 66,* 1301–1311.

Yankelovich, D. (1981). *New rules: Searching for self-fulfillment in a world turned upside down.* New York: Random House.

Yates, M., & Youniss, J. (1996). Community service and political-moral identity in adolescents. *Journal of Research on Adolescence, 6,* 271–284.

Ylllö, K. A. (1993). Through a feminist lens: Gender, power, and violence. In R. J. Gelles & D. R. Loseke (Eds.), *Current controversies on family violence* (pp. 47–62). Newbury Park, CA: Sage.

Yonas, A., & Owsley, C. (1987). Development of visual space perception. In P. Salapatek and L. Cohen (Eds.), *Handbook of infant perception* (Vol. 2). Orlando, FL: Academic Press.

Youngblade, L. M., & Dunn, J. (1995). Individual differences in young children's pretend play with mother and sibling: Links to relationships and understanding of other people's feelings and beliefs. *Child Development, 66,* 1472–1492.

Youngjohn, J. R., & Crook, T. H. III. (1996). Dementia. In L. L. Carstensen, B. Edelstein, & L. Dornbrand (Eds.), *The practical handbook of clinical gerontology* (pp. 239–254). Thousand Oaks, CA: Sage.

Youngjohn, J. R., Beck, J., Jogerst, G., & Caine, C. (1992). Neuropsychological impairment, depression, and Parkinson's disease. *Neuropsychology, 6,* 149–158.

Zahn-Waxler, C., Friedman, R. J., Cole, P. M., Mizuta, I., & Hiruma, N. (1996). Japanese and United States preschool children's responses to conflict and distress. *Child Development, 67,* 2462–2477.

Zahn-Waxler, C., Radke-Yarrow, M., Wagner, E., & Chapman, M. (1992). Development of concern for others. *Developmental Psychology, 28,* 126–136.

Zappert, L. T. (1996). Psychological aspects of sexual harassment in the academic workplace: Considerations for forensic psychologists. *American Journal of Forensic Psychology, 14,* 5–17.

Zaslow, M. J., & Hayes, C. D. (1986). Sex differences in children's responses to psychosocial stress: Toward a cross-context analysis. In M. E. Lamb, A. L. Brown, & B. Rogoff (Eds.), *Advances in developmental psychology* (Vol. 4). Hillsdale, NJ: Erlbaum.

Zelazo, N. A., Zelazo, P. R., Cohen, K. M., & Zelazo, P. D. (1993). Specificity of practice effects on elementary neuromotor patterns. *Developmental Psychology, 29,* 686–691.

Zelazo, P. R. (1993). The development of walking: New findings and old assumptions. *Journal of Motor Behavior, 15,* 99–137.

Zick, C. D., & McCullough, J. L. (1991). Trends in married couples' time use: Evidence from 1977/78 and 1987/88. *Sex Roles, 24,* 459–488.

Zigler, E., & Finn-Stevenson, M. (1992). Applied developmental psychology. In M. H. Bornstein & M. E. Lamb (Eds.), *Developmental psychology: An advanced textbook.* Hillsdale, NJ: Erlbaum.

Zigler, E., & Hall, N. W. (1989). Physical child abuse in America: Past, present, and future. In D. Cicchetti & V. Carlson (Eds.), *Child maltreatment: Theory and research on the causes and consequences of child abuse and neglect.* New York: Cambridge University Press.

Zimberg, S. (1985). Principles of alcoholism psychotherapy. In S. Zimberg, J. Wallace, & S. B. Blume (Eds.), *Practical approaches to alcoholism psychotherapy* (pp. 3–22). New York: Plenum.

Zimiles, H., & Lee, V. E. (1991). Adolescent family structure and educational progress. *Developmental Psychology, 27,* 314–320.

Zmuda, J. M., Cauley, J. A., Kriska, A., Glynn, N. W., Gutai, J. P., & Kuller, L. H. (1997). Longitudinal relation between endogenous testosterone and cardiovascular disease risk factors in middle-aged men: A 13-year follow-up of former Multiple Risk Factors Intervention Trial participants. *American Journal of Epidemiology, 146,* 609–617.

Zsembik, B. A., & Singer, A. (1990). The problem of defining retirement among minorities: The Mexican Americans. *The Gerontologist, 30,* 749–757.

Zuckerman, C. (1997). Issues concerning end-of-life care. *Journal of Long-Term Home Health Care, 16,* 26–34.

CREDITS

This page constitutes an extension of the copyright page. We have made every effort to trace the ownership of all copyrighted material and to secure permission from copyright holders. In the event of any question arising as to the use of any material, we will be pleased to make the necessary corrections in future printings. Thanks are due to the following authors, publishers, and agents for permission to use the material indicated.

FIGURE CREDITS

CHAPTER 1

6: Cartoon Reprinted by permission of King Features Syndicate, Inc. Copyright © 1993 by King Features Syndicate.
24: Figure adapted from *The Child: Development in a Social Context,* by Claire B. Kopp and Joanne B. Krakow, p. 648. Copyright © 1982 Addison-Wesley Publishing Co., Inc. Used with permission of the publisher.

CHAPTER 2

54: Figure from "Genetic Aspects of Intelligent Behavior," by I. I. Gottesman. In N. R. Ellis (Ed.), *Handbook of Mental Deficiency,* p. 255. Copyright © 1963 Norman R. Ellis. Reprinted with permission.
64, 68: Figures from *Before We Are Born, Fourth Edition,* by K. L. Moore and T. V. N. Persaud, p. 130. Copyright © 1993 W. B. Saunders. Reprinted with permission.

CHAPTER 3

87: Cartoon Reprinted by permission of King Features Syndicate. Copyright © 1994 by King Features, Inc.
95: Figure from *Normal and Abnormal Development of the Nervous System,* by R. J. Lemire, J. D. Loeser, R. W. Leech, and E. C. Alvord, Jr., p. 236. Copyright © 1975 J. B. Lippincott Company. Reprinted with permission.
104: Figure from "Specificity of Practice Effects on Elementary Neuromotor Patterns," by N. A. Zelazo, P. R. Zelazo, K. M. Cohen & P. D. Zelazo, 1993, *American Psychologist, 49,* 686–691. Copyright © American Psychological Association. Reprinted with permission.
109: Figure adapted from figure 3.21 p. 201 from "Pattern Perception in Infancy," Chapter 3 pp. 133–234 by Philip Salapatek. In L. B. Cohen and P. Salapatek (Eds.), *Infant Cognition: From Sensation to Perception.* Copyright © 1975

Academic Press Inc. Reprinted [adapted] by permission.
116: Figure based on *Autism: Explaining the Enigma* by Uta Frith.

CHAPTER 4

133: Based on "Object Performance in 3½- and 4½-month-old Infants," by R. Baillargeon, 1987, *Developmental Psychology, 23,* 655–664. American Psychological Association.
148: Cartoon B.C. © 1993. Reprinted by permission of Johnny Hart and Creators Syndicate, Inc.
152: Figure from "The Child's Learning of English Morphology," by J. Berko, 1958, *Word, 14,* 150.

CHAPTER 5

167: Figure based on "Cross-cultural Patterns of Attachment: A Meta-Analysis of the Strange Situation," by M. H. Van Uzendoorn, P. M. Kroonenberg, 1988, *Child Development, 59,* 147–156.
188: Figure from "Process Analysis of Spatial Aptitude," by J. W. Pellegrino and R. V. Kail. In R. J. Sternberg (Ed.) *Advances in the Psychology of Human Intelligence, Vol. 1,* p. 316. Copyright © 1982 Lawrence Erlbaum Associates, Inc. Reprinted with permission.
191: Figure from "A Schematic Processing Model of Sex Typing and Stereotyping in Children," by C. L. Martin and C. F. Halverson, 1981, *Child Development, 52,* p.1121. Copyright © 1981 Society for Research in Child Development, Inc. Reprinted with permission.
194: Cartoon THE FAR SIDE © 1984 Farworks, Inc./Dist. by Universal Press Syndicate. Reprinted with permission. All rights reserved.

CHAPTER 6

215: Figure based on data from "Familial Studies of Intelligence: A Review," by T. J Bouchard and M. McGue, 1981, *Science, 212,* p. 1056.

225: Figure based on data from the Third International Math and Science Study, 1997.
226: Figure based on data from the National Adult Literacy Survey (Kirsch et al., 1993).

CHAPTER 7

239: Cartoon B.C. © 1994. Reprinted by permission of Johnny Hart and Creators Syndicate, Inc.
241: Figure based on data from "A Comparison of Childrearing Practices Among Chinese, Immigrant Chinese, and Caucasian-American Parents," by C. C. Lin and V. R. Fu, 1990, *Child Development, 61,* 429–433.
242: Figure based on data from "Patterns of Competence and Adjustment Among Adolescents from Authoritative, Authoritarian, Indulgent, and Neglectful Families," by S. D. Lamborn, N. S. Mounts, L. Steinberg & S. M. Dornbusch, 1991, *Child Development, 62,* 1049–1065.
259: Figure based on data from "Peer Preputation in Middle Childhood as a Predictor of Adaptation in Adolescence: A Seven-Year Follow-up," by R. Morison and A. S. Masten, 1991, *Child Development, 62,* 991–1007.
261: Cartoon © 1995 Martha F. Campbell. Reprinted with permission.
263: Figure based on data from "Long-term Effects of Repeated Exposure to Media Violence in Childhood," by L. R. Huesmann and L. S. Miller, 1994. In L. R. Huesmann (Ed.), *Aggressive Behavior: Current Perspectives.* Plenum Publishing Group.

CHAPTER 8

278: Figure adapted from *Growth, Maturation, and Physical Activity,* by R. M. Malina and C. Bouchard, 1991. Human Kinetics Academic.
279: Figure from "Puberty," by W. A. Marshall and J. M. Tanner. In J. Falkner and J. M. Tanner (Eds.), *Human Growth: A Comprehensive Treatise, Second Edition, Vol. 2: Postnatal Growth, Neurobiology,* p.196. Copyright © 1962 Plenum

Publishing Corporation. Reprinted with permission.

286: Figure based on data from "Cross-Sectional Age Changes in Ego Identity Status During Adolescence," by P. W. Meilman, 1979, *Developmental Psychology, 15,* 230–231.

290: Figure based on data from *The Teenage World: Adolescents' Self-Image in Ten Countries,* by D. Offer, E. Ostrov, K. I. Howard, R. Atkinson, 1988. Plenum Publishing Group.

294: Cartoon LAUGH PARADE, © 1985. Reprinted courtesy of Bunny Hoest and Parade Magazine.

296: Table adapted and reproduced by special permission of the Publisher, Psychological Assessment Resources, Inc., 16204 North Florida Avenue, Lutz, FL 33549 from the *Self-Directed Search Professional Manual* by John L. Holland, Ph.D. Copyright © 1985 by PAR, Inc. Further reproduction is prohibited without permission from PAR, Inc.

297: Figure modified and reproduced by special permission of the Publisher, Consulting Psychologists Press, Inc., Palo Alto, CA 94303 from the **Strong Interest Inventory®** General Occupational Themes Profile for Robin Byrd. Copyright © 1994 by The Board of Trustees of the Leland Stanford Junior University. All rights reserved. Printed under license from the Stanford University Press, Stanford, CA 94305. Further reproduction is prohibited without the Publisher's written consent. The Strong Interest Inventory and SII are registered trademarks of Stanford University Press.

303: Figure courtesy, Rape Treatment Center, Santa Monica Hospital.

305: Figure data from *Monitoring the Future Study,* 1997.

CHAPTER 9

330: Figure based on data from "Health and Behavorial Consequences of Binge Drinking in College," by H. Wechsler, A. Davenport, G. Dowdall, B. Moeykens, & S. Castillo, 1994, *Journal of the American Medical Association, 272,* 1672–1677.

337: Figure from "The Course of Adult Intellectual Development," by K. W. Schaie, 1994, *American Psychologist, 49,* 304–313. Copyright © American Psychological Association. Reprinted with permission of the author.

338: Figure from "The Course of Adult Intellectual Development," by K. W. Schaie, 1994, *American Psychologist, 49,* 304–313. Copyright © American Psychological Association. Reprinted with permission of the author.

340: Figure from "Organization of Data on Life-Span Development of Human Abilities," by J. L. Horn. In L. R. Goulet and P. B. Baltes (Eds.), *Life-Span Developmental Psychology: Research and Theory,* p. 463. Copyright © 1970 Academic Press. Reprinted with permission.

344: Figure from "Reasoning on Social Dilemmas Varying in Emotional Saliency: An Adult Developmental Study," by F. Blanchard-Fields, 1986, *Psychology and Aging, 1,* 325–333. Copyright © 1986 American Psychological Association. Reprinted with permission of the author.

351: Figure based on data from "Culture and Moral Judgment: How Are Conflicts Between Justice and Interpersonal Responsibilities Resolved?" by J. G. Miller and D. M. Bersoff, 1992, *Journal of Personality and Social Psychology, 62,* 541–554.

354: Figure from *The Me I Know: A Study of Adult Identity,* by S. K. Whitbourne. Copyright © 1986 Springer-Verlag Publishing. Reprinted with permission.

355: Cartoon PEANUTS reprinted by permission of United Feature Syndicate, Inc.

CHAPTER 10

368: Cartoon THE FAR SIDE © 1980 Farworks, Inc./Dist. by Universal Press Syndicate. Reprinted with permission. All rights reserved. Figure from "Age and Sex Differences in Satisfying Love Relationships Across the Adult Life Span," by M. N. Reedy, J. E. Birren, and K. W. Schaie, 1981, *Human Development, 24,* 52–66. Copyright © 1981 S. Karger AG, Basel. Reprinted with permission.

370: Figure from "International Preferences in Selecting Mates: A Study of 37 Cultures," by D. M. Buss et al., 1990, *Journal of Cross-Cultural Psychology, 21,* 5–47. Copyright © 1990 by Sage Publications, Inc. Reprinted by permission of Sage Publications, Inc.

371: Figure from "Through a Psychological Lens: Personality Traits, Personality Disorders, and Levels of Violence," by K. D. O'Leary. In R. J. Gelles and D. R. Loseke (Eds.), *Current Controversies on Family Violence,* 7–30. Copyright © 1993 by Sage Publications, Inc. Reprinted by permission of Sage Publications, Inc.

372: Figure from "Through a Psychological Lens: Personality Traits, Personality Disorders, and Levels of Violence," by K. D. O'Leary. In R. J. Gelles and D. R. Loseke (Eds.), *Current Controversies on Family Violence,* 7–30. Copyright © 1993 by Sage Publications, Inc. Reprinted by permission of Sage Publications, Inc.

380: List from "Marriages Made to Last," by J. Lauer and R. Lauer, 1985, *Psychology Today, 19,* 22–26.

385: Figure from *Marriage and Family Development, 6th Edition,* by E. M. Duvall and B. C. Miller. Copyright © 1985 Harper & Row. Reprinted by permission of Addison Wesley Longman Educational Publishers, Inc.

385: Figure from *Career, Women, and Childbearing: A Psychological Analysis of the Decision Process,* by C. Wilk. Copyright © 1986 Van Nostrand Reinhold. Reprinted with permission.

392: List from "Perceived Causes of Divorce: An Analysis of Interrelationships," by M. B. Cleek

and T. A. Pearson, 1985, *Journal of Marriage and the Family, 47,* 179–191.

395: Figure based on data from Table 4 in "Relationships Between Fathers and Children Who Live Apart: The Father's Role After Separation," by J. A. Seltzer, 1991, *Journal of Marriage and the Family, 53,* p. 79. Copyrighted © 1991 National Council on Family Relations, 3989 Central Ave. NE, Suite 550, Minneapolis, MN 55421. Used by permission.

CHAPTER 11

405: Figure from *Career Motivation in Mid-life Managers,* by A. Howard and D. W. Bray. Paper presented at the meeting of the American Psychological Association, Montreal, August 1990.

420: Figure from U. S. Department of Labor, 1997.

430: Figure from U. S. Department of Labor, 1997.

434: Cartoon HI AND LOIS, © 1993. Reprinted with special permission of King Features Syndicate.

CHAPTER 12

446: Cartoon © Lynn Johnston Productions Inc./Dist. by United Features Syndicate, Inc.

455: Figure from "Aging and Cognitive Changes," by N. W. Denney. In B. B. Wolman (Ed.), *Handbook of Developmental Psychology,* p. 821. Copyright © 1982. Reprinted by permission of Prentice-Hall, Inc., Upper Saddle River, N.J.

463: Figure adapted from "The Anatomy of Generativity," by D. P. McAdams, H. M. Hart & S. Mzruna, 1998, p. 7. In D. P. McAdams & E. de St. Aubin (Eds.) *Generativity and Adult Development: How and Why We Care for the Next Generation.* Copyright © 1998 by the American Psychological Association. Adapted by permission of the author.

469: Figure from "My Children and Me: Midlife Evaluations of Grown Children and of Self," by C. D. Ryff, Y. H. Lee, M. J. Esses & P. S. Schmutte, 1994, *Psychology and Aging, 9 (2),* 195–205. Copyright © 1994 by the American Psychological Association. Reprinted by permission of the author.

471: Cartoon © Lynn Johnston Productions Inc./Dist. by United Features Syndicate, Inc.

CHAPTER 13

488: Cartoon THE FAR SIDE © 1991 Farworks, Inc./Dist. by Universal Press Syndicate. Reprinted with permission. All rights reserved.

503: Cartoon GARFIELD © 1994 Paws, Inc. Reprinted with permission of Universal Press Syndicate. All rights reserved.

505: Cartoon BLONDIE, © 1993. Reprinted with special permission of King Features Syndicate.

506: Figure from "Aging, Spatial Performance, and Spatial Competence," by K. C. Kirasic and G. L. Allen. In N. Charness (Ed.), *Aging and Human Performance*, 191–223. Copyright © 1985 John Wiley & Sons, Ltd. Reprinted by permission of John Wiley & Sons, Ltd.

510: Figure data based on "Creativity Productivity: A Predictive and Explanatory Model of Career Trajectories and Landmarks," by D. K. Simonton, 1997, *Psychological Review, 104*, 66–89.

511: Figure data based on "Creativity Productivity: A Predictive and Explanatory Model of Career Trajectories and Landmarks," by D. K. Simonton, 1997, *Psychological Review, 104*, 66–89.

CHAPTER 14

530: Cartoon DENNIS THE MENACE used by permission of Hank Ketcham and © by North America Syndicate.

532: Figure from "Ecology of the Aging Process," by M. P. Lawton and L. Nahemow. In C. Eisdorfer and M. P. Lawton (Eds.), *The Psychology of Adult Development and Aging*, 619–674. Copyright © 1973 American Psychological Association. Reprinted with permission of the author.

537: Figure from "Possible Selves in Adulthood and Old Age: A Tale of Shifting Horizons," by C. D. Ryff, 1991, *Psychology and Aging, 6*, 286–295. Copyright © 1991 American Psychological Association. Reprinted with permission.

547: Cartoon PEANUTS reprinted by permission of United Feature Syndicate, Inc.

549: Figure from "Relationship Classification Using Grade of Membership Analysis: A Typology of Sibling Relationships in Later Life," by D. T. Gold, M. A. Woodbury, and L. K. George, 1990, *Journal of Gerontology: Social Sciences, 45*, 43–51. Copyright © 1990 Gerontological Society of America. Reprinted with permission.

551: Cartoon DOONESBURY © 1997 by Gary Trudeau. Reprinted by Universal Press Syndicate. All rights reserved.

556: Figure from National Aging Information Center, 1997.

564: Figure from Federal Election Commission, 1998.

576: List from President's Commission for the Ethical Study of Problems in Medicine and Biomedical Behavioral Research.

CHAPTER 15

579: Figure copyright © 1995 California Medical Association. Reprinted with permission.

581: Cartoon FAMILY CIRCUS, © 1993. Reprinted with special permission of King Features Syndicate.

588: Figure from *Adult Development and Aging, Second Edition*, by J. C. Cavanaugh, Brooks/Cole Publishing, 1993.

594: Figure from "The Role of Anticipatory Bereavement in Older Women's Adjustment to Widowhood," by C. D. Hill, L. W. Thompson, and D. Gallagher, 1988, *The Gerontologist, 28*, 792–796. Copyright © 1990 Gerontological Society of America. Reprinted with permission.

596: Figure from "Older Adult Family Stress and Adaptation Before and After Bereavement," by F. N. Norris and S. A. Murrell, 1987, *Journal of Gerontology: Social Sciences, 42*, 606–612. Copyright © 1990 Gerontological Society of America. Reprinted with permission.

597: Figure from "Older Adult Family Stress and Adaptation Before and After Bereavement," by F. N. Norris and S. A. Murrell, 1987, *Journal of Gerontology: Social Sciences, 42*, 606–612. Copyright © 1990 Gerontological Society of America. Reprinted with permission.

602: Figure from "Retrospective Assessment of Marital Adjustment and Depression during the First Two Years of Spousal Bereavement," by A. Futterman, D. Gallagher, L. W. Thompson, S. Lovett, and M. Gilewski, 1990, *Psychology and Aging, 5*, 277–283. Copyright © 1990 American Psychological Association. Reprinted with permission.

PHOTO CREDITS

viii: © Laura Dwight/Photo Edit
x: © David Grossman
xii: © Bachman/Photo Edit
xiv: Rebecca Cooney/Actuality

CHAPTER 1

1: © Robert Brenner/Photo Edit
7: Mathias Oppersdorff/Photo Researchers, Inc.
11: (top) © Jeff Greenberg/Photo Edit
11: (bottom) Chad Slattery/Tony Stone Images
12: (right) © David Young-Wolff/Photo Edit
12: (left) © Robert Brenner/Photo Edit
16: Corbis-Bettmann
17: Corbis-UPI/Bettmann
19: Corbis-Bettmann
20: (top) Chuck Painter/News and Publications Service, Stanford University
20: (bottom) Corbis-Bettmann
22: © Michael Newman/Photo Edit
23: © David Young-Wolff/Photo Edit
26: © Michael Hayman/Stock, Boston
37: © Amy C. Etra/Photo Edit
39: (right) Mathias Oppersdorff/Photo Researchers, Inc.
40: Chad Slattery/Tony Stone Images

CHAPTER 2

42: Courtesy of the Tiger Woods Family
43: (all except background) Courtesy of the Tiger Woods Family
43: (background) © Jeff Christensen/Gamma-Liaison

44: © Stephen Agricola/The Image Works
46: (right) Francis Leroy/Custom Medical Stock
46: (left) Ken Edward/Science Source/Photo Researchers, Inc.
47: (top) Biophoto Associates/Science Source/Photo Researchers, Inc.
50: (bottom) © Comstock/Mike & Carol Werner
52: © Laura Dwight
55: Robert Kail
57: © Lennart Nilsson, A CHILD IS BORN, Dell Publishing Company
59: (bottom far left) © Lennart Nilsson, A CHILD IS BORN, Dell Publishing Company
59: (top) © Lennart Nilsson, A CHILD IS BORN, Dell Publishing Company
59: (bottom near right) © Lennart Nilsson, A CHILD IS BORN, Dell Publishing Company
64: K. L. Jones/LLR Research
70: (top) Richard Hirneisen/Medichrome
74: Lawrence Migdale/Photo Researchers, Inc.
75: Margaret Miller/Photo Researchers, Inc.
77: (bottom) Biophoto Associates/Science Source/Photo Researchers, Inc.
78: (top) © Comstock/Mike & Carol Werner
78: (bottom) Robert Kail
79: Lawrence Migdale/Photo Researchers, Inc.

CHAPTER 3

82: © Laura Dwight/Photo Edit
84: Robert Kail
85: Innervisions
89: Robert Kail
95: (top) Photo Edit
96: Alexander Tsiaras/Stock, Boston
97: (top) "Maturational Changes in Cerebral Function in Infants Determined by FDG Positron Emission Tomography." Copyright 1986 American Association for the Advancement of Science.
97: (bottom) Peter Cade/Tony Stone Images
100: Dexter Gormley
102: © Laura Dwight/Photo Edit
103: (top) Rick Browne/Stock, Boston
103: (bottom) Mitch Reardon/Photo Researchers, Inc.
107: (top) © Dion Ogust/The Image Works
107: (bottom) © Michael Tamborrino/Medichrome
111: Innervisions
115: (top) PT Santana/Tony Stone Images
116: © Robert Brenner/Photo Edit
118: Robert Kail
119: (left) Innervisions
119: (right) Robert Kail
120: (left) Peter Cade/Tony Stone Images
120: (right) PT Santana/Tony Stone Images

CHAPTER 4

122: © Robert Brenner/Photo Edit
125: © Shmuel Thaler/Jeroboam

127: © Laura Dwight
130: (top) © Tony Freeman/Photo Edit
130: (bottom) © Tony Freeman/Photo Edit
136: © Ann Chwatsky/Jeroboam
137: (top) Courtesy, Dr. Carolyn Rovee-Collier
137: (bottom) © Mike Mazzaschi/Stock, Boston
138: © Tony Freeman/Photo Edit
140: Elie Bernager/Tony Stone Images
142: © David Young-Wolff/Photo Edit
144: © Eric A. Wessman/Stock, Boston
145: © Lew Merrim/Monkmeyer Press
146: © Dreyfuss/Monkmeyer Press Photo
147: Barbara Filet/Tony Stone Images
149: Corbis-UPI/Bettmann
150: © David Young-Wolff/Photo Edit
151: © 1994 Don Perdue/Children's Television Workshop
153: Susan Johns/Photo Researchers, Inc.
154: © Tony Freemann/Photo Edit
156: Barbara Filet/Tony Stone Images
157: (left) © Ann Chwatsky/Jeroboam
157: (right) © Laura Dwight

CHAPTER 5

160: © Laura Dwight
164: Photo Edit
166: © Laura Dwight
170: © Boulton-Wilson/Jeroboam
172: (left) © Laura Dwight
172: (center) © Michael Newman/Photo Edit
172: (right) © Laura Dwight
173: © Peter Southwick/Stock, Boston
174: Robert Kail
175: © David Young-Wolff/Photo Edit
177: © David M. Grossman
178: (top) © Tony Freeman/Photo Edit
178: (bottom) © Laura Dwight
179: © Mary Kate Denny/Photo Edit
181: © Frank Siteman
182: (top) © Lawrence Migdale
182: (bottom) © Martin Adler/Panos Pictures
185: © Amy Etra/Photo Edit
187: © David Young-Wolff/Photo Edit
189: © Ariel Skelley/The Stock Market
190: © Goodwin/Monkmeyer Press Photos
192: © Denise Marcotte/Stock, Boston
195: (top right) Robert Kail
195: (top left) © David M. Grossman
195: (bottom) © Laura Dwight
196: © Ariel Skelley/The Stock Market
198: (bottom) © Laura Dwight
199: © Lennart Nilsson, from A CHILD IS BORN, Dell Publishing Company
199: Innervisions
199: (bottom) © David Young-Wolff/Photo Edit

CHAPTER 6

200: Globe Photos
201: (bottom) CORBIS/Neal Preston

201: (top right) CORBIS/Neal Preston
201: (center near right) CORBIS/Neal Preston
201: (background) John Barrett/Globe Photos, Inc. © 1998
202: © Michael Newman/Photo Edit
205: Richard Hutchings/Photo Researchers, Inc.
208: © David Young-Wolff/Photo Edit
213: © Bob Daemmrich/The Image Works
216: © Myrleen Ferguson/Photo Edit
219: (top) © Okoniewski/The Image Works
221: Becky Huffman/Resources and Residential Alternatives, Inc.
222: © Russell D. Curtis/Jeroboam
223: © Tony Freeman/Photo Edit
227: © Richard Hutchings/Photo Edit
228: © Myrleen Cate/Photo Edit
229: (bottom) © M. Siluk/The Image Works
229: (top) © David M. Grossman
230: © David M. Grossman
232: (bottom) © Bob Daemmrich/The Image Works
232: (top) © Myrleen Ferguson/Photo Edit
233: © David M. Grossman

CHAPTER 7

236: © Bob Daemmrich
239: (bottom) © Jean Hangarter/The Picture Cube
240: © James L. Shaffer/Photo Edit
244: (bottom) © Myrleen Ferguson Cate/Photo Edit
244: (top) Charles Thatcher/Tony Stone Images
246: © Bachmann/Photo Edit
249: © Billy E. Barnes/Jeroboam
250: © Dennis MacDonald/Photo Edit
251: © Alan S. Weiner/Gamma Liaison Network
255: © David Young-Wolff/Photo Edit
257: (top) © Mary Kate Denny/Photo Edit
257: (bottom) Richard Hutchings/Photo Researchers, Inc.
261: © David Young-Wolff/Photo Edit
262: Ray Ellis/Photo Researchers, Inc.
265: © Tony Freeman/Photo Edit
266: © 1994 Richard Termine/Children's Television Workshop
271: © David Young-Wolff/Photo Edit
272: © Daemmrich/Stock, Boston
273: © Bachmann/Photo Edit
274: (left) © David Young-Wolff/Photo Edit
274: (right) Richard Hutchings/Photo Researchers, Inc.

CHAPTER 8

276: David Young-Wolff/Tony Stone Images
280: © Byron/Monkmeyer Press Photo
282: © David Young-Wolff/Photo Edit
284: © Richard Hutchings/Photo Edit
286: © Spencer Grant/Photo Edit
287: © Myrleen Ferguson/Photo Edit

291: © Douglas/The Image Works
292: (top) © David Young-Wolff/Photo Edit
292: (bottom) © Billy E. Barnes/Photo Edit
294: (bottom) Photo Edit
296: © Michael Newman/Photo Edit
300: © Vincent Dewitt/Stock, Boston
301: © M. Granistsas/The Image Works
306: © Richard Hutchings/Photo Edit
307: © Dennis McDonald/Photo Edit
312: (left) © Byron/Monkmeyer Press Photo
312: (right) © Vincent Dewitt/Stock, Boston
313: (left) © David Young-Wolff/Photo Edit
313: (right) © Myrleen Ferguson/Photo Edit
314: © Dennis McDonald/Photo Edit
316: (top) © Myrleen Ferguson/Photo Edit
316: (bottom) © Myrleen Ferguson/Photo Edit
317: (bottom) © David Young-Wolff/Photo Edit
317: (top) © Alan S. Weiner/Gamma Liaison Network

CHAPTER 9

318: © Nubar Alexanian/Woodfin Camp & Associates
319: (left) Courtesy of Mrs. Fields' Corporate
319: (center near right) AP/Wide World Photos
319: (top right) © Nubar Alexanian/Stock, Boston
319: (bottom left) AP/Wide World Photos
320: Dale Durfee/Tony Stone Images
322: Photo Edit
323: © Patrick Ward/Stock, Boston
324: © B. Stitzer/Photo Edit
325: (top) © Michael Newman/Photo Edit
325: (bottom) Lori Adamski Peek/Tony Stone Images
327: © Ian Tomlinson/Allsport
328: © Fabian Falcon/Stock, Boston
329: (top) © Billy E. Barnes/Stock, Boston
329: (bottom) © Mike Mcgovern/The Picture Cube
331: © Gary A. Conner/Photo Edit
333: (top far left) © Lawrence Migdale/Stock, Boston
333: (top far right) © Michael Newman/Photo Edit
333: (bottom) Photo Edit
335: Brian Bailey/Tony Stone Images
336: © Laura Dwight/Photo Edit
341: © R. Lord/The Image Works
342: © Bachmann/Photo Edit
343: Don Smetzer/Tony Stone Images
345: © Antonio Ribeiro/Gamma Liaison Network
346: Frank Siteman/Tony Stone Images
347: © Richard Ellis/Sygma
348: © E. Baitel/P. Landmann/Gamma Liaison Network
349: © J. Nordell/The Image Works
350: © N. Gans/The Image Works
353: Kaluzny/Thatcher/Tony Stone Images

356: © Steve Skjold/Photo Edit
358: (left) Brian Bailey/Tony Stone Images
358: (right) © Bachmann/Photo Edit
359: (bottom) © Patrick Ward/Stock, Boston
359: (left) Don Smetzer/Tony Stone Images
359: (top) © N. Gans/The Image Works

CHAPTER 10

362: © Michelle Bromwell/Photo Edit
365: Leland Bobbe/TonyStone Images
366: © Billy E. Barnes/Photo Edit
373: © R. Lord/The Image Works
375: © B. Bachmann/The Image Works
376: Bruce Ayres/Tony Stone Images
378: Bruce Ayres/Tony Stone Images
380: © Frank Siteman/The Picture Cube
381: © Laura Dwight/Photo Edit
382: © Frank Siteman/Monkmeyer Press Photo
383: © Amy Etra/Photo Edit
387: © Myrleen Ferguson/Photo Edit
388: © Michael Newman/Photo Edit
389: © Paul Conklin/Photo Edit
393: © Robert Brenner/Photo Edit
394: (top) © Stephen Agricola/Stock, Boston
394: (bottom) © Bob Daemmrich/Stock, Boston
397: © David Young-Wolff/Photo Edit
398: (right) Bruce Ayres/Tony Stone Images
398: (left) © Billy E. Barnes/Photo Edit
399: (left) © Frank Siteman/Monkmeyer Press Photo
399: (right) © Michael Newman/Photo Edit

CHAPTER 11

402: © Michael Newman/Photo Edit
404: Paul Chesley/Tony Stone Images
407: AP/Wide World Photos
409: © Gish/Monkmeyer Press Photo
410: © Laima Druskis/Stock, Boston
412: © David Lassman/The Image Works
413: B Seitz/Photo Researchers, Inc.
415: © Tom McCarthy/Photo Edit
416: © Michael Newman/Photo Edit
417: © Michael Newman/Photo Edit
418: Dan Bosler/Tony Stone Images
419: (left) AP/Wide World Photos
419: (right) AP/Wide World Photos
421: © John Coletti/Stock, Boston
423: © Richard Lord/The Image Works
426: © Kerbs/Monkmeyer Press Photo
428: © Crandall/The Image Works
429: © Frank Siteman
431: © M. Greenlar/The Image Works
432: © Michael Newman/Photo Edit
436: Ken Fisher/Tony Stone Images
437: © Bob Daemmrich/Stock, Boston
439: (top far left) B. Seitz/Photo Researchers, Inc.
439: (top far right) © Michael Newman/Photo Edit

439: (bottom) © Richard Lord/The Image Works
440: (left) © Michael Newman/Photo Edit
440: (right) Ken Fisher/Tony Stone Images

CHAPTER 12

442: © John Eastcott/Yva Momatiuk/The Image Works
444: © Amy Etra/Photo Edit
445: Laurence Monneret/Tony Stone Images
448: © Sestine/LaPira Ita/Gamma Liaison Network
449: © Esbin/Anderson/The Image Works
450: © Robert Brenner/Photo Edit
451: © Melanie Brown/Photo Edit
452: © Tom McCarthy/Photo Edit
456: © Bill Aron/Photo Edit
458: (top near left) © David Weintraub/Stock, Boston
458: (top near right) © Tom McCarthy/Photo Edit
458: (center near left) © Michael Newman/Photo Edit
458: (center near right) © Maximilian Stock Ltd./Science Photo Library/Photo Researchers, Inc.
460: © David Young-Wolff/Photo Edit
462: © Charles Gupton/Stock, Boston
464: © Sidney/Monkmeyer Press Photo
467: Walter Hodges/Tony Stone Images
468: © Lawrence Migdale
470: © Tony Freeman/Photo Edit
471: (top) © Tony Freeman/Photo Edit
473: © D. Wells/The Image Works
474: © Bob Daemmrich/The Image Works
475: © Lawrence Migdale/Stock, Boston
477: © Amy Etra/Photo Edit
478: (bottom far left) © Maximilian Stock Ltd/Science Photo Library/Photo Researchers, Inc.
478: (bottom near right) Walter Hodges/Tony Stone Images
478: (top right) © Tom McCarthy/Photo Edit
482: (top) © Gary A. Conner/Photo Edit
482: (bottom) © Tom McCarthy/Photo Edit
483: (right) © Frank Siteman/The Picture Cube
483: (left) © Lawrence Migdale/Stock, Boston

CHAPTER 13

484: © Sygma
485: (background) AP/Wide World Photos
485: (top right) AP/Wide World Photos
485: (center far right) © Charles Steiner/Sygma
485: (bottom) © Jacques Chenet/Woodfin Camp & Associates
486: © Jeff Greenberg/Photo Edit
495: © D. Ogust/The Image Works
497: © Najiah Feanny/Stock, Boston
498: © Howard Sochurek/Medichrome
499: © Rudi VonBriel/Photo Edit
503: (top) Frank Siteman

507: © Daemmrich/The Image Works
509: Zephyr/Custom Medical Stock
512: © Mark Burnett/Stock, Boston
514: © Eastcott/The Image Works
516: © Karen Preuss/The Image Works
518: © Alan Oddie/Photo Edit
520: © Robert Brenner/Photo Edit
522: Courtesy of the Alzheimer's Association
523: (right) © Rudi VonBriel/Photo Edit
523: (left) © Alan Oddie/Photo Edit
524: (left) Zephyr/Custom Medical Stock
524: (right) © Eastcott/The Image Works

CHAPTER 14

528: © Jeff Greenberg/Photo Edit
535: © Nubar Alexanian/Stock, Boston
538: © David Austen/Stock, Boston
540: © Bachman/Photo Edit
541: (bottom) © Al Cook/Stock, Boston
541: (top) © S. O'Rourke/The Image Works
542: Rebecca Cooney/Actuality
543: © Comstock
545: © Michael Newman/Photo Edit
548: © Michael Newman/Photo Edit
550: © Cleo/Photo Edit
552: © David Young-Wolff/Photo Edit
553: © Myrleen Ferguson/Photo Edit
555: © Alan Oddie/Photo Edit
557: Larry Mulvehill/Photo Researchers, Inc.
558: © Jeff Greenberg/Photo Edit
559: © Mary M. Steinbacker/Photo Edit
560: © Lawrence Migdale
563: © Daemmrich/The Image Works
564: AP/Wide World Photos
567: (top right) © Bachman/Photo Edit
567: (top left) © David Austen/Stock, Boston
567: (center far left) © Comstock
568: (left) © Michael Newman/Photo Edit
568: (right) © Jeff Greenberg/Photo Edit

CHAPTER 15

572: John Elk/Tony Stone Images
574: © Michael Newman/Photo Edit
575: © FSP/Gamma Liaison Network
577: Reuters/Archive Photos
581: © John Eastcott/Yva Momatiuk/The Image Works
582: © A. Ramey/Photo Edit
586: © Roos/Gamma-Liaison Network
589: © Thomas Bowman/Photo Edit
590: (center far left) © Bob Daemmrich/Stock, Boston
590: (center near left) © Bob Daemmrich/Stock, Boston
590: (center far right) Ken Fisher/Tony Stone Images
590: (center near right) © Robert Ullmann/Design Concepts
592: © Amy Etra/Photo Edit
593: © Bob Daemmrich/Stock, Boston

NAME INDEX

Abbey, A., 303
Abbey, B. B., 176
Aber, J. L., 251
Ablin, A. R., 593
Aboud, F. E., 271
Abrams, W. B., 520
Ackerman, B. P., 155
Adams, C., 341
Adams, G. R., 326
Adams, K., 467, 472
Adams, M. J., 209
Adams, R. J., 110
Adelman, C., 419
Adler, N., 302
Adler, S., 406
Adlersberg, M., 545
Administration on Aging, 489
Agostinelli, J., 432
Aguinis, H., 422
Ahrons, C., 395
Ainslie, J. J., 303
Ainsworth, M. D. S., 166
Aldwin, C. M., 464, 492, 544
Ales, K. L., 63
Alessandri, S. M., 175
Alexander, J. F., 311
Allen, G. L., 506
Allen, J. P., 301
Allen, K. R., 436
Allen, M. C., 75
Allgeier, E. R., 304
Allgeier, R., 304
Alpern, L., 167
Alwin, D. F., 462
Amato, P. R., 247, 248, 383, 392
American Association of Retired Persons, 491

American Council on Education, 426–427
American Heart Association, 332
American Psychological Society, 490
Anand, K. J., 107
Anastasi, A., 214
Anderson, W. T., 591, 597, 598, 599
Andrasik, F., 451
Andreas, D., 168
Andreatos, M., 148
Andrews, J. A., 306
Angiuld, N., 342, 343
Anglin, J. M., 149
Anthill, J. K., 430
Antonarakis, S. E., 52
Antonovsky, A., 543
Antonucci, T. C., 365, 544, 547, 548
Anyanwu, L., 74
Apgar, V., 75, 86
Appel, M. A., 451
Appelbaum, M. I., 101, 223
Aquan-Assee, J., 255
Aquilino, W. S., 465
Aranda, M. P., 473
Aranya, N., 406
Arber, S., 423
Arbona, C., 418
Arcus, D., 89
Arden, H., 538
Arenberg, D., 461
Arias, I., 373, 374
Arnett, J., 325
Arthur, J., 74
Artis, J. E., 472, 473
Aryee, S., 431, 433, 435

Asher, S. R., 258
Aslin, R. N., 109
Assmann, S., 499
Astone, N. M., 323
Atchley, R. C., 530, 543, 553
Atkinson, M., 153
Atkinson, R., 290
Attie, J., 282
Atterbury, J. L., 61
Attig, T., 581, 582, 583, 592, 593, 594, 595, 599, 602
Atwater, E., 308
Au, T. K., 150
Austin-Lafrance, R., 93
Aviezer, O., 168
Axelson, L. J., 382, 383, 470, 549
Azrin, N. H., 105

Bachman, J. G., 292, 306
Baer, D. M., 19
Bagwell, C. L., 254, 259
Bailey, J. M., 193, 390
Bailey, N., 421
Baillargeon, R., 133
Baker, J. E., 281
Baker, M. D., 498, 501
Baker, T. B., 306
Bakshi, A., 257
Balfour, J. L., 555
Balk, D. E., 583
Ball, J. F., 593
Ball, K., 504, 505
Ball, S., 266
Baltes, M. M., 357
Baltes, P. B., 336, 357, 456, 510, 511, 512
Bammel, G., 437
Bandura, A., 189, 262

Banks, M. D., 109
Baradaran, L. P., 259
Barbee, A. H., 356
Barenboim, C., 268
Barer, B. M., 557
Barfield, R. E., 544
Barkley, R. A., 222, 223, 224
Barling, J., 293, 373, 374
Barnard, K. E., 216
Barnes, G. M., 433
Baron, J. N., 419
Barr, H. M., 64, 69
Barrera, M., Jr., 244
Barrett, G. V., 423
Barry, H., 323
Barton, C., 311
Barton, M. E., 154
Barton, P. E., 227
Bartsch, K., 116, 117
Baruch, G. K., 465
Basham, R. B., 387
Basinger, K. S., 350
Baskett, L. M., 245
Bates, E., 148, 149
Bates, J. E., 239, 259
Baugh, S. G., 410
Baugher, S. G., 563
Baumeister, A. A., 88, 220, 221
Baumrind, D., 241, 242
Bawle, E. V., 64
Beal, C. R., 155
Bean, F., 391
Beardsall, L., 245
Bearison, D. J., 144
Beauchamp, G. K., 107
Beck, A. T., 308, 515, 516
Beck, J., 75, 498
Beck, M., 57
Beck, S., 506

Becker, B. J., 188
Beehr, T. A., 542
Beevers, D. G., 329
Behnke, M., 64
Behrend, D. A., 144
Belgrad, S. L., 155
Belgrave, L. L., 557
Bell, A. P., 299
Bell, M., 522
Beller, M., 188
Belsky, J., 89, 165, 245, 280
Bem, D. J., 300
Bence, S. L., 475
Benda, B. B., 300
Bengtson, V., 464, 468, 554
Benin, M. H., 432
Benson, N. J., 222
Benson, R. C., 63
Bento, S., 168
Bentz, L. S., 61
Berdahl, J. L., 420, 421
Bergman, S., 438
Berk, L. E., 144, 179, 220
Berkman, L., 329
Berko, J., 152
Berkow, R., 331, 515, 520
Berman, W. H., 473
Berndt, T. J., 254, 255
Berninger, G., 154
Berry, J. W., 288
Berry, R. E., 381
Bersoff, D. M., 350
Besharov, D. J., 302
Best, D. L., 187, 464
Bettencout, B. A., 188
Betz, E. L., 417
Betz, N. E., 406, 416
Bhatt, R. S., 137
Bhavnagri, N. P., 180, 181,
    241
Bielby, W. T., 419
Bigler, R. S., 187
Bilezikian, J. P., 446
Bill, J. M., 75
Binger, C. M., 593
Binstock, R. H., 490, 563, 564,
    565
Birch, L. L., 93, 281
Birchmore, D., 509
Bird, G. W., 434
Biringen, Z., 101
Birren, J. E., 368
Black, C. M. D., 282
Black, J. E., 96
Black, S. A., 515
Black-Gutman, D., 271
Blackburn, A. B., 509

Blakeslee, S., 393
Blakley, B. W., 64
Blanchard-Fields, F., 344, 455,
    456
Blieszner, R., 473
Block, J., 462
Bloom, L., 153
Blumstein, P., 377, 378, 379
Blyth, D., 280, 299
Bobak, I. M., 63
Bobrow, D., 193, 390
Bogatz, G. A., 266
Bohannon, J. N., 153
Bond, T. G., 205
Bond, J. T., 430, 431
Bondareff, W., 518
Boodoo, G., 212, 214, 216
Bookstein, F. L., 64
Boone, R. T., 176
Booth, A., 377
Bootzin, R. R., 500
Borden, S. L., 222
Borg, S., 599
Borgen, F. H., 406
Borgida, E., 416
Borlange Consensus Group,
    504
Bornstein, M. H., 180
Bortz, S. S., 501
Bortz, W. M., II, 501
Bosman, E. A., 456, 457
Bossé, R., 436, 544
Bouchard, T. J., 212, 214, 216
Bouman, D., 258
Bowden, J., 522
Bowen, R., 285
Bowen-Woodward, D., 249
Bowlby, J., 163
Boyd, R., 394
Boyer, C. B., 302
Boykin, A. W., 212, 214, 215,
    216
Bozett, F. W., 390
Brabeck, M. M., 416
Brackstone, D., 222
Bradley, R. H., 216
Brady, J. E., 181
Braet, C., 281
Braine, M. D. S., 151, 153
Brainerd, C. J., 132, 138
Brand, E., 249
Brand, R. J., 451
Brandtstädter, J., 357
Branstetter, W. H., 182
Brant, L. J., 497
Braungart, J. M., 55
Bray, D. W., 405, 411, 437

Brazelton, T. B., 74, 86
Bretherton, I., 149, 168
Bridges, C. R., 418
Brigham, J. C., 138
Brim, O. G., Jr., 26
Brinton, L. A., 447
Brioni, J. D., 520
Brody, E. M., 472
Brody, G. H., 245
Brody, N., 212, 214, 216
Brodzinsky, D. M., 205
Broman, C. L., 432
Bromley, D. B., 268
Bronfenbrenner, U., 23
Bronson, G. W., 109
Bronzino, J. D., 93
Brooks, L., 416
Brooks, R. H., 299
Brooks-Gunn, J., 115, 214,
    280, 282, 301
Brophy, J. E., 228, 229, 230
Brougham, R. R., 453
Brown, B. B., 256, 257
Brown, E., 116, 180
Brown, J. R., 176, 245
Brown, K. H., 543
Brown, K. P., 260
Brown, Louise, 57
Brown, R., 209
Browne, A., 373
Bruck, M., 138
Brustrom, J. E., 492
Bryan, J. H., 265
Bryant, B. K., 185
Bryden, M. P., 188
Buchanon, C. M., 248, 249
Buchsbaum, B. C., 582, 599
Buckle, L., 397
Buhrmeister, D., 245, 254
Buichan, B., 413
Bukowski, W. M., 255, 256,
    257, 258, 259
Bulcroft, C., 548
Bullinger, A., 108
Bullock, W. A., 115, 383
Bumpass, L. L., 377, 465
Burchinal, M., 293
Burger-Judisch, L. M., 96
Burgess, D., 416
Buriel, R., 238, 240, 242, 243,
    247
Burke, R. J., 418
Burkhalter, J. E., 602
Burkhauser, R. V., 333
Burman, B., 248
Burns, A., 376
Burr, J. A., 540, 541

Burrus-Bammel, L. L., 437
Bursuck, W. D., 325
Burton, L. M., 476, 554
Busch, J. W., 410
Buss, A. H., 88, 89
Bye, C. A., 522
Byrne, D. F., 270

Caggiula, A., 448
Caine, C., 498
Calasanti, T. M., 542
Calciano, R., 449
Caldwell, B. M., 216
Call, K. T., 292
Callahan, C. M., 557
Callahan, L. F., 333
Callendar, G., 51
Camara, K. A., 248
Camp, C. J., 341, 455, 508,
    520, 522
Campbell, F. A., 217
Campos, J., 101, 111, 174
Campos, R. G., 87
Canfield, R. L., 139
Canter, W. A., 306
Cantor, N., 299
Cantu, C. L., 288
Capaldi, D. M., 249, 300
Carey, G., 310
Carlo, G., 182, 185
Carlson, C. L., 224
Carlson, S. M., 179
Carlson, V., 251
Carr, C. R., 329
Carroll, J. L., 88
Carroll, M., 137
Carroll, R. S., 476
Carroll, S. J., 410
Carskadon, M. A., 290
Carstensen, L. L., 357, 381,
    548, 549
Cartwright, B. S., 179
Casadio, P., 149
Casaer, P., 96
Cascardi, M., 373
Cascio, W. F., 408
Caselli, M. C., 149
Caserta, M. S., 601
Casey, M. B., 189
Caspi, A., 89, 280
Cassidy, E., 559
Cassidy, J., 166
Cassidy, L., 303
Castillo, R., 279
Castillo, S., 330, 331
Castle, J. M., 176
Castro, I. L., 420

Cauley, J. A., 451
Cavanaugh, J. C., 15, 341, 450, 454, 472, 475, 507, 509, 518, 519, 538, 550, 551, 589, 590, 595
Ceci, S. J., 138, 212, 214, 216, 454
Center for Creative Leadership, 419
Centers for Disease Control and Prevention, 328, 329
Chacon, M. E., 93
Chadsey-Rusch, J., 324
Chakraborty, R., 281
Chambré, S. M., 546
Chan, C. G., 542
Chan, H., 542
Chance, G., 108
Chang, C. M., 140
Chao, G. T., 410
Chao, P., 240
Chapman, M., 182
Chapman, P. D., 210, 211
Charness, N., 456, 457
Chase-Lansdale, P. L., 248
Chasteen, A. L., 376
Chatters, L. M., 538
Chavira, V., 287
Chen, S., 89
Chen, X., 89, 259, 260
Chen, Y., 456
Cherlin, A. J., 248, 376, 377, 474, 476
Chin-Sang, V., 436
Chinen, A. B., 511
Chipperfield, J. G., 246
Chiriboga, D., 382
Chisolm, J. S., 103
Chodak, G. W., 449
Choi, J. M., 557
Chomsky, Noam, 153
Chow, J., 251
Christensen, K. M., 107
Chugani, H. T., 97
Church, M. W., 64
Chyi-in, W., 251
Cicchetti, D., 250, 251
Cicirelli, V. G., 548
Cielinski, K. L., 52
Cintra, L., 93
Cipani, E., 220
Clark, E. G., 579
Clark, R. F., 519
Clark, S. L., 474, 475
Clarke, A. D., 216
Clarke, A. M., 216
Clarke, S. C., 75

Cleek, M. B., 391, 392
Clemens, A. W., 470
Clements, M., 381, 382
Clements, W. A., 117
Clifton, R., 108, 132
Clingempeel, W. G., 249
Clinton, Bill, 422, 499
Cloud, J. M., 187
Cluss, P. A., 281
Codding, R., 508
Cohen, G. D., 516
Cohen, K. M., 104
Cohen, S., 329, 452
Coie, J. D., 257
Coke, M. M., 538
Colby, A., 348
Cole, A. K., 167
Cole, D. A., 307
Cole, D. R., 102
Cole, P. M, 175
Cole, T. R., 577
Colella, U., 377
Coleman, C. C., 255
Coleman, L. M., 179
Coleman, M., 396
Colligan, M., 450
Collins, N. L., 369
Collins, W. A., 290
Conger, M., 433
Conger, R. D., 239, 248, 251, 280, 293, 383
Conley, J. G., 63
Connell, C. M., 473
Connidis, I., 549
Connor, L. T., 505
Conover, D. L., 66
Contreras, J., 52
Cooney, T. M., 387, 394, 395, 396
Cooper, J., 191
Cooper, R. P., 147
Corballis, M. C., 102
Corby, N., 449
Cordes, C. L., 413
Corley, R., 216
Cornish, N., 423
Cornman, J. M., 541
Cornoni-Huntley, J., 329
Cornwell, K. S., 102
Corr, C. A., 588, 589
Corr, D. M., 589
Corrigan, P. W., 413
Cosby, A., 409
Costa, P. T., Jr., 406, 461, 462, 465
Costello, E., 448
Costin, S. E., 184

Cotton, S., 430
Coulton, C. J., 251
Council on Ethical and Judicial Affairs, 334
Counts, D., 574
Courage, M. L., 110, 137
Cowan, C. P., 369
Cowan, P. A., 369
Coward, R. T., 471
Cowart, B. J., 107
Cox, D. S., 452
Cox, M., 247
Cox, R., 247, 263
Coyle, M., 74
Craig, K. D., 107
Craig, R. K., 132
Craik, F. I. M., 505
Craton, L. G., 111
Crenshaw, T. M., 260
Crick, N. R., 258
Crimmins, E. M., 556
Crisafi, L., 342, 343
Crispi, E. L., 473
Crnic, K., 75, 89, 387
Crockenberg, S. B., 185
Crook, C., 107
Crook, T. H., III, 498, 499, 517, 518, 519
Crosby, L., 300
Crosignani, P. G., 66
Cross, S., 355, 535
Crouter, A. C., 189
Crowell, J. A., 166
Cruzan, Nancy, 578
Csikszentmihalyi, M., 219
Cuellar, I., 288
Culgin, S., 559
Cumberland, A., 176
Cummings, E. M., 248
Cunningham, F. G., 71
Cunningham, J. D., 430
Cunningham, J. G., 176
Curtin, S. C., 301
Curtis, T., 298, 300
Cutler, S. J., 437
Cutter, M. A. G., 578

Da Silva, M. S., 182
Dale, P. S., 148, 149
Dalla Corta, Rosanno, 448
Dalton, S. T., 376
Damast, A. M., 180
Damon, W., 116
Danforth, J. S., 224
Dannemiller, J. L., 109
Darby, B. L., 69
Darling, N., 243

Darrow, C., 408, 409, 465
D'Augelli, A. R., 299, 300
Davenport, A., 330, 331
Davidson, F. H., 272
Davidson, K. M., 71
Davidson, M. M., 272
Davies, P. T., 248
Davis, B. W., 558
Davis, J. O., 50
Davis, L. B., 107
Davis, L. G., 383
Davis, S. W., 187
Davis, T. L., 131
Dawson, P., 208
Day, C. L., 564
Day, S. X., 296
De Fiebre, N. C., 448, 520
De Haan, L. G., 463
de St. Aubin, E., 463
de Vries, B., 364
De Wolff, M. S., 168
DeAngelis, T., 447, 448
Debanne, S. M., 539
DeBerry, K. M., 288
DeCasper, A. J., 61
Decker, M. W., 520
DeFrank, R., 428
DeFries, J. C., 55, 216
Değirmencioğlu, S. M., 257
Dekovic, M., 260
DeLeon, P. H., 589
Dellas, M., 286
DeLoache, J. S., 129
Deluca, T., 222
Demaris, A., 377
Dement, W. C., 88
Denney, N. W., 454, 455
Dennis, M. G., 103
Dennis, W., 103
Denton, K., 254
Depner, C. E., 394
Derbyshire, A., 112
DeSantis, L., 582, 583
Desjardins, R. N., 146
Desouza, E. R., 422
DeSpelder, L. A., 587
Detweiler, R. A., 389
DeVaryshe, B. D., 310
DeViney, S., 540
Devoe, M., 341
Diamond, A., 51, 463
Diamond, J., 380
Diana, M. S., 299
Diaz-Cintra, S., 93
DiBlasio, F. A., 300
Dickinson, G. E., 581, 582
Diehl, M., 456

Dielman, T., 306
Diessner, R., 348
Dimond, M., 601
DiPrete, T. A., 419
Dittmann-Kohli, F., 336
Dixon, J., 224
Dixon, R. A., 336, 454, 456, 510, 511
Dobash, R. E., 372
Dobash, R. P., 372
Dobbs, J. B., 101
Dobson, S. H., 506
Dockrell, J., 222
Dodge, H., 415, 419
Dodge, K. A., 239, 257, 259
Dohrenwend, B. P., 452
Doka, K. J., 553, 554
Domino, G., 181
Donatelle, R. J., 383
Dong, Q., 246
Donnell, F., 168
Dornbusch, S. M., 242, 243, 248, 249, 292, 293
Dougherty, T. W., 413
Doussard-Roosevelt, J. A., 503
Dowdall, G., 330, 331
Dowling-Guyer, S., 387
Down Syndrome Collaborative Group, The, 52
Downs, A. C., 190
Doyle, A., 272
Draper, P., 280
Druin, D. P., 51
Druzin, M. L., 63
Dryfoos, J. G., 301, 302, 311
Dubois, D. L., 255
Dumas, J. E., 244
Duncan, G. J., 214
Duncan, S. C., 306
Dunn, J., 176, 179, 244, 245, 548
Dunn, N. J., 383, 550
Duvall, E. M., 26, 384
Dwyer, J. W., 471
Dyk, P. H., 326

Eagly, A. H., 188
Earles, J. L., 504, 505
Eaton, W. O., 187, 246
Eccles, J. S., 190
Edelbrock, C., 224
Edelstein, B., 507, 515
Edelstein, S., 476
Edwards, C. A., 257
Edwards, J. R., 187

Edwards, P. E., 188
Egeland, G. M., 66
Eilers, R. E., 148
Eisenberg, N., 182, 183, 184, 185, 242, 243
Eisenbud, L., 192
Ekerdt, D. J., 436, 540, 544
Elder, G. H., Jr., 280, 285, 293, 383, 540
Eldis, F., 64
Elicker, J., 167
Elkind, D., 285
Ellis, M. J., 390
Ellison, C. G., 365
Elmer-DeWitt, P., 71
Emde, R. N., 101
Emerson, P. E., 164
Emery, G., 516
Emery, R. E., 246, 248, 250, 252
Emory, E. K., 74
Engle-Friedman, M., 500
Englund, M., 167
Enns, G. T., 136
Enns, L. R., 187
Enright, R. D., 383
Ensing, D. S., 538
Eppler, M. A., 101
Epstein, D., 500
Epstein, L. H., 281
Erdley, C. A., 258
Erel, O., 248
Erera-Weatherley, P. I., 389
Erickson, M. T., 104
Ericsson, K. A., 456
Erikson, E. H., 13, 162, 284, 325, 379, 410, 534, 535, 537
Erikson, J. M., 534
Ernst, E. K. M., 75
Ervin-Tripp, S., 154
Eskew, R. W., 381
Essex, M. J., 469, 547
Estes, R. J., 428
Etaugh, C., 187
Etzioni, A., 392
Evans, D. R., 543, 544
Eyal, N., 438
Eyler, F. O., 64

Fabes, R. A., 183, 185, 188
Fagen, J., 137
Fagot, B. I., 190
Fairlie, H., 563
Falbo, T., 246
Fantauzzo, C. A., 176

Farrell, M. P., 465, 466
Farver, J. M., 178, 182
Faw, G. D., 221
Fazel, S., 265
Feaster, D. J., 602
Federal Election Commission, 564
Feehan, M., 223
Fegley, S., 292
Fehr, B., 364, 365, 366, 547
Feldhusen, J. F., 219
Feldman, D. C., 428
Feldman, D. H., 219
Feldman, J. M., 507
Feldman, S. S., 287
Feltey, K. M., 303
Feminist Majority Foundation, 419
Feng, W. Y., 89
Fenson, J., 149
Fenson, L., 148, 149
Fenwick, K. D., 108
Feren, D. B., 410
Ferguson, D. L., 288
Fernald, A., 176
Ferrari, M., 104, 215
Feuerstein, R. C., 593
Fiano, K., 74
Fick, D. S., 438
Field, D., 383, 552
Field, T., 97, 154, 165, 387
Fields, R., 306
Fields, V., 472
Filcher, I., 193, 390
Finch, M. D., 292, 356
Fincham, F. D., 248
Fingerman, K. L., 467, 472
Finn-Stevenson, M., 215
Fiore, M., 416
Fischer, M., 223
Fisher, D. A., 71
Fisher, H. E., 374, 391
Fisher, J. E., 516, 517
Fitness, J., 422
Fitzgerald, H. E., 102
Fitzgerald, J. F., 557
Fitzgerald, L. F., 420, 421, 422
Fitzpatrick, M. A., 382
Fivush, R., 137
Flaks, D. K., 193, 390
Flavell, J. H., 132, 205
Flay, B. R., 306
Fleeson, J., 167
Fleg, J. L., 497
Fleishner, J. E., 222
Fletcher, K. E., 223
Fogel, A., 164

Folkard, S., 413
Folkman, S., 450
Forde, V., 93
Foreyt, J. P., 281
Foss, J. W., 508
Fowler, R. C., 308
Fowles, J., 187
Fox, A., 544
Fox, K. M., 522
Fox, N. A., 89, 97, 173
Foxx, R. M., 105
Frame, C. L., 258
Franco, A., 137
Frankenburg, W. K., 101
Franklin, J. C., 294
Franks, M., 471
Frazer, D. W., 498, 501
Fredrickson, B. L., 514, 515
Freedman-Letofsky, K., 553
Freeman, H. P., 333
Freeman, S. J. A., 553
Freer, J. P., 579
Frerichs, F., 423
Freud, Sigmund, 163
Freund, A. M., 357
Friedman, D. E., 430, 431
Friedman, M., 451
Friedman, R. J., 175
Friedman, S., 542
Friend, M., 131
Frieske, D. A., 504, 505, 509
Frieze, I. H., 418
Frohlich, C. B., 182
Froman, L., 426
Frone, M. R., 431, 433
Frost, J. L., 418
Frye, D., 117
Fu, V. R., 241
Fulcomer, M., 438
Fulker, D. W., 55, 216
Fulton, G., 594
Fulton, R., 602
Furman, W., 245, 254
Furstenberg, F. F., Jr., 243, 248, 301, 395, 397, 474, 476
Futterman, A., 601

Gable, S., 164
Gafni, N., 188
Gagnon, J. H., 447
Gaines, C. L., 504, 505
Gaitz, C. M., 435, 437
Gajar, A. H., 325
Galinsky, E., 430, 431
Gall, T. L., 543, 544
Gallagher, D., 515, 594

Gallagher, M., 394, 395
Gallagher-Thompson, D., 601
Galler, J. R., 93
Gallup, G. G., Jr., 397
Ganong, L. H., 396
Gant, N. F., 71
Garasky, S., 246
Garbarino, J., 251
Garcia-Colera, A., 504
Gardiner, K. N., 302
Gardner, H., 212, 213
Garland, A. F., 308
Garmezy, N., 174
Garmon, L. C., 350
Garner, P. W., 245
Garner, W., 452
Garnick, M. B., 449
Garvey, C., 154
Gasper, C., 421
Gassin, E. A., 383
Gatz, M., 357
Gauger, K., 245
Gauze, C., 255
Gavaki, E., 288
Gay, J. E., 328
Gaylord, S. A., 515
Ge, X., 239, 280
Geary, D. C., 226
Geib, A., 303
Gelles, R. J., 371
Gelman, R., 139, 154
Gelman, S. A., 187, 190
Gentry, M., 553
Genzel, C., 107
George, L. K., 462, 538, 548
Gerbner, G., 264
Gergen, K., 592, 593
Gergen, M., 592, 593
Gesser, G., 586
Getchell, N., 101
Gfoerer, J. C., 330
Ghatala, E. S., 208
Giannantonia, C. M., 410
Gibbs, J. C., 185, 348, 350
Gibbs, N. R., 562
Giberson, P. K., 69
Gibran, K., 404
Gibson, E. J., 110
Gibson, G. D., 473
Gibson, K. R., 94
Gibson, R. C., 540, 542, 543
Gignac, M. A. M., 430
Giles, H., 187
Gilewski, M. J., 601
Gilford, R., 549
Gill, J. S., 329
Gill, S. K., 329

Gilligan, C., 349
Gillman, S. A., 437
Gillmore, J., 271
Gillum, B., 462
Gillum, R., 462
Gilmore, D., 323
Gilroy, F. D., 416
Ginn, J., 423
Ginsburg, Ruth Bader, 419
Girgus, J. S., 307
Gisin, G. J., 436
Glamser, F., 436
Glaney, N. T., 602
Glaser, R., 452
Glass, K. C., 472
Gleason, K. E., 168
Glenn, John, 484–485
Glenn, N. D., 381, 397
Glick, I. O., 552, 593
Glick, P. C., 248, 396
Glusman, M., 150
Glynn, N. W., 451
Go, C. G., 492
Goate, A. M., 519
Godkin, M. A., 560
Goff, S. J., 431, 438
Goggin, N. L., 504
Gold, D. T., 548, 549
Gold, Tracey, 282
Gold, Y., 421
Goldberg, W. A., 467
Goldenberg, R. L., 63
Goldman, S. R., 222
Goldsmith, H. H., 89, 168
Goldsmith, L. T., 219
Goldstein, D., 219
Goldstein, E., 410
Goleman, D., 334
Golombok, S., 299
Gomez, R., 224
Goncu, A., 143
Good, T. L., 228, 229, 230
Goodkin, K., 602
Goodman, G. S., 246, 248,
    250, 252
Goodnow, J. J., 240
Goodrick, G. K., 281
Goodstein, L., 303
Goosens, L., 506
Gordon, C., 302, 435, 437
Gordon, S. L., 369, 381
Gotlib, I. H., 307, 308
Gottfried, A. W., 216
Gottlieb, B. H., 430
Gottlieb, L. N., 244
Gottman, J. M., 179, 244, 381,
    549

Goubet, N., 132
Gould, R. L., 465
Gouze, M., 462
Graber, J. A., 280
Grady, J. G., 509
Graff, J., 381
Grajewski, B. A., 66
Grant, L., 557
Gray, C., 216
Gray, J. H., 540, 542, 543
Green, K. E., 286
Green, P. S., 448, 520
Greenberg, B. S., 265
Greenberg, M. T., 75, 387
Greenblatt, J. C., 330
Greene, S., 89
Greene, V. L., 558
Greenhaus, J. H., 418
Greenough, W. T., 96
Greer, J., 548
Gregg, V. R., 350
Greve, W., 357
Grice, H. P., 153
Gridley, K. E., 448, 520
Griffin, L. W., 560
Groisser, D. B., 97, 223
Groome, L. J., 61
Growing, M. K., 412
Gruber, J. E., 63
Grunau, R. V. E., 107
Grusec, J. E., 185
Guacci, N., 547
Guelzow, M. G., 434
Guile, C. A., 281
Guilford, J. P., 219
Gulko, J., 187, 189
Gunnar, M., 168
Gunter, B. G., 432
Gunter, N. C., 432
Guralnick, J. M., 555, 556
Gurtner, J., 228, 229
Gurucharri, C., 271
Gutai, J. P., 451
Gutek, B. A., 435
Gutmann, D. L., 464
Guttmacher, A. F., 63
Gutz, E. R., 329

Haan, N., 512, 564
Haas, L., 431
Hadjistavropoulos, H. D., 107
Haff, M., 550
Hagestad, G. O., 353, 395, 396
Hahn, W., 96
Haight, B. K., 535
Hakim-Larson, J., 341
Hall, D. G., 150

Hall, D. R., 377
Hall, G. S., 289
Hall, N. W., 251
Hallinan, M. T., 255
Halperin, W. E., 66
Halpern, D. F., 188, 212, 214,
    216
Halpern, J., 472
Halpern, L. F., 88
Halverson, C. F., 191
Ham, M., 307
Hamer, D. H., 300
Hamill, S. B., 467
Hamilton, J., 559, 600
Hamlet, S., 420
Hammersmith, S. K., 299
Hammond, M. A., 216
Hamon, R. R., 473
Hamond, N. R., 137
Handfield-Jones, R., 472
Hanis, C., 281
Hansen, D. J., 252
Hansson, K., 377
Happersett, C. J., 542
Hareven, T. K., 467, 472
Harkins, S. W., 499
Harman, C., 168
Harmer, S., 116
Harmon, L. W., 406
Harold, G. T., 248
Harringer, C., 324
Harris, J. A., 63
Harris, J. D., 242, 243
Harris, L. B., 597
Harris, L. J., 102
Harris, M. B., 379
Harris, P. L., 116, 178
Harrison, J., 292
Harrist, A. W., 259
Hart, D., 116, 325
Hart, H., 463
Harter, S., 284, 287
Hartin, A., 75
Hartka, E., 465, 512
Hartup, W. W., 177, 180, 181,
    255
Harwood, R. L., 241
Hatch, L. R., 548
Haugaard, J. J., 246, 248, 250,
    252
Havighurst, R. J., 425
Hayden, M., 341
Hayes, C. D., 187
Hayflick, L., 491, 494, 495
Haynes, O. M., 176, 180
Hayslip, F., 436
Hayward, M. D., 542

Hazan, C., 369
Health Care Financing Administration, 565
Healy, L., 229
Hearold, S., 266
Hedges, L. V., 188
Heesacker, R. S., 416
Heffernan, K., 282
Heidrich, S. M., 455
Heilbrun, G., 463
Heimann, B., 409
Hein, K., 302
Helson, R., 471, 512
Hemesath, K., 382
Henderson, C., 111
Henderson, K. A., 436
Henderson, V. W., 448, 517, 520
Hendler, J., 89
Hendricks, J., 437
Hennon, C. B., 394
Henrietta, J. C., 540, 542
Henshaw, S. K., 301
Herbert, T. B., 452
Herrera, C., 176, 252
Herrera, M. G., 94
Herrling, S., 301
Herrnstein, R. J., 214
Hershberger, S. L., 300
Hertz, R., 430
Hertzog, C., 507
Herzog, A. R., 544
Hetherington, E. M., 247, 248, 249
Hetherington, S. E., 74
Hiatt, S., 111
Hickey, P. R., 107
Hickson, F., 271
Hier, C. M., 509
Higby, H. R., 555
Higgins, D. A., 188
Hill, Anita, 422
Hill, C. D., 593
Hill, E. J., 298, 300
Himsel, A. J., 463
Hinshaw, S. P., 242
Hirsch, B. J., 255
Hirshberg, L. M., 176
Hiruma, N., 175
Hobart, C., 397
Hofer, S. M., 340
Hoff-Ginsberg, E., 148
Hoffman, L. W., 255
Hoffman, M. L., 184, 240
Hogan, D. P., 323
Hogan, N., 582, 583
Hogge, W. A., 67

Hohlhepp, K. A., 381
Holden, G. W., 87
Holland, J. L., 295, 296, 406
Holland, S. B., 61
Hollander, M., 152
Holliday, J., 452
Holmes, E. P., 413
Holstein, M., 577, 589
Holyroad, K. A., 451
Hops, H., 306
Horn, J. L., 336, 339, 340
Horning, R. W., 450
Hornung, R. W., 66
Horvath, J. A., 212, 215
Horwitz, R., 561, 562
Howard, A., 405, 411, 437
Howard, J., 543, 544
Howard, K. I., 290
Howard, M., 302, 303
Howe, M. L., 137
Howe, N., 179
Howes, C., 177, 178
Howland, J., 499
Hoy, E. A., 75
Hoyer, W. J., 457
Hoyles, C., 229
Hoyt, M. F., 599
Hsieh, K., 89
Hu, N., 300
Hu, S., 300
Hudson, J., 137
Hudson, R. B., 565
Huesmann, L. R., 263
Hultsch, D. F., 507, 510, 511
Humphrey, H., 66, 67
Hunsberger, B., 348
Hurrell, J., 450
Hurrell, R. M., 303
Hurst, L., 561, 562
Hurt, L., 421
Huston, A. C., 151, 261, 263, 265, 266, 267
Huttenlocher, P. R., 96
Hutz, C., 422
Huyck, M. H., 366, 464
Hyde, J. S., 188, 300
Hymel, S., 259

Ibrahim, J., 74
Ihinger-Tallman, M., 389
Ikeda, H., 416
Illston, L. H., 565
Indelicato, S., 387
Inder, P. M., 179
Ingraham, M., 545
Inhelder, B., 129, 205
Isabella, R. A., 164

Isacson, A., 550
Ishler, K., 450, 538
Iskra, G. I., 413
Israel, A. C., 174, 223, 252, 281
Ivancevich, J. M., 428, 451
Ivy, D. K., 420
Izard, C. E., 172, 173, 176

Jacklin, C. N., 188, 189
Jackson, B., 447
Jackson, J. S., 542, 544
Jackson, Janet, 200–201
Jacobs, J. E., 190
Jacobs, S., 583
Jacobson, J., 66, 67
Jacobson, S., 66, 67
Jaime, A., 539
Jakobsen, R., 300
James, L. R., 410
James, W., 534
Jamison, R. L., 431
Janke, H. C., 455
Janssens, J. M., 260
Jason, L. A., 306
Jenkings, L., 226, 227
Jenkins, C. L., 430
Jennings, J. M., 505
Jensen, J. L., 100
Jensen, M. D., 63
Jernigan, L. P., 286
Jette, A., 499
Jewell, L., 307
Ji, G., 246
Jiao, S., 246
Jing, Q., 246
Jogerst, G., 498
Johanson, R. B., 74
John, D., 432
Johnson, C., 447
Johnson, C. L., 476, 557
Johnson, D. L., 216
Johnson, E., 377
Johnson, J., 388
Johnson, K. E., 152
Johnson, M. H., 132
Johnson, R. L., 557
Johnson-Laird, P. N., 505
Johnston, J. A., 386
Johnston, L. D., 306
Johnstone, B., 258
Jones, A. P., 410
Jones, C. H., 208
Jones, C. J., 462
Jones, D. C., 176, 184, 245
Jones, F. L., 391
Jones, L. Y., 405

Jordan, A. E., 307
Joseph, G., 193, 390
Judge, K. S., 522
Jung, C. G., 464, 534
Jung, P. C., 147
Jungeblut, A., 226, 227
Juscyk, P. W., 108, 146

Kagan, J., 26, 89
Kahana, E., 558
Kahlbaugh, P. E., 343
Kahn, R. L., 544
Kaijura, H., 107
Kail, R. V., 138, 208, 503, 504, 505
Kaiser, I. H., 63
Kalakoski, V., 284
Kalil, K. M., 63
Kalish, K., 507, 515
Kalish, R. A., 574, 575, 584, 586, 590, 591
Kamerman, S. B., 76
Kandel, D. B., 255
Kanekar, S., 416
Kanter, R. M., 407
Kantrowitz, B., 310
Kaplan, G. A., 555
Kaplan, P. S., 147
Karau, S. J., 188
Karniol, R., 101
Karraker, K. H., 187
Kaslow, F. W., 377
Kastenbaum, R., 574, 575, 582, 583, 584, 586, 589, 590, 591
Katz, L. F., 244
Katz, S., 556
Kausler, D. H., 506
Kavenaugh, R. D., 178
Kawakami, K., 89
Kazdin, A. E., 308
Keane, S. P., 260
Kearns, D., 227
Keefe, K., 255
Kefauver, Estes, 262
Kegan, R., 356
Keith, B., 247, 248
Keller, H., 149
Keller, J. W., 583
Kelley, M. L., 243
Kelloway, E. K., 293, 430
Kelly, J. B., 393
Kelly, J. R., 438
Kelsey, S., 448
Kemper, T., 93
Kendig, H. L., 550
Kendrick, C., 245

Kennedy, G. E., 475
Kennedy-Moore, E., 452
Kenney, R. A., 445
Kenrick, D. T., 192
Kenyon, B., 112
Kerns, K. A., 167
Kerr, M., 258
Kestenbaum, R., 168
Kevorkian, Jack, 577
Keyserlingk, E., 476
Kiecolt-Glaser, J. K., 452
Kiernan, K. E., 248
Kim, C. C., 140
Kimball, M. M., 188, 264
Kimmerle, M., 101
Kimmerle, N. L., 173
King, P. M., 324, 325, 342
King, V., 285
Kingson, E. R., 541
Kingston, P. W., 434
Kinney, J. M., 450, 538, 550, 551
Kinsbourne, M., 96
Kirasic, K. C., 506
Kiritsy, M. C., 223
Kirsch, I. S., 226, 227
Kisilevsky, B. S., 61
Kitchener, K. S., 324, 325, 342
Kitson, G. L., 394
Kittrell, D., 410
Kivett, V. R., 475
Kivnick, H. Q., 474, 475, 534
Klaczynski, P. A., 207
Klapper, J. T., 263
Klass, D., 575, 599
Klebanov, P. K., 214
Klein, N. K., 93
Klepa, L., 435
Klepac, L., 167
Klerman, L. V., 63
Kline, D. W., 499
Kline, E., 408, 409, 465
Kline, R. B., 306
Klock, R., 395, 396
Klohnen, E. C., 463, 466
Kloss, J., 102
Knapp, M. L., 383
Knight, B. G., 473
Knight, G. P., 188
Knowles, M., 459
Kobak, R., 369
Koball, E. H., 434
Koblinsky, S. A., 475
Kochenderfer, B. J., 255
Koenig, H. G., 538
Koff, T. H., 589
Kogan, N., 219

Kohlberg, L., 190, 345, 346, 348
Kok, F. J., 332
Kolata, G., 71, 333, 447
Kolb, B., 95
Koller, S. H., 182
Kolsawalla, M. B., 416
Kolstad, A., 226, 227
Korabik, K., 417
Korbin, J. E., 251
Kornhaber, A., 475
Koskela, K., 428
Kostelny, K., 251
Kovacs, D. M., 255
Kowalski, R. M., 303
Kram, K. E., 409, 410
Kramer, D. A., 341, 342, 343, 456, 511, 512
Kramer, L., 244
Kratochwill, T. R., 239
Krause, N., 452, 538
Krebs, D., 271, 350
Krevans, J., 185
Krieshok, T. S., 418
Kriska, A., 451
Krispin, O., 259
Kroger, J., 286
Kroonenberg, P. M., 166
Krout, J. A., 471
Kuban, D. A., 449
Kübler-Ross, E., 586, 587
Kuczynski, L., 251
Kuhl, P. K., 146
Kuller, L., 448
Kumka, D., 356
Kunkel, D., 265
Kuperminc, G. P., 301
Kupp, K., 292
Kurdek, L. A., 381, 393
Kurtz, D. A., 288
Kurz, D., 394
Kushner, J. H., 593
Kymissis, E., 148

La Vecchia, C., 66
Labouvie-Vief, G., 341, 343, 454
Lacerenza, L., 222
Lachman, M. E., 357, 499
Lachs, M. S., 561, 562
LaCroix, A. Z., 329
Ladd, G. W., 180, 255, 260
LaFreniere, P. J., 244
LaGrandeur, R. M., 63
LaGreca, A. M., 260
Lajer, M., 428
Lamb, M. E., 165, 259

Lamborn, S. D., 242, 243, 256
Lamison-White, L., 563
Lampman, C., 387
Landis, P. K., 497
Lang, J., 329
Lang, S., 168
Langer, E. J., 533, 559
Langlois, J. H., 190
Lankau, M. J., 410
LaRossa, R., 387
Larson, R., 244, 290, 307, 437
Lasker, J., 599
Latack, J. C., 412
Lauer, J., 380
Lauer, R., 380
Lauman, E. O., 447
Laursen, B., 290
Lautenschlager, G., 504, 505
Lawton, M. P., 24, 438, 531, 532, 535
Lay, K., 166
Lazarus, R. S., 450
Le Sieur, K. D., 180, 260
Leahy, J. M., 602
Leana, C. R., 428
Lears, M., 264
Lee, G. R., 393, 549
Lee, S., 226
Lee, T. R., 549
Lee, V. E., 248
Lee, Y. H., 469
Leech, S., 306
Leeds, B., 602
Lei, T., 349, 351
Leicht, M. L., 498, 501
Leichtman, M. D., 138
Leirer, V. O., 509
LeMare, L. J., 205, 271
Lemke, J. H., 437
Lenhardt, M. L., 499
Leon, G. R., 462
Lepper, M. R., 228, 229
Lester, B. M., 74, 86
Lester, D., 391
Levenson, M. R., 544
Levenson, R. W., 381, 549
Levin, J. R., 208
Levin, J. S., 538
Levine, C., 342, 343
Levine, L. E., 115, 116
Levinger, D., 365
Levinson, D. J., 408, 409, 465
Levinson, J. D., 408, 409, 465
Levinson, M., 408, 409, 465
Levitt, A. G., 148
Levitt, M. J., 547
Levy, G. D., 187, 190

Levy, J., 102
Lewinsohn, P. M., 307, 308, 516
Lewis, K. G., 376
Lewis, M., 89, 115, 174, 175
Lewis, R. A., 468
Li, Z., 259
Liben, L. S., 192
Lichtenstein, E., 329
Lichtman, R., 447, 448
Lieberman, M., 348, 393
Liebert, R. M., 181, 265, 266
Liebowitz, M., 374
Lieven, E. V. M., 151
Limber, S., 174
Lin, C. C., 241
Lin, L., 246
Lin, L.-W., 468
Lin, S., 248, 396
Lindgren, S. D., 223
Lindlaw, S., 449
Lindros, E., 327
Linn, M. C., 188
Linton, J., 107
Liss, M. B., 187
List, N. D., 501
Little, J. K., 191
Livesley, W. J., 268
Loehlin, J. C., 212, 214, 216
Logan, J., 470
Logan, R. D., 17
Lohr, M. J., 256, 257
Lomranz, J., 438
Long, R. G., 506
Lopata, H. Z., 601, 602
Loren, F. O., 383
Lorenz, G., 333
Loughlin, G. M., 88
Louis-Guerin, C., 427
Lourenco, O. M., 180
Lovett, M. W., 222
Lovett, S. B., 208
Low, J. A., 61
Lowenthal, M., 382
Löwik, M. R. H., 332
Lozoff, B., 93
Lubach, G. R., 63, 69
Luchini, L., 66
Luchins, D., 413
Ludemann, P. M., 176
Luk, V., 431, 433
Lund, D. A., 601
Lundblad, A., 377
Lundin, T., 595
Luo, T. Y., 420
Luthar, S. S., 219
Lütkenhaus, P., 115

Lyall, W. A. L., 553
Lykken, D. T., 216
Lyle, J., 262
Lynch, M. F., 492
Lynch, M. P., 147
Lyness, K. S., 415, 419
Lyon, G. R., 222
Lyons-Ruth, K., 167
Lytton, H., 189

Maccoby, E. E., 179, 188, 189, 248, 249, 394
MacDermid, S. M., 463
MacDonald, P. C., 71
MacKinnon-Lewis, C., 259
Macklin, E. D., 377
MacLean, W. E., 88
Madaus, J. W., 325
Madden, C., 594
Magley, V. J., 420, 421
Magnuson, V. L., 300
Maguire, M., 176
Maier, S. F., 307
Main, M., 166, 369
Makhijani, M. G., 188
Makin, J. W., 107
Maldonado, R. E., 288
Malinak, D. P., 599
Malinosky-Rummell, R., 252
Malone, J., 373, 374
Mancini, J. A., 549
Mandel, D. R., 108
Mange, A. P., 51
Mange, E. J., 51
Mangelsdorf, S., 168, 174
Manuel, M., 93
Marcia, J. E., 284, 285, 286, 326
Marciano, T. D., 390
Marcoen, A., 506
Marcovit, H., 207
Marcus, G. F., 152
Marek, T., 413
Margolin, L., 382
Mark, M., 153
Markides, K. S., 515
Markley, R. J., 341
Markman, E. M., 154
Markman, H. J., 381, 382
Markow, D. B., 150
Marks, J. S., 328
Markus, H., 354, 355, 535
Markusen, E., 602
Marquis, K. S., 389
Marriot, C., 116
Marsh, H. W., 293
Marshall, E., 72

Marsiglio, W., 299
Martin, C. L., 191, 192
Martin, J. A., 75, 301
Martorell, R., 279
Maruna, S., 463
Marzolf, D., 174
Mas, C. H., 311
Masheter, C., 393, 394, 395
Masi, L., 446
Masloff, Sophie, 170
Massagli, M. P., 540, 541
Masten, A. S., 259
Masterpasqua, F., 193, 390
Matheson, C. C., 178
Mathews, T. J., 75, 301
Matsui, T., 416
Mattern, J. M., 522
Matteson, M. T., 451
Matthews, A. M., 382, 543
Matthews, K., 448
Matthews, M. R., 433
Matthews, R., 382
Matthews, S. H., 547, 552, 553
Maurer, C., 106
Maurer, D., 102, 106, 110
Maxwell, J. W., 549
Mayeaux, E. J., 447
Mayer, E. V., 310
Mayo Clinic, 447, 449
Mayseless, O., 168
Mazeh, T., 411, 425
McAdams, D. P., 462, 463
McBride-Chang, C., 252
McCabe, J. B., 302, 303
McCall, R. B., 91
McCartney, K., 54
McClaran, J., 472
McClelland, J. L., 132
McClenahan, E. L., 257
McClish, D. K., 93
McCloskey, L. A., 179
McClure, B. G., 75
McCollum, S. L., 421, 422
McCord, C., 333
McCormick, C. M., 102
McCrae, R. R., 406, 461, 462
McCrae, S., 377
McCubbin, H., 381
McCullough, J. L., 432
McDonald, H. J., 331, 332
McElroy, J. C., 411
McEwen, B. S., 450
McFadden, S. H., 538
McGee, P. E., 204, 205
McGee, R., 223
McGilly, K., 208

McGivern, J. E., 208
McGue, M., 216
McGuffin, P., 50
McGuire, J. M., 325
McGuire, L. C., 508, 519
McGuire, S. A., 189
McHale, S. M., 189, 245
McKee, B., 409, 465
McKitrick, L. A., 508, 520
McLanahan, S., 381
McManus, I. C., 102
McNally, S., 242, 243
McShane, J., 222
Meck, E., 139
Meenaghan, E. G., 393
Mehta, K. K., 538
Meilahn, E., 448
Mekos, D., 249
Mellon, A. F., 102
Melnick, S., 242
Meltzoff, A. N., 52
Menard, W. E., 509
Mendelbaum, K., 307
Mendelson, M. J., 244
Mendlewicz, J., 307
Mendoza, F., 279
Mennella, J. A., 107
Mennen, K., 421
Meredith, W., 462
Merriman, W. E., 150
Mertz, M. E., 553, 554
Mervielde, I., 281
Mervis, C. B., 152
Metropolitan Area Agency on Aging, 430
Meulmeester, J. F., 332
Meyer, D. R., 246
Meyer, S., 373
Meyer, S. M., 475
Meyer-Bahlberg, H. F. L., 300
Meyers, R., 69
Michael, R. T., 447
Michel, G. F., 101
Mick, L. A., 101
Mikach, S., 193, 390
Mikkelson, C., 593
Milford, M., 324, 430
Milich, R., 224
Miller, B. C., 298, 300
Miller, J. G., 350
Miller, K. F., 140
Miller, L. S., 263
Miller, N., 188
Miller, P. A., 183, 185
Miller, R. B., 382
Miller, S. S., 475
Miller, T. Q., 306, 515

Mills, R. S. L., 185
Mills, T. L., 554
Milsap, R., 465, 512
Minichiello, V., 594
Minkler, M., 476, 552
Mischel, W., 189
Mistry, J., 143
Mitchell, M. C., 331
Mitchell, S., 216
Miura, I. T., 140
Miyake, K., 89
Mize, J., 180, 260
Mizes, J. S., 282
Mizuta, I., 175
Mnookin, R. H., 248, 249, 394
Moane, G., 471
Moats, L. C., 222
Mobily, K. E., 436
Mobley, L. A., 244
Moen, P. J., 472
Moeykens, B., 330
Moffitt, T. E., 280, 309
Molfese, D. L., 96
Molgaard, C. A., 542
Mollnow, E., 67
Monahan, D. J., 558
Monczunski, J., 495
Monker, J., 151
Moon, A., 560
Moon, S., 376
Moon, W., 327
Moore, B. S., 184
Moore, D. W., 559, 561
Moore, K. L., 52, 63
Moorman, J. E., 383
Mora, J. O., 94
Moran, G., 168
Morgan, B., 94
Morgan, J. N., 544
Morgan, S. P., 301
Morgane, P. J., 93
Morioka, K., 471
Morison, R., 259
Morland, K., 63
Morrell, C. H., 497
Morrell, R. W., 509
Morris, J. N., 472
Morrison, A. M., 419
Morrison, D. R., 248
Morrongiello, B. A., 108
Morrow, D. G., 509
Morrow, J., 514, 515
Morrow, P. C., 411
Mortimer, J. T., 292, 356
Morton, D. J., 542
Moshman, D., 207

Mosier, C., 143
Moss, M. S., 438, 601
Moss, S. Z., 601
Mount, M. K., 431
Mounts, N. S., 242, 256, 258
Mroczek, D. K., 544
Muehlenhard, C. L., 303
Mullan, J. T., 472
Mumme, D. L., 176
Munakata, Y., 132
Murphy, C., 499
Murphy, S., 602
Murray, B., 421
Murray, C., 214
Murray, W. E., 66
Murrell, A. J., 418
Murrell, S. A., 593, 595, 596
Murstein, B. I., 368
Mutchler, J. E., 540, 541
Muzio, J. N., 88
Muzzonigro, P. G., 299
Myers, J. F., 472
Myles, J. F., 562

Nachmias, M., 90
Nachtigall, L. B., 329
Nachtigall, L. E., 329
Nadel, L., 64
Naegele, G., 423
Nahemow, L., 24, 532
Naito, M., 117
Nam, S., 547
Namazi, K. H., 538
Napoli, A., 452
Narasimham, G., 207
Nathanson, C. A., 333
National Academy on Aging,
    557
National Aging Information
    Center, 556
National Center on Child
    Abuse and Neglect, 250
National Center for
    Educational Statistics,
    324
National Center on Elder
    Abuse, 560, 561, 562
National Center for Health
    Statistics, 302, 308, 329,
    492, 497, 590
National Institute of Child
    Health and Human
    Development Early
    Child Care Research
    Network, 169–170
National Research Council,
    93, 302

Nawrocki, T., 97
Nazareth, T., 416
Neale, J. M., 452
Neergaard, L., 498
Neisser, U., 212, 214, 216, 353
Nelson, B., 382
Nelson, C. A., 176
Nelson, E. C., 93
Nelson, K., 149, 153
Neugarten, B. L., 353, 474,
    583
Newberry, J., 499
Newcomb, A. F., 181, 254,
    259
Newman, B. S., 299
Newman, L. S., 191
Newport, E. L., 147
Newton, P. M., 465
Nichols-Whitehead, P., 144
Nickman, S. L., 581, 582
Nielson, A. C., 261
Nigg, J. T., 242
Niskanen, L., 428
Nocera, R., 518, 550
Nock, S. L., 393, 434
Nolen-Hoeksema, S., 307
Noll, J. P., 516, 517
Nord, C. W., 395
Norlander, K. A., 325
Normand, C. L., 581
Norris, F. N., 593, 595, 596
Norris, L., 456
Norton, A. J., 383
Norton, M. C., 298, 300
Notarius, C. I., 383
Nowell, A., 188
Noworol, C., 413
Nugent, J. K., 74, 86
Nurius, P., 354, 535
Nurmi, J., 284
Nwokah, E., 164
Nyberg, B., 288
Nydegger, C. N., 468

Oberklaid, F., 188
O'Brien, P. M. S., 74
O'Brien, S., 561, 562
Ochs, A. L., 499
O'Connor, B. P., 559
O'Connor, Sandra Day, 419
Odink, J., 332
Offer, D., 290
Offermann, L. R., 412
Ogletree, R. J., 303
O'Hanlon, A. M., 508
Ohlendorf-Moffat, P., 71
Ohnishi, R., 416

Okagaki, L., 240
Okamoto, Y., 140
Okonski, B., 599
Okun, M. A., 462
Olds, S. W., 558
O'Leary, K. D., 371, 372, 373,
    374
Olian, J. D., 410
Oliver, M. B., 300
Ollendick, T. H., 246
Oller, D. K., 147, 148
Olsho, L. W., 108
Olson, D. H., 381
O'Malley, P. M., 306
Oppenheim, D., 165
Opplinger, R. A., 438
O'Rand, A. M., 542
O'Reilly, A. W., 180
Orlick, T., 181
Ormerod, A. J., 421, 422
Orwoll, L., 512
Osborne, L. N., 248
Osgood, N. J., 552
Ostrov, E., 290
Otten, M. W., 328
Overton, W. F., 207
Owen, G., 602
Owen, M. J., 50
Owsley, C., 111, 504, 505

Pacifice, C., 144
Pacy, B., 312
Padgett, R. J., 153
Padgham, J. J., 299
Pagani, L., 258
Page-Adams, D., 428
Painter, K. M., 180
Palkovitz, R., 387
Pallack, M. S., 589
Palmer, D. J., 245
Palmer, J. R., 329
Palmer, K. M., 454
Pancer, S. M., 348
Papalia, D. E., 558
Parasuraman, S., 418
Parazzini, F., 66
Pargament, K. I., 450, 538
Paris, F. A., 176
Park, D. C., 504, 505, 509
Parke, R. D., 165, 180, 181,
    238, 240, 242, 243, 247
Parker, E. B., 262
Parker, J. G., 252, 255, 256,
    257, 259
Parker, R. A., 464
Parkes, C. M., 552, 593
Parkin, L., 117

Parrot, A., 390
Parrott, T. M., 554
Parten, M., 178
Partington, J., 181
Pascual-Leone, J., 348, 512
Pasley, K., 389
Patel, N., 241
Pattatucci, A. M., 300
Patterson, C. J., 193, 299
Patterson, E. M., 326
Patterson, G. R., 239, 249, 310
Patterson, V., 599
Pattison, E. M., 583, 587, 588
Pavalko, E. K., 472, 473, 540
Pearce, K. A., 454, 455
Pearlin, L. I., 388, 472
Pearson, J. C., 544, 545, 549,
    552, 553
Pearson, J. D., 497
Pearson, T. A., 391, 392
Peddecord, K. M., 542
Pederson, D. R., 168
Pederson, F. A., 387
Pelham, W. E., 224
Penn, G. M., 452
Pennington, B. F., 97, 223
Peplau, L., 369, 379, 381
Perkins, H. W., 597
Perlmutter, M., 144, 509, 512
Perloff, R., 212, 214, 216
Perner, J., 117
Perris, E., 108
Perry, T. B., 254
Perry, W. I., 324, 341
Persaud, T. V. N., 52, 63
Peters, A. M., 152
Petersen, A. C., 282
Peterson, B. E., 463
Peterson, C., 307
Peterson, E. W., 499
Peterson, J., 601
Peterson, L., 184
Pethick, S. J., 148, 149
Petraitis, J., 306
Petrakos, H., 179
Petrus, J. J., 332
Pettit, G. S., 180, 239, 257,
    259, 260
Pfost, K. S., 416
Phelps, J. A., 50
Phelps, M. E., 97
Philliber, S., 301
Phillis, D. E., 388
Phinney, J. S., 287, 288
Piaget, J., 15, 20, 126, 129, 205
Pickens, J., 97, 112
Picot, S. J., 539

Pienta, A. M., 540, 541
Pierce, C. A., 422
Pierce, K., 430
Pilgrim, C., 258
Pillemer, K. A., 559, 560, 561, 562
Pillow, B. H., 208
Pincus, T., 333
Pine, J. M., 149, 151
Pinker, S., 152
Pioli, L., 137
Piotrkowski, C., 420, 421, 583
Pisoni, D. B., 108
Pittenger, K. K. S., 409
Plewis, I., 86, 88
Plomin, R., 22, 50, 55, 89, 91, 216, 224
Plude, D. J., 503
Plumert, J. M., 144
Polit, D., 435
Polit, E. F., 246
Pomeroy, E. C., 593
Ponder, R. J., 593
Poole, M. E., 284
Porter, R. H., 107
Posada, G., 166
Post, F., 331
Poulin-Dubois, D., 112
Poulos, R. W., 181
Poulson, C. L., 148
Powell, M. B., 137
Power, T. G., 241, 243
Powers, S. W., 239
Powlishta, K. K., 179, 187, 189, 272
Pozzi, S., 229
Pratt, A., 348
Pratt, M. W., 348
Pressley, M., 208, 209
Prevor, M. B., 51
Prigot, J., 137
Prior, M., 188
Prochaska, J. O., 329
Pryor, J. B., 422
Putnam, P. H., 176
Pyngolil, M., 447

Qualls, S. H., 498, 514, 515, 516, 518, 519
Quigley, M. W., 545

Rabiner, D., 259
Radford, A., 151
Radke-Yarrow, M., 182
Raffaelli, M., 307
Ragland, O. R., 451
Ragozin, A. S., 387

Rajakumar, G., 448, 520
Ramey, C. T., 216, 217
Ramey, S. L., 216
Ramsay, D., 89, 111
Ramsey, E., 310
Ramsey, F., 93
Ramsey, P. G., 272
Rao, K. V., 377
Raphael, B., 601
Rapoport, R., 436
Rapoport, R. N., 436
Rapport, M. D., 223, 224
Rast, M., 52
Rathunde, K. R., 219
Rawlins, W. K., 365, 366, 548
Rayias, M. F., 176
Read, S. J., 369
Reagan, Nancy, 549
Reagan, Ronald, 517, 549
Recker, G. T., 586
Redman, C. W. E., 74
Reedy, M. N., 368
Reeve, K. F., 148
Reeve, L., 148
Reich, P. A., 150
Reichard, C. C., 508
Reid, H., 300
Reid, S. M., 221
Reis, S. M., 219
Reiss, D., 249
Rende, R., 224
Renzulli, J. S., 219
Repacholi, B., 167, 176
Resnick, G., 248
Resnick, M. I., 449
Resnick, S., 168
Reubens, B., 292
Reyna, V. F., 138
Reynolds, D., 591
Reynolds, S. L., 556
Reznick, J. S., 148, 149
Rhodes, J. E., 306
Rhyne, D., 382
Ricciuti, H. N., 94
Rice, C., 74
Rice, M. L., 151
Rich, C. L., 308
Richards, D. S., 71
Richards, M., 244, 280, 283, 307, 421, 437
Rigby, H., 559
Riggs, D. S., 371
Rightmyer, J., 205
Riley, M. W., 25, 336
Rinaldi, C. M., 179
Riordan, K., 168

Roberto, K. A., 554
Roberts, J. D., 538
Roberts, M. W., 239
Roberts, P., 465
Roberts, R. E., 288
Roberts, W., 182
Robertson, L. S., 187
Robin, A., 306
Robins, P. K., 248
Robinson, J., 472
Robinson, M., 140
Robinson, N. M., 387
Roche, A. F., 279
Rock, S. L., 216
Rodd, Z. A., 397
Rodeheaver, D., 476
Rodgers, J. L., 300
Rodin, J., 533, 559
Roe, K. M., 476
Roffwarg, H. P., 88
Rogers, J., 553
Rogers, K., 293
Rogers, S. J., 383, 392
Rogoff, B., 143
Rogosch, F. A., 250, 251
Romney, D. M., 189
Roodin, P. A., 457
Rooks, J. P., 75
Roopnarine, J., 165
Rosario, M., 300
Roscoe, B., 299
Rose, E., 325
Rose, H., 192
Rose, S. A., 112
Rosen, D., 75
Rosen, T. J., 152
Rosenbaum, A., 373, 374
Rosenberg, E. B., 389
Rosenberg, L., 329
Rosenberg, S. D., 465
Rosenblatt, P. C., 595
Rosenfield, A., 75
Rosengren, K. S., 144
Rosenhan, D. L., 184
Rosenman, R. H., 451
Rosenthal, D. A., 287
Rosin, H. M., 417
Roskies, E., 427
Ross, D., 262
Ross, S. A., 262
Rossi, J. S., 329
Rotenberg, K. J., 310
Roth, W. F., 412
Rothbart, M. K., 89
Rotheram-Borus, M. J., 300
Rotto, P. C., 239

Roughton, E. C., 63, 69
Rounds, J., 296
Rovee-Collier, C., 137
Rowe, D. C., 300
Rowland, C. F., 151
Roxburgh, S., 431
Rubenfeld, M. I., 416
Rubin, K. H., 205, 256, 257, 258, 259, 260, 271
Ruble, D. N., 191
Ruffman, T., 117
Rusch, F. R., 324
Rush, J., 516
Russell, B., 421
Russell, J. A., 176
Russell, M., 433
Rutledge, J. H., 452
Rutter, M., 174
Ryan, E. B., 559
Ryan, N., 327
Rybash, J. M., 457
Rye, S., 292
Ryff, C. D., 355, 469, 536, 537
Rykken, D. E., 447, 449
Ryther, J. S., 147

Sacco, W. P., 308
Saffran, J. R., 147
Sagi, A., 168
Sagy, S., 543
St. James-Roberts, I., 86, 88
Saito, Y., 556
Salomone, P. R., 408
Salthouse, T. A., 37, 503, 504, 505
Salvador, W. A., 244
Salvio, M. A., 500
Sameroff, A. J., 168
Sampson, P. D., 64, 69
Samuelson, L. K., 150
Sanderl, L., 149
Sanders, C. M., 601
Sanderson, L. K., 299
Sanson, A., 188, 224
Santini, D. L., 63
Sapone, F. M., 331, 332
Saunders, C., 589
Saxe, G. B., 7
Scandura, T. A., 410
Scarr, S., 52, 288
Schaffer, D., 63
Schaffer, H. T., 164
Schaffer, W. D., 173
Schaie, K. W., 336, 337, 338, 368, 456, 510
Schairer, C., 447

Schaller, M., 185
Schartz, K. M., 50
Schatz, D. A., 71
Scheibel, A. B., 496
Schein, E. H., 409
Scherman, A., 476
Scherr, P., 329
Schiaffino, K., 473
Schieber, F., 498
Schiedel, D. G., 326
Schiller, M., 168
Schindler, Oskar, 348–349
Schlackman, L. J., 74
Schlegel, A., 323
Schleidt, M., 107
Schmutte, P. S., 469
Schneider, K. T., 421
Schneider, M. L., 63, 69
Schnorr, T. M., 66
Schramm, W., 262
Schubert, D. S. P., 244
Schubert, H. J. P., 244
Schuder, T., 209
Schulenberg, J., 292, 306
Schull, W. J., 281
Schulman, A. D., 553
Schulsinger, F., 281
Schulz, J. H., 565
Schulz, R., 550, 586, 597
Schutter, M. E., 476
Schvaneveldt, P., 298, 300
Schwartz, F., 415, 417, 431
Schwartz, P., 377, 378, 379
Schwartz, R. S., 501
Scott, J., 435, 437
Scott, R. B., 331
Scozzaro, P. P., 416
Searle, S., 435
Sears, P. S., 356
Seccombe, K., 393
See, S. K., 559
Segal, E. S., 501
Segal, N. L., 216
Segall, M., 557
Seidner, L. B., 177
Seifer, R., 52, 168
Seligman, M. E. P., 307
Selman, F. L., 271
Selman, R. L., 269, 270
Seltzer, J. A., 395
Semple, S. J., 472
Sénéchal, M., 151
Serbin, L. A., 112, 187, 189,
    272
Serdula, M. K., 281
Serketich, W. J., 244

Sevy, S., 307
Seymour, J., 329, 331
Shaiko, R. G., 415, 419
Shainess, N., 415
Shanahan, M. J., 292, 293
Shapiro, J. R., 174
Shapiro, S., 329
Shatz, M., 154
Shaver, P., 369
Shaw, B., 516
Shaw, G. M., 63
Shaw, S. F., 325
Sheehy, G., 448
Shehan, C. L., 393
Shell, R., 183, 184
Shelov, S. P., 93
Shelton, B. A., 432
Shema, S. J., 555
Shemway-Cook, A., 100
Sher, T. G., 368
Sherman, M., 308
Sherry, D., 583
Sherwin, B. B., 447, 448
Sherwood, S., 472
Shields, A., 250, 251
Shifren, K., 509
Shin, Y. L., 178
Shipley, M. J., 329
Shirom, A., 411, 425
Shiwach, R., 51
Shmotkin, D., 438
Shneidman, E. S., 587, 588
Shope, J. T., 306
Shotland, R. L., 303
Shullman, S. L., 420, 421
Shuttleworth, C., 416
Shwe, H. I., 154
Siegel, L., 216
Siegler, I. C., 357, 462, 538
Siegler, R. S., 131, 132, 134,
    140, 208
Signorella, M. L., 192
Signorielli, N., 264
Sik, G., 102
Silva, P. A., 89, 280
Silverman, P. R., 581, 582
Silverman, W. K., 281
Simmel, C., 242
Simmons, L. W., 575
Simmons, R., 280
Simon, Theophile, 210, 211
Simons, R. L., 251
Simonsick, E. M., 555
Simonton, D. K., 510, 511,
    512
Simpkins, J. W., 448, 520

Simpson, E. L., 350
Singbeil, C. E., 246
Singer, A., 541
Singh, M., 448, 520
Sinnott, J. D., 341, 342, 343,
    427, 464
Sippola, L. K., 255
Skaff, M. M., 472
Skoglund, R. R., 554
Slaby, R. G., 240
Slate, J. R., 208
Slomkowski, C., 245
Smallish, L., 223
Smart, D., 188
Smith, A. B., 179
Smith, A. D., 504, 505
Smith, C. M., 140
Smith, E. G., 139
Smith, J., 456, 512
Smith, K. R., 552, 553
Smith, L., 563
Smith, L. B., 150
Smith, M., 450
Smith, R. S., 76
Smyer, M. A., 395, 396
Snarey, J. R., 349
Snedeker, B., 292
Snidman, N., 89
Snow, C. W., 109
Snow, M. E., 189
Snyder, C. J., 423
Snyder, L., 149
Sochting, I., 326
Soederberg Miller, L. M., 502,
    503
Soffa, V. M., 448
Solnick, R. L., 449
Sommer, S. M., 433
Sorensen, T. I. A., 281
Soule, W. T., 419
Spector, P. E., 411
Speicher, D. E., 452
Spence, J. T., 240
Spence, M. J., 61
Spetner, N. B., 108
Spier, S. A., 138
Spiro, A., III, 544
Spitze, G., 470
Sporakowski, M. J., 382, 383,
    549
Sporkin, E., 282
Sprafkin, J., 181, 265, 266
Sroufe, L. A., 167, 173
Stalikas, A., 288
Stanford, E. P., 542
Stanovich, K. E., 222

Stapleton, S., 75
Stark, E., 372
Starko, A. J., 220
Staudinger, U. M., 511, 512
Steen, B., 331, 332
Stegink, L. D., 223
Stein, P. J., 388
Stein, A., 137
Steinberg, L., 242, 243, 256,
    258, 280, 289, 292, 293
Steinkamp, M. W., 438
Steinmetz, S. K., 371, 561, 562
Stelmach, G. E., 504
Stenberg, C., 174
Stephens, G. K., 433
Stephens, M. A. P., 471, 473,
    474, 475
Stern, M., 187
Sternberg, K. J., 259
Sternberg, R. J., 212, 213, 214,
    215, 216, 240, 335, 366,
    367, 454
Sterns, H. L., 540, 542, 543
Stevens, A. B., 508
Stevens, N., 255
Stevenson, C. M., 150
Stevenson, H. W., 175, 226,
    228, 229,
    230
Steward, R. J., 418
Stewart, L., 348
Stewart, R. B., 244, 260
Stewman, S., 415, 419
Stice, E., 244
Stifter, C. A., 89
Stigler, J. W., 175, 228, 229,
    230
Stine-Morrow, E. A. L., 502,
    503
Stokes, T. F., 224
Stone, A. A., 452
Stoneman, Z., 245
Stoolmiller, M., 300
Stratton, H. H., 306
Straus, M. A., 371
Strawbridge, W. J., 555
Strayer, J., 182
Streissguth, A. P., 64, 69
Strickland, A. L., 587
Stright, A., 430
Strober, M., 283
Stroebe, M. S., 552, 592, 593
Stroebe, W., 552, 592, 593
Stumbo, P. J., 223
Stunkard, A. J., 281
Su, M., 251

Subich, L. M., 416
Suitor, J. J., 562
Sullivan, H. S., 253
Sullivan, L. W., 49
Sullivan, M. W., 175
Sullivan, S. A., 93
Suls, J., 469
Super, C. M., 94, 103
Super, D. E., 294, 295, 407, 408
Surgeon General, 452
Sussman, M. B., 394
Svejda, M., 111, 176
Swain, S. O., 366
Swan, S., 421
Swaney, K., 296
Swanson, J. L., 415, 416, 432
Swarr, A. E., 280, 283
Sweeker, J., 421
Sweet, J. A., 377
Swenson, C. H., 381
Swiber, M. J., 61
Sykes, D. H., 75
Symanski, E. M., 324

Taber, S., 325
Taffell, S. M., 75
Talaga, J. A., 542
Tamis-Lemonda, C. S., 180
Tang, T. L. P., 421, 422
Tannen, D., 365, 366
Tanner, J. M., 278, 279, 280, 327
Tasker, F., 299
Tate, J. D., 288
Taylor, E. H., 383
Taylor, J., 447
Taylor, J. H., 348
Taylor, M., 179, 187, 190
Taylor, R. J., 538
Teachman, J., 397
Teasdale, T. W., 281
Teitler, J. O., 248
Teixeira, R. A., 255
Tennstedt, S., 499
Terkel, S., 404, 412
Terman, Lewis, 211
Terman, M., 500
Tesch, S. A., 326
Tesch-Römer, C., 499
Teutsch, S. M., 328
Thal, D. J., 148, 149
Thelen, E., 100
Third International Math and Science Study, 225
Thomas, Clarence, 422
Thomas, D. A., 418

Thomas, E., 152
Thomas, G. S., 452
Thomas, J. L., 474, 475, 476
Thomas, N. G., 220
Thompson, D. E., 415, 419
Thompson, E., 377
Thompson, L., 387
Thompson, L. A., 224
Thompson, L. W., 515, 594, 601
Thompson, R. A., 164, 165, 174
Thomson, D. M., 137
Thorne, S., 545
Thun, M. J., 66
Thurnher, M., 382
Tienda, M., 391
Tiffany, D. W., 357
Tiffany, P. G., 357
Tobler, N. S., 306
Toda, S., 164
Toffler, A., 425
Tolson, J. M., 255
Tomasello, M., 154
Tomashoff, C., 282
Tonkiss, J., 93
Toth, S. L., 250, 251
Townsend, A. L., 473
Treiman, R., 209
Tremblay, R. E., 258
Trickett, P. K., 251, 252
Troll, L. E., 46, 464, 468, 545
Tronick, E. Z., 173
Truglio, R., 151
Trujillo, K. M., 453
Tulviste, P., 142
Turner, B. F., 382, 464
Turner, H., 379
Tuttle, R. S., 602
Tyree, A., 373, 374

Uecker, A., 64
Uhlenberg, P., 394, 395, 396
Ullian, D. Z., 190
Ullman, M., 152
Ulrich, B. D., 100
Underwood, B., 184
Unger, O., 177
Uniform Crime Reports for the United States, 309
Updegraff, K. A., 189
Urberg, K. A., 255, 257
Urbina, S., 212, 214, 216
U.S. Bureau of the Census, 169, 323, 328, 376, 377, 379, 391, 490, 565

U.S. Department of Health and Human Services, 328, 450
U.S. Department of Labor, 415, 419, 428, 429, 430, 433
Utman, J. A., 148

Vachon, M. L. S., 553
Vachon, R., 207
Vaillant, G. E., 465
Valdimarsdottir, H., 452
Valencic, K., 522
Valenzuela, M., 94
van den Boom, D. C., 168
Van Haitsma, K., 538
Van Hoose, W. H., 386
van IJzendoorn, M. H., 166, 168
Van Maanen, J., 409
Van Meter, P., 209
Van Rossem, R., 300
Van Tuyl, S. S., 244
Van Velsor, E., 419
Vandell, D. L., 430
VandenBos, G. R., 589
Vandereycken, W., 281
Vandewater, E. A., 466
VanManen, K. W., 354
Vaughan, B. E., 52
Vaughn, B. E., 166
Velie, E. M., 63
Ventura, S. J., 75, 301
Verhaeghen, P., 506
Verma, I. M., 72
Vetrosky, D. T., 332
Vickio, C. J., 594, 595
Viinamaki, H., 428
Villa, R. F., 539
Vinovskis, M. A., 385
Vitaro, F., 258
Vivian, D., 373
Volling, B., 245, 259
Vorhees, C. V., 67
Vosler, N. R., 428
Voyer, D., 188
Voyer, S., 188
Vygotsky, L. S., 141, 144

Wachs, T. D., 54
Wagner, E., 182
Wagner, J., 282
Wagner, N. E., 244
Wagner, R. K., 212, 215, 454
Walbek, N. B., 265
Walberg, H. J., 228, 229, 230
Waldo, C. R., 420, 421

Waldron, H. B., 311
Walk, R. D., 110
Walker, A. J., 387
Walker, L. E. A., 373, 374
Walker, L. J., 348, 350
Wall, S., 538
Wallace, J. I., 501
Wallace, R. B., 329, 556
Wallerstein, J. S., 393
Wallisch, L., 395
Walsh, D. M., 453
Walsh, E. K., 589, 590
Wantz, M. S., 328
Ward, R., 470
Ward, S. L., 207
Wark, G. R., 350
Warren, M. P., 280
Warwick, A., 74
Waters, E., 166, 173
Waters, H. F., 262
Watkins, B. A., 265
Watson, J. A., 475
Watson, John, 15, 19
Wattis, J. P., 329, 331
Waxman, S. R., 150
Weatherby, N. L., 75
Weaver, C. N., 381
Weber, M., 265
Weber, R. A., 547
Wechsler, D., 211, 212
Wechsler, H., 330, 331
Wedel, M., 332
Wegman, M. E., 76, 88
Weibel-Orlando, J., 476
Weinbaum, E., 132
Weinberg, J., 69
Weinberg, M. K., 173
Weinberg, M. S., 299
Weinberg, R., 288
Weinstein, K. K., 474
Weir, J., 149
Weisgerber, K., 416
Weishaus, S., 383
Weisman, A. D., 591
Weisner, T. S., 192
Weiss, R. S., 552, 593
Weldon, B., 446
Wellman, H. M., 116, 117
Wells, Y. D., 550
Welsh, M. C., 97, 223
Wentkowsky, G., 553
Wentzel, K. R., 258
Werker, J. F., 146
Werner, E. E., 76
Werner, H., 100
Wertsch, J. V., 142
Westenbrink, S., 332

Whitall, J., 101
Whitbeck, L. B., 251, 285
Whitbourne, S. K., 325, 327, 352, 354, 356, 376, 405, 445, 464, 495, 496, 499, 549
White, A. T., 411
White, D. R., 272
White, J., 382
White, R. P., 419
Whitfield, M. F., 107
Whithall, S., 116
Whiting, B. B., 188
Whitmer, R. A., 559
Whyte, M. K., 299
Wickrama, G. M., 433
Wicks-Nelson, R., 174, 223, 252
Widkrama, K. A. S., 383
Widmayer, S. M., 154, 387
Wiener, J. M., 565
Wiener, R. L., 421
Wilensky, H. L., 428
Wilk, C., 385
Williams, C., 561, 562
Williams, F. L., 381
Williams, H., 100
Williams, J. E., 187, 464
Williams, K. R., 373
Williams, O. J., 560
Williams, S., 223
Williams, T. M., 263

Williams, W. M., 212, 215
Williamson, D. F., 328
Williamson, G. M., 550
Willinger, M., 88
Willis, S. L., 456, 510
Wills, T. A., 469
Wilson, G. T., 282, 350
Wilson, P. G., 221
Wilson-Mitchell, J. E., 192
Wimbush, D. D., 243
Windle, M., 300, 306
Windle, R. C., 300, 306
Winer, G. A., 132
Wing, R., 448
Wink, P., 512
Winograd, E., 353
Witelson, S. F., 96
Wolf, M. M., 19
Wolf, R. S., 560
Wolfe, D. A., 250
Wolfe, M., 193, 390
Wolfe, R., 514, 515
Wolfson, A. R., 290
Wolfson, C., 472
Wolinsky, F. D., 557
Wolraich, M. L., 223
Wong, J., 102
Wong, P. T. P., 586
Woodbury, M. A., 548
Woodruff-Pak, D. S., 491
Woods, Tiger, 42–43
Woollacott, M. H., 100

Worden, J. W., 582
Worden, W., 592
World Health Organization, 93
Wormley, W. M., 418
Worth, M. R., 387
Wright, D. A., 330
Wright, J., 151
Wright, J. C., 261, 263, 266, 267
Wright, L. K., 550
Wright, P. H., 364
Wu, C., 383
WuDunn, S., 490
Wunsch, J. P., 173
Wykle, M. L., 538, 557
Wynn, K., 139

Xia, Y., 246
Xiaohe, X., 299
Xu, F., 152

Yamagata, H., 415, 419
Yang, B., 246
Yankelovich, D., 405
Yardley, J. K., 431
Yates, M., 285
Yeh, K. S., 415, 419
Ylló, K. A., 372, 373
Yonas, A., 111
Young, A., 466
Young, M. H., 298, 300

Youngblade, J. R., 179
Youngjohn, J. R., 498, 499, 517, 519
Youniss, J., 285

Zahn-Waxler, C., 175, 182
Zaia, A. F., 259
Zappert, L. T., 420
Zarbatany, L., 254
Zarlengo-Strouse, P., 147
Zaslow, M. J., 187
Zelazo, N. A., 104
Zelazo, P. D., 104
Zelazo, P. R., 85, 104
Zezulka, A. V., 329
Zhang, H., 140
Zhao, J. Z., 377
Zhou, Q. Y., 181
Zhu, J., 140
Zick, C. D., 432, 552, 553
Zigler, E., 215, 219, 251, 308
Zimberg, S., 331
Zimiles, H., 248
Zimmerman, J., 415, 417, 431
Zmuda, M., 451
Zoger, S., 593
Zsembik, B. A., 541
Zuckerman, C., 589
Zung, W. W. K., 515
Zupan, B. A., 242
Zwahr, M., 504, 505

SUBJECT INDEX

ABCDE model of friendships, 365
abuse
    child, 250–252
    elder, 560–562
    spousal, 371–374
accidents
    among older adults, 500
    among young adults, 328
accommodation, 125
achievement identity status, 285–286
acquaintance rape, 303–304
acquired immunodeficiency syndrome
    (AIDS), 65, 302, 328
ACTION agency, 545
active euthanasia, 577–578
activities of daily living (ADLs), 456, 555,
    556
activity, of newborns, 86–88, 89
adaptation level, 532
addiction, 331
adolescence, 277–312, 316–317
    age range of, 3
    career development in, 294–297
    delinquency in, 308–311
    depression in, 306–308
    eating disorders in, 281–283
    identity development in, 283–291
    myths about, 289–291
    part-time work in, 292–293
    physical growth in, 278–280
    romantic relationships in, 298–304
    substance abuse in, 305–306
    suicide in, 308
    view of death in, 582–583
adolescent egocentrism, 285
adopted children
    cost of, 386
    identity in transracial, 288–289
    intelligence of, 215, 216, 316
    studies of, 50–51, 389

adult relationships, 363–398
    abusive, 371–374
    divorce and remarriage, 390–397
    family life cycle and, 384–390
    friendships, 364–366
    life-styles and, 375–383
    love, 366–371
adulthood. *See* young adulthood; middle
    adulthood; later adulthood
aerobic exercise, 452–453
African Americans, 11
    health of, and racism, 334
    intelligence testing of, 214–215
    religiosity among, 538–539
    See also culture; ethnicity
age
    dying and, 590–591
    parental, and prenatal development,
    52, 63
    possible selves and, 355
    of viability, 61
age discrimination, 423–424
Age Discrimination in Employment Act
    of 1986, 423
aggression
    in abusive relationships, 371–374
    gender differences in, 188
    See also violence
aging
    biological theories of, 494–495
    demographics of, 488–490
    in middle adulthood, 445–446
    psychosocial, 530–533
    well-being and, 535–537
    See also later adulthood
agreeableness, 461
AIDS, 65, 302, 328
alcohol
    addiction to, 331
    adolescent use of, 305–306

    binge drinking of, 329–330
    prenatal consequences of, 64, 68
Alcoholics Anonymous, 331
alert inactivity, in newborns, 86
alienation, occupational, 412
alleles, 47–48
altruism, 182–186
Alzheimer's disease, 355, 448, 517–522,
    549–550
American Association on Mental Retar-
    dation, 220
American Association of Retired Persons
    (AARP), 545, 564
American Cancer Society, 328,
    491–492
American Heart Association, 332
American Psychiatric Association, 300
American Psychological Association, 300
American Telephone and Telegraph
    (AT&T), occupational priorities
    study by, 405
Americans with Disabilities Act, 324
amniocentesis, 70–71
amnion, 60
amniotic fluid, 60
amyloid, 519
animism, 129
anniversary reaction, 595
anorexia nervosa, 282–283
anoxia, 75
anxiety, death, 585–586
anxiety disorders, 516–517
Apgar score, 86
appearance-reality confusion, 130–132
appraising, 450
Asian Americans, 11
    See also culture; ethnicity
aspirin, prenatal consequences of, 64
assimilation, 125
assortative mating, 368

attachment, 163–171
  with alternative forms of parenting, 388–389
  consequences of, 167–168
  development of, 164
  father-infant, 164–165
  quality of, 168–169
  in adult love relationships, 369, 374
  types of, 165–167
attention-deficit hyperactivity disorder (ADHD), 222–224
attentional processes, 136, 502–503
attentional selectivity, 502–503
authoritarian parenting style, 241, 242–243, 286
authoritative parenting style, 241–243, 286
autonomy, well-being and, 536
autonomy versus shame and doubt stage, 18, 162, 163
autosomes, 47, 52
average children, 258
average life expectancy, 491
avoidant attachment relationships, 166
axons, 94

babbling, 147–148
babies. See infancy; newborns
Babinski reflex, 85
Balanced Budget Act of 1997, 563
Bandura, Albert, social cognitive theory of, 15, 19–20, 189–190, 262
basal metabolic rate, 281
basic cry, of newborns, 87
basic emotions, 172–174
battered woman syndrome, 373
behavior
  altruistic, 182–186
  measuring, 28–31
  prosocial, 182, 265–266
  theory of mind and, 116–118
  Type A and Type B, 451
behavior therapy, 516
behaviorism, 15, 19
beliefs
  about memory, 507
  about personal control, 356–357
  depression and, 515
  See also stereotypes
bereavement, 592, 596–597
  See also grief
bias. See discrimination
Binet, Alfred, 210, 211
binge drinking, 329–330
bioethics, 577
  euthanasia and, 577–580

biological forces, 8, 9–10, 12
  in infancy and early childhood, 198
  in later adulthood, 608
  in school-age children and adolescents, 316
  in young and middle adulthood, 482
biopsychosocial framework, 8–13
  applied to death, 584
Bipartisan Commission on Entitlement and Tax Reform, 563
birth control, 302–303, 447
birth order, 245–246
birth. See childbirth
birth weight, 75–76
blended families, 248–249
blink reflex, 85
bottle-feeding, 93
Bowlby, John, 163–164
brain, 94–97
brain death, 576–577
breast-feeding, 93
Bronfenbrenner, Urie, ecological theory of development of, 15, 23–24
Brown, Louise, 57
bulimia nervosa, 282–283
burnout
  in dual-earner couples, 435
  occupational, 413

caffeine, prenatal consequences of, 64
cancer
  DES-related, 69
  in later adulthood, 501
  nutrition and, 332
  smoking-related, 328
  in young adulthood, 328
cardinality principle, 140
cardiovascular disease, 497–498
  cholesterol and, 332
  estrogen and, 447–448
  stress and, 451
cardiovascular system, aging's effects on, 497–498
career development
  in adolescence, 294–297
  Super's theory of, 294–295, 407–408
  in young and middle adulthood, 407–410, 417–418
  See also occupation; work
career plateauing, 426
caregiving
  for aging parents, 430, 470–474
  attachment and, 168–171
  elder abuse and, 561–562
  spousal, 549–551
  workplace and, 430–431

Carolina Abecedarian project, 216–217
cell bodies, 94
cellular theories of aging, 494–495
centrality, 475
cephalocaudal principle, 60, 92
cerebral cortex, 95
cerebral vascular accidents, 497–498
child abuse, 250–252
child care
  attachment and, 169–171
  employers and, 431
childbirth
  after menopause, 448–449
  approaches to, 73–75
  complications of, 75–76
  cost of, 386
  stages of labor, 73
childhood. See children; early childhood
children
  adopted, 50–51, 215, 216, 288–289, 386, 389
  with attention-deficit hyperactivity disorder (ADHD), 222–224
  cost of raising, 386
  creativity in, 219–220
  death and, 581–582, 599–600
  deciding whether to have, 385–387
  divorce and, 247–248, 394–396
  gifted, 219
  grandparents and, 474–475
  with learning disabilities, 221–222
  malnourished, 93–94
  mentally retarded, 220–221
  relations between middle-aged parents and, 468–470
  school-age, 3, 204–209, 258, 316–317
  See also early childhood; infancy
Children's Television Workshop, 266–267
Chomsky, Noam, 153
chorionic villus sampling, 71
chromosomes, 47
  abnormal, 51–53
  sex, 47, 52–53
chronic obstructive pulmonary disease (COPD), 498
circadian rhythm, 500
climacteric, 447, 448
  See also menopause
clinical death, 576
Clinton, Bill, 422, 499
cliques, 256
cocaine, 64, 69, 305
codominant alleles, 49
cognitive development
  culture and, 134, 141–144

cognitive development (*continued*)
   in middle adulthood, 453–459
   Piaget's stages of, 21, 126
   in school-age children, 204–209
   television's influence on, 266–267
   Vygotsky's ideas on, 141–144
   in young adulthood, 335–344
cognitive development theory, 15, 20–22,
      124–134, 204–207
   basic principles of, 124–126
   concrete operational stage, 21, 126,
      204–205
   formal operational stage, 21, 126,
      205–207
   limits of, 132–134, 207
   preoperational stage, 21, 126,
      129–132, 269
   sensorimotor stage, 21, 126–128, 149
cognitive processes, in later adulthood,
      502–513
cognitive therapy, 516
cohabitation, 376–377
cohort effects, 35
   adult intelligence and, 337–339
colleges
   binge drinking in, 329–331
   demographics of students at, 324–325
   midlife students at, 458–459
color vision, 109–110
commitment, as component of love, 366
communication
   about sexual intent, 303–304
   development of skills for, 153–155
   as element of parental control, 239
comparable worth, 420
competence, 531
   altruism and, 184
   retirement satisfaction and, 543
   of spousal caregivers, 551
competence–environmental press the-
      ory, 15, 24–25, 531–533
complex emotions, 174–175
computers, in schools, 228–229
concrete operational stage, 21, 126,
      204–205
cones, visual, 110
conscientiousness, 461
consumer behavior, television's influence
      on, 264–265
continuity-discontinuity issue, 6–7
continuity theory of psychosocial aging,
      530–531
contraception, 302–303, 447
control
   by parents, 239–241
   personal, 356–357

controversial children, 258
conventional level of moral reasoning,
      347
convergent thinking, 219
cooing, 147
cooperative play, 178–179, 180–182
coping, 450
   with dying, 588
   religiosity/spiritual support for,
      538–539
corpus callosum, 95
correlation coefficients, 32
correlational studies, 31–32, 35
Costa, Paul, Jr., adult personality model
      of, 461–462
counting skills, 139–140
court
   adolescents charged as adults in, 311
   children testifying in, 137–138
covenant marriage, 392–393
creativity
   in adults, 510–511
   in children, 219–220
   versus wisdom, 512
cross-linking, 494–495
cross-sectional studies, 34–35
crowds, 256
crowning, 73
Cruzan, Nancy, 578
crying, by newborns, 86–87
crystallization, 294, 295
crystallized intelligence, 340–341, 456
cultural conservator grandparenting
      style, 475
culture
   cognitive development and, 134,
      141–144
   death and, 574–575
   defined, 10
   handedness and, 102
   heterosexual mate preferences and,
      369–371
   language development and, 146, 153
   moral reasoning and, 350–351
   newborn temperament and, 89
   parenting and, 240–241, 250–251
   play's reflection of, 178, 181–182
   transitions into adulthood and,
      323–324
culture-fair intelligence tests, 214
cytomegalovirus, prenatal consequences
      of, 65

Dalla Corta, Rosanno, 448
date rape, 303–304
dating, adolescent, 298–299

day care. *See* child care
death, 573–603
   brain, 576–577
   causes of, of young adults, 328
   clinical, 576
   dealing with different types of,
      598–603
   defined, 574–577
   expected versus unexpected, 583–594
   sudden infant death syndrome (SIDS),
      88
   views of, throughout life span,
      580–584
   See also dying; grief
death anxiety, 585–586
"Death with Dignity" Act, Oregon,
      577–578
deductive reasoning, 206–207
delinquency, 308–311
dementia, 517
   Alzheimer's disease, 448, 517–522
   pseudodementia, 519
   vascular, 497–498
demographers, 488
dendrites, 94
deoxyribonucleic acid (DNA), 47
dependent variables, 33
depression
   in adolescents, 306–308
   drugs for, 308, 515, 520
   in older adults, 514–516
   spousal death and, 601–602
   as stage in dying, 587
depth perception, 110–111
developmental research, 28–38
   communicating results of, 37–38
   designs for, 31–36
   ethical guidelines for, 36–37
   measurement in, 28–31
developmental theories, 14–27
   cognitive-developmental theories, 15,
      20–23
   defined, 14
   ecological (systems) theories, 15,
      23–25
   learning theories, 15, 18–20
   life-span and life-cycle theories, 15,
      25–26
   psychodynamic theories, 15, 16–18
diethylstilbestrol (DES), 69
differentiation of motions, 100
diffusion identity status, 285–286
disabilities. *See* people with disabilities
discipline
   consistent, 239, 260
   delinquency and, 310

socialization of altruism and, 184–185
See also punishment
discrimination
age, 423–424
sex, 419–420
See also sexual harassment
diseases, prenatal effects of, 65
disorganized (disoriented) attachment relationships, 166
dispositional praise, 185
divergent thinking, 219
divided attention, 503
divorce, 246–248, 391–396
effects on couple, 393–394
family life after, 246–247
grandparenting and, 476
impact on children, 247–248
reasons for, 391–392
relationships with children after, 394–396
risk of, and cohabitation, 377
dizygotic twins, 50, 51
"Do Not Resuscitate" (DNR) medical order, 579–580
docility, 532
domestic violence. *See* abuse
dominance hierarchy, 257
dominant phenotypes, 48, 49
Down syndrome, 51–52, 63, 71, 220, 221
dream formation, as developmental task, 408–409
drinking. *See* alcohol
driving, by older adults, 499, 504–505
drugs
addiction to, 331
adolescent use of, 292–293, 305–306
for Alzheimer's disease, 520
antidepressant, 308, 515, 520
for anxiety disorders, 517
prenatal consequences of, 63–64
See also alcohol
dual-earner couples, 170–171, 432–435
durable power of attorney, 579
dying, 573–603
with dignity, 588–590
euthanasia and, 577–580
life-span developmental perspective on, 590–591
theories of, 586–587
See also death; grief
dysphoria, 514

E-I-E-I-O framework, 508–509, 520
early childhood, 198–200
gender roles and identity in, 186–193
information processing in, 135–140

language development in, 145–155
social interaction in, 177–186
See also children
eating disorders, 281–283
ecological theories, 15, 23–25
ectoderm, 59
education
health and, 333
marital happiness and, 381
See also colleges; schools
ego, 16
ego resilience, 466
egocentrism, 129–130, 269
adolescent, 285
elder abuse, 560–562
electroencephalogram (EEG), 96
Ellison v. Brady, 421
embryo, 59
period of the, 59–60, 68
See also prenatal development
emotionality, of newborn temperament, 89–90
emotions
basic, 172–174
complex, 174–175
integrated with logic, 343–344
recognizing, in others, 175–176
empathy, 182–183
encapsulation, 457
endoderm, 59
environment
genes and, 53–55
impact on life expectancy, 491–492
intelligence and, 215–218
mastery of, 536
nature-nurture issue, 5–6
teratogens in, 65–67
environmental press, 531
epigenetic principle, 17
equilibration, 125–126
Erikson, Erik
psychosocial development stages of, 18, 162–163, 284–285, 325–326, 379–380, 462–463, 534–535
psychosocial theory of, 15, 17–18
estrogen-related symptoms, 447
ethics
in developmental research, 36–37
of euthanasia, 577–580
of in vitro fertilization, 57–58, 448–449
See also moral reasoning
ethnic identity, 287–289, 290–291
ethnicity
caregiving stress and, 473
child care and, 169

grandparenting and, 475–476
health and, 328, 333–334, 492
household labor division and, 432–433
intelligence testing and, 214–215
labels for, 11
literacy levels and, 226
occupational development and, 417–418
older adults and, 489–490, 492, 557, 560
prejudice against, 271–272
religiosity/spiritual support and, 538–539
remarriage and, 396
retirement and, 541, 542–543
singlehood and, 376
teenage pregnancy and, 301
television stereotypes of, 263
unemployment and, 428
ethology, 163
eugenics, 57
European Americans, 11
See also culture; ethnicity
euthanasia, 577–580
exchange theory, 380
exercise, aerobic, 452–453
exosystem, 24
expectations, occupational, 408–409
experience
motor skills and, 102–104
openness to, 406
experimental studies, 33, 35
See also developmental research
expertise, 456–457, 512
explicit memory, 508
expressive style of speech, 149
extended family, 384
external aids to memory, 508
extraversion, 49–50, 461
extremely low birth weight, 75

familial mental retardation, 220
family
after divorce, 246–247
blended, 248–249
delinquency and, 310
extended, 384
nuclear, 384
older adults and, 548–554
work and, 429–435
family life cycle, 384–390
deciding whether to have children, 385–387
stages of, 384–385
family life-cycle theory, 15, 26, 384–385

Family Lifestyles Project, 192
Family and Medical Leave Act, 431
fast mapping, 150
fathers
    divorced, 246, 395, 396
    gender typing by, 189–190
    infants' attachment to, 164–165
    stay-at-home, 171
    See also parents
fertilization, in vitro, 57–58, 386,
    448–449
fetal alcohol syndrome, 64
fetal medicine, 71–72
fetal surgery, 71
fetus
    age of viability of, 61
    period of the, 60–62, 68
fictive grandparenting style, 476
Fields, Debbi, 318–319
filial obligation, 472
fine-motor skills, 99, 101–102
fluid intelligence, 339–341
foreclosure identity status, 285–286
formal operational stage, 21, 126,
    205–207
Foster Grandparents, 545
foster parents, 388, 389
frail older adults, 555–556
fraternal twins, 50, 51
free radicals, 494
free recall test of memory, 506
Freud, Sigmund, 163
    psychoanalytic theory of, 16–17
    psychosexual development stages of,
    17
friendships
    ABCDE model of, 365
    adult, 364–366
    childhood and adolescent, 253–255
    in later adulthood, 544, 547–548
frontal cortex, 95, 96–97

Gardner, Howard, multiple intelligences
    theory of, 212–213
gays
    adolescent sexual orientation of,
    299–300
    couple relationships of, 378–379
    death of partners of, 602
    as parents, 193, 389–390
gender
    adult friendships and, 365–366
    causes of abusive behavior and,
    372–373
    divorce and remarriage and, 392,
    393–394, 395, 396, 397
    health and, 328, 333

household chores and, 432–434, 535
    intellectual and psychosocial charac-
    teristics and, 188–189
    intimacy versus isolation and, 326
    life expectancy and, 492
    love relationship behavior and, 369
    moral reasoning and, 349–350
    occupational selection and, 414–416
    play and, 179–180
    retirement and, 542
    widowhood and, 552–553
gender bias, in workplace, 419–420
gender constancy, 190–191
gender identity, 190–192, 464
gender labeling, 190
gender roles, 186–193, 464
gender stability, 190
gender stereotypes, 187
    about occupations, 415–416
    on television, 263–264
gender-schema theory, 191–192
generativity versus stagnation stage, 18,
    462–463
genes, 47
    Alzheimer's disease and, 519–520
    environment and, 53–55
    inheritance determined by multiple,
    49–50
    inheritance determined by single,
    47–49
    prenatal replacement of, 71–72
    See also heredity
genetic counseling, 69–70, 520
genetic disorders, 51–53, 70–71
genetic engineering, 71–72
genital herpes, prenatal consequences of,
    65
genotypes, 47
    effects of teratogens and, 67–68
    reaction range for, 54
germ disc, 59
gifted children, 219
Ginsburg, Ruth Bader, 419
glass ceiling, 419
Glenn, John, 484–485
Gold, Tracey, 282
grammar, development of, 151–153
grammatical morphemes, 152
grandparents, 474–476, 600
great-grandparents, 553–554
grief, 592–603
    abnormal, 597–598
    with different types of loss,
    598–603
    with expected vs. unexpected death,
    593–594
    of miscarriage, 600

normal, 594–597
    process of, 592–593
    See also death; dying
grief work, 595
groups, peer, 255–258
growth
    of adolescents, 278–280
    of infants, 91–94
    personal, 536
    secular trends in, 279
    See also prenatal development

habituation, 146
handedness, 102
hassles, 450
Head Start program, 216
health
    drinking and, 329–331
    ethnicity and, 333–334
    gender and, 333
    grief's impact on, 597
    in later adulthood, 500–501
    life-style factors in, 328–332
    of newborns, 86
    nutrition and, 331–332, 501
    retirement and, 544
    smoking and, 328–329
    social factors in, 332–333
    stress and, 449–452
    in young adulthood, 328–334
health care
    ethnicity and, 328, 333–334
    life expectancy and, 492
Health Care Financing Administration,
    U.S. Department of Health and
    Human Services, 558
hearing, 108
    integrating sight with, 112–113
    prenatal, 61, 108
    in young adulthood, 327
hemispheres, of brain, 95, 96, 97
heredity
    effects of teratogens and, 67–68
    environment and, 53–55
    handedness and, 102
    height as determined by, 92
    impact on life expectancy, 491
    intelligence and, 215–216
    mechanisms of, 47–51
    nature-nurture issue, 5–6
    studies of twins and adopted children
    and, 50–51
    See also genes
hermorrhages, 497
heroin, prenatal consequences of, 64
heterocyclic antidepressants (HCAs),
    515

heterozygosity, 48
high-density lipoproteins (HDLs), 332
Hill, Anita, 422
Hispanic Americans, 11
    religiosity/spiritual support among,
        539
    See also culture; ethnicity
Holland, John, personality-type theory
    of, 295–297, 406–407
homogamy, 380
homosexuality. *See* gays; lesbians
homozygosity, 48
hope, development of, 163
hormone replacement therapy (HRT),
    447–448, 520
hospices, 588–590
household chores, division of, 432–434,
    545
human development
    biopsychosocial framework for, 8–13
    defined, 1
    recurring issues in, 5–8
    See also developmental theories
human immunodeficiency virus (HIV),
    302
Huntington's disease, 51
hyperactivity. *See* attention-deficit hyper-
    activity disorder (ADHD)

id, 16
identical twins, 50, 51
identity
    ethnic, 287–289, 290–291
    gender, 190–192, 464
    occupation and, 405–406
identity development
    adolescent, 283–291
    in young adulthood, 352–357
identity versus role confusion stage, 18,
    284–285
imaginary audience, 285
imitation, 19–20
immortality through clan, 475
implantation of zygote, 58
implementation, 294, 295
implicit memory, 508
in vitro fertilization, 57–58, 386,
    448–449
incontinence, 518
independent variables, 33
index offenses, 308–309
indifferent-uninvolved parenting style,
    242–243
indulgence, by grandparents, 475
indulgent-permissive parenting style,
    242–243, 386–387
industry versus inferiority stage, 18

infancy, 198–200
    age range of, 3
    growth in, 91–94
    information processing in, 135–140
    language development in, 145–155
    motor skills in, 98–105
    nervous system development in,
        94–97
    nutrition in, 93
    perceptual development in, 106–113
    See also newborns
infant mortality, 76
infant-directed speech, 147
infantilization, 559
information processing
    in infancy and early childhood,
        135–140
    in later adulthood, 502–505
information-processing theory, 15,
    22–23, 135–140
    attention in, 136, 502–503
    general principles of, 135–136
    memory and learning in, 136–138,
        207–209
    quantitative knowledge in, 139–140
initiative versus guilt stage, 18, 162, 163
instrumental activities of daily living
    (IADLs), 556
instrumental orientation, 346
integration of motions, 100
integrity versus despair stage, 18,
    534–535
intelligence
    cohort effects and, 337–339
    crystallized, 340–341, 456
    fluid, 339–341
    heredity and environment and,
        215–218
    practical, 454–456
    theory of multiple, 212–213, 335–336
    training for, in older adults, 509–510
    triarchic theory of, 213, 335
    in young adulthood, 335–341
intelligence quotients (IQs), 211
intelligence testing, 210–211
    culture-fair, 214–215
    reliability and validity of, 211–212
interindividual variability, 336
intermediate care, 557
internal aids to memory, 508
internal belief systems, 515
internal working model, 168
international differences
    in infant mortality, 76
    in life expectancy, 492–493
    in students' academic achievement,
        225–226

interpersonal norms, 347
intimacy
    as component of love, 366
    in friendships, 254, 365-367
    in marriage, 379–380
intimacy versus isolation stage, 18,
    325–326, 379–380
intonation, 147–148
introversion, 49–50
irregular (REM) sleep, 88
irreversibility, 130

Jackson, Janet, 200–201
job satisfaction, 410–413, 425–426
joint custody, 248
Jung, Carl, 465
juvenile delinquency, 308–311

Kaufman Assessment Battery for
    Children (K-ABC), 211
Kefauver, Estes, 262
Keller, Helen, 149
Kevorkian, Jack, 577
kinkeepers, 467
Klinefelter's syndrome, 53
knowledge, quantitative, 139–140
Kohlberg, Lawrence, moral reasoning
    theory of, 15, 22, 191, 346–349
Kübler-Ross, Elisabeth, theory of stages
    of dying of, 586–587

labor, stages of, 73
language development, 145–155
    communicating with others, 153–155
    grammar, 151–153
    speech, 145–151
later adulthood, 487–523, 608–609
    cognitive processes in, 502–513
    creativity and, 510–511
    death conception in, 583–584, 586
    driving in, 504–505
    family in, 548–554
    frailty in, 555–556
    friendships in, 544, 547–548
    health in, 500–501
    living in nursing homes in, 556–559
    marital satisfaction in, 382–383
    mental health in, 513–522
    personality development in, 533–539
    physiological changes in, 495–500
    public policy issues and, 562–566
    retirement in, 540–546
    wisdom and, 511–512
    See also adult relationships; aging
learned helplessness, 307
learning
    in adulthood, 340–341

learning (*continued*)
  information-processing strategies for, 208–209
  lifelong, 457–459
  observational, 19–20
  See also cognitive development; social learning theory
learning disabilities, 221–222
  See also people with disabilities
learning theories, 15, 18–20
leisure activities, 435–438
  consequences of, 437–438
  defined, 435–436
  types of, 436–437
lesbians
  adolescent sexual orientation of, 299–300
  couple relationships of, 378–379
  death of partners of, 602
  as parents, 193, 389–390
life expectancy, 491–493
life review, 534–535
life span, terms for periods of, 3
life stories, 353–354
life-cycle forces, 8, 12–13
life-span constructs, 352–354
life-span perspective, 15, 25–26
  on death, 580–584
  on leisure activities, 437
life-styles
  cohabitation, 376–377
  gay and lesbian couples, 378–379
  health-related factors in, 328–334
  marriage, 379–383
  singlehood, 375–376
lifelong learning, 457–459
lipoproteins
  high-density (HDLs), 332
  low-density (LDLs), 332
listening skills, 154–155
literacy, 226–227
living wills, 579–580
locomotion, 98, 99–101
long-term memory, 208
longevity, 491
longitudinal studies, 34, 35
loss. *See* death
love
  components of, 366
  forms of, 366–367
love relationships. *See* romantic relationships
low-birth-weight newborns, 75–76
low-density lipoproteins (LDLs), 332

McCrae, Robert, adult personalty model of, 461–462

macrosystem, 24
mad cry, of newborns, 87
make-believe play, 178–179
malnutrition, in children, 93–94
marijuana, 64, 305
marriage, 379–383
  covenant, 392–393
  factors promoting stable, 379–380, 383
  in later adulthood, 544–545, 549
  satisfaction with, 381–383
  See also remarriage
Masloff, Sophie, 170
masturbation, 300
mates. *See* spouses
mathematics
  counting skills, 139–140
  gender differences in ability in, 188
maturation, motor skills and, 102–104
maturation rates, adolescent, 280
maximum life expectancy, 491
measurement methods, 28–31
  reliability and validity of, 30
Medicare, 563, 565–566
memory
  implicit and explicit, 508
  in infancy and early childhood, 135–136
  in older adults, 505–510
  secondary and tertiary, 506
  strategies for, 207–209, 508–509, 520–521
  working, 505
men
  middle-age reproductive changes in, 449
  See also fathers; gender
menarche, 278, 279
menopause, 447–449
mental abilities
  primary, 336–339
  secondary, 339–341
mental age (MA), 210
mental hardware, 135
mental health
  in adolescence, 292–293, 300, 306–308
  in later adulthood, 513–522
mental operations, 205
mental retardation, 51–52, 220–221
mental software, 135–136
mentors, 409–410
mesoderm, 59
mesosystem, 24
metabolic theories of aging, 495
metabolism, 281, 332
microsystems, 23–24
middle adulthood, 443–477, 482–483

career development in, 407–410, 417–418
cognitive development in, 453–459
death conception in, 583, 586
family dynamics in, 467–476
health and exercise in, 449–453
intelligence in, 335–341
marital satisfaction in, 382
personality in, 460–466
physical changes in, 445–449
thinking in, 341–344
  See also adult relationships
middle-aged adults, age range of, 3
midlife crisis, 460, 465–466
mind, theory of, 116–118
Minnesota Transracial Adoption Project, 288–289
miscarriage, 52, 71, 600
monoamine oxidase (MAO) inhibitors, 515
monozygotic twins, 50, 51
moral reasoning, 345–351
  culture and, 350–351
  gender differences in, 349–350
moral reasoning theory, 15, 22, 191, 346–349
moratorium identity status, 285–286
Moro reflex, 85
morphemes, grammatical, 152
mothers
  divorced, 394, 396
  lesbian, 193
  working, 170, 430–431
  See also parents; pregnancy
motor skills, 98–105
  defined, 998
  fine, 99, 101–102
  influence of maturation and experience on, 102–104
  locomotion, 98, 99–101
  toilet training, 104–105
  See also psychomotor speed
mourning, 575, 592
  See also grief
multidimensionality of intelligence, 335–336
multidirectionality of intelligence, 336
multiple intelligences theory, 212–213, 335–336
myelin, 96

National Committee to Preserve Social Security and Medicare, 564
National Council of Senior Citizens, 564
Native Americans, 11
  spiritual support among, 539

use of cradle boards by, and infant locomotion, 103
   See also culture; ethnicity
naturalistic observation, 28, 30
nature-nurture issue, 5–6
neglected children, 258
Neonatal Behavioral Assessment Scale (NBAS), 86
nervous system
   development of, in infants, 94–97
   effects of aging on, 496–497
neural plate, 95
neuritic plaques, 496
neurofibrillary tangles, 496
neurons, 94–95, 95–96
   effects of aging on, 496–497
neuroticism, 461
neurotransmitters, 94–95, 496
newborns, 84–90
   activity states of, 86–88
   age range of, 3
   assessing health of, 86
   crying by, 86–87
   hearing, sense of, 61, 108
   low-birth-weight, 75–76
   reflexes of, 85–86, 127
   sleeping by, 86, 87–88
   smell, sense of, 106–107
   sudden infant death syndrome (SIDS) and, 88
   temperament of, 88–90
   touch and pain, sensitivity of, 107
   vision, sense of, 109–111
niche-picking, 54–55
nicotine, 64, 328–329
nonnormative influences, 9, 11
norepinephrine, 307
normative age-graded influences, 9, 10, 11
normative history-graded influences, 9
nuclear family, 384
nursing homes, 556–559
   residents of, 557
   selecting, 557–558
   visiting residents of, 558–559
nutrition
   health and, 331–332
   infant growth and, 93
   in later adulthood, 501
   maternal, and prenatal development, 63

obedience orientation, 346
obesity
   in adults, 332
   juvenile, 281–282
observation, systematic, 28–29, 30
observational learning, 19–20

Observed Tasks of Daily Living (OTDL) test, 456
occupation
   gender differences in selection of, 414–417
   identity and, 405–406
   insecurity related to, 427
   personality-type theory and, 295–297, 406–407
   traditional and nontraditional, 415–416
   See also career development; work
occupational expectations, 408–409
occupational priorities, 405
occupational transitions, 425–428
O'Connor, Sandra Day, 419
old-old adults, age range of, 3
older adults. *See* later adulthood
Older Americans Act, 563
Oncale v. Sundowner Offshore Services, 422
one-to-one principle, 140
only children, 246
openness to experience, 461
operant conditioning, 19
optimally exercised ability, 455
organic mental retardation, 220
osteoporosis, 446, 447
overextension, 151
overregularizations, 152

pain, sensitivity to, 107–108
pain cry, of newborns, 87
Palmar reflex, 85
parallel play, 177, 178
parent-child relations
   in adolescence, 290
   in middle age, 468–470
   reciprocity of, 243–244, 251
parenting
   alternative forms of, 388–390
   childhood rejection and, 260
   cultural differences in, 240–241, 250–251
   dimensions of, 238–241
   by grandparents, 476
   styles of, 241–243, 286–287
parents
   abusive, 250–252
   adoptive, 388, 389
   age of, and prenatal development, 52, 63
   altruism fostered in children by, 184–185
   caring for aging, 430, 470–474
   children's television viewing guidelines for, 265

control by, 239–241
   death of children and, 599–600
   death of, 599
   deciding to become, 385–387
   foster, 388, 389
   gay and lesbian, 193, 389–390
   middle-aged, relations between children and, 468–470
   play as influenced by, 180
   role of, 387–390
   single, 388
   stepparents, 388, 389
   See also fathers; grandparents; mothers
Parkinson's disease, 498–499
passion, as component of love, 366
passive euthanasia, 578–580
patronizing speech, 559
peer groups, childhood and adolescent, 255–258
peer pressure, 257–258
peer relationships, 253–260
   in friendships, 253–255
   in groups, 255–258
   popularity/rejection and, 258–260
people with disabilities
   college attendance by, 324–325
   See also learning disabilities
perception, 106–113
   integrating sensory information for, 111–113
period of the embryo, 59–60, 68
period of the fetus, 60, 68
period of the zygote, 56–59, 68
persistent vegetative state, 577
personal control beliefs, 356–357
personal fable, 285
personal growth, well-being and, 536
personality
   in later adulthood, 533–539
   in middle adulthood, 460–466
   in young adulthood, 352–357
personality traits, adult, 461–462
personality-type theory, 295–297, 406–407
perspective-taking, theory of, 269–271
phase theory of dying, 587–588
phenotypes, 47
   determined by multiple genes, 49–50
   determined by single genes, 47–49
   dominant, 48, 49
   environment and genes as determinants of, 53–55
   genotype reaction range and, 54
   recessive, 48, 49
phenylketonuria (PKU), 51, 53, 71–72
phonemes, 146
phonological processing, 222

physical abuse. *See* abuse

physical growth. *See* growth

Piaget, Jean, cognitive development theory of, 15, 20–22, 124–134, 204–207

placenta, 59, 73

plasticity, 336

play
cooperative, 178, 180–182
development of, 177–180
gender differences in, 179–180
parallel, 177, 178
parental influence on, 180
simple social, 178

polychlorinated biphenyls (PCBs), 66–67, 69

polygenic inheritance, 50

popularity, 258
in peer relationships, 258–260

population pyramid, 488–489

populations, 31

positron emission tomography (PET) scan, 96–97

possible selves, 354–355, 535–536

postconventional level of moral reasoning, 347, 348

postformal thought, 342, 343–344
practical intelligence and, 455–456

"Postponing Sexual Involvement" program, 302–303

poverty. *See* socioeconomic status

power assertion, 240

practical intelligence, 454–456

preconventional level of moral reasoning, 346, 347

pregnancy
after menopause, 448–449
diseases during, 65
drugs during, 63–64
exposure to teratogens during, 63–69
life-cycle forces and, 12–13
medical care during, 71–72, 76
nutrition and stress during, 63
teenage, 301, 302–303
See also prenatal development

prejudice, 271–272

prenatal development, 56–72, 198
diagnosis and treatment during, 69–72
period of the embryo, 59–60
period of the fetus, 60–62
period of the zygote of, 56–59
periods of, 56–62
risk factors during, 63
teratogens' effects on, 63–69
in vitro fertilization and, 57–58

preoperational stage, 21, 126, 129–132, 269

presbycusis, 499

preschoolers, age range of, 3

preterm (premature) infants, 75

primary circular reactions, 127

primary mental abilities, 336–339

private speech, 144

proactivity, 532

processes of thinking, 457

products of thinking, 457

programmed cell death theories of aging, 495

Prophet, The (Gibran), 368, 404

prosocial behavior, 182, 265–266

proximodistal principle, 60

pseudodementia, 519

psychoanalytic theory, 16–17

psychodynamic theories, 15, 16–18

psychological forces, 8, 10, 12
in infancy and early childhood, 198
in later adulthood, 608
in school-age children and adolescents, 316
in young and middle adulthood, 482

psychomotor speed, 503–504

psychosocial aging, theories of, 530–533

psychosocial theory, 15, 17–18
autonomy versus shame and doubt stage, 18, 162, 163
generativity versus stagnation stage, 18, 462–463
identity versus role confusion stage, 18, 284–285
industry versus inferiority stage, 18
initiative versus guilt stage, 18, 162, 163
integrity versus despair stage, 18, 534–535
intimacy versus isolation stage, 18, 325–326, 379–380
trust versus mistrust stage, 18, 162–163

psychotherapy, for treating depression, 516

puberty, 278–280

punishment
in behaviorism, 19
as means of parental control, 240
physical, 250–251
See also discipline

purpose, 163, 536

quantitative knowledge, 139–140

race. *See* ethnicity; culture

racism, health and, 334

Raven's Progressive Matrices, 214

reaction range, 54

reaction time, in older adults, 503–505

Reagan, Nancy, 549

Reagan, Ronald, 517, 549

"reasonable woman" standard, 421, 422

recessive phenotypes, 48, 49

recognition test of memory, 506

referential style of speech, 149

reflective judgment, 342

reflexes, newborn, 85–86, 127

regular (nonREM) sleep, 88

reinforcement, in behaviorism, 19

reinvolvement with personal past, 475

rejection, 258–260

relationships
peer, 253–260
romantic, 298–304, 366–371
well-being and, 536
See also adult relationships

reliability
of intelligence tests, 211
of measurements, 30

religiosity, 538–539

remarriage, 248–249, 396–397

representative sampling, 31

research. *See* developmental research

resistant attachment relationships, 166

respiratory system, aging's effects on, 498

retinal disparity, 111

Retired Senior Volunteer Program, 545

retirement, 540–546
adjustment to, 543–544
defining, 540–541
interpersonal ties and, 544–546
reasons for, 542–543

returning adult students, 324

rites of passage, 323–324

role transitions, marking adulthood, 322–326

romantic relationships
adolescent, 298–304
adult, 366–371

rooting reflex, 85

rubella, prenatal consequences of, 65, 68, 69

sampling, 29, 30, 31

sandwich generation, 467

scaffolding, 142–144, 180

scenarios, 352–354

schemes, 124–125

Schindler, Oskar, 348–349

school-age children, 316–317
age range of, 3
cognitive development in, 204–209
social categories of, 258

schools, 225–231
characteristics of effective, 227–228

computers in, 228–229
international comparisons of, 225–226
literacy levels and, 226–227
popular/rejected children in, 258–260
sex education programs in, 302–303
teachers in, 229–231
See also colleges
scripts, 137
Seattle Longitudinal Study of adult intelligence, 337–339, 510
secondary circular reactions, 127
secondary memory, 506
secondary mental abilities, 339–341
secular growth trends, 279
secure attachment relationships, 166, 167, 168–169
selective serotonin reuptake inhibitors (SSRIs), 515
self-acceptance, well-being and, 536
self-concept, 284
origins of, 115–116
in young adulthood, 356
self-control, delinquency and, 310
self-efficacy, 20
self reports, 29–30
Selman, Robert, perspective-taking theory of, 269–271
selves, possible, 354–355, 535–536
Senior Companions, 545
senses
aging's effects on, 499–500
development of, 106–113
sensorimotor stage, 21, 126–128, 149
sequential research designs, 36
serotonin, 307
Service Corps of Retired Executives (SCORE), 545
Sesame Street, 266
sex chromosomes, 47, 52–53
sex discrimination, 419–420
See also gender
sexual assault, 304
sexual coercion, 303–304
sexual harassment, in workplace, 420–423
sexual orientation, in adolescence, 299–300
sexual relationships. *See* romantic relationships
sexually transmitted diseases, 301–302
siblings, 244–246
birth order of, 245–246
of older adults, 548–549
sickle-cell disease, 46–47, 47–48
sickle-cell trait, 48, 49
sight, 108–111
integrating hearing with, 112–113

Simon, Theophile, 210, 211
simple social play, 178
singlehood, 375–376
skilled nursing care, 557
Skinner, B. F., 15, 19
sleep
irregular (REM), 88
of newborns, 86, 87–88
of older adults, 500
regular (nonREM), 88
smell, sense of, 106–107
smoking, 64, 328–329
sociability, of newborn temperament, 89
social class. *See* socioeconomic status
social clocks, 353
social cognitive theory. *See* social learning theory
social contracts, 347
social convoy, 547
social influence, gender differences in, 188
social isolation, child abuse and, 251
social learning theory, 15, 19–20, 189–190, 262
social referencing, 176
social roles, 187
Social Security, 563, 564–565
social smiles, 173
social system morality, 347
socialization, 237–272
of altruism, 184–185
defined, 237
in family relationships, 238–252
in peer relationships, 253–260
by television, 261–267
understanding others and, 267–272
sociocultural forces, 8, 10–12
in infancy and early childhood, 198
in later adulthood, 608
in school-age children and adolescents, 316
in young and middle adulthood, 482
socioeconomic status
child abuse and, 251
delinquency and, 309–310
health and, 332, 334
intelligence testing and, 214–215
life expectancy and, 491
socioemotional selectivity, 548
somatic symptoms, 447
spaced retrieval, 520–521
spatial ability, gender differences in, 188
specification, 294, 295
speech
development of, 145–155
effective, 154

infant-directed, 147
private, 144
telegraphic, 152
spiritual support, 538–539
spouses
abuse by, 371–374
caretaking of, 549–551
cross-cultural preferences in, 369–371
death of, 600–602
stable-order principle, 140
stage theory of dying, 586–587
stagnation, 463
Stanford-Binet intelligence test, 211
status offenses, 308
stepparents, 388, 389
stepping reflex, 85
stereotypes
gender, 187, 263–264, 415–416
of retirement, 544
on television, 263–264
Sternberg, Robert, triarchic theory of intelligence of, 213, 335
Strange Situation procedure, 165–166
stranger anxiety, 174
stress
alcohol use and, 306
bereavement and, 596–597
of caregiving for aging parents, 472–474
health and, 449–452
maternal, and prenatal development, 63
stress and coping paradigm, 450
strokes, 497–498
Strong Interest Inventory (SII), 296–297
structured observation, 28–29, 30
substance abuse, by adolescents, 292–293, 305–306
sucking reflex, 85
sudden infant death syndrome (SIDS), 88
suicide
adolescent, 308
physician-assisted, 577–578
Super, Donald, career development theory of, 294–295, 407–408
superego, 16
symbolic processing, 128, 149–150
syphilis, prenatal consequences of, 65
systematic observation, 28–29, 30
systems theories, 15, 23–25

task-based theory of dying, 588
tasks, sampling behavior with, 29, 30
taste, sense of, 107
teachers, effective, 229–231
telegraphic speech, 152

television, 261–267
　guidelines for children's viewing of, 265
　influence on attitudes and social behavior, 262–266
　influence on cognition, 266–267
　obesity and, 281
　time children spend watching, 261
temperament
　attachment and, 168–169
　of newborns, 88–90
teratogens, 63–69
　diseases, 65
　drugs, 63–64
　environmental, 65–67
　principles of prenatal influence of, 67–69
Terman, Lewis, 211
terminal buttons, of neurons, 94
tertiary circular reactions, 127
tertiary memory, 506
thalidomide, 63, 67–68
theories. *See* developmental theories
thinking
　adult, 341–344
　convergent, 219
　divergent, 219
　postformal, 342, 343–344
　preoperational, 21, 126, 129–132
　processes of, 457
　products of, 457
　sensorimotor, 21, 126–128
　understanding, of others, 269–271
　See also cognitive development
Thomas, Clarence, 422
time-out, 240
toddlers, 3, 100
　See also early childhood; infancy
toilet training, 104–105
Toilet Training in Less than a Day (Azrin and Foxx), 105
touch, sense of, 107–108
transient ischemic attacks (TIAs), 497
transracial children, 288–289
triarchic theory of intelligence, 213, 335
trust versus mistrust stage, 18, 162–163
turn-taking, conversational, 154
Turner's syndrome, 53
twins, studies of, 50, 51, 215–216
Type A behavior pattern, 451
Type B behavior pattern, 451

ultrasound, 70
umbilical cord, 60

underextension, 151
unemployment, 427–428
　See also retirement
unexercised ability, 454–455
universal ethical principles, 347
universal versus context-specific development issue, 7
U.S. Department of Health and Human Services, Health Care Financing Administration, 558
Useful Field of View (UFOV) measure, 504–505
useful life expectancy, 491

Vacco v. Quill, 578
validity
　of intelligence tests, 211–212
　of measurements, 30
valued elders, 475
variables, independent and dependent, 33
vascular dementia, 497–498
verbal ability, gender differences in, 188
vernix, 84
very low birth weight, 75
video-display terminals (VDTs), as prenatal risk factor, 66
violence
　in spousal relationships, 371–374
　on television, 262–263
　See also aggression
Virginia Longitudinal Study of Divorce and Remarriage, 247
vision, 108–111
　integrating hearing with, 112–113
visual acuity, 109, 327
visual cliff, 110
vocational maturity, 407
voluntarism, by older adults, 545–546
Vygotsky, Lev, 141–144

waking activity, in newborns, 86
walking
　development of, 99–100, 103
　skills involved in, 100
Washington v. Glucksberg, 578
Watson, John, 15, 19
wear-and-tear theory of aging, 494
Wechsler Intelligence Scale for Children-III (WISC-III), 211, 212
weight
　adolescent, 281–283
　birth, 75–76
　infant increase in, 91

well-being, in later adulthood, 535–537
widowhood, 551–553
will
　development of, 163
　living, 579–580
wisdom, 511–512, 539
withdrawal reflex, 85
women
　as caregivers, 430–431, 471, 472–473
　discrimination against, in workplace, 419–423
　middle-age reproductive changes in, 446–449
　occupational selection and development by, 414–417
　See also gender; mothers
Woods, Tiger, 42–43
work, 404–435
　by adolescents, 292–293
　age discrimination in, 423–424
　family and, 429–435
　gender bias in, 419–420
　meaning of, 404–406
　retraining workers for, 426–427
　sexual harassment in, 420–423
　See also career development; occupation
working memory, 208, 505
Working (Terkel), 404

XXX syndrome, 53
XYY complement, 53

young adulthood, 321–358, 482–483
　age range of, 3
　career development in, 407–410, 417–418
　health in, 328–334
　intelligence in, 335–341
　personality in, 352–357
　physical capabilities in, 327–328
　thinking in, 341–344
　transitions to, 322–326
　view of death in, 583, 586
　See also adult relationships
young-old adults, age range of, 3

zone of maximum comfort, 532
zone of maximum performance potential, 532
zone of proximal development, 142
zygote, 58
　period of the, 56–59, 68

TO THE OWNER OF THIS BOOK:

I hope that you have found *Human Development: A Lifespan View,* Second Edition, useful. So that this book can be improved in a future edition, would you take the time to complete this sheet and return it? Thank you.

School and address: _____

Department: _____

Instructor's name: _____

1. What I like most about this book is: _____

_____

_____

2. What I like least about this book is: _____

_____

_____

3. My general reaction to this book is: _____

_____

4. The name of the course in which I used this book is: _____

_____

5. Were all of the chapters of the book assigned for you to read? _____

   If not, which ones weren't? _____

6. In the space below, or on a separate sheet of paper, please write specific suggestions for improving this book and anything else you'd care to share about your experience in using the book.

_____

_____

_____

_____

_____

_____

_____